# FIRST AMENDMENT ANTHOLOGY

# ANDERSON'S
## *Law School Publications*

ADMINISTRATIVE LAW ANTHOLOGY
by Thomas O. Sargentich

ADMINISTRATIVE LAW: CASES AND MATERIALS
by Daniel J. Gifford

APPELLATE ADVOCACY: PRINCIPLES AND PRACTICE
Cases and Materials
by Ursula Bentele and Eve Cary

A CAPITAL PUNISHMENT ANTHOLOGY
by Victor L. Streib

CASES AND PROBLEMS IN CRIMINAL LAW
by Myron Moskovitz

THE CITATION WORKBOOK
by Maria L. Ciampi, Rivka Widerman and Vicki Lutz

COMMERCIAL TRANSACTIONS: PROBLEMS AND MATERIALS
Vol. 1: Secured Transactions Under the Uniform Commercial Code
Vol. 2: Sales Under the Uniform Commercial Code and the Convention on
International Sale of Goods
Vol. 3: Negotiable Instruments Under the Uniform Commercial Code
and the United Nations Convention on International
Bills of Exchange and International Promissory Notes
by Louis F. Del Duca, Egon Guttman and Alphonse M. Squillante

A CONSTITUTIONAL LAW ANTHOLOGY
by Michael J. Glennon

CONTRACTS
Contemporary Cases, Comments, and Problems
by Michael L. Closen, Richard M. Perlmutter and Jeffrey D. Wittenberg

A CONTRACTS ANTHOLOGY
by Peter Linzer

A CRIMINAL LAW ANTHOLOGY
by Arnold H. Loewy

CRIMINAL LAW: CASES AND MATERIALS
by Arnold H. Loewy

CRIMINAL PROCEDURE: TRIAL AND SENTENCING
by Arthur B. LaFrance and Arnold H. Loewy

ECONOMIC REGULATION
Cases and Materials
by Richard J. Pierce, Jr.

ELEMENTS OF LAW
by Eva H. Hanks, Michael E. Herz and Steven S. Nemerson

ENDING IT: DISPUTE RESOLUTION IN AMERICA
Descriptions, Examples, Cases and Questions
by Susan M. Leeson and Bryan M. Johnston

ENVIRONMENTAL LAW
Vol. 1: Environmental Decisionmaking: NEPA and the Endangered Species Act
Vol. 2: Water Pollution
Vol. 3: Air Pollution
Vol. 4: Hazardous Wastes
by Jackson B. Battle, Mark Squillace, Maxine I. Lipeles and Robert L. Fischman

FEDERAL INCOME TAXATION OF PARTNERSHIPS AND OTHER PASS-THRU ENTITIES
by Howard E. Abrams

FEDERAL RULES OF EVIDENCE
Rules, Legislative History, Commentary and Authority
by Glen Weissenberger

*Continued*

FIRST AMENDMENT ANTHOLOGY
by Donald E. Lively, Dorothy E. Roberts and Russell L. Weaver

INTERNATIONAL HUMAN RIGHTS: LAW, POLICY AND PROCESS
Problems and Materials
by Frank Newman and David Weissbrodt

INTERNATIONAL LAW ANTHOLOGY
by Anthony D'Amato

INTRODUCTION TO THE STUDY OF LAW: CASES AND MATERIALS
by John Makdisi

JUSTICE AND THE LEGAL SYSTEM
A Coursebook
by Anthony D'Amato and Arthur J. Jacobson

THE LAW OF MODERN PAYMENT SYSTEMS AND NOTES
by Fred H. Miller and Alvin C. Harrell

PATIENTS, PSYCHIATRISTS AND LAWYERS
Law and the Mental Health System
by Raymond L. Spring, Roy B. Lacoursiere, M.D., and Glen Weissenberger

PROBLEMS AND SIMULATIONS IN EVIDENCE
by Thomas F. Guernsey

A PROPERTY ANTHOLOGY
by Richard H. Chused

THE REGULATION OF BANKING
Cases and Materials on Depository Institutions and Their Regulators
by Michael P. Malloy

A SECTION 1983 CIVIL RIGHTS ANTHOLOGY
by Sheldon H. Nahmod

SPORTS LAW: CASES AND MATERIALS
by Raymond L. Yasser, James R. McCurdy and C. Peter Goplerud

A TORTS ANTHOLOGY
by Lawrence C. Levine, Julie A. Davies and Ted Kionka

TRIAL PRACTICE
Text by Lawrence A. Dubin and Thomas F. Guernsey
Problems and Case Files with *Video* Presentation
by Edward R. Stein and Lawrence A. Dubin

# First Amendment Anthology

Edited by

## Donald E. Lively

Professor of Law
University of Toledo

## Dorothy E. Roberts

Associate Professor of Law
Rutgers, The State University of New Jersey

## Russell L. Weaver

Professor of Law
University of Louisville

ANDERSON PUBLISHING COMPANY

FIRST AMENDMENT ANTHOLOGY

Library of Congress Cataloging-in-Publication Data
First amendment anthology / edited by Donald E. Lively, Dorothy E. Roberts, Russell L.
    Weaver.
        p.  cm.
    Includes bibliographical references.
    ISBN 0-87084-265-X
    1. Freedom of speech—United States.   2. Freedom of the press—United States.   3.
Freedom of religion—United States.   4. United States—Constitutional law—Amendments—
1st.   I. Lively, Donald E., 1947–  . II. Dorothy E., 1956–  . III. Weaver, Russell L.,
1952–  .
KF4770.A75F568   1994
342.73'085—dc20
[347.30285]
                                                                              94-9984
                                                                                 CIP

To Pam, Rico and Rika Lively. D.E.L.

To Iris and Robert Roberts. D.E.R.

To the late Kenneth Walter Weaver, Sr. R.L.W.

# Contents

# Preface

Like others of its genre, this anthology has evolved with the objective of contextualizing and enriching study and understanding of the law. The First Amendment represents what the Supreme Court has characterized as "the matrix, the indispensable condition of nearly every other form of freedom." Palko v. Connecticut, 302 U.S. 319, 327 (1937). With so much of consequence at stake, and resolution frequently driven by choice and prioritization of competing values and interests, it is not surprising that First Amendment literature is characterized by heavy volume, much ideology and considerable passion. As much as, if not more than, other areas of legal commentary, output tends to be as "uninhibited, robust, and wide-open" as the First Amendment itself contemplates.

The extent and quality of First Amendment literature provides a significant challenge to the selection process that ultimately defines an anthology. Content decisions for this anthology have been driven by concern with a work's accessibility to students, capacity to generate critical reflection, and potential for stimulating classroom discussion. The aim of the editing process has been to reconcile imperatives of economy with the breadth and depth of each author's vision and purpose. At the end of each section, a bibliography provides a departure point for further exploration of relevant issues.

The sum of efforts resulting in this anthology includes significant contributions by persons other than the editors. Fran Molnar at The University of Toledo College of Law was the linchpin for coordinating the collection and processing of the materials. Gwen Ausby and Roseann Raniere at Rutgers University School of Law were bulwarks of secretarial strength. Tracie Jackson of The University of Toledo College of Law, Lysette Toro of Rutgers University School of Law and Chris Hutchinson, Kim Rodman and Michael Whiteman of the University of Louisville School of Law provided invaluable research assistance. Each of the editors welcomes reader feedback.

D.E.L.

D.E.R.

R.L.W.

# Part I

# First Amendment Concepts and Ideology

## A. The Value of Expressive Freedom

The meaning of the First Amendment, insofar as the speech and press clauses are concerned, largely is a function of values and context. Not until the early part of this century did the Supreme Court speak directly upon or amplify the meaning of freedom of speech and of the press. The absence of First Amendment litigation, prior to seminal cases generating influential opinions by Justices Holmes and Brandeis and Judge Hand, indicated no unawareness of free expression's value. Draconian measures such as the Sedition Act within a decade of the First Amendment's ratification, and southern legislation criminalizing advocacy of abolitionism, illustrated a keen appreciation of expressive liberty's capacity to unsettle established orders. Despite their implications for expressive freedom, such enactments never were challenged in court. The Federalist inspired Sedition Act was repealed as Jeffersonians swept into the executive and legislative branches. As Justice Brennan put it, the enactment also has been repudiated by "the court of history." *New York Times Co. v. Sullivan*, 376 U.S. 254, 276 (1964). Suppressive regimens of the states, meanwhile, were not constitutionally significant until the Court determined that freedom of speech and of the press were incorporated through the Fourteenth Amendment. *Near v. Minnesota*, 283 U.S. 697, 707 (1931); *Gitlow v. New York*, 268 U.S. 652, 666 (1925).

Development of First Amendment values has been a highly competitive exercise. The debate might be largely academic if, as Justice Black saw it, the First Amendment was perceived as an absolute. *Konigsberg v. State Bar of California*, 366 U.S. 36, 61 (1961). With the Court having rejected the absolutist premise, id. at 49, a fundamental and abiding problem has been discerning what speech is protected and why. Not surprisingly, given how value selection is a prime determinant of the scope of expressive liberty, debate on the subject has been rich and extensive. Alexander Meiklejohn asserted that expressive freedom is valuable as a means of ensuring informed self-government. He thus developed a First Amendment theory of protection for speech essential for informed decision-making by the electorate. Although Meiklejohn eventually expanded his vision of protected speech to include artistic, scientific and educational expression and public discussion of public issues, Robert H. Bork, makes the case for protecting only explicitly political speech. Thomas I. Emerson, although acknowledging the imperative of informed self-government, suggested that expressive liberty is valuable as a means of self-development in contexts transcending a person's relationship to the state. C. Edwin Baker challenges traditional marketplace of ideas notions and urges attention to the relationship between expressive liberty and human freedom. Martin H. Redish asserts that the primary value of expressive freedom is as a means of self-realization.

Alexander Meiklejohn, *The First Amendment Is an Absolute,* 1961 SUPREME COURT REVIEW 245 (1961)*

. . .

## V. THE FREEDOM OF THOUGHT AND COMMUNICATION BY WHICH WE GOVERN

. . . The First Amendment does not protect a "freedom to speak." It protects the freedom of those activities of thought and communication by which we "govern." It is concerned, not with a private right, but with a public power, a governmental responsibility.

In the specific language of the Constitution, the governing activities of the people appear only in terms of casting a ballot. But in the deeper meaning of the Constitution, voting is merely the external expression of a wide and diverse number of activities by means of which citizens attempt to meet the responsibilities of making judgments, which that freedom to govern lays upon them. That freedom implies and requires what we call "the dignity of the individual." Self-government can exist only insofar as the voters acquire the intelligence, integrity, sensitivity, and generous devotion to the general welfare that, in theory, casting a ballot is assumed to express.

The responsibilities mentioned are of three kinds. We, the people who govern, must try to understand the issues which, incident by incident, face the nation. We must pass judgment upon the decisions which our agents make upon those issues. And, further, we must share in devising methods by which those decisions can be made wise and effective or, if need be, supplanted by others which promise greater wisdom and effectiveness. Now it is these activities, in all their diversity, whose freedom fills up, "the scope of the First Amendment." These are the activities to whose freedom it gives its unqualified protection. And it must be recognized that the literal text of the Amendment falls far short of expressing the intent and the scope of that protection. I have previously tried to express that inadequacy:

> We must also note that, though the intention of the Amendment is sharp and resolute, the sentence which expresses that intention is awkward and ill constructed. Evidently, it was hard to write and, therefore, hard to interpret. Within its meaning are summed up centuries of social passion and intellectual controversy,

in this country and in others. As one reads it, one feels that its writers could not agree, either within themselves or with each other, upon a single formula which would define for them the paradoxical relation between free men and their legislative agents. Apparently, all that they could make their words do was to link together five separate demands which had been sharpened by ages of conflict and were being popularly urged in the name of the "Freedom of the People." And yet, those demands were, and were felt to be, varied forms of a single demand. They were attempts to express, each in its own way, the revolutionary idea which, in the slowly advancing fight for freedom, has given to the American experiment in self-government its dominating significance for the modern world

What I said is that the First Amendment, as seen in its constitutional setting, forbids Congress to abridge the freedom of a citizen's speech, press, peaceable assembly, or petition, whenever those activities are utilized for the governing of the nation. In these respects, the Constitution gives to all "the people" the same protection of freedom which, in Article I, § 6(1), it provides for their legislative agents: "and for any speech or debate in either House, they shall not be questioned in any other place." Just as our agents must be free in their use of their delegated powers, so the people must be free in the exercise of their reserved powers.

What other activities, then, in addition to speech, press, assembly, and petition, must be included within the scope of the First Amendment? First of all, the freedom to "vote," the official expression of a self-governing man's judgment on issues of public policy, must be absolutely protected. None of his subordinate agencies may bring pressure upon him to drive his balloting this way or that. None of them may require him to tell how he has voted; none may inquire by compulsory process into his political beliefs or associations. In that area, the citizen has constitutional authority and his agents have not.

Second, there are many forms of thought and expression within the range of human communications from which the voter derives the knowledge, intelligence, sensitivity to human values: the capacity for sane and objective judgment which, so far as possible, a ballot should express. These, too, must suffer no abridgment of their freedom. I list four of them below.

1. Education, in all its phases, is the attempt to so inform and cultivate the mind and will of a citizen that he shall have the wisdom, the indepen-

dence, and, therefore, the dignity of a governing citizen. Freedom of education is, thus, as we all recognize, a basic postulate in the planning of a free society.

2. The achievements of philosophy and the sciences in creating knowledge and understanding of men and their world must be made available, without abridgment, to every citizen.

3. Literature and the arts must be protected by the First Amendment. They lead the way toward sensitive and informed appreciation and response to the values out of which the riches of the general welfare are created.

4. Public discussions of public issues, together with the spreading of information and opinion bearing on those issues, must have a freedom unabridged by our agents. Though they govern us, we, in a deeper sense, govern them. Over our governing, they have no power. Over their governing we have sovereign power.

. . . (T)he authority of citizens to decide what they shall write and, more fundamental, what they shall read and see, has not been delegated to any of the subordinate branches of government. It is "reserved to the people," each deciding for himself to whom he will listen, whom he will read, what portrayal of the human scene he finds worthy of his attention. And at this point I feel compelled to disagree with Professor Kalven's interpretation of what I have tried to say. In his recent article on obscenity, he wrote:

> The classic defense of John Stuart Mill and the modern defense of Alexander Meiklejohn do not help much when the question is why the novel, the poem, the painting, the drama, or the piece of sculpture falls within the protection of the First Amendment. Nor do the famous opinions of Hand, Holmes, and Brandeis. The emphasis is all on the truth winning out in a fair fight between competing ideas. The emphasis is clearest in Meiklejohn's argument that free speech is indispensable to the informed citizenry required to make democratic self-government work. The people need free speech because they vote. As a result his argument distinguishes sharply between public and private speech. Not all communications are relevant to the political process. The people do not need novels or dramas or paintings or poems because they will be called upon to vote. Art and belles-lettres do not deal in such ideas— at least not good art or belles-lettres. . . .

In reply to that friendly interpretation, I must, at two points, record a friendly disavowal. I have never been able to share the Miltonian faith that in a fair fight between truth and error, truth is sure to win. And if one had that faith, it would be hard to reconcile it with the sheer stupidity of the policies of this nation—and of other nations—now driving humanity to the very edge of final destruction. In my view, "the people need free speech" because they have decided, in adopting, maintaining and interpreting their Constitution, to govern themselves rather than to be governed by others. And, in order to make that self-government a reality rather than an illusion, in order that it may become as wise and efficient as its responsibilities require, the judgment-making of the people must be self-educated in the ways of freedom. That is, I think, the positive purpose to which the negative words of the First Amendment gave a constitutional expression. Moreover, as against Professor Kalven's interpretation, I believe, as a teacher, that the people do need novels and dramas and paintings and poems, "because they will be called upon to vote." The primary social fact which blocks and hinders the success of our experiment in self-government is that our citizens are not educated for self-government. We are terrified by ideas, rather than challenged and stimulated by them. Our dominant mood is not the courage of people who dare to think. It is the timidity of those who fear and hate whenever conventions are questioned. . . .

Robert H. Bork, *Neutral Principles and Some First Amendment Problems,* 47 INDIANA LAW JOURNAL 1 (1971)*

. . .

SOME FIRST AMENDMENT PROBLEMS: THE SEARCH FOR THEORY

. . .

I am led by the logic of the requirement that judges be principled to the following suggestions. Constitutional protection should be accorded only to speech that is explicitly political. There is no basis for judicial intervention to protect any other form of expression, be it scientific, literary or that variety of expression we call obscene or pornographic. Moreover, within that category of speech we ordinarily call political, there should be no constitutional ob-

* Copyright 1971 by the Trustees of Indiana University. Reprinted by permission.

struction to laws making criminal any speech that advocates forcible overthrow of the government or the violation of any law.

I am, of course, aware that this theory departs drastically from existing Court-made law, from the views of most academic specialists in the field and that it may strike a chill into the hearts of some civil libertarians. But I would insist at the outset that constitutional law, viewed as the set of rules a judge may properly derive from the document and its history, is not an expression of our political sympathies or of our judgments about what expediency and prudence require. When decision making is principled it has nothing to say about the speech we like or the speech we hate; it has a great deal to say about how far democratic discretion can govern without endangering the basis of democratic government. Nothing in my argument goes to the question of what laws should be enacted. I like the freedoms of the individual as well as most, and I would be appalled by many statutes that I am compelled to think would be constitutional if enacted. But I am also persuaded that my generally libertarian commitments have nothing to do with the behavior proper to the Supreme Court.

In framing a theory of free speech the first obstacle is the insistence of many very intelligent people that the "first amendment is an absolute." Devotees of this position insist, with a literal respect they do not accord other parts of the Constitution, that the Framers commanded complete freedom of expression without governmental regulation of any kind. The first amendment states: "Congress shall make no law . . . abridging the freedom of speech. . . ." Those who take that as an absolute must be reading "speech" to mean any form of verbal communication and "freedom" to mean total absence of governmental restraint.

Any such reading is, of course, impossible. Since it purports to be an absolute position we are entitled to test it with extreme hypotheticals. Is Congress forbidden to prohibit incitement to mutiny aboard a naval vessel engaged in actions against an enemy, to prohibit shouted harangues from the visitors' gallery during its own deliberations or to provide any rules for decorum in federal courtrooms? Are the states forbidden, by the incorporation of the first amendment in the fourteenth, to punish the shouting of obscenities in the streets?

No one, not the most obsessed absolutist, takes any such position, but if one does not, the absolute position is abandoned, revealed as a play on words. Government cannot function if anyone can say anything anywhere at any time. And so we quickly come to the conclusion that lines must be drawn, differenti-

ations made. Nor does that in any way involve us in a conflict with the wording of the first amendment. Laymen may perhaps be forgiven for thinking that the literal words of the amendment command complete absence of governmental inhibition upon verbal activity, but what can one say of lawyers who believe any such thing? Anyone skilled in reading language should know that the words are not necessarily absolute. "Freedom of speech" may very well be a term referring to a defined or assumed scope of liberty, and it may be this area of liberty that is not to be "abridged."

If we turn to history, we discover that our suspicions about the wording are correct, except that matters are even worse. The framers seem to have had no coherent theory of free speech and appear not to have been overly concerned with the subject. Professor Leonard Levy's, work, *Legacy of Suppression*, demonstrates that the men who adopted the first amendment did not display a strong libertarian stance with respect to speech. Any such position would have been strikingly at odds with the American political tradition. Our forefathers were men accustomed to drawing a line, to us often invisible, between freedom and licentiousness. In colonial times and during and after the Revolution they displayed a determination to punish speech thought dangerous to government, much of it expression that we would think harmless and well within the bounds of legitimate discourse. Jeffersonians, threatened by the Federalist Sedition Act of 1798, undertook the first American elaboration of a libertarian position in an effort to stay out of jail. Professor Walter Berns offers evidence that even then the position was not widely held. When Jefferson came to power it developed that he read the first amendment only to limit Congress and he believed suppression to be a proper function of the state governments. He appears to have instigated state prosecutions against Federalists for seditious libel. But these later developments do not tell us what the men who adopted the first amendment intended, and their discussions tell us very little either. The disagreements that certainly existed were not debated and resolved. The first amendment, like the rest of the Bill of Rights, appears to have been a hastily drafted document upon which little thought was expended. One reason, as Levy shows, is that the Anti-Federalists complained of the absence of a Bill of Rights less because they cared for individual freedoms than as a tactic to defeat the Constitution. The Federalists promised to submit one in order to get the Constitution ratified. The Bill of Rights was then drafted by Federalists, who had opposed it from the beginning; the Anti-Federalists, who were really more interested in preserving the rights of state governments against federal power, had by that time lost interest in the subject.

We are, then, forced to construct our own theory of the constitutional protection of speech. We cannot solve our problems simply by reference to the test or to its history. But we are not without materials for building. The first amendment indicates that there is something special about speech. We would know that much even without a first amendment, for the entire structure of the Constitution creates a representative democracy, a form of government that would be meaningless without freedom to discuss government and its policies. Freedom for political speech could and should be inferred even if there were no first amendment. Further guidance can be gained from the fact that we are looking for a theory fit for enforcement by judges. The principles we seek must, therefore, be neutral in all three meanings of the word: they must be neutrally derived, defined and applied.

The law of free speech we know today grows out of the Supreme Court decisions following World War I—*Schenck v. United States, Abrams v. United States, Gitlow v. New York, Whitney v. California*—not out of the majority positions but rather from the opinions, mostly dissents or concurrences that were really dissents, of Justices Holmes and Brandeis. Professor Kalven remarks upon ''the almost uncanny power'' of these dissents. And it is uncanny, for they have prevailed despite the considerable handicap of being deficient in logic and analysis as well as in history. . . .

As a starting point Brandeis went to fundamentals and attempted to answer the question why speech is protected at all from governmental regulation. If we overlook his highly romanticized version of history and ignore merely rhetorical flourishes, we shall find Brandeis quite provocative.

> Those who won our independence believed that the final end of the state was to make men free to develop their faculties; and that in its government the deliberative forces should prevail over the arbitrary. They valued liberty both as an end and as a means. They believed liberty to be the secret of happiness and courage to be the secret of liberty. The belief that freedom to think as you will and to speak as you think are means indispensable to the discovery and spread of political truth; that without free speech and assembly discussion would be futile; that with them, discussion affords ordinarily adequate protection against the dissemination of noxious doctrine. . . . They rec-

ognized the risks to which all human institutions are subject. But they knew . . . that it is hazardous to discourage thought, hope and imagination; that fear breeds repression; that repression breeds hate; that hate menaces stable government; that the path of safety lies in the opportunity to discuss freely supposed grievances and proposed remedies; and that the fitting remedy for evil counsels is good ones.

We begin to see why the dissents of Brandeis and Holmes possessed the power to which Professor Kalven referred. They were rhetoricians of extraordinary potency, and their rhetoric retains the power, almost half a century later, to swamp analysis, to persuade, almost to command assent.

But there is structure beneath the rhetoric, and Brandeis is asserting, though he attributes it all to the Founding Fathers, that there are four benefits to be derived from speech. These are:

1. The development of the faculties of the individual;

2. The happiness to be derived from engaging in the activity;

3. The provision of a safety value [sic] for society; and,

4. The discovery and spread of political truth.

We may accept these claims as true and as satisfactorily inclusive. When we come to analyze these benefits, however, we discover that in terms of constitutional law they are very different things.

The first two benefits—development of individual faculties and the achievement of pleasure—are or may be found, for both speaker and hearer, in all varieties of speech, from political discourse to shop talk to salacious literature. But the important point is that these benefits do not distinguish speech from any other human activity. An individual may develop his faculties or derive pleasure from trading on the stock market, following his profession as a river port pilot, working as a barmaid, engaging in sexual activity, playing tennis, rigging prices or in any of thousands of other endeavors. Speech with only the first two benefits can be preferred to other activities only by ranking forms of personal gratification. These functions or benefits of speech are, therefore, to the principled judge, indistinguishable from the functions or benefits of all other human activity. He cannot, on neutral grounds, choose to protect speech that has only these functions more than he protects any other claimed freedom.

The third benefit of speech mentioned by Brandeis—its safety valve function—is different from the first two. It relates not to the gratification of the individual, at least not directly, but to the welfare of society. The safety valve function raises only issues of expediency or prudence, and, therefore, raises issues to be determined solely by the legislature or, in some cases, by the executive. The legislature may decide not to repress speech advocating the forcible overthrow of the government in some classes of cases because it thinks repression would cause more trouble than it would prevent. Prosecuting attorneys, who must in any event pick and choose among cases, given their limited resources, may similarly decide that some such speech is trivial or that ignoring it would be easiest. But these decisions, involving only the issue of the expedient course, are indistinguishable from thousands of other managerial judgments governments must make daily, though in the extreme case the decision may involve the safety of the society just as surely as a decision whether or not to take a foreign policy stand that risks war. It seems plain that decisions involving only judgments of expediency are for the political branches and not for the judiciary.

This leaves the fourth function of speech—"discovery and spread of political truth." This function of speech, its ability to deal explicitly, specifically and directly with politics and government, is different from any other form of human activity. But the difference exists only with respect to one kind of speech: explicitly and predominantly political speech. This seems to me the only form of speech that a principled judge can prefer to other claimed freedoms. All other forms of speech raise only issues of human gratification and their protection against legislative regulation involves the judge in making decisions of the sort made in *Griswold v. Connecticut*.

It is here that I begin to part company with Professor Kalven. Kalven argues that no society in which seditious libel, the criticism of public officials, is a crime can call itself free and democratic. I agree, even though the framers of the first amendment probably had no clear view of that proposition. Yet they indicated a value when they said that speech in some sense was special and when they wrote a Constitution providing for representative democracy, a form of government that is meaningless without open and vigorous debate about officials and their policies. It is for this reason, the relation of speech to democratic organization, that Professor Alexander Meiklejohn seems correct when he says:

> The First Amendment does not protect a "freedom to speak." It protects the freedom of those activities of thought and communica-

tion by which we "govern." It is concerned, not with a private right, but with a public power, a governmental responsibility.

But both Kalven and Meiklejohn go further and would extend the protection of the first amendment beyond speech that is explicitly political. Meiklejohn argues that the amendment protects:

> Forms of thought and expression within the range of human communications from which the voter derives the knowledge, intelligence, sensitivity to human values: the capacity for sane and objective judgment which, so far as possible, a ballot should express.

He lists four such thoughts and expressions:

> 1. Education, in all its phases. . . . 2. The achievements of philosophy and the sciences. . . . 3. Literature and the arts. . . . 4. Public discussions of public issues. . . .

Kalven, following a similar line, states: "[T]he invitation to follow a dialectic progression from public official to government policy to public policy to matters in the public domain, like art, seems to me to be overwhelming." It is an invitation, I wish to suggest, the principled judge must decline. A dialectic progression I take to be a progression by analogy from one case to the next, an indispensable but perilous method of legal reasoning. The length to which analogy is carried defines the principle, but neutral definition requires that, in terms of the rationale in play, those cases within the principles be more like each other than they are like cases left outside. The dialectical progression must have a principled stopping point. I agree that there is an analogy between criticism of official behavior and the publication of a novel like *Ulysses*, for the latter may form attitudes that ultimately affect politics. But it is an analogy, not an identity. Other human activities and experiences also form personality, teach and create attitudes just as much as does the novel, but no one would on that account, I take it, suggest that the first amendment strikes down regulations of economic activity, control of entry into a trade, laws about sexual behavior, marriage and the like. Yet these activities, in their capacity to create attitudes that ultimately impinge upon the political process, are more like literature and science than literature and science are like political speech. If the dialectical progression is not to become an analogical stampede, the protection of the first amendment must be cut off when it reaches the outer limits of political speech.

Two types of problems may be supposed to arise with respect to this solution. The first is the difficulty of drawing a line between political and non-political speech. The second is that such a line will leave unprotected much speech that is essential to the life of a civilized community. Neither of these problems seems to me to raise crippling difficulties.

The category of protected speech should consist of speech concerned with governmental behavior, policy or personnel, whether the governmental unit involved is executive, legislative, judicial or administrative. Explicitly political speech is speech about how we are governed, and the category therefore includes a wide range of evaluation, criticism, electioneering and propaganda. It does not cover scientific, educational, commercial or literary expressions as such. A novel may have impact upon attitudes that affect politics, but it would not for that reason receive judicial protection. This is not anomalous, I have tried to suggest, since the rationale of the first amendment cannot be the protection of all things or activities that influence political attitudes. Any speech may do that, and we have seen that it is impossible to leave all speech unregulated. Moreover, any conduct may affect political attitudes as much as a novel, and we cannot view the first amendment as a broad denial of the power of government to regulate conduct. The line drawn must, therefore, lie between the explicitly political and all else. Not too much should be made of the undeniable fact that there will be hard cases. Any theory of the first amendment that does not accord absolute protection for all verbal expression, which is to say any theory worth discussing, will require that a spectrum be cut and the location of the cut will always be, arguably, arbitrary. The question is whether the general location of the cut is justified. The existence of close cases is not a reason to refuse to draw a line and so deny majorities the power to govern in areas where their power is legitimate.

The other objection—that the political-nonpolitical distinction will leave much valuable speech without constitutional protection—is no more troublesome. The notion that all valuable types of speech must be protected by the first amendment confuses the constitutionality of laws with their wisdom. Freedom of non-political speech rests, as does freedom for other valuable forms of behavior, upon the enlightenment of society and its elected representatives. That is hardly a terrible fate. At least a society like ours ought not to think so. . . .

We must now return to the core of the first amendment, speech that is explicitly political. I mean by that criticisms of public officials and policies, proposals for the adoption or repeal of legislation or constitutional provisions and speech addressed to the conduct of any governmental unit in the country.

A qualification is required, however. Political speech is not any speech that concerns government and law, for there is a category of such speech that must be excluded. This category consists of speech advocating forcible overthrow of the government or violation of law. The reason becomes clear when we return to Brandeis' discussion of the reasons for according constitutional protection to speech.

The fourth function of speech, the one that defines and sets apart political speech, is the "discovery and spread of political truth." To understand what the Court should protect, therefore, we must define "political truth." There seem to me three possible meanings to that term:

1. An absolute set of truths that exist independently of Constitution or statute.

2. A set of values that are protected by constitutional provision from the reach of legislative majorities.

3. Within that area of life which the majority is permitted to govern in accordance with the Madisonian model of representative government, whatever result the majority reaches and maintains at the moment.

The judge can have nothing to do with any absolute set of truths existing independently and depending upon God or the nature of the universe. If a judge should claim to have access to such a body of truths, to possess a volume of the annotated natural law, we would, quite justifiably, suspect that the source of the revelation was really no more exalted than the judge's viscera. In our system there is no absolute set of truths, to which the term "political truth" can refer.

Values protected by the Constitution are one type of political truth. They are, in fact, the highest type since they are placed beyond the reach of simple legislative majorities. They are primarily truths about the way government must operate, that is, procedural truths. But speech aimed at the discovery and spread of political truth is concerned with more than the desirability of constitutional provisions or the manner in which they should be interpreted.

The third meaning of "political truth" extends the category of protected speech. Truth is what the majority thinks it is at any given moment precisely because the majority is permitted to govern and to redefine its values constantly. "Political truth" in this sense must, therefore, be a term of art, a concept defined entirely from a consideration of the system of government which the judge is commissioned to operate and maintain. It has no unchanging content but refers to the temporary outcomes of the democratic process. Political truth is what the majority decides it wants today. It may be something entirely different tomorrow, as truth is rediscovered and the new concept spread.

Speech advocating forcible overthrow of the government contemplates a group less than a majority seizing control of the monopoly power of the state when it cannot gain its ends through speech and political activity. Speech advocating violent overthrow is thus not "political speech" as that term must be defined by a Madisonian system of government. It is not political speech because it violates constitutional truths about processes and because it is not aimed at a new definition of political truth by a legislative majority. Violent overthrow of government breaks the premises of our system concerning the ways in which truth is defined, and yet those premises are the only reasons for protecting political speech. It follows that there is no constitutional reason to protect speech advocating forcible overthrow.

A similar analysis suggests that advocacy of law violation does not qualify as political speech any more than advocacy of forcible overthrow of the government. Advocacy of law violation is a call to set aside the results that political speech has produced. The process of the "discovery and spread of political truth" is damaged or destroyed if the outcome is defeated by a minority that makes law enforcement, and hence the putting of political truth into practice, impossible or less effective. There should, therefore, be no constitutional protection for any speech advocating the violation of the law. . . .

Thomas I. Emerson, *Toward a General Theory of the First Amendment,* 72 YALE LAW JOURNAL 877 (1963)*

. . .

## I. THE FUNCTION OF FREEDOM OF EXPRESSION IN A DEMOCRATIC SOCIETY

The right of the individual to freedom of expression has deep roots in our history. But the concept as we know it now is essentially a product of the development of the liberal constitutional state. It is an integral part of the great intellectual and social movement beginning with the Renaissance which transformed the Western world from a feudal and authoritarian society to one whose faith rested upon the dignity, the reason and the freedom of the individual. The theory in its modern form has thus evolved over a period of more than three centuries, being applied under different circumstances and seeking to deal with different problems. It is sufficient for our purposes to restate it in its final, composite form, as it comes to us today.

The values sought by society in protecting the rights to freedom of expression may be grouped into four broad categories. Maintenance of a system of free expression is necessary (1) as assuring individual self-fulfillment, (2) as a means of attaining the truth, (3) as a method of securing participation by the members of the society in social, including political, decision-making, and (4) as maintaining the balance between stability and change in the society. We consider these in their affirmative aspects, without regard at this time to the problems of limitation or reconciliation with other values.

### A. Individual Self-Fulfillment

The right to freedom of expression is justified first of all as the right of an individual purely in his capacity as an individual. It derives from the widely accepted premise of Western thought that the proper end of man is the realization of his character and potentialities as a human being. Man is distinguished from other animals principally by the qualities of his mind. He has powers to reason and to feel in ways that are unique in degree if not in kind. He has the capacity to think in abstract terms, to use language, to communicate his thoughts and emotions, to build a culture. He has powers of imagination, insight and feeling. It is through development of these powers that man finds his meaning and his place in the world.

The achievement of self-realization commences with development of the mind. But the process of conscious thought by its very nature can have no limits. An individual cannot tell where it may lead nor anticipate its end. Moreover, it is an *individual* process. Every man is influenced by his fellows, dead and living, but his mind is his own and its functioning is necessarily an individual affair.

From this it follows that every man—in the development of his own personality—has the right to form his own beliefs and opinions. And, it also follows, that he has the right to express these beliefs and opinions. Otherwise they are of little account. For expression is an integral part of the development of ideas, of mental exploration and of the affirmation of self. The power to realize his potentiality as a human being begins at this point and must extend at

* Reprinted by permission of The Yale Law Journal and Fred B. Rothman & Company from *The Yale Law Journal,* vol. 72, pp. 877–956.

least this far if the whole nature of man is not to be thwarted.

Hence suppression of belief, opinion and expression is an affront to the dignity of man, a negation of man's essential nature. What Milton said of licensing of the press is equally true of any form of restraint over expression: it is "the greatest displeasure and indignity to a free and knowing spirit that can be put upon him." . . .

Two basic implications of the theory need to be emphasized. The first is that it is not a general measure of the individual's right to freedom of expression that any particular exercise of the right may be thought to promote or retard other goals of the society. The theory asserts that freedom of expression, while not the sole or sufficient end of society, is a good in itself, or at least an essential element in good society. The society may seek to achieve other or more inclusive ends—such as virtue, justice, equality, or the maximum realization of the potentialities of its members. These problems are not necessarily solved by accepting the rules for freedom of expression. But, as a general proposition, the society may not seek to solve them by suppressing the beliefs or opinions of individual members. To achieve these other goals it must rely upon other methods: the use of counter-expression and the regulation or control of conduct which is not expression. Hence the right to control individual expression, on the ground that it is judged to promote good or evil, justice or injustice, equality or inequality, is not, speaking generally, within the competence of the good society.

The second implication, in a sense a corollary of the first, is that the theory rests upon a fundamental distinction between belief, opinion and communication of ideas on the one hand, and different forms of conduct on the other. For shorthand purposes we refer to this distinction hereafter as one between "expression" and "action." As just observed, in order to achieve its desired goals, a society or the state is entitled to exercise control over action—whether by prohibiting or compelling it—on an entirely different and vastly more extensive basis. But expression occupies a specially protected position. In this sector of human conduct, the social right of suppression or compulsion is at its lowest point, in most respects non-existent.

This marking off of the special area of expression is a crucial ingredient of the basic theory for several reasons. In the first place thought and communication are the fountainhead of all expression of the individual personality. To cut off the flow at the source is to dry up the whole stream. Freedom at this point is essential to all other freedoms. Hence society must withhold its right of suppression until the stage of action is reached. Secondly, expression is normally conceived as doing less injury to other social goals than action. It generally has less immediate consequences, is less irremediable in its impact. Thirdly, the power of society and the state over the individual is so pervasive, and construction of doctrines, institutions and administrative practices to limit this power so difficult, that only by drawing such a protective line between expression and action is it possible to strike a safe balance between authority and freedom.

B. Attainment of Truth

In the traditional theory, freedom of expression is not only an individual but a social good. It is, to begin with, the best process for advancing knowledge and discovering truth.

Considered in this aspect, the theory starts with the premise that the soundest and most rational judgment is arrived at by considering all facts and arguments which can be put forth in behalf of or against any proposition. Human judgment is a frail thing. It may err in being subject to emotion, prejudice or personal interest. It suffers from lack of information, insight, or inadequate thinking. It can seldom rest at the point any single person carries it, but must always remain incomplete and subject to further extension, refinement, rejection or modification. Hence an individual who seeks knowledge and truth must hear all sides of the question, especially as presented by those who feel strongly and argue militantly for a different view. He must consider all alternatives, test his judgment by exposing it to opposition, make full use of different minds to sift the true from the false. Conversely, suppression of information, discussion, or the clash of opinion prevents one from reaching the most rational judgment, blocks the generation of new ideas, and tends to perpetuate error. This is the method of the Socratic dialogue, employed on a universal scale.

The process is a continuous one. As further knowledge becomes available, as conditions change, as new insights are revealed, the judgment is open to reappraisal, improvement or abandonment.

The theory demands that discussion must be kept open no matter how certainly true an accepted opinion may seem to be. Many of the most widely acknowledged truths have turned out to be erroneous. Many of the most significant advances in human knowledge—from Copernicus to Einstein—have resulted from challenging hitherto unquestioned assumptions. No opinion can be immune from challenge.

The process also applies regardless of how false

or pernicious the new opinion appears to be. For the unaccepted opinion may be true or partially true. And there is no way of suppressing the false without suppressing the true. Furthermore, even if the new opinion is wholly false, its presentation and open discussion serves a vital social purpose. It compels a rethinking and retesting of the accepted opinion. It results in a deeper understanding of the reasons for holding the opinion and a fuller appreciation of its meaning.

The only justification for suppressing an opinion is that those who seek to suppress it are infallible in their judgment of the truth. But no individual or group can be infallible, particularly in a constantly changing world.

It is essential to note that the theory contemplates more than a process for arriving at an individual judgment. It asserts that the process is also the best method for reaching a general or social judgment. This is true in part because vitally conditioned by the quality of the individual judgments which compose it. More importantly, the same reasons which make open discussion essential for an intelligent individual judgment make it imperative for rational social judgments. Through the acquisition of new knowledge, the toleration of new ideas, the testing of opinion in open competition, the discipline of rethinking its assumptions, a society will be better able to reach common decisions that will meet the needs and aspirations of its members.

## C. Participation in Decision-Making

The third main function of a system of freedom of expression is to provide for participation in decision-making through a process of open discussion which is available to all members of the community. Conceivably the technique of reaching the best common judgment could be limited to an elite, or could be extended to most members of the society excluding only those who were felt to be clearly unworthy. In its earlier forms the theory was often so restricted. But as the nineteenth century progressed it came to be accepted that all men were entitled to participate in the process of formulating the common decisions.

This development was partly due to acceptance of the concept that freedom of expression was a right of the individual, as discussed previously. But it was also inherent in the logic of free expression as a social good. In order for the process to operate at its best, every relevant fact must be brought out, every opinion and every insight must be available for consideration. Since facts are discovered and opinions formed only by the individual, the system demands that all persons participate. As John Stuart Mill expressed it, "If all mankind minus one, were of one opinion, and only one person were of the contrary opinion, mankind would be no more justified in silencing that one person, than he, if he had the power, would be justified in silencing mankind."

But in addition to these reasons, the right of all members of society to form their own beliefs and communicate them freely to others must be regarded as an essential principle of a democratically-organized society. The growing pressures for democracy and equality reinforced the logical implications of the theory and demanded opportunity for all persons to share in making social decisions. This is, of course, especially true of political decisions. But the basic theory carried beyond the political realm. It embraced the right to participate in the building of the whole culture, and included freedom of expression in religion, literature, art, science and all areas of human learning and knowledge.

In the field of political action, as just mentioned, the theory of freedom of expression has particular significance. It is through the political process that most of the immediate decisions on the survival, welfare and progress of a society are made. It is here that the state has a special incentive to repress opposition and often wields a more effective power of suppression. Freedom of expression in the political realm is usually a necessary condition for securing freedom elsewhere. It is in the political sector, therefore, that the crucial battles over free expression are most often fought. . . .

The crucial point, however, is not that freedom of expression is politically useful, but that it is indispensable to the operation of a democratic form of government. Once one accepts the premise of the Declaration of Independence—that governments derive "their just powers from the consent of the governed"—it follows that the governed must, in order to exercise their right of consent, have full freedom of expression both in forming individual judgments and in forming the common judgment. Together with the argument for freedom of religious belief, this proposition was the one most frequently and most insistently urged in support of freedom of expression.

The proponents of freedom of political expression often addressed themselves to the question whether the people were competent to perform the functions entrusted to them, whether they could acquire sufficient information or possessed sufficient capacity for judgment. The men of the eighteenth century, with their implicit faith in the power of reason and the perfectibility of man, entertained few doubts on this score. Political theorists of the nineteenth and twentieth centuries have been more cautious. And there was some disagreement as to whether the right of political expression could safely be extended to societies which had not reached a certain point in the development of education and culture. But these problems were actually questions concerning the viability of democracy itself. And once a society was committed to democratic procedures, or rather in the process of committing itself, it necessarily embraced the principle of open political discussion.

## D. Balance Between Stability and Change

The traditional doctrine of freedom of expression, finally, embodies a theory of social control. The principle of open discussion is a method of achieving a more adaptable and at the same time more stable community, of maintaining the precarious balance between healthy cleavage and necessary consensus. This may not always have been true, and may not be true of many existing societies. But where men have learned how to function within the law, an open society will be the stronger and more cohesive one.

The reasons supporting this proposition can only be stated here in summary form. In the first place, suppression of discussion makes a rational judgment impossible. In effect it substitutes force for logic. Moreover, coercion of expression is likely to be ineffective. While it may prevent social change, at least for a time, it cannot eradicate thought or belief; nor can it promote loyalty or unity. As Bagehot observed, "Persecution in intellectual countries produces a superficial conformity, but also underneath an intense, incessant, implacable doubt."

Furthermore, suppression promotes inflexibility and stultification, preventing the society from adjusting to changing circumstances or developing new ideas. Any society, and any institution in society, naturally tends toward rigidity. Attitudes and ideas become stereotyped; institutions lose their vitality. The result is mechanical or arbitrary application of outworn principles, mounting grievances unacknowledged, inability to conceive new approaches, and general stagnation. Opposition serves a vital social function in offsetting or ameliorating this normal process of bureaucratic decay.

Again, suppression of expression conceals the real problem confronting a society and diverts public attention from the critical issues. It is likely to result in neglect of the grievances which are the actual basis of the unrest, and thus prevent their correction. For it both hides the extent of opposition and hardens the position of all sides, thus making a rational compromise difficult or impossible. Further, suppression drives opposition underground, leaving those suppressed either apathetic or desperate. It thus saps the vitality of the society or makes resort to force more likely. And finally it weakens and debilitates the majority whose support for the common decision is necessary. For it hinders an intelligent understanding of

the reasons for adopting the decision and, as Mill observed, "beliefs not grounded on conviction are likely to give way before the slightest semblance of an argument." In short, suppression of opposition may well mean that when change is finally forced on the community it will come in more violent and radical form.

The argument that the process of open discussion, far from causing society to fly apart, stimulates forces that lead to greater cohesion, also rests upon the concept of political legitimation. Stated in narrower and perhaps cruder terms, the position is that allowing dissidents to expound their views enables them "to let off steam." The classic example is the Hyde Park meeting where any person is permitted to say anything he wishes to whatever audience he can assemble. This results in a release of energy, a lessening of frustration, and a channeling of resistance into courses consistent with law and order. It operates, in short, as a catharsis throughout the body politic.

The principle of political legitimation, however, is more broadly fundamental. It asserts that persons who have had full freedom to state their position and to persuade others to adopt it will, when the decision goes against them, be more ready to accept the common judgment. They will recognize that they have been treated fairly, in accordance with rational rules for social living. They will feel that they have done all within their power, and will understand that the only remaining alternative is to abandon the ground rules altogether through resort to force, a course of action upon which most individuals in a healthy society are unwilling to embark. In many circumstances, they will retain the opportunity to try again and will hope in the end to persuade a majority to their position. Just as in a judicial proceeding where due process has been observed, they will feel that the resulting decision, even though not to their liking, is the legitimate one.

In dealing with the problem of social control, supporters of free expression likewise emphasize that the issue must be considered in the total context of forces operating to promote or diminish cohesion in a society. By and large, they theorize, a society is more likely to be subject to general inertia than to volatile change. Hence resistance to the political order is unlikely to reach the stage of disorder unless a substantial section of the population is living under seriously adverse or discriminatory conditions. Only a government which consistently fails to relieve valid grievances need fear the outbreak of violent opposition. Thus, given the inertia which so often characterizes a society, freedom of expression, far from causing upheaval, is more properly viewed as a leavening process, facilitating necessary social and political change and keeping a society from stultification and decay. . . .

. . . There can be no ironclad guarantee that in the end a decision beneficial to society will be reached. The process, by encouraging diversity and dissent, does at times tend to loosen the common bonds that hold society together and may threaten to bring about its dissolution. The answer given is that the stakes are high and that the risks must be run. No society can expect to achieve absolute security. Change is inevitable; the only question is the rate and the method. The theory of freedom of expression offers greater possibilities for rational, orderly adjustment than a system of suppression. Moreover, they urge, as the lesson of experience, that the dangers are usually imaginary; that suppression is invoked more often to the prejudice of the general welfare than for its advancement. To this they add that the risks are the lesser evil, that the alternatives are worse, that the only security worth having is that based on freedom.

Thus, the theory of freedom of expression involves more than a technique for arriving at better social judgments through democratic procedures. It comprehends a vision of society, a faith and a whole way of life. The theory grew out of an age that was awakened and invigorated by the idea of a new society in which man's mind was free, his fate determined by his own powers of reason, and his prospects of creating a rational and enlightened civilization virtually unlimited. It is put forward as a prescription for attaining a creative, progressive, exciting and intellectually robust community. It contemplates a mode of life that, through encouraging toleration, skepticism, reason and initiative, will allow man to realize his full potentialities. It spurns the alternative of a society that is tyrannical, conformist, irrational and stagnant. It is this concept of society that was embodied in the first amendment.

C. Edwin Baker, *Scope of the First Amendment Freedom of Speech,* 25 UCLA Law Review 964 (1978)*

This paper develops three theories of the scope of speech protected by the first amendment: two different marketplace of ideas theories, which I will call the *classic model* and the *market failure model,*

* Reprinted with permission.

and a third, the *liberty model.* The classic model depends on implausible assumptions for its coherence. The market failure model is unworkable, dangerous, and inconsistent with a reasonable interpretation of the purpose of the first amendment. Although the Court consistently has used and proclaimed the classic theory and though most modern reformist proposals recommend a market failure model, the liberty model provides the most coherent theory of the first amendment. Adoption of this theory, which delineates a realm of individual liberty roughly corresponding to noncoercive, nonviolent action, would have major, salutary implications for judicial elaboration of the first amendment.

The classic marketplace of ideas model argues that truth (or the best perspectives or solutions) can be discovered through robust debate, free from governmental interference. Defending this theory in *On Liberty,* John Stuart Mill argued that three situations are possible: 1) if heretical opinion contains the truth, and if we silence it, we lose the chance of exchanging truth for error; 2) if received and contesting opinions each hold part of the truth, their clash in open discussion provides the best means to discover the truth in each; 3) even if the heretical view is wholly false and the orthodoxy contains the whole truth, the received truth, unless debated and challenged, will be held in the manner of prejudice or dead dogma, its meaning may be forgotten or enfeebled, and it will be inefficacious for good. Moreover, without free speech, totally false heretical opinions which could not survive open discussion will not disappear; instead, driven underground, these opinions will smolder, their fallacies protected from exposure and opposition. In this model, the value of free speech lies not in the liberty interests of individual speakers but in the societal benefits derived from unimpeded discussion. This social gain is so great, and any loss from allowing speech is so small, that society should tolerate no restraint on the verbal search for truth.

Just as real world conditions prevent the laissez-faire economic market—praised as a social means to facilitate optimal allocation and production of goods—from achieving the socially desired results, critics of the classic marketplace of ideas theory point to factors that prevent it from successfully facilitating the discovery of truth or generating proper social perspectives and decisions. Because of monopoly control of the media, lack of access of disfavored or impoverished groups, techniques of behavior manipulation, irrational response to propaganda, and the nonexistence of value-free, objective truth, the marketplace of ideas fails to achieve the desired results. Therefore, the advocates of the market failure model conclude that objective social realities require state intervention in the speech arena, just as in the economic arena, in order to correct for these market failures, only then will freedom of speech promote socially desirable perspectives and decisions.

The liberty model holds that the free speech clause protects not a marketplace but rather an arena of individual liberty from certain types of governmental restrictions. Speech is protected not as a means to a collective good but because of the value of speech conduct to the individual. The liberty theory justifies protection because of the way the protected conduct fosters individual self-realization and self-determination without improperly interfering with the legitimate claims of others. . . .

### III. THE LIBERTY MODEL

My thesis is that the first amendment protects a broad realm of nonviolent, noncoercive activity. The method for determining the scope of protection proceeds, first, by determining the purposes or values served by protected speech. These values, however, are also served by violent and coercive activities. Thus, I conclude that constitutional protection of speech is justified not merely because of the values served by speech but because freedom of speech serves these values in a particular, humanly acceptable manner, e.g., nonviolently and noncoercively. Describing these methods is the second step of the analysis. Finally, I argue . . . that when nonverbal conduct advances the same values in a relevantly similar manner, the nonverbal conduct should be viewed as speech and should receive protection.

#### A. First Amendment Values or Purposes

In the marketplace theories, a single value—discovery of truth or reaching the "best" societal or individual decision—justified and defined the scope of protection. This focus is too limited. Professor Emerson, probably the most thoughtful and influential first amendment scholar, finds first amendment freedom essential for four values: 1) individual self-fulfillment, 2) advancement of knowledge and discovery of truth, 3) participation in decision making by all members of the society (which "embraces the right to participate in the building of the whole culture"), and 4) achievement of a "more adaptable and hence stable community."

Emerson's list is acceptable. However, it is informative to see that the first value, self-fulfillment, and the third, participation in change, are key values and to understand why conduct promoting these two values ought to receive constitutional protection.

The values of self-fulfillment and participation in change impose somewhat different requirements on

a satisfactory theory. The emphasis on "self" in self-fulfillment requires the theory to delineate a realm of liberty for self-determined processes of self-realization. The participation in change value requires the theory to specify and protect activities essential to a democratic, participatory process of change. Emerson's other two values are derivative. Given that truth is chosen or created, not discovered, advancement of knowledge and discovery of truth are merely aspects of participation in change. Also, one apparently achieves a "more flexible and thereby more stable community" by providing for individual self-fulfillment and participation in change as the key first amendment values.

Why should these two values receive constitutional protection? I will briefly summarize an answer I have advanced elsewhere. Obligation exists only in relationships of respect. To justify legal obligation, the community must respect individuals as equal, rational and autonomous moral beings. For the community legitimately to expect individuals to respect collective decisions, i.e., legal rules, the community must respect the dignity and equal worth of its members. One can elaborate this core truth of social contract doctrines in order to explain both the propriety of and proper limits on utilitarian policies. And determining the proper limits on utilitarian policies is crucial for identifying constitutional rights because having constitutional protection means that the right prevails over preference maximization policies. The justification for welfare maximization policies is that, in decision making, the state should weight each person's concerns *equally*, thereby respecting the worth of each. This required respect for people's equal worth also explains the major limit on adopting welfare maximization policies, i.e., the state's policy must respect people's integrity as rational, equal, autonomous moral beings, it must respect people as ends and not just as means. This requires that people's choices, their definition and development of *themselves*, must be respected—otherwise they become mere objects for manipulation or means for realizing someone else's ideals or desires. This respect for defining, developing or expressing one's self is precisely Emerson's value of self-realization. Moreover, since group decisions significantly influence both one's identity and one's opportunities, respecting people's autonomy as well as people's equal worth requires that people be allowed an equal right to participate in the process of group decision making—which is precisely Emerson's other key value, participation in collective decision making. Without trying to further develop this justification for the centrality of these two values, below I will merely rely on the widely accepted conclusion that *individual self-fulfillment and participation in change are fundamental purposes of the first amendment.* If, however, one accepts the justification offered here, it would help explain why utilitarian balancing does not justify limiting first amendment rights.

## B. Uses of Speech

An exploration of the uses of speech will clarify both *how* and *when* speech contributes to the key values of the first amendment. A complete elaboration of the uses of speech is impossible. But in surveying the uses of speech one must take care not to adopt a too narrow or misguided vision. A very insightful article by Professor Scanlon illustrates the problems resulting from too narrow a vision. Scanlon not only argued "that all protected acts will be 'acts of expression,'" which he defines as "any act that is intended by its agent to communicate to one or more persons some proposition or attitude," but also that "almost everyone would agree" with this conclusion. He is, I think, very wrong in his limitation of the category of properly protected acts although he is, possibly, correct that most would agree to his error.

Scanlon's ready acceptance of a marketplace of ideas theory, as evidenced by his emphasis on the intended communication of propositions or attitudes, illustrates the dominance of this model in our thinking. But his categorization of protected acts of expression is inadequate in three respects. First, it excludes many uses of speech. People continually speak or write without intending any person to hear their speech or see their writing. Moreover, people's "solitary" uses of speech—to record by keeping a diary, to organize by outlining or cataloguing, to understand by problem solving, to amuse or relax by singing or making up a story, to perform a duty by praying, or to order one's behavior by writing oneself a note—contribute to self-fulfillment and often to individual or social change. And, although this fact should not be relevant for determining the scope of the first amendment, the government sometimes attempts to control or regulate these solitary uses of speech—for example, if, as in Orwell's *1984*, the government believes the speech is an aspect of, or contributes to, resistance to the government, or if society considers the speech to be anti-social or immoral, or if the government fears the speech might lead to new knowledge or capabilities, like nuclear weapon or genetic research, that the government wants to control or suppress.

Second, many uses of speech—for example, story telling where the purpose of the story telling is to entertain rather than to promote insight—are best described as the speaker intending to do something. Attempting to force such uses of speech into the category of communicating propositions or attitudes is strained. "The paradox disappears only if we make a radical break with the idea that language always functions in one way, always serves the same purpose: to convey thoughts—which may be about houses, pains, good and evil, or anything else you please."

Third, Scanlon duplicates the marketplace model's emphasis on *content*. The speech is protected if, and because, it contains *propositions* or *attitudes* relevant to public debate. Instead, the first amendment values of *self*-fulfillment and *popular participation* in change emphasize the *source* of the speech in the self, and make the choice of the speech by the self the crucial factor in justifying protection.

In describing an alternative to Scanlon's categorization, Wittgenstein's warning should be kept in mind. He writes:

> But how many kinds of sentence are there? Say assertion, question, and command?—There are *countless* kinds: *countless different kinds of use of what we call "symbols," "words," "sentences."* And this multiplicity is not something fixed, given once for all; but new types of language, *new language-games*, as we may say, *come into existence*, and others become obsolete and get forgotten. . . . Here the term "language-game" is meant to bring into prominence the fact that *the speaking of language is part of an activity, or of a form of life* . . . .

Given this warning, one should realize that the task must be to find characterizations of language uses or forms of life that provide insight into the scope of first amendment protection, not to develop a comprehensive catalogue. Two categories of use, self-expressive and creative, cut across the communicative, noncommunicative dichotomy and closely correlate with the key first amendment values of self-fulfillment and participation in change.

To engage voluntarily in a speech act is to engage in self-definition or expression. A Vietnam war protestor may explain that when she chants "Stop This War Now" at a demonstration, she does so without any expectation that her speech will affect the continuance of war or even that it will communicate anything to people in power; rather, she participates and chants in order to *define* herself publicly in opposition to the war. This war protestor provides a dramatic illustration of the importance of this self-expressive use of speech, independent of any effective communication to others, for self-fulfillment or self-realization. Generally, any individually chosen, meaningful conduct, whether public or private, expresses and further defines the actor's nature and contributes to the actor's self-realization.

Speech is not merely communicative but also creative. The Bible reports: "And God *said*, 'Let there be light;' and there was light." For six days God spoke and named things and by these means created the world. Hannah Arendt reports that, to the ancient Greeks,

> [T]hought was secondary speech, but speech and action were considered coeval and co-equal, of the same rank and the same kind; and. . . finding the right words at the right moment, *quite apart from the information or communication they may convey*, is action. Only sheer violence is mute, and for this reason violence alone can never be great.

And, for Arendt, "to act . . . means to take an initiative, to begin." Through speech and action new worlds are created—"new" because action, which "may proceed from nowhere," "acts upon beings who are capable of their own actions," and thus "action and reaction among men never move in a closed circle. . . ." The practice of the poet parallels Arendt's description of the Greek emphasis on the creative use of speech. A poem, which "should not mean [b]ut be," requires no project but instead a "flicker of the soul." Gaston Bachelard describes the poetic image as "a new being in our language, expressing us by making us what it expresses . . . . Here expression creates being . . . . Through this creativeness the imagining consciousness proves to be, very simply but very purely, an origin."

More mundane practices may provide more convincing evidence of the creative use of language. For example, the creative use of language is particularly prominent in: 1) making up new rules for a game or practice, as well as the language embodying the new rules; 2) coining a word, forming a new verbal image; 3) writing a poem or a play; 4) verbally formulating an analysis in order to "discover" new relationships or possibilities, or a dialogue through which *both* participants gain insights which *neither* possessed before; 5) "creating" or planning a new strategy; 6) persuading another of something; 7) teaching or developing new capabilities in another. The creative aspect, the new aspect of the world which results, varies in these examples. But in each case either the speaker or the listener or both possess something new—new images, new capacities, new opportunities, new amusements—which did not exist before and which were created by people's speech activity. Often the new creation will influence behav-

ior. And in each case the creation has changed the social world, the world of meanings, opportunities, and restraints, in which people live.

Self-expressive and creative uses of speech *more fully and uniformly* promote the two key first amendment values, self-fulfillment and participation in both societal decision making and culture building, than does speech which communicates propositions and attitudes. First, *solitary uses* of speech contribute to self-fulfillment. Also, people's private analysis of their own character or of how to accomplish some goal, or people's practice of singing or of creating or viewing obscenity for private entertainment or relaxation, are all private speech activities which, by changing or defining people, change or modify the culture. Second, *communications* not intended to communicate propositions or attitudes of the speaker—such as story telling intended merely to entertain the listener, or singing intended merely to show the accomplishments of the singer, or group singing or a verbal ritual possibly intended to develop group solidarity—may both contribute to self-fulfillment and affect the culture. Third, self-expressive and creative uses properly exclude some uses that do not promote the key first amendment values but that would be included in Scanlon's market place definition. At first, the broad category of self-expressive acts might appear to include all speech acts. Nevertheless, to the extent that speech is involuntary, is not chosen by the speaker, the speech act does not involve the *self*-realization or *self*-fulfillment of the speaker. Focusing on the self-expressive uses of speech directs the inquiry toward the responsible source, not the content, of the speech. Thus, as I have argued elsewhere, if in modern America commercial advertising does not reflect anyone's voluntary or personal choice this commercial speech should not be constitutionally protected. . . .

## C. The Market Place of Ideas Revisited

One should not too quickly dismiss an analysis which has dominated informed opinion as completely as has the marketplace of ideas theory. I criticized the marketplace of ideas as a method of discovering truth or arriving at the "best" perceptions or values because its effectiveness for achieving these goals seemed dependent on several invalid assumptions. Here, my inquiry considers how protecting a broader range of expressive conduct, how forbidding general prohibitions of substantively valued conduct, blunts the criticism of the classic marketplace of ideas model. If interpreting the first amendment to include this broad protection of nonverbal conduct cures the defects of the marketplace theory, this fact would buttress the defense of this broad interpretation.

Protecting substantively valued conduct from abridgement by general prohibitions makes the hope that people will be able to make the "best" choices more plausible for at least four reasons. First, the classic model assumes that truth is discovered or found. To the extent that reality is created, the theory must be concerned with questions of who and how. Equality of opportunity to create reality provides a possible standard. However, since all conduct, not merely speech, contributes to this creation process, equality of opportunity would require a regime of *strict equality* of all resources *and skills*—a regime as unnecessary as it is inconceivable. Lack of sufficient "wealth" is only one cause of the limits on people's opportunities. In addition, general prohibitions can be used by the majority to entirely suppress opportunities for certain choices. This use of majority power can be more oppressive, more totally limiting, and is usually less justified than are limits on opportunities due to inequality of resource distribution (at least, if the inequality is not too great or if a minimum level of opportunity is guaranteed). Clearly, barring state imposed prohibitions of substantively valued conduct greatly increases opportunities of minorities to develop new realities (this notion replaces objective truth). This broadened liberty eliminates a major method by which the choice process is often limited to prevent peaceful challenges to the existing orthodoxies. Thus, such a ban seems *necessary*, whether or not sufficient, to expand people's opportunities for creating new realities.

Second, the ban on general prohibitions makes the process of creating realities much more democratic. Many people may not have the resources, the skills, or the interest to participate in a rational or political search for the best societal decisions. Most people do have an interest in their own life and their relations with others; also, most have sufficient skill (and, in the liberty model, they also have the right) to pursue their own visions and values. Only by disallowing general prohibitions can everyone, by their choice of activities, participate in the debate and in building the culture.

Third, the liberty to live one's values provides for the possibility that at present, or always, pluralism best meets human needs and goals. Moreover, by allowing this pluralism, change can occur by people living, and finding others to join in living, a set of values. Thus, peaceful, gradual change will have space and opportunity to develop.

Fourth, protecting greater liberty of action breaches the status quo bias of the marketplace of ideas. Mass communications apparently are more effective in reinforcing the status quo than in stimulating criticism. Moreover, face-to-face verbal communication and existing forms of reason typically reflect people's experience of the existing order. Even if various economic or social groups experience the existing order from radically different perspectives and evaluate it differently, that existing order dominates people's logic and perceptions when considering alternatives. By discounting preferences of the majority for limiting conduct, the first amendment protects the possibility of developing new loci of experience which potentially can falsify the existing, dominant perspectives. Moreover, this method of change requires neither violence nor the approval of the dominant societal groups. Just as in the classic market model, the power of new perspectives depends on its voluntary acceptance by people; however, protection of new, nonverbal practices allows people to make a new perspective available in a form where its logic might be coherent, thereby overcoming the status quo bias of mere verbal debate.

This revised theory replaces both the doubtful assumptions of the classic marketplace of ideas theory and its hope for a basically rational discovery of timeless truth with a defense of the legitimacy of a social process of choice. The legitimacy must be defended on at least one of two grounds: Either all people have a right to participate in the individual and social process of *self*-determination or a "better" individual and collective expression of humanity results from this social process because of the increased opportunity of each freely to participate. Either ground justifies protecting people's liberty to engage in substantively valued conduct. Moreover, both imply that eliminating or weakening existing structures of domination that influence or distort people's choices improves the process of developing and expressing values. This concern with reducing domination was the one merit of the market failure version of first amendment theory. Unfortunately, that theory's focus on equality of *speech* opportunities—usually, equality of access to channels of mass communication—belies the fact that only general economic equality would suffice to validate the approach. Because of this theoretical confusion, the market failure theorists fail to realize that providing considerable equality of access to communication channels may be less central to dismantling the existing structure of domination than banning existing restrictions, general prohibitions, or liberty. This confusion illustrates the market failure theory's basic problem; it merges the concepts of equality and liberty which provide separate, although crucial, guidance for describing a just social order.

In addition to highlighting these mistakes of the market failure or equal access theory, the liberty approach avoids the problems which engulf that theory. The liberty model avoids offering the false hope that dissenting positions, even without a real basis in experience, can be shown to be best; instead, it provides for a more realistic method of change from "the bottom up." The liberty model, which protects noncoercive uses of speech and forbids enforcement of general prohibitions on substantively valued behavior, provides clearer, less subjective criteria for proper government action than the market failure model provides. Also, because it guarantees a realm of liberty rather than a properly functioning market, one can correct for perceived infringements of the guarantee by violating the "improper restriction" on liberty rather than taking the possibly violent action needed to get "proper results."

By protecting substantively valued conduct from abridgement by general prohibitions, the liberty model provides for a process of public decision making and a search for, or creation of, truth that avoids the problems and improper assumptions of both the market models. Thus, the liberty model better promotes the key value that justified the classic marketplace of ideas theory of freedom of speech: the value of furthering the search for truth or best premises, a value that, due to a failure of assumptions, the classic theory could not adequately serve. These observations provide convincing support for this liberty theory. . . .

---

Martin H. Redish, *Freedom of Expression: A Critical Analysis* (1984)*

Commentators and jurists have long searched for an explanation of the true value served by the first amendment's protection of free speech. This issue certainly has considerable intellectual appeal, and the practical stakes are also high. For the answer we give to the question, what value does free speech serve, may well determine the extent of constitutional protection to be given such forms of expression as literature, art, science, commercial speech, and speech related to the political process.

There seems to be general agreement that the Supreme Court has failed in its attempts to devise a coherent theory of free expression. These efforts have been characterized by "a pattern of aborted doctrines, shifting rationales, and frequent changes of position by individual Justices." Commentators, by contrast, have been eager to elaborate upon their unified theories of the value of speech. . . .

The position taken here is that the constitutional guarantee of free speech ultimately serves only one true value, which I have labeled "individual self-realization." This term has been chosen largely because of its ambiguity: it can be interpreted to refer either to development of the individual's powers and abilities—an individual "realizes" his or her full potential—or to the individual's control of his or her own destiny through making life-affecting decisions—an individual "realizes" the goals in life that he or she has set. In using the term, I intend to include both interpretations. I have, therefore, chosen it instead of such other options as "liberty" or "autonomy," on the one hand, and "individual self-fulfillment" or "human development," on the other. The former pair of alternatives arguably may be limited to the decisionmaking value, whereas the latter could be interpreted reasonably as confined to the individual development concept.

That the first amendment serves only one ultimate value, however, does not mean that the majority of values thought by others to be fostered by free speech—the "political process," "checking," and "marketplace-of-ideas" values—are invalid. I have not chosen from a list of mutually exclusive possibilities, nor do I argue that the value that I have selected supersedes these alternatives. My contention is that these other values, though perfectly legitimate, are in reality subvalues of self-realization. To the extent that they are legitimate, each can be explained by—and only by—reference to the primary value: individual self-realization. It therefore is inaccurate to suggest that "the commitment to free expression embodie[s] a complex of values."

In this Chapter, I attempt to establish that the first principle—individual self-realization—can be proven, not merely by reference to some unsupportable, conclusory assertions of moral value, but by reasoning from what we in this nation take as given: our democratic system of government. It demonstrates that the moral norms inherent in the choice of our specific form of democracy logically imply the broader value, self-realization. It then concludes that all forms of expression that further the self-realization value, which justifies the democratic system as well as free speech's role in it, are deserving of full constitutional protection.

---

An analysis of the self-realization value must avoid giving it an unduly restrictive interpretation. Any external determination that certain expression fosters self-realization more than any other is itself a violation of the individual's free will, recognition of which is inherent in the self-realization principle. I therefore argue that the Supreme Court should not determine the level of constitutional protection by comparing the relative values of different types of speech, as is the current practice. . . .

In summary, then, my thesis rejects those authorities (1) who believe that the first amendment is multivalued, whether they superimpose a hierarchy upon those values or recognize them as interdependent coequals; (2) who argue that the first amendment is single-valued, with that value being something other than individual self-realization; (3) who, although accepting the self-realization value or its rough equivalent as the sole determinant of free speech, refuse to acknowledge one or more of the various subvalues that derive from it; and (4) who believe that total reliance on something akin to the self-realization value is inconsistent with any form of constitutional balancing process with regard to free speech. . . .

I. Self-Realization and the Democratic Process: Ascertaining the Ultimate Value of Free Speech

A. THE "DEMOCRATIC PROCESS" VALUE

An appropriate way to begin analysis of the self-realization value is, ironically, with a discussion of the theory of free speech perhaps furthest in practical result from that value: the view that the sole purpose of the free speech guarantee is to facilitate operation of the democratic process. Advocates of this position are logically required to establish two propositions: first, that the first amendment facilitates the political process, and second, that the first amendment does not foster any value other than conduct of the political process. Examination of the writings of those expounding this view reveals that they have established the former with considerably greater force than they have established the latter.

As already noted, the original exponent of such a theory was Professor Meiklejohn. He began with the premise that "[g]overnments . . . derive their just powers from the consent of the governed. If that consent be lacking, governments have no just powers." Because government officials in a democracy are merely agents of the electorate, the electorate needs as much information as possible to aid it in performing its governing function in the voting booth. Therefore, "[t]he principle of the freedom of speech springs from the necessities of the program of self government. . . . It is a deduction from the basic American agreement that public issues shall be decided by universal suffrage."

Few would argue with Meiklejohn's logic to this point. If the electoral decisions made by the voters are to be based on anything more than emotive hunches, they need a free flow of information that will inform them not only about the candidates but also the day-to-day issues of government. But what seemed counterintuitive to some was the apparent implication of Meiklejohn's theory that such "nonpolitical" forms of speech as art, literature, science, and education were not protected by the first amendment. Meiklejohn himself ultimately concluded "that the people do need novels and dramas and paintings and poems, 'because they will be called upon to vote.'" He thus included within the category of "political" speech numerous forms of expression that do not appear to have any direct—or arguably even indirect—impact upon the political process. He would presumably give full first amendment protection to both the author and the reader who profess absolutely no interest in the political system, and who have never voted and never will, but who simply enjoy writing or reading good fiction. For this extension of his theory, Meiklejohn has been attacked both by those who believe that the first amendment has no special political basis and by political "purists" who accept Meiklejohn's initial premise about the relationship between the first amendment and the political process, but question the logic of his extension.

Judge Bork begins his analysis with this same premise about the political process, but rigidly limits his conclusion to such speech, thus escaping the attack levelled at Professor Meiklejohn. Judge Bork, however, has great difficulty explaining why the first amendment should be read to protect only political expression.

Judge Bork's first amendment analysis flows from his concern that constitutional interpretation be premised on "neutral principles." The decisions of the Supreme Court "must be controlled by principle, which may be defined as 'reasons with respect to all the issues in a case, reasons that in their generality and their neutrality transcend any immediate result that is involved.' " Judge Bork concludes that only speech serving the political process can be deemed "principled."

The method by which Judge Bork reaches this conclusion may be described as a lesson in the limits of the "neutral principles" concept. It demonstrates all too clearly that if the selection of premises is flawed, "neutral principles" will not prevent a doctrine from being applied in a similarly flawed—albeit "principled" and consistent—manner. Judge Bork begins his analysis by quoting the well-known concurrence of Justice Brandeis in *Whitney v. California*. Brandeis identified what Bork has distilled into four benefits provided by the free speech guarantee: "[t]he development of the faculties of the individual; [t]he provisions of a safety value [sic] for society; and [t]he discovery and spread of political truth." Bork then proceeds to explain why the first three values cannot be considered values of the first amendment under a "principled" analysis.

Since Justice Brandeis's first category is the closest to the concept of individual self-realization urged here, it is most relevant to determine why Judge Bork concludes that this value cannot be thought to lie behind the constitutional guarantee. Although Bork does not deny that free speech may develop individual faculties, he nevertheless believes that the development of an individual's faculties and the happiness derived from engaging in speech

> do not distinguish speech from any other human activity. An individual may develop his faculties . . . from trading on the stock market, following his profession as a river-port pilot, working as a barmaid, engaging in sexual activity, playing tennis, rigging prices or in any of thousands of endeavors. . . . These functions or benefits of speech are, therefore, to the principled judge, indistinguishable from the functions or benefits of all other human activity.

Judge Bork ultimately concludes that Justice Brandeis's fourth category—the search for "political truth"—is the only legitimate ground of the first amendment. This conclusion in turn leads him to adopt a first amendment construction that is quite probably the most narrowly confined protection of speech ever supported by a modern jurist or academic: "Constitutional protection should be accorded only to speech that is explicitly political. There is no basis for judicial intervention to protect any other form of expression, be it scientific, literary or that variety of expression we call obscene or pornographic."

Judge Bork's rationale for including political speech and excluding nonpolitical forms of expression, even if they further the value of self-fulfillment, is that it is logically possible to limit the value served by political speech to "speech." Self-fulfillment, on the other hand, cannot logically be limited to "speech" but must also be taken to include countless forms of action. Judge Bork's conclusion that political speech should be protected is, however, inconsistent with his belief that any acceptable rationale for

free speech must be logically unique to speech. For there are countless actions—such as a bombing by the FALN to protest oppression of Puerto Rico, an assassination of a foreign political leader because of human rights violations in his country, and the breaking of windows at the Iranian Consulate to protest the treatment of Americans in Iran—that can be thought to convey very significant political messages. Those who undertake such activities could argue with a fair degree of persuasiveness that the public attention attracted to such acts is geometrically greater than that which would be received by public statements or pickets. Even if we rejected this argument, however, the issue for Judge Bork is not whether the value in question can be furthered by speech, as well as by conduct, but whether it can *only* be furthered by speech. Bork otherwise could not exclude nonpolitical speech that aids individual self-fulfillment on the ground that conduct may also aid such a goal. It is, therefore, difficult to understand how he can protect political speech, when countless forms of political action could achieve similar results.

Political actions, unlike some of the faculty-developing activities referred to by Judge Bork, have as an essential part of their purpose a communicative aspect. But it is unlikely that Bork would be satisfied with a distinction based on communicative purpose, since he leaves little doubt that he would not choose to protect such actions. In any event, there are numerous non-communicative, nonspeech activities that may be thought to aid in the attainment of political truth. For example, working as a farmer could help one understand the problems and benefits of farm price supports; working as a doctor could do the same with respect to socialized medicine; living in a large urban area and taking public transportation might convince one of the need for greater federal aid to cities and mass transit. Thus, nonspeech activities could aid attainment of knowledge of political truth as much as does any political discourse. Bork's logic therefore must be rejected, because it inescapably results in the content of speech protected by the first amendment being a null set: there is no category of expression that furthers a value or values unique to speech.

If one were to look for an appropriate basis for limiting the protection of the first amendment to "speech," the natural starting place would seem to be the language of the amendment itself, which says nothing about protecting only political speech. What the language does refer to is "speech," and not action. Thus, we need not find a logical distinction between the value served by speech and the value served by conduct in order to justify protecting only speech, for the framers have already drawn the distinction. Whether or not the constitutional language must be read to provide absolute protection to speech, there can be little doubt that it was intended to provide greater protection to speech than to conduct, which is relegated to the fifth amendment's protection against deprivation of "liberty" without "due process of law." Indeed, that the framers deemed it necessary to create a first amendment at all, rather than merely include speech within the other forms of liberty protected by the fifth amendment, indicates that speech is to receive a constitutional status above and beyond that given to conduct.

It is not hard to understand why constitutional protection of speech would be greater than that of conduct. The first amendment may be viewed as a recognition of the overriding importance of developing the uniquely human abilities to think, reason and appreciate. It is true that on occasion noncommunicative conduct may develop these intellectual faculties, and that speech at times may cause harm. But if we were to draw a rough distinction—the kind that must necessarily have been drawn by the framers—we could reasonably decide that speech is less likely to cause direct or immediate harm to the interests of others and more likely to develop the individuals' mental faculties than is purely physical conduct, and that speech thus deserves a greater degree of constitutional protection than does conduct. Bork's assumption that any principled first amendment theory must rely solely on values that are *uniquely* protected by speech effectively removes all categories of speech from the amendment's protection.

## B. DERIVING THE ULTIMATE VALUE

The primary flaw in the analysis of Bork and Meiklejohn is that they never attempt to ascertain what basic value or values the democratic process was designed to serve. Examination of the "process" values inherent in our nation's adoption of a democratic system reveals an implicit belief in the worth of the individual that has first amendment implications extending well beyond the borders of the political world. Indeed, political democracy is merely a means to—or, in another sense, a logical outgrowth of—the much broader value of individual self-realization. The mistake of Bork and Meiklejohn, then, is that they have confused one means of obtaining the ultimate value with the value itself.

The logic employed by Meiklejohn and Bork to reach their conclusion that the protection of speech was designed to aid the political process would have

absolutely no relevance except in a democratic system. For a monarchy or dictatorship to function politically, it of course is not necessary that the general public be able to speak freely or receive information about pressing political questions, because private individuals will have no say in decisions. Even a benevolent dictator would be more likely to allow free expression in traditionally nonpolitical areas such as art, literature, and music than in the political realm. The free speech value emphasized by Meiklejohn and Bork, then, is inherently linked to a democratic form of government.

Democracy is by no means the only system that could have been chosen when our nation was founded. Indeed, it is probably safe to say that the overwhelming majority of organized societies throughout history have not chosen it, even in its most diluted form. It would seem, then, that there must be some values that the founding fathers believed to be uniquely fostered by a democracy, values that succeeding generations of political leaders presumably have shared, since there has been little or no effort to alter substantially our system of government by constitutional processes.

One conceivable value is "consequentialist" in nature: efficiency. One could believe that the results of a democratic system are somehow better than any other system's. Such an argument, however, would be difficult to prove for several reasons. Initially, it would probably be difficult to obtain agreement on the criteria for measuring results. How are we to decide what is "better"? Higher gross national product? More international influence? And better for whom? Elites? A majority? Oppressed minorities? Secondly, it is doubtful that we could establish empirically that throughout history democracies have fared better than other forms of government. After all, we do know that the trains ran on time in Mussolini's Italy; can the Chicago Transit Authority make the same claim? Moreover, it may well be counterintuitive to believe, especially in a modern, highly technological society, that decisions made by the masses or their elected representatives—who are rarely chosen because of any degree of real expertise—would be either the wisest or the most efficient. Finally, it is doubtful that many of us would be anxious to discard democracy even if it were established definitely that an alternative political system was more efficient. It is likely, then, that the values inherent in a democratic system are "process-oriented," rather than related to some objective standard of governmental efficiency.

These "process" values seem to translate into two forms: an "intrinsic" value and an "instrumental'' value. The ''intrinsic'' value is one that is achieved by the very existence of a democratic system. It is the value of having individuals control their own destinies. For if one does not accept the morality of such a proposition, why bother to select a democratic system, in the first place? As Meiklejohn said, ''[i]f men are to be governed, we say, then that governing must be done, not by others, but by themselves. So far, therefore, as our own affairs are concerned, we refuse to submit to alien control.'' The point is so obvious that it requires no further elaboration, except to say that the core concept of ''self-rule'' appears to have formed the cornerstone of every theory of democracy to date. It would seem to be so as a matter of definition.

The second value of a democratic system is labeled ''instrumental,'' because it is a goal to which a democratic system is designed to lead, rather than one that is attained definitionally by the adoption of a democratic system. It is a goal that is associated primarily with ''classical'' (fully participatory) democracy: development of the individual's human faculties. In the words of a leading authority:

> The most distinctive feature, and the principle orienting value, of classical democratic theory was its emphasis on individual participation in the development of public policy. . . . Although the classical theorists accepted the basic framework of Lockean democracy, with its emphasis on limited government, they were *not* primarily concerned with the *policies* which might be produced in a democracy; above all else they were concerned with *human development*, the opportunities which existed in political activity to realize the untapped potentials of men. . . .

My thesis is that: (1) although the democratic process is a means of achieving both the intrinsic and instrumental values, it is only one means of doing so; (2) both values (which, as noted previously, may be grouped under the broader heading of ''self-realization'') may be achieved by and for individuals in countless nonpolitical, and often wholly private, activities; and (3) the concept of free speech facilitates the development of these values by directly fostering the instrumental value and indirectly fostering the intrinsic value. Free speech fosters the former goal *directly* in that the very exercise on one's freedom to speak, write, create, appreciate, or learn represents a use, and therefore a development, of an individual's uniquely human faculties. It fosters the latter value *indirectly* because the very exercise of one's right of free speech does not in itself constitute an exercise of one's ability to make life-affecting decisions as much as it *facilitates* the making of such decisions. This conceptual framework indicates that the appropriate scope of the first amendment protection is much broader than Bork or Meiklejohn would have it. Free speech aids all life-affecting decisionmaking, no matter how personally limited, in much the same manner in which it aids the political process. Just as individuals need an open flow of information and opinion to aid them in making their electoral and governmental decisions, they similarly need a free flow of information and opinion to guide them in making other life-affecting decisions. There thus is no logical basis for distinguishing the role speech plays in the political process. Although we definitely need protection of speech to aid us in making political judgments, we need it no less whenever free speech will aid development of the broader values that the democratic system is designed to foster. . . .

## Bibliography

*The Value of Expressive Freedom*

Alexander, Lawrence A. & Horton, Paul, *The Impossibility of a Free Speech Principle*, 78 Northwestern University Law Review 1319 (1983).

Blasi, Vincent, *The Checking Value in First Amendment Theory,* 1977 American Bar Foundation Research Journal 521 (1977).

Bollinger, Lee C., *The Tolerant Society* (1986).

Cass, Ronald A., *The Perils of Positive Thinking: Constitutional Interpretation and Negative First Amendment Theory*, 34 UCLA Law Review 1405 (1987).

Farber, Daniel A., *Free Speech Without Romance: Public Choice and the First  Amendment*, 105 Harvard Law Review 554 (1991).

Greenawalt, Kent, *Free Speech Justifications*, 89 Columbia Law Review 119 (1989).

Kalven, Jr., Harry, *The New York Times Case: A Note on "the Central Meaning of the First Amendment,"* 1964 Supreme Court Review 191 (1964).

Post, Robert C., *The Constitutional Concept of Public Discourse: Outrageous Opinion, Democratic Deliberation and* Hustler Magazine v. Falwell, 103 Harvard Law Review 601 (1990).

Richards, David A.J., *Free Speech and Obscenity Law: Toward a Moral Theory of the First Amendment*, 123 University of Pennsylvania Law Review 45 (1974).

Scanlon, Thomas, *A Theory of Freedom of Expression*, 1 Philosophy & Public Affairs 204 (1972).

Schauer, Frederick, *Must Speech Be Special?*, 78 Northwestern University Law Review 1284 (1983).

Schlag, Pierre, Freedom of Speech As Therapy, 34 UCLA Law Review 265 (1986).

Sherry, Suzanna, An Essay Concerning Toleration, 71 Minnesota Law Review 963 (1987).

Shiffrin, Steven, The First Amendment and Economic Regulation: Away From a General Theory of the First Amendment, 78 Northwestern University Law Review 1212 (1983).

Shiffrin, Steven, The First Amendment and Romance (1990).

Tribe, Laurence H., Toward a Metatheory of Free Speech, 10 Syracuse University Law Review 237 (1978).

Wellington, Harry H., On Freedom of Expression, 88 Yale Law Journal 1105 (1979).

## B. Origins

The articles in this section analyze the history of the First Amendment. Gerald A. Berlin's book review *Leonard Levy: Legacy of Suppression* discusses Leonard Levy's position that freedom of speech "had almost no history as a concept or a practice prior to the First Amendment or even later." Leonard W. Levy's article, *The Legacy Reexamined*, 37 Stanford Law Review 767 (1985), responds to critics of his first book, *The Legacy of Suppression*. Levy concedes that "after the enactment of the Stamp Act, in 1765, American newspapers *practiced* freedom of the press," but sticks to his original thesis that "neither the American Revolution nor the framers of the first amendment intended to abolish the common law of seditious libel." William T. Mayton's *From a Legacy of Suppression to the "Metaphor of the Fourth Estate,"* 39 Stanford Law Review 139 (1986), contends that "in the body of his work about speech, it seems to me that Levy has incorrectly assessed some important constitutional and historical materials."

Gerald A. Berlin, Book Review: *Leonard W. Levy, Legacy of Suppression,* 72 YALE LAW JOURNAL 631 (1963)*

The doctrine of seditious libel derives from the English common law. It maintains that the mere expression of critical opinions which disturb the public repose by holding the government up to contumely constitutes a crime. By definition, then, the doctrine is incompatible with the notion of a truly open society, where presumably any citizen is free to express any opinion of the government, no matter how unpopular, as long as the expression does not immediately and directly result in an incitement to crime.

It has long been a school boy's copy book maxim, let alone a fundamental postulate in the constitutional interpretation of the meaning of free speech, that a major objective of the American Revolution and of the enactment of the First Amendment was to repeal the English common law of seditious libel and install in its stead freedom of speech and press. Judges, from Holmes to Brandeis to Black and Douglas, and constitutional historians, from Madison to Schofield and Chafee have iterated and reiterated the concept. Nor would the concept appear to be something manufactured and distributed by latter day libertarians for their own purposes. For one can assume that if contrary authority existed, the decisions of our time restricting free speech and assembly, or dissents to those decisions protecting them, would have employed it.

Now comes Dean Leonard W. Levy and alleges that the king has no clothes. It is his contention that this entire host of distinguished jurists and constitutional commentators was plainly wrong in concluding that the Bill of Rights, at the time of its adoption, embodied a wide latitude for freedom of expression. On the contrary, he argues that only after the Jeffersonians, when still a minority party, were obliged to defend themselves against the Federalist Sedition Act of 1798, did a broad libertarian freedom of speech and press emerge in the United States. Moreover, once in power, the Jeffersonians were as intolerant of political criticism as the Federalists. Levy insists, in fact, that freedom of speech as an independent concept was virtually unheard of at the time of the framing of the Bill of Rights.

That freedom had almost no history as a con-

cept or a practice prior to the First Amendment or even later. It developed as an offshoot of freedom of the press, on the one hand, and on the other, freedom of religion—the freedom to speak openly on religious matters. But as an independent concept referring to a citizen's personal right to speak his mind, freedom of speech was a very late development, virtually a new concept without basis in everyday experience and nearly unknown to legal and constitutional history or to libertarian thought on either side of the Atlantic prior to the First Amendment . . . .

This thesis, which is as disturbing as it is astonishing, requires more than a cursory summation. Its origins lie well back in English and American Colonial sources. According to the common law as taught by Blackstone, freedom of the press meant simply protection against restraint prior to publication; there was no protection subsequent to publication for seditious or licentious utterances. During the Colonial period the law of sedition was enforced widely and harshly, though chiefly by the provincial legislators. The executive officials and courts in the colonies were far less involved in tracking down nonconformist opinions. The Zenger trial, Levy suggests, was so notorious in part because, as a judicial proceeding, it was a relatively isolated phenomenon.

Nor did Blackstone's common law of criminal libel include the defendant's right to introduce the truth of the libel as a defense or his right to have the jury rather than the judge decide if the words were criminal. These limitations on freedom of speech and of the press greatly exercised the libertarians. Indeed, almost their sole preoccupation in the Eighteenth Century, both in England and America, was with these two notions. Apparently it did not occur to them that the truth of an opinion is not susceptible to proof, and that juries in dealing with truth's purveyors are no more likely to withstand prevailing prejudices than judges. After examining a stupefying array of Court decisions, newspaper accounts, statutes, trial records, treatises, pamphlets, correspondence, and other primary and secondary sources, Levy concludes that the libertarians of that day never even remotely approached the presupposition now so commonly associated with the framing of the First Amendment, namely, that it is not possible criminally to assault the government by mere words. The great libertarian figures of two centuries, from the Star Chamber to the American Revolution, in both countries are examined: in England, William Walwyn, John Locke, "Cato," Roger Williams, John Lilburne and John Wilkes; in America, William

* Reprinted by permission of The Yale Law Journal and Fred B. Rothman & Company from *The Yale Law Journal,* vol. 72, pp. 631–638.

Penn, Alexander MacDougall, Peter Zenger and his attorney, Andrew Hamilton, and Benjamin Franklin. Only one of this group—either explicitly or by implication—disavowed the doctrine of seditious libel. The others did not even acknowledge the right to call for the peaceful overthrow of the Government. Indeed, the great majority of them explicitly embraced the validity of the doctrine. Madison and Jefferson, otherwise so voluble, remained totally silent on the question until well after the First Amendment had been framed. Among this exalted line only Jeremy Bentham stands in unequivocal opposition. True, some lesser English figures—Furneaux, Kippis and Ratcliffe—did attack the application of seditious libel to religious freedom, but not the doctrine *per se*. The debate on the Bill of Rights during the ratification, so Levy's argument continues, was conducted with vague rhetorical references to freedom of the press but without precise definition as to the meaning of that freedom. Neither the great Bill of Rights advocates, such as Jefferson, Patrick Henry, Elbridge Gerry, Richard Henry Lee, and George Mason, nor the newspapers, pamphlets, or the ratifying convention debates provide insight. Probably most of the founding fathers were satisfied that existing common law adequately protected the freedoms in question. At the most, they would have demanded the right to show truth as a defense and to have the jury determine the whole question of libel. Levy thinks that much of the whole Bill of Rights controversy and rather happenstantial wording of the First Amendment itself as finally enacted was a consequence of the political struggle between those favoring strong state and those favoring strong central government. He puts it thus:

> But the history of the ratification indicates no passion on the part of anyone to grind underfoot the common law of liberty of the press. Indeed the history of the framing and ratification of the First Amendment and the other nine scarcely manifests a passion on the part of anyone connected with the process. Considering its immediate background, our precious Bill of Rights was in the main the chance result of certain Federalists, having been reluctantly forced to capitalize for their own cause the propaganda that had been originated in vain by the Anti-Federalists for ulterior purposes. Thus the party that had first opposed a Bill of Rights inadvertently wound up with the responsibility for its framing and ratification, while the party that had at first professedly wanted it discovered too late that its framing and ratification were not only embarrassing but inexpedient.

And so it was not until seven years after the Bill of Rights was framed that the theory now conventionally accepted as American libertarianism emerged. It coincides with the passage of the Sedition Act of 1898 under the Adams administration. The Act made "any false, scandalous and malicious" publications against the government a criminal offense. Truth was a defense and a jury could determine the entire criminal libel. Fearing a Federalist victory in 1800 through a one-party press and the stifling of political criticism and consequent control of public opinion, the Jeffersonian party's writers "were driven to originate so broad a theory of freedom of expression that the concept of seditious libel was, at last, repudiated," Madison, Gallatin, Hay, St. George Tucker, and others, when they attacked the constitutionality of the Sedition Act, constantly avowed among other things that there could be no libel of a free republican government; that the intent of the Framers was to supersede the laws of sedition; that the First Amendment freedoms were absolute with respect to the United States; and that they had been purposely left undefined so as not to limit future generations. Tucker, significantly, included these theories in the edition of Blackstone which he edited, and which, says Levy, was for many years thereafter the standard edition of the American bench and bar. It is these assertions which eventually became woven into our constitutional tradition.

In sum, the noble American libertarian theory is itself the creation of historical revisionism—a revisionism engendered by political imperatives of the day.

The thesis of *Legacy of Suppression*, then, is a somber one. How well does it stand up? A number of considerations will engage the thoughtful reader.

First, there is the language of the Amendment itself, "Congress shall make no law . . . abridging the freedom of speech, or the press . . . ." Could anything be more explicit? A whole body of judicial writing asserts that no amount of historical interpretation or logical inference can surmount the absolute sweep of those words: if the English language had any meaning to the Framers, Congress could abridge *no* speech, including seditiously libelous speech. Such an assertion, however, not only ignores the complete absence of any sources to indicate any intention of the Framers to make the Federal protection absolute, but most certainly fails to explain the advent of the Sedition Act within only seven years after the Amendment's framing. The latter circumstance alone would appear conclusive of the issue. An argument based on the plain meaning of the Amendment's words becomes still more dubious when we note that the Framers did not have the slightest intention of restricting the states' power to deal with seditious libel. (This would explain, though it would hardly justify, the prosecutions of Jefferson's administration.) Unless one is prepared to argue, as Mr. Justice Jackson has done, that the Federal government has narrower latitude than the states in seditious libel matters, the Framers' attitude toward the states may by implication be read back into their strictures on the federal government. But in the continuing debate over the extent to which the word "liberty" in the due process clause of the Fourteenth Amendment embodies the freedom of speech of the First, this distinction, suggested by Mr. Justice Jackson, has yet to find any takers on the Court.

Second, there is the short shrift that Levy gives to the influence of such English thinkers as Bentham, and of Furneaux, Kippis, Ratcliffe, Erskine, and Dawes. For Bentham, it is sufficient that he dealt with the question only as a passing abstraction, not as an actual problem; for the others, that they restricted themselves to religious controversy. True, the history of religious liberty is indissociable from the history of freedom of expression; but where the commentaries, as here, stopped short of addressing themselves to the extent of governmental power, it can scarcely be said in the absence of further proof that they somehow must have created the new and radically heightened political awareness necessary to outlaw seditious libel.

Third, the question has been raised whether sufficient attention has been given by Levy to public feeling and political climate at the time of the framing. The obvious reply is that if popular political expression is not found in the writings and public records of the day, which Levy has so meticulously examined, the feelings probably did not exist in any large measure. Nevertheless, one cannot but wonder whether there might not have been a significant amount of popular feeling behind the (unsuccessful) attempt in the Pennsylvania Assembly in 1788 to institute impeachment proceedings against two judges for convicting a newspaper publisher of seditious libel, and if so, what inspired it.

Finally, Levy has been accused of misrepresenting what Chafee really said in his great classic, *Free Speech in the United States*. Chafee considers seditious libel and the Bill of Rights at length in the very first chapter and he concedes that the Framers "say very little about its exact meaning." Nonetheless, he concludes that a consideration of all the factors "leaves the Blackstonian interpretation . . . without a leg to stand on." No, it is not fair to say that Levy has distorted Chafee's conclusions.

If, as has been said, the writing of history is a determination of the weight of the evidence, then, all things considered, there can be no doubt that Levy's case must stand as proven beyond all reasonable doubt. If such a conclusion is more appropriately arrived at by a professional historian than by a practicing attorney, it nevertheless gives rise to two searching questions that are bound to trouble a historian, a lawyer, or anyone else who is concerned about free speech in the United States. One, how is it that the assumptions which Levy demolishes have existed unchallenged until now? The other, do the implications of the book portend dire consequences for a liberal interpretation of free speech?

The first question, to which Levy does not address himself at all, is dealt with more easily. There were no seditious libel cases considered by the Supreme Court between the 1798 Sedition Act and the cases arising out of the 1917-1918 Espionage Acts. During those four generations, the towering authority of Madison, the father of the Bill of Rights, and of Jefferson, coupled with the writings of the other Jeffersonian Democrats, had made their impact. Had not Madison actually participated in the drafting of the Amendment, and therefore did he not know whereof he spake? Then came Holmes, joined by Brandeis, and in a line of significant free speech cases lent their own immense authority to the endorsement of the Madison-Jefferson legend. By the time such great constitutional authorities as Schofield and (particularly) Chafee had also endorsed the legend, perhaps with more fervor than research, the canonization of the concept of absolute free speech was complete. In other words, the legend has existed because of its original power and nobility, because of the length of the subsequent period during which there was no case to challenge it, and because the stature of the great judges and commentators of our day embraced the legend overshadowed the inadequacy of their scholarly inquires into the nature of its origin. Thus did it spring and remain full blown in our constitutional jurisprudence.

But Levy says:

No citizen, and certainly no jurist worthy of his position, would or should conclude his judgment on either a constitutional question or a matter of public policy by an antiquarian examination of the original meaning of the freedom of speech-and-press clause.

Well, whatever eminent liberal judges would or should do about the freedom of speech-and-press clause, they have certainly not hesitated to conclude their judgments both on constitutional questions and on public policy matters by an antiquarian examination of the original meaning of the establishment clause of the First Amendment. Consider Mr. Justice Black's decision in the *Everson* and the New York Regents *Prayer* cases and, particularly, Mr. Justice Rutledge's dissent in *Everson*. Maybe the Black and Rutledge historical analyses are correct. But what if they are subsequently proven to be otherwise? To what extent is the integrity of the judicial process undermined? It is difficult to conceive a more stark warning against this type of constitutional construction than *Legacy of Suppression*.

More important is the second question, Does the book seriously damage the case for free speech? This much is plain, it does not help the cause. Whether it will wreak mischief remains to be seen. Hopefully, the American libertarian tradition is now so well established that reformulation at this late date of the notions of the greatness of its origins can have little effect on it. One assumes that the faith of the believer has not been irreparably shattered by the discovery of the Dead Sea Scrolls. Conversely, those judges who have sought to abridge political activity short of overt acts have found it possible to do so without the necessity of elaborate historical justification. And latterly there has developed what some observers believe is a distinct tendency to "balance" freedom of expression out of any real meaning.

Yet it does not do, on the basis of such considerations, to take the thesis of this work lightheartedly. Who can deny, for example, the role that historical re-evaluation of original Scriptural texts eventfully played in bringing about the Reformation? No, the devout free speech believer, after such a book as this, must find his refuge in Tertullian's adage, "Certum est, quia impossibile est."

---

Leonard W. Levy, *The Legacy Reexamined,* 37 STANFORD LAW REVIEW 767 (1985)*

In my book, *Legacy of Suppression*, I challenged the conventional wisdom about the intent underlying the press clause of the first amendment. I argued that historical evidence showed that while the clause was meant to restrain the federal Congress absolutely, it was not intended to restrain the states or the federal courts. I further argued that even if the amendment

* 1985 by the Board of Trustees of the Leland Stanford Junior University.

had a broader reach, the "freedom of the press" it originally protected was freedom from licensing, censorship, and other forms of prior restraint. It did not protect the press from subsequent punishment for its publications. Specifically, it was not meant to eliminate the law of seditious libel.

I remain convinced that the revolutionary generation did not seek to wipe out the core idea of seditious libel, that the government may be criminally assaulted by mere words, that the legislatures were more suppressive than the courts, that the freedom of political expression remained quite narrow until 1798 (except for a few aberrant statements), that English libertarian theory usually stayed in the vanguard of American theory, that the Bill of Rights in its immediate history was in large measure a lucky political accident, and that the first amendment was as much an expression of federalism as of libertarianism. I still contend that tarring and feathering a Tory editor because of his opinions shows a rather restricted meaning and scope of the freedom of the process. Indeed, one may ask whether there was free speech during the Revolutionary era if only the speech of freedom was free.

But *Legacy of Suppression* is scarcely beyond criticism. The most common fault found by knowledgeable reviewers was that it paid insufficient attention to press practices. Those critics were right. In researching *Legacy*, I scanned hundreds of issues of colonial, revolutionary, and early national newspapers looking for discussions of freedom of the press. The discussions I found reflected only stunted understandings, but I was oblivious to the fact that after the enactment of the Stamp Act, in 1765, American newspapers *practiced* freedom of the press. Their pages screamed out scathing denunciations of public men and measures.

The legal definition of seditious libel remained what it had been from the time of Hawkins to Mansfield—malicious, scandalous falsehoods of a political nature that tended to breach the peace, instill revulsion or contempt in the people, or lower the citizenry's esteem for its rulers. But the scope of actual political discourse had widened so greatly that seditious libel was reduced to a narrow category of verbal offenses against the government, its officials, and its policies. Prosecutions were infrequent and the press was habitually scurrilous.

State governments realized that prosecutions might fail or backfire because critics often represented strong factions or influential citizens. Moreover, (except in a time of crisis, such as Shay's Rebellion) the populace tended to distrust an administration that sought to imprison its critics. Indeed, the press could not have endured as calumnious and hostile as it was without public support. For the most part, people understood that scummy journalism unavoidably accompanied the benefits to be gained from a free press. They also seemed to understand that critics vented unfavorable opinions in order to excite a justifiable contempt for the government and that to prosecute those critics would be to immunize from criticism public officials who probably deserved to be disliked or distrusted. That was the teaching of *Cato's Letters* and the Zenger case. The actual freedom of the press had slight relationship to the legal conception of freedom of the press as a cluster of constraints.

In short, the law threatened repression, but the press conducted itself as if the law scarcely existed. The American experience with a free press was as broad as the theoretical inheritance was narrow. The obvious conclusion from this, which I failed to draw in *Legacy*—and which none of my critics drew—is that the framers of the press clauses of the first state constitutions and of the first amendment could only have meant to protect the press as they knew it. In other words, they constitutionally guaranteed the *practice* of freedom of the press. They did not adopt its legal definition as found in Blackstone or in the views of the libertarian theorists. By freedom of the press, the framers meant a right to engage in rasping, corrosive, and offensive discussions on all topics of public interest. A narrow understanding of the common law definition had become unsuitable for a republican nation. Although libertarian theory had not caught up with press practice, that practice established a foundation for the new libertarianism that would emerge after the Sedition Act.

I do not gracefully accept my acknowledgment that the press of the new nation functioned as if the law of criminal libel hardly mattered. My principal thesis—that neither the American Revolution nor the framers of the first amendment intended to abolish the common law of seditious libel—remains unchanged. The argument that freedom of political expression existed as a fact and therefore undermines the thesis of *Legacy of Suppression* is an odd one in some respects, on all fours with the proposition that the existence of so many heretics during the reign of Bloody Mary proves there was a great deal of freedom of religion, despite the fires at Smithfield. I am interested, to use an analogy, in the concept of crime, and therefore do not find crime-rate statistics to be helpful. In our own time, obscenity is illegal, although we live in a society saturated by it and witness few prosecutions. So too the rarity of prosecutions for seditious libel and the existence of an unfettered press do not illumine the scope and meaning of freedom of the press or the law on freedom of the press.

· · ·

## I. MAYTON'S NEW UNDERSTANDING

### A. Federalism and Delegated Powers

The Antifederalists urged the states not to ratify the Constitution in part because it lacked a bill of rights. The members of the Constitutional Convention had omitted a bill of rights because they believed that it would be superfluous. As I wrote in *Legacy*:

> The Federalists who expressed themselves on the subject unanimously concurred in stating that Congress, or the "general government," had no power whatever to legislate in a manner violative of personal liberties, no power, for example, to legislate on matters respecting speech or press unless to protect literary property by enacting copyright laws. A bill of rights, as Hamilton argued, would be a bill of restraints on national powers, but "why declare that things shall not be done which there is no power to do? Why, for instance, should it be said that the liberty of the press shall not be restrained, when no power is given by which restrictions may be imposed." The Framers intended a federal system of government to exercise only such powers as were specifically enumerated or were necessary and proper to carry out those enumerated. It followed that the power to punish for criminal libels was denied to the United States in the minds of the Framers. They had vested no such power and intended that none be exercised or abused. In other words, the Framers believed that even without an express limitation such as that later imposed by the First Amendment, Congress was bereft of authority to restrict freedom of speech or press in any manner.

· · ·

If the framers were right in 1787, Mayton, though derivative, is also right; the first amendment, indeed, the entire Bill of Rights, need not have been added to the Constitution, and it "contributed to a misinterpretation of the original scheme" of constitutional protections. By this reasoning, the unamended Constitution extended strong protections against infringements of religious liberty, the right to counsel, and due process of law. It also strongly protected citizens against unreasonable searches and seizures, compulsory self-incrimination, and cruel and unusual punishments. In fact, it extended strong protection to every right mentioned in the Bill of Rights.

The American people of 1787 understood, however, that they were entitled to an explicit reservation of their rights against government, that a bill of rights is a bill of restraints upon government, and that people may be free only if the government is not. They understood a point that escapes Mayton: If the crime of treason required a tight, written definition, other rights required explicit definitions too. Those who demanded a bill of rights had the better argument if only because of the Framers' obvious inconsistencies. The Constitution explicitly protected some rights, but not others. Moreover, a strong argument could be made that everything not reserved had been delegated to the national government by implication. As James Wilson declared:

> A bill of rights annexed to a constitution is an enumeration of the powers reserved. If we attempt an enumeration, everything that is not enumerated is presumed to be given. The consequence is, that an imperfect enumeration would throw all implied powers into the scale of the government and the rights of the people would be rendered incomplete.

That theory causes the argument from structuralism to self-destruct. Moreover, as proponents of a bill of rights contended, delegated powers, especially when implemented by the necessary and proper clause, might be exercised in a way to abridge reserved rights. It was James Madison and not some Antifederalist demagogue who—in a speech that is a running refutation of Mayton's structuralism argument—urged Congress to recommend amendments that would protect "the great rights of mankind," and declared that Congress might employ general warrants in the enforcement of its tax measures. And Antifederalists, answering *The Federalist* 84 and Wilson's State House Yard speech, warned that Congress might abridge the freedom of the press by taxing the press or, in the absence of a restraint upon Congress, by enacting a sedition act.

## B. The Treason Clause

Mayton argues that the Framers intended the treason clause to prevent seditious libel prosecutions by protecting dissident speech in two ways: First, by requiring an overt act, the clause prevents speech alone from constituting treason. Second, by eliminating a historical English category of treasonous offenses—"compassing or imaging the king's death"—it prohibits punishment of speech as "constructive treason." Mayton relies for his proof "on the processes of drafting and ratifying the original Constitution" and asserts that "[t]hese processes were such as to force a break with the historical

practices of both seditious libel and constructive treason." But Mayton offers little historical evidence to prove his points about the treason clause, perhaps because such evidence does not exist. Moreover, even if he were correct about the history, and speech could not be punished as treason, that would not prevent the prosecution of speech as some other crime.

Nothing in the records of the Constitutional Convention bears out Mayton's historical thesis, so it is not surprising that he offers no proof as to the drafting of the treason clause. As for ratification, he has one pertinent but slight piece of evidence. In North Carolina, Richard Dobbs Spaight observed that under the treason clause complaints or writings alone could not constitute treason. This is the only evidence purporting to prove that the Framers intended the treason clause to prohibit prosecutions for seditious libel. Mayton attempts to bolster his argument by referring to statements by James Wilson, James Madison, James Iredell, and George Nicholas. None of these statements, however, construed the treason clause as a protection of free speech or even referred to free speech. Mayton also relies upon the work of Willard Hurst, who concluded that the treason clause was meant to be a free speech provision. But despite Hurst's illustrious reputation, he asserted the proposition without proving it. Hurst referred only to the ratification debates in North Carolina and Virginia, showed only Spaight making the nexus between free speech and the treason clause, and conceded that even in 1798, when the constitutionality of the Sedition Act was at issue, only John Taylor in the Virginia Assembly relied on the treason clause to oppose the Sedition Act. Neither the Jeffersonians in the Congress, nor Madison and Jefferson in the Virginia and Kentucky Resolutions, nor Madison in his attack on the Sedition Act in his *Report* of 1799-1800 suggested that the treason clause prohibited sedition laws. Yet Mayton confidently declares: "The recorded discussion of the treason clause shows a common understanding of the clause as a free speech provision."

Describing the treason clause as a free speech protection is not baseless, if one really believes that there is a possibility of Congress designating dissident speech as treason. In the seventeenth century some dissident speech could be punished under the rubric of "compassing or imaging the king's death," a branch of constructive treason. Because the treason clause embraces only overt acts, it prevents dissident speech from being construed as treason. Mayton makes this point by focusing on the overt acts provision of the treason clause, although he might just as well have focused on the clause's definition of treason: levying war against the United States or adhering to its Enemies, giving them Aid and Comfort. Mayton's agenda, however, requires that he lay a basis for his claim that speech, as contrasted with overt acts, should be constitutionally immune from prosecution.

But the treason clause does not prevent the prosecution of dissident speech or press, because the government can charge an offense other than treason. Mayton approvingly quotes *Legacy* for the assertion that "[u]tterances once held to be treasonable became wholly assimilated within the concept of seditious libel" by the early eighteenth century. This assimilation mooted the issue of dissident speech being treason. In any case, the clause prevents the government from prosecuting dissident speech as treason, but not from prosecuting dissident speech. The treason clause did not prevent the Sedition Act and was not the basis for a constitutional attack on that act. Nor did the clause prevent prosecutions for constructive treason having nothing to do with dissident speech. John Adams and Thomas Jefferson drafted a model treason act in 1776, but the two also drafted the first American articles of war, which punished by courts-martial any "traitorous or disrespectful words" against the authority of the United States or of a state in which the offender might be quartered. The latter document remained in effect until 1806, when Jefferson was President. At one point a staunch Jeffersonian in Congress denounced the provision against "traitorous" words as a second sedition law. Congress responded by substituting "contemptuous" for "traitorous" but extended the offense to include criticisms of the President. An authoritative historian of military law, asserting that the right to use "contemptuous" words against the President and Congress "is of the essence of civil liberties of a citizen," has compared this provision to the Sedition Act. Nonetheless, the article proscribing contemptuous and disrespectful words against the government or the President shows that the treason clause did not protect dissident speech. The primary function of the treason clause is to prevent treason convictions for overt acts that fall short of levying war or adhering to the nation's enemies. Given the Constitution's definition of treason, any overt *acts* not squaring with that definition would constitute constructive treason; Mayton conveys the inaccurate impression that constructive treason referred only to dissident speech. If the treason clause ended constructive treason, as he asserts, the reason is that the courts have thwarted the government's promiscuous interpretations of the Constitution's definition of treason.

Mayton wrongly concludes that eliminating the old treason of compassing the death of the king denied to Congress the power to suppress speech by devising constructive treasons. The crime of compassing the king's death "continued [in England] through the ratification of the United States Constitution." Mayton mentions trials in England in 1794 and concludes that the framers "specifically" blocked such suppression of political dissent by enacting the treason clause. But Mayton's chronology is wrong, his cause-and-effect analysis is wrong, and he has no proof for his thesis about the purpose of the treason clause other than the remark by Spaight. The crime of compassing the king's death had effectively died out in England long before the framing of the Constitution. The most recent case involving a prosecution for compassing the king's death occurred in 1663. Mayton cites none more recent.

In any case, compassing the king's death could not possibly have been a crime in republican America. The United States dropped that category of treason, not as a result of the treason clause having as its object the protection of dissident speech, but as a result of the Declaration of Independence. Denying the authority of the Crown and laying a legal foundation for prosecutions of dissident Tory speech added to the reasons for dropping that category of treason.

Mayton seems to place his emphasis on constructive treason and compassing the king's death because he wants to justify his assertion that the overt act test is the proper test for prosecutions of speech. He attempts to demonstrate the existence of a consensus that an overt acts requirement foreclosed the possibility that dissident speech could be prosecuted under the treason clause. But the historical record is not as conclusive as Mayton portrays it. The Statute of Treasons of 1352 included the crime of compassing the king's death but required an "overt act." This fact leads Mayton to state: "Speech, in and of itself, was not however, generally thought to constitute treason or 'an overt act' . . . ." But that was no longer true by the time of Henry VIII, when, as Mayton notes, treason statutes were enacted "without the overt act requirement and aimed at dissident speech." Forgetting this, Mayton then constructs an eccentric history of the rise of seditious libel, casting the Star Chamber as the villain, and tells us that seditious libel was created as a new crime that "did not fall under the English Statute of Treasons and thereby evaded the overt act limitation." *Twyn's Case* in 1663, which Mayton describes, and *Sidney's Case* in 1683, which he doesn't mention, proved that speech and writings had become overt acts for which a person could be prosecuted under the law of treason. *Pine's Case* of 1629 is Mayton's authority for the rule that speaking disrespectful words about the king was not treason. The rule of *Sidney's Case*, however, is that the deliberate act of writing the words, even if unpublished, is an overt act proving the treason.

Nonetheless, Mayton relies on the overt acts test to prove that the unamended Constitution structurally extinguished the power of the United States to punish the crime of seditious libel. A close reading of his sources shows that they do not prove what he claims they do. For example, he says that James Wilson "described seditious libel" as an unwarranted attempt by the Star Chamber to wrest libel law to the purpose of the ministers. Neither in the passage cited nor anywhere else did Wilson refer to seditious libel. Wilson made no reference to words against government or government officials or to anything else that might be described as "seditious libel." He referred only to the fact that the "malicious defamation of any person" was a common law crime. Mayton does not distinguish between criminal libel, based on malicious defamation of a person, and seditious libel, based on malicious defamation of the government, its measures, or its officers.

Mayton's structuralism argument, based on the principle of federalism and the treason clause, is an artificial construct based on inferences that enable one to prove whatever one pleases by abstract logic. If appropriate historical evidence does not matter, we could embellish the structuralism argument almost at will.

Mayton's structuralism thesis sets forth the treason clause as a free speech guarantee that established an overt acts test for determining the criminality of words, thus overturning the doctrine of seditious libel. That thesis is as valid and convincing as would be structuralism arguments spun out of the guarantee clause, the legislators' free speech clause, and the privileges and immunities clause. The value of those arguments from the standpoint of logic may be considerable (which I doubt); but as revelations of the original meaning of the free press, they are worthless, absent historical proofs from 1791 and earlier.

## II. A LEGACY OF IDEALISM?

Mayton's section on "a legacy of idealism" purports to dismiss about 150 pages of intensive analysis of eighteenth century thought on freedom of the press that I presented in *Legacy of Suppression*, even while drawing on—and distorting—that analysis. The eighteenth century political philosophy to which the framers of the Constitution were heirs did not, as Mayton claims, reject the doctrine of seditious libel. Such a rejection did not occur until the 1790s, after the framing of the Constitution. Nor was the overt acts test—to determine when the government has infringed "a forbidden zone of speech"—"establish[ed]" in the eighteenth century. "Establish" conveys a sense of permanency not mere advocacy or suggestion; in neither law nor theory did the overt acts requirement become established as a test for the criminality of political speech either in the eighteenth century or afterwards. By the close of that century it was still a rarely endorsed or advocated principle.

Mayton states that in the eighteenth century, "notions about the incompatibility of democratic government with the suppression of political speech were strong and well known." He documents this, however, not with evidence from 1735 or 1776 or 1787, but from Madison's *Report* of 1799-1800 and some remarks by Sir James Fitzjames Stephen. Mayton does not seem to recognize that Madison frequently changed his mind regarding freedom of the press. In 1788 he switched from opposing to supporting a bill of rights, and in early 1799 he favored state prosecutions for criminal libel, but by the close of that year favored only private damage suits. Given Madison's record of switching, and absent proof that in 1789 he held the views expressed later, Mayton's reliance on Madison's later views as revelations of his earlier ones is anachronistic. Mayton's reliance on the writings of James Fitzjames Stephen is also misguided. Stephen did not examine eighteenth century political philosophy and was not summarizing an eighteenth century viewpoint; he was presenting his own liberal Victorian viewpoint. Stephen's chapter on seditious libel, which summarized only case law and treatise writers, does not mention a single instance of the repudiation of the doctrine of seditious libel. In fact, Stephen concluded his section on seditious libel in the eighteenth century with a discussion of Fox's Libel Act of 1792, which allowed English juries to decide whether the words used by a defendant constituted seditious libel.

Mayton offers not a fig leaf of evidence to cover his naked assertion that eighteenth century thought rejected the doctrine of seditious libel. He quotes no sources from before 1794 that say anything that amounts to a rejection of that doctrine. *Legacy* quoted many people rejecting the doctrine, both in England and America, after the adoption of the first amendment, but not before.

. . .

Mayton begins his discourse on eighteenth century political philosophy with a description of Spinoza's theory of free speech. Mayton neglects to discuss the significant exceptions that Spinoza made to his principle that words should not be punished. The state, Spinoza wrote, has the "right to treat as enemies all men whose opinions do not, on all subjects, entirely coincide with its own," although, properly, it should punish only politically injurious speech—the equivalent of a sedition act. All "opinions would be seditious . . . which by their very nature nullify the compact by which the right of free action was ceded." Encouraging the people to disagree with their rulers, counseling civil disobedience, advocating the enactment of laws by unconstituted authority, or teaching against the keeping of contracts were, for Spinoza, exceptions to his rule that only overt acts, rather than mere words, should be punishable. Even Spinoza, for all his tolerance, drew the line at seditious utterances, which he construed as tantamount to seditious acts.

According to Mayton, John Trenchard and Thomas Gordon (writing in the 1720s as "Cato"), and James Alexander "objected to laws against speech because of their indeterminacy." But Mayton offers no proof to support this; and he cannot, because it is false. He also alleges that Cato argued that government could not legitimately wield a power over public speech. In fact, Cato argued that it could.

Cato declared that he did not wish to be misunderstood as arguing for the uncontrolled liberty of men to calumniate each other or the government. He stated: "Libels against the Government . . . are always base and unlawful," especially when untrue, and should be punished as an abuse of liberty so long as England's "very good laws" were "prudently and honestly executed, which I really believe they have for the most part been since the Revolution." In a related essay, Cato reinforced the thought by saying, "I do agree, when the natural and genuine Meaning and Purport of Words and Expressions in libellous Writings carry a criminal Intention, that the Writer ought not to escape Punishment by Subterfuge or Evasion . . . ." Perhaps, as I pointed out in *Legacy*, these are mere genuflections that served to keep Cato on the safe side of the existing law. Cato believed that the law of criminal libel was neither good nor prudently executed, indeed, that it proved quite dangerous to public liberty and good government. He disapproved of prosecutions for libel except in extreme cases and even then only under a law which did not penalize criticism whose validity was demonstrable. But he would not have violated the law even if he had said outright that seditious libel was a Star Chamber doctrine that should be abandoned. So it is unlikely that his statements favoring punishment of seditious libel were insincere.

Alexander, the editor of the *New York Weekly Journal*, wrote the articles for which John Peter Zenger, the paper's printer, was indicted for seditious libel. I praised Alexander as the greatest American libertarian theorist of the colonial period; he masterminded Zenger's defense, and after being disbarred by Chief Justice James DeLancey, secured the legal services of Andrew Hamilton, whom he briefed. Alexander also wrote the report of the case that made it live in our history. The Zenger defense did not rely on a repudiation of the law of seditious libel, at least not of its core concept that the government can be criminally assaulted by words alone. Rather, the defense relied on an appeal to the members of the jury that they should decide whether the publications were libelous, and should acquit Zenger if they believed the publications to have been true. Neither Alexander nor Hamilton rejected the doctrine of seditious libel. In 1733 Alexander wrote that anyone who spoke "irreverently and disrespectfully of Magistrates . . . was and is, always will be, criminal . . . ." A year later, Alexander commented: "[Some printers] abused the press with impunity, and I cannot understand how any honest man can see anything, especially a thing essential to the preservation of the Constitution, abused with great satisfaction." He conceded that "abuses that dissolve society and sap the Foundation of Government are not to be sheltered under the Umbrage of the Liberty of the Press." The Hamilton-Alexander trial argument granted that "nothing ought to excuse a man who raises a false charge or accusation, even against a private person, and that no manner of allowance ought to be made to him who does so against a public magistrate." Hamilton never conducted a frontal assault on the concept of seditious libel. He praised criticism of a "bad administration" or an "arbitrary government," but did not defend the lawfulness of criticism of a good or just government. So too, Alexander conceded in his 1737 essay on freedom of speech that "to infuse into the minds of the people an ill opinion of a just administration, is a crime that deserves no mercy . . . ."

Another of Mayton's witnesses is Ben Franklin. Mayton states that Franklin did not even support state prosecutions for seditious libel, because he favored only state laws providing civil remedies for defamation. In the essay by Franklin that Mayton discusses, however, Franklin did not mention defamation of the government except to say in passing that those guilty of it should be tarred and feathered. During a lifetime in politics and publishing, Franklin never criticized the doctrine of seditious libel. On the contrary, he actively supported the prosecution of William Smith and William Moore in 1758 by championing their "kangaroo" trial—by the assembly—for breach of parliamentary privilege in the form of seditious libel. Franklin never endorsed or advocated the view that a republican government and the law of seditious libel are incompatible. If, as Mayton said, Franklin's essay of 1789 disapproved of anything approximating seditious libel laws, Federalist advocates of the Sedition Act would not have quoted Franklin as if he supported their view. Jeffersonians, incidentally, did not dispute the point.

At the Pennsylvania ratifying convention, James Wilson, a great Framer, declared "that there is given to the general government no power whatsoever concerning [the press] . . . ." Mayton relies on this quote, but then quickly moves on. Wilson, however, did not stop at that point. In reply to Antifederalist charges that federal judges might proceed under federal statutes punishing libels, Wilson continued:

> I presume it was not in the view of the honorable gentleman to say that there is no such thing as libel or that the writers of such ought not to be punished. The idea of the liberty of the press is not carried so far as this in any country—*what is meant by liberty of the press is that there should be no antecedent restraint upon it*; but that every author is responsible when he attacks the security or welfare of the *government*, or the safety, character and property of the individual.
>
> With regard to attacks upon the public, the mode of proceeding is by a prosecution. . . .

Wilson's statement leaves no doubt that he believed the law of seditious libel to be in force, because he spoke of the legal responsibility of writers who attacked the security or welfare of the government, and he added that for such attacks the remedy was prosecution. He believed that the federal courts had jurisdiction over seditious libel, because in the same statement he referred to Article III of the Constitution, which describes the judicial power of the United States. No one at the Pennsylvania convention denied Wilson's exposition of the law.

Mayton declares accurately that James Iredell of North Carolina denied that Congress could legislate on the press except to make copyright law. Mayton does not state, however, that in the same paragraph of the same essay Iredell praised England as a place "where the press is as free as ourselves." And, despite his approving quotation from a 1799 circuit court opinion on the treason clause by Justice Iredell, Mayton does not disclose that in the same opinion Iredell expounded a Blackstonian view of the free press clause of the first amendment. According to Mayton, Iredell's view that Congress or the general government had no power over the press represented a "consensus" that "included those opposed to the Constitution." The remark is obtuse because most Antifederalists warned that were the Constitution ratified, Congress would suppress the press. Mayton

does not understand that the reason Wilson and the Federalists reiterated that Congress had no power over the press is that they were refuting an Antifederalist charge; nor does Mayton understand that the first amendment was added to the Constitution to allay the public's fear, aroused by that charge, that Congress would and could harm a free press. The elementary fact is that Antifederalists and Federalists shared no consensus about the power of the United States.

In a different sense Mayton is right. Richard Henry Lee, a major Antifederalist leader, and James Iredell represented a consensus in the sense that both believed that the meaning of a free press clause should be sought in England. England was Lee's model, for he believed that the common law adequately protected freedom of the press. In England, he declared in his "Federal Farmer"—the most widely read and influential Antifederalist tract—the people had obtained the Magna Carta, the power of taxation, the 1689 Bill of Rights, "and, as an everlasting security and bulwark of their liberties, they fixed . . . the freedom of the press." That is, in 1694, Parliament allowed the expiration of the laws requiring the prior restraint of the press, and the press had been free ever since. That was the Blackstonian view, the basis of the consensus.

Mayton relies quite heavily on the Statute of Religious Freedom, enacted by Virginia in 1785, because it explicitly embodied the overt acts test. But neither Jefferson, the author of the bill, nor Madison, who secured its passage, nor Virginia, the state that enacted it, applied the overt acts test to political opinions. The test applied to religious opinions only.

Jefferson had first proposed a religious liberty provision in 1776, when drafting a constitution for Virginia. The first two drafts of his 1776 religious liberty clause suggest the narrowness of his thinking on the scope of *political* expression. The initial draft, after declaring that no person should be compelled to frequent or maintain any religious service or institution, added "but seditious behavior [is] to be pun[ish]able by civil magistrate[s] acc[or]d[in]g to the laws already made or hereafter to be made." On reconsideration, he bracketed but did not delete this phrase. In his second draft, Jefferson again revealed his impulse to punish politically unacceptable opinions: "*But [the liberty of religious opinion] shall not be held to justify seditious preaching or conversation against the authority of the civil government.*" Again, on reconsideration Jefferson bracketed the quoted words. He apparently groped for a way to insure the unfettered right to propagate religious opinion without relinquishing the power of the state to curb dangerous political expression and without permitting freedom for seditious opinions under the guise of religious expression. In the end Jefferson omitted the restrictive clause from the third and final draft, possibly because he recognized that the task at hand was to guarantee religious liberty rather than to acknowledge the unquestioned power of the state to prosecute seditious libels. The right to religious liberty, moreover, was the one above all others to which he was most deeply devoted, and he was willing to take risks to insure it.

Significantly, Jefferson never applied the overt acts test to political opinions. Although his own religious faith was deeply held, he felt quite indifferent about that of others. In his *Notes on the State of Virginia*, which he began in 1780, Jefferson remarked that whether his neighbor said that there were twenty gods or none, "neither picks my pocket nor breaks my leg." But political opinions could pick his pocket or break his leg: He worried about permitting religiously founded opinions "against the civil government"; he supported political test oaths; he denied civil rights to nonjurors; and he was ready to imprison carriers of "traitorous opinions" in times of crisis. In 1783, when proposing a new constitution for Virginia, Jefferson exempted the press from prior restraints but provided for prosecution in cases of false publication. In 1788, when urging Madison to support a bill of rights to the new federal Constitution, Jefferson made the same recommendation. Madison construed this recommendation in its most favorable light, observing: "The Exemption of the press from liability in every case for *true facts* is . . . an innovation and as such ought to be well considered." Yet, after such consideration, Madison did not add the truth-as-a-defense principle to the amendment on the press which he offered when proposing a federal bill of rights to Congress. Yet Madison's phrasing appeared too broad for Jefferson, who stated that he would be pleased if the press provision were altered to exclude freedom to publish "false facts . . . affecting the peace of the confederacy with foreign nations." Such a clause would have great suppressive possibilities in the context of a foreign-policy controversy like Jay's treaty, the Louisiana Purchase, or the Embargo Acts.

Jefferson's threshold of tolerance for hateful political ideas was less than generous, and he intended his great statute to protect only beliefs about religion. "The declaration that religious faith shall go unpunished," he wrote in 1788, "does not give impunity to criminal acts dictated by religious error."

Finally, Mayton distorts my thesis that a new libertarianism emerged after the passage of the Sedition Act, alleging, without evidence, that it already existed prior to 1789. The new libertarianism rejected the principles of the Zenger defense, which had epitomized the liberalism of the eighteenth century on the issue of freedom of the press. The new libertarianism finally realized that those principles insufficiently protected the press, because the Sedition Act, its infamous reputation notwithstanding, incorporated Zengerian principles. Mayton, however, presents the Sedition Act as embodying for the first time the principles of Blackstonianism, as if no one previously had supported subsequent punishment for licentious or malicious misuse of the freedom of the press. On one brief comment by Spaight, Mayton erects a thesis about the treason clause being a free speech provision. In the process, he ignores dozens of comments by theorists, legalists, printers, and constitutionmakers acknowledging that freedom of the press meant only no prior restraints, or that freedom of the press did not immunize seditious libel. In the sense that Blackstonianism implied that seditious libel was a crime, the Sedition Act embraced Blackstonianism and the new libertarianism repudiated it. What was new about the new libertarianism was the outright rejection of the very concept of seditious libel. The new libertarianism asserted that free republican government and the crime of seditious libel were incompatible even at a state level. It repudiated the old distinction between licentiousness and liberty, abandoned the requirement of proving malice as being of little use to a defendant in a political trial, assaulted the claim of truth-as-a-defense on the ground that the truthfulness of political opinions could not be proved, and perhaps most significantly, discarded reliance on the jury as a defense against prosecutorial and judicial bias. The new libertarianism relied on the overt acts test; although the test was not new, invocation of it in cases of political opinion was.

---

William T. Mayton, *From a Legacy of Suppression to the "Metaphor of the Fourth Estate,"* 39 Stanford Law Review 139 (1986)*

In an article recently published in this review and entitled *The Legacy Reexamined*, Leonard Levy reaffirmed his well-known thesis that the first amendment as adopted "substantially embodied the Blackstonian definition [of freedom of speech and the press] and left the law of seditious libel in force." At the same time, and in the larger part of the article, Levy

---

* © 1986 by the Board of Trustees of the Leland Stanford Junior University.

was sharply critical of ideas that I have expressed about the structural protections of speech and the press offered by the Constitution. In this criticism, however, and indeed in the body of his work about speech, it seems to me that Levy has incorrectly assessed some important constitutional and historical materials.

The flaws that I see in Levy's work have to do with a certain understanding of the first amendment. This understanding is of that amendment as first of all a "positive and absolute reservation" in favor of speech and the press of certain institutional and organizational arrangements of the original, unamended Constitution. This understanding is quite different than that of a first amendment that establishes only an amorphous right to speak—a right that might then be defined, as Levy does, by reference to the doctrine of seditious libel.

In response to Levy's criticism, I will first briefly describe the structural arrangements that the first amendment preserves. These arrangements, and the ideas they serve, are not novel; nor may they now, at a time when speech is relatively free, seem especially pressing. Their immediacy, however, is substantiated by Professor Blasi's important and recently developed thesis of a first amendment kept lean and trim and "targeted for the worst of times."

## I. THE PROCESS OF RIGHTS

To a large extent, the protection we today afford speech and the press is in terms of the *rhetoric* and process of rights. The rhetoric is usefully compelling: The "right to speak" evokes a regard for speech and the values that it serves. James Madison, the principal author of our Bill of Rights, made just this point about rhetoric, and offered it as a primary justification for a positive declaration of rights. But Madison also felt that the *process* of rights has its problems, and that in the sense of strong legal protections these problems might reduce a declaration of rights to ineffectual "parchment barriers."

In terms of process, a right is a check available to an individual against a power held by government. This check ordains no substantive result. Rather, it simply compels an assessment by the courts of the propriety of government power in the context of the asserted right. In the case of speech, this judicial assessment invites a "conflict between the rights of a particular speaker as an individual and the competing interests of the community as a whole." In this conflict, speech has at inopportune times been the loser. Judges, while always extolling the importance of a right to speak, have sacrificed that right—perhaps to majoritarian sentiment, perhaps to undifferentiating

fear, and perhaps to unfocused and poor guesses about public policy.

These breakdowns support Madison's point that in the context of democratic institutions, the protections offered by a jurisprudence of rights may be reduced to ineffectual "parchment barriers." Once a democratic body gains the *power* to suppress speech so as to serve the public good, judicial protection of an individual's right to speak—in the face of the popular support that often accompanies that power—is difficult. Not impossible or improbable, but difficult.

Of as much concern as a weak form of judicial review is the problem that much of the suppression of which government is capable may altogether evade that review. Many individuals, as well as the institutional press, are not sufficiently hardy to withstand the rigors and costs of litigation. They therefore choose not to speak, and thus their right to speak is empty. Besides this self-censorship, there are a number of more directly suppressive governmental activities that also evade review, including suppression by police spies, informers, and *agent provocateurs*. Self-censorship and police suppression are in turn enhanced by a characteristic of laws against speech. These laws tend to be intrinsically overbroad and indeterminate. Given this overbreadth, laws against speech create a "pall" of self-censorship and political surveillance, where judicial review is unavailable, and where a "right" to speak is therefore oxymoronic.

A rights-oriented approach to speech invites and accommodates familiar problems of balancing, self-censorship, and political surveillance. But is there a way of avoiding or diminishing these problems? Perhaps. Rather than conceding the government's power to suppress speech and then falling back on a jurisprudence of rights to limit that power, why not a first concern, indeed a discipline, of denying such power. In fact, such a denial of power is a first concern of the United States Constitution.

## II. THE "AMERICAN IDEA" OF SPEECH

The original unamended Constitution protected speech, but not by denoting a right. Instead, this protection was by limitations and dispersals of the government's power over speech, and this was what James Madison meant when he referred to the "American idea of [speech]." In its main parts, this idea does not seem the result of a grand political philosophy of the framers. Rather, it seems more a product of certain necessities of its time—certain social conditions, federalism, and the demands of the ratification process—and for that a better Idea.

One determinant of the "American idea" of speech and government was that in the society that approved the Constitution the press had in practice become free. It was robust and flourishing, a frequent and trenchant critic of public matters and public officials. As Merrill Jensen has pointed out, "[n]o government institution, political faction, or individual was [then] free from attacks such as few newspapers today would dare to print." Also, the society in which the press flourished had an important sense of community, and a desire to preserve that sense of community was a reason for the Constitution's federalism. At the same time, the English experience of a press throttled by central government—by royal prerogative and central bureaucratic control—in the case of speech no doubt reinforced the general American distrust of centralized governmental power.

Symbiotically, these things—a robust press, a strong sense of community, and a distrust of centralized power—all came together. The Constitution had to be ratified where this symbiosis was strong, by "conventions of the people" assembled in the states, and these people would not likely accept a constitution that gave the new national government the power to curtail their lively freedom of expression.

As the debate about speech under the proposed Constitution was joined, the federalists argued that the Constitution's preservation of this freedom of speech and the press lay in its disarming the new national government of a power over speech. This theory started at the constitutional convention in Philadelphia, where the assembly moved to add to the Constitution the declaration that "the liberty of the Press should be inviolably observed." But after the explanation that "[t]he power of Congress does not extend to the Press," that motion was defeated.

Following the convention, the premises of the proffered Constitution's "no power" guarantee were explained, this time to the people, in the crucial ratification debates. As propounded in these debates, in "theory and practice . . . government, with special [limited] powers . . . is better than a government with general powers and special exceptions." Part of this theory was that a list of "special exceptions" (rights) would inevitably be incomplete. Another part was that the very listing of a right, especially of a right to speak, might be used to infer a governmental power with respect to the substance of that right. Also, there was Madison's concern that in the context of democratic institutions, a bill of rights might be reduced to ineffectual "parchment barriers." "In Virginia," Madison said, "I have seen the bill of rights violated in every instance where it has been opposed to a popular current."

These premises all supported the protection of speech through limitation of the national government's power. Accordingly, James Wilson, in the ratification debates in Pennsylvania, explained that "it will be found that there is given to the general government no power whatsoever concerning [the press]; and no law, in pursuance of the Constitution can possibly be enacted to destroy that liberty." Assurances such as these were repeated throughout the ratification process. Thus, it seems clear that the Constitution was ratified on the understanding that the national government had no power over speech. In fact, this understanding was stated explicitly in Virginia, where the Constitution was approved by a resolution that formally stated the following understanding about speech:

> Whereas the powers granted under the proposed Constitution are the gift of the people, and every power not granted thereby remains with them, . . . and, among other essential rights, liberty of conscience and of the press cannot be cancelled, abridged, restrained, or modified, by any authority of the United States.

This protection of speech and the press was unconditional. The framers, however, had not failed to see that speech might cause injury that a government might legitimately seek to redress. Government might, for instance, seek to suppress speech injurious to reputation or speech that might lead to bodily injury (e.g., conspiracy to murder). But in the allocation of powers upon which the Constitution was built, this sort of injurious speech was to be addressed by the states in the exercise of their residual police power. And that allocation, as Madison explained, "account[ed] for the policy of binding the hands of the federal government."

These grants and limitations of power were the "American idea" of speech and government, and the first amendment, as added to the Constitution, was not meant to change it. As that amendment's principal author, James Madison, explained: "no power whatever over the press was supposed to be delegated by the Constitution, as it originally stood, and . . . the amendment was intended as a positive and absolute reservation of it." This purpose is carried out by the text of the amendment, as it denies power by prescribing that "Congress shall make no law . . . ." Indeed, the various relations and forces, the practicalities and the exigencies, that I have described were caught in a nutshell in 1799 by George Hay, and then tied to the first amendment:

The federal government had been organized,

and its operation had commenced, some time before the [first] amendment became a part of the constitution. During this period, the press *was free*, from any control. . . . The measures of the government were subjects of general discussion, and were stated sometimes truly, sometimes falsely, at the discretion of the writer. Nothing that was said, however false, however scandalous, could be noticed by the government. In this state of things, a clause is added to the Constitution, which declares that the freedom of the press shall not be abridged. In other words the press shall continue to enjoy that total exemption from legislative control, which at this moment it possesses.

A reasonable question is whether this understanding that political speech, "however false and however scandalous," could not be "noticed" by the federal government is anachronistic. It might be inasmuch as today, the limited powers structure upon which that understanding of speech depends has largely been abandoned. In the case of speech, though, abandoning the limited powers is especially inconsistent with the Constitution, as by its first amendment the document makes a special case— "Congress shall make no law"—for speech.

Also, an application of the first amendment's no power command remains useful and viable. It may diminish the costs (of self-censorship and police suppression) associated with standing laws against speech. In this regard, the emphasis of a limited powers mode of review is that of nullifying illegitimate assertions of power by voiding those laws that provide the occasion for self-censorship and police suppression.

In terms of viability, a no power approach provides tougher and more jural directions for the courts. Instead of requiring judges to balance a speaker's interests against societal interests (which directly exposes judges to "popular currents"), a limited powers mode of review involves the drier and more abstract determination of whether, *ex ante*, government had the power to act according to its view of the public interest. In this mode of review, the courts should in the case of speech, and outside the economic sphere of *McCulloch v. Maryland*, simply not apply the implied powers doctrine. At the very least, they should *not*, as Marshall stated in *McCulloch*, defer to a congressional implication of a power over speech.

Finally, the power limiting "Congress shall make no law" part of the first amendment is especially consistent with a first amendment lean and trim and targeted for the worst of times. Its application is in the zone of greatest danger, that of suppression of dissident speech at the hands of central government. And in this zone it is strongly backed by what Professor Blasi so persuasively argues is essential to an amendment strong enough for the worst of times: it is backed by history and the intent of the framers.

## III. SEDITIOUS LIBEL

The original understanding about speech and American government has another significance in that it refutes Leonard Levy's assertion that the first amendment "substantially embodied the Blackstonian definition [of a freedom of speech and the press] and left the law of seditious libel in force." In the limitations of power that the first amendment guarantees, there is simply no room in which seditious libel may survive. The amendment did not embody seditious libel; it buried it.

As he reaffirmed that on matters of "law and theory" he was right in *The Legacy*, Levy dissected the arguments that I present in many ways, but the ways that count are presented in two parts, one on intellectual history and the other on structuralism. In his arguments involving intellectual history, Levy focuses mainly on the work of three prominent framers: James Madison, the most influential of the Constitution's framers and the principal author of the Bill of Rights; James Wilson, who in legal theory was second only to Madison; and the framer who was also the great practitioner of a free press, Benjamin Franklin. Levy has, I believe, incorrectly portrayed the work of these men.

## IV. MADISON, WILSON, AND FRANKLIN ON SPEECH AND THE PRESS

In my work, I relied on Madison at several points in identifying the original understanding of the protections afforded speech under the Constitution. Levy finds fault in that, stating: "Mayton does not seem to realize that Madison frequently changed his mind regarding freedom of the press," and that "[g]iven Madison's record of switching," my reliance on Madison is "anachronistic."

Madison, writing in 1799 what no doubt remains the most penetrating, comprehensive, and authoritative assessment of the relation of American government to speech, directly addressed and completely disassembled the idea that the first amendment as enacted embodied the Blackstonian view of freedom of the press. Madison first explained that freedom of expression was an essential implication of the democratic structure established by the Constitution. He then noted (1) the key role of the ratification process, (2) the fact of a free and flourishing press, and (3) the importance of the press issue during the ratification debates. He noted that in these debates assurances were made that the new government had been disarmed of the power to interfere with the press, particularly through the law of seditious libel, and that this was the "actual meaning of the instrument [the Constitution]." What was the relation of the first amendment to this guarantee of the original Constitution? It was, Madison said, that "the amendment was intended as a positive and absolute reservation of [power over the press]."

Madison's assessment of the "actual meaning of the instrument" destroys Levy's seditious libel thesis, and Levy disputes that assessment. He does so indirectly, on the grounds that, given "Madison's record of switching," his 1799 writings cannot be taken as evidence of what he really thought in 1789 when the Constitution was ratified, nor in 1791, when the first amendment was added. The "record of switching" that Levy relies upon, however, is simply nonexistent. Instead Madison's work is all of a piece, and Levy presents only a small amount of scarcely credible evidence, more sophistry than substance, to the contrary.

In *Legacy of Suppression*, Levy says that "if Madison's views of 1800 represented his earlier understanding, it passes belief that he would have remained silent in the Virginia ratifying convention of 1788 when George Nicholas, one of his closest supporters, defined the freedom of the press as the absence of a licensing act." Levy relies on Madison's silence rather than his explicit assertions. But historical method gives little import to silence, particularly in the context of a multi-member discussion such as the Virginia ratification debates. Further, on examination, Nicholas' remarks simply do not, as Levy suggests, support a Blackstonian definition of the liberty of the press under the Constitution. Rather, the opinion that Nicholas expressed was consistent with Madison's own view of the structural protections afforded speech and the press by the proffered constitution.

Actually, in the Virginia ratification debates, Madison was not completely silent on speech and the press. As discussed above, the Virginia ratification convention formally stated its understanding that "the powers granted under the proposed Constitution are the gift of the people, and every power not granted thereby remains with them . . . liberty . . . of the press cannot be cancelled, abridged, restrained, or modified, by any authority of the United States." Madison subscribed to that resolution. Further, in the Virginia debates Madison addressed that resolution's limited powers basis, and said that "[t]here cannot be a more positive and unequivocal

declaration of the principle of the adoption [of the resolution]—that every thing not granted is reserved."

In 1791, as the Bill of Rights was added to the Constitution, Madison, consistent with his profound belief that the best and first line of protection of liberty was in a limitation of power, explained that such a declaration of rights should not imply an assumption of governmental power with respect to them. In his draft of the Bill of Rights, he specifically guarded against that possibility.

Madison continued to express his structuralist views in subsequent debates. In 1794, after the Whiskey Rebellion, a resolution was introduced in Congress to censure "the self-created societies which have risen up in some parts of the Union, misrepresenting the conduct of Government." In the House of Representatives, Madison objected:

> When the people have formed a Constitution, they retain those rights which they have not expressly delegated. . . . Opinions are not the objects of legislation . . . [I]f we advert to the nature of Republican Government, we shall find that the censorial power is in the people over the Government, and not in the government over the people.

The motion to censure was defeated.

Some five years later Madison wrote his great report on speech, seditious libel, and the Constitution. Madison was a man of considerable intellect and not likely to waver on these matters and, as the record shows, he did not. Indeed, he was a profound and consistent structuralist on issues of speech and government.

In the case of James Wilson, Levy says that Wilson's views (1) "cause the argument from structuralism to self-destruct," and (2) "align him with Blackstone." But on destructing structuralism, Levy has surely called Wilson as a hostile witness: Wilson was in fact the most ardent of structuralists. His "state yard" speech in Pennsylvania, which circulated from Portland, Maine to Augusta, Georgia, was a wholly structural and ultimately persuasive response to the charge that the new Constitution provided insufficient protection for liberty of the press. In that speech, Wilson's bottom line was that "the proposed system possesses no influence whatever upon the press."

As evidence of Wilson's antipathy to structuralism, Levy offers Wilson's statement that

> A bill of rights annexed to a constitution enumerates the powers that are reserved. If we attempt such an enumeration, then everything

that is not enumerated is presumed to be given. Thus, an imperfect enumeration throws all implied powers into the scale on the government's side and renders the rights of the people incomplete.

Levy offers this statement in support of what he calls the "strong argument . . . that everything not reserved had been delegated to the national government by implication." If this unusual argument were true, then it would be essential that a right to speak be reserved, and so it might be that Wilson's "theory" causes "structuralism to self-destruct."

This argument, however, considerably distorts Wilson's position. That position, strongly stated, was that national power was not to be taken "from tacit implication, but from the positive grant expressed in the instrument of union." It was from this premise that Wilson argued that "the proposed system possesses no influence whatever upon the press." Indeed, in the statement that Levy offers, Wilson's actual points were (1) that the enumeration of rights was dangerous because the enumeration might not be complete, and (2) that the enumeration in and of itself implied that government had power with respect to those rights not enumerated. In the address from which Levy lifts the statement, Wilson's conclusion, exactly contrary to that imputed by Levy, was that the better protection of liberty was in structuralism and limitation of powers, rather than in a scheme of rights.

As for Levy's attempts to align Wilson with Blackstone, we should keep in mind Wilson's view that "the proposed system possesses no influence whatever upon the press"—not a view that conforms to the Blackstonian vision, under which the government uses the criminal law to suppress speech critical of government or governmental officials. Against this view, Levy relies on a 2-sentence paragraph with, at best, an ambiguous meaning. The paragraph Levy on which relies comes from the ratification debates in Pennsylvania, where Wilson, in answering a question about the liberty of the press under the proposed constitution, replied that "there is given to the general government no power whatsoever concerning it; and no law in pursuance of the Constitution can possibly be enacted to destroy that liberty."

After stating his "no power" position, Wilson immediately turned to a related question: "[I]f a law *should be made* to punish libels, and the judges should proceed under that law, what chance would the printer have of an acquittal?" In response to this "what if" question, Wilson first seemed to be correcting the questioner on the law of seditious libel:

I presume it was not in the view of the honorable gentleman to say that there is no such thing as a libel or that the writers of such ought not to be punished. The idea of the liberty of the press is not carried so far as this in any country—what is meant by liberty of the press is, that there should be no antecedent restraint upon it; but that every author is responsible when he attacks the security or welfare of the government or the safety, character, and property of the individual.

Wilson then addressed the procedural question put to him, and explained that federal procedures were as good as state procedures on the subject of the press. But having already explained that the federal government had no power to make laws on the subject, he ended his discourse on procedures with the qualifier, "*if* [the federal government] *had the power* to make laws on this subject."

Levy, lifting Wilson's description of seditious libel out of its context, presents it as an unqualified endorsement of seditious libel—notwithstanding the fact that Wilson surrounded the description with disclaimers of power in the manner of seditious libel. With some license, Levy also infers from this description that "Wilson, in fact, favored prosecuting perpetrators of seditious libel." In attempting to dismiss my own (and others') discussion of the hypothetical context of Wilson's statement, Levy says that the framers were not generally in the business of speaking hypothetically. That is true, of course, *generally* they were not.

Finally, Levy calls upon Ben Franklin, and finds in him the same sinister implications that he winnows out of Madison and Wilson. Levy places Franklin in the seditious libel camp and claims that he "recommended harsh treatment for anyone calumniating the government or affronting its reputation." In the writing to which Levy refers, however, Franklin stated his general position as being that "If by the *Liberty of the Press* were understood merely the Liberty of discussing the Propriety of Public Measures and political opinions, let us have as much of it as you please." Thereafter, by means of a nimble parody (in which Levy finds sinister implications), Franklin argued for a state remedy (as opposed to self-help) for injuries to reputation:

My proposal then is, to leave the liberty of the press untouched, to be exercised in its full extent, force, and vigor; but to permit the *liberty of the cudgel* to go with it *pari passu*. Thus, my fellow-citizens, if an impudent writer attacks your reputation, dearer to you perhaps than your life, and puts his name to the charge, you may go to him as openly and break his head. If he conceals himself behind the printer, and you can nevertheless discover who he is, you may in like manner way-lay him in the night, attack him behind, and give him a good drubbing. Thus far goes my project as to *private* resentment and retribution. But if the public should ever happen to be affronted, *as it ought to be*, with the conduct of such writers, I would not advise proceeding immediately to these extremities; but that we should in moderation content ourselves with tarring and feathering, and tossing them in a blanket.

If, however, it should be thought that this proposal of mine may disturb the public peace, I would then humbly recommend to our legislators to take up the consideration of both liberties, that of the press and that of the *cudgel*, and by an explicit law mark their extent and limits; and, at the same lime that they secure the person of a citizen from *assaults*, they would likewise provide for the security of his *reputation*.

From this light and sensible argument for state remedies for "security of reputation," Levy rather heavy-handedly inferred that Franklin "recommended harsh treatment for anyone calumniating the government."

In *The* Legacy *Reexamined*, Levy imposes on Franklin the burden of positively renouncing seditious libel, saying that "Franklin never endorsed or advocated the view that a republican government and the law of seditious libel are incompatible." If Franklin had to meet that burden, he certainly endorsed a proposition, that of "liberty of discussing the propriety of public measures and political opinions," that is wholly inconsistent with the doctrine of seditious libel. And as Clinton Rossiter has explained, Franklin rejected that doctrine in his life's work as a printer.

## V. STRUCTURALISM

Levy also criticizes what he calls my "structural arguments" and my use of the Constitution's treason clause as part of these arguments. As the treason clause is not exactly a familiar member of the free speech family, I will respond to Levy's criticism by starting with it.

The treason clause, as it acknowledges the historic power to protect the "established order of government," limits that power as follows:

Treason against the United States, shall consist only in levying War against them, or in adher-

ing to their Enemies, giving them Aid and Comfort. No Person shall be convicted of Treason unless on the Testimony of two Witnesses to the same overt Act, or on Confession in open Court.

On its surface, this clause bears no apparent relation to freedom of speech. Yet just under this surface lies a significant and largely unrecognized constitutional safeguard of free speech, the complexities of which require a fuller discussion than is possible here. These complexities may be summarized by reference to the history and dynamics of "constructive treason."

In Anglo-American history, the power that treason represents—to punish those who would injure the state—has been directed not only to acts against the state (e.g., moving weapons into place) but also to dissident speech. Treason as it included speech was generally referred to as constructive treason, and this treason was limited early in 1352 by the English Statute of Treasons. This statute's limitation of constructive treason included a condition, carried over in the United States Constitution, that the state can establish treason only upon a showing of an "overt act"—and by this condition dissident speech in and of itself could not be a crime.

The Statute of Treasons, however, often failed to stop the crown and parliament from creating new constructive treasons and thereby continuing to subject dissident speech to criminal prosecution. A primary reason for this failure was factional politics. In *Pleas of the Crown*, Sir Matthew Hale wrote of "things so carried by factions and parties . . . that this statute [the Statute of Treasons] was little observed." In America, the framers, "admonished" by these consequences of factional politics, established the treason clause as a constitutional barrier against such abuse. In this context, Madison's short reference to the treason clause in *Federalist* No. 43 is easily understood:

[A]s new fangled and artificial treasons have been the great engines by which violent factions, the natural offspring of free government, have usually wreaked their alternate malignity on each other, the convention have, with great judgment, imposed a barrier to this peculiar danger, by inserting a constitutional definition of the crime.

Thus the first sentence of the treason clause tightly defines treason to exclude constructive treason. This protection is doubled in the clause's second sentence by the overt act condition, a condition that through its procedural terms exempts dissident "thoughts and attitudes" from criminalization.

In his criticism, Levy says that I argue that the "framers intended the treason clause to prevent seditious libel prosecutions by protecting dissident speech" and he then disputes that argument. Actually, my argument was that the framers intended generally to disarm the national government of its power over speech, and that that disarmament eliminated the power that seditious libel represents. In regard to seditious libel, I saw the treason clause as a part of this disarmament.

Levy does, however, dispute of the treason clause in the terms that I have described it. In this regard, his first criticism is that even if speech could not be punished as treason, that "would not prevent the punishment of speech as some other crime." The appropriate response to this is the obvious one, that it is an aggravated instance of substance over form to say that a constitutional barrier to punishment of dissident speech may be avoided simply by manipulating labels.

From a sounder foundation, Levy asserts that nothing in the records of the constitutional convention supports my "historical thesis" and that it is therefore "not surprising that [I] offered no proof as to the drafting of the treason clause." I offered no evidence from the Convention pertaining to the treason clause because, as I said, those debates were sketchy and related largely to the demarcation of federal and state authority over treason. But once the treason clause is read in light of the historical background of constructive treason, the proof is in the text itself, in the studied way in which it continued and added to the protections against political suppression offered by England's Statute of Treason.

Turning next to the ratification debates, Levy finds the evidence from them too thin. He credits as "slight evidence" Richard Dobbs Spaight's explanation, in the North Carolina debates, that the clause shielded "any man who will complain of oppressions, or write against [its] usurpation" from prosecution for treason. Otherwise, Levy says, the ratification debates "neither construed the treason clause as a protection of free speech or even referred to free speech."

True, other than Spaight's explanation of the clause, the ratification debates do not specifically refer to the treason clause and speech. But surely Madison's description of the clause as a barrier to the "new fangled and artificial treasons" which are the "great engines" of factional dispute can only be understood as a reference to the clause as a barrier against constructive treason. George Nicholas' description of the clause as "doing away with the objection that the most grievous oppressions might happen under color of punishing crimes against the general government" carries a similar import. Moreover, even if these explanations are thin standing alone, they gain substance through their consistency with the historical background of the clause.

Apart from the treason clause, Levy also criticizes my general structural argument about limitations and disbursements of power from the standpoint of the Bill of Rights. Departing for the moment from his own general skepticism about the intent behind the Bill of Rights, Levy says that in 1787 the people wanted and "were entitled to an explicit reservation of their rights against government." With regard to speech, he notes that such a reserved right might be a useful check on implied powers. But while these observations are true and sensible, they are inconsequential in terms of the structural guarantees against which Levy argues. These structural guarantees are compatible with a declaration of rights and indeed are reinforced by the check on implied powers that such a declaration affords.

Also, Levy's claim that a perceived need for a bill of rights defeats the structuralism argument involves a telling non sequitur. He writes that "if the crime of treason required a tight, written definition, other rights required explicit definitions too." This reasoning, however, does not distinguish between the nature of powers and rights. Making treason a crime involves a power, and liberty benefits when a power is tightly defined. As James Wilson explained, "the limited power of punishment in cases of *treason* show that the current runs *strong* in favor of *humanity* and security to every individual." On the other hand, liberty may be diminished if a right is too tightly defined.

CONCLUSION: THE "METAPHOR OF THE FOURTH ESTATE"

The "law and theory" that Levy has propounded about the Constitution's protection of speech is fundamentally flawed. Its flaws derive in part from Levy's failure at times to distinguish private from public offenses and federal from state suppressions when marshalling evidence. There is, however, another, greater flaw. Toward the end of The Legacy *Reexamined*, Levy says that "[i]n a different sense Mayton is right." While I do not wish to say that he errs in saying that I am right, I do think that he errs profoundly in the "sense" that he favors. This sense is that "the meaning of the free press clause should be sought in England," where the right was applied against a government with general power and with a history of central control of the press. In this context, Levy's discussion of the dimensions of the right to speak and the effort to gain a greater role for the jury in protecting that right may be pertinent. But this sense of speech and government is off-point in the context of what Madison described as "the American idea of it:" a press left alone and, in being left alone, performing those functions that we value in a democratic society.

The way in which such a left-alone press serves these functions is described by the master printer of colonial times, Ben Franklin, in his *Apology for Printers*. In this work of practical epistemology, Franklin wrote that "the opinions of men are as various as their faces," that so long as the press is left alone to make a dollar it will print these various opinions, and that "when Truth and Error have fair play, the former is always an overmatch for the latter." The quality of the debate generated by a free press was noted in 1788 in the *Pennsylvania Gazette*: "The wise and the good are more dissentient on political topics than any other. Therefore the variety of opinions on the proposed constitution shouldn't surprise us, nor should we regret the diversity of sentiment, that will ensure our safety, if regulated by reason, integrity and moderation." But not regulated by the state: The framers were determined to preserve the press by disabling government of the power to disturb it.

. . .

## Bibliography

*Origins*

Alexander, James, *A Brief Narrative of the Case and Trial of John Peter Zenger* (2d ed. 1972)

Anderson, David A., *The Origins of the Press Clause*, 30 UCLA Law Review 455 (1983)

Anderson, David A., *Levy v. Levy*, 84 Michigan Law Review 777 (1986)

Berns, Walter, *Freedom of the Press and the Alien and Sedition Laws: A Reappraisal*, 1970 Supreme Court Review 109 (1970)

Carroll, Thomas F., *Freedom of Speech and of the Press in the Federalist Period: The Sedition Act*, 18 Michigan Law Review 615 (1920)

Chafee, Jr., Zechariah, *Free Speech in the United States* (1942)

Duniway, Clyde A., *The Development of Freedom of the Press in Massachusetts* (1906)

Hamburger, Philip, *The Development of the Law of Seditious Libel and the Control of the Press*, 37 Stanford Law Review 661 (1985)

Levy, Leonard W., *Legacy of Suppression* (1960)

Mayton, William T., *Seditious Libel and the Lost Guarantee of a Freedom of Expression*, 84 Columbia Law Review 91 (1984)

Van Alstyne, William, *Congressional Power and Free Speech: Levy's Legacy Revisited*, 99 Harvard Law Review 1089 (1986)

## C.  The Nature of Speech

The concept of speech has proved to be elusive and vexing to courts and commentators. Even for advocates of First Amendment absolutism, line-drawing often has proved inevitable as evidenced by Justice Black's distinguishing of speech and conduct. Such a distinction, especially when action is symbolic, has inspired significant debate and extensive literature. C. Edwin Baker asserts that distinguishing between expression and action is a function of unclear purpose and crabbed interpretation. Melville B. Nimmer urges deemphasis of a speech-conduct dichotomy in favor of attention to the quality of regulatory interest. Kent Greenawalt focuses upon the flag-burning cases in considering whether regulatory interests unrelated to speech can be separated from content concern.

C. Edwin Baker, *Scope of the First Amendment Freedom of Speech,* 25 UCLA LAW REVIEW 964 (1978)*

. . .

### IV. Protection of Action

If one concludes that the first amendment does not protect all speech, the literalist argument that all speech and *only* speech is protected loses force. Nevertheless, no accepted criteria exist to evaluate claims of first amendment protection of nonverbal conduct. I think, however, that a persuasive argument for protection of a particular type of conduct could be made by showing that: 1) the experience conduct furthers key first amendment values; 2) protection of this type of conduct is essential for an adequate realization of these values; 3) this conduct and protected verbal conduct promote first amendment values in a relevantly similar manner, and 4) principled lines can identify which conduct should be protected in what ways. My discussion will attempt to meet these four requirements.

### A. The Inadequate Expression-Action Dichotomy

Professor Emerson's approach to delineating the scope of protection relies on a fundamental distinction between "expression" and "action," a categorization which "must be guided by consideration of whether the conduct partakes of the essential qualities of expression or action, that is, whether expression or action is the dominant element." Emerson explains how to make a determination of essential qualities: "The concept of expression must be related to the fundamental purposes of the system [of freedom of expression] and the dynamics of its operation." If protection of such "expression" meets the four criteria I have suggested, and if "expression" can be successfully identified, my inquiry can come to an end.

Unfortunately, neither identifying protected "expression" by determining the conduct's contribution to the purposes of the system nor by using common sense to distinguish between expression and action works. Clearly, the four central values of the first amendment found by Emerson, or the two key ones, self-fulfillment and participation in change, can be, and frequently are, furthered by many types of conduct—including violent, coercive action or other conduct generally thought properly subject to collective control. Thus, in themselves, these values cannot

define or delineate spheres of protected expression and unprotected action.

The common sense distinction, relying on the essential qualities of expression and action, operates less to divide the world of behavior than to indicate the perspective of the person doing the dividing. If the distinction is between "expressing" and "doing," most conduct falls into both categories. Most consciously undertaken actions are at least self-expressive; and many—a political assassination, a hairstyle, a knife placed behind another's back—can be primarily intended to communicate something to others. Contrarily, people routinely use verbal conduct to do something—to write a poem, to command the troops, to test the student, to create a mood, to threaten an enemy, to make a promise. In considering behavior, an observer can choose to focus on either what is done (other than expressing) or what is expressed. The choice of focus will be subjective: Either culture or personal idiosyncrasy, but not logical analysis, will determine the choice. One might "give comfort" to a friend or to an enemy (of the state). If expression, but not action, is constitutionally protected, the determination of which element dominates in acts that "give comfort to an enemy" will likely depend on whether one believes the acts should be protected, not on the essential nature of the acts.

Not only does neither technique of distinguishing expression and action work, but since both verbal and nonverbal conduct advances first amendment values, the purpose of the distinction is unclear. Moreover, only an extremely crabbed reading of other clauses of the first amendment will be consistent with implementing an expression-action dichotomy. If religion plays a significant role in one's life, its free exercise normally will require doing or abstaining from certain conduct. And people typically assemble and associate to multiply their power in order to do something. Nevertheless, even if his "expression-action" dichotomy is not very helpful, Emerson consistently makes very perceptive analyses of concrete situations; and these analyses frequently appear to make a different distinction: whether or not the conduct is, or is intended to be, coercive or physically injurious to another. All Emerson's examples of unprotected conduct, "action," involve coercion or injury to or physical interference with another or damage to physical property. These acts cause harm in a manner quite different from the way protected conduct causes harm. In the case of protected conduct, the supposed harm results from the assimilation of messages by an independent agent, the listener, and from the acts of that independent agent.

. . .

---

* Reprinted with permission.

Expressive political protests sometimes involve acts of physical obstruction like lying down in front of troop trains, blocking traffic in a city, or pouring blood over files. Emerson argues that these must be considered "action" and that to characterize them as "expression" would destroy the distinction between "expression" and "action." Neither the physical activity nor the motives of the actor distinguish these "action" cases from draft card burning, which Emerson characterizes as expression. Rather, Emerson classifies the first examples of civil disobedience "action" because the "[c]ivil disobedience attempts to achieve results through a kind of coercion or pressure . . . ." However, burning a draft card, unlike failing to carry a draft card, does not involve coercing or directly injuring or physically obstructing any person or government activity. This fact apparently explains why Emerson concludes that the expression element clearly predominates in draft card burning. . . .

Emerson's examples indicate that the relevant question is how the conduct advances the key first amendment values; the conduct that advances the actor's values should be protected unless it is "coercive" or physically injurious or intended to be improperly obstructionist. But a principled description of this distinction between protected and unprotected conduct must be developed.

B. Interference with the Rights of Others

The logic of Emerson's examples suggests John Stuart Mill's conclusions concerning liberty in general (as opposed to Mill's special defense of freedom of speech). Mill argued:

> [T]he sole end for which mankind are warranted, individually or collectively, in interfering with the liberty of action of any of their number is self-protection . . . . [T]he only purpose for which power can be rightfully exercised over any member of a civilized community, against his will, is to prevent harm to others . . . . The only part of the conduct of anyone for which he is amenable to society is that which concerns others.

Unfortunately, the lack of criteria for determining when a person's behavior "harms" others or when a person's manner of acting "concerns others" prevents Mill's formulation from indicating when liberty should be protected. If "feeling harmed" or having one's interactions with others unfavorably "affected" count as criteria for "harm" or for being properly "concerned," then any action, no matter how privately undertaken, can be of concern to others, can harm others. Given that both one's public

and private activities influence, develop, or "change" one's personality or capacities or inclinations, and since one's personality and capacities affect one's interactions with others, both one's private and public activities may cause frustration of others' desires (i.e., may "harm" them). Even one's private yoga exercises or obscenity readings contribute to the culture and affect interpersonal relations in ways that may lessen some people's opportunities to realize their desires. Thus, harm to others can not be our touchstone. In order to preserve any area of liberty one must show that either certain harms or certain ways of causing harms cannot justify certain restrictions on liberty. . . .

Rules can directly prevent a person from fulfilling her desires in either of two ways. First, some rules restrict a person's liberty by giving to another the opportunity or decision authority one wants for oneself. I will call these allocation rules. Second, other rules deny a certain decision authority or opportunity to all people. I will call these rules general prohibitions. . . .

General prohibitions restrict liberty in a different and frequently more objectionable manner than do allocation rules. By excluding everyone from making certain decisions, they limit individual choice more than do allocation rules. General prohibitions let the majority directly control minorities; in contrast, allocation rules allow both the majority and minority to use their resources in ways they desire. Allocation rules define the context for both egotistic projects and interpersonal cooperation while general prohibitions unnecessarily restrict individual and cooperative initiatives. General prohibitions that prevent people from engaging in substantively valued behavior unnecessarily restrict people's opportunity to engage in fulfilling activities. Moreover, by completely denying the opportunity to engage in certain activities in which new logics or perspectives or values could gain coherence, general prohibitions drastically limit the possibility of popular participation in change. For these reasons, I will conclude that many general prohibitions violate the first amendment. To reach this conclusion, I must first distinguish between two ways of valuing behavior. Then, I will describe the first amendment restriction on the use of general prohibitions and defend this limit against various objections, particularly "efficiency" or utility maximization arguments. Finally, I will note how this conclusion clarifies the structure of traditional first amendment arguments.

An actor may or may not positively value a specific aspect of her behavior that others find offensive. Presumably, the person who chooses to read pornography, unless she happens to be a Supreme Court Justice, values this "polluting" activity. (The term "polluting" will be used to refer to any activity that others find offensive and that they would prefer to exclude from the community.) Contrarily, owners of a steel plant or of an automobile that emits exhaust pollutants normally do not value polluting the air per se. Polluting the air is an undesired consequence, a subsidiary result, of their preferred behavior.

These two examples, pornography and air pollution, illustrate how the polluter can value a polluting activity either substantively or instrumentally. Since prohibiting the activity forecloses the possibility of anyone undertaking it, if the activity is substantively valued, the prohibition wholly prevents a specific form of self-fulfillment or self-realization. Contrarily, if the polluting activity is only instrumentally valued, prohibiting the pollution operates the same as an allocation rule. That is, the prohibition may affect an individual's wealth or the cost of a desired form of fulfillment, but the prohibition does not prevent one who has sufficient resources (or has the assistance of others who have rights to the needed resources) from undertaking the desired activity. . . .

I conclude that if a general prohibition limits instrumentally valued behavior, it operates like an allocation rule permissibly used to implement the community's substantive and distributional objectives. Also, if a few people, by engaging in a substantively valued polluting activity, could nullify the consequences of the choice of many people not to engage in such an activity, a general prohibition may be appropriate as a means to prevent domination. Generally, however, *when a general prohibition applies to substantively valued behavior, it is an unconstitutional abridgement of freedom of speech or expression*. This conclusion is based on the following two observations: 1) substantively valued conduct is inherently expressive and clearly contributes to the two key first amendment values of self-fulfillment and participation in change; 2) general prohibitions forbid behavior that promotes first amendment values in the same manner as protected speech—i.e., in a noncoercive manner. In fact, the evils of general prohibitions and coercive acts correspond. Like coercive acts, imposition of general prohibitions enables those who favor the rule to make use of others (if the rule requires specified conduct) or to avoid the bother of others (if it forbids specified activities) and, thereby, to treat others as means. General prohibitions also unnecessarily restrict individual liberty, and thereby, like coercive acts, disrespect individual autonomy. In contrast to the corresponding evils of coercion and general prohibitions is the way that the

notion of coercion and allocation rules intertwine. By defining and then forbidding invasions of a person's realm of decision-making authority, allocation rules provide the necessary context in which an act can be coercive; indeed, allocation rules are required by the grammar of coercion.

Like unconstitutional restrictions on verbal conduct, general prohibitions restrict expressive conduct that operates noncoercively to advance self-fulfillment and popular participation in change. But before accepting the conclusion that general prohibitions of substantively valued conduct are unconstitutional abridgements of first amendment rights, one must be convinced that the justifications typically offered for general prohibitions are unpersuasive—an issue to which I now turn.

Justifications for general prohibitions normally take one of three forms. General prohibitions are valuable because they: 1) define and help form a community; 2) result from a valuable group process of choice; 3) promote efficiency or welfare maximization. . . .

The efficiency argument notes that people who substantively desire to act in a manner others find offensive often would agree to abandon the offensive behavior and accept a restraint on their liberty if paid an amount that those offended would be willing to pay. For example, those opposed to air or pornographic pollution might be willing to pay the polluters an amount that the polluters would be willing to accept for ceasing their pollution. However, difficulties and expenses in negotiating and carrying out the transactions prevent them from occurring. In this situation, a general prohibition, although burdening some, may increase the general level of preference satisfaction, i.e., may correct for the market failure and be efficient. . . .

. . . [E]fficiency or welfare maximization may be a particularly incoherent justification for general prohibitions of substantively valued conduct. Certain activities that decrease the satisfaction of existing preferences may help create a better society where people will have "better" preferences than exist at present. Efficiency calculations must presuppose, but cannot justify, some particular, usually existing, tastes or desires as the ones to be satisfied. Until some set of preferences is assumed, efficiency has no evaluative criteria. But if change is to be subject to human choice, if human self-determination is possible, then a central issue is determining what preferences are best. Thus, since efficiency analysis cannot justify its reliance on any set of preferences, it has no criteria with which to guide the choice. No intrinsic quality of *existing* tastes justifies their fulfillment always being the dominant concern. In fact, to paraphrase Mill's faith in people as progressive beings, the merit of change must be evaluated not in terms of whether it fulfills existing tastes but in terms of whether it improves the type of people we are. And, as Professor Tribe has argued, the major choices facing us as a people are those that will determine who and what we will be. If human integrity and responsibility require that people be free to decide (or participate in deciding) what or who they will be, then, when evaluating the process of change, it is a logical mistake to evaluate choices in terms of how well they satisfy existing preferences; rather, one must either evaluate change in terms of the legitimacy of the *process* or evaluate the political and ethical *content* of the change. This second type of evaluation corresponds to many people's practice of subjecting their attitudes and activities to ethical or political criticism. As for legitimacy of the process, the irrelevance of an efficiency analysis that takes as given the key issue in dispute could explain why many intuitively conclude that the first amendment should (absolutely?) protect a process of change from limitations justified by mere utilitarian calculations (i.e., balancing). This logical irrelevance of efficiency arguments for justifying general prohibitions should not be surprising if one accepts my earlier argument that the state is justified in adopting utility maximization as state policy only when necessary to carry out the state's obligation to treat all members as deserving equal respect as autonomous moral beings. Efficiency arguments must be irrelevant until the liberty rights of autonomous beings, particularly the right of self-determination, are assured protection.

One added argument suggests why general prohibitions are objectionable. The idea that we need, and sometimes have had, progressive change, suggests that the legal structuring of the process of change ought to protect those elements which could be progressive, and which, without protection, would be restricted. Identifying progressive elements is, of course, difficult. However, two factors indicate that barring general prohibitions of substantively valued conduct increases the chances of protecting progressive elements. Since a key aspect of general prohibitions is to suppress value realization that is contrary to majority or status quo values, one would expect popular support for precisely those general prohibitions that attempt to suppress those progressive practices which conflict with current regressive orientations. More important, our ethical and political judgments and concepts typically reflect presently shared values and logic. Theorists such as Robert Unger argue that the confidence we should have in our judgments depends on the extent to which these shared values are formed under circumstances of nondomination. Since general prohibitions characteristically involve dominating minorities on the basis of current majority interests and values, they undermine the legitimacy of the very values they promote. Contrarily, by banning general prohibitions of substantively valued conduct, we decrease majority domination and increase the legitimacy of relying on the shared judgments that do exist. By allowing minorities to live their values even when the present majority finds the behavior offensive, society protects an important process for peaceful change of tastes and values while decreasing the conditions of domination.

These criticisms of efficiency justifications for general prohibitions complete the argument for barring the state from enforcing general prohibition of substantively valued expressive conduct. The above criticisms highlight many aspects of conventional first amendment analysis. Typical attempts to justify laws prohibiting specific expressive activity rely on: 1) predictions that the activity will lead to future violations of allocations rules—e.g., the speech creates a clear and present danger to lawlessness, pornography leads to sex crimes; 2) predictions that the activity will affect the actors or observers in detrimental ways, thereby corrupting the cultural climate and negatively affecting friendships and interpersonal relations—e.g., public sales or use of obscenity and public use of vulgar language undermines the desired moral tone of the community; 3) disapproval of the values or attitudes expressed by the activity—e.g., flag burning, wearing long hair, draft card burning, representing unpatriotic attitudes.

Well-developed defenses of free speech meet each claim. First, the classic objection to the bad tendency test for restricting speech is that the state can forbid the violation of the allocation rule but cannot prohibit the speech using a general prohibition. . . .

Similarly, classic first amendment analyses reject the other two "efficiency" arguments for restricting people's noncoercive activities: Either the expressive activities will have a socially undesirable influence on people's personality and their behavior or the expression is itself offensive to the majority. These arguments are rejected on the ground that the majority must respect individuals' choices about their own values and not force them to falsify their values. This position is, of course, a straightforward application of the principle that the state must respect people's integrity and autonomy. Again, classic first amendment arguments repeat our objection to efficiency justifications for general prohibitions. . . .

Melville B. Nimmer, *The Meaning of Symbolic Speech Under the First Amendment*, 21 UCLA LAW REVIEW 29 (1973)*

## INTRODUCTION

In recent years the courts have been confronted with an increasingly persistent and troubling question: Does communication by conduct rather than by words constitute "speech" within the first amendment's guarantee of freedom of speech? That conduct may be expressive of ideas has long been acknowledged in other areas of the law. But should communicative conduct constitute symbolic speech in the first amendment sense, and if so, should it be entitled to protection which is coextensive with that granted to verbal speech? The status of communicative conduct, as with most free speech questions, is usually presented in an emotion-laden context: Does the burning of a flag, or of a draft card, constitute a first-amendment-protected activity? Is the act of marching in a public demonstration (as distinguished from the placards which the marchers carry) a form of protected "speech"? Is a school or other governmental regulation of hair styles an abridgement of freedom of speech? Although the lower federal and state courts frequently have wrestled with all of these questions, the United States Supreme Court, thus far, has failed to rule on many of the specific issues, such as flag desecration and hair styles. Of greater significance, the Supreme Court has yet to articulate a theoretical base which explains the status of symbolic speech under the first amendment. It is the purpose of this Article tentatively to suggest the outlines of such a theoretical base.

## I. "SPEECH" WITHIN THE MEANING OF THE FIRST AMENDMENT

### A. Nonverbal and Verbal Expression

. . .

Any attempt to disentangle "speech" from conduct which is itself communicative will not withstand analysis. The speech element in symbolic speech is entitled to no lesser (and also no greater) degree of protection than that accorded to so-called pure speech. Indeed, in one sense all speech is symbolic. At this moment the reader is observing black markings on paper which curl and point in various directions. We call such markings letters, and in groups they are referred to as words. What is being said in this sentence is meaningful only because the reader recognizes these markings as symbols for particular ideas. The same is true of oral speech which is simply the use of symbolic sounds. Outside of the science fiction realm of mind-to-mind telepathic communication, all communications necessarily involve the use of symbols. . . .

But because all expression necessarily requires the use of symbols, it does not necessarily follow as a matter of logic that first amendment protection is or should be available for all symbolic expressions. It might be argued that "speech" within the meaning of the first amendment should encompass only those particular expressions in which the symbols employed consist of conventional words. The Supreme Court, along with most of the nation, would find such a restrictive reading of the first amendment to be unacceptable. It is not without significance that the Court, in a first amendment context, often uses the word "expression" as the equivalent of speech. Most would agree that it is the freedom to express ideas and feelings, not merely the freedom to engage in verbal locutions, which constitutes the core meaning of the first amendment. Holmes' "free trade in ideas" may not be reduced to mere trade in words. It is the *ideas* expressed, and not just a particular form of expression, that must be protected if the underlying first amendment values are to be realized.

### B. Emotive and Cognitive Expression

Is the first amendment marketplace of "ideas" limited to those ideas which are intellectual in content? Surely it is clear that there is no such limitation. The Supreme Court has held the first amendment to be applicable to ideas whether their content be "social, political, esthetic [or] moral." The emotive content of expression can be fully as important as the intellectual, or cognitive, content in the competition of ideas for acceptance in the marketplace. Men are moved at least as much by emotion as they are by logic and reason in determining their course of conduct. To allow the state either to permit or forbid expressions which appeal to emotion, while refraining from censorship of expressions which appeal to intellect (even if such a dichotomy were possible), would be to permit the state an important measure of control over the popular decision-making process. The Supreme Court in *Cohen v. California* stated:

> We cannot sanction the view that the Constitution, while solicitous of the cognitive content of individual speech, has little or no regard for that emotive function which, practically speaking, may often be the more important element of the overall message sought to be communicated.

* Reprinted with permission.

Of course, most communications encompass both cognitive and emotive content. The point made by the Court in *Cohen* was that if the cognitive component is protected by the first amendment, the expression may not be suppressed by reason of its emotive component. Thus, since the expression "I hate the draft" would be protectible, the state could not proscribe a statement with the same cognitive content because of its more offensive emotive form.

But even if a communication is substantially devoid of all cognitive content, its emotive content is surely protectible. It would be shocking to conclude that symphonic compositions or nonrepresentational art could be the subject of governmental censorship. Both are fully within the ambit of the first amendment notwithstanding their lack of both verbal and cognitive content.

## II. WHEN IS CONDUCT "SPEECH"?

. . . Although "speech" may consist of conduct which is both nonverbal and noncognitive, it is unacceptable to conclude that any nonverbal, noncognitive conduct may be regarded as symbolic speech. A further element must be added to the mix before conduct may be considered to be speech. Whatever else may or may not be true of speech, as an irreducible minimum it must constitute a communication. That, in turn, implies both a communicator and a communicatee—a speaker and an audience. The right to engage in verbal locutions which no one can hear and in conduct which no one can observe may sometimes qualify as due process "liberty," but without an actual or potential audience there can be no first amendment speech right. Nor may the first amendment be invoked if there is an audience but no actual or potential "speaker." Conduct by inanimate objects (a clap of thunder) or by animals (a dog wagging its tail) may convey meaning to observers, but unless there is a human communicator intending to convey a meaning by his conduct, it would be odd to think of it as conduct constituting a communication protected by the first amendment.

Before inquiring as to how an intent to convey meaning may be shown, we should first ask what it is to convey meaning by conduct. A given act may constitute a cause which results in both meaning and nonmeaning effects. If I race my car at 80 miles per hour the nonmeaning effect of this act is that I am physically present at a distant location within a remarkably short period of time. The meaning effect, assuming there is at least one person to observe my conduct, is to produce the impression in the mind of the observer that I am speeding, and perhaps that I am driving recklessly, I am breaking the law, and

so forth. The meaning effect is a signal that registers in the mind of at least one observer. The nonmeaning effect is not dependent upon the reaction of other minds.

As previously indicated, symbolic speech requires not merely that given conduct results in a meaning effect, but that the actor causing such conduct must intend such a meaning effect by his conduct. How can we know whether a given actor intends that his conduct shall have such a meaning effect? It has been suggested that in order to qualify as protectible symbolic speech "the conduct should be assertive in nature [which] will generally mean that the conduct is a departure from the actor's normal activities and cannot adequately be explained unless a desire to communicate is presumed." Judging symbolic speech by such an "assertive" standard is unfortunate on several grounds. In casual conversation rarely are we consciously aware of an intent to communicate. If asked why we said what we did, we might finally explain that the words were uttered because we intended to communicate a certain idea, but this explicit intent would not have been conscious when the words were spoken. Similarly, the meaning effect of nonverbal conduct may not be consciously intended, and yet such intent may be very real. Moreover, conduct which is intended (consciously or otherwise) to produce a meaning effect may well not be "a departure from the actor's normal activities." When each morning I select the particular apparel to wear for the day, I may consider whether it will be a hot or cold day, whether it is likely to rain, and a number of other factors. To the extent that my choice of wearing apparel for the day is dictated by such considerations, my concern is with a nonmeaning effect, i.e., my physical comfort. But if in making my choice I also consider (as most people do) how this particular ensemble will "look," I am then concerned with the impression to be made in the mind of others, whether cognitive, emotive, or both. To that extent I am concerned with the meaning effect of my conduct in wearing certain clothes. Such an intent may well be unconscious, and it is certainly not a departure from my usual intent, nor from the activities which express such intent.

Beyond these objections to an assertive standard, there is the always present difficulty of determining subjective intent—in the present case an intent to achieve what we have here called a meaning effect. This difficulty is compounded when dealing with highly controversial issues, which are the usual milieu of first amendment cases.

There is, in addition, quite a different problem presented if the availability of first amendment protection for symbolic speech is to turn on the determination of the actor's intent to create a meaning effect by his conduct. It may be very clear that the actor intends to communicate a message by his conduct, and yet we may not wish to regard such conduct as protectible under the first amendment. Political assassination illustrates this point. Sirhan Sirhan's murder of Robert Kennedy in one sense could certainly be called symbolic speech. By the act of killing, Sirhan wished to convey a message to the world concerning the asserted Palestinian grievances against Israel. But obviously this conduct is not and should not be protected by the first amendment simply because (in the *O'Brien* opinions' phrase) "the person engaging in the conduct intends thereby to express an idea."

Thus, two separate problems dealing with the significance of the actor's intent to communicate by conduct have been posed. First there is the issue of the circumstances under which proof of such intent should be regarded as a necessary condition to the recognition of conduct as protectible symbolic speech. Assuming such proof, there is the second issue of when such proof should be regarded a sufficient condition for such recognition. The resolution of both of these problems may be found by a consideration of the state's interest in suppressing or regulating the actor's conduct.

## III. THE DISTINCTION BETWEEN NON-SPEECH AND ANTI-SPEECH INTERESTS

Recall the distinction made previously between the meaning effect and the nonmeaning effect of a given act. The meaning effect refers to the signal registered in the mind of a nonparticipating observer of the act. The nonmeaning effect is the physical effect of the act unrelated to the mental reaction of nonparticipating observers. As used here, a nonspeech interest is an interest by the state in suppressing or regulating a nonmeaning effect. In contrast, an anti-speech interest is an interest by the state in suppressing or regulating a meaning effect.

### A. The Status of Conduct Opposed by a Non-Speech Interest

The Supreme Court noted in *O'Brien* that the state interest in suppressing conduct must be "unrelated to the suppression of free expression." That is to say, the state must have a nonspeech rather than an anti-speech interest. The Sirhan case is illustrative of this point. Although Sirhan clearly intended to communicate a message by his act of assassination, the state's reason for punishing the conduct was due to the nonmeaning effect, i.e., the death of a human being. The state was not thereby attempting to suppress the meaning effect having to do with Sirhan's rather obscure point about the Middle East, nor even the more direct meaning effect relating to the shock shared by millions of television viewers observing the killing of a respected political figure.

It may tentatively be concluded that if the state can pose a non-speech interest as the basis for suppressing conduct, then such conduct should not be regarded as protectible under the first amendment even if the actor clearly intends such conduct to communicate a message—that is, to have a meaning effect. This disposes of the actor's intent both as a necessary condition and as a sufficient condition. But this general conclusion must be qualified in several significant respects.

### 1. Overnarrow Statutes

In the last several decades the overbroad statute has become a familiar concept. Such a statute is constitutionally defective because in its breadth of coverage it is capable of abridging both protected and unprotected speech activities. The Supreme Court has ruled that such a statute is invalid even as against one who might have been subject to punishment under a narrowly drawn statute.

Statutes which purport to regulate communicative conduct on the ground of a non-speech interest, i.e., a state interest that is unrelated to the content of the idea communicated, may exhibit a defect that lies at the end of the spectrum opposite to that of overbreadth. Such a statute may be called overnarrow. The statute in *O'Brien* is a case in point. The defendant, who engaged in draft card burning as a protest against the Vietnam War, was convicted of knowingly destroying and mutilating his draft card and of changing it by burning it. The defendant claimed that the statute prohibiting such conduct was unconstitutional because it was enacted to abridge free speech and because it served no legitimate legislative purpose. The Supreme Court did not expressly acknowledge that draft card burning constitutes a form of speech. But, "on the assumption that the alleged communicative element in O'Brien's conduct is sufficient to bring into play the First Amendment," the Court pointed out that "when 'speech' and 'nonspeech' elements are combined in the same course of conduct, a sufficiently important governmental interest in regulating the nonspeech element can justify incidental limitations on First Amendment freedoms." The Court found precisely such a non-speech governmental interest in that it concluded that "the continuing availability to each registrant of his Selective Service certificates substantially furthers the smooth and proper functioning of the system that

Congress has established to raise armies." Thus, the state's non-speech interest in the efficient functioning of the Selective Service System was held to justify the punishment of any conduct which negates the objective of "availability" to the registrant of his draft card. It is to be noted, however, that the statute under which the defendant was convicted does not render criminal any conduct which results in the "unavailability" or nonpossession of a draft card. Only if unavailability results from knowing mutilation, destruction, or change is it subject to punishment under the statute in issue. A draft card may be equally unavailable if the registrant simply decides not to carry it with him, leaving it in a place where it will not be readily available to him.

Assuming, then, a sufficient causal relationship between the availability of draft cards and the proper functioning of the Selective Service system, the statute is nevertheless objectionable because it attempts to punish conduct which may result in non-availability only in those circumstances when such conduct is of such a nature that it can result in a meaning effect (by acts of mutilation or destruction) and not when nonavailability is the result of conduct which creates no meaning effect (e.g., a failure to carry on one's person). In that sense the statute is "overnarrow."

There are at least two alternative grounds for invalidating an overnarrow statute. First, it may be said to create a conclusive presumption that in fact the state interest which the statute serves as an anti- rather than a non-speech interest. If the state interest asserted in *O'Brien* were truly the non-speech interest of assuring availability of draft cards, why did Congress choose not to prohibit any knowing conduct which leads to unavailability, rather than limiting the scope of the statute to those instances in which the proscribed conduct carries with it a speech component hostile to governmental policy? The obvious inference to be drawn is that in fact the Congress was completely indifferent to the "availability" objective, and was concerned only with an interest which the *O'Brien* opinion states is impermissible— an interest in the suppression of free expression. Though generally an assessment of legislative motives is a slippery undertaking which the courts rightly avoid, the overnarrow statute constitutes an objective manifestation of such motive that avoids the shoals of subjective determination of the legislative state of mind.

The other ground for invalidating an overnarrow statute lies in a combination of equal protection and free speech considerations. An overnarrow statute is what Professor Tussman and ten Broek, in their clas-

sic article on equal protection, called "under-inclusive." That is to say,

> all who are included in the class are tainted with its mischief [e.g., not having a draft card available], but there are others also tainted whom the classification does not include [e.g., those for whom their draft cards are unavailable for reasons other than mutilation, destruction, or change by burning]. Since the classification does not include all who are similarly situated with respect to the purpose of the law [e.g., availability of draft cards], there is a prima facie violation of the equal protection requirement of reasonable classification.

But the underinclusive statute is not necessarily defective on equal protection grounds alone. The Supreme Court has often reasoned that a legislature is entitled to attack a problem a step at a time. It was Mr. Justice Douglas, speaking for the Court, who said: "It is not a requirement of equal protection that all evils of the same genus be eradicated or none at all." But the overnarrow statute, as here defined, is an underinclusive statute where the only evils of a given genus which are eradicated are those which carry with them a meaning effect, which is to say, a speech component, while the unregulated evils within the same genus are without any such speech component. In such circumstances the courts should find a classification no less impermissible under the equal protection clause than would be one based upon race, and should find as well an invalid abridgment of freedom of speech.

2. The Required Causal Relationship Between Communicative Conduct and the Asserted Non-Speech Interest

In *O'Brien* the Supreme Court articulated the principle which determines when symbolic speech may be the subject of governmental regulation. The Court said:

> [W]e think it clear that a government regulation is sufficiently justified if it is within the constitutional power of the Government; if it furthers an important or substantial governmental interest; if the government interest is unrelated to the suppression of free expression; and if the incidental restriction on alleged First Amendment freedoms is no greater than is essential to the furtherance of that interest.

As will be argued, this statement is seriously defective with respect to the causal relationship between expressive conduct and the evil which the asserted non-speech interest is intended to avert. Yet, this was the central issue in *Tinker v. Des Moines* in which the Court upheld the wearing of black armbands as symbolic speech. In that case the school authorities suspended certain students for wearing black armbands in protest of the Vietnam War, contrary to school regulations which forbade the wearing of such armbands. If only the quoted statement from *O'Brien* is examined, it might be concluded that the students' first amendment rights were not violated. That is, it is certainly "within the constitutional power" of the state authorities to regulate conduct within the classroom; the anti-armband regulation "furthers an important or substantial governmental interest" in that it "furthers" the state interest in maintaining order and discipline within the school system—undoubtedly an "important" and "substantial" government interest; that interest is by hypothesis "unrelated to the suppression of free expression"; and finally, it may be concluded that the restriction on first amendment freedoms "is no greater than is essential to the *furtherance*" of the interest in order and discipline. The operative words here are "furthers" and "furtherance." Of course, prohibiting the wearing of black armbands will in some degree "further" the interest in order, and since any lesser restriction would derogate from such "furtherance," it follows that the restriction on black armbands wearing is "essential" to such "furtherance." What this analysis ignores is that it is not sufficient that the abridgment of speech "further" a non-speech interest. Absent such abridgment there must be, at the very least, a material and substantial interference with the non-speech interest. In *Tinker*, the Court held that "where there is no finding and no showing that engaging in any of the forbidden conduct would '*materially and substantially* interfere with the requirements of appropriate discipline in the operation of the school,' the prohibition cannot be sustained."

Though this principle was applied in *Tinker*, that it was not applied in *O'Brien*, another symbolic speech case, can only be explained by a reluctance to accord to symbolic speech the full protection which would obviously be applicable to verbal speech. The fact that verbal speech may "further" lawless action is not sufficient to preclude first amendment protection unless such speech is "likely" to produce such action, and further, that such action be rendered "imminent" by reason of the speech. That an idea is expressed by conduct rather than by words cannot justify greater suppression of the idea unless the countervailing threat to the non-speech interest is thereby increased.

It is important at this point to distinguish between communicative conduct where the nonmeaning effect is in and of itself objectionable, and communicative conduct where the nonmeaning effect is itself unobjectionable, but may in turn cause other nonmeaning effects which may be objectionable. An example of the former is a political assassination. In such a case the immediate nonmeaning effect is itself objectionable, and hence no question arises as to the likelihood that such communicative conduct will materially and substantially affect a non-speech interest. Contrast this with draft card burning where (if one ignores the meaning effect of such conduct) the burning of the draft card per se is unobjectionable. The interest there to be preserved, according to the Court in *O'Brien*, is "the smooth and proper functioning of the system that Congress has established to raise armies." Conduct which results in the unavailability of draft cards is not objectionable in itself, unlike political assassination. It is objectionable only because of other conduct to which it might lead. It is here that it becomes important to focus upon the nature of the causal relationship between the immediate nonmeaning effect and the objectionable conduct. In *O'Brien* the Court found it sufficient that the suppression of the communicative conduct "furthers" the "smooth and proper functioning" of the Selective Service system. There is no need here to question the validity of this factual conclusion, although others have done so. The point to be made is that it should not be sufficient that suppression of expressive conduct may "further" a non-speech interest, any more than suppression of verbal speech may be justified simply because this "furthers" a non-speech interest. Unless it in fact materially and substantially interferes with the non-speech interest, or is likely imminently to do so, the suppression of communicative conduct constitutes an abridgment of first amendment rights.

B. The Status of Conduct Opposed by an Anti-Speech Interest

If the state's regulation of conduct is based upon an anti-speech interest, several consequences should follow. First, with reference to the issue of the actor's intent to communicate, something in the nature of an estoppel is created. Of course, as a minimum the actor at trial must claim that his conduct was intended to achieve a meaning effect, i.e., to communicate. Otherwise, no first amendment issue is raised. But such a claim by an actor should be conclusively presumed as proven if the state's interest in opposing the conduct lies in the suppression of the meaning which the actor claims he intended to convey. The state should not be heard to deny the actor's claim that the conduct in question was intended to communicate if the state acted in order to suppress such a communication.

Another consequence should follow when an actor's claim that his conduct was intended to communicate is coupled with an opposing state interest that is anti- rather than non-speech. This in itself should establish that the conduct in question constitutes symbolic speech. But having concluded that in such circumstances that which is being regulated is speech and not conduct, does it necessarily follow that it is entitled to first amendment protection? Only slight probing will disclose difficulties with this conclusion. For example, it is clear that the state interest in avoiding an incitement to violence is caused by the meaning effect of the speech. Yet, if the violence is sufficiently likely and imminent as a result of the speech, then the state interest will prevail over the speech. Other anti-speech state interests will, in given contexts, justify the suppression of speech. Because, as argued above, symbolic speech should receive no lesser protection than that accorded to verbal speech, it does not follow that it should receive greater protection. In given contexts symbolic speech may be overbalanced by a given state anti-speech interest. If, however, the asserted or actual anti-speech state interest is simply an ideological commitment to a given view of the world, whether it be political, ethical, aesthetic, or otherwise, this is not an interest that will justify abridgment of the right to express a commitment to a contrary view, whether such expression is by words or conduct. This must be true if we regard as more than rhetoric Mr. Justice Jackson's oft-quoted injunction: "[N]o official, high or petty, can prescribe what shall be orthodox in politics, nationalism, religion, or other matters of opinion or force citizens to confess by word or act their faith therein." . . .

---

Kent Greenawalt, *O'er the Land of the Free: Flag Burning As Speech,* 37 UCLA LAW REVIEW 925 (1990)*

. . .

## I. TEXAS V. JOHNSON AND THE RESPONSE

Last June the Supreme Court held, five to four, that Gregory Johnson's conviction under a Texas statute punishing flag desecration violated the first amendment guarantee of free speech. Johnson and other

---

* Reprinted with permission.

demonstrators during the 1984 Republican National Convention had protested Republican policies and dramatized the dangers of nuclear war. Johnson set a stolen American flag burning. He was convicted under a penal section entitled "Desecration of Venerated Object," which forbade intentionally or knowingly desecrating a state or national flag. To "desecrate" meant to "deface, damage, or otherwise physically mistreat in a way that the actor knows will seriously offend one or more persons likely to observe or discover his action."

Judged by attention and notoriety, Johnson was a major case. Newspapers widely reported the opinions under leading headlines, and the result upset many people. Politicians and columnists spoke their minds. President Bush expressed dismay at what the Court had done, and, echoing campaign themes, appealed to the values of the flag. He spurred a serious effort to amend the Constitution that gained great momentum in Congress. A revision of the federal law on flag destruction, which proponents claimed could withstand constitutional challenge, deflected, at least temporarily, the effort to amend the Constitution.

Despite these trappings of importance, the case is trivial by some measures. Not many people want to burn flags. The decision does not affect lives in the manner of *Brown v. Board of Education* and *Roe v. Wade*. The case lacks great doctrinal significance because it represents an application of existing first amendment doctrines. It does not protect some fundamental liberty of action. If our country did not permit its flag to be desecrated, it would not be much less free and democratic.

. . . A critic might respond that plenty of serious issues face American democracy; obsession about flag burning panders to an uninformed public and reflects cowardice about confronting hard problems. The critic would be right. Still, wide agreement exists on broadly liberal premises about the boundaries of speech and protest. That people worry so much about this narrow form of political expression, rather than the substance of messages of political dissent, suggests a firm understanding in support of a wide range of political expression.

## II. FIRST AMENDMENT PRINCIPLES

First amendment analysis of flag burning cases proceeds in three stages. First, is flag burning a free speech problem at all? Second, if so, what is the standard for judging the constitutionality of the state's effort to make it criminal? Third, what is the outcome under that standard?

### A. Why Free Speech Is Involved

Does someone convicted for flag burning have

a claim that he was engaged in free speech? One conceivable position would be that only writing and speaking, as well as perhaps art and music, count as expression under the first amendment. All other (or ordinary) acts would fall outside the protection of the free speech and free press clauses. It is easy to see why the Court has long rejected this position. As Nimmer pointed out, speaking and writing themselves are communications by symbols; if the significance of an ordinary act is to express an idea, the act should be treated similarly.

Oversimplifying to a modest degree, the Court indicates that the issue of coverage turns on the communicative nature of Johnson's act. It refers to an earlier flag case that asks whether "[a]n intent to convey a particularized message was present, and [whether] the likelihood was great that the message would be understood by those who viewed it." As Nimmer explained, it is not enough that conduct convey some meaning to observers; under such a standard every act seen by others would qualify for first amendment protection. It also is not enough that an actor have a subjective aim to communicate.

The unworkability of using a subjective criterion alone is evident when one reflects on prosecutions for public nudity. A college student who streaks across campus on a dare may have no message he is trying to communicate consciously. A person who sits nude in cold weather in front of City Hall in protest of treatment of the homeless has an obvious message. What of bathers who are nude on a relatively secluded part of a public beach in the summer? Some simply enjoy bathing and sunning nude. A few may find the sensation unpleasant, but wish to upset prudish restrictions. Most have more complex motivations. They enjoy bathing nude. They also disapprove of the restrictions they are violating and take appearing nude as a kind of implicit statement against the restrictions. Let us suppose that on a particular day all the bathers expect to be seen by each other and by a few members of the larger public. None have signs around their necks or next to their towels explaining why they are nude. An observer cannot know why any one person is nude. We can quickly understand why any serious constitutional test for conviction should not turn on a particular bather's subjective motivation, discoverable only after the fact and difficult then to determine with confidence.

This illustration suggests a possible further limit to conduct protected by the first amendment—that communication be the conduct's dominant aim. It may be that those who break laws of which they do not approve wish in part to communicate their disapproval, and are so understood by others; but it is doubtful that such ordinary lawbreaking should qualify for serious first amendment scrutiny. . . .

## B. The Constitutional Level of Scrutiny

The second stage of analysis is determining the constitutional level of scrutiny. This was the important stage in *Johnson*, and it is at this stage where the new federal statute *might* yield a different outcome. The critical question for the second stage is whether application of a law will be governed by the formulation in *United States v. O'Brien* or by some more demanding standard.

O'Brien was convicted for publicly burning his draft card. Congress had recently enacted a provision forbidding destruction of draft cards. . . . Few doubted that the dominant aim of Congress was to restrict public burning of draft cards by protesters against the Vietnam War. Refusing to look beyond language to underlying purpose, however, the Court treated the statute as not directed at communication. Assuming, after initial equivocation, that the communicative element of O'Brien's conduct brought the first amendment into play, the Court then elaborated a test for such circumstances. A government regulation otherwise within constitutional power is sufficiently justified "if it furthers an important or substantial governmental interest; if the governmental interest is unrelated to the suppression of free expression; and if the incidental restriction on alleged First Amendment freedoms is no greater than is essential to the furtherance of that interest." Requiring that the government have a *substantial* interest, not any plausible interest, and demanding that the restriction of expression be no greater than is essential to further the interest, the Court seemed to set a fairly stringent balancing test that goes well beyond the "rational basis" review that applies to any statute. *O'Brien* sounds as if those engaging in communicative acts are getting significant protection even if a statute is not directed at communication.

In practice, the *O'Brien* test has worked out differently. In *O'Brien* itself the Court accepted thin claims that granting a right to burn draft cards would interfere with the effective administration of the draft. In no later case has the Court actually held that a defendant's communicative activity was protected against application of a law not directed at communication. Since Johnson's prospects would have been poor had the Court used only the *O'Brien* test, the inquiry whether the Texas provision was directed at communication was of major importance. Thus, also, it is critically important whether the Court will determine that the new federal statute is directed at communication.

Some of what the Supreme Court says in *Johnson* on this subject, and some of what two district courts say in reviewing the new federal statute, is a bit confusing. An initial effort at categorization may be clarifying. One way in which a law may be directed at communication is in distinguishing between good messages and bad ones. This is what is known as viewpoint discrimination. Since the government should not be in the business of preferring some messages to others, viewpoint discrimination rightly has been seen as highly threatening to free speech values and is considered to be invalid absent an extremely strong justification. Another way in which a law might be said to be directed at communication is by penalizing communicative acts that have harmful consequences, with harm judged independently of acceptance or rejection of the message. A law forbidding communications that are highly likely to cause deep emotional upset or to trigger violent responses is of this sort. We may call this harmful reaction regulation. A third way in which a law conceivably might be said to be directed at communication is when it protects the communicative value of something. We may call this symbol protection. It is incorrect to suppose that such a law inevitably must be aimed at acts which are themselves communicative. Suppose a country's flag is one solid color, bright red. To protect the symbolic force of that color, the state forbids any human use of bright red except in the flag. No walls or cars can be painted bright red, no clothes can be dyed bright red. The law aims to protect the communicative force of a symbol, but it is not aimed particularly at communicative acts.

Viewpoint discrimination, harmful reaction regulation, and symbol protection are the three critical categories for Johnson and for appraisal of the new federal law. Laws may be directed at communication in at least two other ways as well. Statutes may treat certain subject matters differently from others; they may restrict advertising or communications about sex to an extent greater than communications about politics or religion. Finally, laws may restrict particular methods of communication, such as billboards or demonstrations, more than other methods. Subject matter regulation is not at issue for flag burning. Method restriction is involved. . . .

Assuming that the basis for people's taking offense is the message communicated, the Court does not immediately conclude that strict scrutiny of the statute is required. It asks instead whether the state has an interest behind its prohibition on flag burning that is unrelated to the suppression of expression. If the state had such an interest, it would apparently

succeed in achieving the more relaxed scrutiny of *O'Brien*. One asserted state interest was the prevention of violence. The Court points out that offense is often not followed by violence and that first amendment decisions closely circumscribe when speech may be punished because of a likely violent reaction. Much controversial speech causes offense, and states cannot forbid all offensive speech because violence may occasionally result. This is standard first amendment doctrine, and the Court rightly eliminates prevention of violence as a basis for the Texas statute.

The Court seems to assume, however, that if the statute had applied only when violence was highly likely, it would not have been directed at expression. That assumption involves a serious confusion, one that obscures what is at issue when offense is caused. Someone who reacts violently at a communication initially feels offense and anger. The content of the message triggers violence, just as it triggers offense. If the state's genuine wish is to prevent violence or offense, it can say it does not really care about the content of the communication; it wants only to prevent an independent harm, physical harm or emotional upset. Without quite resolving the point, the *Johnson* Court expresses doubt that "a desire to prevent a violent audience reaction is 'related to expression' in the same way that a desire to prevent an audience from being offended is 'related to expression.'" But plainly the *relations* are similar. The *differences* are that preventing violence is usually a more important state interest and that [it] is less likely to be a cover for suppressing unpopular messages.

We need to recognize that the relations to expression are similar, because we should be open to the possibility that deep offense alone may sometimes be the basis for restriction on speech. . . .

Having disposed of violence prevention as a possible basis for the statute, the *Johnson* Court turns to another asserted state justification, that of preserving the flag as a symbol of nationhood and national unity. The Court says that the state's interest is related to expression. It suggests that the state's concern is that flag desecration will cause people to stop believing that the flag stands for nationhood and national unity or that we enjoy unity as a nation. "These concerns blossom only when a person's treatment of the flag communicates some message. . . ." Since Johnson's "political expression was restricted" because he expressed dissatisfaction with the country's policies, the "State's asserted interest in preserving the special symbolic character of the flag" must be subjected to the " 'most exacting scrutiny.' "

The Court's analysis on this point flows too smoothly. It treats application of the Texas law like application of a law that forbids displaying within fifty feet of an embassy signs that tend to bring that foreign government into "public odium" or "public disrepute." That law, struck down in *Boos v. Barry*, was a straightforward regulation of content; it was viewpoint discrimination. Displaying near the Soviet embassy a sign praising the Soviet Union or neutral toward it is not criminal; displaying a highly critical sign is criminal. But was viewpoint discrimination really involved in the Texas statute? Suppose people constantly dragged flags through the mud and used them to light campfires. The strength of the flag as a symbol might well diminish if people continually treated it shabbily. And its strength as a symbol could be damaged even if people mistreated it in demonstrations in favor of nationhood and national unity. Thus, the threat to the flag as a symbol of nationhood and national unity does not flow only from mistreatment that casts doubt on whether the flag represents national unity, whether national unity exists, or whether national unity of the sort we have is desirable. It is just this point that leads Justice Stevens to say in dissent that "[t]he content of respondent's message has no relevance whatsoever to the case." Nevertheless, the most offensive instances of shabby treatment are probably those that in some way attack the government, national unity, or the idea of the flag; and this type of attack was an aspect of Johnson's causing offense. Further, most people who wish to treat the flag shabbily knowing that what they do will offend others will be people with just such antiestablishment messages. In effect, the Texas law impinges much more heavily on people with these messages than on others. The *Johnson* Court oversimplifies by assuming that an effort to preserve the flag as a symbol of national unity *must* be directed at communications against that idea; but its conclusion that the interest of Texas is aimed against such communications is sound.

## C. Application of the Standard to Johnson

In the third stage of first amendment analysis, the Court has little difficulty determining that Texas has failed to meet "the most exacting scrutiny." The government may not prohibit the expression of an idea simply because it is disagreeable. Nor may the government preclude messages from being expressed in particular ways chosen by those who want to express the ideas. People are normally free to choose how they will express themselves. The government may not restrict symbols to be used for a limited set of messages. . . .

## D. The New Federal Statute

. . .

The Flag Protection Act of 1989 provides that anyone who "knowingly mutilates, defaces, physically defiles, burns, maintains on the floor or ground, or tramples upon" a United States flag is guilty of a crime. The Act excepts actions to dispose of worn or soiled flags. Congress defeated efforts to amend the bill to cover only public acts; the law covers acts committed in private as well as in public. The idea underlying the statute is plain enough. The definition of the crime is removed as far as possible from focusing on communicative acts. The objective is to have this statute treated like the draft card statute in *O'Brien*. If it is treated as a statute not directed at communication that happens to interfere with some acts of symbolic speech, the *O'Brien* test will apply when communicative flag burning is punished. That standard of scrutiny is much more lenient than strict scrutiny. It is the drafters' aspiration that convictions will be upheld.

. . .

What of doctrinal coherence? The Court might distinguish *Johnson* because the federal government has a legitimate interest in the flag's physical integrity per se or because the government's aim to preserve the flag as a national symbol is different somehow from the similar purpose that Texas asserted.

The government's interest in preserving the physical integrity of the flag might be put as some kind of property interest or as a sovereignty interest. In his *Johnson* dissent, Chief Justice Rehnquist draws on a case giving exclusive use of the word "Olympic" to the United States Olympic Committee. He suggests that the government may have a similar limited property right in the flag. Later he mentions an opinion by Justice Fortas urging that private ownership of a flag is subject to special burdens and responsibilities. However, those who burn flags are not trying to take a "free ride" on the work of others as are those who use the word "Olympic" for their own endeavors. And the only conceivable property interest the government has in privately owned flags is to protect the flag as a symbol. The House of Representatives pressed the sovereignty interest before district courts considering dismissal of prosecutions of people who burned flags in protest against passage of the new Act. The courts recognized that any sovereignty claim in flags comes down to a claim to protect the flag as a symbol. The property and sovereignty arguments dissolve into an argument that the government should be able to preserve the flag's symbolic power.

The Senate argued to the district courts that the federal law's aim to preserve the flag as a symbol differs from that urged by Texas. The idea is to preserve the flag as an embodiment of diverse views and not as a representative of any one view. What principles must be accepted if this argument is to be the vehicle by which strict scrutiny is to be avoided? The Court must decide: (1) that the interest of protecting the flag as a symbol does not establish that the law is aimed at communicative acts; (2) that protecting the flag as a symbol does not impermissibly discriminate between forms of expression; and (3) that the aim to protect the flag as a symbol by penal legislation is not itself an impermissible or highly suspect aim to favor certain ideas.

In *Johnson*, the Court assumes that only acts with a message could threaten the flag as a symbol of nationhood and national unity. Suppose it were right. The federal law prohibits some acts that are noncommunicative, but if its underlying purpose to protect the flag as a symbol concerns only communicative acts, the law is directed at speech. As I have noted, the *Johnson* Court is wrong on this point. Noncommunicative acts can tarnish the flag as a symbol. So the purpose of preserving the flag as a symbol does reach some defacing and destruction of the flag that is noncommunicative. But the correlation between forbidden acts that pose the threat and those meant to communicate is very high; moreover, the legislative history contains overwhelming evidence that Congress was concerned about those who intentionally show disrespect for the flag. Despite the absence of any surface reference to communicative acts, the purpose of the law is to inhibit expression. Although I shall not make the argument, I believe that purpose is so clearly establishable here that it should not be disregarded by the courts.

Whether a simple aim to preserve the flag as a symbol discriminates in favor of certain views or forms of expression is a harder question. District Judge Rothstein notes that the new law suppresses the views of those who want to express themselves by destroying the flag. But that could be said of any restriction on a form of expression. The law against destruction of draft cards suppresses those who want to express themselves that way; a law against billboards suppresses those who want to speak through billboards. That form of discrimination alone does not trigger strict scrutiny. Because most of those who want to destroy flags have antiestablishment messages, the law might be understood as discriminating against such messages, but perhaps this high correlation alone should not be enough to trigger strict scrutiny.

The most complex question is whether an aim to protect the flag as a symbol is an impermissible or highly suspect objective for penal legislation in and of itself. This question is a critical one for provisions directed against flag misuse as well as flag destruction, for provisions meant to guard against trivialization as well as symbolic rejection. Let us suppose that most of the acts a legislature is worried about are not hostile expressive acts at all; it fears that various uses or misuses of the flag will dilute its force. Recall the example of a law forbidding people to use the bright red color for any purpose, the aim being to preserve the symbolic force of that color in the flag. One may argue that the government can have a flag, that it can promote reverence for the flag, and that its aim to do that by laws limiting use are a permissible means. On the other hand, one may argue that special protection for a communicative symbol with particular content, however vague, is itself a kind of viewpoint discrimination. As Professor Nimmer put it, the flag symbolizes the nation and to "preserve respect for a symbol *qua* symbol is to preserve respect for the meaning expressed by the symbol." The argument to this effect is strong enough to distinguish this case from one in which the government's interest in preventing behavior has nothing to do with communication. The Court said in *O'Brien*, disregarding legislative history that showed an aim to stop protesters from burning draft cards, that the government's interest in preserving draft cards was unrelated to expression. That could not be said about the government's interest in preserving flags. At a minimum, the aim is to preserve the powerful expressive force of the flag. Thus, the *O'Brien* test does not seem apt. But "most exacting scrutiny" may not be right either. The aim to keep intact expressive symbols people have come to care about, and that the government regards as a positive force, is not the same as an aim to suppress messages because of their content. If the only challengeable aspect of the new federal law were its attempt to preserve the flag as a symbol, perhaps some test more rigorous than what *O'Brien* has come to mean, but less rigorous than most exacting scrutiny, would be appropriate.

I have concluded that *Johnson* was a more complicated case than the majority indicated but that an application of standard first amendment principles supports the Court's result. The challenge to the new federal statute is closer to the border. A purpose to preserve the flag as a symbol is not necessarily aimed at communicative acts. Preserving the physical integrity of the flag has some value independent of the reason why a flag might be destroyed. But the value has to do with communication, positive "flag com- munication." Further, the new federal law, by the particular actions it covers and as indicated by its legislative history, is dominantly aimed at hostile communication. Measured against coherent doctrine rather than likely outcome, the result of cases considering the new law should be the same as in *Johnson*.

. . .

## Bibliography

*The Nature of Speech*

Alexander, Lawrence & Horton, Paul, *The Impossibility of a Free Speech Principle*, 78 Northwestern University Law Review 1319 (1984)

Alfange, Dean, Jr., *Free Speech and Symbolic Conduct: The Draft-Card Burning Case*, 1968 Supreme Court Review 1 (1968)

Emerson, Thomas I., *First Amendment Doctrine and the Burger Court*, 68 California Law Review 422 (1980)

Henkin, Louis, *On Drawing Lines*, 82 Harvard Law Review 63 (1968)

Loewy, Arnold H., *The Flag-Burning Case: Freedom of Speech When We Need It the Most*, 68 North Carolina Law Review 65 (1989)

Michelman, Frank, *Saving Old Glory: On Constitutional Iconography*, 42 Stanford Law Review 1337 (1990)

Tushnet, Mark, *The Flag-Burning Episode: An Essay on the Constitution*, 61 University of Colorado Law Review 39 (1990)

Werhan, Keith, *The O'Briening of First Amendment Methodology*, 19 Arizona State Law Journal 635 (1987)

West, Robin, *Foreword: Taking Freedom Seriously*, 104 Harvard Law Review 43 (1990)

## D. The Nature of the Press

Debate over the scope and function of the speech and press clauses has proceeded despite any consensual definition of the press itself. How the press is understood is critical in determining what the First Amendment protects. A medium that does not qualify as part of the press has no constitutional significance, as was the case for motion pictures until the middle of this century. Significant too is whether the press clause has meaning separate from the speech clause. An understanding of the press clause as independently significant provides the premise for arguments that the press has special privileges, immunities, and access rights not afforded to the general public by the speech clause. Justice Potter Stewart advances a structural definition of the press that favors a preferred First Amendment status. David Lange proposes a functional definition opposed to special First Amendment treatment. Justice William Brennan, Jr. advocates First Amendment standards for the press that dependent upon whether it is performing a "speech" or "structural" function.

Potter Stewart, *"Or of the Press,"* 26 HASTINGS LAW JOURNAL 631 (1975)*

. . .

Surprisingly, despite the importance of newspapers in the political and social life of our country the Supreme Court has not until very recently been called upon to delineate their constitutional role in our structure of government.

Our history is filled with struggles over the rights and prerogatives of the press, but these disputes rarely found their way to the Supreme Court. The early years of the Republic witnessed controversy over the constitutional validity of the short-lived Alien and Sedition Act, but the controversy never reached the Court. In the next half century there was nationwide turmoil over the right of the organized press to advocate the then subversive view that slavery should be abolished. In Illinois a publisher was killed for publishing abolitionist views. But none of this history made First Amendment law because the Court had earlier held that the Bill of Rights applied only against the Federal Government, not against the individual states.

With the passage of the Fourteenth Amendment, the constitutional framework was modified, and by the 1920's the Court had established that the protections of the First Amendment extend against all government—federal, state, and local.

The next fifty years witnessed a great outpouring of First Amendment litigation, all of which inspired books and articles beyond number. But, with few exceptions, neither these First Amendment cases nor their commentators squarely considered the Constitution's guarantee of a Free Press. Instead, the focus was on its guarantee of free speech. The Court's decisions dealt with the rights of isolated individuals, or of unpopular minority groups, to stand up against governmental power representing an angry or frightened majority. The cases that came to the Court during those years involved the rights of the soapbox orator, the nonconformist pamphleteer, the religious evangelist. The Court was seldom asked to define the rights and privileges, or the responsibilities, of the organized press.

In very recent years cases involving the established press finally have begun to reach the Supreme Court, and they have presented a variety of problems, sometimes arising in complicated factual settings.

In a series of cases, the Court has been called upon to consider the limits imposed by the free press guarantee upon a state's common or statutory law of libel. As a result of those cases, a public figure cannot successfully sue a publisher for libel unless he can show that the publisher maliciously printed a damaging untruth.

The Court has also been called upon to decide whether a newspaper reporter has a First Amendment privilege to refuse to disclose his confidential sources to a grand jury. By a divided vote, the Court found no such privilege to exist in the circumstances of the cases before it.

In another noteworthy case, the Court was asked by the Justice Department to restrain publication by the *New York Times* and other newspapers of the so-called Pentagon Papers. The Court declined to do so.

In yet another case, the question to be decided was whether political groups have a First Amendment or statutory right of access to the federally regulated broadcast channels of radio and television. The Court held there was no such right of access.

Last Term the Court confronted a Florida statute that required newspapers to grant a "right of reply" to political candidates they had criticized. The Court unanimously held this statute to be inconsistent with the guarantees of a free press.

It seems to me that the Court's approach to all these cases has uniformly reflected its understanding that the Free Press guarantee is, in essence, a *structural* provision of the Constitution. Most of the other provisions in the Bill of Rights protect specific liberties or specific rights of individuals: freedom of speech, freedom of worship, the right to counsel, the privilege against compulsory self-incrimination, to name a few. In contrast, the Free Press Clause extends protection to an institution. The publishing business is, in short, the only organized private business that is given explicit constitutional protection.

This basic understanding is essential, I think, to avoid an elementary error of constitutional law. It is tempting to suggest that freedom of the press means only that newspaper publishers are guaranteed freedom of expression. They *are* guaranteed that freedom, to be sure, but so are we all, because of the Free Speech Clause. If the Free Press guarantee meant no more than freedom of expression, it would be a constitutional redundancy. Between 1776 and the drafting of our Constitution, many of the state constitutions contained clauses protecting freedom of the press while at the same time recognizing no gen-

---

eral freedom of speech. By including both guarantees in the First Amendment, the Founders quite clearly recognized the distinction between the two.

It is also a mistake to suppose that the only purpose of the constitutional guarantee of a free press is to insure that a newspaper will serve as a neutral forum for debate, a "market place for ideas," a kind of Hyde Park corner for the community. A related theory sees the press as a neutral conduit of information between the people and their elected leaders. These theories, in my view, again give insufficient weight to the institutional autonomy of the press that it was the purpose of the Constitution to guarantee.

In setting up the three branches of the Federal Government, the Founders deliberately created an internally competitive system. As Mr. Justice Brandeis once wrote:

> The [Founders'] purpose was, not to avoid friction, but, by means of the inevitable friction incident to the distribution of the governmental powers among three departments, to save the people from autocracy.

The primary purpose of the constitutional guarantee of a free press was a similar one: to create a fourth institution outside the Government as an additional check on the three official branches. Consider the opening words of the Free Press Clause of the Massachusetts Constitution, drafted by John Adams:

> The liberty of the press is essential to the security of the state.

The relevant metaphor, I think, is the metaphor of the Fourth Estate. What Thomas Carlyle wrote about the British Government a century ago has a curiously contemporary ring:

> Burke said there were Three Estates in Parliament; but, in the Reporters' Gallery yonder, there sat a Fourth Estate more important far than they all. It is not a figure of speech or witty saying; it is a literal fact—very momentous to us in these times.

For centuries before our Revolution, the press in England had been licensed, censored, and bedeviled by prosecutions for seditious libel. The British Crown knew that a free press was not just a neutral vehicle for the balanced discussion of diverse ideas. Instead, the free press meant organized, expert scrutiny of government. The press was a conspiracy of the intellect, with the courage of numbers. This formidable check on official power was what the British Crown had feared—and what the American Founders decided to risk. . . .

It is quite possible to conceive of the survival of our Republic without an autonomous press. For openness and honesty in government, for an adequate flow of information between the people and their representatives, for a sufficient check on autocracy and despotism, the traditional competition between the three branches of government, supplemented by vigorous political activity, might be enough.

The press could be relegated to the status of a public utility. The guarantee of free speech would presumably put some limitation on the regulation to which the press could be subjected. But if there were no guarantee of a free press, government could convert the communications media into a neutral "market place of ideas." Newspapers and television networks could then be required to promote contemporary government policy or current notions of social justice.

Such a constitution is possible; it might work reasonably well. But it is not the Constitution the Founders wrote. It is not the Constitution that has carried us through nearly two centuries of national life. Perhaps our liberties might survive without an independent established press. But the Founders doubted it, and, in the year 1974, I think we can all be thankful for their doubts.

---

David Lange, *The Speech and Press Clauses,* 23 UCLA Law Review 77 (1975)*

Are there important differences in the protection provided by the speech and press clauses of the first amendment? Two distinguished commentators have suggested recently that there are. In a law review article, Professor Melville Nimmer has argued that a speech-press "duality" is suggested by the text of the amendment itself and by recent Supreme Court opinions. He is joined in this view by Mr. Justice Stewart who has suggested, in a speech delivered at the Yale Law School, that the difference is between the individual freedom of expression secured by the speech clause and the institutional freedom protected by the press clause. The views of Professor Nimmer and the Justice do not entirely coincide, but there is enough common ground between them to justify essentially common analysis. As I shall explain, I am persuaded that the first amendment ought not to be read the way Professor Nimmer and the Justice

* Originally published in 23 UCLA L. Rev. 77. Copyright 1975, The Regents of the University of California. All rights reserved.

propose. However that may be, it is at least clear that they have succeeded in isolating issues of immense importance which deserve far more careful attention than they have had during the development of our first amendment tradition.

## I. TOWARD A SPEECH-PRESS "DUALITY": TWO VIEWS

The first amendment forbids abridgement of "the freedom of speech, or of the press." Professor Nimmer and Justice Stewart both observe that unless the separate references to "speech" and "press" convey separate meanings, the Framers have left us with a "constitutional redundancy." Though neither is prepared to rest his argument on this observation alone, their subsequent discussions are to some extent impelled by this initial truism. . . .

It should be said that Justice Stewart's remarks at Yale were primarily in defense of a vigorous, partisan press. His views, though interesting, might have seemed unremarkable had he not explicitly championed the separate constitutional status of the press. Most students of the first amendment would agree that one of its chief theoretical justifications is the advancement of the electorate; and all would surely agree that there is a permissible gulf between "free expression" and "successful expression." Yet these observations alone would not justify particular reliance on the press clause, and, as will be seen, "freedom of the press" does not seem to have had quite the institutional connotations in the eighteenth century that Justice Stewart suggests. Moreover, the brevity of his remarks prevents him from explaining why the press clause might be of separate importance today.

Professor Nimmer, on the other hand, provides a somewhat fuller development of the thesis. He is less certain than Justice Stewart that the Framers meant to distinguish between freedom of speech and a free press. As he concedes, the terms "freedom of speech" and "freedom of the press" were used interchangeably at the time the first amendment was adopted. He also concedes that recent Supreme Court opinions emphasizing "the press" may have employed language which was simply inadvertent or ambivalent even when it seemed most clear. . . .

## II. THE ORIGINS OF SPEECH AND PRESS

It is true, of course, that the Framers have left us language in the first amendment which justifies the present debate—language which, under almost any view one takes, is less than clear. Either it has occasioned some two hundred years of potential misunderstanding or it simply seems redundant. Of the two, the latter is more probable, for the fact is (as

Professor Nimmer himself notes) that the terms "freedom of speech" and "freedom of the press" were used quite interchangeably in the eighteenth century, particularly so among persons who were interested in the terms at a conceptual level.

Justice Stewart appears to believe that the Framers meant explicitly to recognize a "fourth institution outside the Government as an additional check on the three official branches." He may be correct, but in fairness one must insist that the evidence in favor of his view is not entirely persuasive. The partisan press did provide a source of restraint upon government, but it does not seem to have been organized in quite the way Justice Stewart appears to suppose. Instead, the press was partisan because much of it was directly in the service of opposing power factions. This did lead to criticism of authority, sometimes in daring and amusing fashion. Thomas Jefferson, for example, employed a journalist to attack the policies of Washington's party while Jefferson was himself Washington's Secretary of State. But this was scarcely institutional partisanship on the part of the press itself. Burke's "fourth estate" still lay ahead in England as well as in this country. The partisan press bore little relationship to the later "penny press," and still less to the press of Hearst and Pulitzer or the "free and responsible press" of today. In short, the institutional press apparently envisioned by Justice Stewart had scarcely been born. . . .

## III. DISTINGUISHING SPEECH FROM THE PRESS IN CONTEMPORARY AMERICAN LIFE

. . .

At first reading, Justice Stewart seems explicit. He thinks of the organized press, of the business, the institution. He refers in his speech to "the publishing business," but it seems clear that he would include broadcasters and perhaps other representatives of the mass media as well. Thus, for example, in his dissenting opinion in *Branzburg v. Hayes* he acknowledges "the first amendment rights of mass circulation newspapers and electronic media to disseminate ideas and information. . . ." It is not clear, however, who might be excluded from the press as he views it. Is "the lonely pamphleteer" protected by the press clause? What of the novelist and the film maker? The "underground press?" The traditional, if perhaps unthinking, answer of the Court would appear to be that they are included. And Justice Stewart's own opinions have not suggested clear disagreement with that response. Yet none of these is necessarily a part of the mass media and some, by definition, have virtually no institutional identification. Is it a misreading, after all, to suppose that Justice Stewart means to define the institutional press in terms of structure? Would he define it in terms of role or function instead? Again in his opinion in *Branzburg*, he seems to suggest something of the sort when he describes the nature of the reporter's claim to privilege:

> The reporter's constitutional right to a confidential relationship with his source stems from the broad societal interest in a full and free flow of information to the public. It is this basic concern that underlies the constitution's protection of a free press . . . because the guarantee is "not for the benefit of the press so much as for the benefit of all of us."

If it is function, rather than structure, which defines the press, the definition again is at least approximately compatible with the conceptual relationship between speech and press. But a definition expressed in terms of function seems equally at odds with Justice Stewart's emphatic references to the organized mass media and with his insistence that the first amendment libel privileges do not apply to individuals. With misgivings, then, one is forced to conclude either that the Justice does not know himself what he means by "the press" or, more probably, that he has not yet had the occasion to express himself fully.
. . .

Problems in definition, then, are the first obstacle to providing separate constitutional status for speech and the press. In fairness, it should be said again that neither Justice Stewart nor Professor Nimmer can be faulted for not surmounting this obstacle. They have succeeded admirably in isolating the idea of separate rights and their observations are truly proactive. It may be that further debate will yield definitions which will lend somewhat greater clarity to the meaning of the press. It is not altogether impossible to define "the press." We do so every day for many general purposes and, less frequently, for the purpose of defining legal consequences as well. But it is still unlikely, in my opinion, that we will succeed in defining the press in ways which will prove satisfactory in recognizing separate rights under the press clause. The problem comes to this: If the press is defined broadly enough to include the pamphleteer and the underground, the definition also will have to approach speech so closely that the exclusion of speech will often seem arbitrary and unjustified. We will have, in Justice Stewart's words, "a structural provision," but with no distinct structure. If, on the other hand, the pamphleteer and the underground are excluded, the result is perverse; these are two elements in the contemporary press

which the Framers themselves would have recognized. Alternatively, I suppose, each element in the speech-press spectrum might be examined individually, sometimes gaining the protection of the press clause and sometimes not. That may make sense as a general approach to the first amendment, but it is not clear that distinctions between speech and the press should be advanced that way. In fact, to make a system like that work—that is, to recognize overriding differences between speech and the press without particular regard for structure—it would be necessary to emphasize functions and, more important, to assign them values or weight. And that is just where the real uncertainties began.

## IV. RECONCILING SPEECH AND THE PRESS

Let us suppose, however, that adequate definitions are possible. Let us also suppose that the debate is still open—that is to say, that the Framers have given us no clear mandate concerning the question of separate press status under the first amendment. Finally, let us suppose, as we must, that separate status for the press will mean an array of privileges or responsibilities distinct from the rights accorded under the speech clause. That does not mean that individuals within the press will not also be protected by "freedom of expression," as Justice Stewart notes, but merely that the "press *qua* press" will somehow be set apart. It would be helpful if we knew how much apart, but in the circumstances that is not possible and, in any event, it is not essential. What I wish to present here are two frankly speculative observations about what we can ultimately expect if we do elect to recognize separate constitutional status for the institutional press. If these observations are correct, they identify distinct threats to freedom of expression which can best be avoided by serious efforts to reconcile, rather than to distinguish, the freedoms of speech and press.

### A. The Danger for a Free Press

In the first place, I doubt that the institutional press will remain secure for very long if it is set apart from speech. Divorcing speech from the press means ripping away the essential underpinnings of the press as well. Justice Stewart himself has acknowledged that a free press is guaranteed "not for the benefit of the press so much as for the benefit of all of us." One would expect as much. It is not an easy matter to demonstrate the value of an independent press which is not essentially identified with the people it serves. Freedom of the press in the best of times is insecure. Its survival depends ultimately on the confidence and goodwill of the people who support it. If they have serious reason to suppose that they are separated from it, or worse, at odds with it, the most powerful press cannot rest easy. Having lost its constituency, it will have lost its reason for being as well.

This is not to suggest that the press is likely to be put down by armed revolt or anything half so satisfyingly dramatic. Instead, my speculation is that it will simply be nibbled to death by gnats—that is, it will finally fall victim to an unending stream of complaints coupled with unceasing demands for greater responsibility. Responsibility in this context is likely to mean balance, objectivity, or fairness. Justice Stewart seems quite correct when he implies that the first amendment demands none of these from the press. But the plain fact is that an increasing number of people do. . . .

B. The Danger for Free Speech

My second speculation is that individual interests in speech may be even more seriously threatened by separate constitutional status. With no distinct institutional identification—and now without claim to immediate theoretical alliance with the press—they may find it more difficult to stand up against the constraints which a mass society inevitably finds it convenient to impose. I do not wish to appear excessively pessimistic. We are, after all, remarkably tolerant as nations go. Most of us understand, at least sometimes, that "one man's vulgarity is another's lyric." But how much of this tolerance has resulted from our emphasis on freedom of expression? What will we risk if the emphasis is shifted, for example, from "expression" to "media" and "nonmedia" speech? . . .

. . . Public issues can be debated with as much force among individuals as in the press. Indeed, in my experience, journalists themselves are infinitely more "robust, uninhibited and wide open" in private conversation than they are in print or on the air. And understandably so. They must realize that the mass press does not originate ideas; it spreads them around, shaping, leveling, and smoothing them in the process, somewhat the way a road grader moves sand. The process has its uses, to be sure, but someone must still dig. And in the field of human ideas and their original expression, that function belongs first to individuals. Consider the facts in *New York Times Co. v. Sullivan*: an editorial advertisement; a suit against four individuals and the *New York Times*. Does anyone seriously suppose that the advertisement originated with those individuals and the *Times*? In a limited sense, it did; the advertisement's recurring theme was borrowed from an editorial *The Times* itself had published ten days earlier. But where

did the ideas in that editorial and the advertisement come from? They came from the streets of Orangeburg and Montgomery and "a host of other cities in the South;" from demonstrations and songs and speeches of protest; from impassioned sermons in the Ebenezer Baptist Church; in short, from these and hundreds of other acts of individual courage in the pursuit of the democratic dialogue until, having well begun and only then, these individuals could fairly expect others to "heed their rising voices." There are many lessons in this case, but among the most important is the example set by speech—speech in league with the other freedoms guaranteed by the Constitution, yes, but still, emphatically, speech. Should the protection of the libel cases be extended to individual speech? I do not understand how it can be denied in any categorical manner. Nonmedia speech is always the antecedent of media speech. Of course, there are occasions when nonmedia speech is trivial, as there is much which is trivial in the press. It may be sensible, in the interest of private reputation, to ask, before imposing liability, just what the defendant said—or even who the victim was, as *Gertz* proposes. But if public issues are to be debated, it is not sensible to treat two speakers differently merely on the ground that one proposes to speak privately while another intends to use the media. No presupposition can justify that; we have no way of knowing how far the private communication will carry or which of the two will prove to be the more enduring. Today, the private letters of Madison, Jefferson and Adams are among our public treasures. But who really cares what it was that John Peter Zenger published? . . .

Again, then, I submit that the goal of first amendment theory should be to equate and reconcile the interests of speech and press, rather than to separate them. This is scarcely to suggest a new theory; there are as many examples of how this might be done as there have been cases referring to "freedom of expression" or turning on "freedom of speech and press." If anything "new" is needed, it is probably a clearer understanding of the risks which may be incurred when the reference point is something less than these concepts. Balancing interests within the framework provided by the speech and press clauses may be necessary if the larger interests of both are to be advanced. But balancing speech against the press itself is neither necessary nor desirable.

CONCLUSION

Most risks are worth taking in some circumstances. But it is not clear that the risks posed by separate constitutional status for the mass press are justified. The Framers themselves do not seem to have contemplated it. More than fifty years of litigation have not suggested it, at least until now. And even now its purpose does not seem evident. If it is to provide real analytical clarity, then it seems equally clear that it can do so only at the expense of individual interests which have long been protected. As Mr. Justice White wrote in *Branzburg v. Hayes*:

> Sooner or later, it would be necessary to define those categories of newsmen who qualified . . . , a questionable procedure in light of the traditional doctrine that liberty of the press is the right of the lonely pamphleteer who uses carbon paper or a mimeograph just as much as of the large metropolitan publisher who utilizes the latest photocomposition methods. . . . Freedom of the press is a "fundamental personal right" which "is not confined to newspapers and periodicals. It necessarily embraces pamphlets and leaflets. . . . The press in its historic connotation comprehends every sort of publication which affords a vehicle of information and opinion."

Professor Nimmer may prove to be correct when he says that this "is an idea whose time is past due." But until these objections can be answered, I think this is one idea we can afford to keep waiting.

----

William J. Brennan, Jr., *Address,* 32 RUTGERS LAW REVIEW 173 (1979)*

As money is to the economy, so the press is to our political culture: it is the medium of circulation. It is the currency through which the knowledge of recent events is exchanged; the coin by which *public* discussion may be purchased.

This analogy, of course, cannot be pressed too far. Unlike a medium of circulation, which receives the passive valuation of others, the press is active, shaping and defining the very arena in which events assume their public character. In this the press performs a tripartite role. It chooses which events it will publicize; it disseminates to a greater or lesser extent, selected information about these events; and it adopts toward these events attitudes which are often instrumental in forming public opinion.

These functions are of manifest importance for

the political life of the Nation. A democracy depends upon the existence of a *public* life and culture, and in a country of some 220 millions, this would scarcely be possible without the press. I believe now, and have always believed, that, insofar as the First Amendment shields the wellsprings of our democracy, it also provides protection for the press in the exercise of these functions, for, as I said in an opinion for the Court many years ago: the guarantees of the First Amendment "are not for the benefit of the press so much as for the benefit of all of us. A broadly defined freedom of the press assures the maintenance of our political system and an open society.". . .

Under one model—which I call the "speech" model—the press requires and is accorded the absolute protection of the First Amendment. In the other model—I call it the "structural" model—the press' interests may conflict with other societal interests and adjustment of the conflict on occasion favors the competing claim.

The "speech" model is familiar. It is as comfortable as a pair of old shoes, and the press, in its present conflict with the Court, most often slips into the language and rhetorical stance with which this model is associated even when only the "structural" model is at issue. According to this traditional "speech" model, the primary purpose of the First Amendment is more or less absolutely to prohibit any interference with freedom of expression. The press seen as the public spokesman *par excellence*. Indeed, this model sometimes depicts the press as simply a collection of individuals who wish to speak out and broadly disseminate their views. This model draws its considerable power—I emphasize—from the abiding commitment we all feel to the right of self-expression, and, so far as it goes, this model commands the widest consensus. In the past two years, for example, the Court has twice unanimously struck down state statutes which prohibited the press from speaking out on certain subjects, and the Court has firmly rejected judicial attempts to muzzle press publication through prior restraints. The "speech" model thus readily lends itself to the heady rhetoric of absolutism.

The "speech" model, however, has its limitations. It is a mistake to suppose that the First Amendment protects *only* self-expression, only the right to speak out. I believe that the First Amendment in addition fosters the values of democratic self-government. In the words of Professor Zechariah Chafee, "[t]he First Amendment protects . . . a social interest in the attainment of truth, so that the country may not only adopt the wisest course of ac-

----

* Reprinted with permission of Rutgers Law Review.

tion but carry it out in the wisest way.'' The Amendment therefore also forbids the government from interfering with the communicative processes through which we citizens exercise and prepare to exercise our rights of self-government. The individual right to speak out, even millions of such rights aggregated together, will not sufficiently protect these social interests. It is in recognition of this fact that the Court has referred to ''the circulation of information to which *the public is entitled* in virtue of the constitutional guaranties.''

Another way of saying this is that the First Amendment protects the structure of communications necessary for the existence of our democracy. This insight suggests the second model to describe the role of the press in our society. This second model is structural in nature. It focuses on the relationship of the press to the communicative functions required by our democratic beliefs. To the extent the press makes these functions possible, this model requires that it receive the protection of the First Amendment. A good example is the press' role in providing and circulating the information necessary for informed public discussion. To the extent the press, or, for that matter, to the extent that any institution uniquely performs this role, it should receive unique First Amendment protection.

This ''structural'' model of the press has several important implications. It significantly extends the umbrella of the press' constitutional protections. The press is not only shielded when it speaks out, but when it performs all the myriad tasks necessary for it to gather and disseminate the news. As you can easily see, the stretch of this protection is theoretically endless. Any imposition of any kind on the press will in some measure affect its ability to perform protected functions. Therefore this model requires a Court to weigh the effects of the imposition against the social interests which are served by the imposition. This inquiry is impersonal, almost sociological in nature. But it does not fit comfortably with the absolutist rhetoric associated with the first model of the press I have discussed. For here, I repeat, the Court must weigh the effects of the imposition inhibiting press access against the social interests served by the imposition. . . .

# Bibliography

*The Nature of the Press*

Abrams, Floyd, *The Press is Different: Reflections on Justice and the Autonomous Press*, 7 Hofstra Law Review 563 (1979).

Anderson, David A., *The Origins of the Press Clause*, 30 UCLA Law Review 455 (1983).

Bezanson, Randall, *The New Free Press Guarantee,* 63 Virginia Law Review 731 (1977).

Bollinger, Lee C., *Images of a Free Press* (1991).

Levy, Leonard W., *Emergence of a Free Press* (1985).

Lewis, Anthony, *A Public Right to Know About Public Institutions: The First  Amendment As Sword*, 1980 Supreme Court Review 1 (1980).

Nimmer, Melville B., *Introduction—Is Freedom of the Press a Redundancy: What Does It Add to Freedom of Speech?*, 26 Hastings Law Journal 639 (1975).

## E. Prior Restraint

Prior restraint represents perhaps the oldest, and for many the most noxious, method of expressive management. The Supreme Court's original sense was that the First Amendment was primarily concerned with "laying no previous restraints upon publications." *Near v. Minnesota*, 283 U.S. 697, 713 (1931). Since then, it has determined that a system of prior restraint is presumptively unconstitutional and carries a heavy burden of justification. *New York Times Co. v. United States*, 403 U.S. 713, 714 (1971)(per curiam). Given exceptions to the presumption including commercial speech, and the nation's system of licensing broadcasters, it is evident that not all systems of prior restraint are at constitutional risk. The negative doctrinal reaction to prior restraint, however, denotes a powerful response to a legacy of formal and heavy-handed speech control relating back to English licensing schemes abolished in the late seventeenth century. The controversy over prior restraint thus revolves around whether one of the most fundamental distinctions in First Amendment doctrine reckons with a real difference. Thomas I. Emerson advances the traditional First Amendment position disfavoring prior restraint. John Calvin Jeffries, Jr. suggests that attention to the form of regulation diverts attention from real reasons for or against expressive control and that speech interests themselves might benefit from a primary focus upon substance. Vincent Blasi inquires into whether prior restraint presents unique risks to expressive liberty and concludes that special attention to that method of speech control is warranted.

Thomas I. Emerson, *The Doctrine Of Prior Restraint,* 20 LAW AND CONTEMPORARY PROBLEMS 648 (1955)*

The concept of prior restraint, roughly speaking, deals with official restrictions imposed upon speech or other forms of expression in advance of actual publication. Prior restraint is thus distinguished from subsequent punishment, which is a penalty imposed after the communication has been made as a punishment for having made it. Again speaking generally, a system of prior restraint would prevent communication from occurring at all; a system of subsequent punishment allows the communication but imposes a penalty after the event. Of course, the deterrent effect of a later penalty may operate to prevent a communication from ever being made. Nevertheless, for a variety of reasons, the impact upon freedom of expression may be quite different, depending upon whether the system of control is designed to block publication in advance or deter it by subsequent punishment.

In constitutional terms, the doctrine of prior restraint holds that the First Amendment forbids the Federal Government to impose any system of prior restraint, with certain limited exceptions, in any area of expression that is within the boundaries of that Amendment. By incorporating the First Amendment in the Fourteenth Amendment, the same limitations are applicable to the states.

Several features of the doctrine should be observed at the outset. In the first place, the doctrine deals with limitations of form rather than of substance. The issue is not whether the government may impose a particular restriction of substance in an area of public expression, such as forbidding obscenity in newspapers, but whether it may do so by a particular method, such as advance screening of newspaper copy. In other words, restrictions which could be validly imposed when enforced by subsequent punishment are, nevertheless, forbidden if attempted by prior restraint. The major considerations underlying the doctrine of prior restraint, therefore, are matters of administration, techniques of enforcement, methods of operation, and their effect upon the basic objectives of the First Amendment.

Moreover, the doctrine of prior restraint is, in some important respects, more precise in its application than most of the other concepts that have developed out of the First Amendment. It does not require the same degree of judicial balancing that the courts have held to be necessary in the use of the clear and present danger test, the rule against vagueness, the doctrine that a statute must be narrowly drawn, or the various formulae of reasonableness. Hence, it does not involve the same necessity for the court to pit its judgment on controversial matters of economics, politics, or social theory against that of the legislature. This is not to say that the doctrine of prior restraint is clear-cut, simple, and easy to apply. It is not. Further, it is subject to exceptions. But it does raise somewhat different problems, and ones perhaps more susceptible to judicial solution than those with which the Supreme Court appears to have been overwhelmed in dealing with aspects of the First Amendment. . . .

I
DEVELOPMENT OF THE DOCTRINE

The doctrine of prior restraint grew out of the historical setting in which one of the early battles for freedom of expression was fought. The invention of printing in the fifteenth century and its rapid development in the sixteenth and seventeenth centuries opened vast possibilities for the communication of ideas in all fields of thought and action. Prevailing doctrines of spiritual and temporal sovereignty made it inevitable that control over the new medium of expression should be gathered firmly in the hands of the ruling authorities.

As early as 1501, Pope Alexander VI, in a bull which prohibited unlicensed printing, applied the technique of prior restraint as a means of control. In England—the immediate source of our doctrine of prior restraint—printing first developed under royal sponsorship and soon became a monopoly to be granted by the Crown. For almost two centuries, a stream of royal proclamations, Star Chamber decrees, and Parliamentary enactments, constantly increasing in complexity, shackled the art and the business of printing and publication.

The Licensing Act of 1662 illustrates the scope of the system. Not only were seditious and heretical books and pamphlets prohibited, but no person was allowed to print any material unless it was first entered with the Stationers' Company, a government monopoly, and duly licensed by the appropriate state or clerical functionary. Further, no book was to be imported without a license; no person was permitted to sell books without a license; all printing presses had to be registered with the Stationers' Company; the number of master printers was limited to twenty, and these were to be licensed and to furnish bond;

* Reprinted with permission of Duke University School of Law.

and sweeping powers to search for suspect printed matter in houses and shops, except the houses of peers, were granted. In this form, the licensing laws, renewed and augmented from time to time, continued through most of the latter half of the century.

In 1695, when the current licensing law expired, the House of Commons declined to extend it. The House of Lords voted for renewal but, when the Commons insisted, acquiesced. Thus the licensing system, in all important respects, lapsed. It was never revived.

It is interesting to note that the demise of the licensing system appears to have occurred not so much because of broad opposition in principle to any curtailment of free expression, but rather because the system in operation had become generally unwieldy, extreme, and even ridiculous. . . .

Furthermore, it is important to observe that, although the system of prior restraint was allowed to lapse, the law against seditious libel and blasphemy remained unaffected and was, indeed, applied with increasing frequency and severity as a form of subsequent punishment for expression considered hostile to state or church.

Developments in America paralleled, with some lag, the situation in England. By the second decade of the eighteenth century, the licensing laws had broken down.

In the course of the eighteenth century, freedom of the press from licensing came to assume the status of a common law or natural right. Blackstone summarized the law in a famous passage:

The liberty of the press is indeed essential to the nature of a free state; but this consists in laying no *previous* restraints upon publications, and not in freedom from censure for criminal matter when published. Every free man has an undoubted right to lay what sentiments he pleases before the public; to forbid this, is to destroy the freedom of the press; but he publishes what is improper, mischievous or illegal, he must take the consequences of his own temerity

Such was the situation when, in 1791, the First Amendment was drafted, adopted by Congress, and ratified by the states. The struggle over the licensing laws was certainly not forgotten. And there can be little doubt that the First Amendment was designed to foreclose in America the establishment of any system of prior restraint on the pattern of the English censorship system. Indeed, it was argued in some quarters that this was the sole purpose of the First Amendment and that, following Blackstone, it was not intended to embrace subsequent punishment of

publications. Not until the twentieth century did the Supreme Court finally settle this issue in favor of the broader interpretation of the First Amendment. But the doctrine that no previous restraint of publication could stand against the First Amendment was never challenged. Thus, the concept was elevated to the status of constitutional principle. . . .

### III
### THE NATURE OF PRIOR RESTRAINT

. . .

For purposes of our analysis, we will consider primarily those characteristics of prior restraint which mark the most common forms of communications affected by the first, or executive, type of restraint.

*Breadth*: A system of prior restraint normally brings within the complex of government machinery a far greater amount of communication than a system of subsequent punishment. It subjects to government scrutiny and approval *all* expression in the area controlled—the innocent and borderline as well as the offensive, the routine as well as the unusual. The machinery is geared to universal inspection, not to scrutiny in particular cases which are the subject of complaint or otherwise come to the attention of prosecuting officials. The pall of government control is, thus, likely to hang more pervasively over the area of communication, and more issues are likely to be resolved against free expression.

*Timing and delay*: Under a system of subsequent punishment, the communication has already been made before the government takes action; it thus takes its place, for whatever it may be worth, in the market place of ideas. Under a system of prior restraint, the communication, if banned, never reaches the market place at all. Or the communication may be withheld until the issue of its release is finally settled, at which time it may have become obsolete or unprofitable. Such a delay is particularly serious in certain areas—such as in motion pictures—where large investments may be involved.

*Propensity toward an adverse decision*: A system of prior restraint is so constructed as to make it easier, and hence more likely, that in any particular cause the government will rule adversely to free expression. A communication made is a *fait accompli*, and the publisher has all the practical advantages of that position. A government official thinks longer and harder before deciding to undertake the serious task of subsequent punishment—the expenditure of time, funds, energy, and personnel that will be necessary. Under a system of prior restraint, he can reach the result by a simple stroke of the pen. Thus, in one case, the burden of initial action falls upon the government; in the other, on the citizen. Again, once a communication has been made, the government official may give consideration to the stigma and the troubles a criminal prosecution forces upon the citizen. Before the communication has been issued, however, such factors would not enter the picture. For these and similar reasons, a decision to suppress in advance is usually more readily reached, on the same facts, than a decision to punish after the event.

*Procedure*: Under a system of prior restraint, the issue of whether a communication is to be suppressed or not is determined by an administrative rather than a criminal procedure. This means that the procedural protections built around the criminal prosecution—many of which are constitutional guarantees—are not applicable to a prior restraint. The presumption of innocence, the heavier burden of proof borne by the government, the stricter rules of evidence, the stronger objection to vagueness, the immeasurable tighter and more technical procedure—all these are not on the side of free expression when its fate is decided.

Further, the initial decision rests with a single government functionary rather than with a jury. Those who framed the First Amendment placed great emphasis upon the value of a jury of citizens in checking government efforts to limit freedom of expression. While the jury probably plays less of a role in this age of popular conformity, it, nevertheless, still continues to furnish an important safeguard against the abuses of officialdom.

Finally, the net effect of using the administrative process is to place primary responsibility for judging the communication upon an executive official rather than in the courts. Judicial review of administrative action is limited in scope, tends to bow before administrative expertise, and is frequently unavailable in practice. Thus, sensitive issues of free expression are decided largely by a minor bureaucrat rather than through an institution designed to secure a somewhat more independent, objective, and liberal judgment.

*Opportunity for public appraisal and criticism*: A system of prior restraint usually operates behind a screen of informality and partial concealment that seriously curtails opportunity for public appraisal and increases the chances of discrimination and other abuse. Decisions are less likely to be made in the glare of publicity that accompanies a subsequent punishment. The policies and actions of the licensing official do not as often come to public notice; the reasons for his action are less likely to be known or publicly debated; material for study and criticism are less readily available; and the whole apparatus of

public scrutiny fails to play the role it normally does under a system of subsequent punishment. All this may have certain advantages from some points of view. In cases of alleged obscenity, for instance, publicity may serve to give much wider circulation to a publication ultimately condemned. And in some cases, individual citizens may not desire or benefit from greater publicity. In the long run, however, the preservation of civil liberties must rest upon an informed and active public opinion. Any device that draws a cloak over restrictions on free expression seriously undermines the democratic process.

*The dynamics of prior restraint*: Perhaps the most significant feature of systems of prior restraint is that they contain within themselves forces which drive irresistibly toward unintelligent, overzealous, and usually absurd administration. One factor is the ability and personality of the licenser or censor. As Milton long ago observed,

> If he be of such worth as behoves him, there cannot be a more tedious and unpleasing journey-work, a greater loss of time levied upon his head, than to be made the perpetual reader of unchosen books and pamphlets . . . we may easily foresee what kind of licensers we are to expect hereafter, either ignorant, imperious, and remiss, or basely pecuniary.

No adequate study seems to have been made of the psychology of licensers, censors, security officials, and their kind, but common experience is sufficient to show that their attitudes, drives, emotions, and impulses all tend to carry them to excesses. This is particularly true in the realm of obscenity, but it occurs in all areas where officials are driven by fear or other emotion to suppress free communication.

Further, it is necessary to keep in mind not only the character structure of the licenser, but the institutional framework in which he operates. The function of the censor is to censor. He has a professional interest in finding things to suppress. His career depends upon the record he makes. He is often acutely responsive to interests which demand suppression—interests which he himself represents—and not so well attuned to the more scattered and less aggressive forces which support free expression.

All this is true to some extent, of course, with regard to prosecutors who participate in the administration of systems of subsequent punishment. But such a prosecutor normally does not focus on a single problem in the way a licenser does. Nor does he wield comparable power. The long history of prior restraint reveals over and over again that the personal and institutional forces inherent in the system nearly always end in a stupid, unnecessary, and extreme suppression.

*Certainty and risk*: It is frequently argued that a system of prior restraint affords individual citizens greater certainty in the law with less risk of serious consequences. Under such a system, it is said, an individual can find out what is permitted and what is forbidden without incurring the danger of criminal or similar sanctions in the event his interpretation of the law is erroneous. For this reason, some publishers prefer licensing systems to systems based on subsequent punishment. And this has been a factor in the establishment of private systems of censorship, such as exist in the motion picture industry and now in the comic book industry. From the point of view of some individuals, there is much to be said for these considerations. But from a public or social point of view—the interest of society as a whole in free expression—the argument is, in the long run, dubious. For it means, under most circumstances, less rather than more communication of ideas; it leaves out of account those bolder individuals who may wish to express their opinions and are willing to take some risk; and it implies a philosophy of willingness to conform to official opinion and a sluggishness or timidity in asserting rights that bodes ill for a spirited and healthy expression of unorthodox and unaccepted opinion.

*Effectiveness*: A system of prior restraint is, in general, more readily and effectively enforced than a system of subsequent punishment. Undoubtedly it is true that both systems depend ultimately upon the application of penal sanctions. But there are noteworthy differences. A penal proceeding to enforce a prior restraint normally involves only a limited and relatively simple issue—whether or not the communication was made without prior approval. The objection to the content or manner of the communication need not be demonstrated. And furthermore, the violation of a censorship strikes sharply at the status of the licenser, whose prestige thus becomes involved and whose power must be vindicated. Systems of subsequent punishment can, of course, be enforced to the hilt; but in practice, this rarely occurs or is limited to short periods of time.

All in all, therefore, we much conclude that in a democratic society, such as ours, a system of prior restraint based upon executive approval will operate as a greater deterrent to free expression and cause graver damage to fundamental democratic rights than a system of subsequent punishment. This is, of course, not invariably so. A system of subsequent punishment, applying severe criminal sanctions in the first instance, may prove a greater obstruction to

legitimate expression where ruthlessly enforced. This could be true particularly in a highly organized and repressive state. But in the looser confines of an open society, it will normally not be the case. For purposes of the judicial process—which would find it difficult to make refined distinctions between the operation of the two systems in each particular instance—this powerful tendency of prior restraint becomes a factor of critical and definitive importance.

These, then, are some of the considerations which underlie the doctrine of prior restraint. They are the reasons why the doctrine is not simply an arbitrary historical accident, but a rational principle of fundamental weight in the application of the First Amendment. All of them do not apply in every situation. And other factors, relating to the particular form of restraint and the particular area of communication, must obviously be taken into account. But they furnish the basic framework within which the doctrine of prior restraint must be judged. . . .

## V
## CONCLUSION

The doctrine of prior restraint, while growing out of historical circumstances, finds its rationale today in the grievous impact which systems of prior restraint exert upon freedom of expression. The form and dynamics of such systems tend strongly towards over-control—towards an excess of order and an insufficiency of liberty. The doctrine does not require a choice between regulation or no regulation. It simply forbids a particular method of control which experience has taught tends to create a potent and unnecessary mechanism of government that can smother free communication. These tendencies in systems of prior restraint are even more dangerous today in view of the growing pressures for preventive controls over many forms of expression. Thus, the perils that presently threaten democratic rights in this country confirm the basic soundness of the rule against prior restraint. . . .

---

Vincent Blasi, *Toward a Theory of Prior Restraint: The Central Linkage,* 66 MINNESOTA LAW REVIEW 11 (1981)*

## I. THE INQUIRY

The doctrine of prior restraint embodies a temporal preference. Acts of expression that could be sanctioned by means of criminal punishment or a civil damage award may not be regulated "in advance." The factor of timing, however, cannot serve to distinguish methods of regulation as neatly as this statement would seem to imply. In addition to a retrospective impact relating to punishment or compensation, criminal prohibitions and civil liability rules are meant to have a prospective impact—to deter speakers from engaging in harmful acts of expression in the future. If impact on speech before the moment of its dissemination is not by itself a basis for distinguishing methods of speech regulation, what then is it that makes a law a prior restraint? And why are prior restraints disfavored at all?

In this essay I revisit the issue introduced by *Near:* should the injunction, as a general matter, be regarded as a particularly repressive method of regulating speech, akin to the historically disfavored administrative licensing system? The question is of importance in first amendment theory because the modern doctrine of prior restraint would be thrown into disarray should one of its two central props be removed. That denouement may be all to the good. Perhaps there has been too much reliance in recent times on the rhetoric of prior restraint as a substitute for more discriminating analysis. Before the analogy between injunctions and licensing systems is rejected, however, a careful examination of its possible validity seems appropriate, particularly on so fitting an occasion as this fiftieth anniversary celebration of *Near v. Minnesota.*

## II. NEAR v. MINNESOTA

. . .

## III. COMMON FEATURES OF LICENSING SYSTEMS AND INJUNCTIONS: BEGINNING THE SEARCH FOR A RATIONALE

### A. THE PROTOTYPES

There are many kinds of licensing systems and several types of injunctions. Variations in detail within these broad forms of regulation can be significant. First amendment analysis would be complicated to the point of paralysis, however, if each peculiar variant had to be assessed in relation to every other variant before a "general" presumption could be applied to certain of the variants. Instead, as is often true in legal analysis, some generalizing based on prototypes is both unavoidable and efficacious. Only if the common prototypes of the speech-restrictive injunction and licensing system cannot be shown to share significant and unique common features can it be said that the concept of prior restraint lacks coherence. . . .

### B. POINTS OF COMPARISON

Initially, it is worth noting what licensing systems and injunctions do *not* have in common. A licensing system is objectionable in part because it subjects a wide range of expression to scrutiny: a film licensing board typically requires the submission of all films that are to be exhibited in the jurisdiction, a parade permit ordinance requires all would-be marchers to apply. That is not true of all, or even most, injunctions. Normally, even the broadest of injunctions binds only certain designated speakers whose past or proposed speech activities have engendered unusual official concern.

Licensing systems are also troublesome because the initial decision to disallow speech is made by an administrative officer who specializes in suppression, and who will be held accountable for the harmful consequences of any communicative activity that is given approval. Moreover, under the typical licensing procedure there is no adversary hearing before the administrative officer who decides in the first instance whether to allow or suppress the speech. In contrast, injunctions are issued by courts of general jurisdiction after full adversary hearings.

Injunctions are sometimes considered dangerous to liberty because violations of their terms can be punished expeditiously in contempt proceedings. This might have been a major consideration in the days when persons charged with contempt of court enjoyed none of the basic rights, such as trial by jury, that are available to defendants in criminal prosecutions. Today, however, the rights of the accused in the two proceedings are substantially similar. Any differences that remain—and the major difference would seem to be that contempt charges are adjudicated with much less pretrial delay cannot be a basis for linking injunctions with licensing systems because the standard enforcement mechanism for a licensing system is a criminal prosecution for speaking without the required permit.

In the same vein, injunctions might be thought to be governed by an undesirable logic of rigid enforcement because the decision to prosecute persons who disobey them typically is made by the issuing judges, who may be overly sensitive to perceived affronts to their authority, rather than by district attorneys, who must always decide whether the violation of a law is serious enough to justify the commitment of limited prosecutorial resources. Again, this feature, while arguably significant, is not one shared by licensing systems. Persons who violate permit requirements are sanctioned only if a district attorney determines that prosecution is warranted in light of the seriousness of the offense and competing pressures on the criminal docket.

What then is it that licensing systems and injunctions have in common that unites them in the mind of the first amendment theorist? I can think of five potentially important features that appear on the surface to be shared by licensing systems and injunctions, and appear not to be shared, at least to the same extent, by criminal laws and civil liability rules: (1) the tendency, when the practical dynamics of the scheme are considered, to induce persons to engage in an unusually high degree of self-censorship of constitutionally protected expression; (2) the adjudication of constitutional claims at a time and in a manner that produces a formal, abstract quality of decision making; (3) the tendency to be used too readily; (4) an unusual capacity to distort the way audiences respond to communications; and (5) implicit premises that are antithetical to the philosophy of limited government. If any one or combination of these features turns out on close analysis to be notably more characteristic of both licensing systems and injunctions than of the standard "subsequent" sanctions on speech, and also significant in terms of first amendment values, we would have the beginnings of a theory of prior restraint.

## IV. SELF-CENSORSHIP

### F. CONCLUSION

I have examined five different sources of self-censorship and have made some speculative judgments regarding the importance of each under the various major methods of speech regulation. It is time to return to the ultimate question relating to self-censorship as a rationale for prior restraint doctrine: do licensing systems and injunctions that are governed by the collateral bar rule have in common the tendency to engender significantly more self-censorship than criminal prohibitions and civil liability rules? My answer is no. I do not believe the sources of self-censorship . . . are likely, in general, to have more of an inhibiting effect on potential speakers than the sources of self-censorship that are distinctive to the subsequent punishment regimes.

Criminal prohibitions and civil liability rules often leave potential speakers uncertain about what they can say with impunity. Generalized prohibitions almost always contain inherent ambiguities that even strict due process doctrines must tolerate. More importantly, traditional doctrines of fair notice in criminal cases and fault in civil actions require at most that defendants be informed about their statutory and common-law obligations, not the limits of their constitutional rights. Under the subsequent punishment regimes, the prescribed procedure for having one's rights adjudicated is to engage in the prohibited activity, risking incarceration, fine, or liability in damages should the constitutional judgment be adverse. Were declaratory judgments and injunctions against prosecution and civil suit more readily available, this source of uncertainty could be minimized. One thoughtful commentator has even argued that prospective speakers should perhaps enjoy a first amendment right to such anticipatory remedies. Until such an innovative right is recognized, however, or advance definitive rulings become available without constitutional compulsion, a considerable amount of self-censorship can be expected in the subsequent punishment regimes due to the uncertainties inherent in their procedures. Injunctions and licensing systems are far less problematic on this score because under those regimes the definitive adjudications take place before the speakers must decide whether or not to engage in the disputed communicative activities.

I am also inclined to give weight to the factor of severity of sanctions. Even though sentences for contempt of court and speaking without a permit can be substantial, both types of offenses typically are punished lightly. Perhaps sentencing patterns are influenced to some extent by the fact that the defendants are often persons whose communicative activities would not warrant prosecution but for the need to make credible the prohibition on self-help. Whatever the cause, if sanctions tend to be more severe under subsequent punishment systems, self-censorship should be more pronounced as a result.

In light of the ways in which subsequent punishments may cause *more* self-censorship than the prior methods of regulation, the case for building a theory of prior restraint on the self-censorship rationale depends on identifying some distinctive features of injunctions and licensing systems that can be expected to cause large amounts of self-censorship. I have considered several characteristics of injunctions and licensing systems that might be supposed to engender self-censorship, but on examination only two, the burden of initiative and delay, can be said in net effect to impose serious and distinctive self-censorship costs in certain contexts. Moreover, for both the burden of initiative and delay, the predictable self-censorship effects are confined to either a relatively narrow class of potential speakers or to a worst-case scenario that depends on a major alteration of current regulatory patterns. Neither of those dangers of self-censorship should be dismissed as negligible, but for purposes of comparison they would seem not to outweigh the self-censorship risks that derive from the greater uncertainties and more severe sanctions of the subsequent punishment regimes.

## V. ADJUDICATION IN THE ABSTRACT

If the common denominator of self-censorship is not a basis for a general presumption against licensing systems and injunctions, we must look to other features shared by the two methods of speech regulation. One phenomenon common to licensing systems and injunctions governed by the collateral bar rule is what might be termed adjudication in the abstract. Under both systems, the final authoritative judicial decision regarding the legal status of a disputed communication takes place before the moment of initial dissemination. That typically is not true under the subsequent punishment regimes. . . .

First, if the governing first amendment test for the speech at issue is one that turns on consequences (clear and present danger, for example), the necessity for speculation permits groundless fears to figure in the rationale for suppression. If the judgment were made at a later stage, the data from initial dissemination could on occasion serve to dispel such fears. The distorting influence of groundless fears is likely to be compounded, moreover, in disputes over such matters as diplomatic and military secrets and street demonstrations, when the government may have control over the only witnesses who possess the information and expertise required to speculate intelligently about the dangers.

No doubt on occasion the need to speculate regarding the impact of the speech will work to the advantage of first amendment claimants: communicative activities that might have seemed harmless in the abstract will sometimes generate consequences that provide a rationale for holding the speakers civilly or criminally liable. A central tenet of modern first amendment theory, however, is that under conditions of uncertainty regarding consequences, both regulatory officials and judges tend to overestimate the dangers of controversial speech. Unless that tenet is to be abandoned, it makes sense to consider the net effect of adjudication before initial dissemination to be detrimental to speakers so far as the assessment of dangers is concerned. . . .

Second, the dissemination of speech may create public opinion pressures that can exert a healthy influence on the formulation and application of first amendment standards. How warmly one responds to this consideration depends on attitudes regarding judicial independence, the autonomy of legal reasoning, and the like. In the realm of civil liberties, moreover, it is not always the case that the force of public opinion aids the cause of freedom. Nevertheless, there will be some cases, particularly those involving exposes of governmental abuse, where judges inclined to suppress speech would be constrained by public opinion if the populace could be made aware of the contents of the speech in dispute. Seldom will such public awareness generate political and social pressures to suppress speech that are not already felt or anticipated by judges who must decide first amendment disputes.

Third, once a communication is disseminated it becomes to some extent a *fait accompli*. The world is a slightly different place; perceptions regarding what is tolerable are altered. Not only can the effects of the speech not be undone, views regarding the desirability of those effects will be influenced by the common human tendency to find virtue in the status quo. This phenomenon too may influence the formulation and application of doctrine in the direction of permitting more speech.

Finally, a judge's determination whether speech is constitutionally protected is likely to be influenced by the fact that, in the case of adjudication before dissemination, a permissive decision can result in the judge being held responsible for any adverse consequences that ensue from the expressive activity. If a protest march disintegrates into a riot, the judge who ordered the issuance of the parade permit will be criticized. If the publication of a book the CIA tried unsuccessfully to enjoin should result in the assassination of a covert agent, the judge who denied the injunction will be held responsible. One could argue that this is nothing more than the prospective accountability that most other decision makers must endure. In the realm of judicial interpretation of the first amendment, however, the caution inducing constraints that bind bureaucrats and politicians may be viewed as undesirable. . . .

In sum, licensing systems and injunctions have in common the adjudication of disputes regarding controversial communications at a time prior to the initial dissemination of the speech in question. Such adjudication tends to have an abstract quality because courts are then insulated from some of the pragmatic considerations that influence adjudication under the subsequent punishment regimes. There are reasons, deriving from certain fundamental perspectives on the first amendment that are widely shared among modern theorists, for viewing those pragmatic influences as salutary. The common feature of adjudication in the abstract thus provides one reason for linking together licensing systems and injunctions at the center of a general theory of prior restraint.

## VI. OVERUSE

So far we have examined how prior and subsequent systems of regulation compare in terms of their impact on potential speakers and on judges called upon to adjudicate the legal status of particular communications. Another dimension to consider is the impact of the various systems on the behavior of persons who seek to accomplish the suppression or sanctioning of speech. This is a diverse class of actors that includes legislators who work for speech-restrictive legislation, police officers who arrest speakers or try to deter speech by threats, licensing officials, prosecutors, and private persons who bring lawsuits against speakers. I shall refer to this group collectively as regulatory agents. It is possible that injunctive and licensing systems are undesirable simply because they tend in operation to be too fully utilized by regulatory agents—too often invoked to generate prohibitions that are too often enforced. If it is important that the regulation of speech be only an occasional, exceptional event, any system that tends by virtue of its efficiencies or internal dynamics to be either casually or pervasively employed may for that reason alone properly be saddled with an adverse presumption designed to ensure that the system is used only in isolated, compelling situations. . . .

Injunctions are issued and permit applications are denied "by a stroke of the pen." In both cases, the process is expeditious. Certain procedures and evidentiary burdens limit how readily and pervasively those systems can be employed by regulatory agents, but checks of that sort do not fundamentally alter the essentially expeditious character of the prior regulatory regimes. . . .

Not only are there no major burdens to force licensing officials to make priority judgments, there may be bureaucratic dynamics that encourage casual, routine invocation of the power to regulate expression. Licensing officials typically are selected because of their knowledge and concern about the social interests the regulatory system is designed to protect—crowd control, for example, or conventional mores regarding sexual depiction. These officials can be expected to begin their chores with a predisposition to regulate expression. The experience of ruling upon numerous permit applications, moreover, is hardly likely to heighten what little appreciation such persons may have for the value of free expression. When the phenomenon of prospective accountability is added to the calculus, it seems inevitable that regulatory impulses of low or intermediate intensity would be pursued by most licensing officials absent some sort of doctrinal check deriving from a theory of prior restraint.

Under the subsequent punishment regimes, in contrast, the process by which regulatory impulses are implemented is far more complicated, drawn out, and interlaced with disincentives. The passage of a criminal statute requires a majority vote in two separate representative bodies (except in Nebraska). The traditional practice of committee deliberation slows down the process and often provides an opportunity for political minorities (including proponents of strong speech rights) to kill or modify proposed legislation. The gubernatorial veto constitutes an additional obstacle. The power to legislate against speech can certainly be abused, but usually only when the preferences of the political community run intensely in the direction of repression. Even then, the cumbersome nature of the legislative process makes it difficult for the regulatory forces to keep up with innovative, adaptive speakers such as pornographers. Injunctions and permit requirements, for which the basic substantive norms are formulated case by case, seem by comparison far more susceptible to both casual and comprehensive use. . . .

To summarize, certain methods of speech regulation lend themselves more than others to frequent and pervasive use. It is not incongruous as a matter of first amendment theory to institutionalize a preference for sparing, selective use of the power to regulate expression. Both in the formulation and the enforcement of prohibitory norms, licensing and injunctive systems are likely to be used more heavily than the subsequent punishment systems. Such a tendency toward overuse unites licensing systems and injunctions in one respect that can figure prominently in a general theory of prior restraint.

## VII. IMPACT ON AUDIENCE RECEPTION

. . .

In short, prior adjudication erects a filter between speaker and audience. Even for the messages that pass through the filter, the communicative process is detrimentally affected by the existence of such a barrier. The impact is difficult to document or predict, but under any theory that values speech largely for its capacity to influence listeners, this filtering phenomenon should be regarded as undesirable.

Under the subsequent punishment regimes, communications are neither delayed nor filtered. The only way in which audience reception might be adversely affected by subsequent methods of regulation is if listeners are themselves made to risk punishment for merely attending communicative events. Such a risk could cause audiences to dwindle. There have been occasions when local prosecutors have arrested viewers of pornographic films, but that practice has met with a chilly judicial reception. Occasionally, observers of protest demonstrations may run the risk of being swept into the prosecutorial net should events get out of hand. But these are aberrational situations. In no systematic way does the possibility of civil or criminal sanctions interfere with the way an audience responds to a speaker's message.

Thus, because they share the feature of adjudication prior to initial dissemination, licensing systems and injunctions seem more likely than the subsequent punishment regimes to have an adverse impact on how audiences perceive communications that are protected under the first amendment. The case for linking licensing systems and injunctions at the center of a theory of prior restraint is made stronger by consideration of this dimension of audience reception.

## VIII. UNACCEPTABLE PREMISES

. . .

Modern analysis of the problem of prior restraint tends not to pay much attention to the question of premises. That tendency was not exhibited by the greatest writer who ever addressed the subject of prior restraint. John Milton's *Areopagitica*, written in the form of a petition to the Long Parliament in 1644, remains the classic exposition on the evils of censorship. Many of the arguments developed by Milton have been appropriated in the behavioral sections of the present analysis. Milton complained, for example, that ideas cannot fairly be judged before they are disseminated. He objected to the cautiousness and insensitivity to learning likely to be displayed by the types of persons who would agree to assume the tedious chores of the censor. He worried greatly about the stifling self-censorship effect of requiring an author to seek out the censor each time a new idea for a revision comes to mind. He feared that audiences are likely to view a writing with skepticism when they cannot be sure that the version they are permitted to read represents the true beliefs of the writer. What strikes the modern reader most, however, upon returning to the *Areopagitica,* is the extent to which Milton's argument rests on his objection to the premises that underly the licensing of speech.

A theme that permeates the essay is the indignity of licensing due to the paternalism inherent in the procedure. In this view, comprehensive censorship is at odds with the conception of the proper relationship between citizen and state that underlays the Puritan revolution and is today a central premise of democratic theory. The key phenomenon appears to be trust. Licensing implies too much distrust of both writers and readers. A censorship system places the state in the role of a suspicious, omnipresent tutor. No system of political authority premised on the consent of the governed can admit the state to that role, whatever the behavioral consequences. . . .

The premise of distrust that so disturbed Milton would seem to underly modern licensing and injunction systems. The decision to adjudicate the legal status of speech in advance of its initial dissemination is almost always spurred by the belief that the public must be denied access entirely to the speech in question. So concerned is the legal system with how audiences might respond to the speech that the considerable advantages of retrospective adjudication are willingly sacrificed. The point of prior regulation is to suppress, not to sanction. Suppression represents a particularly active and absolute form of intervention by the state that would seem to reflect the view that normal, more limited corrective forces, including both the disincentives created by subsequent sanctioning systems and the good sense of the citizenry, cannot be relied upon to control sufficiently the harmful effects of certain communications. To find the normal corrective forces so inadequate to the task, one must distrust deeply the motives of speakers, the wisdom of audiences, or both. . . .

The answer is that in the kind of analysis we are presently engaged in, distrust is a comparative notion. The allocation of authority between the state and the individual is a function not simply of how much trust should be placed in the capacity of private individuals to process communications thoughtfully and responsibly. Distrust of the state, particularly in its censorial capacity, is a fundamental value that informs the first amendment. The decision to adjudicate the legal status of a communication before its initial dissemination embodies a premise of comparative distrust: better trust the regulatory process not to suppress salutary communications than trust the populace to reject or ignore unsalutary ones. To trust the censor more than the audience is to alter the relationship between state and citizen that is central to the philosophy of limited government. . . .

That a premise of comparative distrust of speakers and audiences sometimes operates in the subsequent punishment regimes does not mean, however, that there are no distinctions to be drawn in this respect between prior and subsequent methods of regulation. Once again, the timing of adjudication in relation to the moment of initial dissemination figures prominently in the analysis. There are safety valves in the subsequent punishment systems that reflect both a distrust of the regulatory process and a respect for audiences. Many violations are not prosecuted. Adjudication draws on the benefits of hindsight in evaluating the character of particular communications. Audience reception may also be taken into account.

Adjudicative judgments typically are rendered some months or even years after the moment of initial dissemination, which means the passage of time can allow long-range perspectives to override momentary suppressive passions. Audiences are not trusted completely; some communications are punished in order to decrease the likelihood that future audiences will be exposed to similar messages. But neither is the regulatory process fully trusted; a recognition of the potential for official error and shortsightedness permeates the design of the subsequent punishment procedures.

In contrast, licensing systems and injunctions do not exhibit such concern for the possibility of official error nor such respect for the judgment of audiences. The decision to settle the legal status of a communication before it is ever disseminated to the public is a bold, confident regulatory gesture. No need is felt to observe the actual consequences of the communication. Audience reception is deemed unimportant. . . .

Not only do regulatory methods embody premises regarding the role of controversial speech in the workings of the society as a whole, the choice of a regulatory method also reflects a view regarding the proper role of government in the process by which communications by private parties are formulated and disseminated. Respect by officials for the integrity of the communicative process is an essential attribute of limited government. In order for the power of the state to be kept in check, it is important that the concept of individual autonomy retain practical significance in the workings of the society. There have to be some important endeavors, relating to public as well as private objectives, that individuals are entitled to pursue by virtue of their status as individuals, and not by sufferance of the state. Communicating one's views, particularly with respect to public issues, would seem, in light of our constitutional tradition, to be one of the activities that belongs in this sphere of individual entitlement. And for that entitlement to reinforce the crucial, partly symbolic, concept of individual autonomy, a large measure of control over the details of the activity must remain in the hands of speakers.

One striking feature of licensing and injunctive systems is the ever present possibility, due to the phenomenon of adjudication prior to initial dissemination, that government officials may convince speakers to alter the details of their plans in order to conform to the government's preferences. Licensing officials and other regulatory agents can tell speakers exactly what they need to do to avoid the costs, delays, and stresses of litigation. In the setting of mass demonstrations, it may seem a triumph of social cooperation for speakers to alter their plans marginally in order to accommodate the regulatory priorities of the state. If one thinks of film or book editing, however, the prospect of government prescribed alterations is a cause for concern. Whether the government dictates changes to speakers who have no real bargaining power, or negotiates for alterations in a spirit of give and take, the symbolic division of authority between the state and the individual is upset when the government so intrudes itself into the formulative stages of the communicative process. . . .

## X. CONCLUSION

Under the assumption that the collateral bar rule governs injunctions, the case is convincing for linking together licensing systems and injunctions, and subjecting those methods of regulation to an adverse presumption designed to restrict their use to exceptional situations. Although there is no reason to believe that licensing and injunctive systems cause more self-censorship of constitutionally protected communications than subsequent punishment regimes, the two principal methods of prior regulation should be disfavored because they both must rely upon adjudication in the abstract, they both encourage regulatory agents to overuse the power to regulate, and they both adversely affect audience reception of controversial messages. In addition, licensing and injunctive systems both embody, if only implicitly, certain unacceptable premises regarding the respective spheres of authority of the state and the individual citizen. . . .

John Calvin Jeffries, Jr., *Rethinking Prior Restraint,* 92 YALE LAW JOURNAL 409 (1983)*

. . . *Near* illustrates several aspects of the developing doctrine of prior restraint. Most important is the assumption that terming the statute a prior restraint was doctrinally necessary to its invalidation. The dissent makes the point explicit. For the majority as well, the implicit assumption seems to have been that unless the law could be treated as a prior restraint, thus falling within the protective part of Blackstone's bifurcation, no settled or familiar basis

* Reprinted by Permission of the Yale Law Journal Company and Fred B. Rothman & Company from *The Yale Law Journal,* Vol. 92, pp. 409-537.

would exist for holding the statute unconstitutional. And the statute had to be held unconstitutional. Otherwise, it could become a successful prototype for official suppression of hostile comment—at least of criticism sufficiently intemperate to be called "malicious, scandalous and defamatory." In truth, *Near v. Minnesota* involved nothing more or less than a repackaged version of the law of seditious libel, and this the majority rightly refused to countenance. Hence, there was pressure, so typical of this doctrine, to cram the law into the disfavored category of prior restraint, even though it in fact functioned very differently from a scheme of official licensing. Here there was no license and no censor, no ex parte determination of what was prohibited, and no suppression of publication based on speculation about what somebody might say. Here the decision to suppress was made by a judge (not a bureaucrat), after adversarial (not ex parte) proceedings, to determine the legal character of what had been (and not what might be) published. The only aspect of prior restraint was the incidental fact that the defendants were commanded not to repeat that which they were proved to have done.

The real defect, of course, was the substantive standard for authorizing suppression. The standard of "malicious, scandalous and defamatory" publication that is neither true nor published "with good motives and for justifiable ends" is utterly inconsistent with the fundamental First Amendment principle of free and unfettered political debate. And that inconsistency would persist, and would be equally intolerable, whether the suppression were accomplished by injunction or by criminal prosecution and punishment. The flaw lies in the standard for suppression, not in the form of the proceeding.

Now, one may well wonder whether this carping about categorization is not a bit off point. After all, if the *Near* Court reached the right result, does it really matter that it gave the wrong reason? The answer, I think, is that it does matter, at least that it has come to matter as *Near* has become a prominent feature of the First Amendment landscape—a landmark, as the case is so often called, from which we chart our course to future decisions. And the course indicated by *Near* is not simply to reject the law of seditious libel, whatever the mechanism of enforcement. Today, at least, that message would be everywhere accepted. Instead, *Near* has come to stand for a sort of syllogism about injunctive relief:

Prior restraint of speech is presumptively unconstitutional, even where the speech in question is not otherwise protected.

An injunction is a prior restraint.

Therefore, an injunction against speech is presumptively unconstitutional, even where the speech enjoined is not otherwise protected.

. . .

The Court has yet to explain (at least in terms that I understand) what it is about an injunction that justifies this independent rule of constitutional disfavor. . . .

## II.

. . . At least as applied by the courts, the doctrine is fundamentally unintelligible. It purports to assess the constitutionality of government action by distinguishing prior restraint from subsequent punishment, but provides no coherent basis for making that categorization. In 1955, Professor Emerson said: "There is, at present, no common understanding as to what constitutes 'prior restraint.'" The intervening years have only reinforced that observation. Some prior restraints involve permit requirements; others do not. Some involve injunctions; others do not. Some cases involving neither permits nor injunctions are treated as prior restraints; others are not. The doctrine purports to deal with matters of form rather than of substance, but there is no unity among the forms of government action condemned as prior restraints.

The explanation for this disarray lies in the historic association of "prior restraint" with a declaration of constitutional invalidity and in the consequent impetus to distort doctrine in order to expand protection. Today, such indirection is unnecessary. There is nothing left of the "Blackstonian theory" that the government may do what it will so long as it avoids prior restraint, and hence there is no need to invoke that categorization in order to protect First Amendment freedoms. We are left, therefore, with a doctrine of honored past but contemporary irrelevance—a formulation whose current contribution to the interpretation of the First Amendment is chiefly confusion.

. . . The tyranny of labels is such that all things called by the same name are assumed to have the same features, even where the label has been used for reasons other than descriptive accuracy. As a result, there is a tendency to ascribe to one of the several manifestations of "prior restraint" a line of reasoning applicable only to another and thus to confuse rather than to clarify the underlying questions of First Amendment policy.

An obvious solution to this problem is to redefine the concept, to restrict the frame of reference to a set of structurally similar situations about which doctrinal generalizations can usefully be made. . . .

## A. Administrative Preclearance

Of the various things referred to as prior restraint, a system of administrative preclearance is the most plainly objectionable. Under such a system, the lawfulness of speech or publication is made to depend on the prior permission of an executive official. Ordinarily, publication without such permission is punished as a criminal offense, even where the particular speech in question could not constitutionally have been suppressed. Thus, it is the failure to obtain preclearance rather than the character of the speech itself that determines illegality.

Such a scheme has many vices. The administrative apparatus erected to effect preclearance may screen a range of expression far broader than that which otherwise would be brought to official attention. The relative ease and economy of an administrative decision to suppress may make suppression more likely than it would be without a preclearance requirement. Under a system of administrative preclearance, suppression is accomplished "by a single stroke of the pen." At that point the burden falls on the would-be speaker to vindicate his right. Without administrative preclearance, the government's decision to suppress may be constrained by the time and money required to demonstrate in court an appropriate basis for such action. And the fact that those exercising the authority of preclearance operate in the relative informality of administrative action may tend to shield their decisions from effective public scrutiny. Most important, administrative preclearance requires a bureaucracy of censorship. Persons who choose to fill this role may well have psychological tendencies to overstate the need for suppression. Whether or not this is so, there are powerful institutional pressures to justify one's job, and ultimately one's own importance, by exaggerating the evils which suppression seeks to avoid. As Emerson put it: "The function of the censor is to censor. He has a professional interest in finding things to suppress." And finally, it may well be that a system of administrative preclearance would be enforced more energetically and efficiently than a system of subsequent punishment. Ultimately, both depend on criminal prosecution, but the issues presented for proof under a preclearance requirement may be significantly more manageable.

These and similar arguments have been detailed by Professor Emerson. They deal with matters of timing, process, and institutional structure rather than with the substantive content of speech, and in my view, they fully justify an attitude of special hostility toward preclearance requirements. All of these concerns, however, are linked to a single factor, a factor ordinarily determinative of the constitutional fate of preclearance requirements. That factor is discretion. Where broad discretion is left in the hands of executive officials—as in a statute authorizing denial of a permit for very general reasons—the vices described above loom very large indeed. Where, on the other hand, executive discretion is tightly controlled—as in a statute requiring issuance of a permit on specified showings—the problems of preclearance seem relatively less troublesome. . . .

A rule of special hostility to administrative preclearance is just another way of saying that determinations under the overbreadth doctrine should take account not only of the substance of the law but also of the structure of its administration. The reason that the various features of timing, process, and institutional structure noted earlier are thought to render administrative preclearance requirements especially objectionable is precisely that they increase the prospect of unconstitutional application. Put another way, a system of administrative preclearance is likely to render a restriction of speech operatively, if not formally, overbroad. Narrow, precise, and objective standards are one way of constraining discretion; subjecting its exercise to judicial supervision is another. In either event, the goal is to limit the opportunities for unconstitutional suppression of protected speech, regardless of whether that danger arises from an overly broad statement of the substantive standard for suppression or whether it flows from the overly broad administration typical of a preclearance requirement.

## B. Injunctions

The second major type of prior restraint is the injunction. Ever since *Near*, injunctions have been classed as prior restraints and subjected to the independent presumption of unconstitutionality for which that doctrine calls. In fact, despite its original reference to official licensing, the doctrine of prior restraint today is understood by many people to mean chiefly a rule of special hostility to injunctions. Of course, to the extent that the speech in question is constitutionally protected against suppression by subsequent punishment, it is also secured against suppression by injunction. This result in no way depends on an independent rule against prior restraint. That doctrine has functional significance only where it bars an injunction against speech that constitutionally could be proscribed by the penal law. The issue, therefore, is whether injunctions should be constitutionally disfavored even where they are directed against speech not otherwise protected under the First Amendment.

In this connection, it is instructive to note how different from administrative preclearance injunctions really are. Under a regime of injunctions, there is no routine screening of speech and no administrative shortcut to suppression. The government has to shoulder the entire burden of identifying the case for suppression and of demonstrating in court a constitutionally acceptable basis for such action. Moreover, because an injunction must be sought in open court, the character of the government's claims remains subject to public scrutiny and debate. Most important, the decision to suppress is made by a court, not a censor. Of course, judges are not perfect; sometimes they may err on the side of suppression and enjoin speech without sufficient justification. But the fact remains that judges, unlike professional censors, have no vested interest in the suppression of speech. The institution of the judiciary is peculiarly well suited—in personnel, training, ideology, and institutional structure—to implement the ideals of the First Amendment. . . .

Not only are injunctions unlike administrative preclearance, they are also far more like subsequent punishments than the conventional rhetoric would suggest. In both cases the *threat* of punishment comes before publication; in both cases the *fact* of punishment comes after. The apparent distinction in timing is actually only a shift in the focus of attention. The procedures in an action for criminal contempt—the enforcement phase of the injunctive process—are generally the same as those used in ordinary criminal prosecutions. Proof must be had beyond a reasonable doubt, and the right to trial by jury is guaranteed where the sentence exceeds imprisonment for six months.

On examination, the chief difference between the two schemes turns out to be this: Under a system of injunctions, the adjudication of illegality precedes publication; under a system of criminal prosecution, it comes later. This is a difference, and perhaps for some purposes it matters, but why the timing of the adjudication should affect the scope of First Amendment freedoms is not at all clear. Three related reasons are most frequently advanced.

The first and most common is that an injunction deters speech more effectively than does the threat of criminal prosecution and for that reason should be specially disfavored. Arguments to this effect are found in the opinions of the Supreme Court and in the writings of leading commentators. The idea has been variously expressed but never so pithily as in Alexander Bickel's remark that, "A criminal statute chills, prior restraint freezes." Yet, with all respect to such authority, it is very hard to credit this point.

It may be true, as many have asserted, that an injunction, because it is particularized, immediate, and concrete, may impinge more forcefully on the consciousness of the individual enjoined than would a more generalized and impersonal threat of criminal prosecution. But that tells only half the story, and the wrong half at that. An injunction may be more effective at stopping the activity at which it is aimed, but it is also more narrowly confined. There is less risk of deterring activities beyond the adjudicated target of suppression—activities plainly outside the injunctive ban but arguably within the necessarily more general prohibition of a penal law. And many find even an uncertain prospect of criminal conviction and punishment sufficient incentive to steer well clear of arguably proscribed activities. In terms, therefore, of the system of free expression and of the aggregate of arguably protected First Amendment activity that might be inhibited under these regimes, it is anything but clear that injunctions are more costly. As Professor Barnett put it: "[T]he pinpointed freeze of a narrowly drawn [judicial] . . . order might produce less refrigeration overall than the broader chill of threatened subsequent punishment . . . ."

That point is strongly reinforced when one remembers that it is only the possibility of *erroneous* deterrence that should be the subject of concern. To the extent that the activity suppressed, whether by injunction or by criminal prosecution, is outside the protection of the First Amendment and within a legitimate sphere of legislative action, efficient inhibition is a good thing. It is only excessive deterrence, erroneous deterrence, deterrence that impinges on the substance of First Amendment freedoms, that is to be decried. In that respect, it seems entirely plausible that the specifically targeted commands of an injunction are actually likely to be *less* threatening to the system of freedom of expression than the inevitably more general proscriptions of a penal statute.

Two additional reasons for regarding injunctions as especially deleterious to speech are really only variations on the theme of efficient deterrence. One is that suppression by criminal prosecution is preferable to suppression by injunction because the latter characteristically delays publication, at least for several days, even if the ban ultimately is lifted. The result is a loss in the immediacy of speech, and in some cases an accompanying loss in its value. The other contention is that criminal prosecution is preferable because it allows the disputed material to be published at least once and thus to enter the marketplace of ideas. An injunction, by contrast, is said to prevent the information from ever being made public.

Both of these contentions enjoy wide currency, but neither withstands scrutiny. Both are based on the implicit assumption that the deterrent impact of penal statutes is felt in those cases in which prosecution is brought. Of course, the opposite is true. Every violation of the penal law is, by hypothesis, a case of failed deterrence. Effective deterrence occurs when the violation never takes place. And in some cases, deterrence will be effective. Thus, while an injunction may delay publication for several days, the prospect of penal sanctions may delay publication forever. And while those publications that become subjects of criminal prosecution do become part of the marketplace of ideas, those that are deterred by the threat of penal sanctions never do. There is, in short, no necessary or dependable relation between the forni of suppression and any identifiable measure of violence to First Amendment interests. . . .

The conclusion that I draw from all this is embarrassingly modest. It is not that injunctions are preferable to subsequent punishment as a mechanism for suppression of speech, though that may be true in some cases. Nor would I assert that there is never a case in which injunctive relief should be specially disfavored. In some situations (the election-eve gambit comes to mind) an injunction may be differentially destructive of First Amendment values, just as in others (perhaps regulation of obscenity) it may prove differentially protective. My only point is to question the broad and categorical condemnation of injunctions as a form of "prior restraint."

In my view, a rule of special hostility to administrative preclearance is fully justified, but a rule of special hostility to injunctive relief is not. Lumping both together under the name of "prior restraint" obscures rather than clarifies what is at stake in these cases. In the context of administrative preclearance, talking of prior restraint is unhelpful, though not inapt. A more informative frame of reference would be overbreadth, the doctrine that explicitly identifies why preclearance is specially objectionable. In the context of injunctions, however, the traditional doctrine of prior restraint is not merely unhelpful, but

positively misleading. It focuses on a constitutionally inconsequential consideration of form and diverts attention away from the critical substantive issues of First Amendment coverage. The result is a two-pronged danger. On the one hand, vindication of First Amendment freedoms in the name of prior restraint may exaggerate the legitimate reach of official competence to suppress by subsequent punishment. On the other hand, insistence on special disfavor for prior restraints outside the realm of substantive protection under the First Amendment may deny to the government an appropriate choice of means to vindicate legitimate interests. In my view, neither risk is justified by any compelling reason to continue prior restraint as a doctrinally independent category of contemporary First Amendment analysis.

### III.

The burden of the preceding discussion is to suggest that the conventional doctrine of prior restraint should be retired from active service in First Amendment adjudication. Its historic role in protecting freedom of expression has been superseded by the expanded substantive coverage of the First Amendment and by the development of other, and more apt, techniques for implementing that guarantee. Moreover, continuing uncertainty as to what is actually meant by "prior restraint" and the accelerating tendency to invoke that phrase in a wide variety of dissimilar cases have undermined whatever usefulness the doctrine may have had in explaining or predicting results. Most regrettable of all is the demonstrated potential of the words "prior restraint" to confound and deflect rather than to guide and clarify the analysis of important questions of First Amendment policy. . . .

In sum, therefore, I suggest that in confronting these and similar questions the conventional doctrine of prior restraint be laid to one side. In my judgment, that doctrine is so far removed from its historic function, so variously invoked and discrepantly applied, and so often deflective of sound understanding, that it no longer warrants use as an independent category of First Amendment analysis.

## Bibliography

*Prior Restraint*

Barnett, Stephen R., *The Puzzle of Prior Restraint*, 29 Stanford Law Review 539 (1977).

Denbeaux, Mark P., *The First Word of the First Amendment*, 80 Northwestern University Law Review 1156 (1986).

Freedman, Monroe, H., & Starwood, Janet, *Prior Restraints on Freedom of Expression by Defen-*

*dants and Defense Attorneys: Ratio Decidendi v. Obiter Dictum*, 29 Stanford Law Review 607 (1977).

Goodale, James C., *The Press Ungagged: The Practical Effect on Gag Order Litigation of Nebraska Press Association v. Stuart*, 29 Stanford Law Review 497 (1977).

Hunter, Howard O., *Toward a Better Understanding of the Prior Restraint Doctrine: A Reply to Professor Mayton*, 67 Cornell Law Review 283 (1982).

Lively, Donald E., *Securities Regulation and Freedom of the Press: Toward a Marketplace of Ideas in the Marketplace of Investment*, 60 Washington Law Review 843 (1985).

Mayton, William T., *Toward a Theory of First Amendment Process: Injunctions of Speech, Subsequent Punishment, and the Costs of the Prior Restraint Doctrine*, 67 Cornell Law Review 245 (1982).

Murphy, William, *The Prior Restraint Doctrine in the Supreme Court: A Reevaluation*, 51 Notre Dame Law Review 898 (1976).

Sack, Robert D., *Principle and Nebraska Press Association v. Stuart*, 29 Stanford Law Review 411 (1977).

Schmidt, Jr., Benno C., *Nebraska Press Association: An Extension of Freedom and Contradiction of Theory*, 29 Stanford Law Review 431 (1977).

Scordato, Martin, *Distinction Without a Difference: A Reappraisal of the Doctrine of Prior Restraint*, 68 North Carolina Law Review 1 (1989).

# Part II

# Speech Classification
# and Content Regulation

## A.  Categorizing Speech

First Amendment jurisprudence over the course of this century has evolved a hierarchy of speech forms. The spectrum of expressive freedom comprehends highly favored speech pertaining to governance, less protected speech such as commercial or indecent expression and defamation of public officials and public figures, and unprotected speech such as obscenity and fighting words. Crucial to a scheme that rejects absolutism and factors in degrees of regulatory interest is the phenomenon of balancing. Frederick Schauer discusses how the speech classification process may be an outcome-determinative factor. John Hart Ely maintains that balancing expressive and regulatory interests is a positive and inevitable First Amendment process. Pierre Schlag offers a philosophically grounded defense of balancing.

Frederick Schauer, *Categories and the First Amendment: A Play in Three Acts* 34 VANDERBILT LAW REVIEW 265 (1981)*

## I. PROLOGUE: THE CONCEPT OF CATEGORY

Categories are the tools of systematic thinking. They enable us to organize our ideas, to draw analogies, and to make distinctions. In this respect categories are important in law because they are important in life. Categories, however, have a special prominence in legal reasoning, to a great extent because effective reasoning by example requires the creation and use of categories through which the lessons of the past can be channelled into service as precedent for the problems of the future. Legal rules not only prescribe results, but they also create (or recognize) the categories of conduct to which the rules apply. Without categories there could be no rules.

All of this no doubt appears trivially true. Yet it is necessary to state the obvious, for failure to recognize the importance of categories, or failure to appreciate the importance of categorization, can and has led to the kind of platitudinous overgeneralization that is inconsistent with tight legal reasoning. Nowhere is this more apparent than in first amendment adjudication, in which the term "categorization" has unfortunately been used to refer to a specific technique of first amendment analysis, a technique most often presented as an alternative to "balancing." Casting first amendment theory as a choice between these alternatives, however, masks the full importance of categories in the structure of first amendment doctrine. This problem is not alleviated by showing, as Professor Ely has done, that categorization and balancing can be consistent and complementary, for even this approach focuses on but one aspect of the way in which categories are relevant to free speech problems.

I would thus like to cast aside any preconceptions about categorization as a first amendment technique and look instead at the way in which thinking about categories in general can help us to think clearly about a number of hard problems in first amendment methodology. One pervasive difficulty is that the term "categorization" is in this context ambiguous, since at least three distinct aspects of first amendment theory can be and have been referred to as "categorization." These three aspects of categorization, although separate, are related in an important and logi-

cal way. They are like three acts of the same play, and they provide the foundation for the tripartite structure of this Article. . . .

## II. ACT ONE: THE QUESTION OF COVERAGE

Not every case is a first amendment case. This is hardly a controversial observation, but it reveals that the first amendment is itself a category, or, more accurately, that it covers a category of behavior. The boundaries of this category are frequently contested, and they are unclear even when there is general agreement as to broad principles. Yet the first amendment constrains only *some* governmental ends, and only *some* governmental means. It is not a universal prohibition on governmental action, and if it is to mean anything at all some boundary must circumscribe its coverage, however fuzzy that boundary may be. Thus, only a certain category of behavior is covered by the first amendment. It can therefore be helpful to look at the question of first amendment coverage as a category question: What marks off the category covered by the first amendment from those other categories of conduct that do not implicate free speech analysis?

. . .

Delineating the category of "speech," determining what counts as "speech" for first amendment purposes, is implicit in every first amendment case. The question only comes to the surface, however, when the accepted or proposed category of "speech" diverges from the meaning of the word "speech" in ordinary language. . . .

. . .

Is the category of speech to be congruent with the denotation of the ordinary meaning of the word "speech," or is the word "speech" in the first amendment to be defined as a piece of technical language, whose definition is derived from the underlying theory of the first amendment? This choice between the ordinary language approach and the technical language approach is in turn contingent upon a more pervasive question of constitutional theory: Is constitutional language in general a form of technical language, to be interpreted in its unique context and with reference to its particular purposes, or is it ordinary language, to be interpreted by applying the ordinary language, or "dictionary," definitions of the terms it contains? It seems clear that only the former approach is defensible, but I do not wish to argue the point here. Rather, I want to explore the implications of the latter approach in the particular context of the first amendment, proceeding by the method of *reductio ad absurdum*; that is, what happens if

---

* Reprinted with permission.

we try to interpret the word "speech" in the first amendment as meaning what it means in ordinary language—what it means to the "man in the street"?

If we do define "speech" by reference to Webster's dictionary, then many distinctly discordant cases would be considered first amendment cases, a circumstance occasioned by the pervasiveness of language (speech) in almost every facet of human activity. . . . Not only do we fix prices with speech, but we also make contracts with speech, commit perjury with speech, discriminate with speech, extort with speech, threaten with speech, and place bets with speech. Is it possible to say that all of these cases and many more are covered by the first amendment?

If we do say that all of these cases are *covered* by the first amendment, we then must have a way of holding that these activities are not *protected* by the first amendment unless of course we want to say that the first amendment makes, for example, all of contract law, most of antitrust law, and much of criminal law unconstitutional. This distinction can be made without doing undue violence to the text by saying that the first amendment is not even in its language absolute—in other words, that *the freedom of* speech does not encompass freedom to fix prices, breach contracts, make false warranties, place bets with bookies, threaten, extort, and so on. But why doesn't it? It is not because these activities necessarily constitute something that looks like a clear and present danger or because the laws against such activity represent a compelling governmental interest. Verbal gambling, for example, is commonly thought to be unpleasant and undesirable (at least by legislatures), but it is bizarre to say that verbal betting presents a clear and present danger or a compelling interest in a way that racial epithets, advocacy of violent revolution, and disclosure of confidential government documents do not. If no first amendment and principle of free speech existed, would we say that a telephone bookie operation constitutes a greater danger of harm than the march of the American Nazi Party in Skokie? I doubt it very much.

· · ·

The literalist is presented with a parallel problem in reference to those acts that are not speech in the ordinary language sense but are speech in the constitutional sense—armband wearing, communicative clothing, oil painting, political contributions, photography, and so on. If these activities count as speech because they share relevant similarities with speech, then some attributes of speech must serve to trigger the guarantees of the first amendment. If that is so, then some verbal acts may not share these attributes, and thus are not "speech" in the constitutional sense. What emerges from all of this is the conclusion that the constitutional definition of the word "speech" carves out a category that is not coextensive with the ordinary language meaning of the word "speech." When we define the word "speech," we are categorizing. This occurs regardless of the source of the definition, and in this sense categorization is implicit in any approach to the theory or structure of the first amendment.

In considering the boundaries of the category covered by the first amendment, I have been looking somewhat unnaturally at the single word "speech." It is perhaps more sensible to look not at the word but at the phrase, asking whether a given act was included within "the freedom of speech." If that act were included, then it would be within the prohibition on abridgement, leaving for the second level of inquiry the question of what is an abridgement. Under this approach not every act of speech would be covered by the first amendment's prohibition on abridgement; only those acts that come within "the freedom of speech" would be covered. Here we substitute for the question, "What is speech?" the question, "What is 'the freedom of speech'?"

In one respect this alternative technique produces no change, for "the freedom of speech" is not the same as "the freedom of action" or "the freedom of contract." This second approach collapses into the first, for the initial question must still be, "What is 'speech'?" It is this category question that comes first in any first amendment case, regardless of what happens with speech once it is found. We must always first ask, "Is this speech?," regardless of whether we are going to determine thereafter if it is the type of speech that we deem to be free, protect absolutely, protect only strongly, or subject to a "balancing of the interests."

In another respect, however, the question of whether to look at the word "speech" in isolation as opposed to looking at the entire phrase, "the freedom of speech," does produce an important distinction. In setting the boundaries of the category of conduct encompassed by the first amendment, those approaches commonly referred to as "definitional" combine close attention to defining the boundaries of the category with a desire to grant absolute protection within those boundaries. The theories of Meiklejohn, Frantz, Emerson, and Nimmer, for example, all define "the freedom of speech" in their own purpose-oriented way (with which there is nothing wrong) and then argue that conduct falling within the contours of the category is absolutely protected.

These "definitional-absolutist" theories treat all

nonprotected speech identically. They treat especially harmful political speech ("Go burn down the draft board—NOW!!," uttered in front of an angry mob of torchbearing antidraft protestors fifty yards from the draft board) the same way as extortion, contract law, and advice or encouragement in the commission of a nonpolitical bank robbery. If we look at the reasons for the exclusion of these utterances from first amendment protection, however, we see that especially harmful political speech is excluded because of the extent and the immediacy of the danger; discussing the wisdom of burning down draft boards at a peaceful teach-in is protected. Yet contract law, antitrust law, and the like are excluded for reasons having little if anything to do with the extent or the imminence of the danger. They are excluded, and properly so, because they have nothing to do with what the concept of free speech is all about.

In thus trying to preserve an enclave of absoluteness, the definers must then construct a theory that treats irrelevant (to the first amendment) speech like verbal betting in the same way as relevant but unprotected speech like incitement to burn down draft boards. Reductionism, the urge to reduce complex phenomena to overly simple formulae, has been a pitfall throughout legal theory, and no less so in relation to the first amendment. The efforts to create one formula that will generate an area of absolute protection have been heroic, but they have failed in one of two ways. Either they have, like Professor Emerson's distinction between expression and action, simplified things to such an extent that the resultant formula has little if any analytical or predictive value, or they have, like the Meiklejohn interpretation, achieved consistency and workability at the expense of excluding from coverage much that a full theory of freedom of speech ought to include.

. . .

Defining an area of absolute protection is likely to be impossible for two main reasons. First, it is unlikely that any one theory can explain the concept of free speech, and no reason necessarily exists to suppose that it could. Freedom of speech need not have any one "essential" feature. It is much more likely a bundle of interrelated principles sharing no common set of necessary and sufficient defining characteristics. It is quite possible that the protection of political discussion and criticism, the aversion to censorship of art, and the desire to retain open inquiry in science and other academic disciplines, for example, are principles not reducible to any one common core. Any attempt to do so is likely to be

both banal and to distort all of the principles involved. The standard jurisprudential and linguistic metaphor of the core and the fringe is useful in its place, but it is harmful if it leads us to search for only one core when there may in fact be several, or many.

The second difficulty in attempting to build all of the exceptions and qualifications into our definition of a right absolute in strength is that we simply do not know what all the exceptions and qualifications might be. Lacking omniscience, we can at best imperfectly predict the future. Rights whose shape incorporates all exceptions and qualifications would be extremely rough tools for dealing with the uncertainties of the future. Instead, we wisely achieve finer tools for future use by combining a relatively vague definition of the coverage of the right (for example, all speech of public importance or all discussion) with a relatively vague specification of the weight of the right (for example, that it prevails in all cases in which the justification for the restriction is not a clear and present danger of great magnitude). . . .

. . .

The theoretical and practical difficulties of a definitional-absolutist approach should not blind us to the importance of the coverage question even when the strength of the protection is less than absolute. If we look, for example, at the theory of the first amendment that focuses on the purposes of the governmental action—we might call this the *O'Brien*-Scanlon-Ely-Tribe theory—we find the full strength of the first amendment's prescriptions reserved for those governmental actions that are "aimed at communicative impact." Although this theory quite properly looks at the totality of the governmental action rather than at some isolated description of the objects of that action, the theory still requires a description of the category of coverage. Laws against price fixing, extortion, perjury, and solicitation to garden-variety, nonpolitical crimes are all "aimed at communicative impact," yet these too are laws intuitively and correctly held to be outside the coverage of the first amendment. This is not to say that the theory based on governmental action "aimed at communicative impact" is incorrect. On the contrary, that theory is a great contribution to understanding the structure of the first amendment and to providing guidance for judicial resolution of a wide variety of hitherto troublesome cases. The theory is incomplete, however, unless it provides some guidance, derived again from the deep theory of the principle of free speech, in determining what species of communicative impact are covered and what species of communicative impact are not. In this respect we once again must answer the question that started all of this: What is "speech" in the constitutional sense?

At this point it is necessary to note two different ways of dealing with this question. In defining the category of coverage of the first amendment, we have a choice between "defining in" and "defining out." . . .

The "defining in" approach assumes both that we can construct a workable definition reflecting the deep theoretical premises of the concept of free speech and that such a definition can be taught to those who matter—the judges who must both apply it and refine its imprecision. If either of these assumptions is unwarranted, it may be preferable to adopt the alternative approach of "defining out." Here we initially construct a coarse and intentionally overbroad definition that is simple enough to be learned and applied easily and broad enough to encompass the full range of plausible theoretical justifications for a principle of freedom of speech. Some examples of such a category might be "all communications," or "everything that is 'speech' in ordinary language," or "all public discourse." Having created this intentionally overinclusive category, we then carve out subcategories of noncoverage, to take care of contract law, perjury, extortion, and so on. These subcategories too must be conceived within the framework of a theory of free speech, although the focus here is negative (no reason to grant special protection against the power of government) rather than positive (grant special protection here because . . .).

. . .

In the context of the choice between defining in and defining out, it seems to follow that we can avoid more errors of underinclusion by defining out rather than defining in. Thus, perhaps the preferable course is to begin with the presumption that all communication is covered by the first amendment and then create areas of noncoverage, regarding which the burden of proof of nonapplicability of first amendment principles can be met.

. . .

## III. ACT TWO: THE VARIETIES OF SPEECH

Our first look at categorization and the first amendment focused on the first amendment as itself constituting a category. From this perspective the conclusion that categorization in this sense is unavoidable was inevitable. The question now is whether we can or should go further in the process of categorization; that is, does the category of conduct covered by the first amendment in turn contain further subcategories? Having concluded that the first amendment covers a particular set of circumstances, do we then apply a uniform test to determine whether the first amendment protects the act, or do we apply differing tests depending upon the subcategory within the first amendment into which the particular case falls?

Hostility toward the creation of subcategories within the first amendment has been a pervasive, albeit not invariably determinative, theme in contemporary free speech doctrine. This hostility can be embodied in a bipolar structure of no protection and full protection. "Full protection" refers not necessarily to absolute protection but only to the maximum level of protection that the first amendment provides, which may, for example, be only the use of some form of a "clear and present danger" standard. If we were to refuse to recognize any subcategories within the first amendment, we would determine first whether the facts of the case fell outside or inside the coverage of the first amendment. If they fell outside, there would be no protection, at least not by the first amendment. If they fell inside, the full protection of the first amendment, however much that might be, would attach to the conduct in question. Implicit in this all-or-nothing approach is an extreme reluctance to assign differing values to the speech that is covered by the first amendment. The works of Shakespeare have the same first amendment value as *Playboy*, which in turn has the same first amendment value as wearing a black armband or arguing for the virtues of Nazism.

At bottom this conscious refusal to subcategorize is founded in the belief that first amendment protection should not turn on whether a statement is on one side or the other of a particular question. If an argument for the roundness of the Earth is protected, then arguments for flatness are protected to the same extent. If arguments for capitalism are to be protected, then so too must arguments for socialism. Moreover, as can be seen from cases like *Brandenburg* and *Skokie*, if arguments for racial equality are protected, so are arguments for racial hatred and intolerance. Certainly there can be little quarrel with this, for the decision not to allow free speech protection to turn on the point of view adopted by the speaker goes to both the epistemological and political cores of free speech theory.

. . .

Still, at least four arguments can be marshalled in favor of categorization within the first amendment. First, if we take the "full protection within" rule as the standard, there may be pressure to keep troublesome categories completely outside. When the choice is all or nothing, the difficulties of "all" may lead courts to choose "nothing." Thus, it may be that one of the reasons for the historical exclusion of commercial advertising was the potential for problems, especially in terms of truth and falsity, that would exist if commercial advertising were treated in the same manner as advocacy of adultery or the single tax. If the creation of a separate category within the first amendment is precluded, a tempting solution is merely to keep the speech that would constitute that category outside first amendment protection. Similar observations seem also applicable to the pre-*New York Times* exclusion of defamatory speech from the coverage of the first amendment.

Second, not all forms of speech are necessarily amenable to the same analytic approach. The tests and tools created to deal with the likes of *Brandenburg*, *Whitney*, *Schenck*, and *Debs*, for example, may not be those most appropriate for dealing with problems of a quite different kind. Neither false advertising nor false attacks on private reputation fit easily into anything even close to a "clear and present danger" formula—nor, for that matter, does speech that offends rather than causes harm in a narrower sense. We are accustomed to thinking in terms of levels of protection, but it may be that different categories of speech should be treated *differently*, which does not necessarily entail more or less.

Third, and somewhat related to the second argument, most first amendment theory is formulated around the "advocacy" paradigm. When statements of fact are concerned, for example, many of the skeptical presuppositions of the first amendment are either irrelevant or highly attenuated. It is true that many statements of fact contain statements of opinion as well as that factual determinations are often erroneous, but the differences between "this car has a six-cylinder engine" and "socialism is wonderful" are apparent to all but the most resolute skeptic. Some people may have so little confidence in their own factual judgments that they always sit down gingerly for fear that the chair they see is only an apparition, but we hardly need tailor first amendment doctrine around them. It may be, therefore, that appropriate categories could recognize the differences in the extent to which first amendment principles are applicable to the variety of speech acts, of which advocacy and factual description are but two.

Finally, the refusal to categorize is frightfully counter-intuitive. Many commentators have strongly criticized Justice Stevens' observation in *Young v. American Mini Theatres, Inc.* that "few of us would march our sons and daughters off to war to preserve the citizen's right to see 'Specified Sexual Activities' exhibited in the theaters of our choice"; but he was right. We would not, if that were all we were protecting. The difficulty comes in describing the behavior, and therefore the category of behavior, at the appropriate level of generality, but most people do believe that there are "commonsense differences" between different categories of utterances. Moreover, most people believe that some categories are more important than others, with great agreement about many questions of relative worth. Political argument is simply more important than "Specified Sexual Activities," and *Hamlet* is simply better literature than "Dance with the Dominant Whip" or "Cult of the Spankers." Anyone who holds otherwise is just plain wrong. Of course, things are not this simple. Our commonsense categories have fuzzy edges, and there is much more agreement that Hamlet is good literature and "Dance with the Dominant Whip" is bad literature than there is about in which category to put *Memoirs of a Woman of Pleasure* or George Carlin's "Seven Dirty Words" monologue. While we might be quite confident in saying that political argument is more important than idle gossip about absent acquaintances, the relative merits of political argument, art, ancient history, and philosophy are far more debatable.

. . .

First, a subcategory must have some relationship to a permissible first amendment purpose. Legal categories are not natural in the way that other categories may be. Human beings create legal categories to serve a purpose, and the category can be no more permissible than the purpose. It should be apparent here that offensiveness *simpliciter* as a category is hardly consistent with most of the antimajoritarian premises of the first amendment. A wide range of utterances, such as "God is dead," "Hitler was a great man," and "The American flag is a symbol of oppression," are quite likely to cause offense to many people, yet *Young* and *Pacifica* do not (it is hoped) indicate that any of these utterances may in any way be restricted. If so, it is more than mere offense that is the defining feature of this subcategory. It is offense of a certain kind, or offense plus something more. If it is offense of the sexual or scatological variety, the continuing validity of Cohen is called into question, for Carlin's words were no more likely to stimulate than were Cohen's. On the other hand, perhaps the definition of the subcategory is in terms of sexual or scatological offense combined with an absence of "important" content. Again, however, it is hard to discern why Carlin's commentary about language is less important than Cohen's commentary about the Selective Service System, and it is equally hard to discern why a radio broadcast is more intrusive than activity in the courthouse lobby. I cannot imagine why one could not switch off the radio, but there may be quite good reasons for having to remain with Cohen in the courthouse. Turning off a radio is much easier than averting your eyes from someone who is in the same room. Just try it sometime.

This criticism of *Pacifica* is hardly novel, and I do not wish to belabor the matter here. The point I wish to make is that the creation of a category must be justified by reasons underlying the features distinguishing that category from others. When those reasons are not applied in all cases in which they are, by their own terms, applicable, then the attempt to create a category has misfired. In traditional terminology we would say that the category-creating case was unprincipled. It is, however, impossible for a case to be unprincipled in isolation. What makes a case unprincipled is the refusal in future cases to treat cases alike within the articulated category. If *Cohen, Spence v. Washington*, and their ilk are to survive, then *Pacifica* and *Young* have not created a subcategory at all. If *Cohen, Spence*, and others are to be overruled or limited on the authority of *Young* and *Pacifica*, then *Young* and *Pacifica* have indeed created a subcategory within the first amendment that is to be treated differently. In that case *Young* and *Pacifica* could no longer be taken to be unprincipled, but would simply be wrong. There *is* a difference.

. . . When, as with "offensiveness," the category is so inherently and extremely indeterminate and so linguistically ill-defined, a serious risk exists that the category will in practice be misapplied, and a powerful argument therefore arises against the creation of the category. In the first amendment, as in all of law, the task of the judge is to classify the particular facts of the case within the appropriate category. Increasing the number of categories may involve an increased risk of misclassification, even if the categories are theoretically sound. When the error of misclassification is likely to occur in derogation of constitutionally preferred values, categorization in the sense of creating additional subcategories is a technique to be employed with only the greatest of caution.

For these reasons the notion of a presumption is once again useful, just as it is useful in choosing between "defining in" and "defining out." If we accept the principle that the first amendment seeks to protect that which may at first sight (or even upon further reflection) seem worthless, then we must guard against the pressure to create subcategories that will leave to judges in a particular case the determination of either the truth or the social utility of a covered communicative act. We can accomplish this

best by creating a presumption, albeit rebuttable, against the creation of subcategories within the first amendment. When, as in the case of commercial advertising and defamation, it can be affirmatively demonstrated that it is possible to create a subcategory that is consistent with the theoretical foundations of the first amendment, that is capable of principled definition and application, and that is sufficiently determinate that the dangers of incorrect application are manageable, then the presumption against creating subcategories may be overcome. The subcategory foreshadowed by *Young* and *Pacifica* is particularly unfortunate because it exhibits none of these features. Thus, it is a compound error, for any one of these factors should be sufficient to defeat the proposed subcategory.

## IV. ACT THREE: RULES

Having determined that a set of facts lies within the coverage of the first amendment and having placed those facts within the appropriate subcategory of the first amendment, the question finally arises of just how we will decide the case, or, more accurately, how the judge will decide the case. It is at this stage that we can no longer escape facing up to the recurrent question of ad hoc balancing. The question at this stage is what the rules of guidance for the judge will look like within a given first amendment category.

. . .

The choice comes down to the amount of flexibility we wish to allow the judge to deal with a particular case whose existence we did not and quite possibly could not have foreseen. If we grant little or no flexibility, we increase the likelihood of anomalous results, the inevitable consequence of attempting to fit the unanticipated future into categories based on suppositions that did not include that event. We can, of course, accommodate the possibility of unanticipated future cases by granting greater flexibility to the judge, who can then look at how the interests are reflected in the particular case and reach what he perceives to be the proper accommodation of those interests.

This flexibility, though, entails two substantial costs. A problem of notice can occur because the more flexibility that the trial court has, the less certain anyone can be in advance of the likely result in a particular case. Lack of predictability in the law is always troublesome, and it is even more so when the inevitable caution that unpredictability yields will induce self-censorship ("chilling") of that which may very well be important. Moreover, the judge might just decide incorrectly. The greater the flexibility that is built into the governing standards, the less the judge is constrained by rules even for the type of case we can anticipate. The less the judge is constrained, the more likely there are to be errant results.

It is by now hardly a novel observation that particularized balancing of interests by the judge in respect to the case at hand (ad hoc balancing) is not a technique with a monopoly on the weighing of interests. We balance when we formulate rules for mechanical or categorical application. Nor is it a simple question of a choice between balancing at the rulemaking level or at the level of application. There is a spectrum rather than a dichotomy. The question is not *whether* to permit judges to balance in the particular case, but rather *how much* authority the governing rule should allocate to the judge to take account of the particular circumstances of the case at hand. Although this allocation could take place in the form of a specific grant of authority, it is much more common for it to exist implicitly in the degree of specificity of the governing rule.

When categorization is presented as a first amendment technique in opposition to balancing, what is in fact being advocated is the establishment of rules leaving little if any discretion to the judge in the particular case. The more a rule predetermines the outcome that flows from easily determinable facts, or the more a rule excludes certain facts from consideration by the judge, the less discretion is available to the judge and the more we can call the rule categorical. . . .

. . .

In seeking answers to these questions pertaining to the appropriate blend of guidance and discretion, it is important to remember that there is no necessary correlation between the approach employed and the strength of the first amendment protection. Although ad hoc balancing has traditionally been associated with a puny first amendment and categorical rules with a powerful one, it could have been and still could be otherwise. It is possible, after all, to devise rigid rules that give little respect to free speech considerations. Consider, for example, a rule that said no first amendment protection was available when the speaker advocated violation of the law. What is or is not considered advocacy may in some cases be a close question. That is beside the point, however, for such a rule is substantially more categorical than the *Brandenburg* rule, which requires a contextual and therefore ad hoc determination of likely effect as well. Similarly, it could have been the case that all judges with the power to balance the interests in the particular case had, even with little guidance or

restriction of their discretion, found in favor of the speaker and against the restriction. If that had been our history, then the reflexive association of ad hoc balancing with limited first amendment protection might never have arisen. . . .

It is thus behavioral observation and speculation far more than inexorable logic that dictates the extent to which categorical rules should narrow the range of judicial choice. That does not mean, however, that we have nothing on which to base the choice. Experience can guide us, and in this respect the virtues of particularized balancing are often quite hard to see. Freedom of speech is a long-term value not always fully appreciated in the case at hand. In order fully to accommodate this long-term interest, we must often make what at first sight appear to be discordant short-term decisions. Moreover, as Professor Emerson has most notably reminded us, freedom of speech is a value that runs counter to many of our intuitions. Psychological forces, if there are such things, run in favor of suppression. In a particular case the asserted governmental interest will often look far more appealing or even compelling than the first amendment interest. As a result, it is not at all surprising that discretion-limiting rules have traditionally provided far more in the way of first amendment protection than has particularized balancing. . . .

. . .

The choice of the appropriate point between unguided judicial discretion and rigid verbal rules, then, must be influenced not only by the balance between predictability and flexibility for unforeseen cases, but also by the psychological factors relating to the likely outcome of that discretion. It is a decision that takes place *within* a given first amendment subcategory. In turn, the decision to create subcategories takes place *within* the process of delineating the category of coverage of the first amendment. Each categorization decision takes place within another, somewhat like those sets of Russian wooden dolls. Each categorization decision, like each doll, can stand alone if necessary, but the full impact is achieved in the way they all fit together. . . .

John Hart Ely, *Flag Desecration: A Case Study in the Roles of Categorization and Balancing in First Amendment Analysis*, 88 HARVARD LAW REVIEW 1482 (1975)*

On three occasions over the past few years the

---

* Reprinted with permission.

Supreme Court on one narrow ground or another, has avoided definitively ruling on the constitutionality of convictions for politically inspired destruction or alteration of the American Flag. The most recent decision, *Spence v. Washington*, does not seem to approach such a ruling, at least if one ignores the various irrelevancies with which the Court hedged its opinion. But logical or not, the qualifications are part of the opinion, and one must assume that the Court finds the issue troubling. At first glance, however, it is hard to see why. Laws prohibiting flag desecration quite obviously inhibit political expression, and the state's interest in doing so—at least when the flag is owned by the person doing the disfiguring, and that is how these cases come up—seems scarcely articulable, let alone strong. The Court's hesitancy, one gathers, stems at least in part from its 1968 decision in *United States v. O'Brien*, upholding a conviction for draft card burning. And indeed the act of burning a flag does look a lot like the act of burning a draft card, which makes it difficult to deny the surface plausibility of the interference that the former can also be proscribed. The plausibility is mostly on the surface, however. Indeed, once certain ambiguities in the test *O'Brien* set forth are resolved—in the only way that is defensible or even remotely consistent with other, virtually contemporaneous decisions—the case will be seen to argue rather strongly *against* the constitutionality of such laws.

## I

The "crux of the Court's opinion" in *O'Brien* was that:

> [A] governmental regulation is sufficiently justified. . .[1] if it furthers an important or substantial governmental interest; [2] if the governmental interest is unrelated to the suppression of free expression; and [3] if the incidental restriction on alleged First Amendment freedoms is no greater than is essential to the furtherance of that interest.

Whatever *O'Brien's* other merits or demerits, the Court is surely to be commended for here attempting something it attempts too seldom, the statement of a coherent and applicable test. The test is not limited to cases involving so-called "symbolic speech." (One conclusion that should emerge from this Comment is that that is one of its virtues.) The test is, however, limited in the sense that it is incomplete. The fact that a regulation does not satisfy criterion [2] does not necessarily mean that it is unconstitutional. It means "only" that the case is switched onto another track and an approach other than that indicated in criterion [3] will be employed, a categorizing approach elaborated in other decisions of the late Warren period, which is in fact substantially more demanding than the approach indicated in criterion [3]. Criterion [3] is also incomplete as described in *O'Brien*. In practice its application involves a choice between different conceptions of its standard, a choice made by reference to factors neither *O'Brien* nor any other Supreme Court decision has yet made explicit. This variability in the content of criterion [3] is important; it reduces the reliability of what at first might seem to be the most restrictive element of *O'Brien's* test, and thus highlights the significance of what is in fact critical—the "switching function" performed by criterion [2]. It is to criterion [3] that we first look.

## II

Criterion [3]'s requirement that the inhibition of expression be no greater than is essential to the furtherance of the state's interest strikes a familiar chord: "less restrictive alternative" analysis is common in constitutional law generally and in first amendment cases in particular. But there is always a latent ambiguity in the analysis, and *O'Brien* brought it to the surface. Weakly construed, it could require only that there be no less restrictive alternative capable of serving the state's interest *as efficiently as it is served by the regulation under attack*. But as I have noted elsewhere, in virtually every case involving real legislation, a more perfect fit involves some added cost. In effect, therefore, this weak formulation would reach only laws that engage in the gratuitous inhibition of expression, requiring only that a prohibition not outrun the interest it is designed to serve.

Further language in the *O'Brien* opinion, and the holding of the case, indicate that this is the strongest form of less restrictive alternative analysis in which, under the circumstances, the Court was prepared to engage. Coupled with the trivial functional significance the Court attached to criterion [1]'s critical word "substantial," however, this turned out to be no protection at all: legislatures simply do not enact wholly useless provisions. It is therefore no surprise to discover that earlier cases protecting more traditional forms of expression (such as the distribution of handbills), although they too purported to apply a sort of less restrictive alternative test, gave it a significantly stronger meaning. The point of these cases, in contradistinction to *O'Brien*, was that the absence of gratuitous inhibition is *not* enough. For in banning the distribution of handbills, municipalities pursue a goal unconnected with the inhibition of expression, the reduction of litter, and they do so without placing any gratuitous limits on expression: the entirety of an anti-handbill ordinance serves the goal of reducing litter. Such cases thus suggest that the existence of possible alternative approaches—such as more trash cans and an anti-littering ordinance—triggers a serious balancing of interests: the question is whether the marginally greater effectiveness of an anti-handbill ordinance relative to alternative means of litter control justifies the greater burden on communication. In order to clear room for effective expression, the Court was saying, cities will simply have to put up with some litter, to be satisfied with less than optimal vindication of the interest they are pursuing, unconnected with expression though it is.

It is not entirely clear what the Court will do, or indeed what it should do, about resolving this apparent discontinuity in its approach to the less restrictive alternative analysis. Bringing the handbill and kindred cases into line with *O'Brien* would go a long way toward eviscerating the first amendment. Given the state's perfectly legitimate and expression-unconnected interests in keeping thoroughfares clear and controlling crowds, noise and litter, an approach that rejected only the gratuitous inhibitions of expression could effectively close altogether such traditional channels of communication as pamphleteering, picketing and public speaking. But bringing *O'Brien* into line with the handbill cases' balancing version of the less restrictive alternative analysis has a parade of horribles all its own. Suppose *O'Brien* had convinced the Court to void his draft card burning conviction on the ground that the government's interest could be fairly well, if not quite as well, served by some alternative means. (The alternative most often suggested by critics of the decision is enforcement of the regulation requiring continued possession of one's draft card.) But then suppose that O'Brien or someone else chose symbolically to flout *the possession requirement.* (The most dramatic way of doing this would probably be by publicly burning one's draft card.) It is difficult to see why he could not successfully defend this case on the theory of the prior one, namely that his expression is being inhibited for no very good reason, in that the interests served by the possession requirement too can be fairly well, if not quite as well, served by alternative means. (Governmental maintenance of several sets of records and the increased use of mailings and television reminders like those used for alien registration suggest themselves.) That case having been won, someone turning eighteen might make a public point of refusing to register for draft in the first place, arguing in his defense that the system can get along fairly well (if not quite as well) without his contacting his draft board, since the information the board needs is all readily available without his sending it to them. The point by now is clear, and it is, of course, a point that is not limited to the context of the draft: universalizing the balancing approach of the handbill cases would seem at least potentially to establish the constitutional right symbolically to break any law, or perhaps it is only any "little" law, so long as its purposes can be fairly well served, as of course, they almost always can, by alternative means. . . .

. . . [I]t seems likely that the Court will continue, either explicitly or implicitly, to distinguish between familiar and unorthodox modes of communication in deciding whether genuinely to balance in evaluating less restrictive alternatives or rather simply to assure itself, as it will always be able to, that no gratuitous inhibition of expression has been effected. In any event, the question of how to accommodate freedom of expression with the state's various expression-unconnected interests is, and will remain, an extremely difficult one. . . .

### III

The two sorts of review we have been discussing—the "no gratuitous inhibition" approach that upheld the draft card burning law, and the balancing approach that has been employed in cases involving more familiar forms of expression—do differ significantly. That is not, however, because the latter is especially protective of expression (in fact it is notoriously unreliable) but rather because the former, honestly applied, will invalidate nothing. There was, of course, a time when balancing was sufficient to satisfy a majority of the Court as a general approach to the first amendment. But that was hardly the attitude of the Warren Court, at least in its later years. During the very period when *O'Brien* was decided, the Court was making clear its dissatisfaction with a general balancing approach, indicating that only expression fairly assignable to one of an increasingly limited set of narrowly defined categories could be denied constitutional protection. Thus in *Brandenburg v. Ohio*, decided a year after *O'Brien*. A unanimous Court, invalidating the Ohio Criminal Syndicalism Act, indicated that:

> [T]he constitutional guarantees of free speech and free press do not permit a State to forbid or proscribe advocacy of the use of force or of law violation except where such advocacy is directed to inciting or producing imminent lawless action and is likely to incite or produce such action.

There is in *Brandenburg* no talk of balancing, let

alone of a simple prohibition of gratuitous suppression: the expression involved in a given case either does or does not fall within the described category, and if it does not it is protected. (O'Brien's expression, it is hardly necessary to add, did not fall within the described category, and no one claimed it did.) Quite obviously the Court of the late Warren period had two radically different first amendment approaches for what it saw as two significantly different sets of problems. Something about O'Brien's case caused the Court to adopt an approach much less protective of first amendment interests than that put forth in *Brandenburg*.

The explanation for this difference is not that Brandenburg was actually talking—moving his mouth and uttering words—whereas O'Brien was expressing himself nonverbally. *Tinker v. Des Moines School District*, decided nine months after *O'Brien*, involved the suspension of school children for wearing black armbands to protest the Vietnam War. The protest's target was very much the same as that in *O'Brien*; the setting, the classroom rather than the post office steps, was if anything more fragile; the penalty was milder; and most important for present purposes, the communication was, again, entirely nonverbal. Yet the Court did not hesitate a moment: this was, it announced—without supporting argument or any attempt to distinguish *O'Brien*—"the type of symbolic act that is within the Free Speech Clause of the First Amendment. . . . It was closely akin to 'pure speech' which, we have repeatedly held, is entitled to comprehensive protection . . . ." Comprehensive protection is certainly what it was given, and the suspensions were reversed. The Court is still unable to account very convincingly for the difference between *O'Brien* and *Tinker*, but the contrast in tone between the two opinions, to say nothing of the result, could hardly be starker. Similarly, in *Cohen v. California*, decided in 1971, the Court reversed the conviction of a young man, obviously a latter Billy Budd, who found he could adequately convey his feelings only by parading about in a jacket that said "Fuck the Draft." Rejecting the dissenters' claim that "Cohen's absurd and immature antic"— so far one must assume no disagreement—"was mainly conduct and little speech," the Court employed, and in the process importantly clarified, the categorization approach it had adopted in *Brandenburg*. . . .

## IV

The distinction between cases like *O'Brien* on the one hand and cases like *Tinker* and *Cohen* on the other can, in fact, be found in the *O'Brien* opinion

itself, but you have to hunt around a bit to find it. The Court give us at least one false lead—suggesting early on thats perhaps O'Brien's act was not "speech" at all and therefore simply not covered by the first amendment:

> We cannot accept the view that an apparently limitless variety of conduct can be labeled "speech" whenever the person engaging in the conduct intends thereby to express an idea.

Although the Court did not ultimately rely on this distinction, it nonetheless deserves some attention. It has received the endorsement of scholars who must command respect, and the fallacy that underlies it is one that has similarly infected other, apparently more subtle, approaches to the problem of "symbolic speech." . . .

. . . [B]urning a draft card to express opposition to the draft is undifferentiated whole, 100% action and 100% expression. It involves no conduct that is not at the same time communication, and no communication that does not result from conduct. Attempts to determine which element "predominates" will therefore inevitably degenerate into question-begging judgments about whether the activity should be protected.

. . .

## V

When the Court in *O'Brien* gets around to what is obviously intended as the definitive statement of its test—specifically in what I have designated criterion [2]—it gives us something substantially more helpful:

> [A] governmental regulation is sufficiently justified . . . if it furthers an important or substantial governmental *interest [that] is unrelated to the suppression of free expression*. . . .

Here the Court shifts from ontology to teleology. It abandons its earlier suggestion that the constitutional answer can be found by examining O'Brien's act— either to determine whether it is really expression or conduct, for of course it is both, or to identify which aspects of the act is being regulated, for of course they both are—and suggests instead an inquiry into whether the governmental interest or interests that support the regulation are related to the suppression of expression.

Obviously this approach is not self-defining: it can, for one thing, be interpreted in a way that will guarantee that its demand can always be satisfied. Restrictions on free expression are rarely defended on the ground that the state simply didn't like what the defendant was saying; reference will generally be made to some danger beyond the message, such as a danger of riot, unlawful action or violent over-throw of the government. Thus in *Brandenburg* the state's defense was not that the speech in question was distasteful, though it surely was, but rather that speeches of that sort were likely to induce people to take the law into their own hands. The reference of *O'Brien*'s second criterion is therefore not to the ultimate interest to which the state is able to point, for that will always be unrelated to expression, but rather to the causal connection the state asserts. If, for example, the state asserts an interest in discourag-ing riots, the Court will ask why that interest is impli-cated in the case at bar. If the answer is (as in such cases it will likely have to be) that the danger was created by what the defendant was saying, the state's interest is not unrelated to the suppression of free expression within the meaning of *O'Brien*'s criterion [2]. The categorization approach of cases like *Bran-denburg* and *Cohen*, rather than (either variant of) *O'Brien*'s criterion [3] is therefore in order, and the regulation will very likely be invalidated. The critical question would therefore seem to be whether the harm that the state is seeking to avert is one that grows out of the fact that the defendant is communi-cating, and more particularly out of the way people can be expected to react to his message, or rather would arise even if the defendant's conduct had no communicative significance whatever.

There may be a temptation to conclude that one has seen all this before, or at least its functional equivalent, in the shopworn distinction between "regulation of content" and "regulation of time, place and manner." That would be a mistaken equa-tion, however, and one with severe costs for free expression. For the state obviously can move, and often does, "simply" to control the time, place or manner of communication out of concern for the likely effect of the communication on its audience. Thus in *Tinker* the state regulated only the place and manner of expression—no armbands in school—but it did so, or at least this is the account most favorable to the state, because it feared the effect that the mes-sage those armbands conveyed would have on the other children. (Had the armbands lacked communi-cative significance, there would have been no way to defend or even account for the regulation.) The regulation at issue in *Cohen* might well be styled by a resourceful prosecutor as simply a restriction on the manner of expression, but perhaps it can also be regarded as a restriction on content. But this brand of ontology, like the others we have seen, is as irrele-vant as it is unintelligible. *O'Brien*'s second criterion is no more concerned with "what sort of regulation it really is" than with "what it is that is really being

regulated''; the critical point in *Cohen*, as in *Tinker*, is that the dangers on which the state relied were dangers that flowed entirely from the communicative content of Cohen's behavior. Had this audience been unable to read English, there would have been no occasion for the regulation.

*O'Brien* was different. The interests upon which the government relied were interests, having mainly to do with the preservation of selective service records, that would have been equally threatened had O'Brien's destruction of his draft card totally lacked communicative significance—had he, for example, used it to start a campfire for a solitary cookout or dropped it in his garbage disposal for a lark. (The law prohibited all knowing destructions, public or private.) Perhaps the Court should have engaged in some serious balancing, but its refusal even to con-sider the categorization approach appropriate to cases like *Brandenburg* and *Cohen* was quite correct. *O'Brien* is more like *Prince v. Massachusetts*, in which the Court upheld the application of the state's labor law to a child distributing Jehovah's Witness literature. Obviously the state was thereby regulating expressive activity, but the evil it was trying to avert was one that would have been equally implicated had the child been engaged in work with no communica-tive component whatever. Similarly, by employing what amounts to a balancing test to permit some municipal regulation of sound-trucks, the Court surely permits some restriction of expression. But again, the values the state seeks to promote by such regulation, values of quiet and repose, would be threatened as much by meaningless moans and static (which is usually how it comes out anyway) as by a political message. And although I am not aware that the Court has ever decided such a case, it seems clear that it would refuse to extend constitutional protection to the right to interrupt a public speaker, even by the most coherent and trenchant of political commentary. For the values the state seeks to protect by forbidding interruption, the right of the originally scheduled speaker to have his say and of his audience to listen, are not geared to the message of the inter-rupter or even to the fact that he has a message. Interruption that expresses disagreement with the speaker threatens those values, to be sure, but no more than they would be threatened by a chant of "Chocolate Mousse" of a chorus of *South Side Shuf-fle* on the slide trombone.

Sorting out free speech issues along these lines should have salutary consequences for freedom of expression. The debate on the first amendment has traditionally proceeded on the assumption that cate-gorization and balancing—and I am using this as a generic term to encompass all approaches (including "clear and present danger") that consider the likely effect of the communication—are mutually exclusive approaches to the various problems that arise under the first amendment. The categorizers or "absolutists," were surely right that theirs was the approach more likely to protect expression in crisis times. But just as surely, an all-encompassing categorization approach could be made to look awfully silly, indeed to confess error, by demonstrations that there were contexts in which a refusal to admit the possibility of balancing was simply untenable. The sound-truck cases furnished a familiar example: "I understand that you would protect sound-trucks. But what about a hospital zone? What about the middle of the night? Surely you wouldn't let a mayoral candidate aim a bullhorn at your window at three in the morning. Surely you have to balance, or employ a clear and present danger test, at *some* point."

The argument is convincing—in context. But what the decisions of the late Warren era began to recognize is that categorization and balancing need not be regarded as competing general theories of the first amendment, but are more helpfully employed in tandem, each with its own legitimate and indispensable role in protecting expression. The fact that one would balance where the evil the state would avert does not grow out of the message being communicated— thereby balancing away the right to use a bullhorn at three in the morning, to shout "Boo!" at a cardiac patient, or to firebomb the induction center in protest against the draft—does not, the Court began to understand, commit him to a balancing approach to the constitutionality of a Criminal Syndicalism Law.

The categorizers were right: where messages are proscribed because they are dangerous, balancing tests inevitably become intertwined with the ideological predispositions of those doing the balancing—or if not that, at least with the relative confidence or paranoia of the age in which they are doing it—and we must build barriers as secure as words are able to make them. That means rigorous definition of the limited categories of expression that are unprotected by the first amendment. But in order thus to protect what really is in need of and amenable to such protection, we must first set to one side, by determinate principle rather than hunch, those situations to which such a categorization approach will inevitably prove unsuited. The Court has made a clear start in this direction, and it is a good one.

## VI

State laws typically extend American flags two separate sorts of protection. One provision, and it is this that is generally referred to as the "desecration" provision, is likely to provide that "[n]o person shall publicly mutilate, deface, defile, defy, trample upon, or by word or act cast contempt upon any such flag. . . ." . . . [S]uch statutes proscribe only ideologically charged acts, and beyond that, only acts charged with a particular set of ideological outlooks. The state's defense, consequently, must be geared to the unusual danger of that set of sentiments; such a defense will of necessity relate to the suppression of expression within the meaning of *O'Brien's* second criterion. That in turn implies that the categorization approach *Brandenburg* and *Cohen* is appropriate. Since such laws obviously are not tailored to reach only expressions of incitement to immediate lawless action, or any other presently recognized category of unprotected expression, they must fall.

The other sort of provision typically employed, sometimes called an "improper use" provision, outlaws affixing to the flag any "word, figure mark, picture, design, drawing or advertisement of any nature," or publicly displaying any flag so embellished. The law is thus ideologically neutral on its face, and would proscribe the superimposition of "Buy Mother Fletcher's Ambulance Paint" or even "It's a Grand Old Flag" as fully as it would the addition of a swastika. Such "improper use" provisions are more complicated constitutionally than the ideologically tilted "desecration" provisions. . . .

What has not yet been sufficiently noted is that although improper use statutes do not single out certain messages for proscription, they *do* single out one set of messages, namely the set of messages conveyed by the American flag, for protection. That, of course, is not true of a law that generally prohibits the interruption of speakers: such a law is neutral not only respecting the content of the interruption but also respecting the content of the messages interrupted. The distinction suggests that the definition we have thus far given *O'Brien's* second criterion, as referring to situations where the harm the state seeks to avert is one that arises from the defendant's communication, may have been incomplete. An adjustment of our earlier elaboration of that criterion so as to encompass the case in which the government singles out a specific message or set of messages for protection would fit the cases more comfortably— and in particular, would provide firmer ground for the decision in *Spence*. That it is also required by the sense of the criterion seems clear too, given the functional similarity, in terms of "the free marketplace of ideas," between singling certain messages out for prohibition and singling certain messages out for protection. Orthodoxy of thought can be fostered not simply by placing unusual restrictions on "deviant" expression but also by granting unusual protection to expression that is officially acceptable. An "improper use" statute, neutral respecting the message it would inhibit though it may be, is not analogous to a law prohibiting the interruption of speeches. It is, at best, analogous to a law prohibiting the interruption of patriotic speeches, and that is a law that is hardly "unrelated to the suppression of free expression."

Pierre J. Schlag, *An Attack on Categorical Approaches to Freedom of Speech,* 30 UCLA LAW REVIEW 671 (1983)*

. . .

## I. THE PROBLEM OUTLINED: THE ABSENCE OF KNOWLEDGE

The failure of categorical theorists to present acceptable approaches to the first amendment is merely a symptom of more general problems that confront liberal political philosophy. The problems are rooted in the inability to establish a secure understanding of human nature and, therefore, to define satisfactorily the scope of liberty that should be preserved for the individual.

* * *

## II. CRITIQUE OF LIBERAL POLITICAL PHILOSOPHY

In the absence of secure knowledge concerning the extent to which human interests are shared, liberal political philosophers take a "middle course," allowing some collective decisionmaking while preserving broad areas of individual choice. Thus, liberal political philosophy is grounded on the premise that the state ought to leave individuals alone to establish and pursue their ends and values, a position I call the "Premise of Individualism." This position may be based on the view that the set of needs, desires, and dispositions shared by human beings is limited. Alternatively, it may be based on the view that, to the extent shared needs, desires, and dispositions cannot be determined, a broad realm of individual choice must be preserved in order to allow common interests, if any, to be revealed.

From the Premise of Individualism, liberal politi-

cal thought typically effectuates a divorce between a concept of formal negative liberty and the means to realize this liberty. If the individual is to be left free in large measure to choose her own ends, the state must guarantee an arena where the individual will be free from interference. Liberty is defined formally because it must be defined independently of the multiplicity of different values held by individuals. Similarly, liberty is defined negatively because the multiplicity of different individual values precludes the state from guaranteeing or providing for the realization of all of these values. In divorcing formal negative liberty and the means of its realization, liberal political philosophy accords liberty a superior position. These two crucial steps lead to a number of difficulties.

* * *

### B. Which Liberties to Choose?

Even if it were possible to distinguish liberty from the means of its realization and to determine the proper amount of social resources to devote to liberty, liberal political philosophers face the difficulty of determining which liberties ought to take precedence over others. The problem is that almost any interest can be framed as a liberty interest. Given that liberties collide, some principle must be found to enable a choice between competing liberties.

* * *

### C. Providing a Mediating Principle to Relate Abstract Liberties to Concrete Social Practices

Even if liberal political philosophy could adequately ascertain the relative importance of liberties, it would still be necessary to provide some mediating principle to connect the abstract liberty to its real world forms. For instance, if we believe that commercial speech ought to be protected because it leads to self-realization, then we must find an operational or descriptive category of speech which corresponds fairly well to the types of commercial speech which lead to self-realization. It is not sufficient to define a liberty that ought to be granted protection if this liberty does not correspond to readily identifiable social practices. A mediating principle thus serves to relate a normative category to an operational category. It would be too much to ask for perfect correspondence between a normative and an operational category. On the other hand, it would hardly be improper to criticize a theory on the grounds that its normative categories deviate too much from available operational categories. Can liberal political philosophy provide a mediating principle to determine whether a given activity falls within a defined liberty?

---

* Reprinted with permission.

In accordance with the Premise of Individualism, the formal character of liberty precludes recourse to the individual's motivation or to the particular value or purpose the individual attaches to his activity. One alternative for liberal political philosophy would be to determine whether a liberty interest (e.g., freedom of speech) protects a particular social practice (e.g., advertising, pamphleteering, outdoor concerts, etc.). If various social practices could be determined to fall inside or outside the liberty interest, then liberal political philosophy would be able to define a liberty such that its normative scope coincides with real world forms. This solution does not work for two reasons. First, there is no guarantee that actual social practices will correspond to the normative scope of defined liberties. For example, it is quite possible that half of all advertising contributes to a first amendment value, such as self-realization, while the other half does not. While we may be able to suggest a normative distinction between these two halves, there is no guarantee that when we turn to the real world we can meaningfully distinguish the two. Second, because liberal political philosophy leaves individuals alone to pursue their own ends and values, it is unlikely that a given social practice serves a homogeneous normative value. The value attached to a social practice differs depending on the individual's values and ends; there is no necessary transcendent value which attaches to any social practice. Moreover, given that liberal political philosophy refuses to subject the bulk of social experience to collective decisionmaking and that individuals place a manifold of different and often conflicting values on the same social practices, any connection between a particular social practice and liberty becomes, as a practical matter, exceedingly problematic.

A mediating principle is required of a theory purporting to define freedom of speech by reference to any abstract categories of protected speech precisely because there is no necessary correspondence between the normative definition of liberties and social practices. The question is not whether judges ought to be allowed discretion in making judgments; clearly, this is unavoidable. Rather, the question is whether it is legitimate and possible to constrain judicial discretion by means of abstract, categorical descriptions of protected realms of speech.

The absence of any satisfactory mediating principle in a liberal theory of liberty thus leaves normative categories of protected activity which cannot easily be related to real world forms. Without a mediating principle, it will be impossible in many cases to determine whether a given social practice engages the liberty interest so as to warrant protection.

## III. THE IMPACT OF THE DIFFICULTIES INTRINSIC TO LIBERAL POLITICAL THOUGHT ON FIRST AMENDMENT THEORY

. . . [The liberal] approach leaves three basic problems unresolved: a) Which liberties to choose and their priority ranking; b) A principle distinguishing liberty from the means of its realization; and c) A mediating principle to relate abstract liberties to concrete social practices.

A satisfactory first amendment theory must confront these three issues. As will be seen, categorical theories fail because they are too abstract and too reductionist to delineate the boundaries between the rights of individuals vis-a-vis each other and vis-a-vis the collective. In essence, categorical approaches do violence to the Premise of Individualism.

### A. Choosing and Ranking the Speech Liberties

Almost all justifications advanced for freedom of speech fall within two camps. One view justifies freedom of speech as an essential attribute of the individual. The other justifies freedom of speech on instrumental grounds as a means to some end.

### 1. Individuality

There is a sense in which freedom of speech can best be characterized as a part of constitutional safeguards that permit the existence of the individual: along with other constitutional provisions, the first amendment grants certain freedoms designed to preserve the notion of the individual as the relevant political unit. These freedoms are designed to give each individual a certain degree of autonomy, recognizing that without this constitutional commitment to non-interference with personal autonomy, the individual would cease to exist as an individual. If individuality is viewed as an end in itself, then the state must recognize a limited arena in which the human being can externalize herself in ways which are within her control.

### 2. A means to an end

While the basic freedoms protected in the Bill of Rights are to some extent founded on what it means to be an individual, they are also grounded on instrumental concerns. These freedoms are important because of the good effects they have on the collective welfare or the good effects they have for individuals. Hence, we have theories of the first amendment based on the marketplace analogy, on participation in the political process, and on promotion of the individual exercise of rational judgment. The instrumental justification focuses not so much on what is necessary for a person to exist as an individual, but rather upon what people ought to be allowed to do with their individuality. The instrumentalist justification thus rests on the view that absent protection of certain liberties, some goods will not be available in sufficient quantity.

### 3. The definitional difficulty

One of the difficulties facing freedom of speech theory lies in the circularity of the task. The scope and content of freedom of speech must ultimately rely upon a description of existing social practices and legal entitlements. Yet social practices and legal entitlements must themselves be scrutinized to determine whether they are related to, or perhaps interfere with, freedom of speech. In pursuing these two inquiries, one can ask either why certain speech should be protected or why it should not. In either case, categorical theories of the first amendment prove unsatisfactory, for they fail to account for and indeed submerge the three major problems of liberal political philosophy.

Categorical definitions of protected speech are plausible only if there is either a single normative value served by freedom of speech or if the several normative values served by the first amendment happen to coincide in terms of the categories they prescribe. That there is no agreement among the commentators on one value served by the first amendment is clear. The values advanced by the commentators are generally some variation of the following: the search for truth, self-realization, participation in peaceful change, and the functioning of the democratic process.

I assume that some variant of the values advanced by the commentators discussed herein has appeal in some concrete cases. The Premise of Individualism, however, deprives liberal political philosophy of any secure vantage point from which to decide which normative value should be recognized. Thus, rejection in the abstract of any of the values advanced is exceedingly problematic. For the same reason, any ranking of the normative values is also problematic. A categorical theory embodying a single normative value will seem appealing from a normative standpoint only if it appears to be highly abstract and potentially all encompassing—in other words, only to the degree to which it fails to compel any particular result. For that reason, such a theory will be rejected. On the other hand, a categorical theory which is appealing because it appears to compel results in concrete cases will not gain adherence because its normative boundaries will be too narrow. Finally, the possibility that a categorical theory could encompass a number of different normative values

is not a realistic one: each normative value would compass the realm of protected speech differently. The very inelegance of a calculus of categories based on a multiplicity of normative values suggests that the wrong edifice is being built.

### B. The Speech Liberty vs. The Means to Realize the Speech Liberty

A theory that seeks to draw a line between freedom of speech and the means to realize freedom of speech in a categorical manner necessarily fails for two reasons. First, speech is multi-faceted; one cannot apply a formal rule across the board because a given type or form of speech may be more or less bound up with the means of its realization. There is no constant, bright line between form and substance in first amendment analysis. Rules which govern time, place, and manner have a definite impact on what it is that can be said. Rules that are said to affect speech only incidentally also have an effect on what it is that is said. For example, zoning ordinances bear upon architecture and thus can curtail certain artistic statements. Similarly, scholarly discussion of symbolic speech is full of questions about whether individuals should be able to co-opt certain matters as symbols to communicate for their own ends.

The second problem is one of determining what impact a burden is likely to have on the speaker. Not all speakers are situated similarly in terms of access to the resources necessary to engage in speech. A relatively minor burden on one class of speakers may be tantamount to an outright prohibition when applied to others. Despite this disparate impact, a categorical theory must draw a rigid, abstract line dividing the speech liberty from the means to engage in speech. In drawing such a line, a categorical approach leaves speakers (and listeners) of lesser means unprotected from the imposition of government burdens. The very existence of this rigid line tracking a liberty/means distinction does more than impact differently on types of speech, speakers, and listeners. It also issues a clear indication to the state of permissible methods for suppressing undesirable speech or speakers and similarly announces to the most well-off speakers how they might restructure their speech to fall within the protection afforded by the categories established.

By virtue of the rigidity and high level of abstraction with which the categories are drawn, categorical theories serve to obscure and insulate these problems. Indeed, categorical theories in effect replicate the unjustified and arbitrary distinction between liberty and the means to realize liberty offered by liberal political philosophy.

## C. The Need for a Mediating Principle

The categories established by any categorical theory are, to some degree, normative: they define protected areas of speech in terms of underlying justifications (i.e., what speech ought to be protected). There is no reason to suppose that such normative categories immediately identify real world forms or that the normative significance of certain categories necessarily coincides with their operational significance. For example, while we may call certain speech items "commercial speech" for purposes of according a certain level of protection to such speech, there is no guarantee that the "commercial speech" we are talking about in our normative theory coincides with what we call "commercial speech" in the everyday world.

As categories necessarily have normative origins, some principle must be advanced to enable the classification of real world speech into the taxonomy. Two such principles are utilitarianism and majoritarianism, but, as we have seen, both are unsatisfactory. We might be tempted to base the mediating principle on a "minimalist perspective." For example, if political speech is protected, we would like to ask the individual who is claiming a right of free speech whether, in his language, the speech he claims is protected would be considered political speech. This approach, however, does not work. First, inasmuch as the individual has an interest in his speech, there is good reason to doubt his veracity when he responds, "Yes, my speech is political." Second, when the individual claims that his speech is political, he may not be speaking the same language we are, and his reasons for claiming that the speech is political may have nothing to do with the reasons we protect political speech. Thus, it is not clear that we should recognize that individual's language as a legitimate basis for decision.

\* \* \*

## D. A Positive and Negative Suggestion

As previously discussed, the Premise of Individualism leads to three major problems for liberal political philosophy. In turn, liberal political philosophy and its Premise of Individualism are the expression of a particular form of social organization, one where normative and aesthetic values are held to be matters of individual choice, and where these multiple values have not congealed to coincide neatly with social practices.

Given this view of liberal democratic society, the relationship between facts and values can be approached in several ways that will not coincide with each other: the normative value of an activity may be judged in terms of the activity's content, source, manner, and effect—together, the "parameters." Because of the fragmentation of value and practice in a liberal democratic society most of us would be unwilling to relate an abstract normative value, such as "the search for truth," "peaceful change," "self-realization," or "self government," to activities without allowing ourselves recourse to at least these four parameters. Recourse to the four parameters is even more pressing if we admit that all of these values inform the meaning of the first amendment. To be sure, the normative evaluation of a particular activity X may ultimately turn upon reference to only one parameter (for instance, content), but when forced to operate at a higher level of abstraction—for example, in deciding what types of speech ought to be protected by the first amendment—recourse to each of the four parameters appears to be warranted in at least some circumstances. Various conceptions of equality likewise require consideration of these four parameters in some circumstances. I will begin by arguing that the four parameters are relevant and necessary in terms of the positive and negative results we would want in first amendment cases.

The *content* of speech is relevant because speech about certain matters—for example, political speech—may be central to the democratic process. From the negative perspective, speech which is not about anything (e.g., the phone book), or speech in which the speech content is minimal relative to other functions (e.g., architecture) may deserve less or no protection. It is difficult to see how one could justify denying protection to speech absent an examination of its content.

The *manner* in which speech affects the world is relevant inasmuch as one of the reasons for the protection accorded to speech, as opposed to other activities, is its generally nonintrusive character. One generally does not have to listen if one does not want to. The impact of speech, in contrast to that of other activities, generally involves the voluntary entry of the spectator into the arena of activity. From the negative perspective, however, certain modes of speech may intrude upon others simply because of the manner in which it produces effects. The pure effect of some speech may be perfectly lawful and unimpeachable, while the way in which that speech produces effects may be objectionable. Blackmail and extortion, for example, seem to fall within this category.

The *source* of speech and its relation to speech are also relevant. Part of the reason for protecting speech stems from our view of how speech is produced. The relation between thought (in its broadest sense) and speech seems to compel us to view speech as the primary medium for the self-realization of the individual. From the negative perspective, to the extent that certain speech does not emanate from an individual but from some artificial institution, such as a corporation or a government, there may be less reason to accord constitutional protection.

The *effect* of speech is likewise relevant. Indeed, there are several theories that ground freedom of speech on the effects it has on individuals or the collective. Some speech, on the other hand, must be left unprotected or less protected because of its effects. For example, some speech that invades privacy fits within this description.

Finally, to the extent that various conceptions of equality play a central role in first amendment analysis, all parameters are relevant. Professor Karst demonstrates that equality requires an examination of the impact of state regulation on the content of speech. He also demonstrates that an examination of the manner in which speech affects the world is necessary if we are to observe principles of equality. The source of speech is also crucial to equality concerns to the extent that the first amendment protects speakers as well as viewpoints. Finally, the effect of speech, the fact that speech competes with speech, also bears directly on equality concerns.

It is difficult to conceive of these four parameters combined in one coherent, categorical theory. There will be cases in which one or more of the parameters are implicated to a greater extent than the others. Decisions about whether to protect certain types of speech might require different levels of concern to be accorded to any of the four parameters. Ultimately, the parameters require four separate inquiries into why speech should or should not be protected. The inquiries should proceed not on an abstract level, but rather in the context of particular cases. In contrast to categorical approaches, these parameters do not seek to compel conclusions. Rather, the parameters identify areas of inquiry that a court might examine in determining whether and how a given activity is related to the values underlying freedom of speech.

\* \* \*

## V. TOWARD A NEW APPROACH TO FREEDOM OF SPEECH: DOING WITHOUT CATEGORICAL RULES

\* \* \*

If we take the three major problems of liberal political philosophy seriously, then any approach, not just categorical approaches, might appear to be precluded in a liberal democracy. On the contrary, the success of theory depends in large part on the tasks it sets for itself. In light of this realization, there are two options for theory. First, theory can become strategic and try to undermine the status quo. Such a course would be undertaken not because the theory is true, but because adopting the theory will disguise or undermine the bases of present contradictions. Second, the claims of theory to truth can be lessened, and our expectations of theory can be restated and reformed.

The former approach, whether in the name of the reactionary right or the radical left, is a form of intellectual domination which is to be condemned—not because it is domination (that would require an examination of the objects dominated), but because (almost surely) it will not work to alter the status quo in the ways desired. The strategic suggestion that courts should adopt a particular categorical approach, and even further that the courts' adoption of this categorical approach will result in the realization of certain values, has several flaws: 1) it overestimates the power of ideas, generally; 2) it overestimates the power of courts and of the law to impose a rational order on the political and social structure to conform to the values advanced by the court; 3) it underestimates the ability of relatively privileged individuals, groups, enterprises, institutions, and governmental actors to adjust their activities to conform to the rules announced by the courts, while negating the substantive values advanced; and 4) it underestimates the possibility that the strategic character of the categorical approach will be discovered and its mystifying aim exposed.

\* \* \*

This brings us to the second possible approach to developing a first amendment theory: restating and reforming the tasks of theory. The three major problems of liberal political philosophy preclude categorical approaches as a method of analysis—both as a matter of theoretical cogency and as a means of informing decision in concrete cases. If we take the three problems seriously, and if we reject strategic defenses of categorical theories, then the only tack to take (short of nihilism) is to redefine our expectations of theory. In short, I suggest that an acceptable theory would have to recognize and treat the three major problems in a rational manner reflecting the fragmented state of the culture. This requires a theory recognizing: (1) that the definition of the scope and content of protected liberties is problematic; (2) that the relation of liberty to the means of its realization is incapable of being resolved in the abstract given the artificiality of an abstract separation of individual activities into a means and end component; and (3) that the relation of real world facts to normative values is complex and largely indeterminate.

Once these three problems are taken seriously, the goal of theory is to outline a method that provides the tools with which to respond to the three problems. No approach can guarantee good or better outcomes in terms of substantive court decisions. Nevertheless, a theory that takes into account the three major problems of liberal political philosophy will avoid the pitfalls that disregard of these problems creates. The pitfalls of ignoring these problems as manifested in categorical approaches can be capsulized as an artificial restriction of meaning (descriptively and normatively), a general mucking up of judicial language, and counterproductive results.

In the service of preferred first amendment values, categorical theories artificially restrict the realm of protected activities that serve those values and, at the same time, expand the realm of protection to activities that have a dubious relation to those values. The reason is simple: if one is to develop a categorical approach to serve certain preferred first amendment values, then categories can only be established by simplifying the manner in which facts relate to value. I submit that each of the four parameters—content, source, manner, and effect—describes a particular way in which facts can relate to value. A categorical approach cannot take all four parameters into account in formulating categories without developing a highly inelegant calculus of categories—a calculus whose very inelegance would itself counsel against the development of abstract categories.

Because categorical theories attempt to simplify the way in which facts can relate to values, categorical theories often fail to compel outcomes in concrete cases. The reason, again, is simple: in any given case, what we perceive to be the significant relation of facts to values may well depend upon a parameter (e.g. source, content, etc.) which lies outside the categorical framework advanced. Sooner or later, the categorical framework loses the meaning which it initially might have had as concerns extrinsic to the framework are smuggled into its abstract terminology.

Still, categorical approaches pretend to compel outcomes in concrete cases. This feature of categorical approaches also robs first amendment theory of meaning. The danger of categorical approaches is that to some extent they present the courts with prepackaged justifications for particular outcomes. By advancing categories which purportedly compel conclusions, the courts are relieved of the responsibility

of judgment: the only failure of a court under a categorical approach is a misclassification, a clerical error akin to a postman misplacing a letter. To be sure, the act of classifying is in a sense an exercise of judgment. But, in another sense, it is not. If categorical theories pretend to compel decisions in concrete cases, but in fact do not, then the court's exercise in classification becomes simply a cover for attaching certain consequences (protection or non-protection) to certain activities on the basis of concerns never articulated and, therefore, never judged.

Indeed, to the extent that courts feel bound by a given categorical approach, they must develop and articulate facts that will allow the categorical approach to compel a decision. The danger is that in any given case the facts may not allow the categorical approach to compel a conclusion one way or the other. When this happens, a premium is placed on the court's characterization of the facts. Thus, in some cases categorical approaches will cause courts to distort the facts so that the categorical approach may yield an outcome (i.e., protection or non-protection).

In effect, by placing such a premium on the characterization of facts in tough cases, categorical approaches destroy the meaning inherent in the common law method of adjudication and artificially restrict the judicial language. Categorical approaches short-circuit the language of common law adjudication because the facts underlying court decisions become superfluous. What is relevant is how the facts are characterized in precedent. And that, in turn, depends on the categorical approach under which the precedent was established. In short, under a categorical approach, precedent is robbed of its value, and comparison of the present case to precedent cannot be expected to yield any insights or value distinctions that are not already included in the ruling categorical approach. Not only are courts thereby deprived of the meaning and insight that common law adjudication might yield, but also their decisions risk becoming increasingly divorced from the way in which people view facts, values, and the relation between the two. This is not to say that courts should necessarily view facts, values, and their relation in accordance with a common consensus. Rather, if a court chooses to speak in a foreign language, this choice should not be simply the incidental result of an artificial restriction of judicial language.

Closely associated with the point that categorical approaches place an undue premium on the characterization of facts so as to validate the ruling categorical approach is the argument that categorical approaches prevent courts from articulating and developing facts which might be relevant to the preferred substantive values observed by courts. Because categorical approaches often serve to enshrine one substantive value to the exclusion of other equally unimpeachable (or impeachable) values, and because categorical theories grossly simplify the way in which facts can relate to values, categorical approaches deprive courts of factual information ab initio. By restricting the places where the courts might look to justify their decisions in terms of values, facts, and their relation, decisional law becomes increasingly divorced from the objects it is intended to regulate and thus from the values that it ostensibly observes. The disregard for particularity inherent in the categorical approach is thus likely to result both in decisions protecting first amendment rights where the values ostensibly supporting the first amendment are not implicated and in decisions denying first amendment rights where no legitimate community interests are implicated.

What is more, categorical approaches hypostatize the culture. They do not take seriously the fact that culture is evolving, that substantive first amendment values become more or less important depending upon the content of the culture, that the ways in which these values are implicated in social practice or individual activities are subject to change. In short, categorical approaches hold out the false promises that the judiciary has arrived at a state of knowledge, that the culture can be rationally ordered, and that all that remains is for the courts to classify the parts of the culture into the taxonomy. The problem with this approach, apart from its falsehood, is that it is self-validating and, to a large extent, serves to insulate the courts from the real, if not the true, facts.

The final vice of categorical approaches is that they underestimate their own power on the culture. Categorical theories are offered to translate some preferred first amendment values into reality. All categorical theories, however, fail to assess the effect their adoption would have on the process of translation. Given that courts have some influence on the culture, as soon as a categorical approach is adopted, we would expect to see powerful individuals, enterprises, institutions, and governmental actors restructure their conduct in response to the categorical framework in order that the same ends pursued before might be realized still. A categorical theory is thus always out of date. The only way to relate values to reality is to take into account the changes brought about in this relation by the very fact that the courts

decide cases. The high degree of abstraction and the rigidity of categorical approaches in effect prevent categorical theories from taking into account this "feedback" effect of court decisions on values, facts, and their relation. This "feedback" problem affects all theory; the measure of theory is not whether it avoids the "feedback" problem, but whether it provides a mechanism to deal with the feedback problems. The very ambition of categorical approaches to compel outcomes by means of an abstract and rigid first amendment analysis precludes a serious consideration of the "feedback" problem within their frameworks. Therefore it would be no surprise if categorical approaches systematically failed to advance the values they hold dear.

In sum, if we are to take the three problems of liberal political philosophy seriously, we must reject categorical approaches. The measure of a satisfactory theory must be restated and reformed in terms of these three problems. One thing we can ask of courts is to make clear their stance in relation to these problems.

\* \* \*

The appeal of the four parameters approach lies in the fact that each describes a way in which facts can relate to value. The parameters point to varying types of inquiries that courts might make in attempting to show and justify a relation between facts and value. It may be that in one area of first amendment jurisprudence only one of the parameters seems to pose the crucial relation. In other areas of first amendment jurisprudence, all four parameters may provide the basis for arguments that the activity ought or ought not to be protected. The four parameters simply point to routes of inquiry. That any of these routes in a given area of first amendment jurisprudence will lead nowhere seems likely—but at least that will be knowledge gained. The four parameters approach is to be defended not on the grounds that it will produce better decisions (it may not), but rather on the grounds that it will permit decisions that are based upon a realistic appraisal of the fragmented state of the culture. The approach will permit decisions based on facts as opposed to the twisting of phenomena to fit preordained categories. The approach will require a court to articulate its value preferences. In short, the four parameters approach will permit, though not compel, a more rational division of the powers of the community and the rights of the individual.

\* \* \*

# Bibliography

*Categorizing Speech*

Aleinikoff, T. Alexander, *Constitutional Law in the Age of Balancing*, 96 Yale Law Journal 943 (1987)

Fallon, Richard H., Jr., *A Constructivist Coherence Theory of Constitutional Interpretation*, 100 Howard Law Review 1189 (1987)

Farber, Daniel A., *Content Regulation and the First Amendment: A Revisionist View*, 68 Georgetown University Law Journal 727 (1980)

Nagel, Robert F., *The Formulaic Constitution*, 84 Michigan Law Review 165 (1985)

Schauer, Frederick, *The Second-Best First Amendment*, 31 William & Mary Law Review 1 (1989)

Shiffrin, Steven, *The First Amendment and Economic Regulation: Away from a General Theory of the First Amendment*, 78 Northwestern University Law Review 1212 (1983)

Shiffrin, Steven, *Liberalism, Radicalism, and Legal Scholarship*, 30 UCLA Law Review 1103 (1983)

Stone, Geoffrey R., *Content Regulation and the First Amendment*, 25 William & Mary Law Review 189 (1983)

Tribe, Laurence H., *Constitutional Calculus: Equal Justice or Economic Efficiency?*, 98 Harvard Law Review 592 (1985)

Van Alstyne, William, *A Graphic Review of the Free Speech Clause*, 70 California Law Review 107 (1982)

Williams, Susan H., *Content Discrimination and the First Amendment*, 139 University of Pennsylvania Law Review 615 (1991).

## B. Political Expression

These articles analyze the special rank of political expression and the tension between that status and the "clear and present danger" doctrine. Frank R. Strong analyzes the demise of the "clear and present danger" test. Gerald Gunther examines how Judge Hand's correspondence with Justice Holmes helped change the latter's approach to freedom of expression problems, especially the "clear and present danger" test. Ernest Freund argues that it is inappropriate to prosecute individuals merely for stating their opinions. He uses the *Debs* case to illustrate his point. Harry Kalven, Jr. assesses Justice Black's impact on the theoretical underpinnings of First Amendment doctrine.

Frank R. Strong, *Fifty Years of "Clear and Present Danger": From Schenck to Brandenburg—and Beyond*, 1969 SUPREME COURT REVIEW 41 (1969)*

The fiftieth anniversary of the "clear and present danger" test is not a happy one for it. Commentators no less than Justices have been undertaking to inter the test for some little time. Hailed at the outset as the interpretational device for effective realization of First Amendment liberties, the danger test has lost favor to the point where the Court only irregularly admits to its employment, and there are few who would grieve at its total demise.

*Brandenburg v. Ohio*, decided at the end of the last Term of the Warren era, is significant on the doctrine's current status among sitting Justices. The decision was announced in a per curiam opinion of a length and importance that in normal practice would be written for the Court and attributed to an individual Justice. In this opinion there is assiduous avoidance of any reference to, let alone admitted employment of, the "clear and present danger" test.
. . .

. . .

The weakness of the danger test is shown by attempted reliance upon it as a complete constitutional solvent. No such role was originally conceived for it. In its beginning it scarcely purported to rise to a constitutional level at all. For a unanimous Court in *Schenck v. United States*, Mr. Justice Holmes employed it essentially as a rule of evidence. Under a statute prohibiting interference with war effort, speech could be punished only on evidence of clear and present danger that that speech would lead to the evil which Congress had sought to forbid by the Espionage Act.

This technical usage of the test was turned against Holmes by the majority in *Gitlow v. New York*, involving the New York statutory prohibition of advocacy of criminal anarchy:

It is clear that the question in such cases [as this] is entirely different from that involved in those cases where the statute merely prohibits certain acts involving the danger of substantive evil, without any reference to language itself, and it is sought to apply its provisions to language used

by the defendant for the purpose of bringing about the prohibited results. . . . In such cases it has been held that the general provisions of the statute may be constitutionally applied to the specific utterance of the defendant if its natural tendency and probable effect was to bring about the substantive evil which the legislative body might prevent. . . . [T]he general statement in the *Schenck Case* . . . was manifestly intended, as shown by the context, to apply only in cases of this class, and has no application to those like the present, where the legislative body itself has previously determined that the danger of substantive evil arising from utterances of a specified character.

It is familiar knowledge that the distinction was washed out by *Dennis*: the opinion for the Court elected the "Holmes-Brandeis rationale" despite *Gitlow*. Yet the distinction continued long enough into the period during which the danger test was used in an attempt to resolve issues of validity to produce the conflict, manifest in *Dennis* and later, between those insisting on jury determination of clear and present danger and those declaring that the making of that judgment was a question of law for the court. That the origin of the danger test was basically a rule of evidence must account for this conflict. For, as one acute commentator has observed: "Juries are not supposed to declare statutes unconstitutional. Such a practice (and it might have come about in the Dennis case if Douglas had had his way) would be consistent neither with practical wisdom nor with American judicial tradition." It can be added that juries are not supposed to rule statutes (or other forms of governmental action) constitutional. This is the essential teaching of the Court's continued insistence upon the doctrine of constitutional fact.

. . .

Elevated to constitutional level, the danger test, retaining much of its original evidentiary flavor, became a device whereby, for legislation to pass constitutional muster, it must be demonstrated that a permissible objective of government is imminently and substantially threatened. Permissible objectives were identified without analysis as "certain substantive evils" with respect to which government possessed some authority. Yet by the new test government was empowered to take action only on proof of the immediacy of serious peril to one or more of those substantive evils. . . .

. . .

In the initial case involving Harry Bridges and

the *Los Angeles Times*, Mr. Justice Black, after an interesting employment of the technical distinction taken in *Gitlow* to buttress support for the use of the danger test, asserted: "What finally emerges from the 'clear and present danger' cases is a working principle that the substantive evil must be extremely serious and the degree of imminence extremely high before utterances can be punished." By this test every one of the four challenges to state contempt citations has been sustained.

. . .

*Terminello v. Chicago*, decided at the close of the 1940's, marked the apogee in the employment of the danger test under the *Abrams-Whitney* formulation. There all the Justices who addressed themselves to the merits agreed on the applicability of the test to the validity of conviction of a Chicago priest for a virulent address, before eight hundred persons, protested by an "angry and turbulent" crowd of "about one thousand persons" gathered immediately outside the auditorium. Reversing the conviction, Mr. Justice Douglas for the Court, explained that "a function of free speech under our system of government is to invite dispute." . . .

With this Mr Justice Jackson took issue in a dissent (joined by Justice Burton and the views of which Justice Frankfurter declared he shared):

> Rioting is a substantive evil, which I take it no one will deny that the State and the City have the right and the duty to prevent and punish. Where an offense is induced by speech, the Court has laid down and often reiterated a test of the power of the authorities to deal with the speaking as also an offense. "The question in every case is whether the words *used are used in such circumstances* and are of *such a nature* as to create a *clear and present danger* that they will bring about the substantive evils that Congress [or the state or city] has a right to prevent." [Emphasis supplied.] Mr. Justice Holmes in *Schenck v United States*, 249 U.S. 47, 52. No one ventures to contend that the State on the basis of this test, for whatever it may be worth, was not justified in punishing Terminello. In this case the evidence proves beyond dispute that danger of rioting and violence in response to the speech was clear, present and immediate. If this Court has not silently abandoned this longstanding test and substituted for the purposes of this case an unexpressed but more stringent test, the action of the State would have to be sustained.

. . .

In the hour of its greatest test, against the tough opponent of national security at mid-twentieth century, the rule of clear and present danger lost its bid for general acceptance as a requirement that for state or federal restriction of speech to be vaild it must be shown that a legitimate objective of government is imminently and substantially imperiled. Mr. Justice Black saw this clearly. . . . Even on the "radical assumption . . . that petitioners although not indicted for the crime of actual advocacy, may be punished for it . . . the other opinions in this case show that the only way to affirm these convictions is to repudiate directly or indirectly the established 'clear and present danger' rule." In a separate dissent Mr. Justice Douglas made a case for the proposition that communism in this country is only a bogeyman. But the demonstration was unresponsive to the majority's position that the danger test in the formulation brought to the argument by petitioners was inapplicable.

In retrospect, *Dennis* has the dubious distinction of bringing to a head the paradox that the Holmes-Brandeis formulation of the danger test as a constitutional solvent would satisfy but few. To be sure, it is employed occasionally, as is attested by its reappearance in the last of the contempt cases. It will even turn up in surprising contexts, as where Mr. Justice Harlan, concurring in *Garner v. Louisiana*, invoked it after explicit reference back to Holmes in *Abrams* and Brandeis in *Whitney*. But to many it became, after *Dennis*, largely or wholly unsatisfactory because either too virile or overly weak. Extrajudicially, Mr. Justice Brennan not long ago limited it to the contempt cases and those involving subversive action. Professor Freund had earlier thought even this went too far. Although finding the formulation "a useful criterion of illicit speech where the social harm apprehended from the speech would flow from the effect of the ideas conveyed," he regarded it as "not appropriate where the harm is such that a corrective could not be sought through countervailing speech: contempt of court, pornography, and political activities by civil servants are examples."

. . .

In the second *Konigsberg* classic confrontation between absolutist and balancing theories of First Amendment interpretation, Mr. Justice Harlan for the majority sought to ground the latter partly on the proposition "[t]hat the First Amendment immunity for speech, press and assembly has to be reconciled with valid but conflicting governmental interests . . ." [I]t was "the sudden transformation of the 'clear and present danger test' in *Dennis v. United States*" that equated it with the balancing test; "diluted and weakened by being recast in terms of this 'balancing' formula, there seems to me to be much room to doubt that Justice Holmes and Brandeis would even have recognized their test."

The Frankfurter concurrence in *Dennis* is clearly cast in terms of essential equivalency between "clear and present danger" and "careful weighing of conflicting interests." . . .

. . .

A full decade before the fateful decision in *Dennis* one of the ablest of commentators had sensed in the danger test a quality that would not make difficult its assimilation into the concept of balancing. Professor Wechsler observed:

> Speech or assembly may be repressed or limited when it gives rise or is intended to give rise or may reasonably be thought by the legislature to give rise to a genuine danger of some substantive evil which the state has a right to prevent, unless the evil is not great enough to warrant the suppression of speech or assembly as a means to its prevention, or to say the same thing in a different way, unless the speech or assembly is justified by some end which outweighs the evil which it admittedly threatens. But if this is the clear and present danger test for which liberals have fought and bled, it needs no argument to show that the formula which it provides is only a formula; that it does little more than to state the general principle of justice which would be accepted in evaluating any legislation which interferes with individual freedom. The use to which freedom is put must threaten social interests; the danger inherent in the threat must not be outweighed by an affirmative good which the behavior entails. In short, what the clear and present danger test can do, and all it can do, is to require an extended judicial review in the fullest legislative sense of the competing values which the particular situation presents. And the scope of that judicial review may be limited by what is in effect a presumption of validity, or a deference to legislative judgment, at least where the legislation condemns specific doctrine or specifically described types of meetings.

Despite, therefore, employment of the Holmes-Brandeis brand of danger test from *Herndon v. Lowry* through the 1940's to the very year of *Dennis*, there was latent an element about it that would not make difficult its assimilation into the concept of balancing, as balancing came to be practiced and understood by Frankfurter in *Dennis* and by Harlan

in *Konigsberg II*. Most commentators now assume a balancing role for the danger test. " 'Clear and present danger' is, to be sure, essentially a balancing formula," one has recently observed. Professor Karst has insisted:

> The clear-and-present danger test, even with its original emphasis on the immediacy of the threatened harm, was always a "balancing" test. The Justices who used the language of clear-and-present-danger did not shrink from making the legislative judgments which are inescapable in our systems of judicial review.

Professor Kalven is the exception in continuing to distinguish "balancing [from] any form of clear and present danger."

Metamorphosed into a balancing formula, "clear and present danger" fares no better as a test for satisfactory delineation of constitutional boundaries. Clearly unsatisfactory to the absolutists, it has, as well, deficiencies for those to whom balancing is necessary. Commentators are, for one, critical of it as an adequate vehicle for balancing. Paul Freund has often been quoted on this point:

> Even where it is appropriate, the clear-and-present-danger test is an oversimplified judgment unless it takes account also of a number of other factors: the relative seriousness of the danger in comparison with the value of the occasion for speech or political activity; the availability of more moderate controls than those the state has imposed, and perhaps the specific intent with which the speech or activity is launched. No matter how rapidly we utter the phrase "clear and present danger," or how closely we hyphenate the words, they are not a substitute for the weighing of values. They tend to convey a delusion of certitude when what is most certain is the complexity of the strands in the web of freedom which the judge must disentangle.

Citing this passage, another commentator more recently observed that "to sophisticated balancers" clear and present danger as a balancing formula

> suggests a simplification of the problem, an incomplete enumeration of the factors involved in balancing. This distortion is at a minimum in face-to-face situations. Yet, even there, external factors are not typically considered, and little play is given to a relative evaluation of the significance of the speech or the seriousness of the evil. In short, less freedom is given the judge than the balancers prefer.

The hazards of inadequate consideration of factors pertinent to the balancing operation are well illustrated by Mr. Justice Black's dissent in *Barenblatt*, in which he was joined by Chief Justice Warren and Mr. Justice Douglas:

> But even assuming what I cannot assume, that some balancing is proper in this case, I feel that the Court after stating the test ignores it completely. At most it balances the right of the Government to preserve itself, against Barenblatt's right to refrain from revealing Communist affiliations. Such a balance, however, mistakes the factors to be weighed. In the first place, it completely leaves out the real interest in Barenblatt's silence, the interest of the people as a whole in being able to join organizations, advocate causes and make political "mistakes" without later being subjected to governmental penalties for having dared to think for themselves. . . .
>
> Moreover, I cannot agree with the Court's notion that First Amendment freedoms must be abridged in order to "preserve" our country. That notion rests on the unarticulated premise that this Nation's security hangs upon its power to punish people because of what they think, speak or write about, or because of those with whom they associate for political purposes. The Government, in its brief, virtually admits this position when it speaks of the "communication of unlawful ideas." I challenge this premise, and deny that ideas can be proscribed under our Constitution.

A further deficiency lies in the limitations of the type of balancing with which the diluted danger test has fused, even when that form takes into account all relevant factors of private right and public interest. This type, now known as ad hoc balancing, although ably defended, has in the present decade come under growing criticism. That criticism finds in ad hoc balancing a congenital infirmity. Because of the decisional character of the juristic process by which the weighing is done, no facet of speech, press, or assembly is protected if the intensity of the governmental interest is deemed "on balance" to override the private values in opposition. Mr. Frantz is mordaciously critical:

> If the arguments employed to justify balancing are carried to their logical conclusion, then the Constitution does not contain—and is not even capable of containing—anything whatever which is unconditionally obligatory. Defendants in criminal cases can be tried in secret, or held incommunicado without trial, can be denied knowledge of the accusation against them, and the right to counsel, and the right to call witnesses in their own defense, and the right to trial by jury. Ex post facto laws and bills of attainder can be passed. Habeas corpus can be suspended, though there is neither rebellion nor invasion. Private property can be taken for public use without just, or any, compensation. Suffrage qualifications based on sex or race can be reinstituted. Anything which the Constitution says *cannot* be done *can* be done, if Congress thinks and the Court agrees (or is unwilling to set aside the congressional judgment) that the interests thereby served outweighed those which were sacrificed. Thus the whole idea of a government of limited powers, and of a written constitution as a device for attaining that end, is at least potentially at stake.

Unable on the other hand to accept in naked form Mr. Justice Black's absolutist approach to interpretation of the First Amendment, these critics opt for what they describe as definitional balancing, some of them urging that this is actually what Mr. Justice Black is getting at in his rejection of ad hoc balancing. In definitional balancing, weighing takes place, yet the juristic process is said to be significantly different:

> To be sure, a judge who is obliged to formulate a new rule of law must consider what its advantages and disadvantages would be and weigh them against the advantages and disadvantages of the possible alternative rules which might be adopted. For example, if the judge is asked to decide whether the first amendment protects the refusal to state one's political affiliations, he must take into consideration the possible dangers to political freedom and other values of denying such protection. And he must also consider whether protecting that refusal would strip the government of power which may be needed for legitimate, nonrepressive purposes. Mr. Justice Black provided an example of this type of "balancing" when, in order to decide whether the first amendment protects a right to anonymous publication, he took into consideration the possible social values of anonymous publication as indicated by the role such publications have played in the past, and the danger of repressing controversial views if identification of the proponents were required. But, though the mental process by which a judge determines what rule

to adopt can be described as "balancing," this does not make it the same as balancing, independently of any rule, to determine what is the best disposition to make of a particular case. Deciding the scope to be accorded a particular constitutional freedom is different from deciding whether the interest of a particular litigant in freely expressing views which the judge may consider loathsome, dangerous, or ridiculous is outweighed by society's interest in "order," "security," or national "self-preservation."

In a concluding footnote Frantz leaves to others the major task of determining "how constitutionally protected speech should be defined," offering only the suggestion that the "starting point" be the Meiklejohn thesis that "freedom of speech is essential to self-government." Professor Emerson laid the groundwork for this task through his excellent formulation of the function of freedom of expression in a democratic society. Professor Nimmer's recent article, following Emerson in embracing definitional balancing as a viable theory of the First Amendment, finds it properly applied by the Court in *Times* but not in *Time*. In the present context it is not necessary to stop to judge the validity of the Nimmer conclusions on either decision, in contrast with those of the Court majority or indeed of the Justices in dissent. The significant feature is the intellectual process employed by both Court and commentator in defining the contours of the First Amendment.

The difference in approach to constitutional interpretation is marked. Professor Kalven, who it will be recalled has not followed others in viewing balancing as equivalent to any form of the danger test, immediately observed of the *Times* opinion: "There is not a word of clear and present danger or of balancing." Expanding on the significance of these omissions, he subsequently said of the danger test:

Whether the rewriting of [the clear and present danger test] by Judge Hand in the *Dennis* case or the persistent attack on it as a constitutional formula by Mr. Justice Frankfurter or the perplexities of the newer speech issues or the sheer inadequacy of the formula itself caused its decline may be unclear. But it is clear that, as of the judgment in the *Times* case, it has disappeared. It did not occur to the Court to test the Alabama law before it in terms of clear and present danger, although barely a decade before, in *Beauharnais*, appeal to the test was the principal argument of the defendant. (It was one of the astute and successful gambles of the Wechsler brief that it did not argue the

case in terms of clear and present danger.) The measure of the conceptual revolution promulgated by the *Times* case is that the Alabama law is found unconstitutional, not because there is no clear and present danger of a substantive evil in defendants' speech, but because the law looks too much like punishment for seditious libel.

There was one mention of the clear-and-present danger test in the majority opinion. It occurred in a reference to *Pennekamp v. Florida* when the Court analogized the problem of defamation with that of contempt of court by publication. It would seem that the contempt problem is at least a sibling if not a twin to the one presented in the *Times* case. The former involves defamation of a specific public official, a judge. It might have been expected, therefore, that the same solution would fit both problems. But the modern Supreme Court decisions on the contempt problem—*Bridges*, *Craig* and *Pennekamp*—all rely for their disposition on the clear-and-present danger test. And as recently as 1962, in *Wood v. Georgia*, the Court adhered to this approach in disposing of a contempt case. The contempt cases make the Court's silence in the *Times* case on the viability of the clear-and-present danger test all the more deafening.

Immediately prior to the *Times* decision, the fashionable First Amendment test was what Professor Emerson called "ad hoc balancing." This formula, which he dates from the *Douds* case in 1950, has been the subject of several celebrated debates within the Court, especially between Justices Black and Harlan. The controversy has centered on large issues about absolutes and the proper role of judicial review. Professor Emerson, a critic of the balancing formula, has defined it "The formula is that the court must, in each case, balance the individual and social interest in freedom of expression against the social interest sought by the regulation which restricts expression."

It is scarcely a novel suggestion that the law of defamation with its strict liability on the one hand and its complex of offsetting privileges on the other is a prime example of balancing the interest in freedom against the social interest sought by inhibiting communication. It is this balancing that in fact generates the bulk of the law in this area and the special fascination that it has derives from the precision and detail with which the common law has struck the balance in different situations. The issue before the Court in the *Times* case, therefore, would have been peculiarly meet for the application of the balancing formula. Again the failure to speak to the issue, either in the Court's opinion or Mr. Justice Black's concurrence, suggests the necessity for its re-evaluation.

The Court's contemporaneous opinion in *Garrison v. Louisiana*, extending the *Times* principle to criminal libel of public officials, bears out the Kalven analysis. The judicial balancing is of the definitional, not the ad hoc, type:

> Truth may not be the subject of either civil or criminal sanctions where discussion of public affairs is concerned. . . . [O]nly those false statements made with the high degree of awareness of their probable falsity demanded by *New York Times* may be the subject of either civil or criminal sanctions. For speech concerning public affairs is more than self-expression; it is the essence of self-government.

On the other hand:

> [T]he use of the known lie as a tool is at once at odds with the premises of democratic government and with the orderly manner in which economic, social, or political change is to be effected. Calculated falsehood falls into that class of utterances which "are no essential part of any exposition of ideas, and are of such slight social value as a step to truth that any benefit that may be derived from them is clearly outweighed by the social interest in order and morality. . . ." *Chaplinsky v. New Hampshire*, 315 U.S. 568, 572. Hence the knowingly false statement and the false statement made with reckless disregard of the truth, do not enjoy constitutional protection.

Advocates of definitional, as opposed to ad hoc, balancing can find Court support for their views not alone in the line of libel cases but, as well, in the longer line of obscenity decisions. The unsatisfactoriness in results achieved from *Roth-Alberts* to *Stanley v. Georgia* does not mitigate from the fact that the Court has been at work attempting to define the reach of First Amendment liberties in the morals area. And there is Chief Justice Warren's footnote disclaimer of ad hoc balancing at the close of his opinion for the Court in *United States v. Robel*. . . .

Such trends in Court commitment and commentator critique would appear to spell the end of the line for "clear and present danger" after a half-century of vicissitudes. This, whether or not the weakened danger test was fully fused by *Dennis* into ad hoc balancing. It is therefore not surprising to find a funereal atmosphere permeating the fiftieth anniversary of "clear and present danger." But the current tearless farewells take no account of still another

facet in the life of "clear and present danger," a facet with a great potential future if definitional balancing is to be the standard approach to resolution of First Amendment boundaries. For, while definitional balancing draws the constitutional line generically, by determining the meaning of constitutional guarantees for different classes of situation (*e.g.*, price regulation, control of obscenity), another step is essential to disposition of any individual case. That step involves a judgment on whether legislation or other governmental action under challenge bears a sufficient nexus to objectives of government determined, through the definitional process, to be consistent with the reach of constitutional restriction. Clearly, the tightness of the nexus that is required will have a direct bearing on the outcome in a given context of validity or invalidity. Thus requirement of but a rational nexus would result in little invalidity. By a metamorphosis no more strained than those earlier experienced, "clear and present danger" could transform into a requirement in First Amendment litigation of a strong demonstration of constitutionality that would force governmental respect for the protected civil interests of the individual.

Although expressed in the conjectural, as a role that "clear and present danger" could play in the future, there is considerable basis in the decided cases for such a development. Origins can be traced back to the 1938 decision in the first *Carolene Products* case. Congressional prohibition of the movement of filled milk in interstate commerce was sustained against Due Process challenge because "regulatory legislation affecting ordinary commercial transactions is not to be pronounced unconstitutional unless in the light of the facts made known or generally assumed it is of such a character as to preclude the assumption that it rests upon some rational basis within the knowledge and experience of the legislators." But to this statement was appended what has become the famous "footnote four," the first two paragraphs of which, with omission of citations, read:

> There may be narrower scope for operation of the presumption of constitutionality when legislation appears on its face to be within a specific prohibition of the Constitution, such as those of the first ten amendments, which are deemed equally specific when held to be embraced within the Fourteenth. . . .

> It is unnecessary to consider now whether legislation which restricts those political processes which can ordinarily be expected to bring about repeal of undesirable legislation, is to be subjected to more exacting judicial

scrutiny under the general prohibitions of the Fourteenth Amendment than are most other types of legislation. . . .

. . .

In *Barnette*'s repudiation of *Gobitis*, which followed six weeks after *Murdock*, Mr. Justice Jackson did not employ the new phrase. But its essence pervaded his opinion and the tie with "clear and present danger" was present, when he put the matter this way:

> Much of the vagueness of the due process clause disappears when the specific prohibitions of the First become its standard. The right of a State to regulate, for example, a public utility may well include, so far as the due process test is concerned, power to impose all of the restrictions which a legislature may have a "rational basis" for adopting. But freedoms of speech and press, of assembly, and of worship may not be infringed on such slender grounds. They are susceptible of restriction only to prevent grave and immediate danger to interests which the State may lawfully protect.

Three years later, at the hands of Justice Rutledge, although for a sharply divided Court, this distinction in judicial rule was explained explicitly in terms of the "preferred freedom" theory:

> The case confronts us again with the duty our system places on this Court to say where the individual's freedom ends and the State's power begins. Choice on that border, now as always delicate, is perhaps more so where the usual presumption supporting legislation is balanced by the preferred place given in our scheme to the great, the indispensable democratic freedoms secured by the First Amendment. Cf. *Schneider v. State*, 308 U.S. 147; *Cantwell v. Connecticut*, 310 U.S. 296, *Prince v. Massachusetts*, 321 U.S. 158. That priority gives these liberties a sanctity and a sanction not permitting dubious intrusions. And it is the character of the right, not of the limitation, which determines what standard governs the choice. Compare *United States v. Carolene Products Co.*, 304 U.S. 144, 152–153.

The evolutionary relation between "clear and present danger" and the "preferred freedom" theory is thus quite clear. As Dean McKay has observed:

> [I]t appears essential to recognize at least that the original formulation of the clear and present danger test by Justice Holmes in *Schenck v. United States* was a recognition that

when first amendment values are involved, the otherwise permissible prohibitions which government might impose are to be examined in a different context and measured by a more critical standard. This, then, is the essence of the preferred position—the exercise of judgment to protect first amendment freedoms in a variety of ways.

On the other hand, it was not clear for a time that the theory of the preferred place of the First Amendment articulated a concept different from the Holmes-Brandeis formulation of the danger test as a full and distinct solvent for constitutional issues involving speech and related guarantees. This is evident from the passage in the Rutledge opinion in *Collins* which immediately follows the paragraph already quoted:

> For these reasons any attempt to restrict those liberties must be justified by clear public interest, threatened not doubtfully or remotely, but by clear and present danger. The rational connection between the remedy provided and the evil to be curbed, which in other contexts might support legislation against attack on due process grounds, will not suffice. These rights rest on firmer foundation. Accordingly, whatever occasion would restrain orderly discussion and persuasion, at appropriate time and place, must have clear support in public danger, actual or impending. Only the gravest abuses, endangering paramount interests, give occasion for permissible limitation.

Of those five sentences, the first, fourth, and fifth sound in terms of the Holmes-Brandeis test. Independently, they might be taken to imply the repudiation for First Amendment matters of the "any tendency" test of the *Gitlow* majority. Yet, linked by the second and third sentences a different meaning could be intended. These sentences place the concept of "clear and present danger" in an entirely new context. That context is an associational one, as is true under the Holmes-Brandeis view. But it is now a matter of essentially qualitative, rather than quantitative, connection.

For a Court again divided, Mr. Justice Black had three weeks earlier, in *Korematsu v. United States*, made a direct linkage between the concepts of "clear and present danger" and nexus:

> In the light of the principles we announced in the *Hirabayashi* case, we are unable to conclude that it was beyond the war power of Congress and the Executive to exclude those of Japanese ancestry from the West Coast war area at the time they did. True, exclusion from

the area in which one's home is located is a far greater deprivation than constant confinement to the home from 8 P.M. to 6 A.M. Nothing short of apprehension by the proper military authorities of the gravest imminent danger to the public safety can constitutionally justify either. But exclusion from a threatened area, no less than curfew, has a definite and close relationship to the prevention of espionage and sabotage. The military authorities, charged with the primary responsibility of defending our shores, concluded that curfew provided inadequate protection and ordered exclusion. They did so, as pointed out in our *Hirabayashi* opinion, in accordance with Congressional authority to the military to say who should, and who should not, remain in the threatened areas.

The new function of the test is here clearer than in *Collins*. To withstand constitutional attack, the challenged governmental action must be shown to be closely and intimately connected with a permitted objective of government.

The requirement of an immediate or tight nexus for constitutionality dooms legislative restrictions and prohibitions cast in embracive terms. In this characteristic it contrasts with the rational nexus test, which because of its looseness ensures constitutionality on the meager showing of an iota of possible connection between the governmental action under attack and some permissible objective of government. Adoption of the test of "clear and present danger" nexus for First Amendment issues therefore requires that policy formulations, whether by court, city council, state assembly, or Congress, must be tightly drafted to guarantee that their thrust is confined to objectives that government is free to attain.

. . .

. . .

Gerald Gunther, *Learned Hand and the Origins of Modern First Amendment Doctrine: Some Fragments of History*, 27 STANFORD LAW REVIEW 719 (1975)*

. . .

The letters printed here span a period of less than

3 years, from the summer of 1918 to the spring of 1921. According to the traditional view of the intellectual history of the first amendment, that brief span is ample to encompass all high points of the formative years: in 1918, the crest of prosecutions under the World War I Espionage Act; in the spring of 1919, the Supreme Court's raising of the banner of the "libertarian" clear and present danger test in *Schenck v. United States*; in the fall of 1919, the elaboration of that standard in Holmes' *Abrams* dissent; at the end of 1920, the publication of the book that was to guide speech-protective thinking for a generation, Zechariah Chafee, Jr.'s *Freedom of Speech*. But these letters cannot be viewed adequately in their historical and legal contexts without reaching back a year earlier, to the summer of 1917, when Learned Hand decided *Masses Publishing Co. v. Patten*. For it was in *Masses* that Hand first articulated the alternative approach to freedom of expression problems that he urged upon Holmes before *Schenck* and that he adhered to throughout these letters, even after Holmes' *Abrams* dissent.

To what extent may Congress suppress criticism of government? For more than a century after the demise of the Sedition Act of 1798, there was little occasion for federal courts to confront that question. But soon after America's entry into World War I, Congress revived the issue by enacting the Espionage Act of 1917. The Act did not purport to prohibit seditious libel in so many words, but its administrators soon sought to achieve that effect. The most important provisions were directed at those who "willfully cause or attempt to cause insubordination, disloyalty, mutiny, or refusal of duty, in the military or naval forces of the United States" and those who "willfully obstruct the recruiting or enlistment service of the United States." And another section declared publications violating those provisions "nonmailable." As Postmaster General Albert Sidney Burleson—and soon, prosecutors—read the statute, criticism of government policies could constitute the prohibited interference with military activities if disruption was the natural and reasonable effect of the dissident speech.

One of the first publications to feel the bite of the new law was Max Eastman's *The Masses*, "a monthly revolutionary journal" with a circulation of over 20,000. Thomas G. Patten, the New York Postmaster, acting under orders of the Postmaster General, notified *The Masses* early in July that its forthcoming issue would be excluded from the mails under the Espionage Act. *The Masses* promptly sought a preliminary injunction against Patten. As a result of that motion, Learned Hand became one of the first judges required to interpret the Act. His decision of July 24, 1917—less than 6 weeks after enactment of the law—granted the injunction.

It was a remarkable decision—remarkable even decades later; especially remarkable given the practical and doctrinal climate of the times, so strikingly inhospitable to dissent. Radicals preaching pacifism, conscientious objection, or worse, were anathema in wartime America. And constitutional interpretation offered no shelter. There was doubt that the first amendment applied to postpublication sanctions: the Supreme Court's sparse announcements had embraced the Blackstonian view that freedom of expression was protected solely against prior restraint. And beyond that niggardly view of the first amendment, many Court statements appeared to give the government virtually total discretion in controlling the mails. Moreover, the Government's arguments for suppressing speech under a statute prohibiting acts such as interference with recruiting reflected the customary legal thinking of the day: punishability of speech turned on its probable effect or tendency, on assessments of causation and consequences; talk of the "natural and reasonable effect of the publication" was a characteristic way of framing the question. Most of those who viewed such a standard as too speech-restrictive did not quarrel with the emphasis on guessing about the consequences of speech. Their rejoinder to arguments about bad tendencies and probable effects was to urge a narrower, closer cause-effect relationship represented by formulations such as "direct and immediate"—or "clear and present danger."

B. Hand's contribution in Masses.

Hand's analysis stepped outside of that framework. He conceded that speech could indeed cause effects harmful to the war effort; but he did not think that tightening the required chain of causation was an apt or effective method of protecting speech. To second-guess enforcement officials about probable consequences of subversive speech was to him a questionable judicial function: judges had no special competence to foresee the future. Moreover, even if predictions about the consequences of words were thought to be appropriate court business, the task would ordinarily fall not to the judge but to the jury, a body reflecting majoritarian sentiments unlikely to be conducive to the protection of dissent in wartime.

Hand's solution to the problem of an appropriate and effective judicial role was to focus on the speaker's words, not on their probable consequences. Instead of asking in the circumstances of each case whether the words had a tendency or even a probabil-

ity of producing unlawful conduct, he sought a more "absolute and objective test" focusing on "language"—"a qualitative formula, hard, conventional, difficult to evade," as he said in his letters. What he urged was essentially an incitement test, "a test based upon the nature of the utterance itself": if the words constituted solely a counsel to law violation, they could be forbidden; all other utterances were permissible. As he put it in *Masses*:

> [T]o assimilate agitation, legitimate as such, with direct incitement to violent resistance, is to disregard the tolerance of all methods of political agitation which in normal times is a safeguard of free government. The distinction is not a scholastic subterfuge, but a hard-bought acquisition in the fight for freedom. . . . If one stops short of urging upon others that it is their duty or their interest to resist the law, it seems to me one should not be held to have attempted to cause its violation.

It was an extraordinarily speech-protective interpretation of the Espionage Act. On its face, it was only statutory interpretation: Hand raised no doubts about the scope of congressional power; he purported to be dealing simply with legislative purpose. But it was legislative purpose read in the context of constitutional values—values expressed in a manner as noble as any we have on the books. In the *Masses* case itself, that articulation of values was simply used to justify the narrow interpretation of the statute. But that Hand's position on the scope of permissible dissent in a free society became for him a constitutional norm as well emerges quite clearly from his letters. His statement of democratic values is notable for several reasons: the *Masses* articulation contrasts sharply with the lack of similar sensitivity in Holmes' early confrontations with the same issues in *Schenck* and the companion cases in the spring of 1919; Hand's eloquence bears comparison with Holmes' much-quoted words when he at last began to exhibit a similar awareness in the *Abrams* dissent in the fall of 1919; and, most important, the values emphasized by Hand in *Masses* inspired his partially successful appeals to Holmes before *Abrams* and his continuing disagreements with Holmes in the post-*Abrams* letters.

Hand's technique in *Masses*, though statutory interpretation in form, was in substance an effort at judicial delineation of areas of protected speech. Criticism and agitation that fell outside of the narrow bounds of direct incitement or advocacy of illegal action should be immune from suppression, no matter what the circumstances, no matter what the changing perceptions of impassioned juries. This delineation did not rest simply on judicial fiat: Hand justified it as rooted in values that he saw as essential to a free society—values that his judicial responsibility authorized him to articulate candidly and forcefully.

. . .

The "normal assumption of democratic government," the "use and wont of our people," or, as Hand put it earlier in the opinion, the "right to criticize either by temperate reasoning, or by immoderate and indecent invective, which is normally the privilege of the individual in countries dependent upon the free expression of opinion as the ultimate source of authority"—those were the sources of the values articulated in *Masses*. They were sources derived from history and philosophy—especially the latter. Hand's invocation of history was essentially impressionistic: he actually had little acquaintance with the history of American civil liberties, or indeed with American history generally. His inclinations in his historical reading ran to Europe. It was the underpinning of philosophy and political theory that truly ran deep: in the eloquent articulation of values, the voice was that of Billings Learned Hand, Harvard undergraduate specializing in philosophy, and Learned Hand, lawyer and judge of an inescapably philosophical bent of mind.

But how were those values to be translated into effective law by a judge skeptical of the speech-protective capacity of doctrine, yet persuaded that doctrine might do some good? If an adequate legal standard "could become sacred by the incrustations of time and precedent," he suggested in one of his letters, "it might be made to serve just a little to withhold the torrents of passion to which I suspect democracies will be found more subject than for example the whig autocracy of the 18th century." For Hand, the best hope for avoiding the "suppression of the free utterance of abuse and criticism of the existing law, or the policies of the war," lay not in analogies to the law of criminal attempts or to legal doctrines of causation, but rather in an "objective" scrutiny of the challenged speech to determine whether the words in question were those of incitement or counselling to illegal action:

> [T]here has always been a recognized limit to such expressions, incident indeed to the existence of any compulsive power of the state itself. One may not counsel or advise others to violate the law as it stands. Words are not only the keys of persuasion, but the triggers of action, and those which have no purport but to counsel the violation of law cannot by any

latitude of interpretation be a part of that public opinion which is the final source of government in a democratic state. . . . To counsel or advise a man to an act is to urge upon him either that it is his interest or his duty to do it. While, of course, this may be accomplished as well by indirection as expressly, since words carry the meaning that they impart, the definition is exhaustive, I think, and I shall use it. Political agitation, by the passions it arouses or the convictions it engenders, may in fact stimulate men to the violation of law. Detestation of existing policies is easily transformed into forcible resistance of the authority which puts them in execution, and it would be folly to disregard the causal relation between the two. Yet to assimilate agitation, legitimate as such, with direct incitement to violent resistance, is to disregard the tolerance of all methods of political agitation which in normal times is a safeguard of free government.

"Direct incitement," "direct advocacy" of illegal action—these were the strict standards Hand insisted upon. They were standards focused more on the content than on the effect of the speech. They were standards that would have protected much of the unpopular speech condemned by the prevailing doctrines—and by Holmes' clear and present danger test of the *Schenck* era. For Hand, the question was not whether "the indirect result of the language might be to arouse a seditious disposition, for that would not be enough," but whether "the language directly advocated resistance to the draft."

The libertarian nature of this standard is illustrated by Hand's application of it to passages in *The Masses* praising conscientious objectors and those, like Emma Goldman and Alexander Berkman, who were in jail for conspiring to induce persons not to register for the draft. To most judges—including the circuit court of appeals that reversed Hand, and to Justice Holmes in the spring of 1919—admiration of such "martyrs" encouraged emulation and contributed at least indirectly to violation of law; and that was enough to justify punishment. Not so for Hand. He conceded that the "martyrs" were indeed held up "to admiration, and hence their conduct to possible emulation." And he noted: "It is plain enough that the paper has the fullest sympathy for these people, that it admires their courage, and that it presumptively approves their conduct. . . . [M]oreover, these passages, it must be remembered, occur in a magazine which attacks with the utmost violence the draft and the war." Still, it was not enough, for the objective standard was not satisfied:

That such comments have a tendency to arouse emulation in others is clear enough, but that they counsel others to follow these examples is not so plain. Literally at least they do not, and while, as I have said, the words are to be taken, not literally, but according to their full import, the literal meaning is the starting point for interpretation. One may admire and approve the course of a hero without feeling any duty to follow him. There is not the least implied intimation in these words that others are under a duty to follow. The most that can be said is that, if others do follow, they will get the same admiration and the same approval. Now, there is surely an appreciable distance between esteem and emulation; and unless there is here some advocacy of such emulation, I cannot see how the passages can be said to fall within the law. If they do, it would follow that, while one might express admiration and approval for the Quakers or any established sect which is excused from the draft, one could not legally express the same admiration and approval for others who entertain the same conviction, but do not happen to belong to the society of Friends. . . . Surely, if the draft had not excepted Quakers, it would be too strong a doctrine to say that any who openly admire their fortitude or even approved their conduct was willfully obstructing the draft.

. . .

What emerges from Hand's 1918 letter is the credo that spurred his doctrinal implementations in *Masses* and thereafter—a credo Holmes was unable to accept until late in the following year, and was never able to implement as effectively. "Opinions are at best provisional hypotheses, incompletely tested. . . . So we must be tolerant of opposite opinions or varying opinions by the very fact of our incredulity of our own." So Hand insisted in the face of Holmes' defense of the right of the majority to suppress the minority. Deference to majoritarianism was ordinarily central to Hand's beliefs as well; but in the area of freedom of expression, he could not follow that customary guide. Yes, silencing "the other fellow when he disagrees" was indeed "a natural right," but it was not a right that society and the law could afford to acquiesce in:

Only, and here we may differ, I do say that you may not cut off heads . . . because the victims insist upon saying things which look against Provisional Hypothesis Number Twenty-Six, the verification of which to date

may be found in its proper place in the card catalogue. Generally, I insist, you must allow the possibility that if the heads are spared, other cards may be added under that subtitle which will have, perhaps, an important modification.

It was a Hand argument strikingly similar to the hallowed defense of free speech that Holmes ultimately presented in his *Abrams* dissent:

Persecution for the expression of opinions seems to me perfectly logical. If you have no doubt of your premises or your power and want a certain result with all your heart you naturally express your wishes in law and sweep away all opposition. . . . But when men have realized that time has upset many fighting faiths, they may come to believe even more than they believe the very foundations of their own conduct that the ultimate good desired is better reached by free trade in ideas—that the best test of truth is the power of the thought to get itself accepted in the competition of the market, and that truth is the only ground upon which their wishes safely can be carried out. That at any rate is the theory of our Constitution.

That "theory of our Constitution" had not yet revealed itself to Holmes in 1918. Then, he could see only the "perfectly logical" aspects of persecuting dissenters. The "but," the qualification about the uncertainty of received opinions and the need for a free trade in ideas that Hand urged in 1918, was not yet congenial to Holmes. Yet, characteristically, Holmes tried to meet Hand's 1918 argument with the assertion that "I agree with it throughout." A year later, after *Schenck* and *Debs*, Holmes would wholly fail to see any difference between his standard and Hand's *Masses* alternative. But in June 1918, he did admit to one difference from Hand, one "qualification"—an all-important one. Free speech, he insisted, "stands no differently than freedom from vaccination." And that, of course, could be readily overridden by the majority, as the decision Holmes had joined 13 years earlier, in *Jacobson v. Massachusetts*, had made clear. In Holmes' letter, the overriding emphasis is on what Hand called the "natural right" to kill the opponent.

In short, Holmes was not truly ready to "agree" with Hand that majorities legitimately may be curbed. He believed that the majority's right is all; there is no recognition of any limitation on that "natural right" stemming from the uncertain nature of "truth" or the demands of a democratic society. As

Holmes saw it in 1918, occasions "when you cared enough" to stop the dissident might indeed be rare, "but if for any reason you did care enough you wouldn't care a damn for the suggestion that you were acting on a provisional hypothesis and might be wrong. That is the condition of every act."

Within months, the philosophical battlelines drawn between Holmes and Hand were to be translated into concrete doctrinal differences. In March 1919, it fell to Holmes to write for the Supreme Court in its first encounters with the provisions of the Espionage Act of 1917 that Hand had tried to construe narrowly in *Masses*. These encounters produced the first statement of the clear and present danger test.

But the clear and present danger test of the spring of 1919 was not a useful libertarian doctrine. Rather, it was little more than a manifestation of the philosophical underpinnings revealed by Holmes in June 1918—a philosophy that would recognize no real justification for limiting the right of the majority to "kill" the dissident minority. And perceiving no such justification, Holmes understandably—and to Hand's regret if not surprise—found no compelling reason to elaborate satisfying doctrinal safeguards for free speech.

. . .

Indeed, to Holmes in *Schenck*, the applicability of the first amendment to postpublication sanctions was still in doubt. All he would concede was that it "well may be that the prohibition of laws abridging the freedom of speech is not confined to previous restraints, although to prevent them may have been the main purpose." And all he could offer by way of analogy was the inapt "shouting fire in a theatre" example. He concluded: "If the act [speaking, or circulating a paper], its tendency and the intent with which it is done are the same, we perceive no ground for saying that success alone warrants making the act a crime." What "intent" had to do with a constitutional test purportedly focusing on the consequences of speech was never made clear, here or in later cases.

In *Schenck*, at least, the antiwar documents that provoked the prosecution were "circulated to men who had been called and accepted for military service." That was not true in either *Frohwerk* or *Debs*; but Holmes showed no greater hesitation about affirming the convictions in those cases. In *Frohwerk*, he added to the "shouting fire" analogy the equally inapt point that men like Hamilton or Madison would not have found suppression of the "counselling of a murder" to be an abridgment of free speech. And

when it came to the permissible interpretation of the defendants' words, Holmes' approach was in particularly striking contrast to Hand's strict, language-oriented analysis in *Masses*. *Frohwerk*, for example, had deplored draft riots in language, as Holmes put it, "that might be taken to convey an innuendo of a different sort." And the position of Holmes' later defenders that clear and present danger contained a strong immediacy element in the spring of 1919 is hard to credit when one reads in *Frohwerk* that "it is impossible to say that it might not have been found that the circulation of the paper was in quarters where a little breath would be enough to kindle a flame."

But the spring 1919 case most clearly insensitive to free speech concerns, and the one that aroused the strongest contemporary protests, was the prosecution of the Socialist leader and soon-to-be presidential candidate, Eugene V. Debs. As Holmes described Debs' speech, its main theme "was socialism, its growth, and a prophecy of its ultimate success." But Holmes added: "[I]f a part or the manifest intent of the more general utterance was to encourage those present to obstruct the recruiting service and if in passages such encouragement was directly given, the immunity of the general theme may not be enough to protect the speech." Again, as in *Frohwerk*, Holmes was willing to speculate about damaging innuendoes: "[Debs] said that he had to be prudent and might not be able to say all that he thought, thus intimating to his hearers that they might infer that he meant more. . . ." Other parts of the speech, Holmes added, "had only [an] indirect though not necessarily ineffective bearing on the offenses alleged." Yet from these fragments, Holmes concluded, a jury could find "that one purpose of the speech, whether incidental or not does not matter, was to oppose not only war in general but this war, and that the opposition was so expressed that its natural and intended effect would be to obstruct recruiting." Again, "natural tendency and reasonably probable effect"—a formulation hardly different from that of the Government in the wartime prosecutions or of the Second Circuit in *Masses*—was enough to send Debs to jail. As Harry Kalven recently reminded us, it was "somewhat as though George McGovern had been sent to prison for his criticism of the [Vietnam] war." *Schenck* is rightly read together with *Debs* (and with *Frohwerk*); and Kalven was right to find that the Holmes of these cases "shows no sensitivity to accommodating a tradition of political dissent, a sensitivity which had so characterized Hand's opinion two years earlier in [*Masses*], and makes no effort to suggest the parameters of improper criticism of the war."

. . .

Clear and present danger, like "natural and probable consequences," was a test of causation, a test calling for guesses about the future impact of words. As in *Masses*, Hand does not disagree that words may have practical consequences; rather, he denies that mere risk of consequences can justify legal culpability:

In nature the causal sequence is perfect, but responsibility does not go pari passu. I do not understand that the rule of responsibility for speech has ever been that the result is known as likely to follow. It is not—I agree it might have been—a question of responsibility dependent upon reasonable forecast. . . . The responsibility only began when the words were directly an incitement.

Hand suggested this as a test validated by history. But as in *Masses*, it was not truly a standard that rested on extensive reading in American history. Rather, it was a legal standard that was primarily a reflection of Hand's appreciation of free speech values.

But there was far more than the detached philosopher behind the incitement approach. It was an approach prompted, too, by Hand's practical awareness of the risks to speech if juries were permitted to punish on the basis of guesses about intent or reasonable consequences:

All I say is, that since the cases actually occur when men are excited and since juries are especially clannish groups . . . it is very questionable whether the test of motive is not a dangerous test. Juries won't much regard the difference between the probable result of the words and the purposes of the utterer. In any case, unless one is rather set in conformity, it will serve to intimidate—throw a scare into—many a man who might moderate the storms of popular feeling. I know it did in 1918.

This practical concern, and the reference to Postmaster General Burleson's "legal irresponsibility" in terrorizing some of the press, reveal some important differences between Hand and Holmes. In Holmes, one finds the detached observer, the ironical philosopher of the June 24, 1918, letter. Holmes is the Olympian, relatively unconcerned stoic watching mankind fight its battles from afar. There were ample detachment and skepticism in Hand's makeup as well. But there was also greater feeling, greater concern with what we now call "chilling effects," greater agony about the real-life impact of legal doctrine. It is a difference well illustrated by the respec-

tive reactions of Hand and Holmes to prosecutions such as that of Debs. Both were sideline observers; but Hand cared more about the injuries inflicted in the arena. Neither supported the prosecutions; but while Holmes viewed them simply as additional illustrations of mankind's follies, to Hand they were genuine tragedies.

Holmes' quite different perspective on the appropriate legal standards emerges clearly from his reply to Hand's comment on *Debs*. The basic theme of his answer to Hand is accurately stated at the beginning of the letter: in response to Hand's advocacy of a word-oriented incitement test—in contrast to a cause-and-effect orientation—Holmes states: "I don't quite get your point." And as if to emphasize Holmes' lack of awareness of distinctions quite plain to more concerned contemporary observers, he responds to Hand's reference to incitement by quoting the full clear and present danger test from *Schenck*, adding the remarkable comment: "I don't see how you differ from the test as stated by me."

But it is the final portion of the passage that may best illustrate the primitiveness of Holmes' first amendment thinking at that time. Holmes points out that Hand had after all agreed in *Masses* that words may constitute a violation of the statute, without proof of an actual obstruction. And he adds: "So I don't know what the matter is, or how we differ so far as your letter goes." But very much was the matter. Of course Hand agreed that words could sometimes be punishable. Virtually all commentators agreed on that point. But Holmes thought that shared premise was the end of the problem. In fact, it was only the beginning. The real challenge was to articulate a standard that, while reaching some words, would protect most criticism of government. The *Masses* incitement test was one such effort. Clear and present danger at the time of *Schenck*, it seems evident, was not. How could it be, when Holmes simply failed to see the problem?

IV. The Abrams Dissent and Hand's Continued Adherence to the Masses Approach, 1919–21

Eight months after the *Schenck* trilogy, Justice Holmes began to get the point: in *Abrams v. United States*, he put forth his now famous elaboration of first amendment doctrine. It was as if the message of critics such as Learned Hand were having a delayed impact; but it was only a partial impact. Holmes' dissent in *Abrams* is a classic primarily because of its eloquent concluding passages, with their emphasis on the "free trade in ideas" as "the theory of our Constitution." Those passages are indeed a response to the first part of Hand's message: the need to appreciate the values of free speech, the legitimate claim of free speech to special legal protection. But as to the second part of the Hand message, on the need for adequate doctrinal implementation of free speech values, the Holmes dissent is considerably less satisfying. And Hand clearly was not satisfied.

Justice Clarke's majority opinion affirming the conviction of the defendants in *Abrams* dismissed the constitutional objections as "definitely negatived" by *Schenck* and *Frohwerk*. And it is indeed difficult to perceive any significant differences in tenor between the Clarke opinion and those of Holmes in the spring. But Holmes, joined by Brandeis, now dissented. There were two strands to his argument; and his dissent does not fully disentangle the strands. In part, Holmes rested on statutory interpretation; in part, he relied on constitutional argument—clear and present danger infused with a new immediacy element.

The statutory argument arose because the *Abrams* defendants had been charged under the 1918 amendments to the Espionage Act, not under the 1917 provisions applied in *Masses* and the *Schenck* trilogy. Among the new offenses designated in the May 1918 amendments was urging the curtailment of the production of materials necessary to the prosecution of the war with Germany, with intent to hinder the prosecution of that war. Holmes managed to read a strict specific intent requirement into that provision. The *Abrams* defendants were "anarchists" who had urged a general strike to oppose American military intervention against the Russian revolution. Stopping war production to impede American forces in Russia might indeed have the effect of interfering with the war with Germany; but, Holmes insisted, since the German war was not the immediate target of the defendants, the requisite specific intent had not been shown. Learned Hand had some difficulty with that reading of the intent requirement, as two of his letters to Chafee illustrate.

But the statutory issue was not the critical one. It was the elaboration of clear and present danger as a constitutional test that made the *Abrams* dissent doctrinally significant. Holmes insisted that the *Schenck* trilogy was "rightly decided":

> I do not doubt for a moment that by the same reasoning that would justify punishing persuasion to murder, the United States constitutionally may punish speech that produces or is intended to produce a clear and imminent danger that it will bring about forthwith certain substantive evils that the United States constitutionally may seek to prevent.

Again, the inapt "persuasion to murder" analogy of *Frohwerk* appears. And once more, intent and

actual risks are alternative ingredients, without any explanation of the relevance of intent to a standard emphasizing the dangerous consequences of words. But despite the continuing obscurity in Holmes' approach, some passages at last injected a genuine immediacy ingredient into clear and present danger and sharply distinguished Holmes' *Abrams* requirements from the remote consequences adequate for conviction under a "bad tendency" standard:

> It is only the present danger of immediate evil or an intent to bring it about that warrants Congress in setting a limit to the expression of opinion where private rights are not concerned. . . . I think that we should be eternally vigilant against attempts to check the expression of opinions that we loathe and believe to be fraught with death, unless they so imminently threaten immediate interference with the lawful and pressing purposes of the law that an immediate check is required to save the country.

. . .

Writing to Holmes, Hand simply acknowledged his appreciation of finding added judicial support for his own special concern for speech. With Holmes' short reply, the Hand-Holmes correspondence about the first amendment ended: Hand thought it pointless to pursue his advocacy of the *Masses* approach vis-a-vis Holmes. But that he did not abandon it and indeed elaborated it is the clear message of the remaining correspondence, with Zechariah Chafee, Jr.

. . .

[I]n *Brandenburg v. Ohio*, the Warren Court built on *Yates* and *Scales* to produce its clearest and most protective standard under the first amendment. And *Brandenburg* continues to be adhered to by the Burger Court. *Brandenburg* rests ultimately on the insight Learned Hand urged without success at the end of World War I. The *Brandenburg* per curiam emphasized that laws affecting first amendment rights "must observe the established distinction between mere advocacy and incitement to imminent lawless action." That was hardly an "established" distinction. Indeed, that was precisely the distinction Holmes has sought to discredit in the *Gitlow* dissent with the deprecating comment: "Every idea is an incitement." An incitement-nonincitement distinction had only fragmentary and ambiguous antecedents in the pre-*Brandenburg* era; it was *Brandenburg* that really "established" it; and, it was essentially an establishment of the legacy of Learned Hand.

In one sense, *Brandenburg* combines the most protective ingredients of the *Masses* incitement emphasis with the most useful elements of the clear and present danger heritage. As the Court summarized first amendment principles in *Brandenburg*—purporting to restate, but in fact creating—:

> [T]he constitutional guarantees of free speech and free press do not permit a State to forbid or proscribe advocacy of the use of force or of law violation except where such advocacy is directed to inciting or producing imminent lawless action and is likely to incite or produce such action.

The incitement emphasis is Hand's; the reference to "imminent" reflects a limited influence of Holmes, combined with later experience; and the "likely to incite or produce such action" addition in the *Brandenburg* standard is the only reference to the need to guess about future consequences of speech, so central to the *Schenck* approach. Under *Brandenburg*, probability of harm is no longer the central criterion for speech limitations. The inciting language of the speaker—the Hand focus on "objective" words—is the major consideration. And punishment of the harmless inciter is prevented by the *Schenck*-derived requirement of a likelihood of dangerous consequences.

And so, via Justice Harlan and the Supreme Court majority at the end of the Warren era, the language-oriented incitement criterion, so persistently urged by Hand in *Masses* and in these letters, has become central to the operative law of the land. *Brandenburg* is the most speech-protective standard yet evolved by the Supreme Court. Learned Hand would no doubt be surprised, and surely pleased, at this belated vindication. In 1921, Hand could not "help wondering whether a good many years from now when you are old and I am dead," his *Masses* contribution might seem trivial. *Masses*, he anticipated, would vanish. Its test might be seen as "some false coin." But Learned Hand's analysis was precious metal, never "false coin"; the problem always lay in the eyes of the appraisers. Hand made sense in 1917 and 1918, in 1920 and 1921. Now, we have come to appreciate it.

---

Ernst Freund, *The Debs Case and Freedom of Speech,* 40 THE UNIVERSITY OF CHICAGO LAW REVIEW 239 (1973)*

After the affirmance of his conviction by the Su-

---

preme Court, Mr. Debs issued a statement to the effect that the real issue, the constitutionality of the Espionage law, had not been decided, and such seems to be the general impression. As a matter of fact the decision raises inevitably the question of the freedom of agitation in war time. The offense of which Debs was convicted was obstruction of recruiting; the acts proved were a violent attack upon the war, its motives and objects, and the approval of the conduct and attitude of persons who had been convicted of like offenses; and from this evidence the jury was permitted to find a tendency and an intent to obstruct recruiting. There was nothing to show actual obstruction or an attempt to interfere with any of the processes of recruiting. How can it be denied that the upholding of such a finding upon such evidence involves the question of the limits of permissible speech? If verbal or written opposition to the war, however violent or unwarranted, can be stretched to mean a form of obstruction, then Congress strikes at utterances as effectually through punishing obstruction as though it punished utterances directly. Not only is to this extent the restraint of speech clearly sanctioned by the Supreme Court, but it is made to rest on judicial interpretation rather than upon legislation.

I shall not attempt to determine what in the way of restraint is possible under the First Amendment. A narrow historic view (rather discountenanced by Justice Holmes) may confine freedom to the prohibition of censorship. Even so, with the post office under the control of the government, and in the absence of a clear and explicit constitutional right to the free and equal use of the postal service, Congress has it in its power to render the free expression of opinion harmless for immediate political purposes by denying mail facilities. It is therefore useless to over-emphasize the substantive limitations of the constitution; the real securities of rights will always have to be found in the painstaking care given to the working out of legal principles.

So long as we apply the notoriously loose common law doctrines of conspiracy and incitement to offenses of a political character, we are adrift on a sea of doubt and conjecture. To know what you may do and what you may not do, and how far you may go in criticism, is the first condition of political liberty; to be permitted to agitate at your own peril, subject to a jury's guessing at motive, tendency and possible effect, makes the right of free speech a precarious gift. Our practice has been so tolerant of political liberty and license that we have had no occasion to consider these things; Justice Holmes takes the very essentials of the entire problem for granted, and intimates that they are conceded even by the defendant.

On the continent of Europe, a harder and more recent struggle for the freedom of the press and for constitutional government in general induced a very much more scientific scrutiny of these fundamentals of penal responsibility, and instead of the illusory simplicity of our doctrines we find elaborately specified criteria of guilt. Over a hundred years ago Royer-Collard, the foremost exponent of the old-time French liberalism, in discussing a proposed law on the press, declared that in the matter of political offenses the recognition of such a thing as indirect provocation, i.e., implied or inferential incitement, spelled arbitrary power. This view finally gained acceptance, and the present French press law recognizes only direct provocation which has reference to some definite and particular criminal act, and punishes even direct provocation not resulting in actual crime only in connection with specified aggravated offenses. It is true that certain kinds of provocation are specially dealt with, and among these the incitement to military insubordination; and the German Penal Code has a general offense of direct incitement to disobedience to the laws; but the vagueness of definition that characterizes the Espionage Act, finds, I believe, no parallel in modern foreign legislation.

The Debs case itself illustrates most clearly the arbitrariness of the whole idea of implied provocation. A violent, if you please, a seditious speech is made; a docile jury finds a design to obstruct recruiting, and the finding is conclusive because the court does not consider it inconsistent with possibility. What are the intrinsic probabilities? An experienced speaker like Debs knows the effect of words. He must have known that, while he might keep alive and even create disaffection, his power to create actual obstruction to a compulsory draft was practically nil, and he could hardly have intended what he could not hope to achieve; in fact it is difficult to conceive of a form of obstruction that can be opposed to a compulsory draft. I know of only one reported case of direct counselling not to report for military service when ordered so to do, and Judge Amidon in directing a verdict of acquittal in a recent case remarked upon the scarcity of overt acts, stating that all judicial decisions had dealt with the use of language. The inherent obstacles in the way of planning or carrying out obstruction certainly add to the intrinsic improbability of the imputed design. Yet Justice Holmes would make us believe that the relation of the speech to obstruction is like that of the shout of Fire! in a crowded theatre to the resulting panic! Surely implied provocation in connection with political offenses is an unsafe doctrine if it has to be made plausible by a parallel so manifestly inappropriate.

It is well known that the Constitution in guaranteeing free speech makes no difference between peace and war time; if it did it would still be enormously difficult to formulate war time restraints as rules of law. On the continent of Europe the matter is handled by unregulated and arbitrary executive power, and the Prussian constitution expressly permits the suspension of the normal guarantees of freedom of speech and press in the emergency of war. The Espionage act is a crude piece of legislation, and, if it is the best that can be done, illustrates the inherent difficulties of the subject. For arbitrary executive, it practically substitutes arbitrary judicial power; since a jury's findings, within the limits of a conceivable psychological nexus between words and deeds, are beyond scrutiny and control; and while the jury may have been a protection against governmental power when the government was a thing apart from the people, its checking function fails where government policies are supported by majority opinion. We fluctuate between constitutional immunity and common law uncertainty; the common law of political crimes was loose and arbitrary in the extreme, and, having fallen into gradual desuetude, has undergone no change or improvement in a hundred years. It was owing to this feature of it that the idea of a federal common law was altogether repudiated; but the criminal legislation of Congress, to which no adequate thought has ever been given, revives and perpetuates the defects of the common law.

It even aggravates them, for sedition at common law is merely a misdemeanor, while congressional legislation, by failing to differentiate offenses according to the kind of culpability and grading only according to the maximum duration of punishment, causes every offense that is punishable by a sentence of imprisonment exceeding one year to assume the character of a felony. I do not speak of the draconic sentences imposed; they are clearly only "in terrorem," and since every one knows that they will not be carried out in full, they fail to terrorize and merely serve to create animosity and bitterness with reference to our processes of justice. But stamp a man like Debs or a woman like Kate O'Hare as felons, and you dignify the term felony instead of degrading them, and every thief and robber will be justified in feeling that some of the stigma has been taken from his crime and punishment.

Now that the war is virtually over, the Espionage act ceases to be effective, but since in time of war

the voice of reason is not heard, or if heard is mis-
construed, this is the time to protest against its legal
unsoundness, and in the long run sound law cannot
be inimical to sound policy. A country can ill spare
the men who when the waves of militant nationalism
run high do not lose the courage of their convictions.
If that was true in Germany, it cannot be untrue of
America. The peril resulting to the national cause
from toleration of adverse opinion is largely imaginary; in any event it is slight as compared with the
permanent danger of intolerance to free institutions.
Fortunately public opinion in this country would not
stand for the kind of legal terrorism that was practiced, for instance, in Italy. A certain amount of
social terrorism must be accepted as inevitable; and
if public opinion demands the prosecution of scurrilous and indecent attacks upon the cause for which
a nation is fighting, local powers are adequate for
that purpose.

No doubt a considerable public opinion also demands a federal prosecution of such attacks as were
made by Debs and La Follette; but a wise government would have resisted that pressure. That sentiment has been gratified by creating an enormous
amount of dissatisfaction, a dissatisfaction born of
the conviction that what was prosecuted and punished
was not action, but opinion. As in the case of all
political persecution, the cause of the government
has gained nothing, while the forces of discontent
have been strengthened, and have been given an example of loose and arbitrary law which at some time
may react against those who have set it. Toleration
of adverse opinion is not a matter of generosity, but
of political prudence.

. . .

Harry Kalven, Jr., *Upon Rereading Mr. Justice
Black on the First Amendment,* 14 UCLA LAW
REVIEW 428 (1967)*

. . .

In both the popular and the professional eye, Justice Black has inherited the mantle of Holmes and
Brandeis. The amendment now bears his personal
trademark as it once did theirs. It is, therefore, in-

structive to note how much easier they had it in that
relatively short and relatively tranquil span from
*Schenck v. United States* to *Near v. Minnesota* and
*Stromberg v. California.* They were not asked to test
classic notions of freedom of speech against group
defamation, labor picketing, obscenity, congressional committees, sound trucks, public issue picketing, sit-ins, or that large array of direct and indirect
sanctions imposed upon the domestic Communist
movement.

To review Mr. Justice Black's thirty years of service to the first amendment, therefore, is to review
all of the contemporary problems of free speech. It
requires, and deserves, a book. I cannot attempt
more here than to comment selectively on a few of
the impressions I have had upon rereading Justice
Black on the first amendment.

I.

To begin with, he passes a major test for a great
judge on free speech issues. He displays the requisite
passion. The requirement is not so much a question
of arguing for the preferred position thesis; it is
rather that the judge respond to the fact at this is not
just another rule or principle of law. Mr. Justice
Black has for thirty years always risen to the occasion
when a free speech issue was at stake; he has always
been vigilant and concerned. And as a result his style
has often had the appropriate eloquence, although he
never perhaps quite matches Holmes, Hand, Brandeis, or Jackson.

Listen once more to the moving conclusion of his
dissent in *Dennis v. United States,* written now some
fifteen years ago:

> Public opinion being what it now is, few will
> protest the conviction of these Communist pe-
> titioners. There is hope, however, that in
> calmer times, when present pressures, pas-
> sions, and fears subside, this or some later
> Court will restore the First Amendment liber-
> ties to the high preferred place where they be-
> long in a free society.

Nine years later in *Communist Party of the United
States v. Subversive Activities Control Bd.,* Justice
Black opened his dissent in even more somber tones:

> I do not believe that it can be too often repeated
> that the freedoms of speech, press, petition,
> and assembly guaranteed by the First Amend-
> ment must be accorded to the ideas we hate
> or sooner or later they will be denied to the
> ideas we cherish. The first banning of an asso-
> ciation because it advocates hated ideas—
> whether that association be called a political
> party or not—marks a fateful moment in the

history of a free country. That moment seems to have arrived for this country.

And he brought the opinion, perhaps the most extensive first amendment opinion he has written, to a close in that case with the following comment:

> I would reverse this case and leave the Communists free to advocate their beliefs in proletarian dictatorship publicly and openly among the people of this country with the full confidence that the people will remain loyal to any democratic government truly dedicated to freedom and justice—the kind of government which some of us still think of as being "the last best hope of earth."

Often the depth of his concern is shown by the flash of irony. There is the last sentence of his dissent in *Beauharnais v. Illinois*, where the Court had upheld group defamation laws: "If there be minority groups who hail this holding as their victory, they might consider the possible relevancy of this ancient remark: Another such victory and I am undone!" And there is his exasperation with the majority decision in *In re Summers*, upholding the refusal to admit a conscientious objector to the practice of law in Illinois:

> It may be, as many people think, that Christ's Gospel of love and submission is not suited to a world in which men still fight and kill one another. But I am not ready to say that a mere profession of belief in that Gospel is a sufficient reason to keep otherwise well-qualified men out of the legal profession . . . .

Or again, and in much the same vein, there is his observation in *In re Anastaplo*, another bar admission case where the petitioner had in his initial application noted the right of revolution as a constitutional principle and had refused to answer questions about Communist affiliation:

> And I think the record clearly shows that conflict resulted, not from any fear on Anastaplo's part to divulge his own political activities, but from a sincere, and in my judgment correct, conviction that the preservation of this country's freedom depends upon adherence to our Bill of Rights. The very most that can fairly be said against Anastaplo's position in this entire matter is that he took too much of the responsibility of preserving that freedom upon himself.

It is characteristic of the depth of his concern over freedom of speech that it should find one of its most eloquent and sustained expressions in a case not normally thought of as in the first amendment family, *Carlson v. Landon*. The case involved provisions of the Internal Security Act affecting the deportability of resident aliens who were members of the Communist Party. The precise issue was whether the Attorney General could keep the aliens in custody without bail pending a determination of their status. Justice Black in a lengthy dissent, arguing a variety of other grounds, found the vice to be in part a violation of the first amendment:

> As previously pointed out, the basis of holding these people in jail is a fear they may indoctrinate people with Communist beliefs. To put people in jail for fear of their talk seems to me an abridgement of speech in flat violation of the First Amendment. I have to admit, however, that this is a logical application of recent cases watering down constitutional liberty of speech. I also realize that many believe that Communists and "fellow travelers" should not be accorded any of the First Amendment protections. My belief is that we must have freedom of speech, press and religion for all or we may eventually have it for none. I further believe that the First Amendment grants an absolute right to believe in any governmental system, discuss all governmental affairs, and argue for desired changes in the existing order. This freedom is too dangerous for bad, tyrannical governments to permit. But those who wrote and adopted our First Amendment weighed those dangers against the dangers of censorship and deliberately chose the First Amendment's unequivocal command that freedom of assembly, petition, speech and press shall not be abridged. I happen to believe this was a wise choice and that our free way of life enlists such respect and love that our Nation cannot be imperiled by mere talk. This belief of mine may and I suppose does influence me to protest whenever I see even slight encroachments on First Amendment liberties. But the encroachment here is not small. True it is mainly those alleged to be present or past "Communists" who are now being jailed for their beliefs and expressions. But we cannot be sure more victims will not be offered up later if the First Amendment means no more than its enemies or even some of its friends believe that it does.

This last example of his style serves as a summary of a basic philosophy which reappears in many opinions: Freedom of speech is indivisible; unless we protect it for all, we will have it for none. It is a sign of weakness to control speech; only democracies can afford the gallant gamble on utter freedom of speech—it is too dangerous for tyranny. The choice for freedom of speech is a choice made once and for all by the Founding Fathers and is not subject to reassessment in light of current anxieties. It is a profoundly wise choice.

# Bibliography

*Political Expression*

Auerbach, Carl A., *The Communist Control Act of 1954: A Proposed Legal-Political Theory of Free Speech,* 23 University of Chicago Law Review 173 (1956)

Coase, R.H., *The Market for Goods and the Market for Ideas,* 64 American Economic Review 384 (1974)

Emerson, Thomas I., *Toward A General Theory of the First Amendment,* 72 Yale Law Journal 877 (1963)

Greenawalt, Kent, *Speech and Crime,* 1980 American Bar Foundation Research Journal 645 (1980)

Posner, Richard A., *Free Speech in an Economic Perspective,* 20 Suffolk University Law Review 1 (1986)

Schauer, Frederick, *Must Speech Be Special?,* 78 Northwestern University Law Review 1284 (1983)

Tribe, Laurence H., *Toward a Metatheory of Free Speech,* 10 Southwestern University Law Review 237 (1978)

Wright, R. George, *A Rationale from J.S. Mill for the Free Speech Clause,* 1985 Supreme Court Review 149 (1985)

## C. Defamation and Privacy

Speech that injures reputation was entirely unprotected until the second half of this century, when the Supreme Court determined that public officials and figures must prove actual malice as a condition for recovery. *New York Times Co. v. Sullivan*, 376 U.S. 254, 279–80 (1964). The consequent need to factor the First Amendment into the traditional law of tort was driven in significant part by circumstance. The actual malice standard requirement hardened standards that otherwise would have enabled southern officials to trade on trivial mischaracterizations as a means of trying to put the civil rights movement out of business. The result in *Sullivan* fortifies the theory that progress under the First Amendment in significant part has been a function of the struggle for racial justice. Harry Kalven, Jr., *The Negro and the First Amendment* (1965). The constitutional recasting of defamation law eventually generated second thoughts, including those of Justice White who later questioned the actual malice standard's wisdom. Two decades after subscribing to it, White concluded that the actual malice standard afforded insufficient reputational protection and allowed "the stream of information about public officials and public affairs [to be] polluted." *Dun & Bradstreet, Inc. v. Greenmoss Builders Inc.*, 472 U.S. 749, 769 (1985) (White, J., concurring). Kalven applauded the *Sullivan* decision as an accounting for the central meaning of the First Amendment, insofar as it enhanced protection of political speech. Arlen W. Langvardt criticizes the Supreme Court's work in the area of defamation on grounds that the principles it has evolved are fuzzy and confusing. Rodney A. Smolla questions the distinction between public and private controversies that may be critical for purposes of determining whether a public figure exists. Diane Leenheer Zimmerman suggests that First Amendment developments significantly have consumed traditional tort law.

Harry Kalven, Jr., *The New York Times Case: A Note on "The Central Meaning of the First Amendment,"* 1964 SUPREME COURT REVIEW 191 (1964)*

. . .

On occasion the Supreme Court hands down a decision in which past doctrine intersects present events in so complex a way as to be the despair of the commentator, not only because its portent is almost beyond prediction, but also because it opens so many avenues for inquiry. Just such a decision was *New York Times Co. v. Sullivan* in which the Court unanimously held that a libel judgment rendered under Alabama law was violative of First Amendment principles and, therefore, of the Fourteenth Amendment.

Since the case involved a rare instance of measuring the common law of defamation by constitutional standards, it clamors for a careful determination of how much of that traditional body of tort law is affected by it. And for the torts teacher, it has the dizzying consequence of transmuting a part of his domain—one that he traditionally does not reach until the last day of the semester—into constitutional law, the Valhalla of the law school curriculum. Moreover, even a cursory examination of the case reveals that the decision was responsive to the pressures of the day created by the Negro protest movement and thus raises the question so frequently mooted whether the Supreme Court has adhered to neutral principles in reaching its conclusion.

. . .

Certain . . . facts must be deemed relevant to the disposition of the issues.

First, the connection of the *Times* with Alabama could scarcely be more marginal: of the 650,000 published copies of the issues containing the advertisement, only 394 were distributed in Alabama, of which 35 were circulated in Montgomery County. The publication, addressed primarily to a national audience, was all but invisible in the community in which plaintiff was claiming harm to his reputation.

The defamatory import presented an inverse instance of what has become known in the law of defamation as the "wrong-thinking minority problem." The problem usually arises when an assertion about the plaintiff would not be considered defamatory by

right-thinking people, *e.g.*, that the plaintiff has Jewish or Negro blood. The rule has been that the court will run the risk of ratifying the prejudice rather than pass on the issue whether the statement ought to have damaged the plaintiff. The plaintiff is entitled to have his reputation protected even among people who do not have "proper" values. The irony in the *Times* case is that the statements of police brutality and harassment would offend those with the "right" values. What is doubtful is that such allegations did, in fact, offend an Alabama audience, in light of the current exacerbations of the civil rights controversy.

This quirk to one side, there was the difficulty of connecting the statements made by the defendant with the plaintiff, an issue that loomed large in the Supreme Court's handling of the case. Quotation of the two offending paragraphs in the advertisement can spotlight this difficulty:

> In Montgomery, Alabama, after students sang "My Country, 'Tis of Thee" on the State Capitol steps, their leaders were expelled from the school, and truckloads of police armed with shotguns and tear-gas ringed the Alabama State College Campus. When the entire student body protested to state authorities by refusing to re-register, their dining hall was padlocked in an attempt to starve them into submission.
>
> . . .
>
> Again and again the Southern violators have answered Dr. King's peaceful protests with intimidation and violence. They have bombed his home almost killing his wife and child. They have assaulted his person. They have arrested him seven times—for "speeding," "loitering" and similar "offenses." And now they have charged him with "perjury"—a *felony* under which they could imprison him for *ten years* . . . .

The plaintiff argued that as head of the police and responsible for their activities, he was, by inference, charged with: (1) ringing the campus with armed police; (2) arresting Dr. King for spurious offenses. This step, if not compelling, is at least not utterly artificial. Plaintiff claimed further, however, that because these two items referred to him, he would also be understood as one of the persons responsible for: (3) padlocking the dining room and starving the students; (4) bombing the King home; (5) assaulting King; and (6) charging him with perjury. It would seem more reasonable to assume that the "they" referred to in the second quoted paragraph was intended to suggest no specific persons but rather the "Establishment" in which the plaintiff's role would be only incidental. Indeed, both paragraphs would seem to be concerned with such an amorphous group rather than individuals such as the plaintiff.

On a second reading then, there are statements invisibly published in plaintiff's community, which refer to him only by a strained construction of their language, and which, given the mood of the day, would not likely be considered defamatory by a southern audience. It is this marginal harm that the jury added up to $500,000 damages. . . .

. . . In several nagging particulars, the statements are not absolutely accurate; they reveal an inaccuracy characteristic of hastily drawn newspaper advertisements of this nature. The roster of inaccuracies is something like this: (1) The dining hall was never padlocked. (2) The students did not refuse to reregister. (3) Less than the entire student body protested. (4) The student leaders were not expelled for the protest on the capitol steps. (5) The police at no time literally ringed the campus. (6) Although the police did appear near the campus on three occasions, it was never in connection with the protest at the capitol. (7) Dr. King had not been arrested seven times. (8) The charge that Dr. King was assaulted was flimsy and was based on a single controverted instance of some years before. Nonetheless, almost every allegation had a core of truth. Dr. King had been arrested four times. Police had been deployed near the campus in large numbers. Student leaders had been expelled for taking part in sit-in demonstrations. Most of the student body had protested. The protest had taken the form of boycotting classes.

It is tempting to say that the falsity reduces itself to a charge that Dr. King was arrested seven times rather than four. And that the students sang "My Country 'Tis of Thee," when in fact they sang the national anthem. But the other points are not so trivial. And it would prove a disturbing exercise to see what would be left of the first quoted paragraph if all the facts were stated with absolute precision. Since it is characteristic of the common law of defamation to measure the defense of truth against very stringent standards, the conclusion that the falsity of the statements was harmless would not comport with established legal tests.

Perhaps an additional fact has to be taken into consideration. That is that other Montgomery County officials and the Governor of Alabama had also decided that the advertisement defamed them and four additional libel suits were pending seeking judgments against the *Times* for an additional 2.5 million dollars.

On the second reading of the facts, the inescapable impression is that, although the Alabama law had not been distorted to achieve the result, Alabama somehow pounced on this opportunity to punish the *Times* for its role in supporting the civil rights movement in the South. The judgment, along with the others that were bound to follow, represented a powerful blow in the South's counterattack. In the civil war that is being waged in the courts as well as elsewhere, the political importance of the case could not be ignored.

One problem among the many that the Court faces in cases of this kind is attributable to the fact that it cannot, like the man in the street, simply state the result that it likes. There may be compelling reasons for decision that it cannot offer publicly without jeopardizing its role and image as a court. The "hard" cases of constitutional law demand high judicial statesmanship. In the *Times* case, the Court was prepared to pay the high price of destroying a considerable part of the common law of defamation. Whether the price was too high must be determined by the adequacy of the contribution it has made to First Amendment doctrine.

. . .

## V. The Opinion: A Second Reading

The exciting possibilities in the Court's opinion derive from its emphasis on seditious libel and the Sedition Act of 1798 as the key to the meaning of the First Amendment. My thesis is dependent on four propositions. First, that the importance of the free-speech provision of the Constitution rests on the rejection of seditious libel as an offense. Second, that constitutional history and the traditional analysis had relegated the concept of seditious libel to a curiously unimportant place, although the nagging question of the constitutionality of the Sedition Act of 1798 had never properly been put to rest. Third, that the special virtue of the *Times* opinion is its restoration of seditious libel to its essential role, thus suddenly and dramatically changing the idiom of free-speech analysis and resolving the question of the constitutionality of the Sedition Act. Finally, that the effect of the *Times* opinion is necessarily to discard or diminish in importance the clear-and-present danger test, the balancing formula, the two-level speech theory of *Beauharnais* and *Roth*, and the two-tier theory of different effects of the First Amendment on federal and state action. If I am right, the *Times* case represents a happy revolution of free-speech doctrine. Or, to put the matter differently, analysis of free-speech issues should hereafter begin with the significant issue of seditious libel and defamation of government by its critics rather than with the sterile example of a man falsely yelling fire in a crowded theater.

My first proposition need not detain us long. The concept of seditious libel strikes at the very heart of democracy. Political freedom ends when government can use its powers and its courts to silence its critics. My point is not the tepid one that there should be leeway for criticism of the government. It is rather that defamation of the government is an impossible notion for a democracy. In brief, I suggest, that the presence or absence in the law of the concept of seditious libel defines the society. A society may or may not treat obscenity or contempt by publication as legal offenses without altering its basic nature. If, however, it makes seditious libel an offense, it is not a free society no matter what its other characteristics.

My second proposition, the denigration of the importance of seditious libel in establishing First Amendment principles, is more difficult to establish. Perhaps it is only the accident of the sequence in which the speech cases have come to the Court, combined with the fact that the Court never had the sedition laws before it, that leaves the impression of its disregard of seditious libel and its fascination with the clear-and-present danger formula and balancing. Perhaps it is because we have not used functional categories in working out the theory of free speech. In any event, we do not start with the notion that seditious libel is clearly beyond the power of government and develop our ideas from that proposition.

Certainly, the logic of the clear-and-present danger test does not foreclose the matter. It leaves the status of seditious libel in doubt. It does not suggest that severe criticism of government policy could never be sufficiently dangerous. Indeed, one might cite *Schenck*, *Debs*, and *Abrams* as three cases in which the Court itself reached the opposite conclusion.

Moreover, until its disposition by the *Times* case, the status of the Sedition Act of 1798 remained an open question. It has been a term of infamy in American usage, but sober judgments about its constitutionality have been few indeed. Many distinguished commentators—Corwin, Hall, and Carroll, for example—regarded the Sedition Act as constitutional, and Story might also be numbered among them. Even Chafee, who makes a strong case for the unconstitutionality of the Act in the opening chapter of his classic, seems willing to leave the question unresolved. More recent researches by Crosskey and Levy have demonstrated how awkward a problem the Sedition Act presents. My point, for the moment, is not to choose the better view of the history of the First Amendment and the Sedition Act, but rather to call attention to the fact that for over 150 years it was not thought necessary to establish the status of

the Act as a first step in getting to the meaning of the First Amendment. It was thus possible for the Espionage Act of 1917, as amended in 1918, to contain sections that oddly echoed the idiom of seditious libel: language intended to bring the form of government of the United States . . . or the Constitution . . . or the flag . . . or the uniform of the Army or Navy into contempt, scorn, contumely, or disrepute.'' And it was possible for the Government solemnly to urge that the Sedition Act was constitutional in its argument in the *Abrams* case in 1919.

Then there was the performance of the Court in 1952 in *Beauharnais v. Illinois*, where the majority, in an opinion by Mr. Justice Frankfurter, upheld the constitutionality of a group-libel statute. One might have expected that, in dealing with a question of the application of defamation to comments about a public issue—the alleged activities of Negroes moving into white neighborhoods, the principal task of the Court would be to distinguish group libel from seditious libel. Yet the majority opinion is virtually silent on the point.

I turn, then, to the third proposition concerned with the meaning of the Court's opinion in the *Times* case. I suggest that the critical statement in Mr. Justice Brennan's opinion is: ''If neither factual error nor defamatory content suffices to remove the constitutional shield from criticism of official conduct, the combination of the two elements is no less inadequate. This is the lesson to be drawn from the great controversy over the Sedition Act of 1798, 1 Stat. 586, which first crystallized a national awareness of the central meaning of the First Amendment. See Levy, Legacy of Suppression (1960), at 258 *et seq.* . . .'' There follows an extended discussion of the ''great controversy,'' with appropriate quotations from Madison whose views the Court summarizes thus: ''The right of free public discussion of the stewardship of public officials was thus, in Madison's view, a fundamental principle of the American form of government.''

The Court then, for the first time in its history and some 166 years after the enactment of the Sedition Act, turned squarely to the issue of its constitutionality. The answer was that ''the attack upon its validity has carried the day in the court of history.'' The opinion cited Jefferson, Calhoun, Holmes, Brandeis, Jackson, Douglas, Cooley, and Chafee and concluded: ''These views reflect a broad consensus that the Act, because of the restraint it imposed upon criticism of government and public officials, was inconsistent with the First Amendment.''

The Court did not simply, in the face of an awkward history, definitively put to rest the status of the Sedition Act. More important, it found in the controversy over seditious libel the clue to "the central meaning of the First Amendment." The choice of language was unusually apt. The Amendment has a "central meaning"—a core of protection of speech without which democracy cannot function, without which, in Madison's phrase, "the censorial power" would be in the Government over the people and not "in the people over the Government." This is not the whole meaning of the Amendment. There are other freedoms protected by it. But at the center there is no doubt what speech is being protected and no doubt why it is being protected. The theory of the freedom of speech clause was put right side up for the first time.

Although the total structure of the opinion is not without its difficulties, it seems to me to convey, however imperfectly, the following crucial syllogism: The central meaning of the Amendment is that seditious libel cannot be made the subject of government sanction. The Alabama rule on fair comment is closely akin to making seditious libel an offense. The Alabama rule therefore violated the central meaning of the Amendment.

If the opinion can be read in this way, what emerges as of large importance is the generous sweep of the major premise and not the application of it to the point of defamation law involved in the *Times* case. The touchstone of the First Amendment has become the abolition of seditious libel and what that implies about the function of free speech on public issues in American democracy. The drama of the *Times* case then is that the Court, forced to extricate itself from the political impasse that was presented to it, did so by returning to the essence of the First Amendment to be found in its limitations on seditious libel. It gets to very high ground indeed.

. . .

## VI. Truth, Falsity, and Freedom of Speech

The Court's confrontation of the relevance of truth to a constitutional doctrine of free speech, closely related as it is to the idea of seditious libel, requires further consideration. Here again Mr. Justice Brennan's observations are refreshing because they far transcend in importance the resolution of the specific issue before the Court.

The question may be asked: Does the constitutional protection of freedom of speech simply establish the right to utter the truth? History makes clear that this would be no inconsiderable freedom. Certainly there are various interesting limitations in contemporary law on the immunity of truth tellers. The critical question, however, is whether falsity must not also be protected. The classic defenses of freedom of speech have all suggested that the truth should not be used to discriminate between permissible and impermissible speech, at least at the level of ideas. More recently the point has been effectively put by Alexander Meiklejohn: "The vital point . . . is that no suggestion of policy shall be denied a hearing because it is on one side of the issue rather than another. . . . These conflicting views may be expressed, must be expressed, not because they are valid, but because they are relevant." . . .

What has been less clear was the vulnerability to legal discipline of false statements of fact. And it was to this issue that Mr. Justice Brennan spoke with such force in the opinion in the *Times* case. False statements of fact, at least on public issues, are apparently to be afforded constitutional protection. Two different rationales were tendered in support of this proposition. There was stress on the likelihood that errors of fact will be made. The Court, thus, approvingly quoted from *Cantwell*'s behavioral dictum: "To persuade others of his own point of view, the pleader, as we know, at times resorts to exaggeration, to vilification of men who have been or are prominent in church or state, and even to false statement." The Court went on to state: ". . . erroneous statement is inevitable in free debate, and . . . must be protected if the freedoms of expression are to have the 'breathing space' that they 'need . . . to survive.' " Once again we are reminded that the national commitment is to debate on public issues that is "uninhibited, robust, and wide open."

The Court is also moved, however, by the difficulty of proving truth in these matters, and of putting the speaker to the risk of proof before fallible judges, juries, or administrative officials. In dealing with this proposition, the Court, put together *Smith v. California* and *Speiser v. Randall* to suggest a new category of invalid regulations: laws that tend to inhibit freedom of speech by generating a kind of "self-censorship." Thus, the bookseller in *Smith*, if left under so loose a requirement of scienter of obscenity, would tend to restrict the books he sells to those he has inspected. The law would then set off a chain reaction of self-censorship "affecting the whole public, hardly less virulent for being privately administered." And the citizen seeking tax exemption in *Speiser*, confronted with the loyalty test there involved which left the burden of proof on the applicant, would become comparably reticent. "The man who knows that he must bring forth proof and persuade another of the lawfulness of his conduct necessarily must steer far wider of the unlawful zone than if the State must bear these burdens." So too in the *Times* case, the "critic of official conduct" would be deterred from uttering what was in fact true "because of doubt whether it can be proved in court or fear of the expense of having to do so." Thus the special vice of such a law is that it introduces a self-censorship that invades the zone of permissible and lawful speech. From these three cases, all written by Mr. Justice Brennan, emerges a fascinating and promising judicial utilization of psychology.

It must be recognized, of course, that a reason implicit in the breadth of the protection afforded speech is due to the judicial recognition of its own incapacity to make nice discriminations. It reflects a strategy that requires that speech be overprotected in order to assure that it is not underprotected. In any event, the *Times* opinion is as great a contribution to the issue of the relevance of truth to protected speech as it is to the issue of the relevance of the doctrine of seditious libel.

VII. Where Are They Now?

. . .

B. Balancing

Immediately prior to the *Times* decision, the fashionable First Amendment test was what Professor Emerson called "ad hoc balancing." This formula, which he dates from the *Douds* case in 1950, has been the subject of several celebrated debates within the Court, especially between Justices Black and Harlan. The controversy has centered on large issues about absolutes and the proper role of judicial review. Professor Emerson, a critic of the balancing formula, has defined it: "The formula is that the court must, in each case, balance the individual and social interest in freedom of expression against the social interest sought by the regulation which restricts expression."

It is scarcely a novel suggestion that the law of defamation with its strict liability on the one hand and its complex of offsetting privileges on the other is a prime example of balancing the interest in freedom against the social interest sought by inhibiting communication. It is this balancing that in fact generates the bulk of the law in this area and the special fascination that it has derives from the precision and detail with which the common law has struck the balance in different situations. The issue before the Court in the *Times* case, therefore, would have been peculiarly meet for the application of the balancing formula. Again the failure to speak to the issue, either in the Court's opinion or Mr. Justice Black's concurrence, suggests the necessity for its re-evaluation.

The point, however, is even stronger. In substance, the Court adopted as its constitutional principle the so-called minority view of *Coleman v. MacLennan*, an old Kansas case that Mr. Justice Brennan quoted with approval. *Coleman* contains a stunning, extensive opinion by Justice Burch of the Kansas Supreme Court. The Burch opinion may well be the most elaborate, careful, extended act of balancing in the history of American law. It is one long, able dialogue on the problem. If ever a case was appropriate for the application of the balancing test, the *Times* case was. But, from the Court, only silence.

The silence here, however, does not suggest the same result as the silence accorded the clear-and-present danger test. It means only that the balancing cases have been treated as having too wide an application. The philosophic debate over balancing has overshot the actual area of controversy. Whatever the Court may have said, it has never used the balancing formula except in a limited type of speech case, a category in which the *Times* case did not fall.

A distinction must be drawn between cases in which legal sanctions are imposed for the specific purpose of restricting speech and those in which the control of speech is a by-product of government action that is otherwise permissible. *Douds, Bates*, and *Konigsberg*, for example, did not involve the direct application of a sanction intended to deter speech. It is in these cases that the Court has sought to solve the problems before it by some effort to balance the state's acknowledged interest against the resulting interference with speech. It seems to me that in this regard Mr. Justice Harlan has been clearer than Mr. Justice Black as to the precise scope of the issue. Mr. Justice Harlan would not balance in the ordinary case, but only in these curiously oblique speech cases where he sees no way to avoid it. Mr. Justice Black, on the other hand, often appears to treat the issue as if it involved a reappraisal of all First Amendment cases. And he insists that if there is any governmentally initiated interference with speech, however unintended and however slight, the action is unconstitutional.

I do not mean here to pass judgment on which of the Justices has the better of the argument, but only to stress that the speech issue involved in the *Times* case is different in kind from those in which the Court has utilized its balancing formula. The intended function of the tort law was to discipline certain kinds of speech. The importance of the silence of the *Times* case on the balancing test is that it cuts it down to its appropriate size.

There is, of course, a sense in which the Court did indulge in balancing. It did not go the whole way and give an absolute privilege to the "citizen-critic." It left open the possibility of liability where the defendant's actions were the result of actual malice. Like Justice Burch, therefore, it has balanced the two obvious conflicting interests. Nonetheless, the idiom of balancing was eschewed in the *Times* case not only by the majority but by the concurring opinions as well.

## C. The Two-Level Theory

Beginning with *Chaplinsky*, in 1942, and emerging as the central point of *Beauharnais* in 1952 and *Roth* in 1957, the Court developed a special technique for fitting certain kinds of free-speech problems into the constitutional framework. The technique consisted of dividing speech into two categories: that which is worthy enough to require the application of First Amendment protection and that which is beneath First Amendment concerns. The litany of lower-level speech, so often quoted from *Chaplinsky*, runs as follows: "There are certain well-defined and narrowly limited classes of speech, the prevention and punishment of which has never been thought to raise any Constitutional problem. These include the lewd and obscene, the profane, the libelous, and the insulting or fighting words." This passage had served the Court well in disposing of the problem of group libel in *Beauharnais* and of obscenity in *Roth*. It is not quoted in the *Times* case.

In this instance, however, the point is not passed over in silence. The plaintiffs had urged as a principal argument in defense of the judgment that libel was not constitutionally protected. The Court confronted the issue directly and disposed of it firmly: ". . . 'mere labels' of state law" cannot control constitutional judgment; "libel can claim no talismanic immunity from constitutional limitations. It must be measured by standards that satisfy the First Amendment." No matter how speech is classified, there must still be First Amendment consideration and review. No category of speech is any longer beneath the protection of the First Amendment. Had the *Times* case preceded *Roth*, for example, *Roth* could not have been written the way it was, although the decision might have been the same. Obscenity, too, it would seem, "can claim no talismanic immunity from constitutional limitations."

The special logic of *Chaplinsky*, *Beauharnais*, and *Roth* may well disappear now that the *Times* opinion is on the books. The two-level theory may, in any event, have been the consequence of an attempt to avoid the clear-and-present danger test. Now that that test has been obliterated, there may no longer be a need for the special technique developed to deal with it.

· · ·

## IX. Conclusion

· · ·

The closing question, of course, is whether the treatment of seditious libel as the key concept for development of appropriate constitutional doctrine will prove germinal. It is not easy to predict what the Court will see in the *Times* opinion as the years roll by. It may regard the opinion as covering simply one pocket of cases, those dealing with libel of public officials, and not destructive of the earlier notions that are inconsistent only with the larger reading of the Court's action. But the invitation to follow a dialectic progression from public official to government policy to public policy to matters in the public domain, like art, seems to me to be overwhelming. If the Court accepts the invitation, it will slowly work out for itself the theory of free speech that Alexander Meiklejohn has been offering us for some fifteen years now.

---

Arlen W. Langvardt, *Media Defendants, Public Concerns, and Public Plaintiffs: Toward Fashioning Order from Confusion in Defamation Law,* 49 UNIVERSITY OF PITTSBURGH LAW REVIEW 91 (1987)*

## I. INTRODUCTION

For the past twenty-three years the Supreme Court has wrestled with the ever-present problem of determining the extent to which the first amendment must play a role in the law of defamation. The Court's defamation decisions during that time centered around a perceived need to effect a proper balancing of speakers' first amendment freedoms of speech and press and the legitimate interests that those who are the subjects of others' statements have in preserving their respective reputations and good names. The path toward such a balance has been both irregular and interminable.

Such balancing attempts have led to the adoption of different governing constitutional standards, depending upon the status of the plaintiff. The constitutional requirements have been held to differ depending upon whether the plaintiff falls within the

---

* Reprinted with permission.

public official-public figure arena or instead is a private figure. Despite this development, the extent of the first amendment's reach into the common law of defamation has remained unclear and has become the subject of debate among members of the Supreme Court.

The Court continues to disagree over whether the status oriented rules lead to a proper balancing of conflicting reputational interests and first amendment rights. In addition, the Court has contributed to the ongoing uncertainty in defamation law by providing ambiguous, and sometimes conflicting, signals concerning whether the defamation defendant's status as a member or nonmember of the media must be thrown into the calculus. Similar indications have been given by the Court concerning whether first amendment considerations are triggered only when the defamatory speech involves a matter of public concern, and concerning whether the plaintiff bears the burden of proving the falsity of the defamatory speech. The most recent major defamation decisions, Dun & Bradstreet, Inc. v. Greenmoss Builders, Inc., and Philadelphia Newspapers, Inc. v. Hepps, have contributed significantly to the lack of clarity and certainty in the constitutional law of defamation. Dun & Bradstreet mandates that an inadequately defined ''public concern'' standard be factored into the defamation analysis with respect to private figure plaintiffs and certain constitutional fault requirements. Hepps, with its imposition of a proof of falsity requirement on the plaintiff in some defamation cases, is laudable because of the result reached. Nevertheless, it is troubling because of certain public concern-private concern and media-nonmedia problems which the plurality opinion briefly suggests but leaves essentially unexplored and unresolved.

This Article will examine the increasingly blurry yet technical constitutional law of defamation, in light of the unsettling effects of Dun & Bradstreet and the somewhat positive but, on balance, negative contributions of Hepps. In particular, the discussion and analysis will focus on three questions that linger after Dun & Bradstreet and Hepps and that deserve satisfactory answers if the constitutional law of defamation is to become more certain and clear. . . .

. . .

## III. THE PROOF OF FALSITY QUESTION: LIMITED PROGRESS TOWARD EFFECTING ORDER

. . .

### A. The Court's Tentative But Meaningful Steps

The Hepps ruling of proof of falsity is in large part commendable, although arguably too restrictive in scope. At least as to the proof of falsity question, the Court took tentative but meaningful steps toward effecting some sense of order in an otherwise confusing constitutional law of defamation. The proof of falsity holding is consistent with two common threads that tie together the Court's previous defamation decisions: first, the concept that, under the first amendment, true speech is fully protected from being the subject of a successful defamation action, and second, the idea that in order to achieve proper protection of first amendment freedoms, even some false speech must be considered protected.

Full first amendment protection from defamation liability for true speech would not be fulfilled by a requirement that the defamation defendant must prove the truth of his statements in order to escape liability. Under such a rule, defendants could be held liable even though they spoke truthfully, if they were not able to prove the truth of their statements. In addition, potential speakers would decide not to exercise their first amendment free speech rights, even as to true statements, out of fear that if a defamation action were brought against them and they were not able to prove the truth of their statements, they could be held liable for a sizeable amount of damages. A rule requiring a defamation plaintiff to prove falsity, as enunciated in Hepps, is a substantial step toward eradicating those constitutionally suspect results.

Hepps is also consistent with the thrust of the constitutional decisions that preceded it. The New York Times actual malice requirement has been read to include an implicit requirement that the public official plaintiff and the public figure plaintiff must prove the statement's falsity in addition to the defendant's fault in making the statement. Furthermore, a proof of falsity requirement is implicit in Gertz's imposition of a fault requirement in private figure plaintiff cases. The actual language used in New York Times and Gertz should be read in the context of the constitutional considerations that prompted the decisions. When such cases are read in that fashion, a requirement that the plaintiff prove falsity must be seen as part of the landmark New York Times and Gertz decisions and as part of what continues to be a necessary constitutional requirement in the law of defamation. The imposition of a constitutional requirement that the plaintiff prove falsity does not inflict a crushing blow upon the private figure plaintiff's interest in protecting his reputation. Indeed, the plaintiff ordinarily is the party in the more favorable position to present evidence bearing upon the actual truth or falsity of a statement made about him.

Another virtue of the Hepps proof of falsity ruling

is that it promotes some degree of consistency in a body of law that is not always consistent and has become increasingly technical in its content. By requiring private figure plaintiffs (at least those in cases involving statements of public concern made by a member of the media) to prove falsity, the Court is requiring the same falsity burden be imposed on public officials and public figures. There are enough technical dividing lines and rules in the constitutional law of defamation. For instance, there are the public official, public figure, and private figure classifications; the varying fault requirements attached to those classifications; the varying degrees of fault that private figure plaintiffs must prove to obtain punitive damages; the newly mandated distinctions between statements of public concern and statements of private concern; and the distinction between media defendants and nonmedia defendants. Consequently, consistency on the proof of falsity issue, at least as to public official plaintiffs, public figure plaintiffs, and private figure plaintiffs in public concern cases, is a welcome sight. . . .

## B. The Case For Extending the Hepps Rule to All Defamation Actions

Despite the positive steps taken in Hepps concerning the proof of falsity issue, the Court's approach to the issue is not without flaws. The Court's preoccupation with references to the media suggests the unsettling prospect that the vague media-nonmedia distinction may be looming just beyond the horizon, at least in the minds of some members of the Court. There is no justification for treating nonmedia defendants differently from media defendants in terms of the proof of falsity issue, unless one is willing to accept the suspect premise that in the defamation context the respective first amendment interests of media and nonmedia defendants are so different that they justify the imposition of a radically different proof of truth or falsity rule, or that the plaintiff's interest in protecting his reputation is greater when an allegedly false and defamatory statement has been made by a nonmedia defendant as opposed to when such a statement has been made by a media defendant.

Neither of these notions withstands analysis. In the defamation setting, the first amendment interests of media and nonmedia speakers are essentially coextensive. Even if the respective interests are different, this does not justify treating the two classes of defendants inconsistently with regard to the proof of truth or falsity matter. Further, the plaintiff's interest in protecting his reputation is the same, regardless of the status of the defendant. Since the first amendment

interests of media and nonmedia speakers are essentially the same, and since the plaintiff's reputation interest is no greater in the nonmedia context than in the media context, there is no reason for the plaintiff, in the nonmedia defendant case, to receive the benefit of a rule requiring the nonmedia defendant to carry the burden of persuasion concerning the truth of his statements. The Hepps Court was too cautious by insisting on confining its proof of falsity holding to media defendant cases and by expressly avoiding the question of whether the same rule would apply to nonmedia defendant cases. Regardless of the defendant's media or nonmedia status, the rule should be that the plaintiff bears the burden of proving falsity.

Another flaw in Hepps lies in the Court's insistence on confining the decision to private figure plaintiff cases involving statements on matters of public concern. This is troubling for two reasons. First, the Court in Dun & Bradstreet set forth vague contours of the public concern requirement. Second, the Court in Hepps made no effort to clarify "public concern."

There is, at best, a shaky foundation for the notion that the public concern-private concern determination contemplated by Dun & Bradstreet and Hepps will be made reasonably and consistently by lower courts. Assuming, however, that one is willing to accept such notion, it is difficult to see how even the apparently less significant first amendment value of speech on matters of private concern is accorded proper recognition by a rule requiring the defendant to prove the truth of his statement in order to escape defamation liability. The Court has noted the serious first amendment disorders inherent in a rule that places upon the speaker the obligation to prove the truth of his statements if he wishes to escape liability. Unless the Court wishes to regard speech on matters of private concern as wholly without first amendment protection, a step even the Dun & Bradstreet plurality was not inclined to take, the rule requiring the plaintiff to prove falsity must be extended beyond the public concern context to cases involving statements of private concern.

. . .

## IV. THE MEDIA-NONMEDIA QUESTION: PERSISTENT CONFUSION

Another aspect of defamation law is whether the defendant's media or nonmedia status is of any constitutional significance. The Court's approach to this question illustrates the conflicting signals emitted, and the resulting confusion wrought, in recent defamation decisions.

## A. How the Uncertainty Developed

In Hepps, the majority expressly confined its holding to cases involving media defendants. The Court reserved judgment on whether the rule it enunciated would apply in a case involving a nonmedia defendant. However, the two concurring Justices who helped to form the five-member majority expressed their views that the proof of falsity rule should apply without regard to whether the defendant was a member or nonmember of the media. The media-nonmedia preoccupation of three-fifths of the Hepps majority made its way into the decision a mere ten months after at least five Justices, in the various opinions in Dun & Bradstreet, had expressed disapproval of a media-nonmedia distinction.

The Dun & Bradstreet-Hepps combination is not the first time the Court has given vague hints on the media-nonmedia issue. Since New York Times, and especially since Gertz, there has been a question whether the constitutional rules engrafted on the common law of defamation apply only when the defendant is a member of the media. In these cases, the Court has offered conflicting indications on whether such a distinction exists. Lower courts, understandably, have split on the question.

. . .

## B. The Necessity of Rejecting the Media-Nonmedia Distinction

. . .

Various considerations point to a conclusion that the applicability of the constitutional aspects of defamation law should not hinge on the defendant's being a member of the media. Among these considerations is the important role of the freedom of speech clause in the overall first amendment scheme. Although it is possible to argue that the media has a special status under the Constitution because the press, as an institution, is guaranteed freedom by the first amendment, the intent of the Framers with regard to the speech and press clauses is unclear. Even if one accepts the notion of special constitutional status for the press, however, it does not necessarily follow that the organized media, by virtue of the press clause, is entitled to preferred treatment as compared to what is given to nonmedia defendants in the constitutional law of defamation. The public, whether part of the press or not, plays a key role in the process of creating an informed and advanced society. The freedom of speech clause must be regarded as having been premised on the principle that nonmedia speakers and media speakers serve an educative, opinion-shaping function. Otherwise, there would have been no need in the first amendment to include both the freedom of speech and freedom of press clauses. As the Court has observed, the function of providing useful, significant, and desired information cannot be regarded as the exclusive province of the press.

New York Times and Gertz, with their various references to both freedom of the press and freedom of speech, appeared to recognize the considerations mentioned above. The repeated references in these cases to the freedom of speech clause justify the conclusion that ''media-type'' terms were employed in New York Times and Gertz simply because the cases involved media defendants, and that the constitutional fault requirements enunciated in these cases should apply regardless of the defendant's media or nonmedia status. In order to regard cases such as New York Times and Gertz as merely ''free press'' cases whose fault requirements apply only in media defendant cases, one either must ignore the freedom of speech references in the opinion or adopt the curious notion that the freedom of speech clause discriminates among speakers and affords some speakers more protection than it does others.

To restrict the applicability of the constitutional fault requirements to media defendant cases would be to grant the media a preferred status carrying with it rights not granted to nonmedia speakers—something the Court has not been willing to do in other first amendment cases. In the nondefamation context, the Court has refused to give the press special rights and privileges not available to the public in general. . . .

. . .

The freedom of the press clause, which is to protect the press, would not be diminished, let alone destroyed, by the application of the same constitutional rules in all defamation cases regardless of the defendant's media or nonmedia status. Nothing would be taken away from the press under this approach. Rather, there would be a recognition, at least with regard to defamation liability, that the constitutional interests of media and nonmedia defendants are identical, and that such defendants, therefore, should be treated alike in terms of the constitutionally mandated proof of falsity and fault burden that must be carried by the plaintiff.

There are other considerations that cut against a media-nonmedia distinction in the constitutional aspects of defamation. If the constitutional fault rules were not regarded as applicable in a nonmedia defendant case, liability without fault would apply. The imposition of such liability on a nonmedia defendant would run contrary to the risk shifting concept underlying strict liability, because nonmedia defendants generally would be less able to pay and shift the costs of judgments entered against them than would media defendants. Yet nonmedia defendants would be held liable more readily than would media defendants because of the natural effects of the enhanced burden imposed on plaintiffs when the fault requirements are made part of the elements that must be proved. Further, a false and defamatory statement published by a media defendant has a greater potential for doing widespread harm to the plaintiff's reputation than does the typical false and defamatory statement by the nonmedia defendant because of the broader circulation the media defendant's statement would get. Nevertheless, if a media-nonmedia distinction were part of the constitutional law of defamation, the nonmedia defendant would be held liable much more readily than would the media defendant. Consequently, a media-nonmedia distinction is fundamentally unsound.

A media-nonmedia distinction also would occasion the practical difficulty of determining whether the defendant in fact was a member of the media. Such a determination would not be especially troublesome in typical cases. It would result, however, in inconsistent outcomes for sources such as specialized publications with a narrow audience, company newsletters, trade union publications, credit reports, handbills and brochures distributed by a group, and pamphlets handed out by the proverbial "lonely pamphleteer."

Courts inevitably would draw constitutionally suspect lines based on such factors as the size of the speaker's communications operation, the nature and scope of the publication, the extent of its circulation, and the sort of audience at which it is aimed. None of these factors is likely to lead to reliable, fair, and constitutionally sound results. Further, given the rapid technological developments that have taken place and will continue to take place in the communications field, a media-nonmedia distinction could become increasingly hazy and difficult to apply. These various classification problems would be avoided by an abandonment of any media-nonmedia distinction in the constitutional law of defamation.

## V. PUBLIC CONCERNS AND PUBLIC PLAINTIFFS: AVOIDING FURTHER CONFUSION

It is difficult to come away from a reading of the Dun & Bradstreet and Hepps decisions without acquiring a sense that further change is forthcoming in the constitutional law of defamation. In restricting its proof of falsity holding to cases involving matters of public concern, the Hepps majority followed the

lead of Dun & Bradstreet, which reintroduced the public concern concept in the context of what a private figure plaintiff must prove to recover presumed or punitive damages. It is not yet clear whether the effect of the public concern requirement extends beyond the proof of falsity issue decided in Hepps and the presumed and punitive damages issue dealt with in Dun & Bradstreet, so as to eliminate all fault requirements from the private figure-private concern case. There is support for each view on the question.

Besides raising a question about the extent of the public concern requirement's effect on private figure plaintiff cases, the Dun & Bradstreet-Hepps preoccupation with matters of public concern suggests a question that goes beyond the private figure contexts of these cases. The question is whether, in cases involving public official or public figure plaintiffs, the constitutional fault and proof of falsity rules previously imposed on such plaintiffs are to be regarded as inapplicable if the defendant's statement did not deal with a matter of public concern. Both Dun & Bradstreet and Hepps contained statements hinting at the disconcerting prospect of a new focus on the public concern-private concern determination even in public official and public figure cases. As part of its retracing of the Court's previous defamation decisions, the Hepps majority noted that "[w]hen the speech is of public concern and the plaintiff is a public official or public figure, the Constitution clearly requires the plaintiff to surmount a much higher barrier before recovering damages from a media defendant than is raised by the common law." Certain public concern references in Dun & Bradstreet were very broad and arguably unrestricted to the private figure plaintiff context. . . .

### A. The Vague Public Concern Concept

. . .

No meaningful standard is provided by the content, form, and context test set out in Dun & Bradstreet. This test amounts to little more than an implied assertion by the plurality that no stated standards are necessary to guide courts in making the public concern-private concern determination, because judges will know a matter of public concern when they see it. The problem associated with such an unprincipled approach to the public concern question is twofold. First, although judges often may recognize a matter of public concern when they see it, there is no assurance they will recognize it often enough. Second, inconsistent determinations on the now-important public concern concept will likely result. When the nature and extent of the plaintiff's damages and the defendant's liability are dependent on the public concern-private concern determination, the first amendment interests of speakers are poorly served by the vague public concern standards articulated by the Supreme Court in Dun & Bradstreet and Hepps.

It is inevitable that the essentially standardless Dun & Bradstreet-Hepps approach to the public concern question will lead to ad hoc determinations on the constitutionally suspect bases of the relative value or importance of speech. Judges necessarily will consider their own personal notions of value or importance, and those personal ideas will not always coincide with those of the public, or even those of other judges. The resulting uncertainty and inconsistency on the public concern question will likely lead to the chilling of first amendment freedoms. Speakers, uncertain of where the seemingly arbitrary public concern line will be drawn, may elect to remain silent out of fear of the consequences that could result if what appears to them to be true turns out to be false and, according to the Court, only a matter of private concern.

Perhaps the term public concern defies definition in any meaningful sense. If that is so, it is no solution, given the first amendment infirmities of the nebulous public concern requirement, to hope that lower courts will somehow divine their way to results that are constitutionally adequate. Assuming public concern cannot be defined usefully, the solution effecting a vastly more reliable protection of the first amendment interests of speakers is to opt for a set of fault requirements hinging on the status of the plaintiff—as was the situation after Gertz and its constitutional predecessors but before Dun & Bradstreet. An approach that focuses on the status of the plaintiff comes closer to achieving predictable, constitutional results than does the Dun & Bradstreet-Hepps approach which considers not only the status of the plaintiff, but also a nebulous public concern-private concern element.

. . .

B. The Unsuitability of Requiring Public Concern Determinations in the Public Plaintiff Context

Of all the potential ramifications of the renewed public concern focus exemplified by the Dun & Bradstreet and Hepps decisions, the most troublesome is the prospect that the public concern-private concern determination will be explicitly required, even in public plaintiff cases, as one of the triggering factors in determining whether the plaintiff must satisfy the constitutional proof of fault requirements. Although the Court has not definitely stated that such a determination will be required in cases involving plaintiffs who are public officials or public figures, the thrust of Dun & Bradstreet and Hepps and some of the language employed therein indicate otherwise. In particular, Hepps, with its reference to "[w]hen the speech is of public concern and the plaintiff is a public official or public figure," compels the conclusion that the Court envisions requiring both a public plaintiff (public official or public figure) and a statement dealing with a matter of public concern for the actual malice burden to be appropriate.

The actual malice burden for public officials and public figures was developed against a backdrop of furthering the interest in promoting free debate on issues of significance to the public. Both New York Times Co. v. Sullivan and Curtis Publishing Co. v. Butts devoted discussion to the presence of public issues under the facts of the cases. Nevertheless, in neither of these cases, nor in any case prior to the Dun & Bradstreet-Hepps duo, did the Court explicitly state that the actual malice fault requirement would not apply if it somehow could be shown that the offending statements, though they were about a public plaintiff, were of only private concern. The primary focus of New York Times and Butts was on the status of the plaintiff, not on the subject matter of the speech. This focus has been confirmed by the Court in the public plaintiff cases in which the actual malice rule was applied without discussion of any supposedly required public concern-private concern element.

In short, although the roots of New York Times and Butts may connect these two cases with the public issue setting, the status of the plaintiff has been regarded as the actual determining factor with regard to whether the plaintiff must prove actual malice. If, as the Hepps majority would have us believe, the public concern-private concern determination has been required for twenty-three years in public plaintiff cases, the opinions of the Court during this interval have been strangely silent about the public concern element. The reason the public plaintiff cases have not mentioned the public concern element is that New York Times and Butts have been regarded by the Court as establishing an actual malice rule that is triggered by the presence of one factor, a public plaintiff. An attempt now by the Court to require the public concern determination in the public plaintiff context would amount to a cutting back on, and substantial reworking of, the actual malice rule as it has evolved over the years. A weakening of the actual malice rule, or even an outright abandonment of the New York Times approach, would meet with the approval of at least some members of the Court, but the constitutional wisdom of such course of action is minimal at best and nonexistent at worst.

The requirement of a public concern-private concern determination in the public plaintiff context would be both impractical and unworkable. The difficulties associated with making the public concern-private concern determination in a case involving a private figure plaintiff would be present to an even greater degree if courts were expected to make meaningful decisions about whether a statement dealt with a matter of only private concern even though it pertained to a public official or public figure—the sort of person about whom the public would have a keen interest. Indeed, labeling a case as public plaintiff-private concern would be a contradiction in terms. If the Court wishes to embark on the previously uncharted course of requiring such determinations in the public plaintiff context, inconsistent results would ensue, as would a chilling of first amendment freedoms. Potential speakers would refrain from speaking freely about public officials and public figures, out of fear that a false statement made innocently about such a party would lead to devastating financial consequences for the speaker, if the court determined that the speaker's statement dealt only with a matter of private concern and therefore did not trigger application of the actual malice rule. Such uncertainty is especially troublesome in the public plaintiff setting if the Court continues to avoid setting a public concern standard and maintains the vague description of what sorts of speech fall within the public concern realm.

With regard to cases involving plaintiffs who are public officials, constitutionally sound determinations of public concern and private concern will be impossible, as the Court should have difficulty abandoning certain long established principles. It is true that in New York Times, the actual malice rule was imposed on public officials with regard to cases in which the defendants' statements pertained to such plaintiffs' "official conduct." In later cases, however, the Court quite properly gave a very broad scope to what constitutes official conduct. Garrison v. Louisiana was the first of the cases to consider the "official conduct" language of New York Times. The Court observed, in Garrison, that the actual malice rule was not rendered inapplicable by the fact that the public official plaintiff's private reputation, as well as his public reputation, was harmed by the defendant's statement. Continuing with language highlighting the fallacy underlying the Court's current inclination to require the public concern-private concern determination in public plaintiff cases, the Garrison opinion stated that the actual malice rule

protects the paramount public interest in a free flow of information to the people concerning public officials, their servants. To this end, anything which might touch on an official's fitness for office is relevant. Few personal attributes are more germane to fitness for office than dishonesty, malfeasance, or improper motivation, even though these characteristics may also affect the official's private character. . . .

The message of Garrison and Monitor Patriot [v. Roy] is unmistakable and appropriate, given the content of the first amendment. Virtually anything in the defendant's statement that some members of the public could regard as bearing upon the public official's or political candidate's fitness for office should trigger operation of the actual malice rule in a defamation action brought by a public official or political candidate on the basis of such statement. Many things that could be considered matters of private concern in a private figure plaintiff case cannot be regarded as matters of private concern in a case involving a public official or political candidate as plaintiff, because even such matters could bear, in the view of some members of the public, on such person's fitness for office. By entering the public arena, the public official and political candidate effectively abandon, for purposes of defamation law, what ability they may have had to claim that certain matters were of only private concern, because of the breadth of the "fitness for office" doctrine contemplated by Garrison and Monitor Patriot.

Requiring the public concern-private concern determination in the public official context would amount to an impermissible retreat from the constitutionally sound 'fitness for office' doctrine previously adhered to by the Court. Of course, if the Court is bent on requiring such determinations, it would seem capable of fashioning a set of rules dealing with how a statement about a public official somehow can be considered only a matter of private concern. Any such set of rules would not, however, adequately come to grips with the fundamental notion, recognized by the Court in Garrison and Monitor Patriot, that courts should not be making judgments concerning whether a certain matter is important enough or public enough for citizens properly to take into account in determining whether someone is fit for public office. The first amendment demands that the individual citizen be free to make his or her own determinations about what to consider in deciding whether a particular person should hold office. To that end, when a speaker's statement contains something that listeners or readers may find pertinent in that regard, the public official or political candidate should be required to prove actual malice in a defamation action based on such statement.

. . .

## VI. CONCLUSION

The Court's recent decisions in Dun & Bradstreet and Hepps have raised more questions than they have answered and have been essentially inadequate additions to defamation law's constitutional legacy. These decisions are the product of a Court that has become increasingly less focused in its approach to a complicated body of law. In future defamation decisions, the Court should resist the temptation to make the defamation waters muddier than they already are. Specifically, the Court should follow the lead of Hepps and extend its rule requiring the plaintiff to prove falsity in all defamation cases, regardless of whether the defendant's statements dealt with a matter of public concern or private concern, and regardless of the media or nonmedia status of the defendant. Furthermore, the Court should decide the media-nonmedia issue instead of backing away from it. This issue should be decided by clearly rejecting any media-nonmedia distinction in the constitutional law of defamation.

In addition, the Court should recognize the artificiality, uncertainty, and unworkability of the public concern doctrine it announced in Dun & Bradstreet and Hepps. The Court should not extend the application of that doctrine to eradicate the basic fault requirement imposed on private figure plaintiffs or alter the basis for requiring public plaintiffs to prove actual malice. If the Court instead insists on perpetuating the public concern doctrine, it must develop the boundaries and contours of that doctrine, so that what constitutes the all-important public concern will be more readily discernible.

---

Rodney A. Smolla, *Dun and Bradstreet, Hepps, and Liberty Lobby: A New Analytical Primer on the Future Course in Defamation Law,* 75 GEORGETOWN LAW JOURNAL 1519 (1987)*

## I. INTRODUCTION

. . .

Reforming the law of defamation has become a prominent topic of national conversation, as high vis-

* Reprinted with permission of the publisher, © 1987 The Georgetown Law Journal Association and Georgetown University.

ibility libel suits . . . pit powerful public plaintiffs against powerful media outlets, leaving in their wake a flurry of commentary critical of the modern defamation system. Because of the apparent lack of any coherent consensus on the Supreme Court as to what the first amendment rules for defamation ought to be, and the proliferation of proposals for dramatic alternations in the law of torts, the law structuring the procedure for providing legal redress for reputational injury is in a period of unprecedented flux.

The Supreme Court's most recent contributions to this dialogue are particularly perplexing. In three recent decisions, Philadelphia Newspapers, Inc. v. Hepps, Anderson v. Liberty Lobby, Inc., and Dun & Bradstreet, Inc. v. Greenmoss Builders, Inc., the Court made significant alterations in the complex matrix of first amendment rules that have been gradually superimposed on the common law of libel and slander since New York Times Co. v. Sullivan. The recent alternations in Hepps, Liberty Lobby, and Dun & Bradstreet were relatively small, and all three decisions are striking in their painstaking care to articulate as narrow a holding as possible. The irony of this precision is that the very narrowness of the holdings, when juxtaposed with the broad potential implications of the cases, has thrown the already confused law of defamation into yet deeper levels of chaos.

In the last two years it has become increasingly difficult to discern exactly what the states are free to do with the torts of slander and libel. The Court has deconstitutionalized and returned to the common law some aspects of defamation, and has constitutionalized and withdrawn from the common law other aspects. In each case, however, the Court has left unclear how much it has given and how much it has taken away. At a time in which the law of defamation is so deeply dissatisfying to plaintiffs and to defendants, and calls for reform are gaining increasing support, this doctrinal uncertainty is especially damaging, for it so clouds the picture that intelligent judgments about the future course of defamation become almost impossible to make.

One of the worst by-products of the confusion in constitutional defamation law is that it distracts attention from thoughtful management of the tort side of the system. So much legal ingenuity and energy is consumed in determining what states are constitutionally free to do, that the question of what states ought to do with the freedom they have tends to get lost in the shuffle.

A states' rights reflex appears to be at work. Because federal intervention through first amendment rules has benefited defendants, states tend to respond automatically with pro-plaintiff choices whenever those first amendment restrictions are cut loose. If defamation is increasingly to return to the common law, then it should be shaped to reflect evolving modern common law principles, which presumably ought to reflect social policies sensitive to valid interests of both plaintiffs and defendants. The rules for defamation should make sense in light of the overall structure of the tort system, they should be consistent with the developing mission of the law of torts, and they should be synchronized with both the broad theoretic structure of the tort system and with the operation of other specific torts.

· · ·

## II. THE SUPREME COURT'S MOST RECENT CONTRIBUTIONS

### A. HEPPS

· · ·

In a significant victory for the press, one that may well have caught Court watchers by surprise, the Court [in Hepps] held that the Constitution requires the burden of proof of truth or falsity to be placed on the plaintiff.

· · ·

The holding in Hepps leaves a number of important burden of proof questions unresolved. In emphasizing the media status of the defendant, the Court left open the burden of proof rule when nonmedia defendants are involved. Presumably, public officials would bear the burden of proof as plaintiffs in media and nonmedia cases alike. New York Times Co. v. Sullivan, it should be remembered, was both a media and a nonmedia case; Commissioner Sullivan sued not only the Times but also four individual black ministers who had signed the advertisement. The burden of proof in the remaining types of nonmedia cases, involving public figure and private figure plaintiffs, however, remains somewhat problematic.

Hepps also fails to establish the burden of proof when the subject matter of the speech does not involve an issue of public concern. If the preoccupation with the "issue of public concern" exhibited in both Hepps and Dun & Bradstreet, Inc. v. Greenmoss Builders, Inc. evolves into the dominant analytic principle of the modern law of defamation, then the burden of proof, even in public official and public figure cases, could conceivably be placed on defendants when the speech involves private issues. Again, because it is unclear whether the "issue of public concern" test is to be the gatekeeper for any first amendment protection, this area remains unresolved.

Hepps is, however, an important victory for the press, a victory that was by no means foreordained. Many Americans equate defamatory charges made by the media as at least symbolically equivalent to criminal charges instituted by the state, and from that equation conclude that the victim (the "accused") should be deemed innocent until proven guilty. Something is grossly amiss, this line of reasoning goes, when the defendant is given license to drag someone through the mud and then force the hapless victim to clear himself if he can. . . .

In a case presenting a configuration of speech and plaintiff like the one we face here, and where the scales are in such an uncertain balance, we believe that the Constitution requires us to tip them in favor of protecting true speech. To ensure that true speech on matters of public concern is not deterred, we hold that the common-law presumption that defamatory speech is false cannot stand when a plaintiff seeks damages against a media defendant for speech of public concern.

Under Hepps, therefore, ties go to the press. This resolution extracts a substantial cost. Hepps is only meaningful in cases in which the media has misbehaved. By hypothesis, the power of Hepps lies in its protection of stories concerning matters of public interest that were negligently, recklessly, or intentionally prepared, since the fault requirements of Gertz and New York, Times must be satisfied at the threshold in cases involving public plaintiffs or private plaintiffs and public speech.

In theory, Hepps invites the unscrupulous publisher who does not believe in the truth of the story but is confident that at any trial the truth would ultimately prove unknowable, to go ahead and publish. Even assuming that some publishers are sufficiently amoral and brazen to make this calculation, however, there are many other practical disincentives to publishing such a story. If litigation does ensue, it will be costly whether won or lost, and the uncertainties of trials are such that the niceties of the burden of proof allocation may give way to the vengeance of the outraged jury. Realistically, however, Hepps does provide safe harbor for at least some sloppy, unprofessional journalism. The powerful message of the majority opinion is that this social subsidy must be paid to give breathing space to good journalism, journalism that is aggressive, insistent, conscientious, but sometimes wrong. For defenders of the press, Hepps, for all its limitations and wrinkles, is a crucial victory.

In summary, Hepps indicates that plaintiff bears the burden of proof on the issue of truth or falsity in the following types of cases:

(1) Media defendant cases involving public of-

ficials or public figures and issues of public concern.

(2) Media defendant cases involving private figures and issues of public concern.

Hepps leaves the burden of proof issue open in the following cases:

(3) Media defendant cases involving public officials or public figures and issues of private concern.

(4) Media defendant cases involving private figures and issues of private concern.

(5) Nonmedia defendant cases involving public officials or public figures and issues of public concern.

(6) Nonmedia defendant cases involving private figures and issues of public concern.

(7) Nonmedia defendant cases involving public officials or public figures and issues of private concern.

(8) Nonmedia defendant cases involving private figures and issues of private concern.

The wisest choice in those cases left open by Hepps (cases three through eight) is to place the burden of proof on the plaintiff, creating one uniform rule for all defamation cases. . . .

The[] judgments in Hepps have only slightly diminished force when the speech is not about issues of public concern. Private truth is as valuable as public truth; for most of us the private facts of our family lives, workplaces, schools, churches, and neighborhoods are as vital as the more public facts of politics, are, and science.

More significantly, the "innocent until proven guilty" aphorism should actually operate to place the burden on the plaintiff and not the defendant if we intend defamation rules to be consistent with the rest of the law of torts. The traditional tort rule in every area except defamation is that because the plaintiff is invoking the heavy machinery of state power against a fellow citizen, the plaintiff bears the burden. The defendant is deemed innocent of tortious activity until proven guilty. Defamation has survived in some jurisdictions as an exception to this rule only because of the psychological transposition of roles that defamation suits invite. The plaintiff is thought of as the accused rather than the accuser, for it is the plaintiff's reputation at stake. But this logic does not justify the exception, because tort law routinely places the burden of proof on plaintiffs when interests every bit as precious as reputation are being litigated. The common law exception for defamation simply cannot withstand logical scrutiny.

. . .

## C. DUN & BRADSTREET

. . .

### 1. The Meaning of the "Matters of Public Concern" Standard Used in Dun & Bradstreet

. . .

It is extremely important to keep the "matters of public concern" standard articulated in Dun & Bradstreet separate from the term of art "public controversy" that is part of the "vortex public figure" Gertz test. By definition, any private figure plaintiff has already failed to thrust himself voluntarily into a public controversy—had he done so, he would be deemed a public figure. If anyone who did not fall into the public figure classification could automatically claim that the speech involved did not implicate matters of public concern, then the negligence standard in Gertz would never apply as a constitutional minimum because Gertz as reinterpreted by Dun & Bradstreet imposes the negligence requirement only in private figure/public speech cases.

Dun & Bradstreet clearly held no such thing; it did not establish an all or nothing regime. Rather, it segregated from the universe of cases involving private figures those containing defamatory speech about matters of public concern. This means that the "public concern" standard may include speech that is "public" even when the plaintiff is "private." Whereas the public controversy formulation is linked to the plaintiff's voluntary participation in the public arena, the public concern test looks primarily to the speech itself. . . .

### 2. Meshing the "Public Concern" Standard with the Public Figure/Private Figure Dichotomy

Dun & Bradstreet was a private figure plaintiff case and arguably has no impact on cases involving public officials and public figures. What constitutional standard now applies when the plaintiff is a public official or public figure but the speech involves a private matter bearing no connection to the public official's performance or fitness for duty, or no connection to the plaintiff's public figure status? This is arguably not a very significant problem, since defamatory speech about public officials or all-purpose public figures will almost always qualify as a matter of public concern. If, however, some topics remain private matters for public officials and all-purpose public figures and are therefore outside the ambit of the actual malice test, does Dun & Bradstreet authorize skipping over the negligence standard and imposing strict liability? The answer could be yes. If the speech is outside the scope of comment on public officials on public figures for which the actual malice test applies, and the speech is not about a matter of public concern, the private figure standard—strict liability—might apply.

A counterargument can be made, however, that Dun & Bradstreet should be limited to private figure cases on the theory that the Court's analysis of the case was never meant to, and simply does not fit into the public official/public figure framework. Remembering that Gertz described all-purpose public figures as plaintiffs who "occupy positions of such persuasive power and influence that they are deemed public figures for all purposes," there does not seem to be any room for carving out exceptions to the actual malice standard for such plaintiffs. And if the all-purpose public figure is always subject to the actual malice test, it does not seem logical that public officials would be subject to any less expansive coverage.

Nevertheless, the implications of Dun & Bradstreet have yet to be worked out; it seems at least possible that for certain purely private matters, defamatory speech involving public officials and all-purpose public figures could revert below the Gertz negligence standard all the way to strict liability. For the reasons discussed below, however, any move to strict liability should be rejected, whatever the configuration of speech and plaintiff.

## III. FAULT STANDARDS

## V. A NEUTRAL READING OF DUN & BRADSTREET, AND THE STRICT LIABILITY QUESTION

As Justice Powell was careful to emphasize in the opening paragraph of Dun & Bradstreet, only the Gertz presumed and punitive damages rules were technically before the Supreme Court. Thus, the question whether the Gertz fault rules are also swept away in cases not involving matters of public importance remains open. More specifically, Dun & Bradstreet fails to answer conclusively this question: May a state impose common law strict liability standards in cases involving private figure plaintiffs and defamatory speech not involving matters of public concern, or does the Gertz prohibition on liability without fault continue to apply to all private figure cases? . . .

The plurality opinion contained a number of clues indicating that the Justices joining the opinion would probably not overturn a decision by a state to return to strict liability in private figure cases not involving speech of public concern. First, throughout the opinion, Justice Powell's language slipped from the narrow formulation of the issue before the Court to a broader phrasing of the question in terms of whether the Gertz rule was controlling. This phraseology suggested that Powell would abandon all of Gertz, not just its damage rules, in such cases. Second, Justice Powell's opinion was an important signal because it quoted with approval language from the Oregon Supreme Court's decision in Harley-Davidson Motorsports, Inc. v. Markley, the leading state court decision applying strict liability in a private figure nonmedia situation. The Court also cited with approval Denny v. Mertz, a Wisconsin Supreme Court decision that held that all the Gertz protections were inapplicable when a private figure sued a nonmedia defendant.

Finally, applying Justice Powell's analytic structure on the damages issues to the strict liability question, it is evident that he would permit strict liability in such cases. His methodology was simply to balance the importance of the type of speech involved against the state's interest in applying the common law rule. He strongly downgraded the constitutional significance of speech not involving matters of public concern. The only significant question was whether the state's interest in applying its common law strict liability rule was as strong as its interest in applying its common law presumed and punitive damages rules. . . .

. . . The state's interest in the strict liability rule appears much stronger than the state's interest in awarding punitive damages on something less than actual malice. The strict liability principle goes to the essence of the tort at common law, representing the state's interest in protecting the defamed individual's dignity and easing the path to compensation. The punitive damages rule has only the purposes of punishment and deterrence to support it. From a plaintiff's perspective the strict liability standard is probably of greater aid in vindicating reputation than the common law punitive damages rule, which still requires proof of common law malice.

When comparing the state's interest in permitting presumed damages to its interest in applying strict liability, the analysis is somewhat more complex. Both rules clearly further the state's general interest in providing effective remedies for defamation. The two rules complement each other at common law and work to facilitate a plaintiff's recovery.

The presumed damages rule, however, has an additional ground to support it that the strict liability rule does not: the difficulty of proof. Whereas there is some common sense to the notion that harm to reputation is often present but cannot be seen or proven, there is no comparable difficulty with proving the existence or nonexistence of negligence, a routine issue in tort cases.

This potential distinction may be regarded by many courts as too thin to justify any difference in the constitutional treatment of the two rules. On the one hand, given the already broad constitutional definition of "actual harm," the additional bonus given a plaintiff through the presumed harm rules may be overrated, since few plaintiffs have found the actual harm requirement a complete barrier to recovery, if it is a barrier at all.

The requirement of proving negligence, however, may at times be a substantial impediment. Defendants may often have a monopoly on the information necessary to establish fault, and a plaintiff's efforts to prove negligence may often be frustrating and costly. If one views Dun & Bradstreet as something of an exercise in federalism, returning to the states greater power to superintend state defamation law, then strict liability may well be seen as a powerful plaintiff's weapon that in many cases serves the state's interests as much or more than presumed harm rules. Viewed in these terms, a neutral reading of Dun & Bradstreet could legitimately treat the case as opening the door to a return by states, if they wish, to strict liability standards, at least in private figure cases not involving defamatory speech related to matters of public concern.

## B. THE CASE AGAINST THE RETURN TO STRICT LIABILITY IN ANY AREA OF DEFAMATION

To concede that Dun & Bradstreet may permit states the freedom to return to strict liability in certain cases is not to concede that such a doctrinal regression is desirable. A return to strict liability in any aspect of the law of defamation would be a regrettable mistake; a number of powerful arguments counsel against such a move. The arguments against adoption of strict liability may be put to dual service. First, they provide rationales both for not interpreting Dun & Bradstreet as authorizing strict liability and for adopting one uniform national federal "floor" negligence rule in all defamation cases not subject to actual malice principles. Second, if one assumes the worst (from the media's perspective)— that Dun & Bradstreet frees states from federal constitutional compulsion with regard to liability rules in some circumstances, such as private figure/private speech cases—then the arguments discussed below may be marshaled to argue against a move to strict liability as a matter of state law.

### 1. The Common Law Strict Liability Standard Was an Anomaly Even Prior to New York Times

The common law rule of strict liability for defamation was an anomaly within the overall structure of tort law even before New York Times began to constitutionalize defamation. Scholars disagree as to whether the primary liability rule prior to the coher-

ent emergence of the body of law we now call "torts" was strict liability or negligence. With the industrial revolution and the birth of the law of torts as an independent doctrinal system, the lines of demarcation became quite clear. The dominant liability rule in America was negligence. The full intellectual weight of common law theorists from Holmes to Cardozo to Hand stood behind the proposition that the cumbersome machinery of the state should not transfer injury losses from the victim to the tortfeasor unless the victim could bear the burden of proof that the tortfeasor was at fault.

The tort system did have limited areas in which strict liability displaced the negligence principle. Strict liability was principally reserved for activity that could be classified as ultrahazardous or abnormally dangerous. Tests for strict liability may have varied slightly in verbal formulation from state to state, but the essential requirements remained the same. The activity had to be uncommon, and it had to be an activity in which a high risk of harm could not be eliminated even through the observance of extraordinary care.

In an analytic structure dominated by negligence, the strict liability standard for defamation stuck out like a sore thumb, existing purely because of the inertia of history. It was an island of strict liability in a sea of negligence, out of harmony with the rest of the landscape. None of the traditional justifications for strict liability applied to defamation law. Speech was not uncommon; quite to the contrary, it was as common as breathing, indistinguishable from the thousands of routine activities of social life to which the negligence rule applied. Nor was speech by any measure abnormally dangerous or ultrahazardous in the graphic and physical sense of other strict liability applications. There was no plausible analogy to dynamite blasting, keeping ferocious animals, or building reservoirs. Strict liability for defamation was never defended by anyone on these grounds since such an attempt would have been ridiculous. . . .

### 2. The Analogy to Modern Products Liability Standards is Inappropriate

If strict liability for defamation cannot fit comfortably into the tort system's traditional classification of an ultrahazardous activity, it may nonetheless be compatible with a more modern manifestation of strict liability—products liability law. Perhaps the irony of defamation's peculiar place in the system has come full circle, so that a return to the past becomes a move back to the future, not anachronistic but avant-garde. Indeed, there are superficial similarities between defamatory falsehoods disseminated by media outlets and defective products produced by manufacturers. . . .

However, the superficial attractiveness of drawing a parallel between defamation and products liability dissolves on closer analysis.

Distinguishing Tangible from Intangible Injury. . . . A look at the broad expanse of tort rules in areas other than defamation indicates that the use of strict liability for defamation would run directly contrary to the following rough and ready theorem for all tort law: the less tangible the injury, the higher the level of fault required to state a prima facie case. The rules for cases involving injuries other than physical harm to persons and property, such as emotional and economic harm, almost invariably require conduct more egregious than mere negligence.

. . .

The Flaw in the "Defective Product/Unreasonably Dangerous" Analogy. Equating defamation with strict products liability is inappropriate because the central operative standard in products cases, the notion of a defect unreasonably dangerous to the user or consumer, is not strict liability in any pure sense, and is not equivalent to strict liability when used in the defamation context. Tort theorists, practicing attorneys, and judges have for a long time recognized that to some degree the term "strict liability" in products law is a misnomer. In the fast lanes of products litigation, involving alleged design defects and failure to warn theories, strict liability principles and negligence principles merge to form a hybrid standard that includes fault principles. . . .

The Irony of the Analogy in Nonmedia Cases. Strict products liability rules have generally been applied only to entities within the chain of commercial distribution of new products. Remote manufacturers, primary manufacturers, distributors, wholesalers, and retailers have all been trapped in the net of strict liability rules. Generally speaking, however, the private market for products (for instance, the sale of used lawnmowers and automobiles in local want ads) has not been subject to strict products liability. Legal recourse for the injured victim in private transactions is normally limited to whatever the law of contracts or fault related tort rules (fraud, for example) provides.

To the extent that a state attempts to impose strict liability on nonmedia speakers but not on media speakers, an occasional pre-Dun & Bradstreet choice and a very possible post-Dun & Bradstreet option, the state actually reverses its normal pattern. Imposing strict liability on nonmedia speakers but not on media speakers is like excusing General Motors for a defect in a new Chevrolet while holding strictly liable the private seller who sells it through the newspapers a year later. This inequity, of course, may be corrected in two ways: by ignoring the media/nonmedia distinction and imposing strict liability in all cases in which it is otherwise permissible, or by ignoring the media/nonmedia distinction and imposing strict liability in none of these cases. For the reasons expressed in this section, the more logically consistent choice is never to impose strict liability.

Self-Censorship as the Cost Avoidance Response. The final reason for rejecting the analogy to strict products liability applies primarily to the media, and goes to the unique nature of the industry. The press faces different market incentives and disincentives than do most other industries, because of factors unique to the dissemination of information. Manufacturers of tangible products respond to the imposition of strict liability rules by accepting the liability as a cost of doing business, and if necessary by increasing the costs of their products. Strict products liability may force manufacturers to internalize costs, but it normally should not cause manufacturers to drop product lines altogether. The media, however, may respond to strict liability in a manner not at all socially desirable—by avoiding all controversy and selling a watered down product. . . .

## IV. A FINAL SUBJECT OF DOCTRINAL CONFUSION—THE MEDIA/NONMEDIA DISTINCTION

In the aftermath of Gertz there was considerable debate over whether the holding ought to be applied to media and nonmedia speakers alike. Several states specifically held Gertz inapplicable to nonmedia defendants when the plaintiff was a private figure. When the plaintiff was a public official or public figure, however, decisions generally held that the actual malice standard governed even against nonmedia defendants.

Rejecting the media/nonmedia distinction altogether, some decisions found Gertz applicable even to cases involving private figure plaintiffs and nonmedia defendants. The Supreme Court, in Hutchinson v. Proxmire, stated in a footnote that the applicability of the actual malice standard of New York Times in the nonmedia context remained an open issue.

For a fleeting moment, Dun & Bradstreet seemed to have ended the debate. Arguably, a majority of the Justices in Dun & Bradstreet either explicitly or implicitly rejected the media/nonmedia distinction. The plurality opinion of Justice Powell rested on the "public concern" test rather than the media/nonmedia distinction, and at one point Justice Powell stated that the Gertz protections were not "justified solely by reference to the interest of the press and broadcast media in immunity from liability." . . .

Hepps threw the apparent resolution of Dun & Bradstreet into disarray. As previously noted, the majority opinion by Justice O'Connor expressly treated the issue as open, and conspicuously framed the issue before the Court as a case involving a private figure plaintiff, public speech, and a media defendant. Only Justice Brennan, in a brief concurrence joined by Justice Blackmun, pressed the point, arguing as he had in Dun & Bradstreet that the maintenance of a media/nonmedia distinction is irreconcilable with the first amendment principle that the value of speech does not depend on the identity of the speaker.

The best educated guess, however, is that the Court will ultimately reject the media/nonmedia distinction. Dun & Bradstreet, which superimposes the "matters of public concern" analysis upon the public figure/private figure dichotomy, seems to have been the Court's substitute for a media/nonmedia distinction. To add a media/nonmedia distinction would complicate matters beyond all manageability. Significantly, the distinction has several vocal and vigorous opponents on the Court, but no openly professed defenders—at most a majority seem disinclined to face the issue.

· · ·

## VI. CONCLUSION

If it is true that the Supreme Court is gradually allowing the states to govern more and more aspects of defamation through common law, then it is also true that states should consider the overall common law system of which defamation is a part in making doctrinal choices concerning its development. If defamation is to become, once again, more a part of the family of torts than the family of constitutional law, then it should be made to live in harmony with the rest of the tort family.

---

Diane L. Zimmerman, *Requiem for a Heavyweight: A Farewell to Warren and Brandeis' Privacy Tort,* 68 CORNELL LAW REVIEW 291 (1983)*

## INTRODUCTION

In 1890, Samuel Warren and Louis Brandeis

stirred the American legal community with a ringing call to arms to protect the hapless citizenry against the truthful exposure of their personal affairs on the pages of the "yellow press." Warren and Brandeis dubbed the protection they proposed a "right to privacy," and described it as the right "to be let alone." Their advocacy of this new tort created a minor revolution in the development of the common law.

Nonetheless, even after ninety years, the real impact of that revolution on legislatures and courts is hard to evaluate. Depending upon the biases of the viewer, the article's effect could be said to exemplify the power, the impotence, or even the perniciousness of legal scholarship. Those who assert that the impact of the article demonstrates the power of scholarship point out that the Warren-Brandeis argument led most states in this country to recognize a right to recover in tort for the wrongful public exposure of private information, as well as for a wide range of other invasions of privacy.

The impotence argument contends, however, that despite the ever-increasing number of claims under the Warren-Brandeis theory, plaintiffs rarely win. One frustrated judge exclaimed in an impassioned dissent that if a right to be protected against the publication of truthful information indeed existed within his state, his colleagues should honor it "by more than lip service."

Finally, one can argue that the Warren-Brandeis contribution has actually had a pernicious influence on modern tort law because it created a cause of action that, however formulated, cannot coexist with constitutional protections for freedom of speech and press.

The constitutional dilemma posed by the Warren-Brandeis tort inevitably implicates the companion problem of the failure of this branch of law to protect plaintiffs. The confusion that has attended the effort to create a firm legal contour for the tort merely reflects the inherent difficulty under the first amendment of treating truthful speech as tortious. The Warren-Brandeis tort posits a legal power to control the flow of information about one's self to other people— the right to govern authoritatively both the nature of personal information exposed to public view and the conditions under which others may discuss those personal facts. Yet even the most enthusiastic advocates of a right to privacy, including Warren and Brandeis, recognized that any absolute protection of such an interest would intolerably hamper human discourse.

From the outset, advocates of privacy have thus faced a dual, and sometimes internally inconsistent, task. On the one hand, they needed to develop a philosophical basis to support the right through an exploration of why a civilized and humane society should recognize and protect an interest in controlling public discussion of personal information. On the other hand, they had to protect free speech by creating numerous defenses and narrowing the scope of the privacy tort, so that much personal information could circulate without penalty.

The challenge of harmonizing privacy with free speech has attracted many outstanding scholars of tort and constitutional law. The moral force of the privacy argument has compelled most commentators to attempt to entrench the private-facts tort firmly in modern law. They have stated the case in favor of the Warren-Brandeis right of privacy eloquently and forcefully. In their attempt to justify the tort, however, they have often underplayed its serious constitutional problems and have overlooked the fact that genuine social values are served by encouraging a free exchange of personal information. This article seeks not to restate what has already been argued so well in favor of the private-facts tort, but, by presenting the opposite view, to encourage a re-evaluation of the prevailing doctrine. Is it possible that the seemingly elegant vessel that Warren and Brandeis set afloat some nine decades ago is in fact a leaky ship which should at long last be scuttled?

. . .

## II

## THE HISTORY OF PROTECTING TRUTHFUL SPEECH

### A. The Framers' Intent: A Study of Truth as a Defense to Defamation Preceding the Adoption of the First Amendment

The history of the common law of defamation provides a useful point of departure for analysis. Although not dispositive, that history may shed some light on the meaning of the first amendment and on the intent of its framers—to the extent that any such intent may be discerned—and provide some insight into the impropriety of treating truthful speech as tortious. The long tradition of allowing defamation actions that preceded the adoption of the Bill of Rights, coupled with the uniform acceptance of such causes of action by the original states, suggest that the framers could not have expected the first amendment to prohibit the punishment of false and injurious speech. Privacy, in contrast, was not a recognized interest at the time the Bill of Rights was adopted. And nothing in the history of the common law suggests even a tacit acceptance on the part of the framers of civil liability for accurate but personally embarrassing speech. England has never recognized the tort of invasion of privacy. Even the precedents relied on by Warren and Brandeis in 1890 protected privacy interests only as an incident to the recognition of some other independent interest, such as a property right.

Indeed, despite some confusion in the sources, English and early American law seemed affirmatively to protect truthful but discreditable speech, at least from civil liability. English sources, from the earliest up until the adoption of the common law by the United States, recognized truth as an absolute defense in tort actions for defamation. The defense was not technical; rather, it seems to have reflected the prevailing view that sound social policy precluded legal recognition of the harm caused by speaking the truth.

. . .

### B. The Supreme Court's Protection of Truthful Speech in Modern Case Law

#### 1. The Fault Standard in Defamation Cases Requires a Defense of Truth

Supreme Court decisions over the course of the twentieth century suggest that the Court shares the historical understanding that the first amendment protects truthful speech in all but the most extreme situations. As recently as 1979, Chief Justice Burger, after reviewing a wide range of the Court's first amendment opinions, concluded that "state action to punish the publication of truthful information can seldom satisfy constitutional standards."

The most illuminating line of Supreme Court cases on the question of when, if ever, states may provide damage awards for truthful but embarrassing communications are the libel and false-light privacy cases beginning in the 1960s. Both lines of cases deal with tort law and involve interests roughly comparable to those at stake in the private-facts cases. In addition, these opinions are the first in which the Court deals directly with the theoretical implication of truth and falsity for the scope of constitutional protection of speech.

The Court's decisions in New York Times Co. v. Sullivan and its progeny leave little doubt that truth should be considered a constitutionally mandated defense, at least in the context of common law tort actions for harmful speech. The Court has declared the Sullivan line of cases to rest upon the premise that false speech can be regulated because it has no constitutional value. In Gertz v. Robert Welch, Inc., the Court confirmed that proposition:

> Neither the intentional lie nor the careless error materially advances society's interest in "uninhibited, robust, and wide-open" debate

on public issues. . . . They belong to that category of utterances which "are no essential part of any exposition of ideas, and are of such slight social value as a step to truth that any benefit that may be derived from them is clearly outweighed by the social interest in order and morality."

Because the Court finds false speech constitutionally valueless because it does not contribute to public debate or a search for truth, it follows logically that its opposite—accurate speech—must deserve substantial protection. The Court, therefore, would presumably regard state laws restricting free exchange of accurate speech with skepticism, if not outright disapproval. . . .

. . .

## III

## COMPETING INTERESTS IN THE PRIVATE-FACTS TORT

In his Cox [Broadcasting Corp. v. Cohn] concurrence, Justice Powell distinguished between the interests underlying defamation and those underlying private-facts actions: "causes of action grounded in a State's desire to protect privacy generally implicate interests that are distinct from those protected by defamation." In so doing, he left open the possibility that those undefined privacy interests might be so substantial as to justify liability for true speech despite the Gertz rule. Justice Powell thus raises a critical question about the precise nature and weight of the asserted state interest in permitting a cause of action for truthful but embarrassing disclosures of private facts.

The Court in Smith v. Daily Mail Publishing Co. made it very clear that state action infringing on the fundamental rights of speech and the press must pass strict judicial scrutiny. The Court reviewed a West Virginia statute making it a criminal offense to publish the name of someone charged as a juvenile offender and concluded—at least as to matters of "public significance," "[I]f a newspaper lawfully obtains truthful information . . . then state officials may not constitutionally punish publication of the information, absent a need to further a state interest of the highest order."

At present, few clues exist to determine what constitutes a "state interest of the highest order" in the privacy-tort area. The Court did not need to weigh interests in its libel decisions because it found that deliberate falsehoods were totally outside the purview of the first amendment, and that negligent falsehoods do not contribute anything important to the free marketplace of ideas. Since this speech was not

protected, the Court did not need to decide if the interest in regulating it was a "state interest of the highest order." But even if the weight of the states' interest in providing redress for libel were an issue, the ancient common law history of protecting individuals from defamation provided the Court with a basis for finding the states' purpose sufficiently substantial. History provides no equivalent support for the Warren-Brandeis notion of a protection for the right to privacy. That interest, therefore, will have to swing alone on the scales of justice without the heavy thumb of a thousand years of Anglo-American legal development to lend it bulk.

A. The Substantiality of the Interests Protected By the Privacy Tort

. . .

How . . . could a state convince the Court that the interest protected by the private-facts tort outweighs the constitutional interest in free speech? Presumably, it would need first to be able to articulate the reasons that justify creation of a legal remedy for unwanted revelations about the self, and that might be difficult to do.

The commentators are in considerable disagreement over how to describe the purposes of this tort. Dean Prosser, for example, suggested that the tort protects two interests: an interest in freedom from emotional distress, and an interest in preventing reputational injury. Other commentators contend that the tort protects only against emotional harm, and ignore or deny the relevance of reputational injury to these privacy cases. Bloustein rejects both the reputational and emotional distress arguments, and responds that the tort, in preserving some "right to be let alone," really protects "individual dignity and integrity," and prevents the loss of "individual freedom and independence."

The factual situations which have generated law suits in this area of tort law give but small aid in choosing among these theories. Some cases clearly involve both reputational harm and the probable infliction of substantial amounts of mental distress; plaintiffs in those suits seek to recover to some extent for the damage to their standing in their communities. But other cases may involve only one, or none, of these elements. . . .

. . . What these plaintiffs do seem to have in common is a dislike of being talked about by the general public, and a willingness to use the courts to complain about it—ironically, even when the probable result is further publicity for the supposedly "private" facts at issue. That a dislike of publicity emerges as the surest common denominator of the private-facts cases is not surprising. After all, a dislike of publicity is exactly what impelled Warren and Brandeis to suggest the creation of the privacy right in the first place. When weighed against the social and constitutional costs of preventing such publicity, however, a legal action to support such a distaste is not highly compelling. Even if one were to assume that each case involved at least emotional injury and damage to dignity and that many also involve reputational harm, it remains unclear whether preventing such harm is a social interest of sufficient magnitude to give the states a right to limit free speech.

## 1. The Problems Associated with Compensating Emotional Harm

Regardless of the source of the injury, a tort recovery based solely or largely on claimed psychological harm (within which I would include emotional distress and possibly injuries to dignity) hardly rests on firm legal ground. Traditionally, courts were extremely reluctant to compensate plaintiffs for emotional harms except as an adjunct to awards of damages for other injuries that the courts deemed more concrete and easier to value. . . .

The risk that damages awarded for emotional distress may exceed the harm done is acceptable in some areas of tort law because the law wants to discourage the underlying behavior. When the alleged injury results from speech, however, the threat of uncontrolled jury verdicts poses an entirely different problem. The Constitution seeks to encourage speech except in rare and especially egregious forms. As the Supreme Court has recognized, the risk of large, speculative damage awards chills desirable as well as undesirable speech, and does so as effectively as can the threat of a prison sentence or criminal fine.

## 2. A Case for the Positive Value of Gossip

The privacy tort not only poses problems of definition and damages, but also rests upon a dubious assumption that society has a greater interest in protecting certain details of an individual's life than in protecting the values on which our traditional constitutional preference for unrestricted speech depends. A closer examination raises serious doubts, however, as to whether our society in reality has ever placed so high a value on protecting an individual's reputation, dignity or emotional security from the assaults of true disclosures.

The literature on privacy has emphasized the social and philosophical bases supporting the notion that law should protect against publication of private facts. What is "private" has been variously defined by courts and commentators, but in the aggregate includes a wide range of data about individuals' character, personality, and social behavior. The privacy literature, however, has rarely acknowledged a contrary body of evidence, casting doubt on the preeminent value of privacy and suggesting that the communication of information about such personal matters may serve a useful and productive social function. To the extent that this expression has worth, arguments for its suppression need serious reconsideration.

History, religious doctrines, literature, and the social sciences are replete with examples that suggest our society is at least ambivalent about the weight to assign to interests in personal privacy when they compete with the value of truthfulness about the character and activities of our neighbors. . . .

The reasons behind such ambivalence are easily uncovered. Most of us have some personal traits or indiscretions that we would prefer to remain unknown. We may also believe, as a matter of ethics, religious training, or simple good manners, that it is wrong, unkind or vulgar to make certain revelations about others. Yet, we at least tacitly recognize that the cohesiveness and durability of any social organization depends upon the ability of its members to evaluate each other accurately and to use their observations to exert, modify, or develop social controls.

Two sources support this assertion. First, social scientists in this century have developed both an understanding of the constructive functions of gossip and a recognition of its universality in human communities. Second, history suggests that we have intuitively appreciated the benefits of free exchange of gossip for a long while and that our understanding of its value may well have been a major force in the extraordinary reluctance of the English common law to develop legal sanctions against truthful speech. . . .

### a. Gossip from a Historical Perspective. . . .

Historians' accounts of the structure of English society support the notion that gossip, although occasionally irksome, was on the whole perceived as having genuine social value. Stone maintains that during the period from 1500 to 1800, close observation by one's neighbors, servants, and members of the extended kinship group was an immutable fact of life for rich and poor alike. Living conditions and prevailing social mores led people to expect little privacy, even in the home. Even sexual intimacies were somewhat public events. Not surprisingly, prying, observing, and gossiping about the behavior of others were commonplace, and the ecclesiastical courts entertained an active trade in denunciations of misbehavior and sexual peccadillos. In addition to the controls exerted by the church, the secular authorities and neighbors themselves used devices from stocks to skimmingtons to chastise observed deviations from behavioral norms. A society so dependent on gossip as a form of social control understandably would be reluctant to discourage truthful speech by making it a basis of liability in a defamation action. . . .

b. The Function and Persistence of Gossip in Contemporary Life.

Superficial differences, of course, do exist between contemporary practices and those of early England and America. Spying through keyholes and chinks in walls is now as unacceptable as maintaining dunking stools and public whippings. Our mobile and industrial society offers opportunities for anonymity unimagined by inhabitants of the small, cohesive towns and villages of rural England and early America. Yet, contemporary communities still enjoy considerable knowledge about the private lives of individual members, and still use that knowledge to preserve and enforce social norms. This appears to be true across all social strata, in urban neighborhoods as well as in small towns and rural areas. To a large extent, the development of modern popular journalism paralleled the growth of less intimate communities. The press, therefore, when it provides information about the private lives of both famous and ordinary people, could be viewed merely as performing a traditional function that no longer can be accomplished by person-to-person gossip alone.

Moreover, gossip—the exchange of personal information about character, habits and lifestyles—does not merely serve as an instrument of social control. Students of the phenomenon claim that gossip, and the rules governing who participates and who is privy to what information about whom, helps mark out social groupings and establish community ties. By providing people with a way to learn about social groups to which they do not belong, gossip increases intimacy and a sense of community among disparate individuals and groups. Gossip may also foster the development of relationships by giving two strangers the means to bridge a gap of silence when they are thrown together in a casual social situation. . . .

The private-facts tort is thus both constitutionally and practically untenable. A serious effort to enforce a general right to be free of unwanted publicity about private facts would probably be as successful as the attempt to enforce temperance through the ill-fated eighteenth amendment, or the effort to use the law to prevent extramarital sexual intercourse.

. . .

. . . [A] state can justify a content-based regulation of speech, such as the private-facts tort, only if it can demonstrate a clearly defined harm and a compelling interest in its prevention. But the nature of the harm done by publication of private facts has continued for almost a century to elude more than vague, subjective definition. Furthermore, because society has a powerful countervailing interest in exchanges of accurate information about the private lives and characters of its citizenry, a compelling case for a general right to suppress such exchanges is difficult to construct. Many decades ago, a commentator on the budding tort of invasion of privacy cautioned that publicity about our private affairs may be among the "impertinent and disagreeable things which one may suffer" but which do not "amount to legal injuries such as courts may redress." However uncomfortable that conclusion is, it may well have turned out to be right.

IV

THE POSSIBILITY THAT A NARROW RIGHT TO RECOVER FOR PUBLICATION OF PERSONAL FACTS COULD BE PRESERVED, CONSISTENT WITH CONSTITUTIONAL VALUES

Even those writers most sensitive to the constitutional thorniness of the private-facts tort have nonetheless insisted that it could be so shaped as to salvage a cause of action for those plaintiffs who suffer particularly painful publicity. For the sake of argument, let us assume that some particular facts are so intimate and revealing that their disclosure would probably cause most individuals serious distress and strain their relationships with others. Let us also assume that compensation of these individuals for that harm is a sufficiently substantial state interest to justify limitation of the defendant's right of free speech. At the same time, common sense and concern that free speech not be choked off at the roots require some limits on the extent to which communications can be made tortious. Courts and legislatures must therefore face the difficult process of delineating standards that permit recovery in serious cases, while not also encouraging costly litigation over injuries that are more trivial.

This narrowed tort would have to be defined precisely and clearly enough that a publisher would have fair warning of the approximate location of the line between protected and unprotected revelations. Although the Supreme Court has consistently refused to rule that any speech—including accurate speech—is absolutely protected by the Constitution, the Court has also been equally insistent that the Constitution condemns vague regulation. The Court has stated repeatedly that vague proscriptions against speech may chill the willingness of individuals and the media to take part in those communicative activities that are clearly protected by the first amendment. The Court has developed the doctrines of vagueness and overbreadth to address this concern. . . .

The problem of finding clear and precise demarcations between protected and unprotected speech in the private-facts area actually occupied the attention of judges and scholars even before the Supreme Court began developing modern free speech law. No court has wanted to grant plaintiffs carte blanche to veto what could be said about them by mass communicators. Yet, after all the years devoted to the task, no one has yet developed a set of satisfactory and uniformly applied definitional standards. . . .

## CONCLUSION

After ninety years of evolution, the common law private-facts tort has failed to become a usable and effective means of redress for plaintiffs. Nevertheless, it continues to spawn an ever-increasing amount of costly, time-consuming litigation and rare, unpredictable awards of damages. In addition, this "phantom tort" and the false hopes that it has generated may well have obscured analysis and impeded efforts to develop a more effective and carefully tailored body of privacy-protecting laws.

Many of the most troubling privacy questions today arise not from widespread publicizing of private information by the media, but from electronic eavesdropping, exchange of computerized information, and the development of data banks. Much of this information, which individuals supply as a necessary prerequisite to obtaining important benefits like credit, medical care, or insurance, can cause serious harm, even if circulated only to one or two unauthorized recipients. Privacy law might be more just and effective if it were to focus on identifying (preferably by statute) those exchanges of information that warrant protection at their point of origin, rather than continuing its current, capricious course of imposing liability only if the material is ultimately disseminated to the public at large. . . .

More thought should also be given to increasing the use of legal sanctions for the violation of special confidential relationships, in order to give individuals greater control over the dissemination of personal information. The lawyer-client relationship provides a useful model. A client who hires an attorney expects the attorney to keep confidential all disclosures made by the client in the course of the professional relationship. Breach of this duty gives rise to an action for damages. The contractual duty of confidentiality puts both parties on notice of the communica-

tions to be protected and the rights and responsibilities that the relationship creates.

States have only intermittently recognized rights of contractual confidentiality in other relationships. Contractual or quasi- contractual notions of confidentiality, of course, can pose major constitutional dilemmas of their own, particularly when the government is one of the parties to the contract and the scope of the information to be controlled is broad. In the context of private commercial and professional services, however, a careful identification of particularly sensitive situations in which personal information is exchanged, and an equally careful delineation of the appropriate expectations regarding how that information can be used, could significantly curtail abuses without seriously hampering freedom of speech. At the very least, this possibility merits considerably more thought as an alternative to the Warren-Brandeis tort than it has received thus far.

. . . As centuries of experience have shown, many of the most important aspects of human relationships are beyond the reach of the law and must work themselves out in the imprecise laboratory of manners and mores. Some human problems are impervious to legal solution because they involve social ideals that do not readily translate into intelligible legal theory; some elude legal resolution because we cannot clearly identify and balance the relevant social and moral values; and we refuse to resolve some human problems by law because we are unwilling to bear the cost that legal solutions would impose. Perhaps the problem identified by Warren and Brandeis has been incapable of resolution in the courts because, after nearly a century of experience, it has proved woefully vulnerable on all three counts. If so, it is probably time to admit defeat, give up the efforts at resuscitation, and lay the noble experiment in the instant creation of common law to a well-deserved rest.

---

Russell L. Weaver & Geoffrey Bennett, *Is The New York Times "Actual Malice" Standard Really Necessary? A Comparative Perspective,* 53 LOUISIANA LAW REVIEW 1153 (1993)*

In *New York Times Co. v. Sullivan*, the United States

---

Supreme Court extended First Amendment guarantees to defamation actions. Many greeted the Court's decision with joy. Alexander Meiklejohn claimed that the decision was "an occasion for dancing in the streets." He believed that the decision would have a major impact on defamation law, and he was right. After the decision, many years elapsed during which "there were virtually no recoveries by public officials in libel actions."

The most important component of the *New York Times* decision was its "actual malice" standard. This standard provided that, in order to recover against a media defendant, a public official must demonstrate that the defendant acted with "malice." In other words, the official must show that the defendant knew that the defamatory statement was false or acted in reckless disregard for the truth. The Court adopted this standard because it felt that free and robust debate inevitably generates erroneous statements, and that some degree of error must be tolerated in order to provide "breathing space" for free expression.

But the *New York Times* decision may no longer be providing the breathing space that it once did. Recent studies suggest that libel litigation in the United States is increasing and that defamation awards occur more frequently and in much larger amounts. Such information prompted Professor Richard Epstein of the University of Chicago Law School to observe recently that "the onslaught of defamation actions is greater in number and severity than it was in the 'bad old days' of common law libel, as is evidenced by data collected by the Libel Defense Resource Center, which shows a steady increase in defamation suits notwithstanding *New York Times*."

Not only is libel litigation on the increase, but the cost of that litigation has become prohibitive. This is due, in part, to the fact that the actual malice standard encourages plaintiffs to seek extensive discovery of editorial decision-making processes. Such discovery, which is the only way to determine whether a defendant acted knowingly or recklessly, is quite costly. *Herbert v. Lando*, discovery lasted for eight years and cost CBS between $3 million and $4 million in legal fees. Cases like these have prompted some commentators to argue that the Court should provide even greater protection to newspapers and broadcasters including, possibly, a ban on libel suits by public officials.

Despite these dire assessments, it is possible to argue that the *New York Times* decision still provides adequate protection to libel defendants. Indeed, one might even argue that it provides too much protec-

tion. British defamation law is significantly more restrictive than U.S. law. Indeed, after the *New York Times* decision was rendered, English politicians considered whether to adopt a similar standard and declined to do so. They felt that the actual malice standard was unnecessary, and they left in place existing law which allows plaintiffs to more easily recover against media defendants than in the United States. As a result, British plaintiffs have been able to recover substantial judgments against newspapers and broadcasters. Nevertheless, the British press seems to be free and robust. England has plenty of newspapers, including tabloids and scandal sheets. Moreover, throughout Britain, there seems to be more concern about the need to control the press, in an effort to prevent "irresponsible journalism," than there is about the need for an actual malice standard.

The British situation raises questions about the need for an actual malice standard in the United States. This question is not purely academic. If the standard is not necessary, then a strong argument can be made for eliminating it. Every defamation case involves a conflict between the public interest in free speech, and the state interest in providing redress to those who have been defamed. The Supreme Court recognized the existence of these conflicting interests in *Gertz v. Robert Welch, Inc.*: "[W]e believe that the *New York Times* rule states an accommodation between [free speech concerns] and the limited state interest present in the context of libel actions brought by public persons." If the actual malice standard is not essential to insure breathing space for free expression, then it should be abandoned.

In an effort to explore these conflicting views of the *New York Times* decision, this article compares how the British media functions under Britain's more restrictive defamation laws with how the U.S. media functions under the actual malice standard. It does so based on interviews with reporters, editors, defamation lawyers, and others involved in the media in an effort to understand how they decide which stories to publish, and to gain some understanding of how libel laws affect editorial decisionmaking.

. . .

## II. English Defamation Law

British defamation law is inconsistent with many of the fundamental principles articulated in the *New York Times* decision.

### A. Standards Governing Damage Awards Against Media Defendants

Britain provides limited protection to the press and media when they criticize governmental officials. In order to recover, plaintiffs need only show that the press or media made defamatory statements that referred to them or that reasonable people would regard as referring to the plaintiffs. In theory, an additional requirement exists—that the statements must have been maliciously published. But this requirement is, in the words of a leading commentator, "purely formal." "Though the word [maliciously] is usually inserted in the plaintiff's statement of claim, no one takes any notice of it at the trial except for the purpose of inflating damages where there has been spite or deliberateness."

The media and press do have a privilege of fair comment. But the scope of this right is severely limited; it protects only assertions of opinion, and not assertions of fact. This is an important distinction. If, for example, the press believes that the government has been involved in illegal or improper conduct, proceeds cautiously in gathering its evidence, and accuses governmental officials of misconduct, it still might be held liable in defamation if its factual assertions are incorrect. Britain recognizes privileges other than fair comment, but virtually all of them require that all reporting be fair and accurate.

From time to time, those in the British press and media have called on British officials to adopt what they refer to as the "Sullivan defense." For example, following the announcement of a large defamation judgment against a media defendant, an editorial in the *Financial Times* pointedly argued that the government should provide the press with greater protection:

> [T]he observer of the English libel scene may reasonably cast envious eyes across the Atlantic, for US law relating to libel suits is much more solicitous about press freedom and less protective of the defamed than is English law. US laws require private plaintiffs to prove at least that the defendant publisher has been negligent with respect to the falsity of the words used
>
> . . . .
>
> . . .

English law has so far made only a half-hearted attempt to cope with the problem of inaccuracies in reporting by newspapers. Section 4 of the Defamation Act 1952 is an exception to the rule that whoever libels another is strictly liable unless he proves the substantive truth of his statement, and incorporates the notion of unintentional defamation. But the provision is cumbersome in its phraseology and has in practice been resorted to very infrequently.

Without a more generous application of the principle that there should be no legal remedy if the libel is unintentional, the press in England will continue to be vulnerable to constant and expensive litigation. If, as is expected, the Court of Appeal sends the Private Eye case back for a fresh assessment of damages, it will at least give an impetus for reform of the libel laws, to the general benefit of publishing.

In another editorial in the *Financial Times*, a journalist argued that "instead of resisting legislative proposals recently prompted and designed to protect the individual from the outcrop of irresponsible journalism, the Government would do better to ensure the proper balance between the public right to freedom of the press and the rights of the private citizens."

But the British government has generally been unresponsive to these pleas. In a 1991 report, the Supreme Court Procedure Committee reviewed British defamation law, and considered whether England should adopt the *New York Times* defense. It did so at the prompting of the British media, and it did so with full recognition that the *New York Times* defense "has led to a fundamental distinction between defamation law, as applied within that jurisdiction [the United States], and its English counterpart." But the Committee decided not to recommend in favor of the *New York Times* defense. In its view, adoption of such a defense would encourage "irresponsible" journalism:

> Standards of care and accuracy in the press are, in our view, not such as to give any confidence that a "Sullivan" defence would be treated responsibly. It would mean, in effect, that newspapers could publish more or less what they like, provided they were honest, if their subject happened to be within the definition of a "public figure". We think this would lead to great injustice. Furthermore, it would be quite contrary to the tradition of our common law that citizens are not divided into different classes. What matters is the subject-matter of the publication and how it is treated, rather than who happens to be the subject of the allegations.

In the Committee's view, "the media are adequately protected by the defenses of justification and fair comment at the moment, and it is salutary that these defenses are available to them only if they have got their facts substantially correct."

## B. Damage Awards

Because Britain does not have an actual malice standard, British politicians and public figures have been quite successful in their efforts to bring defamation actions against the press and media. In 1987, a senior conservative politician, Norman Tebbitt, brought suit against the BBC for attributing to him the statement, "Nobody with a conscience votes Conservative." He also brought suit against Lawrence Knight, President of the National Union of Mineworkers, for making the same statement. Against the BBC, Tebbitt received £ 2,000 plus costs.

In 1986 five Conservative Members of Parliament (MPs) brought suit against the BBC for allegations made in its *Panorama* program. The allegations linked the MPs to extreme racist groups that were allegedly trying to infiltrate the Tory Party. In the program, the BBC used pictures of the National Front, of Nazi regalia, and of music associated with fascism. The BBC settled the suits. Two MPs received approximately £ 300,000 in damages and legal fees plus an apology. The other MPs received undisclosed sums.

Even though the suits listed above involved substantial sums, each seems relatively modest in comparison with Jeffrey Archer's judgment against *The Star* newspaper. Archer, a famous author and playwright, was also a Deputy Chairman of the Conservative Party. *The Star* alleged that Archer had paid a prostitute £ 70 to have intercourse with him. Archer sued *The Star* and won £ 500,000—a record amount for a defamation action in Britain.

But Archer's record did not last for long. A short time later, Sonia Sutcliffe was awarded £ 600,000 in a libel action against *Private Eye*. This award included both compensatory and punitive damages. *Private Eye* alleged that Mrs. Sutcliffe, the wife of the "Yorkshire Ripper," had been paid £ 250,000 by the *Daily Mail* to publish an account of her married life with Mr. Sutcliffe. Interestingly, even though the story was inaccurate, *Private Eye*'s counsel later alleged that it had some elements of truth. He claimed that Mrs. Sutcliffe had been paid £ 25,000 by the *Daily Mail* in a roundabout way, although he failed to specify the motive for the payment.

## III. The Effect of Britain's Defamation Laws

How do Britain's libel laws affect the press and media? Based on the *New York Times* decision and its discussion of the need for an actual malice standard, one might expect the British press to be fairly timid as compared to the U.S. press. There is no "breath-ing space" for errors. The threat, indeed the fact, of large judgments (e.g., the *Archer* and *Sutcliffe* judgments) should have a chilling effect on the newspapers and broadcasters. But does the theory comport with reality?

## A. At First Glance: A Robust Media

At first blush, the British press and media seems to be remarkably robust. Britain has several recognized, quality newspapers including *The Guardian, The Independent*, and *The Times* (London). Britain also has an array of tabloids including the *Daily Star, Daily Mirror, Sport, Sunday Sport, Sun*, and *News of the World*, and in-between papers like the *Daily Mail* and *Express* that occupy a position leaning towards the quality end of the market.

Britain also has *Private Eye* magazine, a satirical magazine which often takes on the British royal family, as well as politicians and others who might be regarded as members of the establishment. National Public Radio (U.S.) described *Private Eye* in the following way: "Every other week the British establishment gets a nasty case of the jitters. That's because a new edition of the satirical magazine *Private Eye* hits the stands. Reputations are rubbished with glee, official hypocrisy exposed with delight." National Public Radio went on to state that: "[E]ven though it [*Private Eye*] still looks like it's laid out by badly hung-over undergraduates, it has become an institution, the gadfly buzzing the heads of state."

Despite Britain's restrictive libel laws, the British press frequently makes hard-hitting allegations against British politicians and public figures. Illustrative is the following article that was published in *Private Eye*:

> The arrogant, picket line crossing Labour member for Sheffield Attercliffe, Clive Betts, is a 42-year-old bachelor and professional politician who, like so many MPs in the People's Party, has never had to endure the sweat of a job in the real world outside politics.
> In becoming a powerless backbencher, however, Betts has suffered a humiliating fall from grace after spending five years as leader of Sheffield city council. But that is nothing to the humiliation poll taxpayers have endured during his tenure as head of Britain's fourth-ranked provincial local authority.
>
> Betts managed to achieve everything the Tories warned would follow a Labour general election victory: gross financial mismanagement engineered by a blundering executive setting high taxes with little return for the public, accompanied by the usual dollop of spineless but

"worthy" posturing. It was no coincidence that Sheffield hosted Labour's ill-fated Nuremburg victory rally nine days before it lost the general election.

British newspapers also publish accusations about nonpoliticians. Similarly hard-hitting articles can be found in other newspapers. In a recent article, the *Daily Mirror* claimed that a "DEVIL-worshipping sex fiend dubbed the Mongol Warrior was being hunted last night over the murder of gentle barmaid Harvell."

The British tabloids give virtually unceasing attention to the British royal family often portraying it in an unfavorable light. For example, The Sun reported on a book about the marriage of Prince Charles and Princess Diana:

The 158-page book by Andrew Morton is described as "shocking" because it tells the truth.

*Charles is portrayed as uncaring and unloving, both as a husband and as a father to sons William and Henry.*

The book contains details of an alleged suicide attempt by the Princess, and fresh information about Charles's friendship with Camilla Parker Bowles.

Moreover, in publishing these allegations, some papers seem relatively unconcerned about the threat of defamation suits. National Public Radio described *Private Eye* as follows:

While *Private Eye* has earned respect for its investigative journalism, it's also been roundly criticized for some fairly shoddy practices — among them, printing as fact gossip and rumor. Editor Ian Hislop frankly admits that he takes a rather cavalier attitude to the concept of fact checking.

Since the British press publishes fairly hard-hitting articles on a regular basis, it might seem that Britain's failure to adopt an actual malice rule has had no real effect on the British press. British newspapers may be subject to libel actions from time to time, and they may end up on the wrong end of judgments or settlements, but they appear not to be profoundly affected by such judgments or settlements. On the contrary, they seem to carry on in a remarkably robust fashion and to regard libel actions as a business hazard that must be accepted as a cost of doing business rather than as a significant restriction on their coverage.

Some British editors go so far as to suggest that the U.S. press is, itself, far too timid. Ian Hislop,

editor of *Private Eye*, flatly stated in a recent interview:

Hislop: The Americans are always very keen on fact checking. I've had a lot of lectures on fact checking.

Goldfarb: What have they said?

Hislop: They say, "You really should get a lot of interns and have them sit in a row and go through every piece and ring people up and say, is this true?" There is a problem in the area we work in—which is a fairly gray area, the area of printing stories which people don't want printed about themselves—is that they will say, "No, it isn't true."

So, based on a preliminary analysis, one might question whether the *New York Times* decision was correctly decided. The British experience seems to indicate that an actual malice standard may not be necessary to a free press. Indeed, the British experience might suggest that, even without such a standard, the press can be fairly robust and aggressive.

## B. Probing Deeper

But is this view of the British press accurate? Do British editors really feel free to make hard-hitting allegations? Or is the image of a free and robust press and media somewhat deceiving? In an effort to ascertain the impact of Britain's libel laws, we conducted extensive interviews with newspaper reporters, editors, and defamation lawyers in both the United States and Britain.

The interviews suggested that the appearance projected by the British media is, at best, misleading. The British media frankly admits that defamation laws have a significant impact on its coverage. Every British editor and defamation lawyer we interviewed expressed serious concerns about the state of British law. A company solicitor felt that British law gave plaintiffs an "easy run" by making papers "guilty [of defamation] until proven innocent." One editor complained that even quite small errors could lead to judgments. Thames Television's counsel suggested that defamation cases are high risk because juries almost always find against media defendants, even though only the strongest cases are ever litigated. Thames' counsel also complained that defamation cases often result in relatively large judgments. Although Britain restricts recoveries in personal injury cases, it does not impose similar restrictions in defamation cases. This results in the anomaly that, even though a plaintiff who suffers personal injury might recover, say, £50,000 for a serious injury, the same person might receive as much as £ 500,000 if he is defamed. This situation partly reflects the fact that England handles the two types of cases differently from a procedural perspective. Personal injury cases are now invariably dealt with by a judge sitting alone who relies on his own experience as well as on amounts awarded in prior cases. By contrast, defamation is one of the few areas of the law where juries are still the norm. Not surprisingly, some have suggested that the use of juries be curtailed in the interest of cost and efficiency.

British newspapers and broadcasters receive fairly large numbers of defamation complaints. Even quality newspapers, which are less inclined to sensationalize, regularly receive letters from solicitors regarding their coverage. These letters can average two or more per week. If the paper or broadcaster feels that a statement was inaccurate, it will usually offer to retract the statement and may offer to pay a small amount of damages. Some papers make such retractions in response to about one-third of the letters they receive. Of course, some matters cannot be settled and result in litigation, something which occurs about ten percent of the time.

These letters and suits have had a dramatic effect on the functioning of British newspapers and broadcasters. Hislop, who expressed such flippancy about fact checking, has been dramatically affected. As noted earlier, *Private Eye* suffered a £600,000 judgment in the Sonia Sutcliffe case. Following the judgment, Hislop expressed concerns about the ruinous nature of the judgment in an interview with *Morning Edition*:

Bob Edwards: *Private Eye* has a circulation of about 200,000.

Ian Hislop: That's right.

Bob Edwards: Can you begin to afford this kind of settlement?

Ian Hislop: No, obviously not.

Nevertheless, Hislop expressed optimism that his readers would help bail him out:

Bob Edwards: You're trying to raise the money to cover this, aren't you, right now?

Ian Hislop: Yes, and we are desperately trying to get our readers to cough up.

Bob Edwards: And how's that going?

Ian Hislop: Well, there's a lot of money coming in, which is very good news. I am hopeful we're going to raise it and I am hoping that we will win our appeal on the grounds that this is a perverse award. But I'm not sold on the fact that the law will bail us out. I have

very little confidence in the law. I have a feeling that our readers might be more reliable than the workings of the legal system.

At present, *Private Eye* continues to publish.

The threat of defamation actions affects day-to-day news coverage. As a rule, the media finds that the most efficient way to avoid retractions and damage settlements is by acting with extreme caution. Newspapers and broadcasters can insure themselves against defamation losses, but few find it feasible to do so. Insurance is often expensive, and usually carries a very high deductible, so all publishers find that the best way to protect themselves is through careful reporting.

But the thoroughness of the review process is startling. Most newspapers and broadcasters have teams of lawyers who review each day's paper or program for material that might be defamatory. The *Guardian*, for example, has several lawyers who review each day's paper before it is published. *The Times* has an in-house staff of three solicitors who perform this task and also employs a barrister who comes in during the evening to make spot checks. Thames Television has two lawyers who spend up to seventy percent of their time on defamation issues. These two lawyers cannot review all programs, but they try to review as many as they can, and they make a special point of reviewing high-risk investigative programs.

If a lawyer flags an article as potentially defamatory, a secondary review process is then triggered. At most newspapers, editors (and sometimes lawyers) meet with reporters who wrote the story in an effort to determine the basis for allegations. Throughout the process, the focus is on legal sufficiency. Counsel for News International stated that he focuses on three basic issues: (1) Is the statement true? (2) Can he prove it? and (3) Is the person mentioned likely to file suit? Other organizations use similar criteria.

All media organizations indicated that, as a matter of journalistic ethics, they did not want to print or broadcast anything that is untrue. But all stated that they were not able to publish everything that they believed was true. Most focused on whether, if their organization was called on to account for a story, it would have legally admissible evidence with which to defend itself. At Thames Television, one of the solicitors meets with the editor and reporter in an attempt to determine the basis for any allegations that are made. This is a cooperative process under which the solicitor tries to understand and accommodate the needs of program makers.

But the process is also pragmatic. Editors consider whether, even if evidence is admissible, the sources are willing to go "into the box" and testify. Editors might be reluctant to rely on evidence learned from a source they cannot expose, or who is likely to go "wobbly." Editors will also consider whether information was learned under the "lobby system," and is therefore deemed to be off the record, and whether the subject of the article is someone who is likely to sue. Some individuals are particularly litigious. As to these individuals, editors are less inclined to take risks.

After considering this melange of factors, editors decide whether to publish. This decision is often a "team" decision involving the editor and the reporter as well as, perhaps, the head of the department. This process can produce a variety of results. Although editors sometimes decide to scrap a piece, this option is rarely chosen. More commonly, editors try to save a piece by rewriting or altering it in a way that will limit their exposure. In rewriting a piece, editors may delete segments that are not legally supportable, present the subject in a more balanced fashion, or change a statement of fact to an opinion in order to make the statement a "comment" and thereby invoke the privilege of fair comment.

Even though few stories are scrapped, Britain's defamation laws take an inevitable toll on political reporting. Editors will print allegations against public officials, but they rarely do so except when there is strong supporting evidence. One editor referred to the Wilbur Mills' tidal basin incident that occurred in the United States. He suggested that the facts in that case were so strong that, had a similar incident occurred in Britain, it would have been widely reported and the subject of much comment. Indeed, the British Wilbur would probably have been the subject of much derisive comment.

However, a very different picture emerges when British editors are asked about a case like Watergate. That case was slow developing and was initially based on inside sources who were unwilling to be named. In some instances, sources were unknown even to the reporters themselves, and were unwilling to be publicly revealed. Thus, it was difficult for editors and publishers to produce legally admissible evidence substantiating their allegations of misconduct. Nevertheless, the Watergate story was published in the United States. Would the same type of story have been reported in England? British editors and defamation lawyers uniformly stated that, without legally admissible evidence, they would have been unable to print such allegations. Even the *Sun* newspaper, one of the tabloids, suggested that it would have been "reluctant to run" such a story.

Moreover, if a libel suit had been brought, news sources might have "dried up." The sources, who in the Watergate case were governmental insiders, might have feared retaliation and refused to provide further information. As a result, the investigation might not have continued to conclusion and the full extent of the scandal might never have been revealed.

The "chilling" effect of British defamation law is dramatically revealed by the case of Robert Maxwell, the British publishing magnate who died mysteriously off the coast of the Canary Islands in 1992. Following his death, it was discovered that he had suffered serious financial reverses. In addition, he had looted his companies, thereby causing major losses to British pensioners. Some have suggested that Maxwell's financial problems would have come to light earlier except for Maxwell's litigious nature, which caused the British press to be reluctant to make allegations against him. As a result, the extent of Maxwell's problems were not revealed until after his death.

British editors and lawyers flatly stated that they were well aware of Maxwell's litigious nature, and that they were quite careful about their reporting on him. One defamation lawyer stated that the British media was "scared" of Maxwell because he used the libel laws "savagely." Another lawyer indicated that he routinely demanded proof that "one hundred percent" of all allegations made against Maxwell were accurate. Alistair Brett, Company Solicitor for the London *Times*, flatly stated that Maxwell was quick to serve defamation writs, and that he would do so if the newspaper got so much as a word wrong.

British editors confirmed that Maxwell's litigious nature affected their reporting on him. Repeatedly, the media indicated that Maxwell's threats had a chilling effect which prevented them from publishing allegations that could not be proved easily in court. Publishers would make allegations against Maxwell when they had strong evidence to support their allegations. But when the media lacked compelling proof, it would not publish. Thus, the media withheld items that would have been aired against someone who was less litigious. Editors were much more willing to print allegations against Rupert Murdoch, another British publishing magnate, who is less litigious. The net effect is that many things that were known about Maxwell went unreported, including his financial reverses.

Of course, some British papers may regard defamation judgments as simply a cost of doing business, and therefore may engage in aggressive investigative reporting despite the threat of liability. Perhaps these papers sensationalize, even though they know that they are taking risks, in order to gain a competitive advantage. They hope they can net enough additional revenue to pay defamation claims and still make a profit. The tabloids themselves suggest that they do not engage in such cost-benefit analysis. Thomas Crone, the Legal Manager for News International, which owns *The Sun*, claims that the risk from defamation actions is simply too great. In addition, he claims that it is difficult to predict which stories will produce major circulation increases. There are fantastic stories which produce no significant increase in sales.

Britain's defamation laws do, however, have one positive effect: they encourage newspapers and broadcasters to make sure their reporting is evenhanded. Because they fear the possibility of liability, British editors tend to check and recheck their stories. In addition, they tend to rewrite articles to make sure their coverage is balanced. For example, the *Guardian* appears to be particularly careful about balance. If the *Guardian* has contrary information in its possession, it is likely to place that information closer to the beginning of the piece rather than at or near the end.

A recent study by the Guild of British Newspaper Editors supports these conclusions. The Guild surveyed regional newspapers. Eighty percent of those who replied to the Guild's questionnaire were weekly or biweekly publications, and thirty-eight percent of those responding distributed their papers for free, suggesting that the respondents represented a somewhat different segment of the market than the national dailies. Based on this difference, one might surmise that weekly and biweekly publications, especially those that are distributed for free, would be involved in far less libel litigation than the national dailies. This surmise was partially borne out by the fact that most respondents replied that they had suffered either no increase or only a slight increase in the number of defamation complaints leveled against them. Nevertheless, those who did complain to the newspapers were more likely to have consulted a lawyer first rather than to have approached the newspaper directly. Interestingly, the responding newspapers indicated that defamation complaints most commonly involved court reporting and, although a majority of respondents planned to continue reporting on judicial proceedings, ten papers had chosen to reduce their coverage in this area. In addition, thirteen titles, seven percent of the sample, had received libel writs during 1991 although none proceeded to trial. Of the actions that were settled, the highest payment was for £ 20,000. Twenty-five percent of the respondents indicated that they sought prepublication advice more frequently in 1991 than in prior years.

. . .

## C. Exploiting Privileges

Because of their fear of defamation suits, British newspapers and broadcasters have become remarkably adept at finding "safe" ways to get material into print. They report freely on the British royal family, which rarely sues for defamation. They also report fairly freely on cabinet ministers who, by custom, cannot sue for defamation without first gaining clearance. Of course, this custom provides publishers with only a limited reprieve. Once ministers relinquish their cabinet posts, they are free to sue regarding defamatory statements made while they were in office.

The British media also takes advantage of various privileges including the absolute privileges for accurate reporting of parliamentary debates and judicial proceedings. Indeed, many hard-hitting pieces are carefully sculpted pieces based on statements rendered in privileged contexts.

The British media's tendency to base allegations on testimony heard in courts or in parliament is somewhat disturbing. Obviously, it is desirable for the media to report what transpires in these two contexts. But in a free society, one would prefer to have a more robust media that does its own investigations and reports freely the results. Obviously, Britain does have investigative journalists. However, as the Watergate and Maxwell examples suggest, Britain's press reports less freely.

To its credit, the British press is remarkably adept at manipulating and taking advantage of the various privileges. When newspapers gain information about a scandal, but feel they do not have enough legally admissible evidence to support their allegations, they sometimes ask an MP to raise the matter during "question time" in Parliament. The press is then free to report on the question and the response, if any. If the paper feels strongly enough about a matter, they might ask an MP to schedule a matter for an "early day motion"—a motion suggesting that a matter has troubling implications and should be investigated.

But despite the British press' resourcefulness, it is unable to report on many matters of public interest. The press must have sufficient evidence of wrongdoing before it can ask an MP to ask a question or to file an early day motion. Of course, part of the problem is that some of the most important allegations seem fairly preposterous in the beginning. This was true of Watergate until a sufficient mass of proof was developed. But how is the proof to be developed under England's system? Absent sufficiently credible support, MPs might be reluctant to ask questions for fear they might not be taken seriously.

## IV. Comparison to the United States

Once the British interviews were complete, we then interviewed U.S. editors, reporters, and defamation lawyers in an effort to find out whether they functioned differently than their British counterparts.

### A. The Doomsday Scenario

Although we believed that U.S. newspapers and broadcasters would be much more relaxed about the possibility of defamation suits, there was reason to suspect that our belief was wrong. The *New York Times* decision did not terminate libel litigation. On the contrary, many continued to sue. Some plaintiffs felt wronged and hoped they would prevail, but many who did not necessarily expect to prevail had nevertheless filed libel actions. There were many reasons. Some of these plaintiffs were economically motivated. They hoped to gain modest settlements from defendants who wished to avoid the cost of litigation. But others were motivated by non-economic factors such as the hope of clearing their names.

Some argue that libel litigation continues unabated, and indeed is on the increase. As one commentator noted, "[A]n astonishing shift in cultural and legal conditions has caused a dramatic proliferation of highly publicized libel actions brought by well-known figures who seek, and often receive, staggering sums of money."

Even though there were virtually no recoveries in the first years after *New York Times* was decided, that situation has now changed. . . .

Because the threat of litigation continues to exist, one might speculate that U.S. libel laws force editors to engage in a degree of self-censorship. Obviously, any litigation can be expensive. But libel litigation is particularly expensive. The actual malice standard encourages plaintiffs to seek extensive discovery of editorial decision-making processes. This discovery can take years and cost millions of dollars to complete. In addition, defendants lose many defamation cases at the trial court level. Even though they win most of these cases on appeal, they must bear the cost of the appeal. Moreover, the number of judgments that are sustained on appeal has increased.

Because of these risks, one might suspect that U.S. editors would not be free and uninhibited in their coverage. Even editors who believe they will ultimately prevail in a libel action may be deterred from publishing hard-hitting allegations fearing the costs of defending a possible action. Some publishers

may be well financed sufficiently that they are undeterred by these potential costs, and are willing to publish notwithstanding the threat of litigation. But many small publishers would be devastated by a large award. Moreover, even some large publishers indicate their uneasiness by requiring authors to agree to indemnify the publisher in the event of a defamation action. These agreements may encourage the authors themselves to engage in self-censorship.

### B. The Interviews

These dire assessments of the state of U.S. libel were not, however, borne out by the interviews. U.S. editors are concerned about the threat of defamation actions and the possibility of adverse judgments, but they are far less concerned about this possibility than their British counterparts. For example, Bob Edwards of National Public Radio's Morning Edition flatly stated that defamation laws had no impact on his coverage. Others agreed. In fact, only one interviewee, a lawyer for a major network, expressed any serious concerns about the impact of U.S. defamation laws.

The reason U.S. newspapers and broadcasters are less concerned about defamation is because they are threatened with suit, and actually sued, far less frequently than their British counterparts. The *Louisville Courier-Journal* is, for example, sued only once every two years or so. The *Washington Post* receives three or four letters a year from lawyers threatening suit, but is rarely sued. Although the *New York Times* may receive one letter a month from lawyers, it is sued only about once a year. Bob Edwards was unable to state whether National Public Radio had ever received threatening letters or had been sued. David Gelber, the Executive Producer of the CBS program *60 Minutes*, has only been sued twice in his eight years with that program.

Editors and producers in the United States are not so relaxed that they ignore the possibility of defamation liability. But, because the threat of suit is much lower, they often tend to be more worried about other matters (e.g., journalistic accuracy and integrity) than they are about the threat of liability. Producers and editors stated that for professional reasons, they want to report accurately. Even if there is no threat of liability, they want to avoid publishing something that is untrue or that cannot be supported by hard evidence. Thus, at times, they know things they do not report. But the primary reason for withholding such information is that the editors are concerned about the ethics of publishing it. They also fear that questionable allegations might diminish their credibility or harm their standing in the community.

Some argue that it is difficult to differentiate between what is done for reasons of journalistic integrity and what is done for fear of defamation liability. For example, David Gelber, producer of CBS's *60 Minutes*, stated that few situations would arise when he might be fearful of liability when he would not also have concerns about whether he was being fair as a journalist. Others agreed, arguing that, if they live up to journalistic ideals, they have little to fear in terms of defamation liability.

These attitudes are reflected in the day-to-day functioning of U.S. newspapers and broadcasters. Unlike the British, U.S. newspapers and broadcasters do not have teams of lawyers that comb through copy searching for material that may be defamatory. Most papers and broadcasters allow editors and producers to decide for themselves whether material is potentially defamatory and whether to involve counsel. If an editor or producer feels comfortable with a piece, he may publish or air it without any input from counsel.

When U.S. editors or producers involve their lawyers, they use a process that is similar to that used by their English counterparts. The attorney examines the statement and examines the reporter's sources in an effort to ascertain whether there is adequate evidence to support the assertion. In some instances, the attorney may urge the paper to do additional investigative work. In other instances, the lawyer may recommend that part of a piece be rewritten or softened or that an effort be made to present something in a more balanced way. Nevertheless, if there is adequate evidence to support a claim, something will be printed or broadcast even though it contains hard-hitting allegations.

Thus, the possibility of defamation suits has some impact on reporting. But most interviewees indicated that the impact was minimal. Few editors or producers reported that they had ever killed a story for fear of defamation liability. Moreover, few indicated that they were unable to make a statement for fear of liability. They were often reluctant to rely entirely on confidential sources. In addition, if they had inadequate support for a piece, they might seek additional support. Alternatively, they might soften a statement or attempt to present it in a more balanced way. But there was a very good chance that the allegation would still be made.

Even those who have been defendants in defamation litigation do not seem unduly chilled by the threat of additional litigation. Brian Ross, an NBC correspondent, suffered a $24 million plus defamation judgment that was ultimately overturned on appeal. Nevertheless, he felt that libel laws do not unduly affect news coverage. Ross admits that he suffered many sleepless nights while the litigation was pending. But he was lucky in that his employer continued to support him: he received a contract renewal as well as generous raises. Today the judgment has little effect on his reporting. He is less inclined to rely on confidential sources, but he still reports what he believes to be true. Nevertheless, Ross worries that a more timid journalist might be affected by such an ordeal.

Is there a Maxwell parallel in the United States—a particularly litigious individual who scares newspapers and stunts their coverage of him? The simple answer is no. Some media reported that they receive threats designed to discourage them from airing allegations. For example, CBS's *60 Minutes* is routinely threatened that it will be sued regarding stories that it plans to air. But these threats do not have much effect on coverage. In rare instances, editors will soften or alter stories to protect themselves, but they rarely kill a story. Moreover, they do not seem to fear any particular individual like the British media feared Maxwell.

During the course of the interviews, we payed particular attention to the major television networks. Those outside the networks warned us that reporters at the networks often complain about their pieces being "lawyered to death." The interviews revealed that, although the networks seem to be somewhat more concerned about defamation issues, defamation laws do not have a major impact on their coverage. Indeed, network sources did not seem unduly concerned about the possibility of defamation suits. This lack of concern stems from the fact that the networks are infrequently sued. For example, NBC may be threatened with suit as often as once a week, but ninety percent of the complainants do not file suit. One producer stated that, although he had been sued, he had never been to court. The same is true at CBS, which indicated that defamation does not "come up all that much." CBS gets a lot of angry letters and responses, but it is sued infrequently.

The networks also indicated that they never "kill" a story because of defamation concerns. They may rewrite a story, but they rarely make major changes. Producer Stephen Friedman flatly stated that defamation law has very little effect on what he airs. Indeed, he spends less than three hours a month doing prepublication review of broadcasts for defamatory material. ABC claims that it will air allegations it believes to be true, even though it fears it may lose in court. Discussions with correspondents seemed to confirm these statements.

CBS's house counsel suggested that defamation

laws do have a significant effect on reporting. He felt that the processes described above—of seeking additional sources and rewriting—have a significant chilling effect. His major complaint was that defamation laws impose significant additional work on editors, producers, and lawyers. Nevertheless, he felt that most pieces are approved without alteration and are not extensively edited or rewritten. In the final analysis, CBS is still able to "put forth what needs to be put forth."

There are some significant differences between the national networks and other media outlets. The networks tend to air a number of investigative pieces which are more likely to contain defamatory material. These investigative pieces are scrutinized more carefully than other programs. Both ABC and NBC regularly engage in prepublication review of investigative pieces. But even when network lawyers are concerned about an investigative piece, they rarely kill that piece, although they might rewrite it to some extent, as suggested earlier. Moreover, they rarely make major changes if a reporter's claims are supportable.

Even though few complained about pieces "being lawyered to death," many complained about journalists who felt they could publish anything. Stephen Friedman stated that some journalists believe they can air anything they want simply because they are journalists. Carl Stern, a reporter for NBC News, agreed.

U.S. journalists who publish and broadcast overseas seem to be somewhat more conservative than those who publish in the United States. This conservatism is understandable. CNN, for example, broadcasts around the world. To the extent that plaintiffs have a choice, they will sue CNN in a foreign country. As a result, if the absence of an actual malice standard has a "chilling" effect on journalism, one would suspect that overseas broadcasters might be "chilled" in some cases by the threat of an English defamation action.

But the interviews revealed that, by and large, foreign laws do not unduly affect U.S. overseas coverage. The *Washington Post* and *New York Times* indicated that they use almost the same procedures and criteria for overseas publications and broadcasts that they use for domestic ones. In only rare instances do they soften a story for the overseas market. Interestingly, neither organization was threatened by Robert Maxwell regarding their coverage of him, and both treated him no differently than they treated anyone else. CNN is a little more cautious about its coverage. Again, its primary concern is with journalistic accuracy and with "getting it right." But, at the same time, because CNN broadcasts constantly to all parts of the globe, it is more cautious about the threat of defamation suits. In addition, CNN is much more likely to have lawyers routinely engage in prepublication review of its broadcasts.

### V. CONCLUSION

. . .

The British experience provides interesting insights into the impact of the absence of the actual malice standard. Interestingly enough, that contrast suggests that the Supreme Court's original conclusions regarding the need for an actual malice standard were essentially correct. By contrast to the U.S. media, the British media is far more timid. British reporting seems to be "chilled" by prevailing defamation laws, and the British press does not appear to be as free and robust as the U.S. press. Correspondingly, the U.S. media seems to believe that it has more "breathing space" for errors as indicated by its operating procedures and its statements. U.S. editors seem more concerned about journalistic accuracy and integrity than they do about the threat of liability.

# Bibliography

*Defamation and Privacy*

Anderson, David A., *Libel and Press Self-Censorship*, 53 Texas Law Review 422 (1975)

Ashdown, Gerald G., *Of Pubic Figures and Public Interest: The Libel Law Conundrum*, 25 William & Mary Law Review 937 (1984)

Beth, Loren P., *Group Libel and Free Speech*, 39 Minnesota Law Review 167 (1955)

Bezanson, Randall P., *The Libel Tort Today*, 45 Washington & Lee Law Review 535 (1988)

Daniels, Diana M., *Public Figures Revisited*, 25 William & Mary Law Review 957 (1984)

Epstein, Richard A., *Was New York Times v. Sullivan Wrong*, 53 University of Chicago Law Review 782 (1986)

Franklin, Marc A., *Public Officials and Libel: In Defense of New York Times Co. v. Sullivan*, 5 Cardozo Acts & Entertainment Law Journal 51 (1986)

Hill, Alfred, *Defamation and Privacy Under the First Amendment*, 76 Columbia Law Review 1205 (1976)

Ingber, Stanley, *Defamation: A Conflict Between Reason and Decency*, 65 Virginia Law Review 785 (1979)

Monaghan, Henry P., *Constitutional Fact Review*, 85 Columbia Law Review 229 (1985)

Nimmer, Melville B., *The Right to Speak from Time to Time, First Amendment Theory Applied to Libel and Misapplied to Privacy*, 56 California Law Review 935 (1968)

Schauer, Frederick, *Public Figures*, 25 William & Mary Law Review 905 (1984)

Smolla, Rodney A., *Let the Author Beware: The Rejuvenation of the American Law Libel*, 132 University of Pennsylvania Law Review 1 (1983)

Zimmerman, Diane Leenheer, *False Light Invasion of Privacy: The Light that Failed*, 64 New York University Law Review 364 (1989)

## D. Commercial Expression

Commercial speech until the mid-1970s was an entirely unprotected species of expression. Acknowledging that the public's "interest in the free flow of commercial information may be [at least] as keen . . . [as] his interest in the day's most urgent political debate," the Supreme Court eventually determined that such expression fell within the First Amendment's ambit. Virginia State Board of Pharmacy v. Virginia Citizens Consumer Council, 425 U.S. 748, 763 (1976). Case law and literature since have focused upon the extent to which commercial speech should be protected. C. Edwin Baker believes that the lesser protection given to commercial speech is justified because that speech is profit driven and does not necessarily reflect "the speaker's value choice or prejudice." Steven Shiffrin disagrees. He argues that "almost all of the commentators have looked at the 'commercial speech' problem through the lens of commercial advertising," and claims that this perspective has distorted the debate. Burt Neuborne argues for a "hearer-centered" approach to commercial speech, and suggests that it provides a strong justification for protecting some commercial speech. Lawrence Alexander and Daniel A. Farber engage in a debate over what types of commercial speech deserve special protection. Thomas H. Jackson and John Calvin Jeffries, Jr. argue that the First Amendment guarantee of freedom of speech and press should not extend to commercial speech. Their position is that the speech clause was only intended to protect only "certain identifiable values" such as self-government.

C. Edwin Baker, *Commercial Speech: A Problem in the Theory of Freedom*, 62 Iowa Law Review 1 (1976)*

Since the Supreme Court's 1942 decision denying first amendment protection to the distribution of a commercial advertising handbill, the denial of protection to commercial speech has been a major anomaly in first amendment theory. The commercial speech exception has continually eluded theoretical justification, as well as precise definition. . . .

. . .

## I. LIBERTY: THE KEY TO THE FIRST AMENDMENT

Any argument for or against including particular types of activity within the category of first amendment protected speech will embody some notion of why speech is constitutionally protected. Some theories attribute the special constitutional status of speech to its instrumental role in seeking truth, recognizing universally agreed upon values, and changing people's attitudes. For these theories, the importance of speech lies in its *content*. However, a focus on content not only fails to distinguish commercial speech from protected speech, but also fails to emphasize a possibly more important aspect of speech— its use to advance self-interest and its role in self-realization. It is the thesis of this Article that the crucial parameters of first amendment theory in general, and the commercial speech doctrine in particular, are the *source* and *purpose* of speech rather than the *content* of speech. Before delineating the distinction between a self-interested and a profit-oriented source which structures and justifies the commercial speech exception, it is instructive to examine the constitutionally crucial "self-interest" aspect of speech.

Speech performs a multitude of functions. It may be used to communicate one's position, to convince, to induce desired behavior in another, to describe, to direct, to entertain or amuse, to investigate, analyze, or plan. Protected speech is not merely instrumental in searching for absolute truth, in trying to discover universally agreed upon values, or in attempting to influence the activities of the state. It often expresses how the speaker would choose to structure the world or the immediate environment. It expresses the speaker's *Weltanschauung* or worldview; when the speaker attempts to persuade, to plan, or to organize, speech may be used as a means of structuring the world in accordance with the speaker's desires. Alternatively, the speaker may employ speech to aid the listener in developing an orientation toward the world. Myths and tales help create and maintain the content of our social world. The common feature of all of these activities is that the impulse to discover, create, or maintain exists within the individual or group of individuals. Speech is central to the individual's activity of discovery and creation; it is necessary for the individual's choice or habit in maintaining the social world.

Professor Emerson has attempted to summarize the commonly accepted values and functions of our system of freedom of expression. He finds that the system is essential (1) as a means of assuring individual self-realization, (2) as a process for advancing knowledge and discovering truth, (3) as a method of providing for participation in decision making (particularly with respect to political decisions, but also including participation in building the entire culture), and (4) as a method for achieving a more adaptable and hence more stable community. At first glance, only the first function is self-focused. Self-realization is possible when the expression is a manifestation of the self for which the mind must be free. On closer analysis, however, the second function is performed because people's real commitments and hypotheses are tested against each other in a spirit of inquiry; the third because, through expression, a person's individual and personal commitments become relevant contributions to collective choices; and the fourth when a person's real commitments and tendencies enter into the mechanism of governmental and societal decision making. *Only by existing as a manifestation of the self, and the self's choices and commitments, can speech serve these essential functions.*

Reaction to speech is reaction to the intended meaning of one as mediated through the consciousness of another. Speech, unlike violence, which is always mute, depends for its effect on acceptance and agreement. Both the myth and the political harangue shape the world by being accepted; both our use of language and the meaning of language require agreements in forms of life, for words only have uses and meaning within social practices or forms of human interaction. *As long as speech represents the freely-chosen expression of the speaker while depending for its power on the free acceptance of the listener, freedom of speech represents a charter of liberty for noncoercive action.* Even beyond elections and political campaigns, freedom of speech is both a person's most important political "tool" or instrument and the most democratic political practice possible. Everybody's speech counts. Speech implants the individual's stamp on the world and maintains that world—and while speech requires a common, plural world for its existence, the source of specific speech is in principle the individual.

Once the way speech performs its function of being a manifestation of self is recognized, the justification and scope of the listener's "right to know" becomes clear. As a manifestation of the self, speech deserves protection even if it is not used to communicate with others. Often, however, communication is used to stimulate change. If first amendment protection is granted in part in order to protect a process of change based on noncoercive, freely adopted activities, then the willing listener as well as the speaker can claim a personal interest in this protected process of change and must be allowed to receive the willing communications of the speaker. Moreover, the speaker may have a right to demand that the government not interfere with his or her attempt to communicate with even unwilling listeners, although this right only applies in situations where state interference would also prevent some communications with potentially willing listeners. Both parties' interest in the communication is protected. Thus, the first amendment, which operates as a restraint on the government's interference with the realm of individual liberties, does not give the listener any right other than to have the government not interfere with a willing speaker's liberty. Any other interpretation of the listener's rights could conflict with the speaker's liberty and would improperly require the government to make more information or different opinions available to the listener.

It is worth reemphasizing that, despite the purpose for which speech is employed, the motivation for it normally comes from the speaker and from the speaker's own interests. The speech is rooted in "self-interest"—whether the interest is to discover, to change or to maintain the world; whether the goal is achieved by organizing one's own perceptions or by changing others; whether one's "interests" are narrowly selfish, generally altruistic, or more complexly organized. Assuming that acceptance forms the basis of the power of speech, the fact that verbal activity is motivated by self-interest (or even selfish interests) is no reason to frown upon it or to limit it. Self-interest is, in fact, a normal and valuable aspect of speech.

## II. COMMERCIAL SPEECH AND INDIVIDUAL LIBERTY

Intuitively, many have thought that the profit-motivated speech of the marketplace of commodities does not deserve the same status as speech in the marketplace of the mind. However, in order to identify commercial speech and then justify excluding it from constitutional protection on the basis of its profit orientation, one must explain why the "profit" motive is, in principle, any different from other self-interested motives which are generally present in protected uses of speech, and which even provide part of the rationale for protecting speech. If motivational or structural differences between profit-oriented and self-interested speech do not exist, the profit orientation of commercial speech does not provide a principled basis for denying commercial speech constitutional protection—even if "profit motive" could be operationalized sufficiently to define a category.

### A. Commercial Speech in Modern America

1. Importance of the Economic and Social Order

. . .

In a possessive market society, where "value" represents commodity or exchange value, the failure to exploit one's resources in the most efficient manner necessarily leads to a decrease in the value of these resources. If one does not always strive to increase profits or to increase capital, the profit-making value of what one has at present may, because of competition, decrease and then disappear. The value of property or capital depends on its ability to return a profit—to reproduce itself with a surplus. For example, if Firm A stops changing in accord with the requirements of a profit orientation while other firms continue to change, Firm A will eventually be driven out of business. Because it will be unable to reproduce itself without a loss, the value of its capital will eventually decline to zero. As C.B. MacPherson has shown, systematic orientation by an enterprise within a possessive market society toward anything but profits will eventually result in its destruction. Although this analysis does not apply in all societies, it particularly applies to a possessive market society. Thus, within such a society, the individual must strive for more and more, business must be oriented toward efficiency and profits, and non-economic regulations will merely impose a constraint to be integrated into the profit calculus rather than supplant the profit motive. State regulation normally will lead not to collapse but, like a technological factor, to additional costs which must be internalized by all similarly situated firms.

Certain institutional features make such profit-oriented behavior both possible and necessary. For example, although a profit-maximizing stance could either be individually adopted by enterprises or required by law for all enterprises, without competition and the existence of a settled market for business inputs and outputs, the economic structure could not require or enforce such a profit-oriented stance. Likewise, only the development of modern accounting methods makes possible rational calculations concerning the profitability of various courses of action. For the purposes of this Article, the particular significance of the separation of the enterprise from the household for capitalist or profit-oriented behavior merits careful examination.

### 2. The Distinction Between the Profit-Making Enterprise and the Household: Freedom of Choice

As economic behavior becomes increasingly oriented toward the formally rational pursuit of profits, one should expect, and historically one finds, that the household or consumption-oriented arenas of life are increasingly, and more radically, separated from the profit-making enterprise. Without the legal and budgetary separation between the household and the business enterprise—usually physical separation occurs as well—efficiency calculations could not be made, risk could not be as well controlled, and profitability or unprofitability would be less evident. For example, an "unprofitable" family store may be subsidized by cheap family labor, unless owning and operating the store is considered a form of consumption. Logically, the separation makes possible a more rational orientation towards profits. Historically, this legal and budgetary separation uniquely occurred in the West—and, it has been argued, is integrally related to the rise of the capitalist industrial economy in the West. However, not only is this separation instrumentally important, it also affects the resulting forms of life which, like any structure of interaction, must themselves be "valued." The separation allows and requires activity within the economically productive and allocative sphere of life to be increasingly divorced from the individual values of the actors and, instead, to be instrumentally oriented toward the one structurally required goal—profits. The economic actors are given no choice but to pursue profits.

. . .

The obvious implication for commercial speech in the foregoing economic model—that the enterprise's speech is directed toward increasing profits—has never been challenged by critics of the commercial speech exception. More importantly, the key feature of the model, often ignored in the commentary, is that the profit orientation is *externally imposed* on the capitalist enterprise by the market. The enterprise has no specific goal other than instrumental rationality—the increase of profits. Any other goal would

detract from that rationality, would partially reintegrate the household and the enterprise, and would effect a merger of substantive and instrumental reason. Given the household-enterprise separation, commercial speech is in principle separate from the speaker's decisions about the world or investigations into its nature. Ideally, the content, the form, and particularly the intensity and direction of the propagation of commercial speech is determined by calculating its positive contribution to profits. A standard given and enforced by the structure of the competitive market rather than the speaker's value choice or prejudice lies at the source of commercial speech.

### B. Profit-Induced Behavior: The Lack of Both Individual Choice and Value-Neutrality

### 1. The Rationale for Regulation

Despite the fact that commercial speech is not rooted in individual choice and thus fails to serve the important functions of protected speech, it still might escape regulation if it remained neutral or irrelevant to the major decisions facing us as individuals and collectives. Defenders of the market and its commercial practices claim that the market takes individual and group preferences and predilections—the subjective values of consumers—as given, and that the instrumental rationality of the market—its competitive pursuit of profits—merely aids in the realization of *otherwise* decided upon ends. Because market practices including commercial speech are both useful and value neutral, they merit first amendment protection.

However, commercial speech is in no sense irrelevant or value free. Not only does it help to mold the world, it molds the world in very particular ways. The conventional wisdom concerning modern America is reflected in C.B. Macpherson's observation that "the market system . . . creates the wants which it satisfies." Macpherson goes on to argue:

> There is no reason to expect that the wants and tastes which [the market] satisfies will reflect or permit that full development of the individual personality which is the liberal-democratic criterion of the good society.

Speaking anthropomorphically, commercial speech is directed toward creating the world as "profit" requires. This profit-directed orientation has a number of implications. Profit requires a constant increase in our desires. In addition, the desires stimulated have particular characteristics—they must be those satisfied by objects or services which can be sold by the enterprise without impeding the stimulation of tastes on which the sales of its other products depend. With all other factors held constant, profit can advance best by stimulating the most cheaply aroused desires. Stimulation of these types of taste clearly involves the movement of the social world in specific directions determined by profit-dictated value choices. "Profit" strives to create or reinforce certain images of humans which are useful for profit's purposes. However, no one need believe or decide that the world is better if these desires are created. How "profit" wants the world to be bears no necessary relation to how any individual wants it to be. To allow "profit" to vote is to depreciate human freedom.

. . .

However, neither the management, the owners, nor the workers of the distillery need have any belief in the content of the commercial advertisement. It is not necessary that anyone associated with the distill-ery believe that the activities advocated would make for a better social world. The only necessary belief about the advocated activities is that their promotion will increase profits. Both the content and the context of the whiskey company's speech is relevant to the company only to the extent that its speech is the most effective available method to increase profits. The failure to adopt the most profit-stimulating speech is a business mistake. The company's president, other employees, and stock and bond owners could very well all be teetotalers who personally oppose the use of alcohol, although certain human psychological characteristics would militate against this situation. Moreover, within the structure of the commercial enterprise, their personal commitment to the activity advocated is irrelevant. Rather than evaluate the ad-vocacy in terms of any personally adopted criteria, they are to consider the advocacy entirely from the technical perspective of sales and profit. *The domina-tion of profit, a structurally required standard, breaks the connection between speech and any vi-sion, or attitude, or value of the individual or group engaged in advocacy*. Thus, the content and form of commercial speech cannot be attributed to individual value allegiances.

Although no necessary relationship exists between the personal beliefs of those connected by either ownership or labor to the whiskey company and the content of its commercial speech, a high correlation between the two might be expected. Both psychologi-cal and structural factors promote a coalescence of the personal beliefs of the speaker and the implica-tions of the particular commercial speech. Psycholo-gists claim that the existence of psychological tenden-cies reduces dissonance between value contradictory behavior or attitudes in individuals. A more balanced

state results when one's personal beliefs correspond with one's business speech or behavior. Reduction of dissonance could take the form of increasing one's private belief in the values communicated by the en-terprise. This form of dissonance reduction is most likely when the economic actors view their involve-ment in the enterprise as voluntary. Even without dissonance theory, this psychological effect might be expected, given a reinforcement system within the enterprise which rewards manifestations of private belief in enterprise policy.

Structurally, everything else being equal between two potential jobholders, if one agreed and the other disagreed with the values promoted by the enterprise, and if both placed some value on integrating their beliefs with their behavior, the one who agreed with the enterprise's values could be employed more cheaply than the other. Consequently, assuming the existence of job competition, that person would be the one hired.

However, neither the psychological nor the struc-tural reasons for expecting a correspondence between private beliefs and the enterprise's speech suffice to show that the speech can be attributed to the values of individuals. The commercial speech would be the same regardless of the individual's values. The prop-osition that commercial speech cannot be attributed to individual free choice is explained not by the fact that psychological factors determine or influence the individual's beliefs—some would hold that this is al-ways the case—but by the fact that the individual's beliefs, however formed, do not determine the speech. Structurally, the employment situation may merely result in hiring the person who disagrees with the enterprise's message the least. Although wide-spread disagreement with the enterprise's speech might incidently affect profitability calculations since higher wages may be necessary to attract needed em-ployees, in a capitalist market system the profitability calculations still determine the speech.

## 2. Arguments Against Regulation

One may not immediately accept the argument that advertising, given the sway of the profit motive, tends toward the creation of a world which is not the product of individual choice. Three counter-arguments seem particularly plausible. First, when the value implications of pursuing profits are con-trary to someone's personal values, that person will determine the costs and benefits of the behavioral requirements of pursuing profits in light of personal values, and will then freely adopt a chosen course of action. Second, even though the pursuit of profits and the corresponding advertising substantively affect the types of people and society that result, these substantive value implications are implicit in maximum want satisfaction, itself a neutral or, at least, a generally shared and dominant value. Third, even if the effects of commercial speech cannot be defended on the basis of neutral or universally shared values, many persons do adopt the substantive values implicit in commercial speech. Freedom, within the scope of the first amendment, means that these persons should be free to articulate that which embodies their values. These counter-arguments fail, however, to withstand careful scrutiny.

The first argument presumes that, in the presence of a conflict between the dictates of profit and the personal values of the individuals comprising, managing, or owning the enterprise, these individuals can choose which of these two interests to follow. This hypothesis must be considered within a specific historical and socio-economic context. If competition or law either enforces or requires profit-oriented behavior, the hypothesis must be rejected. Since failure to pursue profits, in the societal model described herein, results in a decrease or elimination of the "value" of the enterprise, even an irrational *attempt* to pursue these other values would soon come to an end. In *Leviathan*, Thomas Hobbes demonstrated a precise understanding of this observation about modern market man. The individual must have a "perpetual and restless desire of power after power" or ever more profit *even though he may be "content with a moderate power"* because the value of the enterprise will diminish unless he continues to pursue profit: "he cannot assure the power and means to live well, which he hath present, without the acquisition of more."

The second argument—that ever greater want satisfaction is a neutral or a virtually universal and overriding value and that, therefore, commercial speech, which serves this value, merely promotes a desired form of the social world—has a certain persuasive force. In the possessive market, the profit or maximization orientation serves as the paradigm of rationality as well as the key to the system's dynamism. Such a system of coordination, it is argued, takes into account and adjusts all the conflicting values of the participants. A major merit of this system, and the reason it is value neutral (according to its apologists) is that it begins by accepting individual values as given. However, this starting point obscures the process of change and the development of values. Moreover, the account is descriptively inadequate. The economic enterprise does not passively accept individual values as given. In order to increase profits, the enterprise attempts to create and manipulate

values. It does this by stimulating particular desires. In this dynamic process, some potential values or desires are necessarily ignored; others are undermined or distorted.

Severe criticism can and has been leveled against this process of cost-benefit manipulation of values. Even if a "value" gain would result from cutting down our greatest redwood forests and replacing them with properly advertised plastic Disney trees, reasons have been advanced why this move should not be taken. People of this generation and succeeding generations have an interest in participating in the substantive processes whereby the values through which they define themselves are created and chosen. Neither our legal-political structures and obligations nor our economic structures can be adequately evaluated solely in terms of their contribution to the satisfaction of endless desires. These structures and obligations also constitute what we are, and contribute to determining what our values and desires will be. Given the constitutive aspects of these structures, any defense of freedom as self-determination or any vision of the person as being the subject of the human will, necessarily implies that people should have a right to choose the form and determine the boundaries of the economic, as well as the political, system. Since economic forms tend to create certain types of persons, self-determination requires that the existence and extent of economic forms be subjected to group choice.

The practice of making decisions solely in order to increase want satisfaction could not be accepted if persons have a right in the strong sense, or a duty, to take other considerations into account. Recent commentary has attempted to show that we may have *obligations* toward the environment requiring actions that may be contrary to the goal of maximum want satisfaction. If such obligations exist, they could provide a reason for regulating the attitude-creating aspects of commercial speech as well as other profit-oriented activities of economic enterprises. However, the source or basis of such an obligation must be explained before one can assume that the existence of that obligation can serve as an adequate reason for a society to act contrary to utilitarian dictates. Interestingly, like the reasons for limiting commercial speech, the existence of this type of obligation may be implicit in the idea of self-determination.

In another article, this writer has argued that the justification of legal obligation requires the recognition of rights which place limits on communal attempts to maximize want satisfaction. Members of the legal community can legitimately demand that the legal order treat them equally as free, autonomous, rational human beings. Such treatment implies the recognition of certain rights. One basic right required in order to justify legal obligation in general (and implicit in the political practices and theory of democracy) is a right to participate in choosing or determining what we will be. Such a right must include a right to create or recognize obligations which are not justified on want satisfaction grounds—for example, obligations toward the environment which interfere with market practices and circumscribe utility-maximization policies.

Without further pursuing this theoretical argument, it is possible to note the existence and acceptance of values contrary to maximum want satisfaction. Laws creating victimless crimes are more concerned with the way we, as individuals and communities, ought to live than with maximization of utility. Even advocates of decriminalization of these crimes frequently do not base their arguments on utilitarian grounds. Our chosen educational and social processes imply that ease of stimulation should not be the primary criterion for the development of tastes and values. The desires most readily stimulated in a given person depend in part on the person's upbringing, and possibly on the biological aspects of the person's constitution. When controversies concerning child-rearing practices exemplify not only lack of knowledge about the effects of various practices but also lack of agreement as to how these effects should be evaluated, one must conclude that the issues involved are not limited to determining which practices will result in the most happiness, but extend also to determining the types of persons we want to be. Moreover, increasing evidence suggests that neither happiness, nor a sense of freedom, nor any other important human goal closely correlates with a maximum satisfaction of market-simulated desires. Neither a concept of humanity which centers on an interest in self-determination nor the actual state of existing social practices will allow the maximum creation and satisfaction of wants to be viewed as a universally accepted or neutral value.

Despite its value implications, should not commercial speech be protected for those who want it? The first amendment should protect not only advocacy but freedom to practice beliefs, unless those practices operate "coercively" on others. Only such a broad, pluralistic view of the first amendment provides protection for the peaceful creation of societal alternatives and for democratic participation in change. Often the creation of revisionist or dissenting views requires a group or sect, or community, to provide stimulus and support. Only actual groups through their forms of interaction can give coherence

and vitality to alternative concepts and categorizations; only actual groups can provide a home for converts to alternative ideas and a base for promoting those ideas. This view of the first amendment suggests that those who so desire should be free to sell and advertise as they wish. However, the "desire" to use commercial speech is insufficient to justify protection. As an individual right, the first amendment protects an individual's expression of his or her allegiances. It protects one's expression of one's "self." This interpretation of first amendment protection can serve as a guide for its extension to commercial speech.

The allegiances of a speaker in the commercial realm may be either to the existence of a profit-oriented commercial realm, or to the expected sociopolitical effects of the speech, or to the desired commercial transaction and profit. It has been argued above that an individual's involvement in commercial speech practices is, in principle, not a criterion for the presence of either the first or second of these hypothesized allegiances. Although a correlation between such involvement and these allegiances may exist, there is no necessary connection between them. Most important, the speech is in no way dependent upon the existence of the correlation. Moreover, regulation of commercial speech is perfectly consistent with an individual having either or both of these allegiances and promoting them in practice with protected speech. For example, one can write a book rather than an advertisement extolling the virtues of drink. Thus, protection of commercial speech is unnecessary and may be irrelevant for the protection of these possible allegiances.

The third hypothesized allegiance, the desire to make a sale and profit, appears qualitatively different from other kinds of value commitments. The other allegiances represent substantive commitments. However, making a sale has only instrumental value. The self is expressed through living allegiances to substantive, not to instrumental, values. Although a person may express expertise or capability through effective instrumental activity, the exercise of the skill, not the instrumental goal, is the important element. And, of course, the created structure of society will affect the specific opportunities for demonstrating personal capacities. The first amendment protects the expression of people's substantive values. Nevertheless, if the state is allowed to promote or protect any system of order, it must have power to regulate instrumental activities—the activities whose meaning and consequences are often largely determined by the social structure.

Hidden complexity may lie behind this simple distinction between the substantive value commitments of individuals and the instrumental goal of making a profit. In our society, where the sense of self is frequently precarious and insecure, and where comparison with others and social recognition frequently serve to mold one's sense of personal identity, many people find their affirmation and personal fulfillment in making money, in making a profit, in being "successful" in their economic activities. In fact, prominent theorists have correlated the historical development of western industrial capitalism with the spread of the attitude that economic success is evidence of personal worth.

Even if the frequent criticism of this economic success notion of self-fulfillment and of the society which encourages it is accepted as valid, and even if such a society promotes only a truncated notion of the self, members of that society may substantively value the profit-making activity. Nevertheless, the argument for constitutional protection of profit-making activities fails. One's opportunities for self-fulfillment, as well as one's concept of it, are greatly affected not only by chance, natural endowments, and personal effort, but also by the form of the existing social order. The opportunities for success in instrumental activity are determined by that social order.

For example, the opportunity for a pianist either to make money or to please others is affected by such factors as the kind of education given youth, and the way the prevailing system of property rights allows or prevents music teachers, performers, and even instrument makers to require payment for the various positive effects of their activities. The individual's claim for protection of action manifesting substantive values cannot extend to a prohibition on the conscious structuring of instrumental opportunities. Such a prohibition would imply that no collective choices could be made with respect to the institutional and social forms of our society. Since *any* definition of personal or property rights involves collective choices, prohibiting societal choices affecting the instrumental consequences of behavior is not only a denial of the freedom to be involved in decisions concerning the kind of world one wants to live in, but, since some such definitions must exist, is, from the start, incoherent. To the extent that one's self-fulfillment comes merely through success in instrumental activity, one's claim to freedom to pursue this form of success must be limited by the framework resulting from collective choice. Thus, in failing to represent any substantive value of the speaker, the third allegiance, the goal of making sales and profits, has no claim to protection as a part of the first amendment.

Beyond the conclusion that commercial speech does not promote individual or human sovereignty, one further comment seems appropriate. Powerful arguments have been advanced which indicate that the commercial practices of a possessive market society operate to deny most people real freedom of choice in many significant decisions; that market practices operate to decrease both the totality and equality of human power to exercise human capacities; and that other socio-economic structures would allow for a more just and more democratic society. Individual freedom, it is argued, may be increased by regulating these value-laden market practices in accordance with the democratic choices of the smallest subdivision of the polity capable of effectively making and implementing such choices. According to such an analysis, the commercial sphere should be marked off as especially appropriate for restructuring by the polity, not in order to maximize welfare but in order to expand freedom.

In the preceding discussion, the proposition that commercial speech is justifiably excluded from constitutional protection on the basis of its profit orientation was examined. The profit motive and other self-interested motives which are generally present in protected uses of speech were seen to be quite dissimilar. And while the content of expression in an advertising context, for example, is often indistinguishable from expression protected in another context, such content-equivalence is constitutionally irrelevant. Within a capitalist market structure, the content of commercial speech is not the expression of individual choice or individual value commitments. Therefore, commercial speech legitimately can be regulated for virtually the same reasons that speech, even revolutionary speech, is protected—in order to expand the realm of freedom.

. . .

## IV. POLITICAL SPEECH OF THE COMMERCIAL ENTERPRISE

If all of the enterprise's profit-oriented communications are treated as unprotected commercial speech, the category may appear to be too large. For example, a private utility company publicizing the advantages of free enterprise and encouraging popular opposition to a local TVA type development, or a company contributing funds to the political campaign of a "free trade" candidate, are both engaged in political speech which many would assume the first amendment should protect. Moreover, fairness may require that the utility company's speech be protected since the speech of the individual who advocates public power cannot be abridged. Although business considerations may dictate the content of such speech, the utility company's "political" speech appears qualitatively different from, for example, a shampoo advertisement. The courts have already suggested a distinguishing criterion: one should ask whether the speech does no more than merely propose a private commercial transaction. The two corporate messages can be distinguished by determining whether the speech is directed toward influencing private commercial transactions and is made by a potential party to such transactions.

Although "proposing a private commercial transaction" is a serviceable distinction, the real problem is finding a rationale or justification for the distinction consistent with the principled argument for denying protection to the shampoo or liquor ads. The clearly commercial advertisements should be denied protection, not because these advertisements have less importance or different political and social effects than protected speech, but because their source was, in principle, not rooted in individual choice or freedom. The crucial consideration is not the content of the speech but whether the speech can be attributed to the choice of a free agent.

The possible motivations structurally attributable to the "political commercial speech" show that it must be included within the category of commercial speech. When a private individual or group advocates public power, thereby expressing views about how the socio-economic world ought to be organized, either a broadly or narrowly *self-interested* motive can be attributed to the speaker. If, however, the speech of the private power company or the export-import company is carefully examined, several motivational bases for these business' "political" speech are plausible: (1) The speech may represent the management's judgment that the company's income, profits, and stability would be reduced or endangered by the introduction of public power. This would be a typical profit-oriented motive. (2) The speech may represent the management's personal social and political beliefs. (3) The management may be speaking in behalf of the stockholders or owners who personally favor free-enterprise power production, either because of ideological beliefs or because of their economic self-interest.

The first account, based on a profit orientation, admits that the existing conditions of economic organization determine the content of the speech. As long as the company does not use fraudulent or unlawful means, pursuing a profit orientation is often socially approved. However, this orientation implies the substantive manipulation and creation of values which do not originate in either individual or collective vi-

sions or decisions about what humanity should be, but which instead are rooted in the technical conditions of profit maximization. In such a situation, allowing for human choice requires that the authority to control this speech be located where choices can be based on substantive values and constitutive concerns—in other words, in the political realm.

According to the second account the speech merely represents the management's personal prejudices or values. This account is not likely to be advanced in a world where the use of corporate funds to fulfill management's personal desires, rather than to aid management in carrying out its fiduciary duties, is normally described as either taxable compensation or illegal conversion. The mere coalescence of the employee's views and the enterprise's speech, considered earlier, is not a basis for attributing the speech to the individual's views. Any situation in which corporate "political speech" is properly attributable to management's personal prejudices involves an incomplete separation or a partial merger of productive and consumptive activities of the enterprise and the household. The sociological premise of this Article has been that these spheres are normally separated in the economic enterprises of a developed capitalist economy. In fact, possibly the most important function of the modern corporation is to legally formalize this separation. Consequently, the separation of the household or consumptive sphere from the enterprise or profit-making sphere appears to be a general feature of the existing order. Nevertheless, in cases in which it is lawful to spend corporate funds for this purpose, and in which such an attribution factually exists, the speech should receive first amendment protection subject to the constraint that the cost of the speech be characterized as income for those corporate participants to whom such speech is attributed.

The third account—that the speech represents the *personal* values of the owners or stockholders—also denies any clear separation of the realm of personal values from the economic enterprise. In fact, in some instances the two are not separate. Many associations are formed to advance the specific values of individuals and their visions of the world. Among them are most non-profit organizations, alternative life-style communes, and political organizations. Some associations such as political parties and labor unions are formed to advance various substantive goals formulated usually by a semi-political process. However, modern business corporations normally cannot be, and are not expected to be, oriented toward such substantive goals, at least where the achievement of the substantive aims are expensive and do not secure profits. Even when it also is concerned with a degree of investment and institutional security, the business corporation is primarily oriented toward profit maximization. Thus, a declaration that the "political speech" is "personal" rather than "business"—that it is designed to advance specifically approved substantive ends rather than the instrumental end of profit—would be inconsistent with the business' normal institutional role. Of course, if the owners or stockholders in fact approve and are willing to help pay for the substantive message, then it should be viewed as personal speech and receive first amendment protection. The cost of the speech would then represent income to those owners rather than a business expense of the corporation. An appropriate way to overcome the presumption that the speech of the large business corporation is "commercial" would be to require that the "personal" speech be financed through the voluntary contributions of owners or shareholders, possibly by requiring them to sign over part of their dividends. Without such evidence of individual approval, a profit-oriented motive would be attributed to the speaker, in which case the government would have power to regulate or prohibit commercial political speech.

. . .

The preceding analysis is reflected in federal statutory law. Existing regulations of corporate "political" speech can only be understood and constitutionally defended if speech attributed to the enterprise—to a profit motive—is not constitutionally protected. However, because of the difficulty in determining the motivational source of corporate political speech, devices have been created allowing such speech to be attributed to the personal choice of individuals and, consequently within the ambit of first amendment protection. As noted above, tax deductions are allowed for business expenses, which represent the cost of profit-oriented activities. However, no deductions are allowed for a business' grassroots lobbying for legislation or for any type of support of political candidates. Disallowing deductions for the corporation's profit-motivated "political speech" places a differentially greater burden on one specific component of the enterprise's various profit-directed activities—its political speech. Placing a special burden on constitutionally protected speech, of course, would be unconstitutional. Thus, our tax laws apparently embody the assumption that commercial political speech is not protected by the first amendment.

Another example of existing regulation is the legal ban on corporate political campaign expenditures or contributions. In *Buckley v. Valeo*, the Court struck down limits on an individual's expenditures for polit-

ical speech, and expressed constitutional concerns about the limits on contributions—doubts which were only alleviated by the reasonableness of these limits and the lack of limits on expenditures. By analogy, the legislative power to completely prohibit corporate contributions and campaign expenditures would hardly be sustainable unless this corporate speech activity were not protected by the first amendment.

Neither the contribution ban nor the tax rule differentially burden or limit speech if the speech is attributable to individual allegiances rather than to profit dictates. To disallow the tax deduction for corporate grassroots lobbying is to charge the owners for the speech, thereby attributing the speech to them rather than to the business. Corporate funds can be used for political contributions only if the corporation's owners or employees first receive the money and then, if they wish, return the money to a political fund. This technique first assures an independent "personal" judgment and, second, treats the money as the income of the person who uses it for political speech purposes. To the extent that formal legal provisions work, the law prohibits political speech by the enterprise *qua* enterprise—surely an impermissible effect if commercial "political" speech is to receive first amendment protection—but allows the enterprise, or committees, or funds which it sets up, to offer political speech or make contributions when the funds used, and decisions made, can be structurally attributed to the owners or employees rather than to the market-induced profit motive.

Including "political" commercial speech within the category of unprotected commercial speech does not necessarily imply that while a person is involved in "economic" activities or in the economic sphere all of the person's speech is unprotected. The commercial speech category is based on the historically relative, and necessarily incomplete, separation of the enterprise from the household or budgetary unit. Because of the lack of separation of the household and the enterprise, the commercial speech category applies to neither a feudally organized economic world nor to marginal areas of modern economic life which have not been rationalized by market processes. Moreover, numerous visions of the future, and some present attempts at restructuring life, involve recognizing and subjecting to human decision the substantive and constitutive values inherent in economic activity and organization. Economic activity would then be determined by conscious and democratic decision and commitment rather than by the alien market-imposed standards of technical rationality. If the present disjunction of substantive and technical rationality were eliminated, no separate category of commercial speech would remain. Even at present, in some important areas of the economic world, speech can and often does address or manifest the values or visions of the speakers; labor organizations represent a clear example. Even demands for higher wages do not quite fit the profit-oriented model. The conditions of employment clearly relate to substantive, although often self-interested, values of the worker. Therefore, the commercial speech exception cannot serve to justify governmental power to regulate labor-organizing or speech activities. Only that speech rooted in the profit-oriented requirements of the enterprise fails in principle to exhibit individually chosen allegiance to personal values.

. . .

Thomas H. Jackson and John Calvin Jeffries, Jr., *Commercial Speech: Economic Due Process and the First Amendment,* 65 VIRGINIA LAW REVIEW 1 (1979)*

Until very recently, the Supreme Court refused to apply the first amendment to "commercial speech." Although the Court never has defined that concept with precision, its meaning is reasonably settled. "Commercial speech" refers to business advertising that does no more than solicit a commercial transaction or state information relevant thereto. Both content and context are critical to this classification. Editorial advertising is not commercial speech, and neither is a discussion of goods or services in a news account or consumer guide. Ordinary business advertising, however, is commercial speech, and as such it has long been thought to fall outside the guaranteed freedom of speech and press.

At bottom, the doctrine of commercial speech rests on a clean distinction between the market for ideas and the market for goods and services. In the realm of ideas, the first amendment erects stringent safeguards against governmental restraint. In the economic sphere, by contrast, the majoritarian political process controls. Under the doctrine of commercial speech, ordinary business advertising is part and parcel of the economic marketplace and therefore is

excluded from the protections of the first amendment.

As a result, commercial speech has been subject to numerous restrictions that would be unconstitutional if applied to "speech" of a different sort. For example, advertisements may be banned as offensive, even though they are manifestly not obscene, and they may be condemned as misleading, even though they contain no false statement of fact. In some cases, the federal authorities have actually required corrective advertising to undo the supposed misconceptions engendered by past efforts. Government commonly may demand that advertisements include certain information, display specific warnings, or use approved product descriptions, even where these requirements are not necessary to avoid inaccuracy or deception. The federal government also may suppress advertising of illegal products and all broadcast advertising of some legitimate products, most notably cigarettes. These illustrations suffice to suggest the pervasive legal regulation of business advertising. That such restraints have long been assumed constitutional is tribute to the prevalence of the notion that commercial speech is something apart from the freedom of speech and press guaranteed by the first amendment.

In its 1976 decision in *Virginia State Board of Pharmacy v. Virginia Citizens Consumer Council, Inc.,* the Supreme Court rejected that notion. Earlier decisions had presaged the demise of the commercial speech exception, but all were explicable on other grounds. As the Court itself recognized, however, *Virginia Board of Pharmacy* was a paradigm case of commercial speech, and the invalidation of the restrictive statute therefore was all the more telling. Virginia law prohibited any licensed pharmacist from advertising prescription drug prices. Consumers challenged this provision by asserting that it interfered with their first amendment right to receive and with pharmacists' first amendment right to convey such price information. In holding that price advertising was not outside the first amendment, the Court rejected the central premise of the commercial speech doctrine—namely, that business advertising that does no more than solicit a commercial transaction may be regulated by government on the same terms as any other aspect of the marketplace. Instead, the Court equated ordinary business advertising with constitutionally protected speech. Although noting that commercial speech may be restricted in some ways in which noncommercial speech may not be, the Court withdrew the regulation of commercial advertising from the arena of political choice and reserved it to review by the judiciary under the aegis of the first amendment.

We believe that *Virginia Board of Pharmacy* was decided wrongly. In our view, the first amendment guarantee of freedom of speech and press protects only certain identifiable values. Chief among them is effective self-government. Additionally, the first amendment may protect the opportunity for individual self-fulfillment through free expression. Neither value is implicated by governmental regulation of commercial speech. Thus the justifications supporting judicial abrogation of political choice to uphold the guarantees of the first amendment do not extend to commercial speech. Although disallowing state interference with commercial advertising serves other values that merit careful legislative considerationaggregate economic efficiency and consumer opportunity to maximize utility in a free marketthese values are not appropriate for judicial vindication under the first amendment. We therefore suggest that the line of development begun by *Virginia Board of Pharmacy* should be cut short.

. . .

## II.  FIRST AMENDMENT PRINCIPLES AND COMMERCIAL SPEECH

Measured in terms of traditional first amendment principles, commercial speech is remarkable for its insignificance. It neither contributes to self-government nor nurtures the realization of the individual personality. Thus, although business advertising may play an important role in ordering the marketplace, it falls outside the accepted reasons for protecting the freedom of speech.

In the first place, commercial speech has no apparent connection with the idea of individual self-fulfillment. Whatever else it may mean, the concept of a first amendment right of personal autonomy in matters of belief and expression stops short of a seller hawking his wares. Professor Emerson himself asserts that commercial soliciting and similar activities "fall within the system of commercial enterprise and are outside the system of freedom of expression." Also, the Court in *Virginia Board of Pharmacy*, despite an exhaustive canvas of the reasons for its decision, did not identify drug price advertising as a form of protected self-expression by the pharmacist. In fact, the Court contradicted any such rationale by correctly "assuming" that "the advertiser's interest is a purely economic one." Thus, whatever its other effects, governmental regulation of commercial speech does not invade the concept of a first amendment right of a personal fulfillment through self-expression. Judicial abrogation of legislative control over commercial speech cannot be justified on this ground.

Governmental regulation of commercial advertising also does no violence to the protection of political speech. Conceptually, the irrelevance of commercial speech to the political speech principle is a mere truism, at least from the speaker's standpoint, because "commercial speech" is defined in part by the absence of political significance. "[S]peech which does 'no more than propose a commercial transaction'" omits, by definition, any expression essential to self-government. For this kind of communication, the structure of representative democracy yields no inference of inviolability because commercial speech concerns economic rather than political decisionmaking. Furthermore, in this case, at least, experience confirms reason. The typical newspaper advertisement or television commercial makes no comment on governmental personnel or policy. It does not marshall information relevant to political action, nor does it focus public attention on questions of political significance. Indeed, ordinary commercial advertising is generally so bland as to be irrelevant even to those antecedent questions of value or attitude that may underlie political opinion.

The point seems plain enough and would require no belaboring were it not for some rather curious pronouncements by the Court in *Virginia Board of Pharmacy*. As a starting proposition, the Court accurately noted what was not in issue:

> Our pharmacist does not wish to editorialize on any subject, cultural, philosophical, or political. He does not wish to report any particularly newsworthy fact, or to make generalized observations even about commercial matters. The "idea" he wishes to communicate is simply this: "I will sell you the X prescription drug at the Y price."

On first glance, the statement could not be more clear. The Court is saying that price advertising has nothing to do with political speech or even with the exposition of cultural or philosophical ideas, and most of the Court's analysis proceeds on that basis. Had the case involved political commentary or the publication of newsworthy information, the result would have been commonplace, and there would have been no occasion for the groundbreaking assertion of first amendment protection for speech of purely commercial import.

Having initially assessed the problem correctly, the Court then muddies the waters. The Court rightly avoids any effort to force price information into the concept of political expression by the speaker. With respect to the listener, however, the Court apparently could not resist trying to associate price advertising with the protection of political speech. That attempt begins with the familiar observation that the ready availability of commercial information fosters the efficient allocation of resources in a free market economy. The opinion then continues as follows:

> And if it [the free flow of commercial information] is indispensable to the proper allocation of the resources in a free enterprise system, it is also indispensable to the formation of intelligent opinions as to how that system ought to be regulated or altered. Therefore, even if the First Amendment were thought to be primarily an instrument to enlighten public decisionmaking in a democracy, we could not say that the free flow of information does not serve that goal.

The striking indirection of phrasing suggests that the Court may be a little doubtful of this argument, as well it should be. While an unrestrained flow of commercial advertising may be essential to the efficient functioning of a free market economy, neither commercial advertising nor a free market economy is essential to informed political decisionmaking.

Simply put, the Court's argument, if its cautiously negative approach may be called that, is a non sequitur. It apparently rests on the assertion that because regulation of the free enterprise system is a matter of political choice, commercial advertising that plays a part in the functioning of the free enterprise system is *for that reason* politically significant speech. But in terms of relevance to political decisionmaking, advertising is neither more nor less significant than a host of other market activities that legislatures concededly may regulate. Political decisionmaking does not depend any more on knowing that "I will sell you the X prescription drug at the Y price" than it does on the ability of pharmacists to charge different prices for the same product in the first place. The decisive point is the absence of any principled distinction between commercial soliciting and other aspects of economic activity. This identity of interests belies the Court's cautious attempt to support the constitutionalization of commercial speech not as a matter of economic right but as a manifestation of political speech. The correct conclusion is the one with which the decision began: The role of price advertising in ordering the marketplace does not bring it within the political speech principle of the first amendment.

A related line of argument posits a purely strategic rationale for protecting commercial speech. The thrust of this view is not that commercial speech, as such, is politically significant but rather that constitutional protection for commercial advertising is necessary to make effective the guarantee of free political debate. In other words, this argument concerns the practical administration of the distinction between commercial and political speech and not the theoretical scope of the political speech principle itself.

The starting point is the accepted proposition that constitutionally protected speech does not lose that status merely "because money is spent to protect it." The distinction between protected and unprotected communication does not depend solely on conveyance for payment but rests on a mixed question of context and content: Does the advertisement discuss an issue relevant to self-government, or does it merely solicit a commercial transaction? The Court in *Virginia Board of Pharmacy* apparently believed that this inquiry would prove difficult, if not debilitating. "[N]o line," the Court suggested, "between publicly 'interesting' or 'important' commercial advertising and the opposite kind could ever be drawn."

Certainly, the Court is right in perceiving that there is no self-executing rule for determining the limits of the political speech principle in the context of business advertising. The specter of linedrawing, however, is seldom sufficient reason to abandon the inquiry entirely. As Mr. Justice Rehnquist pointed out in dissent, it is one thing to speculate that some future case may require a refined and subtle judgment in applying the commercial speech doctrine. It is quite another thing to take this observation as a springboard for the wholesale displacement of legislative authority even where no such ambiguity exists. To withdraw an entire field from legislative competence simply because doing so obviates the need for some more careful inquiry in the future puts the constitutional cart before the horse and contradicts all the usual arguments for restraint in the exercise of judicial review. Generally speaking, at least, respect for the concept of a representative democracy demands that intrusion into the legislative process on grounds of judicial expedience be sparingly used.

Of course, there may be exceptions. Conceivably, a difficulty in linedrawing could become so intractable and pervasive as to render the distinction itself untenable. To protect the constitutional rights in those cases, the sensible solution would be to abandon the inquiry or restructure the rule of decision. As the Supreme Court itself has observed in another context, it may sometimes be necessary to protect constitutionally irrelevant communication "in order to protect speech that matters." While there may be situations in which this kind of rule is ultimately justified, respect for the majoritarian political process requires that a purely strategic abrogation of legislative choice not be undertaken in advance of necessity.

That necessity was entirely absent in *Virginia Board of Pharmacy*. The case concerned the purported desire of the pharmacist to make a purely commercial statement to a prospective buyer. Because that statement does not remotely suggest an intractable linedrawing problem, the Court resorted to a hypothetical to suggest that the difficulty might nevertheless arise. "Our pharmacist," said the Court, "could cast himself as a commentator on store-to-store disparities in drug prices, giving his own and those of a competitor as proof." That hypothetical is as close as the Court comes to explaining why the lack of a bright line at the boundary of commercial speech justifies withdrawal of the entire field from legislative competence. The implication is that a legislative policy of restricting commercial speech would be impossible to administer and hence ineffectual. The Court apparently fears that advertisers could evade the legislative restraint by garnishing their advertisements with political commentary. If this proved correct, overruling the doctrine of commercial speech would be largely a formality. There would be no real curtailment of legislative power but only a facilitation for advertisers to do directly that which the Constitution guarantees them the right to do by subterfuge and indirection.

This argument founders on at least two grounds. First and foremost, it is belied by experience. The record in this case, for example, does not indicate that any pharmacist in fact had tried to avoid the legislative restriction by posing as a commentator on store-to-store disparities in drug prices. The Court points to no evidence of an unsolvable problem; indeed, the Courts' example is pure speculation. The absence of any previous problem of this sort is highly significant. After all, a rule distinguishing commercial from political speech is not an untried possibility. Quite to the contrary, the exclusion of commercial speech from the protections of the first amendment has been an established feature of constitutional doctrine for more than thirty years. During that era legislatures imposed a wide variety of restraints on commercial advertising. Presumably, the parties adversely affected by such regulation have had ample incentive to evade its impact, and their efforts to do so should have presented to the courts exactly the kinds of linedrawing problems discussed above.

The remarkable fact, of course, is the absence of historical experience of this sort. *Valentine v. Chrestensen* itself involved an attempted subterfuge, but the Court did not find any particular difficulty in making the distinction required by that case. Subsequent decisions have touched on one or another aspect of the commercial speech doctrine, but neither the volume nor character of past litigation reveals any inordinate judicial difficulty in applying the traditional rule. Even Professor Emerson has acknowledged that "the problem of differentiating between commercial and other communication has not in practice proved to be a serious one." The impression derived from study of prior experience is that of a rule widely understood, though not everywhere accepted a rule attacked not for instability or unintelligibility but for reaching results thought by some to be undesirable.

One reason for this rather quiet history is a purely practical consideration of the sort often overlooked in theoretical debate. It concerns the assumed propensity of affected parties to try to evade legal restraints on commercial speech by clothing their business messages in political commentary or social debate. Good reason exists to regard this as an unreal picture. After all, the businessman's first purpose is to make money, and advertising costs money. Ordinarily, the businessman will advertise or not according to his estimate of the expected return on that investment. When the law restricts his ability to advertise, he will try to avoid that constraint if he thinks it would be profitable to do so. The kinds of disguises and stratagems that would be necessary to portray commercial advertising as political speech, however, are very likely to render the advertising itself less effective. Economic self-interest would often counsel against any elaborate ruse to convey a forbidden commercial message. As a result, the legislative policy underlying a limitation on commercial speech is not likely to be defeated in practice by the subtle problems that abstract speculation may suggest.

Second, one must recognize that *Virginia Board of Pharmacy* in fact does not resolve whatever difficulties do inhere in the need to distinguish "commercial speech" from speech protected by the first amendment. The Court in that case explicitly stated that commercial speech, although now assimilated to the protections of the first amendment, is not entitled to the same level of protection accorded other kinds of "speech." Even after *Virginia Board of Pharmacy* then, commercial speech must be distinguished from traditionally protected speech to determine the level of first amendment protection a particular communication will receive. Whatever linedrawing problems may have been encountered under the old doctrine thus are simply carried forward in a different context.

In summary, *Virginia Board of Pharmacy* is inexplicable under traditional first amendment principles. Ordinary business advertising does not advance the goal of individual self-fulfillment through free expression, nor does it contribute to political decisionmaking in a representative democracy. Commercial advertising simply is not relevant to either of these commonly accepted bases for construing the first amendment. Moreover, there is no evidence of a strategic necessity to protect constitutionally irrelevant speech "in order to protect speech that matters." Both reason and experience suggest that the distinction between commercial speech and protected speech is relatively easy to maintain. Finally, we are at a loss to identify any other comprehensible understanding of the first amendment that would require protection of commercial speech. That is not to say, of course, that *Virginia Board of Pharmacy* is unsupported by any intelligible perception of public policy but only that the decision is responsive to values far removed from those that plausibly might be associated with a constitutional guarantee of the freedom of speech.

## III. COMMERCIAL SPEECH AND ECONOMIC LIBERTY

In light of the irrelevance of traditional first amendment concerns to commercial advertising, it is not surprising that the Court in *Virginia Board of Pharmacy* spent relatively little effort trying to explain its decision in those terms. Instead, the opinion emphasized the adverse economic effects of Virginia's ban against drug price advertising. The Court saw this restriction as an invasion of two basic values of economic liberty. The first is the opportunity of the individual producer or consumer to maximize his own economic utility. The second is the aggregate economic efficiency of a free market economy. The Court correctly perceived that the suppression of drug price advertising is likely to impair both of these values.

In discussing maximization of individual utility, the Court began with the "assumption" that the advertiser's interest "is a purely economic one." While, as the Court noted, this factor does not disqualify the advertiser's claim to first amendment protection, neither does it provide a reason for giving such advertisements constitutional protection. A more potent consideration was the interest of the individual consumer. As the Court pointed out, a "consumer's interest in the free flow of commercial information . . . may be as keen, if not keener by far, than his interest in the day's most urgent political debate." The Court went on to describe with feeling and eloquence the impact of a price advertising ban on individual consumers:

Those whom the suppression of prescription

drug price information hits the hardest are the poor, the sick, and particularly the aged. A disproportionate amount of their income tends to be spent on prescription drugs; yet they are the least able to learn, by shopping from pharmacist to pharmacist, where their scarce dollars are best spent. When drug prices vary as strikingly as they do, information as to who is charging what becomes more than a convenience. It could mean the alleviation of physical pain or the enjoyment of basic necessities.

By voiding the legislative restriction on drug price advertising the Court hoped to enable individual consumers to spend their "scarce dollars" more effectively.

The Court's economic analysis is surely correct. In the competitive economic model, a seller advertises only if he believes it to be more efficient than an alternative expenditure of similar resources. A ban against price advertising increases the costs of obtaining price information and makes it less likely that the consumer's choices will be well informed. Because the marginal cost of acquiring more information at some point exceeds the marginal benefits of obtaining such information, the reduction of less costly sources of information means that a consumer (now more "uninformed" than would otherwise be the case) will pay more than is "necessary" (in a world of less costly information). On the evidence in this case, the consumer may pay as much as seven times more. The result is an unnecessary reduction in consumer purchasing power, and for the person of limited means, a decrease in the "alleviation of physical pain or the enjoyment of basic necessities." The ban, of course, may increase the welfare of pharmacists as a class but only by effecting a wealth transfer from consumers to pharmacists.

The Court also perceived that this impairment of individual economic opportunity has adverse implications for aggregate efficiency:

So long as we preserve a predominantly free enterprise economy, the allocation of our resources in large measure will be made through numerous private economic decisions. It is a matter of public interest that those decisions, in the aggregate, be intelligent and well informed.

When consumers choose ignorantly, an inefficient allocation of societal resources is likely. While the ultimate results of legislative interference with the competitive market are difficult to predict, it seems plausible to assume that the consequence of a reduced flow of information will lead to some situational monopolies that would not exist if advertising were un-restricted. Most economists are willing to assume that the existence of some monopoly power likely will lead to a lower level of aggregate economic efficiency than would otherwise be the case.

As a matter of public policy, both of these considerations are significant. The opportunity of the individual consumer to maximize his own utility by making well-informed economic choices is important, particularly in the context of medical care. Moreover, the nation plainly has an interest in promoting allocative efficiency in the economy as a whole that interest lies at the heart of the federal antitrust laws. Generally, one might regret any governmental action that invades these interests without some clearly off-setting benefit to the public good.

Virginia claimed such an offsetting benefit in the maintenance of professionalism among pharmacists. The state argued that unlimited advertising would lead to aggressive price competition in the preparation and sale of prescription drugs. Such competition, feared the state, would drive the conscientious pharmacist out of business and endanger the survival of the neighborhood pharmacy. Despite these arguments, the Court was not persuaded of the merits of Virginia's law. The Court found no direct or necessary relation between drug prices and professional standards. The pharmacist whom the advertising ban enables to charge more than the competitive price may or may not provide superior service. Moreover, the Court thought it significant that pharmacists in any event were subject to close regulation explicitly addressed to maintaining professional standards.

While the state's arguments are not inherently implausible, one may well agree with the Court that Virginia's ban against drug price advertising contributed less to the professionalism of pharmacists than to their wealth. Certainly, the legislation benefited small, inefficient pharmacies that could not compete effectively with larger concerns if price advertising were allowed. In other words, the advertising ban operated to insulate certain sellers from the competitive marketplace and thus to achieve special advantage for the owners of small pharmacies. Whether this legislation also redounded to the benefit of the public at large seems more doubtful. The Court, at least, seems to have viewed Virginia's law as nothing more or less than a classic case of special interest legislation inconsistent with any disinterested understanding of the public good.

The issue is not free from doubt, but on balance, the *Virginia Board of Pharmacy* opinion seems persuasive in demonstrating the unwisdom of Virginia's law against drug price advertising. No reason exists to doubt the Court's assessment that the advertising ban would inhibit competition and lead to artificially high drug prices, and, although the point is certainly arguable, the Court may also be right to discount the purported contribution of economic inefficiency to high professional standards. These concerns undoubtedly are sufficient grounds to warrant criticism of Virginia's policy and opposition to its continued enforcement. It is surprising to discover, however, that these economic considerations add up to a *constitutional* impediment to legislative control of the marketplace. It is all the more startling to be told, as *Virginia Board of Pharmacy* announces, that the source of that constitutional restraint is the first amendment. One might have thought, as the Court has so often proclaimed, that demanding judicial review of economic legislation was a concern of the past. Even if that tradition were to be revived, one would expect to find the constitutional safeguards of economic liberty to be housed within the flexible contours of due process of law. Instead, economic due process is resurrected, clothed in the ill-fitting garb of the first amendment, and sent forth to battle the kind of special interest legislation that the Court has tolerated for more than forty years. In short, the Supreme Court has reconstituted the values of *Lochner v. New York* as components of freedom of speech. This renovation of discredited doctrine is far more troublesome than commentators have been willing to admit and warrants thorough reconsideration.

Were it not for the first amendment trappings, this revivification of *Lochner* would no doubt excite substantial opposition. At the very least, it would be recognized as a contradiction of the heretofore settled idea that the Constitution tolerates extensive regulation of the economy. Various decisions have reiterated that proposition in a host of different contexts. For example, government constitutionally is free to restrict production of a good, to determine the prices and conditions of sale, and even to ban certain items from the marketplace. Government also has the authority to limit access to a profession, to prescribe wages and conditions of employment, and even to outlaw certain lines of work. Additionally, government may distort the free market economy by licensing a monopoly, by creating other barriers to entry, or by subsidizing public competition to private industry. In all of these ways, government may regulate and affect commercial transactions. According to *Virginia Board of Pharmacy*, however, government may not suppress the solicitation of commercial transactions in the form of business advertising. That kind of regulation is supposedly barred by the first amendment, even though it does not implicate the traditionally accepted meanings of freedom of speech. The problem, says the Court, is that the ban against drug price advertising impairs the economic welfare of the individual consumer and contributes to aggregate economic inefficiency. These values are also implicated, however, by every one of the laws mentioned above. Every kind of legislative restraint on the operation of the free market economy may be used to favor one group at the expense of the public at large and thus to further one or another social objective by encouraging an economically inefficient allocation of resources.

Indeed, such results are commonplace. Price supports for farm products raise the price of bread and maintain an inefficient concentration of resources in food production. Minimum wage laws add to unemployment, especially among young and unskilled workers, and distort the aggregate labor market. Exactly the same values that are impaired by Virginia's ban against drug price advertising are also invaded by these and most other instances of governmental regulation of the economy. Of course, countervailing social objectives often may justify governmental displacement of the free market, and we are very far from suggesting that regulation of the market is necessarily, or even presumptively, undesirable. The point is, rather, that such judgments are properly left to popularly elected legislatures. In terms of constitutional values, price supports, minimum wage laws, and advertising bans are utterly indistinguishable. Constitutional objection to such laws stands or falls on precisely the ground asserted in *Lochner v. New York* and repeatedly repudiated in the decades since then.

Exactly the same point can be made in terms of the familiar notion that the greater power normally includes the lesser. Nothing in the federal Constitution bars a state from legislating prescription drug prices, even if the prices were set significantly higher than those that would prevail in a competitive market. Ancillary to such action, the state might also forbid commercial advertising of prescription drugs at any price other than that authorized by law. Given the authority to set prices in the first place, there is nothing remarkable in the extension of legislative control to price-advertising. After all, if it is illegal to sell the X drug at the Y price, then no legitimate reason can be found to advertise such a sale. The typical business advertisement speech that does "no more than solicit a commercial transaction" serves no valid purpose when the underlying transaction is forbidden by law. The Supreme Court apparently has accepted this reasoning and has indicated its readiness to uphold legislative regulation of commercial advertising "incidental to a valid limitation on economic activity."

The significance of this analysis lies in its application to the instance in which the legislature has not exercised its "greater power" over the underlying economic activity. Thus, for example, the legislature rationally might conclude that the sale of cigarettes should be allowed but that advertising should be banned to discourage new users. In such a case, according to the reasoning of *Virginia Board of Pharmacy*, governmental control over price advertising would offend the first amendment. This conclusion only makes sense if one assumes a first amendment value in the advertising of cigarettes independent of its role in encouraging or facilitating the sale of cigarettes. The latter transaction the government concededly has the power to forbid or control. If independent first amendment significance did exist in this instance, it would also exist when the state has declared the underlying transaction unlawful. So, for example, some legitimate function would arise for the advertisement, "I will sell you the X drug at the Y price," even where the sale is forbidden by law. That no such independent purpose in fact can be identified confirms the hypothesis that the significance of ordinary business advertising lies entirely in its relation to the contemplated economic transaction. It follows that such advertising should be subject to governmental regulation on the same terms as any other aspect of the marketplace.

The point can be put more vividly by comparing *Virginia Board of Pharmacy* with *North Dakota State Board of Pharmacy v. Snyder's Drug Stores, Inc.* The latter case involved a North Dakota statute requiring that the holder of a permit to operate a pharmacy be a "registered pharmacist in good standing" or "a corporation or association, the majority stock in which is owned by registered pharmacists in good standing." *Snyder's Drug Stores, Inc.* was denied a permit because no evidence existed that the majority stock of the parent corporation was held by registered pharmacists. A state court held this requirement unconstitutional under the authority of *Liggett Co. v. Baldridge.* In that 1928 decision, the Supreme Court had invalidated a Pennsylvania law requiring 100% ownership of pharmacies by licensed pharmacists. Reconsidering the question in 1974, the Court unanimously overruled *Liggett* and reinstated the North Dakota statute, noting that "oppos[ing] views of public policy are considerations for the legislative choice." Only two terms later, the Court held unconstitutional Virginia's ban against drug price advertising. Of course, the Virginia case involved "speech," but the identity of interests in the two cases reveals the bankruptcy of this reversion to nonfunctional definitionalism.

Both Virginia and North Dakota defended their laws as appropriately designed to maintain high professional standards in the practice of pharmacy. Virginia's announced purpose was to facilitate provision of professional services by inhibiting effective price competition. North Dakota said it was promoting the same goal by prohibiting ownership by cost-cutters who would not share a professional's devotion to duty over profit. In both cases, however, the legislation is more easily understood as benefiting small, inefficient pharmacies against drugstore chains and other would-be competitors. North Dakota approached that problem directly, while Virginia merely made it difficult for large discount houses to realize their competitive advantage. The predictable result of both laws is to make prescription drug prices higher than would otherwise be the case and thus to effect a wealth transfer from consumers to pharmacists. All the economic evils identified by the Court in *Virginia Board of Pharmacy* are present as fully in the North Dakota case, yet not a single justice voted to strike the latter statute. This outcome cannot be attributed to judicial enthusiasm for North Dakota's brand of special interest legislation. Rather, it reflects a profound and hitherto consistent regard for legislative authority over economic affairs. That deference has been shown not only in *North Dakota State Board of Pharmacy* but also in numerous other modern decisions upholding laws that were arguably unwise, unfair, or opposed to the public interest. No deference was found in *Virginia Board of Pharmacy* because that case happened to involve something called "speech." As we have tried to show, that statute had nothing to do with any intelligible understanding of the meaning of the first amendment. Its invalidation under that rubric constitutes an unwarranted, and probably unintended, resurrection of economic due process in the guise of the freedom of speech.

Finally, the Court in *Virginia Board of Pharmacy* carefully noted that the guarantees of the first amendment do not apply to commercial speech with their usual force. Indeed, the Court emphasized that not all commercial advertising would receive constitutional protection; only "truthful and legitimate commercial information" would be protected. Government remains free to purge commercial advertising of speech that is deceptive or misleading or perhaps merely unverifiable. This result is entirely sound, for only mischief would flow from constitutional abrogation of the government's ability to prevent commercial

fraud. The distinction between "truthful and legitimate" information and other kinds of speech, however, does suggest how far *Virginia Board of Pharmacy* has gone in standing traditional first amendment doctrine on its head. The political speech principle scarcely is limited to empirically verifiable or demonstrably true statements. The rhetoric of any political campaign bears witness to the constitutional tolerance for speech that fairly might be termed deceptive or misleading. The core evil that the first amendment seeks to avoid is official determination of the truth or falsity of political opinion. Nothing could be more hostile to the traditional understanding of the freedom of speech than governmental evaluation of the deceptiveness of political statements. Yet nothing could be more palpably wrongheaded than the extension of this approach to protect deceptive or misleading solicitations of commercial transactions. The Court has recognized the difference and announced its willingness to allow suppression of misleading commercial speech. That seeming contradiction once again shows how far ordinary business advertising is removed from the traditional concerns of the first amendment and how plainly the freedom of speech has been diverted to serve the entirely unrelated values of individual economic liberty and aggregate economic efficiency.

. . .

---

Steven Shiffrin, *The First Amendment and Economic Regulation: Away from a General Theory of the First Amendment*, 78 NORTHWESTERN UNIVERSITY LAW REVIEW 1212 (1983)*

. . .

Each commercial speech case the Court has considered has involved advertising or the proposal of a commercial transaction, and almost all of the commentators have looked at the "commercial speech" problem through the lens of commercial advertising. The collective myopia has distorted something quite important: the commercial speech that has been beneath the protection of the first amendment for all

---

these years has not been confined to commercial advertising.

. . .

By looking at speech made pursuant to commercial transactions, however, we examine only the tip of the iceberg. Commercial actors such as corporations do not speak only to propose commercial transactions, to advertise, or even to influence the outcome of initiatives. Corporations speak to the press, for example, about their corporate future, regulated by the securities laws, to their shareholders about their future, regulated by still other aspects of the securities laws, to their employees, subject to the labor laws, to their competitors, subject to the antitrust laws, government officials, with an eye on the lobbying laws, and their lawyers, their accountants, their bankers, and their suppliers, subject to a host of government regulations. Some of these same corporations are banks, airlines, or public utilities subject to other layers of regulation. Most such regulation has been thought to be economic regulation of speech that is beneath the protection of the first amendment. Most of the speech I have described above does not propose a commercial transaction. Yet some of it could be characterized as relating solely to the economic interests of speaker and audience—to borrow a phrase casually introduced by the Court in *Central Hudson*. What is its status? Is it beneath the protection of the first amendment under *Valentine*? That is, is *Valentine* alive and well except for a small part of what the Court previously deemed unprotected? Or is some (much?) of this speech entitled now to full first amendment protection because it does not meet the definition of commercial speech? How should we think about it?

. . .

Seventeen years ago Kenneth Karst wrote a tribute to Harry Kalven that would steer us in another direction. Karst celebrated "the advantages of thinking small." He praised Kalven for recognizing that if we do not think small we run the risk of deciding cases on the basis of empty abstractions. "To make a balancing approach meaningful, we must think in narrower terms, recognizing that the strengths of the competing interests may vary in new contexts. That is precisely the sort of thing that Professor Kalven does so well." Even following Karst and Kalven, we might want to create rules that exclude much commercial speech from the protection of the first amendment. Before deciding upon rules, however, we would need to take account of the range of speech involved.

. . .

## The Commentators, Commercial Speech, and Free Speech Theory

### Divorcing Commercial Speech from the First Amendment

Many first amendment commentators would counsel the courts to stay out of the commercial speech area. . .

*The Politically Based Approach.*—Jackson and Jeffries begin with the assumption that the commercial speech that has long been considered to be beneath the protection of the first amendment is "business advertising that does no more than solicit a commercial transaction or state information relevant thereto." With this understanding, they proceed to argue that free speech has nothing to do with commercial speech. In their view, the first amendment protects "only certain identifiable values." The principal value is effective self-government. It is possible, they observe, that the amendment protects the opportunity for individual self-fulfillment through free expression, though they are not comfortable with that idea and assume it only for purposes of argument. The two principles of self-government and individual self-fulfillment, they say, "capture in reliable summary the dominant conceptions of the meaning of freedom of speech." In their view, "neither value is implicated by government regulation of commercial speech." And Jackson and Jeffries "are unable to discover—in the opinion of the Court, in the secondary literature, or in our own reflections—any other principle that would bring the protection of commercial speech within the scope of the first amendment."

To the contrary, John Stuart Mill's emphasis on the role of free speech in the discovery of truth and on the fallibility of the government in regulating speech is a prominent theme in the secondary literature, not to mention its frequent appearances in the opinions of the Court. That fact should at least give one pause before conceding the reliability of the Jackson-Jeffries glossary of first amendment values. Additional doubt arises when one remembers that Kenneth Karst and Ronald Dworkin emphasize equality, dignity, and respect as principal values of the first amendment. One can question whether Karst's and Dworkin's concepts are captured in a summary that itself does not distinguish between individual self-fulfillment and autonomy. These considerations can be saved for discussion of Professor Baker's work, however, since he gives them more detailed treatment.

. . .

Jackson and Jeffries are on their strongest ground when they argue that a politically based approach to the first amendment would dictate a different result in *Virginia Pharmacy*. Politically based approaches to the first amendment, of course, have long been criticized for their inability to define the scope of "political." Commentators either define political speech too narrowly, excluding literature, art, and science from the first amendment, or define political speech broadly enough to include these areas, an approach that exaggerates the role of literature, art, and science in politics and offers no principled way to justify other exclusions. Jackson and Jeffries believe that they need not tackle the problem of defining political speech in order to handle the problem of commercial speech. Whatever the scope of a politically based approach, it surely does not "include 'speech' irrelevant to the processes of political decisionmaking, or so tenuously connected as to be no more useful in the formation and reformation of political opinions than the experience of life itself."

What of *Virginia Pharmacy*'s claim that drug price advertising is relevant to the political process? Jackson and Jeffries have a relatively easy path to pursue here. Price advertising is simply not political speech. In terms of relevance to political decisionmaking, "advertising is neither more nor less significant than a host of other market activities that legislatures concededly may regulate." The same can be said about the role of commercial information in fostering the efficient allocation of resources. Their argument here seems right on target. It was strange indeed for the Court to suggest that the first amendment has been Chicago-school economics travelling incognito for all these years. This suggestion looks a little less strange, of course, if the pursuit of truth is counted as one of the purposes of the first amendment. It is easy enough to say, however, that price advertising is removed from political debate.

Jackson and Jeffries have a more difficult time with the Court's contention that an individual advertisement may be of general public interest. The Court points to such examples as an artificial fur manufacturer promoting its product as an alternative to the extinction of furbearing mammals by its competitors, or a domestic producer advertising its product as an alternative to imports. There is a straightforward way to handle these examples. One could candidly admit that the content of commercial advertising sometimes has political significance, and proceed to argue that sorting out such advertisements on a case-by-case basis presents risks of arbitrary decisionmaking and uncertainty—speech might be commercial one day and political the next, creating the concomitant difficulty of determining how long an issue is political—and that commercial advertising is so rarely political that a general refusal to make these inquiries would not seriously interfere with political debate. Has the nation's political debate turned much at all on the content of product advertisements? Advocates could find occasional examples, but putting aside institutional advertising, commercial advertisements rarely contribute to political dialogue. Recognizing that *some* commercial speech is relevant to political dialogue seems more palatable, however, than pretending (as the Court does in *Central Hudson*) that speech advocating the consumption of electricity in the midst of a national debate about energy is "related solely to the economic interests of the speaker and its audience." Admitting that commercial speech is occasionally relevant to political issues also seems more palatable than the way in which Jackson and Jeffries handle the Court's artificial fur and domestic manufacturer examples.

In a move that preserves their textual claim that commercial speech has nothing to do with political speech, Jackson and Jeffries consign the Court's examples to a footnote in which they argue that government can regulate such speech because the government could outlaw the underlying activity. "The problem with the examples used in *Virginia Board of Pharmacy*, therefore, is that it is difficult to justify protection of a means to an end primarily on the ground of its ability to achieve that end, when the end itself may be freely dispensed with." Indeed it is. But the examples mentioned in *Virginia Pharmacy* were not offered to show that advertising achieves a particular end. They were designed to support the separate argument that commercial advertising may be of general or public interest. The best Jackson and Jeffries can do here is try to argue that the speech can be regulated nonetheless, but they cannot maintain a squeaky-clean separation between commercial advertising and political speech.

Beyond Commercial Advertising.—If it is difficult to fashion a neat dichotomy between commercial advertising and political speech, it is impossible to maintain a commercial/political distinction when one moves beyond advertising to other categories of "commercial" speech. Let us first focus upon what most would regard as a sacred cow. Surely the first amendment has nothing to do with the securities laws, or at least so we have long assumed. In *Ohralik v. Ohio State Bar Association*, the Court went out of its way to explain that "[n]umerous examples could be cited of communications that are regulated without offending the First Amendment, such as the exchange of information about securities . . . [or]

corporate proxy statements. . . .'' That is the Court's present bottom line, but it glosses over a significant doctrinal problem which makes the distinction between commercial and political speech impossible to maintain.

Suppose the chief executive of General Motors wants to give a speech at a press conference. He or she wants to talk about the future of the company, future production plans and expected sales, expected areas of difficult competition, and the potential for successes and failures in meeting that competition. Would such a speech be political or commercial? There are certainly commercial aspects to the speech. People will likely buy and sell General Motors stock in response to it. But the executive is not proposing a commercial transaction or advertising cars. Rather, the speech is about the economic future of General Motors.

Analyzing the political aspects of the encounter is somewhat more complicated than it would be if the speech were to be given by a car manufacturer in Eastern Europe. The political character of the speech would then be obvious since the speaker would be an appointed government official announcing the government's hopes and expectations. Some might be tempted to say that what is political there is non-political here, but that retort is glib.

Look first at the executive's speech through the lens of American libel law. In casting the decisive vote to extend the protection of *New York Times Co. v. Sullivan* to public figures, Chief Justice Warren recognized that "increasingly in this country, the distinctions between governmental and private sectors are blurred . . . . It is plain that although they are not subject to the restraints of the political process, 'public figures,' like 'public officials' often play an influential role in ordering society." Even if the libel perspective were not available, it would be quite difficult to maintain that the remarks of a major auto executive are irrelevant to the political process. The fate of elected public officials often turns on the degree of inflation or unemployment, or more generally on economic conditions. The decisions of major corporate executives obviously affect economic conditions. Public officials have never been blind to this. They have tried to threaten, to subsidize, to regulate, and to persuade businesses to serve the public interest. They have talked of a partnership between business and government because there is one. If we shift our example from the auto industry to the defense industry, the point is even more obvious. The Lockheed executive's expectations for the future depend in large measure on his or her expectations about what government officials are likely to do in the future, and insights on that point are of political moment. The same is true of auto executives and many others. In short, if Jackson and Jeffries were to maintain that a first amendment that covered only political speech would be irrelevant to the speech of corporate executives about the future of their companies, they would be forced to fall back on a simplistic model of politics.

Moreover, if the position would be a hard one for Jackson and Jeffries to take, it would be even harder for the Court to do so. Having opined that a pharmacist's public statements of drug prices are political because they serve to allocate resources in the economy, what room for maneuver could the Court find if it were confronted with the fact that bankers routinely examine the statements of corporate executives in deciding how productive resources shall be invested?

All this comes home to roost in the securities laws. For years the SEC has taken various positions as to what corporate executives could talk about without exposing their companies to crushing liability under the securities laws. Today the Commission purportedly encourages executives to make statements about the Company's future, but the form of the Commission's "encouragement" is such that a lawyer is likely to advise a corporate executive that serious risks attach to making future projections. Moreover, for many years the SEC discouraged executives from making projections. If the analysis so far is correct, for many years the SEC has been regulating speech that is important to the political process—*without any first amendment scrutiny*. On Jackson's and Jeffries' own premises, even if they are right about *Virginia Pharmacy*, there are strong grounds for questioning the sagacity of the "commercial speech" doctrine.

The same set of questions arises when government regulates union or corporate elections. Here the regulations vary. The NLRB, for example, has vacillated for many years about the scope of its power to act when it finds that a representation election has been influenced significantly by the misleading statements of an employer. Similarly, the SEC regulates the content of proxy materials in corporate elections to screen out misleading statements. By contrast, a federal administrative agency surely could not screen out "misleading" statements made by a candidate for political office, or dictate other sanctions, even if it found the statements to be deceptive or misleading.

Even if one were prepared to cling to the idea that elections of those who command substantial productive resources are non-political, however, a separation between the political and the commercial could not be easily made here, either. For example, suppose a shareholder submits a proposal for the proxy materials suggesting that the corporation should not invest in South Africa, Israel, or the Middle East. Better yet, suppose the shareholder submits a proposal that would bar the corporation from using treasury funds to give contributions to any Republican or to solicit funds for any fund that gives money to Republicans. Suppose the shareholder opposes a proposed slate of directors because they are Republicans and argues that Republicans have always done a poor job of managing the productive resources of the economy. Even if one assumes that corporate elections are generally non-political, the spectacle of the SEC editing proxy materials on the basis of what is true or false on matters of domestic and foreign policy should at least cause first amendment eyebrows to lift.

The union context is equally interesting. The debate over whether to unionize is a debate about the sources of power that should govern an important part of an employee's life. The debate often may turn on matters of general political interest. Moreover the union often works as lobbyist in the legislative process and as participant in the electoral process. At the same time, unions are bargaining to sell the services of their members at the highest price. In that sense they are "commercial" entities. Similarly, the content of the employers' speech often may involve statements that relate to matters of general political interest. When discussion focuses on how power ought to be distributed in the workplace, we might regard the discussion as inherently political. In any event, many union campaigns involve the most volatile of political issues. If those committed to a politically based conception of the first amendment were to consign labor law to a status beneath first amendment protection, they could not plausibly defend the consignment on the ground that such speech was irrelevant to the processes of political decisionmaking.

The approach that Jackson and Jeffries champion, then, is not well suited to support the conclusion that all economic regulation should be beneath first amendment protection. Even if one accepts their assumption that the first amendment is exclusively concerned with political speech, there is good reason to think that much so-called economic regulation touches speech of political importance. The case they marshal, however strong in the commercial advertising area, seems to cut the other way when one steps back to examine more of the territory than they and other commentators have typically examined.

Confronting The Underlying Premises.—I have accepted the underlying wisdom of a politically based approach to the first amendment, to this point, arguing only that its scope reaches somewhat further than Jackson and Jeffries might want to allow. In retort, those authors could retreat to a narrow conception of politics, a strategy followed by Judge Bork, but one that they have left open. In any event, Jackson and Jeffries are building from Bork's general interpretation of the first amendment. It is that interpretation I now want to criticize. My aim is to establish that the premises of the politically based approach are unacceptable.

In understanding the politically based approach that Jackson and Jeffries, BeVier, and Bork follow, it is important to recognize that their approach derives from a particular theory of the judicial role as much as from a theory of freedom of speech. It owes as much to Herbert Wechsler as it does to Alexander Meiklejohn. As Bork develops the argument, the starting point is that the Court must not be a "naked power organ" and must formulate principled positions because if "the judiciary really is supreme, able to rule when and as it sees fit, the society is not democratic." His idea is that the judiciary can properly function as a counter-majoritarian force that confronts majority tyranny only by resort to "certain enduring principles believed to be stated in, and placed beyond the reach of majorities by, the Constitution." If the judiciary functions in this way, Bork is prepared to say that society has consented to be ruled undemocratically to that extent. If, on the other hand, the judiciary imposes its own value choices, the Court "necessarily abets the tyranny either of the majority or of the minority." The Court must govern according to principle, then, because the constitutional and popular assumptions that give the Court power demand that it so function.

"[L]ed by the logic of the requirement that judges be principled," Bork concludes that constitutional protection should be afforded only to political speech. What about literature or speech that is otherwise conducive to the development of the faculties of an individual, to happiness, or to the spread of truth? First amendment analysis cannot countenance any of these goals because "[t]hese functions or benefits of speech are . . . to the principled judge, indistinguishable from the functions or benefits of all other human activity. He cannot, on neutral grounds, choose to protect speech that has only these functions more than he protects any other claimed freedom." Such values and others like them raise questions about expediency, prudence, and how to rank the means of human gratification. Therefore, according to Bork, these questions are best suited for resolution by legislatures, not judges.

Freedom of political speech, on the other hand, Bork asserts is implicit in the representative democracy formed by the Constitution: "The first amendment indicates that there is something special about speech. We would know that much even without a first amendment, for the entire structure of the Constitution creates a representative democracy, a form of government that would be meaningless without freedom to discuss government and its policies."

Nonetheless, Bork contends that only explicitly political speech deserves protection. Any other view, he argues, would lead to unprincipled decisions; and that is that. All other speech is open for regulation by city councils, legislatures, town mayors, and the like. "Freedom of non-political speech rests, as does freedom for other valuable forms of behavior, upon the enlightenment of society and its elected representatives. That is hardly a terrible fate. At least a society like ours ought not to think so."

Bork's position breathes new vitality into the old cliche about the tail wagging the dog. Instead of first exploring the concept of freedom of speech in light of our history and traditions, and then paying attention to judicial responsibilities in light of that exploration, he interprets freedom of speech in a way that services a pre-conceived judicial role. As Bork puts it: "[W]e are looking for a theory fit for enforcement by judges." If the tail is to wag the dog, if we are to define freedom of speech by the judges' role, rather than the other way around, one at least expects a powerful showing about the theory of the judicial role. I shall argue that Bork's showing is deficient, but first, some of the underbrush needs to be cleared away. By invoking the term "principle" to cloak his theory, Bork's position enjoys a rhetorical advantage it does not deserve. To be opposed to a principle or a principled interpretation suggests that one is unprincipled, lacking integrity. One can be stock full of integrity, however, and favor entirely different ways of looking at the judicial role. Indeed, it is not clear that any Justice of the Supreme Court has ever adopted Bork's view of the judicial role; certainly no Justice of the Supreme Court has ever adopted anything close to Bork's theory of freedom of speech. Bork would not contend they all lacked integrity. He would contend, however, that their exercise of power has been illegitimate.

Before addressing the heart of the legitimacy claim, it is helpful to note what Bork rejects. Some might think that the history leading up to the adoption of the first or fourteenth amendments is a legitimate interpretative source, and Bork would endorse that position—to a point. The history is somewhat inconclusive, but it is at least clear that prior restraints were regarded as an interference with freedom of the press whether or not the restrained publication was political in character. Bork chooses to ignore this history, citing Leonard Levy only for the conclusion that "[t]he framers seem to have had no coherent theory of free speech and appear not to have been overly concerned with the subject." What is remarkable here is the idea that, because the framers had no coherent theory, we should ignore the particular evils with which they were concerned. Certainly, one might have thought that the particular evils of concern should be taken into account in the building of theory. But no, "[w]e are . . . forced to construct our own theory of the constitutional protection of speech."

Not only does Bork give no weight to the particular evils that concerned the framers, he also disregards a massive body of judicial precedent. Bork puts the point gently: "I am, of course, aware that this theory departs drastically from existing Court-made law. . . ." He does not explore the jurisprudential implications of that departure. In BeVier's development of a politically based first amendment theory, heavily influenced by Bork, she spells out the implications of this disregard for precedent. "[T]he only legitimate sources of constitutional principle are the words of the Constitution itself, and the inferences that reasonably can be drawn from its text, from its history and from the structure of government it prescribes." In BeVier's theory, precedent is not a legitimate source of principle. Therefore, precedent is not a legitimate source of constitutional interpretation.

. . .

Extremist positions are sometimes right, of course, and in any event they deserve to be treated on the merits. The heart of Bork's position is a theory about legitimacy and democracy. "[A] Court that makes rather than implements value choices cannot be squared with the presuppositions of a democratic society." A person who endorses a court that does so "if he is candid . . . must admit that he is prepared to sacrifice democratic process to his own moral views."

Bork confuses support of institutions with support of the views they endorse, drains substance from the idea of democracy, underestimates the role of making value choices in his own theory, and does not answer the problem of legitimacy that he purports to solve. First, one who supports the proposition that a court should make value choices is not necessarily advancing his or her own moral views, let alone sacrificing the democratic process to those views. My own moral views, for example, would have been advanced if the Court had not used the first amendment as a weapon to interfere with legislative efforts to combat inequality in cases like *Miami Herald Publishing Co. v. Tornillo*, *Buckley v. Valeo*, and *First National Bank of Boston v. Bellotti*. Yet I can support the legitimacy of the Court's act of making value choices even if I condemn the particular choices that it makes.

Second, Bork's conception of democracy is shallow. He adopts a neo-Madisonian model, assuming that "in wide areas of [American] life majorities are entitled to rule for no better reason [than] they are majorities," but also recognizing that "[t]here are some things a majority should not do to us no matter how democratically it decides to do them." Bork appears to recognize the dilemma that "neither the majority nor the minority can be trusted to define the freedom of the other." The dilemma is purportedly resolved by resort to the fiction of consent. According to Bork, we have consented to majority rule subject to Supreme Court restrictions pursuant to Bork's particular conception of principle. If our history were the guide to consent, it would be more accurate to say that we have consented to some electoral accountability in parts of the system, less in others, and almost none in others. We would have consented to majority rule subject to Supreme Court restrictions pursuant to a theory of interpretation that gives weight to considerations of language, history, intent, structure, precedent, power, and policy. In fact, we may or may not have consented to any of this. Consent here is a theological device.

What is missing from Bork's analysis is a satisfactory explanation of why majority "tyranny" is any more legitimate than majority rule tempered by minority "tyranny." Lurking behind Bork's devotion to principle, one suspects, is a commitment to relativism and to utilitarian preference-maximizing. Those who resist relativism and utilitarian preference-maximizing in favor of a different moral view, for example, a natural rights view or one of its variations, can characterize the institution of majority rule as a "naked" and illegitimate "power organ." They can also regard majority rule as undemocratic or illegitimate when it fails to respect basic human rights. In short, Bork's claim of legitimacy ultimately rests on question-begging. Indeed, Bork disregards the very concept of rights he purports to interpret. So understood, Bork's case for a politically based interpretation of the first amendment, and for abandoning first amendment protection for art, literature, philosophy, and science has not been made. If a case for excluding commercial speech from first amendment protection is to be made, it must come from an under-

standing of first amendment values, not from reflection about the judicial role.

Politically based theories contain one final argument relevant to the commercial speech question that merits consideration. It is an argument designed to refute the suggestion that self-expression, self-realization, or the like are legitimate first amendment values. The argument against values like self-expression is of general academic interest because it has been attractive in one form or another to scholars such as Scanlon, Schauer, and Wellington, along with the politically based theorists Bork, BeVier, and Jackson and Jeffries. Refuting the politically based theorists' argument, of course, will make a nice bridge to Professor Baker's position because he is at the opposite pole, believing that self-expression is the only value protected by freedom of speech.

The argument begins with the premise that freedom of speech is in the Constitution as a special right. Therefore, speech must have some unique property that distinguishes it from conduct. The search for first amendment theory (alternatively, a principled approach to the first amendment) is the search for that unique property. Bork's search, of course, ends with the discovery of the political functions of speech. He rules out individual development as a first amendment value because it does "not distinguish speech from any other human activity." Self-development can take place through work, jogging, "or in any of thousands of endeavors." The premise of this argument is strange, and an example quickly shows the problem. Suppose we took the same premise and applied it to other amendments in the Bill of Rights. The fourth amendment protects against unreasonable searches and seizures; therefore, there must be something special about that provision, and we would have to look for the unique property that would separate it from the other parts of the Constitution. Privacy could not be a value underlying the fourth amendment because other amendments advance privacy; the same for property, equality, dignity, and the like.

The premise is wrong in at least two respects. First, there is no reason to assume at the outset that speech is dramatically unique. It might be a part of a larger view of how human beings flourish or a subcategory of a larger value or set of values. Such a reading of the amendment, for example, might emerge from an elaboration of the structure of the Constitution. Second, and more important, for our purposes, there is no reason to suppose that the uniqueness of freedom of speech flows from a single value or perspective. It could well be that speech is different from conduct in that speech more or less combines many values in a particular way we do not generally find in conduct. As Kent Greenawalt has explained, the fallacy of Bork's line of argument is its failure to acknowledge that

> speech may well be thought to promote development or happiness in different ways (or more consistently) than nonspeech activities, that speech may be thought generally not to possess the offsetting disadvantages of many other activities, and that legislatures may be thought particularly likely to forbid speech with insufficient reason. In other words, substantial justifications could exist for affording explicit constitutional protection to expression even if the basic justifications for liberty of expression coincided with the basic justifications for permitting a broader range of liberty generally.

A summary of the objections to a politically based approach to the first amendment in general and to the commercial speech problem in particular can now be set forth. Even if the Court adopted a politically based approach to the first amendment, the Court could not exclude all commercial speech from first amendment protection unless it gave the term "political" an exceedingly narrow definition. More important, a politically based approach to the first amendment abandons history, precedent, and important values in pursuit of a legitimacy that is founded on controversial question-begging. Finally, the exclusion of self-expression from the values underlying the first amendment is based on similar question-begging. The politically based approach to first amendment analysis is not irrational. It does ask us to "think large" by adopting an extremist position in regard to the judicial role and freedom of speech. The politically based theorists offer the security of a monistic position, but root this position too far from our traditions and institutions to be taken seriously. An exploration of the implications of a politically based theory, however, suggests that even through its limited perspective, some commercial speech might deserve a measure of first amendment protection. Even if we were to adopt that way of looking at free speech problems, the category of commercial speech would be too abstract to be serviceable. Some commercial speech would deserve protection; some would not.

. . .

Persons, Baker observes, do not weigh arguments like rational decisionmakers. They are passionate beings influenced by their experience and their environment. They will believe what they want to believe.

Drawing from the sociology of knowledge, Baker claims that "[p]eople's perspectives and understandings are greatly influenced, *if not determined*, by their experiences and their interests, both of which reflect their location in a specific, historical socioeconomic structure." Moreover, the marketplace is stacked. It disproportionately represents dominant economic groups who tend to favor the status quo on fundamental issues. Even if it were somehow possible to correct the marketplace to address these failures, there would, according to Baker, be no reason to assume that truth for everyone should be the same. If truth is created, people's expressive experience itself may be as important as speech in arriving at their own private truth. Moreover, serious problems plague efforts to correct marketplace failures.

. . .

Commercial Speech: Applying an Eclectic Approach

*True Commercial Speech.*—In analyzing the difficulties associated with state regulations of true commercial speech, *Virginia State Board of Pharmacy v. Virginia Citizens Consumer Council* is an excellent place to start. In that case, consumers maintained that their audience rights had been violated by a regulation that prohibited pharmacists from informing the general public of their drug prices. The regulation did not prohibit false speech, nor was there any good argument that the speech would mislead the audience. The state was trying to prevent the dissemination of admittedly true information.

From one perspective, *Virginia Pharmacy* is an uncommonly easy case. The first amendment is at least in part designed to further the process of arriving at the truth. When the state tries to prevent the dissemination of truth, it is time to demand justification. Looking at Baker's marketplace arguments in this context highlights their excessively abstract character. What, for example, would it mean to say in this context that objective truth does not exist? Are we to doubt that pharmacists exist? Drugs? Prices? The debate about truth may provide interesting coffee house conversations, but here the government obviously seeks to prevent speakers from telling the truth to consumers. Philosophical debates about the nature of truth are out of place in this context and provide a fragile foundation for denying audience rights.

More interesting attempts to avoid the truth argument in *Virginia Pharmacy* would argue that the truth at issue in that case is not the kind of truth with which the first amendment is concerned. One tactic might be to argue that the marketplace was designed to protect ideas, not factual information. This, however, is a dangerous line. Even Jackson and Jeffries could not take the fact/idea dichotomy seriously. Even under their restricted approach, government ordinarily could not prevent speakers from communicating non-defamatory *facts* about political actors. Nor is this an argument Baker would make because it forces case-by-case content analysis of messages to determine which speech content falls in the idea category and which speech does not. My reaction to this particular argument is to admit that drug prices are not ideas and to admit that they are irrelevant to the political process, but to insist that audience rights do not depend upon some connection to general marketplace theory, or to the political process or, as Baker would have it, to the presence of a speaker making speech choices free of profit domination. The Court should invoke first amendment scrutiny whenever the government seeks to prevent the truth from being disseminated.

Nonetheless, many commentators have a rather strong intuition that pharmacist drug advertising is far afield from genuine first amendment values. Many insist that information on drug prices simply is not the kind of "truth" we are worried about protecting. What is the source of that intuition? The answer to this question is somewhat complicated. First, I suggest that the intuition is not based just on subject matter. If the government tried to stop *Consumer Reports* or an academician from publicizing comparative drug prices, I suspect the intuition that first amendment values were not present would quickly vanish. Yet when a pharmacist hawks his or her wares, the intuition is present. The combination of a particular profit motive and of subject matter triggers that intuition. I am not sure it is possible to give a full account of the intuition, but something like this may be involved: the first amendment is heavily concerned with protecting matters of general concern or public interest. When the government interferes with the dissemination of truth by a commercial advertiser, rather than by the media or by an individual speaking to the public who has no profit motive in the product advertised, there is no particular reason to think that the speech is of general or public interest. Moreover, we have no general basis to believe that the government is operating from an unhealthy bias, as we might if it interfered with the press or an individual generally unencumbered with a profit motive in the particular product. Notice that this argument need not assume that the first amendment is *exclusively* concerned with matters of general concern or of public interest. It can concede that the first amendment is concerned with individual self-expression and with vital human relationships whether or not of general or public interest, but posit that neither value is implicated in *Virginia Pharmacy*.

Whether or not one has sympathy for the principle that the first amendment has special concern for matters of general or public interest, however, that principle does not really fit here, despite contrary intuitions. There is a significant difference between holding that some categories of commercial speech are not of general or public interest and allowing the state selectively to bar particular factual statements such as those in *Virginia Pharmacy*. Whether or not some categories of commercial speech are generally bereft of general or public interest, there is no good reason to believe that true commercial statements that the state would like to suppress are similarly innocuous. I would let arguments about the nature of the truth involved go to the weight of the free speech interest, not to its existence.

Strongly connected to the truth argument is another matter to be weighed on the first amendment side of the balance in *Virginia Pharmacy*, and we can borrow from Professor Baker in making the argument despite the fact that he contends the decision is wrong, while I contend it is right. According to Baker, human beings have the right to speak because they are entitled to be treated by government as equal and autonomous agents. Similarly, human beings are entitled to the same treatment when they are members of audiences. In *Virginia Pharmacy*, the purpose of the state's restriction was to keep drug price information from human beings for fear that they would make bad decisions on the basis of the information. From this perspective, the problem with the *Virginia Pharmacy* regulation is not that it offends the efficient functioning of the marketplace; rather, it offends the concept of human dignity. The problem is less that consumers would be deprived of valuable information; the problem is that when government prevents willing speakers from speaking the truth to audiences in order to manipulate their decisionmaking, it engages in an especially offensive form of paternalism. If the government tells me that I cannot read Mobil Oil's literature, I should have a first amendment right to object whether or not I have any desire to read the literature (irrespective of the rights of Mobil Oil and wholly apart from whether truth will emerge in the marketplace of ideas). Any such regulation would offend the value of respect owed to persons.

I need to insert two immediate qualifications. First, the concepts of dignity and respect are often overused and will not assist us in resolving most of the most interesting first amendment conflicts. For example, the values of respect and dignity weigh on both sides of the defamation-free speech conflict, the privacy-free speech conflict, and even the personal security-free speech conflict. Staring at words like respect, dignity, and autonomy will not produce answers to such conflicts. Recognizing the limited problem-resolving power of these concepts, however, ought not to blind us to their enormous importance, particularly in cases like *Virginia Pharmacy*.

Second, respecting people is not the same as respecting the choices that people make. We may show our respect for a hopeless drug addict by administering involuntary medical care. Paternalism is not always wrong even when adults are the recipients. Paternalism, however, is risky business; it needs more justification than was provided in *Virginia Pharmacy*.

Under an eclectic approach, however, justification is always a possibility when first amendment values are impinged upon, and that principle operates even when the government seeks to suppress the truth. Any idea that the first amendment automatically protects the dissemination of truth is simply specious. The libel laws, for example, afford a defense of "truth," but republication of a defamatory utterance is not considered true unless the defamatory sting of the statement is true. To be sure, there are defenses, some constitutionally based, some based in common law privileges. There are many occasions under the libel laws, however, when the press is not free to publish the truth. Moreover, the public disclosure of embarrassing private facts is often tortious and without first amendment protection, although the Supreme Court has suggested that the question is still open. Similarly, labor unions are not free to publicize true facts about a secondary employer's connection to a labor dispute even though they may use pickets to communicate other facts about the same employer. The list of permissible abridgments is not infinite, but the point has been made: we prohibit the dissemination of a lot of truth for various reasons. Indeed, the test adopted by the Court in *Central Hudson Gas & Electric Corp. v. Public Services Commission* makes it clear that the Court will permit suppression of the truth if substantial state objectives are furthered in the least restrictive way. Meeting such a test might not always mean that the disadvantages in suppressing truth have been outweighed, but the test is flexible enough to permit maneuver when necessary.

Although there is much room for criticism here, the courts have not always been wrong in permitting the state to outlaw the dissemination of truth. Speech is important, but so are the values of privacy, security, and reputation. Although we might question

many of the specific accommodations in this area, the problems lie in particular contexts; the process of making accommodations is appropriate. It is tempting here to march through the commercial speech cases in an effort to show that speech interacts with other values in complicated ways and to suggest that many other factual combinations are possible. It is enough to note that the state interests introduced in the commercial speech context have included a desire to protect competition in the drug industry, the promotion of racial equality, and the preservation of energy. Daniel Farber, I would suggest, is right on the money when he observes:

> [A] state could claim any number of possible justifications, each potentially requiring separate treatment. . . . [W]hen the regulation impinges upon the flow of truthful information, the situation should be analyzed under general first amendment theory, whatever that may turn out to be. The best approach to the topic is probably to discuss the problems on a case-by-case basis, just as the Court is forced to confront them.

*False and Misleading Commercial Statements.*— The regulation of false and misleading commercial statements raises many of the most difficult questions in first amendment law. Confronting some of those questions requires a firm conception of the place of so-called marketplace values in first amendment theory. Marketplace values are related to a basic fear about government bias in regulating speech. Discussion of marketplace values will lead us to a discussion of the kind of bias with which we are concerned, and the questions of whether such a bias is either necessary or sufficient to trigger marketplace values. That discussion will suggest several other important variables. One such variable is the mode of dissemination. A consideration of that aspect will invite a reconsideration of the much-discussed question of whether the press is special.

Marketplace Theory: General Considerations.— In attempting to clarify the so-called marketplace argument it is helpful to turn back to John Stuart Mill. Mill has been charged with saying a lot of stupid things he never said. In fact, his "marketplace" argument was quite limited. His basic claim was that it was not useful for government to prohibit speech merely because it was false. Mill thought it was useful to prohibit speech only when it was likely to cause harm or, more precisely, harm to the interests of others. For example, Mill had no objection to libel laws. If speech caused harm, Mill's approach was to ask whether restricting it, on balance, was likely to promote utility. If it would promote utility, the restriction should be enacted. In modern terms, Mill was a balancer. He entertained no pie-eyed notions about the value of truth. If the dissemination of truth were likely to cause significant harm, nothing in Mill's writings suggests that he would oppose sanctions. Similarly, Mill had no romantic conceptions about truth emerging in the marketplace of ideas. Instead, Mill propounded a thesis that Frederick Schauer has stressed in his recent writings: there is no good reason to think that government has a monopoly on truth. If government intervenes to prevent speech, simply on the basis that it is false, without more, there are reasons to fear that the government acts out of bias or in an effort to repress minorities. As Mill put it, there is no reason to suppose that government is infallible.

It is instructive to recognize that in many respects, C. Edwin Baker is a latter day Mill. His whole first amendment project is designed to implement Mill's vision. The difference, however, is that Baker opposes ad hoc balancing. He wants clean lines. He would substitute "coercion" for Mill's "harm." Like Mill, Baker would permit unrestricted freedom for speakers so long as they do not cause harm to others. Unlike Mill, Baker would permit speakers to cause harm to others until the speech became coercive. Like Mill, Baker hopes that if speakers are granted a zone of liberty, they will set examples that others might follow in building a better society. Baker's attack on the marketplace theory should not disguise his basic agreement with Mill on these common premises: a distrust of government's ability to define truth, a search for rules that will grant dissenters a generous measure of freedom, and a hope, but not a guarantee, that the lives of dissenters will serve as models for a progressive future.

The difficulty comes in applying these abstractions. Perhaps the principal area of government concern is the prevention of fraudulent speech. If I take your money by telling lies, in Mill's terms, I have harmed you. In Baker's terms, I have coerced you by not treating you with the respect I owe you as an equal. I can trick you in many ways: I can lie about the future of my corporation to drive up the price of its stock, about the product I sell, about various facts to get your proxy in a stock sale, about what my union will do for you in return for your dues, about why you should not join a union in order to keep my company's costs down, about what I will do as a politician to get contributions for my campaign, about my role as a religious leader to get contributions for my church, and about my soothsaying abilities to persuade you to pay for my predictions.

In many of these areas I may be negligent or careful, but wrong. Whatever my motivation, I harm you when, in reliance on my false statements, you act to your detriment. Similarly, in order to prevent harm, states have enacted a series of licensing statutes that prevent people from charging money for giving legal advice, investment advice, real estate counsel, and the like without state approval. Indeed, most states prohibit giving free legal advice without a license. When the state regulates in any of these areas, it asserts its ability to know the truth and its unwillingness to let truth emerge in an unregulated marketplace.

We are, of course, more comfortable about letting the states' notions of truth or "expertise" prevail in some of these areas than in others. The first point to notice is that economic harm is not in and of itself sufficient to justify the absence of first amendment scrutiny. If the state were to license politicians or ministers in order to prevent persons from being hoodwinked into contributing their money to those who make false statements, the first amendment surely would pose a bar.

The Court itself made this clear in *Thomas v. Collins*, a case in which the state regulation was less offensive. The state of Texas merely sought to register a paid union organizer who was in the business of soliciting persons to purchase the services of a union, or to join a union, depending on your characterization. In fact, both characterizations are correct, and the Court so recognized. The Court firmly denied that "the First Amendment safeguards are wholly inapplicable to business or economic activity," observed that "regulation . . . aimed at fraud . . . must not trespass upon the domains set apart for free speech and free assembly," and insisted that no clear conclusion could automatically be drawn from the simple fact that the individual receives compensation for speaking. The Court affirmed that "in the circumstances of our times the dissemination of information concerning the facts of a labor dispute must be regarded as within that area of free discussion that is guaranteed by the Constitution. . . ."

*Thomas* is a difficult case, but the Court is on firm ground when it posits that the exchange of money in a transaction is not a sufficient condition for the obliteration of first amendment protections. States consequently cannot tell religious or political peddlers that they can distribute their materials so long as they do not ask for money.

*Thomas* thus highlights an uncomfortable truth, namely, that special subject matter categorizations are unavoidable. It is clearly unconstitutional to license political speakers and ministers, but most of us assume that licensing lawyers, psychiatrists, real estate agents, and investment advisors is not unconstitutional. Yet lawyers, psychiatrists, real estate agents, and investment advisors are speaking or writing for money; so are politicians, ministers, and union solicitors. It would, of course, be possible to argue that the first amendment prohibits government licensing of lawyers; it is easy to see how the argument would go. My point is that those who want no content discrimination would have to go at least that far. For those unwilling to go that far, the problem is not only how to draw the lines, but how to justify the lines drawn.

As an eclectic approach suggests, a number of variables interact in complex ways. To show how complicated the issues are we ought to continue our consideration of one part of the balance to be struck, that is, the way marketplace values figure in several different contexts. The marketplace argument is obviously powerful in some of these cases. We have grave doubts about the government's ability to define truth, even about matters of fact, in the political arena and in religion. To repeat a prior point, suspicions are triggered not merely because of content. Although no one supposes the FTC is infallible, we have significantly less doubt about government's capacity to define truth when it moves against a deceptive advertiser who makes an allegedly false statement about its own or another's product, than we do when the government moves against a source that has no profit motive in the sale of a product. The first amendment will ordinarily bar the latter action even if the false statement were the same one that had been made by an advertiser. Consider, again, for example, an injunction action against a consumer magazine or an author of a book who has no financial interest in the product discussed. The first amendment would prevent such an injunction because we fear that the government has no other reason for restricting the publication except a desire to suppress a certain version of truth.

There are enormous complications here that we ought not to smooth over. There are problems of identifying the type of bias we are concerned with and there are problems of sorting out how important a role such bias should play in the marketplace part of the balance.

Truth and Bias in Marketplace Theory.—First, the presence of a matter of general or public interest or even a matter of political importance in a speaker's presentation need not suggest the presence of the kind of government bias we are worried about, although first amendment values might otherwise be involved. Return, for example, to the SEC's regulation of statements by corporate executives about a corporation's future. I argued earlier that those statements are of political importance. Nonetheless, it is unlikely that SEC regulation of such statements has been infected with the same kind of bias we ordinarily worry about when the government regulates political speech. There do not seem to be grounds for believing that partisan interests have influenced the scope and kind of regulation in such a case, as there would be if a Political Exchange Commission regulated political campaign speeches. Even if worrisome bias is absent, government action may implicate first amendment values nonetheless. In its best light, the government, without partisan bias, is here suppressing speech of political, social, and economic importance. To make the case even more difficult, the speech at issue is not false; the government's concern is that it will mislead. The speech would be valuable to many (for example, investment advisors) and harmful to others (many of the uneducated small investors). If the marketplace theory values truth for its own sake wholly apart from concern about bias, there is a case for heightened scrutiny of the regulation.

There is some reason to believe that the SEC regulation would not survive any such scrutiny. Consider the two most obvious responses the SEC could offer. The first is that the SEC has expertise to which the Court should defer; the second is that the SEC has a compelling governmental interest in its regulations.

Some might put the first argument entirely beyond the pale. It is reminiscent of *Gitlow v. New York*, and if anything is clear, some would say, it is that courts should not defer to legislative or executive determinations about how to weigh first amendment values. This general posture might be subject to some qualification when an administrative agency with demonstrable expertise is especially sensitive to first amendment concerns. The Court has on occasion apparently been impressed by this possibility when the FCC has taken positions on broadcast regulations. But the argument for deference would be less persuasive when the agency could not make such a case. I certainly do not pose as an expert on securities regulation, but there is some evidence to suggest that a case for the SEC would be difficult to make. Distinguished commentary suggests that the SEC in many areas has framed its regulations with an eye to protecting the small investor while subordinating concern for the allocative inefficiency of its regulations. Indeed, the commentary is often less generous than that. Observers of the SEC criticize the regulations for not directly advancing the goal of protecting the small investor and, sometimes, for being incoherent. No one, so far as I am aware, contends that the

SEC is especially sensitive to first amendment values or even that the value of allocative efficiency is a compelling interest. Given that the Court has paid so little deference to the SEC's interpretation of the securities laws, there seems less reason to defer to the SEC's assessment about how SEC regulations implicate first amendment values.

What then of the SEC's substantial government interest, namely, that projections about the future of a company have the potential to mislead unsophisticated investors? The attempt to justify regulation by reference to this interest is precisely what the commentators' criticism is all about. Most small investors' information about a corporate executive's speech (and certainly about information contained in documents filed with the Commission) comes through their brokers, whose opinions are in large part influenced by the reactions of other investment advisors and of institutional investors. Much of that reaction is quickly reflected in the market price of the stock. If the corporate executive does not give the speech (or does not put the projection in a document filed with the SEC), the small investor and the economy do not get the benefit of the information and are misled to that extent. The market price will not reflect information that is not available. However one comes out on the issue, there are excellent grounds for wondering why SEC statements that speech is misleading should be given great deference when the State Bar of Arizona's similar assessments are not.

Let us suppose then that the SEC's past or present regulation of corporate projections might not satisfy heightened scrutiny analysis. Let us also assume that utterly toothless scrutiny is inappropriate. If the dissemination of truth has some first amendment value, we will afford this value no protection if government agencies can entirely avoid scrutiny by saying they are regulating "misleading" speech. To suppose, however, that the courts should invoke some *very strict* scrutiny is to suppose that, in all contexts, the general value of information or truth that the corporate executive seeks to disseminate presumptively outweighs the value of protecting small investors. I see no reason for creating such an abstract hierarchy or for making that choice. Anyone who is confident that one such value is significantly more important than the other ought to speak out. This is not a decision the first amendment has "made for us." It is one we must make for ourselves.

The Court made such a decision in the defamation area. The complex set of rules produced in *Gertz v. Robert Welch, Inc.*, right or wrong, resulted from an appreciation that the protection of truth was im-

portant but that the protection of reputation also was important. The Court wisely avoided discussion of levels of scrutiny because any resort to such abstractions would have constitutionalized reductionism. *Gertz* reflects the balancing methodology Mill called for in the middle of the nineteenth century. Indeed, the problem of defamation in the commercial arena further illustrates the theme of this section. Typically, state regulation of commercial defamation gives rise to no general concern of partisan bias. Consider, for example, the case of a commercial supplier of credit information that defames a person applying for credit. If the first amendment requirements outlined in *Gertz* apply, there is something clearly wrong with the first amendment or with *Gertz*. The interests in individual self-expression, autonomy, and the like are not present here or are present in only an attenuated way. The constitutional interest in affording strategic protection to these defamatory falsehoods in order to encourage investment in credit information suppliers is not impressive. Nor are there general grounds for concern about government bias. Affording constitutional protection here would trivialize the first amendment.

Nonetheless, it would be a mistake to conclude that commercial defamation law is always bereft of first amendment interest. Competitive commercial advertising is an important example in which first amendment values loom large despite the absence of any particular concern about government bias. Take the case of trade defamation. A competitor makes derogatory statements about another's product. The marketplace seems greatly unbalanced here. Billions are spent making affirmative claims about products; much less is spent in opposing them. Here we need to afford some strategic protection for falsehoods in order to encourage the dissemination of truth. If *Gertz* is to apply generally to statements about persons on the assumption that the public has a "right to know," there is a strong case for suggesting that similar protection should apply to statements about products.

I mean to make only tentative claims in this section. The conclusions I reach in each of the specific areas discussed are of little concern. It is important, however, to separate the marketplace concern about bias from the concern for having as much truth or information as possible in the marketplace, because the latter concern could trigger first amendment scrutiny even when there is no reason to be concerned about government bias.

The Possibility of Benign Bias.—As Shown above, there is room for inquiry as to whether the presence of a government bias is *necessary* to trigger marketplace values. In this section, I want to suggest that the presence of a partisan government bias might not be *sufficient* to trigger any strict form of scrutiny. Consider again the NLRB's on-again-off-again policy of setting aside representation elections in circumstances in which the misleading or false statements of an employer have allegedly influenced the outcome. Presumably the Board is pro-union in some years, and is not in other years. Nonetheless, it is not obvious that first amendment values are necessarily compromised in this context by the presence of bias. If it were national policy to encourage the formation of labor unions, for example, and a particular board consistently interpreted the facts surrounding representation elections in a pro-union fashion, the first amendment implications would not be clear. Even if we think of representation elections as political (or not commercial) and public (or not private), the presence of government bias, without more, might be irrelevant to any first amendment point. That, of course, would not be the case if a National Political Relations Board were to favor Democrats over Republicans in elections for the House of Representatives.

Suppose, on the other hand, the Board were to favor employers over prospective unions in representation election cases. It would then be necessary to consider the relationship between freedom of association and unions. It is at least arguable that employees have a first amendment right to form unions and to engage in collective bargaining. If government intervenes to prevent such associations out of bias against them, first amendment values appear to be strongly implicated. From this perspective, government intervention to encourage associations like unions does not interfere with first amendment values, but intervention to oppose such associations does interfere with those values.

However one decides this issue, trying to determine whether speech in the union context is political, commercial, or an example of political economy is a witless exercise. The existence of regulation in a political context need not betray an underlying governmental bias, nor is the existence of governmental bias in a free speech context necessarily a constitutional problem. We may sometimes consider bias to be constitutionally benign.

The Difficulty of Recognizing Bias.—Sometimes even malignant bias is so deeply entrenched in our society that it becomes respectable. Most scholarly disciplines have decades to their discredit in which quite reasonable approaches were "out of fashion" or "wrong" and not pursued. Determining when marketplace values should cancel attempts by the

state to regulate fraud is obviously a tricky business. Whatever confidence we might muster about our decisions as to government regulation of political or religious fraud must diminish when we leave such traditional territory; there are gray areas and hard cases. In developing this point, I shall rely on an example that I suspect will be controversial. In many states fortune-telling is outlawed. Some fortune-tellers have raised first amendment arguments, only to meet the brisk refrain that charlatans and quacks who engage in fraud are not entitled to the protection of the Constitution.

No doubt, the vast majority of people and certainly the vast majority of academics think fortune-tellers are quacks, at best; frauds, at worst. Indeed, academics typically have a strong emotional stake in opposing psychic phenomena. They are genuinely threatened by the thought that fortune-tellers might be right. There is a literature in the scientific community, for example, arguing that any scientist who attempts to apply normal scientific methodological techniques to test the alleged psychic abilities of individuals is *not* involved in scientific research. Science, it seems, tests claims that comply with contemporary scientific paradigms. Galileo had similar opponents.

Yet Galileo was right, and fortune-tellers are quacks, many would say, and it is time to turn back to marketplace theory. Marketplace theory does not rest on confidence in the market; it rests on distrust of government. Government is not to define the truth for us. We are to define our view of truth, and should be able to present that truth to others free of government interference. Fortune-tellers make an ontological or epistemological claim that is contrary to what most people believe and to what most people want to believe. Whether or not we must define the religion clause broadly to include the activities of fortune-tellers (and that itself is an interesting question), fortune-tellers' claims to free speech protection are hardly frivolous. To be sure, the state interest in protecting people from fraud is also not frivolous. But the consumers of fortune-tellers pay little money to receive many things—they get attention and a sympathetic ear; they are entertained; and they get stories to tell their friends. The state's consumer protection efforts here are founded on an enormous lack of respect for consumers. I suspect the urge to censor plays a stronger role than the desire to protect the public. Marketplace values, individual self-expression, respect, dignity, and the like weigh heavily here, and the state's interest, however well-pedigreed, seems relatively insubstantial in this context. This seems to be one of the few areas where *caveat emptor* is a useful phrase.

The fortune-telling example illustrates, I hope, an important point. Malignant bias in the fraud context is necessarily a function of historical and social context. It cannot be resolved by formula. Once *Thomas* made clear that the fraud label was not a talisman for the automatic eradication of first amendment values, the formidable task of drawing lines among subject matter categories could not be escaped. The fortune-telling example also nicely captures the general point that a range of first amendment values might interact in very different and complicated ways with interests the state seeks to advance. In that sense, the example presents a significant challenge to the building of first amendment theory.

*The Special Place of the Press.*—Another uncomfortable truth emerges from an analysis of the fraud issue—the press does have a special place in first amendment analysis. Many have argued (and I agree with them) that the press has made a tactical error in contending so frequently that it should be entitled to special privileges denied to others. It was a tactical error to rely so heavily on the argument that the press was special in *Zurcher v. Stanford Daily*, for example. Moreover, there are strong arguments to support the view that the press should have no special privileges in the defamation context. In the view of many, the press clause simply means that the freedom of speech guaranteed in the Constitution does not diminish when someone uses a printing press in the act of speech.

Yet the regulation of fraud presents at least one area in which the press is special. Consider SEC regulation of investment advisors. In order to combat fraud in the securities market, the SEC has cumbersome registration provisions for investment advisors. Investment advisors, however, do not only give advice over the telephone. They sometimes communicate to their clients in writing. If they have enough clients, they send out newsletters. The extreme case, of course, is the person who writes a column in the *Wall Street Journal*. I suspect that most people would regard it as a clear first amendment violation if the SEC required financial columnists in major newspapers to comply with SEC registration requirements. At the same time, most would not have initially balked at requiring investment advisors who communicate in person, by telephone, or through informal notes to register. The problem is to determine when the "informal notes" become the press. Is it enough that the authors label their notes "newsletters"? Presumably not.

A body of law exists in which judges have attempted to draw lines. One major difficulty is that in order to make decisions about the character of the "publisher," judges have found it appropriate to conduct discovery on how the purported investment advisor makes decisions, what his or her financial holdings are, with whom he or she consults, what his or her sources of compensation are, and the like.

Again, my purpose is not to resolve this issue but to suggest that lines must be drawn. The same problems can arise in psychiatry, law, real estate, and elsewhere unless it is constitutional to prevent people from writing about law in a newspaper without bar certification, about psychiatry without a degree, and so on. Finally (I cannot resist), would those who uphold fortune-telling laws advocate outlawing the astrology column in the local newspaper?

The urge to make the press special comes in part because we think the danger of exploitation is greater when the speech is not exposed to public view. We may not entertain romantic expectations about truth emerging in the marketplace, but if we ensure that people give bad advice publicly, there is a greater opportunity for someone to respond.

Yet there may also be an element of special privilege for the press in current first amendment doctrine. The doctrine of prior restraint may have been designed to put the press on an equal footing. People could speak or write without a license and that ought not to change merely because they used a printing press. Yet we now license a good deal of speech (for example, of lawyers), and those licenses are clearly prior restraints. So we have turned the law upside down. To speak you sometimes need a license; to use the press you almost never do. A doctrine designed to create equality for the press has evolved into one that gives it a special place.

*Discriminating Against Commercial Speech in the Time, Place, and Manner Context.*—Even if commercial speech were equated with commercial advertising, it would still be the case that the commercial speech problem is an abstraction that includes several distinct problems. These include the problems of when government can prohibit the dissemination of truth, what the limits are upon government power to suppress the false and the misleading, and the extent to which government can limit dissemination of advertising in circumstances in which it has permitted non-commercial speech. The last of these problems is perhaps the most interesting because it challenges what many regard as fundamental in free speech theory. Martin Redish states the problem in strong terms: "[I]f the first amendment means anything it is that the level of constitutional protection cannot vary on the basis of differing viewpoints." Indeed, Redish finds it "doubtful that an arm of the state should have the authority to decide for the individual that certain means of mental development are better than others." He argues, therefore, that we cannot justify any differences in our treatment of commercial speech and non-commercial speech on the premise that "some forms of speech are more valuable than others." One should not read too much into Redish's doubt that the "state should not have the authority to decide for the individual that certain means of mental development are better than others." He would freely concede that the state rightly makes such decisions daily. For example, the state compels education, and selects curriculum and textbooks. In so doing, the state decides for the individual that "certain means of mental development are better than others." Indeed, as I argue elsewhere in detail, the state necessarily makes such decisions in deciding what rights will exist, in accommodating clashes between rights, in designing systems of property rights, and so on. The state appropriately makes content decisions about what is best suited to belong in its libraries and its museums. The state then of necessity makes decisions about what is best suited for mental development and about what kind of people we ought to be.

The fighting issue is whether that form of decisionmaking should extend to prevent private actors from communicating. To a large extent, the equal value principle has already been breached. Obscenity regulation presents a clear example. The very test used to determine whether speech is obscene calls upon judges to determine what is or is not of literary, artistic, political, or scientific value. Similarly, the standard argument the Court makes to explain various categorical exclusions of speech from first amendment protection is that some categories of speech are "no essential part of any exposition of ideas, and *are of such slight social value as a step to truth that any benefit that may be derived from them is clearly outweighed* by the social interest in order and morality."

Nor is the breach in the equal value principle confined to speech that is deemed to be outside the protection of the first amendment. In determining whether there is a "public" controversy for purposes of establishing the status of a libel plaintiff, the Court clearly looks to the normative value of the subject matter. In *Time, Inc. v. Firestone*, the subject matter surrounding the plaintiff's divorce had attracted much media attention, nonetheless, there was no "public" controversy. I suppose that translates to the proposition that Palm Beach gossip has enough first amendment *value* to warrant some protection for the media under *Gertz*, but not enough to warrant a malice test.

Does all this mean that there is no equal value principle? Not at all. Everyone presumably agrees that it is not desirable as a general matter to have judges making decisions that turn on the value of the speech. Some, like Redish, would never permit such decisions. Others would permit judges to make decisions that depend upon the value of speech some of the time, but not without regret. If and when the value principle is to be breached, the breach should be noted and accompanied by significant justification.

That justification has not been sufficiently articulated in the commercial speech area. In *Ohralik*, the Court crisply observed that commercial speech occupies a "subordinate position in the scale of First Amendment values." Commentators like Redish, of course, disapprove. Yet many individuals and communities have the intuition that commercial speech is not as important or valuable as non-commercial speech. In time, place, and manner contexts alone, communities have barred commercial leafletting, while permitting non-commercial leafletting, prohibited commercial door-to-door soliciting, while permitting similar non-commercial activity, and outlawed commercial off-site billboards, while permitting non-commercial off-site billboards. It is surely worth exploring the intuitions that might support a subordinate position for commercial speech and to inquire into how much damage, if any, the subordinate position doctrine has wrought.

Let us ask first why communities make such distinctions and later examine the first amendment implications of what they have done. If one focuses upon the personal interest people have in the communications, it seems hard to draw a distinction. Product advertisements may provide important information to individuals or call their attention to matters of importance to them. So may political or religious speech. Academics and intellectuals may profess a greater interest in ideological matters, but academics and intellectuals are probably not the constituencies such laws were designed to serve.

More interesting as a basis for the discrimination is the idea that commercial speakers are lining their pockets, seeking profit, and treating people as objects for exploitation while political and religious speakers are advancing a cause and seeking genuine personal contact. Obviously, this rationale is both overinclusive and underinclusive. Some who sell products regard their activities as socially productive, as a mission, or a cause. Some politicians and religious folk are exploiting and out to make money. Despite the overgenerality of the commercial/non-commercial stereotypes, they contain some appeal as a general matter. Those who sell pots and pans are not ordinarily engaged in an ideological pursuit; the Jehovah's Witnesses surely are.

An interesting test of the distinction based on profit-seeking is presented by the decision *Breard v. Alexandria*, in which a door-to-door solicitor was selling many kinds of magazines. The Court in *Breard* put the solicitor on the commercial side of the line because the solicitor had no cause and was representing many who had no cause. When the issue concerns misleading statements, the profit motive associated with the press does not place it in the commercial category. In the door-to-door context, however, the profit motive seems to put the press seller on the commercial side.

It may be that the commercial/non-commercial distinction goes no deeper than this, but at least in some communities, there appears to be a more fundamental basis for the distinction, whatever its relationship to first amendment values might be. The concern, if articulated with some passion, might go like this:

We live in a society in which citizens are daily confronted with massive amounts of commercial advertising. Millions of children educated in schools purportedly promoting humane values return to their homes to watch state subsidized commercial television for four hours a day. Adults watch that same television often for longer periods. Persons of all ages leave their homes to encounter commercial billboards and to confront leaflets hawking wares of every description. By organizing a property structure making this possible, America undeniably promotes a system of values. Americans are taught to be materialistic, to be hedonists, to pursue profit. Instead of being taught to ask who they really are and how their identity is constituted by their relationships, their projects and commitments, they are taught to ask what they want to own. Their identity is defined by their consumption desires.

People with widely differing political perspectives criticize this commercial environment. Opposition to a society in which persons are viewed as appropriate objects for commercial manipulation is a prominent theme in the writings of both conservatives and Marxists. Indeed, the opposition to a society in which people are viewed as means and not as ends is also a central theme of liberals from Kant to John Stuart Mill. More important, I would suggest that the commercial/non-commercial distinction in time, place, and manner contexts is supported by communities whose environmentally oriented citizens have internalized these anti-commercial themes in a powerful way.

Enter the first amendment. The initial first amendment retort would be that citizens of these communities would like to suppress commercial speech precisely because they do not consider it as valuable as other speech, and that the first amendment stands for the proposition that the value of ideas is to be fought out in the marketplace. Ideas are not open to suppression in the marketplace merely because they are deemed offensive. Moreover, it could be argued that the anti-commercial argument is deeply paternalistic. If people want to internalize or promote materialistic values, they ought to be free to do so.

Perhaps they should, but this conventional first amendment response does not admit the difficulty of the issue and is unduly romantic. It calls up the picture of a rational individual making informed choices, and downplays the extent to which the inputs in a culture influence the beliefs of the persons within that culture. Looking at the matter in the aggregate, it is certain that the children born, for example, in San Francisco in the coming year will grow up with quite different views and perspectives than those born in Jackson, Mississippi. This is not to deny free will or free choice. It is not to invoke a conspiracy theory. It is only to affirm that the inputs into a culture have a major influence in value formation.

Certainly the inputs promoting materialism in American culture are quite strong. Living in a society in which children and adults are daily confronted with multiple communications that ask them to purchase products inevitably places emphasis on materialistic values. The authors of the individual messages may not intend that general emphasis, but the whole is greater than the sum of the parts. Even if it were not, the parts add up to a loud materialist chorus.

Moreover, the promoters of the materialist message benefit from an almost classic case of market failure. Advertisers spend some sixty billion dollars per year to disseminate their messages. Those who would oppose the materialist message must combat forces that have a massive economic advantage. Any confidence that we will know what is truth by seeing what emerges from such combat is ill placed. The inequality of inputs is structurally based.

Yet arguments about market failure have limited appeal to the current Court. The Court rejected such arguments when it was said that the media dominated the market, when the wealthy were thought to control candidates' political campaigns, and when corporations were said to dominate initiative campaigns. After all the factors are sifted and weighed, the reality becomes apparent: the lesser status for commercial speech flatly contradicts conventional first amendment principles. To the extent that we accept the subordinate position of commercial speech, we do not believe in the first amendment—at least not the conventional stereotype of the first amendment, or Redish's first amendment, or the ACLU's first amendment.

Instead, lurking throughout first amendment doctrine are renunciations of the equal value principle, and difficult compromises. What is important is that the courts should be forced to face up to the significance of the compromises that they make. At the same time, it is important to recognize that the compromises, while theoretically significant, have been small compromises. The subordinate position for commercial speech does not deny anyone the right to promote a materialist message. Indeed, in addition to overtly ideological speech, current commercial speech doctrine protects commercial advertising from any general state prohibition. As a practical matter, the subordinate position of commercial advertising simply permits greater community control of the time, place, and manner of its dissemination. Nor is any damage wrought by the subordination of commercial advertising likely to create any pressure to carve out pockets of non-protection for political speech. This latter point is related to the Court's perspective in *Ohralik*. The lesser position for commercial speech is designed to avoid "dilution . . . by a leveling process, of the force of the Amendment's guarantee" with respect to non-commercial speech. Arguably, the creation of a first amendment hierarchy makes the equal value principle more secure in the areas that count the most. In any event, however troublesome the compromise may be, it is something less—a great deal less—than a wholesale abandonment of constitutional ideals.

. . .

Burt Neuborne, *The First Amendment and Government Regulation of Capital Markets*, 55 BROOKLYN LAW REVIEW 5 (1989)*

. . .

Legal disputes about speech in the United States have arisen in the context of seven subject matter areas: religion, politics, science, aesthetics, con-

sumer affairs, labor relations, and capital formation. Until recently, a structural divide in first amendment theory provided effective protection to speech about religion, politics, science, and art, but no protection at all to speech about consumer affairs, labor relations, or capital formation. During the past decade, the Supreme Court has shattered the symmetry of that structural divide by affording significant, albeit limited, first amendment protection to speech about consumer affairs.

. . .

## I. THE DISTINCTION BETWEEN SPEAKER-CENTERED AND HEARER-CENTERED FIRST AMENDMENT DOCTRINE

Forty-seven years ago, in *Chrestensen v. Valentine*, a divided panel of the Second Circuit ruled that the first amendment protected commercial speech. The circuit's prescience was vindicated more than a generation later when the Supreme Court ruled in *Virginia Pharmacy Bd. v. Virginia Consumer Council* that price advertising by pharmacists merited first amendment protection; but not before an interregnum of more than thirty years during which a bright line distinction in first amendment theory between "political" and "commercial" speech provided significant protection for speech about religion, politics, science, or aesthetics, but virtually no protection for speech about consumer choice, labor relations, or capital formation.

The bright line distinction between "political" and "economic" speech erected in *Valentine v. Chrestensen* ensured that intellectuals would receive significant protection against government interference with a free market in their ideas, but that virtually no protection would exist against government control of the information markets for economic, as opposed to intellectual, goods. Fifteen years ago, Ronald Coase challenged the legitimacy of first amendment doctrine that insulated the "business" of intellectuals from government interference, but subjected everyone else's "business" to pervasive control by the government.

Whatever the validity of Coase's contention that a bright line first amendment divide between "political" and "economic" *speech* reflects a not-so-subtle bias in favor of the intelligentsia, he was, I believe, quite wrong in his insistence that no meaningful difference exists between "political" and "economic" *speakers*. As Jerome Frank pointed out in his dissent from the panel's opinion in *Chrestensen*, the germinal conception of first amendment protection enunciated by Justices Holmes and Brandeis, and developed by the Supreme Court during the ensuing two decades, was designed to compel the majority to tolerate speakers whose beliefs about religion or politics impelled them to controversial forms of self-expression.

The common denominator that ties the Court's seminal speech cases together is a concern with societal toleration of expression driven by religious or political conscience; a concern that is generally absent from most "economic" speech settings. While the traditional hearer-centered justifications for the free speech principle were dutifully cited by Holmes and Brandeis, it was, I believe, toleration of and respect for the inherent dignity of a conscientiously driven speaker, together with a deep mistrust of the government's capacity to apportion political or religious toleration fairly, that drove the early free speech cases. It is no coincidence that the language chosen by Holmes and Brandeis stressed the foolishness of the speech at issue; the weakness of the speakers; the lack of any real threat posed by the speech; the historic tendency to intolerance and overreaction in religion and politics; and the disproportionately severe nature of the sentence. Even more significantly, it is no coincidence that the substantive doctrine, the clear and present danger test, that emerges from the Holmes-Brandeis analysis is a doctrine that protects primarily weak and vulnerable speakers of conscience. Constitutional protection under the clear and present danger doctrine varies inversely with the power of the speaker. When a speaker becomes too effective, we have not hesitated to override the hearer-centered underpinnings of free speech at the point where the toleration level of the society is exceeded by the perceived threat latent in unpopular political, religious, or aesthetic speech.

It is fair to assert that throughout the formative period of our free speech heritage—from Milton's plea for unlicensed printing to Locke's plea for religious toleration; from the Holmes-Brandeis dissents to Justice Jackson's majestic articulation of the toleration principle in *West Virginia State Bd. of Educ. v. Barnette*; from the halting recognition of artistic freedom in *United States v. One Book Called Ulysses* to Justice Harlan's sophisticated protection of offensive speech in *Cohen v. California*—the paradigm beneficiary of the free speech principle has been a vulnerable speaker of conscience, impelled to speak out by the demands of humanity, yet subject to waves of unnecessarily harsh parochial intolerance. While the long-term interests of hearers are cited to justify protecting the speaker, the primary source of judicial concern in the early free speech cases was the establishment and defense of breathing space—toleration—for the speaker's capacity for self-expression.

Such an assertion is controversial and, concededly, intuitive. It is also broader than necessary for the purposes of my thesis. All that is necessary to support my argument is a recognition that a concern for the toleration of speakers of conscience played a significant role in the evolution of free speech theory. I argue that its role was dominant. There is no doubt, however, that it was, at a minimum, significant.

. . .

As long as we equated free speech protection with forced toleration of a conscientiously motivated speaker, Coase's complaint that it was unfair to distinguish between "political" and "economic" speakers was beside the point. A toleration based, speaker-centered vision of the first amendment can offer little solace to speakers who are not engaged in self-expressive speech. Nonanthropomorphic speakers like corporations or labor unions, with no self to express, are deemed fair game for censorship. Humans not engaged in self-expressive speech are similarly poor candidates for speaker-centered protection.

Predictably, the logically derivable attributes of a speaker-centered first amendment coincide closely with first amendment doctrine under the structural divide established in *Valentine v. Chrestensen*. Speech that implicates religious or political conscience receives the highest level of protection, subject to a disturbing tendency to collapse when fear or hysteria saps society's capacity for toleration. Speech involving aesthetics and science enjoys significant, but somewhat lesser, protection, because we sense, rightly or wrongly, that such speech is somewhat less linked with conscientiously driven self-expression than is speech about religion or politics. Speech involving topics with no discernible link to the self-expressive development of the human personality receives no protection at all; neither do speakers without an anthropomorphic self to express. Protection, when available though, is intense, since it flows from respect for the speakers' right to say what they want; not the listeners' interest in hearing what they need.

. . .

Before Coase's criticism of *Valentine v. Chrestensen* could bear fruit, therefore, the first amendment universe had to be expanded beyond the classical speaker-centered analysis characterized by the *Skokie* decision—an analysis that acknowledges hearers only grudgingly and then generally to reinforce the speaker's interest—to a multiparticipant speech universe where the interests of all participants in the speech process can be identified and accommodated.

. . .

## II. THE CONTOURS OF HEARER-CENTERED SPEECH PROTECTION

### A. The General Contours of The Doctrine

Hearer-centered speech protection of economic speech rests upon two strong props and one weaker one. Its strongest prop is the recognition that hearers have a powerful interest in receiving information that enhances their capacity for informed choice. Once such an interest is borrowed by commercial speakers lacking a traditional speaker interest of their own, it triggers first amendment protection and may be overborne, if at all, only by a very powerful showing of societal need. However, the "informed choice" rationale is subject to two significant internally generated checks. First, by definition, an informed choice rationale is consistent with government censors deciding whether a given exercise of commercial speech will, in fact, impede informed choice because it is false or misleading or incomplete. Second, government censors remain free to argue that merely because information is accurate, it does not necessarily enhance the likelihood of genuinely wise decision making by hearers. Thus, left to itself, the informed choice rationale has the capacity to degenerate into a highly paternalistic doctrine that licenses government censors to manipulate information flow in the name of enhancing the social desirability of the hearer's ultimate choice.

The tendency toward paternalism latent in the informed choice rationale should be kept in check by the second strong prop underlying hearer-centered speech protection: recognition that the free flow of information enhances autonomous decision making by hearers. Unlike the concept of "informed" decision making, "autonomous" decision making may lead a hearer to do something that seems silly or, even, self-destructive to a government censor. But the toleration based respect for individual dignity that fuels speaker-centered speech protection should also lead to a refusal to permit the government to manipulate hearers into "preferred" choices by controlling the flow of information to them. In both settings, respect for the dignity of individuals should assure them the ability to make lawful choices that appear quite foolish to the government censor.

Unlike the speaker-centered toleration rationale, it is possible, at least in theory, for a government censor to distinguish commercial speech that enhances the capacity for autonomous decision making from speech that impedes it. Thus, while the toleration principle in a speaker-centered setting leads to a prophylactic insistence on protecting virtually all "wrong" political or religious speech (like Nazi race baiting) because it is self-affirming, the hearer-centered variant of the toleration principle—respect for autonomous decision making—should permit a government censor to block speech which is demonstrably of no use in making an autonomous decision. It is this distinction between the role of toleration in a speaker-centered setting and toleration in a hearer-centered setting that justifies the government in banning false and misleading commercial speech, but forbids the government from banning false and misleading religious or political speech.

The need to distinguish between commercial speech that enhances informed and/or autonomous choice and speech that impedes such choice implicates the third and weaker prop underlying the commercial speech doctrine: skepticism of the government's ability to perform acceptably as a censor. Under a speaker-centered, toleration based rationale, our mistrust of the government's competence to decide whose speech to tolerate and whose to suppress leads to an almost absolute prophylaxis that forbids the banning of even clearly false speech that has no conceivable benefits for hearers. Should the same skepticism about competence preclude government regulators from deciding that a given message fails to enhance either informed or autonomous choice and, therefore, does not qualify for hearer-centered speech protection? I think not. Unlike a speaker-centered setting, government speech regulators in a hearer-centered system would not be deciding whose "wrong" speech to tolerate. Rather, they would be gauging the value of speech in enhancing a hearer's capacity for informed or autonomous choice. Although a healthy skepticism should surround any attempt by the government to assess the value of speech, the process of measuring instrumental value is less openly subjective than the selective apportionment of toleration that takes place in a speaker-centered setting. Accordingly, so long as the government censor's persuasion burden is significant and so long as the government is utterly disabled from the kinds of self-interested censorship decisions that are banned in speaker-centered settings, a government regulator in a hearer-centered setting should not be disabled from demonstrating that a given message diminishes a hearer's capacity for informed and autonomous choice and is, therefore, unprotected.

The Supreme Court's commercial speech cases fall neatly into three categories that parallel the three props. The easiest cases involve commercial speech that is concededly choice enhancing both in the informed and autonomy senses of the word, but that the government seeks to suppress in order to advance some other legitimate social interest. In *Virginia Pharmacy Bd. v. Virginia Consumer Counsel*, for example, the price information at stake was concededly of value to hearers in making an informed choice about the purchase of nonprescription drugs and making an autonomous choice about where and whether to purchase at all.

. . .

The centrality of the choice-enhancing nature of speech to a hearer-centered first amendment gives rise to a second, slightly more difficult category. This category involves settings in which a government censor has determined that a given message does not enhance legitimate choice, either because the choice is unlawful or because the information is actually or potentially false, deceptive, or misleading. If the choice that would be enhanced by a given commercial message is itself unlawful, the analysis is not difficult. The commercial speaker generally lacks the toleration based interest in protecting self-affirming expression that underlies the traditional advocacy of illegal action cases. The hearer lacks a significant interest in receiving information enhancing unlawful choice. Since neither the speaker nor the hearer can assert a first amendment interest, commercial speech whose sole effect is the enhancement of unlawful choice is subject to suppression. Thus, in *Pittsburgh Press Co. v. Pittsburgh Commission on Human Relations*, the Court upheld a ban on sex-specific employment advertisements in a newspaper.

However, if the choice that is enhanced by commercial speech is lawful, the issue is somewhat more difficult. If the censor is right in branding the speech as false, deceptive, or misleading, neither of the strong hearer-centered props supporting commercial speech protection are available to the speaker, since false commercial speech actually impedes both informed and autonomous choice. The hard question is how to decide whether the censor's negative assessment of the speech is correct. The real issue raised by the "false and misleading" cases, therefore, is the strength of the third and weaker prop-skepticism about the government's ability to make fair and accurate judgments concerning the choice-enhancing nature of speech in an economic context. How much deference should be paid to a censor's assertion that a given commercial message is actually or potentially false or misleading?

The Court has demonstrated an unfortunate tendency to take at face value a government censor's assertion that a given exercise of commercial speech, or an entire category of commercial speech, is actu-

ally or potentially false and misleading without considering whether the censor was competent to make such a judgment; whether the censorship decision was potentially self-interested; or whether the prediction of potential harm is too speculative. Thus, in *Friedman v. Rogers*, the Court upheld a Texas ban on the use of trade names in the practice of optometry because the Texas Board of Optometry had determined that consumers might be misled about the identity of the personnel in a particular location. While *Friedman* is a close case, I believe that it was wrongly decided for two reasons. First, no serious investigation of the potential for consumer confusion was undertaken by the government censor. In fact, trade names often provide consumers with a choice-enhancing assurance of a uniform level of service based upon reputation. Second, the decision to censor was made by a self-interested segment of the optometry profession that was using its control of the optometry board as a means to ward off unwanted competition. Censorship decisions by such self-interested bodies, especially when they are not based on persuasive data, should not enjoy deference.

Despite its deferential posture, however, when the form or content of commercial speech does not pose a credible danger to a hearer's capacity for informed choice, the Court has rejected attempts by well-meaning censors to brand entire categories of speech as false or misleading. Thus, in *Bates*, the Court declined to accept the argument that lawyer advertising is inherently misleading because it can never convey the necessary nuances. Similarly, in *In re R.M.J.*, the Court invalidated an attempt by Missouri to impose rigid prophylactic rules on the form of lawyer advertising because the restrictions were broader than necessary. And, in *Zauderer v. Office of Disciplinary Counsel*, the Court struck down a ban on the use of illustrations in a lawyer's advertisement offering to represent Dalkon Shield victims. In the absence of a showing that the commercial illustration was itself choice impeding, the Court declined to uphold a flat ban merely because future illustrations might be misleading. On the other hand, since the advertisement in *Zauderer* offered to represent victims free of charge for a contingent fee, the Court upheld a requirement of forced disclosure of possible liability for costs and expenses. Most recently, in *Shapero v. State Bar of Kentucky*, the Court struck down a flat ban on solicitation letters aimed at targeted categories of potential clients. Thus, as long as the proper degree of skepticism and a sufficiently significant burden of justification are maintained, the "false or misleading" speech cases are consistent with effective hearer-centered speech protection.

The third and most difficult category of Supreme Court commercial speech cases involve settings in which a government censor concedes that a given message enhances informed and autonomous decision making by hearers, but fears that the informed, autonomous decision may be a socially undesirable one. In order to enhance socially desirable decision making, therefore, the government censor prohibits the speech precisely because of its choice-enhancing nature.

On one level, this third category of cases—I call them "social engineering cases"—present the same concerns about the competence of government censors raised by the "false and misleading" cases. When the government censor's conception of social good is clouded by self-interest and majoritarian bias, it is entitled to little or no weight. Moreover, even when no structural impediment to respecting the censor's judgment exists, the burden of demonstrating the causal nexus between the censored speech and socially undesirable decision making by hearers should rest squarely on the government.

On a second level, the stakes are far higher in these social engineering cases; for, if the hearer's interest in informed and autonomous decision making can be trumped by a government censor's decision to subordinate autonomous decision making to the censor's conception of socially desirable behavior, a hearer-centered approach to speech protection becomes a paternalistic trap that invites the government to use the selective manipulation of information as a tool of social control. The social engineering cases must be distinguished from cases like *Pittsburgh Press*, in which the only choice involved was forbidden by law. In the social engineering cases, society has not elected to make the choice unlawful or to place other constraints on its exercise. Rather, it seeks to deter socially undesirable but lawful choices by prohibiting speech which provides accurate information to hearers about the existence and nature of the choice.

. . .

## B. The Application of Hearer-Centered Free Speech Doctrine to Regulation of Speech in the Capital Markets

Protection of speech about capital formation will ordinarily be quintessentially hearer-centered. In the absence of a self-expressive, toleration based speaker, the vast bulk of capital formation speakers must generally rely on the interests of their hearers in receiving information that enhances the hearers' capacity for informed and autonomous choice as the sole basis for first amendment protection. In addi-

tion, capital formation speakers may deploy only a weak version of the prophylactic mistrust of the government's competence to censor.

Under such a hearer-centered analysis, government censorship in the capital markets blocking the free flow of information that enhances informed and autonomous choice almost certainly violates the first amendment unless the censorship can be justified by an overwhelming social need. Similarly, when the government asserts that particular speech about capital formation is unprotected because it impedes informed and autonomous choice, the government bears the significant burden of establishing the correctness of its assertions. Finally, the government is obliged to demonstrate that speech-limiting prophylactic procedures it has adopted to protect future hearers (like prior restraints and restrictions on the form and timing of speech) are genuinely necessary to preserve the hearers' interests in informed and autonomous decision making. In the absence of such a showing, the government's insistence upon widespread prior restraints and highly restrictive controls on the form and timing of speech relevant to choice is vulnerable to first amendment challenge. However, if the government can establish that a given message adversely affects hearers' interests in informed or autonomous choice, no first amendment objection to suppressing the speech exists. Moreover, when speech restrictive procedures and regulations can be defended as genuinely—not speculatively—necessary to preserve hearers' interests in informed and autonomous choice, they do not violate the first amendment. Finally, no serious first amendment objection to forced disclosure exists so long as the disclosures are demonstrably necessary to preserve hearers' capacity for informed and/or autonomous choice.

Having developed a theoretical model of hearer-centered free speech at great—some might say interminable—length, I propose to look at Securities and Exchange Commission (SEC) regulation of speech in the capital markets. First, I will discuss the relatively few existing cases that have sought to resolve first amendment challenges to existing SEC regulations from the standpoint of hearer-centered free speech. Second, I will attempt a discussion of the procedural methods used by the SEC to regulate information flow—primarily prior restraints and restrictions on the form and timing of speech—and hazard a guess as to the factors that should determine their constitutionality. Finally, I will attempt a general overview of the four principal areas of SEC speech regulation: (a) licensing and regulation of investment newsletters; (b) control of proxy solicitations and tender offers; (c) regulation of information flow in the primary capital formation market; and (d) management of information flow in the secondary capital markets.

. . .

## 2. Hearer-Centered Analysis of SEC Procedural and Substantive Regulations

The harder question is the extent to which the emergence of a hearer-centered first amendment analysis alters traditional thinking about the SEC's power to brand particular speech as actually or potentially harmful to hearers, and its power to adopt Draconian procedural constraints on speech to guard against the possibility of future harm to hearers.

Attempts by the SEC to brand certain speech as harmful to hearers and, thus, to exclude it from hearer-centered speech protection, raise two related issues. First, how much deference should a reviewing court give to a SEC assessment that a particular communication is, in fact, harmful to hearers; and, even more fundamentally, how does a reviewing court decide who the relevant "hearers" are?

One point appears to emerge forcefully from the commercial speech cases: a mere allegation by the SEC that speech is potentially misleading should not be sufficient to justify its suppression. As with any attempt to censor speech that is arguably protected by the first amendment, the SEC should bear a heavy burden of justification that deflects error in favor of freedom, not control. Thus, the tragi-comic story of the SEC's decision to ban corporate estimates of earnings projections from the primary and secondary capital markets for years because the information was "soft" should never be repeated under a hearer-centered first amendment analysis.

The deference question is merely a restatement of how much skepticism should exist toward the government's competence to act as a censor in a particular context. A high level of skepticism translates into a very low level of deference. A low level of skepticism translates into almost total deference. I have suggested that two versions of skepticism exist in our first amendment tradition. In the toleration based, speaker-centered area, powerful distrust of the government's capacity to apportion toleration fairly leads to a set of prophylactic rules disabling the government from deciding what political, religious, scientific, or aesthetic speech should be tolerated. In a hearer-centered system, a weaker skepticism about the government's ability to make the empirical assessments needed to decide whether a given communication is choice enhancing or choice impeding has led to greater deference to government attempts to censor allegedly harmful commercial speech.

Recent scholarship casts real doubt on the assumption that government censors can be trusted in the commercial speech area. Whether or not one accepts the postulate of "public choice" theoreticians who view all government behavior as an attempt to aid one group at the expense of its rivals, it is clear that problems ranging from the bureaucratic imperative of any regulatory body to expand its power, to well-documented examples of capture of regulatory agencies by a regulated industry, to sheer incompetence should lead to a healthy skepticism about any attempt by a government bureaucrat to manage speech. Perhaps the most important effect of the importation of hearer-centered first amendment protection into the SEC's world will be to force the SEC to carry a significant burden of justification whenever it brands speech as harmful to hearers. Mere good faith speculation should not suffice. Mere fear of future harm should not suffice.

Closely connected with the level of deference and standard of review is the question of what form SEC speech regulation may take in the future. Traditionally, the agency has used a radical prophylactic approach to speech—banning all speech that might be harmful to someone, some day. The classic SEC approach applies an interlocking set of prior restraints and restrictions on the form and timing of speech to minimize the possibility of harmful speech, despite its concededly restrictive effect on much speech that would be of use to hearers.

The validity of the SEC's routine use of the most drastic alternative in regulating speech in the capital markets rests on a single support—the assumption that almost total deference must be paid to SEC judgment about whether radical prophylaxis is necessary to prevent hearers from being injured by speech that impedes their capacity for informed, autonomous choice. That assumption rests, in turn, upon an almost total suspension of disbelief about the incapacity of the government to make judgments about the management of information flow.

As with the deference paid to government judgment that a particular message is false or misleading, the introduction of hearer-centered free speech analysis into the SEC's domain should lead to a more skeptical approach to the SEC's assertion that draconian rules on prior restraint, timing, and form are genuinely necessary to protect the hearers' capacity for choice. While the Supreme Court has been reluctant to disturb a government judgment that a particular form of speech is, in fact, false or misleading, the Court has not hesitated to invalidate restrictions that suppress concededly useful speech as part of a prophylactic assault on potentially harmful speech.

In fact, Justice White's concurrence in *Lowe v. SEC* is precisely such a refusal to permit unnecessarily restrictive speech regulation.

One important caveat should be noted: I do not believe that courts will—or should—invalidate SEC censorship in the capital market area because the form of a regulation is too draconian when the result of such a decision would be to permit a speaker to disseminate information that is, in fact, harmful to the hearers' capacity for informed, autonomous choice. Such a speaker possesses no cognizable free speech interest and cannot articulate any hearer interest to borrow. Accordingly, whether expressed as jus tertii, standing, overbreadth, or as a decision on the merits, such a speaker should not be heard to complain that the SEC's choice of prior restraint, timing rules, or restrictions on form are unjustified as applied to the speaker. No reason exists in a hearer-centered free speech setting to provide false and misleading speakers with a windfall because the SEC constable has blundered in choosing the wrong form of regulation.

However, if unnecessarily restrictive SEC censorship rules are applied to stifle speech that would be useful to hearers today in the name of protecting hearers tomorrow, I believe that it is the courts' duty under a hearer-centered first amendment system to strike the prophylactic censorship rules down. This duty exists unless the SEC is able to persuade a reviewing court that the prophylactic restrictions are genuinely necessary to protect current hearers against false and misleading speech.

The ability of the SEC to satisfy such a substantial burden of justification will rest less on a court's respect for the SEC's claimed expertise than on a conception of who the hearer is in a capital market free speech case. In a sense, talking about hearer-centered free speech doctrine without a precise picture of the hearer's characteristics is like a Russian omelet without the blintz. Yet, much of the disagreement over the wisdom, and now the constitutionality, of much SEC regulation of speech in the capital markets rests on a fundamental disagreement over the nature of the hearer.

The SEC's vision of a hearer is an unsophisticated naif who is thinking about investing in the capital market and who requires substantial protection on both a substantive and procedural level if this naif is to be able to make an informed and autonomous choice. On a substantive level, this hypothetical hearer must be shielded from information that the hearer lacks the sophistication to understand and discount. On a procedural level, virtually all speech much be filtered through SEC censors to be certain that nothing is said that might mislead the hypothetical novice investor. The net result is a massive paper jam at the SEC headquarters and a stylized, often meaningless, set of official documents from which most interesting assertions have been purged. This censorship, together with a set of restrictions on the timing and form of nonofficial communications that virtually guarantees that little of interest will be said in either the official or unofficial documents, induces sophisticated investors to operate black markets in information.

The polar opposite of the SEC's vision of the novice prospective investor is the highly sophisticated investor, either a market professional or a canny amateur counseled by one. Measured by the standard of such a sophisticated market professional, most of the more radically prophylactic SEC rules are, at best, unnecessary, and, at worst, positively harmful because they dry up much information that could be useful to a sophisticated hearer.

Although it is probably impossible to describe a "typical" capital speech hearer, the reality appears to be far closer to the sophisticated investor model than to the SEC's Arcadian vision of Main Street America engaged in romantic, capitalist risk taking. As the Supreme Court recognized in *Basic Inc. v. Levinson*, the nation's capital markets do not function like a Mom and Pop candy store. They operate as highly sophisticated information processing machines that rapidly assimilate date to price stock through efforts of market professionals. Thus, while there is clearly room for rules designed to protect unsophisticated investors, a regulatory structure predicated on a market consisting almost exclusively of unsophisticated investors leads to censorship overkill. In the absence of first amendment considerations, government regulators are free, within the loose bounds set by the fifth amendment, to adopt prophylactic rules designed to protect the most vulnerable at the expense of others more able to fend for themselves. But when the ground rules are changed by the introduction of hearer-centered free speech protection, the government may not deny certain hearers access to information of use to them in making informed and autonomous choice in order to protect the lowest common denominator of potential hearers, at least not in the absence of an overwhelming showing of necessity. At a minimum, prophylactic censorship rules must be tailored to zero in on vulnerable hearers while permitting more sophisticated hearers free access to the information. Indeed, in the context of the contemporary capital market, it is possible that the SEC cannot even establish the continued existence of its paradigmatic unsophisticated hearer.

Stripped of its unchecked regulatory power, the SEC's traditional viselike grip on speech in the capital markets must be harmonized with hearer-centered free speech protection in four contexts. The SEC's regulation of investment newsletters should be radically reduced. While no impediment exists to the continued policing of the accuracy of the contents of investment newsletters, including the use of narrowly tailored prior restraints forbidding genuinely false and misleading material, the imposition of broad prophylactic censorship aimed at preventing potentially misleading speech in future newsletters should be doomed. Regardless of whether the prophylaxis is based on a SEC mistrust of the character of the speaker as in *Lowe*, or a desire to protect particularly vulnerable hearers, or a desire to provide hearers with even more information as in *Wall Street Publishing Institute*, the censorship should fail unless it is linked precisely to the correction of demonstrably false or misleading information.

The SEC's overregulation of proxy solicitations and tender offers is similarly vulnerable to hearer-centered free speech analysis. As the SEC's position in *Long Island Lighting* illustrates, the commission asserts total control over all speech that is "reasonably calculated" to affect the outcome of a proxy fight. Although the commission's aggressive position dodged a bullet in *Long Island Lighting*, it is vulnerable on at least two levels. First, the commission's assertion of the right to pass on the truth of all assertions made in the context of a proxy battle that are "reasonably calculated" to affect the outcome is indefensibly overbroad. When, as in the LILCO setting, the proxy fight turns on issues that fall within traditional toleration based speaker-centered free speech protection, the government lacks the power to certify political assertions as true or false. Although regulations assuring that both sides in the dispute have an opportunity to make their respective cases would survive both a speaker-centered and a hearer-centered challenge, attempts to impose the SEC's version of the truth in the corporate political arena can be no more successful than any other well-intentioned attempt by the government to police the usefulness or accuracy of political speech.

Moreover, even when proxy solicitations involve purely commercial speech that does not trigger the speaker-centered toleration principle, the stifling procedural constraints imposed by the SEC in the hope of heading-off potentially false and misleading speech cannot survive a hearer-centered analysis. Although a regulation requiring that all proxy solicitations be deposited with the SEC prior to distribution would probably be valid, a requirement that the material be affirmatively approved before dissemination is far too broad. At most, the SEC might be given a brief period to file an objection, but, unless the government could establish the falseness of the assertions, no basis exists for restraining its dissemination. At that point, the existence of potent subsequent sanctions for false or misleading proxy material and the availability of flexible equitable remedies capable of providing adequate post hoc relief are sufficient to protect the hearers' interest in receiving truthful and complete information. Moreover, SEC restrictions on the form and timing of proxy solicitations and tender offers, especially the type of "indirect" solicitation involved in *Long Island Lighting*, can no longer be defended by referring to a fictitious unsophisticated hearer who must be shielded from robust debate for the hearer's own good.

Third, the SEC's intense regulation of speech in the primary capital market must be measured against hearer-centered free speech protection. At least four aspects of the SEC's primary market speech regulations raise serious first amendment issues: (1) forced disclosure by the issuer; (2) prior SEC approval of each registration statement and prospectus; (3) restrictions on the contents of the registration statement and the prospectus; and (4) restrictions on the form and timing of pre- and post-prospectus promotional speech.

To the extent SEC forced disclosure rules surrounding registration statements and prospectuses are necessary to permit informed and autonomous investor choice, they pose no first amendment problems in a hearer-centered setting. Although the *Wall Street Institute* decision is a reminder that there are limits to the SEC's desire to force the disclosure of *all* useful information, the common sense test adopted by the Supreme Court in *Basic Inc. v. Levinson* should provide guidance as to the limits of forced disclosure. A requirement that new issues be described in a standardized document deposited with the SEC containing information necessary to an informed investor choice poses no serious hearer-centered speech issues. The requirement of a registration statement and prospectus containing standardized data assures a common denominator of information that will be generally available to investors, and the obligation to deposit the registration statement and prospectus with the SEC prior to issuance of stock provides the SEC with an opportunity to deal with patently false and misleading material before it is transmitted to hearers.

However, two important qualifications on the SEC's power over primary capital formation speech must be noted. First, the SEC's ability to delay issuance pending approval of a registration statement and prospectus should be strictly limited in time. Whether the ten-day period that applies in other settings is sufficient in the capital market area is a matter for discussion. But there should be a time limit, and a short one at that. The existing practice that permits the SEC to start the twenty-day clock anew each time it suggests the alteration of a registration statement gives the agency a virtually unlimited power to use delay as a potent censorship weapon.

Second, the SEC's ability to block a prospectus based on an allegation of false or misleading data should depend on the SEC's affirmative duty to persuade a reviewing court that the speech restriction is genuinely necessary to protect a hearer's ability to make an informed and autonomous choice about whether to purchase the stock. Thus, in order to obtain a prior restraint on initial issue speech, the SEC should be required to take the initiative to obtain judicial approval of the censorship within a strictly limited period of time. Passivity or undue delay by the SEC should release the registration statement and prospectus for dissemination, subject, of course, to subsequent sanctions for false and misleading statements.

Moreover, it is impossible to square existing SEC restrictions on the scope and timing of pre- and post-prospectus promotional speech involving new issues with a hearer-centered theory of free speech. Banning all prefiling promotional speech and limiting post-prospectus speech to anodyne tombstone announcements is a parody of the robust flow of information that ought to characterize primary capital market speech.

By reducing speech about new stock issues to the level of simplicity that is allegedly necessary to protect widows and orphans, the SEC virtually guarantees that the officially sanctioned sources of information will be of limited use to more sophisticated investors who make up the bulk of primary capital market hearers. Indeed, the predictable result of drying up officially sanctioned sources of information about new issues has been to create a black market in unsanctioned information in the form of rumors and insider generated tips. Although it is the farthest thing from the SEC's mind, the net effect of SEC overregulation of speech in the primary capital market may well have been to increase the capacity of insiders to manipulate the market to their advantage by the use of selective, unsanctioned, and unattributed leaks. Thus, while restrictions on false and misleading pre- and post-prospectus speech pose no serious free speech problems, the routine use of broad prophylactic restrictions on the scope and timing of

accurate promotional activity in the primary capital markets should not withstand hearer-centered first amendment scrutiny.

On the other hand, the requirements of systematic forced disclosure, coupled with subsequent sanctions for false and misleading statements, that characterize current SEC regulation of speech in the secondary capital markets does not appear to violate the first amendment. So long as the forced disclosure is limited to information that is genuinely necessary to permit hearers to make informed and autonomous choices, the regulations enhance hearer-centered free speech. Moreover, to the extent the SEC seeks to enjoin false and misleading speech in the secondary market, hearer-centered speech is not threatened as long as the SEC is required to establish its allegations affirmatively under a significant burden of persuasion.

---

Lawrence Alexander & Daniel A. Farber, *Commercial Speech and First Amendment Theory: A Critical Exchange*, 75 NORTHWESTERN UNIVERSITY LAW REVIEW 307 (1980)*

### Lawrence Alexander

In *Commercial Speech and First Amendment Theory*, Professor Daniel Farber considered the level of first amendment protection afforded to commercial speech and concluded that a lower level of protection is justified for speech employed in the sale of products than for political speech. After all, the law of contractual liability for fraud and misrepresentation has not provoked any serious first amendment challenge. In his article, Professor Farber argues:

> So long as a regulation relates to the contractual function of the utterance, the regulation should not be subjected to the intensive scrutiny required when a regulation directly implicates the first amendment function of language. Thus, the problem is to devise a test which will distinguish between regulations involving the first amendment, informative aspect of advertising and those involving its non-first amendment, contractual aspect.

Professor Farber goes on to illustrate the application of his test to false and deceptive advertising and to affirmative disclosure requirements. It is at the end of his article, when he deals with *Ohralik v. Ohio State Bar Association*, that he raises the point that is the subject of my concern. In a footnote, Professor Farber attempts to distinguish *Ohralik*, in which the United States Supreme Court upheld the disciplining of an attorney for soliciting tort clients, from its companion case, *In re Primus*, in which the Court held unconstitutional the application of a state's antisolicitation rules to solicitation by the American Civil Liberties Union (ACLU) in a civil rights suit. Professor Farber justifies the different outcomes as follows:

> The difference in approaches is consistent with the theory propounded in this article. In *Primus*, unlike *Ohralik*, the Court found that the contemplated litigation itself was an expression of first amendment associational activity. Consequently, the formation of agreements to bring suit in *Primus* was itself subject to some measure of first amendment protection, unlike the typical commercial speech case, in which the state has a free hand in regulating the contractual relationship between the parties. Although the state's interest in *Primus* focused on what this article has called the contractual aspect of the speech, the state interest nonetheless directly implicates first amendment values and cannot be considered wholly unrelated to the suppression of free expression.

In an earlier article on commercial speech, I raised "the question of the validity of bans on advertising transactions which are legal but which are nonetheless deemed undesirable." That question, I wrote, "raises such basic issues as why the government . . . may be paternalistic regarding the purchase of goods but may not be paternalistic regarding information about those goods, as the Court in *Virginia State Board [of Pharmacy v. Virginia Citizens Consumer Council, Inc.*, 425 U.S. 748 (1976)] said it may not be." Professor Farber seems to suggest that the government *should* be allowed to regulate, freer from first amendment constraint, advertising of transactions it could constitutionally prohibit or restrict. On the other hand, he maintains that if a transaction is itself constitutionally protected, the accompanying advertising should receive strong first amendment protection.

With all due respect, I think Professor Farber has come up with the wrong solution to the issues I raised in my earlier article. If advertising accompanying the sale of products receives a certain level of first amendment protection, any additional constitutional

protection the advertising receives as a result of the constitutionally favored status of the transaction itself should derive from whatever constitutional provision protects the transaction, not from the first amendment.

Consider advertising regarding the terms and conditions for performance of an abortion. A woman's right to obtain an abortion is constitutionally protected by the due process clause of the fifth and fourteenth amendments. Does it make sense to say that the ordinary laws regarding contractual liability, fraud, and duress in the execution of contracts for the sale of goods and services are subject to stricter *first amendment* scrutiny when the service sold is an abortion rather than, say, housecleaning? If stricter scrutiny is called for at all, it must be as the result of the impact of the law of contract on the obtaining of an abortion, an impact that implicates the due process clause rather than the first amendment.

Of course, sometimes the sale of the product itself and not just the accompanying advertising will be protected under the first amendment rather than under some other constitutional provision, if it is protected at all. The sale of a book on politics or religion is a good example. Even here, however, it would seem that the first amendment analysis of advertising accompanying contracts of sale and the first amendment analysis of the content of the book should be kept distinct. In some cases that may be difficult—consider, for example, an advertisement such as, "This book will guarantee you the happiness that comes from glimpsing the Eternal Truth." In most cases, however, it will not.

With respect to cases like *Ohralik* and *Primus* a court would be ill-advised to begin comparing contracts to undertake personal injury litigation with contracts to undertake civil rights litigation if the object is to define the limits of first amendment protection of attorney solicitation. Professor Farber makes two unwarranted assumptions regarding *Ohralik* and *Primus*. First, he assumes that suits for personal injuries have little constitutional protection and therefore may be eliminated or severely restricted by the state. Thus, if "the greater includes the lesser," the state may restrict solicitation of clients for such suits. Second, he assumes that the Court would, or at least should, have decided *Ohralik* and *Primus* as it did even if the ACLU had solicited the tort clients in *Ohralik* and the solicitation in *Primus* had been conducted face-to-face in the client's home.

The distinction Professor Farber draws between the two cases based upon the first amendment associational rights implicated by the ACLU's involvement in *Primus* blurs a bit if we consider the following hypothetical solicitation. An attorney with a non-profit organization called Citizens United for Bodily Integrity (CUBI) speaks at a meeting of homeowners who are concerned about a rash of hit-and-run accidents in their neighborhood, and he offers to represent a woman at the meeting in a suit against a drunken driver who ran a stop sign and knocked her off her bicycle. In *Primus*, an ACLU attorney addressed a meeting of women who had been sterilized as a condition for receiving public assistance medical payments, and the attorney later offered to represent one of the women in a suit against the physician who had performed the sterilization. On one level, the hypothetical suit contemplated by the CUBI attorney and the ACLU suit in *Primus* are tort actions for personal injuries, although the ACLU action could also be phrased in constitutional terms. On another level, solicitations by the hypothetical CUBI attorney and the ACLU fall within the penumbra of associational rights protected by the first amendment that seemed to concern the Court in *Primus*. Only if suits for personal injuries somehow lack constitutional significance would the CUBI solicitation be distinguishable from the ACLU solicitation in *Primus*.

It is doubtful that suits for personal injuries lack constitutional significance. It is also doubtful that *Ohralik* and *Primus* would have been distinguishable to the Court but for the facts that Primus solicited for the ACLU and Ohralik solicited face-to-face for his own profit. Although I have difficulties with these bases for a first amendment distinction, difficulties well-expressed by others, I have more difficulty with Professor Farber's distinction based on the constitutional status of the two contemplated lawsuits.

There is something almost irresistible about the "greater includes the lesser" approach in constitutional law. The approach surfaced in the heyday of the "right-privilege" distinction and is again manifested in the Supreme Court's two-step approach to procedural due process. My question remains, however: why may the government paternalistically ban the sale of certain products but not paternalistically ban their advertisement? Although Professor Farber's general distinction between ordinary speech and contractual speech, which distinction is the main focus of his article, is useful, his answer to my question—government may paternalistically ban or restrict the advertising of transactions it may paternalistically ban or restrict—is unsupported by either the case law or any first amendment rationales. Although I do not wish to maintain that the first amendment is hermetically sealed off from the other constitutional provisions, it is those latter provisions, not the first amendment, that hold the key to my riddle.

*Daniel Farber*

Before I respond to Professor Alexander's comments, perhaps a brief recapitulation is in order. The thesis of my article, *Commercial Speech and First Amendment Theory*, was that advertising serves two distinct functions. It serves both as the initial stage in the creation of a contractual relationship and as a means of communicating product information. That is, an advertisement serves both a contractual function like that of a formal offer and an informational function like that of a consumer report. Although the informational function is protected by the first amendment, the contractual function generally is not so protected because commercial contracts are subject to virtually plenary state regulation. Attempts to regulate the contractual function of commercial speech, however, have spillover effects on the informative function. These spillover effects necessitate first amendment scrutiny under the balancing test enunciated in *United States v. O'Brien*. With this background in mind, Professor Alexander's comments and my responses should be clearer.

Professor Alexander raises three separate points. First, he takes issue with my reading of the opinions in the attorney solicitation cases, *Ohralik v. Ohio State Bar Association* and *In re Primus*. Second, he believes that my analysis of these cases implies that government may "paternalistically" ban advertising about purely commercial transactions based on its power to ban the transactions themselves. Finally, he believes that the constitutional status of the underlying transaction should be irrelevant to the first amendment analysis of advertising. In general, these areas of disagreement do not detract from the more important areas of our agreement about the usefulness of distinguishing the contractual function of commercial speech from its informational function.

Let me begin with our narrowest area of disagreement. Professor Alexander appears to argue that the only distinction between *Primus* and *Ohralik* is factual: the ACLU lawyer in *Primus* did not engage in face-to-face solicitation as did the personal injury lawyer in *Ohralik*. The opinions in the two cases clearly reveal, however, that the Supreme Court found a more fundamental distinction between these cases. The opinion in *Ohralik* stresses that the lawyer was engaging in a "business transaction," and that since speech undertaken as part of a business transaction "occurs in an area traditionally subject to government regulation," such speech enjoys lesser constitutional protection. As the Court viewed *Primus* however, the ACLU lawyer's offer to represent a potential civil rights client was not simply part of a business transaction. The Court held that the ACLU lawyers were engaged in a kind of associational activity implicitly protected by the first amendment. Indeed, this was the precise ground on which the Court in *Primus* distinguished *Ohralik*. The regulation in *Primus* was subjected to greater scrutiny because, "[i]n the context of political expression and association, . . . a State must regulate with significantly greater precision." Given the Court's view of the different constitutional status of the litigation activities involved in the two cases, the dissimilar treatment of the cases is entirely understandable. In both cases the state's goal was to regulate the making of offers, but in *Primus* the resulting agreement was itself thought to enjoy constitutional protection while in *Ohralik* it was an ordinary business transaction. Of course, it is arguable that the Court is mistaken in holding that some litigation-related agreements are subject to greater constitutional protection than others. After *Ohralik* and *Primus* however, the Court appears to have taken a clear position on the matter.

Beyond the question of the correct reading of these cases, Professor Alexander argues that my analysis indicates that the state is always free to suppress information about transactions whenever the state could constitutionally ban the transactions themselves. My discussion of *Primus* was not intended to indicate this view. Neither *Ohralik* nor *Primus* involved an attempt to justify a deliberate decision to prevent information from reaching consumers. Hence, neither case raises the issue of whether purposeful, "paternalistic" attempts to suppress information are ever justifiable. As I indicated elsewhere in my article, the Court's apparent view that all attempts to suppress information are *per se* invalid gives me some qualms, but I certainly do not mean to adopt the contrary view of *per se* validity.

It does seem to me, however, that paternalistic bans on advertising are more *clearly* unconstitutional when the underlying transaction is itself immune from regulation. For example, in *Bigelow v. Virginia*, the Court was confronted with a Virginia ban on abortion advertising as applied to an advertisement for a New York abortion referral service. The Court acknowledged that the right to travel protected the interest of a Virginia resident in traveling to New York for this service. This finding is directly relevant to the first amendment analysis of the advertising ban under the *O'Brien* balancing test. As I argued in my article, the *O'Brien* test is appropriate when a government regulation implicates a course of conduct involving both "speech" and "nonspeech" elements. To pass this test, the statute must, among other factors, be necessary to achieve a permissible state goal. The state's asserted goal in *Bigelow* was

to prevent Virginia residents from using the New York referral service. Essentially, this amounted to an attempt to prevent the exercise of the constitutional right to travel to New York to use the service. This goal is clearly impermissible, and the statute therefore failed the *O'Brien* test. This does not necessarily mean that a direct right to travel claim would have succeeded. The newspaper probably would not have had standing to raise the travel rights of its audience. Furthermore, no direct penalty on travel was involved. Hence, the case did not fall within the relatively small class of cases that have been subjected to heightened scrutiny under the right to travel rationale. The right to travel was nevertheless relevant to assessing the legitimacy of the state's interest once scrutiny under the first amendment was triggered.

As this example illustrates, the *O'Brien* test is incompatible with Professor Alexander's view that the nature of the underlying transaction is irrelevant to first amendment analysis. In order to pass muster under *O'Brien*, a regulation must significantly further a government interest that is "unrelated to the suppression of free expression" and is otherwise within the government's power. If the state's goal is to affect the underlying transaction, the analysis will be influenced greatly by the constitutional status of that transaction. If the underlying transaction is itself protected by the first amendment or by some other constitutional provision, a court must decide if the state interest in regulating that transaction is constitutionally permissible. This is simply not a problem in most cases involving advertising for normal commercial transactions. In these cases, we can usually take for granted the legitimacy of the state's interest in regulating the underlying commercial transaction, and simply apply the *O'Brien* test in considering whether the means chosen by the state impermissibly intrude on the informational function of the advertising.

Although the first amendment test used in *O'Brien* makes the nature of the underlying transaction a highly relevant factor, this is not due to any peculiarity of the *O'Brien* test. Under any first amendment test that involves an appraisal of competing individual and governmental interests, the nature of the underlying transaction will always be relevant. If the underlying transaction is itself constitutionally protected, this will generally diminish the state's interest in regulating speech relating to the transaction and strengthen the individual's interest in receiving information about the transaction. Nevertheless, the restriction on the state's power derives not from whatever constitutional provision protects the underlying transaction, but from the first amendment itself. Ignoring the constitutionally protected nature of the underlying transaction as an important component of any first amendment analysis, as Professor Alexander proposes, would significantly weaken the first amendment protection accorded to all forms of speech.

In conclusion, I would simply like to reiterate that I view our area of agreement as more significant than any of these disagreements. My primary purpose was to argue for a distinction between regulations aimed at the unique contractual function of commercial speech as a means of making offers, and those aimed at the informational function that commercial speech shares with other forms of speech. In my view, the *O'Brien* test is proper for contractually based regulations, but regulations aimed at the informational function need stricter scrutiny. If I understand him correctly, Professor Alexander finds this analysis useful, and I am gratified at our apparent agreement on this point.

# Bibliography

*Commercial Expression*

Alexander, Lawrence, *Speech in the Local Marketplace: Implications of* Virginia  State Board of Pharmacy v. Virginia Citizens Consumer Council, Inc. for Local Regulatory Power, 14 San Diego Law Review 357 (1977)

Coase, R.H., *Advertising and Free Speech*, 6 Journal Legal Studies 1 (1977)

Farber, Daniel A., *Commercial Speech and First Amendment Theory*, 74 Northwestern  University Law Review 372 (1979)

Lively, Donald E., *The Supreme Court and Commercial Speech: New Words with an Old  Message*, 72 Minnesota Law Review 289 (1987)

Redish, Martin H., *Product Health Claims and the First Amendment: Scientific Expression and the Twilight Zone of Commercial Speech*, 43 Vanderbilt Law Review 1433 (1990)

Redish, Martin H., *The First Amendment in the Marketplace: Commercial Speech and  the Values of Free Expression*, 39 George Washington Law Review 429 (1971)

# E.  Obscenity and Pornography

As a prime variant of unprotected expression, obscenity can be regulated even if harm is uncertain or speculative. The categorically unprotected status of obscenity was illuminated by the Supreme Court's observation that ''(i)t is not for us to resolve empirical uncertainties underlying state legislation, save in the exceptional case where the legislation plainly impinges upon rights protected by the Constitution itself.'' *Paris Adult Theatre I v. Slaton*, 413 U.S. 49, 60 (1973). Despite the technical absence of a real controversy, given no need for the state to justify regulation of obscenity, literature for and against such speech control has been notable for its volume and intensity. Traditionally, the most vexing problem in the area of obscenity has been one of definition. That intractable difficulty prompted Justice Stewart's memorable observation that he might never intelligently describe obscenity, but ''I know it when I see it.'' *Jacobellis v. Ohio*, 378 U.S. 184, 197 (1964)(Stewart, J., concurring). It also led Justice Brennan from authorship of the Court's basic position on obscenity in *Roth v. United States*, 354 U.S. 476 (1957) to repudiation of it in *Paris Adult Theatre I v. Slaton*, 413 U.S. 49, 113 (1973)(Brennan, J., dissenting). William B. Lockhart and Robert C. McClure suggest that the benefits of regulating obscenity are slight compared with the cost it extracts from literary freedom. Louis Henkin equates obscenity with sin and thus considers regulation as a means of accounting for public morality. Catharine A. MacKinnon proposes a redirection of regulatory concern to pornography's capacity for abasing and dominating women. Cass R. Sunstein focuses upon concepts of viewpoint neutrality and their relevance to pornography control. Nadine Strossen challenges the premise of a monolithic feminist perspective upon pornography.

William B. Lockhart and Robert C. McClure, *Literature, The Law of Obscenity, and the Constitution,* 38 MINNESOTA LAW REVIEW 295 (1954)*

. . .

## B. FREEDOM OF EXPRESSION FOR SEX IN LITERATURE

Whatever may be its limits, constitutional protection to freedom of expression must be held to apply to literature dealing with sex problems and behavior as well as to literature dealing with other social and economic problems. It is not conceivable that the Supreme Court will ever hold this vast and significant area of human thought and conduct to be unprotected territory, in which speech and writing are subject to unrestricted governmental suppression. Sex has always occupied too important and dominant a place in literature and in human interest and concern to be impliedly excluded from the broadly stated First Amendment freedoms.

While the Supreme Court has never had occasion to deal explicitly with this issue, it has made abundantly clear in other connections that constitutional freedom of expression applies to all subject matter of human thought, interest, and concern. In *Thornhill v. Alabama*, dealing with freedom to communicate viewpoints on labor disputes, Mr. Justice Black, speaking for an all but unanimous Court, said:

> "The freedom of speech and the press guaranteed by the Constitution embraces at the least the liberty to discuss publicly and truthfully *all matters of public concern* without previous restraint or fear of subsequent punishment. The exigencies of the colonial period and efforts to secure freedom from oppressive administration developed a broadened conception of these liberties as adequate to supply the public need for *information and education with respect to the significant issues of the times. . . .* Freedom of discussion, if it would fulfill its historic function in this nation, must embrace *all issues about which information is needed or appropriate to enable the members of society to cope with the exigencies of their period* [italics supplied]."

. . .

And in *Pennekamp v. Florida*, protecting freedom to discuss judicial action, the Court emphasized:

"Free discussion of the *problems of society* is a cardinal principle of Americanism—a principle which all are zealous to preserve [Italics supplied]."

Literature dealing with various aspects and problems of sex and sex behavior relates to a significant "field of human interest" and "public concern." Such literature deals with some of the basic "problems of society." Certainly this is an area in which there is "public need for information and education" to permit intelligent grappling with these problems.

In the decisions quoted above, the particular issues related to expressions in the field of labor and the administration of justice, but it is clear that the Court had no thought of limiting freedom of expression to these and kindred subjects. Indeed, a few years later an unsuccessful attempt was made to limit freedom of expression to such subjects when counsel for the state suggested in *Winters v. New York* that freedom of the press only applies to interference with religion and with "the free expression of ideas on political or economic matters." In its opinion holding too vague and indefinite a statute forbidding the massing of stories of bloodshed and lust, the Supreme Court rejected this suggestion, saying:

> "We do not accede to appellee's suggestion that the constitutional protection for a free press applies only to the exposition of ideas. The line between the informing and the entertaining is too elusive for the protection of that basic right. Everyone is familiar with instances of propaganda through fiction. What is one man's amusement, teaches another's doctrine. Though we see nothing of value in these magazines, they are as much entitled to the protection of free speech as is the best of literature. . . . They are equally subject to control if they are lewd, indecent, obscene or profane."

Here is an express ruling that magazines dealing with crime and lust are not automatically excluded from constitutional protection, though their publication can be controlled "if they are lewd, indecent, obscene or profane"—whatever that may mean. Of course there are limits on the literary treatment of sex, just as there are limits on the expression of ideas on other subjects, and our major concern in the following pages is how to determine that limit without harmful repression of freedom of expression on a subject of great public interest, concern, and importance. But the point we make here, without discussing the limitations, is that literature dealing with sex problems and sex behavior is entitled to constitutional freedom of expression.

---

* Reprinted with permission.

That literature on sex problems, practices, and behavior deals with a subject of great public interest and concern is amply demonstrated by the widespread public interest in the two recent Kinsey studies dealing with the sexual behavior of the human male and female. Not only did these studies become best sellers, but they became the subject for extensive comment and discussion in both popular and professional writings. Even before these studies were published, Walter Lippman pointed out man's "immense preoccupation with sex" and the "immense urgent discussion of sex throughout the modern world." It is common knowledge that in recent years there has been wide distribution and sale in this country of books and other publications dealing with many aspects of sex, sex problems, and sex behavior from a great many points of view—psychology, sociology, anthropology, education, birth control, marital relations, sex instruction, and sex techniques.

Here is an area of life that immediately concerns all of mankind. It creates problems that vitally affect most individuals. It is an area in which man has often groped in the dark, because of periodic taboos on intelligent discussion. The ready response in recent years to the wider distribution of literature dealing with this area demonstrates great interest in and serious concern with problems that so closely affect the lives of all, and the widespread desire for more information, light, and understanding. There are many differing and conflicting viewpoints and opinions concerning the place that sex should play in the life of individuals, and what is acceptable human conduct. This is exactly the type of subject matter on which freedom of expression is essential—because of this great human interest and the great variety of viewpoints. Unrestricted censorship over the expression of ideas in this area would defeat the very purpose of the guarantees of free expression—that men shall be free to express themselves on, and to consider and choose between, conflicting viewpoints in matters of vital concern to themselves.

Not only must constitutional freedom of expression apply to literature dealing with sex problems and sex behavior, but it must apply regardless of the form the literature takes—whether it be fiction, poetry or non-fiction. It is axiomatic that fiction and poetry are important vehicles for the conveyance of ideas. Fiction not only reaches readers that resist non-fiction, but it is often the best method of expressing some kinds of ideas, or for explaining and portraying human behavior. But this point needs no belaboring, for the Supreme Court has clearly recognized that the freedom of expression guaranteed by the Constitution covers fiction and entertainment, as well as more serious works. . . .

## D. APPLICATION OF THE [CONSTITUTIONAL] STANDARD TO OBSCENITY CENSORSHIP

### 1. Values of a Free Literature: Consequences of Obscenity Censorship

The values of a free literature are of course the same as those of any other form of expression. Indeed, the need to protect freedom of literature in book form is even greater than the need to protect it in other forms. For a book, as publisher Curtice Hitchcock once wrote, ". . .has always been the means which the community uses for the testing and development of new and pioneering ideas in the arts, in the sciences, and in the philosophies. To tamper with freedom of expression in book form, therefore, is the most dangerous exercise of interference with freedom of thought which can be imagined." This of course is self-evident with respect to expository and argumentative literature. But it is not so apparent in fiction and poetry—at least to the censorious; for the private censorship groups, the police and prosecuting officers, and sometimes judges too do not seem to have much love for imaginative literature or appreciation and understanding of its nature and function.

Fiction and poetry, like all other forms of art and expression are vehicles for the conveyance of ideas. They differ from other forms of art and expression in the use of their own peculiar means of communication. Sometimes this is obvious, as in A.P. Herbert's well-known novel *Holy Deadlock*, which was written to ridicule the English divorce law and to generate support for its amendment. But the use of fiction and poetry for the communication of ideas is not always so apparent. For it is not necessarily the function of fiction and poetry to teach or instruct or to argue, in the usual sense in which these words are used. This does not mean that the reader learns nothing from fiction and poetry; he does learn, but he learns "in the fashion that is art's unique own."

But what is "the fashion that is art's unique own"? Harold C. Gardiner, S.J., the perceptive and intelligent literary critic of *America* magazine, tells us that he learns from fiction by its truth of fact and its truth of ideal, that he finds "truth through the door of beauty." . . .

Irwin Edman also tells us how the reader learns from fiction and poetry. The chief functions of art, he says, are the intensification, clarification, and interpretation of experience. Experience is intensified by arresting the reader's sensations, focusing his attention upon his own emotions so that he can know them for what they are. Experience is clarified by setting emotions and random impressions in a pattern so as to make their meaning clear to the reader. And experience is interpreted, simply because any work of art necessarily carries in it the artist's view of life and his criticism of that phase of experience he has selected for treatment. To the reader:

"The great and simple appeal of fiction is that it enables us to share imaginatively in the fortunes of these created beings without paying the price in time or defeat for their triumphs and frustrations. One moves with them in lands where one has never been, experiences loves one has never known. And this entrance into lives wider and more various than our own in turn enables us more nicely to appreciate and more intensely to live the lives we do know."

And this imaginative sharing in the fictitious lives of others helps to give the reader an understanding of unfamiliar problems and modes of life and to foster development of the personal quality the psychologists call "empathy"—the ability to put one's self imaginatively into the other fellow's shoes.

Love and desire and jealousy are among the basic human emotions that give rise to the conflict and tension essential to fiction and poetry. And since sex lies at the root of these and other similar emotions, it is a significant and necessary ingredient of most imaginative literature, and requires broad freedom for the manner in which it may be treated; for only with the freedom to experiment in the manner of treating sex in imaginative literature are authors and poets able to produce their best works. Sex is also significant in its own right; for it is one of the most important elements of all human experience. As such, it demands freedom for rational discussion, scientific investigation, and education. Yet these are the very social values of sex that censorship of obscenity jeopardizes, especially when the censorship is indiscriminate.

And censorship of obscenity has almost always been both irrational and indiscriminate. Perhaps the best explanation for this fact lies in the personal characteristics of the censor. He is rarely an educated person who understands and appreciates the nature and function of imaginative literature. He is often an emotionally disturbed and intemperate person with a paranoid personality. His attention is focused on smut, and since he looks for it, he finds it everywhere. Indeed, his continued existence may depend on his ability to turn it up. In either case, he is so much interested in smut that he cannot, even if he had the ability, see the good at all.

The effects of obscenity censorship upon authors and publisher are of course difficult to ascertain. Yet the lack of definiteness in any standard of obscenity, the absence of even a uniform indefinite standard applicable throughout the nation, and the constant threat of prosecution instigated by some local smuthound cannot help but have a repressive effect upon authors and publishers. H.L. Mencken's description of his problems as an editor is illuminating:

"[A]s a practical editor, I find that the Comstocks, near and far, are oftener in my mind's eye than my actual patrons. The thing I always have to decide about a manuscript offered for publication, before ever I give any thought to its artistic merit and suitability, is the question whether its publication will be permitted—not even whether it is intrinsically good or evil, moral or immoral, but whether some roving Methodist preacher, self-commissioned to keep watch on letter, will read indecency into it. Not a week passes that I do not decline some sound and honest piece of work for no other reason. . . ."

Though Mencken wrote this description in 1917 and the law of obscene literature has changed very much since then, the problems of a publisher today, faced with the current wave of censorship across the country, are probably not very much different. And the publisher's fears are likely to be transmitted in even greater degree to the author. For the author is ordinarily less able to bear the financial risk involved in a book that might be suppressed as obscene, and his contract with the publisher may even contain a clause that "The author hereby guarantees . . . that the work . . . contains nothing of a scandalous, an immoral or a libelous nature." The inevitable tendency is to make the serious author timid, to cramp his mind so that the books he is not afraid to write will fall far below the level of his abilities. And society, as a consequence of the anxiety to suppress smut at all costs, may lose the values of important literary, scientific, and educational contributions. In their place it may have a distorted literature, unfaithful to life, and perhaps even a blacking out of rational public discussion of social problems of immense public importance.

### 2. "Evils" Claimed to Justify Obscenity Censorship: Balancing the Interests

These significant values that arise out of freedom to write and to read literature without restrictions as to theme or materials, and the substantial losses to society that inevitably result from most censorship aimed at "obscenity," must be balanced against the evils thought to justify the suppression of literature attacked as "obscene.". . .

. . . Professor Chafee has observed that obscenity is a "complex idea" that includes several "real or supposed social injuries." In the main these injuries relate to various effects upon individual readers. The offensive or shocking effect upon the reader is occasionally suggested as among the evils aimed at, but the effects usually mentioned are danger of stimulating impure sexual thoughts, or sexual conduct contrary to the laws or accepted moral standards of the community. In addition to these supposed effects upon individuals, another evil sometimes mentioned is the danger that literature challenging or questioning the accepted moral standards of the community might actually bring about a change in the commonly accepted standards. The relative weight that should be attached to each of these evils when thrown into the balance against the loss to society from this kind of censorship requires critical consideration.

### a. Changing Community Moral Standards

Only slight consideration need be given to the contention that literature challenging or questioning the currently accepted moral standards of the community should be suppressed because of the danger that it may in time influence those moral standards through changing laws or customs, as distinct from influencing individuals to deviate from the currently accepted standards. If this purpose were not so apparent in the materials advocating censorship, in the type of books occasionally censored, and in some of the judicial decisions applying censorship laws, it would hardly merit discussion. Not only is this purpose inconsistent with the fundamental reasons for freedom of expression, but the causal relationship between such literature and a change in the general moral standards is far too tenuous to satisfy the constitutional standard of "clear" or "probable" danger. . . .

. . . Back of this fundamental freedom [of expression] lies the basic conviction that our democratic society must be free to perfect its own standards of conduct and belief—political, economic, social, religious, moral—through the heat of unrepressed controversy and debate. The remedy against those who attack currently accepted standards is spirited and intelligent defense of those standards, not censorship. . . .

Even if there were substantial danger that one book, or several books, would actually bring about a change in the currently accepted moral standards, this still would not be a sufficient evil to justify repression of the book. . . . If that were a justification, then freedom of expression would be guaranteed only when it could make no difference. But it is not amiss to point out also that the standards of society are changed neither quickly nor as the result of a single force. Changes in moral standards are necessarily slow and gradual, the result of many interrelated forces. Perhaps a book may be a minor factor in a change of the generally accepted standards, but this will only occur if many other factors also concur in bringing this about. The "probable effect" of any book attacking current moral standards is that it may cause a brief stir and discussion among a relatively small portion of the population, and then be placed on the shelves without causing any perceptible change in the accepted standards. . . .

### b. Offensiveness

Professor Chafee has suggested that one of the injuries sought to be prevented by obscenity laws is "offensiveness, which links indecency to profanity and public drunkenness." . . .

This harm—if it is a harm—is relatively minor for two reasons. In the first place, few who read literature that might offend the sensitive will in fact be offended, for the sensitive seldom read such literature—unless they are looking for the shock. Those who dislike or are offended by such literature need not, and ordinarily do not, read it. If by accident they start to read a book that turns out to be offensive, there is no obligation to continue reading. In this respect, literature containing words, scenes, or ideas likely to offend some readers is quite unlike publicly spoken obscenity from which there may often be no escape. For the offensive materials are confined within the covers of a book, and need not be brought to life unless it is the reader's desire to do so.

In the second place, for the relatively few readers who will be offended by what they read, the shock to their sense of decency and propriety is really a very trivial harm, standing by itself. Those who quite accidentally read a book containing unexpected scenes or words of a nature shocking to them may at the worst become momentarily embarrassed, and perhaps outraged or distressed that such a book should be available to the innocent reader. Any such emotional reaction is of relatively short duration, and causes no serious or lasting harm. . . .

### c. Stimulating Sex Thoughts

The basic evil aimed at by obscenity censorship is protection of the moral standards of individuals, stated usually in very broad and inexact terms, even by those who would reduce the excesses of censorship. While the classic obscenity test in *Hicklin*, which would ban literature believed to have a "tendency . . . to deprave and corrupt those whose minds are open to such immoral influences" has been largely discredited, even the most liberal opinions still talk in broad terms of whether "the book as a whole has a libidinous effect'' whether its ''dominant effect'' is ''to promote lust'', or whether ''the likelihood that the work will so arouse the salacity of the reader'' outweighs its merits. Without attempting to be precise, these and countless other statements relating to the ''effect'' of literature in determining the issue of obscenity appear to be concerned both with the effect upon the *mind* of the reader and the effect upon his *conduct*. There is no attempt to separate these two, as indeed would be impossible in appraising the effect of a book; nor is there any clear indication in typical statutes or court decisions whether the ultimate evil sought to be prevented is *conduct* inconsistent with the existing moral standards, or whether the ''evil'' of lustful sex *thoughts*, independent of any risk of translating those thoughts into action, is also a purpose of obscenity censorship.

Is ''corrupting'' the reader's mind with sex thoughts, independent of any risk that these may be translated into action inconsistent with the current moral standards, in itself a sufficient evil to justify censorship of literature? Without devoting much time to this question, because whatever the answer we are immediately driven to consider the stimulation of sex thought into sex conduct, it should suffice to suggest briefly four reasons for a real doubt that, standing alone, the stimulation of sex thoughts is a sufficient evil to justify censorship.

First, the creation of normal sexual desires is, in itself, neither immoral nor contrary to the accepted sex standards. The stimulation of thoughts and ideas about sex, even creating the desire for sexual intercourse, may often be in the public interest. For example, education in sexual practices that will make for more satisfying marital relations, or an exposition of the delights that can come from the perfect mating of a man and wife in a physical and spiritual union, may well make for more stable family relationships, and encourage a young man to marry rather than to experiment in unmarried love. Even books that make love attractive when it happens to be illicit may have a beneficial effect on some by attracting young people to marry rather than to seek sex pleasures outside of wedlock.

The second reason is that independent of the danger of inducing or encouraging sex conduct inconsistent with accepted moral standards, the harm that can result from the stimulation of sex thoughts is relatively trivial in the case of the normal person. Sex thoughts are perfectly natural, without them men and women would be abnormal. The failure of pro-censorship literature or court opinions to analyze the harm that can come from stimulation of sex thoughts, independent of stimulating action, may indicate that this is really not an important factor. But what are the possible harms? Some of the religious advocates of censorship say that sex literature ''darkens the mind'' and ''corrupts the heart,'' but they do not attempt to indicate just what this harm is, apart from its effect on conduct. Basic to religious thinking is the emphasis that lustful thoughts are as great a sin as lustful acts; this talk of corrupting the mind probably is derived from the religious duty to think noble thoughts. Certainly it is entirely appropriate for the *church* to discourage reading that turns the mind from spiritual to carnal thoughts, but under our constitutional system the *government* can scarcely claim authority to impose controls on literature for the purpose of directing men's minds always from the physical interests of life towards more spiritual and worthy thoughts. Another possible evil is that excessive preoccupation with sex thoughts may perhaps divert the mind from more important subjects, such as the study of law, but to ban literature in order to turn the mind into more productive or useful channels would be unthinkable. Again, literature dealing with sex may further stimulate the abnormal thinking of those already mentally unbalanced, who can be set off on abnormal tangents in innumerable ways. Disregarding at this point the effect on outward conduct, the insignificant and generally indefensible character of these ''evils'' that may result from stimulating sex thoughts emphasizes the overwhelmingly greater weight of the values to society of freedom in literature.

Assuming that the non-action ''evils'' that may result from stimulation of thoughts and desires on sex are worthy of some weight in the constitutional balancing of interests, there is a third reason why the danger to worthwhile thinking cannot justify censorship; it is that the causal relationship between literature dealing with sex and the composite sex thoughts and desires of an individual is likely to be extremely tenuous. So many non-literary stimuli to sex thoughts and desires are constantly thrown at mankind, and are ordinarily so much more powerful in arousing sex thoughts and desires, that in most cases literature touching on the subject is an exceedingly minor factor. Thus, even if these ''evils'' from sex thoughts and desires are entitled to some weight, the relative unimportance of literature in stimulating such thoughts only serves to point up the overwhelmingly greater weight of the value of freedom to write and to read in this area.

Finally, if the purpose of obscenity censorship is really to control the kind of thoughts people have in this important area of human life, this invades dangerous territory constitutionally. The state can properly be concerned with controlling action that harms society, but ordinarily it must stop short of what men think and believe. In the area of sex morals, the Supreme Court recognized this long ago in connection with polygamous marriage, and in more recent days it has been emphasized in connection with political problems. It seems unlikely there should be or could be any difference with respect to ideas or thoughts on sex problems generally. We conclude, therefore, that the possibility of stimulating sex thoughts and desires, independent of the danger of stimulating objective conduct inconsistent with current standards, seems altogether inadequate to justify the losses to society that result from interference with literary freedom in this area.

### d. Stimulating Sex Conduct

The primary evil aimed at by obscenity censorship is the danger that through stimulating sexual desire obscene literature will lead to sexual conduct that is illegal or otherwise inconsistent with current moral standards. Preventing deviation from the community standard in sexual matters is sufficiently important to society that the danger of such deviation, if established, would doubtless be given great weight by the Court. If it were established that reading a certain book would, in fact, induce normal persons to engage in sexual conduct that seriously deviates from the accepted community standards, there can be little doubt of the constitutional power to ban the circulation of the book among the general public. But our major difficulty arises because it is impossible to know that the book will have that effect; instead, the effect of any book upon the action of normal individuals is in the realm of prophecy. Therefore, as regards this primary evil asserted in support of obscenity censorship, the constitutional issue is not whether the evil, if established, is serious enough. The issue is whether the possibility that a particular book, or type of book, will adversely affect the moral conduct of the normal reader is sufficiently great to constitute the "clear danger" needed to outweigh the social values of the free distribution of the book and the harm to society that would result if this type of book were subject to censorship.

In appraising the actual effect of literature upon the sex conduct of the reader, there is a great deal of talk and very little factual data upon which to base a fair judgment. The advocates of obscenity censorship simply assume, with no attempt at proof, that reading about sex is a primary cause of sexual deviation. Those who oppose censorship point out that its advocates have "never proved their case," that censorship "scorns facts" and "substitutes guesses for findings." On both sides there is much heat and little light on this critical question. Both grasp at straws for lack of any dependable information on the effect of reading upon the sex conduct of the reader. . . .

### E. A CONSTITUTIONAL STANDARD FOR OBSCENITY CENSORSHIP

. . .

The constitutional standard in obscenity censorship cannot be reduced to any formula. As in the case of all policy judgments involving significant conflicting interests, a sound decision here requires the careful balancing of all relevant factors bearing on (a) the losses to society that may result from censoring the book, and (b) the harms to society that may result from not censoring it. Major values to be weighed in arriving at this policy judgment are three: (1) The values to society of freedom of expression through literature, and the importance to this freedom of avoiding governmental action that tends to discourage freedom to read and write in important areas of human interest, including sex. (2) The value to society of the particular book or work of literature under attack. (3) The value to society of avoiding the harmful effect on sex conduct that might reasonably result from reading the book in question, but weighed heavily against this value must be the recognition that we have very little dependable information or knowledge with respect to the effects of reading on human conduct in this area. In weighing these major values in particular cases the following considerations may often be determinative.

We believe the constitutional standard requires that a book be judged as a whole, rather than by isolated words or passages. Statutes that authorize a finding of obscenity based only on a part of the book are to that extent unconstitutional, as are judgments of obscenity similarly based. It is not possible for a court to give the requisite consideration to the value of a book, or to the effect of suppressing the book upon freedom of expression in literature, without considering the entire book and the relationship of the disputed passages to its theme. To permit a book to be condemned as obscene solely because of isolated words or passages ripped from the total structure of the work would result in depriving society of the value of the particular book, and the value of freedom of expression through literature, without judicial consideration of the value of what is being destroyed. . . .

But in weighing the value of a particular book, the requirement that the book be judged as a whole is not alone enough to give adequate protection to society's interest in literature, or to insure adequate consideration and understanding by the courts of the value of the book in question. Something more is required to give sufficient emphasis to the aesthetic, scientific, educational and other social values of the book, and to enable the courts to appraise these values intelligently. If, for instance, the particular book is a work of fiction or poetry, it is important that it be viewed with a sympathetic appreciation and understanding of the nature and function of imaginative literature. Here, the appraisal of literary critics is indispensable, for without it, judges are forced to assume the role of literary critics themselves—a role that few courts, if any, are competent to play. Much the same observation applies to nonimaginative literature as well. . . .

We believe the constitutional standard requires that in making determinations as to the probable effect of a book on sex conduct, courts must take account of the unsatisfactory state of a human knowledge concerning the effect of literature relating to sex. With our present inadequate knowledge on this subject, a court would probably not now be justified in taking the position that a legislature is entirely wrong in basing obscenity legislation on the premise, usually unstated, that reading some kinds of literature probably affects the sex conduct of some readers. Obscenity censorship of literature cannot be rejected in toto on the ground that the effect of obscenity on sex conduct is too uncertain. But in view of the importance to society of adequate protection for freedom of expression in literature, courts are obliged to give careful consideration to whether there is any real and substantial danger that a particular book will bring about anti-social sex conduct. Certainly, in view of the good reasons for doubting that literature relating to sex has any such effect, courts should never make the assumption—so common in past adjudications—that any literature labeled "obscene" has an adverse effect on sex conduct. Such an assumption violates a court's constitutional obligation to protect freedom of expression. . . .

Louis Henkin, *Morals and the Constitution: The Sin of Obscenity*, 63 COLUMBIA LAW REVIEW 391 (1963)*

The several cases in which the Supreme Court of

the United States has examined obscenity legislation under the light of the Constitution have unloosed a torrent of writing—official, legal, psychological, and lay. The many words have reflected and evoked passion; they have not brought clarity to the constitutional questions or to the social questions. They have not spoken to a common effect; they have not joined issue. The Supreme Court itself has split and splintered in variegated opinions and doctrines. Students of the Court's work have cast stones at some Justices, or at all of them. Those who make the obscenity laws and those who enforce them, and others who vigilantly support their hands, have welcomed the Court's decisions with a spate of metaphor about the poison of obscenity and its fearful consequences for man and child. "Libertarians" have deplored another breach in the constitutional bulwark against repression.

At risk of adding yet another tongue to Babel, I venture a few pages with modest purpose. I wish to focus on a small point, but one of constitutional consequence. To me it seems that the unusual confusion—more prevalent than in discussions of other attempts of government to regulate forms of expression—is due in large measure to misapprehension of the concern and the interest that inspire government to regulate obscenity. Specifically, I believe, despite common assumptions and occasional rationalizations, that obscenity laws are not principally motivated by any conviction that obscene materials inspire sexual offenses. Obscenity laws, rather, are based on traditional notions, rooted in this country's religious antecedents, of governmental responsibility for communal and individual "decency" and "morality."

If I am correct about the origins and purposes of obscenity legislation, much of the constitutional discussion about the control of obscenity seems out of focus. Concentration on whether obscenity may—or may not—incite to unlawful acts aims beside the mark. The question, rather, is whether the state may suppress expression it deems immoral, may protect adults as well as children from voluntary exposure to that which may "corrupt" them, may preserve the community from public, rampant "immorality." This different question may receive the same or a different answer; clearly, the path and the guide posts, the facts sought, the issues considered, and the doctrine applied may be very different. Indeed, this inquiry might today command attention even to a question that must have appeared insubstantial earlier in the history of the Constitution: the authority of government under the Constitution to adopt "morals legislation," to suppress private, individual indul-

* Reprinted with permission.

gence which does no harm to others, in the name of traditional notions of morality.

The proper issues of obscenity regulation, I believe, do not lead constitutional lawyers deep into the penumbra in which speech moves toward unlawful action; they demand, rather, forthright and sophisticated exploration of the claims of "unsophisticated" morality and of the community's authority to maintain standards of "decency" and to prevent the corruption of individual character and morals. . . .

## I. THE PURPOSES OF OBSCENITY REGULATION

One cannot, of course, demonstrate beyond doubt a single aim of obscenity regulation. Motives and purposes for legislation are notoriously elusive, ambiguous, and multifarious. The fear that obscenity may induce crime is one occasional reason or rationalization for regulation. Perhaps some legislators enacting or re-enacting traditional laws against obscenity have this reason in mind. At bottom, there are other, authentic motives for obscenity laws.

Clearly, "obscenity," and other concepts to which it is frequently joined in legislation, include at least some expressions that do not relate at all to "incitement" to illegal action. For one instance—too often concealed by the emphasis on sex in discussions of obscenity—the accepted definition of obscenity includes not only the sexual but the scatological. Surely the latter does not lead to any unlawful act: it may be emetic; it is not aphrodisiac.

"Sexual obscenity," too, is regulated for purposes unrelated to fear that it may lead to "sex crimes." Obscenity—sexual or scatological—is forbidden, in large part, not because it incites but because it offends. A state forbids obscenity—and nudity, "indecent exposure," graffiti—as it forbids public fornication and public excretion, because it is offensive to others. The state seeks to suppress or abate these noxious emanations on grounds akin to traditional notions of "nuisance." While "nuisance" may here be a metaphor—and metaphor has tended to obscure rather than clarify constitutional analysis—this kind of obscenity legislation has a social purpose to protect others from the impact of acts or expressions offensive to them.

. . .The accepted definition of obscenity, as that which "appeal[s] . . . to prurient interest," makes no assumption that it will incite to any action. The history of obscenity legislation points, rather, to origins in aspirations to holiness and propriety. Laws against obscenity have appeared conjoined and cognate to laws against sacrilege and blasphemy, suggesting concern for the spiritual welfare of the person

exposed to it and for the moral well-being of the community. Metaphors of "poison" and "filth" also emphasize concern for the welfare of the one exposed and the atmosphere of the community. A "decent" community does not tolerate obscenity. A "decent" man does not indulge himself with obscene materials.

The moral concern of the community may consist of several different strands frequently entangled beyond separation. Obscenity is immoral, an individual should not indulge it, and the community should not tolerate it. In addition, obscenity, like other immoral acts and expressions, has a deleterious effect on the individual from which the community should protect him. Obscenity is bad for a man, and the concern is not for his "psyche," his mental health. Obscenity is bad for character. It "corrupts" morals, it corrupts character. Character, of course, bears on behavior, but the corruption feared, it should be emphasized, has a very unclear, very remote, and problematic relation to a likelihood that he will commit any particular unlawful act or indeed any unlawful act at all, immediately or in the future.

This concern of the state for the "character" and "morals" of the person exposed is particularly evident in the plethora of laws designed to prevent the "corruption of youth." Among other evil influences, obscenity, it is assumed, may "corrupt" a child. The state assists parents who seek to prevent this corruption, or may even act in loco of those parents who are remiss in protecting their own children. The Supreme Court built constitutional doctrine on these assumptions when it held that Michigan could not "reduce the adult population of Michigan to reading only what is fit for children." Again, the corruption of youth by obscenity is deemed to have some immeasurable effect on character and personality; it is not believed to "incite" to any particular actions now or in the future. While in regard to youth it has always been assumed that government has special responsibility and authority, laws adopted for their protection reflect assumptions and attitudes about obscenity not inapplicable to the regulation of obscenity for adults.

Society intervenes because it is immoral for a person to indulge in obscenity and because obscenity corrupts morals and character of man or child. Either purpose is aimed at saving the "user" from his own indulgence, however private and discreet. But if indulgence in obscenity is prevalent, the prevalence becomes notorious, and the immoral activity takes on a public character and offends "public order." The state may seek to eradicate even isolated, clandestine obscenity; it is concerned in particular to suppress commercial exploitation in order to reduce the public disorder, as well as to protect individuals from their own moral weakness by preventing the spread of the moral infection.

Communities believe, and act on the belief, that obscenity is immoral, is wrong for the individual, and has no place in a decent society. They believe, too, that adults as well as children are corruptible in morals and character, and that obscenity is a source of corruption that should be eliminated. Obscenity is not suppressed primarily for the protection of others. Much of it is suppressed for the purity of the community and for the salvation and welfare of the "consumer." Obscenity, at bottom, is not crime. Obscenity is sin.

## II. OBSCENITY REGULATION: THE RELEVANT CONSTITUTIONAL INQUIRY

If obscenity laws are seen primarily as "morals legislation," if a principal purpose of these laws is to protect, from himself, the person who wishes to indulge, and to maintain the moral "tone" of a community, constitutional discussion of such laws would seem to deserve emphasis different from that which has preoccupied the judges and the writers. Immediately, we would move aside discussion based on the assumption that "unlawful action" incited by obscene materials is the "evil" at which obscenity laws are directed. These writings bear the mark of the particular time in the history of constitutional adjudication when the obscenity cases made their way up to the Supreme Court. For the principal cases raising the issue of freedom of communication in recent years have involved "speech" found to be part of a pattern of subversive action believed to endanger the safety of the nation. . . .

The evils at which the state aims are not unlawful action, but indecency and corruption of morals. Of these evils, the dangers assumed are clear and immediate. The impact of "nuisance" obscenity on others is indubitable and immediate. The immorality of indulgence even in private obscenity, the state may believe, is clear; the consequences of widespread indulgence and commercial exploitation on prevailing "decency" are present and certain.

Clear and present danger of unlawful action is a relevant inquiry on only one view—that the state cannot suppress obscene materials for the "moral" purposes we have suggested, that it can regulate forms of expression, including those falling within the definition of the obscene, only if they are "brigaded with action," only if they incite, say, to rape or other violence, or perhaps to adultery or fornication. . . .

If minority views have mistaken the moral purposes of obscenity legislation, or dismissed them, without consideration, as constitutionally impermissible, prevailing views too have failed to attend to moral foundations of obscenity laws in framing issues and building doctrine. To the majority of the Supreme Court in Roth v. United States, the purpose of the legislation was apparently irrelevant. The Court asserted that "obscenity is not within the area of constitutionally protected speech or press." It seemed to reach that conclusion by reading "freedom of speech" in the first amendment as having an important qualification: the speech protected by the Constitution is only that which has some "redeeming social importance." Obscenity, the Court said, has none. The Court supported this reading of the Constitution by reference to history: obscenity was not intended to be included in the freedom of speech protected by the first amendment and in the liberty which the states could not deny without due process of law. Since the constitutional language does not protect obscenity, and was not intended to protect obscenity, there is no need to ask what is the purpose of legislation or whether it has any purpose at all. "Clear and present" danger, of unlawful action or of some other evil consequence, is also irrelevant. So is, presumably, any consideration of "preferred" freedom, or the weight to be given to the interest of the speaker, or the interest of society in his freedom to speak or in his particular speech.

That the Supreme Court's approach leaves too much to be desired has been suggested by others, beginning with the Justices who did not join the Court's opinion. Critics have questioned the Court's reading of constitutional language and of history. They have thought to trace circles in the Court's reasoning, and to identify questions that it seemed to beg. Some of the criticism might be met by reducing the reference to "redeeming social importance" from doctrine to rationalization, from a constitutional standard to an explanation of a historical exception. Roth, then, does not limit the protection of the first amendment to speech having social importance; Roth asserts simply that as a matter of historic interpretation the general phrases of the first and fourteenth amendments did not purpose to deny to government the authority to suppress that which is obscene. Those to whom history is not a whole answer may support the decision by suggesting that it reflects the attitude of a majority of the Court in other "speech cases"; the Court, invoking history, is asserting that expression is not ipso facto immune to regulation for social ends, that obscenity is a proper object of social regulation, that in the balance of freedom and authority under the scrutiny of the Constitution the public's interest in suppressing obscenity outweighs the exponent's freedom of expression.

These restatements of the Roth doctrine may provide more respectable doctrine; they do not justify disregard of the special character of obscenity laws as "morals legislation." The claims of history, generally, are subject to the caveat that laws and practices accepted as valid when a constitutional provision was adopted may yet be found invalid in the light of later readings of an organic, creative Constitution. In regard to "morals laws," in particular, one may ask that the Court consider whether moral assumptions and assertions of a past day necessarily survive as exceptions to freedom today. The Court accepts "appeal to prurient interest" as the test for permissible limitations of obscene materials under the Constitution. If this is asserted as the traditional meaning of obscenity, the Court does not appear to re-examine its continuing validity as a constitutional standard. If it is a new test, the Court does not distinguish it from past notions of obscenity and justify it as presently valid to effect purposes presently permissible to the community. Should not the Court ask why may the state today outlaw obscenity? What governmental purposes, valid today, are these laws designed to effectuate? Are the means proper to these purposes? History, surely, does not foreclose argument that in new light old laws reveal no reasonable foundations, or are based on irrational or false assumptions.

. . . Since the Court—like most statutes—does not distinguish between proscription of the most private indulgence in obscenity and social attack on public obscenity or organized commercial exploitation, the claims of authority appear to rest strictly on the historic concern for private morality. The nonrational, nonutilitarian aims of "morals legislation," like obscenity laws, might well have weight quite different from other historically accepted regulations of speech that have a social, utilitarian purpose, e.g., libel laws. On the other balance, the Court dismisses obscenity as utterly without "redeeming social importance." It does not consider that there may be "social importance" to expressions or words even if they do appeal predominantly to prurient interest. It does not ask: whether regulation of obscenity may have a deterrent and limiting effect on other expressions not themselves obscene; whether there are social values in leaving all individuals free to express, others free to receive, without external limitations and without the shadow of the censor and the vigil of the heirs of Comstock; whether, like other attempts to regulate "the morals" of adults and to save them from themselves (e.g., Prohibition), efforts to deal with obscenity by law may produce greater evils, and may even aggravate the very evils at which these laws are directed. . . .

## III. THE CONSTITUTIONAL CLAIMS OF PRIVATE "IMMORALITIES"

It has been suggested that the Supreme Court has read obscenity out of the protection for expression in the first and fourteenth amendments without asking whether the "moral" character of obscenity laws continues to justify that historical exception today, or whether the moral aims of these laws may properly outweigh the freedoms suppressed. I venture now to suggest that the moral purpose and motive of obscenity legislation—and of other prevalent laws aimed at private indulgence in "immoral" activity—may invite inquiry of yet a different, fundamental order.

We lay aside now claims of freedom to communicate, even the obscene; we are concerned, instead, with claims of the "consumer" to freedom and privacy to indulge in what others may deem immoral. The authority of the state, under the Constitution, to enact "morals legislation"—laws reflecting some traditional morality having no authentic social purpose to protect other persons or property—has always been assumed; it has deep roots, and it has seemed obvious and beyond question. It may now be respectable to ask whether indeed the state may adopt any "morals legislation." And if it be concluded that morals legislation is not ipso facto beyond the state's power, can one avoid asking: what morality the state may enforce; what limitations there are on what the state may deem immoral; how these limitations are to be determined?

In doctrinal terms, one may present these as several constitutional questions, not wholly discrete. For the sake of clarity, I declare them as hypotheses to be examined:

*First*: even if the "freedom of speech" protected by the first and fourteenth amendments does not include a freedom to communicate obscene speech, suppression of obscenity is still a deprivation of liberty or property—of the person who would indulge in it, at least—which requires due process of law. Due process of law demands that legislation have a proper public purpose; only an apparent, rational, utilitarian social purpose satisfies due process. A state may not legislate merely to preserve some traditional or prevailing view of private morality.

*Second*: due process requires, as well, that means be reasonably related to proper public ends. Legislation cannot be based on unfounded hypotheses and assumptions about character and its corruption.

*Third*: morals legislation is a relic in the law of our religious heritage; the Constitution forbids such establishment of religion. . . .

A. Morals as a Legislative Concern—The Requirements of Due Process

The relation of law to morals has been a favored preoccupation of legal philosophers for a thousand years; in the history of American law the relevance of that relation to constitutional limitations has lain unexamined behind discussions of the scope and the limits of government. That morals were the concern of government was assumed, not explored, in discussions of the reaches of the "police power" limited by substantive "due process of law."

May the state, under our Constitution, legislate in support of "morals"? The question may take us back to another: What are the purposes for which the state may legislate under the Constitution? That question, in other contexts, once deeply troubled the Supreme Court. Not too many years ago the Court seemed to assume that by the law of nature and by social contract government was given limited powers for limited purposes. Freedom was the rule; government had to justify itself, and the justifications had to satisfy the Constitution. The state could, of course, legislate to protect one from his neighbor. Perhaps the whole function of government was to assure that, in regard to one's liberty as well as one's property, *sic utere tuo ut alienum non laedas*. But government also had other purposes, among them the regulation of morality. . . .

No one seemed disposed to doubt that the legitimate purposes of government included the preservation of morals, public or private. All law indeed may have appeared as an implementation of accepted morality; no one seriously suggested that laws for the preservation of "morals" might not have the clear justification which is obvious in laws having a social purpose of protecting the person or property of others. Morals legislation, like social legislation, might have appeared equally rooted in "the law of nature," which had respectable credentials in the history of American law. It was obvious that the state could forbid persons to enter into a usurious contract, to gamble, to drink intoxicating liquors, to be a prostitute, to visit a prostitute, to commit fornication or adultery with another willing adult, to enter into a polygamous marriage, to utter obscenity, profanity, immorality in act or word. Clearly, too, the state could declare the morality that determined "public policy," relied on in various contexts to frustrate consensual arrangements.

If the challenge had been seriously pressed, some utilitarian reason for these laws might have been found. But they would have been rationalizations and might have been recognized as such. In truth, the legislation reflected traditional morality, and the preservation of this morality was an unquestioned purpose of government. If the Supreme Court glanced at the authority of the state to enact such legislation, it blended moral and utilitarian bases for the legislation in indisputable justification.

Today, a court would probably not begin with the assumption that government has defined purposes and corresponding "inherent," "natural" limitations. The only limitations on the state, a court might say, are the prohibitions of the Constitution—specific, like those few in the original Constitution, or more general, like those in the Civil War amendments. If one would today examine embedded assumptions about morals legislation, the question, then, is not whether legislation for decency and morality is within the accepted powers of government; we must ask, rather, whether such legislation deprives one to whom it applies of "liberty or property" without due process of law. But if that question looks very different from the one that might have been asked in the nineteenth century, it may be less different than it looks. For some of the "inherent" limitations on the police power may still be with us in notions that the state may legislate only for a "public purpose." And "due process" still requires some link in reason between purpose and the means selected by the legislature to achieve that purpose. We may state the question, then, as whether morality legislation deprives one of liberty or property without due process of law. The subsidiary questions may still be: Is the state's purpose in "morality legislation" a proper public purpose? Are the means used to achieve it "reasonable"?

Emphasis on "public purpose" has usually been intended to exclude legislation for the special interest of some private person or group. Morals legislation presumably does not serve a strictly "private purpose," even if some groups seem more concerned about morals legislation than is the community at large. The beneficiaries of this legislation, it is assumed, are each citizen and the whole community. But is every "non-private" purpose a proper public purpose of government? Can the state legislate, not to protect the person or property of others or to promote general economic or social welfare, but to protect and promote "morals," particularly morals reflected—or violated—in private activity?

Perhaps the question can have no provable answer. Supporters of legislation like obscenity laws may urge that government has always legislated in support of accepted morality, and may challenge those who would deny the authority of government to find anything in the Constitution that would take it away. But supporters of the past do not have the only word. Others will stress that the due process clause has intervened, and that it requires government to be reasonable, in purpose as well as in means to achieve the purpose. One may even accept the right of the state to impose restrictions on the individual for his own good—by preventing his suicide, or forcing medical aid, or compelling education; in the context of society, these are "rational" ends, reasonably achieved. But how can "morals," a nonutilitarian, non-rational purpose, be "reasonable"? Could government conjure up some new (or old), nonsocial principle of morality and impose it by law? Could a state forbid me to go to an astrologer—or require me to go to one or abide by his conclusions? And if history is invoked, does the fact that some behavior has been deemed "immoral" in the past—by some, even a violation of "natural law"—render it forever a proper object of legislative prohibition? Is it sufficient to justify legislation that such acts continue to be regarded as "immoral," "sinful," "offensive" by large segments of the community? Or does the due process clause, in this context too, serve to protect individuals from the irrationalities of the majority and of its representatives?

One may ask, it is suggested, whether any nonutilitarian morality can be a reasonable public purpose of legislation. But purpose aside, due process requires also that the means to achieve that purpose be not unreasonable. Of course, means and purposes are not discrete categories, and purposes may themselves be means to other purposes. But assuming that the preservation of private morals continues to be a proper purpose of government, obscenity legislation, in particular, raises the further question whether suppression of obscenity is reasonably related to the morality that the state seeks to preserve.

The question may be clarified if one compares obscenity laws to other morals legislation, e.g., laws against incest. Incestual relations have indubitably been deemed "immoral," at least since Biblical times. If the state may suppress what is immoral, there can be no doubt about the validity of laws against incest. Exposure to obscenity, on the other hand, is at most a derivative, secondary "immorality." In itself, it has no ancient roots; presumably, it would have been condemned, or frowned on, as inconsistent with admonitions to be holy and to avoid pagan abominations. In modern times, obscenity has been condemned in large part because it corrupts morals or character. Since, I have said, corruption of morals or character has no clear relation to any unlawful acts, or even acts that could be made unlawful, what evidence is required of the state, or what assumptions permitted to it, to support the conclusion that obscenity corrupts morals? What are these "morals" and this "character," and what does their

corruption mean? And if we accept the concept of "morals" as well as their corruption, how does one decide whether the state is reasonable in its conclusion that indulgence in obscenity does or does not effect this "corruption" of these "morals"?

The Constitution does not enact legal positivism; it does not enact natural law. Due process, I hypothesize, requires that the state deal with the area of the reasonable and deal with it reasonably. It is proper to ask whether the preservation of a nonsocial morality is within the realm of the reasonable, whether concepts like "private morality" and its corruption are subject to logic and proof inherent in reasonableness and rationality. These, of course, are not merely technical requirements of constitutional jurisprudence. They suggest that the Constitution renders unto government the rational governance of the affairs of man in relation to his neighbor; only if government is kept within this domain can it be limited government, subject to constitutional requirements of rational, reasonable action administered by an impartial judiciary. It is only by confining government to what is reasonable that the Constitution and the courts can protect the individual against the unreasonable. Private "morals," and their "corruption," and what "corrupts" them, as differently conceived, have profound significance in the life of a nation and of its citizens. But they are not in the realm of reason and cannot be judged by standards of reasonableness; they ought not, perhaps, to be in the domain of government.

Civilized societies, including ours, have increased the area of government responsibility to protect one against his neighbor. The authority of government to protect us from ourselves is less clearly recognized today, except when injury to ourselves may in turn have undesirable social consequences; although, we have suggested, one may justify—within the limits of the "rational"—governmental efforts to prevent suicide, or compel health measures, "for the individual's own good." When we deal not with physical injury to ourselves but with "sin," respectable and authoritative voices are increasingly heard that there exists "a realm of private morality and immorality which is, in brief and crude terms, not the law's business." Should not the Supreme Court today, or tomorrow, consider whether under the Constitution some morality, at least, may be not the law's business and not appropriate support for legislation consistent with due process of law?

. . .

## IV. CONCLUSION

. . .

Of course, it should be clear, I have asserted

hypotheses for further consideration. That the government may act only for social purpose, for the protection of persons and property, is doctrine easy to state, and perhaps no more difficult to apply than some other constitutional doctrine. But the right of the state to legislate in the field of morals, to deprive the citizen of liberty or property for the sake of accepted notions of morality, is deeply part of our law; some will argue that is beyond question or need for justification. It asks much of the Supreme Court to tell legislators, and communal groups behind them, that what has long been deemed the law's business is no longer, that even large majorities or a "general consensus" cannot have their morality written into official law. And a reluctant Court can find support in history, and some among the philosophers. . . .

What is important is that the underlying questions be recognized and considered, in the context of concrete cases, in the light of new facts, new insights, new views of morality, new readings of the Constitution. Obscenity laws, at least those directed at private adult acts done privately, provide the Supreme Court an occasion to recognize and wrestle with the problem of morals legislation under the Constitution. If the Court will not look afresh at obscenity laws, particularly in its private aspects, other morals legislation may soon afford the Court another occasion. It is time to begin to examine—if only in order to justify—the right of constitutional government to legislate morality which has no secular, utilitarian, or social purpose. It is time to attempt to define and articulate the extent to which the religious antecedents of our values may continue to motivate our governments in the enactment and enforcement of law. The Court, one may hope, will begin to attempt to disentangle and separate crime from sin in a secular country having warm feelings toward its religions and its religious ancestry, and having the strong conviction that the wall between Church and State is a good fence making good neighbors.

Catharine A. MacKinnon, *Pornography, Civil Rights and Speech*, 20 HARVARD CIVIL RIGHTS-CIVIL LIBERTIES LAW REVIEW 1 (1985)*

. . .

. . . In pornography, there it is, in one place, all

* Reprinted with permission of the President and Fellows of Harvard College. © (1985) Harvard Civil Rights Civil Liberties Law Review.

of the abuses that women had to struggle so long even to begin to articulate, all the *unspeakable* abuse: the rape, the battery, the sexual harassment, the prostitution, and the sexual abuse of children. Only in the pornography it is called something else: sex, sex, sex, sex, and sex, respectively. Pornography sexualizes rape, battery, sexual harassment, prostitution, and child sexual abuse; it thereby celebrates, promotes, authorizes, and legitimizes them. More generally, it eroticizes the dominance and submission that is the dynamic common to them all. It makes hierarchy sexy and calls that "the truth about sex"' or just a mirror of reality. Through this process, pornography constructs what a woman is as what men want from sex. This is what the pornography means. . . .

Pornography constructs what a woman is in terms of its view of what men want sexually, such that acts of rape, battery, sexual harassment, prostitution, and sexual abuse of children become acts of sexual equality. Pornography's world of equality is a harmonious and balanced place. Men and women are perfectly complementary and perfectly bipolar. Women's desire to be fucked by men is equal to men's desire to fuck women. All the ways men love to take and violate women, women love to be taken and violated. The women who most love this are most men's equals, the most liberated; the most participatory child is the most grown-up, the most equal to an adult. Their consent merely expresses or ratifies these preexisting facts.

The content of pornography is one thing. There, women substantively desire dispossession and cruelty. We desperately want to be bound, battered, tortured, humiliated, and killed. Or, to be fair to the soft core, merely taken and used. This is erotic to the male point of view. Subjection itself with self-determination ecstatically relinquished is the content of women's sexual desire and desirability. Women are there to be violated and possessed, men to violate and possess us either on screen or by camera or pen on behalf of the consumer. On a simple descriptive level, the inequality of hierarchy, of which gender is the primary one, seems necessary for the sexual arousal to work. Other added inequalities identify various pornographic genres or sub-themes, although they are always added through gender: age, disability, homosexuality, animals, objects, race (including anti-semitism), and so on. Gender is never irrelevant.

What pornography *does* goes beyond its content: It eroticizes hierarchy, it sexualizes inequality. It makes dominance and submission sex. Inequality is its central dynamic; the illusion of freedom coming together with the reality of force is central to its working. Perhaps because this is a bourgeois culture, the victim must look free, appear to be freely acting. Choice is how she got there. Willing is what she is when she is being equal. It seems equally important that then and there she actually be forced and that forcing be communicated on some level, even if only through still photos of her in postures of receptivity and access, available for penetration. Pornography in this view is a form of forced sex, a practice of sexual politics, an institution of gender inequality.

From this perspective, pornography is neither harmless fantasy nor a corrupt and confused misrepresentation of an otherwise natural and healthy sexual situation. It institutionalizes the sexuality of male supremacy, fusing the erotization of dominance and submission with the social construction of male and female. To the extent that gender is sexual, pornography is part of constituting the meaning of that sexuality. Men treat women as who they see women as being. Pornography constructs who that is. Men's power over women means that the way men see women defines who women can be. Pornography is that way. Pornography is not imagery in some relation to a reality elsewhere constructed. It is not a distortion, reflection, projection, expression, fantasy, representation, or symbol either. It is a sexual reality.

. . .

. . . [T]he experience of the (overwhelmingly) male audiences who consume pornography is therefore not fantasy or simulation or catharsis but sexual reality, the level of reality on which sex itself largely operates. Understanding this dimension of the problem does not require noticing that pornography models are real women to whom, in most cases, something real is being done; nor does it even require inquiring into the systematic infliction of pornography and its sexuality upon women, although it helps. The way in which the pornography itself provides what those who consume it want matters. Pornography participates in its audience's eroticism through creating an accessible sexual object, the possession and consumption of which *is* male sexuality, as socially constructed; to be consumed and possessed as which, *is* female sexuality, as socially constructed; and pornography is a process that constructs it that way.

The object world is constructed according to how it looks with respect to its possible uses. Pornography defines women by how we look according to how we can be sexually used. Pornography codes how to look at women, so you know what you can do with one when you see one. Gender is an assignment made

visually, both originally and in everyday life. A sex object is defined on the basis of its looks, in terms of its usability for sexual pleasure, such that both the looking—the quality of the gaze, including its point of view—and the definition according to use become eroticized as part of the sex itself. This is what the feminist concept "sex object" means. In this sense, sex in life is no less mediated that it is in art. One could say men have sex with *their image* of a woman. It is not that life and art imitate each other; in this sexuality, they *are* each other.

To give a set of rough epistemological translations, to defend pornography as consistent with the equality of the sexes is to defend the subordination of women to men as sexual equality. What in the pornographic view is love and romance looks a great deal like hatred and torture to the feminist. Pleasure and eroticism become violation. Desire appears as lust for dominance and submission. The vulnerability of women's projected sexual availability, that acting we are allowed (i.e. asking to be acted upon), is victimization. Play conforms to scripted roles. Fantasy expresses ideology, is not exempt from it. Admiration of natural physical beauty becomes objectification. Harmlessness becomes harm. Pornography is a harm of male supremacy made difficult to see because of its pervasiveness, potency, and, principally, because of its success in making the world a pornographic place. Specifically, its harm cannot be discerned, and will not be addressed, if viewed and approached neutrally, because it *is* so much of "what is." In other words, to the extent pornography succeeds in constructing social reality, it becomes invisible as harm. If we live in a world that pornography creates through the power of men in a male dominated situation the issue is not what the harm of pornography is, but how that harm is to become visible.

## II.

Obscenity law provides a very different analysis and conception of the problem. . . . Feminism doubts whether the average gender-neutral person exists; has more questions about the content and process of defining what community standards are than it does about deviations from them; wonders why prurience counts but powerlessness does not, and why sensibilities are better protected from offense than women are from exploitation; defines sexuality, and thus its violation and expropriation, more broadly than does state law; and questions why a body of law which has not in practice been able to tell rape from intercourse should, without further guidance, be entrusted with telling pornography from anything less. Taking the work "as a whole" ignores that which the victims of pornography have long known: Legitimate settings diminish the injury perceived to be done to those whose trivialization and objectification it contextualizes. Besides, and this is a heavy one, if a woman is subjected, why should it matter that the work has other value? Maybe what redeems the work's value is what enhances its injury to women, not to mention that existing standards of literature, art, science, and politics, examined in a feminist light, are remarkably consonant with pornography's mode, meaning, and message. And finally—first and foremost, actually—although the subject of these materials is overwhelmingly women, their contents almost entirely comprised of women's bodies, our invisibility has been such, our equation as a sex *with* sex has been such, that the law of obscenity has never even considered pornography a woman's issue.

Obscenity, in this light, is a moral idea; an idea about judgments of good and bad. Pornography, by contrast, is a political practice, a practice of power and powerlessness. Obscenity is ideational and abstract; pornography is concrete and substantive. The two concepts represent two entirely different things. Nudity, excess of candor, arousal or excitement, prurient appeal, illegality of the acts depicted, and unnaturalness or perversion are all qualities that bother obscenity law when sex is depicted or portrayed. Sex forced on real women so that it can be sold at a profit to be forced on other real women; women's bodies trussed and maimed and raped and made into things to be hurt and obtained and accessed and this presented as the nature of women in a way that is acted on and acted out over and over; the coercion that is visible and the coercion that has become invisible—this and more bothers feminists about pornography. Obscenity as such probably does little harm. Pornography is integral to attitudes and behaviors of violence and discrimination which define the treatment and status of half the population.

### III.

At the request of the city of Minneapolis, Andrea Dworkin and I conceived and designed a local human rights ordinance in accordance with our approach to the pornography issue. We define pornography as a practice of sex discrimination, a violation of women's civil rights, the opposite of sexual equality. Its point is to hold accountable, to those who are injured, those who profit from and benefit from that injury. It means that women's injury—our damage, our pain, our enforced inferiority—should outweigh their pleasure and their profits, or sex equality is meaningless.

We define pornography as the graphic sexually explicit subordination of women through pictures or words that also includes women dehumanized as sexual objects, things, or commodities, enjoying pain or humiliation or rape, being tied up, cut up, mutilated, bruised, or physically hurt, in postures of sexual submission or servility or display, reduced to body parts, penetrated by objects or animals, or presented in scenarios of degradation, injury, torture, shown as filthy or inferior, bleeding, bruised, or hurt in a context that makes these conditions sexual. Erotica, defined by distinction as not this, might be sexually explicit materials premised on equality. We also provide that the use of men, children or transsexuals in the place of women is pornography. The definition is substantive in that it is sex-specific, but it covers everyone in a sex-specific way, so is gender neutral in overall design.

. . .

To define pornography as a practice of sex discrimination combines a mode of portrayal that has a legal history—the sexually explicit—with an active term central to the inequality of the sexes—subordination. Among other things, subordination means to be placed in a position of inferiority or loss of power, or to be demeaned or denigrated. To be someone's subordinate is the opposite of being their equal. The definition does not include all sexually explicit depictions *of* the subordination of women. That is not what it says. It says, this which *does* that: the sexually explicit which subordinates women. To these active terms to capture what the pornography *does*, the definition adds a list of what it must also contain. This list, from our analysis, is an exhaustive description of what must be in the pornography for it to do what it does behaviorally. Each item in the definition is supported by experimental, testimonial, social, and clinical evidence. We made a legislative choice to be exhaustive and specific and concrete rather than conceptual and general, to minimize problems of chilling effect, making it hard to guess wrong, thus making self-censorship less likely, but encouraging (to use a phrase from discrimination law) voluntary compliance, knowing that if something turns up that is not on the list, the law will not be expansively interpreted.

The second half of the definition, by itself, would be a content regulation. But together with the first part, the definition is not simply a content regulation. It is a medium-message combination that resembles many other such exceptions to first amendment guarantees.

. . .

This law aspires to guarantee women's rights consistent with the first amendment by making visible a conflict of rights between the equality guaranteed to all women and what, in some legal sense, is now the freedom of the pornographers to make and sell, and their consumers to have access to, the materials this ordinance defines. Judicial resolution of this conflict, if they do for women what they have done for others, is likely to entail a balancing of the rights of women arguing that our lives and opportunities, including our freedom of speech and action, are constrained by—and in many cases flatly precluded by, in, and through—pornography, against those who argue that the pornography is harmless, or harmful only in part but not in the whole of the definition; or that it is more important to preserve the pornography than it is to prevent or remedy whatever harm it does.

In predicting how a court would balance these interests, it is important to understand that this ordinance cannot now be said to be either conclusively legal or illegal under existing law or precedent, although I think the weight of authority is on our side. This ordinance enunciates a new form of the previously recognized governmental interest in sex equality. Many laws make sex equality a governmental interest. Our law is designed to further the equality of the sexes, to help make sex equality real. Pornography is a practice of discrimination on the basis of sex, on one level because of its role in creating and maintaining sex as a basis for discrimination. It harms many women one at a time and helps keep all women in an inferior status by defining our subordination as our sexuality and equating that with our gender. It is also sex discrimination because its victims, including men, are selected for victimization on the basis of their gender. But for their sex, they would not be so treated.

. . .

## A.

The first victims of pornography are the ones in it. To date, it has only been with children, and male children at that, that the Supreme Court has understood that before the pornography became the pornographer's speech, it was somebody's life. This is particularly true in visual media, where it takes a real person doing each act to make what you see. This is the double meaning in a statement one ex-prostitute made at our hearing: "[E]very single thing you see in pornography is happening to a real woman right now." Linda Marchiano, in her book *Ordeal*, recounts being coerced as "Linda Lovelace" into performing for "Deep Throat,'" a fabulously profitable film, by abduction, systematic beating, being

kept prisoner, watched every minute, threatened with her life and the lives of her family if she left, tortured, and kept under constant psychological intimidation and duress. Not all pornography models are, to our knowledge, coerced so expressly; but the fact that some are not does not mean that those who are, aren't. It only means that coercion into pornography cannot be said to be biologically female. The further fact that prostitution and modeling are structurally women's best economic options should give pause to those who would consider women's presence there a true act of free choice. In the case of other inequalities, it is sometimes understood that people do degrading work out of a lack of options caused by, say, poverty. The work is not seen as not degrading "for them" because they do it. With women, it just proves that this is what we are really for, this is our true nature. I will leave you wondering, with me, why it is that when a woman spreads her legs for a camera, what she is assumed to be exercising is free will. Women's freedom is rather substantively defined here. And as you think about the assumption of consent that follows women into pornography, look closely some time for the skinned knees, the bruises, the welts from the whippings, the scratches, the gashes. Many of them are not simulated. One relatively soft core pornography model said, "I knew the pose was right when it hurt." It certainly seems important to the audiences that the events in the pornography be real. For this reason, pornography becomes a motive for murder, as in "snuff" films in which someone is tortured to death to make a sex film. They exist.

. . .

As part of the relief for people who can prove this was done to them, our law provides an injunction to remove these materials from public view. The best authority we have for this is the *Ferber* case, which permits criminal prohibitions on child pornography. That case recognized that child pornography need not be obscene to be child abuse. The Court found such pornography harmful in part because it constituted "a permanent record of children's participation and the harm to the child is exacerbated by circulation." This was a film, by the way, largely of two boys masturbating. The sensitivities of obscenity law, the Court noted, were inapt because "a work which, taken on the whole, contains value may nevertheless embody the hardest core of child pornography." Whether a work appeals to the prurient interest is not the same as whether a child is physically or psychologically harmed to make it.

Both of these reasons apply to coerced women.

Women are not children, but coerced women are effectively deprived of power over the expressive products of their coercion. Coerced pornography should meet the test that "the evil to be restricted . . . overwhelmingly outweighs the expressive interests, if any, at stake." . . . Unless one wishes to retain the incentive structure that has introduced a profit motive into rape, pornography made this way should be able to be eliminated.

### B.

We also make it actionable to force pornography on a person in employment, education, in a home, or in any public place. The person who was forced cannot, under this part of the law, reach the pornography, but they can reach the perpetrator or institution that does the forcing. In our hearings we heard the ways in which pornography is forced on people. Children, it is used to show how to perform sex acts, to duplicate exactly these so-called natural childish acts; women on men's jobs, to intimidate them into leaving; women in women's jobs, to have or set up a sexual encounter; prostitutes or wives, so they will know what a natural woman is supposed to do. In therapy, it is seen as aiding in transference, i.e., submitting to the therapist; in medical school, it desensitizes doctors so that when patients say they are masturbating with a chicken or wondering if intercourse with a cow will give them exotic diseases, the doctor does not react. In language classes, it becomes material to be worked over meticulously for translation. It is used to terrorize children in homes, so they will keep still about its use in the rape of their mothers and sisters: Look at this, if you tell, here's what I'll do to you. Sometimes it ends there; some children "only" have the pornography forced on them. Some of them later develop psychological difficulties that are identical to children who had the *acts* forced on them. Do a thought-act distinction on that one.

Women who live in neighborhoods where pornography is concentrated, much of it through state and local legal action called "zoning," report similar effects on a broad scale. Because prostitutes know what others seem to have a lot staked on denying, which is that pornography makes men want the real thing, they sometimes locate around it. This means that any woman there can be taken as a prostitute, which is dangerous enough if you are a prostitute, but becomes particularly dangerous if you do not mean to deliver. The threat of sexual harassment is constant. . . .

### C.

Specific pornography directly causes some assaults. Some rapes are performed by men with paper-

back books in their pockets. One young woman testified in our hearings about walking through a forest at thirteen and coming across a group of armed hunters reading pornography. As they looked up and saw her, one said, "There is a live one." They gang-raped her at gunpoint for several hours. One native American woman told us about being gang-raped in a reenactment of a videogame on her. . . .

Received wisdom seems to be that because there is so little difference between convicted rapists and the rest of the male population in levels and patterns of exposure, response to, and consumption of pornography, pornography's role in rape is insignificant. A more parsimonious explanation of this data is that knowing exposure to, response to, or consumption of pornography will not tell you who will be reported, apprehended, and convicted for rape. But the commonalities such data reveal between convicted rapists and other men are certainly consistent with the fact that only a tiny fraction of rapes ever come to the attention of authorities. It does not make sense to assume that pornography has no role in rape simply because little about its use or effects distinguishes convicted rapists from other men, when we know that a lot of those other men do rape women; they just never get caught. In other words, the significance of pornography in acts of forced sex is one thing if sex offenders are considered deviants and another if they are considered relatively nonexceptional except for the fact of their apprehension and incarceration. Professionals who work with that tiny percentage of men who get reported and convicted for such offenses, a group made special only by our ability to assume they once had sex by force in a way that someone (in addition to their victim) eventually regarded as serious, made the following observations about the population they work with. "Pornography[.] is the permission and direction and rehearsal for sexual violence." "[P]ornography is often used by sex offenders as a stimulus to their sexually acting out." It is the "tools of sexual assault," "a way in which they practice" their crimes, "like a loaded gun," "like drinking salt water," "the chemical of sexual addiction." They hypothesize that pornography leads some men to abusiveness out of fear of loss of control that has come to mean masculinity when real women won't accept sex on the one-sided terms that pornography gives and from which they have learned what sex is. "[Because pornography] is reinforcing, [and leads to sexual release, it] leads men to want the experience which they have in photographic fantasy to happen in 'real' life." "They live vicariously through the pictures. Eventually, that is not satisfying enough and they end up acting out sexually." "[S]exual fantasy represents the hope for reality." These professionals are referring to what others are fond of terming "just an idea."

. . .

### D.

To reach the magnitude of this problem on the scale it exists, our law makes trafficking in pornography—production, sale, exhibition, or distribution—actionable. Under the obscenity rubric, much legal and psychological scholarship has centered on a search for the elusive link between pornography defined as obscenity and harm. They have looked high and low—in the mind of the male consumer, in society or in its "moral fabric," in correlations between variations in levels of anti-social acts and liberalization of obscenity laws. The only harm they have found has been one they have attributed to "the social interest in order and morality." Until recently, no one looked very persistently for harm to women, particularly harm to women through men. The rather obvious fact that the sexes *relate* has been overlooked in the inquiry into the male consumer and his mind. The pornography doesn't just drop out of the sky, go into his head and stop there. Specifically, men rape, batter, prostitute, molest, and sexually harass women. Under conditions of inequality, they also hire, fire, promote, and grade women, decide how much or whether or not we are worth paying and for what, define and approve and disapprove of women in ways that count, that determine our lives.

If women are not just born to be sexually used, the fact that we are seen and treated as though that is what we are born for becomes something in need of explanation. If we see that men relate to women in a pattern of who they see women as being, and that forms a pattern of inequality, it becomes important to ask where that view came from or, minimally, how it is perpetuated or escalated. Asking this requires asking different questions about pornography than the ones obscenity law made salient.

Now I'm going to talk about causality in its narrowest sense. Recent experimental research on pornography shows that the materials covered by our definition cause measurable harm to women through increasing men's attitudes and behaviors of discrimination in both violent and nonviolent forms. Exposure to some of the pornography in our definition increases normal men's immediately subsequent willingness to aggress against women under laboratory conditions. It makes normal men more closely resemble convicted rapists attitudinally, although as a group they don't look all that different from them to start with. It also significantly increases attitudinal

measures known to correlate with rape and self-reports of aggressive acts, measures such as hostility toward women, propensity to rape, condoning rape, and predicting that one would rape or force sex on a woman if one knew one would not get caught. This latter measure, by the way, begins with rape at about a third of all men and moves to half with "forced sex."

. . .

Pornography stimulates and reinforces, it does not cathect or mirror, the connection between one-sided freely available sexual access to women and masculine sexual excitement and sexual satisfaction. The catharsis hypothesis is fantasy. The fantasy theory is fantasy. Reality is: Pornography conditions male orgasm to female subordination. It tells men what sex means, what a real woman is, and codes them together in a way that is behaviorally reinforcing. This is a real five-dollar sentence but I'm going to say it anyway: Pornography is a set of hermeneutical equivalences that work on the epistemological level. Substantively, pornography defines the meaning of what a woman is by connecting access to her sexuality with masculinity through orgasm. The behavioral data show that what pornography means *is* what it does.

. . .

### E.

It is worth considering what evidence has been enough when other harms involving other purported speech interests have been allowed to be legislated against. By comparison to our trafficking section, analytically similar restrictions have been allowed under the first amendment, with a legislative basis far less massive, detailed, concrete, and conclusive. Our statutory language is more ordinary, objective, and precise, and covers a harm far narrower than its legislative record substantiates. Under *Miller*, obscenity was allowed to be made criminal in the name of the "danger of offending the sensibilities of unwilling recipients, or exposure to juveniles." Under our law, we have direct evidence of harm, not just a conjectural danger, that unwilling women in considerable numbers are not simply offended in their sensibilities, but are violated in their persons and restricted in their options. Obscenity law also suggests that the applicable standard for legal adequacy in measuring such connections may not be statistical certainty. The Supreme Court has said that it is not their job to resolve empirical uncertainties that underlie state obscenity legislation. Rather, it is for them to determine whether a legislature could reasonably have determined that a connection might exist between the prohibited material and harm of a kind in which the state has legitimate interest. Equality should be such an area. The Supreme Court recently recognized that prevention of sexual exploitation and abuse of children is, in their words, "a governmental objective of surpassing importance." This might also be the case for sexual exploitation and abuse of women, although I think a civil remedy is initially more appropriate to the goal of empowering adult women than a criminal prohibition would be.

Other rubrics provide further support for the argument that this law is narrowly tailored to further a legitimate governmental interest consistent with the interests underlying the first amendment. Exceptions to the first amendment—you may have gathered from this—exist. The reason they exist is that the harm done by some speech outweighs its expressive value, if any. In our law, a legislature recognizes that pornography, as defined and made actionable, undermines sex equality. One can say—and I have—that pornography is a causal factor in violations of women; one can also say that women will be violated so long as pornography exists; but one can also say simply that pornography violates women. Perhaps this is what the woman had in mind who testified at our hearings that whether or not pornography causes violent acts to be perpetrated against some women is not her only issue. "Porn is already a violent act against women. It is our mothers, our daughters, our sisters, and our wives that are for sale for pocket change at the newsstands in this country." *Chaplinsky v. New Hampshire* recognizes the ability to restrict as "fighting words" speech which, "by [its] very utterance inflicts injury. . . ." Perhaps the only reason that pornography has not been "'fighting words'"—in the sense of words which by their utterance tend to incite immediate breach of the peace—is that women have seldom fought back, yet.

Some concerns close to those of this ordinance underlie group libel laws, although the differences are equally important. In group libel law, as Justice Frankfurter's opinion in *Beauharnais* illustrates, it has been understood that individuals' treatment and alternatives in life may depend as much on the reputation of the group to which such a person belongs as on their own merit. Not even a partial analogy can be made to group libel doctrine without examining the point made by Justice Brandeis, and recently underlined by Larry Tribe: Would more speech, rather than less, remedy the harm? In the end, the answer may be yes, but not under the abstract system of free speech, which only enhances the power of

the pornographers while doing nothing substantively to guarantee the free speech of women, for which we need civil equality. The situation in which women presently find ourselves with respect to the pornography is one in which more *pornography* is inconsistent with rectifying or even counterbalancing its damage through speech, because so long as the pornography exists in the way it does there *will not be more speech by women*. Pornography strips and devastates women of credibility, from our accounts of sexual assault to our everyday reality of sexual subordination. We are deauthorized and reduced and devalidated and silenced. Silenced here means that the purposes of the first amendment, premised upon conditions presumed and promoted by protecting free speech, do not pertain to women because they are not our conditions. Consider them: individual self-fulfillment—how does pornography promote our individual self-fulfillment? How does sexual inequality even permit it? Even if she can form words, who listens to a woman with a penis in her mouth? Facilitating consensus—to the extent pornography does so, it does so one-sidedly by silencing protest over the injustice of sexual subordination. Participation in civic life—central to Professor Meiklejohn's theory—how does pornography enhance women's participation in civic life? Anyone who cannot walk down the street or even lie down in her own bed without keeping her eyes cast down and her body clenched against assault is unlikely to have much to say about the issues of the day, still less will she become Tolstoy. . . .

For those of you who still think pornography is only an idea, consider the possibility that obscenity law got one thing right. Pornography is more act-like than thought-like. The fact that pornography, in a feminist view, furthers the idea of the sexual inferiority of women, which is a political idea, doesn't make the pornography itself into a political idea. One can express the idea a practice embodies. That does not make that practice into an idea. Segregation expresses the idea of the inferiority of one group to another on the basis of race. That does not make segregation an idea. A sign that says "Whites Only" is only words. Is it therefore protected by the first amendment? Is it not an act, a practice, of segregation because of the inseparability of what it means from what it does? *Law* is only words.

The issue here is whether the fact that the central link in the cycle of abuse that I have connected is words and pictures will immunize that entire cycle, about which we cannot do anything without doing something about the pornography. As Justice Stewart said in *Ginsburg*, "When expression occurs in a setting where the capacity to make a choice is absent, government regulation of that expression may coexist with and *even implement* First Amendment guarantees.'' I would even go so far as to say that the pattern of evidence we have closely approaches Justice Douglas' requirement that ''freedom of expression can be suppressed if, and to the extent that, it is so closely brigaded with illegal action as to be an inseparable part of it.'' Those of you who have been trying to separate the acts from the speech—that's an act, that's an act, there's a law against that act, regulate that act, don't touch the speech—*notice here* that the fact that the acts involved are illegal doesn't mean that the speech that is ''brigaded with'' it, cannot be regulated. It is when it *can* be.

. . .

The most basic assumption underlying first amendment adjudication is that, socially, speech is free. The first amendment says Congress shall not abridge the freedom of speech. Free speech, get it, *exists*. Those who wrote the first amendment *had* speech—they wrote the Constitution. *Their* problem was to keep it free from the only power that realistically threatened it: the federal government. They designed the first amendment to prevent government from constraining that which if unconstrained by government was free, meaning *accessible to them*. At the same time, we can't tell much about the intent of the Framers with regard to the question of women's speech, because I don't think we crossed their minds. It is consistent with this analysis that their posture to freedom of speech tends to presuppose that whole segments of the population are not systematically silenced, socially, prior to government action. If everyone's power were equal to theirs, if this were a non-hierarchical society, that might make sense. But the place of pornography in the inequality of the sexes makes the assumption of equal power untrue.

. . .

Cass R. Sunstein, *Pornography and the First Amendment*, 1986 DUKE LAW JOURNAL 589 (1986)*

. . .

## II. LOW-VALUE AND HIGH-VALUE SPEECH

. . .

Although the harms generated by pornography are

_____

* Reprinted with permission.

serious, they are insufficient, standing alone, to justify regulation under the usual standards applied to political speech. After *Brandenburg v. Ohio*, speech—not including obscenity—cannot be regulated because of the harm it produces unless it is shown that the speech is directed to produce harm that is both imminent and extremely likely to occur. Moreover, the Court has rejected the notion that this showing can be made by linking a class of harm with a class of speech; it is necessary to connect particular harms to particular speech. These doctrinal conclusions will not be questioned here, although they do have powerful adverse implications for antipornography legislation. If current standards are applied, a particular pornographic film or magazine might be beyond regulation unless the harms that result from the particular material are imminent, intended, and likely to occur. Demonstrating this, of course, will be hard to do.

But acceptance of these doctrinal conclusions does not resolve the question of the constitutionality of antipornography regulation. The Court has drawn a distinction between speech that may be banned only on the basis of an extremely powerful showing of government interest, and speech that may be regulated on the basis of a far less powerful demonstration of harm. Commercial speech, labor speech, and possibly group libel, for example, fall within the category of ''low-value'' speech. Whether particular speech falls within the low-value category cannot be determined by a precise test, and under any standards there will be difficult intermediate cases. But in determining whether speech qualifies as low-value, the cases suggest that four factors are relevant.

First, the speech must be far afield from the central concern of the first amendment, which, broadly speaking, is effective popular control of public affairs. Speech that concerns governmental processes is entitled to the highest level of protection; speech that has little or nothing to do with public affairs may be accorded less protection. Second, a distinction is drawn between cognitive and noncognitive aspects of speech. Speech that has purely noncognitive appeal will be entitled to less constitutional protection. Third, the purpose of the speaker is relevant: if the speaker is seeking to communicate a message, he will be treated more favorably than if he is not. Fourth, the various classes of low-value speech reflect judgments that in certain areas, government is unlikely to be acting for constitutionally impermissible reasons or producing constitutionally troublesome harms. In the cases of commercial speech, private libel, and fighting words, for example, government regulation is particularly likely to be based on legitimate reasons. Judicial scrutiny is therefore more deferential in these areas.

The exclusion of obscene materials from first amendment protection, in contrast, stems largely from an act of definition. Obscene materials, to the Court, do not count as "speech" within the meaning of the first amendment. But this definitional distinction can be viewed as reflecting the same considerations that define the low-value speech category. If the materials are defined narrowly, only nonpolitical and noncognitive material will be prohibited. The limitation of obscenity law to speech not having "serious literary, artistic, political, or scientific value" fits comfortably with this understanding.

This four-factor analysis is, of course, controversial. The distinction between political and nonpolitical speech, for example, is often unclear and may ultimately depend on the political view of the decisionmaker. The difficulty inherent in such line drawing, moreover, may support abandoning any attempt to do so. Perhaps more importantly, distinctions between cognitive and emotive aspects of speech are thin and in some respects pernicious. Furthermore, approaches based on the purpose of the speaker are troublesome for familiar reasons. Finally, freedom of speech might be thought to promote self-realization and, on that ground, attempts to make distinctions among categories of speech might be questioned.

But it would be difficult to imagine a sensible system of free expression that did not distinguish among categories of speech in accordance with their importance to the underlying purposes of the free speech guarantee. A system that granted absolute protection to speech would be unduly mechanical, treading unjustifiably on important values and goals: consider laws forbidding threats, bribes, misleading commercial speech, and conspiracies. Any system that recognizes the need for some regulation but does not draw lines could be driven to deny full protection to speech that merits it—because the burden of justification imposed on the government would have to be lightened in order to allow regulation of, for example, commercial speech, conspiracies, and private libel. By hypothesis, that lighter burden would have to be extended across-the-board. The alternative would be to apply the standards for political speech to all speech, and thus to require the government to meet a test so stringent as to preclude most forms of regulation that are currently accepted. In these circumstances the most likely outcome would be that judgments about low-value would be made tacitly, and the articulated rationales for decisions would fail to reflect all the factors actually considered relevant by the court.

Once it is accepted that distinctions should be drawn among different categories of speech, the question becomes one of identifying an appropriate basis for those distinctions. The issue is complex, and it will be possible only to outline some of the important considerations here. First, the distinction between political and nonpolitical speech is well-established, and properly so. The distinction protects speech that serves a central function of the first amendment and precludes regulation where it is most likely to be based on impermissible or disfavored justifications.

The distinction between cognitive and noncognitive speech is more difficult to defend. This is so not only because of the existence of difficult intermediate cases, but also because the very concept of communication is badly misconceived if it is understood as an appeal to rational capacities alone. But any attempt to distinguish among categories of speech must start with an effort to isolate what is uniquely important about speech in the first place. Speech that is not intended to communicate a substantive message or that is direct solely to noncognitive capacities may be wholly or largely without the properties that give speech its special status. Subliminal advertising and hypnosis, for example, are entitled to less than full first amendment protection. Listeners or observers will frequently draw messages from speech or conduct, whether or not it has a communicative intent; the fact that a message may be drawn does not mean that the speech in question has the usual constitutional value.

Under this approach, or any plausible variation, regulation of pornography need not be justified according to standards applicable to political speech. The effect and intent of pornography, as it is defined here, are to produce sexual arousal, not in any sense to affect the course of self-government. Though comprised of words and pictures, pornography does not have the special properties that single out speech for special protection; it is more akin to a sexual aid than a communicative expression. In terms of the distinctions made among classes of speech, pornography is low-value speech not entitled to the same degree of protection accorded other forms of speech.

In one respect, however, the feminist case for regulation of pornography might seem, quite paradoxically, to weaken the argument for regulation. The feminist argument is that pornography represents an ideology, one that has important consequences for social attitudes. Speech that amounts to an ideology, one might argue, cannot be considered low-value, for such speech lies at the heart of politics. If pornography indeed does amount to an ideology of male supremacy, it might be thought to be entitled to the highest form of constitutional protection.

But an argument along these lines is based on a misconception of what entitles speech to the highest form of protection. Child pornography, for example, may reflect an ideology, but this did not compel the Court to hold in *New York v. Ferber* that child pornography is constitutionally protected. Indeed, most categories of low-value speech—fighting words, commercial speech, obscenity—amount in some respects to an ideology. In commercial speech, for example, there is an implicit ideology in favor of market-ordering, and perhaps some sort of ideology involving the product advertised. But that fact does not justify a conclusion that courts should accord such speech the highest level of constitutional protection.

Whether particular speech is low-value does not turn on whether the materials contain an implicit ideology; if it did, almost all speech would be immunized. The question instead turns more generally on the speaker's purpose and on how the speaker communicates the message. The pornographer's purpose in disseminating pornographic materials—to produce sexual arousal—can be determined by the nature of the material. And any implicit "ideology" is communicated indirectly and noncognitively. A distinction along these lines has become an integral part of the Supreme Court's commercial speech doctrine. Paid speech addressed to social issues receives full first amendment protection; paid speech proposing specific commercial transactions receives less protection despite any implicit political statement such speech may contain. A contention that the purpose of the speech is to transmit an ideological message is easily overborne by the nature of the speech itself. Furthermore, the purpose of the speaker is central to the question; someone who burns a draft card for the purpose of protesting a war is in a very different position from someone who burns a draft card as part of a general program of arson, even if the action of the latter is taken to have expressed an ideology to bystanders. There are, moreover, differences between ideological argument in favor of free markets, or of domination of women by men, and commercial and pornographic speech. The differences have to do with both purposes and effects. For pornography is particular, the cognitive element, to the extent that there is one, operates at a subconscious level; the message is communicated indirectly. Hypnosis, whether or not voluntary, does not amount to constitutionally protected speech, or to speech that is entitled to the highest level of first amendment concern;

this conclusion holds even if the hypnotist's message has some ideological dimension. The example is extreme, but it suggests that the fact that speech communicates a message is not a sufficient reason to accord it the highest level of constitutional protection.

These considerations suggest a conventional, two-stage argument for the regulation of pornography. First, pornography is entitled to only a lower level of first amendment solicitude. Under any standard, pornography is far afield from the kind of speech conventionally protected by the first amendment. Second, the harms produced by pornographic materials are sufficient to justify regulation. Admittedly, there will be difficult intermediate cases and analogies that test the persuasiveness and reach of the argument. The crucial point, however, is that traditional first amendment doctrine furnishes the basis for an argument in favor of restricting pornography, and that such an argument can be made without running afoul of the weak version of the notion of neutral principles. . . .

## III. THE PROBLEM OF VIEWPOINT DISCRIMINATION

The only federal court of appeals that has faced a challenge to antipornography legislation found it unnecessary to examine either the issue of low-value categorization or the issue of harms. In *American Booksellers Association v. Hudnut* the United States Court of Appeals for the Seventh Circuit invalidated antipornography legislation on the ground that it discriminated on the basis of viewpoint. In the court's view, the Indianapolis ordinance amounted to "thought control," since it "establish[es] an approved view of women, of how they may react to sexual encounters, [and] . . . of how the sexes may relate to each other." Under this decision, which the Supreme Court summarily affirmed, neither the problem of low-value nor the problem of harm is relevant.

This basic approach is familiar in first amendment law. Modern doctrine distinguishes among three categories of restrictions: those that are based on viewpoint, or that single out and suppress particular opinions concerning a particular subject, those that are based on content, or that regulate any speech concerning a subject, regardless of viewpoint; and those that are both content- and viewpoint-neutral. The most intense constitutional hostility is reserved for measures that discriminate on the basis of viewpoint, even though such measures may suppress less speech than do other sorts of restrictions. Thus, for example, a statute that prohibits all speech on billboards stands a far greater chance of constitutional success than a statute that prohibits speech on billboards that is critical of Republicans. . . .

The United States Court of Appeals for the Seventh Circuit concluded that the Indianapolis antipornography legislation was viewpoint-based and that its defenders failed to meet [their] burden of justification. The legislation, in the court's view, singled out for suppression a particular point of view by aiming at the portrait of male-female relations reflected in some sexually graphic material. One portrait is ruled out; the other is permitted. The issue of harm is irrelevant when restrictions based on viewpoint face a per se rule of illegality.

The initial response to a claim that antipornography legislation is viewpoint-based should be straightforward. The legislation aimed at pornography as defined here would be directed at harm rather than at viewpoint. Its purpose would be to prevent sexual violence and discrimination, not to suppress expression of a point of view. Only pornography—not sexist material in general or material that reinforces notions of female subordination—is regulated. Because of its focus on harm, antipornography legislation would not pose the dangers associated with viewpoint-based restrictions. The government, in effect, would have concrete data to back its legitimate purposes.

This approach is supported by a recent decision that was handed down by the Supreme Court in the same week that it summarily affirmed the Indianapolis case. In *City of Renton v. Playtime Theatres, Inc.*, the Court was faced with a statute that prohibited the showing of sexually explicit motion pictures within 1000 feet of any residential zone, single- or multiple-family dwelling, church, park, or school. The Court concluded that the statute was content-neutral because it was aimed not at the substantive message of the speech, but at its secondary effects on crime rates, property values, neighborhood quality, and retail trade. The statute's apparent content-based character, according to the Court, was not troubling because the statute could be justified by reference to these secondary effects. It might be said that *Renton* involves regulation on the basis of content rather than viewpoint—a point taken up below—but it is not clear how that conclusion is relevant to the issue of whether harms rescue a statute from skepticism about government motivation. Although the *Renton* decision is questionable on its facts, the Court's willingness to look at possible neutral justifications is sound and coexists uneasily with the outcome in *Hudnut*.

A response to this line of reasoning—and to the *Renton* analogy—would be to point out that view-point-based restrictions are frequently defended by reference to harm, and that the possibility of such defenses has not been thought to rescue the restrictions from severe constitutional scrutiny. For example, the government's defense of a law prohibiting people from criticizing a war effort in the presence of soldiers is not that it has any hostility toward the speaker's point of view, but that it is seeking to regulate something that could seriously prejudice the war effort. Despite this claim, the restriction is properly subject to the stringent standards applicable to viewpoint-based restrictions. The reason is straight-forward: notwithstanding the possible invocation of harm, the government is attempting to bypass deliberative processes of the community. "More speech" and direct regulation of unlawful conduct should be the preferred remedy for harms. The risks of factional tyranny and self-interested representation are sufficient to justify imposing on government a heavy burden of showing that "more speech" and direct regulation of unlawful conduct are inadequate responses to the harm.

Harm-based justifications thus do not foreclose an attack on pornography legislation as viewpoint-based. Yet one may question the very applicability of the notion of "viewpoint discrimination" in this context. First amendment law contains several categories of speech that are subject to ban or regulation even though they are viewpoint-based in the same sense that antipornography legislation is said to be. The most obvious example can be found in labor law.

Courts have held that the first amendment permits the government to prohibit employers from speaking unfavorably about the effects of unionization in the period before a union election if the unfavorable statements might be interpreted as a threat. In the leading case, the employer had suggested that the firm was not financially strong, that any strike would result in a plant closing, and that many employees would have a hard time finding alternative employment. Regulation of such speech is unquestionably viewpoint-based, for employer speech favorable to unionization is not proscribed. Similarly, regulation of bribery turns not only on content but also on point of view; one may not offer $100 to tempt a person to commit murder, although a $100 offer to build a fence is permissible. Prohibitions of "fighting words" might be similarly understood. False or misleading commercial speech, as well as television and radio advertisements for cigarettes and casinos, are regulable, even though all are based on viewpoint.

Moreover, one may doubt whether the courts would invalidate a statute forbidding advocacy of the use of unlawful force to overthrow the government in circumstances in which the standards of *Brandenburg v. Ohio* were met, even if the statute did not also forbid advocacy of the use of unlawful force to perpetuate the existing government. Such a statute is viewpoint-based because the speaker's point of view triggers statutory sanctions. More generally, the existing law of obscenity may readily be regarded as viewpoint-based. The line drawn by statutes implementing *Miller* necessarily distinguishes between messages on the basis of social attitudes toward sexual mores.

These and other apparently viewpoint-based statutes are upheld because they respond, not to point of view, but to harms that the government has power to prevent. In regulating labor speech, the Court indicated that the government was aiming not at viewpoint but at coercion of employees. The existence of genuine and substantial harm allayed concern about impermissible motivation. Significantly, the Court was sensitive to disparities in power that gave employer speech particular authority. The notion that the Labor Management Relations Act interfered with a well-functioning marketplace of ideas thus seemed absurd.

In the area of bribes, threats, and fighting words, the government is also attempting to combat obvious harms. Analysis of suppression of speech advocating the immediate and violent overthrow of the government would be similar: the government is attempting to eradicate a harm, not attempting to impose a particular point of view. Bans on false or misleading commercial speech, cigarette advertising, or casino gambling are analyzed in substantially the same way. In the obscenity context, the reasoning is more obscure, but the central point remains: in some contexts, statutes that appear to be viewpoint-based are justified and accepted because of the harms involved. The harms are so obvious and immediate that claims that the government is attempting to silence one position in a "debate" do not have time even to register.

One might go further and suggest that the distinction between content-based and viewpoint-based restrictions is at best elusive and more likely nonexistent—and that the distinction itself will depend on viewpoint. Obscenity, commercial speech, fighting words, and perhaps even labor speech are said to involve viewpoint-neutral restrictions because the "viewpoint" of the speaker is deemed irrelevant to regulation. But the line drawn by the regulation does, in all these contexts, depend on point of view. One does not "see" a viewpoint-based restriction when the harms invoked in defense of a regulation are obvious and so widely supported by social consensus

that they allay any concern about impermissible government motivation. Whether a classification is viewpoint-based thus ultimately turns on the viewpoint of the decisionmaker.

It is for this reason that obscenity law is regarded as viewpoint-neutral and antipornography law as viewpoint-based. Obscenity law, particularly insofar as it is tied to community standards, is deemed "objective" because the class of prohibited speech is defined by reference to an existing social consensus. Antipornography legislation is deemed "subjective" because the prohibited class of speech is defined by less widely accepted values favoring the protection of the relatively powerless. But this distinction between objectivity and subjectivity is hard to sustain. Indeed, one could imagine a world in which the harms produced by pornography were so widely acknowledged and so generally condemned that an antipornography ordinance would not be regarded as viewpoint-based at all.

All this suggests that the problem of identifying impermissible viewpoint regulation is far more complex than it at first appears. Regulation based on point of view is common in the law. The terms "viewpoint-based" and "viewpoint-neutral" often represent conclusions rather than analytical tools. In the easy cases, they serve as valuable simplifying devices. But in the hard cases, further analysis is needed. Specifically, three factors help identify impermissible viewpoint-based legislation.

The first factor is the connection between means and ends, a recurrent theme in constitutional law. If the harm invoked is minimal, or if it is implausible to think that the regulation will remedy the harm, it will be more likely that the regulation is in fact based on viewpoint. The second factor is the nature of the process by which the message is communicated. Regulation of harms that derive from types of persuasion appealing to cognitive faculties is presumptively disfavored; more speech is the preferred remedy here. Regulation of antiwar speeches in the presence of soldiers is impermissible because any harm that results is derived from persuasion. More speech should be the solution. Finally, whether the speech is low- or high-value is also relevant. The low-value issue, therefore, is not made irrelevant on the ground that antipornography legislation discriminates on the basis of viewpoint. The viewpoint issue depends, in part, on whether the speech is low-value. Viewpoint-based regulation of high-value speech raises especially intense concerns about government motivation.

Under these criteria, antipornography legislation is defensible. First, the means-ends connection is quite close. Such legislation could be tightly targeted to the cause of the harm: the production and dissemination of portrayals of sexual violence. Second, the "message" of pornography is communicated indirectly and not through rational persuasion. The harm it produces cannot easily be countered by more speech because it bypasses the process of public consideration and debate that underlies the concept of the marketplace of ideas. Finally, pornography falls in the general category of low-value speech. Under these circumstances, antipornography legislation should be regarded not as an effort to exclude a point of view, but instead as an effort to prevent harm. In this respect, the best analogy is to labor speech—with the important caveat that labor speech, which touches public affairs, is far closer to the heart of first amendment concern than is pornography.

The task, in short, is to sort out permissible and impermissible viewpoint discrimination, and to explain the circumstances in which discrimination arguably on the basis of viewpoint should be permitted. It is important in this respect that efforts to regulate pornography, as defined here, do not interfere with deliberative processes at all. By hypothesis, pornography operates at a subconscious level, providing a form of social conditioning that is not analogous to the ordinary operation of freedom of speech. What is distinctive about pornography is its noncognitive character; though it amounts to words and pictures, its purposes and effects are far from the purposes and effects that justify the special protection accorded to freedom of speech. In these circumstances, the response to the claim of viewpoint discrimination is that antipornography legislation does not pose any of the dangers that make discrimination on the basis of viewpoint so troublesome. The three factors identified above—means-ends connection, nature of the process by which the "message" is communicated, and low-value—point in this direction.

This three-factor analysis does have important limitations. Not all materials having a noncognitive appeal are unprotected; communication, whether or not political, is almost always a mixture of cognitive and noncognitive effects. Nor should viewpoint-based restrictions survive constitutional scrutiny in every case in which secondary harms can be identified. Finally, the harms invoked to defend antipornography legislation are not sufficient to justify regulation of political speech, broadly defined. It is the peculiar features of pornography that justify regulation: the low-value status of the speech, the powerful showing of harm, and the nature of the process by which the message is communicated. For this reason the case for antipornography legislation survives the weak version of the requirement of neutral principles.

## IV. SUBSTANTIVITY, FORMALITY AND THE FREE SPEECH GUARANTEE

The argument thus far has been somewhat technical, and it operates within the framework of traditional first amendment doctrine. But proponents of antipornography legislation argue not only that such legislation will combat related harms, but also that restrictions on pornography will promote freedom of speech. At first glance, the argument is mysterious. Conventional first amendment doctrine is based on the assumption that restrictions on speech cannot promote freedom of expression. As we shall see, that assumption ultimately stems from a belief that serious threats to free expression come mostly or exclusively from the public sphere, and that one should always distinguish the public and private spheres for purposes of first amendment analysis.

The argument that antipornography legislation can promote free speech touches on more fundamental issues than have been discussed here thus far. Essentially, the claim is that an attack on antipornography legislation represents legal formalism akin to Professor Wechsler's attack on *Brown v. Board of Education*. In both cases an abstract notion of equality is decisive, though a substantive examination of issues of power and powerlessness would lead to a conclusion that the abstract notion is untenable. Wechsler's view that *Brown* produced a conflict between two coequal sets of associational preferences now appears quite odd. The argument ignores issues of substantive power that make the social meaning—the purposes and effects—of the associational preferences of blacks altogether different from that of the associational preferences of whites. Similarly, first amendment doctrine that refuses to examine issues of substantive power and substantive powerlessness might be thought to generate an indefensible system of expression.

More concretely, the argument goes, the pornography industry is so well-financed, and has such power to condition men and women, that it has the effect of silencing the antipornography cause in particular and women in general. The silencing involved is not the kind of silencing associated with totalitarian regimes. Instead, women who would engage in "more speech" to counter pornography are denied credibility, trust, and the opportunity to be heard—the predicates of free expression. The notion that "when she says no, she means yes"—a common theme in pornography—thus affects the social reception of the feminist attack on pornography. Understood in this way, the case for antipornography legislation is a version of the arguments derived from the famous footnote in *United States v. Carolene*

*Products*. Legal intervention is required because of a maldistribution of private power that interferes with a well-functioning political marketplace. Akin to the view that correction of market failures is a valid basis for governmental intervention, the argument might be understood as a variation of traditional justifications for affirmative action. . . .

The *Lochner*-like approach that underlies the Court's rejection of attempts to promote first amendment values through the regulation of powerful private actors . . . appears to stem from an amalgam of three factors: (1) the view that disparities in private power do not significantly interfere with a well-functioning system of free expression; (2) the perception that if government is permitted to intervene on behalf of groups deemed powerless, lines will be impossible to draw, and government will be licensed to act for impermissible reasons; and (3) the belief that if some people—even if they have disproportionate power—are not permitted to speak, a genuine impairment of freedom results, even if that impairment is made in the interest of equality. . . .

These considerations suggest that as a general rule, inquiries into substantive powerlessness should not be used to defend restrictions on expression. But the issue is a difficult one, and the tentative character of the conclusion should be emphasized. . . . As we have seen, pornography operates at a subconscious level; its influence is hard to match through "more speech." Ideological counterargument cannot easily compete with the process by which pornography communicates its message. Moreover, pornography is far afield from the core of the first amendment. I conclude that examining substantive differences in power as a basis for regulation of pornography is appropriate in this context, and helps the case for regulation, even if we ought to avoid such an examination as a general rule.

In sum, first amendment doctrine reflects a strong version of the notion of neutral principles. With the important exception of *Red Lion [Broadcasting Company v. FCC]*, issues of substantive power and powerlessness are avoided. Despite its *Lochner*-like quality, this general approach is sound. But it poses substantial disadvantages as well as benefits; and in some narrow contexts, its disadvantages are sufficiently great, and its benefits sufficiently doubtful, to justify a departure from the general principle. Regulation of pornography is such a context. . . .

I conclude that the skepticism about antipornography legislation is based on a simultaneous undervaluation of the harm pornography produces, a misapplication of conventional doctrines requiring viewpoint-neutrality, and—perhaps most important—an overvaluation of the dangers posed by generating a somewhat different category of regulable speech bound to have some definitional vagueness. At least as the notion is used here, antipornography legislation should produce important social benefits without posing significant threats to a well-functioning system of free expression.

---

Nadine Strossen, *A Feminist Critique of "the" Feminist Critique of Pornography*, 79 Virginia Law Review 1099 (1993)*

## INTRODUCTION: THE FEMINIST ANTI-CENSORSHIP MOVEMENT

Over the past decade, some feminists—led by Andrea Dworkin and Catharine MacKinnon—have had great influence in advancing the theory that certain sexually oriented speech should be regulated because it "subordinates" women. They have labeled this subset of sexually explicit speech "pornography" to distinguish it from the separate subset of sexually explicit speech that the Supreme Court has defined as proscribable "obscenity." This Essay counters the Dworkin-MacKinnon pro-censorship position with an argument grounded in feminist principles and concerns. . . .

Because I am offering a feminist critique of the efforts by the Dworkin-MacKinnon faction of feminism to regulate the expression they label "pornography," I use the term as they do, which is to refer to sexually explicit speech that allegedly "subordinates" women. I emphasize that such speech "*allegedly*" is subordinating, because that subjective characterization is one with which many women, feminists, authors, and artists disagree. To highlight the problematic nature of the term "pornography," I put it in quotation marks throughout this Essay. . . .

My analysis . . . attempts to correct an imbalance existing in both the popular perception and the legal discussion of the "pornography" issue. Encouraged by oversimplified, extremist, divisive pronouncements by feminist pro-censorship leaders, there is a widespread misperception that if you are a feminist—or a woman—you must view "pornography" as misogynistic and "detrimental" to women. And you must favor censoring it.

. . .

---

* Reprinted with permission.

## III. CENSORING "PORNOGRAPHY" WOULD UNDERMINE WOMEN'S RIGHTS AND INTERESTS

. . .

The principal negative effects that censoring "pornography" would have upon feminist values, which this Section discusses, are the following:

1. Any censorship scheme would inevitably encompass many works that are especially valuable to feminists.

2. Any censorship scheme would be enforced in a way that would discriminate against the least popular, least powerful groups in our society, including feminists and lesbians.

3. Censorship is paternalistic, perpetuating demeaning stereotypes about women, including that sex is bad for us.

4. Censorship perpetuates the disempowering notion that women are essentially victims.

5. Censorship distracts from constructive approaches to countering anti-female discrimination and violence.

6. Censorship would harm women who make their living in the sex industry.

7. Censorship would harm women's efforts to develop their own sexualities.

8. Censorship would strengthen the power of the religious right, whose patriarchal agenda would curtail women's rights.

9. By undermining free speech, censorship would deprive feminists of a powerful tool for advancing women's equality.

10. Sexual freedom, and freedom for sexually explicit expression, are essential aspects of human freedom; denying these specific freedoms undermines human rights more broadly.

### A. Any Censorship Scheme Would Inevitably Encompass Many Works That Are Especially Valuable to Feminists

The ACLU's brief in Hudnut noted the adverse impact of "pornography" censorship on feminist concerns. It explained that the Dworkin-MacKinnon model law, by proscribing sexually explicit depictions of women's "subordination," outlawed not only many valuable works of art and literature in general, but also many such works that are particularly important to women and feminists:

Ironically, much overtly feminist scholarly material designed to address the same concerns prompting the [ordinance] would fall within [its] sweeping definition of pornography. Prominent examples include Kate Millett's *The*

*Basement*, a graphic chronicle of sexual torture; . . . works on rape, wife beating and domestic violence; court testimony and photographic evidence in rape and sexual assault cases; works like [Susan] Brownmiller's *Against Our Will: Men, Women and Rape*; and psychiatric literature describing sexual pathologies and therapeutic modalities. Indeed, *Pornography: Men Possessing Women*, a work by Andrea Dworkin, one of the ordinance's original drafters, contains . . . so many . . . passages graphically depicting the explicit sexual subordination of women that it could easily be pornographic under the ordinance.

I have been told that Andrea Dworkin acknowledges that much of her own work would be censored under her model law, but that she considers this "a price worth paying" for the power to censor other works that would also be viewed as "pornography." Even assuming that Andrea Dworkin or other advocates of censoring "pornography" do in fact take this position, they certainly do not speak for all feminists on this point. Many may well believe that works such as Dworkin's, by depicting and deploring violence and discrimination against women, make invaluable contributions to redressing those problems.

The sweeping breadth of the Dworkin-MacKinnon model anti-"pornography" law is not the accidental result of poor drafting. To the contrary, their proposed law well reflects their view of the problem, and hence of its solution. In an exchange with Catharine MacKinnon, Professor Thomas Emerson made this point, as follows:

As Professor MacKinnon emphasizes, male domination has deep, pervasive and ancient roots in our society, so it is not surprising that our literature, art, entertainment and commercial practices are permeated by attitudes and behavior that create and reflect the inferior status of women. If the answer to the problem, as Professor MacKinnon describes it, is government suppression of sexual expression that contributes to female subordination, then the net of restraint must be cast on a nearly limitless scale. Even narrowing the proscribed area to depictions of sexual activities involving violence would outlaw a large segment of the world's literature and art.

### B. Any Censorship Scheme Would Be Enforced in a Way That Discriminate[s] Against the Least Popular, Least Powerful Groups in Our Society, Including Feminists and Lesbians

Vague censorship laws always rebound against the

groups that hope to be "protected" by them. This is because such laws are enforced by the very power structure against which the disempowered censorship advocates seek protection. Given that the laws' vague and open-ended terms require the enforcing authorities to make subjective, discretionary judgments, it should not be surprising that these judgments are unsympathetic to the disempowered and marginalized. . . .

Censorship of "pornography," defined by Dworkin and MacKinnon as the sexually explicit depiction of women's "subordination," necessarily vests in government officials the power to impose on others their views about what forms of sexuality are politically or morally correct. The criteria for assessing "subordination" under the Dworkin-MacKinnon model statute accentuate the problem of vesting open-ended, discretionary power in enforcing authorities. These vague criteria are merely invitations for subjective, value-laden interpretations.

Because of the inherently subjective nature of determinations as to which sexually explicit imagery is pleasurable or otherwise positive, it is antithetical to feminism to impose censorship schemes that deprive individual women (and men) of the right to make these determinations for themselves. As Feminists for Free Expression stated in its letter to the Senate Judiciary Committee opposing the Pornography Victims' Compensation Act:

> It is no goal of feminism to restrict individual choices or stamp out sexual imagery. Though some women and men may have this on their platform, they represent only themselves. Women are as varied as any citizens of a democracy; there is no agreement or feminist code as to what images are distasteful or even sexist. It is the right and responsibility of each woman to read, view or produce the sexual material she chooses without the intervention of the state "for her own good." We believe genuine feminism encourages individuals to make these choices for themselves. This is the great benefit of being feminists in a free society.

Even beyond the significant danger that censoring "pornography" poses to individual sexual choices in general, such censorship poses a special threat to any sexual expression that society views as unconventional. Censors would likely target "pornography" that conveys pro-feminist or pro-lesbian themes, because of its inconsistency with "traditional family values" or conventional morality. For example, "pornography" "may convey the message that sexuality need not be tied to reproduction, men,

or domesticity." It may extol sex for no reason other than pleasure, sex without commitment, and sexual adventure.

Years ago, feminist writer Erica Jong predicted that the enforcement of any "pornography" censorship scheme would probably target expression by and about feminists and others who challenge prevailing cultural norms, such as gay men and lesbians: "Despite the ugliness of a lot of pornography, . . . I believe that censorship only springs back against the givers of culture—against authors, artists, and feminists, against anybody who wants to change society. Should censorship be imposed . . . feminists would be the first to suffer." . . .

Jong's predictions came to pass in Canada, after the 1992 Canadian Supreme Court decision . . . , which empowered the government to prosecute sexually explicit expression that is "degrading" or "dehumanizing" to women. One of the first targets of the new law was a lesbian and gay bookstore, Glad Day Bookstore, and a magazine produced by lesbians for lesbians. Not surprisingly, the police, prosecutors, and other government officials viewed this lesbian imagery as degrading. They did not so view violent, misogynistic imagery. Other actions on the part of Canadian authorities that hold censorship power reflect similar attitudes. . . .

The Canadian experience has proven the sadly prophetic nature of Erica Jong's warnings in a particularly ironic development. Pursuant to their newfound authority to interdict at the border material that is "degrading" or "dehumanizing" to women, Canadian customs officials have confiscated several feminist works that Canadian bookstores sought to import from the United States, including two books that were written by Andrea Dworkin herself! . . .

## C. Censorship is Paternalistic, Perpetuating Demeaning Stereotypes about Women, Including that Sex is Bad for Us

Ironically, the Dworkin-MacKinnon effort to extirpate sexually explicit expression that, in their view, perpetuates demeaning stereotypes about women, itself perpetuates such demeaning stereotypes. One subordinating stereotype that is central to the feminist censorship movement is that sex is inherently degrading to women.

To emphasize that the feminist pro-censorship position rests upon traditional, stereotypical views disapproving sex and denying women's sexuality, anticensorship feminists have characterized their own views as "pro-sex." The basic contours of these opposing "anti-sex" and "pro-sex" positions— which are linked, respectively, to the pro- and anti-censorship positions—are delineated by three feminist scholars and activists as follows:

> Embedded in [the feminist pro-censorship] view are several . . . familiar themes: that sex is degrading to women, but not to men; that men are raving beasts; that sex is dangerous for women; that sexuality is male, not female; that women are victims, not sexual actors; that men inflict "it" on women; that penetration is submission; that heterosexual sexuality, rather than the institution of heterosexuality, is sexist.
> . . . It's ironic that a feminist position on pornography incorporates most of the myths about sexuality that feminism has struggled to displace.
>
> . . . .
>
> . . . Underlying virtually every section of the [Dworkin-MacKinnon model law] there is an assumption that sexuality is a realm of unremitting, unequaled victimization for women. . . . But this analysis is not the only feminist perspective on sexuality. Feminist theorists have also argued that the sexual terrain, however power-laden, is actively contested. Women are agents, and not merely victims, who make decisions and act on them, and who desire, seek out and enjoy sexuality.

The "anti-sex" position of the pro-censorship feminists essentially posits a mutual inconsistency between a woman's freedom and her participation in sexual relations with men. For example, both Dworkin and MacKinnon have argued that, in light of society's pervasive sexism, women cannot freely consent to sexual relations with men. Dworkin makes this point in the most dramatic and extreme terms in her book *Intercourse*, which equates all heterosexual intercourse with rape.

In contrast to the "anti-sex," pro-censorship view that women's freedom is undermined by their sexual relations with men, the "pro-sex," anti-censorship position regards these phenomena as mutually reinforcing. Anti-censorship, "pro-sex" feminist Ann Snitow captured this contrast well:

> Ti Grace Atkinson [a pro-censorship, "anti-sex" feminist] says, "I do not know any feminist worthy of that name who, if forced to choose between freedom and sex, would choose sex." [But] [w]hile women are forced to make such a choice we cannot consider ourselves free. . . .

The feminist pro-censorship movement inverts central tenets of the feminism of the 1960s and 1970s, which criticized the idea that sex degrades women as reflecting patriarchal, subordinating stereotypes. Like labor laws that many states passed in the early twentieth century, to "protect" women in the workplace, censorship of "pornography" also aims to shelter women from our presumed innate vulnerability. As the Supreme Court said in a 1973 decision upholding women's equality rights, such "protective" legislation reflected attitudes of "romantic paternalism" that, in practical effect, "put women, not on a pedestal, but in a cage." . . .

### D. Censorship Perpetuates the Disempowering Notion that Women Are Essentially Victims

Just as the pro-censorship movement views women as inevitably being victims in sexual matters, that movement also perpetuates the stereotype that women are victims in a more general sense. For example, feminist law professor Carlin Meyer has noted the pro-censorship feminists' "general tendency to view women as actually, not merely portrayed as, submissive—as acted upon rather than acting; as objects of male will rather than subjects able to challenge or change cultural norms."

As Cathy Young has observed, it is considered strategically advantageous from some perspectives to depict women as victims: "Victimhood is [p]owerful. Both feminists and antifeminists see advantages in keeping women down."

On the other hand, though, growing numbers of feminists are recognizing that purveying the view of women as victims can backfire against gender equality. This increasing realization was described by a female journalist as follows:

> On issues from domestic violence to pornography, feminists are rethinking their emphasis on women as victims—and looking for new legal and political approaches to enable women to force social change. Fifteen years ago, Elizabeth Schneider helped develop the legal argument that battered women who killed husbands who had abused them for years were the victims, not the aggressors. Now she worries [that] battered women are victims of their victim status. [She said:] "Courts and society have glommed onto the victim image. . . . But it's a two-edged sword. Many battered women lose custody of their children because judges see them as helpless, paralyzed victims who can't manage daily life. And if a woman seems too capable, too much in charge of her life to fit the victim image, she may not be believed."

### E. Censorship Distracts from Constructive Approaches to Reducing Discrimination and Violence against Women

Like all censorship schemes, the feminist proposal to censor "pornography" diverts attention and resources from constructive, meaningful steps to address the societal problem at which the censorship is aimed—in this case, discrimination and violence against women. Feminist advocates of censoring "pornography"—along with feminist opponents of such censorship—are concerned about the very real, very disturbing societal problems of discrimination and violence against women. The focus on censoring "pornography," though, diverts attention from the root causes of discrimination and violence against women—of which violent, misogynistic "pornography" is merely one symptom—and from actual acts of discrimination and violence.

For those with a more complex analysis of the manifold causes and reflections of women's inferior societal status, the Dworkin-MacKinnon focus on "pornography" is at best myopic, and at worst blinding. As Canadian feminist Varda Burstyn has written:

> [T]here has been, among the antipornography feminists, a series of subtle shifts in ideas about the forms and causes of women's oppression. From an appreciation of the multidimensional reality of masculine dominance, vocal feminists have been increasingly narrowing their focus to one dimension: . . . pornography. Women's attention has been diverted from the causes to the depictions of their oppression.

The Dworkin-MacKinnon tunnel-visioned focus on "pornography" overlooks the many complex factors that contribute to sexism and violence against women in our society. As Professor Meyer observes:

> It seems implausible, to say the least, that pornography is more centrally responsible either for rendering erotic or for making possible the actualization of male violence against women than are the ideologies and practices of religion, law, and science. These institutions far more deeply and pervasively undergird male domination of women.

Furthermore, she notes, the Dworkin-MacKinnon focus on "pornography" as a central cause of sexism and violence also "under-emphasize[s] . . . institutions and practices—such as sports and militarism—in which male bonding in physically aggressive pursuits seems inevitably to spill into an erotica which ultimately targets women."

Proponents of censorship in all contexts have designed their censorship regimes to advance some important societal goal. In operation, though, censorship always is at best ineffective and at worst counter-productive in terms of actually advancing that goal. The reason is that, by focusing on expressions of the problem, censorship targets symptoms rather than causes; it does not address either the problem's root causes or its actual manifestations. Consequently, censorship distracts from more constructive, more effective approaches.

. . .

### F. Censorship Would Harm Women Who Make a Living in the Sex Industry

The Dworkin-MacKinnon approach to sexually oriented expression would undermine the interests of women who choose to make their living in the sex industry in several respects. Most obviously, by seeking to ban major aspects of this industry, the Dworkin-MacKinnon regime would deprive women of an option that many now affirm they have freely chosen.

Moreover, as even feminist censorship advocates recognize, the practical impact of their approach would not be to prevent the production of sexually explicit expression altogether, but rather simply to drive that production underground. In consequence, the women who participate in producing sexually oriented materials would be more subject to exploitation and less amenable to legal protection. The Dworkin-MacKinnon approach also deprives women who pose for sexually explicit works of an important tool for guarding their economic and other interests because it deems women incompetent to enter into legally binding contracts regarding the production of such works.

In contrast, under a non-censorship regime, individual women, or organized groups of women, could seek improved compensation and other working conditions, to protect their health, safety, and welfare, through contractual negotiations. Additionally, governmental regulation could provide these protections for sex industry workers.

For the foregoing reasons, it is not surprising that virtually all of the organized workers in sex trades have opposed schemes to censor "pornography." It is also not surprising that sex industry workers widely perceive the feminist anti-"pornography" movement as censuring their occupational choices and undermining their interests both in making such choices and in improving their terms and conditions of employment. As stated by Dr. Leonore Tiefer, a professor of psychology who specializes in clinical and research work on sexuality: "These women have appealed to feminists for support, not rejection. . . . Sex industry workers, like all women, are striving for economic survival and a decent life, and if feminism means anything it means sisterhood and solidarity with these women."

## G. Censorship Would Harm Women's Efforts to Develop Their Own Sexuality

As each successive wave of the women's movement has recognized, sexual liberation is an essential aspect of what has been called "women's liberation." Feminist law professor Carlin Meyer explains that the Dworkin-MacKinnon analysis strongly supports the conclusion that gender equality and sexual freedom are closely interconnected:

> If [feminist advocates of censoring "pornography"] are right that sex is central to patriarchal control of women, then freedom to explore it is crucial to women's ability to achieve change. Precisely to the extent that sexuality has historically been a crucial site of repression and oppression for women, it is critically important to women's liberation.

Conversely, throughout history, opponents of women's rights have sought to limit the production and dissemination of information about women's sexuality. By censoring sexually explicit words and imagery, the Dworkin-MacKinnon movement shores up the efforts of its right-wing allies to deprive women of information important to developing their own sense of sexual and gender-role identity. On an even more basic level, such censorship schemes would deprive women of vital information concerning sexuality and health. Accordingly, feminist anthropologist Carole Vance predicted that if the Pornography Victims' Compensation Act were adopted, conservatives would utilize it to target sexuality educators, sexologists, and HIV/AIDS educators.

Dr. Leonore Tiefer, who believes that "women are in more danger from the repression of sexually explicit materials than from their expression," grounds that conclusion in large part on the fact that such materials are especially important for women's "struggl[e] to develop their own sexualities. . . ." She explains:

> We need the freedom for new female sexual visions to inspire our minds and practices away from the ruts worn by centuries of religious inhibition, fear of pregnancy and disease, compulsory heterosexuality, lies and ignorance of all kinds.
>
> . . . Female sexuality is a joke without freely available information and ideas.

Censoring "pornography" would also stultify discussions and explorations of female sexuality by women, including by female artists. As one woman artist stated: "Censorship can only accentuate the taboos that already surround women's open exploration of their sexuality. There are too many other obstacles now in place to women becoming artists or writers, or even speaking out publicly, without inviting the judicial control of censorship."

## H. Censorship Would Strengthen the Religious Right, Whose Patriarchal Agenda Would Curtail Women's Rights

. . . [T]he traditional, right-wing groups that have exercised much political power since 1980 have lent that strength to the feminist pro-censorship faction by using its rhetoric in an attempt to justify various censorship measures. The feminist and right-wing advocates of censoring "pornography" have a symbiotic relationship. Thus, just as the right-wing activists have reinforced the influence of the pro-censorship feminists, so too, the pro-censorship feminists have strengthened the political power of the religious right.

History teaches that such a symbiotic relationship between those who view themselves as social reformers and those with more traditional values redounds to the reformers' disadvantage. Professor Walter Kendrick concludes his powerful study of "pornography" in modern culture with the following lament about the failure of current feminist censorship advocates to heed these historical lessons:

> The most dismaying aspect of the feminist anti-pornography campaign is its exact resemblance to every such effort that preceded it, from . . . that of Comstock and all the Societies for the Suppression of Vice, to the modern vigilantism of Leagues and Legions of Decency. . . . If the twisted history of "pornography" shows nothing else, it shows that forgetfulness of history is the chief weapon in the armory of those who would forbid us to see and know.

The Dworkin-MacKinnon faction has ignored the specific lesson from this history: that when women's rights advocates form alliances with conservatives over such issues as "pornography" or "temperance," they promote the conservatives' anti-feminist goals, relegating women to traditional sexual and gender roles. Feminist historian Judith Walkowitz drew this conclusion. She wrote an award-winning book about such a misalliance between feminists and traditionalists in late nineteenth century England, when both groups sought to protect young girls from prostitution. Warning contemporary feminists to be wary of repeating their foremothers' mistakes, Walkowitz stressed that the earlier feminists' "efforts were ultimately taken over by a repressive coalition that passed sweeping sexual legislation that repressed women. That provides a lesson for politics today."

. . .

## I. By Undermining Free Speech, Censorship Would Deprive Feminists of a Powerful Tool for Advancing Women's Equality

Because free speech is a powerful tool for advancing women's equality, and because censorship consistently has been used to undermine women's rights, advocates of such rights have far more to lose than to gain from any censorship scheme. For example, free speech has proven to be an effective ally even of feminism's anti-"pornography" faction; they and others have successfully used "pornography" itself, as well as other expression, to counter misogynistic attitudes.

### 1. Anti-"Pornography" Movement's Use of "Pornography"

. . . [O]ne positive impact of free speech in the women's rights context . . . [is] the fact that anti-"pornography" activists have effectively utilized their free speech rights—including, specifically, the right to display "pornography"—to galvanize public concern about the ongoing problems of anti-female discrimination and violence, and to heighten public awareness that some sexually oriented expression may convey misogynistic messages. To the extent that censorship would make such images less visible, the protest against sexism would be weakened. . . .

### 2. Effect of Debriefings in Laboratory Studies Regarding the Impact of Exposure to "Pornography"

The social science studies as to whether there is any causal connection between exposure to "pornography" and the commission of actual violence against real women demonstrate another positive impact of free speech protection specifically for "pornography." Extensive and widely cited experiments by Edward Donnerstein and other researchers involved intensively exposing male college students to violent, misogynistic, sexually oriented films, depicting women as welcoming rape. Shortly after this concentrated exposure, the experimental subjects temporarily revealed attitudinal changes that made them more receptive to adverse stereotyping of women, including the "rape myth" that women really want to be raped. However, when the researchers followed the massive exposure to these violent,

misogynistic films with debriefing sessions in which the college men were exposed to materials dispelling the rape myth, the net impact of their exposure to the full range of expression (both the violent, misogynistic films and the pro-feminist material) was striking—the college men had more positive, less discriminatory, and less stereotyped attitudes toward women than they had before the experiment. Moreover, the combined exposure to misogynistic and feminist materials reduced negative attitudes even more effectively than exposure to the latter alone.

The efficacy of "counterspeech" to mitigate the temporary attitudinal impact of exposure to violent "pornography" has been demonstrated by several studies. In fact, the Surgeon General's Report that was specifically requested by the Meese Pornography Commission recognized that such educational strategies could effectively counteract any negative attitudinal impact that viewing violent "pornography" might temporarily have.

The foregoing experience in the "pornography" context is completely consistent with a central tenet of U.S. free speech jurisprudence: that the appropriate antidote to speech with which we disagree, or which offends us, is more speech. Consistent with this general premise and with his own experimental findings, Professor Donnerstein has concluded, "Censorship [of "pornography"] is not the solution. Education, however, is a viable alternative."

### 3. Free Speech Consistently Has Been an Important Ally of the Women's Rights Movement; Censorship Consistently Has Been Its Enemy

There is a broader reason why free speech is especially precious to feminists: . . . feminists, like all who seek social change and equality, are especially dependent on free expression. Conversely, those who seek to repress women's rights consistently have used censorship as their tool. This has been true from the nineteenth-century Comstock Act, which banned the distribution of information about birth control, to the recently revoked "gag rule," which banned the dissemination of information about abortion at federally funded family planning clinics.

Significantly, these censorship efforts often have linked the suppression of sexually oriented material with the suppression of material important to women's rights—namely, information regarding women's health and reproductive freedom. For example, the Comstock Act banned both sexually oriented material and material related to contraception or abortion. Accordingly, the writings of feminist and birth control advocate Margaret Sanger were banned under that law as "obscene." Sanger's campaign to convey accurate sexual information began in 1912 with two articles in a New York City newspaper. The first, entitled "What Every Mother Should Know," ran without incident, but the Post Office barred the second, "What Every Girl Should Know." It contained no information on birth control, but postal officials were offended by Margaret Sanger's explanation of venereal disease and her use of words such as "gonorrhea" and "syphilis." Consequently, the newspaper's next issue contained the following announcement: "What Every Girl Should Know: 'NOTHING! By order of the Post Office Department.'"

The use of censorship laws aimed at sexually explicit expression to stifle information about women's sexuality, women's health, and women's reproductive choices has continued to the present day. In addition to the "gag rule's" censorship of accurate information about abortion, frequent targets of censorship efforts include such feminist health guides as *Our Bodies, Our Selves*. . . .

J. Freedom for Sexually Explicit Expression Is an Essential Aspect of Human Freedom; Restricting It Undermines Human Rights More Broadly

What is at issue in the effort to defend freedom for those who choose to create, pose for, or view "pornography" is not only freedom for this particular type of expression, but also freedom of expression in general. Ultimately, though, the stakes are even higher. . . . [S]exual expression is an integral aspect of human freedom more broadly. Accordingly, as [Gary Mongiovi] reminds us, "[a]ttempts to stifle sexual expression are part of a larger agenda directed at the suppression of human freedom and individuality more generally."

Throughout history, down to the present day, the suppression of sexually explicit speech characterizes regimes that repress human rights in general. As writer Pete Hamill commented:

> Recent history teaches us that most tyrannies have a puritanical nature. The sexual restrictions of Stalin's Soviet Union, Hitler's Germany and Mao's China would have gladdened the hearts of those Americans who fear sexual images and literature. Their ironfisted puritanism wasn't motivated by a need to erase sexual inequality. They wanted to smother the personal chaos that can accompany sexual freedom and subordinate it to the granite face of the state. Every tyrant knows that if he can control human sexuality, he can control life.

Like all groups who seek equal rights and freedoms, women and feminists have an especially important stake in securing human rights in general.

Therefore, they should be especially reluctant to hand over to government what history has proven to be an important tool for repressing human rights: the power to censor sexually explicit speech. Given the pro-censorship feminists' powerful critique of the patriarchal nature of government power, it is especially ironic—and tragically misguided—that their censorship scheme would augment that very power.

. . .

CONCLUSION

In light of the numerous adverse effects that censoring "pornography" would have on women's rights and interests, those who advocate such censorship ostensibly on feminist rationales have a heavy burden of proof indeed. The only alleged justification they offer is the claim that censoring "pornography" will reduce violence and discrimination against women. This claim rests on three assumptions, all of which must be established to substantiate the asserted justification: 1) that the effective suppression of "pornography" would significantly reduce exposure to sexist, violent imagery; 2) that censorship would effectively suppress "pornography"; and 3) that exposure to sexist, violent imagery leads to sexist, violent behavior. In fact, each of these assumptions is fatally flawed.

First, given the pervasive presence of sexist, violent imagery in mainstream American culture, most such imagery would remain intact, even if "pornography" could be effectively suppressed. Moreover, because the mainstream imagery is viewed by far more people than is "pornography," and because it has the stamp of legitimacy, it has a greater impact on people's attitudes. Therefore, if it is true—as the feminist censorship advocates assert—that exposure to sexist, violent imagery leads to sexist, violent, conduct, such conduct would still be triggered, even if "pornography" could be effectively suppressed.

Second, "pornography" could not be effectively suppressed in any event. As feminist censorship advocates themselves have recognized, any censorship regime would simply drive "pornography" underground, where it might well exercise a more potent influence on its viewers.

For the foregoing reasons, even assuming for the sake of argument that exposure to sexist, violent imagery caused anti-female discrimination and violence, censoring "pornography" would make, at best, an insignificant contribution to reducing these problems. At worst, censorship could actually aggravate these problems, since some evidence indicates that censorship could augment any aggressive responses that some viewers might have to "pornography." The conclusion that the costs of "pornography" censorship outweigh its putative benefits, in terms of women's rights, is reinforced by the lack of evidence to substantiate the alleged causal link between exposure to "pornography" and misogynistic discrimination or violence.

The speculative, attenuated benefits of censoring "pornography," in terms of reducing violence and discrimination against women, are far outweighed by the substantial, demonstrable costs of such a censorship regime in terms of women's rights. Throughout history, to the present day, censorial power has consistently been used to stifle women's sexuality, women's expression, and women's full and equal participation in our society. This pattern characterizes even—indeed, especially—censorial power that is wielded for the alleged purpose of "protecting" women.

As is true for all relatively disempowered groups, women have a special stake in preserving our system of free expression. For those women who find certain "pornographic" imagery troubling, their most effective weapon is to raise their voices and say so. Moreover, as illustrated by the tactics of various feminist anti-"pornography" groups, one essential component of their message is the very "pornographic" imagery they decry. By effectively using such imagery not to promote women's "subordination," but rather, to rally public outrage against misogynistic violence and discrimination, these activists illustrate why feminists should defend freedom of speech even for expression they find abhorrent.

. . .

## Bibliography

*Obscenity and Pornography*

Dworkin, Andrea, *Against the Male Flood: Censorship, Pornography, and Equality*, 8 Harvard Women's Law Journal 1 (1985)

Downs, Donald, *The Attorney General's Commission and the New Politics of Pornography*, 1987 American Bar Foundation Research Journal 641 (1987)

Emerson, Thomas I., *Pornography and the First Amendment: A Reply to Professor MacKinnon*, 3 Yale Law & Policy Review 130 (1985)

Gey, Steven G., *The Apologetics of Suppression*, 86 Michigan law Review 1564 (1988)

Hoffman, Eric, *Feminism, Pornography and the Law*, 133 University of Pennsylvania Law Review 497 (1985)

Kalven, Harry, Jr., *The Metaphysics of the Law of Obscenity*, 1960 Supreme Court Review 1 (1960)

Katz, Al, *Privacy and Pornography: Stanley v. Georgia*, 1969 Supreme Court Review 203 (1969)

Lockhart, William B. & McClure, Robert C., *Censorship of Obscenity: The Developing Constitutional Standards*, 45 Minnesota Law Review 5 (1960)

MacKinnon, Catharine A., *Not a Moral Issue*, 2 Yale Law & Policy Review 321  (1984)

Nahmod, Sheldon H., *Artistic Expression and Aesthetic Theory: The Beautiful, the Sublime and the First Amendment*, 1987 Wisconsin Law Review 221 (1987)

Post, Robert C., *Cultural Heterogeneity and the Law*, 76 California Law Review 297 (1988)

Richards, David A.J., *Free Speech and Obscenity Law: Toward a Moral Theory of the First Amendment*, 123 University of Pennsylvania Law Review 45 (1974)

Schauer, Frederick, *Speech and "Speech"—Obscenity and "Obscenity": An Exercise in the Interpretation of Constitutional Language*, 67 Georgetown Law Journal 899 (1979)

Sherry, Suzanna, *An Essay Concerning Toleration*, 71 Minnesota Law Review 963 (1987)

## F. Hate Speech

The debate over hate speech regulation largely has been framed in the context of race, although it is relevant to gender and the experience of other minorities and outcast groups. The controversy implicates fundamental guarantees of liberty and equality. With values of expressive freedom and equal protection at stake, and generally pitted against each other, the controversy is fueled by powerful concerns and imagery. The debate over racist speech focuses upon a modern reckoning with the nation's racially significant legal and moral legacy. Preceded by the accommodation of slavery at the republic's inception, the defeat of slavery, establishment and maintenance of formal systems of maintaining racial advantage, the prohibition of formal segregation and discrimination, and general preclusion of remedial racial preferences, the racist speech control agenda claims a linkage to two centuries of reckoning with racial injustice. Kenneth L. Karst offers a useful backdrop to the debate by facing considerations of power, perceptions, expectations, and achievement potential. Richard Delgado proposes that hate speech causes real harm to its victims that should provide the basis for a tort action and urges the prioritization of equality interests over the liberty interests of those who would inflict stigmatic harm. Nadine Strossen warns against speech restrictive schemes, especially as they tend to undermine minority interests, and touts the virtues of expressive liberty and education in accounting for equality interests and aims. Donald E. Lively questions the utility and priorities of racist speech management. One significant article, authored by Mari J. Matsuda, is not excerpted because the author denied permission necessary for republication. It is referenced, however, in the bibliography.

Kenneth L. Karst, *Boundaries and Reasons: Freedom of Expression and the Subordination of Groups*, 1990 UNIVERSITY OF ILLINOIS LAW REVIEW 95 (1990)*

Expression is power. By assigning meanings to our experience, expression defines much of our world. In our social order expression draws the boundaries that divide us into groups, with momentous effects on our individual identities. If you doubt the power of expression, ask yourself what meanings come to mind when someone you don't know is identified as black, or gay, or a woman—and then consider where those meanings came from. The freedom of expression is the freedom to contribute to the social definition of other people, and to contribute to our own self-definition as well. For every one of us, then, the freedom of expression holds a promise, but it also carries a threat.

America has always been a nation of many peoples, and throughout our history the most insistent demands for suppression of speech typically have arisen out of clashes at our cultural boundaries. When a subordinated group challenges a dominant community of meaning, those expressions are bound to arouse strong emotions, for they threaten the individual identities of the people who live inside the boundaries of the dominant culture. Yet, when the civil rights movement began, the most influential understanding of the freedom of expression assumed a model of the first amendment that evoked quite a different image: citizens sitting around a table, deliberating and exchanging views with the utmost civility, reasoning together toward the civic truth that would decide public issues.

This model of civic deliberation seems apt for a polity in which virtually all major values are shared and disagreements mainly concern ways and means. If the model has plausibility as a picture of the first amendment's core, surely the reason is that American society has always included communities of this kind, and we have all witnessed civic discussions in the deliberative mode. But any American who reads the newspapers and watches television also knows that a persistent theme in our polity is deep cultural conflict. At the cultural boundaries, expression typically is not deliberative, and often is not civil. . . .

* Reprinted with permission of the *University of Illinois Law Review*. Copyright held by The Board of Trustees of the University of Illinois.

. . . By the time the civil rights movement had run its course, the Supreme Court had made clear that the first amendment reached far beyond the limits of the civic debate mode. More recently, however, some Justices and some commentators have given the mode of civic deliberation new influence by arguing that hate literature—such as group libel or pornography—deserves little or no first amendment protection because, in one way or another, it is not the civic speech of Reason. . . .

A view of the first amendment narrowly focused on the civic speech of Reason can have effects outside the scope of the first amendment, hindering judges from seeing the importance of expressive values in other constitutional claims to liberty and equality. . . .

## I. BOUNDARIES AND REASONS

A. The First Amendment and the Speech of Reason

. . .

If you assume that the freedom of speech is designed for reasoned civic discussion, you may find it easy to conclude that Unreason should be suppressed. And what kinds of expression do we consign to the category of Unreason? Of course: speech that rejects the common sense of what "we all know" (where "we" are those who share the conventional wisdom), and modes of expression (like *Chaplinsky's* intemperate preaching of Jehovah's Witnesses' doctrine) that go against the dominant cultural grain. Ignoring that our own perspectives are perspectives, "we" simply think of them as neutral and abstract Reason.

The civic speech of Reason is a thin layer that has crystallized atop the vast pool of a dominant culture's "cultural unconscious"—the very condition that causes us to treat deviations from "normal discourse" as irresponsible, perverse, irrational. Mostly, we use the speech of Reason to announce and defend choices we have made in a process in which Reason has played a minor role. Mostly, too, we apprehend our culture in ways that have little to do with articulated Reason. . . .

## II. EXPRESSION, SUBORDINATION, AND LIBERATION

A. Labeling and Silencing the Unreasonable Outsider

. . .

Disloyalty and deceit are only two among many kinds of Unreason that outsiders are said to display. Other charges are equally familiar. Their speech is "Political" (self-serving rather than civic-spirited); it is incoherent; it addresses the wrong questions; it is emotional; it appeals not to Reason but to baser elements in our nature. One or another of these charges of Unreason has been fastened on every group denied full participation in American life—typically by way of rationalizing the group's exclusion. In particular, charges like these will be familiar to any reader who is black or female.

The subordination of outsiders and their identification with Unreason are both rooted in fear, and fears come to us early. To be introduced to a culture is to enter a community of meaning. Because the most influential part of anyone's acculturation is founded on interpersonal rituals that are heavily charged with emotion, the meanings we learn become part of our senses of who we are. When we encounter people who have been acculturated to assign different meanings to behavior, our lack of understanding may lead us to mistrust them. Worse, we are likely to project on them the image of the Other, a negative identity that we want to repress in ourselves. Men, to protect their masculine identities, fear the feminine in themselves and seek to repress it. Similarly, whites repress the parts of themselves they see as black; heterosexuals repress the part of themselves that is homosexual—and so on, through the whole catalogue of differences that are socially defined as important.

It is no accident that each of these negative identities is founded on social categories defining a system of dominance and subordination. The internal repression and the external suppression reinforce each other. For example, whites have easily developed a strong attachment to the assumptions underlying white supremacy, and readily fear the loss of identity that may emerge from a reordering of the status of blacks. This is a potent combination: fear of the unknown; fear of our own negative identities; and fear for the loss of position. A challenge from a subordinate group is readily taken as a threat to our very selves.

The means of subordination of black people in America have always included two techniques that lie in the realm of expression: labeling and silencing. Each technique has reinforced the other. From the earliest days of European and American enslavement of Africans, racism and slavery went together as "twin aspects of a general debasement" of black people. By the late eighteenth century, when a growing spirit of egalitarianism necessitated an apology for slavery, the argument was founded on a theory of the innate biological inferiority of blacks. In this view blacks as a group represented not Reason but "innocent nature"; they were called moral children who lacked the capacity for self-determination. If

blacks were to achieve even minimally satisfactory lives, the argument concluded, they needed the benevolent control of whites.

The most extreme version of the racist apology for slavery placed blacks at the margin of humanity, as bestial creatures "utterly devoid of reason." . . .

After slavery had been abolished and after Reconstruction had come and gone, race remained a central signifier of group status and personal identity, in the North as well as the South. Yet it was the Southern system of Jim Crow that drew the color line most sharply. Black people had gained formal citizenship, and yet, as in the time of slavery, the whole system of expression was rigged against them. Their own freedom of expression was severely limited, while Jim Crow gave free circulation to the messages that maintained their subordination. . . .

Today, too, the freedom of expression is closely linked with group status. There is no surprise when a subordinated group's claim to equal citizenship stirs passions within the group and among those who are culturally dominant. Such a claim challenges deeply rooted assumptions about proper roles, and thus touches everyone's sense of self. The personal is political, and vice-versa. The political order strongly influences our modes of personal behavior, our modes of thinking, even our modes of feeling. And the status of various groups in society, which is a matter of power and thus of politics, is strongly influenced by the personal. The subordination of black Americans (or any other group) is crucially affected by the images of the Other tucked away in the heads of the dominant group—and often in the heads of those who are subordinated. Emancipation is not just something that happens in the material world; it also takes place in people's minds. Before the labeling and the silencing end, the images of the Other must be transformed, and the construct of Reason made more inclusive.

## B. Identity and the Expressions of Liberation

A group's escape from subordinate status is accomplished primarily through persuasion: first the persuasion of the group's own members, then the persuasion of others. Usually, in these contexts, we think of persuasion as advocacy, but that kind of expression is only part of the story. At least as important is the expression through which individual members of subordinated groups work out their own self-definition. One meaning of "the personal is political" is that the group can take its place in the community of equal citizens only if millions of its individual members redefine themselves. Every expression of a claim to equal citizenship is, to some extent, self-validating. . . .

For subordinated groups, the aims of liberating expression include not just specific governmental actions but the reacculturation of scores of millions of people. Free expression is at the heart of this process, but the expression we need most lies outside the focus of the civic deliberation model of the first amendment. To create institutions that encourage listening to the narratives of inclusion, we shall have to transcend that model's limits. . . .

To end group subordination, then, we need not a more reasoned public debate but a more inclusive conversation. Given this objective, we should also question the "civic" aspect of the traditional conception of the first amendment's "core." Considering all the ways in which the personal is political, it is artificial to conclude that private speech is less deserving of constitutional protection than is speech directed to questions the Supreme Court has chosen to call "matters of public concern." What sort of focused debate on a specific public issue is of greater public concern than the myriad expressions in unfocused private conversations that will add up to the liberation of women, or blacks, or lesbians and gay men from subordination?

To focus the constitutional freedom of expression on the speech of Reason, in the mode of civic deliberation, makes the freedom almost useless when cultures collide. Usually, it is outsiders who have to invoke the first amendment; the insiders who do the suppressing are sure to say that Reason has nothing to do with the case. In American history, the hand of the censor has always fallen disproportionately on speakers and writers who are members of racial or ethnic or religious minorities. What good is a constitutional protection centered on deliberative Reason for the outsiders whose messages are labeled Unreason and whose methods are not deliberative? The civic debate model's impoverished understanding not only clouds our view of the functions of freedom of expression but also threatens the liberating expression of subordinated groups—including, as we shall now see, women.

## III. THE OBJECTIFICATION OF "WOMAN" AND THE EXPRESSION OF WOMEN

### A. Women, Expression, and the Taming of Nature

Women, too, have worn the label of Unreason ever since the idea of Reason made its appearance in Western thought. Indeed, from the earliest human societies to our own times, Nature has been seen as female, and women have represented Nature, the disorderly earth spirit that men must tame if civilization is to flourish. Men's fear of women has centered on women's sexuality and maternity, which must be conquered and controlled, lest they engulf Reason

and all its works. One explanation for this need is that men have wanted the assurance of offspring: not only assurance that they would have children, but assurance that the children were their own. But that explanation is just one illustration of a larger concern. Men are worried not only about their identity as fathers but about their identity as men. . . .

For a boy to become a man, he must differentiate himself from women—or, more accurately, from the social construct of "woman." The view of woman as dangerous, as needing control, is directly connected to men's need to control the "woman" in themselves. Men define femininity as what they must not be: delicate, timid, passive, receptive, dependent, domesticated. The construct of woman becomes the Other, the abstract image of the negative identity a man must repress. . . .

The labeling that equates women with unreasoning Nature has, of course, taken the form of express written argumentation. But far more important contributions to the labeling of women as objects have been made by other expressive means, and many of those means make little or no use of the printed word. Here, in parallel to the case of racial subordination, the propagation of the traditional construct of woman and the silencing of women's own expression have been closely connected. And, in similar parallel, both the labeling and the silencing have grown out of a pervasive social system interweaving governmental and private action: what Robert Cover, describing the system of Jim Crow, called the "resonance of society and politics.". . .

Boys, after all, still find their gender identity in separation from their mothers; men still reassure themselves about their masculinity by seeking to control the feminine within them. The basic psychic conditions for projecting a man's negative identity on the abstraction, "woman," are as they were before. True, the legal status of women has changed fundamentally. True, too, women's opportunities in the world are greatly increased. Yet it is difficult for any woman, whatever her educational level or career or income, simply to ignore the demands of femininity in its traditional definition. The male reader might try to imagine how it feels to be told every day that, in the eyes of roughly half the people you meet, you are not just yourself, but also the projection of an abstract image of Otherness centered on notions of the sexuality and maternity of "woman." The communications that label you as an object may not be explicit, but they are clear and inescapable. In the media of the popular culture, from women's magazines to pornography, the messages often are explicit. So they are, with regularity, on the street. And what will your answer be when the men whistle?

Are you better able to articulate a reasoned response than the judge was when those demonstrators raised their fists in the courtroom? Labeling and silencing go together. . . .

C. The Literatures of Hate and the Speech of Reason

From the earliest times, Anglo-American law has recognized the power of words to hurt people. Even in a time of expanded first amendment protections, much of the law of defamation remains secure against constitutional attack. For two decades after Justice Murphy casually located libel outside the bounds of protected speech, the Court gave no hint that it might depart from that dictum. Indeed, in *Beauharnais v. Illinois* the Court upheld a criminal conviction for distributing a racist leaflet that portrayed, as the state law put it, depravity, criminality, unchastity, or lack of virtue of a class of citizens, of any race, color, creed or religion which said publication exposes [such citizens] to contempt, derision, or obloquy. . . .

Today the value of the *Beauharnais* decision as a precedent is extremely doubtful. Yet if defamatory words can hurt individuals, it seems plain—especially now that the civil rights era has heightened our awareness of the harms of stigma—that the defamation of a racial or religious group can hurt the group's members. In an era that takes *Brown v. Board of Education* for granted, it is no surprise that some writers have argued for reviving group libel laws, and defended their constitutionality on communitarian grounds.

These arguments have come mainly from the academy, and have not yet been translated into a mobilized political movement. In contrast, another kind of hate literature is under vigorous political attack in legislative halls across the country. Some feminists, viewing pornography as a central cause of the subordination of women, have proposed a legislative response. A model ordinance authored by Catharine MacKinnon and Andrea Dworkin would provide civil remedies against the production and distribution of pornography, the coercion of actors and models into performing for the producers of pornography, and the forcing of pornography on unwilling viewers. This ordinance barely failed to secure passage in Minneapolis, but a modified version was adopted in Indianapolis. The lower federal courts promptly held the ordinance unconstitutional, and the Supreme Court affirmed that decision summarily, without opinion.

The leading feminist proponents of antipornography legislation see pornography not as a side effect of the sexualization of women's subordination but as the central means by which women's sexuality is socially constructed—and thus the central cause of

their silencing and subordination. Thus, they argue, pornography falls outside the first amendment's protection because it is not an idea but a "practice" of subordination, "the essence of a sexist social order, its quintessential social act."

If this argument fails as a justification for censorship, it is a grand failure, one that illuminates a large and vitally important area of human interaction. Several of the argument's insights are indispensable to any serious effort to end the subordination of women: that sexuality is a social construct; that the construct is formed by the interaction of speech and other expressive conduct; that stigma—the association of women's sexuality with their subordination—is a group harm that deserves both recognition and remedy; and that women's control over their own sexuality and maternity is crucial to their liberation from group subordination. . . .

Group libel and pornography each respond to a sense of inadequacy, but the two types of hate literature are circulated differently. Where the defamation of racial or religious groups is driven by the felt inadequacies of its distributors, today's pornography is largely driven by the inadequacies of its consumers, with most distributors simply profiting from that demand and seeking to increase it. In neither case will the elimination of the literature cause the underlying sense of inadequacy to disappear. Anxious hatemongers, thwarted in purveying their racist leaflets, can find plenty of other ways to express their fear and hate, as the Ku Klux Klan and the Nazis have made clear. And anxious men, thwarted in the consumption of pornography, can find substitute symbols of sexual objectification not just in magazine ads or on television but in every woman they see.

Although the politics of antipornography laws and of group libel laws diverge sharply, the two kinds of laws pose several common problems under existing first amendment doctrine. In both, for example, the definitions of the regulated categories of speech inevitably raise difficult issues of vagueness and overbreadth. Even more serious, under conventional doctrine, is the objection that both kinds of law effectively censor the content (even the viewpoints) of messages in areas of public interest. Some defenders of the constitutionality of both group libel and antipornography laws have sought to respond to this latter concern by defining their way out of the problem. These commentators argue either that the expression in question is not "speech" within the first amendment's protection or that it amounts to low value speech that can be regulated on lesser justifications than would be required for regulations of speech within the amendment's "core." Central to these arguments is Justice Murphy's understanding of the first amendment as centered on the reasoned deliberation of citizens in search of truth about matters clearly defined as public issues.

Perhaps, when Justice Murphy issued his *Chaplinsky* catalogue of types of unprotected speech, he thought he was trading away some possible applications of the first amendment in order to preserve a strong form of the freedom of expression in civic debate. It is even more likely that Justice Brennan had this strategy in mind when in 1957 he defined obscenity outside the scope of the first amendment. If he assumed that the courts would allow some regulation of literature in the name of preserving public morals, the strategy was plausible. Isolating obscenity would protect the civic speech of Reason from the corrosive effects on first amendment doctrine of decisions upholding morals regulation. We have no reason to believe that this maneuver has fostered the expression of historically subordinated groups. But for women and for the members of racial and ethnic minorities a first amendment doctrine that offers less protection to "low value" speech is not just unhelpful; it is dangerous.

For minority groups, surely Murphy's dictum will play out in a corollary to Murphy's Law: suppressions that *can* happen *will* happen. Dissenting in *Beauharnais v. Illinois,* Justice William O. Douglas made this gloomy prophecy:

> Today a white man stands convicted for protesting in unseemly language against our decisions invalidating restrictive covenants. Tomorrow a negro will be hailed before a court for denouncing lynch law in heated terms. Farm laborers in the West who compete with field hands drifting up from Mexico; whites who feel the pressure of orientals; a minority which finds employment going to members of the dominant religious group—all of these are caught in the mesh of today's decision.

Justice Hugo Black, dissenting in the same case, ended on the same note:

> If there be minority groups who hail this holding as their victory, they might consider the possible relevancy of this ancient remark: "Another such victory and I am undone."

No lawyer who has lived through the decades since the *Beauharnais* decision can read these warnings without recognizing their striking relevance to a wide range of cases in which minority groups have invoked the first amendment against efforts to suppress messages and methods that the dominant majority labeled as Unreason.

No doubt the state can constitutionally punish those who coerce actors and models into participating in the production of pornography, and at least some who force pornography on unwilling consumers. But women who are claiming their equal citizenship should think twice about pressing the argument that pornography is not protected speech, or that it is "low value" speech because it is not "cognitive," not the speech of Reason. Calling sexual imagery low value speech perfectly suits a strategy aimed at getting women out of the workplace and back into the traditional roles of housewife and mother—that is, under male protection. Such a strategy is already a central part of the agenda of the New Right, which has trained its impressive political weaponry on sex education, the dissemination of information about birth control and abortion, and the explicit treatment of sexuality in the media.

Surely, as antipornography laws proliferate, some of the primary targets for censorship by injunction will be feminist sexual imagery: writing and films created by women artists, offering new and egalitarian visions of sexuality, and aimed at ending the "social context of ignorance and shame" that male-oriented pornography needs if it is to thrive. Some of these forms of expression would be called pornographic, not just by the New Right or by antipornography feminists, but by the feminist writers and filmmakers who produce them. Carefully examining the statements of such artists, Robin West makes the unassailable point that this "good pornography" seeks to transform our understanding of sexual difference and sexual relations. By changing people's views of the world, these artists aim to undermine the institutions (notably, institutions forcing "the family" into the New Right's restrictive definition) that deny or confine women's sexuality.

Such a transformation would recognize what Ann Snitow aptly calls the "frightening malleability of gender," and would recognize women as sexual actors, not passive victims. Furthermore, as West points out, these artists can count on the female half of their audience to see their work from a perspective that is not male-centered: "Women who consume pornography see (and seek) *ideas* in pornography, even if men do not." This line of argument reduces to rubble the notion that pornography is "noncognitive." It also illustrates how the bounds of Reason—defined, as always, by the dominant group's conventional wisdom—can be expanded when an "outsider" gets to offer her own meanings, to create her own definitions.

D. Listening Beyond the Pale

. . .

The central concern of the civic deliberation model of the first amendment is the speech of Reason in public debate; in this model judicial attention focuses on ideas, not speakers. The "citizen as ruler," deliberating toward civic truth, needs access to a free marketplace of ideas. When Alexander Meiklejohn looked at the marketplace, he saw not the sellers but their wares: "What is essential [in the town meeting] is not that everyone shall speak, but that everything worth saying shall be said." When we consider the uses of expression in reaching a more inclusive definition of the community of equal citizens, this vision of the first amendment seems much too narrow. A theory of free speech limiting its conception of "ideas" to the civic speech of Reason will be of little help when the purpose of expression is to reach the fears that underlie group subordination. To be a "citizen as ruler," first you must be a citizen, a full member of the polity. The metaphor of the marketplace is a distraction unless we remember how important it is to assure not only that every idea be heard but that everyone have a booth. The problem of listening to people we have labeled as the Other is not so much freedom for "opinions that we loathe" as freedom for the groups that we fear. To cross the boundaries policed by fear, we need to develop the common language that grows out of doing things together, to build on shared understandings that may or may not have originated in the dominant group's version of Reason.

Whatever else a community may be, it includes the mutual communication among its members that they accept each other as people who belong. A strong freedom of expression is not an impediment to the integration of a multicultural nation. Rather it is essential, not just for the proper settlement of public issues, not just for the tolerance of hateful ideas, but for the day-to-day, one-to-one personal interchanges on which the sense of belonging to a national community ultimately depends. Undeniably, expression is power. But it is a mistake to think of power only as domination. Power is also capacity. The power of expression includes the capacity to expand the boundaries of our national community.

---

Charles R. Lawrence III, *If He Hollers Let Him Go: Regulating Racist Speech on Campus*, 1990 DUKE LAW JOURNAL 431 (1990)*

. . .

## INTRODUCTION

. . .

The "double consciousness" of groups outside the

ethnic mainstream is particularly apparent in the context of this controversy. Blacks know and value the protection the first amendment affords those of us who must rely upon our voices to petition both government and our neighbors for redress of grievances. Our political tradition has looked to "the word," to the moral power of ideas, to change a system when neither the power of the vote nor that of the gun are available. This part of us has known the experience of belonging and recognizes our common and inseparable interest in preserving the right of free speech for all. But we also know the experience of the outsider. The Framers excluded us from the protection of the first amendment. The same Constitution that established rights for others endorsed a story that proclaimed our inferiority. It is a story that remains deeply ingrained in the American psyche. . . .

. . . I fear that by framing the debate as we have—as one in which the liberty of free speech is in conflict with the elimination of racism—we have advanced the cause of racial oppression and have placed the bigot on the moral high ground, fanning the rising flames of racism. Above all, I am troubled that we have not listened to the real victims, that we have shown so little empathy or understanding for their injury, and that we have abandoned those individuals whose race, gender, or sexual orientation provokes others to regard them as second class citizens. These individuals' civil liberties are most directly at stake in the debate. . . .

## I. BROWN v. BOARD OF EDUCATION: A CASE ABOUT REGULATING RACIST SPEECH

The landmark case of *Brown v. Board of Education* is not a case we normally think of as a case about speech. As read most narrowly, the case is about the rights of black children to equal educational opportunity. But *Brown* can also read more broadly to articulate a principle central to any substantive understanding of the equal protection clause, the foundation on which all anti-discrimination law rests. This is the principle of equal citizenship. Under that principle "every individual is presumptively entitled to be treated by the organized society as a respected, responsible, and participating member." Furthermore, it requires the affirmative disestablishment of societal practices that treat people as members of an inferior or dependent caste, as unworthy to participate in the larger community. The holding in *Brown*—that racially segregated schools violate the equal protection clause—reflects the fact that segregation amounts to a demeaning, caste-creating practice.

The key to this understanding of *Brown* is that

the practice of segregation, the practice the Court held inherently unconstitutional, was *speech. Brown* held that segregation is unconstitutional not simply because the physical separation of black and white children is bad or because resources were distributed unequally among black and white schools. *Brown* held that segregated schools were unconstitutional primarily because of the *message* segregation conveys—the message that black children are an untouchable caste, unfit to be educated with white children. Segregation serves its purpose by conveying an idea. It stamps a badge of inferiority upon blacks, and this badge communicates a message to others in the community, as well as to blacks wearing the badge, that is injurious to blacks. Therefore, *Brown* may be read as regulating the content of racist speech. As a regulation of racist speech, the decision is an exception to the usual rule that regulation of speech content is presumed unconstitutional. . . .

A. The Conduct/Speech Distinction

Some civil libertarians argue that my analysis of *Brown* conflates speech and conduct. They maintain that the segregation outlawed in *Brown* was discriminatory conduct, not speech, and the defamatory message conveyed by segregation simply was an incidental by-product of that conduct. This position is often stated as follows: "Of course segregation conveys a message but this could be said of almost all conduct. To take an extreme example, a murderer conveys a message of hatred for his victim. [But], we would not argue that we can't punish the murder—the primary conduct—merely because of this message which is its secondary by-product. This objection to my reading of *Brown* misperceives the central point of the argument. I have not ignored the distinction between the speech and conduct elements of segregation by mistake. Rather, my analysis turns on that distinction. It asks the question whether there is a purpose for outlawing segregation that is unrelated to its message, and it concludes the answer is "no."

If, for example, John W. Davis, counsel for the Board of Education of Topeka, Kansas, had been asked during oral argument in *Brown* to state the Board's purpose in educating black and white children in separate schools, he would have been hard pressed to answer in a way unrelated to the purpose of designating black children as inferior. If segregation's primary goal is to convey the message of white supremacy, then *Brown*'s declaration that segregation is unconstitutional amounts to a regulation of the message of white supremacy. Properly understood, *Brown* and its progeny require that the systematic group defamation of segregation be disestablished.

Although the exclusion of black children from white schools and the denial of educational resources and association that accompany exclusion can be characterized as conduct, these particular instances of conduct are concerned primarily with communicating the idea of white supremacy. The non-speech elements are by-products of the main message rather than the message simply a by-product of unlawful conduct.

The public accommodations provisions of the Civil Rights Act of 1964 provide another example illuminating why laws against discrimination are also regulation of racist speech. The legislative history and the Supreme Court's opinions upholding the Act establish that congress was concerned that blacks have access to public accommodations to eliminate impediments to the free flow of interstate commerce, but this purpose could have been achieved through a regime of separate-but-equal accommodations. Title II goes further; it incorporates the principle of the inherent inequality of segregation, and prohibits restaurant owners from providing separate places at the lunch counter for "whites" and "coloreds." Even if the same food and the same service are provided, separate-but-equal facilities are unlawful. If the signs indicating separate facilities remain in place, then the statute is violated despite proof that restaurant patrons are free to disregard the signs. Outlawing these signs graphically illustrates my point that anti-discrimination laws are primarily regulations of the content of racist speech.

Another way to understand the inseparability of racist speech and discriminatory conduct is to view individual racist acts as part of a totality. When viewed in this manner, white supremacists' conduct or speech is forbidden by the equal protection clause. The goal of white supremacy is not achieved by individual acts or even by the cumulative acts of a group, but rather it is achieved by the institutionalization of the ideas of white supremacy. The institutionalization of white supremacy within our culture has created conduct on the societal level that is greater than the sum of individual racist acts. The racist acts of millions of individuals are mutually reinforcing and cumulative because the status quo of institutionalized white supremacy remains long after deliberate racist actions subside.

It is difficult to recognize the institutional significance of white supremacy or how it *acts* to harm, partially because of its ubiquity. We simply do not see most racist conduct because we experience a world in which whites are supreme as simply "the world." Much racist conduct is considered unrelated to race or regarded as neutral because racist conduct maintains the status quo, the status quo of the world as we have known it. Catharine MacKinnon has observed that "to the extent that pornography succeeds in constructing social reality, it becomes invisible as harm." Thus, pornography "is more act-like than thought-like." This truth about gender discrimination is equally true of racism.

Just because one can express the idea of message embodied by a practice such as white supremacy does not necessarily equate that practice with the idea. Slavery was an idea as well as a practice, but the Court recognized the inseparability of idea and practice in the institution of slavery when it held the enabling clause of the thirteenth amendment clothed Congress with the power to pass "all laws necessary and proper for abolishing all badges and incidents of slavery in the United States." This understanding also informs the regulation of speech/conduct in the public accommodations provisions of the Civil Rights Act of 1964 discussed above. When the racist restaurant or hotel owner puts a "whites only" sign in his window, his sign is more than speech. Putting up the sign is more than an act excluding black patrons who see the sign. The sign is part of the larger practice of segregation and white supremacy that constructs and maintains a culture in which non-whites are excluded from full citizenship. The inseparability of the idea and practice of racism is central to *Brown's* holding that segregation is inherently unconstitutional.

Racism is both 100% speech and 100% conduct. Discriminatory conduct is not racist unless it also conveys the message of white supremacy—unless it is interpreted within the culture to advance the structure and ideology of white supremacy. Likewise, all racist speech constructs the social reality that constrains the liberty of non-whites because of their race. By limiting the life opportunities of others, this act of constructing meaning also makes racist speech conduct.

## B. The Public/Private Distinction

There are critics who would contend that *Brown* is inapposite because the equal protection clause only restricts government behavior, whereas the first amendment protects the speech of private persons. They say, "Of course we want to prevent the state from defaming blacks, but we must continue to be vigilant about protecting the speech fights, even of racist individuals, from the government. In both cases our concern must be protecting the individual from the unjust power of the state."

At first blush, this position seems persuasive, but its persuasiveness relies upon the mystifying properties of constitutional ideology. In particular, I refer to the state action doctrine. By restricting the application of the fourteenth amendment to discrimination implicating the government, the state action rule immunizes private discriminators from constitutional scrutiny. In so doing, it leaves untouched the largest part of the vast system of segregation in the United States. The *Civil Rights Cases*, in which this doctrine was firmly established, stands as a monument preserving American racial discrimination. Although the origin of state action is textual, countervailing values of privacy, freedom of association, and free speech all have been used to justify the rule's exculpation of private racism.

In the abstract, the right to make decisions about how we will educate our children or with whom we will associate is an important value in American society. But when we decontextualize by viewing this privacy value in the abstract, we ignore the way it operates in the real world. We do not ask ourselves, for example, whether it is a value to which all persons have equal access. And we do not inquire about who has the resources to send their children to private school or move to an exclusive suburb. The privacy value, when presented as an ideal, seems an appropriate limitation on racial justice because we naively believe that everyone has an equal stake in this value.

The argument that distinguishes private racist speech from the government speech outlawed by *Brown* suffers from the same decontextualizing ideology. If the government is involved in a joint venture with private contractors to engage in the business of defaming blacks, should it be able to escape the constitutional mandate that makes that business illegal simply by handing over the copyright and the printing presses to its partners in crime? I think not. And yet this is the essence of the position that espouses first amendment protection for those partners.

In an insightful article considering the constitutional implications of government regulation of pornography, Frank Michelman has observed that the idea of state action plays a crucial, if unspoken, role for judges and civil libertarians who favor an absolute rule against government regulation of private pornographic publications (or racist speech), even when that expression is causative "of effects fairly describable . . . as deprivations of liberty and denials of equal protection of the laws." He notes that judges and civil libertarians would not balance the evils of private subversions of liberty and equal protection against the evils of government censorship because "the Constitution, through the state action doctrine, in effect tells them not to. Michelman suggests that the state action doctrine, by directing us to the text of the fourteenth amendment, diverts our attention from the underlying issue whether we should balance the evils of private deprivations of liberty against the government deprivations of liberty that may arise out of state regulations designed to avert those private deprivations.

When a person responds to the argument that *Brown* mandates the abolition of racist speech by reciting the state action doctrine, she fails to consider that the alternative to regulating racist speech is infringement of the claims of blacks to liberty and equal protection. The best way to constitutionally protect these competing interests is to balance them directly. To invoke the state action doctrine is to circumvent our value judgment as to how these competing interests should be balanced.

The deference usually given to the first amendment values in this balance is justified using the argument that racist speech is unpopular speech, that, like the speech of civil rights activists, pacifists, and religious and political dissenters, it is in need of special protection from majoritarian censorship. But for over three hundred years, racist speech has been the liturgy of America's leading established religion, the religion of racism. Racist speech remains a vital and regrettably popular characteristic of the American vernacular. It must be noted that there has not yet been satisfactory retraction of the government-sponsored defamation in the slavery clauses, the Dred Scott decision, the black codes, the segregation statutes, and countless other group libels. The injury to blacks is hardly redressed by deciding the government must no longer injure our reputation if one then invokes the first amendment to ensure that racist speech continues to thrive in an unregulated private market. . . .

## II. RACIST SPEECH AS THE FUNCTIONAL EQUIVALENT OF FIGHTING WORDS

. . .

Face-to-face racial insults, like fighting words, are undeserving of first amendment protection for two reasons. The first reason is the immediacy of the injurious impact of racial insults. The experience of being called "nigger," "spic," "Jap," or "kike" is like receiving a slap in the face. The injury is instantaneous. There is neither an opportunity for intermediary reflection on the idea conveyed nor an opportunity for responsive speech. The harm to be avoided is both clear and present. The second reason that racial insults should not fall under protected speech relates to the purpose underlying the first amendment. If the purpose of the first amendment

is to foster the greatest amount of speech, then racial insults disserve that purpose. Assaultive racist speech functions as a preemptive strike. The racial invective is experienced as a blow, not a proffered idea, and once the blow is struck, it is unlikely that dialogue will follow. Racial insults are undeserving of first amendment protection because the perpetrator's intention is not to discover truth or initiate dialogue but to injure the victim.

The fighting words doctrine anticipates that the verbal "slap in the face" of insulting words will provoke a violent response with a resulting breach of the peace. When racial insults are hurled at minorities, the response may be silence or flight rather than a fight, but the preemptive effect on further speech is just as complete as with fighting words. Women and minorities often report that they find themselves speechless in the face of discriminatory verbal attacks. This inability to respond is not the result of oversensitivity among these groups, as some individuals who oppose protective regulation have argued. Rather, it is the product of several factors, all of which reveal the non-speech character of the initial preemptive verbal assault. The first factor is that the visceral emotional response to personal attack precludes speech. Attack produces an instinctive, defensive psychological reaction. Fear, rage, shock, and flight all interfere with any reasoned response. Words like "nigger," "kike," and "faggot" produce physical symptoms that temporarily disable the victim, and the perpetrators often use these words with the intention or producing this effect. Many victims do not find words of response until well after the assault when the cowardly assaulter has departed.

A second factor that distinguishes racial insults from protected speech is the preemptive nature of such insults—the words by which to respond to such verbal attacks may never be forthcoming because speech is usually an inadequate response. When one is personally attacked with words that denote one's subhuman status and untouchability, there is little (if anything) that can be said to redress either the emotional or reputational injury. This is particularly true when the message and meaning of the epithet resonates with beliefs widely held in society. This preservation of widespread beliefs is what makes the face-to-face racial attack more likely to preempt speech than are other fighting words. The racist name-caller is accompanied by a cultural chorus of equally demeaning speech and symbols. . . .

One of my students, a white, gay male, related an experience that is quite instructive in understanding the inadequacy and potential of the "fighting words'' doctrine. In response to my request that students describe how they experienced the injury of racist speech, Michael told a story of being called "faggot" by a man on a subway. His description included all of the speech inhibiting elements I have noted previously. He found himself in a state of semi-shock, nauseous, dizzy, unable to muster the witty, sarcastic, articulate rejoinder he was accustomed to making. He suddenly was aware of the recent spate of gay-bashing in San Francisco, and how many of these had escalated from verbal encounters. Even hours later when the shock resided and his facility with words returned, he realized that any response was inadequate to counter the hundreds of years of societal defamation that one word—"faggot"—carried with it. Like the word "nigger" and unlike the word "liar," it is not sufficient to deny the truth of the word's application, to say, "I am not a faggot." One must deny the truth of the word's meaning, a meaning shouted from the rooftops by the rest of the world a million times a day. Although there are many of us who constantly and in myriad ways seek to counter the lie spoken in the meaning of hateful words like "nigger" and "faggot," it is a nearly impossible burden to bear when one encounters hateful speech face-to-face.

But there was another part of my discussion with Michael that is equally instructive. I asked if he could remember a situation when he had been verbally attacked with reference to his membership in a superordinate group. Had he ever been called a "honkie," a "chauvinist pig," or "mick"? (Michael is from a working class Irish family in Boston.) He said that he had been called some version of all three and that although he found the last one more offensive than the first two, he had not experienced—even in that subordinated role—the same disorienting powerlessness he had experienced when attacked for his membership in the gay community. The question of power, of the context of the power relationships within which speech takes place, must be considered as we decide how best to foster the freest and fullest dialogue within our communities. . . .

## III. KNOWING THE INJURY AND STRIKING THE BALANCE: UNDERSTANDING WHAT IS AT STAKE IN RACIST SPEECH CASES

. . .

The argument most commonly advanced against the regulation of racist speech goes something like this: We recognize that minority groups suffer pain and injury as the result of racist speech, but we must allow this hatemongering for the benefit of society as a whole. Freedom of speech is the lifeblood of our democratic system. It is a freedom that enables us to persuade others to our point of view. Free speech is especially important for minorities because often it is their only vehicle for rallying support for redress of their grievances. We cannot allow the public regulation of racist invective and vilification because any prohibition precise enough to prevent racist speech would catch in the same net forms of speech that are central to a democratic society.

Whenever we argue that racist epithets and vilification must be allowed, not because we would condone them ourselves but because of the potential danger that precedent would pose for the speech of all dissenters, we are balancing our concern for the free flow of ideas and the democratic process and our desire to further equality. This kind of categorical balance is struck whenever we frame any rule—even an absolute rule. It is important to be conscious of the nature and extent of injury to both concerns when we engage in this kind of balancing. In this case, we must place on one side of the balance the nature and extent of the injury caused by racism. We also must be very careful, in weighing the potential harm to free speech, to consider whether the racist speech we propose to regulate is advancing or retarding the values of the first amendment.

### A. Understanding the Injury Inflicted by Racist Speech

There can be no meaningful discussion about how to reconcile our commitment to equality and our commitment to free speech until we acknowledge that racist speech inflicts real harm and that this harm is far from trivial. I should state that more strongly: To engage in a debate about the first amendment and racist speech without a full understanding of the nature and extent of the harm of racist speech risks making the first amendment an instrument of domination rather than a vehicle of liberation. Not everyone has known the experience of being victimized by racist, misogynist, and homophobic speech, and we do not share equally the burden of the societal harm it inflicts. Often we are too quick to say we have heard the victims' cries when we have not; we are too eager to assure ourselves we have experienced the same injury, and therefore we can make the constitutional balance without danger of mismeasurement. For many of us who have fought for the rights of oppressed minorities, it is difficult to accept that—by underestimating the injury from racist speech—we too might be implicated in the vicious words we would never utter. Until we have eradicated racism and sexism and no longer share in the fruits of those forms of domination, we cannot justly strike the balance over the protest of those who are dominated. My plea is simply that we listen to the victims. . . .

## C. Asking Victim Groups to Pay the Price

Whenever we decide that racist hate speech must be tolerated because of the importance of tolerating unpopular speech we ask blacks and other subordinated groups to bear a burden for the good of society—to pay the price for the societal benefit of creating more room for speech. And we assign this burden to them without seeking their advice, or consent. This amounts to white domination, pure and simple. It is taxation without representation. We must be careful that the ease with which we strike the balance against the regulation of racist speech is in no way influenced by the fact the cost will be borne by others. We must be certain that the individuals who pay the price are fairly represented in our deliberation, and that they are heard. . . .

Derrick Bell has noted that often in our constitutional history the rights of blacks have been sacrificed because sacrifice was believed necessary to preserve the greater interests of the whole. It is not just the actual sacrifice that is racist but also the way the "whole with the greater interests" gets defined. Today in a world committed to the ideal of equality, we rarely notice the sacrifice or how we have avoided noticing the sacrifice by defining the interests of whites as the whole, "the regular." When we think this way, when we see the potential danger of incursions on the first amendment but do not see existing incursions on the fourteenth amendment, our perceptions have been influenced by an entire belief system that makes us less sensitive to the injury experienced by non-whites. Unaware, we have adopted a world view that takes for granted black sacrifice. . . .

## IV. "WHICH SIDE ARE (WE) ON?"

However one comes out on the question of whether racist hate speech should be artificially distinguished from other fighting words and given first amendment protection, it is important to examine and take responsibility for the effects of how one participates in the debate. It is important to consider how our voice is heard. We must ask ourselves whether, in our well-placed passion for preserving our first amendment freedoms, we have been forceful enough in our personal condemnation of ideas we abhor, whether we have neglected our alliances with victims of the oppressive manifestations of the continuing dominance of these ideas within our communities and within ourselves.

At the core of the argument that we should resist all government regulation of speech is the ideal that the best cure for bad speech is good speech, and ideas that affirm equality and the worth of all individuals ultimately will prevail over racism, sexism, homophobia, and anti-semitism because they are better ideas. This is an empty ideal—one that invites those injured or appalled by hate-speech to call for restrictions on speech—unless those of us who fight racism are vigilant and unequivocal in that fight.

There is much about the way many civil libertarians have participated in the debate over the regulation of racist speech that causes the victims of that speech to wonder which side they are on. Those who raise their voices in protest against public sanctions of racist speech have not organized private protests against the voices of racism. It has been people of color, women, and gays who have held vigils at offending fraternity houses, staged candlelight marches, counter-demonstrations and distributed flyers calling upon their classmates and colleagues to express their outrage at pervasive racism, sexism, and homophobia in their midst and to show their solidarity with its victims.

Traditional civil libertarians have been conspicuous largely in their absence from these group expressions of condemnation. Their failure to participate in this marketplace response to speech with more speech is often justified, paradoxically, as concern for the principle of free speech. When racial minorities or other victims of hate speech hold counter-demonstrations or engage in picketing, leafletting, heckling, or booing of racist speakers, civil libertarians often accuse them of private censorship, of seeking to silence opposing points of view. When both public and private responses to racist speech are rejected by first amendment absolutists as contrary to the principle of free speech, it is no wonder that the victims of racism do not consider them allies. . . .

There is also a propensity among some civil libertarians to minimalize the injury to the victims of racist speech and distance themselves from it by characterizing individual acts of racial harassment as aberrations, as isolated incidents in a community that is otherwise free of racism. When those persons who argue against the regulation of racist speech speak of silencing a few creeps" or argue that "the harm that censors allege will result unless speech is forbidden rarely occurs," they demonstrate an unwillingness even to acknowledge the injury. Moreover, they disclaim any responsibility for its occurrence. . . .

When the ACLU enters the debate by challenging the University of Michigan's efforts to provide a safe harbor for its black, hispanic, and Asian students (a climate that a colleague of mine compared unfavorably with Mississippi in the 1960s), we should not be surprised that non-white students feel abandoned. When we respond to Stanford students' pleas for protection by accusing them of seeking to silence all who disagree with them, we paint the harassing bigot as a martyred defender of democracy. When we valorize bigotry we must assume some responsibility for the fact that bigots are encouraged by their newfound status as "defenders of the faith." We must find ways to engage actively in speech and action that resists and counters the racist ideas the first amendment protects. If we fail in this duty, the victims of hate speech rightly assume we are aligned with their oppressors.

We must also begin to think creatively as lawyers. We must embark upon the development of a first amendment jurisprudence that is grounded in the reality of our history and contemporary experience (particularly the experiences of the victims of oppression). We must eschew abstractions of first amendment theory that proceed without attention to the dysfunction in the marketplace of ideas created by the racism and unequal access to that market. We must think hard about how best to launch legal attacks against the most indefensible forms of hate speech. Good lawyers can create exceptions and narrow interpretations limiting the harm of hate speech without opening the floodgates of censorship. We must weigh carefully and critically the competing constitutional values expressed in the first and fourteenth amendments. . . .

. . . Most importantly, we must continue this discussion. It must be a discussion in which the victims of racist speech are heard. We must be as attentive to the achievement of the constitutional ideal of equality as we are to the ideal of untrammeled expression. There can be no true free speech where there are still masters and slaves.

Richard Delgado, *Campus Antiracism Rules: Constitutional Narratives in Collision*, 85 NORTHWESTERN UNIVERSITY LAW REVIEW 343 (1991)*

. . .

## I. FRAMING THE ISSUE

Persons tend to react to the problem of racial

* Reprinted by special permission of Northwestern University School of Law, Volume 85, Issue 2, *Northwestern University Law Review*, pp. 345–48, 361–63, 364, 365–66, 367–69, 371–72, 374–75, 376, 378–82, 383–86 (1991).

insults in one of two ways. On hearing that a university has enacted rules forbidding certain forms of speech, some will frame the issue as a first amendment problem: the rules limit speech, and the constitution forbids official regulation of speech without a very good reason. If one takes that starting point, several consequences follow. First, the burden shifts to the other side to show that the interest in protecting members of the campus community from insults and name-calling is compelling enough to overcome the presumption in favor of free speech. Further, there must be no less onerous way of accomplishing that objective. Moreover, some will worry whether the enforcer of the regulation will become a censor, imposing narrow-minded restraints on campus discussion. Some will also be concerned about slippery slopes and line-drawing problems: if a campus restricts this type of expression, might the temptation arise to do the same with classroom speech or political satire in the campus newspaper?

Others, however, will frame the problem as one of protection of equality. They will ask whether an educational institution does not have the power, to protect core values emanating from the thirteenth and fourteenth amendments, to enact reasonable regulations aimed at assuring equal personhood on campus. If one characterizes the issue *this* way, other consequences follow. Now, the defenders of racially scathing speech are required to show that the interest in its protection is compelling enough to overcome the preference for equal personhood; and we will want to be sure that this interest is advanced in the way least damaging to equality. There are again concerns about the decisionmaker who will enforce the rules, but from the opposite standpoint: the enforcer of the regulation must be attuned to the nuances of insult and racial supremacy at issue, for example by incorporating multi-ethnic representation into the hearing process. Finally, a different set of slopes will look slippery. If we do *not* intervene to protect equality here, what will the next outrage be?

The legal analysis, therefore, leads to opposite conclusions depending on the starting point. But there is an even deeper indeterminacy: both sides invoke different narratives to rally support. Protectors of the first amendment see campus antiracism rules as parts of a much longer story: the centuries-old struggle of Western society to free itself from superstition and enforced ignorance. The tellers of this story invoke martyrs like Socrates, Galileo, and Peter Zenger, and heroes like Locke, Hobbes, Voltaire, and Hume who fought for the right of free expression. They conjure up struggles against official censorship, book burning, witch trials, and communist blacklists. Compared to that richly textured, deeply stirring account, the minority-protector's interest in freeing a few (supersensitive?) individuals from momentary discomfort looks thin. A textured, historical account is pitted against a particularized, slice-of-life, dignitary one.

Those on the minority-protection side invoke a different, and no less powerful, narrative. They see a nation's centuries-long struggle to free itself from racial and other forms of tyranny, including slavery, lynching, Jim Crow laws, and "separate-but-equal" schools. They conjure up different milestones—Lincoln Emancipation Proclamation, *Brown v. Board of Education*; they look to different heroes—Martin Luther King, the early Abolitionists, Rosa Parks, and Cesar Chavez, civil rights protesters who put their lives on the line for racial justice. Arrayed against that richly textured historical account, the racists' interest in insulting a person of color face-to-face looks thin.

One often hears that the problem of campus antiracism rules is that of balancing free speech and equality. But more is at stake. Each side wants not merely to have the balance struck in its favor; each wants to impose its own understanding of what is at stake. Minority protectors see the injury of one who has been subject to a racial assault as not a mere isolated event, but as part of an interrelated series of acts, by which persons of color are subordinated, and which will follow the victim wherever she goes. First amendment defenders see the wrong of silencing the racist as much more than a momentary inconvenience: protection of his right to speak is part of the never-ending vigilance necessary to preserve freedom of expression in a society that is too prone to balance it away.

My view is that both stories are equally valid. Judges and university administrators have no easy, a priori way of choosing between them, of privileging one over the other. They could coin an exception to free speech, thus giving primacy to the equal protection values at stake. Or, they could carve an exception to equality, saying in effect that universities may protect minority populations except where this abridges speech. Nothing in constitutional or moral theory requires one answer rather than the other. Social science, case law, and the experience of other nations provide some illumination. But ultimately, judges and university administrators must *choose*. And in making this choice, we are in uncharted terrain: we lack a pole star. To gain a sense of the scope of the problem, the next Part reviews recent events at leading universities and reactions to those events. . . .

## III. INTERNATIONAL PERSPECTIVES

. . .

The debate surrounding campus antiracism rules swirls around a number of issues that have empirical components—questions that might be answered yes or no. Can free speech continue to exist in a society that prohibits one of its forms? Will one type of regulation lead to another, or conversely, will enforcement inevitably be turned against minorities? Are laws limiting racist speech effective compared with other approaches to controlling racism? The debate about campus rules has proceeded largely in an empirical vacuum. Although one must always be cautious in drawing conclusions from the experiences of other cultures, those experiences may nevertheless suggest answers to these questions.

### A. International Conventions and Declarations

Many countries have condemned discrimination and racial violence. This condemnation has taken a number of forms, including international treaties and conventions, many enacted in response to the atrocities inflicted upon Jews and other minorities during World War II. For example, the Universal Declaration of Human Rights provides that persons are entitled to protection from discrimination *and* its incitement. The European Convention for the Protection of Human Rights and Fundamental Freedoms and the American Declaration of the Rights and Duties of Man provide similar protections. The Convention on the Prevention and Punishment of the Crime of Genocide requires states to prohibit "direct and public incitement" to commit that crime. The International Covenant on Civil and Political Rights, which affirms freedom of expression, nevertheless states that "advocacy of national, racial or religious hatred that constitutes incitement to discrimination, hostility or violence shall be prohibited by law."

The most important and specific piece of antiracism legislation, however, is the International Convention on the Elimination of All Forms of Racial Discrimination. Signed by 104 states, the Convention provides that:

> The concern of the United Nations with the promotion and protection of human rights and fundamental freedoms is an expression of the ever-increasing interest of the international community in ensuring that these rights and freedoms shall be enjoyed by all human beings everywhere. . . . [R]acial discrimination has been and is considered to be one of the most odious of human rights violations.

The Convention's central provision is article 4, which requires member countries to criminalize dissemination of hate propaganda and all organizations that incite racial discrimination. The General Assembly adopted this article only after heated debate, yet most signatory nations have followed its mandate in enacting national legislation.

1. *Great Britain*. . . . The Race Relations Act of 1965 was the culmination of several earlier attempts to broaden and conform British law to international trends. The Act created a new offense for persons who:

> with intent to stir up hatred against any section of the public . . . distinguished by colour, race or ethnic or national origins—. . . publish[] or distribute[] written matter which is threatening, abusive or insulting; or . . . use[] in any public place or at any public meeting words which are threatening, abusive or insulting, being matter or words likely to stir up hatred. . . .

. . .

The new Act permits a constable to arrest without a warrant "anyone he reasonably suspects is committing an offense under this section." Moreover, unlike earlier versions, the statute prohibits private as well as public behavior. The Attorney General, however, must still consent to prosecutions. Although many are still unsatisfied with the law, few advocate doing away with it altogether. In the meantime, British courts interpret the Act narrowly to minimize conflict with free speech. . . .

2. *Canada*.—Like Great Britain, Canada has developed a panoply of measures to protect minorities against racism. These include the Constitutional Charter of Rights, the Canadian Bill of Rights, certain provisions of the Canadian Criminal Code, and ten provincial human rights codes. . . .

Canada's national criminal code prohibited hate speech as early as June 1970. A 1965 Report of the Special Committee on Hate Propaganda provided the impetus for Canada's current legislation. Parliament commissioned the Report in an attempt to understand the origin and activity of various hate organizations in the country. Out of the Report's recommendations and the desire to harmonize Canada's legislation with international standards, Canada enacted House of Commons Bill C-3 which recognizes four types of hate speech as crimes: advocating genocide, public incitement of hatred, willful promotion of hatred, and spreading false news. The first was the least controversial; it merely carries out Canada's responsibilities to legislate the provisions of the United Nations Convention on Genocide. The second, public incitement of hatred, drew fire; one of the criticisms

is that the reaction of the audience dictates whether or not an offense has occurred. The third and fourth provisions, wilful promotion of hatred other than in a private conversation and spreading false news, have been rarely applied.

Each of the offenses is subject to a number of defenses—all designed to protect free expression—which together with the requirement of the Attorney General's consent to prosecute are designed to limit the likelihood of abuse. Although a few civil libertarians continue to express concern, criticism generally has been muted. One commentator has observed that when hate laws were first proposed, the Canadian Civil Liberties Association raised the spectre of the slippery slope, yet, they have been applied sparingly, and little discernible weakening of commitment to free speech has occurred. As in Great Britain, the remaining debate concerns how broad or narrow the rules should be, details of their effectuation, and defenses to charges brought under them.

3. *Other Countries*.—As has been seen, anti-hate speech legislation generally takes one of three forms: laws against group libel, breach of the peace, and incitement to racial hatred. . . .

4. *Summary*.—As previously noted, one must extrapolate cautiously from the experience of other societies. Moreover, what holds true of a nation may not hold true for a university, whose peculiar interests may make anti-hate speech legislation either more or less defensible. Still, it would be a mistake to ignore the experience of Canada, a nation whose constitutional approach to regulation of speech resembles our own; or that of Great Britain, with whom we share a long common-law tradition. With these provisos, some cautious generalizations are possible. The acceptance and effectiveness of laws against hate speech depend on a constellation of social and historical conditions. In Scandinavia, the laws have remained untested and unchallenged. In Britain and Canada, antiracism laws met with initial resistance, which has largely subsided. In these and other countries which have implemented anti-hate legislation, there appears to have been little of a snowball effect towards censorship. Thus, it is evidently possible to regulate the more vicious forms of race-hate speech, while remaining committed to free expression.

The debate surrounding campus antiracism rules has not only proceeded in an empirical vacuum, ignoring the experience of other countries; it has also proceeded in a theoretical one, blind to the insights of social scientists who have studied race and racism. Critics of antiracism rules, for example, often assert: (i) that rules forbidding racist remarks will simply cause racism to go underground or surface in a more virulent form; (ii) that racist speech serves as a pressure valve, allowing prejudiced individuals to blow off stream harmlessly; (iii) that punishing racist speech is ineffective because it does not deal with the "root" causes of racism; and (iv) that the harm of a racial insult is de minimis. For their part, defenders of anti-hate rules maintain that racial speech causes serious harm to the psyche and educational prospects of its, victims, with little if any documentation of these effects. Social science research sheds light on these and other assertions central to the debate about antiracism rules. . . .

## B. Controlling Racism

Unlike with racism's etiology, there is relative agreement on the part of social scientists on how to control its expression. Much prejudice is situational—individuals express it because the environment encourages or tolerates it. The attitude may be relatively constant, but most of us express it selectively—at times we hold it in check, at other times we feel freer to express it in action. The main inhibiter of prejudice is the certainty that it will be remarked and punished. This "confrontation theory" for controlling racism holds that most individuals are ambivalent in matters of race. We realize that the national values—those enshrined in the "American Creed"—call for fair and respectful treatment of all. But the fair-mindedness of our public norms is not always matched by our private behavior. During moments of intimacy we feel much freer to tell or laugh at an ethnic joke, to make a racist or sexist remark.

Rules, formalities, and other environmental reminders put us on notice that the occasion requires the higher formal values of our culture. The existence of rules forbidding certain types of racist acts causes us not to be inclined to carry them out. Moreover, threat of public notice and disapproval operates as a reinforcer—the potential racist refrains from acting, out of fear of notice and sanction. The confrontation theory is probably today the majority view among social scientists on how to control racism. Most who subscribe to this approach hold that laws and rules play a vital role in controlling racism. According to Allport, they "create a public conscience and a standard for expected behavior that check *overt* signs of prejudice." Nor is the change merely cosmetic. In time, rules are internalized, and the impulse to engage in racist behavior weakens.

The current understanding of racial prejudice thus lends some support to campus antiracism rules. The mere existence of such rules will often cause members of the campus community to behave in a more egalitarian way, particularly when others may be watching. Even in private settings, some people will refrain from acting because the law has set an example. Those whose prejudice is associated with authoritarianism will do so because the rules represent society's legitimate voice.

Further, social science casts doubt on both the "hydraulic" theory of racism, according to which controlling racism in one arena will simply cause it to crop up somewhere else, and the theory that racist remarks are relatively harmless. A large body of literature shows that incessant racial categorization and treatment seriously impair the prospects and development of persons of minority race, deepen rigidity and set the stage for even more serious transgressions on the part of persons so disposed.

## V. CONSTITUTIONAL PARADIGMS

. . .

### A. A First Amendment View

The first amendment appears to stand as a formidable barrier to campus rules prohibiting group-disparaging speech. Designed to assure that debate on public issues is "uninhibited, robust, and wide open," the first amendment protects speech which we hate as much as that which we hold dear. Yet, racial insults implicate powerful social interests in equality and equal personhood. When uttered on university campuses, racial insults bring into play additional concerns. Few would question that the university has strong, legitimate interests in (i) teaching students and teachers to treat each other respectfully; (ii) protecting minority-group students from harassment; and (iii) protecting diversity, which could be impaired if students of color become demoralized and leave the university, or if parents of minority race decide to send their children elsewhere. . . .

Much speech . . . is unprotected. The issues are whether the social interest in reining in racially offensive speech is as great as that which gives rise to these "exceptional" categories and whether the use of racially offensive language has speech value. . . .

Our system of free expression serves a number of societal and individual goals. Included are the personal fulfillment of the speaker; ascertainment of the truth; participation in democratic decisionmaking; and achieving a balance between social stability and change. Applying these policies to the controversy surrounding campus antiracism rules yields no clear result. Uttering racial slurs may afford the racially troubled speaker some immediate relief, but hardly seems essential to self-fulfillment in any ideal sense. Indeed, social science writers hold that making racist remarks impairs, rather than promotes, the growth of the person who makes them, by encouraging rigid, dichotomous thinking and impeding moral development. Moreover, such remarks serve little dialogic purpose; they do not seek to connect the speaker and addressee in a community of shared ideals. They divide, rather than unite.

Additionally, slurs contribute little to the discovery of truth. Classroom discussion of racial matters and even the speech of a bigot aimed at proving the superiority of the white race might move us closer to the truth. But one-on-one insults do not. They neither state nor attack a proposition; they are like a slap in the face. By the same token, racial insults do little to help reach broad social consensuses. Indeed, by demoralizing their victim they may actually reduce speech, dialogue, and participation in political life. "More speech" is rarely a solution. Epithets often strike suddenly, immobilizing their victim and rendering her speechless. Often they are delivered in cowardly, anonymous fashion—for example, in the form of a group against a single victim, rendering response foolhardy. Nor do they help strike a healthy balance between stability and social change. Racial epithets could be argued to relieve racial tension harmlessly and thus contribute to racial stability, but this strained argument has been called into question by social science.

Yet racial epithets *are* speech, and as such we ought to protect them unless there is a very good reason for not doing so. A recent book by Kent Greenawalt suggests a framework for assessing laws against insults. Drawing on first amendment principles and case law, Greenawalt writes that the setting, the speaker's intention, the forum's interest, and the relationship between the speaker and the victim must be considered. Moreover, abusive words (like kike, nigger, wop, and faggot) are punishable if spoken with intent, cause a harm subject to formulation in clear legal language, and form a message essentially devoid of ideas. Greenawalt offers as an example of words that could be criminally punishable, "You Spick whore" uttered by four men to a woman of color at a bus stop, intended to humiliate her. He notes that such words can have long-term damaging effects on the victim and have little if any cognitive content; that which the words have may be expressed in other ways.

Under Greenawalt's test, narrowly drawn university guidelines penalizing racial slurs might withstand scrutiny. The university forum has a strong interest in establishing a nonracist atmosphere. Moreover, most university rules are aimed at face-to-face remarks that are intentionally abusive. Most exclude classroom speech, speeches to a crowd, and satire published in a campus newspaper. Under Greenawalt's nonabsolutist approach, such rules might well be held constitutional.

The first amendment perspective yields no clear-cut result. Society has a strong interest in seeing that expression is as unfettered as possible, yet the king of expression under consideration has no great social worth and can cause serious harm. Unfortunately, looking at the problem of racist speech from the perspective of the equality-protecting amendments yields no clearer result.

Equality and equal respect are highly valued principles in our system of jurisprudence. Three constitutional provisions and a myriad of federal and state statutes are aimed at protecting the rights of racial, religious, and sexual minorities to be free from discrimination in housing, education, jobs, and many other areas of life. Moreover, universities have considerable power to enact regulations protecting minority interests. Yet the equality principle is not without limits. State agencies may not redress breaches by means that too broadly encroach on the rights of whites, or on other constitutional principles. Rigorous rules of intent, causation, standing, and limiting relief circumscribe what may be done. New causes of action are not lightly recognized; for example, the legal system has resisted efforts by feminists to have pornography deemed a civil rights offense against women.

Moreover, courts have held or implied that a university's power to effectuate campus policies, presumably including equality, is also limited. Cases stemming from efforts to regulate the wearing of armbands, what students may publish in the school newspaper, or their freedom to gather in open areas for worship or speech have shown that individual liberty will sometimes subordinate an institution's interest in achieving its educational objectives—students do not abandon all their constitutional rights at the schoolhouse door. According to the author of a leading treatise on higher education law, rules bridling racist speech will be found constitutional if there is a local history of racial disruption; if the rules are narrowly tailored to punish only face-to-face insults and avoid encroaching on classroom and other protected speech; if they are consistently and even-handedly applied; and if due process protections such as the right to representation and a fair hearing are present. . . .

## VI. RECONCILING THE FIRST AND FOURTEENTH AMENDMENTS: STIGMA-PICTURES AND THE SOCIAL CONSTRUCTION OF REALITY

### A. Class Subordination and the Problem of Concerted Speech

As the analysis to this point has shown, neither the constitutional narrative of the first, nor of the thirteenth and fourteenth, amendments clearly prevails in connection with campus antiracism rules. Judges must choose. The dilemma is embedded in the nature of our system of law and politics: we want and fear both equality and liberty. This Part offers a solution to the problem of campus antiracism rules based on a post-modern insight: the speech by which society "constructs" a stigma picture of minorities may be regulated consistently with the first amendment. Indeed, regulation may be necessary for full effectuation of the values of equal personhood we hold equally dear.

The first step is recognizing that racism is, in almost all its aspects, a class harm—the essence of which is subordination of one people by another. The mechanism of this subordination is a complex, interlocking series of acts, some physical, some symbolic. Although the physical acts (like lynchings and cross burnings) are often the most striking, the symbolic acts are the most insidious. By communicating and "constructing" a shared cultural image of the victim group as inferior, we enable ourselves to feel comfortable about the disparity in power and resources between ourselves and the stigmatized group. Most civil rights law, of necessity, contributes to this stigmatization: the group is so vulnerable that it requires social help. The shared picture also demobilizes the victims of discrimination, particularly the young. Indeed, social scientists have seen evidence of self-hatred and rejection of their own identity in children of color as early as age three.

The ubiquity and incessancy of harmful racial depiction are thus the source of its virulence. Like water dripping on sandstone, it is a pervasive harm which only the most hardy can resist. Yet the prevailing first amendment paradigm predisposes us to treat racist speech as an individual harm, as though we only had to evaluate the effect of a single drop of water. This approach—corresponding to liberal, individualistic theories of self and society—systematically misperceives the experience of racism for both victim and perpetrator. This mistake is natural, and corresponds to one aspect of our natures—our individualistic selves. In this capacity, we want and need liberty. But we also exist in a social capacity; we need others to fulfill ourselves as beings. In this group aspect, we require inclusion, equality, and equal respect. Constitutional narratives of equal protection and prohibition of slavery—narratives that encourage us to form and embrace collectivity and equal citizenship for all—reflect this second aspect of our existence.

When the tacit consent of a group begins to coordinate the exercise of individual rights so as seriously to jeopardize participation by a smaller group the "rights" nature of the first group's actions acquires a different character and dimension. The exercise of an individual right now poses a group harm and must be weighed against this qualitatively different type of threat.

First amendment scholar Kent Greenawalt's recent book has made a cautious move in this direction. Although generally a defense of free speech in its individual aspect, his book also notes that speech is a primary means by which we construct reality. Thus, a wealthy and well-regarded citizen who is victimized by a vicious defamation is able to recover tort. His social "picture," in which he has a property interest, has been damaged, and will require laborious reconstruction. It would require only slight extension of Greenawalt's observation to provide protection from racial slurs and hate-speech. Indeed, the rich man has the dominant "story" on his side; repairing the defamation's damage will be relatively easy.

Racist speech, by contrast, is not so readily repaired—it separates the victim from the storytellers who alone have credibility. Not only does racist speech, by placing all the credibility with the dominant group, strengthen the dominant story, it also works to disempower minority groups by crippling the effectiveness of *their* speech in rebuttal. This situation makes free speech a powerful asset to the dominant group, but a much less helpful one to subordinate groups—a result at odds, certainly, with marketplace theories of the first amendment. Unless society is able to deal with this incongruity, the thirteenth and fourteenth amendments and our complex system of civil rights statutes will be of little avail. At best, they will be able to obtain redress for episodic, blatant acts of individual prejudice and bigotry. This redress will do little to address the source of the problem: the speech that creates the stigma-picture that makes the acts hurtful in the first place, and that renders almost any other form of aid—social or legal—useless.

## B. Operationalizing the Insight

Could judges and legislators effectuate this Article's suggestion that speech which constructs a stigma-picture of a subordinate group stands on a different footing from sporadic speech aimed at persons who are not disempowered? It might be argued that *all* speech constructs the world to some extent, and that every speech act could prove offensive to someone. Traditionalists find modern art troublesome, Republicans detest left-wing speech, and some men hate speech that constructs a sex-neutral world. Yet race—like gender and a few other characteristics—is different; our entire history and culture bespeak this difference. Thus, judges easily could differentiate speech which subordinates blacks, for example, from that which disparages factory owners. Will they choose to do so? There is cause for doubt: low-grade racism benefits the status quo. Moreover, our system's winners have a stake in liberal, marketplace interpretations of law and politics—the seeming neutrality and meritocratic nature of such interpretations reassure the decisionmakers that their social position is deserved.

Still, resurgent racism on our nation's campuses is rapidly becoming a national embarrassment. Almost daily, we are faced with headlines featuring some of the ugliest forms of ethnic conflict and the spectre of virtually all-white universities. The need to avoid these consequences may have the beneficial effect of causing courts to reflect on, and tailor, constitutional doctrine. As Harry Kalven pointed out twenty-five years ago, it would not be the first time that insights born of the cauldron of racial justice yielded reforms that ultimately redounded to the benefit of all society. . . .

Nadine Strossen, *Regulating Racist Speech on Campus: A Modest Proposal?* 1990 DUKE LAW JOURNAL 484 (1990)*

. . .

INTRODUCTION

. . .

Because civil libertarians have learned that free speech is an indispensable instrument for the promotion of other rights and freedoms—including racial equality—we fear that the movement to regulate campus expression will undermine equality, as well as free speech. Combating racial discrimination and protecting free speech should be viewed as mutually reinforcing, rather than antagonistic, goals. A diminution in society's commitment to racial equality is neither a necessary nor an appropriate price for protecting free speech. Those who frame the debate in terms of this false dichotomy simply drive artificial wedges between would-be allies in what should be a common effort to promote civil rights and civil liberties. . . .

What is disquieting about Professor Lawrence's article is not the relatively limited Stanford code he

defends, but rather his simultaneous defense of additional, substantially more sweeping, speech prohibitions. The rationales that Professor Lawrence advances for the regulations he endorses are so open-ended that, if accepted, they would appear to warrant the prohibition of *all* racist speech, and thereby would cut to the core of our system of free expression.

Although Professor Lawrence's specific proposed code appears relatively modest, his supporting rationales depend on nothing less immodest than the abrogation of the traditional distinctions between speech and conduct and between state action and private action. He equates private racist speech with governmental racist conduct. . . . Professor Lawrence apparently acknowledges that, if accepted, his theories could warrant the prohibition of *all* private racist speech. Moreover, although he stresses the particular evils of racism, he also says that "much of my analysis applies to violent pornography and homophobic hate speech." Thus, Professor Lawrence himself demonstrates that traditional civil libertarians are hardly paranoiac when we fear that any specific, seemingly modest proposal to regulate speech may in fact represent the proverbial "thin edge of the wedge" for initiating broader regulations. . . .

Two problems arise from the disharmony between the breadth of the racist speech regulations endorsed by Professor Lawrence and the harm that inspires them. First, this disparity underscores the rules' ineffectiveness. The regulations do not even address much of racist speech, let alone the innumerable other manifestations of racism which—as Professor Lawrence himself stresses—pervade our society. Second, this disharmony encourages the proponents of hate speech regulations to seek to narrow the gap between the underlying problem and their favored solution by recommending broader regulations. For example, Professor Mari Matsuda recently proposed a substantially more restrictive hate speech regulation on the theory that such a regulation is needed to redress the harm suffered by hate speech victims. Professor Lawrence has indicated his approval of Professor Matsuda's approach. And the wedge widens. . . .

I. SOME LIMITED FORMS OF CAMPUS HATE SPEECH MAY BE REGULABLE UNDER CURRENT CONSTITUTIONAL DOCTRINE

. . .

B. Particular Speech-Limiting Doctrines Potentially Applicable to Campus Hate Speech

In addition to the foregoing general principles, Professor Lawrence and other proponents of campus

---

hate speech regulation invoke three specific doctrines in an attempt to justify such rules: the fighting words doctrine; the tort of intentional infliction of emotional distress; and the tort of group defamation. As the following discussion shows, the Supreme Court has recognized that each of these doctrines may well be inconsistent with free speech principles. Therefore, these doctrines may not support any campus hate speech restrictions whatsoever. In any event, they at most would support only restrictions that are both narrowly drawn and narrowly applied.

1. Fighting Words. The fighting words doctrine is the principal model for the Stanford code, which Professor Lawrence supports. However, this doctrine provides a constitutionally shaky foundation for several reasons: it has been substantially limited in scope and may no longer be good law; even if the Supreme Court were to apply a narrowed version of the doctrine, such an application would threaten free speech principles; and, as actually implemented, the fighting words doctrine suppresses protectible speech and entails the inherent danger of discriminatory application to speech by members of minority groups and dissidents.

Although the Court originally defined constitutionally regulable fighting words in fairly broad terms in *Chaplinsky v. New Hampshire,* subsequent decisions have narrowed the definition to such a point that the doctrine probably would not apply to any of the instances of campus racist speech that Professor Lawrence and others seek to regulate. . . .

In accordance with its narrow construction of constitutionally permissible prohibitions upon "fighting words," the Court has overturned every single fighting words conviction that it has reviewed since *Chaplinsky.* Moreover, in a subsequent decision, the Court overturned an injunction that had been based on the very word underlying the *Chaplinsky* conviction.

For the foregoing reasons, Supreme Court Justices and constitutional scholars persuasively maintain that *Chaplinsky's* fighting words doctrine is no longer good law. More importantly, constitutional scholars have argued that this doctrine should no longer be good law, for reasons that are particularly weighty in the context of racist slurs. First, as Professor Gard concluded in a comprehensive review of both Supreme Court and lower court decisions that apply the fighting words doctrine, the asserted governmental interest in preventing a breach of the peace is not logically furthered by this doctrine. He explained that:

> [I]t is fallacious to believe that personally abusive epithets, even if addressed face-to-face to

the object of the speaker's criticism, are likely to arouse the ordinary law abiding person beyond mere anger to uncontrollable reflexive violence. Further, even if one unrealistically assumes that reflexive violence will result, it is unlikely that the fighting words doctrine can successfully deter such lawless conduct.

Second, just as the alleged peace-preserving purpose does not rationally justify the fighting words doctrine in general, that rationale also fails to justify the fighting words doctrine when applied to racial slurs in particular. As Professor Kalven noted, "outbursts of violence are not the necessary consequence of such speech and, more important, such violence when it does occur is not the serious evil of the speech." Rather, as Professor Lawrence stresses, the serious evil of racial slurs consists of the ugliness of the ideas they express and the psychic injury they cause to their addressees. Therefore, the fighting words doctrine does not address and will not prevent the injuries caused by campus racist speech.

Even if there were a real danger that racist or other fighting words would cause reflexive violence, and even if that danger would be reduced by the threat of legal sanction, the fighting words doctrine still would be problematic in terms of free speech principles. As Professor Chafee observed, this doctrine "makes a man a criminal simply because his neighbors have no self-control and cannot refrain from violence." In other contexts, the Court appropriately has refused to allow the addressees of speech to exercise such a "heckler's veto."

The fighting words doctrine is constitutionally flawed for the additional reasons that it suppresses much protectible speech and that the protectible speech of minority group members is particularly vulnerable. Notwithstanding the Supreme Court's limitation of the doctrine's scope, Professor Gard's survey reveals that the lower courts apply it much more broadly. Since the Supreme Court only reviews a fraction of such cases, the doctrine's actual impact on free speech must be assessed in terms of these speech-restrictive lower court rulings. Professor Gard concluded that, in the lower courts, the fighting words doctrine "is almost uniformly invoked in a selective and discriminatory manner by law enforcement officials to punish trivial violations of a constitutionally impermissible interest in preventing criticism of official conduct." Indeed, Professor Gard reported, "it is virtually impossible to find fighting words cases that do not involve either the expression of opinion on issues of public policy or words directed toward a government official, usually a police officer." Even more disturbing is that the reported cases indicate that blacks are often prosecuted and convicted for the use of fighting words. Thus, the record of the actual implementation of the fighting words doctrine demonstrates that—as is the case with all speech restrictions—it endangers principles of equality as well as free speech. That record substantiates the risk that such a speech restriction will be applied discriminatorily and disproportionately against the very minority group members whom it is intended, to protect. . . .

2. Intentional Infliction of Emotional Distress. A committee report that the University of Texas is currently considering recommends the common law tort of intentional infliction of emotional distress as a basis for regulating campus hate speech. This doctrinal approach has a logical appeal because it focuses on the type of harm potentially caused by racist speech that universities are most concerned with alleviating—namely, emotional or psychological harm that interferes with studies. In contrast, the harm at which the fighting words doctrine aims—potential violence by the addressee against the speaker—is of less concern to most universities.

Traditional civil libertarians caution that the intentional infliction of emotional distress theory should almost never apply to verbal harassment. A major problem with this approach is that, the innate vagueness of the interest in preventing emotional injury to listeners suggests that any attempt at judicial enforcement will inevitably result in the imposition of judges' subjective linguistic preferences on society, *discrimination against ethnic and racial minorities,* and ultimately the misuse of the rationale to justify the censorship of the ideological content of the speaker's message.

Again, as was true for the fighting words doctrine, there is a particular danger, that this speech restrictive doctrine also will be enforced to the detriment of the very minority groups whom it is designed to protect. . . .

3. Group Defamation. Professor Lawrence does not elaborate on either the constitutionality or efficacy of the group defamation concept, yet he approvingly notes others' alleged support for it. The group defamation concept, however, has been thoroughly discredited by others.

First, group defamation regulations are unconstitutional in terms of both Supreme Court doctrine and free speech principles. . . .

Statements that defame groups convey opinions or ideas on matters of public concern, and therefore should be protected even if those statements also injure reputations or feelings. The Supreme Court recently reaffirmed this principle in the context of an individual defamation action, in *Milkovich v. Lorain Journal Co.*

In addition to flouting constitutional doctrine and free speech principles, rules sanctioning group defamation are ineffective in curbing the specific class of hate speech that Professor Lawrence advocates restraining. Even Justice Frankfurter's opinion for the narrow *Beauharnais* majority repeatedly expressed doubt about the wisdom or efficacy of group libel laws. Justice Frankfurter stressed that the Court upheld the Illinois law in question only because of judicial deference to the state legislature's judgment about the law's effectiveness.

The concept of defamation encompasses only false statements of fact that are made without a good faith belief in their truth. Therefore, any disparaging or insulting statement would be immune from this doctrine, unless it were factual in nature, demonstrably false in content, and made in bad faith. Members of minority groups that are disparaged by an allegedly libelous statement would hardly have their reputations or psyches enhanced by a process in which the maker of the statement sought to prove his good faith belief in its truth, and they were required to demonstrate the absence thereof.

One additional problem with group defamation statutes as a model for rules sanctioning campus hate speech should be noted. As with the other speech-restrictive doctrines asserted to justify such rules, group defamation laws introduce the risk that the rules will be enforced at the expense of the very minority groups sought to be protected. The Illinois statute upheld in *Beauharnais* is illustrative. According to a leading article on group libel laws, during the 1940s, the Illinois statute was "a weapon for harassment of the Jehovah's Witnesses," who were then "a minority . . . very much more in need of protection than most." Thus, a rule based on the group defamation theory provides no guarantee that it will not be used against minorities.

C. Even a Narrow Regulation Could Have a Negative Symbolic Impact on Constitutional Values

. . .

Even assuming that a regulation could be crafted with sufficient precision to survive a facial constitutional challenge, several further problems would remain, which should give any university pause in evaluating whether to adopt such a rule. . . . First, because of the discretion entailed in enforcing any such rule, they involve an inevitable danger of arbitrary or discriminatory enforcement. Therefore, the rule's implementation would have to be monitored to ensure that it did not exceed the bounds of the regulations' terms or threaten content- and viewpoint-neutrality principles. The experience with the University of Michigan's rule—the only campus hate speech rule that has an enforcement record—graphically illustrates this danger.

Second, there is an inescapable risk that any hate speech regulation, no matter how narrowly drawn, will chill speech beyond its literal scope. Members of the university community may well err on the side of caution to avoid being charged with a violation. . . .

Further, in light of constitutional constraints, any campus hate speech policy inevitably would apply to only a tiny fraction of all racist expression, and accordingly it would have only a symbolic impact. Therefore, in deciding whether to adopt such a rule, universities must ask whether that symbolic impact is, on balance, positive or negative in terms of constitutional values. On the one hand, some advocates of hate speech regulations maintain that the regulations might play a valuable symbolic role in reaffirming our societal commitment to racial equality (although this is debatable). On the other hand, we must beware of even a symbolic or perceived diminution of our impartial commitment to free speech. Even a limitation that has a direct impact upon only a discrete category of speech may have a much more pervasive indirect impact—by undermining the first amendment's moral legitimacy. . . .

## II. PROFESSOR LAWRENCE'S CONCEPTION OF REGULABLE RACIST SPEECH ENDANGERS FREE SPEECH PRINCIPLES

. . .

### A. The Proposed Regulations Would Not Pass Constitutional Muster

. . .

#### 2. The Regulations Will Chill Protected Speech

. . .

In the recent wave of college crackdowns on racist and other forms of hate speech, examples abound of attempts to censor speech conveying ideas that clearly play a legitimate role in academic discourse, although some of us might find them wrongheaded or even odious. For example, the University of Michigan's anti-hate speech policy could justify attacks on author Salman Rushdie because his book, *The Satanic Verses,* was offensive to Muslims.

Such incidents are not aberrational. Any anti-hate speech rule inescapably entails some vagueness, due to the inherent imprecision of key words and concepts common to all such proposed rules. For example, most regulations employ one or more of the following terms: "demeaning," "disparaging," "harassing," "hostile," "insulting," "intimidating," and "stigmatizing." Therefore, there is real danger that even a narrowly crafted rule will deter some expression that should be protected—especially in the university environment. In particular, such a rule probably will "add to the silence" on "gut issues" about racism, sexism, and other forms of bias that already impede interracial and other intergroup dialogues.

Additionally, it must be recognized that silencing certain expressions may be tantamount to silencing certain ideas. As the plaintiff in *Doe v. Michigan* argued:

[T]he policy . . . is an official statement that at the University of Michigan, some arguments will no longer be tolerated. Rather than encourage her maturing students to question each other's beliefs on such diverse and controversial issues as the proper role of women in society, the merits of particular religions, or the moral propriety of homosexuality, the University has decided that it must protect its students from what it considers to be "unenlightened" ideas. In so doing, the University has established a secular orthodoxy by implying, among other things, that homosexuality is morally acceptable, [and] that . . . feminism [is] superior to the traditional view of women. . . .

The Michigan plaintiff was victimized directly by the "pall of orthodoxy" that the University's anti-hate speech policy cast over the campus. As a graduate student specializing in behavioral psychology, he felt that the rule deterred him from classroom discussion of theories that some psychological differences among racial groups and between the sexes are related to biological differences, for fear of being charged with racial or sexual harassment. . . .

. . .

#### 1. Protection of Speech Advocating Regulable Conduct

. . .

## III. PROFESSOR LAWRENCE'S RATIONALES FOR REGULATING RACIST SPEECH WOULD JUSTIFY SWEEPING PROHIBITIONS, CONTRARY TO FREE SPEECH PRINCIPLES

. . .

### A. Brown and Other Cases Invalidating Governmental Racist Conduct Do Not Justify Regulating Non-Governmental Racist Speech

Professor Lawrence intriguingly posits that

*Brown v. Board of Education, Bob Jones University v. United States,* and other civil rights cases justify regulation of private racist speech. The problem with drawing an analogy between all of these cases and the subject at hand is that the cases involved either *government* speech, as opposed to speech by private individuals, or *conduct,* as opposed to speech. Indeed, *Brown* itself is distinguishable on both grounds.

1. The Speech/Conduct Distinction. First, the governmental defendant in *Brown*—the Topeka, Kansas Board of Education—was not simply saying that blacks are inferior. Rather, it was treating them as inferior through pervasive patterns of conduct, by maintaining systems and structures of segregated public schools. To be sure, a by-product of the challenged conduct was a message, but that message was only incidental. Saying that black children are unfit to attend school with whites is materially distinguishable from legally prohibiting them from doing so, despite the fact that the legal prohibition may convey the former message.

Professor Lawrence's point proves too much. If incidental messages could transform conduct into speech, then the distinction between speech and conduct would disappear completely, because *all* conduct conveys a message. To take an extreme example, a racially motivated lynching expresses the murderer's hatred or contempt for his victim. But the clearly unlawful act is not protected from punishment by virtue of the incidental message it conveys. And the converse also is true. Just because the government may suppress particular hate messages that are the by-product of unlawful conduct, it does not follow that it may suppress all hate messages. Those messages not tightly linked to conduct must still be protected.

Professor Lawrence's argument is not advanced by his unexceptionable observation that all human activity may be described both as "speech" and as "conduct." All speech entails some activity (e.g., the act of talking) and all conduct expresses some message. First, this fact does not justify treating any speech-conduct as unprotected; second, it does not justify eliminating protection from the particular class of speech-conduct that Professor Lawrence deems regulable. . . .

2. The Private Action/State Action Distinction

. . .

Professor Mari Matsuda has argued that the government's failure to punish private hate speech could be viewed as state action insofar as this failure conveys a message that the state tolerates such speech.

Because the Court construes the establishment clause as prohibiting government action that conveys a message of state support for religion, establishment clause cases constitute instructive precedents for evaluating Professor Matsuda's argument. . . . The Court declared, "[T]here is a crucial difference between *government* speech endorsing religion, which the Establishment Clause forbids, and *private* speech endorsing religion, which the Free Speech and Free Exercise Clauses protect." Paraphrasing this language and applying it to the campus hate speech context, one could say, "There is a crucial difference between *government* speech endorsing racism, which the Equal Protection Clause forbids, and *private* speech endorsing racism, which the Free Speech Clause protects." . . .

Professor Lawrence also makes the persuasive point that there is no absolute distinction between state and private action in the racist sphere, insofar as private acts of discrimination (as well as government acts) also are unlawful. This point, however, raises the other distinction discussed above—the distinction between words and conduct. Civil libertarians vigorously support the civil rights laws that make private discriminatory acts illegal, but that is a far cry from making private *speech* illegal. The *Bob Jones* case, upon which Professor Lawrence seeks to rely, illustrates these distinctions. What was objectionable there was the government conduct that supported and endorsed the private racist conduct—namely, the government's making of financial contributions, through the tax system, to racially discriminatory private educational institutions. Moreover, even if a private university could be prohibited from taking discriminatory actions—in the case of Bob Jones University, barring interracial marriage and dating—it still could not be prohibited from *advocating* such actions. The ACLU amicus brief in the *Bob Jones* case made precisely these points in countering the University's claim that withdrawing its tax benefits would violate its first amendment rights. The ACLU argued, and the Court agreed, that the University was still free to urge its students not to engage in interracial marriage or dating, and this was as far as its first amendment rights extended. Prohibited racist acts are no different from other prohibited acts. The government may punish the acts, but it may not punish words that advocate or endorse them. . . .

## IV. PROHIBITING RACIST SPEECH WOULD NOT EFFECTIVELY COUNTER, AND COULD EVEN AGGRAVATE, THE UNDERLYING PROBLEM OF RACISM

A. Civil Libertarians Should Continue to Make Combating Racism a Priority

Despite Professor Lawrence's proffered justifications for regulating a broader spectrum of racist speech, he in fact advocates regulating only a limited category of speech. Thus, even Professor Lawrence's views of regulable speech, although broader than those of the Supreme Court or traditional civil libertarians, would allow most racist speech on campus.

I do not think it is worth spending a great deal of time debating the fine points of specific rules or their particular applications to achieve what necessarily will be only marginal differences in the amount of racist insults that can be sanctioned. The larger problems of racist attitudes and conduct—of which all these words are symptoms—would remain. Those who share the dual goals of promoting racial equality and protecting free speech must concentrate on countering racial discrimination, rather than on defining the particular narrow subset of racist slurs that constitutionally might be regulable.

I welcome Professor Lawrence's encouragement to civil libertarians to "engage actively in speech and action that resists and counters the racist ideas the first amendment protects." But Professor Lawrence need not urge traditional civil libertarians to "put[ ] at least as much effort and as many resources into fighting for the victims of racism as we put into protecting the rights of racists." The ACLU, for example, puts far more effort and resources into assisting the victims of racism than into defending the rights of racists. . . .

In light of these efforts, Professor Lawrence's suggestion that "the call for fighting racist attitudes and practices rather than speech [is] 'just a lot of "cheap talk"' is a cheap shot. In particular, it is noteworthy that the ACLU affiliates that have brought lawsuits challenging campus hate speech regulations also have undertaken specific efforts to counter campus and societal racism. Moreover, the charge of "cheap talk" more appropriately might be leveled at those who focus their attention on hate speech regulations. Such regulations may appear to provide a relatively inexpensive "quick fix," but racist speech is only one symptom of the pervasive problem of racism, and this underlying problem will not be solved by banning one of its symptoms. . . .

## C. Banning Racist Speech Could Aggravate Racism

For several reasons banning the symptom of racist speech may compound the underlying problem of racism. Professor Lawrence sets up a false dichotomy when he urges us to balance equality goals against free speech goals. Just as he observes that free speech concerns should be weighed on the pro-regulation, as well as the anti-regulation, side of the balance, he should recognize that equality concerns weigh on the anti-regulation, as well as the pro-regulation, side.

The first reason that laws censoring racist speech may undermine the goal of combating racism flows from the discretion such laws inevitably vest in prosecutors, judges, and the other individuals who implement them. One ironic, even tragic, result of this discretion is that members of minority groups themselves—the very people whom the law is intended to protect—are likely targets of punishment. . . .

The general lesson that rules banning hate speech will be used to punish minority group members has proven true in the specific context of campus hate speech regulations. . . .

. . . During the approximately one year that the University of Michigan rule was in effect, there were more than twenty cases of whites charging blacks with racist speech. More importantly, the only two instances in which the rule was invoked to sanction racist speech (as opposed to sexist and other forms of hate speech) involved the punishment of speech by or on behalf of black students. Additionally, the only student who was subjected to a full-fledged disciplinary hearing under the Michigan rule was a black student accused of homophobic and sexist expression. . . .

Professor Lawrence himself recognizes that rules regulating racist speech might backfire and be invoked disproportionately against blacks and other traditionally oppressed groups. Indeed, he charges that other university rules already are used to silence anti-racist, but not racist, speakers. Professor Lawrence proposes to avoid this danger by excluding from the rule's protection "persons who were vilified on the basis of their membership in dominant majority groups." Even putting aside the fatal first amendment flaws in such a radical departure from content- and viewpoint-neutrality principles, the proposed exception would create far more problems of equality and enforceability than it would solve.

A second reason why censorship of racist speech actually may subvert, rather than promote, the goal of eradicating racism is that such censorship measures often have the effect of glorifying racist speakers. Efforts at suppression result in racist speakers receiving attention and publicity which they otherwise would not have garnered. As previously noted, psychological studies reveal that whenever the government attempts to censor speech, the censored speech—for that very reason — becomes more appealing to many people. Still worse, when pitted against the government, racist speakers may appear as martyrs or even heroes.

Advocates of hate speech regulations do not seem to realize that their own attempts to suppress speech increase public interest in the ideas they are trying to stamp out. Thus, Professor Lawrence wrongly suggests that the ACLU's defense of hatemongers' free speech rights "makes heroes out of bigots"; in actuality, experience demonstrates that it is the attempt to *suppress* racist speech that has this effect, not the attempt *to protect* such speech.

Banning racist speech could undermine the goal of combating racism for additional reasons. Some black scholars and activists maintain that an antiracist speech policy may perpetuate a paternalistic view of minority groups, suggesting that they are incapable of defending themselves against biased expressions. Additionally, an anti-hate speech policy stultifies the candid intergroup dialogue concerning racism and other forms of bias that constitutes an essential precondition for reducing discrimination. In a related vein, education, free discussion, and the airing of misunderstandings and failures of sensitivity are more likely to promote positive intergroup relations than are legal battles. The rules barring hate speech will continue to generate litigation and other forms of controversy that will exacerbate intergroup tensions. Finally, the censorship approach is diversionary. It makes it easier for communities to avoid coming to grips with less convenient and more expensive, but ultimately more meaningful, approaches for combating racial discrimination. . . .

## V. MEANS CONSISTENT WITH THE FIRST AMENDMENT CAN PROMOTE RACIAL EQUALITY MORE EFFECTIVELY THAN CAN CENSORSHIP

. . .

In the context of countering racism on campus, the strategy of increasing speech—rather than decreasing it—not only would be consistent with first amendment principles, but also would be more effective in advancing equality goals. All government agencies and officers, including state university officials, should condemn slavery, de jure segregation, and other racist institutions that the government formerly supported. State university and other government officials also should affirmatively endorse equality principles. Furthermore, these government representatives should condemn racist ideas expressed by private speakers. In the same vein, private individuals and groups should exercise their first amendment rights by speaking out against racism. Traditional civil libertarians have exercised their own speech rights in this fashion and also have defended the first amendment freedoms of others who have done so.

In addition to the preceding measures, which could be implemented on a society-wide basis, other measures would be especially suited to the academic setting. First, regardless of the legal limitations on rules barring hate speech, universities should encourage members of their communities voluntarily to restrain the form of their expression in light of the feelings and concerns of various minority groups. Universities could facilitate voluntary self-restraint by providing training in communications, information about diverse cultural perspectives, and other education designed to promote intergroup understanding. Members of both minority and majority groups should be encouraged to be mutually respectful. Individuals who violate these norms of civility should not be subject to any disciplinary action, but instead should be counseled. These educational efforts should be extended to members of the faculty and administration, as well as students. Of course, universities must vigilantly ensure that *even* voluntary limits on the *manner* of academic discourse do not chill its *content*.

In addition to the foregoing measures, universities also should create forums in which controversial race-related issues and ideas could be discussed in a candid but constructive way. Another possibility would be for universities to encourage students to receive education in the history of racism and the civil rights movement in the United States and an exposure to the culture and traditions of racial and ethnic groups other than their own. Consistent with free speech tenets, these courses must allow all faculty and students to express their own views and must not degenerate into "reeducation camps." . . .

It is particularly important to devise anti-racism strategies consistent with the first amendment because racial and other minority groups ultimately have far more to lose than to gain through a weakened free speech guarantee. History has demonstrated that minorities have been among the chief beneficiaries of a vigorous free speech safeguard. . . .

The civil libertarian and judicial defense of racist speech also is based on the knowledge that censors have stifled the voices of oppressed persons and groups far more often than those of their oppressors. Censorship traditionally has been the tool of people who seek to subordinate minorities, not those who seek to liberate them. As Professor Kalven has shown, the civil rights movement of the 1960s depended upon free speech principles. These principles allowed protestors to carry their messages to audiences who found such messages highly offensive and threatening to their most deeply cherished views of themselves and their way of life. . . .

The foregoing history does not prove conclusively

that free speech is an essential precondition for equality, as some respected political philosophers have argued. But it does belie Professor Lawrence's theory that equality is an essential precondition for free speech. Moreover, this history demonstrates the symbiotic interrelationship between free speech and equality, which parallels the relationship between civil liberties and civil rights more generally. Both sets of aims must be pursued simultaneously because the pursuit of each aids the realization of the other. . . .

## CONCLUSION

. . .

An exaggerated concern with racist speech creates a risk of elevating symbols over substance in two problematic respects. First, it may divert our attention from the causes of racism to its symptoms. Second, a focus on the hateful message conveyed by particular speech may distort our view of fundamental neutral principles applicable to our system of free expression generally. We should not let the racist veneer in which expression is cloaked obscure our recognition of how important free expression is and of how effectively it has advanced racial equality.

Donald E. Lively, *Reformist Myopia and the Imperative of Progress: Lessons for the Post-Brown Era*, 46 Vanderbilt Law Review 865 (1993)*

## I. INTRODUCTION

Over the course of two centuries, constitutional law has evolved as both a source and ratification of moral development. The processes of constructing and interpreting the nation's charter have established a unique window through which it is possible to glimpse the fundamental concerns of bygone and present eras and the competition of values and ordering of priorities that define the society. A survey of the complete record discloses innumerable conflicts of law and morality that have arisen, been resolved and exist now primarily as historical reference points. It also reveals significant business that remains unfinished. Even as the nation has developed and reinvented itself, fundamental problems of race have endured as a seemingly immutable and intracta-

ble feature of its cultural landscape. Race was a crucial factor when the union was formed, and later when it ruptured and was reconstructed. It has persisted as an agent of profound division, confoundment and nonresolution. . . .

Contemporary agendas for further racial progress, at least those assuming an interventionist or management role for government, typically have as a premise the redefinition of power or reallocation of privilege. Such a strategy should not be surprising in a society that persistently has stressed group identity and used it to define status and distribute advantage. As a departure point for meaningful progress beyond formalism, and notwithstanding historical support for it, the management of group advantage, has elicited significant misgiving with respect to its potential for achievement. What is now the lost constitutional cause of affirmative action consumed nearly a generation's worth of political and intellectual energy. Even if the Court had proved more receptive to remedial racial preferences, affirmative action strategy required heavy investment of reformist capital for what would have been relatively limited returns. A significant lesson of affirmative action's constitutional failure is not just that it may stigmatize in its own way or facilitate bouts of racial politics that minorities are destined to lose. The Court itself has instructed that the management of group advantage by redistributing burdens and benefits is inconsonant with the equal protection guarantee. For many architects of racially significant reformist strategy, the Court's message has been lost or ignored. Even as preferential proposals and policies were undone by the Court's insistence upon a color-blind Fourteenth Amendment, reformist energy renewed itself in similar group-restrictive terms. Like the agenda for racial preferences, the case for special protection from racist speech has proposed a special allocation of constitutional interests.

The philosophy of racist speech management denotes a relatively insular, underdeveloped, and perilous effort to account for the harms it identifies and progress it envisions. Such a criticism does not undervalue the harm that may be attributed to racially stigmatizing expression. It may be conceded that the injury is as real and profound as proponents of regulation maintain, and that the First Amendment has been qualified for less trenchant reasons. Even factoring a discount for the charge that it is easier to oppose regulation in the abstract, when one has not borne the brunt of assaultive racist speech, the case for racist speech control is ultimately unpersuasive because it lacks general historical perspective, is underinclusive, and suffers from disproportionality. It

* Reprinted with permission of the Vanderbilt Law Review.

ignores the limited returns and indulgence of imagery that ensue when legal change is uncoupled with coextensive moral development. The strategy for hate speech control overlooks the record of like methods over the course of this century that were either unsuccessful or counterproductive. Bypassed also is the fact that in a functionally segregated society, the points of interracial contacts are relatively scarce and the beneficiaries of regulation constitute a relatively discrete subgroup. A particularly awkward reality is that abasing intraracial expression represents a more extensive and profound source of harm. Given the broad contours and consequences of racism that await reckoning, attention to a relatively narrow slice of racist injury betrays a poor distribution of reformist resources. . . .

## II. RACIST SPEECH MANAGEMENT AND THE LESSONS OF HISTORY

The case for regulating racist speech has been presented in terms that implicate a broad spectrum of law and its sources. Racist speech management has been supported, by reference to the law of torts, of the constitution, and of nations. A common premise of regulatory exponents is that racist expression constitutes a verbal assault that profoundly injures its victims. As Charles Lawrence has described it, such speech represents an "instantaneous . . . slap in the face that generates injury rather than dialogue." Mari Matsuda characterizes hate speech as one of several "implements" of racism that "work in coordination, reinforcing existing conditions of domination." From the stigmatizing consequences of racist speech, Lawrence has deduced a harm that implicates Fourteenth Amendment interests and necessitates a formal sanction.

Much criticism of racist speech management has been clothed in the First Amendment. Commentators have devoted substantial attention to demonstrating why such control is generally vague, overbroad, and inimical to constitutional and regulatory objectives. If the harm attributed to racist expression is as profound and real as regulatory advocates maintain, however, a facially sound case for speech control might be constructed. Relevant case law establishes that freedom of speech is not an absolute. The Court has allowed states to abridge the First Amendment to the extent that either a compelling reason is established for regulation or the speech at issue is classified as unprotected.

Insofar as racist speech causes identifiable harm, it is possible and even principled to maintain that it is without "significant social value" and, like obscenity or fighting words, should not be protected.

Alternatively, it may be argued that regulatory interests should be balanced against First Amendment demands. Even assuming that concerns with overbreadth and precision could be satisfied, the regulatory agenda represents a dubious exercise that misreads history at various levels. Recent Fourteenth Amendment history discloses a profound animus toward group-referenced policy that establishes special status or immunity. First Amendment history indicates a tendency to transform minority protective rules into methodologies that consolidate the dominant group's advantage. The history of constitutional law, even when profound minority concerns are at stake, evidences a pattern of resistance and underachievement in accounting for them. Against that confluence of historical tendencies, the risk is not just that asking so little will result in achieving so little, but that apparent gain will be transformed into real loss. . . .

Resistance to redistributive or selective justice, although fixed and even overstated, has not deterred theoretical creativity in support of racist speech management. A serious effort exists, as noted previously, to establish racist speech control as a logical extension of the *Brown* legacy. Apart from any problems that may exist in establishing that connection, a strategy that ties into *Brown* may assume too much about its imagery and too little about its achievements. The meaning and significance of *Brown* rest not just with the decision, which speech control advocates reference, but with its fate over the course of four decades. What began in 1954 as an epochal exercise in redefining the Constitution, and recrafting the society it governs, has yielded results that at best are uncertain and debatable and at worst delusionary and damaging. A generation of public school students experienced little if any benefit from desegregation, which primarily begot widespread evasion, delay, and resistance. When the Court finally demanded real compliance and achievement, the perception of actual change on a national scale precipitated opposition and backlash—first in the political process and then in constitutional principle. Thereafter, the potential for social engineering through the Fourteenth Amendment was curtailed by interpretations that limited the conditions for, scope of, and duration of relief. By the 1990s, *Brown's* insistence upon elimination of segregation "root and branch" had been reduced to a demand for eradication of segregation "to the extent practicable."

For all the powerful imagery that the *Brown* decision and its early progeny project, a final record of performance that includes an educational system "as separate and inherently unequal . . . in the future . . . as . . . in the past" represents a model of significant underachievement. Striking down official segregation was an apt and belated exercise in interpreting the Constitution. Beyond that accounting for formalism, and given its ultimate unwinding by constitutional limiting principles, the legacy of *Brown* is important for the insight it provides into the relative value society has put on racial appearance and reality. The desegregation decision generally is one of the most revered in the Court's history, causing even conservative interpretivists awkwardness in squaring their theories of review with its result. The imagery it projects, however, enables society to hide from the underlying reality left untouched. Like the touting of color-blindness, in an era of pervasive group-consciousness, the largely cosmetic and formal achievements of the *Brown* era suggest a real peril to reformism that may expect too much from innovation or redirection of the law. Regulation of racial wrong has proved vexingly different from the sanctioning of almost any other civil or criminal activity, given well-established habits of and easily identified opportunities for circumventing legal demands. The *Brown* experience itself evidenced those tendencies and thus presents a dubious model for attempted reform of speech habits. Mere enactment of a law prohibiting offensive expression does not alter the predictability of subsequent equivocation toward and accommodation of the identified evil. By attempting to imitate the perceived success of *Brown*, racist speech management assumes the danger of achievement that is more illusory than real.

While Fourteenth Amendment history has been unresponsive to group claims and concerns, for the most part, First Amendment history evidences that speech management strategy actually may be inimical to minority interests. In dissenting from a decision upholding group libel laws in *Beauharnais v. Illinois*, Justice Black warned: "Another such victory and I am undone." As Justice Black saw it, prohibition of expression that degraded, slurred, or offended minorities was more likely to imperil than protect them. The record of speech management over the past half century generally bears out his concern. Libel law, a decade after *Beauharnais*, was invoked in an effort to put the civil rights movement out of business in the South, much like abolitionists were shut down there more than a century earlier. The fighting words doctrine, although conceived as a means of deterring expression provokes a retaliation or breach of the peace, likewise has a history of being turned against minorities.

Evidence suggests that the resurrection of hate speech regulation will not reverse those historical trends. To guard against such misdirection, and the transformation of protective into oppressive methodology, it has been suggested that racist speech regulation should cut only one way. As so conceived, anti-hate speech laws would be enforced only when the victim of degrading speech

is a minority. The very urging of such a double standard, contemporaneous with clear constitutional trends against race-dependent attention or protection, suggests an exercise that not only is unattuned to recent trumpetings of constitutional color-blindness but is insular and disinterested in the lessons of history or considerations of practicality. The limited aims of group-referenced speech control arise at a time when "after several hundred years of class-based discrimination, . . . the Court is unwilling to hold that a class-based remedy for that discrimination is permissible." They are a focal point of forums and conferences, even as individuals are saddled with the near impossible burden of proving they are specific "victims of discrimination" in a society where "racism . . . has been so pervasive that none . . . has managed to escape its impact." From constitutional principle that "ignores the fact that for several hundred years Negroes have been discriminated against, not as individuals, but rather solely because of the color of their skins," a message exists that meaningful progress requires a significantly grander moral and legal vision than the relatively discrete concern with and attack on racist speech. Stubborn touting of it as part of a reformist methodology suggests the possibility at least of a commitment primarily toward maintaining life-support for a pet academic theory instead of contributing to the cause of meaningful progress. . . .

Given the general failure of the racist speech control movement to factor in the most directly relevant aspects of history, it is not a shock to find obliviousness to long-term patterns of racially significant legal and moral development. Two centuries of racial reckoning disclose a national consistency in ordering priorities and underachieving through the law. Abolition of slavery, like subsequent racially significant reforms, accomplished a change in form as racist energy was redirected toward creation of an equivalent system in fact. Despite the Fourteenth Amendment's subsequent eradication of the Black Codes, a system of peonage survived into the early part of this century. Official segregation was established as a methodology not only for maintaining racial separation but consolidating group advantage. The eventual determination that "separate is inherently unequal," as noted previously, eliminated overtly racist policy but was qualified in a way that enables discrimination to operate subtly or unconsciously without constitutional significance. Historical patterns of legal reform and consequent rerouting of racist impulses indicate an established model of limited change that is more eager to account for appearance than to compel real progress. Successful enactment of hate speech laws promises a hollow victory to the extent it redirects racism into more secretive and insidious enterprises. Methods that yield such results and taunt history denote poor strategy and undermine confidence in the wisdom of those responsible for it. At risk in the debate over racist speech regulation is not only the efficacy of policy but the credibility of those reformists whose priorities evidence practical disengagement, lack of perspective, and inept allocation of resources.

## III. MANIPULATING REALITY TO FIT THE CAUSE

The case for racist speech management is troubling not only for its deficient historical perspective but for its lack of perspective or honesty in describing the problem. For all of the attention that racist hate speech has elicited in current law and literature, it is a relatively marginal source of stigmatization and subordination. Reformist fixation upon expression suggests that anger, even though legitimate, has consumed judgment, clouded vision, and displaced interest in inspiring meaningful change. In a society that remains functionally segregated, many traditionally disadvantaged minorities have limited if any contact across racial lines. The imagery and conditioning effects of television, in contrast, are absorbed in virtually every household in the nation. Contemporary prime-time programming contains more series and shows featuring Blacks than ever. The phenomenon is a function in part of the fact that black households watch considerably more television than white households. The images communicated by television, according to various researchers, tend "to reinforce social dominance and control with respect to preferred social relations between the races." The institutionalization of demeaning stereotypes as a mainstream source of profit generates and indulges caricatures and misperceptions that are communicated and digested in a voluntary but largely non-interactive process. Without an effective defense mechanism or competing source of definition, trade in stigmatization is compounded and is largely validated by programming strategy and viewer choice.

The nation's heritage of racism includes the awkward reality that most verbal racial blows are incidental to intragroup rather than intergroup experience. Missing from modern concern with stigmatizing speech, however, is any attention to the subcultural usage of class-conscious terminology referenced to racial physiognomy. Traditionally, the acceptability of trading in certain race-sensitive terms has depended upon the racial identity of their source. The distinction does not determine necessarily the risk of injury. Investment in the notion that harm is determined by the speaker's identity, moreover, subscribes to and perpetuates more racial, if not racist, mythology. Racially demeaning speech within a group actually may be especially effective in stigmatizing and reinforcing pernicious stereotypes. The childhood experience of Justice Clarence Thomas has been offered as a classic example in support of that point. Raised in a formally segregated society, Justice Thomas as a child regularly was taunted and belittled by other blacks because of his thick lips, kinky hair and dark skin.

Such intragroup differentiation, calculated to fortify an internal class and status hierarchy, discloses an especially perverse aspect of racism. The fact that the victimizers themselves are victimized by an especially perverse twist of racism's legacy makes the injury no less serious. To the extent stigmatizing speech is an evil that must be controlled, moreover, constitutional principle affords no support for distinguishing on the basis of source. Whether a provable linkage between intragroup verbal degradation and injury exists in Justice Thomas's case, the perils of internal verbal warfare are bypassed largely by legal literature that focuses on interracial damage. Regulatory attention that is incremental and limited to cross-cultural incidents responds to deeply etched and easily recognized aspects and consequences of racism. It also may result from group sensitivity, poor perception, or dishonesty. Even if merely reflecting a historical conditioning process that induces recognition of and response to bright racial lines, narrowly framed speech management theories conveniently respect rather than challenge those divisions. The oversight, if not a function of unawareness, seems to represent a theory concerned more with posturing than achievement. . . .

## IV. OVERBLOWN INTERESTS AND MISALLOCATED RESOURCES

· · ·

Measured against the backdrop of past challenges to racial disadvantage and injustice, not to mention the dimensions of modern problems, recent initiatives to reckon with the nation's legacy of racism fall short both with respect to vision and breadth. The push for racial preferences during the past few decades was vulnerable to objection that it was too narrow in both its conception and its potential for achievement. The case for affirmative action, however, at least attempted to reference itself to group-wide interests. Even acknowledging the possibility that the benefits of racially preferential policies may accrue primarily to a discrete subgroup, one commentator has offered the defense that a single policy choice should not exclude broader reformist responses and thus should not be condemned simply for limited focus or achievement. The argument of nonexclusivity might be satisfactory if the resources for change were unlimited. Fending off the underinclusiveness charge is more difficult, however, when higher group-wide priorities exist and reformist resources are limited. Unlike the concept of racial preferences as a means of ensuring economic opportunity, which has the relative luxury of defending itself against claims that it is a tactic for subgroup advantage, the case for racist speech regulation has not managed effectively to reference itself to a clear group-wide interest. It is a strategy that misallocates reformist resources without even a claim to group-wide service.

It is conceivable that the inverted priorities, denoted by the limited aims and benefits of the racist speech regulation movement, may be understood as a function of factors beyond the control of reformists who otherwise would pursue broader change. In response to such a contention, one must be acknowledged that constitutional standards in recent years have limited substantially the capacity of the equal protection guarantee as an agent of change. Modern law and society reflect real animus toward official management of racial disadvantage, whether effected through desegregation processes or through racially preferential policies. Constitutional case law, in addition to rejecting the group accounting methodologies of racial preferences and racist speech regulation, has established motive requirements that function as seemingly indefeasible impediments to further constitutional challenges of discrimination. Social critics also have identified a sense of "racial fatigue" which, as experienced by other generations that effected limited change but found race a still intractable problem, has established an inertia of disinterest, resignation, or indifference. Even acknowledging that circumstances are not perfect for racial vision and change (that more comprehensively account for group interests), the reality is that conditions for racial progress never have been ideal. If reformist energy historically had been harbored pending a welcoming signal, or nonresistant environment, official segregation might be absent from the record only because slavery never was defeated. . . .

Broad achievement under the law is dependent not just upon identifying the racially disadvantaged status of a group (as affirmative action strategy did) or the victimized circumstance of a subgroup (as racist speech management initiatives do). If further progress is to be attained at a level that seriously reckons with the nation's unfinished racial business, it must be generated with a grander vision and the identifiable potential for a wider impact. A useful starting point for legal reformists would be to swear off narrowly targeted strategies that primarily stress victimization, offer limited possibilities of return, and do not have broad spectrum relevance. It also is essential to understand that limited intellectual and material resources exist for pursuing racially significant change. The unwise and potentially counterproductive strategy for regulating racist speech, although impressive in its academic polish and sophistication, might not have been pressed so seriously if tested against some real world sense and perspective. Had they performed a reality check first, the architects and exponents of racist speech management theory might have pondered the preference of disadvantaged groups with respect to whether energies should be dedicated toward primary impediments to development and opportunity or the relatively marginal phenomenon of interracial dialogue or monologue. Assuming that the choice is as simple as it would seem, and that overwhelming support would exist for the broader vision, the challenge for legal reformists is to rise above the discouraging trends of recent constitutional jurisprudence, not be consumed by anger or lesser priorities, and avoid battles that by their relatively incidental nature indicate that the greater war has been lost.

Instead of picking relatively small fights of their own convenience, or defined largely by their own experience, reformists must confront stubbornly the obstacles that truly impede the evolution of further racial progress under the law. The most crippling constitutional blow of the post-*Brown* era, largely foreclosing interpretive progress beyond an accounting for formalism, has been the installment of discriminatory intent requirements as a condition for establishing an equal protection violation. Motive-based criteria are to modern reckoning with racial disadvantage and discrimination what the separate but equal doctrine was to constitutional progress from the late nineteenth through the middle twentieth century. Although history discloses confirmed habits of resistance to progress, as noted previously, it also provides inspiration for contesting and even undoing unjust social orders.

The legal challenge to desegregation was a prolonged exercise that eventually succeeded because of its unwavering focus, tireless effort, and effective marketing of its ideals. As the primary barrier to reckoning with modern incarnations of discrimination, motive-referenced standards are the progeny of past legal methods for securing racial advantage. Like segregation before them, motive-based criteria are an apt and ripe target for a massive legal challenge. It took nearly four decades, in a more intimidating social environment, for the challenge to official segregation to express itself in a tactical fashion. In half that amount of time, since the Court invested in motive-based inquiry, legal reformists have responded to the overarching equal protection challenge of the time in generally underwhelming fashion. Rather than conceiving strategies of litigation and education targeted toward the defeat of principles that indulge subtle and unconscious discrimination, reformist energy is being diverted into and dissipated by causes that are generally lost and would have limited significance even if successful. It may be an ominous sign for the future that as the process of framing strategic goals and development has progressed from circumstances of real human peril to the relative comfort of academic tenure, policy vision and strategy have become correspondingly uninspired and insular. The phenomenon of parochialism and interest stratification is reminiscent of John Hart Ely's concern, expressed as a critique of fundamental rights development, with "a bias in constitutional reason in favor of the values of the upper middle, professional class from which most lawyers . . . and for that matter most moral philosophers are drawn.''

Focusing attention and energy upon the real impediment to further progress, and thereby adapting the model for defeating segregation to modern needs, responds to Charles Lawrence's plea ''to think creatively as lawyers.'' It represents such thinking, however, with a sense of proportionality. Creative thought by itself, as recent reformist efforts demonstrate, does not ensure wise policy or useful results. Racist speech management in particular, although creative, also is distinguished by a lack of vision and failed sense of marketability that risks tainting the historically profound movement for racial justice with the debatable and perhaps trendy agenda of political correctness. Unlike abolitionism, which managed to insinuate itself into mainstream politics, and the anti-segregation movement, which diligently cultivated legal and moral support, speech management theory has succeeded primarily in dividing traditional reformist allies.

Especially crucial to thinking that is both creative and productive may be a reacquisition of the capacity for not thinking like a lawyer. . . . It is tempting to regard modern advocacy of racist speech classification as the artfully crafted work of individuals who thrived in the professional education process but, in so doing, sacrificed the perspective, understanding, and other aspects of intelligence and emotion that would make their talents especially useful in reckoning with society's compounding legacy of racial disadvantage. A revitalized sense of context and proportion at least might improve the chances for shrewder allocation of reformist resources in the future.

Creative thought, if it is to be bridled with real achievement, must factor in considerations other than legal theory and analytical prowess. Crucial to the ends of progress is an effective marketing strategy for selling change. Consistent with the advice given many law students—that a significant market exists for their skills beyond the legal profession—a need exists outside the legal for the perspective, public sensitization, and moral development that legal reformists can supply. Regardless of how aptly a strategy for legal change is conceived and developed, it may be largely for naught if sufficient attention also is not devoted to elevating levels of social awareness. Teaching a constitutional law class affords quick insight into the reality that the vast majority of law students, until exposed to modern equal protection doctrine, have no idea that a daunting barrier exists to proving discrimination. A safe inference would be that if a relatively well-educated class of prospective professionals is largely oblivious to that reality, the society at large has little if any clue that modern discrimination is mostly above the law. Like the evils of segregation before, the unfairness of mod-

ern legal standards now is a tale that needs to be told well. Effective narration may require some armchair advocates to enhance their exposure to and engagement in real world diversity, however, rather than define their pluralistic credentials on the basis of the relatively limited differences among professionals. Real appreciation of, and accounting for, cultural pluralism in the end is denoted not just by filling faculty positions with persons of like professional training but by a broader mix of actions, decisions and involvement that more meaningfully confirm a person's or institution's life. . . .

For any cause, selling change is a crucial prerequisite of change itself. History illustrates why social awakening is essential for any racially pertinent change that may be achieved by law. The latter half of this century has included two racially significant demands by the legal system for social and moral change. In *Brown*, the Court required dismantlement of formal segregation. Later, it prohibited racial preferences even for remedial purposes. Both decisions, despite their constitutional demands, have legacies demonstrating that the challenge of moral reform is at least as daunting as the task of legal change. A review of post-*Brown* litigation discloses the pervasiveness of resistance to the redefined imperatives of equal protection. Notwithstanding the recent demand for constitutional color-blindness, one need go no farther than a faculty hiring meeting at countless American law schools to witness an exercise in group prioritization and effective repetition of *Brown's* aftermath guided only by a different moral compass.

Creative thinking in its broadest sense also requires identifying and seizing advantage when opportunity presents itself. Trying to rework the magic of *Brown*, by making its theory relevant to modern problems, is an odd enterprise when the past two decades of relevant jurisprudence essentially have gutted it. In retrospect, *Brown* and its progeny represent a classic exercise in the treatment of symptoms rather than causation. Racist speech management likewise inclines toward results that account more for the appearance than the actuality of social change. Peculiar too is the willingness to reinvest in a premise that indulges the imagery of achievement and reinforces habits of reliance on what history suggests will be unkept promises or inadequate resolve. Further appeals for special attention or protection miss a key lesson of the nation's racial legacy that the desegregation experience has reinforced. If the purpose of speech regulation is to safeguard against further victimization, it seems, as one observer has put it, ''somewhat self-defeating to appeal to the sense of the majority'' as a strategy of accounting for minority rights. Indications are that neither the present nor future of a society that rewards individual achievement and advantage will differ much from the past, at least with respect to anyone's or any group's willingness to qualify or restrain self-interest as a condition for redistributing power, status, and justice. The case for managing group interests, apart from reflecting on incompetent strategy, trades both in the imagery of patronization and the reality of false hope. What is missed by legal intellectuals, seduced by the allure of formalistic manipulation and discovery, is effectively articulated by grass-roots social critics who—having witnessed the underachievement of desegregation and broken promises of urban redevelopment—''don't expect whites to do anything for blacks.'' Appeals for official management of group interest are viewed skeptically from such a perspective that sees ''[t]he only reason we could ever have to be a supplicant before another group [as being] our own lack of self-respect and belief in ourselves.'' Even in a system burdened by the legacy of discrimination, a group or individual strategy that prepares for emerging opportunities may prove more useful in the long run than trading in victimization or attempting to squeeze progress from *Brown* ever could be. More useful than pleas for special attention or protection may be strategies that trade in group identity for purposes of pooling resources and investing them in group benefiting ways. The lifetime training of minorities in multiculturalism, and the dominant race's tendency toward maintaining its insularity, presents at least one foreseeable possibility for inverting traditional group advantage. In an increasingly globalized existence that rewards cultural adaptability, not to mention a nation itself that is becoming increasingly diversified, minorities possess an advantage that the market should reward if modern incarnations of discrimination are effectively discerned and uprooted.

Inventorying group strength and identifying group advantage represents a strategy for progress that draws upon the brokering and leveraging methodologies that an opportunity society touts by emphasizing self-responsibility, it seriously tests the society's professed commitment to comprehensive color blinding. Acceptance of the spoken rules for individual or group development, thus, must be met by the legal system's commitment to recontour its standards so that those who invest in the system and its credibility still are not denied their rewards as a result of vestigial prejudice or discrimination. Legal change even if achieved, moreover, represents an essentially technical accomplishment of the craft, unless responsibility is also assumed for the educational groundwork that makes real social reform possible. Time and energy spent trying to control the way people speak is time and energy lost from the grander challenge to how they think. Even armed with the best of vision and strategy, efforts to redefine the future may not preclude a further extension of history that perpetuates race as its most intractable problem. Although society's development to date might not encourage betting against such a future, an agenda of narrow or insular goals and underdeveloped strategy makes the prospect a bankable certainty. . . .

## V. CONCLUSION

. . .

Four decades after *Brown*, at the termination point of the desegregation era, it is time to begin framing and communicating the broader vision of future racial progress. With all deference to the *Brown* era, it is essentially over and further achievement rests not with revisiting its real or presumed glories but learning from the multi-faceted strategy that begot it. Legalistic creativity that trumpets the connection of a peripheral concern to a bygone principle and era is a poor substitute for any vision of wholesale progress. Fundamental to any achievement in a morally competitive context is an intelligent and informed understanding of the market. A strategy that lacks perspective, ignores history, risks counterproductivity, and affects a relative few is a difficult commodity to sell. A more worthy successor to past struggle and achievement is an agenda framed as broadly as the problem it confronts and seeking change that makes a real difference.

## Bibliography

*Hate Speech*

Bartlett, Katharine T. & O'Barr, Jean, *The Chilly Climate on College Campuses: An Expansion of the "Hate Speech" Debate*, 1990 Duke Law Journal 574 (1990).

Byrne, J. Peter, *Racial Insults and Speech Within the University*, 79 Georgetown Law Journal 399 (1991).

Delgado, Richard, *Words That Wound: A Tort Action for Racial Insults, Epithets and Name-Calling*, 17 Harvard Civil Rights-Civil Liberties Law Review 133 (1982).

Gard, Stephen W., *Fighting Words as Free Speech*, 58 Washington University Law Quarterly 531 (1980).

Gates, Jr., Henry Louis, *Let Them Talk*, The New Republic, September 20 & 27, 1993.

Greenawalt, Kent, *Insults and Epithets: Are They Protected Speech?*, 42 Rutgers Law Review 287 (1991).

Jones, Charles H., *Equality, Dignity and Harm: The Constitutionality of Regulating American Campus Ethnoviolence*, 37 Wayne Law Review 1383 (1991)

Kretzmer, David, *Freedom of Speech and Racism*, 8 Cardozo Law Review 445 (1987).

Lively, Donald E., *Racist Speech and the Management: The High Risks of Low Achievement*, 1 Virginia Journal of Law and Social Policy 1 (1993).

Mazzaro, Toni M., *Equality and Freedom of Expression: The Hate Speech Dilemma*, 32 William & Mary Law Review 211 (1991).

Matsuda, Mari, J., *Public Response to Racist Speech: Considering the Victim's Story*, 87 Michigan Law Review 2320 (1989).

Post, Robert C., *Racist Speech, Democracy, and the First Amendment*, 32 William & Mary Law Review 267 (1991).

Rubenstein, William, *Since When is the Fourteenth Amendment Our Route to Equality?: Some Reflections on the Construction of the Hate Speech Debate from a Lesbian/Gay Perspective*, 2 Law & Sexuality 19 (1992).

Schwartz, Deborah R., *A First Amendment Justification for Regulating Racist Speech on Campus*, 40 Case Western Reserve 1 Review 733 (1989).

Sherry, Suzanna, *Speaking of Virtue: A Republican Approach to University Regulation of Hate Speech*, 75 Minnesota Law Review 933 (1991).

Smolla, Rodney A., *Rethinking First Amendment Assumption About Racist and Sexist Speech*, 47 Washington & Lee Law Review 171 (1990).

## G.  Use of Government Funds

Expenditure of government money for purposes of subsidizing or facilitating speech or expressive activity has emerged as a significant First Amendment issue in the final decades of the twentieth century. Implicated in the debate are the existence and extent of governmental power and the principle that the state cannot discriminate on the basis of content. A central issue is whether the government, even if without authority to regulate individual choices and decisions, can influence them pursuant to subsidies or other benefits. Kathleen M. Sullivan rejects distinctions that have evolved between penalties and nonsubsidies, arguing instead for an alternative approach grounded in the systemic effects that conditions have on the exercise of constitutional rights. In a number of First Amendment contexts, Richard A. Epstein examines the government's power to impose conditions upon benefits that it could not establish pursuant to direct regulation. Dorothy E. Roberts criticizes official control of knowledge as a means of oppressing and maintaining the dependence of subordinated groups.

Kathleen M. Sullivan, *Unconstitutional Conditions*, 102 HARVARD LAW REVIEW 1413 (1989)*

The doctrine of unconstitutional conditions holds that government may not grant a benefit on the condition that the beneficiary surrender a constitutional right, even if the government may withhold that benefit altogether. It reflects the triumph of the view that government may not do indirectly what it may not do directly over the view that the greater power to deny a benefit includes the lesser power to impose a condition on its receipt. Consensus that the better view won, however, has not put an end to confusion about its application. To the contrary, recent Supreme Court decisions on challenges to unconstitutional conditions seem a minefield to be traversed gingerly. Just when the doctrine appears secure, new decisions arise to explode it. This Article seeks to make the footwork easier by exploring and reconceiving the doctrine's underlying theoretical foundation. . . .

## II. UNCONSTITUTIONAL CONDITIONS AS COERCION

Directly and through metaphors of duress or penalty, the Court has repeatedly suggested that the problem with unconstitutional conditions is their coercive effect. Yet the Court's unconstitutional conditions rulings display serious inconsistencies in their account of coercion. The Court has never satisfactorily refuted the argument that offers of conditioned benefits expand rather than contract the options of the beneficiary class, and so present beneficiaries with a free choice. Even assuming that the choice such offers present is less than free, the Court has never developed a coherent rationale for determining when such offers rise to the level of "coercion." . . .

First, although the Court frequently treats coercion as a matter of mere description or measurement—conditions become unconstitutional when they "pass the point at which 'pressure turns into compulsion'"—such an empirical account of coercion is unsustainable. As accounts of interpersonal coercion in both private law and moral philosophy make clear, any useful conception of coercion is irreducibly normative. Without a theory of autonomy, utility, fairness, or desert, one cannot tell when choice has been wrongfully constrained. Such normative accounts of coercion are peculiarly elusive in the unconstitutional

conditions context, however, because they cannot be derived from the post-1937 Constitution itself. Moreover, even a satisfying normative theory of coercion would give only an incomplete account of unconstitutional conditions. Conditions on benefits, like other government actions, can burden constitutional rights even when they do not rise to the level of coercion. . . .

### C. Limits of Coercion

Even if there were a consensus on the normative baseline characterizing coercion, two difficulties in applying a coercion approach to the unconstitutional conditions context would remain. First, government, in contrast to any given individual, crucially shapes the background against which conditional offers are made. Second, coercion does not exhaust the range of unconstitutional government action; government can infringe rights through various other modes. Any focus solely on whether conditions coerce government beneficiaries will thus inevitably be too narrow.

1. Features of Government.—In several respects, government poses greater danger than private parties of coercion, however defined. First, government has compulsory taxing and taking powers and a monopoly on legitimate violence. Second, government has pervasive influence; it is far more difficult to avoid encounters with government than with other individuals. As post-New Deal constitutional law recognizes, government determines the distribution of wealth both by regulatory action and inaction.

In themselves, however, these facts do not make all government offers coercive. Government plays a variety of roles: not only regulator but also employer, contractor, proprietor, insurer of last resort, buyer, and seller, to name a few. Moreover, government's coercive power base should not be confused with the coercive effect of its actions: offers of subsidies depend on the coercive power to tax, and offers of exemptions from regulation derive from the coercive power to regulate, but conditions attached to benefits do not on that basis necessarily coerce the beneficiary.

Third, and more troubling, is government's considerable monopoly power over many benefits it provides. To be sure, private competition with government exists to varying degrees, sometimes as a matter of constitutional right. The extent to which competition disciplines government, however, should not be overestimated; as Justice Powell wrote in a different context, "[a] state frequently will respond to market conditions on the basis of political rather than economic concerns." Moreover, government frequently attaches conditions to those benefits whose

* Reprinted with permission.

supply government overwhelmingly dominates. Finally, although the political process itself involves bargaining, government typically offers benefits to individual beneficiaries on a take-it-or-leave-it basis.
. . .

2. Modes of Infringement.—Recall that the entire analogy to coercive interpersonal offers arose in an effort to refute the argument that unconstitutional conditions are in fact consensual. From a less defensive perspective, however, the entire focus on "coercion" of constitutional rightholders appears anomalous. Constitutional rights impose upon government far broader obligations of restraint than the mere obligation not to coerce citizens in the exercise of their liberties. In other words, coercion is not typically a prerequisite to the unconstitutionality of government action in the first place.

On the contrary, government action that inhibits freedom but falls short of "coercion" has long been held in numerous contexts to infringe constitutional rights. As Justice Stewart once noted in the context of the right to jury trial, "[a] procedure need not be inherently coercive in order that it be held to impose an impermissible burden upon the assertion of a constitutional right"; it is enough that it exert a lesser deterrent effect. To take some familiar examples, speech has been held to be burdened not only when the speaker is threatened with jail but when he is required to obtain a license, reveal his identity, or confine his speech to media that leave no litter on the public square. Indeed, the first amendment doctrines of vagueness and overbreadth identify a mere "chilling effect" as a burden on protected speech. The Court has likewise held the right to abortion infringed not only when abortion is made a crime, but when it is burdened by regulations that impose excessive expense or delay, or that even seek to tip the scales of information about reproductive choice in favor of the government's preference for childbirth.

To be sure, coercion is the essence of violation of *some* constitutional rights, such as the right against compelled self-incrimination protected by the fifth amendment. But few, if any, other constitutional rights share this character. The liberties implicated in unconstitutional conditions problems far more typically can be burdened even if the rightholder is not "coerced." The view that only coercion unconstitutionally burdens rights such as speech and free exercise of religion follows from a mistaken conception of government neutrality toward such rights. Government neutrality here cannot consist of pure inaction, and therefore restraint from "coercion." At a minimum, government must affirmatively create and maintain some preconditions for the exercise of autonomy by the rightholder—for example, by protecting speakers from mob veto. Although the extent of this affirmative obligation is deeply controversial, it should at least be clear that government can sometimes burden a right by eliminating the minimal preconditions for its exercise. . . .

In the end, then, the very indefiniteness of the Court's "coercion" reasoning in unconstitutional conditions cases suggests an important insight: namely, that focusing on coercion alone misses the point. There is good reason to turn elsewhere in a search for the rationale of unconstitutional conditions doctrine, both because the necessary baselines are elusive, once government benefits in this context are conceded to be gratuitous, and because government, which differs significantly from any given individual, can burden rights to autonomy through means other than coercion. Coercion thus begins rather than ends the inquiry.

## III. UNCONSTITUTIONAL CONDITIONS AS CORRUPTION

The difficulties of patrolling the elusive border between coercion and voluntary exchange prompt consideration of a second, wholly different approach to unconstitutional conditions problems. This approach asks not whether the condition coerces the beneficiary, but instead whether the government's proposal reflects illegitimate legislative process, and should therefore be condemned even if the offeree is free to refuse it. Metaphors of extortion, bribery, manipulation, and subterfuge that surface in the cases often suggest this approach. But the Court has never provided a theory to explicate these metaphors, and thus to distinguish legitimate from illegitimate government proposals.

The Court's recurrent focus on the "germaneness" of condition to benefit comes closest to providing possible foundation for such a theory. Thinkers as otherwise divergent as Robert Hale and Justice Scalia have suggested that the legitimacy of a government proposal depends upon the degree of relatedness between the condition on a benefit and the reasons why government may withhold the benefit altogether. The more germane a condition to a benefit, the more deferential the review; nongermane conditions, in contrast, are suspect. Germaneness also figures in the "greater-power-includes-the-lesser" debate and the current "penalty/nonsubsidy" distinction in the cases. Any distinction so important to the outcome of the cases ought to have an explanation. The cases and commentary, however, say remarkably little about why germaneness should matter.

At first glance, "germaneness" in this context might seem to refer simply to the standard means-ends rationality review characteristic of all claims of violation of constitutional right. But that is not the case; the two inquiries serve different functions. The standard inquiry into means-ends rationality in constitutional review asks whether, at the appropriate level of scrutiny (minimal, heightened, or strict), the government's action is justified by a sufficient (rational, close, or necessary) relationship to a sufficient (legitimate, substantial, or compelling) government end. Unconstitutional conditions cases have used the germaneness inquiry to resolve a different, prior question: does attachment of the condition to the benefit burden a constitutional right? In other words, in unconstitutional conditions cases, the degree of germaneness helps to determine at the threshold what level of government justification would suffice to uphold a condition, not whether the government has provided that justification. Specifically, the Court has held that nongermane conditions trigger closer scrutiny than germane conditions pressuring the same rights. . . .

## C. Limits of Germaneness

Three difficulties plague efforts to ground the germaneness approach to unconstitutional conditions in civic republican or public choice theories. First, both theories are deeply controversial and have been subject to various forms of global critique. For example, the notion of reviving civic republicanism in the contemporary United States has been criticized as overly optimistic about the common good as a regulative ideal in a heterogeneous society, and as insufficiently protective of rights transcending political process. Likewise, public choice theory has been criticized for overestimating the extent to which politics is driven by rent-seeking as opposed to other motivations such as altruism or ideology. These broad controversies, however, will not receive extended discussion here.

Second, germaneness theories founder on the extreme malleability of the concept of germaneness itself. Germaneness to the purpose of a benefit depends crucially on how broadly or narrowly that purpose is defined. For example, conditioning food stamps on nonparticipation in labor strikes may be interpreted either as a nongermane condition mixing welfare policy with labor policy, or as a condition germane to welfare policy because it arguably limits subsistence to those least able to avoid need. Likewise, the condition invalidated in *Nollan* may be interpreted either as nongermane to the provision of visual access to the sea, as the majority held it was,

or as germane to a more general state interest in facilitating public use and enjoyment of the beach, as the dissent argued. Moreover, a legislative package's complexity in itself need not signal a lack of the deliberation that civic republicanism requires, or fail to express the genuine majority preference that public choice theory seeks to facilitate. The excision of strikers from the food stamp program or abortion patients from Medicaid could plausibly reflect deliberation more than logrolling, and the majority may actually have preferred no program at all to a program lacking these conditions. The very definition of germaneness is thus contested and dependent on further normative assumptions.

Third and most important, civic republican and public choice theories of germaneness are both significantly over- and underinclusive in relation to unconstitutional conditions problems. They are overinclusive because the problem of mixing agendas extends far beyond conditions that affect constitutional rights. Corruption in either model might infect not merely rights-affecting conditions on benefits, but virtually any kind of legislation that inappropriately intertwines issues. In short, the civic republican and public choice models give no special weight to the fact that unconstitutional conditions problems involve pressure on constitutional rights. If the simple fact of divergence between condition and benefit signals a deficit in deliberation, then republican premises would condemn as equally corrupt laws that tied highway funds to anti-abortion measures or to a ban on turnip sales; mixed agendas are problematic whether rights-affecting or not. Similarly, the public choice theorist who deplores the existence of vote trading should not care whether constitutional rights or some other currency is traded in the political marketplace; the key defect is that there is vote trading at all.

Civic republican and public choice theorists thus focus on unjust redistribution in politics, regardless of whether the medium of redistribution involves pressure on preferred constitutional liberties. To a civic republican such as Sunstein, transfers are unjust if they embody special rather than public interests. To a public choice theorist such as Epstein, powerful factions should not be allowed to capture rent through abuse of public monopolies, and citizens should not be compelled to pay into a public protection scheme more than they have a chance of getting out. Such theories, however, intersect only fortuitously with the particular forms of pressure on rights at issue in unconstitutional conditions cases. A focus on controlling government abuse in the distribution of benefits makes the question whether a condition burdens a preferred constitutional liberty secondary or even unnecessary. Conditions with equal effects on constitutional rights will stand or fall depending on whether they reflect the factional rent-seeking each theory targets.

Germaneness theories suffer from underinclusiveness in relation to unconstitutional conditions problems as well as overinclusiveness. In particular, they fail to explain why *germane* burdens on constitutional rights should be regarded as benign. Minimum rate schedules equally curtail the trucker's economic liberty whether imposed to conserve highways or to protect powerful entrenched business interests; yet germaneness theory subjects schedules enacted for one purpose and not the other to strict scrutiny. Likewise, the government arguably impairs interests protected by the takings clause equally when it uses its leverage over building permits to exact surrender of *either* a viewing spot *or* a lateral passageway. In either event, the government may have zoned restrictively in the first place with the goal of trading back variances for free coastal access in the future—an arguable abuse of the zoning power. And in either event, the government accomplishes a "taking" without the visibility or political checks that normally flow from approving expenditures to compensate overt exercises of the eminent domain power.

The over- and underinclusiveness of germaneness theories in relation to unconstitutional conditions problems reflect a common theme: germaneness has more to do with disciplining governmental activity according to some independent norm of appropriate legislative process than it does with protecting constitutional rights. Not surprisingly, then, germaneness theories fail to resolve unconstitutional conditions problems.

## IV. UNCONSTITUTIONAL CONDITIONS AS COMMODIFICATION

Unconstitutional conditions doctrine has a third possible theoretical explanation: that some constitutional rights are inalienable, and therefore may not be surrendered even through voluntary exchange. This approach identifies the harm in unconstitutional conditions as the commodification of rights—the treatment of rights as transferable objects.

Inalienability arguments, unlike coercion and germaneness arguments, rarely appear in the unconstitutional conditions cases, and appear in only slightly more developed form in the commentary. As a matter of common sense, however, unconstitutional conditions doctrine plausibly appears to be a species of inalienability rule. Furthermore, inalienability theories have been richly elaborated in the context of

private market relationships; possible applications of such theories to the unconstitutional conditions context deserve exploration. . . .

### B. Theories of Inalienability

Four different sorts of theory defend inalienability rules in private market contexts: theories of paternalism, efficiency, distribution, and personhood. Paternalism arguments deny that an individual is necessarily the best judge of whether an exchange is in his or her best interest. Both efficiency arguments and distributive arguments, unlike paternalistic arguments, assume that individuals can best judge their own interests. Efficiency arguments seek to remove obstacles, such as market imperfections, to the expression of those interests; distributive arguments seek to transfer power or wealth between groups without changing or overriding their perception of their own interests. Arguments from personhood hold that some things are inalienable because they are too centrally constitutive of identity to be treated as commensurable with other objects and thus as tradeable. . . .

### C. Limits of Inalienability

Each of the arguments for inalienability just sketched faces problems in translation from the market to the constitutional context. In the end only the distributive strand helps to capture the problem with unconstitutional conditions, and even the distributive argument must be recast to fit this context.

The first problem undercuts both the paternalism and personhood strands: the rights pressured in unconstitutional conditions cases inherently give special protection to decisional autonomy. Because these rights protect the decision itself, the distinction between exercise of a right and its waiver or sale is blurred. The less clear the distinction, the more barring sale will interfere with rather than protect the seller's rights. Scrutiny of the reasons one chooses to worship or not, or to carry a pregnancy to term or abort, for example, appears inconsistent with protecting individual sovereignty over the decision. A decision to give up worshipping on the Sabbath is normally protected whether grounded in philosophical reflection or prompted by venal motives to work for wages on that day instead. Declaring a constitutional right nonrelinquishable for the rightholder's own good thus contradicts the premise of the rightholder's exclusive jurisdiction over those questions.

Put another way, making decisions inalienable creates duties. For example, in barring people from selling themselves into slavery or from renting their wombs or kidneys, the state simultaneously declares rights to free labor or bodily integrity inalienable, and creates duties not to become a slave or an organ bank. But such duty-creation is inappropriate for constitutional liberties that consist of freedom *for* potential private decisions, rather than freedom *from* them. To oblige the exercise of speech or privacy rights would misconstrue their meaning. If the right to divulge the secrets of government employment is deemed inalienable—for example, in order to prevent government from insulating itself from public criticism—is Snepp then obliged to speak? If the abortion right is deemed inalienable—for example, in order to equalize the power relationship between men and women on the whole—are pregnant women obliged to choose abortion?

A second problem undercuts efficiency arguments for inalienability in the unconstitutional conditions context. Efficiency arguments presuppose a uniquely desirable end state or equilibrium normally produced by private transactions; such arguments defend inalienability where necessary to produce a more efficient result than the market. But it is difficult to conceive of any equivalent metric for measuring the success of a regime of preferred constitutional liberties—that is, of a constitutional surrogate for efficiency. To be sure, market metaphors have sometimes animated constitutional discourse, most famously in Justice Holmes' image of "free trade in ideas": "the best test of truth is the power of the thought to get itself accepted in the competition of the market." Others have defended different conceptions of an appropriate equilibrium or end state for free speech: for example, "enrich[ed] public debate."

Such end-state theories, however, give incomplete accounts of the value of constitutional liberties. In some sense all "individual" rights may be understood to serve collective values. The right of "privacy," for example, not only promotes freedom for individual self-definition and personality formation, but also serves as a check on totalitarianism by preventing the state from fashioning persons in a single orthodox mold. The protection of private property rights serves the social value of encouraging wealth-creation as well as the value of individual security. But exclusive focus on these social values would ignore persistent constitutional conceptions of freedom as autonomous moral agency and of justice as respect for individuals' choices for their own lives: self-actualization for one who speaks or is conscientiously silent, self-government for one who affiliates with political organizations, or self-definition for one who engages in sex, marriage, or childbearing. Moreover, even if equilibria such as "enriched public de-

bate" in the speech context were appropriate, inalienability rules standing alone are hardly guaranteed to promote them.

Third, all of these inalienability arguments share a more basic and undermining flaw: they ask the wrong question. The unconstitutional conditions cases ask not whether a constitutional right is inalienable in general, but rather whether it may be relinquished to *government*. It is one thing to choose atheism or sign a secrecy agreement in response to a private inducement; it is another matter for government to induce either result. The special problems of government purchase may require restrictions on the transfer to government of privately alienable rights. Both polar positions in the existing commentary miss this point: the free-alienability argument errs by assuming that government is no different from any other "buyer" of rights; structural arguments for the wholesale inalienability of rights prove too much.

If government is the problem, declaring rights generally inalienable is not the solution. Such problems demand not a general theory of blocked exchanges, but a particularized theory for determining when to block surrender of preferred constitutional liberties to government. Because distributive arguments for inalienability turn on the particular identities or features of the classes involved in an exchange, and on their relative power, they point in a helpful direction for unconstitutional conditions analysis. But the problem of giving such arguments more specific content in this context remains. . . .

## V. A SYSTEMIC ACCOUNT OF UNCONSTITUTIONAL CONDITIONS

This Part argues for an alternative approach grounded in the systemic effects that conditions on benefits have on the exercise of constitutional rights. Such an approach starts from the proposition that the preferred constitutional liberties at stake in unconstitutional conditions cases do not simply protect individual rightholders piecemeal. Instead, they also help determine the overall distribution of power between government and rightholders generally, and among classes of rightholders. . . .

### A. Constitutional Liberty as Distribution

A systemic approach to unconstitutional conditions problems recognizes that constitutional liberties regulate three relationships: the relationship between government and rightholders, horizontal relationships among classes of rightholders, and vertical relationships among rightholders. As the following sections argue, rights-pressuring conditions on government benefits potentially skew all three.

Such an approach has important advantages over coercion, germaneness, and inalienability theories in illuminating unconstitutional conditions problems. Unlike coercion and inalienability theories, a systemic approach emphasizes the distinctive role of government: citizens' transactions with government require different analysis than interpersonal transactions, an analysis that focuses not on individuals but on the balance of power and freedom in the polity as a whole. Unlike germaneness theories, the approach here focuses on constitutional liberties and the values they serve, not on norms of legislative process. Moreover, a systemic approach helps to resolve the apparent paradox of consent in unconstitutional conditions cases, and to avoid the pitfalls of theories that require a showing that a particular beneficiary has been coerced. Individuals who waive constitutional rights in exchange for government benefits, even if uncoerced, might undervalue the structural values those rights serve. Individuals lack both the information and the stake necessary to assess the value of their own exercise of rights to third parties and to the polity as a whole. A systemic approach can bar government from redistributing rights even if affected individuals consent.

Finally, by focusing on distributive concerns, a systemic approach acknowledges that unconstitutional conditions cases raise issues of equality as well as liberty. This should come as no surprise; it is a familiar principle in a wide variety of constitutional contexts that, even if government has no obligation to provide something, distributive concerns constrain it if it chooses to do so. The fundamental rights branch of equal protection doctrine furnishes obvious examples: although the Constitution does not compel states to institute democratic voting or criminal appeals, the equal protection clause forbids them from permitting differentials in wealth to determine access to such procedures if instituted. Likewise, the doctrine of selective prosecution holds that, even though no one has a right to the benefit of nonprosecution for a crime, and random underenforcement is not constitutionally objectionable, everyone has a right not to be singled out on the basis of race, national origin, religion, or political viewpoint. Similarly, a municipality need not permit speech on public property outside the traditional public forum, but if it does so, it "may not *condition* . . . speech on obtaining a license or permit from a government official in that official's boundless discretion." And although land use decisionmaking is otherwise discretionary with states and cities, they may not delegate it to a church because to do so threatens political oppression through a union of civil and ecclesiastical control.

1. Preserving Private Ordering.—The set of preferred constitutional liberties characteristically affected in unconstitutional conditions cases functions to preserve spheres of autonomy. Government may not directly command or forbid actions protected by individual rights of speech, association, or reproductive privacy, for example, because these decisions belong in the realm of private ordering rather than government control. Unconstitutional conditions doctrine protects that private ordering by preventing governmental end-runs around the barriers to direct commands.

Preserving autonomous private decision-making not only promotes self-determination by rightholders; it also checks the power of the state. Ensuring that decisions about rights remain to the greatest extent possible a matter of private ordering preserves an equilibrium between public and private spheres. The boundary between public and private spheres, of course, is not natural or prepolitical, but rather a social construct. While the *content* of private ordering will thus vary with the substantive theory that underlies it, unconstitutional conditions doctrine responds to a constant fear that government will tend to use the strategic manipulation of gratuitous benefits to aggrandize public power. On this view, government overreaches when it offers benefits in order to gain leverage over constitutional rights. The state may have many good reasons to deal out regulatory exemptions and subsidies, but gaining strategic power over constitutional rights is not one of them.

Nightmares about state encroachment will vary depending on the reasons private ordering is valued and governmental tyranny is feared. Those principally concerned with the defense of old property against the regulatory state, for example, will fear a different scenario than those who worry about welfare-state control over recipients of new property. . . .

2. Ensuring Government Evenhandedness.—Unconstitutional conditions inherently classify potential beneficiaries into two groups: those who comply with the condition and thereby get better treatment, and those who do not. This discrimination raises a second kind of distributive concern whenever the content of a liberty includes some equality principle or entitlement to government neutrality. Targeting of benefits can destroy such equality or neutrality as readily as can imposition of harms: for example, government can skew political speech, association, and the system of representation they support whether it jails Democrats or offers cash bounties to Republican converts.

Which constitutional rights entail such obligations of government evenhandedness? Speech is the paradigm example. If government could freely use benefits to shift viewpoints in a direction favorable to the existing regime, democratic self-government would be undermined. The view that government must treat speakers evenhandedly underlies the Court's consistent statements in unconstitutional conditions challenges that benefit conditions predicated on viewpoint discrimination are void: government may not "'a[m] at the suppression of dangerous ideas'" by buying them out any more than by punishing them. The religion clauses also plainly impose on government an obligation of neutrality, however, difficult the question of whether government has fulfilled it. For example, state aid to parochial education appears not neutral but preferential to religion if measured against a common-law baseline (no aid), but neutral if measured against a welfare-state baseline (universal public education supported by general taxation)—at least up to the point that government spends equivalent sums per capita on public and parochial students alike. Whether rights other than those protected by the first amendment entail similar obligations of evenhandedness is more controversial. For example, *Roe v. Wade* may be interpreted either as requiring government neutrality on reproductive choice, or as merely barring criminalization and its equivalents while leaving government free to express its preference for childbirth over abortion in other ways.- Wherever obligations of government evenhandedness are central to a right, however, conditions on a benefit designed to prefer one otherwise constitutionally protected choice to another will pose a danger.

This observation does not depend upon any affirmative government obligation to subsidize or otherwise equalize access to rights. Government's skewing effects on an existing distribution can be recognized and restrained even if inequality among rightholders remains. Just as antitrust law can recognize and reduce relative monopoly power without seeking to realize perfect competitive equilibrium as the necessary result, a right against government distortion need not entail a right to government equalization. This second distributive argument for unconstitutional conditions doctrine stresses that some equity conditions restrain government even in a constitutional order founded on negative rather than positive liberty.

3. Preventing Constitutional Caste.—The third sort of systemic concern underlying unconstitutional conditions doctrine focuses on vertical rather than horizontal redistribution among rightholders. This argument does not aim to ensure evenhandedness among classes that would choose to exercise their rights *differently* before the government intervention. Rather, it attempts to prevent hierarchy among classes that, without the government intervention, would make the *same* choice. This strand recognizes that background inequalities of wealth and resources necessarily determine one's bargaining position in relation to government, and that the poor may have nothing to trade but their liberties. From the perspective of *liberty*, all conditions on benefits may look alike: government pressures the speech of the indigent through conditions on welfare no more or less than it pressures the speech of the rich through conditions on capital gains tax benefits or oil depletion allowances. From the perspective of *equality*, however, the two measures may have quite different effects.

The fundamental rights branch of equal protection doctrine provides useful analogies here. In decisions such as *Skinner v. Oklahoma* and *Zablocki v. Redhail*, the Court held that some rights—such as the rights to procreate and to marry—are too fundamental to be distributed according to a system of constitutional caste. If embezzlers are to be spared the knife, so must chicken thieves; if the well-off can remarry, the poor must be permitted to do the same. Such rulings may be read merely as perfecting legislative process by requiring universalization of burdens and benefits. Alternatively, these decisions may be read as judging some rights too important to be reserved for selected privileged groups.

Where rights have this character, conditions on benefits that affect their exercise can pose a similar danger of hierarchy. For example, conditioning welfare benefits on contribution of body organs to a public organ bank, or aid to mothers with dependent children on their service as surrogate mothers in a public program to remedy infertility, would unconstitutionally create a donor caste. This argument does not depend on either the view that such exchanges are "coerced" by the desperation of poverty, or the view that body parts or gestational services are generally inalienable.

A straightforward application of such equality arguments to the abortion funding cases, for example, would reverse the outcome. Government cannot universally criminalize abortion, nor universally burden it with heavy restrictions, at least in the first trimester. The only difference between such general bans and the selective subsidization of childbirth but not abortion for indigent women is the class affected. Dependency on government defines the class here. But what the government cannot restrict for all, it may not restrict for those over whom it has special leverage because of their dependency—especially where the displacement of private alternatives creates special responsibility. To hold otherwise would sanction a two-tier system of constitutional rights—a system of constitutional caste.

### B. Applying a Systemic Approach

If unconstitutional conditions pose problems of improper redistribution, strict review must apply beyond cases of "coercion," "penalty," or "nongermaneness." A systemic approach deemphasizes the form conditions may take; it recognizes that government can as readily aggrandize excessive power or maldistribute power among rightholders through selective subsidization as through conditions that more obviously restrict liberty. Cases drawing a distinction between permissible "nonsubsidies" and impermissible "penalties" often miss just this point. A focus on systemic relationships, requires strict review of a broader range of conditions.

An appropriate test would subject to strict review any government benefit condition whose primary purpose or effect it to pressure recipients to alter a choice about exercise of a preferred constitutional liberty in a direction favored by government. Put another way, it would require strict review any time a government benefit condition redistributed, or was intended to redistribute, power to government or among rightholders in violation of any of the three distributive concerns discussed above in Section V.A. . . .

2. Justifying Conditions on Benefits.—Some may fear that liberal identification of rights-pressuring conditions on benefits as infringements might invalidate them too readily. By definition, a finding that a preferred liberty has been infringed triggers strict review. Strict review, however, is not always fatal— a point illustrated, for example, by the Court's limited toleration of affirmative action plans in the face of strict equal protection scrutiny, or approval of restrictive abortion regulations after the point of viability. Likewise, nothing about the doctrine of unconstitutional conditions rules out the possibility that some conditions or selective subsidy schemes designed to pressure rights will be upheld in compelling cases. Indeed, the nature of the government benefit involved will sometimes furnish uniquely strong justifications absent in the case of "direct" regulation.

For example, a requirement that government employees never reveal information acquired on the job undoubtedly pressures expressive rights, whether an employee works for the CIA or as a custodian at the National Archives. The existence of pressure on the right does not depend on the degree of private competition in the labor market; the government has equal censorial intent in jobs with and without private-sector substitutes. In most cases, the condition should be struck down, but in some cases, compelling justification will easily save it. For example, if the existence of the state requires national security, national security requires espionage, and espionage requires secrecy, then secrecy agreements have a compelling justification as a condition of employment as a spy. Thus, the outcome in *Snepp v. United States* was acceptable—not because Snepp's rights were not pressured, but because there was compelling justification for pressuring them. . . .

## VI. CONCLUSION

The doctrine of unconstitutional conditions was invented by a laissez-faire Court bent on dismantling progressive legislation that reduced the liberty of corporations, but then perpetuated by a Court seeking strong protections for personal liberties. The doctrine occupies a demilitarized zone between different substantive theories of constitutional law because it identifies a powerful technique of government manipulation. Across quite different contexts, modes of deploying this technique bear strong structural similarities. The similarities have hardly engendered agreement, however, on the constitutionality of conditions across the board. . . .

This Article has sought to provide a better account of unconstitutional conditions doctrine. It has argued that the doctrine guards against a characteristic form of government overreaching and thus serves a state-checking function. Furthermore, it bars redistribution of constitutional rights as to which government has obligations of evenhandedness. Finally, it prevents inappropriate hierarchy among rightholders.

These three distributive themes provide a theoretical foundation for subjecting all conditions on benefits that pressure certain preferred liberties to the same strict scrutiny that such rights receive when burdened directly. This strict scrutiny both preserves spheres of private ordering from government domination and ensures that citizens receive appropriately evenhanded treatment from government. Not anchored in any one substantive vision of the Constitution, this theory sweeps broadly across the spectrum of situations in which government, through conditions on benefits, burdens preferred liberties. Since some of these burdens may ultimately survive strict scrutiny, this theory does not compel the conclusion that government may *never* burden a preferred liberty. By recognizing the dangers posed by such burdens, however, it seeks to bolster the role of the Constitution as a barrier protecting individuals from the state.

Richard A. Epstein, *The Supreme Court, 1987 Term—Foreword: Unconstitutional Conditions, State Power, and the Limits of Consent*, 102 HARVARD LAW REVIEW 4 (1988)*

## I. INTRODUCTION

### A. A Ubiquitous Problem

. . .

The problem of unconstitutional conditions arises whenever a government seeks to achieve its desired result by obtaining bargained-for *consent* of the party whose conduct is to be restricted. There is, for example, an ordinary first amendment issue when the government seeks to impose prior restraints on publication. That question is transformed into an unconstitutional conditions issue when a government benefit is conditioned upon acceptance of prior restraint. Similarly, there is only a traditional equal protection claim when the government imposes heavier criminal penalties on blacks than it does on whites or vice versa. The unconstitutional conditions overlay comes into play only when the government sells goods or services to blacks on more onerous contract terms and conditions than those it offers to whites.

There is a special conceptual problem with the doctrine of unconstitutional conditions, however, that does not arise in connection with ordinary constitutional limits on government powers. Why does the doctrine exist at all? Why should there be any limitation at all on a system of government power that rests on the actual consent of the individuals whose rights are thereby abridged? To be sure, even the system of free markets recognizes some limitations upon the principle of consent in ordinary contracts between private individuals. Duress, force, misrepresentation, undue influence, and incompetence may be used to set aside contracts that otherwise meet the normal requirements of offer, acceptance, consideration, and consent. But none of these conventional grounds accounts for the doctrine of unconstitutional conditions, which comes into play only after all these conventional hurdles to consensual union have been overcome.

The analogies to ordinary contract law thus give rise to a persistent puzzle that can be formulated in both conceptual and practical terms. . . . [I]f a state can exclude a foreign corporation, why can it not admit the corporation subject to whatever conditions it wishes to impose? Sometimes the puzzle is stated in terms of a greater and a lesser power. The greater power to exclude might be said to include the lesser power to admit on condition.

The objection to the doctrine of unconstitutional conditions can also be stated in functional terms. How can striking workers complain that they have not received benefits to which they have no absolute entitlement? The state has made an offer that any worker may choose to accept or reject. There has been no use or threat of force. As long as individuals know what is best for themselves, they can enter into only those bargains that leave them better off after than before. Some workers have taken the bargain and others have cast it aside. All workers are free to make whatever decisions they choose, but must live with the consequences of their decisions once made. The same point could be made about the case of race. Blacks cannot complain, because they are better off with the bargains they made than they were before the state contracted with either blacks or whites.

These examples appear to justify the doctrine of unconstitutional conditions as a half-conscious adaptation of the classical Pareto superiority test used in modern welfare economics to evaluate alternative social states. As originally developed, the Pareto criterion attempted to make social judgments about alternative states of the world without resorting to problematic interpersonal comparisons of utility. It avoided the necessity and awkwardness of such comparisons by prescribing a test that allowed each person to compare his own private welfare before and after the legal change. Thus if no person in state A is worse off than he was in state B, and at least one person is better off in state A than he was in state B, then state A must be judged as superior to state B. The criterion of judgment is social in the sense that the welfare of every individual is taken into account, yet the stringent condition that no person be worse off in state A than in state B obviates the need for any comparison of welfare across separate persons.

The Pareto formula has often been attacked for being too restrictive of the type of social changes that it allows. Nonetheless, where the relevant universe involves only two self-interested parties, any voluntary agreement or grant satisfies the test, for the agreement is formed only if it makes both sides better off than before, given that each is the best judge of his own welfare. The use of this Pareto formula presupposes that the status quo ante is the baseline against which shifts in individual welfare are measured. Thus when people reject a bargain or grant

---

* Reprinted with permission.

offered by the state, they are no worse off than they were before. When they accept the bargain or grant on condition, they are better off. Either way, they are not in a position to complain. The state for its part is treated (and this assumption will become controversial) as though it were a single person that knows its own preferences, measured against the same baseline of the status quo ante. If its bargain or grant is rejected, then it will be no worse off than before; if that grant or condition is accepted, then it will be better off. Either way the stringent Pareto conditions are satisfied so that there is no reason to worry about the terms and conditions that the government attaches to its bargain or grant. No matter what its outcome, the proposed transaction appears unassailable. . . .

The importance of the unconstitutional conditions doctrine has brought forth an extensive array of academic literature to explain and justify it. The received writing sensibly recognizes the essential place that the doctrine occupies in modern constitutional law, but it makes far less sense when it attempts to explain how the doctrine arises or what it does. In part, the difficulties arise from the persistent efforts to make unconstitutional conditions cases resemble duress or coercion cases, as is made evident by the discussion of differences between "penalties" or "fines" on the one hand, and "subsidies" or "benefits" on the other. Yet if common law duress were present in these cases, the recipient of the grant would be able to attack the offending condition without resorting to any special doctrine of unconstitutional conditions. As long as the condition is obtained by coercion or duress, it can be set aside as a matter of right, regardless of its content. In contrast, the doctrine of unconstitutional conditions is directed toward the substance of various conditions, regardless of the course of negotiations between the individual recipient and the state.

The balancing tests commonly suggested by commentators show that the doctrine of unconstitutional conditions cannot be explained by analogy to common law coercion. This balancing is not evidentiary, as courts are not asked to weigh different sorts of evidence that might indicate whether a certain gesture is an implied threat of the use of force. Rather, its close involvement with the substantive terms and conditions of the statute—for example, whether the use of state highways is conditioned upon agreeing to service of process in all cases, or only in those arising out of use of the highways—distances us from the process-oriented issues that dominate ordinary duress cases. But without a strong substantive theory that explains both the use and the limits of individual

consent, the use of balancing tests in this context leaves far too much room to the legal imagination. Balancing must be in service of a general theory. It cannot be a substitute for one.

. . .

## II. THE CONCEPTUAL FRAMEWORK

In order to understand the limitations on bargaining, it is best first to sketch how bargains can lead to optimal social results. I thus begin with a brief discussion of perfect competition, and then move on to discuss monopoly, collective action, and externality problems as they occur in private law contexts. Thereafter I shall show how these problems arise in the context of state power.

. . .

### B. The Political Context

The dangers inherent in a system of private contracting often carry over into the political arena. Thus, despite the traditional Hobbesian insistence that the state must exercise a monopoly of force within its jurisdiction in order to prevent the war of all against all, the creation of that monopoly power in the hands of a few public officials itself poses a great danger of abuse. The major task of constitutionalism, therefore, has been to forge a system in which these government excesses are curtailed while leaving the state sufficient power to discharge the necessary tasks of governance. A system of unrestrained political power does a poor job in setting the right balance. In some markets the government has a high degree of monopoly power. It may be the only party that can operate the public roads, issue building permits, or allow firms to do business in corporate form. Unlike the private monopolist, its power cannot be eroded by the entry of new firms, but is perpetuated by a legal prohibition against entry by new rivals. The risks of resource misallocation identified in private transactions carry over to the political area as well. There is an obvious need for limitations on the direct use of coercion. By the same token, if the monopoly and necessity cases are any guide, there are obvious reasons to limit the capacity of the government to bargain with its individual citizens. Just as the dockowner in the private necessity case is limited to a fixed rate of return when the dock is used by others and forbidden from imposing collateral or unrelated conditions on that use, so too the state, when it provides resources of which it is the sole supplier, should be limited both in the concessions that it may exact from private owners and in the conditions it may impose on them.

Similarly, government action often creates the risk of collective action problems. As a single unified entity, the state may be able to make offers to widely dispersed individuals who find themselves faced with a prisoner's dilemma game. Each person acting alone may think it in his interest to waive some constitutional right, even though a group, if it could act collectively, would reach the opposite conclusion. By barring some waivers of constitutional rights, the doctrine of unconstitutional conditions allows disorganized citizens to escape from what would otherwise be a socially destructive prisoner's dilemma game.

Finally, the problem of externalities as it arises from majority rule must be taken into account. The state is an association of a large number of individuals with diverse interests and inconsistent desires. Yet it must make decisions that bind them all. In principle it would be ideal if all collective decisions could be made by unanimous consent, which would forestall the problem of the majority exploiting the minority. But any unanimous consent requirement would lead to government paralysis, because any single individual would be in a position to bargain strategically by holding out for a lion's share of the gain from social action. For better or for worse, some system of majority rule is a necessary evil, and one that forces us to confront explicitly the expropriation problem in the political context.

Left unregulated by constitutional limitations, a majority could use a system of taxation and transfers to secure systematic expropriation of property. Taxes could be used to purchase property, which could then be conveyed to some preferred groups via "bargain sales," at a fraction of its true value. There would be no exploitation of the happy buyer, but there would be a risk that the state as trustee would have abused its power in relation to the other citizens it represents, all of whom received less than fair value in exchange for the property transferred. This pattern of abuse would result not only in a systematic deprivation of the interests of some citizens but also in an overall efficiency loss, as the controlling group will not only expend resources to obtain the transfer, but will be willing to acquire the property even when they value it less than the state did. The legal system tries to combat this problem through the use of the public trust doctrine. Standing alone, the problem is not one of unconstitutional conditions because there is no effort to take advantage of the happy parties who prosper from doing business with the state.

Externalities, however, become entwined with the problem of unconstitutional conditions when the state seeks to grant benefits or make contracts subject to conditions that some individuals find far more onerous than others. To be sure, conditions will not be imposed if everyone is hurt equally by them, but they may become part of a system of contracts or grants if they work to the benefit of a dominant faction and against the interests of others. . . .

## C. Citizen Misconduct

Thus far, all attention has been directed toward potential misconduct by government officials. But there is no reason to assume that government officials are any more self-interested than are the citizens with whom they do business. Thus the risk of strategic behavior is *bilateral*. In private dealings, any party to a complex transaction can engage in strategic behavior, and so too in the area of political action. Just as the government may seek to exploit the individual, so too a citizen may try to exploit the government. The flip-side, therefore, to the doctrine of unconstitutional conditions is the idea of "compelling state interest," which appears throughout all constitutional analysis. Typically the doctrine of unconstitutional conditions does not interfere with government bargains designed to prevent individual exploitation of some common pool assets. . . .

## D. Judicial Implementation of the Unconstitutional Conditions Doctrine

1. First Principles.—The analysis of any unconstitutional conditions problem requires an assessment of the relative strength of the three risks of abuse that can arise when the state bargains with its citizens. But even after the relevant factors are set out, several pieces of the puzzle must still be put in place.

The first piece concerns the extent to which the Supreme Court will undertake this review of government behavior. Here, as in other contexts, the answer is heavily dependent upon its attitude toward the behavior of government officials. The private law response to monopoly, collective action problems, and externalities reflects the assumption that individuals will seek to maximize their own private returns, given the external constraints under which they labor. Its legal rules therefore have been set to minimize the likelihood that they will be able to achieve some private gain at some net social cost. To be sure these assumptions are overdrawn. There are many individuals who will come to the aid of those who are in trouble, without so much as the thought of payment to themselves. Many people would never think of abusing their partnership control to cheat their partners. These cases are important for any overall assessment of human nature, but they are not the cases against which the legal rules are directed. Honest and honorable people do behave well regardless of the legal framework in which they act. The law must be directed against that fraction of the total population for whom self-interest is the sole beacon of conduct. For such people, the assumptions of the law fit all too well with the behavior that the law seeks to control.

The question what to make of human nature carries over to the constitutional context with equal significance. If it is assumed that government officials and the private parties who influence them are prone to the corrosive influence of self-interest, then the legal rules should strictly scrutinize whatever behavior they undertake. If the direct use of government coercion is subject to serious constitutional scrutiny, then government bargains should be subject to a similar level of scrutiny. The doctrine of unconstitutional conditions thus becomes an inseparable part of constitutional law, attendant to any and all exercises of government power. Alternatively, if government officials are assumed to act with benevolent motives when they regulate, then they should be assumed to act with similar motives when they contract. The low level of scrutiny found under rational basis review would carry over from regulation to bargains, and the doctrine of unconstitutional conditions would play only a marginal role in our legal firmament.

There are today many competing general constitutional visions, which bear on the question of how courts should regard government figures. Some theories stress the virtues of republican self-government; others the satisfaction of "dignitary" interests; still others the protection of economic liberty or the niceties of utilitarian calculation. Other constitutional theories rest upon the sanctity of private property and the fear of the democratic excesses of the populist masses. For present purposes, the correctness of the basic orientations is not the critical point. The various theories only direct attention to those areas in which the political process is viewed with distrust. It is precisely in those areas that the doctrine of unconstitutional conditions will take root and flourish.

In this connection, the constitutional fault line of the past-1937 period poses the same problem for the doctrine of unconstitutional conditions that it does for direct forms of government regulation. The weak protection of property and contract is juxtaposed with a strong suspicion of government regulation of preferred freedoms, such as speech and religion, and the government use of suspect classifications, such as those based upon religious and political views. Today there remains, to a lesser degree than before, an erratic fear of political aggrandizement by one state at the expense of another, or of the states at the expense of the federal government.

This hierarchy of legal rights makes the doctrine of unconstitutional conditions especially difficult to apply to complex modern statutory schemes that implement explicit or implicit transfers of wealth for purposes now regarded as unquestionably legitimate—for example, to regulate land use, or to help the needy or unemployed. Yet these programs, whether by regulation or taxation, often effect such transfers along forbidden lines, such as political or religious affiliation. Frequently, the question arises how to disentangle these two distinct strands of a single statutory scheme, subjecting each to its appropriate level of review—minimal scrutiny for ordinary rights, strict scrutiny for fundamental rights and suspect classifications. The coerced transfer of property from A to B may be allowed today in general economic areas, but it will not be tolerated along (say) religious or political lines. Where the state seeks those forbidden objectives through contracting, its actions will be met with the same hostility as when it proceeds through direct regulation or taxation. In such contexts, we find the continued, indeed expanded, vitality of the doctrine of unconstitutional conditions in modern times.

2. Second Best.—The doctrine of unconstitutional conditions is also beset with the serious problem of being a "second best" approach to controlling government discretion. In many cases, the Supreme Court has held that Congress or the states have absolute discretion with regard to matters such as allowing foreign corporations to do business within the state or allowing commercial vehicles to use public highways. This discretion increases the risks associated with monopoly, collective action problems, and externalities in a wide variety of bargaining contexts. In some cases, the doctrine of unconstitutional conditions is used to "take back" some of the power which had been conferred upon government officials in the first instance. In principle, the doctrine's application would be unnecessary if the Court had restricted the scope of the government power in the first instance.

Often the unsatisfactory nature of the doctrine of unconstitutional conditions arises from its status as a mop-up doctrine where other forms of constitutional restraint have been abandoned. Within these contexts, it is often very difficult to decide whether the doctrine does more harm than good. When the government is told that it cannot bargain with individuals, the empirical question arises whether government will deny them a useful benefit altogether, or grant them the benefit without the obnoxious condition.

. . .

## V. PUBLIC ROADS AND HIGHWAYS

If the federal government has always had an effective legal monopoly over the instrumentalities of interstate transportation, then similarly state governments have long enjoyed a powerful local monopoly over public highways and roads. It should come as no surprise, therefore, that the doctrine of unconstitutional conditions also emerged in cases where the state demanded the release of constitutional rights as the price of access to public highways. *Frost & Frost Trucking Co. v. Railroad Commission* shows the halting and ineffective development of the doctrine in the context of classic state economic regulation. *City of Lakewood v. Plain Dealer Publishing Co.,* decided this past Term, raises parallel issues in a first amendment context, thus resulting in a more forceful application of the doctrine. The framework of analysis is similar in the two areas, even if the protected constitutional rights differ. The first inquiry is to determine the extent of the government's monopoly power in its control of public highways. The second inquiry is to determine the extent to which the conditions imposed upon entry or use are designed to upset the competitive balance between rival users. The third inquiry, which is the flip side of the second, is to determine whether the restrictions in question are designed to control against opportunistic behavior by individual citizens in their use of the common pool asset, the public roads. . . .

## B. Freedom of Speech and the Highways: Lakewood

The doctrine of unconstitutional conditions as generalized in *Frost* involved access to public highways for economic uses. *Frost* was decided when the Court still afforded moderately strong constitutional protection of economic liberties, as shown by its willingness to probe into the state's asserted police power justification. With the waning of judicial concern with economic affairs, the regulatory issues raised in Frost dropped out of later cases. At the same time, *Carolene Products* and its progeny dictated a higher level of scrutiny for legislation impinging upon fundamental rights or employing suspect classifications. The doctrine of unconstitutional conditions migrated with the flow, and thus became entwined with modern issues of religion, speech, and equal protection.

The public highway cases were thus transformed into the "public forum" cases, and the renewed level of higher scrutiny once again proceeded from a presumption of distrust of legislative and executive behavior. Before this new orientation was adopted, there was some judicial support, again voiced by Justice Holmes, for the categorical position that the state owns the highway or park and therefore can exclude speakers at will. But this absolutist position quickly fell when it was decided that state title to the public highways did not allow it to bar the distri-

bution of literature, or to subject it to any special prior restrictions, license tax, or permits. The end run tolerated in the context of economic regulation would not be allowed here.

This welcome retreat from the principle of absolute public ownership limits the need for the doctrine of unconstitutional conditions, but does not render it entirely unnecessary. There is often a capacity limitation—if not for lonely leafleteers on public roads and streets, then surely on public fairgrounds—that becomes critical as the demands on public space rise. Someone has to decide who will gain access and who will not. Given the level of scrutiny applied to such decisions, the issue of unconstitutional conditions should have been expected to reappear in the modern context of the public forum, and it did, in last Term's decision in *City of Lakewood v. Plain Dealer Publishing Co.*

Lakewood's ordinance gave the town mayor the discretion to decide which newspaper companies would receive annual, nonassignable permits to place its newsracks on public property. . . . The issue of unconstitutional conditions arose when it was urged that the City was under no obligation to allow any newsracks at all on public streets, and could therefore make the right to place racks on public roads subject to whatever conditions the City wished to impose. . . .

The sound first amendment limitations on discretion do not . . . answer all the questions of what newsracks, if any, must be placed upon public property. Surely the first amendment does not require that any newspaper company be allowed to place its racks on public property at will, without paying any fee at all. Public streets and roads are still a form of commons, and one risk associated with the maintenance of any commons is its overexploitation by private users who do not fully take into account the costs that their own behavior imposes upon other members of the public. Strategic behavior by the mayor is only one form of abuse; excessive use by the newspaper companies must be reckoned with as well, which is why decisions preventing excessive noise and other similar nuisances have survived to the present day, under the rule that allows for appropriate "time, place and manner" restrictions.

Because of this dual hazard, there is surely some reason to allow the City to restrict the number of newsracks on public property, and perhaps even to confine them to certain locations within the town. *Lakewood* did not pass, for example, on whether a total ban on newsracks in residential areas would be constitutional. There is, of course, the risk that restrictions on the locations and number of newsracks could also be more severe than appropriate. Such a restriction might be attacked in extreme cases—for example, if the ordinance restricted all newsracks in order to punish one particular newspaper. Yet a facial attack on such a statute is surely out of place; some concrete evidence of official misconduct should be required. More generally, there comes a point at which the capacity to control government abuse diminishes, while the gains from controlling that abuse are small. Then it is time to quit, under the first amendment just like anywhere else. The simple rule that the town can determine the number and location of newsracks, but must allocate them by some nondiscretionary means goes a very long way toward controlling the most obvious forms of abuse.

It is instructive to note that the first amendment principles applicable in this case are drawn from those developed in connection with the economic liberties cases. The concern with conditional admission to the roads that animated *Frost* had to do with implicit redistribution of wealth among separate common carriers, and across different sectors of the trucking business. The restrictions against excessive weight and the like were routinely allowed in order to control against the exploitation of a common resource by a single user. If that economic model had applied, *Lakewood* would have come out the same way even without resort to first amendment principles. Indeed under the economic liberties framework, it would not be enough to guard against the possibility of favoritism to firms within the class of newspapers. It would also be necessary to worry about a reciprocal risk: whether newspapers as a class received a subsidy from the rest of the public at large in the form of below-market rents of public space. . . . The demise of economic liberties means in essence that we have to worry about only one form of error, the imposition of undue restrictions, but can ignore implicit subsidies to the newspaper companies. Government misconduct probably has far greater impact in the context of road regulation than it does in the context of speech. But whatever the Court's shortcomings in its protection for economic liberties, *Lakewood* itself is a welcome and correctly decided case.

## VI. THE POLICE POWER

. . .

### B. Commercial Speech and the Morals Head of the Police Power

. . . In *Posadas de Puerto Rico Associates v. Tourism Co.,* Puerto Rico wished to encourage tourists to come to Puerto Rico to gamble. It did not make gambling illegal for local citizens, but it did prevent any local advertisement of gambling on the island proper, leaving Posadas, a Holiday Inn franchisee, free to advertise its gambling facilities on the mainland. It was conceded that the control of gambling fell within the traditional "morals" head of the police power of the state, so that the state could have made gambling illegal had it so chosen. In upholding the statute, Justice Rehnquist implicitly rejected the doctrine of unconstitutional conditions when he argued that Puerto Rico's plenary power to ban gambling itself gave it the lesser power to license gambling, subject to the condition that the licensee accept a ban on local advertisement—itself a limitation on a first amendment right. Do first amendment principles require that such advertisements be tolerated, given the decision to allow the gambling itself? . . .

*Posadas* is extremely difficult to make sense of because the statute, as applied to both Puerto Ricans and to visitors, can plausibly be characterized either as a traditional exercise of the police power or as an attempt by Puerto Rico to exploit those within its borders. The unconstitutional conditions inquiry in Posadas is . . .: should the Court require the bundling of the two issues—casino gambling and casino advertising—in order to forestall the political abuse that threatens commercial speech?

Perhaps it should. One advantage of the bundling is that the advertising ban, permissible only if gambling itself is banned, is of no consequence: who would advertise what he could not sell? This means that governments and citizens would not become comfortable with large bureaucracies whose sole function is to suppress or regulate speech. Yet in another sense this linkage is very hard to sustain. One reason to legalize gambling is simply damage control. It is better that people not gamble, not only for their own personal character, but also for the corrosive effect gambling has on family and business obligations. Nonetheless, it is just too costly to try to control gambling by criminal sanctions. Better therefore to legalize the "disfavored" activity, which can then be taxed to keep participation within reason. Disfavored activities, moreover, need not be treated like all other business activities. Advertisement stimulates business, so it might be proper for a state to decide that, while it should not ban gambling, it should nonetheless moderate its growth by banning advertising. Surely if the issue were the legalization of marijuana and other drugs, a respectable argument could be made to allow their sale, subject to a general tax and to prohibitions or restrictions on advertising, which, because of advertising's public visibility, should be reasonably easy to enforce. In effect we have adopted such a strategy with respect to cigarettes, which are sold, heavily taxed, and subject to advertisement restrictions, at least on television and radio. Given the absence of any coherent social attitude toward gambling (or toward drugs, alcohol, tobacco, or prostitution), courts should exercise some deference to state restrictions on such activities, which fall within the traditional "morals" head of the police power as it relates to *both* property and speech.

Nonetheless there are reasons to doubt that the regulation at issue in *Posadas* meets that test. The social disruptions of gambling, if real, should be manifest in all its forms. When the state seeks to divide markets—with local customers directed toward the state's own lottery, and well-heeled out-of-state customers toward its posh casinos—it looks as if the anticompetitive motives dominate the protective motives. Forcing an all-or-nothing choice between banning all advertisement or banning none allows the state to pursue its legitimate police power objectives without running the risk of rigging local markets. . . . Justice Rehnquist might have been correct in insisting that the doctrine of unconstitutional conditions is inapplicable to the connection between gambling and advertising. But the explicit discrimination between government-run and privately run gambling raises the prospect of abuse that calls for a stronger use of unconstitutional conditions in its equal protection guise.

There is a second element of *Posadas* that is still more disturbing. Present law freely allows general economic regulation of all sorts and descriptions. Under Justice Rehnquist's logic, the power to ban an activity implies the power to ban its advertisement. It follows, therefore, that first amendment protections afforded commercial speech can be no greater than the meager protections given to economic liberties. In order to provide adequate protection for speech, then, it becomes necessary to build a Maginot line between the relaxed attitude toward economic liberties and the stricter scrutiny on matters of speech. The doctrine of unconstitutional conditions again serves as a second-best tool to limit the ominous implications of the modern economic liberties cases. But this larger problem, and the horribles it suggests, would disappear if we returned to the older cases on occupational freedom, requiring the state to show a strong justification before banning any ordinary commercial activity.

. . .

## VIII. GOVERNMENT BENEFITS

. . .

### A. Tax Exemptions and Freedom of Speech

One way for the government to influence the pattern of private activities is through the imposition of selective taxes. People are less willing to engage in those activities that are taxed than in those that are not. The flip side of this power is the provision of tax exemptions, which have the reverse effect upon the pattern of activities. People are more likely to engage in activities that are exempt from taxes than in those that are not. The incentive effects of tax rules are evident across the entire spectrum of economic activities, although they normally receive almost no constitutional examination under the prevailing rational basis test. If direct regulation proceeds largely without constitutional interference, then there is no reason to subject taxation to any higher level of review. The situation is quite the opposite when speech is affected. Here taxation and exemptions have the same effect as they do in other contexts, and are subject to the same high levels of scrutiny imposed on direct regulations generally. What is true of taxes is also true of exemptions.

*Speiser v. Randall* is an early manifestation of the problem, and it shows how the conditions attached to a tax exemption can properly be struck down on first amendment grounds. The California Constitution provided that World War II veterans were entitled to property tax exemptions only if they signed an oath stating that they did not advocate the overthrow of the governments of the United States or California by force or violence, or aid of hostile foreign states in time of war. The state argued that it could give its "privilege" or "bounty" to whomever it saw fit. On this view, the exemption would withstand constitutional challenge even if a statute that sought to punish the same conduct by fine or imprisonment did not. Justice Brennan characterized the statute as though it was tantamount to a "fine," and struck it down accordingly, for the want of the proper procedural protections. The doctrine of unconstitutional conditions is implicated because the benefit conferred by the exemption is conditioned on the willingness of individual taxpayers to adhere to certain political views. The selective tax exemption, no less than a selective tax, necessarily results in a redistribution of wealth and political influence from those who are unwilling to sign the oath to those who are. It may well be that the general property tax exemption for veterans is proper, but redistribution on grounds of political belief generally is not. Coercive tax burdens cannot be waived selectively for those whose views conform to the dominant political position, any more than additional taxes can be imposed on those whose views do not. State gifts work as much of an illicit redistribution of wealth and power as state fines. . . .

The question of tax exemptions came up in a somewhat more difficult form in the recent case of *Arkansas Writers' Protect, Inc. v. Ragland*, a case decided in the 1986 Term. Here the statutory structure was more complicated. Arkansas exempted from its general sales tax the "[g]ross receipts or gross proceeds derived from the sale of newspapers" and from certain types of magazines, including "religious, professional, trade and sports journals and/or publications printed and published in this State." The plaintiff's general-purpose magazine fell into neither of these two categories, and hence had to pay the tax.

*Arkansas Writers' Project* again raises the problem of unconstitutional conditions because Arkansas did not have to give any publication an exemption. Thus, the sole issue was whether the state could condition the exemption on the willingness of a magazine to publish material of a particular subject matter. The statute would have been a manifest violation of the first amendment if it had tied the exemption to the adoption of any particular viewpoint, which it did not. Nonetheless, the statute did single out certain types of publications for benefits that other types of magazines were denied. By changing the relative costs of producing various kinds of magazines, the statute in effect brought about a mix of publications different from the one that would have arisen under either a tax-free world or one with a uniform tax on all types of publications. As a matter of marketplace economics, these distortions deviate from the competitive ideal, and could be condemned on those grounds alone. But with the waning of economic liberties as a constitutional doctrine, this argument can be directed only to the legislature, not to the courts. Indeed, Justice Scalia would have upheld the tax because he regarded *Arkansas Writers' Project* as an economic regulation case, scarcely distinguishable from other cases of selective exemption that have thus far survived constitutional attack.

Nonetheless, the evident connection between the exemption and speech makes this clearly a first amendment case. In this context, it is hard to demonstrate how any economic misallocation leads to an unwanted distortion in the marketplace of ideas, especially one that could be seized upon by political actors to advance their own interests. Still, the Court was correct to strike the statute down because there was so little to be said on its behalf. A uniform system of exemptions could end all objection to the statute without requiring a detailed analysis of its content, while still allowing the state to advance newspapers and magazines as against other activities. In the unlikely event that a uniform exemption created a budget shortfall, the state could adopt a partial uniform exemption as necessary to meet its revenue requirements. Finding the condition attached to the exemption unconstitutional thus achieves the right result, even in a case that seems to present only limited opportunities for government abuse.

The same analysis yields different results in the earlier case of *Regan v. Taxation with Representation (TWR)*, in which a system of charitable exemptions was challenged on the ground that it could not be applied to moneys raised for lobbying activities. The taxpayer in *TWR* was a political organization that attacked two provisions of the Internal Revenue Code that failed to grant it tax-exempt status, and that failed to grant deductions to its contributors. The unconstitutional conditions challenge came in two parts. The first was that it was impermissible to attach any limitations restricting the ability of otherwise exempt organizations to participate in lobbying. The second part was that it was impermissible to permit veterans' organizations to operate free of the restrictions made applicable to other political groups.

Justice Rehnquist, speaking for the majority, rejected both challenges, relying heavily upon the norm of "broad discretion" in taxing matters. "This Court has never held that Congress must grant a benefit such as TWR claims here to a person who wishes to exercise a constitutional right." But this account suppresses the equal protection component of the argument. The objection is not to the failure to grant the subsidy, as such, but to granting the subsidy to charitable organizations while denying it to lobbying organizations.

Properly formulated, the critical question is whether this broad type of condition creates any distortion in the political process. It is doubtful that it does, even when the statute is tested against the more demanding first amendment standards of scrutiny. The religious, political, and educational activities exempted under the statute cover the full range of activities without subject matter or viewpoint discrimination, and the ban on lobbying is imposed at the same high level of generality. The differences in tax treatment may well induce some moneys to go into, say, academic work that would otherwise go into direct lobbying, but it is hard to see what political groups, if any, would gain systematic advantage from this effect. Here, unlike the tax exemption situation posed by *Arkansas Writers'*, there seems to be a powerful government counterweight on the other side. One great peril in political life today is that the broad discretion of federal and state government over economic affairs increases the potential gains to partisan activities, of which lobbying is only the most visible. Why that conduct must be subsidized, even if charitable organizations are subsidized, is therefore something of a mystery. The doctrine of unconstitutional conditions should be invoked precisely when the conditions attached to government action increase the risk of political polarization, the opposite of the case when lobbying efforts proceed without tax dollars. The distinction between lobbying and charitable activities thus survives even a higher level of constitutional scrutiny.

The standard of review becomes far more important on the second question: whether veterans' organizations alone should receive preferred tax status for their lobbying activities. Justice Rehnquist, still employing a degree of judicial deference, simply noted that all veterans organizations qualified regardless of their views. If veterans groups only had disagreements among themselves on issues of no concern to others, a tax subsidy to them might not affect the denial of a parallel subsidy to other organizations. But although these groups may differ among themselves on some issues, they must surely act in concert on others, where they operate in direct competition with unsubsidized lobbying groups. In these cases the differential tax treatment does distort the outcome of the political process in ways that the first amendment and the equal protection clause should preclude. It appears therefore that Congress at least should be put to the all-or-nothing choice of granting exemptions to all lobbying organizations or to none.

I reach that conclusion with a fair bit of trepidation, lest Congress take the bait and extend the tax benefit to all lobbying groups, including the vast number that are totally unconcerned with veterans' activities. Lobbying may well be a protected constitutional right, but in a system of limited government it is not one that is either deserving of or entitled to a political subsidy.

. . .

Dorothy E. Roberts, *Rust v. Sullivan and the Control of Knowledge*, 61 GEORGE WASHINGTON UNIVERSITY LAW REVIEW 587 (1993)*

. . .

### Introduction

The Supreme Court in *Rust v. Sullivan* upheld the regulations that prohibit employees of Title X-funded clinics from discussing abortion with their patients. The Court rejected the First and Fifth Amendment challenges brought by clinics and their doctors, reasoning that the regulations were merely a constitutional refusal by government to subsidize the delivery of abortion information. According to the majority, the "government is not denying a benefit to anyone, but is instead simply insisting that public funds be spent for the purposes for which they were authorized." Although the regula-

tions subsequently were repealed, the *Rust* decision remains a powerful defense of government restrictions on speech.

This Article is about the struggle over knowledge. It examines how the Court in *Rust* aligned with the side of the powerful on two fronts. We live in a society in which poor Black communities are isolated geographically in inner cities and excluded from the benefits of society. *Rust* upheld regulations that deliberately withheld from women in these communities knowledge critical to their reproductive health and autonomy. By promoting ignorance among these women, the Court erected one more layer of the "structural entrapment" that keeps poor Black women at society's margins. The Court's reasoning also excluded them from the concern and compassion of the rest of society, by portraying Title X patients as undeserving of the care to which affluent women are entitled simply because poor women are dependent on the government's charity. The Court's logic foreclosed the possibility of an alternative constitutional interpretation that requires affirmative protection of Title X patients' right to self-determination. Poor women of color live in communities hidden from sight. The Court's legal discourse hides them from the mind, as well.

This Article has two goals. The first is to critique the Court's First Amendment analysis in *Rust*. The Court's rhetoric, which focused on the abstract equality of ideas, masked the violence that the regulations inflicted upon women. It failed to recognize that the government's control of knowledge available to poor Black women not only suppresses an idea, it also represses a people. My second goal is to use this analysis as the foundation for an alternative vision of the government's role in nurturing individual liberty and achieving racial justice. I am more interested in the way that we think about dependency and government control of knowledge than in manipulating current First Amendment doctrine to reach a more desirable outcome. My particular task is to articulate an affirmative government obligation to provide abortion counseling to Title X patients. I see this project as part of the broader inquiry into the relationship between constitutional liberties and the distribution of wealth. Rather than present a generalized entitlement theory, however, I defend a narrower claim by people dependent on government aid to a particular resource—information necessary for self-determination. It is my hope that my explanation of this particular claim to information will illuminate the need to change the negative constitutionalism that has supported unjust relationships of power.

. . .

## II. Critique of *Rust's* First Amendment Analysis

The contest in *Rust* rested on two First Amendment

* Reprinted with the permission of The George Washington Law Review © 1989.

theories—the marketplace of ideas and the unconstitutional conditions doctrine. Both theories assert that the aim of the Constitution's guarantees is government neutrality. This focus on neutrality cannot illuminate the regulations' injury to Black women because it fails to recognize the significance of speech and government restrictions on speech within the context of relationships of power.

## A. The Marketplace of Ideas

. . .

Both sides in *Rust* viewed the regulations as government participation in the market's public debate on abortion. The point of contention was whether interjecting the government's antiabortion viewpoint distorted an otherwise rational and fair marketplace. Petitioners argued that the government's participation in the marketplace potentially could drown out other viewpoints. The government failed to see any distortion of the marketplace at all but saw merely the government's effort to add its voice to the debate. The test that both the majority and the dissent used to answer the question of government distortion was whether the regulations violated the principle of viewpoint neutrality. The danger in the regulations was that they breached the touchstone of First Amendment doctrine—"equality of status in the field of ideas." By refusing to fund family-planning projects advocating abortion, petitioners argued, the government targeted a particular ideological viewpoint and forced doctors to be instruments for fostering public adherence to the opposite orthodoxy. This First Amendment analysis focused on the individual and on ideas. The constitutional evil was perceived as suppression of abortion advocacy. The right at stake was the individual's right to be free from imposition of the state's viewpoint.

One weakness of the marketplace approach is that constitutional answers can vary, depending on the delineation of the "marketplace." Petitioners presented the marketplace as the limited forum in which poor and low-income women can obtain medical counsel and information—in other words, the Title X project itself. This marketplace is monopolized entirely by the government. Petitioners' construction of the marketplace recognized that poor communities have fewer resources to challenge the government-sponsored view. Respondents, on the other hand, described the government as a participant in a bigger marketplace of diverse ideas.

An analogy in respondents' brief illustrates this distinction. Respondents likened the regulations to a government grant to produce a television documentary that discusses family-planning techniques, but not abortion. The government may decide simply not to enter the market of abortion documentaries. In respondents' hypothetical, a lack of absolute control over the available information is what makes the government a market participant rather than a regulator of expression. Other producers remain free to present alternative views, including documentaries about abortion.

The government's analogy, however, mischaracterized the regulations' overwhelming impact on patients' access to abortion information. Nor was the proper analogy a solely government-owned station that forces all citizens to imbibe the state's message. The hypothetical that more accurately illustrates the injustice of the regulations is a society where the dispossessed only have access to a government television channel that broadcasts limited, misleading—even harmful—information, while the privileged have their pick of channels that provide a wealth of information.

Petitioners' focus on neutrality among abstract ideas also limited the force of their argument. The logical extension of this neutrality perspective is that government must stay out of the marketplace of ideas altogether and fund no viewpoint, or it must fund each and every viewpoint equally. This approach has two immediate shortcomings. First, the Court pointed out that petitioners' assertion would mean that, if government chooses to subsidize one protected view, it also must subsidize all counterpart views. If the government sponsored programs aimed at dissuading people from drinking alcohol, for example, it must also fund programs that encourage drinking. State funding of messages promoting racial harmony would require funding for hate speech. This logical extension of the neutrality argument is undesirable both because the costs are prohibitive and because we do want the government to be somewhat selective in its funding decisions.

Second, under the neutrality approach, the constitutional wrong was that the government suppressed only one of two reproductive options—abortion and not childbirth. The government's "neutral" elimination of all pregnancy counseling would remedy this viewpoint discrimination. The government's total retreat from the marketplace of reproductive information, however, would have a devastating impact on the health of poor women. Thus, neither solution to the problem framed as viewpoint discrimination—government funding of all viewpoints or government funding of none—adequately addresses the harm caused by the regulations.

The marketplace of ideas assumes not only a marketplace in which ideas trade freely, but also one which is open to all citizens who seek knowledge. It is based on the fiction that prohibiting government restrictions on access to knowledge is enough to ensure access to everyone. The negative protection against government interference alone, however, overlooks the effect of existing inequalities of resources in the marketplace. It also ignores that many people are silenced by social domination on the basis of race, gender, and class. A laissez-faire market inevitably will produce an exchange of ideas dominated by those with the most economic and social power. The monopoly of mass media ownership and the difficulty of organizing participation by less powerful groups compound marketplace failures. Government involvement may be necessary to counterbalance the overwhelming communications power wielded by corporate and wealthy interests. The poor often must depend on the government to express or subsidize their views. Thus, government intervention may broaden, rather than distort, the spectrum of views expressed. . . .

It is important to rethink the fixation on viewpoint neutrality by considering the social and political context of government speech. An alternative approach examines the effect of government control of information on relationships of social power. It does not allow us to use the shield of neutral principles in order to avoid confronting inequalities in the power to communicate. This view rejects the illusion that we can achieve knowledge without the taint of power. Rather, it purposefully examines how the relationship between knowledge and power operates in our society. It asks how knowledge functions to secure the powerful and how it might serve to liberate the oppressed. This analysis reveals the real evil of the regulations: The government's control of knowledge not only suppresses an idea, it represses a people. This inquiry then calls us to determine what information is essential for self-determination and demands that the government provide this information to people who are dependent on government aid.

## B. Unconstitutional-Conditions Doctrine

The other theory framing the First Amendment analysis in *Rust* is the unconstitutional-conditions doctrine. This doctrine provides that the government may not condition the conferral of a benefit on the beneficiary's surrender of a constitutional right, although the government may choose not to provide the benefit altogether. The doctrine rests on a negative vision of the Constitution. It presumes that the state has no affirmative obligation to fund the exercise of rights, but asks whether its conditional offer of a benefit requires stricter scrutiny than its denial of the benefit.

Both sides in *Rust* accepted the premise that "[n]o one has a right to a subsidy for the exercise of rights to speech and privacy." Petitioners argued, however, that once the government had chosen to subsidize family planning, it could not exact adherence to its antiabortion orthodoxy through the imposition of view-

point-based conditions on its largesse. The Court rejected petitioners' unconstitutional-conditions argument on the ground that the regulations did not deny a benefit to anyone, nor did they prevent grantees from engaging in First Amendment activities outside the scope of the federally funded project. The regulations simply required that Title X funds be spent on the purpose for which they were intended—establishing and operating projects that provide preventive family-planning services.

Framing the First Amendment problem as an unconstitutional condition is also a demand for government neutrality. This approach recognizes the potential for government use of conditions on benefits to prefer one constitutionally protected viewpoint over another. As the Supreme Court noted in *Speiser v. Randall*, "the denial of [funding] for engaging in certain speech necessarily will have the effect of coercing the claimants to refrain from the proscribed speech. The denial is 'frankly aimed at the suppression of dangerous ideas.'" As with the marketplace-of-ideas model, inequalities of communications power caused by social and economic disparities are beyond the doctrine's reach.

One failing of the unconstitutional-conditions approach in *Rust* is that it focused on the wrong distinction. The doctrine classifies potential beneficiaries into two groups: those who comply with the condition and receive the benefit and those who do not. The critical inequality created by the regulations was not between those provided with government aid—i.e., clinics that do not advocate abortion—and those denied aid—i.e., clinics that do. The violence of the decision was not suffered by the physicians whose speech was restricted, but by their patients, the third-party beneficiaries of Title X. Moreover, the violence did not consist solely of the distinction the government made between ideologies. Rather, the regulations' injustice lies in the distinction they allow between the powerful—who attempt to control knowledge—and the dispossessed whose status is maintained through that control.

The tortured history of the unconstitutional-conditions doctrine also raises questions about its utility as a test of constitutional legitimacy. Scholars have noted the use of the doctrine to justify irreconcilable decisions. Different justices have manipulated the doctrine to achieve desired results based on their respective substantive ideals. The doctrine was "invented by a laissez-faire Court bent on dismantling progressive legislation that reduced the liberty of corporations, but then perpetuated by a Court seeking strong protections for personal liberties." The Court more recently has disregarded the doctrine, as it did in *Rust*, to weaken these very protections.

Kathleen Sullivan defends the unconstitutional-conditions doctrine as a useful method for identifying "a characteristic technique by which government appears not to, but in fact does burden . . . liberties." The state, however, appears not to burden liberties by conditioning benefits only if we accept the premises of the action/inaction and positive/negative rights discourse. The unconstitutional-conditions doctrine explains the harm of government conditions within the constraints of this discourse; thus, abandoning the prevailing use of these dichotomies would dispense with the need for the doctrine altogether. We would then face squarely the critical question ignored by the Court: How can the government justify its denial of information to people who rely on government aid? By addressing directly the issue of dependency and the opportunity it creates for oppressive government control of knowledge, we may develop a stronger claim to the government's affirmative obligations.

. . .

### III. Oppression and the Control of Knowledge

The regulations banned from publicly funded clinics information vital to a woman's well-being, autonomy, and participation in the community. From the perspective of the people most affected, the regulations deliberately promoted ignorance among poor Black women. They are an example of the control of knowledge that helps to maintain the existing structure of racial domination.

To understand the political implications of the state's promotion of ignorance, it is helpful to look at theories about oppression and the control of knowledge. The Brazilian scholar Paulo Freire illuminated the relationship between education and oppression in his book, *Pedagogy of the Oppressed*. Freire defines oppression as any situation in which one person hinders another's pursuit of self-affirmation as a responsible person, thus interfering with "man's ontological and historical vocation to be more fully human." The chief preoccupation of oppressors is to prevent the oppressed from taking steps to change their status. It is in the interest of those in power to keep the oppressed in a state of "submerged consciousness," impotent to critique and transform their situation. The powerful are so afraid that critical thinking will lead to revolution that they instinctively use any means, including physical violence, to keep the oppressed from this enterprise.

The most critical weapon of oppressors, then, is the control of knowledge. Those in power control knowledge in three interconnected ways: They attempt to determine social meaning; they reinforce their dominance through education; and they stifle sources of information available to subordinated groups. These

methods of oppression may operate outside the conventional political and legal processes. Their repressive function is not always curtailed by legal doctrines, such as the marketplace-of-ideas and unconstitutional-conditions doctrines, which promote neutrality. The most potent instruments of domination go unnoticed in opinions such as *Rust v. Sullivan*.

\* \* \*

### IV. Knowledge and Dependency

#### A. Government Gratuities and the Meaning of Dependency

In his groundbreaking article, *The New Property*, Charles Reich described a critical feature of the dominant conception of government aid, which he termed the "gratuity principle." This principle holds that because "[g]overnment largess has often been considered a 'gratuity' furnished by the state[,] . . . the state can withhold, grant, or revoke the largess at its pleasure." The gratuity principle accords to government in its role as dispenser of public funds the same status as a private giver. The recipients hold this wealth conditionally rather than absolutely, subject to confiscation by the state. The gratuity principle thus creates a feudal relationship between the government and grantees: "Just as the feudal system linked lord and vassal [through] a system of mutual dependence, obligation, and loyalty, so government largess binds man to the state."

The gratuitous nature of state assistance to the poor is an important feature of oppression. Paulo Freire explained how state aid in the context of oppression always manifests itself in a false generosity: It never goes beyond the oppressor's "attempt to 'soften' [its] power . . . in deference to the weakness of the oppressed." The government's charity does not change the underlying power structure that sustains and justifies the state's mercy. Rather, "[a]n unjust social order is the permanent fount of this 'generosity', which is nourished by death, despair, and poverty." Freire distinguished this false generosity of oppression with the true generosity that enables liberation: "True generosity consists precisely in fighting to destroy the causes which nourish false charity."

The dependent status of the poor in America is reinforced by an ideology that separates and stigmatizes them as morally weak and "different from us." Recent discourse increasingly has attributed the problems of the poor to their own behavior and has based poverty reform on correcting their social deviance through programs such as workfare—requiring welfare recipients to work for their benefits—and mandatory paternity laws. The rhetoric of poverty categorizes people who receive government aid as either "deserving" or "undeserving." The deserving are considered entitled to government assistance either because their impoverished condition resulted from forces beyond their control or because they earned benefits through previous work. The undeserving, on the other hand, have no claim to public funds because they are considered responsible for their plight. Thus, the public views disaster relief, disability benefits, and social security as entitlements, while it views welfare as charity.

Black women on welfare are considered "undeserving" because of both their race and their gender. Blacks have experienced the precarious state of dependence more than any group in America—a condition Patricia Williams describes as "defining blacks as those who ha[ve] no will." As slaves, they were deemed chattel owned by others with virtually no protection by the law. Their physical and mental well-being—indeed their very lives—were subject to the whim of white masters, as well as the brutality imposed by law. Slavery inflicted, in addition to individual white masters' violence, the terrorism of the entire state. Because Blacks remain subordinate to whites in many ways—for example, many Blacks' dependency on the welfare system for survival—Black nationalist scholars have characterized the modern Black experience as a form of domestic colonialism. Poor Black women's reliance on government welfare makes them particularly vulnerable to government control of their reproductive decisions. The popular mythology about the social degeneracy of Blacks and the causes of their poverty places the poor Black community within the "undeserving" category of the poor. The distinction between deserving and undeserving poor is constructed according to gender, as well as race. Men are entitled to compensation by social insurance programs for their prior participation in the labor force, while women—especially single mothers—are treated as dependent clients of the welfare system. As unpaid caregivers, many women lack the relationship to the work force necessary to entitle them to benefits. In addition, society blames them for perpetuating poverty by deviating from the norm of marriage to a male breadwinner.

This categorization of those who receive government assistance profoundly affects the way we view dependency. Because social welfare programs are based on mere altruism, rather than any sense of collective obligation, it is likely that in times of economic hardship the "undeserving poor" will lose what meager support they have. Dependency on the part of the "undeserving" has come to signify a lack of entitlement to the basic conditions of human dignity and membership in society. The current ideology of poverty, race, and gender links this form of reliance on the government with the forfeiture of a claim to constitutional protection. Our society does not recognize any injury in violating the autonomy of the propertyless.

It tolerates laws such as the regulations at issue because it cannot imagine poor Black women as self-determining people, seeing them as having no will.

. . .

## C. Dependency and the Control of Knowledge

The state's false generosity and the dependency it fosters combine with the control of knowledge to perpetuate hierarchies of power. The gratuitous nature of government aid ensures continued dependency on the government, which, in turn, allows the state greater control over what knowledge is made available to dispossessed communities. Government charity merely placates the poor, rather than providing the knowledge and other resources necessary to change their status. Freire explains, "[i]ndeed, the interests of the oppressors lie in 'changing the consciousness of the oppressed, not the situation which oppresses them'; for the more the oppressed can be led to adapt to that situation, the more easily they can be dominated.". . .

These coordinated tools of power are at work in the *Rust* decision. The Court held in *Rust* that poor women of color are not entitled to knowledge that the rest of society deserves. It reasoned that their constitutional entitlement is to rely on the conditional generosity of the state, rather than to change the material conditions of their lives. The *Rust* decision keeps these women in a state of ignorance that makes it more likely that they will adapt to social control of their reproduction. Both methods—the state's false generosity and the promotion of ignorance—serve to entrench the poor Black community further into the structure of oppression.

. . .

## VI. LIBERATION THEORY: THE GOVERNMENT'S AFFIRMATIVE DUTY TO PROVIDE INFORMATION

. . .

A liberation theory would be aimed at ending the oppressive control of knowledge available to the Black community and ensuring the information necessary for Black emancipation. The preceding examination of dependency and the control of knowledge suggests two features of a liberating constitutional vision: It would recognize the importance of information for self-determination, and it would place an affirmative obligation on the government to provide this information to people who are dependent on government funds. . .

Information about reproduction is especially critical to women's self-determination. The denial of information about abortion deprives women of the knowledge necessary to take control of their lives and to transform their own reality. The systematic, institutionalized denial of reproductive freedom has been a principal means of Black women's subjugation throughout their history in America. A liberating constitutionalism would invalidate the promotion of ignorance among poor Black women that denies them control over their reproduction and would seek to provide the information necessary for them to experience true reproductive liberty.

Both liberal and republican constitutional theory support a government duty to provide information. Constitutional scholars belonging to both schools have suggested First Amendment approaches rejecting the abstract focus on ideas that characterized the *Rust* opinion. Rather, their systemic models analyze the role of freedom of speech within the social structure and in relation to a broader vision of social justice.

Liberal scholars have argued that the aim of freedom of expression is to ensure individual autonomy. This model argues that individual liberty, rather than the free trade of ideas, deserves protection from government interference. It values expression, not because it leads to the "truth," but because it fosters the individual's self-determination. Under this view, government censorship is the primary evil because it "stunts the individual's growth as a human being and shows disrespect for the individual's ability to make her own informed decisions." This approach suggests that the government's power to restrict speech should be subject to special scrutiny where it is used to influence constitutionally protected choices, such as the decision to terminate a pregnancy. The regulations violate the liberty model of free expression because they impermissibly infringe upon poor women's autonomy, denying women information critical to a decision that will significantly impact the course of their lives. Abortion counseling respects a woman's autonomy by providing her with the information necessary to make a decision about pregnancy that best contributes to her well-being.

Civic republicanism centers on citizens' participation in collective deliberation. Rather than rely on individual rights to protect against wrongful state action, republicans propose continuing dialogue within the community as the methodology for achieving the common good. Republican theory justifies free speech as the foundation for self-government through deliberative democracy. This conception of the First Amendment, associated with Thomas Jefferson and Alexander Meiklejohn, ensures the ability of citizens to fulfill their decisionmaking role as the true rulers in a republican society. It is premised on the belief that intelligent determination of public issues re-

quires widespread and informed popular deliberation. Free speech allows citizens to gather the information necessary to make rational decisions about public issues and to communicate with others in the deliberative process.

. . .

This republican model of free speech supports the government's obligation to provide abortion counseling. The regulations degrade the citizenship of poor Black women by limiting their ability to participate in the public sphere. A constitutional guarantee of the necessities for republican self-government would invalidate the regulations' obstruction of information critical to the public debate on abortion and to citizens' knowledge of their rights. . . .

The liberal and republican models of the constitutional role of information are strengthened by recognizing the connection between the control of knowledge and racial subordination. Acknowledging this connection enhances the First Amendment analysis in two ways. First, it complicates the fear that both liberalism and republicanism have concerning the concentration of power in the corporate economy and bureaucratic state as the primary threat to human freedom. Both the liberal protection of the individual against the state and the republican protection of the majority against self-interested government ignore the context of social power, defined by race, gender, and economic status, in which these conflicts occur. The state is not a monster that strikes arbitrarily simply to enhance its might. Rather, it wields its power in ways that have historically supported the subordination of particular groups of people. The alienation of all citizens in the capitalist, bureaucratic state cannot explain the particularly brutal oppression of the Black community. The liberal and republican approaches also discount the possibility of using the power of government to destroy illegitimate social domination.

Second, the connection between knowledge and subordination brings into question the faith that both liberalism and republicanism have in an ideal government process, a faith that neglects the need to eradicate these forms of subordination. Republicanism relies on the notion that reasoned deliberation, divorced from private interests, will lead to community consensus as to the common good. The republican reliance on dialogue may provide insufficient protection against repression of minorities. The model of civic deliberation presents the danger that outsiders' freedom of expression will be sacrificed on the basis of the dominant group's perception of the common good. Subordinated voices typically have been silenced on the ground that their speech is not worthy of participation in the public debate. When a subordinated group challenges the social order it is more likely to generate violent conflict than reasoned deliberation.

The history of racial domination in America demonstrates that Blacks are particularly vulnerable to exclusion. For most of American history, Blacks were barred by law from civic participation, including voting, holding public office, and serving on juries. . . . The common good is an elusive goal when one group defines its interests in terms of the continued subordination of another. Liberation is a precondition for true republicanism.

Liberalism depends on neutral government decisionmaking that protects rational individual choice. The experience of group oppression, however, teaches that the dehumanization of the individual is connected to the subordination of the group. The individual's ability to make autonomous decisions is circumscribed by the material conditions of her life, including the community to which she belongs. For members of subordinated communities, protecting individual autonomy necessarily involves the struggle for group liberation. These individuals recognize a positive aspect of group membership that corresponds with communitarians' faith that "freedom might encompass an ability to share a vision of a good life or a good society with others." In contrast to the liberal emphasis on individual freedom, many Blacks see their historically created community as the basis for social identity and the source of liberation. The existence of liberating aspects of both liberalism and communitarianism affirms the inevitable interdependence of individual autonomy and community membership-"the affirmation of free human subjectivity against the constraints of group life, along with the paradoxical countervision of a group life that creates and nurtures individuals capable of freedom."

The systemic nature of racism in American society suggests that rational processes will fail at social transformation without a more deliberate eradication of racial subordination. Liberal and republican theories do not address the invidious potential for government to perpetuate racial subordination by controlling knowledge available to the Black community. The power to control knowledge not only limits individual women's ability to engage in self-determining activity, it also keeps entire communities of people in ignorance. This critical nexus between freedom of speech and racial equality strengthens the affirmative claim to information. . . .

## Bibliography

*Use of Government Funds*

Bittker, Boris I., & Kaufman, Kenneth M., *Taxes and Civil Rights: "Constitutionalizing" the Internal Revenue Codes*, 82 Yale Law Journal 51 (1972)

Delgado, Richard, *The Language of the Arms Race*, 64 Boston University Law Review 961 (1984)

Kamenshine, Robert D., *The First Amendment's Implied Political Establishment Clause*, 67 California Law Review 1104 (1979)

Kreimer, Seth L., *Allocational Sanctions: The Problem of Negative Rights in a Positive State*, 132 University of Pennsylvania Law Review 1293 (1984)

McConnell, Michael W., *Unconstitutional Conditions: Unrecognized Implications for the Establishment Clause*, 29 San Diego Law Review 255 (1989)

Rosenthal, Albert J., *Conditional Federal Spending and the Constitution*, 39 Stanford Law Review 1103 (1987)

Sullivan, Kathleen M., *Unconstitutional Conditions and the Distribution of Liberty*, 26 San Diego law Review 327 (1989)

Sunstein, Cass R., *Why the Unconstitutional Conditions Doctrine is an Anachronism (with Particular Reference to Religion, Speech, and Abortion)*, 70 Boston University Law Review 593 (1990)

Yudof, Mark G., *Politics, Law, and Government Expression in America* (1983)

# Part III

# Regulation of Modern Media

## A. Prelude: Media Specific Concern

When the First Amendment was framed and ratified, the only element of the press was the medium of print. Over the course of the twentieth century, the press consistently has reinvented itself as a function of technology. The medium of broadcasting, which was beyond even the imagination of the First Amendment's architects, is now the nation's dominant medium. The presence and influence of electronic media are being further compounded by the evolution of cable, wireless, and satellite technology. As the traditional print media developed photojournalistic capability and acquired an industrial nature in the late nineteenth century, social critics expressed concern with the press' impact. Louis D. Brandeis and Samuel D. Warren preview regulatory premises referenced to the media's intrusive nature. Concern with the quality of the mass media's output, articulated by Brandeis and Warren, is reiterated by Alexander Meiklejohn. Their observations and reservations reflect caution about the role of electronic media that has persisted in defining regulatory objectives and constitutional standards.

Louis D. Brandeis & Samuel D. Warren, *The Right to Privacy*, 4 HARVARD LAW REVIEW 193 (1890)*

THAT the individual shall have full protection in person and in property is a principle as old as the common law; but it has been found necessary from time to time to define anew the exact nature and extent of such protection. Political, social, and economic changes entail the recognition of new rights, and the common law, in its eternal youth, grows to meet the demands of society. Thus, in very early times, the law gave a remedy only for physical interference with life and property, for trespasses *vi et armis*. Then the "right to life" served only to protect the subject from battery in its various forms; liberty meant freedom from actual restraint; and the right to property secured to the individual his lands and his cattle. Later, there came a recognition of man's spiritual nature, of his feelings and his intellect. Gradually the scope of these legal rights broadened; and now the right to life has come to mean the right to enjoy life—the right to be let alone; the right to liberty secures the exercise of extensive civil privileges; and the term "property" has grown to comprise every form of possession—intangible, as well as tangible. . . .

This development of the law was inevitable. The intense intellectual and emotional life, and the heightening of sensations which came with the advance of civilization, made it clear to men that only a part of the pain, pleasure, and profit of life lay in physical things. Thoughts, emotions, and sensations demanded legal recognition, and the beautiful capacity for growth which characterizes the common law enabled the judges to afford the requisite protection, without the interposition of the legislature.

Recent inventions and business methods call attention to the next step which must be taken for the protection of the person, and for securing to the individual what Judge Cooley calls the right "to be let alone." Instantaneous photographs, and newspapers enterprise have invaded the sacred precincts of private and domestic life; and numerous mechanical devices threaten to make good the prediction that "what is whispered in the closet shall be proclaimed from the house-tops." For years there has been a feeling that the law must afford some remedy for the unauthorized circulation of portraits of private persons and the evil of the invasion of privacy by the newspapers, long keenly felt, has been but recently discussed by an able writer. The alleged facts of a somewhat notorious case brought before an inferior tribunal in New York a few months ago, directly involved the consideration of the right of circulating portraits; and the question whether our law will recognize and protect the right to privacy in this and in other respects must soon come before our courts for consideration.

Of the desirability—indeed of the necessity—of some such protection, there can, it is believed, be no doubt. The press is overstepping in every direction the obvious bounds of propriety and of decency. Gossip is no longer the resource of the idle and of the vicious, but has become a trade, which is pursued with industry as well as effrontery. To satisfy a prurient taste the details of sexual relations are spread broadcast in the columns of the daily papers. To occupy the indolent, column upon column is filled with idle gossip, which can only be procured by intrusion upon the domestic circle. The intensity and complexity of life, attendant upon advancing civilization, have rendered necessary some retreat from the world, and man, under the refining influence of culture, has become more sensitive to publicity, so that solitude and privacy have become more essential to the individual; but modern enterprise and invention have, through invasions upon his privacy, subjected him to mental pain and distress, far greater than could be inflicted by mere bodily injury. Nor is the harm wrought by such invasions confined to the suffering of those who may be made the subjects of journalistic or other enterprise. In this, as in other branches of commerce, the supply creates the demand. Each crop of unseemly gossip, thus harvested, becomes the seed of more, and, in direct proportion to its circulation, results in a lowering of social standards and of morality. Even gossip apparently harmless, when widely and persistently circulated, is potent for evil. It both belittles and perverts. It belittles by inverting the relative importance of things, thus dwarfing the thoughts and aspirations of a people. When personal gossip attains the dignity of print, and crowds the space available for matters of real interest to the community, what wonder that the ignorant and thoughtless mistake its relative importance. Easy of comprehension, appealing to that weak side of human nature which is never wholly cast down by the misfortunes and frailties of our neighbors, no one can be surprised that it usurps the place of interest in brains capable of other things. Triviality destroys at once robustness of thought and delicacy of feeling. No enthusiasm can flourish, no generous impulse can survive under its blighting influence. . . .

Alexander Meiklejohn, *Free Speech and Its Relation to Self-Government* (1948)*

. . . When all that concerns our argument has been felt and said, the stark fact remains that the First Amendment is a negation. It protects. It forbids interference with something. And that protection can have value only as the "something" which is protected has value. What, we must ask, would be the use of giving to American citizens freedom to speak if they had nothing worth saying to say? Or—to state the principle less baldly—surely it is true that the protection of public discussion in our nation takes on an ever-increasing importance as the nation succeeds in so educating and informing its people that, in mind and will, they are able to think and act as self-governing citizens. And this means that far deeper and more significant than the demand for the freedom of speech is the demand for education, for the freeing of minds. These are not different demands. The one is a negative and external form of the other. We shall not understand the First Amendment unless we see that underlying it is the purpose that all the citizens of our self-governing society shall be "equally" educated.

I cannot, in these closing pages, discuss the methods, the successes and failures, of our national education—though my argument is only a fragment unless that is done. It is essential, however, to mention one typical failure which, since it has to do with the agencies of communication, falls within the field of our inquiry. The failure which I have in mind is that of the commercial radio.

When this new form of communication became available, there opened up before us the possibility that, as a people living a common life under a com-

mon agreement, we might communicate with one another freely with regard to the values, the opportunities, the difficulties, the joys and sorrows, the hopes and fears, the plans and purposes, of that common life. It seemed possible that, amid all our differences, we might become a community of mutual understanding and of shared interests. It was that hope which justified our making the radio "free," our giving it the protection of the First Amendment.

But never was a human hope more bitterly disappointed. The radio as it now operates among us is not free. Nor is it entitled to the protection of the First Amendment. It is not engaged in the task of enlarging and enriching human communication. It is engaged in making money. And the First Amendment does not intend to guarantee men freedom to say what some private interest pays them to say what, as citizens, they think, what they believe, about the general welfare.

As one utters these words of disappointment, one must gratefully acknowledge that there are, working in the radio business, intelligent and devoted men who are fighting against the main current. And their efforts are not wholly unavailing. But, in spite of them, the total effect, as judged in terms of educational value, is one of terrible destruction. The radio, as we now have it, is not cultivating those qualities of taste, of reasoned judgment, of integrity, of loyalty, of mutual understanding upon which the enterprise of self-government depends. On the contrary, it is a mighty force for breaking them down. It corrupts both our morals and our intelligence. And that catastrophe is significant for our inquiry, because it reveals how hollow may be the victories of the freedom of speech when our acceptance of the principle is merely formalistic. Misguided by that formalism we Americans have given to the doctrine merely its negative meaning. We have used it for the protection of private, possessive interests with which it has no concern. It is misinterpretations such as this which, in our use of the radio, the moving picture, the newspaper and other forms of publication, are giving the name "freedoms" to the most flagrant enslavements of our minds and wills. . . .

# Bibliography

*Prelude: Medium Specific Concern*

Barnouw, Eric, *The Golden Web* (1969)

Emery, Edward, *The Press and America* (1962)

Robinson, Glen O., *The Federal Communications Commission: An Essay on Regulatory Watchdogs*, 64 Virginia Law Review 169 (1978)

Simmons, Steven, *The Fairness Doctrine and the Media* (1978)

## B. Redistributing Expressive Opportunity

The evolution of new communications technologies has profoundly influenced the First Amendment's scope and direction. Freedom of the press has become a medium specific concept. As the Supreme Court has put it, the "'differing natures, values, abuses and dangers' of each method" of communication necessitate a "'law unto itself.'" *Metromedia, Inc. v. City of San Diego*, 453 U.S. 490, 501 (1981) quoting *Kovacs v. Cooper*, 336 U.S. 77, 97 (1949, (Jackson, J., concurring). Although broadcasting has become the nation's dominant medium, it is afforded less constitutional protection than traditional print media. Spectrum scarcity—the problem of fewer actual frequencies than potential broadcasters—has been cited as the basis for detailed broadcasting regulation in the form of licensing, structural and content controls. Traditional perceptions of a scarcity problem have engendered a new set of First Amendment rights accruing to viewers and listeners, as their right to receive diverse expression has been prioritized over editorial autonomy. Pursuant to such an understanding, regulation struck down when applied to print media has been upheld with respect to broadcasting. As even newer media such as cable have emerged, the challenge has been to determine whether their First Amendment status should be defined by the print or broadcast model. Jerome Barron suggests that, in a mass media culture, the public should have a right of access affording them real speaking opportunities. Lee C. Bollinger argues that it is acceptable to regulate newer media such as broadcasting, provided traditional media remain unfettered. Lucas A. Powe challenges the basic premises of modern broadcast regulation. Mark S. Fowler and Daniel L. Brenner maintain that constitutional interests and regulatory aims are best served by free market principles. Stanley Ingber stresses the risks of a First Amendment model favoring editorial management over autonomy. Daniel Brenner and a student note argue respectively for and against the redistribution of First Amendment rights appurtenant to cable.

Jerome A. Barron, *Access to the Press—A New First Amendment Right*, 80 HARVARD LAW REVIEW 1641 (1967)*

There is an anomaly in our constitutional law. While we protect expression once it has come to the fore, our law is indifferent to creating opportunities for expression. Our constitutional theory is in the grip of a romantic conception of free expression, a belief that the "marketplace of ideas" is freely accessible. But if ever there were a self-operating marketplace of ideas, it has long ceased to exist. The mass media's development of an antipathy to ideas requires legal intervention if novel and unpopular ideas are to be assured a forum—unorthodox points of view which have no claim on broadcast time and newspaper space as a matter of right are in poor position to compete with those aired as a matter of grace.

The free expression questions which now come before the courts involve individuals who have managed to speak or write in a manner that captures public attention and provokes legal reprisal. The conventional constitutional issue is whether expression already uttered should be given first amendment shelter or whether it may be subjected to sanction as speech beyond the constitutionally protected pale. To those who can obtain access to the media of mass communications first amendment case law furnishes considerable help. But what of those whose ideas are too unacceptable to secure access to the media? To them the mass communications industry replies: The first amendment guarantees our freedom to do as we choose with our media. Thus the constitutional imperative of free expression becomes a rationale for repressing competing ideas. First amendment theory must be reexamined, for only by responding to the present reality of the mass media's repression of ideas can the constitutional guarantee of free speech best serve its original purposes.

. . .

II. OBSTACLES TO ACCESS: THE CHANGING TECHNOLOGY OF THE COMMUNICATIONS PROCESS

. . .

. . . Many American cities have become one newspaper towns. This is a "disquieting" development for American journalist J. Russell Wiggins since "[t]his noncompetitive situation puts it within

the power of the monopoly newspaper to suppress facts at its discretion . . . ."

Mr. Wiggins suggests that the economics of newspaper publication—rising costs of everything from newsprint to labor—may be a more significant cause of the withholding of news than conspiratorial efforts of publishers. Less sympathetic to the mass media in evaluating the practical obstacles which confront the group seeking an adequate forum for its opinion is Marshall McLuhan's view that the very nature of modern media is at war with a point of view orientation. McLuhan observes that each medium engenders quite different degrees of participation. The new modes of communication engage us by their form rather than by their content; what captivates us is the television screen itself. In his view the electronic media which have eclipsed the typographical age entail a high degree of nonintellectual and emotional participation and involvement. We have become mesmerized by the new forms of communication to the point of indifference to their content and to the content of the older media. The electronic media which dominate modern communications are, in McLuhan's analysis, ill suited to the problem of making public issues meaningful.

Another commentator on communications, Dan Lacy, has explained this indifference to content somewhat differently. More critical than popular obsession with the forms of technological advance is the dull emphasis on majoritarian values which characterizes of our media, old and new. . . .

The aversion of the media for the novel and heretical has escaped attention for an odd reason. The controllers of the media have no ideology. Since in the main they espouse no particular ideas, their antipathy to all ideas has passed unnoticed. What has happened is not that the controllers of opinion, Machiavellian fashion, are subtly feeding us information to the end that we shall acquiesce in their political view of the universe. On the contrary, the communications industry is operated on the whole with an intellectual neutrality consistent with V.O. Key's theory that the commercial nature of mass communications makes it "bad business" to espouse the heterodox or the controversial.

But retreat from ideology is not bereft of ideological and practical consequences. In a commentary about television, but which applies equally well to all mass media, Gilbert Seldes has complained that, in a time demanding more active intelligence than has ever before been necessary if we are to survive, the most powerful of all our media are inducing inertia. The contemporary structure of the mass media direct media away from rather than toward opinion-

---

* Reprinted with permission.

making. In other words, it is not that the mass communication industry is pushing certain ideas and rejecting others but rather that it is using the free speech and free press guarantees to avoid opinions instead of acting as a sounding board for their expression. What happens of course is that the opinion vacuum is filled with the least controversial and bland ideas. Whatever is stale and accepted in the status quo is readily discussed and thereby reinforced and revitalized.

The failures of existing media are revealed by the development of new media to convey unorthodox, unpopular, and new ideas. Sit-ins and demonstrations testify to the inadequacy of old media as instruments to afford full and effective hearing for all points of view. Demonstrations, it has been well said, are "the free press of the movement to win justice for Negroes. . . ." But, like an inadequate underground press, it is communications medium by default, a statement of the inability to secure access to the conventional means of reaching and changing public opinion. By the bizarre and unsettling nature of his technique the demonstrator hopes to arrest and divert attention long enough to compel the public to ponder his message. But attention-getting devices so abound in the modern world that new ones soon become tiresome. The dissenter must look for ever more unsettling assaults on the mass mind if he is to have continuing impact. Thus, as critics of protest are eager and in a sense correct to say, the prayer-singing student demonstration is the prelude to Watts. But the difficulty with this criticism is that it wishes to throttle protest rather than to recognize that protest has taken these forms because it has had nowhere else to go.

## III. MAKING THE FIRST AMENDMENT WORK

The Justices of the United States Supreme Court are not innocently unaware of these contemporary social realities, but they have nevertheless failed to give the "marketplace of ideas" theory of the first amendment the burial it merits. Perhaps the interment of this theory has been denied for the understandable reason that the Court is at a loss to know with what to supplant it. But to put off inquiry under today's circumstances will only aggravate the need for it under tomorrow's.

### A. Beyond Romanticism

There is inequality in the power to communicate ideas just as there is inequality in economic bargaining power; to recognize the latter and deny the former is quixotic. The "marketplace of ideas" view has rested on the assumption that protecting the right of expression is equivalent to providing for it. But

changes in that communications industry have destroyed the equilibrium in that marketplace. While it may have been still possible in 1925 to believe with Justice Holmes that every idea is "acted on unless some other belief outweighs it or some failure of energy stifles the movement at its birth," it is impossible to believe that now. Yet Holmesian theory is not abandoned, even though the advent of radio and television has made even more evident that philosophy's unreality. A realistic view of the first amendment requires recognition that a right of expression is somewhat thin if it can be exercised only at the sufferance of the managers of mass communications.

Too little attention has been given to defining the purposes which the first amendment protection is designed to achieve and to identifying the addresses of that protection. An eloquent exception is the statement of Justice Brandeis in *Whitney v. California* that underlying the first amendment guarantee is the assumption that free expression is indispensable to the "discovery and spread of political truth" and that the "greatest menace to freedom is an inert people." In *Thornhill v. Alabama* Justice Murphy described his view of the first amendment:

> The exigencies of the colonial period and the efforts to secure freedom from oppressive administration developed a broadened conception of these liberties as adequate to supply *the public need for information and education with respect to the significant issues of the times.* . . . Freedom of discussion, if it would fulfill its historic function in this nation, must embrace all issues about which information is needed or appropriate to enable the members of society to cope with the exigencies of their period.

That public information is vital to the creation of an informed citizenry is, I suppose, unexceptionable. Both Justices recognize the importance of confronting citizens, as individual decision makers, with the widest variety of competing ideas. But accuracy does demand one to remember that Justice Brandeis was speaking in *Whitney*, as was Justice Murphy in *Thornhill*, of the constitutional recognition that is given to the necessity of inhibiting "the occasional tyrannies of governing majorities" from throttling opportunities for discussion. But is it such a large constitutional step to take the same approach to non-governing minorities who control the machinery of communication? Is it too bold to suggest that it is necessary to ensure access to the mass media for unorthodox ideas in order to make effective the guarantee against repression?

Another conventionally stated goal of first amendment protection—the "public order function"—also cries out for recognition of a right of access to the mass media. The relationship between constitutional assurance of an opportunity to communicate ideas and the integrity of the public order was appreciated by both Justice Cardozo and Justice Brandeis. In *Palko v. Connecticut* Justice Cardozo clearly indicated that while many rights could be eliminated and yet "justice" not undone, "neither liberty nor justice would exist . . . [without] freedom of thought and speech" since free expression is "the matrix, the indispensable condition, of nearly every other form of freedom." If freedom of expression cannot be secured because entry into the communication media is not free but is confined as a matter of discretion by a few private hands, the sense of the justice of existing institutions, which freedom of expression is designed to assure, vanishes from some section of our population as surely as if access to the media were restricted by the government.

Justice Brandeis, in his seminal opinion in *Whitney*—one of the few efforts of a Supreme Court Justice to go beyond the banality of the "marketplace of ideas"—also stressed the intimacy of the relationship between the goals of a respect for public order and the assurance of free expression. For Brandeis one of the assumptions implicit in the guarantee of free expression is that "it is hazardous to discourage thought, hope and imagination; that fear breeds repression; that repression breeds hate; that hate menaces stable government; that the path of safety lies in the opportunity to discuss freely supposed grievances and proposed remedies . . . ." I would suggest that the contemporary challenge to this "path of safety" has roots in the lack of opportunity for the disadvantaged and the dissatisfied of our society to discuss supposed grievances effectively.

The "sit-in" demonstrates that the safety valve value of free expression in preserving public order is lost when access to the communication media is foreclosed to dissident groups. It is a measure of the jaded and warped standards of the media that ideas which normally would never be granted a forum are given serious network coverage if they become sufficiently enmeshed in mass demonstration or riot and violence. Ideas are denied admission into media until they are first disseminated in a way that challenges and disrupts the social order. They then may be discussed and given notice. But is it not the assumption of a constitutional guarantee of freedom of expression that the process ought to work just the other way—that the idea be given currency first so that its proponents will not conclude that unrest and violence alone will suffice to capture public attention? Contemporary constitutional theory has been indifferent to this task of channeling the novel and the heretical into the mass communications media, perhaps because the problem is indeed a recent one.

### B. The Need for a Contextual Approach

A corollary of the romantic view of the first amendment is the Court's unquestioned assumption that the amendment affords "equal" protection to the various media. According to this view new media of communication are assimilated into first amendment analysis without regard to the enormous differences in impact these media have in comparison with the traditional printed word. Radio and television are to be as free as newspapers and magazines, sound trucks as free as radio and television.

This extension of a simplistic egalitarianism to media whose comparative impacts are gravely disproportionate is wholly unrealistic. It results from confusing freedom of media content with freedom of the media to restrict access. The assumption in romantic first amendment analysis that the same postulates apply to different classes of people, situations, and means of communication obscures the fact, noted explicitly by Justice Jackson in *Kovacs v. Cooper*, that problems of access and impact vary significantly from medium to medium: "The moving picture screen, the radio, the newspaper, the handbill, the sound truck and the street corner orator have differing natures, values, abuses and dangers. Each, in my view, is a law unto itself, and all we are dealing with now is the sound truck." . . .

An analysis of the first amendment must be tailored to the context in which ideas are or seek to be aired. This contextual approach requires an examination of the purposes served by and the impact of each particular medium. If a group seeking to present a particular side of a public issue is unable to get space in the only newspaper in town, is this inability compensated by the availability of the public park or the sound truck? Competitive media only constitute alternative means of access in a crude manner. If ideas are criticized in one forum the most adequate response is in the same forum since it is most likely to reach the same audience. Further, the various media serve different functions and create different reactions and expectations—criticism of an individual or a governmental policy over television may reach more people but criticism in print is more durable.

The test of a community's opportunities for free expression rests not so much in an abundance of alternative media but rather in an abundance of opportunities to secure expression in media with the largest impact. . . .

## C. A New Perspective

The late Professor Meiklejohn, who has articulated a view of the first amendment which assumes its justification to be political self-government, has wisely pointed out that "what is essential is not that everyone shall speak, but that everything worth saying shall be said"—that the point of ultimate interest is not the words of the speakers but the minds of the hearers. Can everything worth saying be effectively said? Constitutional opinions that are particularly solicitous of the interests of mass media—radio, television, and mass circulation newspaper—devote little thought to the difficulties of securing access to those media. If those media are unavailable, can the minds of "hearers" be reached effectively? Creating opportunities for expression is as important as ensuring the right to express ideas without fear of governmental reprisal.

The problem of private restrictions on freedom of expression might, in special circumstances, be attacked under the federal antitrust laws. In *Associated Press v. United States*, involving an attempt to exclude from membership competitors of existing members of the Associated Press in order to deprive them of the use of the AP's wire service, Justice Black wrote for the Court that nongovernmental combinations are not immune from governmental sanction if they impede rather than expedite free expression:

> [The First] Amendment rests on the assumption that the widest possible dissemination of information from diverse and antagonistic sources is essential to the welfare of the public, that a free press is a condition of a free society. Surely a command that the government itself shall not impede the free flow of ideas does not afford non-governmental combinations a refuge if they impose restraints upon that constitutionally guaranteed freedom. . . . *Freedom to publish is guaranteed by the Constitution, but freedom to combine to keep others from publishing is not. Freedom of the press from governmental interference under the First Amendment does not sanction repression of that freedom by private interests.*

Despite these unusual remarks this opinion reflects a romantic view of the first amendment, for Justice Black assumes the "free flow of ideas" and the "freedom to publish" absent a combination of publishers. Moreover, this was an unusual case; antitrust law operates too indirectly in assuring access to be an effective device.

But the case is important in its acknowledgment that the public interest, here embodied in the antitrust statutes, can override the first amendment claims of the mass media; it would seem that the public interest in expression of divergent viewpoints should be weighed as heavily when the mass media invoke the first amendment to shield restrictions on access. . . .

Our constitutional theory, particularly in the free speech area, has historically been inoperative unless government restraint can be shown. If the courts or the legislature were to guarantee some minimal right to access for ideas which could not otherwise be effectively aired before the public, there would be "state action" sufficient to support a claim by the medium involved that this violated its first amendment rights. However, the right of free expression is not an absolute right, as is illustrated by *Associated Press*, and to guarantee access to divergent, otherwise unexpressed ideas would so promote the societal interests underlying the first amendment as perhaps to outweigh the medium's claim. Nor is the notion of assuring access or opportunity for discussion a novel theory. In *Near v. Minnesota ex rel. Olson* Chief Justice Hughes turned to Blackstone to corroborate the view that freedom from prior restraint rather than freedom from subsequent punishment was central to the eighteenth century notion of liberty of the press. This concern with suppression before dissemination was doubtless to assure that ideas would reach the public. "'Every freeman has a undoubted right to lay what sentiments he pleases before the public; to forbid this, is to destroy the freedom of the press; but if he publishes what is improper, mischievous or illegal, he must take the consequence of his own temerity.'"

The avowed emphasis of free speech is still on a freeman's right to "lay what sentiments he pleases before the public." But Blackstone wrote in another age. Today ideas reach the millions largely to the extent they are permitted entry into the great metropolitan dailies, news magazine, and broadcasting networks. The soap box is no longer an adequate forum for public discussion. Only the new media of communication can lay sentiments before the public, and it is they rather than government who can most effectively abridge expression by nullifying the opportunity for an idea to win acceptance. As a constitutional theory for the communication of ideas, laissez faire is manifestly irrelevant.

The constitutional admonition against abridgment of speech and press is at present not applied to the very interests which have real power to effect such abridgment. Indeed, nongoverning minorities in control of the means of communication should perhaps be inhibited from restraining free speech (by the denial of access to their media) even more than governing majorities are restrained by the first amendment—minorities do not have the mandate which a legislative majority enjoys in a policy operating under a theory of representative government. What is required is an interpretation of the first amendment which focuses on the idea that restraining the hand of government is quite useless in assuring free speech if a restraint on access is effectively secured by private groups. A constitutional prohibition against governmental restrictions on expression is effective only if the Constitution ensures an adequate opportunity for discussion. Since this opportunity exists only in the mass media, the interests of those who control the means of communication must be accommodated with the interests of those who seek a forum in which to express their point of view.

## IV. NEW WINDS OF CONSTITUTIONAL DOCTRINE: THE IMPLICATIONS FOR A RIGHT TO BE HEARD

### A. New York Times Co. v. Sullivan: A Lost Opportunity

The potential of existing law to support recognition of a right of access has gone largely unnoticed by the Supreme Court. Judicial blindness to the problem of securing access to the press is dramatically illustrated by *New York Times Co. v. Sullivan*, one of the latest chapters in the romantic and rigid interpretation of the first amendment. . . .

The constitutional armor which *Times* now offers newspapers is predicated on the "principle that debate on public issues should be uninhibited, robust, and wide-open, and that it may well include vehement, caustic, and sometimes unpleasantly sharp attacks on government and public officials." But it is paradoxical that although the libel laws have been emasculated for the benefit of defendant newspapers where the plaintiff is a "public official," the Court shows no corresponding concern as to whether debate will in fact be assured. The irony of *Times* and its progeny lies in the unexamined assumption that reducing newspaper exposure to libel litigation will remove restraints on expression and lead to an "informed society." But in fact the decision creates a new imbalance in the communications process. Purporting to deepen the constitutional guarantee of full expression, the actual effect of the decision is to perpetuate the freedom of a few in a manner adverse to the public interest in uninhibited debate. Unless the *Times* doctrine is deepened to require opportunities for the public figure to reply to a defamatory attack, the *Times* decision will merely serve to equip the press with some new and rather heavy artillery

which can crush as well as stimulate debate. . . .

### B. Ginzburg v. United States: The Implications of The "Commercial Exploitation" Doctrine

The *Times* decision operates on the assumption that newspapers are fortresses of vigorous public criticism, that assuring the press freedom over its content is the only prerequisite to open and robust debate. But if the *raison d'etre* of the mass media is not to maximize discussion but to maximize profits, inquiry should be directed to the possible effect of such a fact on constitutional theory. . . .

Whether the mass media suffer from an institutional distaste for controversy because of technological or of economic factors, this antipathy to novel ideas must be viewed against a background of industry insistence on constitutional immunity from legally imposed responsibilities. A quiet truth emerges from such a study: industry opposition to legally imposed responsibilities does not represent a flight from censorship but rather a flight from points of view. Points of view suggest disagreement and angry customers are not good customers.

However, there is emerging in our constitutional philosophy of the first amendment a strain of realism which contrasts markedly with the prevailing romanticism. The much publicized case of *Ginzburg v. United States* contains the seeds of a new pragmatic approach to the first amendment guarantee of free expression. In *Ginzburg* the dissemination of books was held to violate the federal obscenity statute not because the printed material was in itself obscene but because the publications were viewed by the Court "against a background of commercial exploitation of erotica solely for the sake of their prurient appeal." The books were purchased by the reader "for titillation, not for saving intellectual content."

The mass communications industry should be viewed in constitutional litigation with the same candor with which it has been analyzed by industry members and scholars in communication. If dissemination of books can be prohibited and punished when the dissemination is not for any "saving intellectual content" but for "commercial exploitation," it would seem that the mass communications industry, no less animated by motives of "commercial exploitation," could be legally obliged to host competing opinions and points of view. If the mass media are essentially business enterprises and their commercial nature makes it difficult to give a full and effective hearing to a wide spectrum of opinion, a theory of the first amendment is unrealistic if it prevents courts or legislatures from requiring the media to do that which, for commercial reasons, they would be otherwise unlikely to do. Such proposals only require that the opportunity for publication be broadened and do not involve restraint on publication or punishment after publication, as did *Ginzburg* where the distributor of books was jailed under an obscenity statute even though the books themselves were not constitutionally obscene. In a companion case to *Ginzburg*, Justice Douglas remarked that the vice of censorship lies in the substitution it makes of "majority rule where minority tastes or viewpoints were to be tolerated." But what is suggested here is merely that legal steps be taken to provide for the airing and publication of "minority tastes or viewpoints," not that the mass media be prevented from publishing their views. . . .

## V. IMPLEMENTING A RIGHT OF ACCESS TO THE PRESS

The foregoing analysis has suggested the necessity of rethinking first amendment theory so that it will not only be effective in preventing governmental abridgment but will also produce meaningful expression despite the present or potential repressive effects of the mass media. If the first amendment can be so invoked, it is necessary to examine what machinery is available to enforce a right of access and what bounds limit that right. . . .

Constitutional power exists for both federal and state legislation in this area. Turning first to the constitutional basis for federal legislation, it has long been held that freedom of expression is protected by the due process clause of the fourteenth amendment. The now celebrated section five of the fourteenth amendment, authorizing Congress to "enforce, by appropriate legislation" the provisions of the fourteenth amendment, appears to be as resilient and serviceable a tool for effectuating the freedom of expression guarantee of the fourteenth amendment as for implementing the equal protection guarantee. Professor Cox has noted that our recent experience in constitutional adjudication has revealed an untapped reservoir of federal legislative power to define and promote the constitutional rights of individuals in relation to state government. When the consequence of private conduct is to deny to individuals the enjoyment of a right owned by the state, legislation which assures public capacity to perform that duty should be legitimate. Alternatively, legislation implementing responsibility to provide access to the mass media may be justified on a theory that the nature of the communications process imposes quasi-public functions on these quasi-public instrumentalities.

It is interesting to note that the late Professor Meiklejohn did not anticipate the new uses that the long dormant section five of the fourteenth amendment could be put in order to implement in a positive manner the great negatives of section one of the fourteen amendment. Consequently, he believed that the only solution to what I have styled the romantic approach to the first amendment was by way of constitutional amendment. Mr. W.H. Ferry of the Center for Democratic Institutions has made public Professor Meiklejohn's despair at the unintended result which had been wrought by the first amendment—freedom of the press had become an excuse for the controllers of mass communication to duck responsibility and to exercise by default the same censorship role which had been denied the government. Mr. Ferry says that shortly before his death Professor Meiklejohn proposed, in an unpublished paper for the Center, that the first amendment be revised by adding the following:

> In view of the intellectual and cultural responsibilities laid upon the citizens of a free society by the political institutions of self-government, the Congress, acting in cooperation with the several states and with nongovernmental organizations serving the same general purpose, shall have power to provide for the intellectual and cultural education of all of the citizens of the United States.

What is especially interesting about Professor Meiklejohn's suggested addition is the depth of its criticism of contemporary first amendment theory. However, it is not necessary to amend the first amendment to attain the goal of greater access to the mass media. I do not think it adventurous to suggest that, if Congress were to pass a federal right of access statute, a sympathetic court would not lack the constitutional text necessary to validate the statute. If the first amendment is read to state affirmative goals, Congress is empowered to realize them. My basic premise in these suggestions is that a provision preventing government from silencing or dominating opinion should not be confused with an absence of governmental power to require that opinion be voiced. . . .

## VI. CONCLUSION

The changing nature of the communications process has made it imperative that the law show concern for the public interest in effective utilization of media for the expression of diverse points of view. Confrontation of ideas, a topic of eloquent affection in contemporary decisions, demands some recognition of a right to be heard as a constitutional principle. It is the writer's position that it is open to the courts to fashion a remedy for a right of access, at least in the most arbitrary denial of space, hence securing an effective forum for the expression of divergent opinions.

With the development of private restraints on free expression, the idea of a free marketplace where ideas can compete on their merits has become just as unrealistic in the twentieth century as the economic theory of perfect competition. The world in which an essentially rationalist philosophy of the first amendment was born has vanished and what was rationalism is now romance.

---

Charles D. Ferris and James A. Kirkland, *Fairness—The Broadcaster's Hippocratic Oath*, 34 CATHOLIC UNIVERSITY LAW REVIEW 605 (1985)*

Sixteen years ago, the Supreme Court unanimously upheld the Fairness Doctrine in *Red Lion Broadcasting Co. v. FCC*. Over forty years ago, the Court held that public interest regulation of broadcasters is fully consistent with the first amendment. Both of these venerable holdings, though consistently reaffirmed by the Court, are now under concerted attack by broadcasters and those who have taken up their cause. The volume and vigor of these attacks, however, exceed their merit. The case for the Fairness Doctrine and the similar provisions affecting political broadcasting is stronger now than it was when the Supreme Court decided *Red Lion*.

The power of television broadcasters in providing the public with information on political, social, and cultural issues and current events is indisputable. Broadcasting now outdistances other media of communication by a wide margin. This growth in power parallels the recent growth of independent political groups, known as political action committees (PACs). PACs are presently willing and able to devote their immense resources to media campaigns to advocate their limited political agendas. As a result, the risk that broadcasters and wealthy interests could monopolize our national dialogue, recognized in *Red Lion*, looms larger than ever before.

Critics of the fairness rules often overlook the fact that broadcasters possess this power not by their own efforts, but because the government has granted them the privilege of using a portion of the spectrum

---

* Reprinted with permission.

as trustees for the public. Without government allocation of the spectrum, no one could broadcast effectively, as the chaotic experience in the infancy of radio demonstrated. Requiring broadcasters to air diverse views on important issues, and provide access opportunities for political candidates, is the quid pro quo our society expects for the broadcaster's use of the public airways. These requirements, however, are no greater than the requirements imposed by the canons of journalistic ethics. The fairness rules are thus, quite simply, the Hippocratic Oath of broadcasters. Just as doctors are expected responsibly to exercise their power over life and death, so too are broadcasters expected responsibly to exercise their power in our national dialogue. This article will defend the Fairness Doctrine as a sensible accommodation of the first amendment rights of broadcasters, and the right of the public both to present its various viewpoints and to receive an evenhanded presentation of important issues.

. . .

## II. THE RIGHTS AND RESPONSIBILITIES OF BROADCASTERS

Both the *Red Lion* and *CBS* cases recognize that broadcasters have unique responsibilities to serve the public interest. Broadcasters are "'public trustees' charged with the duty of fairly and impartially informing the public audience." The trustee concept, with its concomitant responsibilities, dates back to the origins of radio. The early experience with radio showed that with unfettered competition for use of the airwaves, no one could effectively broadcast; all were drowned out. As a result, the broadcasting industry unanimously demanded government allocation of the public airwaves. In responding to the demands of the broadcasters, the Federal Communications Commission (FCC or Commission), and its predecessor, the Federal Radio Commission (FRC), allocated the spectrum to a limited number of applicants. Congress wisely chose the "public interest" as the criterion for selection of those who would receive this valuable privilege. Significantly, the FRC, in one of the first actions under the public interest standard, required broadcasters to devote a reasonable amount of time to coverage of issues of public importance.

Requiring broadcast licensees to inform the public in return for the grant of a valuable privilege was, and still is, a fair bargain. Indeed, the dramatic increase in the power of broadcasters in modern times makes the case for the fairness rules all the more compelling. Secretary of Commerce Herbert Hoover recognized the risk of domination of the broadcast medium by a few voices even prior to the passage of the Radio Act of 1927. He testified that "we can not allow any single person or group to place themselves in [a] position where they can censor the material which shall be broadcasted to the public."

Sixty years later, the domination of broadcasting by the three television networks is an economic fact of life. The networks have the resources to take advantage of the pronounced economies of scale in the development and distribution of programming, which are particularly pronounced in the area of news programming. As a consequence, the networks supply the vast majority of the programming to their affiliates.

The advent of new technologies capable of transmitting video programming has not reduced the dominance of the networks. As one network executive recently observed, the development of these technologies merely "underscore[s] the singular role of network television—which remains our only true mass medium—as the only shared experience that crosses over all the differences that characterize this vast and varied nation." Cable television and the other new video outlets cited by critics of broadcast regulation are insignificant by comparison. The "video cornucopia" envisioned by these critics is, indeed, many years away.

Exotic technologies such as Multipoint Distribution Systems and Satellite Master Antenna Television together presently reach less than one percent of the population. Even cable television only reaches slightly more than one-third of all households while a majority of the twenty largest United States cities remain unwired for cable. More importantly, cable television today is primarily a new means of delivering programming. Cable has not yet become a sufficiently important source of original and diverse programming to reduce the American public's dependence on the three commercial networks for their news and information. Instead, today's cable systems are dependent upon the networks for their livelihood. Cable television systems in many communities carry as many as six network-affiliated stations, whose programs necessarily overlap. Any other programming carried by cable and other systems is generally sports or movies, not informational programming. Even the emergence of a cable offering such as the Cable News Network does not, by itself, significantly affect the preeminent position of the networks.

The dominance of television in our national dialogue thus continues unabated. Recent studies of how the population receives its news show clearly the magnitude of this dominance. The vast majority of the population depends primarily upon traditional television for news, while over forty percent of the population relies exclusively on television for news. Studies also indicate that television is the main source of information on national political campaigns and issues.

The Fairness Doctrine simply requires that television, as the dominant means of mass communication, cover public issues and candidates, and cover them in a fair and balanced fashion. These requirements are all the more important in light of the recent rise of independent political groups, known as political action committees or PACs. These organizations have at their disposal great financial resources for advocacy of their limited interests. The number of PACs has mushroomed, as have their total expenditures in the political arena.

The fairness and political broadcasting rules limit the risk that such wealthy special interest groups will drown out those groups with less financial resources. Under the Fairness Doctrine, sale of time to a PAC triggers a broadcaster's obligation to air contrasting views by including opposing viewpoints in a program, by selling advertising time to opposing groups, or by offering free time to opposing groups. In addition, the Commission has held that where broadcasters sell time to supporters of one candidate to air, for example, negative advertisements against an opposing candidate, the supporters of the opposing candidate must be afforded an equal opportunity to purchase time to air their views. Independent political action committees actually supporting a particular candidate are thus prevented from circumventing the rules requiring broadcasters to afford equivalent opportunities to opposing political candidates. . . .

The Fairness Doctrine and political broadcasting rules thus temper the power of broadcasters by requiring them to exercise their power responsibly. The rules prevent a single-minded pursuit of profit that could lead broadcasters to ignore important and controversial issues or viewpoints by providing airtime only to wealthy candidates or to the highest bidders for advertising time. These responsibilities, which critics of the fairness rules claim to be so onerous, are no greater than those required by journalistic ethics and sound journalistic practice. For instance, Group W, owner of several broadcast stations, made this point succinctly in comments to the FCC: "The Fairness Doctrine . . . has never caused Group W to treat issues in any manner other than it would have done based on reasons of good journalistic practice." Similarly, the Code of Ethics, Standards and Practices of the National Broadcast Editorial Association provides that "it is the duty and the obligation of every radio and television station to present editorials on issues of public significance in order to serve the needs and interests of the community." One can only wonder why broadcasters are so intent on repealing standards that simply require ethical conduct.

The rules, however, do more than restate accepted journalistic ethics. They also insulate broadcast journalists from external pressures and allow them to act as their conscience dictates. When pressured by established powers or advertisers in a community to suppress coverage of a controversial political issue or to support their particular points of view, a broadcaster can simply point to the obligations imposed by the Fairness Doctrine.

The fairness rules provide for broadcaster responsibility by setting broad standards of conduct that leave broadcasters with great editorial freedom in day-to-day coverage of the news. As a matter of policy, the FCC has shown great deference to the good faith judgments of broadcasters in meeting their obligations under the Fairness Doctrine. The latitude allowed broadcasters is so great that the FCC will question a broadcaster only when the "station's position is so 'off the wall' that no reasonable person could accept it." For example, in 1980, the FCC requested only twenty-eight broadcasters to respond to Fairness Doctrine and political broadcasting complaints, even though the Commission received an estimated 20,000 complaints in all. A grand total of six cases were decided against the station involved. In cases such as these, where coverage is found inadequate, the remedy, however, is not "censorship." Rather, the broadcaster is simply advised to meet its fairness obligations through additional programming.

The Commission's deference to broadcasters in this area is no accident. The courts have carefully protected the rights of broadcasters, and have scrutinized the FCC's decisions more closely than those of other regulatory agencies. In addition, the courts have held that the FCC's deferential policies are required in light of the first amendment interests of broadcasters. Fears that FCC regulation could escalate to "censorship" are, therefore, clearly unfounded.

Given the Commission's deferential policies and the actual reality of enforcement, broadcasters' claims that the fairness rules "chill" or otherwise intrude upon editorial discretion do not ring true. Indeed, broadcasters have produced no evidence of a chilling effect. In 1974, after two years of study consuming thousands of staff hours, the FCC concluded that there was "no credible evidence of a chilling effect." Again, in 1984, the National Asso-

ciation of Broadcasters, presumably after an exhaustive search, could produce only a few instances of a supposed chilling effect. Furthermore, the "chill" argument ignores the first part of the Fairness Doctrine, which requires broadcasters to devote a reasonable amount of time to important issues. By saying they are "chilled," broadcasters, in effect, admit noncompliance with this part of the doctrine. It is also strange that critics of the fairness rules believe that a pattern of violations of one part of the rules is a good argument for repeal of all of the fairness rules. In any event, it is more probable that if any chilling effect is present, it results from economic incentives and not from the minimal standards of fairness imposed by the Fairness Doctrine. The simple fact is that coverage of controversial issues is not as profitable as airing "sitcoms" or blooper shows, and advertisers are reluctant to support controversial programming. If anything, the Fairness Doctrine and political broadcasting rules provide an antidote to this chilling effect.

The fairness rules thus provide our society with a sensible accommodation of conflicting rights and values. The rules vindicate the public interest in information on issues and candidates, and in a fair presentation of this information, by setting broad standards of acceptable conduct. Within these guidelines, editors have broad discretion in selecting material without fear of government reprisal or censorship. If a broadcaster is unsure of his responsibilities, he or she can simply provide for more air time on a particular issue.

The alternatives to these rules are far worse. Our democracy and Constitution are founded on the belief that those with great power must be held accountable for their actions. This attitude pervades our society, and broadcasters would be naive to think that it does not extend to them as well. The fairness rules are a minimally intrusive means of enforcing some level of broadcaster accountability. Repeal of these rules, on the other hand, would feed popular perceptions of the unchecked power of the press. Repeal would also run counter to the high value the public places on fairness. Indeed, a recent survey of public opinion indicated that by a wide margin, people believe that freedom of expression means that all views on important issues should be available, not freedom of the institutional press from regulation. The fairness rules ensure that these public expectations are met. Without the rules, broadcasters increasingly would be vulnerable to public suspicion of a hidden agenda or some secret bias.

Such public sentiment in support of fairness cannot be ignored. Distrust and suspicion of broadcasting will manifest itself one way or another, most likely in ways far more harmful to the media than the fairness rules. As Fred Friendly, former president of CBS, observed in the context of the Westmoreland libel case:

> It is a basic law of physics and journalism that to create a pressure-cooker climate without the safety valve is to ensure a destructive force inexorably destined to explode. Freedom of the press is a protection, a safety valve, for all citizens, not just those lucky enough or rich enough to control the levers of communication power.

Juries already return most libel verdicts against the media, often for millions of dollars. The burdens imposed by the Fairness Doctrine are minuscule compared to the staggering costs of defending libel suits. Worse still, growing public dissatisfaction may eventually lead to imposition of far more burdensome governmental regulations, such as mandatory access requirements.

## III. THE FIRST AMENDMENT AND THE FAIRNESS RULES

The Fairness Doctrine and political broadcasting rules embody a delicate balance of three competing first amendment values: the public's interest in the free flow of information, the interests of speakers other than media owners in presenting their views to the public, and the editorial freedom of broadcasters. Critics of the rules nonetheless argue that the rules violate the first amendment. These critics view the first amendment narrowly, focusing solely on the supposed right of the broadcaster to be free from governmental interference. In doing so, they not only ignore other first amendment values, but also ignore the threat to these values posed by concentration of media control in the hands of the few. This is a real threat in the context of broadcasting. Government intervention under the circumstances is not only permissible, but truly essential to meaningful freedom of expression. The Supreme Court recognized this need in no uncertain terms in *Associated Press v. United States*:

> It would be strange indeed, however, if the grave concern for freedom of the press which prompted adoption of the First Amendment should be read as a command that the government was without power to protect that freedom. . . . That Amendment rests on the assumption that the widest possible dissemination of information from diverse and antagonistic sources is essential to the welfare of the public, that a free press is a condition of a free

society. Surely a command that the government itself shall not impede the free flow of ideas does not afford non-governmental combinations a refuge if they impose restraints upon that constitutionally guaranteed freedom. Freedom to publish means freedom for all and not for some.

The fairness rules protect, first and foremost, the public's right of access to diverse viewpoints. *Red Lion* provided one of the Court's strongest pronouncements of the public's right to "receive suitable access to social, political, esthetic, moral and other ideas and experiences." It was, however, by no means the first. As early as 1923, the Supreme Court recognized that access to knowledge must be protected. Since then, the Court has vindicated the right of access to diverse ideas in a variety of contexts. The value of this access cannot be doubted. Exposure to different and even disturbing viewpoints helps us to better refine our own views and understand those around us. As Justice Brennan said of students, "access [to ideas] prepares [them] for active and effective participation in the pluralistic, often contentious society in which they will soon be adult members." The process of self-government also requires that citizens be fully informed of competing viewpoints.

The fairness rules also serve first amendment values in a way that is often overlooked. The rules have created substantial opportunities for expression by those "who wish to exercise their freedom of speech even though they are not members of the press." The political broadcasting rules accomplish this goal directly by providing candidates with an enforceable right of reasonable access to the airwaves, as well as a right to equal opportunities. Additionally, the Fairness Doctrine indirectly creates similar opportunities for expression by nonmedia speakers. While the doctrine does not require that a broadcaster provide airtime to individuals or groups in order to meet its fairness obligations in any particular case, the Commission has recognized that broadcasters should, as one means of complying with fairness obligations, allow speakers to present their own views directly to the public.

Aside from these general statements of policy, the Fairness Doctrine . . . created significant opportunities by providing individuals and community groups with leverage in their informal requests to broadcasters for coverage of opposing views on critical issues. Through such discussions, groups and individuals have obtained free and paid advertising time, as well as opportunities to appear on news programs and talk shows. Without the Fairness Doctrine, it is doubtful that many broadcasters would even discuss reasonable requests from individuals or groups seeking to present their views. In recent congressional hearings, several groups testified that, if not for the Fairness Doctrine, they would not have been granted access to broadcasting facilities. The Fairness Doctrine has thus served well to ensure that a broadcaster presents "those views and voices which are representative of his community and which would otherwise, by necessity, be barred from the airwaves."

The free speech of individuals outside the press is also central to the right of freedom of expression under the first amendment. As Justice Brennan observed in *CBS v. Democratic National Committee*:

> [T]he First Amendment must therefore safeguard not only the right of the public to *hear* debate, but also the right of individuals to *participate* in that debate and to attempt to persuade others to their points of view. And, in a time of apparently growing anonymity of the individual in our society, it is imperative that we take special care to preserve the vital First Amendment interest in assuring 'self-fulfillment' [of expression] for each individual. For our citizens may now find greater than ever the need to express their own views directly to the public, rather than through a governmentally appointed surrogate, if they are to feel that they can achieve at least some measure of control over their own destinies.

Fostering individual speech by guaranteeing access to broadcast media not only lends dignity and provides fulfillment to the individual, but also serves society by adding new, and potentially important, views to social discourse. Society derives an even more clear and direct benefit from affording opportunities to political candidates. As the Supreme Court stated in *CBS v. FCC*, "it is of particular importance that candidates have the . . . opportunity to make their views known so that the electorate may intelligently evaluate the candidates' personal qualities and their positions on vital public issues before choosing among them on election day."

The first amendment rights of the public and speakers outside the media justify the responsibilities of broadcasters as trustees for the public. Critics of the rules nonetheless argue that the broadcast industry is the same as the print industry, and hence, the government must, under the first amendment, treat both industries the same. Broadcast stations, they argue, often outnumber newspapers, which remain unregulated. These critics, however, have improperly identified the relevant market for comparison as simply newspapers, rather than the print media as a whole. In any given locality, an individual has access to hundreds, if not thousands, of newspapers, magazines, and newsletters, not to mention an unlimited number of books. By comparison, broadcast outlets remain relatively scarce. New technologies have not alleviated this scarcity. Even if new technologies do reduce the scarcity of electronic outlets, the crucial importance of broadcasting in our national dialogue places the fairness rules beyond constitutional challenge. . . .

## IV. CONCLUSION

The passage of time has not made the wisdom of the *Red Lion* decision obsolete. Regulation is still needed to ensure that the public has access to competing views on important issues. The electronic media will continue to be dominated by a few voices for the foreseeable future. The rise of political action committees presents a new and serious threat to balanced discussion. Creative use of the fairness rules by individuals and groups outside the media to gain access to broadcast facilities further strengthens the case for the rules.

The fairness rules remain our least intrusive means of guaranteeing accountability, responsibility, and diversity in our most important medium of mass communications. The Fairness Doctrine and political broadcasting rules are thus important symbols not only of our society's commitment to full and fair debate, but also of our commitment to freedom of expression for all individuals and groups. In a perfect world, a marketplace free of governmental involvement might provide opportunities for all to speak, and allow all important viewpoints to be heard. If new technologies or changed circumstances at some point bring this possibility closer to reality, governmental intervention in general and the fairness rules in particular may become anachronisms. For the present, and for the foreseeable future, however, these rules cannot be abandoned without leaving the "marketplace of ideas" in the hands of the few and the powerful.

---

Lee C. Bollinger, Jr., *Freedom of the Press and Public Access: Toward a Theory of Partial Regulation of the Mass Media*, 75 MICHIGAN LAW REVIEW 1 (1976)*

During the past half century there have existed in

---

* Reprinted with permission.

this country two opposing constitutional traditions regarding the press. On the one hand, the Supreme Court has accorded the print media virtually complete constitutional protection from attempts by government to impose affirmative controls such as access regulation. On the other hand, the Court has held affirmative regulation of the broadcast media to be constitutionally permissible, and has even suggested that it may be constitutionally compelled. In interpreting the first amendment, the Court in one context has insisted on the historical right of the editor to be free from government scrutiny, but in the other it has minimized the news director's freedom to engage in "unlimited private censorship" and has exalted the "right of the public to receive suitable access to social, political, aesthetic, moral and other ideas and experiences." The opinions in each area stand apart, carefully preserved through a distinctive core of precedent, analysis and idiom.

The purpose of this article is to examine critically these decisions and to explore whether there is any rational basis for limiting to one sector of the media the legislature's power to impose access regulation. The article takes the position that the Court has pursued the right path for the wrong reasons. There is a powerful rationality underlying the current decision to restrict regulatory authority to broadcasting, but it is not, as is commonly supposed, that broadcasting is somehow different in principle from the print media and that it therefore is not deserving of equivalent first amendment treatment. . . .

There has recently been a dramatic outpouring of articles addressing the issues associated with access regulation in the press. This literature demonstrates the dual constitutional nature of regulation: It can be at once a valuable, indeed essential, means of redressing the serious inequality in speech opportunities that exists today within the mass media *and* a dangerous deviation from our historical commitment to a free and unfettered press. The problem, therefore, is formulating a constitutional approach that captures the benefits of access regulation yet still minimizes its potential excesses. These first amendment goals, it will be argued, can be achieved by permitting legislative access regulation but sharply restricting it to only one segment of the mass media, leaving the choice of the area of regulation to Congress. Without adequately explaining or perhaps even comprehending its decisions, the Supreme Court has actually reached the constitutionally correct result in refusing to permit government regulation of the print media, but has done this only because Congress had already chosen to regulate the broadcast media.

## I. THE FIRST AMENDMENT AS PORTMANTEAU

In 1974, when the Court considered the constitutionality of access regulation in the print media, it was able to turn to a longstanding constitutional tradition. Our society has generally been committed to the notion that, with a few narrow exceptions, the government should stay out of the business of overseeing editorial discretion in the press. Our historical experience has given rise to a hearty skepticism of the ability of officials to decide, for example, what is "fair" political debate. This skepticism recognizes the corruptibility of government and its seemingly innate desire to magnify whatever power over the press it might possess at a given time. The longstanding conception of the press as a "fourth branch" of government has seemed antithetical to the idea that the state should have power to affect its content. Even the most ardent advocates of access legislation have never sought to claim historical respectability for their proposals; theirs is the argument of changed circumstances.

At issue in *Miami Herald Publishing Co. v. Tornillo* was a Florida statute requiring a newspaper in the state to publish without cost the reply of any candidate criticized in its columns. In a relatively brief and conclusory opinion, the Court surveyed prior print media cases and found implicit in them the proposition that "any . . . compulsion [by the government on newspapers] to publish that which 'reason' tells them should not be published is unconstitutional." Access regulation violates that principle because it intrudes "into the function of editors" and because, as the Court assumed, although there was no evidence on the point, it also creates an impermissible risk of a chilling effect on news content.

What seems so remarkable about the unanimous *Miami Herald* opinion is the complete absence of any reference to the Court's unanimous decision five years earlier in *Red Lion Broadcasting Co. v. FCC*. In that case, the Court upheld two component regulations of the Federal Communications Commission's "fairness doctrine," one of which, the so-called personal attack rule, is almost identical in substance to the Florida statute declared unconstitutional in *Miami Herald*. That omission, however, is no more surprising than the absence of any discussion in *Red Lion* of the cases in which the Court expressed great concern about the risks attending government regulation of the print media.

Instead of scrutinizing government regulation of broadcasting in light of the print media cases and our traditional reservations about government oversight of the press, the Court in *Red Lion* regarded broadcasting as a "unique medium" that needed a distinctive first amendment analysis. Specifically, the Court plunged ahead to assert for the first time the incompatibility of a concentrated medium, which is how it characterized broadcasting, with the first amendment goals expressed in the Holmesian metaphor of the "market-place of ideas." The market-place theme as developed in *Red Lion* states that when, as now, the channels of communication are effectively controlled by a few interests, there is the risk that many important voices will be excluded and that, as a consequence, the public will be seriously hampered in its efforts to conduct its affairs wisely. Unless the government intervenes to insure the widespread availability of opportunities for expression within the mass media, the objectives of the first amendment may be frustrated.

. . .

. . . The Court in *Red Lion* introduced a new principle into our first amendment jurisprudence. Essentially, that principle provides that when only a few interests control a major avenue of communication, those able to speak can be forced by the government to share. The initial logic supporting the principle is clear: If it is accepted that a principal objective of the first amendment is to assure the widespread dissemination of various points of view, then any serious constriction of the available methods of communication would seem to justify some remedial action. Applying this logic to broadcasting, the Court found that concentration there justified action *and* that access regulation is an appropriate legislative response.

Equally important, on the other hand, is what the Court has failed to say in its decision on the access regulation. It is clear that the Court has not made explicit just what is so "unique" about the broadcast media that justifies legislative action impermissible in the newspaper context. It is doubtful that the so-called scarcity rationale articulated in . . . *Red Lion* provides an explanation. Certainly the scarcity rationale explains why Congress was justified in devising an allocation scheme to prevent the overcrowding of broadcasting frequencies. It may also serve to explain in part why the television industry is so concentrated. The scarcity rationale does not, however, explain why what appears to be a similar phenomenon of natural monopolization within the newspaper industry does not constitute an equally appropriate occasion for access regulation. A difference in the cause of concentration—the exhaustion of a physical element necessary for communication in broadcasting as contrasted with the economic constraints on

the number of possible competitors in the print media—would seem far less relevant from a first amendment standpoint than the fact of concentration itself.

. . .

. . . Even if we assume greater ease in entering the print media, however, the question remains why the purported openness of the newspaper market should not be considered an important factor in assessing the significance of concentration in the broadcast media. Why, this analysis asks, did the Court in *Red Lion* treat the broadcast media as separate and discrete? Why did the Court, in an exercise similar to defining the "relevant market" in an antitrust case, narrow its focus to a particular segment of the mass media? Why did the Court not say that, so long as people can gain access somewhere within the mass media, there is no need for legislative action in any concentrated branch? The treatment of the broadcast media as discrete constitutes at least implicit acknowledgement that the newspaper and other major print media are also highly restricted. If anyone could set up a major newspaper, would we really care if entry into the broadcast media was physically precluded? Or is the explanation somehow hinged to the nature of the regulatory scheme itself?

The fact is that the Court has never sought to answer the difficult questions relating to the scope of the new constitutional principle. The Court in *Miami Herald* acknowledged the argument that the increased concentration within the newspaper industry constituted changed circumstances justifying affirmative governmental action but offered little in the way of satisfactory explanation. Instead of exploring the relevance for the print media of the new principle developed in broadcasting, the Court merely reiterated the opposing, more traditional, principle that the government cannot tell editors what to publish. It thus created a paradox, leaving the new principle unscathed while preserving tradition.

There thus now exists an unresolved tension between the constitutional themes that have been drawn in the electronic and print media. As will be shown below, however, this does not mean that the tension cannot be resolved.

## II. TOWARD A FIRST AMENDMENT THEORY

. . .

### A. Comparison of the Electronic and Print Media

The customary approach to the disparate treatment of the electronic and print media has been to line them up side by side and see whether there are any differences between them that justify the result. It is implicitly assumed that if broadcasting cannot be distinguished from the print media, it must be treated similarly; if it is different, then it can be regulated to the extent that the differences allow. The scarcity analysis, which focuses exclusively on broadcasting without making express comparisons and which argues that this branch of the communications media possesses a "unique" characteristic of concentration, is one such attempt to isolate a difference that would permit separate treatment. Although that differences apparently should fail the test of materiality, there may be more appropriate distinctions, such as a possible qualitative difference of degree in levels of concentration and a reputed special impact of television on its viewers.

Irrespective of the cause of concentration within each branch of the media, television is in some respects more concentrated than any segment of the print media. There are fewer television stations, for example, than daily newspapers, but even more significantly, fewer interests control the content of television broadcasting than is true within the newspaper industry. In television an oligopoly of three networks commands the attention of a vast percentage of the television audience, while in newspapers the concentration is more dispersed, with monopolization on a local, regional, or more limited, national level.

This might not be regarded as very significant if few people watched television, but, of course, the situation is quite the reverse. In many important respects, television is today the most pervasive medium of communication in our society. Not only does virtually everyone have access to a television set, but more people watch it, even for purposes of obtaining news, and for longer periods, than read the publications of the print media. In addition, television is frequently considered to have a "special impact" on its audience. Thus, many courts and commentators believe television is today the dominant means of influencing public opinion, not only because more people watch it than read newspapers, but also because it possesses some undefined and unquantifiable, but nevertheless unique, capacity to shape the opinions of the viewers in ways unrelated to the merits of the arguments presented. The television medium, it is also said, offers the opportunity to thrust information and ideas onto the audience. Unlike printed publications, which can be avoided by "averting the eyes," television provides the opportunity to force extraneous messages onto audiences gathered for other purposes. This medium, in short, may be the preeminent forum for the discussion of ideas and viewpoints in the society and it may offer opportunities to persuade that cannot be matched elsewhere within the system of expression. The greater concentration of power in television, there-

fore, may arguably represent more serious social and first amendment problems than the situation in the print media.

This line of argument, promising though it may seem, contains several serious problems. First, the analysis fails to explain why the current level of concentration in newspapers, even assuming that it is not as high as that in television, is not sufficiently troublesome by itself to justify governmental intervention. The monopoly status of so many of our community newspapers does not present a happy prospect for the first amendment. Beyond some point, the level of concentration seems to become irrelevant to constitutional doctrine. The question to be asked, therefore, is not whether broadcasting is more concentrated than the print media, but whether both have passed beyond the point of safety for first amendment purposes.

It seems reasonable to believe that, if concentration in broadcasting has passed an acceptable level, concentration in newspapers has also reached a similar level. Are the abuses of journalistic power and one-sidedness more likely in the electronic than in the print media? Is the access for new ideas more problematical in the broadcast than in the print media? Certainly there is no empirical evidence supporting affirmative answers to these questions, and their validity as intuitive propositions is subject to doubt. Television is characterized more by its placidity than by its politicization. Moreover, newspapers are a primary source of news for television, and the print media may instead prove to be the first line of defense against new ideas. Further, it is significant that in television there are three independently owned national networks vying for viewers, a potentially important systemic check against distortion that is lacking in communities with only a single newspaper. Finally, the major networks do control the content of prime-time television, but the major wire services, such as Associated Press and United Press International, similarly control much of the national news reported in newspaper throughout the country, although perhaps to a somewhat lesser degree.

Even more problematical, however, is the alleged special impact of television. Quite apart from any natural suspicions concerning the validity of the claim, given the frequency with which it seems to confront each new medium of communications, the impact thesis is a dangerously amorphous justification for regulation. It provides no clear limits to official authority and invites censorship as well as affirmative regulation. Further, in so far as the thesis rests upon the premise that regulation is more acceptable the greater the audience and the impact, it seems inconsistent with the underlying purpose of the first amendment, which presumably is to protect effective as well as ineffective speech. A comparison of the gross audience figures is, in any event, a clumsy basis on which to gauge the differing effects of various media on the formation of public opinion or policy. Use of such data alone completely ignores the insights of political scientists into the complexity of cognition and decision-making. Finally, there is simply no evidence at the present time to support the proposition that television shapes attitudes and ideas in ways so unprecedented as to require urgent remedial regulation. Thus, until more evidence exists to support the theory, or perhaps until a much wider consensus is formed in its support, it seems wise to avoid relying on the special impact theory.

This discussion does not mean to suggest that the line of analysis focusing on the potential differences between television and newspapers and magazines is unworthy of further investigation. On the contrary, the issues raised are highly important and should continue to command attention. On the whole, however, the arguments presently contain too many doubtful underlying assumptions to support a conclusion that the media are fundamentally different. Differences indeed exist, but they are either too insignificant to justify momentous distinctions in treatment under the first amendment or too broad and vacuous to be persuasive. We must, therefore, conclude that they are the same.

It is at this point that conventional thinking about broadcast regulation largely stops. Once it is determined that the broadcast and print media are constitutionally indistinguishable, then it is concluded that the Court's theory of access regulation is without rational foundation and should be discarded at the earliest opportunity. Such a conclusion possesses a certain legalistic appeal, but it also may be an oversimplification. The very weakness of the scarcity rationale suggests that there is something more here than first meets the eye. The dual treatment of the press has been so long accepted, even by persons known for their sensitivity to first amendment values, that the scarcity rationale may in fact be a convenient legal fiction covering more subtle and important considerations.

It is helpful, therefore, to adopt a less formalistic approach to the problem and to probe beyond normal legal analysis to account for this remarkable constitutional development. For even if broadcasting and the printing press are essentially the same, they nevertheless have different origins, have existed for different periods of time, and one has been controlled from its beginning while the other has been left unrestricted. It is important, in short, that our analysis be sensitive to the historical process through which the present system has developed.

Such an approach reveals two closely interrelated factors that help reconcile the divergent traditions within the press. First, society has long considered broadcasting to be meaningfully different from the print media, and this perception has greatly influenced the decision to allow regulation only in the former. Understanding this perception and its effects is necessary for an appreciation of the complex way in which first amendment theory is implemented and developed. Second, broadcast regulation involves only a part of the press; this fact provides not only an explanation for past treatment by the courts but also offers the most rational basis for future constitutional adjudication in this area.

. . .

## C. The Rationality of Partial Regulation

Ultimately, the Court's decisions on the question of access regulation exhibit fundamental good sense. The good sense, however, derives not from the Court's treatment of broadcasting as being somehow special, but rather from its apparent desire to limit the over-all reach of access regulation. The Court need not, however, isolate the electronic media to achieve this result. Although it is uncertain whether the Court in *Miami Herald* saw it as such, the critical difference between what the Court was asked to do in *Red Lion* and what it was asked to do in *Miami Herald* involved choosing between a partial regulatory system and a universal one. Viewed from that perspective, the Court reached the correct result in both cases.

The central problem in this area results from the complexity of the access issue. The truth of the matter is, as the Court's opinions so plainly, if unintentionally, demonstrate, that there are good first amendment reasons for being both receptive to and wary of access regulation. This dual nature of access legislation suggests the need to limit carefully the intrusiveness of the regulation in order safely to enjoy its remedial benefits. Thus, a proper judicial response is one that will permit the legislature to provide the public with access *somewhere* within the mass media, but not throughout the press. The Court should not, and need not, be forced into an all-or-nothing position on this matter; there is nothing in the first amendment that forbids having the best of both worlds.

Access regulation both responds to constitutional traditions and cuts against them. On the one hand, it helps to make possible the realization of first amendment goals. Unlike attempts to censor types of speech, an access rule is designed to operate in the service of the first amendment. It seeks to neutralize the disparities that impede the proper functioning of the "market-place of ideas," to equalize opportunities within our society to command an audience and thereby to mobilize public opinion, and in that sense to help realize democratic ideals. . . .

Of all the efforts thus far to restructure private arrangements that impinge on the "market-place of ideas," access regulation represents the most directassault, and, consequently, the most dangerous. Although its aims conform to those of the first amendment, the methods of access regulation constitute a significant departure from our traditional constitutional notions concerning the need to maintain a distance between the government and the press, especially on matters directly touching news content. Access regulation carries the greatest potential for altering the press as we have known it and for exposing us to grave risks.

In general, access regulation may have three adverse consequences for the marketplace of ideas. The first is a commonly identified cost of access regulation: It may have a depressing effect on journalistic motivation to engage in discourse on social issues. This cost is presumably greater with some forms of access regulation than with others. The chilling effect associated with the right-of-reply rules is likely much greater than that associated with the requirement that editors publish all advertisements on a nondiscriminatory basis. Even where the chilling effect is thought to be a problem, however, no data exist as to the extent to which the regulation does, in fact, have an inhibiting effect. Nevertheless, in those cases where a significant chilling effect may predictably occur, there is cause for concern, given our general commitment to the idea that debate is more likely to be fruitful if it is "inhibited, robust, and wide-open." The prospect that some regulated editors will choose to forego coverage of some political discussion because of reply requirements need not necessitate rejection of access regulation; its benefits may still outweigh this cost. Such a cost, however, remains a matter of concern, and should be minimized as much as possible.

A second general concern associated with access regulation involves the risk that the administrative machinery required to implement it will be used to force the press into some official line and will undermine its role as a critic and antagonist of government. Although neither *Red Lion* nor *Miami Herald* discussed this risk, the possibility of official misbehavior has been a traditional reason for withholding approval of governmental schemes to "improve" the press. It is a consideration that reflects the sum of our experience and should not be lightly disregarded. Evidence that this risk is still vital may, regrettably, be found in an examination of our recent upheaval in presidential politics.

In the course of the revelations about Watergate, it became known that the executive branch, angered by unflattering remarks, criticism, and disclosures of government secrets, embarked on an extensive campaign to harass the press. A substantial part of the attack apparently involved using administrative machinery to apply pressure on journalists. There were also serious allegations that the executive branch had sought to apply pressure directly on the *Washington Post* by creating difficulties for the *Post's* subsidiary radio stations with the Federal Communications Commission. If there is a Watergate lesson for the first amendment, therefore, it is that we should continue to be extremely wary of making available official machinery for the regulation of the press. Such a regulatory structure would stand as a constant temptation to governmental officials—a source of leverage with which to compel obedience within the press and, in more subtle ways, to manipulate the content of the public debate.

The third potential adverse consequence of access regulation is that it may result in an escalation of regulation. . . . This criticism is one of those stock arguments that suffers badly from overuse. It is easy to dismiss the claim because it is advanced so often in circumstances where it carries no conviction. With respect to access regulation, however, the argument has powerful force and should not go unheeded.

The problem is not simply that regulation will induce irresistible pressure for censorship. The dangers are more subtle and complicated. Access regulation comes in a variety of shapes and sizes. Some forms, like a vigorously enforced fairness doctrine, may lead to utter blandness of content and in this way may permit official manipulation of the news. In addition, it is virtually impossible for the Court to articulate in advance unambiguous standards. Experience with a particular regulation will often be necessary to judge its desirability and constitutionality. It is important to know, for example, how frequently the government will be drawn into conflict with the editors, what financial burdens the administrative procedures will impose on those that are regulated, and whether the administering officials will be prone to misconduct or will exhibit a healthy respect for first amendment freedoms.

By sanctioning the concept of access regulation, the Court can expect administrative experimentation with the various types of regulation. And since clear guidelines cannot be established, there may be constant pressure to expand the regulatory power into impermissible areas. The clamor for greater regulation may itself be used as a weapon to bend the press into line. If what turns out to be improper regulation is imposed, irremediable harm may have already occurred before the Court acts. Similarly, the difficulties in assessing the future consequences of the regulation may lead the Court to sanction conduct that is ultimately very harmful. In both instances, it must be remembered that "[l]egal experiments, once started, cannot be stopped the moment they show signs of working badly."

Viewed in its entirety, therefore, access regulation is both desirable and dangerous. That it raises a constitutional problem of enormous difficulty is reflected in the schizophrenic nature of *Red Lion* and *Miami Herald*. In light of the double-edged character of access regulation, the Court's appropriate response is to affirm congressional authority to implement only a *partial* regulatory scheme. Only with this approach, with a major branch of the press remaining free of regulation, will the costs and risks of regulation be held at an acceptable level. Or, put another way, only under such a system can we afford to allow the degree of governmental regulation that is necessary to realize the objectives of public access.

One advantage of a partial regulatory system is that the unregulated sector provides an effective check against each of the costs of regulation. A partial scheme offers some assurance that information that might not be disseminated by the regulated sector of the press will nevertheless be published by the unregulated press. If, for example, a local broadcast station chooses not to cover a debate between two prominent mayoral candidates because of equal time obligations, then the public will still be informed of the event by the local newspaper. Second, a partial scheme offers some assurance that governmental use of the regulatory authority to bludgeon the press into an official line will not suppress the truth. If, for example, the *Washington Post* had curtailed its Watergate investigations to ward off what it might reasonably have perceived to be governmental pressure to have the licenses of its subsidiary radio stations revoked, other newspapers free of governmental entanglements, such as the *New York Times*, would still have continued the investigation. Finally, such a system gives some assurance that the pressures for and effects of harmful regulation will be cushioned. If, for example, a Vice-President were to urge much more vigorous access regulation in order to ward off criticism of the President, and as a result the regula-

tion sector were to tone down its criticism, the unregulated press would remain active.

Restricting regulation to only a part of the press, however, offers more than a check against these costs. It provides, again through the presence of the unregulated media, a beneficial tension within the system. The unregulated sector can operate to minimize the three costs of regulation. Consider, for example, the chilling effect problem. The publication of news in the unregulated press serves as a competitive prod to the regulated press to publish what it might otherwise omit. Thus, broadcasters may initially have been reluctant to cover Watergate events because of fears of official reprisals and access obligations, but a decision not to cover the story would have been impossible once the print media began exploiting it.

The most significant aspect of a partial regulatory scheme, however, is that it preserves a benchmark— and important link with our constitutional traditions as the Court permits experimentation with regulation. The continuing link with traditional first amendment theory conveys the message that old principles have not been abandoned, and it forces every departure to be more carefully scrutinized and justified. The message is one of adjustment rather than wholesale revision.

One of the more interesting features of our experience with broadcast regulation has been the absence of egregious abuses of power by the FCC. The Commission has, on the whole, been extraordinarily circumspect in the exercise of its powers. It is reasonable to assume that this self-restraint is explained in large part by the constant juxtaposition of the autonomous print media, representing our continued respect for the ideal of a free press, against the regulated broadcasting media. By preserving the unregulated print media, the benchmark against which the reform must continually be measured, even if not explicitly, the Court has furnished a built-in restraint against excesses in regulation.

. . .

The theory of partial regulation mandates, in effect, a system in which the burdens of regulation will be allocated unequally among the various institutions of the press. Those associated with the institutions that Congress chooses to regulate may claim that it is unfair for them to bear the burdens of regulation when their similarly situated counterparts do not. Their claim would be that the scheme of classification is "underinclusive." This claim of unequal treatment may be a factor to be considered in deciding whether to mandate a partial system, but it ought not be determinative for several reasons. First, courts and commentators generally give greater constitutional leeway to an underinclusive rather than an "overinclusive" approach to a general problem, since in underinclusive classifications "all who are included in the class are at least tainted by the mischief at which the law aims . . . while over-inclusive classifications reach out to the innocent bystander, the hapless victim of circumstances or association." Second, the trait that defines the class would not be the content of speech and it would not reflect an official animus against a particular group of people because it would be directed at institutions and not individuals. That is, the classifying trait would be the neutral factor of technology, and not a suspect factor such as race. This means that those individuals indirectly affected would be able to shift to the unregulated media and escape the burden imposed should they find it offensive, and that the opportunity for government to pursue solely political or discriminatory purposes under the guise of the first amendment is minimized.

In seeking to advance first amendment goals, the Court should not be precluded from deciding on a rational basis to limit congressional powers of regulation. There may be more than one claim to "equality" to be considered. Those persons excluded from public debate because of private ownership also have a claim to "equality" in the sense of obtaining an equal opportunity to speak. If a full restructuring of the press to accommodate those claims is too dangerous, then the Court must balance the interests of those excluded from the media against the interests of those members of the press whom Congress will ultimately select to bear the burden of regulation in a partial system. Phrased somewhat differently, it is the first amendment itself that justifies this differential treatment of mass communication technologies.

The analysis of *Red Lion* and *Miami Herald*, therefore, demonstrates the need to maintain a partial regulatory structure for its own sake, What the Court has never fully appreciated is that the very similarity of the two major branches of the mass media provides a rationale for treating them differently. By permitting different treatment of the two institutions, the Court can facilitate realization of the benefits of two distinct constitutional values, both of which ought to be fostered: access in a highly concentrated press and minimal governmental intervention. Neither side of the access controversy emerges victorious. The Court has imposed a compromise—a compromise, however, not based on notions of expediency, but rather on a reasoned, and principled, accommodation of competing first amendment values.
. . .

Mark S. Fowler and Daniel L. Brenner, *A Marketplace Approach to Broadcast Regulation*, 60 TEXAS LAW REVIEW 207 (1982)*

## I. INTRODUCTION

Regulation of radio and television by the Federal Communications Commission remains a frequent target for administrative law reformers. The vague licensing criterion provided by Congress—the standard of "public convenience, interest, or necessity"—has provided a starting point for critics dissatisfied with the last fifty-five years of regulatory performance in this area. In applying this criterion, the Commission has built a series of legal fictions into a regulatory environment altogether different from that faced by the media ventures that preceded radio and television, or those that are now being introduced. . . .

This Article proposes a new direction for governmental regulation of broadcasting in the United States. The ideas raised are not entirely new, but they have been ignored by those who have been busy raising and lowering the drawbridge of licensing. Our thesis is that the perception of broadcasters as community trustees should be replaced by a view of broadcasters as marketplace participants. Communications policy should be directed toward maximizing the services the public desires. Instead of defining public demand and specifying categories of programming to serve this demand, the Commission should rely on the broadcasters' ability to determine the wants of their audiences through the normal mechanisms of the marketplace. The public's interest, then, defines the public interest. And in light of the first amendment's heavy presumption against content control, the Commission should refrain from insinuating itself into program decisions made by licensees.

### A. Economics and Broadcasting

The proposition that consumers are best off when society's economic resources are allocated in a manner that enables people to satisfy their wants as fully as possible permeates all sectors of our economy. Depending on what goods or services are involved, consumer satisfaction is enhanced by freedom of choice in the price, quality, or variety of products. We increase social utility promoting competition, removing artificial barriers to entry, preventing any

* Published originally in 60 TEXAS LAW REVIEW 207 (1982) by the Texas Law Review Association. Reprinted by permission.

one firm from controlling price or eliminating its competitors, and in general establishing conditions that allow the price of goods to be as close as possible to their cost of production.

Although we have relied on free markets to provide most of the goods and services in our society for over 200 years, this has not been the case in the broadcast industry. For a variety of reasons, the Commission has traditionally refused to recognize the undeniable fact that commercial broadcasting is a business. But it is a business, one that faces increasing competition in the years ahead for the eyes and ears of its audience. The first step in a marketplace approach to broadcast regulation, then, is to focus on broadcasters not as fiduciaries of the public, as their regulators have historically perceived them, but as marketplace competitors.

### B. Spectrum Markets

A threshold difficulty in applying a marketplace approach to commercial broadcasting lies in the definition of the market. Broadcasters differ from some other information providers because they receive exclusive use of an assigned frequency; the frequencies reserved for broadcasters are not available for non-broadcasting uses regardless of demand. In a true marketplace, broadcasters would compete with all potential users of the airwaves for the exclusive right to use a particular frequency, just as they must compete with other businesses for land, labor, buildings, equipment, and other factors of production. The spectrum market would consist of those buying and selling rights to use frequencies on an exclusive, protected basis.

. . .

A marketplace approach to exclusive use of radio frequencies would open all positions in the electromagnetic spectrum to bidding by those who want them. As with the allocation of other goods in society, the highest bidder would acquire exclusive rights to a particular frequency. In the fully deregulated marketplace, the highest bidder would make the best and highest use of the resource. R. H. Coase set forth the contours of this approach to the electromagnetic spectrum, and broadcasting in particular, in 1959. Professor Coase observed that producers generally obtain more of a desired resource when buying it on the open market. If forced to bid for unused frequencies or to buy them from existing users, broadcasters would draw the frequencies away from other industries only if they paid more for them, and vice versa. The pricing mechanism would bring the costs of spectrum use in line with those of other factors of production used in broadcasting or any other business.

Commenting on Coase's argument, Professor Harry Kalven concluded that "the perspective is so radical by today's views that although I am persuaded of its correctness, I am not clear how it can be used in public discussion." More than fifty years of regulatory precedent, now compounded by the settled expectations of the public and the broadcasting industry, would make it difficult to conduct an auction of the entire electromagnetic spectrum. . . .

### II. THE TRUSTEESHIP MODEL

Instead of being exchanged as a property right, exclusivity to a radio frequency has been assigned by the Commission on the amorphous "public interest" standard. Broadcaster responsibility officially runs to the viewing public as defined by the Commission, not to shareholders, sponsors, or even the users of the sponsors' products or services who indirectly finance the stations. Two considerable evils have come from this arrangement: "broadcasters take advantage of the public-interest myth to promote a variety of protectionist policies, motivated in fact by economic self-interest . . . [and] . . . the public at large is misled in its perception of the role and function of broadcasting in America." In short, by abandoning a marketplace approach in the determination of spectrum utilization, the government created a tension, in both first amendment and economic terms, that haunts communications policy to this day. . . .

### D. The Flawed Rationales Supporting the Model

1. Defects of the Scarcity Rationale.—Spectrum scarcity always has been the cornerstone of the justification for abandoning the marketplace approach and reducing first amendment protection for broadcasters. The Supreme Court pointed to spectrum scarcity in its ratification of the trusteeship model in *NBC*, and the Court has cited scarcity in some of its other, although not in all, pronouncements supporting Commission content regulation. But the use of spectrum scarcity to justify "public interest" determinations over licensees is fraught with serious logical and empirical infirmities.

First, virtually all goods in society are scarce. In most sectors of the economy, the interplay of supply and demand regulates the distribution of goods. If a good becomes especially scarce, its price is bid up. Ideally the highest bidder will make the best use of the resource. The application of the trusteeship model to broadcasting is a substantial deviation from the ordinary allocation of scarce goods and services in society.

One might argue, however, that deviations from the market should occur with regard to communications media. For instance, in wartime the government might be justified in regulating the amount of newsprint any one paper received. The supply of newsprint could be reduced for newspapers intending to print only comics or other purely entertainment features. But no factors remotely comparable exist in broadcasting today. Yet the trusteeship model results in broadcast regulation that resembles this hypothetical.

Apart from this basic misunderstanding of scarcity, other factors should lead to a rejection of the belief that a condition of true scarcity prevails in broadcasting. Scarcity is a relative concept even when applied to the limited spectrum earmarked for broadcast use. Additional channels can be added, without increasing the portion reserved for broadcast, by decreasing the bandwidth of each channel. Technology is an independent variable that makes scarcity a relative concept. At some point, quality becomes so reduced or costs so great that new channels should not be added. But until that point is reached, saturation of the spectrum has not occurred. The continued evolution of spectrum efficiency techniques makes it difficult to say with certainty that saturation of channels will ever be permanent in any market. . . .

Finally, the scarcity notion also fails to recognize the substitutes for over-the-air distribution. In audio service, cassette and phono disc recordings vie with AM and FM channels and their subcarrier services like Muzak. Cable television, low-power television, multipoint distribution service, cassette and disc, and, in the future, direct broadcast satellites provide substitutes for over-the-air video service in many markets. A five-meter backyard satellite dish can, for those who can afford them, bring in more channels "off the air" than a television antenna picks up in a city with the greatest number of stations on the air.

Nonspectrum-utilizing distribution modes like cable and video cassette provide virtually limitless diversity of scheduling and content. Where new high-capacity cable systems are in place, no scarcity exists with respect to the television spectrum. What may inhibit the number of cable channels, is again, a scarcity of dollars to support advertiser-based or subscription channels. Similarly, choice in video cassette programming is completely determined by what the consumer is willing to spend for software. Thus, the scarcity rationale, as used to justify the regulation of broadcasting in a different manner than other media, misperceives what scarcity is in a free economy. Moreover, it ignores the practical realities that go a long way toward explaining the limited number of channels in some markets.

Even if one assumes that the absence of more television channel space in the largest markets justifies a licensing policy in those markets, this assumption establishes nothing about the form the regulations should take. The trusteeship model endorsed the giant leap from scarcity to the current panoply of federal regulation over all broadcasters, not just those in saturated markets. Logic, however, does not support the assumption that the trusteeship scheme is more likely to maximize consumer welfare, even in markets without available outlets, than would a system relying on the judgment of marketplace players.

### 2. Other Justifications

(a) The "prior grant" theory.—A more rational justification for continued government regulation is the bootstrap argument that rests on broadcasters' enjoyment of "the fruits of a prior government grant." The Supreme Court advanced this rationale in *Red Lion Broadcasting Co. v. FCC* after acknowledging "gaps in spectrum utilization." The Court stated that "the fact remains that existing broadcasters have often attained their present positions because of their initial government selection in competition with others before new technological advances opened new opportunities for further uses." Since the government has aided the market strength of incumbent licensees, it may under the "prior grant" rationale regulate some aspects of the conduct of those licensees in order to guarantee the best service to the public.

This reasoning leads equally well to a market approach as to the trusteeship model, because it does not follow from licensing that the government also must affirmatively regulate licensee conduct. Once the Commission concludes that the best service for the public lies with a market system, where licensees can air programs designed to attract the largest audiences for advertisers or the largest subscriber base, it can refrain from reviewing programming and other licensee decisions. Moreover, now that broadcasting outlets face more competition from new media delivery outlets, activistic "grandfathering" of early licensed stations with trusteeship duties makes even less sense.

(b) *FCC v. Pacifica Foundation: "impact" theories.*—The Supreme Court has identified other reasons for regulating broadcast content under the public interest standard, and they appear most strikingly in *FCC v. Pacifica Foundation.* The Court was confronted with a Commission policy statement prohibiting indecent broadcasting that allegedly applied to the airing of a comedy monologue by George Carlin on an FM nonprofit station in New York City. *Pacifica* upheld the Commission's determination that "indecent" broadcasts, as identified in congressional statutes and defined by the agency, could be punished. The Court minimized the relative first amendment claims of broadcasters as compared to the right of the audience, particularly children, to avoid exposure to offensive materials. The Court noted that "the broadcast media have established a uniquely pervasive presence in the lives of all Americans." Likening reception of offensive broadcast signals to an indecent phone call, the Court surmised that listeners and viewers cannot insulate themselves from offensive program content. Second, the Court concluded that regulation of broadcasting content was justified because broadcasting is "uniquely accessible to children, even those too young to read."

Neither argument, however, adequately distinguishes broadcasting from other mass media. Broadcasting may have a pervasive presence in the "lives of all Americans," but that says very little about the operation of a particular station, which is, after all, the unit of regulation under the licensing scheme. Under the Court's rationale, program producers have a "presence"—measured, for example, by having two or more network series on the air at the same time—far more "pervasive" than the operator of an individual station. Furthermore, it is unlikely that any viewer watches a single station's entire daily broadcast. The assertion of the pervasive influence of individual licensees is a gross exaggeration of the licensees' real impact.

Moreover, other media are also "pervasive." One can hardly argue that a one-newspaper town is not "pervaded," "uniquely," by the orientation of its paper. A blockbuster motion picture, unlike a typical television or radio broadcast, is repeated for weeks on end in a community. Its exhibition is also more likely to pervade the community's consciousness than a single television (or, as in *Pacifica*, a nonprofit FM afternoon) broadcast.

The fact that broadcasting is usually received in the home adds no support to the continued application of the trusteeship model to broadcasting. A large number of television programs probably offend some portion of the home audience. For example, evangelical programs may offend those whose faith is grounded in a different theological perspective, but the annoyance caused to some viewers by these programs hardly justifies government intervention to ascertain where the public interest lies in such matters. The viewer always retains ultimate control over what enters his home; he may choose to turn the channel.
. . .

Undoubtedly many children below the age of literacy watch television. This situation may justify regulation of indecent materials carried over the air. Indecent material can be withheld from distribution to children if it is in the form of print or film, and scheduling of adult programs for late-night viewing can and does give parents more control over what their children watch. But these narrow restrictions do not justify a broad-scale trusteeship approach with its power to grant and revoke licenses based on content, any more than a trusteeship approach should be sustained over bookstores because they might at some point carry indecent materials on their shelves.
. . .

## III. THE MARKETPLACE APPROACH IN BROADCASTING

The reasons articulated by the Commission and the courts for the trusteeship model are hardly convincing, let alone compelling, when poised in a constitutional balance against the rights of broadcasters. Scarcity analysis is theoretically misguided and, in many cases, factually erroneous. Other facets of broadcasting, such as intrusiveness, failure to segregate child and adult audiences, and "captiveness," do not call for government involvement. There is reason to believe that marketplace forces can, and indeed do, affect the success or failure of television programming, just as they affect the content of nonbroadcast media.

A scheme that empowers the Commission to judge content on these speculative rationales should be rejected, for the consequence has been and continues to be a level of first amendment protection for broadcasters that is not simply "different" but substantially weaker than the protection given other media. In the meantime it has led to the exclusion of new entrants who might have met unserved communications needs. A marketplace approach to broadcast regulation, on the other hand, emphasizes the role of new competitors, and new competition among existing firms, to ensure service in the public interest. . . .

### C. The First Amendment and the Marketplace Approach

1. The First Amendment Rights of Listeners and Viewers Under the Speech Clause.—The Supreme Court's recently repeated formulation of the hierarchy of values in broadcasting—that "the right of the viewers and listeners, not the right of the broadcasters . . . *is paramount*"—is central to a first amendment analysis of broadcast regulation. Under this hierarchy, initially set forth in *Red Lion*, the rights of listeners "to receive suitable access to social, politi-

cal, esthetic, moral and other ideas and experiences'' outweigh the first amendment claims of broadcasters when the two conflict. This ranking does not, however, create an individual right of access to broadcast time in any single listener or viewer.

Even before *Red Lion,* the Court had subordinated broadcaster claims of first amendment rights to the public's interest in access to ideas and information and to rules designed to enhance that interest. In *NBC,* where the issue was the independence of station owners from network control, the Court rejected the broadcasters' claim that the licensing criteria established in the chain broadcasting rules offended their freedom of speech.

The *Red Lion* decision addressed the first amendment question more directly. The Court endorsed a right of access to ideas and upheld the Commission's requirement that a radio or television station give an individual time to reply to personal attacks and political editorials. Five years later, in *Miami Herald Publishing Co. v. Tornillo,* the Supreme Court unanimously rejected a similar regulation when applied to a daily newspaper. But the Court in *Tornillo* did not attempt to harmonize the disparate holdings of the two cases.

In *CBS v. FCC,* the Court, relying on *Red Lion,* again concluded that the public interest in access to particular communications outweighed the impact on the editorial functions of the broadcaster. The Court faced a conflict between the broadcaster's first amendment claim and a Commission interpretation concerning presentation of the viewpoints of candidates for federal office under a congressionally created right of ''reasonable'' paid access. The Court noted that a statutory right of access did not preclude broadcasters from presenting any particular viewpoint or program and sustained the Commission's mandate of air time for the Carter-Mondale reelection committee under the reasonable access provisions.

A divided Supreme Court subordinated the broadcaster's constitutional rights in a different manner in *FCC v. Pacifica Foundation. Pacifica* has little to commend its constitutional analysis. The majority lacked support both for its claim that broadcasting ''has received the most limited first amendment protection,'' and also for maintaining that a sound basis for more regulation is the pervasive ''power'' of the electronic media. Yet like the other broadcasting cases, *Pacifica* indicated that the Commission can, indeed should, subordinate a broadcaster's claim to editorial freedom to the perceived needs of the general public for access to expression over the airwaves or (as in *Pacifica)* for protection against harm from such expression.

What do the Supreme Court's repeated holdings on the hierarchy of first amendment interests tell us about a marketplace approach to broadcasting? First, it should be noted that the language of the first amendment protects the right of speech, not the right of access to ideas or even the right to listen. The direct concern of the first amendment is with the active speaker, not the passive receiver. The listener's interest is certainly enhanced by the exercise of the right of free speech, especially where the first amendment is viewed as a tool for self-governance. But listener rights are not the same as the individual's right to speak, and no such rights exist in broadcasting. Thus, it remains unclear exactly what listener interests are protected under the first amendment, aside from the ''values'' spilling over from the exercise of free speech.

Even assuming the existence of a protected right of access to ideas under the first amendment, it is illogical to assume that broadcasting, and broadcasting alone, is the exclusive arena for the exercise of this right, as the language in *Red Lion* might suggest. ''Crucial'' access to ideas pertinent to self-governance or self-fulfillment can be provided by many sources other than the airwaves. Furthermore, broadcasters should not shoulder a broader responsibility for providing important information than other media. The argument that listener access to broadcasting is crucial may prove too much. For if listener rights are deemed ''paramount'' to broadcaster rights, so the rights of newspaper readers should be paramount to the rights of the publishers and editors and the rights of movie patrons superior to those of exhibitors, distributors, and producers. This is the logical result once one stops analyzing the issue in terms of the rights of individuals under the first amendment.

Finally, even assuming that the interest in access to ideas is more pronounced in radio and television than in other media, it does not follow that only governmental regulations can ensure this access. . . .

. . . The commercial broadcaster maximizes profits by providing the service it believes consumers most desire. In choosing a service that maximizes profit, the licensee serves listener interests because the choice of service is geared to attracting the most listeners. The market approach is superior to the alternatives because it does not put the government between the licensee and the listener it is wooing.

Thus, a Commission policy that equates the functions of the marketplace in commercial broadcasting with satisfaction of listener interests finds support in the Court's analysis of the first amendment rights of listeners. Once the Commission concludes that market forces, rather than its own judgments, are most likely to produce programming that best serves the people, the paramount claims set forth in *Red Lion* are satisfied. . . .

2. The First Amendment Rights of Broadcasters Under the Press Clause.—The marketplace approach emphasizes broadcaster discretion as a way to maximize listener welfare. An independent first amendment interest also protects broadcaster discretion from the dictates of the government. As Professor Kalven has sentiently observed:

> We have been beginning, so to speak, in the wrong corner. The question is not what does the need for licensing permit the Commission to do in the public interest; rather it is what does the mandate of the First Amendment inhibit the Commission from doing even though it is to license. . . .

3. Summary—The marketplace approach to broadcast regulation has two distinct advantages from a first amendment perspective. First, it does not conflict with *Red Lion*. In basing editorial and program judgments on their perceptions of popular demand, broadcasters enforce the paramount interests of listeners and viewers. Even if licensees occasionally misperceive the wants of their audiences, the present regulatory system, which is based upon the Commission's judgment of the community's needs, does not ensure a better result. Second, the marketplace approach accords protection to the distinct constitutional status of broadcasters under the press clause. This first amendment interest is, or should be, coextensive with the first amendment rights of the print media, regardless of whether the public is best served by its uninhibited exercise. A broadcaster's first amendment rights may differ from its listeners' rights to receive and hear suitable expression, but once the call is close, deference to broadcaster judgment is preferable to having a government agency mediate conflicts between broadcasters and their listeners.

## V. CONCLUSION

The Communications Act provides the Commission with discretion to translate consumer wants into the programming decisions of broadcasters by invoking marketplace principles. The need for a fresh approach to broadcasting, now spurred by competitive challenges from cable and other video providers, is long overdue. This new approach concludes that broadcasters best serve the public by responding to market forces rather than governmental directives. It restores the broadcasting business to the unregulated status of American en-

terprise generally. In doing so, it also recognizes that content regulation of commercial radio and television is fundamentally at odds with the first amendment status of broadcasting. . . .

---

Lucas A. Powe, Jr., *American Broadcasting and the First Amendment* (1987)*

. . .

Every real Texan knows that when you own something, you control it. This tenet is not only an elemental principle of property law; it seems also to be a principle of human nature. If the government owns the airwaves, there ought to be no argument that broadcasters are duty bound to comply with whatever conditions the government wishes to set for their temporary use of the electromagnetic spectrum. This proposition seems so obvious, so inherently right, that a lay reader will undoubtedly wonder why neither *NBC* nor *Red Lion* devoted a word to it. The answer is that the conclusion of absolute control does *not* always follow from the premise of ownership, and the Court knows this full well.

Others do not recognize the distinction, however, and one often finds language dealing with broadcasters stating that broadcasters are trustees of the public, with a fiduciary duty that must be met. These nice legal terms from the law of trusts suggest the high duty of care that a trustee must exercise in handling someone else's property. When used in the broadcasting context, though, the terms are typically thrown in merely to overwhelm any argument the broadcasters might raise about their own rights; the terms add nothing to the debate and can rise no higher than the initial statement that because the government owns the spectrum, it has the power to regulate all aspects of use.

The reason the Supreme Court has never even nodded toward this justification for regulation is that despite its superficial appeal, the justification rests first on a "bootstrap" argument and second on a legal conclusion that has been decisively rejected. The bootstrap is the ownership conclusion. The idea of "ownership" goes something like this: the government owns the radio frequencies because it has power to regulate their use, and the government has

---

* Reprinted with permission.

power to regulate their use because it owns them. A nifty circle, and it does not break.

Nevertheless, even if the bootstrap argument had validity (and for convenience I have been writing as though it does), it would not, as much of the discussion on public ownership assumes, end all debate there. The government, it so happens, owns lots of things. It owns food stamps, it owns jobs for government workers, it owns parks, and it owns the Post Office, to name just a few. Although the government has occasionally tried to condition welfare benefits (such as food stamps) or government employment on the recipient's promise to forego constitutional rights, the Supreme Court has decisively rejected such attempts.

The government behaves in an unconstitutional manner when it attempts to "purchase" constitutional rights with its handouts. It may ask for many things as quid pro quo, but one thing it is forbidden to request is a citizen's constitutional rights. Whether one turns to speakers in parks or to everyone using the Post Office, the situational is equally clear. Simple ownership of the parks or the Post Office by the government does not provide the slightest power to censor. The government may in fact adopt certain regulations, but these will be tested on the same basis as government regulation of private actors. If the Constitution is a bar, then the regulations fall. Innumerable cases over the past four decades have so held.

Public ownership cannot explain the difference between broadcasting and print, then. Government owns the real property of a park much more obviously than it owns the electromagnetic spectrum, and yet no scheme exists for controlling what is said in parks. The Supreme Court has therefore avoided any reliance on public ownership as justifying broadcast regulation. If the Court moved in that direction, it would face problems of censorship in hundreds of local communities as firmer control over who could use the parks was asserted. Thus the Court, in both *NBC* and *Red Lion*, told its readers that it is because broadcasting is scarce that the government may regulate it in ways that would be inconceivable—and unconstitutional—if applied to the print medium.

The argument of broadcast scarcity has had a talismanic immunity from judicial scrutiny. It is asserted, not explored. When it *is* explored outside the confines of a Supreme Court opinion, scarcity turns out to be rather elusive, in part because the Court is using economic language in a nonsensical way. Broadcast frequencies are indeed scarce; but so are all resources, whether they are trees, ink, or iron ore. The notion of a "nonscarce" resource is simply a contradiction in terms. Probably because of this initial definitional problem, the scarcity argument is hard to pin down. There are a number of different variants of "broadcasting is scarce [and implicitly, print is not]," each of which merits closer analysis.

Only arguments asserting a scarcity that apply to broadcasting but not to print can satisfy the Supreme Court's conclusion. There appear to be five possible types of scarcity argument fitting this formula. The first comes from Justice Frankfurter's *NBC* opinion. Remembering the chaos that occurred after Secretary Hoover abandoned all attempts to regulate stations, Justice Frankfurter noted: "The result was confusion and chaos. With everyone on the air, nobody could be heard." How clearly this situation contrasts with print, where you can write what you wish on your piece of paper, and I can do likewise on mine, and neither of us interferes with the other.

The problem with this form of the argument is that its analogy is wrong. It is true that if everyone broadcasts, no one can be heard. But it is also true that if everyone at a park speaks at the same time, no one can hear and, equally, that if you write your message on a piece of paper and I write mine over it, no one can read your message. In the last two examples, the real-world solutions are that most people listen rather than speak at the park and that our system of property rights prevents the person who does not own the paper from writing over the owner's message. It is not technological scarcity that is at work, but lack of a property mechanism to allocate the rights to broadcast. . . .

During 1984, 782 radio stations and 82 television stations changed hands, for a total price exceeding $2 billion. One must go back to 1975 to find a year in which fewer than two dozen television stations were sold, and to 1972 for a sale of fewer than three hundred radio stations. The government may give the license away initially, but thereafter a free marketplace reigns (subject to pro forma approval of any sale by the FCC). Nothing involving property rights (or scarce property rights, if one prefers) requires a Federal Communications Commission, any more than a property control mechanism with respect to trees and paper requires a Federal Paper Commission. Justice Frankfurter's problem was that he assumed that the normal—in terms of the press, that is, a writer and a reader—was the inevitable. This idea of scarcity is not particularly helpful, for the omission of a property control mechanism for trees and paper would make print just like broadcasting. In other words, the phrasing of the question assumes its answer.

A second form of the scarcity argument also traces its roots to *NBC*. "The plight into which radio fell prior to 1927 was attributable to certain basic facts about radio as a means of communication—its facilities are limited; . . . the radio spectrum simply is not large enough to accommodate everybody. There is a fixed natural limitation upon the number of stations that can operate without interfering with one another." Broadcasting frequencies are inherently limited, but print is not. More trees can be grown; more spectrum cannot be created.

This version of the argument is both right and wrong. It is true that more trees can be grown—but they can't be grown for use *today*. The resources available *now* for print are inherently limited; so are the resources available for broadcasting. Similarly, just as additional trees can be made available for later use, so too can additional frequencies become available. On a single day in 1984 the FCC allocated 684 new FM stations in the lower forty-eight states—two dozen more than the number of stations in the entire country as noted in the Chain Broadcasting Report. We can—and do—add more broadcast stations to service as the technology improves. This aspect of broadcasting development has been rather constant and will continue to be so. The idea of an inherent limitation on broadcasting, with none for print, might have been fine for 1943, but it is untenable today. Furthermore, the FCC has in the past consciously adopted policies that have limited the number of television stations and hindered the development of new technologies that would compete with over-the-air broadcasting. Additional options might have been good for viewers, but the Commission perceived them as harmful to broadcasters. Thus to some extent, the Commission itself can claim some credit for supplying the rationale that keeps its regulation in business.

All other scarcity arguments take *Red Lion* rather than *NBC* as their starting point. One of these uses excess demand as proof that broadcast frequencies are scarce. "Where there are substantially more individuals who want to broadcast than there are frequencies to allocate . . . if one hundred persons want broadcasting licenses but there are only ten frequencies to allocate, . . . only a few can be licensed." Implicitly Justice White was noticing that there is not an excess demand for paper. . . .

The excess demand vanishes as soon as the licenses to broadcast are in private hands. Broadcast licenses today are bought and sold with much greater frequency than are newspaper concerns, and anyone who wants one—and has the money—can buy one.

This market then functions like any other market, with supply and demand finding an equilibrium. Furthermore, as the explication of the next version of the scarcity argument will show, newspapers, because of their scarcity, sell at a greater premium than do broadcast properties.

The next argument, offered with frequency and—given the failure of the other scarcity arguments—ferocity is that whereas anyone can begin a newspaper, not everyone can begin a broadcast station. Like the initial Frankfurter version of the scarcity argument, this one also carries an implicit assumption that answers the very question being asked. Why is it that not everyone can start to broadcast? Simply put, the government will not allow it. In other words, the existing scheme of regulation prevents entry. Under these circumstances, to say that one cannot begin a broadcast station is simply to recite the relevant conclusions of the Communications Act; and to say that anyone can begin a newspaper is to note that there is no Federal Newspaper Entry Act. Thus, this loading of the question fails to advance the analysis. Nevertheless, even with the loaded question it is worth pursuing what would happen in the real world of late-twentieth-century America.

When the co-owned newspapers of Jackson and Hattiesburg, Mississippi, sell for $110 million ($852 per subscriber), one would expect to see new newspapers beginning all the time so that other entrepreneurs could reap similar financial rewards. Even if one could see a newspaper for just the typical $582 per subscriber (the Sunbelt rate is quire a bit higher), one would do quite nicely. But in fact, new newspapers rarely begin. Anyone can start one, but virtually no one does. Why? The answer is simple: the laws of economics. Only the largest of cities are able to support two newspapers. . . .

Believers in broadcast regulation must be believers in scarcity. That is how the Supreme Court has framed the debate and offered the justification. For the true believer, if the Supreme Court says broadcasting is scarce and print is not, well, it just must be so. Others might be deterred by the collapse of the various scarcity theories, but not those wishing to justify regulation: they simply call forth yet another theory of scarcity. If all the former arguments have proven unable to distinguish broadcasting from print on the basis of broadcast scarcity (rather than print scarcity), one final argument still remains: relative scarcity. There are, when compared to print, too few broadcast outlets.

Relative scarcity invites a look at the numbers of outlets. At the end of 1985 there were 1,200 television stations (of which 654 were VHF) and 9,871 radio stations. On the newspaper side there were about 1,750 dailies and 7,666 weeklies. The number of broadcast outlets expend yearly, whereas the number of daily newspapers had been declining for decades.

How should these figures be compared? If the comparison is between broadcast outlets and daily newspapers, the result is clear: newspapers are scarce; broadcasting outlets are not. If the comparison is broadcast outlets to dailies *and* weeklies, then it is a wash. If only dailies are compared against television, then broadcasting becomes somewhat scarcer. However, if VHF stations only are compared to dailies, the dailies come out ahead by quite a margin. . . .

Professor Daniel Polsby noted that only the Supreme Court has had anything good to say about scarcity in the last decade. In the legal literature that is true. Only those born during an era in which scarcity appeared real and permanent have been able consistently to avoid questioning the basis for their conclusions. Outside the legal literature, the belief in scarcity exists—or at least the assertion of scarcity exists—because those who wish to continue broadcast regulation believe that it must exist; otherwise, broadcasters could not be controlled by the government.

This clinging to scarcity does serve a useful purpose. Because the rationale is so untenable, its continued existence demonstrates that there is *something* about broadcasting that leads people to know it must be regulated. The "something" is the reason for continued regulation. We simply await its revelation.
. . .

. . . We should remember that in its infancy, and for almost two centuries thereafter, print was regulated with varying degrees of strictness in England. First monopolies were given, then they were closely supervised. Why? There was money to be made, and the printing press carried with it enormous potential. The rulers didn't know what to make of this new technology, and the easiest way to make sure it did not get out of hand was to keep it under royal scrutiny. After all, it was "unique" and might well upset the status quo.

So too, I think, with American broadcasting. It radiated fear. It was "pervasive," "unique," an "intruder" in our lives. It was—it is—powerful; indeed, it is almost impossible to read an article on broadcasting that does not make that point. To be sure, nice generalities ring out. We watch more; we read less; we're most violent; we're more passive;

events are telescoped to meet our lessened attention span; it changes us in ways we cannot know. But exactly what it does and how it exerts power remain mysteries, even though large numbers of people, many of them very knowledgeable, assure us of its power.

The *New York Times* and the *Washington Post* are powerful, too, but we don't regulate them because of that. Beyond the fact that the Constitution forbids their regulation, the reason we don't regulate is that we have grown used to them. They may be powerful, but we think we know the how and the why. With broadcasting—specifically television (I think we have outgrown the belief that radio is powerful)—we are not as sure what the medium is doing to us, and so we attempt to regulate it to prevent it from doing what we do not know it is doing. We may not know the consequences of introducing television into our homes, but there appears to be a regulatory consensus that we don't want those consequences to get out of hand. We fear broadcasting because we don't understand it as well as we do print. The fear may be irrational, but it is there nevertheless. It does not justify regulation, but it does explain it. It also explains why we can expect that as newer technologies become available to the public there will be an intense desire to keep them under control.
. . .

Cable, unlike even newer technologies, has had an eventful history. Many difficult constitutional issues have been discussed, although most remain unresolved. This lengthy overview of cable's history is an attempt to shed light on the choices being made. It also fully illustrates the reluctance of decision makers to ask constitutional questions. Instead, those questions are left to judges who will bend over backward to sustain whatever status quo government legislates. Cable nicely illustrates the observation of Lee Bollinger that "new technologies of communication are both new battle grounds for renewed fighting over old first amendment issues and focal points for reform efforts."

Some of the First Amendment issues posed by cable regulation after enactment of the Cable Communications Policy Act—such as attempted bans on offensive programming—are quite familiar. Others, such as franchising, *should* be familiar, but technology often dazzles us, making the problem seem all too novel and complex. Still others, such as whether an entity can be partly a full communicator and partly a common-carrier conduit, are genuinely novel. If we can remove technology's blinders, we may be able to avoid the slapped-together legislative compromise that leaves the First Amendment somewhere in the judges' chambers, to be taken out only after decades upon decades of regulation. Otherwise the history of broadcasting, and now of cable, will in all likelihood simply be replayed again and again with newer technologies.

Stanley Ingber, *The First Amendment in Modern Garb: Retaining System Legitimacy — A Review Essay of Lucas Powe's American Broadcasting and the First Amendment*, 56 GEORGE WASHINGTON LAW REVIEW 187 (1987)*

## I. INTRODUCTION: CHANGING TIMES

The bicentennial of the American Constitution is a fitting occasion to reflect upon the inevitable difficulties in interpreting a constitutive document now two hundred years old. How, for example, are we to transform the majestic generalities of the Bill of Rights, conceived as part of eighteenth-century liberal ideology, into concrete mechanisms for confronting the problems of the late twentieth? This challenge is compounded by constitutional claims that arise from fields which modern technology has transformed to an extent unimaginable to our forebears. Just as rapid technological change may disquiet the lives of individuals forced to adapt to it, so it may also unsettle those institutions responsible for interpreting our aging Constitution.

### A. Transforming Communication

Nowhere has technological development been more pronounced than in the field of communications. Yet the First Amendment's freedoms of speech and press emerged from a society where the major forms of public debate were hand-printed leaflets, hand-set newspapers, and speeches in town meetings and public parks. Today these mechanisms, which for most of our country's history provided the primary means of communication, are rapidly being replaced by telephone lines, cable television systems, satellite links, and microwave hookups. Are freedoms designed and initially understood in an eighteenth-century context equipped to resolve conflicts created by contemporary use of sophisticated methods of mass communication?

No one today seriously would argue that lecturing or distributing leaflets at streetcorners are as effective communicative devices as the modern mass media of newspapers and broadcasting. Consequently, many would-be communicators have lost interest in the comparatively inefficient effort of speaking directly to one person or even a handful of people. Access to the mass media, either print or electronic, is crucial to those wishing to disseminate their views widely. Understandably, speakers perceive their expressive rights in terms of access to these mechanisms of mass speech. Yet, monopolistic practices, economics of scale, and an unequal distribution of resources have made it difficult for new ventures to enter the business of mass of communications. Because these factors limit entry to the economically advantaged, voices, which might have been heard in the time of the town meeting and the pamphleteer, today may be effectively quelled.

In addition, our world has become significantly more complex since the formulation of the First Amendment. Technological advances in communication, transportation, and warfare have ended the insularity once provided by distance, forcing us to confront issues or consider factors we were once free to ignore. Moreover, an information explosion now presents us with choices and problems previously inconceivable. The importance of the mass media reflects this added complexity as the individual is increasingly compelled to rely on specialists to gather and analyze data. The media consequently possess great power to suggest and shape articulated thought.

The mass media, thus, are both a societal boon and threat. Media technology can give individuals a window on the world, supplying them with the knowledge and perspectives needed to face the exigencies of our time. That same technology, however, can supply government and private power groups with a potent tool of mass socialization. Therefore, application of the First Amendment's freedom of speech and press to today's mass media, although at times troubling, is essential. . . .

## III. THE UNTOLD STORY: RAMIFICATIONS OF DEREGULATION

The communications industry today is big business. Virtually every means of communicating ideas in today's mass society requires the use of the mass media and expenditure of funds. Total deregulation of broadcasting would require us to rely on the commercial market to select messages, or on the grace of station owners and managers. These media owners and managers, rather than the individual wishing to speak, would determine which persons, facts, and ideas reached the public. Lacking regulation, the mass media would possess awesome power to edit, censor, or prejudice.

Purportedly, the First Amendment is meant to promote free discussions of public policy. The injunction against government regulation is to further this goal, and not to permit private interests to manipulate public discussion or prevent it altogether. Consequently, when private concentrations of power can drastically limit effective communication, one can argue that the First Amendment value of a free exchange of ideas must permit societal protection from private power as well as government power. Otherwise, we are left with a system where, as Professor Stephen Carter observes, only "those willing and able to pay have the ability to spread their messages. Those who lack the money lack the access to do the same; their principal First Amendment right is to listen.". . .

A. The Impact of an Unregulated Market

  1. Limitations of the Real World

. . .

A free press theory founded on the supposition that enforced government noninterference sufficiently protects individual autonomy simply does not conform with present-day realities. In today's world we must confront the reality of the lopsided access to the media that wealth can buy. The concentration of media ownership in relatively few private hands compounds the problem. This concentration of control empowers media owners and managers to limit or prevent the dissemination of messages with which they disagree. To simply continue to protect autonomy by placing a zone of governmental noninterference around the individual or around certain institutions accomplishes little more than to produce public debate dominated, and thus constrained, by the same forces that dominate the social structure. These zones of governmental noninterference do not assure debate that is "uninhibited, robust, and wide-open.

If the essence of free expression is the opportunity of individuals to express themselves and to have their ideas judged principally by their merit, a communications system that increases the relative influence of organizations with large financial resources and shrinks the attention paid to truly individual voices must constitute a net loss of freedom. Once we recognize that private power concentrations, in the same way as government, may manipulate thought, we may well ask whether it matters who controls the manipulative process. The Constitution was written to preserve certain human values. If, however, autonomy is protected to such a degree that those with

significant power to manipulate thought are free from all restraints, then we may have produced a society that will inevitably defeat its own purposes because, ironically, individuals will be unable to exercise their autonomy. We will have, as intellectual historian Isaiah Berlin once wrote, fallen victim to the "suffocating straitjackets" of great liberating ideas. . . .

2. The Market's Value Bias

The initial beneficiaries of deregulation would be broadcast media owners and managers whose power would increase as the "chill" of government oversight thawed. The market, however, supplies its own constraints on both editorial freedom and media access. First, the market, by making the media especially responsive to the needs and desires of certain groups, privileges these select groups. Accordingly, those facts, ideas and perspectives most likely to gain media attention are those appealing to the self-interest of individuals possessing the capital to acquire or own a media outlet, of the mass audience whose patronage provides the economic and political basis for advertising, and of organizations whose commercial payments provide funds for the media. Because all these groups tend to embrace established values and traditional perspectives, media managers and editors are unlikely to disseminate those ideas most challenging to conventional wisdom and the established power structure. Media exposure, accordingly, is wrought with status quo constraints and biases. . . .

Because the broadcasting industry is essentially a business, a second market constraint on the media exists. To the extent that ownership of the communications media is seen as a property interest, media management emphasizes profit-making rather than informing the public. Programming and editorial decisions based on market considerations stress profitability or allocative efficiency rather than the informational needs of the electorate. For businessmen, focusing on production costs and projected revenues is totally justifiable. But there is little reason to assume that decisions based on these factors will also serve to supply citizens with the information and perspectives necessary to make free and intelligent choices about public policy.

Given these inevitable market factors, protection against governmental interference does not guarantee that an individual with something to say will have effective access to an audience. Private interests can thwart the free exchange of ideas allegedly protected by the First Amendment as easily as can government. In short, even if the First Amendment erected a wall between the government and the marketplace of ideas, the mere existence of a mass media controlled largely by interests committed to established values and traditional perspectives limits the forums available for challenging existing power structures.

## B. The Dilemma of Reform

An anomaly exists in our system of free expression. Although the rhetoric surrounding the First Amendment purports to protect all expression, our laws are, at best, essentially indifferent to creating opportunities for expression. Telling an unpopular speaker that he will incur no penalty for his expression is of little value if he has no effective means of disseminating his views. A right that cannot be meaningfully exercised is, after all, no right at all.
. . .

## IV. THE RELATIONSHIP BETWEEN FREE PRESS AND GOVERNMENTAL *LEGITIMACY*

. . .

## C. The Myth and Media Bifurcation

The dilemma of the First Amendment in the modern era is quite plain. System legitimacy requires the appearance of two, quite distinct conditions. First, all individuals must sense they possess the opportunity to meaningfully communicate their beliefs and perspectives and, thereby, possibly influence the populace. They must not feel they are the victims of systematic exclusion. Second, government must not seem to control this communicative process, for if it does, individual judgment may be distorted and the essence of government by consent threatened.

In practice, however, these two conditions conflict. In an age of privately owned channels of mass communication, the individual communicator quickly may appear irrelevant; money may become more important than presentation of divergent perspectives in determining media access, and media mastery may weigh more heavily than appeals to judgment in effective communication. Yet, if government determines that media regulation is required to open communicative channels, the administrative process developed to enforce media access may be abused and governmental manipulation ensue.

The constitutional challenge, therefore, must be to develop strategies that symbolically support and practically protect goals that, at first blush, appear wholly incompatible. Courts need a "philosophy of prudence." . . . Prudent judgments thus lack purity and orderliness. But they work precisely because they appear to acknowledge the value of all opinions in societal conflicts. No one receives a clear victory, but no one suffers crushing defeat. No one feels banned from or extraneous to the decisional process.

As a result, prudent judgments avoid social trauma and chaos, making harmonious progress more likely.
. . .

A fundamental contradiction, . . . exists between two valued traditions: that of liberalism, which focuses on individual autonomy, and that of community, which emphasizes institutions that shape character by inculcating a common conception of good and evil. In bifurcating our legal treatment of the media, we can fulfill part of both goals by dedicating the print media to one tradition and the electronic media to the other. Thus, for two separate sets of reasons, neither of which is based on logic, media bifurcation is explainable.

Neither set of reasons, however, justifies the choice of broadcasting, rather than the print media, as the situs for regulation. . . . Three factors merit discussion. First, the print media in the United States have a history and tradition of crusading against and being protected from governmental interference. Because electronic media have been subject to some governmental control from their inception, there is no tradition of freedom to overcome and there is thus less of an appearance of illegitimate governmental action. If the First Amendment's concern is to maintain the *appearance* of a government prohibited from illegitimate interference of the media, the regulation of broadcasting and not of print makes sense.

Second, unlike popular beliefs surrounding the electronic media, the print media have an unlimited number of frequencies, i.e., printing presses; accordingly, there is no threshold justification for government rationing. The argument that the prohibitive cost of starting a newspaper is analogous to the scarcity of broadcast frequencies in limiting access, therefore justifying state involvement, has not been successful in altering popular or judicial perceptions. Our existing capitalist system of value distribution therefore is preserved: Although the press may be an economically scarce resource, it remains generally available to the wealthy. Market-based scarcity is so endemic to a capitalist system that it remains often invisible—not piercing the public's consciousness. The well-to-do, however, are not equally assured access when dealing with a scientifically scarce resource, the electronic media, that is distributed by a nonmarket process. Because the science of broadcasting media appears to have practical imperatives, market reform—that is, regulation—is not as clearly inconsistent with capitalist principles as is market reform of the print media.

These first two suggested rationales for choosing broadcasting over the print media for regulation both address the *appearance* of governmental involvement. The third potential factor is of a somewhat different order. Certain types of individual behavior, including some kinds of speech, are capable of creating highly impassioned community responses. When considering such behavior, federal courts have been more comfortable with the decisions of federal agencies, such as the FCC, representing national communities, rather than those of state institutions representing secluded local communities. The judicial acceptance of federal regulation of broadcasting and rejection of state regulation of the printed press, therefore, may serve to protect national dominance in the creation of orthodoxy when challenged by locally dominant groups whose views do not conform to those of national elites.

## D. Constitutional Compromise in an Imperfect World

The values embodied in the guarantee of a free press are of great importance to society; yet, in the modern context of a media beset by both sophisticated technology and an unequal allocation of resources, we often find them in conflict. Any effort to satisfy them all, therefore, requires at least a partial abandonment of logic. Instead, one must follow a philosophy of prudence and seek legitimizing constitutional compromises. Although we may never totally fulfill our constitutional aspirations, we also are never required to totally forsake them. As long as the aspirations remain, we have reason to try harder.

This perspective will upset those legal theorists who insist that constitutional judgments must rest entirely on considerations of principle, demanding a purity of reason and logic. Such theorists demand that constitutional law be complete, consistent, and determinate. When the legal process fails to meet these expectations, as is true in the case of freedom of the press and regulation of the mass media, critics often blame the Court's analysis, rather than recognizing that, due to conflicting value goals, the law has limitations as to what it can accomplish.

Such critics, however, spin their ideas at a high level of abstraction. They insist on principles unaffected by the painful complexities and inconsistent goals of human institutions. At heart, these critics are idealists: Unfortunately, we cannot often understand life and language in idealistic terms. Human situations are sufficiently complex and involve so many variables that approaching them at high levels of abstraction often is of little assistance in resolving specific controversies. Realistic constitutional adjudication requires a more practical approach, one concerned with the processes of accommodation needed to more closely align theory and practice. Such adju-

dication must show tolerance for the inevitable gaps separating the ideal from the necessary.

## V. THE IMPACT OF ONGOING TECHNOLOGICAL CHANGE

. . .

### B. The Challenge for the Future: The Convergence of Two Media

If the electronic media merely supplemented the print media, we might take comfort in Professor Bollinger's argument that the divergent judicial traditions for the printed press and for broadcasting serve to ensure that one medium of expression remains totally free of regulation while the other is used as a regulatory laboratory in which government attempts to create rules that accommodate the interests of speaker access and listener edification. But telecommunications today often do, and clearly in the near future regularly will, supplant, rather than merely supplement, the press as the primary means of communication. Instead of the balanced system envisioned by Bollinger, the free press guarantee of the future is in danger of being tied to a tradition protecting a form of speech reduced in significance while a tradition of regulation will cover a form of speech that represents the primary means of communication.

Technological advances are quickly leading to a convergence of the once apparently distinct modes of communication. Given cable television, optical fibers and electronic publishing, it becomes increasingly more difficult to distinguish the print from the electronic media. If networked computers will be the printing presses of the future, and if they are not free of public control, then, as Professor Ithiel Pool fears, "the continued application of constitutional immunities to nonelectronic mechanical presses, lecture halls and man-carried sheets of paper may become no more than a quaint archaism, a sort of Hyde Park Corner where a few eccentrics can gather while the major policy debates take place elsewhere."

From a purely logical perspective, these fears are wholly justified. If cable can be regulated because it competes with over-the-air broadcasting, and if direct satellite broadcasting can be regulated because it uses the airwaves, it would be quite simple to argue for the regulation of newspapers transmitted by microwave or satellite. But again one must reach beyond logic and consider the importance of appearances and the legitimizing myths of individual autonomy and the value-neutral state. Almost surely a distinction will remain between the written word—whether on paper or an electronic screen—and the spoken word. To regulate fully the written word merely because it is telecommunicated is too obviously inconsistent with a tradition of a free press. The symbols of our secular bible—the Constitution—cannot be so flagrantly ignored. The concept of a *free press* must somehow be retained.

The future, however, will entail more than the telecommunication of the written word. The trend against the written word in whatever form is likely to continue; broadcast journalism—the spoken word—is likely to gain even further preeminence. How in such a world, overshadowed by the tradition of broadcast regulation, may the image of a free press survive? The answer, possibly, is to bifurcate the electronic media itself by separating television from radio. . . .

The market factors affecting radio are quite different, as is its industrial structure. Networking is of little importance, and the number of radio stations in each market compels the development of a diversity of formats as each broadcaster attempts to find his niche and program for a targeted audience. . . . Radio deregulation, therefore, may be the future's best hope for preserving the legitimizing image of a free press. Severance of a regulated television from an unregulated radio medium may salvage the First Amendment's third century.

## CONCLUSION

. . .

. . . In our complex society, affected by both sophisticated communications technology and unequal distributions of wealth, one must not blindly accept a communications system which merely converts economic power into political power through the purchase of and dominance over mass media access. Although mass communication channels may inevitably be biased to support entrenched power structures or ideologies, system legitimacy is preserved only if *both* channels of communication appear open to all *and* government appears to avoid systematic manipulation or indoctrination of the individual's perspective. . . .

. . . Ironically, to safeguard the myth and appearance of a free press, one must still consider the all-too-obvious limitations of reality.

The more appropriate response to the dilemma of the First Amendment and the mass media is to develop a system that recognizes the tensions between the conflicting values of the First Amendment and resolves those tensions in a pragmatic way that accommodates conflicts while ensuring furtherance of the values at risk. This Essay attempts such a response.

Note, *Access to Cable, Natural Monopoly, and the First Amendment*, 86 COLUMBIA LAW REVIEW 1663 (1986)*

## INTRODUCTION

The application of the first amendment to cable television has been guided by the Supreme Court's statement that "[e]ach medium of expression . . . must be assessed, for First Amendment purposes by standards suited to it." Despite this directive, however, the first amendment treatment of an emerging technology is always based, at least in part, on the treatment traditionally applied to old technologies. It is in this context that government at all levels has regulated cable television so that speakers other than the cable operators who build and run systems may have guaranteed access to cable facilities. . . .

## I. THE UNCERTAIN CONSTITUTIONAL TREATMENT OF ACCESS

Though the emergence of mass media has created opportunities for all to receive communications that were previously available to a limited audience, there has been no corresponding growth in the number of communicators with access to media facilities. Efforts have been made to remedy this situation, raising difficult constitutional questions. In 1986, after more than a decade of uncertainty, the Supreme Court severely restricted the ability of government to require access to communication facilities. Whether this decision controls in the area of cable television access can only be determined by further analysis of cable as a medium.

### A. The Judicial Struggle Over Access

In 1967 a new theory of the first amendment was proposed, adopting an affirmative view that required access to media for all who wish to speak, despite the generally prohibitive language of the first amendment—"Congress shall make no law . . . abridging freedom of speech, or of the press. . . . The precise definition of access, however, was unclear. Suggestions ranged from reply time for those personally attacked to unrestricted time for presentation of any material at no cost to the speaker. While personal attack rules were applied to broadcasting and, unsuccessfully, to newspapers, access regulations applied to cable have been more general, requiring channel time to be made available either for a fee or free of

* This article originally appeared at 86 COLUM. L. REV. 1663 (1986). Reprinted by permission.

charge. Access programmers, the beneficiaries of the access rules, may present whatever they wish, with no interference from the cable operator.

Historically, the Court's attitude toward access has depended upon the medium involved. In *Red Lion Broadcasting Co. v. FCC*, the Court upheld the Fairness Doctrine, which requires broadcasters to grant reply time to those personally attacked and to cover all sides of important public issues. In *Miami Herald Publishing Co. v. Tornillo*, however, the Court refused to uphold a virtually identical Florida statute that required newspapers to print replies to personal attacks, stating that such regulation cannot be allowed because the imposition on newspaper editors of "a compulsion to publish that which 'reason tells them should not be published' is unconstitutional." The Court's explanation for rejecting newspaper access in the face of its broadcast precedent was that there is a "physical scarcity" of broadcast spectrum and a need for licensing to prevent electronic interference among transmissions. Broadcasters do not own their frequencies—they are trustees for the public. On the other hand, while recognizing that most newspapers are monopolies within their towns, the Court refused to acknowledge economic scarcity as a basis for newspaper regulation in *Tornillo*.

The constitutionality of cable access regulations may depend on whether cable is regarded as an electronic newspaper, a wired broadcaster, or some third entity. Cable exhibits some of the characteristics of each medium. In fact, in two lower court cases which have applied the first amendment to cable access rules, the courts reached opposite conclusions in part because one preferred the newspaper analogy, and the other classified cable as a broadcaster. . . .

## II. BALANCING EDITORIAL DISCRETION AND THE INTEREST IN DIVERSITY

. . .

B. Applying the Balancing Test to Access

1. Defining the Protected Interest: The Editorial Discretion of a Cable Operator.—

. . .

While courts seem willing to protect the editorial discretion of cable operators either to produce their own material or to package programming for distribution over their systems, it has been suggested that not all functions of cable operators are editorial in nature. Instead, when the operator acts as a conduit for the transmissions of others, he is entitled to little, if any, protection under the first amendment, because he is not actually engaged in speech.

While it is true that a cable operator acting as a conduit would not be entitled to the same amount of protection as an editor, the conduit approach is misplaced with regard to cable because the cable operator is always an editor and never merely a conduit. The editorial function in cable is similar to the role of a retailer in selecting goods from a wide variety of sources. In this regard, cable operators perform three editorial functions for their subscribers: they search for the programs that will appeal to their subscribers and gather them together as a package; they evaluate and identify programming by deciding which programs to promote actively; and they organize the programming on their various channels to make selection by their subscribers easy. Conduits, such as a phone company or postal service, are interested only in carrying as many messages as possible, not in carrying the most desired messages since their profitability does not depend on the content of the carried messages.

The view that the function of a cable operator is completely editorial in nature is consistent with recent judicial treatment of cable. The protected interest of cable operators is the selection of programming for their subscribers from a "'rich variety' of options." In fact, the only programming transmitted over cable systems that is selected by editors is that which is mandated by regulation. It would be circular, however, to argue that regulations are justified because operators act as conduits rather than as editors when they present programming that is mandated by the regulations themselves. Even on these channels, operators would act as editors were they not forbidden to do so. . . .

Regarding the total cable package as the product of the editorial function is consistent with the multiple first amendment interests at stake. The most quoted line from the *Red Lion* decision states that "[i]t is the right of the viewers and listeners, not the right of the broadcasters, which is paramount." If this is so, then the editorial function is even more sacred, since the process of editing, like the process of retailing, is to provide the material that viewers are most likely to desire and to organize it in a meaningful fashion for them. Thus, by curtailing the editorial freedom of cable operators, the government is also depriving cable consumers of the right to receive editorial services. Examining the editorial function from the perspective of the cable consumer reinforces the view that the whole cable package is the protected interest.

2. Access Regulations as Incidental Burdens on Speech.—In order for access regulations to come under the *O'Brien* balancing test, they must involve

only incidental burdens upon protected speech. There is no set formula, however, for determining whether a regulation is merely an incidental burden. Typically in *O'Brien* analysis, the government regulates conduct which involves both speech and non-speech. Balancing of interests is proper only if the legislative intent is directed at the non-speech aspect.

The main purpose of access regulations is to enhance the ability of their beneficiaries to communicate, and they burden protected speech only because they cannot be implemented without doing so. Yet the whole concept of access implicates speech. The intent is to enhance the relative voice of speakers other than the cable operator, implying necessarily some diminution in the operator's speech as the direct regulatory goal. Although the purpose of the rules is not to curtail speech, they interfere with the cable operator's ability to present a "total service offering to be extended to subscribers."

If access requirements are not incidental burdens upon protected speech, they will not be evaluated under *O'Brien*. However, any balancing test used to evaluate a direct challenge to access rules will require, at minimum, satisfaction of the *O'Brien* standard. While it is unclear which test is proper, the regulations will fail under any test if they do not serve a substantial governmental interest or if they are not the least intrusive means of serving that interest.

3. The Interest Served by Access Regulations.—Access regulations serve two general purposes: they ensure that the public receives a fair presentation of all issues, and they create an equal opportunity for all to use the tools of mass communication. Providing some chance to use powerful modern tools for all who wish to communicate is not alone a sufficient governmental interest, because it merely advances the private interests of some who wish to communicate at the expense of others. However, creating such opportunity is a legitimate goal when viewed in conjunction with the other purpose of access. "The First Amendment . . . rests on the assumption that the widest possible dissemination of information from diverse and antagonistic sources is essential to the welfare of the public. . . . Freedom to publish means freedom for all and not for some." The reason that there is a governmental interest in providing access to cable is not to ensure a *fair* presentation of all issues directly, but to ensure that communication is presented from a *diverse* group of speakers, on the theory that a fair presentation of issues will be the result.

The Supreme Court has often recognized that diversification of programming sources is a proper interest that may be considered by government in regulating the media. In the cable context, the Court in 1972 upheld early FCC regulations that required cable operators to originate programming, in addition to carrying programming produced by others. This ruling has been interpreted in the lower courts as applying the diversity interest to cable.

The lack of diversity arises because cable is a natural monopoly. Just as the "scarcity rationale" is used to justify regulation of broadcasting, it can also be used to define an interest in regulating cable systems that are controlled by one operator. Though several courts and commentators have argued that the scarcity rationale does not apply to cable because cable can theoretically offer an unlimited number of channels, this argument focuses simply on the number of available channels and ignores the issue of control.

The Supreme Court has ruled that the natural monopoly status of newspapers is not a sufficient justification for imposition of access regulations in that industry. Some commentators argue that this precludes cable access regulations based on a natural monopoly rationale. However, if sufficient differences between the status of natural monopoly in the two media exist, access regulations could plausibly be justified for cable in spite of the irrelevance of natural monopoly in the newspaper context.

Unlike monopolistic newspapers, which exist independent of government influence, cable monopolies involve the government in the process of granting a franchise. If only one company can serve a franchise area, local governments may have a strong interest in making sure that the lone operator will provide the best service, offering a diverse range of programming. Because government decides which of many applicants may receive a franchise, it is forced to choose who may communicate; access regulations, the argument continues, are merely one method of fine-tuning this choice.

In addition, the use of the public rights of way by cable adds a unique aspect to natural monopoly in the industry. The interest of the government in preserving public streets justifies regulations that minimize disruption. Limiting the number of cable franchisees accomplishes this task. Even if cable companies could feasibly compete, the social costs of cable installation and replacement may reduce the optimal number of competitors, so the need to minimize street disruption adds to the costs of allowing many companies to serve an area, exacerbating the natural monopoly status of cable. Thus the efficient number of cable operators encompasses a less diverse group due to disruption of streets. The use of streets by newspapers involves only the running of trucks and the addition of more trucks would increase disruption by a comparatively trivial amount. Access regulations allow more parties to present their programming without the need for extra parties to disrupt the streets by laying their own cables; such a justification for newspaper access is absent.

Thus any diminution in the level of diversity actually caused by natural monopoly may justify governmental countermeasures despite the Court's rejection of economic scarcity as a similar justification for newspaper access. The legally protected status of cable operators' monopolies has historically let the government intrude into cable in ways that would never have been permitted in the newspaper context. This relationship, along with arguable efficiencies from limiting the number of operators, allows government to search for the means to prevent natural monopoly from restricting diversity.

4. The Least Intrusive Means of Ensuring Diversity.—The presence of natural monopoly results in control of an entire cable system by only one company, which decides who may and who may not communicate. Thus, control is not diversified. However, this does not necessarily mean that those who communicate via cable are not a diverse group. Although the cable operator chooses which programmers may communicate over the cable, he does not actually program all channels. His protected speech is his editorial discretion to pick which other parties may communicate over his cables.

Since the interest to be served is diversity, and the reason that there may not be sufficient diversity is natural monopoly, access regulations are only constitutional if natural monopoly can be shown to restrict the amount of diversity. Otherwise, deregulation, not regulation, would be the least intrusive means of ensuring the proper level of diversity. Regulation would either be overbroad or gratuitous.

Those who rely on diversity for wide-ranging access rules ignore the actual function of the cable operator. Rather than reserving all channels for his own communications, he grants access to those other parties who, in the editorial judgment of the operator, will provide the services that viewers desire most. Natural monopoly justifies interference with this process if and only if it results in some diminution of the amount of diversity in cable programming.

## III. DIVERSITY AND THE PROBLEM OF NATURAL MONOPOLY

Justice Holmes once wrote that "the best test of truth is the power of the thought to get itself accepted in the competition of the market." Natural monopoly has the potential to prevent some communicators from even reaching the "marketplace of ideas," thereby limiting the diversity of programming presented over cable television. However, while natural monopoly in other areas may sometimes result in distortion, in the case of cable television it affects only the profitability of systems and not the amount of programming diversity. Cable access regulations in any form must therefore be deemed unconstitutional because they are either gratuitous or overly burdensome, and they are not the least intrusive means of serving a substantial governmental interest.

### A. Diversity in a Competitive Environment

If entry to the cable industry were free and a competitive market existed, cable access regulations probably could not survive the *Pacific Gas* ruling. Therefore, the proper inquiry is to determine those ways in which natural monopoly causes less diversity than that which would exist in a competitive marketplace. If access regulations are the least intrusive method of correcting actual failures, then they should be upheld. If not, then they are not permitted by the Constitution.

1. Competition as a Standard and the lack of Suitable Alternatives.—Before determining whether constitutionally cognizable failures exist under conditions of natural monopoly, it is necessary to establish that competition is the proper benchmark level of diversity. A simple reading of *Pacific Gas* supports such a benchmark. Since access in a competitive market would not survive the ruling, it would be illogical to increase diversity above the competitive level when combatting natural monopoly.

While *Pacific Gas* establishes competition as the constitutional standard, other standards cannot similarly be supported. Though unlimited diversity, if it were possible, might be the ultimate goal of the first amendment, for a diverse group of ideas to be communicated, there must be some limit on programmer diversity. If absolutely equal access to the media were mandated, no private individuals would invest in the media business, since their ability to communicate would be no greater by investing themselves than it would be if others took the risk of investing.

Support for the competition standard is not weakened by its emphasis on economic allocation of cable facilities. Any diversity over and above that which would exist in a competitive environment is, at a minimum, economically inefficient. Mandated diversity would be unlikely to reflect consumers' desires for exposure to original viewpoints. In addition, if true competition existed, cable operators would be unable to discriminate among programmers on the basis of viewpoint without going out of business. Though the notion that economics should dictate the availability of the communications media may at first seem harsh or inequitable, it is undeniable that economic constraints govern access in some fashion no matter which regulations are used. If channel leasing is required, for example, then the price of channel time is an economic constraint. If free access is mandated, then producers are still constrained by the value of their time for production and for developing their talent and experience at communicating. The problem is actually one of who is able to sue what resource and who is not, a problem usually dealt with through market forces.

Deviation from a standard of competition based upon economic inequality would be justified only if the use of another benchmark would actually reduce barriers to effective communication facing economically disadvantaged groups. However, access regulations simply will not be effective in solving problems grounded in economic inequality. There is no necessary correlation between economic circumstances and the desire to communicate something that may not attract an audience. Therefore, fighting economic inequality cannot be used to justify a standard other than a competitive market.

2. The Competition Standard as a Matter of Sound Policy.—The effect of limiting access to those whose programming would exist in a competitive environment is to make sure that the total benefits, such as commercial gain and goodwill generated by access channels, exceed the costs of channel use. Channels would be allocated according to the relative preferences of programmers or viewers. . . .

If market preferences are allowed to dictate the availability of access to a system, then the economic decisions of operators will be identical to their communicative decisions. All editorial decisions of cable operators should by definition be economic; the function of the editor is to determine which programming subscribers are most willing to receive. The editor does so by selecting economically successful programming, or by choosing material that generates goodwill.

Once the economic nature of editorial decisions is recognized, the propriety of the competition standard is not affected by the presence of blank channel capacity. If a cable operator allows channels to remain blank, it is because no material will cover the costs of programming that channel, including often minimal equipment and personnel for the channel as well as more substantial marketing costs. Thus the decision to leave a channel blank is as much a posi-

tive decision regarding programming services as is a decision to present certain material.

Using only programming that would survive in a competitive marketplace as the standard for diversity will not improperly preclude unpopular communications from the use of cable television. If a programmer feels strongly enough that his message should be on cable, he will pay a competitive operator to carry the programming. In a competitive market the operator would not arbitrarily refuse to carry the programming. More importantly, the ability to communicate an unpopular viewpoint presupposes that an audience is listening—otherwise there is no communication. If the programming is not significantly viewed, the programmer will be required to cover all of the costs associated with the distribution of his programming. Material will be carried only if the total benefit to the programmer, to the viewers, or to both is greater than the cost of presentation. Unpopular viewpoints will survive, but only if their proponents feel strongly enough about them to cover the costs of communication. If few viewers are willing to support the presentation, then the programmer should be forced to decide if it is worthwhile to use this particular means of mass communication to reach his relatively small audience. Requiring a cable operator to carry the message without forcing viewers to watch it does not guarantee that it will be communicated. . . .

The cable situation is similar to that of long-distance telephone service before the introduction of antitrust considerations. AT&T owned most of the local phone systems in the country, and competitors in the long distance market demanded and gained access to those local systems. However, there are two major differences between, long distance telephone service and cable television. First, since AT&T owned most local phone systems, it was able to foreclose a large part of the market that other phone companies desired. In contrast, the largest multiple cable system owner serves only eleven percent of the nation's cable subscribers. Second, AT&T controlled an overwhelming share of the long distance market, while twenty-six cable networks reach at least ten million subscribers. Without substantial control of both the programming market and the national market for cable systems, no cable operator could gain market power by dealing exclusively with vertically affiliated programmers.

When cable operators integrate backwards into programming, it is done most often to take advantage of efficiencies, not to preclude competition in the programming market. It is likely that the Supreme Court would find no antitrust violation if refusal to deal were based on genuine economic efficiencies. In addition, since vertical integration due to efficiencies would occur even in a competitive marketplace where no natural monopoly exists, there is no governmental interest in mandating access to counter vertical integration that results in increased efficiency.

The intrusion on the editorial discretion of cable operators of common carrier access rules designed to counter vertical integration would impose a cure where no sickness exists. Cable operators only have incentives to integrate their operations where efficiency would be gained, not where diversity would be lost. Thus there is no interest in countering vertical integration, and any access rules that are justified by integration cannot be valid under the first amendment.

C. Monopoly Profit and the Suppression of Viewpoints

Diversity of programming sources is an important governmental interest, because if it exists, no viewpoints to which the public might want to be exposed will be suppressed. As two early access proponents noted:

> If a handful of communicators dominate the potent television medium . . . , and this handful vigorously promotes one point of view, then their biases are likely to gain wide acceptance . . . not because of their merit, but because of their unnaturally prominent position in the public forum.

This is, in fact, the heart of the cable access problem. Natural monopoly only causes concern if it results in denial of access to those whose use covers the costs of programming the channel. Neither the natural monopoly structure itself nor vertical integration of programmers and cable operators is likely to affect the level of diversity as long as able operators maximize profits. However, if excess profits are earned by the natural monopolists, then it is possible that they will develop goals other than maximization of the cable system's profit. The presence of excess profits creates a substantial governmental interest in countering any reduction in diversity that may result. Notwithstanding the opportunity for suppression of viewpoints and the existence of this interest, however, access regulations are not the least intrusive means of solving the problem.

## CONCLUSION

The first amendment protects a cable operator's editorial discretion from being abridged by the government unless the abridgement will serve at least a substantial governmental interest and the particular regulation is no more intrusive than necessary to serve the interest. Because a cable television system is arguably a natural monopoly within its local service area, government has an interest in assuring that the cable operator does not deprive viewers of the diversity of viewpoints that would exist if there were no natural monopoly.

While monopoly often causes distortions in the market that might alter the amount of diversity available, in the case of cable television, the industry's structure merely shifts wealth and profits rather than altering the programming shown on a system. Although these profits might be used by cable operators to subsidize suppression of particular viewpoints, the excess profits can be eliminated by auctioning the right to operate a system. By doing so, government can ensure that natural monopoly will not reduce the level of diversity without requiring cable operators to grant access to programmers against their editorial judgment. Because less intrusive means are available to serve the government's interest in promoting diversity, access regulations fail under the first amendment.

---

Daniel Brenner, *Cable Television and the Freedom of Expression*, 1988 DUKE LAW JOURNAL 329 (1988)*

. . .

## III. ASSESSING THE ACT'S TREATMENT OF OPERATOR RIGHTS UNDER THE FIRST AMENDMENT

. . .

*A. The Cable Act's Phantom First Amendment Problem.*

The search for the central meaning of the first amendment is like a tour of the Winchester Mystery House. All persons enter through some doors, but other doors have meaning for a few even if they lead to nowhere. John Stuart Mill set forth a principle that enjoys wide acceptance: government should not be entitled to a monopoly over what ideas or arguments the public hears. This concept of a marketplace of ideas recognizes two tenets of a democratic state: government is not infallible, and government

---

* Reprinted with permission of the Duke Law Journal.

cannot be the only provider of news and information. Where one of the mass media, including cable, is concerned, suppression of speech not only offends the medium as a speaker, but also debilitates it as an informer of listeners or readers. The state should not be allowed to use its police power to ban ideas or silence voices. . . .

*C. Access Regulation Under the Act.*

. . . Preliminarily, we need to consider whether the Act's imposition of access channels amounts to impermissible content based regulation of an operator.

1. Noncommercial Access: Government and Educational Channels. As noted earlier, the Cable Act, in addition to creating a catch-all public access category, permits a city to assign channels to educational and governmental entities. The operation of access for educational and government uses seems straightforward enough, although some complications are worth noting.

Cable operators must decide which educational authority in the community will schedule the educational channel. The same is true for the government channel. Channel administration does not pose a content-related problem, but assigning channels to educational and governmental users is arguably a content-based decision, since the categories limit who may use them. "Public", in contrast, theoretically excludes no one. Classification becomes more of a problem if a city council, as franchising authority, assigns the government channel to itself in order to feature those in office.

However, the labels "government" and "educational" are not viewpoint-specific. More importantly, access regulations in general, and these regulations in particular, do not suppress views. They enhance the speech opportunities of those identified by the categories, without diminishing those of any other speaker. And since anyone may address the audience of educational and government channels by using public access, the perceived favoritism bestowed on the two channel groups can be redressed on the third.

Media regulation that is diversity-enhancing can nevertheless further the first amendment, even if it poses some limit on the press. In *Federal Communications Commission v. National Citizens Committee for Broadcasting,* the Court upheld the constitutionality of an FCC rule barring common ownership of a radio or TV station and a newspaper in the same community. The Court rejected the claim that this rule violated the co-owner's first amendment rights. The rule was not content-based, and its purpose and

effect was to promote free speech. Access channel requirements, too, serve a diversity-enhancing goal, as Congress determined, and are not based on the views of the operator.

For local governments, an access channel is a way to maintain communication with the public, a part of the political process long recognized in the form of newsletters. Such channels encourage awareness of civic matters, by opening city councils to public view, for example, and cannot be directly used by the operator to favor a particular political candidate. The operator does not program the channel, and the Act relieves the operator from legal responsibility for what is broadcast. Government and educational channels represent low-cost networks for cities, negotiated by them as part of a franchise package. Whether they are wasteful expenditures that drive up cable subscriber rates without a substantial public benefit (a complaint often raised by cable operators about all forms of access) is a problem separate from whether requiring such channels violates the first amendment in principle.

2. Access Channels Generally. Public access may be viewed as access leased at less than the market price. Given the power of the operator to determine what is a reasonable price for leasing a channel, it is probably easier for a speaker to appear on public access, assuming that a franchise provides for it.

Noncommercial and commercial public access channels generally call for similar first amendment analysis. Even more than educational or governmental access requirements, public access requirements are content-neutral: they are not triggered by the operator's own speech, nor are they based on the speech content of the person seeking their use.

Access channels raise two potential first amendment problems. First, they may take up too many channels, imposing more than an incidental burden on the operator's speech. Second, they may lead to an unacceptable association of the cable operator's expression with that of the access seeker.

a. Number of channels claimed by access. Access channel requirements deny an operator the use of channels for which it would otherwise select program services. Apart from whether that channel selection process should be characterized as editorial, overall channel carriage requirements can be an unreasonable burden under the first amendment. The United States Court of Appeals for the District of Columbia Circuit, in *Quincy Cable TV, Inc. v. Federal Communications Commission,* invalidated the original must-carry rules in part because those rules led operators to dedicate too many channels to local signals, regardless of viewer or operator choice.

The reduction in channel capacity due to required access, however, does not usually approach the degree of control involuntarily ceded under the former must-carry rules. The Cable Act does not specify the number of PEG channels to be used. The operator is free to negotiate the extent of its noncommercial access commitment. And the Act does not bind operators to dedicate cable channels in perpetuity in the face of insufficient access demand. To the contrary, the franchising authority must establish rules to allow the operator to reclaim access channels.

As to leased access, the Act imposes no such requirements on system of less than thirty-six activated channels. Even for systems of 100 channels or more, the requirement does not exceed fifteen percent of channels. And until a written lease is obtained, operators can ignore leased access requirements. In practice, many systems with thirty-six channel-plus systems do not set aside leased access channels until they are demanded. Thus, unlike the inflexible rules annulled in *Quincy*, the market of speakers creates a demand for such channels.

Even so, access obligations could result in exclusion of services that an operator wants to carry and subscribers want to see. There is no complete answer to this objection; however, access channels presumably appeal to some viewers. And cities are free to release operators from all unpaid access obligations in response to subscriber reaction or to exclude them entirely if they turn out to be undesirable. Further, evidence indicates that having ballooning numbers of cable program services may not appeal to viewers. Demand drops off sharply after a subscriber's four or five favorite satellite signals are on a system. Access channels are not necessarily any less desirable to some viewers than the operator's last selected choice. Compare cable service to the Sunday paper. Once a reader has plucked out the four or five sections of most interest, the rest of the paper may have little value. For some readers, "leased access" in the form of advertising circulars or educational catalogues may occupy the same importance as less-favored sections. So too, for cable.

Finally, cities negotiate the required number of channels in the system as part of a franchise, regardless of whether access is required. The burden of access must be viewed in relation to this agreed-upon number of channels. A requirement that places too high a burden on channel discretion, as the FCC's original must-carry rules did, may violate the first amendment. But at some point the impact of access requirements on channel discretion attenuates to where it cannot be said to violate the operator's rights of expression.

b. *Access channels as a private forum problem.* A second objection to access requirements is that, however many channels are taken up, their content always burdens a cable operator's speech. Even though the editorial viewpoints of the operator and the access user are not consciously joined, a form of forced association results. A system may be required to carry extremist political viewpoints or, as in the case of New York City systems, sexually explicit programs. The operator may complain that viewers, who do not understand that the operator's discretion over such channels has been stripped away by the Act, may disconnect from the system, preferring not to subscribe if it risks bringing offensive material into the home. A more pertinent objection for first amendment purposes is that the operator is associated with expression not of its choosing; it should not be required to carry messages that it would not otherwise select. . . .

This protest calls to mind two forum-type cases, *Pacific Gas & Electric Co. v. Public Utilities Commission (PG&E)* and *Miami Herald Publishing Co. v. Tornillo.* In *PG&E*, the Court found that California violated the first amendment rights of a utility when a public commissioner required the utility to include an opposition group's leaflet in "the extra space" of its monthly billing envelope, four times a year in addition to, or in lieu of, the company's newsletter. The plurality decision concluded that an access right could deter the utility from addressing some issues because its comments could trigger a duty response. Alternatively, the plurality decided, forced carriage of the opposition's newsletter might require the utility to address issues raised in it. It struck down the regulation also because it forced the utility to associate with messages with which it disagreed.

*Tornillo* involved a challenge to a Florida newspaper right-of-reply statute. The statute provided that a newspaper that attacked a candidate's character or record could be required to print the candidate's reply in equal space and prominence. *Tornillo* is often cited for rejecting the argument that the *Miami Herald's* "natural monopoly" in the market could give rise to required access to its editorial pages. As significant as that point may or may not be, the case can be read, as it was in *PG&E*, as condemning access requirements because they discouraged the paper from editorializing. If the paper expressed an opinion, the regulation would force it to let other speakers with whom it disagreed use its facilities.

Cable access does not operate like the schemes invalidated in *Tornillo* and *PG&E*. In those cases, the Court thought that the editorial voice of the newspaper and the utility company would be influenced by the access right of an opponent. In cable, the access user is not an opponent, because the user's speech rarely relates to something carried consciously by the operator. Other than adding new ideas—offensive, insightful or tedious—the access user does not influence an operator's agenda. In any case, access rights are not triggered by the operator's decision whether to address an issue. Access is achieved independently of the operator's message. Conversely, access channel use does not force a cable operator to tailor its speech to a user's agenda or to speak when it prefers to remain silent.

By tradition, access channels are not identified as produced by the operator. They are well-known for their potluck character, with anyone allowed to contribute. This situation produces forced association only in that the same operator is involved; access channel speakers are not perceived as having the carrier's imprimatur. They are like "junk" mail that is carried by the U.S. Postal Service or distributed by landlords, surely not produced by them. And the larger truth is that many points expressed on a cable system as part of the operator's programming can stir resentment. Depictions of violence or sex on a movie channel or a controversial interview on a news channel may cause a subscriber to disapprove. To single out cable access channels on the basis of their potential offensiveness is arbitrary.

Cable access also differs from access to broadcasters. Broadcast access means access to an unreclaimable portion of the finite time available for generating revenues. The broadcaster has amassed an audience for its own purpose. The access seeker wants to expose its message to an audience that has been drawn to the broadcaster's programs but that may not be interested in the access message. In cable, there is no similar "piggybacking" with respect to audience. Access users do not intrude on the operator's speech on an originating channel. Viewers watch access channels not because of anything the operator programs, but because of what access users say. This separation diminishes the effect of access channels on the editorial independence of the operator.

Finally, as noted earlier, access requirements can be viewed as a permissible condition of a franchising process in which not all who wish to operate a cable system may do so. Exclusive licensing may be permitted under the first amendment because access can ensure the availability of cable outlets for those excluded. Unlike broadcasting or newspapers, cable entry usually has been limited to one operator. Access is an acceptable diversifying principle that ameliorates this exclusivity.

## Bibliography

*Redistributing Expressive Opportunity*

Bazelon, David L., *FCC Regulation of the Telecommunication Press*, 1975 Duke Law Journal 213 (1975).

Bollinger, Jr., Lee C., *Freedom of the Press and Public Access: Toward a Theory of Partial Regulation of the Mass Media*, 75 Michigan Law Review 1 (1977).

Coase, Ronald, *The Federal Communication Commission*, 2 Journal of Law & Economics 1 (1959).

Levi, Lilli, *Challenging the Autonomous Press*, 78 Cornell Law Review 665 (1993).

Lively, Donald E., *Fear and the Media: A First Amendment Horror Show*, 69 Minnesota Law Review 1071 (1985).

Powe, Jr., Lucas A., *American Broadcasting and the First Amendment* (1987).

Price, Monroe E., *Taming Red Lion: The First Amendment and Structural Approaches to Media Regulation*, 31 Federal Communications Law Journal 215 (1979).

Schmidt, Benno C., *Freedom of the Press vs. Public Access* (1970).

Simmons, Steven, *The Fairness Doctrine and the Media* (1978).

Van Alstyne, William N., *The Mobius Strip of the First Amendment: Perspectives on Red Lion*, 29 South Carolina Law Review 539 (1978).

Weinberg, Jonathan, *Questioning Broadcast Regulation*, 86 Michigan Law Review 1296 (1988).

## C. Indecency and Violence

Content regulation of modern communications media other than print has not been limited to allegedly unique conditions of scarcity. Concern with impact has become increasingly significant in the regulation of broadcasting. Sexually explicit or suggestive program content, or the use of profanity, originally begot a regulatory response consonant with Justice Harlan's sense that "one man's vulgarity is another's lyric." *Cohen v. California*, 403 U.S. 15, 25 (1971). Over the past two decades, government has become more aggressive in policing and punishing indecent expression. Content control has been driven by concern that broadcasting is a pervasive medium uniquely accessible to children. It has been facilitated by an understanding of the expression as having diminished value and of the medium as being less protected. *Federal Communications Commission v. Pacifica Foundation*, 438 U.S. 726, 748-50 (1978). Experience in regulating indecency has provided a reference point for evolving arguments to limit televised violence. Thomas Krattenmaker and L.A. Powe, Jr. examine the implications of the Court's investment in impact theory. Daniel A. Farber maintains that, although government is not entitled to assume the role of moral guardian over acceptable discourse, neither is it absolutely prohibited by the premise of *Cohen v. California* from regulating offensive expression. From case law concerning nude dancing and peep shows, Vincent Blasi identifies what he perceives as "themes and tensions" evolving in the opinions of a conservative federal judiciary.

Thomas G. Krattenmaker and L.A. Powe, Jr., *Televised Violence: First Amendment Principles and Social Science Theory,* 64 VIRGINIA LAW REVIEW 1123 (1978)*

## INTRODUCTION: THE POLITICAL CONTEXT OF TELEVISED VIOLENCE

"Violence is as American as cherry pie." If Rap Brown's assertion is valid, America's three television networks celebrated the Bicentennial with a banner display of Americanism. The networks, however, were out of tune with their viewers because many public organizations, including the American Medical Association (AMA) and the National Parent Teachers Association (PTA), raised loud objections that were taken seriously by politicians and social science researchers alike. Political and academic attention to the level of televised violence and its particular effects on children has produced what popular journals alone cannot—a wealth of studies exploring the relationship between violence on television and antisocial aggression in everyday life, important (if possibly transitory) changes in the programming practices of the networks, and a substantial threat of legislative intervention if the networks' actions do not satisfy their critics.

To view these recent events as an isolated phenomenon, however, would fail to see the staying power of televised violence as a political issue. Indeed, almost since television's entry into American life, politicians, aided by social scientists, have maintained a heavy barrage against the putative effects of televised violence. Twice before Rap Brown uttered his memorable phrase, Senate committees, first under Senator Kefauver and later under Senator Dodd, questioned the relationship of depictions of violence in the mass media to the rising tide of crime, especially juvenile delinquency, in the country. These early efforts produced little beyond pious platitudes. The issue came and went in the 1950s, and Senator Dodd's effort to make it reappear in the early 1960s accomplished little. The spreading violence of the mid-1960s however, generated widespread concern over the causes of violence and social unrest and led to President Johnson's appointment in 1968 of the Eisenhower Commission on the Causes and Prevention of Violence. The commission took a hard look at the mass media, stating that it "is reasonable to conclude that a constant diet of violent behavior on

television has an adverse effect on human character and attitudes. Violence on television encourages violent forms of behavior and fosters moral and social values about violence in daily life which are unacceptable in a civilized society."

. . .

Broadcasters typically respond to such congressional anxiety like any other regulated group. They state they are considering the problem and taking initial steps to alleviate it, then patiently wait, secure in the knowledge that the attention span of Congress and the public does not significantly exceed that of a two-year old. Albert Bandura, one of the leading experimental researchers on the effects of violence on children, understood this when he evaluated the prospects for remedial action: "My general impression is that congressional hearings are sort of like television reruns: same characters, same plot, same outcome." . . .

Events, however, proved Bandura wrong. Just as the issue of violence on television became intertwined with the burning cities in the mid-1960s, in the early 1970s it was fused with obscenity and indecency, or more accurately, programming that seemed to challenge traditional American values. Between 1972 and 1973, complaints to the Federal Communications Commission (FCC) concerning obscenity and indecency increased more than fifteenfold. Decency in broadcasting thus became a pressing problem, and congressmen simply joined it with existing public desire to see less gratuitous violence on television.

. . .

## I. THE SOCIAL SCIENTISTS LOOK AT TELEVISED VIOLENCE

. . .

### A. The Violence Hypothesis: The Positive View

Those who try to study the extent to which viewing violence causes antisocial aggression face an enormous, insoluble dilemma at the outset. Ethical norms properly prevent a researcher from deliberately provoking one person to inflict antisocial or violent acts upon another. Consequently, experimenters must choose scientifically less attractive, but ethically acceptable, means for attempting to measure cause and effect. In the final analysis, this socially imposed constraint on experimentation may well render futile the quest for convincing evidence of the violence hypothesis.

Those active in the field, however, have not generally shared this conclusion. Indeed researchers have displayed remarkable ingenuity in seeking to

---

* Reprinted with permission.

mitigate the effects of their ethical constraints. Some have conducted laboratory experiments that control viewing of television and observe behavior directly, but the "violence" measured consists of harmless acts. Such researchers substitute a different effect for that postulated by the violence hypothesis. Another method is to collect data on viewing habits and peer perceptions of aggressive or violent tendencies. Utilizing this second approach, at least one pair of researchers has measured specific behavioral responses to a program based on a real television series. Finally, others have controlled subjects' viewing habits and then observed a wide variety of postviewing conduct. In the latter two types of studies, the researcher sacrifices control over other possible causes. Whatever the techniques employed, the majority of published accounts have concluded that televised violence causes aggressive behavior, although the results are less positive the less control the researchers have over their subjects.

. . .

## B. A Critical Examination of the Violence Hypothesis

Despite the plethora of social scientists' results pointing toward the conclusion that viewing violent television breeds aggression, methodological faults in studies both in the laboratory and in the real world raise troubling doubts about their utility. These doubts are magnified by several more general flaws common to both kinds of studies. One is left with the uneasy, but inescapable, conclusion that we know little more after these studies than before.

The correlational studies probably are the weakest link in the social scientists' cases. A correlation between viewing violent television and interpersonal aggression is easily established. For example, simply knowing that the poor commit more violent acts and watch more television is enough to permit one to assume that a correlation exists between viewing violence and committing it. Causality, however, is something else: How do we decide whether poverty, or television, or both, or neither *cause* violence?

. . .

Viewed in a similarly critical manner, the studies in natural settings as yet cannot provide definitive conclusions. . . . Such experiments will tell us little until conducted with sufficiently large samples./ Moreover, because a natural setting contains many uncountable variables, such experiments may at most suggest a null hypothesis for the effect of violence on aggression. . . .

One would expect that the strength of the studies utilizing correlation and natural settings is their ability to corroborate the more controlled laboratory experiments. As the above criticisms demonstrate, however, even read in their most positive light these two types of studies cannot provide a compelling case for an attempt to regulate televised violence without the complementary conclusions of the laboratory studies. While the laboratory studies have provided the most positive results linking violent behavior to a diet of aggressive televised fare, the significance of these results may be challenged because of the very nature of the laboratory method.

First and foremost, a laboratory is not a natural environment; subjects may behave differently there than they would elsewhere. For example, the laboratory may affect the way television is viewed. Although research uncovered no definitive studies on the point, one writer has remarked that anyone who believes viewers are passive vegetables in front of the set "'has never watched children watch TV.'" While children "watch" television at home, they may do a number of other things, including leaving the room. A study done for the Surgeon General described the tremendous amount of activity done by a family of four while "watching" the set. The study concluded that between 55% and 76% of the time spent "watching" actually is spent viewing the program. This contrasts with the laboratory experiments where distractions of the home are unavailable.

Further, the films used for the laboratory studies thus far have been either specially made or specifically excerpted from an actual drama. In either case, they lack the complexity and length of a full program interspersed with commercials. Whether this fact might affect results is unclear, especially in light of the gaps in viewing programs at home, but it presents additional differences between the home and the laboratory.

Another difference is that to date all reported testing has been done virtually immediately after viewing. One wonders if the subjects were given additional time after viewing the results might be different. Suppose the subjects had been fed, bathed, and allowed to sleep for ten hours before being confronted with a Bobo Doll or Buss Aggression Machine?

More significant, in none of the laboratory experiments have the subjects been sanctioned for indulging in violent behavior. In the "real world," persons (whether preschoolers or adults) function in a system where violence is formally viewed as antisocial and is frequently punished by a third party or the victim. In reality, a child's viewing of televised violence takes place in the presence of at least one adult about 50% of the time. . . .

In sum, the laboratory data address the question of the effects of viewing television on behavior in a rather oblique manner. At most, the positive results suggest that one forced to view simulated violent television in an artificial setting, angered and frustrated by an experimenter, and subject to no social or interpersonal sanctions for violent behavior will, if deliberately presented with the opportunity, be more likely to engage in such activities as hitting a Bobo Doll or administering greater electrical shocks immediately after viewing such fare than one who has just watched nonaggressive filmed behavior. As the earlier discussion shows, the studies involving correlation and natural settings do not fill the void left by the artificiality of the laboratory processes.

. . .

Finally, and most damaging to proponents of the violence hypothesis, no one yet has been able to suggest an acceptable operational definition of the very kind of behavior sought to be measured: "violence." To be useful as a basis for policymaking, studies of the causes of violence must rest upon a definition incorporating normative, social connotations. To illustrate, if violence is defined simply as a willingness to stand one's ground when physically attacked, it is extremely unlikely that violence caused by television would produce an outcry for increased public regulation. What then can the researcher take as an objectivity observable conception of violence capable of measuring behavior that produces social concern?

. . .

A normative definition of violence agreeable to all and fairly objectively determinable can be derived: the purposeful, illegal infliction of pain for personal gain or gratification that is intended to harm the victim and is accomplished in spite of societal sanctions against it. Whether viewing such behavior simulated on television tends to cause its occurrence in real life seems to be the question about which researchers, regulators, and the public care. Such violence, however, is precisely the sort of behavior that no researcher in a laboratory may seek to cause and that no "real world observer" can hope to witness systemically. The social research to date simply has not left this question unanswered: it has left it unasked.

Perhaps violent fare on television causes harmful, illegal violence in isolated individuals, in identifiable groups (large or small), or throughout society at large. We have, however, seen little convincing evidence that it does. The use of such studies in political debate simply is not justified. When measured against what the evidence truly represents, assertions that the violence hypothesis is supported by "substantial testimony," or that the data now "justify action," or that disputes over the violence hypothesis are "political" rather than "scientific" are premature and utterly unreal. Careful inquiry simply does not support such extravagant conclusions.

. . .

## II. FIRST AMENDMENT CONSIDERATIONS

If Congress or a duly authorized agency such as the Federal Communications Commission found the social science data persuasive despite all the flaws discussed in the previous section and sought to eliminate or reduce the amount of televised violence, the critical issue remains whether the first amendment stands as a barrier to such regulation. Several factors make careful analysis of this issue difficult. First, the range of possible responses by the legislature or agency seems almost limitless. At least five different forms of regulation immediately suggest themselves: (1) ban certain violence completely, (2) limit violence to certain times or days in the week, (3) require that violent programming be balanced by other forms of prosocial programming, (4) provide technical facilities that enable parents to exercise greater control over their children's access to the set, and (5) require that information on the level of violence of programs be disseminated in advance of their broadcast. To assess the extent to which the constitutionally protected rights of freedom of speech and of the press would or should override legislative efforts to deal with televised violence ultimately requires a series of discrete inquiries about these various regulatory techniques.

The need for such an inquiry leads to the second problem: the absence of any established set of doctrinal principles that bear directly on the first amendment issues such rules would implicate. Although one can find both discussions of the problems of effects of media violence on children dating back at least to the 1930s and occasional litigation concerning statutes designed in one way or another to protect children from these displays, the courts have not even begun to develop a specific corpus of law under the first amendment that deals with attempts to shield viewers from the perceived harmful effects of exposure to media violence. This lack of specific cases discussing violence means that analysis must begin with an examination of the general body of first amendment jurisprudence dealing with a variety of statutes that in one way or another seek to protect the public interest from harm that flows from a given type of speech.

The chore of analyzing possible regulations of televised violence is complicated further by the fact that both the cases and the literature provide ample suggestions that general first amendment principles have limited force where the medium regulated is electronic communications or where the rights at issue are those of children. Upon close analysis, these suggestions also seem to lack coherent structures or consistent themes.

To impose some order on this complexity, we find it necessary to begin with a broad inquiry that remains central to analysis of all others: Apart from any special concerns that arise because television or children's rights are involved, how should courts proceed under the first amendment in assessing a challenge to a ban on televised violence enacted because of the concerns voiced by the social scientists?

. . .

. . . [T]he violence hypothesis cannot justify a ban on televised violence. Although the empirical work of the behavioralists purports to demonstrate that the likelihood of harm occurring is quite high, their claims simply are not supported by the evidence. The Court should subject the behavioralists' results to the same scrutiny given assertions that subversive advocacy, false statements, dirty words, and fighting words cause harm. Earlier we engaged in such scrutiny, and as the results demonstrate, consistent application of the first amendment compels both rejection of the conclusions reached by the social scientists and invalidation of any general content ban on televised violence.

Moreover, if the Court refuses to consider the validity of the behavioralists' results and concludes that viewing violence on television does in fact lead to violent behavior, the question then becomes whether the accepted results are a sufficient basis for suppression of televised violence. Even accepting the studies at face value, the Constitution would not be satisfied for two reasons. First . . . the reformulation of *Chaplinsky* has led to a consistent insistence that the harm sought to be avoided by censorship be specific and particularized. The mere possibility that someone might suffer an unidentified harm to reputation or might be tempted to retaliate when confronted with offensive speech is not a sufficient basis for punishing protected speech. By contrast, the social science literature says nothing at all about what kinds of violent portrayals will yield what forms of subsequent harmful aggressive behavior. Indeed, the social scientists have been utterly oblivious to the difficulty of defining violence in a normatively useful fashion. Accordingly, even if violent television pro-grams simulate interpersonal aggression among children, no rational proof exists that such aggression is indeed socially harmful. Indulging the false assumption that all the predicted aggression is harmful and unlawful, we still do not know what specific kind of aggression is to be avoided. Is it children hitting Bobo Dolls, assaulting each other, pushing "HURT" buttons, or playing football rather than chess that is the evil at stake? Without answers to such questions, present doctrine under the first amendment strongly suggests that the empirical findings are insufficient to justify suppression.

Second, except for commercial speech, the various categories of [first amendment] cases . . . in practice all seem to incorporate the mandate of Justices Holmes and Brandeis that censorship is an impermissible sanction unless the harm intended to be avoided is imminent. Again, the behavioralists' publications are not illuminating. The studies utilizing correlation and natural settings seek to measure aggressive behavior over time, but they admittedly lack any evidence of cause and effect. The laboratory studies purport to show only that if subjects are placed immediately after viewing violence in an environment that has no sanctions against aggression, they may behave aggressively (although not necessarily unlawfully or harmfully). These findings are of little value inthe real world, however, where television is typically watched in the home but where the aggression the state seeks to avoid is displayed elsewhere. Some timelag between viewing and aggressive behavior seems inevitable, and this timelag normally is thought to demonstrate the wisdom of punishing actors for what they do rather than speakers for what they say. Although the television program is the initial instigator, the potential aggressor may remember the legal and societal sanctions against his intended act and change his mind. Or he may mention to someone what he intends to do, thus provoking a discussion about the act. And once there is discussion or reflection, we have, by definition, Justice Brandeis's time for more talk. The notion that speech ought not to be banned when normal opportunities exist to convince an actor not to break the law or when the harm may be avoided by further debate seems to us to be the gist of modern first amendment law as it concerns depictions of violence. Thus the existence of this potentiality for dissuasion also should be an obstacle to constitutional regulation of televised violence.

. . .

Writing thirty years ago in *Kovacs v. Cooper*, Justice Jackson vigorously disputed that the case was precedent for any form of communication beyond sound trucks: "The moving picture screen, the radio, the newspaper, the handbill, the sound truck and the street corner orator have differing natures, values, abuses and dangers. Each in my view, is a law unto itself. . ." Probably no medium better illustrates this statement than one Justice Jackson did not include: television. Our earlier discussion of general first amendment principles purposely omitted one factor: the principles at issue may be qualified somewhat when the medium of expression is television.

The reasons for this special treatment are less clear than the fact that it occurs. Over the years a number of rationales have been proffered as to why first radio and then television were distinctive media of communication that require separate treatment under the first amendment. Basically, the available justifications are four: (1) the public owns the airwaves and may do with them as it pleases, (2) television is a medium of unique power, (3) the medium is scarce and thus needs regulation to overcome problems caused by scarcity, and (4) television is such an intrusive medium that its viewers are a quasi-captive audience. A review of each of the theories is necessary to understand the legal context of any attempt to reduce or eliminate violence on television. Furthermore, *FCC v. Pacifica Foundation* marks an important shift in the Court's treatment of the rationales for the special regulation of broadcasting, a shift that may set the tone for regulating the next generation of mass communication.

. . .

*FCC v. Pacifica Foundation* marks the first time any theory other than scarcity has received the official imprimatur of the Court. . . .[S]carcity could not have authorized the result in Pacifica because regardless of whether one thinks the incredible abundance of radio stations in the United States (and especially in New York City) is insufficient, scarcity supports adding voices not banning them. To justify a content ban under the facts in *Pacifica*, a different theory was needed, and none works better than intrusiveness.

As with scarcity, explaining the theory of the intrusiveness of broadcasting is deceptively easy. Radio is everywhere—at the beach, in the car going to and from work or errands, and in almost every room in the home. Intrusiveness is particularly important when radio enters the home, for in the home an individual's "right to be let alone plainly outweighs the First Amendment rights" of any speaker wishing to communicate with him there. *Pacifica* noted further that prior warnings about a program's content

are ineffective because individuals constantly are turning the radio on or off. Persons easily could be exposed unwillingly to a program or even a few words they find offensive, and in one's home one has a right not to be offended.

A closer look at *Pacifica*, however, demonstrates that this simple argument contains several flaws deriving mainly from the majority's cavalier treatment of precedent. For example, all five Justices in the majority agreed that "it is well settled that the First Amendment has a special meaning in the broadcasting context." All of the cases cited to support this statement, however, relied on scarcity as the basis for differential treatment. Nowhere did the majority acknowledge that its use of intrusiveness to ban speech constituted a departure from existing analysis or spoke to issues different from scarcity.

A more significant flaw occurred in the Court's attempt to distinguish *Pacifica* from *Cohen v. California*. Relying on the cases involving offensive language, the Pacifica Foundation argued that the unwilling listener has the duty to avert his ears or turn off the radio just as any unwilling viewer has the duty to avert his eyes from Paul Cohn's offending jacket. Justice Stevens replied: "To say that one may avoid further offense by turning off the radio when he hears indecent language is like saying that the remedy for an assault is to run away after the first blow." Yet if Justice Stevens's rejoinder is correct, it is equally applicable to *Cohen*. Indeed, one might have expected some prominence for *Cohen* in *Pacifica* because presumably the conclusion that Carlin's monologue is protected speech stems from *Cohen* and because no other case is more relevant to the duties of the offended viewers. Despite this, *Cohen* received but a "cf." citation in the text, an accompanying footnote, and a subsequent footnote.

The principal way of avoiding *Cohen* in both opinions comprising the Pacifica majority was to rely on the 1970 opinion of *Rowan v. Post Office Department*, where a unanimous Court upheld a statute giving an addressee the right to demand that his name be removed from mailing lists if he finds the mail sent offensive. The majority in *Pacifica* properly acknowledged that *Rowan* recognized a special status under the first amendment for the home, but it failed to give even a passing glance to *Rowan's* analysis and the specific language of that opinion.

The Court in *Rowan* allowed an unwilling addressee to bar an anxious communicator from sending him letters. Although the principle itself easily may be extended to include speaking as well as writing, *Rowan* paid scrupulous attention to the first amendment rights of everyone in question. The unwilling recipient, asserting a right of privacy in the home, was given that—but no more. He could not bar the speaker from communicating with anyone else. By contrast, *Pacifica*, in focusing its analysis on why children should not be exposed to four-letter words, virtually ignored the first amendment rights of other very willing listeners who wanted to hear George Carlin's monologue on the radio. Justice Stevens's only reference to the rights of those listeners is limited to a footnote telling them to go to a nightclub. Justice Powell at least recognized this problem in his concurring opinion, but he did not attempt to resolve it. Instead, he expressed his hope that in the future the Commission, whose "judgment [as to first amendment] is entitled to respect," would consider the rights of willing as well as unwilling listeners. In the interim, willing listeners could buy a record.

The majority in *Pacifica* not only ignored this important analytical difference between the two cases, but it also pointedly ignored what the Court said in *Rowan*. In sustaining the conclusion that an unwilling recipient could prevent a distributor from sending him unwanted messages, *Rowan* stated that to "hold less would tend to license a form of trespass and would make hardly more sense than to say that a radio or television viewer may not twist the dial to cut off an offensive or boring communication and thus bar its entering his home." *Rowan* thus recognized the obvious: a disgruntled viewer retains a self-help remedy against offensive programming. Placing the radio in the status of an "intruder" as Justice Stevens did does not affect this remedy, especially when, if the radio is an "intruder," it is an intruder purchased (or acquired) by the occupant of the home and turned on by a volitional act of that occupant.

* * *

. . . [T]he rationale of intrusiveness more than overwhelms the suggestion that this is a narrow holding. The very concept of a right in the home that supersedes any first amendment rights of all speakers and all willing listeners is an idea not easily cabined. Until Pacifica, the balance between the home and the first amendment had been struck as in Rowan: government coercively could protect the occupant of a home who objected to speech because of its content only when the rights of no other listeners were affected. Pacifica changes that equation radically for, surprising as it may seem to the majority, significant numbers of people exist who are not offended by Carlin's monologue. The rights of this receptive, unoffended majority are affected drastically. . . .

* * *

In sum, *Pacifica* makes very difficult knowing how the fact of broadcasting a depiction of violence on television would change our general first amendment analysis. The majority went out of its way to invent a transparently unprincipled excuse for refusing to extend some settled first amendment principles to broadcasting. Like *Red Lion Broadcasting Co. v. FCC*, in so doing it carved out a separate niche for broadcasting in first amendment jurisprudence; but it also ignored the first amendment's purpose of ensuring the expression of diverse viewpoints, the underlying principle of *Red Lion*. One reading of *Pacifica* and its finding that the intrusive nature of radio allows greater regulation of broadcasted speech could support the conclusion that if a ban on televised violence can be supported by a plausible—and not necessarily proven or correct—argument, it will be sustained. If the Court's reasoning is pushed to the limit, the data of the social scientists might support regulation of televised violence notwithstanding the generally unconvincing nature of those studies. . . .

Nevertheless, *Pacifica* is susceptible to limitation either as a case involving radio rather than television or, more plausibly, as an extension of the obscenity cases to their outermost limits when children may be involved. If *Pacifica's* statement that it is a limited holding is to be taken seriously, one of these limitations must be invoked. Under either, the fact that television is the medium used for the broadcast ought not to detract from our earlier analysis. Only the future will tell, however, how the Court intends to treat *Pacifica*.

Until someone provides constitutionally acceptable support for the conclusion that television is an intruder in the home, we think it better to treat *Pacifica* in a more limited way. We simply cannot believe that electronic communications—the most prominent means of mass communications in the world today—are to be cut off from the first amendment simply to protect the desires of those who do not wish to watch them. The federal courts and especially the Supreme Court never have abandoned their special solicitude for the first amendment, and we find it unlikely that they will sit happily with large areas of communications isolated from constitutional protection. Accordingly, the majority's invitation to treat *Pacifica* as a limited holding should be accepted, and scarcity, as exemplified by *Red Lion's* emphasis on a consistency with first amendment purposes, should return as the cornerstone of first amendment analysis in the context of broadcasting.

. . . [N]either public ownership nor television's power to communicate would support a content ban on violent programming. Scarcity does not justify a complete ban, although it might support a limitation on the amount of time that could be devoted to such programming if the government could produce persuasive evidence that such programming filled a disproportionate number of programming hours and left alternative tastes substantially unsatisfied. Scarcity does not, however, justify any governmental regulation of violent programs because of their tendency to produce antisocial behavior unless the government can meet the requirements imposed by the first amendment for content regulation of more traditional media. Thus television in and of itself should not make a difference.

Daniel A. Farber, *Civilizing Public Discourse: An Essay on Professor Bickel, Justice Harlan, and the Enduring Significance of Cohen v. California*, 1980 DUKE LAW JOURNAL 283 (1980)*

On April 26, 1968, Paul Cohen was arrested for displaying the slogan "Fuck the Draft" on his jacket. Three years later, the United States Supreme Court reversed his conviction. Justice Harlan himself noted, the case seemed "at first blush too inconsequential to find its way into our books." Yet *Cohen v. California* did not escape notice entirely, for it struck the discerning eye of Professor Harry Kalven "as a helpful, and remarkably gallant, contribution to first amendment theory."

Today, *Cohen v. California* is widely recognized as an important first amendment case. It is commonly considered the leading statement on the validity of prohibitions designed to protect people from involuntary exposure to offensive speech. *Cohen* is generally thought to resolve this "captive audience" issue by placing the burden upon the offended person to look away, at least when he is outside his own home. Only when avoidance is impossible may the state intervene. If this reading of *Cohen* is correct, then the decision is highly relevant to cases like *FCC v. Pacifica Foundation*, which involved a ban on "indecent" broadcasting to protect people who might unwittingly turn on their radios and be shocked by the language. After all, it is argued, turning off the radio would be no more of a burden than looking away from an offensive jacket.

One of the primary purposes of this Essay is to refute the notion that *Cohen* resolved the captive audience problem. I will argue, to the contrary, that the structure of Harlan's opinion shows that *Cohen* is largely irrelevant to this issue. Instead, Harlan's real concern was whether the state had the power to maintain a tolerable climate of thought by purifying public discourse. For Harlan, the question was not frivolous. He had previously been willing to grant the states broad authority in regulating obscenity, in order to protect the moral fabric of society from the effects of "degrading" speech. Yet in *Cohen*, he ultimately concluded that to extend the state's role as moral guardian to areas beyond obscenity was incompatible with first amendment values.

So understood, Justice Harlan's opinion in *Cohen* contrasts strikingly with the views of another great conservative thinker, Professor Alexander Bickel. In his last book, *The Morality of Consent*, Bickel argued that certain kinds of speech—pornography, "filthy and violent rhetoric," and "a kind of cursing, assaultive speech that amounts to almost physical aggression"—erode fundamental social values, thereby creating a climate in which actions otherwise unthinkable become realistic possibilities. He viewed these kinds of speech as a form of pollution of our common moral environment. While aware of the risks, he believed that government should take cautious steps toward dealing with assaultive speech.

Bickel's theory is somewhat removed from current first amendment doctrine, although perhaps less so than when he first wrote. Yet the concerns he voiced are troubling and deserve attention, not only because existing doctrine is subject to change, but also because as citizens, if not as lawyers, we cannot limit our vision strictly to legal doctrine.

This Essay is intended as an exploration of these contrasting views on control of offensive speech.

. . .

## I. AN ANALYSIS OF THE *COHEN* OPINION

The genesis of *Cohen v. California* was an antiwar meeting attended by nineteen-year-old Paul Cohen. Someone else at the meeting inscribed a peace symbol and the phrases "Stop War" and "Fuck the Draft" on his jacket. Although he was not the inscriber, Cohen admittedly was aware of these insignia. On April 26, 1968, he went to the Los Angeles County courthouse to testify in a case that apparently had no relation to the draft or the Vietnam War. When Cohen entered the courtroom, he took off his jacket and stood with it folded over his arm. In the meantime, a vigilant policeman had observed the jacket and had sent the judge a note suggesting that Cohen be held in contempt of court. Evidently, the

* Reprinted with permission.

policeman's theory was either that wearing the jacket in the hall was an act of contempt, or that having it folded over one's arm in the presence of a judge was contumacious behavior. In any event, the judge wisely declined the policeman's invitation to forge new paths in the law of contempt. Thus deprived of judicial reinforcement, the officer waited until Cohen left the courtroom and then arrested him for disturbing the peace.

California's disturbing the peace statute did not easily yield a charge against Cohen. It did prohibit the use of "vulgar, profane, or indecent language within the presence or hearing of women or children"—so far, so good—but unfortunately this part of the statute applied solely to language used in a "loud and boisterous manner." The only other potentially applicable provision was the general prohibition against "maliciously and willfully disturb[ing] the peace or quiet of any neighborhood or person . . . by . . . offensive conduct." The trial judge found this language a sufficient basis for conviction and imposed a sentence of thirty days in jail. This harsh sentence, for what was at most a juvenile prank, is hard to understand except as the consequence of either a puritanical attitude toward Cohen's language or, worse, strong hostility to Cohen's political views. . . .

. . . [T]he California Court of Appeal . . . held that the statute *did* cover Cohen's conduct. The appellate court construed the statute to apply when a person's willful conduct foreseeably provokes others to engage in violence or breach the peace. In the court's view, Cohen was guilty under this test: he had "carefully chose[n] the forum for his views where his conduct would have an effective shock value." Accordingly, the appellate court concluded, he should have known that others might assault him or forcibly remove his jacket to protect women and children from exposure to his "lewd and vulgar language." . . .

On June 22, 1970, the Court agreed to hear the case, postponing consideration of whether it had jurisdiction. The parties presented oral argument in February of 1971, and the Court announced its decision on June 7, 1971. Splitting five to four, the Court reversed the conviction, with Justice Harlan writing for the majority and Justice Black joining the dissent.

Had he not been troubled by the case, Justice Harlan could have disposed of it with little elaboration. The record contained no indication of a violent reaction, actual or threatened, to Cohen's conduct, as required by the lower court's construction of the statute. Hence, the California court had necessarily relied on the questionable presumption that offensive speech is *likely* to cause a violent reaction. Justice

Harlan took only a single paragraph to expose the unconstitutionality of this presumption. Surely, he argued, there cannot be a great many people who would resort to violence at the sight of a four-letter word, and the possible existence of a few persons this easily provoked to violence is not a sufficient justification for a restriction on speech. If it were, anyone who voiced an unpopular viewpoint would face arrest. With this line of reasoning, Justice Harlan dismissed the rationale of the lower court as "plainly untenable."

Justice Harlan was not always averse to disposing of cases on the narrowest of grounds. He could have done so in *Cohen*, based solely on the failure of the statute (as construed to cover only conduct likely to cause a violent reaction) to reach Cohen's conduct without the aid of an unconstitutional presumption. An opinion resting entirely on this narrow ground, however, would not have been intellectually satisfying. The lower court's rationale was too patently meritless to be taken seriously. It can only be understood as a transparent attempt to provide doctrinal support for the traditional taboo on public utterance of certain words. The crux of the case was the legal status of deep-seated societal antipathy for certain four-letter words. Harlan's evident desire to deal with the problem caused him to take a more circuitous approach in resolving the matter.

The opinion begins with an analysis of "various matters which this record does *not* present." Of these, two issues are especially significant for our purposes. The first relates to the locale of the speech. The California court had stressed Cohen's "selection of the public corridor of the courthouse as the place to parade" with his slogan. This appears to be the point of Justice Blackmun's dissent, which dismissed Cohen's action as "mainly conduct and little speech." This characterization makes little sense unless Blackmun thought Cohen was conducting a sort of protest march through the courthouse. Although Justice Harlan probably was sympathetic to this claim of special respect for courts and their environs, he nevertheless rejected it as a basis for upholding the conviction because the statute contained no suggestion of any special restriction on speech within the courthouse. Because of this failure to provide fair notice, the Court held that the conviction could not be supported on the ground that the statute attempted to "preserve an appropriately decorous atmosphere in the courthouse." The Court's failure to rule on the abstract validity of strictures to assure courthouse decorum leaves open the possibility, however, that a narrowly drawn ban on four-letter words within the courthouse would have been acceptable.

The second issue specifically put aside by the Court is the "captive audience" argument, in particular, whether the government could legitimately act to prevent Cohen's offensive language from being thrust upon unwilling viewers. The discussion began with a general exploration of the captive audience problem. Justice Harlan observed that the recognized power of government to prevent intrusion into the sanctuary of the home must be sharply limited elsewhere if it is not to become an instrument for majoritarian repression of dissidents. His proposed test was that "substantial privacy interests" must be invaded in an "essentially intolerable manner." This test obviously leaves unspecified which privacy interests have substance and which invasions can be tolerated. Justice Harlan found the privacy interest in *Cohen* far less substantial than the interest invaded by sound trucks blaring into homes, since people confronted with Cohen's jacket could simply look away. On the other hand, the interest in privacy while walking through the courthouse corridor was at least arguably more substantial than the interest in privacy while "strolling through Central Park." Perhaps it is fair to infer that Harlan found the privacy claim in *Cohen* less than compelling, but it is also clear that he did not find it frivolous. His final decision was to avoid the issue. . . .

With these two issues placed to the side, Harlan found that the case presented a single remaining issue: whether the state could completely outlaw the word "fuck," either on the theory that its use is inherently likely to provoke violence, or on the theory that the states, "acting as guardians of public morality, may properly remove this offensive word from the public vocabulary." As has been shown, Harlan rejected the violence theory as unsupportable, leaving only the second theory, which Harlan restated as an attempt to maintain "a suitable level of discourse within the body politic." This theory represented state censorship in its purest form: it claimed state power to censor offensive words, even when there was no objection and no risk of concrete harm. Not only would this censorship apply as fully to Lenny Bruce speaking to a willing nightclub audience as it would to Cohen, but presumably it would apply to literary works as well. Despite his willingness to grant the states similar power over erotic literature, Harlan was reluctant to expand the established exceptions to the usual rule against content censorship. He concluded, for reasons that will be discussed in connection with Professor Bickel's views, that government control over the public vocabulary was intolerable.

It should be clear by now that Harlan's first amendment methodology did not revolve around the simple issue of constitutional protection for particular conduct. Rather, Harlan first carefully determined what justifications for regulation were properly before the Court and then attempted to determine the sufficiency of those particular justifications. The result of this analysis has been misleading when carelessly used as precedent in later cases. For example, in *FCC v. Pacifica Foundation*, the issue was whether a radio station was entitled to play a record containing a number of four-letter words. At first sight, *Cohen* appears to be powerful precedent on this issue. On closer analysis, however, *Cohen* proves to have little relevance. The Federal Communications Commission's justifications for regulating speech in *Pacifica* turned on the context of the mid-afternoon broadcast, whereas Justice Harlan found that none of the possible context-related justifications were properly presented in *Cohen*. Instead, the issue he did find to be properly presented—and therefore the only issue he decided—was whether the state, acting as a paternalistic guardian of public morality, could ban the use of certain words in all contexts. Because *Pacifica* dealt with context and *Cohen* dealt only with content, *Cohen* contributes little to the issue presented in *Pacifica*.

Although *Cohen* does not resolve all the questions relating to offensive speech, it does answer one basic question: whether the goal of maintaining a minimum quality of public discourse justifies restrictions on offensive speech. Before accepting too readily Harlan's negative answer to this question, however, it is well to consider opposing arguments.

## II. THE DEBATE ON CIVILITY AND RESTRICTIONS ON SPEECH

In the abstract, the balance between the values of free speech and public civility is struck all too easily: free speech must prevail. When confronted with speech that truly offends us, however, we begin to feel the need for a less facile analysis. Cohen's speech is probably not sufficiently offensive to challenge our abstract views on civility and free speech. His underlying message was well within the political mainstream. In retrospect, that message today probably arouses the sympathy even of many people whose political views differed at the time. Moreover, Cohen's language has become considerably more acceptable in what used to be called "polite society."

A much tougher test is posed by the facts of *Village of Skokie v. National Socialist Party* and *Collin v. Smith*. These cases arose from the same circumstances: an attempt by the American Nazi Party to conduct a march in the largely Jewish suburb of Skokie, Illinois. . . .

Both the Illinois Supreme Court and the United States Court of Appeals for the Seventh Circuit were convinced that an affront to our sense of decency did not justify prohibiting the Nazis' march or their display of swastikas. The Seventh Circuit conceded that the Nazis' beliefs are repugnant to our "core values" and to "much of what we cherish in civilization." Nevertheless, under the first amendment, "there is no such thing as a false idea"; even the Nazis are entitled to compete in the marketplace of ideas. The Illinois Supreme Court, while admitting that the sight of swastikas is "abhorrent to the Jewish citizens of Skokie" and that the memories evoked are "offensive to the principles of a free nation," concluded with some reluctance that "it is entirely clear that this factor does not justify enjoining the defendants' speech." Both courts, incidentally, cited *Cohen* extensively.

It is a tribute to both courts that they ruled as they did despite obvious misgivings about the effect of their decisions. The Skokie cases ought to provoke misgivings. We ought not lightly decide to subject survivors of concentration camps to the nightmare of storm troopers marching through the streets. As a society, must we tolerate speech that so grievously offends the most basic values of our civilization?

Several years before Skokie, Professor Alexander Bickel presented a forceful argument that we should not tolerate this kind of speech. At some risk of oversimplification, his basic argument against tolerance may be summarized as follows: the necessary premise of the first amendment is that speech has important consequences. If we believed that "words don't matter, that they make nothing happen and are too trivial to bother with," then little reason would exist to refrain from regulating speech that annoys the majority. Yet, if speech does matter, speech like that of the Nazis must have the capacity for enormous harm. Bickel then addressed and rejected the arguments made by Justices Brandeis and Holmes for tolerating potentially harmful speech. Brandeis, with his usual faith in human nature, argued that further discussion "affords ordinarily adequate protection against the dissemination of noxious doctrine. . . ." In other words, bad ideas will not survive exposure to the marketplace of ideas. Holmes, with *his* usual toughmindedness, purported not to care: "If in the long run [these] beliefs . . . are destined to be accepted by the dominant forces of the community, the only meaning of free speech is that they should be given their chance and have their way." Bickel rejected Brandeis' optimism. In Bickel's view, to assume that further discussion will necessarily lead to the rejection of false ideas was to ignore the lesson

of history that [d]isastrously, unacceptably noxious doctrine can prevail." Nor did Bickel accept Holmes' purported indifference to the final product of the marketplace. Bickel's belief in the marketplace of ideas was not so strong that he was willing to accept the idea of genocide if enough people came to believe in it after full discussion. In his view, ideas such as genocide are not entitled to a fair chance to gain majority support. In short, Bickel was not willing to ignore the risk that truly horrible ideas may triumph in the marketplace.

Bickel saw another harm in tolerating unacceptable speech: he found in expressions such as "fuck the draft" a kind of verbal assault on the audience. He believed also that abusive language creates a moral climate in which antisocial conduct becomes more likely. As in the case of obscenity, he contended that "what is commonly read and seen and heard and done intrudes upon us all, wanted or not, for it constitutes our environment."

To imply that Bickel's appeal was a simple plea for repression, however, would be to misrepresent his views. As always, tension and ambiguity characterized his thoughts. He was keenly aware of the risks created by even the most limited grant of the power of censorship. As a consequence, he sought a workable accommodation rather than a clear resolution of conflicting values. Although his ultimate conclusions were not entirely clear, he seemed inclined toward the following position. First, he believed that we need to "resist the assertion of absolute claims." In particular, we should not acknowledge a positive right to engage in offensive speech, for to do so is to legitimize it. Second, we should control the risks created by restrictive laws through devices like the vagueness and overbreadth doctrines. Third, the very existence of restrictive laws, and "occasional but steady enforcement in aggravated cases," serve the important purpose of providing visible support for our basic social values. In sum, Bickel believed that in regulating this area, the law "walks a tightrope, and runs high risks," but that the effort is worth it, "[f]or the stakes are high.". . .

Harlan makes, in essence, two arguments for tolerance. The first is that banning offensive methods of expression is undesirable in itself. When symbols such as the swastika or four-letter words are banned, the speaker's ability to express his emotions and even his ideas is undesirably limited. Further, banning such speech is inappropriate because the decision to regulate must be based on subjective judgment; "one man's vulgarity is another's lyric." Second, even if offensive speech is not to be protected for its own sake, it must be protected as a necessary side effect of our basic decision to leave control of discourse in the hands of the people rather than the government. In view of the difficulty of line drawing, we cannot afford to open the door to censorship.

As applied to the Nazi march in Skokie, Harlan's first line of argument seems misplaced. While one man's vulgarity may be another man's lyricism, this kind of relativism is misguided when applied to the swastika. Rejecting the swastika is not on the same level of subjective taste as disliking garlic, if one has the slightest belief in the existence of moral standards. Perhaps banning the swastika limits expression of an idea. Bickel is surely right, however, that there is no affirmative societal interest in encouraging the uninhibited propagation of that idea. He is surely also right that genocide is not an issue on which we are prepared to abide by the results of a referendum. While the first amendment may give some protection to the expression of emotion, a person's desire to express vicious racial prejudices deserves no solicitude on our part. If this speech is to be protected, in short, the reason cannot be our concern that the Nazis might lose the opportunity to impart their message and convert new disciples.

Justice Harlan is on stronger ground in arguing that this speech, although worthless, must be tolerated because of the risks created by suppression. An attempt to purge public discourse of everything offensive and obnoxious undoubtedly would drastically impair the "robust and uninhibited" public debate we value. There is also force in Harlan's argument that it is risky to make any exceptions on this point, lest there be no principled stopping place. Finally, he is, one hopes, justified in his faith that our society is strong enough to shrug off the side effects of allowing even the most debased messages their place in the market.

Perhaps Harlan's argument is all the justification for tolerance we should require. Yet somehow it does not fully satisfy. It is true that if we began to make exceptions for especially horrible speech we would have to draw the line somewhere. Still, much of the law consists of rough but workable line drawing. In this situation, the line could be drawn generously enough to allow speech with any conceivable merit. Justice Harlan may be right that the risk, albeit small, is just not worth taking, but this is a rather negative reason for protecting speech. It rejects the practicability, but not the desirability, of suppression. To permit speech we detest would be more palatable if we believed that doing so served some positive purpose, rather than simply the negative one of preventing the slightest leak in the first amendment dike.

. . .

There is at the outset something reassuring and attractive about the notion of limiting discussion of [racist] ideas to the pleasant, civilized atmosphere we associate with academia, while ridding ourselves of crude, vehement expressions of racism. Yet on closer examination there is also something seriously wrong with this idea. Limiting expression of racist views to the calm, heavily qualified statements of scholars would give a completely misleading view of racist thinking. The truth is that racism in our society is far more often characterized by the ugliest of emotions. If many of its expressions are ugly, that is because the attitudes behind those expressions are ugly. The most obnoxious expressions of racism confront us with the offensiveness of the speakers and their ideas. We obtain an important truth from these speakers, although it is not a truth they mean to convey.

In the Skokie cases, if we take away the swastika, we take away the most vivid reminder of just how offensive the Nazis are. We need to be reminded of the consequences of their kinds of "ideas." We also need to be reminded that the Nazis are not just another group of harmless cranks: their views have a deadly potential that we must not be allowed to forget. In short, as in the case of racist invective, to reduce the ugliness of the Nazis' speech would only conceal the real ugliness, the ugliness of their ideas. That truth is too important to suppress merely to maintain our mental equanimity.

What of *Cohen v. California*? For the militarist, perhaps *Cohen* stands on all fours with the Skokie cases. To allow Cohen to use offensive language reinforces the offensiveness of his views. It also reveals the link between those views and rebellion against other American norms. For the rest of us, Cohen's message was within the bounds of the legitimately thinkable, and his use of strong language accurately reflected his views. After all, few things are more offensive than an unjust war.

In short, offensiveness is often an important part of the speaker's message. Use of offensive language reveals the existence of something offensive and ugly, whether in the situation described by the speaker or in the speaker's mind itself. In either event, the language reveals an important though unpleasant truth about the world. Suppressing this language violates a cardinal principle of a free society, that truths are better confronted than repressed. As long as we live in an ugly world, ugly speech must have its forum. We cannot expect to have, nor should we require, true civility in discourse until we achieve civility in society.

### III. CONCLUSION

Justice Harlan narrowed the issues in *Cohen* to a

single question: whether the state has the power to upgrade public discourse by banning offensive speech. He concluded that this power is lacking, a conclusion easy enough to accept in *Cohen*, but more difficult in cases like *Village of Skokie* and *Collin*, where the speech is more offensive and more clearly worthless. In this context, Professor Bickel's arguments become harder to refute. Yet there is much to be said for Harlan's counterargument that the benefits to be gained outweigh the risks created by even the most limited censorship.

The last portion of this Essay has attempted to bolster Harlan's argument with an additional rationale, that the most highly offensive forms of expression communicate an important truth about the offensiveness of the speaker's message. They have a place in the marketplace of ideas because they help the marketplace reject false, ugly ideas by revealing them for what they are. Acceptance of this rationale depends, of course, on a basic confidence in the ability of the people to understand and to act upon what they read and hear. It is this confidence in the American people that Justice Harlan so eloquently expressed in his *Cohen* opinion.

This Essay has stressed throughout the limits on the holding in *Cohen*. While *Cohen* says that offensive speech may not be banned outright, it says little about when such speech can be banned in particular contexts. It offers only limited guidance for determining to what extent government can protect people from involuntary exposure to offensive forms of expression. It does not even assure us that Paul Cohen was entitled to wear his jacket in the courthouse corridor. It does, however, establish one very important principle: the government is not entitled to assume the role of moral guardian and to set the standards of acceptable discourse. Establishment of that principle is an enduring contribution to our legal heritage.

---

Vincent Blasi, *Six Conservatives in Search of the First Amendment: The Revealing Case of Nude Dancing*, 33 William and Mary Law Review 611 (1992)*

## I. INTRODUCTION

The future of political freedom in the United States hardly turns on whether women have a First Amendment right to dance in the nude in bars and

* Reprinted with permission.

peep shows. The future of artistic freedom is perhaps implicated by this question, but only if the law's demand for general principle prohibits judges from treating expressive nudity in those environments as fundamentally different from expressive nudity in ballet performances, museum exhibitions, and films. *Barnes v. Glen Theatre, Inc.* is an interesting and potentially important case not because of the significance of the specific issue it decided, but because it provoked a lively debate among several articulate judicial conservatives. By looking closely at that debate, we may discern some of the themes and tensions that will be played out as the First Amendment enters a period of conservative dominance of the federal judiciary.

. . .

## III. THE BACKGROUND

The First Amendment issue posed by the prohibition of topless dancing reached the United States Supreme Court at an opportune time. The ascendancy of legal conservatism generated by a decade of centrally managed, ideologically screened appointments to the federal bench has given renewed impetus to the claim that the enforcement of morals is a legitimate function of law. The political mobilization of moralists over issues such as abortion, obscenity, and homosexuality has had a carry-over effect that has helped to focus public attention on the full spectrum of sexual practices and attitudes. Some prominent feminists have challenged the premises of libertarianism from the left, claiming that many forms of erotic display and depiction cause serious harm to women. Recently, traditional liberals were provoked and energized when conservative efforts to enforce morality strayed outside the confines of sleazy settings and extended to critically acclaimed museum exhibitions and government funding for avant garde theatre.

. . .

The timing of the *Glen Theatre* litigation helped to sharpen the issues raised by the case for yet another reason. Perhaps the most hotly debated contemporary free speech dispute concerns the wisdom and constitutionality of efforts by university officials, and occasionally by state legislatures, to regulate speech that is perceived by various groups, particularly women and members of racial minority groups, to denigrate, intimidate, or silence their members. On this issue, some conservatives challenge on principle the authority of officials to enforce a morality of personal respect, even as applied to particular instances of speech that are concededly intemperate, degrading, crude, and devoid of any kind of rational exposition. The First Amendment is indivisible, these conservatives say, and hate-speech codes inevitably will be applied indiscriminately. Liberals, on the other hand, seem more comfortable with the enforcement of morality in this context, and less concerned about the expansive potential of the censorial mentality. Can a principled conservative approve the enforcement of morals in the context of erotic dancing but not in the context of group vilification? Can a principled liberal argue that topless dancing is protected by the First Amendment but not the shouting of racial epithets? Important differences between the two categories of speech regulation may exist—hate speech ordinarily is not confined to settings in which every member of the audience has made a choice to receive the message, but hate speech also seems more political in character—but the response of many conservatives to the hate speech issue at least suggests that they do not invariably prefer a narrow interpretation of the First Amendment and do not always take a broad view of the state's power to enforce morality.

As the hate speech issue illustrates, the question of the proper scope of the state's power to enforce morality often is raised in conjunction with the question of what counts as "speech" in the constitutional sense. The ascendancy of conservatives on the federal bench may yield a conception of speech different from that which the courts have developed over the last fifty years. Just as in most contexts conservatives tend to be more concerned with diffuse harms to the moral fabric than are persons of other political persuasions, conservatives tend to emphasize qualities such as excellence, prudence, and civility. The more visceral, rambunctious, or flamboyant modes of communication may strike some conservative judges as outside the ambit of First Amendment concern, and thus not entitled to whatever protective doctrines govern disputes over genuine "speech" . . . Yet the implications of applying First Amendment principles in the realm of artistic expression are not easy to contain. If works of art, presumably including visual art, qualify for constitutional protection, why not artistic dances? Is a painting of a nude displayed in a museum more entitled to consideration under the First Amendment than a nude scene in a ballet or opera? And if a ballerina or a diva can legally disrobe, why not a go-go dancer?

A natural response would be to distinguish varieties of purported artistic expression on the basis of such factors as the presumed motivation of the dancers and their voyeurs and the degree to which the activity under review requires training and skill. Perhaps conservatives who value excellence are more willing than others to make these kinds of judgments, but they are judgments that are bound to turn heavily on the personal values of those who do the judging. In recent years, a central tenet of conservative constitutional thought has been the paramount responsibility of judges not to render decisions that depend heavily on their personal values. This tension between the quest for excellence and the fear of judicial subjectivity helps to make the issue of topless dancing a good test of judicial conservatism.

. . .

Finally, a fascinating aspect of the background to *Barnes v. Glen Theatre, Inc.* is that the most carefully reasoned Supreme Court precedent regarding the First Amendment and the enforcement of morality is *Cohen v. California*, in which Justice John Marshall Harlan, the quintessential judicial conservative, wrote an opinion for the majority holding unconstitutional a state's prohibition on the use of profane words in public. Harlan's opinion relied heavily on the conservative virtue of self-reliance, claiming that "each of us," not the government, has the responsibility to develop and abide by norms of permissible language use. He observed that the defendant's employment of a four letter word was neither legally obscene nor forced upon a captive audience, characteristics shared by the topless dances at issue in *Glen Theatre*. That a judge so conservative and so steeped in civility as Justice Harlan should have found in the First Amendment a bar against the enforcement of a morality of language illustrates how difficult it is to identify an orthodoxy of conservative thought regarding the freedom of speech.

## IV. THE OPINIONS

The *Glen Theatre* litigation caused judges at all levels of the federal judiciary to grapple with the various First Amendment issues raised by Indiana's prohibition of nude dancing. Twelve different judges published opinions. Although some other opinions are worthy of study, particularly those written by Judges Flaum and Coffey in the Seventh Circuit Court of Appeals, I shall examine the opinions written by six judges who have achieved special prominence as contributors to the conservative philosophy of constitutional interpretation. A close look at how each of these judges went about resolving this difficult case may enrich our understanding regarding what the ascendancy of legal conservatism portends for the freedom of speech.

### A. Richard Posner

In the Seventh Circuit, Judges Richard Posner and Frank Easterbrook, longtime colleagues on the University of Chicago Law School faculty and leading lights of the law-and-economics movement, engaged in a debate of a quality one rarely encounters in the pages of the law reports. . . . Despite their many affinities, the two judges sharply and passionately disagreed over whether striptease dancing is "speech" within the meaning of the First Amendment.

Judge Posner focused his analysis on the claim, accepted by the district court, that a striptease dance is "conduct" rather than "expressive activity" and hence outside the ambit of First Amendment concern. Posner called this conclusion "indefensible and a threat to artistic freedom." Perhaps reflecting the conservative economist's unwillingness to employ external criteria to ascribe differential value to personal preferences, Posner was at pains in his opinion to avoid letting class bias or aesthetic evaluation influence his assessment of the legal status of the dancing at issue. He equated for constitutional purposes Darlene Miller's nude dancing in the Kitty Kat Lounge in South Bend with the nude (under Indiana's definition) performance of the Dance of the Seven Veils in a recent production of the opera *Salome* at the Chicago Lyric Opera.

One might suppose that a defining feature of legal conservatism would be the willingness to notice some of the contextual differences between nude dancing in bars and in classical ballet performances. Conservatives pride themselves on their sensitivity to social context and their distrust of abstractions that lump together divergent, distinctive phenomena. Judge Posner duly noted the elements of barroom striptease that might cast doubt on its claim to First Amendment protection.

. . . But he was not persuaded. He recounted the long and varied history of striptease dancing from the satyr plays of ancient Greece to the scandalous performances of Sally Rand, Gypsy Rose Lee, and Isadora Duncan. He found in this history a refutation of the claim that striptease has more the quality of sexual encounter than artistic statement:

> The striptease was not invented in order to place a cultural patina on displays of naked women. Of course, there would be no female stripteases without a prurient interest in the female body; but that is just to say that there would be no erotic art without Eros. Though there is no striptease without some stripping—in today's moral climate, without a great deal of stripping—the dancing and the music are not distractions from the main theme, patched on to fool the censor; they are what make a given female body *expressive* of a specifically sexual emotion. . . .

Having established to his satisfaction that strip-

tease makes a statement, Posner considered the argument that such dancing "is not the *type* of expression that the First Amendment protects, because it is not the expression of ideas or opinions." He concluded that such a limitation on the scope of the First Amendment would have disturbing implications for the arts:

> If the striptease dancing at the Kitty Kat Lounge is not expression, Mozart's piano concertos and Balanchine's most famous ballets are not expression. This is not to suggest that striptease dancing is indistinguishable from these other forms of expression. But they cannot be distinguished on the ground that a piano concerto and a (nonpantomimic) ballet express ideas and a striptease expresses emotion. If the concert and the ballet have meaning—and I do not doubt that there is a meaningful sense in which they do—so has the striptease.

Judge Posner reinforced the point with a detailed analysis of Titian's painting of a voluptuous nude, *Venus with a Mirror*, on permanent display in the National Gallery of Art. . . .

. . .

To fail in the effort to place striptease dancing outside the ambit of First Amendment concern is not necessarily to conclude that such dancing is constitutionally immune from regulation. The State of Indiana argued that even if the striptease is speech in the First Amendment sense, it can be regulated under the state's power to enforce morality. Judge Posner rejected this contention. . . .

. . .

One might ask what is distinctively conservative about the Posner opinion. The proposition that drives his analysis is egalitarian in spirit: vulgar forms of erotic entertainment cannot be made illegal when much of what we call art is also, in essence, erotic entertainment for the better educated classes. Egalitarianism is not a value one usually associates with conservatism. A close reading of Judge Posner's opinion, however, reveals that his concern for equal treatment in the regulation of erotica derives from premises that are indeed conservative.

First, conservative economists are generally skeptical about the capacity of central planners to make interpersonal comparisons of utility, to decide which products provide the most value to consumers. These economists are respectful of the divergent preferences of different consumers and hesitant to base public policy on a centralized decision that one product (such as a particular form of erotic entertainment) has more intrinsic value for most persons than another product (such as a different form of erotic entertainment). In this view, preferences revealed in market behavior provide the best test of consumer value. The market for barroom and peep show striptease seems robust and resilient. Consumer preference is not the only factor to be taken into account—there remain serious questions of external harm, for example—but conservative economists consider consumer preference an important starting point for determining social value. Judge Posner no doubt was drawing on his background as a conservative economist when he wrote: "The Constitution does not look down its nose at popular culture even if its framers would have done so."

Second, the conservative aversion to judicial subjectivity seems to have played a major role in Judge Posner's analysis. He was quite willing to make the personal aesthetic judgment that the striptease dances at issue in the case were performed "with vigor but without accomplishment." . . . But Judge Posner did not believe that aesthetic judgments, his own or those of other judges, ought to play a role in demarcating the boundaries of the First Amendment. . . .

Third, modern conservatives profess a disdain for paternalism, not only for its inefficiency in economic terms but also for its adverse effect on character. Paternalism can be seen as a feudal impulse, a practice that engenders passivity, stasis, and hierarchical relationships, and that discourages experimentation and initiative. This view of the paternalism inherent in censorship seems to have informed Judge Posner's view of the topless dancing case. . . .

. . .

## B. Frank Easterbrook

Possibly provoked by Judge Posner's analysis, Judge Frank Easterbrook devoted most of his opinion to a call for precisely the kind of line drawing that Posner argued is illegitimate. Easterbrook saw differences of constitutional significance between barroom striptease and nude ballet. He considered the First Amendment to be concerned exclusively with the expression of "ideas," "thoughts," and "messages," not "emotions" as such. He disputed Judge Posner's contention that the striptease dances at issue conveyed a message of eroticism to barroom and peep show audiences in a manner comparable to the way such a message might be communicated by serious works of art:

> Sophisticates go to the museum and see Renoir's *Olympia* or to the opera and see a soprano strip during the Dance of the Seven Veils in Strauss' *Salome*. If the First Amendment

protects these expressions, the argument goes, Joe Sixpack is entitled to see naked women gyrate in the pub. Why does this follow? That a dance in *Salome* expresses something does not imply that a dance in JR's Kitty Kat Lounge expresses something, any more than the fact that Tolstoy's *Anna Karenina* was a stinging attack on the Russian social order implies that the scratching of an illiterate is likely to undermine the Tsar.

In defense of his refusal to draw lines between various forms of entertainment, Judge Posner had made much of the point that abstract art and nonprogrammatic music have less of an articulable message than a striptease. Posner labelled as "philistine" the "notion that all art worthy of the name has a 'message.'" He could not believe that under the First Amendment "Beethoven's string quartets are entitled to less protection than *Peter and the Wolf*." Drawing on his own considerable knowledge of the fine arts, Judge Easterbrook responded that for all serious works of art, those in which narrative does not predominate as well those in which it does, there *is* a message in the sense required by the First Amendment. . . . Easterbrook found no real message in striptease: "Barroom displays are to ballet as white noise is to music."

In contrast to Judge Posner's near hypersensitivity concerning the perils of cultural elitism, Judge Easterbrook seemed almost to relish the opportunity to draw lines, "to distinguish serious art from swill." One might be tempted to read into the Easterbrook opinion a judicial embrace of what some conservatives would call standards of excellence. The opinion is more complicated than that. Judge Easterbrook's ambitious effort to distinguish art from entertainment was at least as much the product of his concern about excessive judicial power as any view he may have about popular culture. He did, in fact, say that he would find the nude scene in the musical *Hair* to fall within the protection of the First Amendment.

For Judge Easterbrook, the obligation to interpret the First Amendment requires of a judge the willingness to draw lines, and to do so via the medium of categorical rules. Unless the ambit of First Amendment concern is demarcated with relative clarity, and demarcated in a way that excludes the all-embracing phenomenon of entertainment, courts would wind up evaluating the reasonableness of all legislative attempts to regulate entertainment. That would be substantive due process reincarnate. Judges can best prevent its recurrence "by insisting on categorical rules." With characteristic certitude, Judge Easterbrook explained his categorical understanding of the

First Amendment: "'Conduct' and 'speech' are the principal categories, and observing that distinction is essential if we wish to maintain the boundary between legislative and judicial roles in a democratic society."

. . .

Judge Easterbrook's call for categorical rules must be understood in the context of the modern conservative hostility to judicial review. For Easterbrook, any departure from categorical rules as a mode of legal analysis is likely to expand the power of the judiciary, in the case at hand by expanding the scope of First Amendment coverage. . . . Justices Frankfurter, Harlan, and Jackson were also deeply interested in limiting the role of the judiciary, but they believed the way to do that was to take into account the many variables that might bear on a case, reasoning that a judge aware of the complexity of a dispute would define his role narrowly. If Judge Easterbrook is representative, perhaps several decades of accumulated frustration over judicial activism have led modern legal conservatives to question that judgment and to opt instead for a more categorical approach to constitutional interpretation.

. . .

## C. William Rehnquist

One conservative who cannot be accused of attempting to strengthen the First Amendment by narrowing it is Chief Justice William Rehnquist. His opinion in *Glen Theatre* has precisely the opposite thrust: by finding topless dancing within the ambit of First Amendment concern, Rehnquist tried to seize the occasion to win acceptance for the proposition that the enforcement of morality is a proper basis for limiting the freedom of speech. His effort was only partially successful: only Justices Kennedy and O'Connor joined the Rehnquist opinion. Justices Scalia and Souter went out of their way to avoid having to endorse Chief Justice Rehnquist's proposition. . . .

If the "important or substantial governmental interest" requirement of the *O'Brien* test means something more than "legitimate," more than the minimum regulatory interest that would suffice to justify a law that restricted a liberty other than the freedom of speech, one might suppose that the interest in enforcing morality might have difficulty satisfying the test. Not only is this interest controversial in both scholarly and popular debate, but also claims of moral harm are exceedingly difficult to specify, confine, or calibrate. Because the enforcement of morality is the kind of interest that can be neither

tested nor balanced against competing interests, its invocation is likely to operate as a trump card in constitutional analysis. These problems need not force a judge to adopt as a matter of constitutional interpretation the moral philosophy of Professor Hart in preference to that of Lord Devlin. But in the limited realm of First Amendment adjudication, they might lead a judge to conclude that the otherwise legitimate state interest in enforcing morality ought not to be considered the kind of "important or substantial" governmental interest that can justify the regulation of speech that falls within the ambit of First Amendment concern.

Chief Justice Rehnquist was not persuaded by this line of argument. He recounted the venerable statutory history of morals regulation, in Indiana and elsewhere, and noted also the common law roots of the public indecency concept. Reciting the familiar trilogy of legitimate governmental interests, he refused to relegate morals enforcement to any kind of inferior status as a justification for limiting personal liberty: "[t]he traditional police power of the States is defined as the authority to provide for the public health, safety, and morals." He observed also that the Supreme Court had recognized the legitimacy of moral interests when it upheld state prohibitions on private, consensual homosexuality and obscenity. Pointedly, Rehnquist disclaimed any effort to bolster the interest in morals enforcement with an appeal to instrumental concerns, observing that "the governmental interest served by the text of the prohibition is societal disapproval of nudity in public places and among strangers. The statutory prohibition is not a means to some greater end, but an end in itself."

. . .

The Chief Justice declined to interpret the "unrelated to the suppression of free expression" element of the *O'Brien* test to mean that the harm that justifies the regulation must not be a product of the communicative impact of the activity the state wishes to regulate. Instead, he considered the appropriate inquiry to be whether by regulating the activity the state seeks to prevent a message from reaching an audience. It would be difficult to maintain that the moral objection to nude dancing is not a consequence of the communicative impact of the activity, and Rehnquist did not so maintain. Whether the moral objection relates to a "message" is more open to dispute. Rehnquist found the state's concern broader than that, and hence in his view "unrelated to the suppression of free expression":

> [W]e do not think that when Indiana applies its statute to the nude dancing in these night-

clubs it is proscribing nudity because of the erotic message conveyed by the dancers. Presumably numerous other erotic performances are presented at these establishments and similar clubs without any interference from the state, so long as the performers wear a scant amount of clothing. Likewise, the requirement that the dancers don pasties and a G-string does not deprive the dance of whatever erotic message it conveys; it simply makes the message slightly less graphic. The perceived evil that Indiana seeks to address is not erotic dancing, but public nudity. . . .

The Chief Justice refused to regard striptease dancing as outside the ambit of First Amendment concern, but he qualified his conclusion in a way that might suggest a limitation on the potential sweep of the morality justification. He stated: "nude dancing of the kind sought to be performed here is expressive conduct within the outer perimeters of the First Amendment, though we view it as only marginally so." Perhaps the enforcement of morality is a permissible justification in the realm of the First Amendment only when the activity regulated is "expressive conduct" rather than verbal speech. Or perhaps expressive conduct, nonverbal as well as verbal, is not subject to moral prohibition when the activity is more political, or in some other sense less peripheral, than is nude dancing. That notion might serve to distinguish the flagburning decisions. Perhaps by his comment about marginality, the Chief Justice meant to invoke a distinction between high culture and low culture such that impresarios and museum directors have nothing to fear from the decision in *Glen Theatre*. The logic of the Rehnquist opinion could accommodate some or all of these limitations on the power to enforce morality, but the opinion itself leaves these possibilities of containment unexplored.

. . .

## D. Antonin Scalia

Justice Antonin Scalia also rejected the contention that topless dancing enjoys constitutional protection, but he devoted a good part of his opinion in *Glen Theatre* to an effort to contain the doctrinal implications of that judgment. Like both Chief Justice Rehnquist and Judge Easterbrook, Scalia attributed much significance to the generality of Indiana's prohibition on public nudity. He noted that "Indiana officials have brought many public indecency prosecutions for activities having no communicative element." This generality principle has appealed to Justice Scalia for some time, and recently has been invoked by other conservative judges in a variety of contexts. If ap-

plied indiscriminately, the principle could be used to rewrite a great deal of First Amendment doctrine protective of speakers. It is important, therefore, that Justice Scalia, the judge who has given the principle its fullest articulation and defense, viewed the generality principle as applicable to only one subset of free speech disputes, cases involving the regulation of expressive conduct.

. . .

In *Glen Theatre*, Justice Scalia evinced no desire to employ the generality principle to rewrite First Amendment doctrine on a grand scale. So long as "oral and written speech" is involved, he expressed a willingness to subject state regulation to the traditionally demanding standard of scrutiny without regard to the generality of the prohibition: "When any law restricts speech, even for a purpose that has nothing to do with the suppression of communication (for instance to reduce noise, to regulate election campaigns, or to prevent littering), we insist that it meet the high, First-Amendment standard of justification." Moreover, for nonverbal forms of communication he would apply a comparably stringent level of judicial review "where the government prohibits conduct *precisely because of its communicative attributes*." Interestingly, in the flag burning cases Justice Scalia joined the majority opinions upholding the First Amendment claims of the protesters. Scalia discerned an appropriate way to confine his generality principle by utilizing the familiar distinction between speech and conduct: Laws that restrict "speech" are not saved by the fact that by design and definition they also restrict nonspeech activities; but laws that restrict nonverbal communicative conduct that falls within the ambit of First Amendment concern can be saved by their generality unless "suppressing communication was the object of the regulation of conduct."

. . . Although his opinion is not as explicit on this important point as one would like, Justice Scalia presumably would consider photography, film, painting, and sculpture to be "speech" even when words are not employed, but dance and mime "conduct" even when the gestures are stylized, choreographed, and unmistakably of narrative import. Apparently, the physical immediacy of live, human movement is the essential phenomenon that delimits the boundary of First Amendment concern except when such conduct is prohibited precisely because of the message it conveys. The implication of this analysis is that Justice Scalia would find no First Amendment violation in a state's application of its general public indecency statute against nude ballet (opera is more difficult because a diva might be singing or declaiming while disrobing), but would strike down the enforcement of such a statute against nonobscene depictions of nudes in painting, sculpture, or photography. Strauss's *Salome* is at risk, but Titian's *Venus* is safe.

. . .

Scalia stated his defense of the constitutional legitimacy of morals enforcement in the strongest terms, but he also offered a qualification that explains why he felt a great need to confine the scope of application of First Amendment principles. He said the enforcement of morality is not problematic "absent specific constitutional protection for the conduct involved." By clear implication, Justice Scalia was reluctant to permit morality to serve as a constitutionally sufficient basis for the regulation of activities that qualify as "speech" in the First Amendment sense. . . .

. . .

E. David Souter

. . .

Justice Souter agreed with Judge Posner and Chief Justice Rehnquist, and disagreed with Judge Easterbrook and Justice Scalia, that striptease dancing enjoys "a degree of First Amendment protection." Not all nude display is expression in the First Amendment sense nor is all dancing, ballroom and aerobic dancing for example. But "dancing as a performance directed to an actual or hypothetical audience gives expression at least to generalized emotion or feeling, and where the dancer is nude or nearly so the feeling expressed, in the absence of some contrary clue, is eroticism, carrying an endorsement of erotic experience." Souter conceded that nudity by itself can be expressive. He thought, however, that the First Amendment requires more:

> [T]he voluntary assumption of that condition, without more, apparently expresses nothing beyond the view that the condition is somehow appropriate to the circumstances. But every voluntary act implies some such idea, and the implication is thus so common and minimal that calling all voluntary activity expressive would reduce the concept of expression to the point of the meaningless.

He found the extra dimensions of expression provided by the integration of music, dance, and disrobing sufficient to differentiate striptease from common forms of indecent public exposure.

. . .

Both in his effort to delineate the scope of the First Amendment's concern with expressive conduct and in his effort to confine the domain of the *O'Brien* test, Justice Souter displayed a willingness to search for limiting principles. That aspect of his temperament may also explain why he could not accept Chief Justice Rehnquist's proposition that the state's interest in the enforcement of morality can serve as a justification for restricting activities that enjoy First Amendment protection. After noting his areas of agreement with the Chief Justice's view of the case, Souter said: "I nonetheless write separately to rest my concurrence in the judgment, not on the possible sufficiency of society's moral views to justify the limitations at issue, but on the State's substantial interest in combating the secondary effects of adult entertainment establishments of the sort typified by respondents' establishments."

Justice Souter plainly considers material harms to be the preferable, and possibly the exclusive, basis for restricting First Amendment rights of expression. In the case of striptease dancing, he found those material harms in the possible link between such dancing in certain settings and "prostitution, sexual assault, and associated crimes." Of course, such a causal link is disputable, and certainly was not proven in the record to have existed regarding the particular dances at issue. Moreover, even if prostitutes were shown to have solicited outside the Kitty Kat Lounge or if rapes had been committed by patrons of the *Glen Theatre*, the standard of causation the Court applies to speech at the center of First Amendment concern would not have been satisfied. Presumably no one would claim that the dances of Ms. Miller and Ms. Sutro were "directed to inciting or producing imminent lawless action and likely to incite or produce such action." One reason those who would regulate expression seek the authority to invoke moral justifications is that justifications grounded in claims of material harm are more susceptible to demands for evidence and requirements of temporal proximity.

Justice Souter acknowledged this difficulty with his analysis but proposed a way to avoid the demanding standard of causation that has been a central feature of First Amendment doctrine since the opinions of Holmes and Brandeis. Souter reasoned that although sexually explicit expressive conduct enjoys "a degree of First Amendment protection," it does not warrant the level of protection accorded the most highly valued forms of expression. Twice in his opinion he made this point, each time citing the cases in which the Supreme Court had upheld zoning restrictions on theaters showing sexually explicit but nonobscene films on the basis of a presumed, generalized causal connection between the presence of such theaters and neighborhood deterioration. In one of those cases Justice Stevens, writing for a plurality, said: "[S]ociety's interest in protecting this type of expression is of a wholly different, and lesser, magnitude than the interest in untrammeled political debate." Justice Souter quoted this statement with approval.

Justice Souter's willingness to apply special, less protective First Amendment standards to striptease dancing on the ground "that the protection of sexually explicit expression may be of lesser societal importance than the protection of other forms of expression" raises a number of questions. First, if we are to have such a multitiered First Amendment, perhaps the enforcement of morality ought to be considered a cognizable regulatory interest on the lower tiers. Souter seems to have rejected this course in *Glen Theatre*. He strained to find a sufficient causal connection to material harm in order to avoid having to rely on the morality justification, even when the speech at issue ranks low on his scale of First Amendment value.

Second, if generalized, undocumented claims of causal connection to material harm can justify the regulation of sexually explicit expression, what constitutional principle protects nude ballet, painting, sculpture, and "serious" film? Souter suggested that the likelihood of material secondary effects varies depending on the setting in which the sexually explicit expression is viewed. That variation supplies the elusive principled basis for distinguishing high-culture nudity from its low-life counterpart. . . .

Third, if speculative, delayed effects can sometimes justify the regulation of First Amendment expression "of lesser societal importance," can sexist, racist, and other varieties of stereotyping employed in nonpolitical speech be regulated on account of the long-term harm such speech causes members of the groups so stereotyped? Justice Souter did not address this question, but he defined "secondary effects" in such a way that the diffuse, delayed, but nonetheless potentially substantial consequences of stereotyping would not qualify. If the material harms could result only from "the persuasive effect" of speech, he said, they cannot serve as a justification for regulation under the secondary effects rationale. Only harms that are caused in some other way count as "secondary effects." . . . Souter did not explain how Indiana's requirement that go-go dancers wear pasties and a G-string could be thought, even speculatively, to have any incremental impact on the secondary effects he had posited.

On the evidence of his opinion in *Glen Theatre*,

Justice Souter's brand of judicial conservatism builds on the virtues of careful attention to nuance and context and the disinclination to employ sweeping propositions. That type of conservatism can produce doctrines that are overly complex and judgments that lack courage. On the other hand, humility and patience are conservative virtues of the first order that often correlate with the willingness to notice distinctions and the desire to identify limiting principles. For those who believe that the concept of conservatism speaks to temperament more than to first principles, Justice Souter may better deserve the label than any of his brethren.

Justice Souter may be a true conservative in the sense just described, but his opinion does not leave one convinced that he is a judge worthy of being compared with Justice Harlan in the matter of intellectual self-discipline. Why was Justice Souter so quick to credit without any evidence the claim that nonobscene nude dancing bears a significant causal connection to rape or sexual assault? Why did he not address the troubling point for his rationale that if nonobscene nude dancing might indirectly lead to a higher incidence of sexual assault, so too might live erotic dancing by partially clothed women as well as sexually suggestive depictions and plots in nonobscene films? . . .

F. Byron White

Some might question whether Justice Byron White, the lone member of the Supreme Court appointed by a Democratic president (Kennedy), should be considered a conservative. . . .

With regard to the First Amendment, however, Justice White's credentials as a conservative are impeccable. . . .

In *Glen Theatre*, Justice White wrote a dissenting opinion that Justices Blackmun, Marshall, and Stevens joined. It is noteworthy that a Justice with such a conservative history regarding interpretation of the First Amendment should have concluded that nude dancing enjoys constitutional protection. That Justice White wrote the Court's opinion in *Bowers v. Hardwick*, upholding a state's enforcement of morality against consensual homosexual relations, adds further interest to his dissent in *Glen Theatre*.

It seems that with regard to the effort to criminalize nude dancing, Justice White's longstanding hostility to legal claims of a symbolic, unspecific character worked to the detriment of the state's assertion of regulatory authority. He plainly was skeptical regarding what Indiana hoped to achieve by this law. He noted that "it is impossible to discern the exact state interests which the Indiana legislature had in mind when it enacted the Indiana statute.'' He criticized Chief Justice Rehnquist's opinion for accepting ''societal order and morality'' as a sufficiently specific and informative description of the state's regulatory interest. White then tried to supply the missing specification on his own. The state could not be concerned with protecting unwilling or inadvertent viewers from offense because the dances at issue were performed indoors before willing, fully forewarned audiences. Nor could the state be enforcing a judgment that nudity in the presence of other persons is always indecent or degrading because Indiana asserted no authority or desire to start prosecuting the full range of nude encounters, for example among friends and relatives in homes or among strangers in locker rooms. On this point, Justice White distinguished the Court's prior decisions upholding comprehensive prohibitions, applicable without regard to setting or context, on the destruction of draft cards, the practice of homosexuality, and the smoking of peyote.

Because nudity per se is not the evil to be addressed, Justice White concluded that the rationale for the law must have something to do with the state's desire to protect willing viewers from the impact of the experience of viewing nude figures in certain settings, as contrasted with other settings in which the impact would be different. But what is special, in terms of the impact on viewers, about the setting of a bar or a theater in which nude women perform dances to music? What is special, Justice White concluded, is the erotic message that is conveyed by that variety of nudity:

> Legislators do not just randomly select certain conduct for proscription; they have reasons for doing so and those reasons illuminate the purpose of the law that is passed. . . . The purpose of the proscription in these contexts is to protect the viewers from what the State believes is the harmful message that nude dancing communicates.

The state denied that it sought to prevent the communication of an erotic message by noting that all sorts of erotic dances, including those employing the barest minimum of clothing (pasties and a G-string), remained outside the reach of the law. Nudity, not an erotic message, was the trigger of illegality. Justice White was not convinced: ''The sight of a fully clothed, or even a partially clothed, dancer generally will have a far different impact on a spectator than that of a nude dancer, even if the same dance is performed. The nudity is itself an expressive component of the dance, not merely incidental 'conduct.''''

To conclude that when unpacked analytically the State's interest in ''order and morality'' reduces to an interest in protecting audiences from certain erotic messages still does not prove that the state interest is constitutionally insufficient. Many conservatives would not deny that the harm in nude dancing is indeed in the message it communicates, and would claim that a proper function of government is to prevent the degradation of the society, including the degradation that is caused by certain messages.

This type of argument might appeal to many conservatives, but not to a tough-minded, skeptical conservative like Justice White, who values both analytical precision and proof of harm. He is not impressed by quixotic gestures in defense of morality or speculative judgments regarding the long-term cultural consequences of certain messages. He concluded that both legislatures and judges must have more solid grounding before overriding the First Amendment principle against content regulation. . . .

From Edmund Burke to Michael Oakeshott, leading conservative thinkers traditionally have been skeptical of ideology, partly because a devotion to ideology can lead one to a single-minded pursuit of objectives and a failure to appreciate the complexity of life, the relevance of history, and the efficacy of arrangements that have survived the evolutionary process. Justice White appears to share those sentiments. Not all conservatives would consider the moral objection to public nudity to be an ideology, nor the common practice of nude go-go dancing to be a social institution worthy of respect by virtue of the fact that it has evolved and commands a market. But regulation in the name of morality does often tend to have a zealous quality about it. Moreover, because the exact interests at stake are seldom specified, moral regulation is not easily subjected to the disciplining influence of law. Those characteristics need not trouble a conservative when the activities in dispute enjoy no constitutional protection. However, a conservative who views erotic dancing as a form of ''speech'' within the meaning of the First Amendment has to be troubled by the boundless quality of the moral justification for regulating speech. In turning against moralists the conservative disdain for excess and reductionism and the conservative regard for analytical rigor, Justice White challenged his fellow conservatives to develop an understanding of the First Amendment that is true to their professed principles.

. . .

# Bibliography

*Indecency and Violence*

Albert, James A., *Constitutional Regulation of Televised Violence*, 64 Virginia Law Review 1299 (1978)

Blanchard, Margaret A., *The American Urge to Censor: Freedom of Expression Versus the Desire to Sanitize Society—from Anthony Comstock to 2 Live Crew*, 33 William & Mary Law Review 741 (1992)

Cohen, William, *A Look Back at* Cohen v. California, 34 UCLA Law Review 1595 (1987)

Crigler, John & Byrnes, William J., *Decency Redux: The Curious History of the New FCC Broadcast Indency Policy*, 38 Catholic University Law Review 329 (1989)

Dyk, Timothy D. & Schiffer, Lois, *The FCC, the Congress and Indecency on the Air*, 8 Communications Lawyer 8 (Winter 1990)

Lively, Donald E., *Deregulatory Illusions and Broadcasting: The First Amendment's Enduring Forked Tongue*, 66 North Carolina Law Review 963 (1988)

Post, Robert C., *The Constitutional Concept of Public Discourse: Outrageous Opinion, Democratic Deliberation, and* Hustler Magazine v. Falwell, 103 Harvard Law Review 601 (1990)

Tovey, Morgan W., *Dial-a-Porn and the First Amendment: The State Action Loophole*, 40 Federal Communications Law Journal 267 (1988)

Weinberg, Jonathan, *Broadcasting and Speech*, 81 California Law Review 1103 (1993).

## D. Future Media and the First Amendment

Medium specific First Amendment standards present a looming choice in constitutional models for the future. As media increasingly acquire multidimensional capabilities, it is difficult to define them in traditional terms. To the extent print media use satellite technology to transmit work product from editorial to printing plants, and broadcasters or cable deliver text, traditional lines of distinction already have become blurred. As broadband services provide the basis for interactive communication, the potential exists for renewal of a soapbox society that for much of this century was superseded by the emergence of mass media. Ithiel de Sola Pool expresses his concern that, as technology provides new speaking opportunities, increasingly anachronistic methods of editorial management will survive and dominate media governance. Allen S. Hammond, IV suggests a public forum analysis for emerging broadband communication services as a basis for factoring competing speech interests.

Ithiel de Sola Pool, *Technologies of Freedom*
(1983)*

1. A Shadow Darkens

Civil liberty functions today in a changing technological context. For five hundred years a struggle
was fought, and in a few countries won, for the
right of people to speak and print freely, unlicensed,
uncensored, and uncontrolled. But new technologies
of electronic communication may now relegate old
and freed media such as pamphlets, platforms, and
periodicals to a corner of the public forum. Electronic modes of communication that enjoy lesser
rights are moving to center stage. The new communication technologies have not inherited all the legal
immunities that were won for the old. When wires,
radio waves, satellites, and computers became major
vehicles of discourse, regulation seemed to be a technical necessity. And so, as speech increasingly flows
over those electronic media, the five-century growth
of an unabridged right of citizens to speak without
controls may be endangered. . . .

Although the first principle of communications
law in the United States is the guarantee of freedom
in the First Amendment, in fact this country has a
trifurcated communications system. In three domains
of communication—print, common carriage, and
broadcasting—the law has evolved separately, and in
each domain with but modest relation to the others.

In the domain of print and other means of communication that existed in the formative days of the
nation, such as pulpits, periodicals, and public meetings, the First Amendment truly governs. In well
over one hundred cases dealing with publishing, can-
vassing, public speeches, and associations, the Supreme Court has applied the First Amendment to the
media that existed in the eighteenth century.

In the domain of common carriers, which includes
the telephone, the telegraph, the postal system, and
now some computer networks, a different set of policies has been applied, designed above all to ensure
universal service and fair access by the public to the
facilities of the carrier. That right of access is what
defines a common carrier: it is obligated to serve all
on equal terms without discrimination.

Finally, in the domain of broadcasting, Congress
and the courts have established a highly regulated
regime, very different from that of print. On the

grounds of a supposed scarcity of usable frequencies
in the radio spectrum, broadcasters are selected by
the government for merit in its eyes, assigned a slice
each of the spectrum of frequencies, and required to
use that assignment fairly and for community welfare
as defined by state authorities. The principles of
common carriage and of the First Amendment have
been applied to broadcasting in only atrophied form.
For broadcasting, a politically managed system has
been invented.

The electronic modes of twentieth century communication, whether they be carriers or broadcasters,
have lost a large part of the eighteenth and nineteenth
century constitutional protections of no prior restraint, no licenses, no special taxes, no regulations,
and no laws. Every radio spectrum user, for example, must be licensed. This requirement started in
1912, almost a decade before the beginning of broadcasting, at a time when radio was used mainly for
maritime communication. Because the United States
Navy's communications were suffering interference,
Congress, in an effort at remedy, imposed licensing
on transmitters, thereby breaching a tradition that
went back to John Milton against requiring licenses
for communicating.

Regulation as a response to perceived technical
problems has now reached the point where transmissions enclosed in wires or cables, and therefore causing no over-the-air interference, are also licensed and
regulated. . . .

The mystery is how the clear intent of the Constitution, so well and strictly enforced in the domain
of print, has been so neglected in the electronic revolution. The answer lies partly in changes in the prevailing concerns and historical circumstances from
the time of the founding fathers to the world of today;
but it lies at least as much in the failure of Congress
and the courts to understand the character of the new
technologies. Judges and legislators have tried to fit
technological innovations under conventional legal
concepts. The errors of understanding by these scientific laymen, though honest, have been mammoth.
They have sought to guide toward good purposes
technologies they did not comprehend.

"It would seem," wrote Alexis de Tocqueville,
"that if despotism were to be established among the
democratic nations of our days . . . it would be
more extensive and more mild; it would degrade men
without tormenting them." This is the kind of mild
but degrading erosion of freedom that our system of
communication faces today, not a rise of dictators
or totalitarian movements. The threat in America,
as Tocqueville perceived, is from well-intentioned
policies, with results that are poorly foreseen. The

---

danger is "tutelary power," which aims at the happiness of the people but also seeks to be the "arbiter of that happiness.". . .

The erosion of traditional freedoms that has occurred as government has striven to cope with problems of new communications media would not have surprised Tocqueville, for it is a story of how, in pursuit of the public good, a growing structure of controls has been imposed. But one part of the story would have surprised him, for it tells how a legal institution that he overlooked, namely the First Amendment, has up to now maintained the freedom and individualism that he saw as endangered.

A hundred and fifty years from now, today's fears about the future of free expression may prove as alarmist as Tocqueville's did. But there is reason to suspect that our situation is more ominous. What has changed in twentieth century communications is its technological base. Tocqueville wrote in a pluralistic society of small enterprises where the then new mass media consisted entirely of the printed press which the First Amendment protected. In the period since his day, new and mostly electronic media have proliferated in the form of great oligopolistic networks of common carriers and broadcasters. Regulation was a natural response. Fortunately and strangely, as electronics advances further, another reversal is now taking place, toward growing decentralization and toward fragmentation of the audience of the newest media. The transitional era of giant media may nonetheless leave a permanent set of regulatory practices implanted on a system that is coming to have technical characteristics that would otherwise be conducive to freedom.

The interaction over the past two centuries between the changing technologies of communication and the practice of free speech, I would argue, fits a pattern that is sometimes described as "soft technological determinism." Freedom is fostered when the means of communication are dispersed, decentralized, and easily available, as are printing presses or microcomputers. Central control is more likely when the means of communication are concentrated, monopolized, and scarce, as are great networks. But the relationship between technology and institutions is not simple or unidirectional, nor are the effects immediate. Institutions that evolve in response to one technological environment persist and to some degree are later imposed on what may be a changed technology. The First Amendment came out of a pluralistic world of small communicators, but it shaped the present treatment of great national networks. Later on, systems of regulation that emerged for national common carriers and for the use of

"scarce" spectrum for broadcasting tended to be imposed on more recent generations of electronic technologies that no longer require them. . . .

Today, in an era of advanced (and still advancing) electronic theory, it has become possible to build virtually any kind of communications device that one might wish, though at a price. The market, not technology, sets most limits. For example, technology no longer imposes licensing and government regulation. That pattern was established for electronic media a half-century ago, when there seemed to be no alternative, but the institutions of control then adopted persist. That is why today's alarms could turn out to be more portentous than Tocqueville's.

The key technological change, at the root of the social changes, is that communication, other than conversation face to face, is becoming overwhelmingly electronic. Not only is electronic communication growing faster than traditional media of publishing, but also the convergence of modes of delivery is bringing the press, journals, and books into the electronic world. One question raised by these changes is whether some social features are inherent in the electronic character of the emerging media. Is television the model of the future? Are electromagnetic pulses simply an alternative conduit to deliver whatever is wanted, or are there aspects of electronic technology that make it different from print—more centralized or more decentralized, more banal or more profound, more private or more government dependent?

The electronic transformation of the media occurs not in a vacuum but in a specific historical and legal context. Freedom for publishing has been one of America's proudest traditions. But just what is it that the courts have protected, and how does this differ from how the courts acted later when the media through which ideas flowed came to be the telegraph, telephone, television, or computers? What images did policy makers have of how each of these media works; how far were their images valid; and what happened to their images when the facts changed?

In each of the three parts of the American communications system—print, common carriers, and broadcasting—the law has rested on a perception of technology that is sometimes accurate, often inaccurate, and which changes slowly as technology changes fast. Each new advance in the technology of communications disturbs a status quo. It meets resistance from those whose dominance it threatens, but if useful, it begins to be adopted. Initially, because it is new and a full scientific mastery of the options is not yet at hand, the invention comes into use in a rather clumsy form. Technical laymen, such as judges, perceive the new technology in that early, clumsy form, which then becomes their image of its nature, possibilities, and use. This perception is an incubus on later understanding.

The courts and regulatory agencies in the American system (or other authorities elsewhere) enter as arbiters of the conflicts among entrepreneurs, interest groups, and political organizations battling for control of the new technology. The arbiters, applying familiar analogies from the past to their lay image of the new technology, create a partly old, partly new structure of rights and obligations. The telegraph was analogized to railroads, the telephone to the telegraph, and cable television to broadcasting. The legal system thus invented for each new technology may in some instances, like the First Amendment, be a *tour de force* of political creativity, but in other instances it may be less worthy. The system created can turn out to be inappropriate to more habile forms of the technology which gradually emerge as the technology progresses. This is when problems arise, as they are arising so acutely today.

Historically, the various media that are now converging have been differently organized and differently treated under the law. The outcome to be feared is that communications in the future may be unnecessarily regulated under the unfree tradition of law that has been applied so far to the electronic media. The clash between the print, common carrier, and broadcast models is likely to be a vehement communications policy issue in the next decades. Convergence of modes is upsetting the trifurcated system developed over the past two hundred years, and questions that had seemed to be settled centuries ago are being reopened, unfortunately sometimes not in a libertarian way. . . .

The American case is unique only in the specific feature of the First Amendment and in the role of the courts in upholding it. The First Amendment, as interpreted by the courts, provides an anchor for freedom of the press and thus accentuates the difference between publishing and the electronic domain. Because of the unique power of the American courts, the issue in the United States unfolds largely in judicial decisions. But the same dilemmas and trends could be illustrated by citing declarations of policy and institutional structures in each advanced country.

If the boundaries between publishing, broadcasting, cable television, and the telephone network are indeed broken in the coming decades, then communications policies in all advanced countries must address the issue of which of the three models will dominate public policy regarding them. Public interest regulation could begin to extend over the print media as those media increasingly use regulated electronic channels. Conversely, concern for the traditional notion of a free press could lead to finding ways to free the electronic media from regulation. The policies adopted, even among free nations, will differ, though with much in common. The problems in all of them are very much the same.

The phrase "communications policy" rings oddly in a discussion of freedom from government. But freedom is also a policy. The question it poses is how to reduce the public control of communications in an electronic era. A policy of freedom aims at pluralism of expression rather than at dissemination of preferred ideas. . . .

. . . The specific question to be answered is whether the electronic resources for communication can be as free of public regulation in the future as the platform and printing press have been in the past. Not a decade goes by in free countries, and not a day in the world, without grim oppressions that bring protesters once more to picket lines and demonstrations. Vigilance that must be so eternal becomes routine, and citizens grow callous.

The issue of the handling of the electronic media is the salient free speech problem for this decade, at least as important for this moment as were the last generation's issues for them, and as the next generation's will be for them too. But perhaps it is more than that. The move to electronic communication may be a turning point that history will remember. Just as in seventeenth- and eighteenth-century Great Britain and America a few tracts and acts set precedents for print by which we live today, so what we think and do today may frame the information system for a substantial period in the future.

In that future society the norms that govern information and communication will be even more crucial than in the past. Those who read, wrote, and published in the seventeenth and eighteenth centuries, and who shaped whatever heritage of art, literature, science, and history continues to matter today, were part of a small minority, well under one-tenth of the work force. Information activities now occupy the lives of much of the population. In advanced societies about half the work force are "information processors." It would be dire if the laws we make today governing the dominant mode of information handling in such an information society were subversive of its freedom. The onus is on us to determine whether free societies in the twenty-first century will conduct electronic communication under the conditions of freedom established for the domain of print through centuries of struggle, or whether that great achievement will become lost in a confusion about new technologies.

Allen S. Hammond, IV, *Regulating Broadband Communication Networks*, 9 YALE JOURNAL OF REGULATION 181 (1992)*

## I. INTRODUCTION

The United States is on the brink of yet another communications revolution. This time the revolution is precipitated by the merging of computer, telephone, and fiber optic technologies into broadband communications networks (BCNs). Each of these technologies contributes critical characteristics which, when combined, change the manner in which users will communicate. Computer technology contributes the ability to store, retrieve, manipulate, and control the flow of information. Telephony networking technology contributes the ability to engage in interactive communication. Fiber optics technology contributes the ability to communicate using various types of information integrated over one transmission path or network. BCN technology ultimately allows for the replacement of the currently separate information delivery modes of print, broadcasting/cable, and telephone.

These networks will interconnect many users. Large network providers such as the telephone companies could provide BCNs that are accessible to the general public. Single users or groups of private users will likely own BCNs that connect multiple communications stations in single or multiple locations. BCNs will also support the high speed transmission of integrated voice, data and video information in digital form, which will integrate the transport of voice, data, and video information and promote two-way interaction between users.

These two characteristics transform broadband communications technology into more than the functional sum of the computer, fiber optic, and telephone technologies and more than an extension of the existing publishing, broadcasting, cable, and telecommunications networks. When BCNs interconnect users, the combined technology will change not only the manner in which information is used, but also the manner in which information is communicated. The public will be able to receive, seek out, identify, store, manipulate, compose, alter, filter, and transmit digitized data, print, video, and voice information. Moreover, users will be able to select who receives their information.

Electronic communication will no longer be a predominantly passive mode of interaction conducted via one-way, single-format information streams controlled by a limited number of senders. Instead, communication will be an interactive process conducted via two-way, multiple-format information streams controlled by users of the media. BCNs thus have the potential to shift the locus of control over communication from the privileged government-sanctioned media to a greater portion of the public.

Most important, however, this new control will allow individuals and groups to become electronic speakers and publishers. The ability to determine what information is received, how it is manipulated, and where it is sent allows the user to exercise editorial control over his or her multi-media speech. The user's capacity to send and receive interactively also provides the ability to "assemble" a group electronically. Finally, as the number of speakers increases, the diversity of available information is likely to increase as well.

BCNs have the potential to expand opportunities for speech and assembly dramatically. However, with a faulty regulatory scheme, BCNs could further centralization of control over the means of information transmission. . . .

This article begins to identify BCNs' potential for expanding user speech, access, and assembly rights and concludes that such rights are protected by the First Amendment. The article proceeds to question the appropriateness of applying the current regulatory models of print, broadcast and cable, or common carriage to protect the panoply of speech rights created by BCNS, and concludes that broadband technology demands a new regulatory scheme. . . .

The article concludes by proposing a possible resolution of the constitutional dispute over the regulation of speech. The resolution favors a model in which public and private communication forums coexist. Recognizing a distinction between public and private forums will protect the First Amendment rights of both the providers and the users while limiting the potential for government and private censorship. . . .

## II. HOLDING MARKET AND REGULATORY LINES AGAINST A "SANDSTORM OF SILICON"

. . .

### B. Entry Into the Broadband Marketplace: The Coming Competition In Multi-Media Information Distribution

The use of broadband technology has begun to

erode the market protection previously enjoyed by the traditional information distribution industries. Further, as the technology and information-related distinctions vanish, regulatory protection of the distinct markets no longer makes sense. The removal of these protections will increase opportunities for market entry. Consequently, each industry has a significant stake in controlling the development, deployment, and use of broadband technology.

### C. "A Regulatory Nightmare in the Making"

. . .

Historically, market entry and technological considerations have shaped the distribution of the First Amendment rights between media providers and the public. Media owners in each industry have been accorded First Amendment rights based in part on the ease of entry into each market.

In print, speech was unregulated because it was assumed that anyone could publish. There was no perceived need for the government to assure access.

The initial scarcity of broadcast frequencies made acquisition of the means of transmission more problematic. All those who sought to broadcast could not do so without substantial signal interference, so the government licensed only a few broadcasters. However, by requiring the broadcast licensee to share his or her frequency with the public, government regulation sought to reduce the impact of the broadcasters' control over the channel of communication.

Similarly, cable television franchises were scarce because of the physical limits inherent in the use of public rights of way. The economies of scale exacerbated this physical scarcity. Because all who sought to cablecast could not do so, the cable franchisee was required to share his or her channels of communication with the public.

In telephony, the need for interconnection and economies of scale led to the creation of government-sanctioned monopolies. Government then sought to assure public access by prohibiting discrimination between customers on the basis of facilities or the price paid for the services provided. As a further means of preventing discrimination, regulations deprived the telephone company of any control over the content of the information transmitted.

There is a critical relationship between regulatory policy assumptions regarding market entry and competition and the scope of First Amendment rights afforded media owners. Therefore, any regulation of market entry and competition in broadband should include explicit recognition of its impact on the First Amendment rights of broadband providers and consumers.

Since the lines between publishing, broadcasting and the telephone network are now being broken, the question arises as to which of these three models will dominate public policy regarding the new media. There is bound to be debate with sharp divisions between conflicting interests.

The evolving regulatory "nightmare" provides the Congress, the FCC, and the courts with an opportunity to eschew the piecemeal approach to communications policy, and instead base regulation on the underlying First Amendment premises of communications and telecommunications.

### III. APPLYING AN EIGHTEENTH CENTURY FIRST AMENDMENT TO A TWENTY-FIRST CENTURY TECHNOLOGY

The access afforded by communication technology has traditionally shaped regulation. Since there are supposedly few economic barriers to entry in print, regulation has been sparse. The newspaper owner enjoys almost complete freedom of speech while the public enjoys no right to access.

In broadcast or cable television, spectrum or franchise scarcity limits market entry, and so regulation tries to assure some public access. Broadcasters, for instance, must allow access to political candidates, and cablecasters of a certain size must set aside channels for public or commercial use. Entry into the common carrier market is economically difficult, and so regulators have limited common carriers' speech rights.

The courts have contributed to these models: "applying familiar analogies from the past to their lay image of the new technology, [the judiciary] create[s] a partly old, partly new structure of rights and obligations. For instance, the courts have compared and distinguished broadcasting and print; cable television and print and broadcasting; and direct broadcast satellites and video subscription and print, broadcasting, and common carriage. The courts would likely compare broadband distribution networks to print, broadcasting, cable, and common carriage and regulate BCNs based on an amalgamation of previous regulatory models. . . .

. . . Moreover, technological, physical, or economic scarcity, the primary justification for much of government regulation of electronic mass media, is diminishing as technology creates more potential media outlets. However, interpretations of the First Amendment which emphasize the "private liberty" or print model fail to acknowledge the notion of equality prevalent in American political philosophy.

Moreover, proponents of the "private liberty" model rely on flawed assumptions regarding the marketplace of ideas. . . .

A. Liberty, Equality, and Electronic Speech

. . .

The difficulty with the private liberty model of the First Amendment is what it ignores or dismisses. Large corporations controlling communication through liberal FCC multiple and cross-ownership rules have the power to suppress speech far in excess of that possessed by a private single person. Further, large corporations have suppressed speech when their interests have benefited by suppression. This corporate power is more akin to that wielded by the government than that wielded by the private individual.

Further, the private liberty theory of the First Amendment rests in large part on assumptions about liberty which parallel the flawed theory of free market capitalism. The marketplace theory falsely assumes that bargainers are basically equal in power, that true competition exists, and that all bargainers possess adequate, if not perfect knowledge. The marketplace of ideas also suffers from real world ailments which undermine its effectiveness. "[S]ophisticated and expensive communications technology, monopoly control of the media, access limitations suffered by disfavored or impoverished groups, techniques of behavior manipulation [advertising], irrational responses to propaganda, and the arguable nonexistence of objective truth, all conflict with marketplace ideals.". . .

The abuse of private liberty through the exercise of concentrated media ownership may result in censorship and may frustrate the self-expression and the dissemination of truth essential to a democracy. Nevertheless, an insistence that all citizens must have equality of access to the media may give the government too large a role in controlling speech. The real challenge to Congress, the court, and civil libertarians lies in the development of a regulatory scheme somewhere between absolute liberty and absolute equality. How may we assure both equal access and individual liberty to speak while minimizing the dangers of private speech and government regulation?

B. Mass Communications, Broadband, and the Clash of Competing First Amendment Rights

. . .

There are inherent problems in adapting any of the regulatory schemes applied to preceding technologies to interactive broadband technology. First, except in the case of telephone regulations, the communications regulations govern one-way point to multipoint communication or transmission technologies, not two-way interactive technology. . . .

By contrast, broadband technology contemplates the existence of at least two speakers in an interactive exchange of information. Neither party is passive, as both possess the ability to communicate with one another on any of a variety of subjects. Furthermore, unlike telephony, interactive broadband technology will allow an individual speaker to communicate with large groups of people. Regardless of whether the exchange of information occurs between two or more persons, two or more machines, a person and a machine, or several persons and machines, the critical feature of broadband usage is that both parties may create, package, process, and transmit information. Furthermore, broadband communication need not be limited to voice or data, but also may include video and combinations of voice, data, and video. This capacity for interactive communication through multiple forms of information sets broadband apart from its predecessors.

Although broadband technology combines many of the capacities of its predecessors, broadband technology should not be governed by the conflicting speech regulations applied to these preexisting technologies. Regulatory solutions which work for a technology and information specific network distribution system would create chaos if applied to a single broadband communications distribution system.

1. Print, Personal Liberty, and Broadband

. . .

Application of the print model to broadband networks, while perhaps pleasing to a number of constitutional purists, would deny the public a right of access to the broadband network. The discretion to allow access for private as well as public speech would reside entirely with the owner/carrier. Such a development would wreak havoc upon the relatively well-ordered telecommunications common carrier market and its users. Users would find not only their private and public speech, but also their social and business activities circumscribed by broadband network providers. The same broadband network provider would both own the network and decide who has access to the network and its users. Endowed with this power, a broadband network provider could demand a financial interest in any business seeking to reach subscribers on its network.

Regulating broadband based on the print model

would exacerbate the problems of private censorship and self-serving editorializing sometimes experienced in the print mass media because the broadband network provider would control a greater number of communication channels. The provider would control the public's access to information and other speakers' access to the public. In effect, the broadband network provider would control the scope of individuals' speech, access, assembly, and diversity rights. Subscribers would hear, see, and receive only that information which the provider chose to allow. If the private liberty model is applied to broadband, the promise of broadband technology will be eviscerated, if not destroyed.

2. Personal Liberty Circumscribed by Government Mandated Access

a. Broadcasting and the Public Interest

. . .

Although the broadcast model allows a minimal level of public access, its application to broadband network providers would be problematic. The access provided by the broadcast model is available only to politicians running for federal office and non-federal candidates whose opponents have received air time. Allowing only limited access to a particular class of speakers denies the public direct rights of access, speech, assembly, and diversity.

b. Multi-Channel Video Subscription Technologies and Public Access

. . .

Like extensions of the print and broadcast models, application of the cable model to broadband network providers also has significant problems. The cable model requires some measure of public access. Cable television systems of a certain size must provide commercial leased access channels. However, the cable operator may effectively control the content on the leased access channels via price, tier placement, or the withholding of marketing, billing, or other services. The net effect of a cable operator's control of these variables may be to foreclose effective access to some programmers. This ability to foreclose access supplements the cable operator's power to prevent the transmission of programming services in which it has no financial interest.

Franchising authorities also may require cable systems to provide PEG access channels. The individual members of the public, therefore, may secure limited access to certain cable systems on a nondiscriminatory, first come, first served basis. Public rights to speech and assembly also flow from this limited access. While this right of access is greater than that afforded under the print or broadcast models, an individual's ability to speak may be limited by the imbalance between the number of channels available and the number of people seeking access to them.

The number of channels the cable television owner operates and the leased and mandatory access channels programmed by other parties arguably provide a certain degree of diversity. However, the indirect controls a cable operator can exercise over leased access channels may seriously undermine the diversity which might otherwise be realized. Further, an expanded menu of programs may not constitute meaningful diversity if all the programs are targeted to the same class of potential users.

Unlike broadcasting and cable television, wireless video subscription service owners have no corresponding duties to provide public access. Absent an owner's election to assume common or private carrier status, the public has no access right to the facilities. Thus, although the wireless video subscription systems use the public airways and the electromagnetic spectrum in the same manner as broadcast station licensees, system owners retain complete control over access to this media.

3. Telephony: Equality and Non-Discriminatory Access

Under principles of telecommunications common carriage, the owner of the transmission facilities exercises no editorial control over the content of communications. Thus, in this communications arena, ownership is completely separated from control over the content communicated. Conversations over the public switched telecommunications network are labelled private rather than public because they most often occur between two parties. . . .

In exchange for a fee, the public enjoys non-discriminatory access to the transmission paths on the public switched network. Access is regulated by tariff, a contract between the carrier and the subscriber, which establishes the subscriber's eligibility, class, and charge for telecommunications services. Business and residential subscribers may assemble with others through use of available conference call and teleconferencing features. Data users sharing a common data base or switch also may interact with one another simultaneously.

Interactive telephony comes closest to approximating the scope and flexibility of the information transmission and use which may be achieved through broadband technology. Subscriber access to diverse points of view is constrained only by the interests of other subscribers resident on the system, the technical limitations of the network, and the legal and technical limitations on access to services such as dial-a-porn. However, while telephony provides the public with non-discriminatory access within specific user groups, it does so at the expense of the medium owner who has no corresponding speech rights. . . .

## C. Application of Other Regulatory Theories to Broadband Communications

. . .

### 3. Public and Private Fora

Certain commentators have suggested that the public forum doctrine might provide an excellent tool for allocating speech rights in the context of hybrid technology. They argue that the doctrine is useful where the hybrid technology possesses similarities to existing technologies, as well as unique characteristics of its own. Because the doctrine is not premised on the particular characteristics of a technology, it facilitates the analysis of speech rights in the context of new technologies like broadband. . . .

#### a. Traditional Public and Private Speech Fora

. . .

Under current definitions of public and private fora, media of communication may be argued by analogy to be public fora, quasi-public fora or private fora open to the public. For instance, the public switched networks may be argued to be public fora because traditionally they have been regulated to be open to the public at large on a non-discriminatory basis. Broadcasting and cable television may be argued to be quasi-public fora in that they are designated as open to the public under limited circumstances. By comparison, print media could be categorized as private fora because absent the election of the publisher/owner, print media are not open to the public.

Alternatively, if the use of scarce public resources is the criteria for identifying a public forum, telephony, cable and broadcasting would all be classified as public fora. For example, both telephone and cable television firms make use of public streets and rights of way, and broadcasting makes use of the electromagnetic spectrum.

Under the media-oriented definition of speech fora referenced above, a public forum may be argued to exist where an individual owner or entity has monopoly control over a medium of communication or possesses sufficient economic power to effectively censor messages of others seeking access to the fo-

rum (telephone, cable and arguably broadcasting). A quasi-public forum exists where essentially private facilities are opened to the public for limited purposes, as in the case of broadcasting and cable. A private forum exists where a private individual or entity is not required to open its facilities to the public, but nevertheless elects to do so, as in the case of certain subscription technologies. Print media do not fit neatly into this formulation of the doctrine, because despite their economic status as local monopolies, they are deemed private fora, not subject to any access requirements. . . .

### 4. A New Model for Public and Private Fora

. . .

#### b. Public and Private Fora Defined

. . .

Public fora would be deemed to exist in two major categories, per se public fora and voluntary public fora. Transmission providers possessing natural, physical or economic monopoly power, or possessing essential facilities would be regulated as per se public fora. Monopoly status would be defined by statute and agency regulation, subject to modification or expansion through the adjudication process. Voluntary public fora would consist of entities possessing no monopoly or essential facilities status, but electing to be public fora by making their transmission or speech facilities available to the public for expressive activity.

In either case, public fora would enjoy limited liability for service degradation or outages absent gross negligence or evidence establishing an attempt to censor user speech. The public fora would also enjoy immunity from liability for the content of any user speech carried, presented or displayed over public fora facilities. Finally, the public fora would be eligible for tax incentives and other financial incentives to encourage system and service upgrades.

Private fora would be composed of firms or services without monopoly power or essential facilities. For the most part, these entities would be using dedicated or leased facilities providing service to distinct, specialized users. These entities would provide public notice of their intent to offer private forum services. They would maintain full control over access to their channels and/or networks and full editorial control over any speech conducted through their facilities. Consequently, they would have full liability for any loss of service (subject to their ability to negotiate a lesser liability with users) and full liability for what is said over their facilities. To the extent they rely on interconnection to public fora facilities to provide service, they would have to make available some portion of their transmission capacity to other interconnected entities and users on the public fora networks. . . .

### c. Limitations on Government and Private Censorship

With regard to public fora, government regulation would have to protect owners and users against government and private censorship. Public fora owners would exchange access and content control over significant portions of their facilities for limited liability for the foreseeable and consequential damages arising out of their provision of service. They would also be absolved of liability for the content of user speech. Any residual control of access or speech by public forum owners would be in the form of content-neutral determinations of the adequacy of available channel or network capacity and access or speech queuing. The government would not be authorized to penalize or hold the public forum provider liable for any user-initiated and conducted speech, and a potential public fora user could not be denied access to a public constitutionally neutral criteria.

Public fora owners, through a fully owned subsidiary, would have the right to communicate over their facilities or those of any other public fora. Users of the public fora facilities would be allowed to petition at any time alleging inappropriate censorship activities on the part of public fora owners. Congress and the FCC would develop standards regarding the burden of proof and the burden of going forward in such proceedings.

### D. Summary

Reliance on any of the current regulatory schemes of print, broadcast or common carriage has inherent flaws. Application of these models would ignore the continuous blurring of distinctions between technologies and the information they deliver. Why should the legal status of the same information turn on the manner in which it is delivered? Print may be distributed in hard copy or by wire or microwave, and video may be transmitted over different portions of the electromagnetic spectrum, by wire or by satellite. Nonetheless, the resulting communication is the same.

Furthermore, use of these schemes places too great a burden on one or another class of speakers. Either the public (print) or the owner-speaker (common carrier) finds its respective rights diminished or usurped. Finally, these models do not reflect the full range of broadband technology's interactive capacity and utility. Broadband's capacity to provide interactive communication between individuals or groups of individuals, irrespective of the type of information transmitted, distinguishes it from its predecessors. Extending the capacity for electronic speech to individual users may be the mechanism for equalizing the speech rights of media users and owners.

## IV. TOWARD A NEW THEORY OF ELECTRONIC FIRST AMENDMENT REGULATION FOR BROADBAND TECHNOLOGY

. . .

### A. Steering Between Scylla and Charybdis

. . .

The debate regarding the meaning of the First Amendment remains insoluble in the final analysis because the actual intentions of the collective authors of the First Amendment are not apparent. What has become increasingly clear, however, is that reliance on either an unregulated private speech right or government-arbitrated access can leave substantial portions of the public vulnerable to the specter of censorship. The loss of speech rights is equally detrimental to American society, whether it stems from the abuses of the private press exacerbated by government or market-based inequalities of wealth, or from the ofttimes well-meant actions of an overzealous government. What matters is that speech may be irreparably lost. . . .

The advent of computer augmented broadband switched networks, however, may present American society with a new opportunity to restructure the relationship among the public, private media owners, and the government. In the process of this restructuring, the potential for abuse by private owners and the government may be reduced without losing the benefits of privately-exercised speech or government-mandated public access.

### 1. The Root of the Problem

Under current regulatory schemes, the twin threats of private and government censorship remain high. One source of these threats is the high cost of access to the wire and spectrum technologies and the hierarchical nature and social use of these technologies. Except for telephony, where federal and state governments have sought to make public access affordable, most current technologies require substantial amounts of capital to acquire relatively unfettered access. This is because unfettered access or editorial control has often been viewed as part of the panoply of rights which accompany ownership of the medium.

Most current applications and uses of the technologies are, and have historically been hierarchical or one-way: traveling from an originating point to one or many other points. Put another way, information flows "down stream" from the source. Consequently, the speech rights of owners are further enhanced by the actual nature of the technological application.

The confluence of ownership and origination of the information flow necessarily invites regulation at the source of control, the owner. The owner is the point at which such regulation can be most efficient. This is especially true when the source of control is the focus of the speech right as well. It is this confluence of owner rights and government regulatory efficiencies which creates the constitutional problem. . . .

C. Infrastructure, Access, and Speech

. . .

At a minimum, the broadband infrastructure legislation and policies should recognize that both the private owner of transmission facilities and the public have constitutionally discernable and legitimate First Amendment speech rights. The pronouncements should also acknowledge that current regulatory schemes are incapable of adequately protecting public and private speech rights.

Owner and user speech rights may be protected by resort to a public/private forum regulatory scheme which incorporates a number of regulatory elements of existing models. The FCC should designate a broadband provider as a public forum when it possesses monopoly power via economic, physical, or natural means or via essential facilities. A public forum may also be deemed to exist where private owners choose to hold their media of communication open to the public. In order to protect against private censorship whether for economic or other reasons, public forum broadband providers should exercise their speech rights through separate subsidiaries. These subsidiaries should not receive interconnections or transmission or switching services which are superior to those provided to other comparable speakers.

Thus, where the private owner possesses essential or monopoly facilities which a substantial portion of the public must use (for example, the public switched network), the government would be able to legislate some form of structural public access in exchange for reducing the owner's liability for transmission and user speech. The government would be authorized to preserve the "public" and "open" nature of the facilities. The owner would also have rights of access and speech. Neither the government nor the public would be allowed to regulate on the basis of content.

Under such a regulatory scheme, the non-owning public gains access to the larger telecommunications infrastructure while speaker-owners retain a right of speech circumscribed only when they possess monopoly power or essential facilities. This scheme is arguably consistent with the current thrust of public policy and technological development. It is also flexible enough to accommodate future changes in policy, technology and industry structure as they occur. . . .

# Bibliography

*Future Media and the First Amendment*

Cate, Fred H., *Communications Policy Making, Competition, and the Public Interest: The New Dialogue*, 68 Indiana Law Journal 665 (1993)

Inose, Hiroshi and Pierce, John Robinson, *Information Technology and Civilization* (1984)

Katsh, M. Ethan, *The Electronic Media and the Transformation of Law* (1989)

Sidak, J. Gregory, *Telecommunications in Jericho*, 81 California Law Review 1209 (1993)

Stern, Jill A., Krasnow, Erwin G. & Senkowski, R. Michael, *The New Video Marketplace and the Search for a Coherent Regulatory Philosophy*, 32 Catholic University Law Review 529 (1983)

# Part IV

# Religious Freedom

## A. Constitutional Origins

This section analyzes the extent to which historical considerations influence present understanding of the Establishment Clause. Phillip B. Kurland argues that necessity explains the presence of the religion clauses in the First Amendment and elaborates the factors which created this necessity. Michael E. Smith contends that "[r]eligion had no special constitutional place until after the constitutional revolution of 1937," and that its special status in modern case law reflects primarily policy considerations.

Philip B. Kurland, *Of Church and State and the Supreme Court*, 29 THE UNIVERSITY OF CHICAGO LAW REVIEW 1 (1961)*

. . .

Like most commands of our Constitution, the religion clauses of the first amendment are not statements of abstract principles. History, not logic, explains their inclusion in the Bill of Rights; necessity, not merely morality, justifies their presence there. As Father John Courtney Murray has noted: "Every historian who has catalogued the historical factors which made for religious liberty and separation of church and state in America would doubtless agree that these institutions came into being under the pressure of their necessity for the public peace."

The factors creating this necessity were four, according to Murray. The first was the large number of unbelievers in the community that inserted these guarantees into the Constitution. The second was the great variety of denominations among the believers. Third was the economic factor: "Persecution and discrimination were as bad for business affairs as they were for the affairs of the soul." And last, and least in Murray's estimate, was the influence of the "widening religious freedom in England." There was a fifth of which Murray took no note, but which Professor Jordan put this way:

[I]t seems apparent that very considerable gains had been made in terms of human decency, that men had come to be animated by an increasing sensitivity to human pain and suffering. This significant and obscure development . . . contributed most immediately and notably to the rise of religious toleration. It might be suggested, indeed, that the history of culture can in one sense be interpreted in terms of the rising and falling curve of man's sensitivity to cruelty and of his reaction to needless suffering. There was in religious persecution a very considerable and a very ugly psychological and moral element which must be described as sadism. Innate barbarism relieved and justified itself by the infliction of suffering for what was conceived as a moral end. . . . [T]he mass of men in England came to make a very sharp and important distinction between punishment imposed for the judicially demon-

strable fact of crime and the infliction of punishment for the retention of opinion. This must be regarded as one of the most significant cultural gains in human history. These gains of the human race are painfully and slowly attained and they may be lost before the mass of men realize that they are threatened. Brutality and sadism are deeply rooted in man's nature. They are restrained by no surer sanction than a decent attitude toward the fact of difference, which man's biological nature apparently teaches him to abhor but which his history has taught him he must respect in the interest of sheer survival.

Religious toleration, summed up in the second of the two clauses, was, therefore, necessary to preserve the peace. Separation, represented by the first of the two clauses, was necessary to make such religious freedom a reality. But the separation clause had a greater function than the assurance of toleration of dissenting religious beliefs and practices. To suggest but two lessons of the evils resulting from the alliance of church and state, there was abundant evidence of the contributions of the churches to the warfare among nations as well as the conflict within them and equally obvious was the inhibition on scientific endeavor that followed from the acceptance by the state of church dogma. It is not necessary to suggest that the Francophiles in the American community were dedicated to the anti-clericalism that contributed to the French Revolution, but they certainly were not ignorant of the evils that aroused such violent reactions. For them toleration could hardly satisfy the felt needs; separation was a necessary concomitant. But admittedly separation was a new concept in practice. Toleration had a long English history; separation—conceived in the English writings of Roger Williams—had its beginnings as an historical fact only on the shores of this continent. It is justified in Williams' terms by the necessity for keeping the state out of the affairs of the church, lest the church be subordinated to the state; in Jeffersonian terms its function is to keep the church out of the business of government, lest the government be subordinated to the church. Limited powers of government were not instituted to expand the realm of power of religious organizations, but rather in favor of freedom of action and thought by the people.

Nor were these two concepts closed systems at the time of the adoption of the first amendment. The objectives of the provisions were clear, but the means of their attainment were still to be developed and, indeed, are still in the course of development. Thus, like the other great clauses of the Constitution, the religion clauses cannot now be confined to the application they might have received in 1789.

The utilization or application of these clauses in conjunction is difficult. For if the commands is that inhibitions not be placed by the state on religious activity, it is equally forbidden the state to confer favors upon religious activity. These commands would be impossible of effectuation unless they are read together as creating a doctrine more akin to the reading of the equal protection clause than to the due process clause, *i.e.*, they must be read to mean that religion may not be used as a basis for classification for purposes of governmental action, whether that action be the conferring of rights or privileges or the imposition of duties or obligations. Or, to put it in Lord Bryce's terms: "It is accepted as an axiom by all Americans that the civil power ought to be not only neutral and impartial as between different forms of faith, but ought to leave these matters entirely on one side. . . ." It must be recognized, however, that this statement of the "neutral" principle of equality, that religion cannot supply a basis for classification of governmental actions, still leaves many problems unanswered. Not the least of them flows from the fact that the actions of the state must be carefully scrutinized to assure that classifications that purport to relate to other matters are not really classifications in terms of religion. "[C]lassification in abstract terms can always be carried to the point at which, in fact, the class singled out consists only of particular known persons or even a single individual. It must be admitted that, in spite of many ingenious attempts to solve this problem, no entirely satisfactory criterion has been found that would always tell us what kind of classification is compatible with equality before the law."

. . .

Michael E. Smith, *The Special Place of Religion in the Constitution*, THE SUPREME COURT REVIEW 83 (1983)*

. . .

To the question, What justifies the special constitutional place of religion? perhaps the most straightforward answer is what current commentators would

call "interpretivist." The very language of the Constitution gives religion a special place in Article VI, section 3, and in the First Amendment. Moreover, the framers of the Constitution had urgent reasons for giving religion a special place. Some scholars stress the Enlightenment rationalism of leaders such as Thomas Jefferson. Others emphasize the free church Protestantism of the followers of Roger Williams. Still others argue that the framers had a non-ideological desire to allay potential social conflict.

In reality, however, interpretivism has affected our constitutional practice only to a limited extent. Insofar as the Justices at present maintain the special constitutional place of religion, they do so mainly for present-day policy reasons. Religion had no special constitutional place until after the constitutional revolution of 1937. Before that time, the Supreme Court readily upheld government actions concerning religion that seem highly problematic by present standards. For example, in *Davis v. Beason*, an 1890 case, a Mormon challenged an Idaho statute that required voters to swear that they did not belong to any group that taught or practiced polygamy. The Court rejected the challenge unanimously, saying little more than that "on this point there can be no serious discussion or difference of opinion. . . . Probably never before in the history of this country has it been seriously contended that the whole punitive power of the government for acts, recognized by the general consent of the Christian world in modern times as proper matters for prohibitory legislation, must be suspended in order that the tenets of a religious sect encouraging crime may be carried out without hindrance."

During World War I the draft law exempted as conscientious objectors only members of a "well-recognized religious sect . . . whose existing creed or principles forbid its members to participate in war." When the statutory classification was challenged as a violation of the Religion Clauses of the Constitution, the Court responded unanimously that "we pass [the challenge] without anything but statement . . . because we think its unsoundness is too apparent to require us to do more." By contrast, economic liberty, which at present has no special constitutional place, was perhaps the Supreme Court's most cherished constitutional value between 1890 and 1937.

Indeed, some Justices of the Supreme Court have begun to acknowledge openly that, in their view, the language and history of the Religion Clauses are largely beside the point as compared with present-day policy considerations. Justice White wrote in dissent in *Committee for Pub. Educ. v. Nyquist*:

No one contends that he can discern from the

sparse language of the Establishment Clause that a State is forbidden to aid religion in any manner whatsoever or, if it does not mean that, what kind of or how much aid is permissible. And one cannot seriously believe that the history of the First Amendment furnishes unequivocal answers to many of the fundamental issues of church-state relations. In the end, the courts have fashioned answers to these questions as best they can, the language of the Constitution and its history having left them a wide range of choice among many alternatives. But decision has been unavoidable; and, in choosing, the courts necessarily have carved out what they deemed to be the most desirable national policy governing various aspects of church-state relationships.

Justice Powell was even blunter in his separate opinion in *Wolman v. Walter*: "At this point in the 20th century we are quite far removed from the dangers that prompted the Framers to include the Establishment Clause in the Bill of Rights . . . . The risk [of great harm from financial aid to private religious schools] is remote, and when viewed against the positive contributions of sectarian schools, any such risk seems entirely tolerable. . . ."

Little has been written on the Supreme Court's present-day policy justifications for the special constitutional place of religion. The writings of Professors Kurland and Howe and Father Murray, among others, are full of important perceptions, but they do not treat the subject systematically. The contrast with political speech is especially vivid. There have been many powerful essays, judicial and scholarly, on the justifications for the special constitutional place of the latter.

C. Description of the Inquiry

I shall describe the Supreme Court's articulated justifications for the special constitutional place of religion, concentrating on the views of the Justices since 1937. Before the constitutional revolution of 1937, religion had no special constitutional place. In 1940, however, the Court first ruled that the Free Exercise Clause is applicable against the states, and during the next four years it enforced the Clause rigorously. In 1947, the Court ruled that the Establishment Clause also applies against the states, and it invalidated state aid to religion one year later. The constitutional rules that give religion its special place are the product of these path-breaking decisions.

. . .

II. THE ARTICULATED JUSTIFICATIONS

A. Personal Freedom

Following the constitutional revolution of 1937, the first cases to come before the Supreme Court under the Religion Clauses concerned certain inhibitions on religious behavior, especially that of the Jehovah's Witnesses. At that time, freedom of speech doctrine was already fairly fully developed, and freedom of religion was closely linked to freedom of speech in these early cases. Those challenging government hindrance of religion typically invoked both parts of the First Amendment, and when the Court granted their claims, it sometimes did so on both grounds. Moreover, the Justices explicitly associated the two freedoms with each other. In *Prince v. Massachusetts*, for example, Justice Rutledge wrote for the Court: "All [the liberties of the First Amendment] are interwoven there . . . . [T]hey have unity in the charter's prime place because they have unity in their human sources and functionings. . . . [T]hese variant aspects of personality find inseparable expression in a thousand ways. They cannot be altogether parted in law more than in life."

It is significant that in these cases the Justices offered justifications for the special constitutional place of religion analogous to prevalent freedom of speech justifications. In a most perceptive article on the demise of economic liberty under the Constitution, Professor McCloskey summarized the justifications commonly offered for the special constitutional place of freedom of speech:

> [First] it is sometimes argued that laws limiting freedom of expression impinge on the human personality more grievously than do laws curbing mere economic liberty. . . . The individual has, *qua* individual, "the right to be let alone. . . . [Second,] another suggested rationale looks toward the community rather than the separate individuals within it. Progress, it is said, "is to a considerable extent the displacement of error which once held sway as official truth by beliefs which in turn have yielded to other beliefs.

In the early cases, the Justices emphasized what Professor McCloskey called the community rationale. That is, they repeatedly espoused the view that in order to attain the truth or, if that is a quixotic objective, in order to serve social needs, a free marketplace of ideas is indispensable. Thus on the first hearing of *Jones v. Opelika*, Justice Reed wrote for the Court: "Too many settled beliefs have in time been rejected to justify this generation in refusing a hearing to its own dissentients." Justice Murphy, concurring in *Martin v. Struthers*, stated: "If a religious belief has substance, it can survive criticism . . . with the aid of truth and reason alone. By the same method, those who follow false prophets are exposed." In *West Virginia Bd. of Educ. v. Barnette*, Justices Black and Douglas in concurrence wrote: "If, as we think, [these beliefs] are groundless, time and reason are the proper antidotes for their errors." Concurring in a case two decades later, *McGowan v. Maryland*, Justice Frankfurter stated that with freedom from government intervention, "[religious] beliefs and institutions shall continue, as the needs and longings of the people shall inspire them, to exist, to function, to grow, to wither, and to exert [influence] with whatever innate strength they may contain. . . ."

This justification for the constitutional place of religion has, however, all but disappeared from Supreme Court opinions. Cases in which it might plausibly have been adduced tend to be treated as matters of speech. The major exception is *McDaniel v. Paty*, a freedom of religion case, in which Justice Brennan wrote in concurrence: "The antidote which the Constitution provides against zealots who would inject sectarianism into the political process is to subject their ideas to refutation in the marketplace of ideas and their platforms to rejection at the polls."

Professor McCloskey had doubts about this justification. He conceded that freedom of expression promotes social welfare, especially in a democracy, but insisted that freedom of economic activity, which has no special constitutional place, may be of comparable social value. He observed, for example:

> Few historians would deny that the growth of entrepreneurial and occupational freedom helped to promote material progress in England in the eighteenth and nineteenth centuries and in America after the Civil War. . . . We can refuse to swallow whole the dogmas of nineteenth-century rugged individualism and can still believe that some freedom of occupation and economic choice is also instrumental to the development of [the] self-determining and sensitive citizen-governor.

In the later cases, there has been much greater emphasis on Professor McCloskey's other suggested rationale, the right to be let alone. Intrusion into parts of our psyche, especially the realm of religious belief, may be too painful and destructive of our psychological well-being. We must be spared certain trials of conscience. Thus, as early as *West Virginia Bd. of Educ. v. Barnette*, Justices Black and Douglas, concurring, deplored the "fear of spiritual condemnation" to which the youthful Jehovah's Witnesses were being subjected. Two decades later, in *Braunfeld v. Brown*, Justice Stewart, in dissent, characterized the situation of the Orthodox Jews there as a "cruel choice." In one of the conscientious objector cases, *Welsh v. United States*, Justice Black sided with those "whose consciences, spurred by deeply

held moral, ethical, or religious beliefs, would give them no rest or peace." Writing for the Court in a later conscientious objector case, *Gillette v. United States*, Justice Marshall referred repeatedly to the "hard choice," the "painful dilemma," of the defendants.

Indeed, for years the Supreme Court has endorsed tests that apply this justification in cases involving hindrance of religion. The courts ask whether the dissenter's objection is sincere, and how central it is to the dissenter's religious belief. Most commentators seem to agree that these tests are appropriate if not applied too rigorously.

Nevertheless, Professor McCloskey also objected to this justification. He acknowledged the "inarguable importance" to the human personality of freedom of expression generally but doubted that giving it a special constitutional place reflected the "real preferences of the commonality of mortals. . . . [M]ost men would probably feel that an economic right, such as freedom of occupation, was at least as vital to them as the right to speak their minds. Mark Twain would surely have felt constrained in the most fundamental sense, if his youthful aspiration to be a riverboat pilot had been frustrated by a State-ordained system of nepotism" such as the one upheld by the Supreme Court.

## B. Social Harm

In the earliest hindrance of religion cases, the Justices suggested another set of justifications for the special constitutional place of religion. The alternative justifications, however, were not fully elaborated until the Court began hearing cases concerning government aid to religion, in particular aid to religious education. The justifications offered in these cases were social harms peculiar to religion.

First. The Justices claimed that government action concerning religion is apt to degenerate into persecution. Justice Murphy, dissenting in *Prince v. Massachusetts*, put the point especially forcefully:

> No chapter in human history has been so largely written in terms of persecution and intolerance as the one dealing with religious freedom. From ancient times to the present day, the ingenuity of man has known no limits in its ability to forge weapons of oppression for use against those who dare to express or practice unorthodox religious beliefs.

A majority of the Court adopted the point in *Everson v. Board of Educ.*, where Justice Black summarized the European past as follows: "Catholics had persecuted Protestants, Protestants had persecuted Catholics, Protestant sects had persecuted other Protestant sects, Catholics of one shade of belief had persecuted Catholics of another shade of belief, and all of these had from time to time persecuted Jews.'' Later, in *Engel v. Vitale*, in the course of another historical essay, Justice Black took it as ''historical fact that governmentally established religions and religious persecution go hand in hand.''

By ''persecution,'' Justice Black and the others presumably meant something more than the mere hindrance of religion. Otherwise, in some cases they would have been saying hardly more than that hindrance of religion degenerates into itself. Presumably they meant cruelty, that is, the intentional infliction of a high degree of pain without a defensible justification. Thus, Justice Black, dissenting in *Zorach v. Clauson*, referred to ''zealous sectarians entrusted with governmental power'' who would ''torture, maim and kill those they branded 'heretics,' 'atheists' or 'agnostics.''' Concern about this degree of persecution has disappeared almost entirely from Supreme Court opinions in recent years.

Second. The Justices asserted that government action aiding or hindering religion is particularly damaging to social unity. They commonly linked this concern to the religious diversity of our people. Sometimes they contemplated outright social conflict among religious groups. For example, dissenting in *Board of Educ. v. Allen*, Justice Black claimed: ''The First Amendment's prohibition against governmental establishment of religion was written on the assumption that state aid to religion and religious schools generates discord, disharmony, hatred, and strife among our people. . . .'' At other times they warned against the less dramatic harm of social separatism. Probably the most ardent expression of this concern was Justice Frankfurter's concurring opinion for four members of the Court in *McCollum v. Board of Educ.* No one ever put the point more articulately, however, than Justice Brennan, concurring in *Abington School Dist. v. Schempp*, when he extolled ''the training of American citizens in an atmosphere free of parochial, divisive, or separatist influences of any sort—an atmosphere in which children may assimilate a heritage common to all American groups and religions.'' At still other times, the Justices feared animosity toward government. Thus, writing for the Court in *Engel v. Vitale*, Justice Black claimed that ''whenever government had allied itself with one particular form of religion, the inevitable result had been that it had incurred the hatred, disrespect and even contempt of those who held contrary beliefs.''

Of the justifications for the special constitutional place of religion, fear of social disunity has probably been the one most commonly articulated. Nearly all of the Justices writing on the subject have recited this fear. Some Justices, especially Frankfurter, have adduced hardly any other justification. Moreover, unlike the concern about persecution, this justification continues to be invoked repeatedly. Justice Harlan forcefully asserted the point when he wrote, concurring in *Walz v. Tax Comm'n*, that undue ''government involvement in religious life . . . is apt to lead to strife and frequently strain a political system to the breaking point.'' Indeed, since *Lemon v. Kurtzman* and *Tilton v. Richardson*, under the name ''political entanglement,'' the concern has been raised to an independent test of unconstitutionality in cases involving aid to religion. Justice Brennan has come to rely heavily on this test, as in his recent opinion for the Court in *Larson v. Valente*.

On the other hand, some of its early exponents have begun to express doubts about this test. Dissenting from invalidation of certain aids to religious schools in *Meek v. Pittenger*, Chief Justice Burger argued, ''I see at least as much potential for divisive political debate in opposition to the crabbed attitude the Court shows in this case.'' Likewise, Justice Powell asserted in a separate opinion in *Wolman v. Walter*: ''At this point in the 20th century we are quite far removed from the dangers that prompted the Framers to include the Establishment Clause in the Bill of Rights. . . . The risk . . . even of deep political division along religious lines . . . is remote. . . .'' Even Justice Brennan, an enthusiast for this justification, acknowledged in *McDaniel v. Paty* that it is limited by other constitutional values such as the free marketplace of religious ideas.

As Dean Choper has pointed out, there are strong reasons to agree with Chief Justice Burger and Justice Powell. But even if government aid to religion may still be a source of social strife, that alone does not justify singling it out constitutionally. Proponents of this justification must establish further that religion is significantly more divisive than other sources of social discord, such as economic condition, race, sex, and political ideology. There are strong reasons to think otherwise.

For example, in 1968, Professor Morgan argued cogently that while the potential occasions for political conflict along religious lines were increasing in number, the underlying sources of religious conflict in our country were continuing to abate. He pointed to several developments, including the waning importance of dogma, both religious and atheistic; the willingness of Jews and conservative Protestants to reconsider their commitment to strict separationism; the greater acceptability of the Catholic Church following Vatican II; the increasing social integration of people of different religions and nonreligions; the convergence of Catholic parochial schools and other kinds of American schooling.

. . .

## C. Social Benefit

From almost the first of the cases, it was argued that aid to religion may be socially beneficial and, therefore, constitutional. These arguments moved to the fore in the 1960s with the coming of the second generation of Justices. It is possible that these arguments have had nothing to do with justifying the special constitutional place of religion. They may have asserted no more than that certain government interests limit the principle that government may not aid religion. Likewise, in the one hindrance of religion case cited in this section, *Wisconsin v. Yoder*, the passages quoted may have gone only to show that the government interest in limiting religion was inadequate. But these arguments are typically recited with a fervor appropriate to constitutional values. They constitute a new set of justifications for the principle that government should not hinder religion.

First. The Justices have suggested that the special constitutional place of religion is justified by historical tradition. Religion, including corporate religion, has been deeply entrenched in American social life. The way that government has treated religion has also become deeply entrenched. Traditionally, government has treated religion benignly, without unduly favoring it. Much social harm would be done if legislatures or courts were to disturb such a strong and persistent tradition.

In one of the most renowned passages in the whole line of cases, Justice Douglas, writing for the majority in *Zorach v. Clauson*, espoused this justification: "We are a religious people whose institutions presuppose a Supreme Being. . . . When the state encourages religious instruction . . ., it follows the best of our traditions. For it then respects the religious nature of our people and accommodates the public service to their spiritual needs." Numerous Justices of the second generation have quoted this passage, while others have put the point in their own words. Dissenting in one of the first aid to religion cases, *McCollum v. Board of Educ.*, Justice Reed noted "the many instances of close association of church and state in American society" and added that "many of these relations are so much a part of our tradition and culture that they are accepted without more," and he then argued: "This Court cannot be too cautious in upsetting practices embedded in our society by many years of experience." Dissenting in *Engel v. Vitale*, Justice Stewart asserted:

"What is relevant to the issue here is . . . the history of the religious traditions of our people. He then defended certain aids to religion as calculated "to recognize and to follow the deeply entrenched and highly cherished spiritual traditions of our nation." Even while concurring in a decision invalidating certain aids to religion, *Abington School Dist. v. Schempp*, Justices Goldberg and Harlan asserted: "Neither government nor this Court can or should ignore the significance of the fact that a vast portion of our people believe in and worship God and that many of our legal, political and personal values derive historically from religious teachings." Chief Justice Burger, writing for the Court in *Walz v. Tax Comm'n*, stated: "Few concepts are more deeply embedded in the fabric of our national life, beginning with pre-Revolutionary colonial times, than for the government to exercise at the very least this kind of benevolent neutrality toward churches and religious exercise. . . .

Two of our most profound scholars of the subject also espoused this justification for religion's special constitutional place. In the last section of his published lectures on religion and government in American constitutional history, Professor Howe repeatedly invoked as criteria for interpreting the Religion Clauses "America's way of life," "the presuppositions of our society," "the society's history," "the mandate of a recognized tradition," "the living practices of the American people," "the subtle gradations of past and present reality." Father Murray argued that the Religion Clauses are not theology but only "a matter of prejudice."

[That is, their] origins are in our peculiar context and [their] validity has been demonstrated by the unique course of American history. . . . They are not destitute of reason, but their chief corroboration is from experience. They are part of the legacy of wisdom from the past; they express an ancestral consensus. . . . [O]ther prejudices may obtain elsewhere—in England, in Sweden, in Spain. Their validity in their own context and against the background of the history that generated them does not disturb [our] conviction that [our] own prejudice, within [our] own context and against the background of [our] own history, has its own validity.

Dean Ely has raised troubling objections to the use of tradition as a test for deciding constitutional cases. He doubts that we have any traditions that are specific enough to help in deciding particular cases, and even if we do, he doubts that judges have any special competence to discern these traditions. Ely's point is not uniformly compelling. For example, tradition was an inconclusive guide in the cases involving prayers and religious readings in the public schools, but it seems to have provided a firm basis for upholding tax exemptions for church property.

Second. The special constitutional place of religion is justified by its social functions. The key opinion here is Justice Brennan's concurrence in *Walz v. Tax Comm'n*. He contended that "religious organizations . . . uniquely contribute to the pluralism of American society by their religious activities. . . . [E]ach group contributes to the diversity of association, viewpoint, and enterprise essential to a vigorous, pluralistic society." Moreover, Justice Brennan asserted that through their "public service activities," "religious organizations contribute to the well-being of the community in a variety of non-religious ways, and thereby bear burdens that would otherwise either have to be met by general taxation, or be left undone, to the detriment of the community."

The latter justification was explicitly disavowed by the majority in *Walz v. Tax Comm'n*, but in numerous contemporaneous and later cases involving aid to religious schools, other Justices have argued to the same effect. For example, dissenting in *Committee for Pub. Educ. v. Nyquist*, Chief Justice Burger, referred to the "debt owed by the public" to religious schools and the "wholesome diversity" that they engender. Justice Rehnquist wrote sympathetically of the "service" to the public rendered by parents who send their children to private schools and of their efforts to "keep alive pluralism" in education. Justice White called the private schools "an educational resource that could deliver quality education at a cost to the public substantially below the per-pupil cost of the public schools."

These justifications apparently apply to freedom of association generally. As such, they are subject to the same objection that Professor McCloskey raised against the special constitutional place of freedom of expression: freedom of noneconomic association may promote social welfare, but freedom of economic association, which has no special constitutional place, may be of comparable social value.

Third. The Justices have suggested that religion, particularly corporate religion, may contribute to the development of good personal character. Hinted at in some early opinions, this view was expressed clearly in Chief Justice Burger's opinion for the Court in *Wisconsin v. Yoder*. Referring to the Amish community, he wrote, "Its members are productive and very law-abiding members of society; they reject public welfare in any of its usual modern forms," because the Amish inculcate "habits of industry and self-reliance," "qualities of reliability, self-reliance, and dedication." In short, "the Amish communities singularly parallel and reflect many of the virtues of Jefferson's ideal of the 'sturdy yeoman' who would form the basis of what he considered as the ideal of a democratic society."

### D. Religious Justification

In later cases before the Supreme Court, there appeared clearly for the first time a quite different justification for the special constitutional place of religion, a strictly religious justification. That is, religion's place was justified by the intrinsic value of religion. The justification rests on the foundation of traditional, theistic religion—obedience to God's will.

This justification has been hinted at by several Justices. For example, concurring in *Abington School Dist. v. Schempp*, Justice Brennan contended, for the first of many times, that the rule against aiding religion was partly meant to protect "the devout believer who fears the secularization of a creed which becomes too deeply involved with and dependent upon government."

The only Justice to assert a religious justification at all explicitly, however, was Douglas. Dissenting in *McGowan v. Maryland*, he wrote: "The institutions of our society are founded on the belief that there is an authority higher than the authority of the State; that there is a moral law which the State is powerless to alter; that the individual possesses rights, conferred by the Creator, which government must respect." Likewise, concurring in *Abington School Dist. v. Schempp*, he quoted the following with approval: "This pure Religious Liberty" . . . "declared [all forms of church-state relationships] and their fundamental idea to be oppressions of conscience and abridgments of that liberty which God and nature had conferred on every living soul."

Justice Douglas's views may appear paradoxical. On the one hand, he was a strong advocate of the personal freedom justifications. No Justice of the Supreme Court since 1960 voted more consistently in favor of individual believers. In *Zorach v. Clauson*, he wrote the most famous judicial statement in defense of aid to corporate religion. He alone explicitly sought to justify protecting religion for its own sake. On the other hand, since 1960 his criticisms of corporate religion were by far the harshest of any Justice, and he consistently voted against it.

If his remarks in *Zorach v. Clauson* are put to one side, Justice Douglas's position is reasonably coherent. Justice Douglas was very sympathetic to religion as an individual activity. After 1960 he was very hostile to corporate religion, particularly corporate Christianity and Judaism. What happened to Douglas between *Zorach v. Clauson* and the 1960s? This essay is not concerned with judicial biography, so I shall do no more than to suggest two possibilities. First, he may genuinely have changed his mind about corporate religion in the interim. Second, what he said in *Zorach v. Clauson* may have been an oddity, reflecting political ambition or some other personal impulse.

. . .

B. The Second Generation

1. Social benefit. Many Justices of the second generation have taken substantially different underlying views of religion. They have been more favorably disposed toward corporate religion. They have showed this by espousing different justifications for the special constitutional place of religion. First, they have largely avoided the justifications involving social harm that most clearly disparage corporate religion. Justice Fortas's opinion for the Court in *Epperson v. Arkansas* is the only one by a latter-day Justice to emulate the open hostility of Justices Black and Douglas. Concern about persecution has also largely disappeared from opinions of the second generation of Justices. Some Justices have even begun to question the claim that corporate religion contributes to social disunity.

Second, they have offered new justifications based on the social benefits of corporate religion. These include religion's contribution to social diversity, to public welfare programs, and to the development of good moral character. These justifications are far more favorable to corporate religion even than the personal freedom justifications.

. . .

There is also evidence that some Justices of the second generation may be less sympathetic than their predecessors to individual religion. Dissenting in *Welsh v. United States*, the three Justices who have probably been most favorable to corporate religion, Burger, Stewart, and White, gave a relatively narrow definition of "religious belief" in the conscientious objector statute and defended their definition as constitutional.

. . .

Finally, the Supreme Court of the second generation has not invariably ruled in favor of corporate religion and against individual believers. On the contrary, most of the cases invalidating religion in the public schools and financial aid to religious schools were decided after 1960. The same is true of the cases that have exempted religious dissenters, even those belonging to no religious group, from nonreligious legal requirements.

2. Religious justifications. The social benefit justifications of the second generation of Justices are revealing in another way. The benefits attributed to corporate religion may properly be called secular benefits. Social diversity, public welfare programs, industrious character—these are apt to be regarded primarily as temporal, material goods, not as means of worshiping and obeying God. In other words, even the second generation of Justices seems to have viewed the religion worthy of being protected by the Constitution primarily as a secular activity.

This may be somewhat confirmed by at least one major opinion. Concurring in *Walz v. Tax Comm'n*, Justice Brennan, after reciting the contributions of corporate religion to social diversity and public welfare programs, sought to refute the argument that the means of attaining these benefits are essentially religious: "The means churches use . . . are the same means used by any purely secular organization—money, human time and skills, physical facilities."

The same is true of the personal freedom justifications, insofar as they too imply that religion is beneficial. The advantages attributed to individual, pluralistic religion—psychological well-being and socially useful ideas—are apt to be regarded primarily as temporal, material values. Likewise, the means of achieving these benefits, psychological "space" and competitive ideological markets, are secular processes. Indeed, the very propensity to identify freedom of religion with freedom of speech implies that religion is primarily a secular activity. It assumes that thought and expression, whether in the realm of politics, science, or religion, are basically alike.

. . .

George C. Freeman, III, *The Misguided Search for the Constitutional Definition of "Religion"*, 71 GEORGETOWN LAW REVIEW 1519 (1983)*

. . .

The Founding Fathers' views on the meaning of "religion" cannot easily be gleaned from the sketchy historical record. What little evidence there is, how-

* Reprinted with permission of the publisher, © 1983 The Georgetown Law Journal Association and Georgetown University.

ever, suggests that most of the Founders equated religion with theism. For example, George Mason and James Madison, two of the most prominent figures in the struggle for religious freedom, characterized religion as "the duty which we owe to our Creator, and the manner of discharging it." Benjamin Franklin expressed a similar view when he "esteemed the essentials of every religion" to be, among other things, a belief in "the Diety; [and] that he made the world, and govern'd it by his Providence. . . ." Even the unorthodox Thomas Paine described religion as "man bringing to his Maker the fruits of his heart." Only in the writings of a few, such as Thomas Jefferson, might we find a broader conception of religion. Writing on the passage of the Virginia Bill for Establishing Religious Freedom, Jefferson had this to say: "The bill . . . [was] meant to comprehend, within the mantle of its protection, the Jew and the Gentile, the Christian and Mahometan, the Hindoo, and infidel of every denomination." Even this remark fails to show conclusively, however, that Jefferson's view of religion was not theistic. With its focus on religious freedom, the remark reveals more about Jefferson's views on whose opinions should be protected than it does about his views on whose opinions are religious.

Knowing that the Founding Fathers equated religion with theism is not nearly so important, however, as knowing why they equated the two. Unfortunately, the Founders were almost wholly silent on this point. If any explanation for their equation is possible, perhaps the best is this: In propounding their definition of "religion," the Founders sought simply to describe what religion itself is like, not to prescribe which religion or religions people should practice. Their aim, in other words, was to propound a neutral definition of "religion," one that did not discriminate against any unorthodox believer. At that time in American history, however, all of the unorthodox believers appear to have been theists. Had there been nontheists among them, the Founders, in the interest of neutrality, might very well have conceived of religion in broader terms. This seems especially likely in view of the fact that most nontheistic religions resemble their theistic counterparts in emphasizing the importance of worship, rituals, deities, and the transcendent. In any event, no evidence exists to suggest that the Founders' intention in equating religion with theism was to deny the religious character of nontheism.

Although the Founders might have been willing to include nontheism within the meaning of "religion," the same cannot easily be said for traditional atheism. For while the Founders appear to have been unfamiliar with the views of nontheists, they were neither unfamiliar with nor accepting of the views of traditional atheists. To be sure, the Founders did intend for the religion clauses to protect everyone's right to freedom of conscience, at least from interference by the federal government. The Founders' aim, however, was to protect freedom of conscience only in matters of religion, not freedom of conscience per se. Two sources support this conclusion: The report of the debates over the wording of the religion clauses and the final wording itself. The historical record reveals that the Founders debated ten different versions of the religion clauses before adopting the present wording. Significantly, only the first seven versions containded a specific provision protecting the rights of conscience. The Founders' decision to omit such a provision from the remaining versions can be interpreted in either of two ways. On the one hand, the Founders may have thought a provision protecting freedom of conscience would protect more than freedom of religion and was for this reason objectionable. On the other hand, the Founders may have thought such a provision was redundant, the right to freedom of conscience being subsumable under the right to the free exercise of religion. Neither interpretation supports the view that the Founders sought to protect freedom of conscience per se.

Nor is this view supported by the specific language selected for either the free exercise clause or the establishment clause. What the free exercise clause protects is the free exercise of religion, not the free exercise of conscience. It does this by affording every individual a right to freedom of religion. This right, as a matter of logic, entails both a duty that is imposed on the government and a liberty that is accorded to every individual. To be more explicit, the government has a duty not to restrict or require the practice and support of religion. Every individual, moreover, is at liberty either to practice and support a religion or not to practice and support a religion. Standing alone, however, the free exercise clause does not protect the nonbeliever except by guaranteeing him a right not to practice and support a religion. The clause affords him no right to engage in any other antireligious activities. For a right to engage in these, he must look to other provisions of the Constitution—to the free speech clause, for example.

Justice Harlan maintained that it is the establishment clause that protects the nonbeliever. It does this, he argued, by requiring that the government always treat the nonbeliever and the believer equally. According to this view, the establishment clause may be interpreted, in part, as the nonbeliever's free exercise clause. Justice Harlan never suggested, however, that this view could be derived from the original intent of the Founders. He recommended it for other reasons. As for the original intent, moreover, there appears to be no evidence to suggest that the Founders intended for the establishment clause to be construed as the nonbeliever's free exercise clause. Had they intended for it to be, they simply could have retained some version of the freedom-of-conscience clause.

. . .

# Bibliography

*Constitutional Origins*

Alley, Robert S., *James Madison on Religious Liberty* (1985)

Ahlstrom, Sydney E., *A Religious History of the American People* (1972)

Buckley, Thomas E., *Church and State in Revolutionary Virginia: 1776–1787* (1977)

Cahn, Edmond, *The "Establishment of Religion" Puzzle*, 36 New York University Law Review 1274 (1961)

Howe, Mark, *The Garden and the Wilderness: Religion and Government in American Constitutional History* (1965)

Levy, Leonard W., *The Establishment Clause* (1986)

## B. Defining Religion

These articles deal with the intractable problem of defining religion. Jesse H. Choper argues that, although the definition of "religion" plays . . ."[an] integral role [in] the content to be assigned to the religion clauses," "[g]iving the concept of 'religion' a precise meaning is a formidably complicated task." George C. Freeman III disagrees, arguing that the "[f]ounders equated religion with theism." He critically analyzes many of the other theories that have been advanced.

Jesse H. Choper, *Defining "Religion" in the First Amendment*, 1982 UNIVERSITY OF ILLINOIS LAW REVIEW 579*

## I. INTRODUCTION

Giving the concept of "religion" a precise meaning is a formidably complicated task. Although the first clauses of the Bill of Rights designate "religion" as a subject of special constitutional significance—both prohibiting government from granting it undue assistance and at the same time affording it distinct protection from government regulation—the Supreme Court has never seriously discussed how this term should be defined for constitutional purposes.

Moreover, the scope of religious pluralism in the United States alone has resulted in such a multiplicity and diversity of ideas about what is a "religion" or a "religious belief" that no simple formula seems able to accommodate them all. Scholars have written volumes on the subject without reaching anything approaching agreement. Judicial as well as theological efforts to cabin the notion may take on the appearance of exercises in circularity, proposed definitions using as a starting point comparison to groups or beliefs that are stipulated as being religious. Thus, although a constitutional definition of "religious belief" may be expressed as whether the belief "occupies a place in the life of its possessor parallel to that filled by the orthodox belief in God," or "religion" may be described as "the state of being ultimately concerned," these formulations may be no more useful when applied to specific cases than the words "religious belief" and "religion" themselves. Further, any definition of religion for constitutional purposes that excludes certain beliefs (or groups) that are reasonably perceived or characterized as being religious by those who hold them (or belong to them) may be fairly viewed as judicial preference of some "religions" over others. Indeed, the very idea of a legal definition of religion may be viewed as an "establishment" of religion in violation of the first amendment. These complexities notwithstanding, the definition of "religion" plays as integral a role in the articulation of any well-developed doctrine governing the constitutional separation of church and state as does the content to be assigned to the religion clauses' two substantive terms—"establishment" and "free exercise."

· · ·

## II. THE FREE EXERCISE CLAUSE

Virtually all of the Supreme Court's efforts, modest as they have been, to wrestle with the problem of what constitutes a "religion" or a "religious belief" have occurred in cases presenting claims that properly fall under the free exercise clause rather than the establishment clause.

· · ·

### E. Defining "Religion"

It has been forcefully argued that the free exercise clause should not be read to require any special dispensation for religion from general government rules enacted to serve secular goals. If this view had been accepted, there would be no need to construct a definition of "religion" for these purposes. But the series of decisions just described have chosen to grant religion a special privilege under certain circumstances, a position that I endorse—at least when such an exemption does not itself interfere with anyone's religious liberty and is not outweighed by a sufficiently strong government interest. Thus, the question of how the Court should define "religion" for these purposes must be confronted.

#### 1. Evolution in the Supreme Court

The Justices' first real attempt at a definition of religion came at the end of the 19th century in Davis v. Beason, sustaining a law of the territory of Idaho that disenfranchised any person belonging to an organization that encouraged the practice of polygamy:

> Bigamy and polygamy are crimes by the laws of all civilized and Christian countries. . . . To extend exemption from punishment for such crimes would be to shock the moral judgment of the community. To call their advocacy a tenet of religion is to offend the common sense of mankind. . . . The term "religion" has reference to one's views of his relations to his Creator, and to the obligations they impose of reverence for his being and character, and of obedience to his will.

This passage contains two separate elements. The thrust of its first part—that because the practice of polygamy was (at least then) abhorrent to our culture, it cannot be classified as "a tenet of religion"—confuses the question of what is or is not "religion" (the issue that the Court purported to address) with the question of whether the practice, even if it is a "religious" one, may nonetheless be proscribed by civil authority (the issue that this portion of the

Court's rationale in fact resolved). The second part of the Court's discussion, however, directly considers the relevant problem and, echoing James Madison's perception of religion as "the duty which we owe to our Creator," adopts a theistic definition conforming to the traditions of western Judeo-Christian thought.

As late as 1931, Chief Justice Hughes, joined by Justices Holmes, Brandeis and Stone, opined that "the essence of religion is belief in a relation to God involving duties superior to those arising from any human relation." But by 1944, the Court stepped back, albeit somewhat ambiguously, from the ukase that "religion" requires a belief in God, stating in *United States v. Ballard* that "freedom of religious belief . . . embraces the right to maintain theories of life and of death and of the hereafter which are rank heresy to followers of the orthodox faiths." And in 1961, in *Torcaso v. Watkins*, in the course of invalidating a Maryland provision requiring a declaration of belief in the existence of God as a test for public office, the Court observed that the religion clauses prohibit government support of "those religions based on a belief in the existence of God as against those religions founded on different beliefs," noting that "among religions in this country which do not teach what would generally be considered a belief in the existence of God are Buddhism, Taoism, Ethical Culture, Secular Humanism and others."

The most generous definition that the Supreme Court has given to religion has been in a statutory, rather than a constitutional, setting. In *United States v. Seeger*, the Court interpreted a provision of the Universal Military Training and Service Act that exempted from military service, "those persons who by reason of their religious training and belief are conscientiously opposed to participation in war in any form." "Religious training and belief," was defined by the statute as "an individual's belief in a relation to a Supreme Being involving duties superior to those arising from any human relation, but does not include essentially political, sociological or philosophical views or a merely personal moral code." Seeger claimed to have a religious opposition to war, although he did not believe in God, asserting rather a religious "belief in and devotion to goodness and virtue for their own sakes and a religious faith in a purely ethical creed." Rather than reach the merits of Seeger's constitutional challenge, the Court gave the Act a sufficiently expanded construction to include his beliefs:

> We have concluded that Congress, in using the expression "Supreme Being" rather than the designation "God," was merely clarifying

the meaning of religious training and belief so as to embrace all religions and to exclude essentially political, sociological, or philosophical views. We believe that under this construction, the test of belief "in a relation to a Supreme Being" is *whether a given belief that is sincere and meaningful occupies a place in the life of its possessor parallel to that filled by the orthodox belief in God of one who clearly qualifies for the exemption.* Where such beliefs have parallel positions in the lives of their respective holders we cannot say that one is "in a relation to a Supreme Being" and that the other is not.

The opinion also stated that the statute protected "all sincere religious beliefs which are based upon a power or being, or upon a faith, to which all else is subordinate or upon which all else is ultimately dependent," referring to the writings of modern theologians such as Paul Tillich in support of the view that the concept of a "Supreme Being" is very broad and need not refer to an anthropomorphic entity "out there."

Although *Seeger* was resolved strictly as a matter of statutory interpretation, the decision appeared to have significant constitutional portents, particularly because the Court's straining of the language of the statute—recently described as "a remarkable feat of linguistic transmutation"—was prompted by its desire to "[avoid] imputing to Congress an intent to classify different religious beliefs, exempting some and excluding others . . . . " The complexities surrounding *Seeger's* "functional" approach to defining religion—in contrast to one that emphasizes the "content" of the beliefs that seek constitutional recognition as being "religious"—will concern us shortly. But the *Seeger* definition's promise for attaining constitutional status has been measurably diminished by the Court's subsequent treatment of the problem in *Sherbert* and *Yoder*, which were necessarily grounded in the free exercise clause rather than an act of Congress.

The seminal decision in *Sherbert* did not discuss at any length the type of claimant who was entitled to assert the newly established exemption from general government regulations nor the sort of a claim that may be raised. At several points, however, the Court's opinion seems to underline that Sherbert's position was based on a clearly recognizable, fairly conventional religious precept. Thus, the Court observed that there was no "doubt that the prohibition against Saturday labor is a basic tenet of the Seventh-Day Adventist creed, based on that religion's interpretation of the Holy Bible"; that South Carolina's denial of unemployment compensation burdened "a cardinal principle" of Sherbert's faith; and that "South Carolina may not constitutionally apply the eligibility provisions so as to constrain a worker to abandon his religious convictions respecting the day of rest." All of these declarations have a ring of orthodoxy that is commonly related to worship in the Judeo-Christian tradition.

A more explicitly considered view of religion was expressed in *Yoder*, which emphasized that the free exercise clause's extraordinary exemption was available for only "a 'religious' belief or practice," and then, without clearly specifying the criteria for a definition, nonetheless articulated a relatively cautious approach:

> A way of life, however virtuous and admirable, may not be interposed as a barrier to reasonable state regulation of education if it is based on purely secular considerations; to have the protection of the Religion Clauses, the claims must be rooted in religious belief. Although a determination of what is a "religious" belief or practice entitled to constitutional protection may present a most delicate question, the very concept of ordered liberty precludes allowing every person to make his own standards on matters of conduct in which society as a whole has important interests. Thus, if the Amish asserted their claims because of their subjective evaluation and rejection of the contemporary secular values accepted by the majority, much as Thoreau rejected the social values of his time and isolated himself at Walden Pond, their claims would not rest on a religious basis. Thoreau's choice was philosophical and personal rather than religious, and such belief does not rise to the demands of the Religion Clauses.

The Court then reviewed the record in detail to demonstrate that "the traditional way of life of the Amish is not merely a matter of personal preference, but one of deep religious conviction, shared by an organized group, and intimately related to daily living," stressing that the Amish are an old and established Christian sect, and that their opposition to formal higher education is grounded in Biblical beliefs.

## 2. The Relationship Between Definition and Scope of Substantive Protection

The Court's seemingly guarded attitude in *Sherbert* and its more openly conservative approach in *Yoder*—both cases involving beliefs that could easily be characterized as religious by reference to conventional ideas of Christian orthodoxy—may well have been influenced by the very generous protection those decisions afforded to claims falling within the Court's conception of religion. Indeed, it is fair to question whether the Court would have reached the same results if the claimants' beliefs had not been reinforced by membership in recognized sects or if the Justices had been less familiar with the content of those beliefs.

There is an obvious relationship between the legal definition of religion and the shaping of substantive doctrine under the free exercise clause. In effect, the definition acts as a screening mechanism that determines what claims will be subjected to the substantive "balancing test" that the Court has developed for judging whether an exemption for religion must be granted. Thus, the more inclusive the legal definition of religion, the greater the number and diversity of claims under the free exercise clause that must be considered on the merits. Indeed, one function of arguments for a broad definition of religion—*e.g.* "all that is '*arguably religious*' should be considered religious in a free exercise analysis" so that the free exercise clause may "continue to fulfill its 'historic purpose'"—is the creation of an indirect and textually-based method of obtaining meaningful and expanding judicial protection for "rights of privacy and personhood" despite the Court's reluctance to do so under the rubric of substantive due process.

Nevertheless, a spacious judicial definition of religion need not necessarily lead to greater protection for religious freedom or for other personal liberty. The ultimate reach of the free exercise clause can be expanded or limited by the Court at either the definitional or substantive steps of the process, and it is unlikely that an extremely broad definition of religion will be permitted to coexist with an extremely generous protection of the claims that fall within that definition. The restrictions that the free exercise clause places on government's power to enact neutral, generally applicable regulations governing health, safety, and welfare are marked exceptions to the plenary nature of that authority. Judicial recognition of the fact that, at least under our present system of values, civil government requires that these exceptions be fairly narrow is obvious from the Court's observation in *Yoder* that "the very concept of ordered liberty precludes allowing every person to make his own standards on matters of conduct in which society as a whole has important interests." Thus, the Court's recognition of all conceivably religious claims as falling within the free exercise clause probably would result in a relatively modest degree of substantive protection for them, whereas a more confined definition of religion more readily permits the quite far-reaching protection that the Court has afforded those beliefs.

It should be clear, however, that once a belief is categorized as "religious," it must be accorded the same constitutional refuge as all other such "religious" beliefs; the Court cannot adjust the substantive part of the process to secure the practice of one assertedly "religious" group and reject the same precept of another. For example, in *Yoder*, the Court's grant of an exemption to the Amish but not to those like Thoreau was accomplished on a definitional basis, not on a substantive one. If the Court had defined Thoreau's beliefs as "religious," it would have been faced with the choice of either granting an exemption to all the Thoreaus of the world, as well as to the Amish, or affording no such immunity at all. Indeed, the increased impact on state programs of exempting a wider group might well have led the Court to reach the opposite result on the merits.

### 3. The Seeger-Welsh Formulation

The most thoroughly considered effort by the Supreme Court to define "religion"—albeit, at least technically, in a nonconstitutional context—produced the *Seeger* opinion's standard of "whether a given belief . . . occupies a place in the life of its possessor parallel to that filled by the orthodox belief in God." This guideline as to "whether a conscientious objector's beliefs are religious" was given further content (and elasticity) in *Welsh v. United States*, the opinion announcing the Court's judgment pointing out "that 'intensely personal' convictions which some might find 'incomprehensible' or 'incorrect' come within the meaning of 'religious belief'" if they are "held with the strength of traditional religious convictions." Although the *Seeger* Court expressed the view that this "parallel position" test would be "simple of application," a probe beneath its veneer—especially as more fully articulated in *Welsh*—discloses substantially greater difficulties than the Court's confident language suggests.

One major ambiguity of the *Seeger-Welsh* formulation concerns precisely what "place" God or religion occupies in the life of a member of a conventional religious sect. In fact, a traditional believer's religion does not play a single, ascertainable role in his existence; rather, it may influence his being in a variety of ways—*e.g.*, morally, spiritually, socially, etc. Nor need its influence remain constant; rather, it may change over time. Moreover, even within a given sect, religion will fill different functions in the lives of different members.

More importantly, there appears to be no readily observable line of demarcation between those beliefs that are "parallel" to a belief in God or other orthodox religious precepts and those beliefs that are not. It is true that some parallels can be drawn between the beliefs of, for example, Orthodox Jews, Jehovah's Witnesses, and Catholics. All three involve a belief in God, but that is precisely the parallel that *Seeger* rejected as being too narrow. All three also involve membership in a group that propounds certain moral principles, but this is equally true for the Boy Scouts and the American Bar Association, neither of which is either commonly perceived as a religion or thought to be entitled to the special privileges of the free exercise clause.

There are two distinct paths that may be pursued in adding texture to the *Seeger* "parallel position" formulation's uncertain scope. One is a functional approach that seeks equivalence in the intensity of conviction with which beliefs are held. Another is a content-based approach that searches for analogues in subject matter that are both common and exclusive to concededly religious beliefs. In considering these broad alternatives (and their more specific applications) for defining "religion" for the purpose of the free exercise clause's constitutional immunity from secularly based general government regulations of conduct, it is important to attempt to identify various historic and contemporary values underlying the provision that justify this very special protection. Then the alternatives can be evaluated in light of those values as well as the more general criteria for a legal definition of the term discussed earlier.

### 4. "Ultimate Concerns": A Functional Criterion

As a comparison of the *Davis v. Beason* and *Seeger* opinions reveals, judicial efforts to define religion in the legal context have attempted to keep pace with modern theological ideas. Developing concepts of religion within the Christian tradition have tended to move beyond orthodox concepts of God. Some contemporary theologians, with a significant Christian following, urge secularization as the proper path of the church and social change as the just study of theology. Others, while reaffirming the importance of transcendental faith, have departed from an anthropomorphic concept of a deity. Thus, John A.T. Robinson, the Bishop of Woolwich, in his controversial book, *Honest to God* which was quoted by the Court in *Seeger*, rejects the idea of "a God 'out there,' a God who 'exists' above and beyond the world he made, a God 'to' whom we pray and to whom we 'go' when we die." Paul Tillich identifies faith as "the state of being ultimately concerned," and God as "the ground of all being." The *Seeger*

Court also quoted Tillich's work in support of its holding.

Because of the favorable attention given by the Court to these progressive theologians, several constitutional interpretations of religion have been advocated that are based on the idea of "ultimate concerns," a phrase taken from the writings of Tillich. These proposals look primarily to the functional aspects of religion—its importance in the believer's scheme of things—rather than to its content. Ultimate concerns are to be protected, no matter how "secular" their subject matter may appear to be.

This approach has several attractive features. First, it fulfills the need for a tolerant definition by its capability of including nonconformist, fringe religions as well as known orthodox sects and by its rejection of judicial determinations of whether some beliefs are inherently more "valuable" than others. Even more importantly, respect for deeply held beliefs is plainly a central value underlying the religion clauses. By focusing on the great significance that the belief holds for the claimant, this approach responds to the aversion, discussed more fully below, of confronting an individual with the especially oppressive choice of either forsaking such precepts or suffering the pains of government sanctions.

The virtues of this definition, however, are outweighed by a series of difficulties. First, although Tillich's views may well be the profound expressions of a radical theologian searching for truth, even today they only marginally comprehend "religion" as that term is understood by most theologians or laymen. Moreover, Tillich's writings occupy volumes and are directed at theologians and lay believers, not lawyers. To extract from them the phrase, "ultimate concerns," and instruct judges to apply it as a legal formula seriously underestimates the subtlety of Tillich's thought and overestimates the theological sophistication of the participants in the legal process. For example, although Tillich recognizes that individuals may have such things as nationalism or worldly success as their ultimate concerns, he accords them no special respect, finding them to be idolatrous, because they claim to be ultimate without really being so.

Our experience reveals that ultimate concerns may relate to such matters as science, politics, economics, social welfare, or even recreation—all staples of normal government regulation. For this reason, the "ultimate concerns" approach is at odds with an important historic sentiment that underlies the constitutional protection granted by the religion clauses: that religion comprehends matters with which the government, whose authority is presumptively plenary, is incompetent to interfere. Pursuant to this postulate, religion was to be regarded as a separate realm, to which the first amendment ceded a degree of sovereignty. Because "ultimate concerns," however, pervade virtually all areas of ordinary government involvement, whatever the true importance of such beliefs to the individual or society as a whole, to grant them the special constitutional immunity of the free exercise clause merely because they are strongly held would severely undermine the state's ability to advance the commonweal.

Finally, because of its inherent vagueness, the "ultimate concerns" standard suffers from being based in large measure on psychological factors that are very difficult to administer. The legal process would be confronted with such formidable issues as what an "ultimate concern" really is and how "ultimate" must a concern be in order to qualify as religious. The broad discretion afforded the fact finder, whether judge or jury, poses a significant risk that parochial preconceptions will often prevail to the detriment of claimants with unorthodox principles and that appellate review will be able to correct only the most blatantly arbitrary decisions. Moreover, because the claimant's own characterization of his beliefs will frequently be the sole evidence supporting his position and because success will often depend on the ability to articulate the relationship between deeply held beliefs and a definition whose meaning is only dimly understood, the likely beneficiaries will be both the orthodox believers and those others who are best educated and most articulate.

5. "Extratemporal Consequences": A More Content-Based Criterion

As indicated above, a forceful explanation and pragmatic justification for the free exercise clause's special exemption from otherwise universal governmental regulation is the fact that the commands of religious belief, at least as conventionally perceived, have a unique significance for the believer, thus making it particularly cruel for the government to require the believer to choose between violating those commands and suffering meaningful temporal disabilities. Moreover, although the state may—and sometimes must—make many harsh demands on its citizenry—such as serving in the military, paying taxes, and forbearing from various forms of pleasurable behavior—our traditions, informed by both moral and instrumental concerns, have set certain constitutional, statutory, and common law limits on the reach of government power.

The relationship between religion and this tradition may be illustrated by hypothesizing two objectors to military service. One has sincere conscientious scruples against killing, but they are not claimed by anyone, including the draftee, to be religious. The other's objection is rooted in a deep-seated faith that if he voluntarily kills another human being, this will influence or indeed determine his destiny after death. At the extreme, he may believe that if he does so, his immortal soul will be damned for eternity. Clearly, both will experience severe psychic turmoil if required to kill. But, although there is no sure method of proving it scientifically as an empirical matter, intuition and experience affirm that the degree of internal trauma on earth for those who have put their souls in jeopardy for eternity can be expected to be markedly greater than for those who have only violated a moral scruple.

It must be acknowledged, however, that the state is not exclusively responsible for the concededly grave consequences facing the religious objector to military service. The government has simply presented both draftees with the option of either fulfilling their legal obligation or paying the price of fines, imprisonment, or a loss of government benefits. Because these state-imposed consequences are the same for both objectors, it may be said that there is no special cruelty in punishing the latter. Moreover, at a psychological level, the identical cost may be more comfortably borne by those religionists who can balance it against eternal rather than merely temporal benefits. Indeed, some may believe that martyrdom has independent value in affecting their destiny. Nonetheless, because the burden of *obeying* the law is so severe for the religious objector, our traditions hold that his noncompliance is not as morally culpable as one who disobeys for other reasons. This principle is reflected in the defenses of duress and necessity in the criminal law, excusing or justifying violations when the cost of compliance is higher than an individual can reasonably be expected to bear.

This "special cruelty" factor—that seeks to draw a line beyond which it is unreasonable for society to expect a person to alter or violate his beliefs—is difficult to measure precisely, because the degrees of importance of various individuals' beliefs obviously form a continuous spectrum. Nonetheless, I believe, as the discussion above suggests, that belief in the phenomenon of "extratemporal consequences"— whether the effects of actions taken pursuant or contrary to the dictates of a person's beliefs extend in some meaningful way beyond his lifetime—is a sensible and desirable criterion (albeit plainly far short of ideal) for determining when the free exercise clause should trigger judicial consideration of whether an exemption from general government regulations of conduct is constitutionally required.

The "extratemporal consequences" criterion, which does not focus on the intensity of conviction with which the beliefs are held but rather on the perceived repercussions of their violation, is somewhat more content-based than functional in approach. By tending toward the subject matter of beliefs in this way, it probably conforms more than the "ultimate concerns" approach with the conventional, average-person conception of religion which, although largely intuitive, would generally conclude that a belief in God is religious but a belief in the Republican party is not, no matter how strongly held either of the beliefs may be.

While this approach thus has the virtue of greater common acceptability, the primary disadvantage of adopting a content-based definition of "religion" for constitutional purposes is the danger of parochialism and intolerance—that judges will include conventional orthodoxy in the definition and exclude new, unfamiliar, or "dangerous" beliefs. This is in fact the course that the Supreme Court took in the polygamy cases. Thus, it has been argued that, "[a]t the very point where [content-based efforts to define religion] say, in effect, that a person must hold certain tenets or focus on certain issues in order to come within the constitutional protection, they demonstrate their incapacity to effectuate that protection. They enshrine an orthodoxy within a Constitution designed in part to protect unorthodoxy."

Several considerations, however, support the "extratemporal consequences" precept. First, unlike content-based approaches that center on the specific substance of beliefs—such as a belief in God—it looks only to the ultimate supposed effects of beliefs whatever their peculiar substance may be. In this sense at least, it is sufficiently flexible and capable of growth to include newly perceived and unconventional values.

Second, to the extent that this criterion "enshrines" beliefs of a particular genre, it must be recalled that the dominant purpose of the religion clauses is to single out "religion," as opposed to other systems of belief, and requires that the concept have some minimum content. It should also be remembered that beliefs falling outside this definition (such as those associated with the Universalist, Secular Humanism, Deism and Ethical Culture movements) are not remitted to uncontrolled punishment or persecution. Rather, all individual concerns, opinions, and beliefs receive substantial protection under other constitutional provisions. As a matter of history and necessity, however, the special immunity for *conduct* afforded by the free exercise clause may belong only to a special category of beliefs.

Third, although the content of even the most well-recognized religious belief systems is so varied as to defy any efforts to distill uniform tenets, the extratemporal consequences phenomenon finds support not only in those traditional religions prevalent in our culture but in most of the world's other major sects as well. At present, Christianity, Islam, and most branches of Judaism all believe in some form of divine judgment after death. Various sects of Hinduism and Buddhism teach that each person is to be reincarnated, with the merit accumulated by virtuous acts in this life affecting one's status in the next, and with the possibility of eventual entry into heaven or Nirvana. Moreover, this extratemporal consequences concept already has appeared in major Supreme Court decisions. The *Yoder* opinion, for example, notes that the Old Order Amish "believed that by sending their children to high school, they would . . . endanger their own salvation and that of their children." Similarly, Justices Black and Douglas observed in the *Flag Salute Case* that "compelling little children to participate in a ceremony . . . ends in nothing for them but a fear of spiritual condemnation."

Finally, the extratemporal consequences standard is consistent with a primary goal of the religion clauses—to isolate government from matters that it has neither the power nor competence to control. Because the state can neither perceive nor determine what happens after death, it is particularly appropriate that it have minimal legislative authority to affect what may possibly occur in that realm.

6. "Transcendent Reality": A Possible Criterion

Despite the advantages of the extratemporal consequences test for determining when a system of beliefs qualifies for the special constitutional protection of the free exercise clause, it must be admitted that this criterion is not totally congruent with much that theologians and laymen would include in a definition of religion. Even within the Christian tradition, there are many articles of faith that do not relate directly to any rewards or punishments after death. Belief in the possibility of divine intervention on earth is one example: faith healing, retribution, and answered prayers. Another is the precept, which many find in the teachings of such persons as Saint Augustine and John Calvin, that salvation is the gift of God to His chosen, and is not to be earned by such behavior as good works during life. Under beliefs of this nature, one may act under a religious compulsion that is not at all connected to the achievement of redemption.

Other religions, moreover, may ignore the afterlife consequences of one's acts altogether. Many major religions in their "primitive" stages have been far more concerned with the relationship between the living and the world around them than with the fate of the dead. Some religions that do concern themselves with the deceased often have as their aim to propitiate the spirits of the departed or to prevent them from returning, an attitude towards the dead that is still wide-spread. The indigenous religion of China, for example, is a well-developed system of ancestor worship in which the spirits of dead forebears are regarded as taking an active and continuing role in the well-being of the family. Chinese religion involves strong duties, but does not usually connect them with consequences to follow after death. Thus, although belief in this life as but one phase of existence, with the next phase to be determined by one's actions on earth, is extensive, it is not universal among the world's major religions, nor is it the only important belief of those sects that do hold it.

Admittedly, many beliefs that are generally regarded as religious despite their exclusive bearing on temporal affairs do share a common core with the extratemporal consequences precept. These beliefs are concerned with aspects of reality that are not observable in ordinary experience, but which are assumed to exist at another level. By addressing "basic questions" or perhaps through mystical revelation of the unity of the world, such beliefs tend to infuse reality with transcendent meaning and significance—often through doctrines that explain such phenomena as the creation of the world and the nature of life and death. These aspects of reality may be felt by the believer, but because they cannot be demonstrated as facts, they transcend material experience.

This is confirmed by theological conceptions such as John Robinson's, which substitutes the metaphor of depth for the metaphor of height and views God as "the ultimate depth of all our being, the creative ground and meaning of our existence." Robinson rejects the naturalistic contentions that "God is merely a redundant name for nature or for humanity," and thus affirms the transcendent nature of religion. Similarly, Paul Tillich has written that "the source of this affirmation of meaning within meaninglessness, or certitude within doubt, is not the God of traditional theism but the 'God above God,' the power of being, which works through those who have no name for it, even the name of God."

It may be persuasively argued that *all* beliefs that invoke a transcendent reality—and especially those that provide their adherents with glimpses of meaning and truth that make them so important and so uncompromisable—should be encompassed by the special constitutional protection granted "religion" by the free exercise clause. Such beliefs not only conform to broadly based theological and lay perceptions of religion, but appear to be distinguishable from those more secularly grounded ideologies (such as humanistic pacifism, socialism, or Marxism) that we think of as being concerned largely with observable facts or ordinary human experience, even though the latter sets of beliefs may be as comprehensive and deeply held.

Systems of belief that are grounded in observable facts, about which evidence can be gathered, experts consulted, empirical conclusions drawn, and policies made, fall squarely within the realm of traditional governmental decisionmaking. While individuals may hold strong views on these matters, presumably there is a demonstrably correct answer that civil authority may decree. On the other hand, facts that are not observable in a conventional sense nor empirically verifiable, but are rather unknowable in the physical world, can only be experienced by the believer or taken on faith. No one, including government, can dictate or deny such experiences. Thus, it may be said that beliefs concerned with transcendent reality are outside the regulatory competence of the state.

In many ways, however, transcendental explanations of worldly realities are essentially no different, even in terms of government regulatory competence, than conventional exegeses for temporal outcomes that are based on such "rational" disciplines as economics, political science, sociology, or psychology, or even such "hard" sciences as biophysics, geophysics, or just plain physics. When justifying competing government policies on such varied matters as social welfare, the economy, and military and foreign affairs, there is at bedrock only a gossamer line between "rational" and "supernatural" causation—the former really being little more capable of "scientific proof" than the latter. Moreover, at the level of final decision, even the most frankly utilitarian goals depend ultimately on values—such as good or evil, or even the desirability of human survival—that represent normative preferences rather than rationally compelled choices. Therefore, if government possesses generally plenary authority to regulate the worldly affairs of society—and it surely does under our historical and contemporary political scheme—then its ability to do so should not be restricted because of the nature of the causes, which are all basically unverifiable, that different groups believe will produce consequences that the state seeks to achieve. In addition, from the standpoint of the need for principled adjudicative standards so vital for constitutional decisionmaking by a nonmajoritarian judiciary, there are several other central factors as to

which it appears very difficult, if not impossible, to distinguish transcendental ideologies from those commonly considered to be based on secular premises—the intensity with which the beliefs are held (and the mental anguish resulting from their violation) and the comprehensive scope of the creeds' dogmas. Moreover, from a utilitarian perspective, the intuitive empirical judgment persists that obeying the law at the price of perceived eternal repercussions produces substantially greater psychological suffering than doing so at the cost of compromising scruples with only temporal reactions. Thus, the extreme protection from government power to regulate conduct afforded by the free exercise clause should be reserved for those who believe that departure from certain beliefs will carry uniquely severe consequences extending beyond the grave.

## III. THE ESTABLISHMENT CLAUSE

The Supreme Court has developed a three-part test for assessing alleged violations of the establishment clause. In order to pass constitutional muster, government action (1) must have a secular, rather than a religious purpose, (2) may not have the principal or primary effect of advancing or inhibiting religion, and (3) may not involve "excessive entanglement" between government and religion. Although each prong of this formula requires that content be given to the term "religious" or "religion," the Court has rarely even begun to do so and, when it has, its discussion has usually been very brief and quite conclusory.

Problems arising under the establishment clause have generally fallen into three broad categories. The first involves government financial assistance to religiously affiliated institutions—usually educational facilities. Because virtually all the cases have involved schools or colleges operated under the auspices of organized churches, the Court's focus has been on whether "religion" permeated the educational offering and on what sorts of aid were permissible. In none of these decisions was any definitional issue seriously disputed, the Court's discussion plainly assuming that everyone knew what was "religious" and what was not. A second group of decisions concerns regulatory laws allegedly enacted for religious purposes. In the two most prominent cases in this area, the Court again simply assumed a common understanding of the difference between a legislature's acting for "religious" rather than for "secular" reasons. The third major category implicates religious influences in the public schools. In the several instances here that defenders of the challenged practices claimed that they had a nonsectarian goal, the Court rather summarily rejected the assertions as implausible.

## A. Dual Versus Unitary Definition of "Religion"

In order to accommodate the range of values underlying the religion clauses without subverting the regulatory goals of civil government in modern society, the Court has been urged to adopt a dual definition of religion—an expansive interpretation for the free exercise clause so as to protect "the multiplying forms of recognizably legitimate religious exercise," but a more confined definition for the establishment clause so as to avoid having "all 'humane' programs of government be deemed constitutionally suspect." For example, even though it may be that "a group of gymnasts proclaiming on their trampolines that physical culture is their religion" should fall within the coverage of the free exercise clause, this should not mean that "if Congress, in a particular Olympic year, appropriated funds to subsidize their calisthenics," this would be aid to "religion" in violation of the establishment clause. Similarly, the fact that some people regard Transcendental Meditation to be their religion, thus entitling them to the constitutional immunity of the free exercise clause, should not lead to the conclusion that the establishment clause forbids a public school course in meditation that is offered for its psychologically beneficial effects.

Apart from the objection that the text of the first amendment—"Congress shall make no law respecting an establishment of religion, or prohibiting the free exercise thereof"—makes it grammatically difficult to argue that "thereof" has a different meaning than the word "religion" to which it refers, close examination of the operative doctrines for the religion clauses suggests that a dual definition of religion may not be required to avoid the results feared under a unitary version of the term. Although there is considerable overlap in the purpose and operation of the two provisions—the central function of both being to secure religious liberty—each nonetheless has an identifiable emphasis. In the main, the free exercise clause protects *adherents of religious faiths* from *secularly* motivated government action whose effect imposes burdens on them because of their particular beliefs. When the Court finds a violation of the free exercise clause, this usually means that the law is invalid as applied; all that is required is an exemption for the claimant from the law's otherwise proper operation. In contrast, the principal (although—as we shall see—not the exclusive) thrust of the establishment clause concerns *religiously* motivated government action that poses a danger that *believers* and *nonbelievers* alike will be required to support their own religious observance or that of others. When the Court finds a violation of the establishment clause, this ordinarily means that the offensive law (or part thereof) is invalid in its entirety and may not be enforced at all.

Under these existing principles, the Court may hold that, on balance, the free exercise clause requires an exemption from a generally valid regulation that happens to impose burdens on what the Court concludes to be the "religion" of Transcendental Meditation. But a public school course in meditation does not violate the establishment clause, despite the fact that this course is very helpful to, or parallels that required by, the Transcendental Meditation faith, unless it is shown that the school board's purpose in instituting the course (or the principal or primary effect of its being offered) is to advance religion. The Court has made clear that the establishment clause does not forbid government action simply because it provides some aid to what is conceded to be a "religion," or because there is a coincidence between a legal command and the dictates of a group that comes within the protective coverage of the free exercise clause. That many conventional religious sects adhere to the Ten Commandments—prohibiting such acts as murder, adultery, perjury, theft, disrespect for one's parents, and Sunday labor—does not alone disable the government from legislating on those subjects. "In many instances, the Congress or state legislatures conclude that the general welfare of society, wholly apart from any religious considerations, demands such regulation."

## B. Identifying Legislative Purpose

The crucial question, of course, is how to determine whether the legislative purpose is to further "the general welfare of society" rather than to "advance religion." Just as the free exercise clause should require judicial acceptance of a claimant's bona fide subjective characterization of his beliefs as being "religious" (as that term is defined for constitutional purposes), so, too, this key issue under the establishment clause should ultimately center on the intent of the lawmaking body. Although not dispositive, the crux of this delicate inquiry into why a majority of legislators enacted a particular law is best evidenced by its primary (or independent) effect and should turn not on the fact that some person or group perceives the law's goals or results as being "religious" (which may suffice to afford that person or group the protection of the free exercise clause), but rather on a more general societal perception of the matter. For although there may be occasions when it can be proven that the legislature is consciously pursuing sectarian ends despite a contrary popular understanding, ordinarily the public's perception that "the general welfare of society" is the law's object will powerfully evidence the intent of their elected or appointed representatives.

For example, if a group adopted physical fitness as its religion and believed that practices pursuant thereto had extratemporal consequences, and if an extratemporal consequences definition of religion were accepted for purposes of the free exercise clause, then action (or inaction) dictated by the group's tenets would be comprehended by the free exercise clause. But if this same definition of religion were applied under the establishment clause, the government would not thereby be prohibited from sponsoring physical fitness programs unless it could be shown that the legislative purpose was to advance physical fitness because of its extratemporal consequences. Because, in the absence of unusual evidence to the contrary, most government physical fitness programs are correctly perceived by the public to be directed at health, rather than to extratemporal consequences, no establishment clause problem would be present.

Those few establishment clause decisions of the Supreme Court that consider the issue of how to identify what is "religion" or "religious" are consistent with this approach. As for regulatory laws allegedly enacted for religious purposes, in upholding Maryland's Sunday closing law, the Court found that despite the fact that "the original laws which dealt with Sunday labor were motivated by religious forces," their "present purpose and effect" was to further "the general welfare of society." The Court relied on the fact that secular emphases in language and interpretation had come about, that recent "legislation was supported by labor groups and trade associations," and that "secular justifications have been advanced for making Sunday a day of rest, a day when people may recover from the labors of the week just passed and may physically and mentally prepare for the week's work to come." Thus, even though refraining from work on Sunday is a tenet of major American religious groups, the relevant evidence satisfied the Court that the present legislation was motivated by economic and social considerations. In contrast, in invalidating a state statute prohibiting the teaching of evolution in public schools, the Court concluded that "Arkansas' law selects from the body of knowledge a particular segment which it proscribes for the sole reason that it is deemed to conflict with a particular religious doctrine." Citing newspaper advertisements and letters supporting adoption of the statute in 1928, the Court found it "clear that fundamentalist sectarian conviction was and is the law's reason for existence."

In two of the cases invalidating religious influences in the public schools, the Court—acknowledging the intimate relationship between the Bible and the nation's dominant religious sects—also drew on common understanding of what constitutes "religion" to impeach what it obviously concluded were implausible assertions that there were secular purposes for the challenged practices. In *Abington School District v. Schempp*, the defendant school boards contended that the reading, without comment, of a chapter of the Bible at the opening of the school day served such nonsectarian ends as promoting moral values, inspiring pupil tolerance and discipline, contradicting the materialistic trends of the times, and teaching literature. The Court's brusque reply was that, "surely, the place of the Bible as an instrument of religion cannot be gainsaid." More recently, the Court summarily reversed a decision by the Kentucky Supreme Court which had upheld the practice of posting copies of the Ten Commandments in public school classrooms. The avowed purpose for posting the Ten Commandments was printed at the bottom of each copy: "The secular application of the Ten Commandments is clearly seen in its adoption as the fundamental legal code of Western Civilization and the Common Law of the United States." Observing that the Commandments were not integrated into any study of history, ethics, or comparative religion, but could only have the effect, if any, of inducing students to meditate on, revere, or perhaps obey them, the Court quite peremptorily concluded that "the Ten Commandments is undeniably a sacred text in the Jewish and Christian faiths, and no legislative recitation of a supposed secular purpose can blind us to that fact."

## C. The Relevance of "Effect"

As noted earlier, the Court's three-part establishment clause test holds that a law is invalid if either its purpose *or* its principal or primary effect is to advance religion. Although the establishment clause decisions in the categories of religious influences in the public schools and regulatory laws with allegedly religious motivation have focused almost exclusively on legislative purpose rather than on effects, some rulings have invalidated financial aid to church-related schools or colleges on the ground that despite their bona fide secular purpose the programs' primary effects advanced religion.

The fact that government action which furthers religious interests serves potentially as an independent ground for invalidating a program rather than simply evidencing the legislature's purpose creates substantial problems of judicial prerogative. Such an approach empowers the Court to assess, by means of an ad hoc balancing process, the multiple impacts of legislation, to isolate those that are religious from those that are secular, and then to determine which are paramount, relying ultimately on the Justices' subjective notions of predominance.

Regardless of the deficiencies of this process, however, it need not influence the issue of a dual versus a unitary definition of religion. The hypothetical physical fitness cult discussed previously again provides an illustration. Despite the fact that a government sponsored bodily health program might assist this group in pursuing its concededly religious goals, just as a Sunday closing law undoubtedly aids those conventional religions that require church attendance on their Sabbath, it is extremely unlikely that advancement of the physical fitness faith could be found to be either the "principal" or "primary" effect of the program.

---

George C. Freeman, III, *The Misguided Search for the Constitutional Definition of "Religion"*, 71 GEORGETOWN LAW REVIEW 1519 (1983)*

. . .

Throughout its history, the Supreme Court has had surprisingly little to say about the meaning of "religion." In fact, prior to its 1961 landmark decision in *Torcaso v. Watkins*, the Court had commented on the meaning of 'religion" in only four cases. In the first, *Davis v. Beason*, in 1890, the Court paid tribute to theism: "The term 'religion' has reference to one's view of his relations to his Creator, and to the obligations they impose of reverence for his being and character, and of obedience to his will." The second comment, coming some forty years later, in *United States v. Macintosh*, seconded the tribute: "The essence of religion is belief in a relation to God involving duties superior to those arising from any human relation." In 1944, in *United States v. Ballard*, the Court subtly shifted its position. Without commenting explicitly in the case on the meaning of "religion," the Court implied that

* Reprinted with the permission of the publisher, © 1983 The Georgetown Law Journal Association and Georgetown University.

earlier attempts to equate religion with theism were probably unconstitutional. Religious freedom, said the Court, includes "the right to maintain theories of life and of death and of the hereafter which are rank heresy to followers of the orthodox faiths." In 1953, in *Fowler v. Rhode Island*, the Court again suggested that any attempt to reduce religion to theism is constitutionally suspect: "[I]t is no business of courts to say that what is a religious practice or activity for one group is not religion under the protection of the First Amendment."

With *Torcaso*, the Supreme Court dispelled whatever doubts may have existed about its willingness to conceive of religion in new, and radically different, terms. The dispute in the case arose over a provision in a Maryland statute requiring all public officials to profess a belief in God before assuming office. The Court invalidated the provision on the grounds that the requirement placed Maryland "on the side of one particular sort of believer" and therefore imposed an unconstitutional burden on both nonbelievers and believers whose religion does not rest on a belief in God. In what has become a famous footnote, the Court said of this latter group: "Among religions in this country which do not teach what would generally be considered a belief in the existence of God are Buddhism, Taoism, Ethical Culture, Secular Humanism and others." With this remark, the Court expressly repudiated its earlier attempts to equate religion with theism.

What the Court in *Torcaso* did not do was provide any guidelines for determining which beliefs and practices are rooted in religion. These the Court sought to provide, albeit in the context of statutory interpretation, in *United States v. Seeger*. At issue in *Seeger* was the meaning of the phrase "religious training and belief" in section 6(j) of the Universal Military Training and Service Act of 1948. Section 6(j) guaranteed an exemption from military service to anyone    ·

> who, by reason of religious training and belief, is conscientiously opposed to participation in war in any form. Religious training and belief in this connection means an individual's belief in a relation to a Supreme Being involving duties superior to those arising from any human relation, but does not include essentially political, sociological, or philosophical views or a merely personal moral code.

In the light of this language, the petitioner, Andrew Seeger, did not appear to qualify for an exemption, since his opposition to war was not based on a belief in a Supreme Being. Indeed, Seeger expressed skepticism about the existence of such a Being. He based his opposition to war, instead, on a "religious faith in a purely ethical creed."

Despite strong evidence that Congress intended otherwise, the Court interpreted section 6(j) as guaranteeing an exemption to every religious believer who opposed war in any form, no matter what his religion. Had Congress sought to limit exemptions to traditional theists, the Court reasoned, Congress would have used the word "God" rather than the phrase "Supreme Being" in defining "religious training and belief." This question of congressional intent resolved, the Court then proposed the following test for determining when a belief is a religious belief: "[T]he test . . . is whether a given belief that is sincere and meaningful occupies a place in the life of its possessor parallel to that filled by the orthodox belief in God of one who clearly qualifies for the exemption." Drawing on the writings of several eminent theologians, most notably Paul Tillich, the Court suggested that a belief is "parallel to that filled by the orthodox belief in God" if it is "based upon a power or a being, or upon a faith, to which all else is subordinate or upon which all else is ultimately dependent." Under this view of religious belief, the Court concluded, Seeger's opposition to war was religious; consequently, he could not be denied an exemption.

In the next major draft-exemption case, *Welsh v. United States*, the Court embraced an even more expansive view of the meaning of "religion." The petitioner, Elliott Welsh, insisted that his opposition to war, unlike Andrew Seeger's, was not in any way religious. It arose, said Welsh, from his "reading in the fields of history and sociology." For the government, this meant that Welsh fit into the class of persons Congress had intended to exclude from exemption.

The Court disagreed. In its view, while "a registrant's characterization of his own belief as 'religious' should carry great weight . . . a registrant's statement that his beliefs are non-religious is a highly unreliable guide" for the authorities to use in determining whether those beliefs are within the scope of the exemption. The reason: "Very few registrants are fully aware of the broad scope of the word "religious" as used in § 6(j)." Rather than simply ignoring Welsh's characterization of his beliefs, however, and applying the *Seeger* test to them, the Court went further. Welsh could be denied an exemption, the Court declared, only if his beliefs were not deeply held and did not "rest at all upon moral, ethical, or religious principles but instead rest[ed] solely upon considerations of policy, pragmatism, or expediency." Finding that Welsh's opposition to war could

not be classified under any of the latter three headings, the Court held he was entitled to an exemption.

Since *Welsh*, the Court has commented only twice, and then only in dicta, on the meaning of "religion." In *Wisconsin v. Yoder*, where the right of the Amish to withdraw their children from school after the eighth grade was upheld, the Court expressed doubts about defining religion solely in functional terms, according to how a belief functions in the life of the believer. No one, argued the Court, is entitled to an exemption from reasonable state regulations for "purely secular considerations":

> [T]o have the protection of the Religion Clauses, the claims must be rooted in religious belief. . . . Thus, if the Amish asserted their claims because of their subjective evaluation and rejection of the contemporary secular values accepted by the majority, much as Thoreau rejected the social values of his time and isolated himself at Walden Pond, their claims would not rest on a religious basis. Thoreau's choice was philosophical and personal rather than religious, and such belief does not rise to the demands of the Religion Clauses.

The Court simply asserted in *Yoder*, however, that Thoreau might be classified as a paradigm of the secular believer. The Court made no attempt either to explain or to justify this classification; nor did the Court there expressly repudiate *Torcaso*, *Seeger*, and *Welsh*. More recently, in *Thomas v. Review Board*, the Court similarly asserted that some claims may be "so bizarre" as to be "clearly nonreligious in motivation." At no point, however, did the Court attempt to formulate a standard for distinguishing claims that fall within the "clearly nonreligious" category from claims that do not.

## C. The Circuit Courts

Recently, several circuit courts have also attempted to formulate a constitutional definition of "religion." In *Founding Church of Scientology of Washington v. United States* the United States Court of Appeals for the District of Columbia Circuit held that the Church of Scientology is a religion. Scientologists disavow the supernatural but claim close kinship between their doctrines and the doctrines espoused by Eastern religions, especially Hinduism and Buddhism. Their goal is to improve the spiritual condition of man by ridding the mind of "'engrams,' or patterns imprinted on the nervous system in moments of pain, stress or unconsciousness . . . [that] may produce unconscious or conditioned behavior which is harmful or irrational." The court declared that Scientology's fundamental writings, which espouse this goal, contain "a general account of man and his nature comparable in scope, if not in content, to those of some recognized religions." The court noted, however, that "it might be possible to show that a self-proclaimed religion was merely a commercial enterprise, without the underlying theories of man's nature or his place in the Universe which characterize recognized religions."

In *International Society for Krishna Consciousness, Inc., v. Barber* the United States Court of Appeals for the Second Circuit relied explicitly on the *Seeger* test in finding Krishna Consciousness (ISKCON) to be a religion. The court declared that the *Seeger* test "treats an individual's 'ultimate concern'—whatever that concern be—as his 'religion.' A concern is 'ultimate' when it is more than 'intellectual.' A concern is more than intellectual when a believer would categorically 'disregard elementary self-interest . . . in preference to transgressing its tenets.'" The court then examined "the role that Krishna Consciousness plays in the life of an ISKCON devotee" and concluded that for such an individual "adherence to the sect's theological doctrines is an 'ultimate concern.'" To bolster its conclusion, the court noted that the Krishna philosophy also constitutes a religion "in the more traditional sense" . . . . The court appears to have viewed these traditional elements of religion merely as providing additional evidence that Krishna Consciousness can serve as an ultimate concern. Nowhere in the opinion did the court suggest that an individual can have an ultimate concern only if these traditional elements are present.

One of the most thorough treatments of the meaning of "religion" by a circuit court can be found in the concurring opinion of Judge Adams in *Malnak v. Yogi*. In *Malnak* the United States Court of Appeals for the Third Circuit ruled that the Science of Creative Intelligence—Transcendental Meditation (SCI/TM), as taught in the New Jersey public schools, was a religion. As part of the SCI/TM course, students were required to read a textbook developed by the founder of SCI, a monk, and to bring fruit, flowers, and a white handkerchief to a ceremony in which the teacher chanted and made offerings to a deity. For a majority of the court, such circumstances were sufficient to qualify SCI/TM as a religion. Judge Adams, in his concurring opinion, agreed, but thought the question what constitutes a religion should be discussed at length.

Referring to *Torcaso*, *Seeger*, and *Welsh*, Judge Adams characterized the modern definition of religion as a "definition by analogy": "The modern approach . . . looks to the familiar religions as models in order to ascertain, by comparison, whether the new set of ideas or beliefs is confronting the same

concerns, or serving the same purposes, as unquestioned and accepted 'religions.'" In his view, "[t]here appear to be three useful indicia that are basic to our traditional religions and that are themselves related to the values that undergird the first amendment." The most important of these is "the 'ultimate' nature of the ideas presented." Such ideas are concerned with "the meaning of life and death, man's role in the Universe, [and] the proper moral code of right and wrong." According to Judge Adams, however, an idea is not religious simply because it addresses an ultimate question: "Certain isolated answers to ultimate questions . . . are not necessarily 'religious' answers [e.g., the Big Bang theory], because they lack the element of comprehensiveness, the second of the three indicia." A religion, Judge Adams maintained, "lays claim to an ultimate and comprehensive 'truth.'" The final element in Judge Adams' test concerns the "formal, external, or surface signs that may be analogized to accepted religions." Formal services, ceremonial functions, the existence of clergy, and a structural organization are just a few of the signs that fit into this category. Judge Adams' view regarding these signs is that, while a religion can exist without them, they may provide evidence that a group or belief system is religious.

Shortly after writing his concurring opinion in *Malnak*, Judge Adams again commented on the meaning of "religion" in *Africa v. Commonwealth of Pennsylvania*. Writing this time for the court, Judge Adams rejected the idea, which he had embraced in *Malnak*, that a belief system is religious so long as it addresses ultimate questions in a comprehensive way. . . . Rather than completely rejecting the *Malnak* approach, however, Judge Adams declared that the court would simply revise that approach in accordance with "the framework set forth in *Yoder*." The *Yoder* framework provides that a "way of life, however virtuous and admirable, may not be interposed as a barrier to reasonable state regulation . . . if it is based on purely *secular* considerations; to have the protection of the Religion Clauses, the claims must be rooted in *religious* belief." According to Judge Adams, *Yoder* also provides a satisfactory standard for distinguishing between secular beliefs and religious beliefs: beliefs are secular rather than religious when they "are more akin to Thoreau's rejection of 'the contemporary values accepted by the majority' than to the 'deep religious conviction[s]' of the Amish." Guided by this standard, Judge Adams declared that the petitioner's claim in *Africa* was not rooted in religion and so was not entitled to protection.

In reaching this conclusion, Judge Adams thought it important to describe the facts in *Africa* in some detail. The petitioner in the case, Frank Africa, was a prisoner. He was also a self-proclaimed "Naturalist Minister" of MOVE, a purportedly religious organization that is, in Africa's own words, both "revolutionary" and "absolutely opposed to all that is wrong." In his complaint, Africa argued that the state had abridged his free exercise rights by refusing to provide him with a special raw-foods diet that MOVE requires all of its members to follow. In discussing the diet's significance, Africa stated in a document submitted to the court that "our religious diet is common and uncomplicated because our diet is provided by *God* and already *done*." Africa also suggested that for MOVE members the word "diet" refers to more than just food and drink: "[O]ur religious diet is family, unity, consistency, [and] uncompromising togetherness."

According to Africa, the MOVE diet is not an end in itself but merely a means to achieving the organization's goals. These goals are "to bring about absolute peace . . . to stop violence altogether, to put a stop to all that is corrupt." To achieve these goals, MOVE tries to put its members "in touch with life's vibrations." The organization emphasizes what is "pure," "healthy," and "natural": "Water is *raw*, which makes it *pure*, which means it is *innocent*, *trustworthy*, and *safe*, which is the same as *God*." Furthermore, pursuit of the pure, the healthy, and the natural, through the diet and other means, "is not a one-day thing or a once-a-week thing or a monthly thing" for MOVE members. According to Africa, members

> are practicing [their] religious beliefs all the time: when I run, when I put information out like I am doing now, when I eat, when I breathe. . . . Every time a MOVE person opens their mouth, according to the way we believe, according to the way we do things, we are holding church.

In analyzing Africa's characterization of MOVE as a religion, the court focused on the three indicia initially articulated in Judge Adams' concurrence in *Malnak*: (1) fundamental and ultimate questions, (2) comprehensiveness, and (3) structural characteristics. As to the last of these, the court concluded that "MOVE is not structurally analogous to those 'traditional' organizations that have been recognized as religions under the first amendment." The court reached this conclusion after finding that MOVE conducts no special services, recognizes no official customs, celebrates no religious holidays, lacks an organizational structure, and appears to have "nothing that arguably might pass for a MOVE scripture book or catechism."

The court also concluded that MOVE does not provide its members with a comprehensive world view but encourages them, instead, to embrace "a single governing idea, perhaps best described as philosophical naturalism." The court acknowledged, however, that this conclusion might be open to one serious objection, namely, that a philosophy which emphasizes "[t]he notion that all of life's activities can be cloaked with religious significance," is, in a sense, comprehensive. To this, the court responded:

> Such a notion by itself, however, cannot transform an otherwise secular, one-dimensional philosophy into a comprehensive theological system. It is one thing to believe that, because of one's religion, day-to-day living takes on added meaning and importance. It is altogether different, however, to contend that certain ideas should be declared religious and therefore accorded first amendment protection from state interference merely because an individual alleges that his life is wholly governed by those ideas. . . .

Perhaps the most important part of the court's tripartite analysis concerns MOVE's attitude toward fundamental and ultimate questions. After carefully reviewing the record, the court concluded that "[s]ave for its preoccupation with living in accord with the dictates of nature, MOVE makes no mention of, much less places any emphasis upon, what might be classified as a fundamental concern." The court based this conclusion on the fact that MOVE "recognizes no Supreme Being and refers to no transcendental or all-controlling force . . . [and] does not appear to take a position with respect to matters of personal morality, human mortality, or the meaning of life." Again, though, the court conceded that its conclusion might be mistaken. What troubled the court most was the possibility that "Africa's insistence on 'keeping in touch with life's vibrations' [might be] a form of pantheism," which the court defined as "the doctrine that God is everything and everything is God." The court declined, however, to characterize Africa's beliefs in this way:

> His concerns appear personal . . . and social . . . rather than spiritual and other-wordly. Indeed, if Africa's statements are deemed sufficient to describe a religion under the Constitution, it might well be necessary to extend first amendment protection to a host of individuals and organizations who espouse personal and secular ideologies, however much those ideologies appear dissimilar to traditional religious dogmas.

It was here, in explaining why the court would not classify such ideologies as religious, even if they addressed ultimate questions, that Judge Adams relied on *Yoder*. In that case, he declared, "[t]he Supreme Court would appear to have foreclosed such an expansive interpretation of the free exercise clause." According to the standard proposed in *Yoder*, Thoreau epitomizes the secular, while the Amish epitomize the religious. Thus, to be religious, a belief system must not only address ultimate questions and be comprehensive; it must also have more in common with the belief system of the Amish than with that of Thoreau. In the court's view, since Africa's belief system failed to satisfy this standard, as well as the standards outlined in the tripartite test of the *Malnak* concurrence, Africa could not turn to the religion clauses for protection.

. . .

## II. THE MEANING OF "RELIGION": THE COMMENTATORS

The expansive view of the meaning of "religion" defended by the Supreme Court in *Torcaso*, *Seeger*, and *Welsh* has been thoughtfully discussed by several commentators. Two essays in particular are especially noteworthy. Since both contain an insightful account of the Supreme Court's expansive definition, and since both already have influenced some lower courts and are likely to influence others in the future, both essays are worth examining in some detail. In examining these essays, it will be useful to consider attempts to clarify the meaning of "religion" in terms of functional and nonfunctional definitions.

### A. Functional Definitions

#### 1. The Ultimate Concern Test

The first essay, a student Note, proposes to define religion as "ultimate concern," but only with respect to the free exercise clause. Ultimate concern is an appropriate definition in this context, the Note argues, because such a definition, more than any other, promotes "the core value underlying the free exercise clause—inviolability of conscience." Any narrower definition would be likely to "enshrine an orthodoxy within a Constitution designed in part to protect unorthodoxy." As the Note rightly points out, however, a narrower definition is needed for the establishment clause: "To borrow the ultimate concern test from the free exercise context . . . would be to invite attack on all programs that further the ultimate concerns of individuals or entangle the government with such concerns."

The Note bases its analysis of ultimate concern largely on the writings of the theologian Paul Tillich:

The meaning of the term "ultimate" is to be found in a particular human's experience rather than in some objective reality. Tillich's thesis . . . is that the concerns of any individual can be ranked, and that if we probe deeply enough, we will discover the underlying concern which gives meaning and orientation to a person's whole life. It is of this kind of experience, Tillich tells us, that religions are made; consequently, every person has a religion.

Under this analysis, an ultimate concern is "an act of the total personality, not a movement of a special and discrete part of the total being." It is the "single most important interest in [an individual's] life." This interest might be political, it might be economic, or it might be cultural. Indeed, any interest can serve as an ultimate concern, and "the free exercise clause demands that any concern deemed to be ultimate be protected, regardless of how 'secular' that concern might seem to be."

Two additional remarks in the Note bring the meaning of the term "ultimate concern" into sharp relief. First, the Note states that "[a]n ultimate concern, by definition, cannot be superseded . . . . The [United States v.] *Kauten* court recognized this when it said that religious belief 'categorically requires the believer to disregard elementary self-interest and to accept martyrdom in preference to transgressing its tenets.'" The second remark parallels the first:

Clearly not every belief—not even all those strongly held—constitutes a matter of ultimate concern. . . . An ultimate concern must be unconditional, made without qualification or reservation . . . . This attribute, in large measure an outgrowth of [an act of the total personality], prevents an individual from defining his ultimate concern conjunctively as "X and Y and Z."

Thus an individual can not maintain more than one "ultimate concern." A second would always operate as a condition on the first.

Although the Note's description and defense of the ultimate concern test are incisive, they are far from convincing. To begin, the Note's description of the test is contradictory. In relying on the *Kauten* court's statement that "religious belief categorically requires the believer to disregard elementary self-interest," the Note overlooks the fact that self-interest itself might be an individual's ultimate concern. Perhaps the main objection to protecting the egoist under the free exercise clause is that his ultimate concern is not a moral concern and, therefore, he does not violate his conscience when he acts against his own self-interest. But this objection is unsound. Some philosophers have argued that, however unattractive egoism may be, the theory is, nonetheless, a moral theory. If these philosophers are correct, then acting according to conscience is compatible with acting out of self-interest. Yet, even if these philosophers are wrong, this does not justify denying the egoist the same protection of his ultimate concern that every other individual enjoys. Egoism, like any other ultimate concern, "need not be acceptable, logical, consistent, or comprehensible to others in order to merit First Amendment protection." Moreover, denying egoism protection would be tantamount to discriminating impermissibly against one religion in favor of another. Given these facts, the ultimate concern test must be revised in order to protect the egoist.

Although revising the test in this way may save it from contradiction, other defects still remain. Among these is the fact that the test discriminates unfairly against the individual who has no ultimate concern but who is, nevertheless, strongly committed to certain principles and to a certain way of life. Such an individual might be called an "intuitionist." He is a person "who cannot commit himself to a single moral principle that can be a trump card in all cases." Intuitionist theory has been described as having two features: "[F]irst, . . . a plurality of first principles which may conflict to give contrary directives in particular cases; and second, . . . no explicit method, no priority rules, for weighing these principles against one another." Joel Feinberg sums up the intuitionist's reasons for refusing to embrace a single, ultimate concern by saying that "[t]here are, after all, different degrees of injustice, different amounts and types of evils, and different probabilities in our projections of consequences." Feinberg concludes that "few sensitive persons will be satisfied with a theory that would represent even the difficult problems as simple by declaring in advance that one type of conflicting consideration must always triumph over the other."

The Note's explanation as to why only those people who are ultimately concerned should be protected is that they are the only ones who stand to suffer immense distress if prohibited from acting according to conscience . . . . This explanation is unsatisfactory for at least two reasons. First, the Note's dichotomy between the "intellectual" and the "ultimately concerned" seems highly dubious. Common sense suggests that the world cannot be so neatly divided. Some people, like the intuitionist, may have no ultimate concern yet still will be sorely distraught at having to "follow a distasteful government order,"

especially if that order requires inflicting immediate harm. No doubt, there may be a difference between the distress the intuitionists experience in such situations and the distress experienced by the ultimately concerned in the same situations. Even so, this difference is likely to be a difference in degree rather than a "difference in fundamentality." That is to say, the distress experienced by the intuitionists will, in many cases, more closely resemble that experienced by the ultimately concerned than that experienced by the intellectualist. The Note's explanation is also unsatisfactory for another, even more important, reason: it is inconsistent with the Note's claim that the ultimate concern test is designed to protect the inviolability of conscience. For those who are deeply committed but not ultimately concerned, the test appears to provide no protection whatsoever.

Closely related to this objection is a question that the Note does not sufficiently explore, but which is central to its thesis: Do many, if any, individuals actually have an ultimate concern? The Note asserts that they do and that careful investigation will reveal how an individual ranks his concerns and which concern he holds as ultimate. To see that we have reason to be skeptical of this claim, consider the following. A devout theist maintains that obeying God's law is his ultimate concern. Much to his chagrin, however, the theist is frequently tempted to sin and occasionally succumbs to the temptation. Now, surely the ultimate concern test must not be so inflexible as to disqualify this individual from protection simply because his heart is not always pure and his actions are not always honorable. Allowances must be made, it would seem, both for temptation and for weakness of will. Otherwise, any devout theist who has ever been tempted to sin, much less succumbed to the temptation, could not sincerely claim obedience to God's law as his ultimate concern. Yet, despite appearances, the ultimate concern test, as formulated in the Note, lacks precisely the kind of flexibility such cases require. As the Note declares in describing the test, "an ultimate concern is an act of the *total personality*, not a movement of a special and discrete part of the total being." Given this requirement, if the devout theist deviates even slightly from the chosen path, or is tempted to do so, his commitment to God becomes something other than "an act of the total personality." The theist might be very devout indeed, yet, if he sins or is tempted to, his commitment can only be "a special and discrete part of his total being." The problem, put simply, is that totality admits of no degrees, in either thought or deed. It does not seem unfair to say, therefore, that the individual who is totally committed, if anyone fits this description, is doubtless either a very rare and exceptional person or a dangerous fanatic.

. . .

## 2. An Alternative: The Cardinal Concerns Test

To expand the scope of the free exercise clause, "religion" might be defined as cardinal concerns rather than as an ultimate concern. The result, however, would not necessarily be greater protection for freedom of conscience. Indeed, the result might be even less protection for freedom of conscience.

Imagine a young painter, inspired by Cezanne's example in the Franco-Prussian war, applying for a religious exemption from military service. In defending his right to the exemption, the young man explains that participating in any war would interfere seriously with one of his cardinal concerns, namely, his painting. He readily admits that he is not a pacifist, so that his opposition to participating in war is different from that of the traditional conscientious objector. The painter denies, however, that this difference is relevant. In his view, both he and the traditional objector would have to ignore their cardinal concerns if they participated in a war; he would have to ignore his painting, while the traditional objector would have to ignore his pacifism. What *Torcaso* forbids, the young painter rightly argues, is government discrimination against one form of religious belief in favor of another. Thus, if "religion" were defined as cardinal concerns, the young painter would qualify under existing law for the exemption. So, too, would any individual who could make the requisite showing—any athlete, any entrepreneur, any scholar, any hedonist. To avoid this prospect, Congress might eliminate the religious exemption altogether, and in so doing, eliminate the protection now afforded to traditional conscientious objectors. The Note makes the same point about discretionary exemptions in arguing for a strict ultimate concern test: "When confronted with the choice between accommodating a vast number of religious interests and not accommodating any at all, the legislature may eliminate those discretionary accommodations which now exist for the core religions." Given the likelihood of this result, defining "religion" as cardinal concerns could produce less rather than more protection for freedom of conscience, exactly the opposite effect from that intended.

In cases in which an individual can directly invoke the free exercise clause for protection, instead of having to rely on a discretionary legislative exemption, the result would very likely be the same. As currently construed, the free exercise clause prohibits any law that limits religious liberty, unless the

government can show that the law is "the least restrictive means of achieving some compelling state interest." In the past, this standard has provided fairly broad protection for religious freedom. There is a tension, however, between this standard and the government's interest in not having to accommodate religious interests where "accommodation would 'radically restrict the operating latitude of the legislature.'" If "religion" were defined as cardinal concerns, the operating latitude of the legislature would undoubtedly be seriously jeopardized. Since most laws impinge upon the cardinal concerns of numerous individuals, legislatures would have to spend untold hours reviewing every piece of legislation—trying to anticipate how many individuals a particular law might affect, how the law might affect them, and how the law might be drafted to avoid being struck down under the free exercise clause. Even then, no legislature could be confident that any law it passed would not be widely challenged in the courts. The cost, in terms of efficiency and effectiveness, would surely be enormous. And there would be other costs as well: those the government would incur in defending itself and those courts would incur in hearing the challenges. In light of these potential problems, it seems reasonable to predict that if the cardinal concerns test were adopted the Court would repudiate its current standard for deciding cases under the free exercise clause. A likely replacement, one that would afford minimal protection for freedom of conscience, was recently proposed by Justice Stevens in *United States v. Lee*. Stating there that the current standard is too lenient even under a less expansive definition of "religion," Justice Stevens recommended imposing "an almost insurmountable burden on any individual who objects to a valid and neutral law of general applicability on the grounds that the law proscribes (or prescribes) conduct that his religion prescribes (or proscribes).

. . .

Let us assume, however, that "religion" could be defined as cardinal concerns under the free exercise clause without raising any of the problems discussed so far. One problem would still remain: How to define "religion" under the establishment clause. If "religion" were defined under the establishment clause as cardinal concerns, the result would be "doctrinal chaos": since there is probably no government program that does not promote some cardinal concern, virtually every government program could be deemed an unconstitutional establishment of religion. To avoid this problem, courts could adopt a dual definition of "religion"—a narrow definition for the establishment clause and a broad definition for the free exercise clause. Such a definition would protect freedom of conscience and preserve the government's ability to operate. In doing so, however, it would create another, equally unacceptable, problem: A three-tiered system of ideas. Judge Adams was the first to identify this problem with his concurrence in *Malnak*:

> [A dual definition] would create a three-tiered system of ideas: those that are unquestionably religious and thus both free from government interference and barred from receiving government support; those that are unquestionably non-religious and thus subject to government regulation and eligible to receive government support; and those that are only religious under the newer approach and thus free from governmental regulation but open to receipt of government support.

Judge Adams noted that the ideas classified in the third grouping, those that are "free from governmental regulation but open to receipt of government support," would be in an obviously advantaged position. He found no reason, however, for favoring a newer belief system over an older one: "If a Roman Catholic is barred from receiving aid from the government, so too should be a Transcendental Mediator or a Scientologist if those two are to enjoy the preferred position guaranteed to them by the free exercise clause." Judge Adams' objection provides us with yet another reason for rejecting the cardinal concerns test. . . .

### B. A Nonfunctional Definition

In the second of the two articles to be discussed here, Professor Mansfield rejects the *Seeger* court's functional definition of "religion" and, by implication, the ultimate concern and cardinal concerns tests. Taking a more traditional approach, Mansfield argues that "the fundamental character of the truths asserted . . . is the primary reason for characterizing a belief in these truths as religious." He develops this point more fully by saying:

> A religious belief is first of all a belief, that is to say the affirmation of some truth, reality, or value. In addition, it addresses itself to basic questions to which man has always sought an answer, questions about the meaning of human existence, the origin of being, the meaning of suffering and death, and the existence of a spiritual reality. . . . In this respect . . . [it requires] attention to whether the questions to which the belief addresses itself are of a certain character; it requires attention to the subject

matter of the belief rather than the condition of the believer.

Mansfield's critics have charged that his "definition succeeds only by being so general as to include nearly all belief whatsoever." Nearly everyone, the critics contend, addresses Mansfield's questions at some point in life and answers them in a more or less tentative way. Yet this does not mean that every answer to these questions is a religious answer or that everyone is religious. Someone might conclude that the concept of a spiritual or transcendent reality is unintelligible and that the concept of being is incoherent. This person might view questions about the meaning of life, death, and suffering solely in secular terms. He might affirm some truth about these matters, but the truth he affirms may bear little resemblance to a religious truth. He might believe, for example, that in his case the acquisition of wealth is essential to living a meaningful life. According to Mansfield's definition, this belief arguably would be a religious belief, as would many other beliefs Mansfield probably intended to exclude. When carefully examined, then, Mansfield's definition appears to resemble closely the definition that characterizes cardinal concerns as the essence of religion. Consequently, his definition should be rejected for the same reasons that support rejection of the cardinal concerns definition.

Mansfield's mistake was to focus exclusively on the character of fundamental questions. Had he focused as well on the character of the answers to these questions, he could have avoided the charges of his critics. Had he said, that is, that a religious belief is not merely "the affirmation of some truth" about "the existence of a spiritual reality," but the affirmation of a particular truth about the existence of such a reality—the affirmation that such a reality does in fact exist—his definition would be much more plausible. Had he then added that the religious believer interprets questions about the meaning of life, death, suffering, and the origin of being in light of a belief in a spiritual reality, Mansfield would have provided an account of religious belief quite similar to the accounts provided by many modern theologians and anthropologists.

Even if revised along these lines, however, Mansfield's definition would still be incomplete. At best, it would specify only the conditions that must normally be satisfied, rather than the conditions that must always be satisfied, for a belief or practice to be religious. It would not specify what every definition is supposed to specify, namely, the "essential qualities" of what is defined—in this case, the respects in which all religions are alike. The problem is not that Mansfield's definition, or the revised version of that definition, is less satisfactory than some other definition. Indeed, as far as definitions go, the revised version seems superior to most. The problem is that the very attempt to define "religion" is itself misconceived. There simply is no essence of religion, no single characteristic or set of characteristics that all religions have in common that makes them religions. What we discover when we examine a variety of different religions or different religious belief systems is not a shared essence, but a set of "family resemblances," "a complicated network of similarities overlapping and criss-crossing."

### III. THE MEANING OF "RELIGION": THE SEARCH FOR ESSENCES

#### A. The General Problem

The search for essences, of words and of concepts, goes back at least as far as Socrates. In dialogue after dialogue, Socrates advanced the same thesis: knowing how to apply a word, knowing a word's meaning, entails knowing the necessary and sufficient conditions for its application; if no such conditions exist, the word has no application, no meaning. This thesis rests on the reasonable assumption that there is some quality or collection of qualities common to all things of a certain kind that distinguishes things of that kind from everything else. All acts of courage, for example, while they might differ in some respects, have at least one common quality that distinguishes them from all other acts. We can tell whether a particular act—risking one's life in a war or one's reputation for a just cause—is a courageous act by determining whether the act shares the quality or qualities common only to acts of courage. If the particular act lacks the requisite quality or qualities, it must be an act of some other kind. What is true, moreover, for the concept of courage is true as well for all other concepts. Every concept must share one or more qualities that no other concept possesses if the task of distinguishing between and among concepts is not to be impossible. To be able to distinguish chairs from couches, cars, and charnels, we must know what is unique about chairs. We must know, in other words, what the essence of a chair is.

. . .

#### B. Essence and Religion

At the turn of the century, in his celebrated Gifford Lectures on religious experience, William James stated that "[m]ost books on the philosophy of religion try to begin with a precise definition of what its essence consists of." James vehemently objected to this approach and advised his audience to "admit freely at the outset that we may very likely find no one essence, but many characters which may alternately be equally important to religion." To see that James' advice was sound, let us begin by trying to identify the purpose of religion. Here we would do well to take our cue from Professor Mansfield and Judge Adams and say that the purpose of religion is to provide answers, or a way of arriving at answers, to certain fundamental "Why" questions—most or all of which are thought by the traditional religious believer to be interrelated: "Why is there something rather than nothing? Why are we here? Why is there suffering and evil in the world? Why should we ever act in one way rather than another? Why is any one thing ever more valuable than any other?" Using this purpose of religion as a starting point, we can identify the features common to most traditional Eastern and Western religions, and can then show that no feature is both necessary and sufficient to guarantee that a belief system is religious. The following is a list of relevant features:

1. A belief in a Supreme Being
2. A belief in a transcendent reality
3. A moral code
4. A world view that provides an account of man's role in the universe and around which an individual organizes his life
5. Sacred rituals and holy days
6. Worship and prayer
7. A sacred text or scriptures
8. Membership in a social organization that promotes a religious belief system

Taken together, these features provide us with a paradigm of a religious belief system. A belief system will thus be more or less religious depending on how closely it resembles this paradigm, in the same way that a material object will be more or less a chair depending on how closely it resembles a standard chair.

Starting at the bottom of the list, we can see that the last four features are characteristically religious because of their relation to either or both of the first two features. Sever this relation and the last four features usually lose their religious character. Even in borderline cases, these features are linked to a moral code and a world view. Standing alone or together, the last four features are not *sufficient* to make a belief system religious. Nor is any one of them *necessary* for this purpose: A mystic might avoid affiliation with any religious organization; a primitive religion might sustain itself without any literature; and a Buddhist might not worship, pray, celebrate holy days, or practice any rituals. Thus, to discover what, if anything, is essential to religion, we must focus on the first four features on the list.

Consider, first, belief in a Supreme Being. Making this a necessary feature of a religious belief system would entail denying that most Buddhists and many Hindus are religious. Even making belief in a Supreme Being a sufficient feature of a religious belief system would be odd. Some individuals, like Ivan Karamazov, believe in a Supreme Being but still reject Him. In their view, a Supreme Being does not deserve our love and respect because He allows so many people to suffer for no good reason.

The second possibility, belief in the transcendent, fares no better than belief in a Supreme Being. Many Greeks believed in gods but thought of them as somehow part of the natural order, not as part of any transcendental order. Assuming the Greeks who held this view were religious, belief in the transcendent cannot be a necessary feature of a religious belief system. Similarly, since a Kantian and a Platonist might believe in the existence of the transcendent as a world of "things-in-themselves" or as a realm of essences, but not attach any special significance to this world as, say, Hindus and Christians do, belief in the transcendent cannot be sufficient to make a belief system religious.

When we turn to moral codes and world views, a third option, the result is the same. Since "the Greco-Oriental [religious] mystery cults . . . offer no moral or ethical principles to guide their adherents," neither a moral code nor a world view is necessary for having a religious belief system. Nor is either sufficient for that purpose. No one but a Tillichian, who thinks that religion has an essence and that its essence is having an ultimate concern, is likely to classify such people as Bertrand Russell, A. J. Ayer, and Antony Flew as religious. Although each of these men subscribed to a moral code and held a world view, each also unabashedly rejected religion.

At this point, we might enhance our understanding of a religious belief system by contrasting it with a secular or irreligious belief system. All that the two ordinarily have in common, as paradigms, is a moral code and a world view. The traditional secularist has no interest in the last four features on the list, except perhaps as significant cultural or psychological phenomena. More important, he has no faith in or commitment to a Supreme Being or the transcendent. Indeed, he thinks all statements about a Supreme Being and the transcendent are either unintelligible or vacuous.

The dissimilarities between the traditional secularist and the traditional believer become even more pronounced when we consider the different responses each provides to the fundamental questions noted above. Whereas the traditional believer generally thinks the question "Why is there something rather than nothing?" to be of the utmost importance, the traditional secularist thinks it unintelligible, and so not a genuine question at all. To the question "Why are we here?" the traditional secularist gives a scientific or causal explanation. If the believer is dissatisfied with this answer because it does not tell us why we are here but only how we got here, the secularist contends that the believer is once again asking the pseudo-question, "Why is there something rather than nothing?" The secularist also gives a causal explanation for the existence of suffering and evil in the world. He points to natural disasters, to limited resources, and, perhaps most of all, to limited sympathies. For him, something like the doctrine of original sin is at best an illuminating metaphor. Finally, in discussing why we should ever act in one way rather than another or why some things are more valuable than others, the secularist rejects explanations that the believer finds appealing, explanations that rely on the notion of intrinsic goodness and intrinsic value, or on the notion that goodness and value are somehow divinely or transcendentally underwritten. Roughly speaking, then, the difference between the traditional believer and the traditional secularist is this: The former believes, while the latter does not, that all of the fundamental questions are both genuine and inter-related, that these questions cannot be answered satisfactorily without referring to a Supreme Being or the transcendent, and that an individual's attempt to answer these questions can be facilitated by such activities as worship and prayer.

Between these two extremes lie a variety of borderline cases in which the question "Is the belief system religious or irreligious?" can not be answered unequivocally. Such cases are significant here for two reasons: First, because if they must be classified, they can be classified as either religious or irreligious; and second, because no sharp line can be drawn between such cases and the paradigm cases. These facts are significant because they provide further support for the claim that there is no single feature or set of features that constitutes the essence of religion.

To see this point more clearly, consider the case of the British philosopher R. M. Hare. Hare contends that all religions that rely on the supernatural or the transcendent are based on "superstition." Nevertheless, Hare classifies himself as a Christian, and perhaps justifiably so, since there are important similarities between his views and way of life and those of the traditional Christian. Hare attends church, for example, and emphasizes the importance of the Bible. He also prays, not to anyone or anything, but seemingly as a mode of reflection or meditation. Hare worships, too, although what he worships is not altogether clear. Yet, while these indicia of Christianity are important to Hare, what makes him a Christian, in his view, is his commitment to Christian morality and his faith that embracing this morality will make life worthwhile for him and for others. Against Hare, it might be argued that he cannot be a Christian because he has eliminated from Christianity what is most essential to it, namely, God. Hare responds to this objection by saying:

> The position which I have been defending could be said to be obviously a humanist one, and incompatible with Christianity. But I wonder whether this is still the case. We must reflect that there was a time when it was thought . . . that you cannot be a Christian (at least not a nonheretical one) unless you believe in transubstantiation, or in the immaculate conception, or in the Genesis story of the creation, taken literally. We have to allow that ideas about what is requisite for being said to be a Christian can change, and may change radically and, in the present circumstances, rapidly.

Courts, of course, have no interest in whether or not Hare's belief system is Christian. Their concern is with whether or not it is religious. All the neutral observer can reasonably say, however, is that Hare's is a religious belief system in some important respects but not in others. This is true, moreover, not only in Hare's case; it is true, as well, in the case of the individual who does not pray or worship or attend church but who, like Hare, admires the ethical teachings of the New Testament and who dedicates himself to following them. In all such cases, so long as the individual is concerned with some of the fundamental questions that are central to a religious belief system and looks to religious doctrine for his answers, the neutral observer can do no more than point to similarities and dissimilarities. Wittgenstein described this dilemma when he said: "Philosophy simply puts everything before us, and neither explains nor deduces anything."

It would be a mistake to conclude from these observations, however, that courts are handicapped only by the fact that religious belief systems have nothing in common that distinguishes them from all other belief systems. As William Alston explains, the problem is more complicated:

> Even if we could say exactly which or how

many of the various religion-making characteristics a [belief system] has to have in order to be religious, we would be unable to say with respect to a given characteristic, exactly what degree of it we must have in order to apply the term.

Take the word "transcendence," for example. One prominent scholar, A. H. Maslow, lists thirty-five different kinds of transcendence. These range from "transcendence in the sense of loss of self-consciousness, of self-awareness" and "[t]ranscendence of culture" to "[t]ranscendence [as becoming] divine or godlike, to go beyond the merely human" and "[t]ranscendence [as living] in the realm of Being . . . plateau-living." As these different descriptions suggest, what is true in general for different belief systems is also true in particular for different beliefs about transcendence: some will be religious, others will not, and still others will fall on the borderline. Alston's point is that any careful investigation will show the same to be true for all religious concepts. All are, to some extent, inherently vague.

The problem, though, is even more complicated than Alston's remark suggests. Alston is concerned only with the problem of vagueness. He is not concerned, as well, with the problem of vacuity. This is the problem raised by the contemporary secular atheist. The secular atheist's argument is that the concepts generally thought to be central to religion—the concepts of God, Supreme Being, and transcendence—are not only vague but also vacuous. John Passmore summarizes the atheist's argument this way:

> [P]ositivist arguments [concerning the criteria a proposition must satisfy to be meaningful], if backed by other forms of philosophical reasoning, . . . show that religious statements cannot be used as theologians have commonly wanted to use them—as at once giving us some sort of information about a transcendental Being and serving as a basis for explaining, predicting, describing, justifying forms of human activity. The very fact that it is logically impossible ever to say of a transcendental Being that he is here rather than there and so to refer to a situation as "this" in which he is particularly present—makes them unusable in explaining, predicting, describing and justifying.

Although those who subscribe to this view may be wrong, perhaps profoundly wrong, there appears to be no simple way to show why they are wrong or even that they are wrong. Hence, even if the central concepts of religion are not vacuous, they are considerably more vague than other empirical concepts. What can count as a genuine belief about God, a Supreme Being, or transcendence is far more difficult to determine than what can count as a genuine belief about tangible items such as tables or chairs. This inherent vagueness suggests that the central concepts of religion have little to contribute to the search for the essence of religious belief. And so we return, or should return, to William James, who advised us to abandon the search.

### C. Yoder and Africa

Assuming that the arguments in the previous two sections are sound, and thus that religion has no essence but does have a focus, we are now in a position to consider some of the views expressed in *Wisconsin v. Yoder* and *Africa v. Commonwealth of Pennsylvania*. Judge Adams can be construed as speaking for both courts when he says in *Africa* that a belief system is secular rather than religious if it is "more akin to Thoreau's rejection of 'the contemporary values accepted by the majority' than to the 'deep religious convictions' of the Amish." This view of the meaning of "religion," which neither court attempted to explain or justify, is not only one of the most important views expressed on the subject; it is doubtless one of the most controversial as well. What makes it controversial is not the choice of the Amish as a paradigm of the religious believer. This choice is likely to be widely accepted. What makes it controversial is the choice of Thoreau as a paradigm of the secular believer. This choice must be considered more carefully.

Because Thoreau often criticized institutional religion, some have concluded he was antireligious. The consensus among those who have studied his life and writings, however, appears to be just the opposite. E. B. White, for example, has written that "when he died [Thoreau] uttered the purest religious thought we ever heard. They asked him whether he had made his peace with God and he replied, 'I was not aware we had quarreled.'" Significantly, Thoreau did not utter such thoughts only on his deathbed. Ten years earlier, in 1851, he made the following entry in his journal: "My profession is to be always on the alert to find God in nature, to know his lurking-places, to attend all the oratorios, the operas, in nature." Earlier still, he wrote: "I must not be for myself, but [for] God's work, and that is always good." Had Thoreau simply identified God with the world or with nature, we might wonder whether he should be classified as religious. But Thoreau was no pantheist. As one observer has remarked, "Thoreau's God . . . was a personal God." Although Thoreau may have

thought the universe is part of God, he also thought God is "more than, and is not exhausted by, the universe." Robert Dickens summarizes Thoreau's views on the relation between God and the natural world by saying:

> Thoreau used "Nature" to denote the godly and purposeful aspect of nature, and "nature" he used to denote the external world excluding human beings and their works. He also used "Nature" in an inclusive sense—e.g., as including "nature," though not being limited to "nature." Thus "Nature" transcends "nature," but also includes "nature." Further, God transcends "Nature" and is immanent in "Nature."

In short, then, Thoreau appears to have believed in a personal God, as well as in the transcendent, and to have chosen as his life's profession to be always on the alert for both. Although these views might not make Thoreau a paradigm of the religious believer, they do suggest that the courts made a serious mistake when they chose him as a paradigm of the secular believer.

Far harder to classify is Frank Africa, the self-proclaimed "Naturalist Minister" of MOVE. As a purely descriptive matter, Africa does not appear to be either religious or irreligious. Instead, he appears to fall somewhere in between. Although Africa claims, for example, to believe in God, his conception of God is very different from more traditional conceptions. Here, in his own words, is Africa's conception: "Water is *raw*, which makes it *pure*, which means it is *innocent*, *trustworthy*, and *safe*, which is the same as *God*." It is worth emphasizing here that not every belief in "God" is a religious belief. A belief in the value of rawness and purity does not become a religious belief simply because an individual identifies one or both with God. The same holds true for a belief in the value of innocence, trustworthiness, and safety. In general, a belief in "God" need not be classified as religious unless it plays an integral role in an individual's attempt to answer the "Why" questions that religion itself is concerned with answering.

This is not to say, however, that Africa's claim to hold a belief in God, in addition to other religious beliefs, should be readily dismissed. A sympathetic observer might reasonably conclude that, when viewed in conjunction with his "all-consuming belief in a 'natural' or 'generative' way of life," Africa's belief system is sufficiently similar to pantheism to at least warrant not being classified as irreligious. A sympathetic observer might also conclude that Africa's commitment to "keeping in touch with life's vibrations" forms the basis of a rudimentary world view, "a Weltanschauung, or philosophy, in which a picture of reality is combined with a sense of its meaning and value and with principles of action." Africa appears, for example, to divide the world into two realms. The first consists of the "pure," the "natural," and the "generative." The second consists of the "polluted," the "artificial," and the "perverted." It is because the former supposedly takes precedence over the latter that Africa commits himself to "keeping in touch with life's vibrations." This commitment might be viewed as giving Africa's life a sense of purpose and meaning. It might also be viewed as providing him with principles of action—promoting peace and opposing violence, working hard, and following a strict natural foods diet that is "direct, straight, and true"—that some contemporary theorists might reasonably classify as moral. Other similarities between Africa's belief system and the traditional believer's include the fact that "for MOVE members every day of the year can be considered a religious 'holiday,'" and the fact that while "MOVE members participate in no distinct 'ceremonies' or 'rituals' . . . every act of life itself is [thought to be] invested with religious meaning and significance." In the eyes of a sympathetic observer, all of these similarities are likely to make Africa a borderline case of a religious believer.

In considering these same issues and comparisons, the court in *Africa* reached a different set of conclusions, thereby limiting the types of claims likely to be protected by the religion clauses. Some of the court's conclusions merit at least a brief discussion. Especially noteworthy is the court's conclusion that "MOVE does not appear to take a position with respect to matters of personal morality, human mortality, or the meaning and purpose of life." As the court acknowledged, however, "the matter is not wholly free from doubt." One reason for being skeptical is that the court never explained what it meant by the phrases "personal morality" and "purpose of life." Another reason is that the court never explained why the commitment of MOVE members to "a 'natural' or 'generative' way of life," to "keeping in touch with life's vibrations," can not provide the basis for a personal morality or serve as a purpose of life. What the court did say is that Africa's commitment is not a form of pantheism, since it is not "spiritual or other-worldly." In saying this, however, the court again eschewed explanation. It never said what it meant by "spiritual or otherworldly" or how pantheism could even be otherworldly. Nor did the court explain, apart from mentioning the dubious Thoreau paradigm, why a commitment like Africa's is irreligious simply because it is not other-worldly and not, in any traditional sense, spiritual. R. M. Hare's commitment is certainly not other-worldly, and would seem to be spiritual only in a sense of that term which is broad enough to include Africa's commitment, yet Hare is not irreligious. Very likely, Hare is a borderline case, at least at the present time. What the court failed to show is why Africa should not be classified in exactly the same way.

Of course, even if the court had classified Africa as a borderline case, the inquiry could not have ended with that classification. The court's principal task was to determine if Africa was entitled to protection under the first amendment. To make that determination, the court had to decide whether to classify Africa as religious. Descriptively, that task was incompatible with Africa's being a borderline case. Legally, however, no incompatibility need have existed. Indeed, the fact that Africa was a borderline case means that, as a matter of law, the court might reasonably have classified him either way, depending on what the aims of the religion clauses are and on which classification would best have promoted those aims. Where the court erred was in ignoring the aims of the religion clauses in examining Africa's belief system. What the court did, instead, was turn to the Thoreau paradigm and, after examining Africa's belief system in light of that paradigm, conclude that Africa was not religious. Thus, even if the court reached the right result, it did so for the wrong reasons. Needless to say, though, whether or not the court actually reached the right result is still an open question, one that requires careful scrutiny of the aims of the religion clauses.

Up to this point, the comments on the court's decision in *Africa* have all been critical. The impression this leaves may be misleading. For even though there is much in the decision to criticize, there is also much in the decision to praise. In fact, of all the decisions that attempt to explore and resolve the problems that arise in connection with identifying the meaning of "religion," none comes closer to the heart of the matter than does the decision in *Africa*. The focus in *Africa* on the underlying concerns of traditional believers, the reliance on the use of paradigms, and the emphasis on a thorough development of the facts, taken together, provide a reasonably sound framework for determining which claims are religious and which are not. To be sure, since there is no essence of religion, this framework could be improved by revision along the lines suggested in the previous section. The end result, however, would still be a revised framework, not an entirely new one.

## IV. THE MEANING OF "RELIGION:" THE FIRST AMENDMENT

Two sets of recommendations arise from the preceding discussion of attempts to define "religion." The first set pertains to the establishment clause; the second, to the free exercise clause. These recommendations focus on how courts can decide cases under the religion clauses without relying on a definition of "religion." They are not intended to be exhaustive. To the extent they are useful, their utility lies in the direction they provide for further study.

### A. The Establishment Clause

Gail Merel's distinction between the religious and the irreligious, on the one hand, and the nonreligious, on the other, provides a useful starting point for discussing the establishment clause. Although Merel herself fails to draw a satisfactory distinction, such a distinction can be drawn. Perhaps the best way to conceptualize the nonreligious is to contrast it with the religious and the irreligious. The latter two, in turn, can best be conceptualized in light of the paradigms described above. These paradigms suggest the following rules of thumb. First, government support of an activity is *religious* if the activity is more likely to promote a paradigmatic religious belief system than a paradigmatic irreligious belief system. Second, government support of an activity is *irreligious* if the activity is more likely to promote a paradigmatic irreligious belief system than a paradigmatic religious belief system. Finally, government support of an activity is *nonreligious* if the activity is just as likely to promote either type of paradigmatic belief system.

Although this scheme is rather vague, its vagueness does not render it unmanageable. For knowing that government support of an activity is religious, irreligious, or nonreligious is not the same as knowing whether government support of the activity violates the establishment clause. Two examples will illustrate this point. The first involves government support that is religious; the second involves government support that is nonreligious. When the government bans the use of peyote but allows Navajo Indians to use the drug as part of their sacred ritual, the government is supporting religion. Whether this support violates the establishment clause, however, depends on whether the exemption granted to the Navajo constitutes an impermissible establishment of religion. Similarly, when the government supports a speech and hearing therapy program at a church school by allowing public employees to administer the program, the government is supporting nonreligion. Administering the therapy program is itself just as likely (or no more likely) to promote a paradigmatic religious belief system than it is to promote a paradigmatic irreligious belief system. Yet, even though the government's support is nonreligious, it may still violate the establishment clause. Whether the support does violate the establishment clause depends, once again, on whether the support constitutes an impermissible establishment of religion.

These examples illustrate that the key word in establishment clause cases, particularly in those at the penumbra, is not the word "religion" but the word "establishment." The critical inquiry in such cases is: What constitutes an impermissible *establishment* of religion? To answer this question, courts must look to the aims of the establishment clause. Determining what those aims are is certainly no easy task. Not surprisingly, the subject has generated considerable debate. It is from these debates, however, and from the search for the meaning of "establishment," not from any attempt to define "religion," that the standards for deciding cases under the establishment clause must be sought.

### B. The Free Exercise Clause

Turning from the establishment clause to the free exercise clause, the temptation is surely great to recommend that courts treat the word "religion" in the free exercise clause in much the same way they treat the word "speech" in the free speech clause. Few commentators today argue that courts should interpret "speech" literally. Most contend that the word should be used as a term of art, encompassing such diverse forms of expression as talking, painting, picketing, distributing a handbill, displaying a red flag, wearing a black armband, and marching in a demonstration. Unfortunately, the temptation to recommend that "religion" be treated in a similar way is one that should be resisted. Courts simply cannot use "religion" as a term of art without converting the right to the free exercise of religion into a seemingly illimitable right of personal autonomy.

Under the free exercise clause, then, religion must be given its standard meaning. So, too, must "irreligion." These meanings can be gleaned from the paradigms described above. In most cases, those paradigms will serve courts well. Only in the borderline cases will the paradigms prove unavailing. In those cases, the belief or activity or institution in question, because it appears equally similar to both paradigms, can be reasonably classified as either religious or irreligious. To decide such difficult cases, courts must devise an alternate strategy. One promising possibility would be to construct a wholly different kind of paradigm—a borderline-case paradigm.

A suitable candidate for such a paradigm would be Frank Africa. Imagine, for example, that the Third Circuit improperly denied Africa protection under the free exercise clause. Under these circumstances, other borderline cases could qualify for protection only by having more in common with the religious paradigm than Africa had. Conversely, imagine that the Third Circuit properly denied Africa protection under the free exercise clause. Under these circumstances a different standard would apply: Other borderline cases could qualify for protection only by having more in common with the religious paradigm than Africa had. Whether Africa himself was or was not entitled to protection—and thus whether the former or latter standard should be adopted—depends on what the aims of the free exercise clause are. Only by scrutinizing those aims more carefully, and by resolving any tensions that might exist between them, can courts determine which standard to adopt.

# Bibliography

*Defining Religion*

Delgado, Richard, *Religious Totalism: Gentle and Ungentle Persuasion Under the First Amendment*, 51 Southern California Law Review 1 (1977)

Garvey, John, *Free Exercise and the Values of Religious Liberty*, 18 Connecticut Law Review 779 (1986)

Ingber, Stanley, *Religion or Ideology: A Needed Clarification of the Religion Clauses*, 41 Stanford Law Review 233 (1989)

Kent Greenawalt, *Religion as a Concept in Constitutional Law*, 72 California Law Review 753 (1984).

Note, *Toward a Constitutional Definition of Religion*, 91 Harvard Law Review 1056 (1978)

Weiss, Jonathan, *Privilege, Posture and Protection—"Religion" in the Law*, 73 Yale Law Journal 593 (1964)

## C. Establishment and Exercise Clause Tension

The following articles discuss the conflict between the religion clauses and offer theories of resolution. Douglas Laycock argues that the mere fact that government accommodates religion does not per se violate the Establishment Clause: "[g]overnment support for religion is an element of every establishment claim." Jesse H. Choper suggests that the Establishment Clause should prohibit government action only when driven solely by religious purpose and likely to interfere with religious liberty "by coercing, compromising or influencing religious beliefs."

Douglas Laycock, *Towards a General Theory of the Religion Clauses: The Case of Church Labor Relations and the Right to Church Autonomy*, 81 COLUMBIA LAW REVIEW 1373 (1981)*

Secular regulation of churches has increased substantially in recent years, and litigation over the constitutionality of such regulation has increased as well. Regulation of church labor relations has been a particularly prolific source of litigation. There have been challenges to the National Labor Relations Act, the Fair Labor Standards Act, the Civil Rights Act of 1964, the Federal Unemployment Tax Act, and other statutes affecting church labor policy. A wide variety of religious groups have become involved in such litigation.

. . .

## II. DISTINGUISHING THE ESTABLISHMENT AND FREE EXERCISE CLAUSES

One obstacle to any coherent analysis of the religion clauses is the frequent failure to distinguish between them. Some courts have made no effort to do so. Other courts and commentators have drawn distinctions without a difference, elaborately discussing whether religion was burdened by the state under the free exercise clause, and then whether it was entangled with the state under the establishment clause, with no identifiable difference between "burden" and "entanglement."

The two clauses can be run together this way only at the risk of distorting their meaning. For example, the Seventh Circuit recently said that both clauses have "the identical purpose of maintaining a separation between Church and State." Similarly, in some of the Supreme Court's opinions, "entanglement" seems to represent the full meaning of the religion clauses.

Neither separation nor entanglement, however, is a sufficient principle of decision. As the courts have acknowledged, "total separation" is impossible. Indeed, the separation metaphor can be positively misleading; it has led to the strange notion, so far rejected by the Court, that churches and religiously motivated citizens have no right to engage in political speech. Additional principles must be brought to bear to decide which contacts between church and state

should be permitted and which forbidden. Separate attention to the free exercise and establishment clauses is necessary to identify those principles.

One important source of confusion is the Supreme Court's three-part test for identifying an unconstitutional establishment, first announced in *Lemon v. Kurtzman* and repeated ever since. The *Lemon* test sets forth criteria for validity as follows:

First, the statute must have a secular legislative purpose; second, its principal or primary effect must be one that neither advances nor inhibits religion; finally, the statute must not foster "an excessive entanglement with religion."

Part of the problem is the unstructured expansiveness of the entanglement notion. But the more fundamental error is in the second part of the test: that the primary effect of the statute neither advance *nor inhibit* religion. Many lower courts and commentators, and two Supreme Court Justices, have read that to mean that any measure that inhibits religion in any way raises an establishment question. As a result, the establishment clause threatens to swallow the free exercise clause.

The "inhibits" language has become part of the accepted test for religious establishment through mindless repetition of dicta. The Supreme Court has never explained this language or applied it in a holding. *Lemon* simply cited *Board of Education v. Allen*. *Allen* does not explain the rule, but cites *School District of Abington Township v. Schempp*. *Schempp* does not explain the rule either; it cites *McGowan v. Maryland* and *Everson v. Board of Education*. Those two cases do not support a general rule that any inhibition of religion is an establishment, although they do say that some important kinds of inhibitions are establishments.

. . .

If the establishment clause is construed as I suggest, there is a clear definitional distinction between the two clauses. Government support for religion is an element of every establishment claim, just as a burden or restriction on religion is an element of every free exercise claim. Regulation that burdens religion, enacted because of the government's general interest in regulation, is simply not establishment. Magic words like "entanglement" cannot make it so. Such regulation is properly challenged under the free exercise clause; courts that have analyzed the church labor relations cases in establishment clause terms have invoked the wrong provision.

. . .

---

* This article originally appeared at 81 COLUMBIA LAW REVIEW 1373 (1981). Reprinted by permission.

## III. Free Exercise and the Right to Church Autonomy

### A. *The Three Faces of Free Exercise*

It is commonplace to divide the right to free exercise of religion into the freedom to believe, which is absolute, and the freedom to act, which is necessarily limited. The distinction is accurate as far as it goes, but it does not decide many cases. Freedom to believe is rarely infringed in this country. Nearly all the cases involve freedom to act on religious beliefs, and analytic categories that do not subdivide further are not very helpful.

The free exercise clause protection for religious activity includes at least three rather different kinds of rights. In each category, some claims have been accepted and others rejected; none of these rights is protected absolutely.

One category is the bare freedom to carry on religious activities: to build churches and schools, conduct worship services, pray, proselytize, and teach moral values. This is the exercise of religion in its most obvious sense.

Second, and closely related, is the right of churches to conduct these activities autonomously: to select their own leaders, define their own doctrines, resolve their own disputes, and run their own institutions. Religion includes important communal elements for most believers. They exercise their religion through religious organizations, and these organizations must be protected by the clause.

Third is the right of conscientious objection to government policy. The phrase is most prominently associated with the military draft, but there has also been conscientious objector litigation with respect to war taxes, compulsory education, medical treatment and inoculations, social insurance, Sabbath observance and nonobservance, monogamy, and other requirements that conflict with the moral scruples of certain sects or individual believers. These cases are also within the clause, because one way to exercise one's religion is to follow its moral dictates.

Each of these rights has solid support in the case law, but many courts and commentators think only in terms of conscientious objection. One of the most common errors in free exercise analysis is to try to fit all free exercise claims into the conscientious objector category and reject the ones that do not fit. Under this approach, every free exercise claim requires an elaborate judicial inquiry into the conscience or doctrines of the claimant. If he is not compelled by religion to engage in the disputed conduct, he is not entitled to free exercise protection. Thus, courts have tried to decide whether activities of organized churches were required by church doctrine or were something that the churches did for nonreligious reasons. Courts have even allowed schools to deny student religious groups access to schoolrooms—freely available to other student groups—on the ground that the students' religion did not require prayer and services at the disputed time and place.

This approach reflects a rigid, simplistic, and erroneous view of religion. Many activities that obviously are exercises of religion are not required by conscience or doctrine. Singing in the church choir and saying the Roman Catholic rosary are two common examples. Any activity engaged in by a church as a body is an exercise of religion. This is not to say that all such activities are immune from regulation: there may be a sufficiently strong governmental interest to justify the intrusion. But neither are these activities wholly without constitutional protection. It is not dispositive that an activity is not compelled by the official doctrine of a church or the religious conscience of an individual believer. Indeed, many would say that an emphasis on rules and obligations misconceives the essential nature of some religions.

Moreover, emphasis on doctrine and requirements ignores the fluidity of doctrine and the many factors that can contribute to doctrinal change. A church is a complex and dynamic organization, often including believers with a variety of views on important questions of faith, morals, and spirituality. The dominant view of what is central to the religion, and of what practices are required by the religion, may gradually change. Today's pious custom may be tomorrow's moral obligation, and vice versa.

These characteristics of doctrinal change have two consequences. One is that the officially promulgated church doctrine, on which courts too often rely, is not a reliable indication of what the faithful believe. At best the officially promulgated doctrine of a large denomination represents the dominant or most commonly held view; it cannot safely be imputed to every believer or every affiliated congregation. If an official statement of doctrine has not been revised in recent times, it may be that almost no one in the church still believes it. Occasionally, an official pronouncement is obsolete as soon as it is made: the 1968 papal encyclical forbidding artificial contraception never represented the beliefs of more than a minority of Roman Catholics in the United States. This gap between official doctrine and rank-and-file belief means that courts are prone to err in deciding whether activities of a local church or small group of believers are compelled by conscience.

The complex and open-ended nature of the processes that lead to doctrinal change has a second consequence that is even more important. When the state interferes with the autonomy of a church, and particularly when it interferes with the allocation of authority and influence within a church, it interferes with the very process of forming the religion as it will exist in the future. For example, Professor Howe has shown that state law contributed substantially to the trend toward congregationalism in the early national period, and more subtly, to less rigorous standards of admission to church membership. In the labor relations context, it is impossible to predict the long-term effect of forcing religious leaders to share authority with a secular union, or of substituting one employee for another as a result of a discrimination charge or a union grievance. A number of such substitutions may have a cumulative effect, especially if, as seems likely, there is some bias in the process making them. Employees who are more aggressive and less deferential to authority, and therefore more litigious, are more likely to invoke remedies that result in compulsory replacement of one employee with another. Thus, any interference with church affairs may disrupt "the free development of religious doctrine."

Such government-induced changes in religion are too unpredictable to be avoided on a case-by-case basis. They can be minimized only by a strong rule of church autonomy. The free exercise clause therefore forbids government interference with church operations unless there is, to use the conventional phrase, a compelling governmental interest to justify the interference. Identifying those governmental interests that are sufficient is a complex task that requires further exploration.

## B. Church Autonomy and Entanglement

Anything that I would describe as an interference with church autonomy the Supreme Court might describe as an entanglement. But the two concepts are not interchangeable. "Entanglement" is such a "blurred, indistinct, and variable" term that it is useless as an analytic tool. Sometimes it seems to mean contact, or the opposite of separation; it has also been used interchangeably with "involvement" and "relationship." Sometimes it seems to mean anything that might violate the religion clauses.

In the cases on aid to church schools, where the term has been given specific content, it has been used to describe at least three different phenomena. One is government control of churches—what I have called interference with church autonomy. Government regulation of church operations to assure that money given to church schools is not spent for religious purposes is an entanglement.

The second meaning of entanglement is surveillance, which may be necessary to enforce the rules that prevent diversion of money to religious purposes. These two meanings of entanglement—regulation and surveillance to enforce the regulations—are at least closely related. But the Court has been careful to distinguish them and to give independent significance to the ban on surveillance. In explaining why surveillance is entangling, the Court has not emphasized its tendency to aggravate substantive restrictions on church operations—to shift decisions about how to implement regulations from church to state and press churches to please the state inspector. Rather, it has simply emphasized that surveillance requires contact. And at times, it has seemed more concerned about surveillance than about the substantive restrictions the surveillance would be designed to enforce.

The third meaning of entanglement is quite unrelated to the first two, and the Court has begun to distinguish it by calling it "political entanglement." Political entanglement occurs when a statute is likely to lead to a division of political factions along religious lines. Political entanglement is a private-sector phenomenon that does not in itself involve any church-state contact at all. Of course, if voters divide on religious lines on issues important to a church, the affected church will probably attempt to influence government action. But church lobbying is a constitutionally protected contact between church and state; churches and their members have the same political rights as other citizens and organizations. If a particular form of aid to churches would be constitutional under the first two parts of the Court's establishment clause test, it is hard to see how the aid becomes unconstitutional because of its tendency to incite constitutionally protected lobbying. Fear of such lobbying is like fear of state control of churches: it may be a reason to want an establishment clause, but it is government support, and not religious lobbying, that violates the clause.

"Entanglement" does not clearly communicate any of the Court's three specific meanings. The first meaning is regulation, or interference with autonomy. The second is surveillance or inspection. The third is political division on religious lines. Such gaps between the Court's concepts and its label for them make the label irrelevant or misleading in the process of adjudication.

. . .

By contrast, a right to church autonomy under the free exercise clause focuses on the real interests at stake. The right is the right of churches to make for themselves the decisions that arise in the course of running their institutions. Because the general right is not absolute, it will not always be clear what specific rights are within it. But it is clear what interests weigh on the churches' side of the balance. A union rule and an identical government regulation are equal infringements of church autonomy: both interfere with church control of church institutions.

. . .

## D. Autonomy and Church Labor Relations

Church labor relations rather plainly fall within the right of church autonomy. Deciding who will conduct the work of the church and how that work will be conducted is an essential part of the exercise of religion. In the language of the Supreme Court's autonomy cases, labor relations are matters of "church administration"; undoubtedly, they affect "the operation of churches."

Occasionally, a labor relations law requires a church to violate its official doctrine or collective conscience. These cases present conscientious objection claims as well as church autonomy claims. But it is worth repeating that the right of church autonomy does not depend on conscientious objection.

Churches may object to regulation on church autonomy grounds even when their official doctrine seems to support the regulation. Two examples from the recent church labor relations cases illustrate the point. The Roman Catholic Church has long supported the moral right of workers to organize and bargain collectively, and the moral duty of employers to bargain. Yet most local bishops resisted NLRB jurisdiction over teachers in parochial schools. Similarly, the Seventh Day Adventists resisted the Secretary of Labor's authority to enforce the Equal Pay Act in their schools, even though official church doctrine endorsed equal pay.

There are a variety of possible reasons, all constitutionally legitimate, for these examples of resistance to regulation that arguably reinforces church teaching. These churches may have been hypocritically seeking to exempt themselves from a moral duty they preach to others. Such conduct is not very admirable, but free exercise protection is not limited to churches the government admires. Alternatively, these churches may have resisted government regulation on principle, to avoid creating an adverse precedent that might support some more objectionable regulation in the future.

There is a third possible reason, and it casts further light on the nature of the right to autonomy. Even if government policy and church doctrine endorse the same broad goal, the church has a legiti-mate claim to autonomy in the elaboration and pursuit of that goal. Regulation may be thought of as taking the power to decide a matter away from the church and either prescribing a particular decision or vesting it elsewhere—in the executive, a court, an agency, an arbitrator, or a union. And regulation takes away not only a decision of general policy when it is imposed, but many more decisions of implementation when it is enforced.

For example, the NLRA initially takes away the decision whether to recognize a union. But once there is a union and a duty to bargain, a vast array of decisions that the church could once make autonomously must be shared with the union, and in the event of disagreement, with arbitrators, the NLRB, and the courts. A church might be willing to bargain with an uncertified union over wages and a few key working conditions, but resist NLRB jurisdiction to avoid the Board's expansive list of mandatory bargaining subjects. Forcing church authorities to share control of religious institutions with a labor union may not stir quite the same emotions as forcing them to relinquish control to schismatics. But a common principle is at stake in both cases: each is an interference with church control of church affairs.

Similarly, antidiscrimination laws initially prevent the church from deciding whether to discriminate among its employees and applicants. Many churches may wish to discriminate on the basis of religion, and some on the basis of race, sex, or national origin. Equally important, churches that do not want to discriminate at all are deprived of the chance to define discrimination. Some may oppose unequal treatment of individuals because of race, sex, or national origin, but want to be free to act on any facially neutral basis even if it has disparate impact on racial, sexual, or ethnic groups.

Even churches that accept the full scope of collective bargaining and the government's definition of discrimination may be seriously alarmed at the prospect of secular enforcement. This requires secular tribunals to review the church's comparisons of the responsibility and difficulty of jobs and of the skills, qualifications, and performance of workers; its motives for personnel decisions and the credibility of its claims to have acted for religious reasons; the religious or other necessity for employment practices that have disparate impact; even the effect on workers of its bishops' prayers and Bible readings. Similar review of church personnel decisions is required under the Federal Unemployment Tax Act.

. . .

IV. Balancing Church Autonomy and
Governmental Interests

In the religious observance and conscientious objector cases, the Supreme Court has balanced the citizen's interest in continuing his religious practice against the government's interest in the regulation that restricts him. In *Wisconsin v. Yoder* the Court said that only a state interest "of the highest order and . . . not otherwise served can overbalance" the interest protected by the free exercise clause.

The Court has not yet explicitly balanced interests in a church autonomy case, but sooner or later it will have to do so. A church's legitimate interest in autonomy has few natural limits, but at some point that interest becomes sufficiently attenuated, and the government's interest in regulation sufficiently strong, that neutral regulation for secular purposes becomes consistent with free exercise. This requires a balancing test, but a balancing test tilted in favor of the constitutional right. The government's interest in regulation must compellingly outweigh the church's interest in autonomy.

The balance cannot be struck by drawing a line on a unidimensional continuum, or even by drawing concentric circles around a spiritual epicenter, as one commentator has recently suggested. The spiritual epicenter image implies that the strength of the churches' interest can be measured by a single variable—the centrality, or perhaps the religious intensity, of an activity. This variable is important, but it is not the whole story. It is now possible to identify several important variables, and one other that has been invoked but must be irrelevant.

A. *Internal v. External Relations*

An organization's claim to autonomy is strongest with respect to internal affairs, including relationships between the organization and all persons who have voluntarily joined it. The voluntary nature of religious activity has played a prominent role in church autonomy cases from the beginning. The Court has repeatedly stated that all who join a church do so with the "implied consent" to its government, to which they "are bound to submit." If one is ill-treated by his church, he can leave it; if he feels bound by faith or conscience to stay in, the government can offer him no remedy.

The Court recently called it "the essence of religious faith that ecclesiastical decisions are reached and are to be accepted as matters of faith whether or not rational or measurable by objective criteria. Constitutional concepts of due process, involving secular notions of 'fundamental fairness' or impermissible objectives, are therefore hardly relevant . . . ." The point

is overstated, but the lesson for the secular courts is not: if a church chooses to treat its members unfairly or irrationally, there can be no secular remedy. The state has no legitimate interest sufficient to warrant protection of church members from their church with respect to discrimination, economic exploitation, or a wide range of other evils that the state tries to prevent in the secular economy.

This is not to say that a church and its members may not agree to such protection and make their agreement enforceable in a secular court. . . .

. . .

When the Serbian Orthodox Church in North America negotiated its affiliation with the hierarchy in Belgrade, and insisted on guarantees of independence for the North American diocese, it might conceivably have anticipated disputes and desired adjudication of those disputes in American courts. If so, it should have said so, because such circumstances are rare. The more typical case involves an unforeseen and bitter dispute that arises within a church after many years in which all disputes were successfully resolved internally and no one seriously considered going to a secular court.

Beyond this empirical judgment is a constitutional judgment—that the error of secular adjudication when that was not intended is more offensive to free exercise values than the error of leaving the church alone when it intended to submit to secular adjudication. . . .

. . .

Voluntary affiliation with the group is the premise on which group autonomy depends. If a church member is held in his church involuntarily, he retains all his civil rights and may enforce them in a secular court. Physical imprisonment would be a clear case. The brainwashing and deprogramming cases are a problematic extension of the same idea. The essence of the parents' claims in these cases is that their children are held in cults involuntarily. The voluntariness principle is also relevant to cases involving young children. The Court's tolerance of restrictions on free exercise to protect small children may in part reflect doubts about the validity of their consent.

Courts have intervened to protect church members from serious bodily harm even when they voluntarily submitted. The snake-handling cases are the best examples. Assuming true voluntariness, these results can be explained only on the ground that the state's interest in human life outweighs the snake handler's interest in free exercise. But such balancing must be narrowly limited with respect to internal affairs, or the right to autonomy will be lost.

It is much easier to justify regulation of a church's external affairs. An organization has no claim to autonomy when it deals with outsiders who have not agreed to be governed by its authority. For example, merchants who sell goods to churches do not thereby implicitly consent to not being paid, or to having disputes adjudicated by church courts or without due process. In general, there is no free exercise problem in holding churches responsible to outsiders under the ordinary rules of contract, property, and tort.

The internal-external distinction should not be misapplied in ways that infringe the right to proselytize. Proselytizing is a core function of evangelical religions, and has long been accorded free exercise protection. The non-members, often total strangers, who are approached by proselytizers have a right to be treated as outsiders entitled to the full protection of the law as against someone else's church. But if proselytizing is not to be forbidden altogether, this is a right they must invoke. Until he indicates otherwise, even a stranger implicitly submits to church authority to the extent of agreeing to listen to the proselytizer. Similarly, a church does not forfeit its autonomy by acquiring the means to proselytize more effectively. The District of Columbia Circuit was simply wrong to hold that churches forfeit control over internal affairs to the extent they seek out a broadcasting license.

Church employees have some characteristics of insiders and some of outsiders. Underlying much of the debate over church labor relations are unexamined assumptions about how employees should be classified. In all the litigation that has arisen, employees have been cast as outsiders. Modern labor legislation is designed to aid the worker in the adversary aspect of his relationship with his employer. But there is another aspect to the relationship. Every employee is a fiduciary for his employer. He has agreed to carry out his employer's business, to faithfully perform the tasks assigned him, and to always act in his employer's interest. He may resign at any time, but as long as he stays, he owes a duty of undivided loyalty to his employer. An unskilled laborer may face fewer decisions to which his fiduciary duty is relevant than the corporate president, but the controlling common law principles are the same.

Tension between the adversary and fiduciary aspects of the relationship inheres in all cases of principal and agent. This tension is easy to resolve in theory: the prospective employee is free to deal at arm's length in negotiating terms of employment and deciding whether to become or remain an employee, but once he begins to act as an employee, he is a fiduciary until he resigns.

In practice this breaks down with respect to both time and subject matter. Bargaining is not done once and for all when an applicant accepts employment. An employee can always quit if his employer does not make the job satisfactory to him. More importantly, collective bargaining, strikes, grievances, suits for reinstatement under the NLRA or the Civil Rights Act, and claims for pay or better conditions under the FLSA or OSHA, all allow employees to make arm's length demands without threatening to resign. With regard to subject matter, employees may bargain over matters that would seem to come within any reasonable conception of fiduciary duty.

The courts have recognized that modern collective bargaining seriously conflicts with the fiduciary duty of employee to employer. They have responded by excluding from the NLRA a class of management personnel whose responsibilities make their fiduciary status particularly important. This group is not limited to high ranking executives: it also includes many confidential secretaries, college professors, buyers, production schedulers, time-study personnel, and all persons in labor relations, employment, and personnel departments. In addition, supervisors are excluded by express statutory exception. The Court has said that "both exemptions grow out of the same concern: That an employer is entitled to the undivided loyalty of its representatives."

The Court's acknowledgement that the loyalty of unionized employees is divided apparently means that the NLRA partially preempts the state common law rule that employees owe undivided loyalty to their employer. Four members of the Court do not even contemplate divided loyalty. In their view, a nonmanagerial employee acts "only on his own behalf and in his own interest."

Both common law and statutory labor law offer models for considering whether church employees should be considered as insiders or outsiders in church autonomy cases. But neither is controlling; the question is one of constitutional law. The free exercise of religion includes the right to run large religious institutions—certainly churches, seminaries, and schools, and I would add hospitals, orphanages, and other charitable institutions as well. Such institutions can only be run through employees. It follows at the very least that the free exercise of religion includes the right of churches to hire employees. It surely also follows that the churches are entitled to insist on undivided loyalty from these employees.

The employee accepts responsibility to carry out part of the religious mission. He enters into a continuing relationship with the church in a way that independent sellers of goods and services usually do not. In so doing, he becomes a part of the church. He is not part of the church in the same way as a member, but in some ways he is more important. If an ordinary member deviates from the faith, or fails to comply with some matter of church practice, the church itself may suffer little or no harm. Most churches have many marginal members, and no one relies on them. But churches rely on employees to do the work of the church and to do it in accord with church teaching. When an employee agrees to do the work of the church, he must be held to submit to church authority in much the same way as a member.

It follows that church labor relations are internal affairs, and the state's interest in interfering to protect employees must be judged accordingly. The state may not intervene to protect employees from treatment that is merely arbitrary or unfair; the remedy for that is to resign or renegotiate the terms of employment. Modern labor legislation may have deprived secular employers of the fiduciary duty once owed them by their rank and file employees, but to deprive the churches of that duty would be to interfere with an interest protected by the free exercise clause.

## B. *The Religious Intensity of the Regulated Activity*

I said earlier that anything a church does is an exercise of religion. Even so, its interest in conducting a worship service is clearly greater than its interest in organizing a trip to a baseball game for the church men's club. If the validity of regulation depends on somehow balancing the state's interest against the church's, these differences must be taken into account. This factor will be referred to as the religious intensity of the regulated activity. Religious intensity is the factor described by Professor Bagni's concentric circles around a spiritual epicenter.

Religious intensity is analytically separate from the distinction between internal and external activity. For example, all church labor relations are internal matters, but a priest's job is more intensely religious than a janitor's. Similarly, contracts to purchase goods from merchants are external, but the purchase of communion wafers has more religious significance than the purchase of mop buckets. And proselytizing, one of the most intensely religious activities of all for many sects, becomes an external activity as soon as the listener invokes his right not to listen. The importance of religious intensity stems from the particular subject matter of the free exercise clause. The internal-external distinction, by contrast, will be important in any substantive freedom that includes a right to autonomy.

I have analyzed the religious intensity of church jobs in another journal, distinguishing employees of church-owned commercial businesses from support personnel in intrinsically religious operations (e.g., the church janitor), and both from jobs with intrinsically religious responsibilities. These categories should be thought of as ranges on a continuum. The ranges overlap to a much greater extent than I originally realized.

For example, consider the variety of church-owned commercial businesses. In the extreme case, such a business may be nothing more than an investment; any equally lucrative investment may have served as well, and employees may not even be aware that they are working for a church. This is still religious activity: the funds are being raised for the church. But except for claims of conscientious objection, a claim that it is religiously important that the business be conducted in some particular way is not very compelling. The primary interest is in a profit, the same interest a secular owner would have.

But some church-owned commercial businesses are owned for intrinsically religious reasons or run in intrinsically religious ways. A church may run a large business on a nonprofit basis as a charity; hospitals are common examples. A church may run a business to provide a religious working environment for its members, persons it hopes to proselytize, or persons in need of work. A monastery of contemplative monks should not forfeit its protection under the free exercise clause because it supports itself by selling sausage. A church may run a business to produce goods for use in worship services, or goods that must be produced in accord with some ritual to comply with religious law. Thus, some operations that might be called commercial businesses are an integral part of the religious mission.

Because it is so frequently involved in church labor relations litigation, the job of schoolteacher deserves special attention. Church schools serve multiple purposes. In part, they are simply schools, teaching secular subjects and satisfying the compulsory education laws. In part, they are philanthropic institutions, as when inner-city Catholic schools educate economically disadvantaged Protestant children. But in part, as the Court has emphasized, they are religious institutions, organized to transmit faith and values to succeeding generations. There can be no more important religious function for an institutional church; the very existence of the church depends on its success. And the employees who must carry out this function are the teachers.

There is evidence that religious schools do in fact perform this function. Survey research indicates the

Catholic schools have measurable permanent effects on their graduates' values. These effects are greater than the effects of the substitute religious instruction the church gives to Catholic students who attend public schools. This difference suggests that more than just the religion class is important to the transmission of values in religious schools, and more tentatively, that the Court has been right in its intuitive judgment that faith and values can be incorporated into any subject. Schools run by other churches have not been similarly studied. But some of them, the fundamentalist Protestant schools, strongly espouse the view that religion should be taught in every subject by every teacher.

Not every religious school can or will insist that every teacher actively promote religion. But nearly all will at least require every teacher not to interfere. A religious school might hire a nonbelieving math teacher, but it is not likely to permit him to flaunt his nonbelief, to denigrate the church that runs the school, or to set a bad moral example. Thus, even the nonbelieving math teacher has some intrinsically religious responsibilities. And even for those who would minimize such a teacher's religious function, there is no feasible way to distinguish him from teachers who actively seek to instill religious values, without intolerable litigation over the religious content of each teacher's instruction. Churches have strong claims to autonomy with respect to employment of teachers.

## C. The Nature and Extent of Interference

Church autonomy cases rarely involve government regulation that would prohibit some church activity altogether. More commonly, the government permits the activity to continue but interferes with the church's control of the activity. Some such regulations are more intrusive than others, and this must weigh in any balance. Assessments of intrusiveness must include both qualitative and quantitative elements.

The qualitative element may be thought of as the nature of the interference, or more precisely, the aspect of control interfered with. Whatever the label, the operative question is: What decisions have been taken away from the church? Elsewhere, I have distinguished four kinds of regulations: those that merely increase the cost of operations, those that interfere directly with the way an activity is conducted, those that interfere with selection of those who will conduct the activity, and those that forbid an activity entirely or create incentives to abandon it.

Each kind of interference may vary in severity.

A regulation that raises operating costs fifty percent is obviously more intrusive than one that raises costs five percent. A child labor law is much less intrusive than an EEOC order to reinstate a defrocked priest. Though both restrict the church's freedom to select its own employees, the child labor law leaves an enormous range of discretion; the EEOC order leaves none. Thus, the nature and extent of interference must be considered independently.

## D. A Factor that Does Not Matter: Church Organization

There are recurring suggestions that the right to church autonomy somehow depends on the way in which the church is organized. For example, the Seventh Circuit thought it important to the Catholic teacher union litigation that exclusive control of the schools was vested in the bishop. One danger of this approach is that it forces the courts to consider sensitive theological arguments about the locus of church authority. The more immediate danger is demonstrated by *Roman Catholic Diocese*. There, on reconsideration in light of the Supreme Court's decision exempting church schools, the NLRB again ordered a Catholic high school to bargain. The Court's decision was held inapplicable to schools owned and managed by lay boards of trustees instead of bishops. The Second Circuit quite sensibly denied enforcement. But Congress has made some statutory exemptions depend on whether a religious organization is separately incorporated from its sponsoring church.

The view that forms of church organization matter to the scope of autonomy is partly a misapplication of a class of cases in which secular courts unavoidably inquire into the allocation of authority within a church. A rule of deference to church authority requires courts to identify the authority to whom they will defer. The Supreme Court has placed restrictions on such inquiries. But they cannot be entirely avoided without denying all legal protection to churches and allowing church disputes to be settled by physical force. Once a church dispute reaches the secular courts, the best those courts can do to safeguard church autonomy is to stay out of the merits and defer to the authority recognized by both factions before the dispute arose.

In identifying the authority entitled to deference, the Court found it useful to distinguish hierarchical from congregational churches. In hierarchical churches, the highest ecclesiastical authority to which a dispute has been carried is entitled to deference, not only on the merits, but also on questions of who within the church was empowered to decide the merits and what was decided. This highest ecclesiastical authority can be identified without the "searching . . . inquiry" needed to identify the authority with responsibility for the particular issue, just as a foreigner could easily identify the Supreme Court of the United States as the highest court in the land without understanding the many rules that make lower courts the highest authorities on particular issues. In congregational churches, the highest authority is not so easy to identify. Unavoidably, secular courts are authorized to determine who, under the rules of the church, is entitled to bind it. The hierarchical rule and the congregational rule are formulations of the same basic principle of deference to church authority; the differences reflect application of the principle to slightly different facts.

Some courts, however, accorded congregational churches considerably less autonomy than hierarchical churches. That cannot be what the Court meant. The one thing that everyone agrees the religion clauses mean is that government cannot discriminate among churches. Regulation for congregational churches and autonomy for hierarchical churches would deny free exercise to the former and arguably tend to establish the latter. The right of church autonomy is the right to keep decisionmaking authority over church operations within the church, free of outside control; how that authority is allocated internally is irrelevant. Churches may be hierarchical or congregational, episcopal or democratic, clerical or lay, incorporated or informally associated, a single entity or a network of subsidiaries and affiliates—all are entitled to autonomy by the free exercise clause. Unavoidable secular inquiry into church organization in some cases implementing the right of church autonomy does not justify distinctions based on church organization in determining the scope of the right or the strength of a church's interest in it.

## V. The Limiting Effects of the Establishment Clause

This Article suggests that the free exercise clause frequently requires exemption from government regulation. An important counterargument is that such special treatment for religion would violate the establishment clause. The argument has been frequently made, but never accepted by the Supreme Court. It deserves to be taken more seriously.

An exemption from regulation raises establishment clause problems if it forces nonbelievers to financially support the conscientious objector's religion, as in *Sherbert v. Verner*. There, the Court held that a Sabbatarian who lost her job because she refused to work on Saturday was constitutionally entitled to unemployment compensation. The result was to make the taxpayers pay the costs of her religion, supplying her with the income that her religion precluded her from earning. The Court brushed aside the establishment issue, resolving it by authority but not by reasoned argument. The Court recently decided a similar case on the authority of *Sherbert*.

A different kind of subsidy is given when conscientious objectors are exempted from an onerous duty that must be performed by someone, thus increasing the burden on everyone else. The military draft illustrates the point nicely: if ten thousand conscientious objectors are exempt, then ten thousand others must serve. All nonobjectors are exposed to a greater risk of selection, in part because of their religion, and this shift of burden from objectors to nonobjectors is a form of subsidy.

Some commentators try to make this problem disappear by suggesting that "religion" should be construed broadly for free exercise purposes and narrowly for establishment clause purposes. But this can only be explained by a preference for one clause over the other—a preference with no basis in the Constitution. This is not even a case in which one can argue that the same word was used twice with two different meanings: "religion" appears only once in the first amendment.

Gail Merel has tried to dispose of the problem by distinguishing "irreligion" from "nonreligion." By "irreligion," she means opposition to some or all religious views. She believes that the religion clauses require government neutrality between religion and irreligion: a Jehovah's Witness and an atheist have the same right to proselytize. But there need not be neutrality between religion and nonreligion: a Sabbatarian and a college football fan do not have the same claim to exemption from Saturday work.

Merel's distinction is helpful, but it does not eliminate the tension between the two clauses. It ignores the cases in which an exemption for one religion burdens or extracts a subsidy from all others. No first amendment interest is implicated when the football fan asks for Saturday off because he is a football fan, and any exemption given Sabbatarians is irrelevant to such a request. But assuming state action, there is a first amendment problem when the fan is asked to work an extra Saturday to cover for the Sabbatarian. In the second case, he is not burdened because he is a football fan, but because he is a non-Sabbatarian. He is discriminated against because of his religion or lack thereof. It should not matter whether he observes some other holy day, militantly opposes all holy days, or is completely nonreligious. What matters is that a burden has been shifted because of a difference in religious beliefs.

These cases require further analysis to resolve the square conflict between the apparent meanings of the free exercise and establishment clauses. Possible solutions are a balancing test, deference to Congressional resolution of the conflict in particular cases, or allowing conscientious objectors to hire substitutes. Perhaps cases of direct subsidy, like *Sherbert v. Verner*, should be distinguished from cases where the only subsidy is to transfer a burden imposed by government in the first place, like the military draft.

These difficult problems do not cast doubt on this Article's construction of the free exercise clause. Many conscientious objector claims, and most church autonomy claims, do not involve any form of subsidy. The state does not support or establish religion by leaving it alone. No other organization has to comply with a regulation in place of a church in the way that other draftees must take the place of conscientious objectors. For example, no other employer has to bargain with a church's employees if the church is exempt; those employees simply will not be bargained with.

Nor does the usual church autonomy case present any claim that would require outsiders to subsidize religion. One can imagine exceptions. If the church were allowed to pay wages so low that its employees became public charges, the subsidy would be obvious. But in the absence of such a subsidy, the mere fact that the state does not impose on a church all the costs and burdens it imposes on secular organizations is not an establishment. And the fact that church employees may not earn as much or be as well treated as they would if the church were regulated is not a forced subsidy. Church employees are voluntarily part of the church; they are not to be treated as outsiders. The much noted tension between the two religion clauses simply does not exist in the typical church autonomy case.

. . .

Jesse H. Choper, *The Religion Clauses of the First Amendment: Reconciling the Conflict,* 41 UNIVERSITY OF PITTSBURGH LAW REVIEW 673 (1980)*

. . .

I.

In the main, the Court has tended to view the

Religion Clauses as embodying two independent mandates. Consequently, it has developed separate tests for determining whether government action violates either provision. As for the Establishment Clause, the three-prong test that has evolved is that, in order to pass constitutional muster, government action (1) must have a secular, rather than a religious, purpose, (2) may not have the principal or primary effect of advancing or inhibiting religion, and (3) may not involve "excessive entanglement" between government and religion.

As for the Free Exercise Clause, the Court has made clear that if the purpose of a law "is to impede the observance of one or all religions or is to discriminate invidiously between religions, that law is constitutionally invalid." It is equally plain that a law that attempts to regulate religious *beliefs* is unqualifiedly forbidden. Very few laws, however, single out religion for adverse treatment, deliberately prejudice persons because of their particular religious scruples, or penalize religious *beliefs*. Rather, most issues under the Free Exercise Clause arise when a general government regulation, undertaken for genuinely secular purposes, either penalizes (or otherwise burdens) *conduct* that is dictated by some religious belief or specifically requires (or otherwise encourages) *conduct* that is forbidden by some religious belief. The Court has recognized that while "[the freedom to believe] is absolute . . . , in the nature of things, the . . . [freedom to act] cannot be." In this context, the Court has employed "a balancing process" and ruled that if a government regulation of general applicability burdens the exercise of religion then, in the absence of a state interest "of the highest order," government must accommodate the religious interest by granting it an exemption from the general rule.

Thus, the seemingly irreconcilable conflict: on the one hand the Court has said that the Establishment Clause forbids government action whose purpose is to aid religion, but on the other hand the Court has held that the Free Exercise Clause may require government action to accommodate religion. Unfortunately, the Court's separate tests for the Religion Clauses have provided virtually no guidance for determining when an accommodation for religion, seemingly required under the Free Exercise Clause, constitutes impermissible aid to religion under the Establishment Clause. Nor has the Court adequately explained why aid to religion, seemingly violative of the Establishment Clause, is not actually required by the Free Exercise Clause.

II.

Nearly twenty years ago, I proposed an interpretation of the Establishment Clause for testing the validity of religious practices in the public schools. The interpretation was that such activities should be held unconstitutional if (1) they were *solely religious*, that is, if their "primary" purpose was religious even if "derivative" secular benefits might flow from their promotion of religion, *and* if (2) they were likely to *compromise* or *influence* students' religious beliefs. Under this test, students' religious beliefs are "compromised" if they do something that is forbidden by their religion; their religious beliefs are "influenced" if they engage in religious activities that, although not contrary to their religion, they would not otherwise undertake.

Several years later, I proposed a rule for testing the validity of government financial aid to religious institutions, particularly parochial schools. It reasoned that government expenditures for "solely religious" purposes—as ordinarily evidenced by their "primary" effect even if "derivative" public goals were advanced—result in *coercing* taxpayers to support religion and thereby infringe religious liberty. My approach concluded that government assistance to parochial schools should not be held violative of the Establishment Clause so long as it did not exceed the value of the secular educational services provided by the schools because, in such case, the primary purpose and effect was nonreligious.

Taken together, both proposals encompass a single principle: *the Establishment Clause should forbid only government action whose purpose is solely religious and that is likely to impair religious freedom by coercing, compromising, or influencing religious beliefs.* My main goal in this paper is to suggest why I believe this principle should also be used to resolve the conflict between the Establishment and Free Exercise Clauses.

### III.

It is both appropriate and useful to begin all constitutional interpretation by consulting the historical intent of the Framers. Indeed, perhaps "[n]o provision of the Constitution is more closely tied to or given content by its generating history than the religious clause of the First Amendment." But, as is so often true, "[a] too literal quest for the advice of the Founding Fathers [may be] futile and misdirected," because there is no clear record as to the Framers' intent, and such history as there is reflects several varying purposes.

. . .

Nonetheless, history does "divulge a broad philosophy of church-state relations." One tenet that emerges most clearly is that a central purpose of the Establishment Clause (as well as of the Free Exercise Clause) was to protect religious liberty—to prohibit the coercion of religious practice or conscience, a goal that remains paramount today. "Cruel persecutions," observed the Court in its first major Establishment Clause decision, "were the inevitable result of government-established religions." As Justice Brennan concluded in his influential examination of the Religion Clauses, "[the Establishment and Free Exercise Clauses], although distinct in their objectives and their applicability, emerged together from a common panorama of history. The inclusion of both restraints . . . shows unmistakably that the Framers of the First Amendment were not content to rest the protection of religious liberty exclusively upon either clause."

The practice perceived by the Framers as perhaps the most serious infringement of religious liberty sought to be corrected by the Establishment Clause was forcing the people to support religion by the use of compulsory taxes for purely sectarian purposes. Thus, Madison abhorred obliging "a citizen to contribute three pence only of his property" for nonsecular ends; Jefferson insisted that "to compel a man to furnish contributions of money for the propagation of opinions which he disbelieves, is sinful and tyrannical;" and the Court has repeatedly expressed this basic ideal by confirming that the Establishment Clause means at least that "[n]o tax in any amount, large or small, can be levied to support any religious activities or institutions, whatever they may be called, or whatever form they may adopt to teach or practice religion." While public subsidy of religion may not directly influence people's beliefs or practices, it plainly coerces taxpayers either to contribute indirectly to their own religions or, worse, to support sectarian doctrines and causes that are antithetical to their own convictions. As a matter of both historical design and present constitutional policy, the Establishment Clause forbids so basic an infringement of religious liberty.

### IV.

My proposals—based on the principle that the Establishment Clause should forbid government action whose purpose is religious and that is likely to impair religious freedom—sought to fulfill the central aim of the Religion Clauses: protection of religious liberty. Before exploring how this principle may help resolve the tension between the Establishment and Free Exercise Clauses, I should like briefly to compare my proposals to the paths the Court has taken in the past two decades.

With respect to religious practices in the public

schools, most of the results reached by the Court—invalidating "on-premises" released time, and prayer and Bible reading programs—have been in accord with my approach; but the Court's rationale, at least read literally, has been somewhat at variance with it. My proposed standard would forbid public school practices only when sectarian purpose is coupled with an infringement of religious liberty—*i.e.*, when it is shown that religiously motivated programs such as released time, Bible reading, and prayer will likely compromise or influence religious beliefs. Under the Court's articulated test, however, religious purpose alone condemns the programs. I have already indicated how this position raises severe problems in reconciling the tension between the Establishment and Free Exercise Clauses, and I shall expand on this shortly. At this point, however it is enough to observe that although the Court has *stated* in its major opinions in this area that coercion of religious belief—which is central under my proposal—is unnecessary for an Establishment Clause violation, it has often carefully catalogued the coercive elements of the programs that it has held invalid. Indeed, in *Zorach v. Clauson*, in which the Court upheld an "off-premises" released time program, the Court effectively conceded that the program's purpose was religious, but emphasized, wrongly in my view, that it involved no "coercion to get public school students into religious classrooms." Thus, on closer examination, I find substantial consonance between the Court's approach and my own.

With respect to aid to parochial schools, however, I must take considerably less comfort both from what the Court has said and also from what it has done. Under my proposal, since spending public funds for religious purposes is, as has been discussed, a form of religious coercion, the Establishment Clause would forbid government aid to church-related schools if the money were used for sectarian ends. A state appropriation that would be used in this way would be government action for religious purposes with the consequent threat to religious freedom. If it could be shown, however, that the state receives full secular value for its money, then its expenditure would be for a nonreligious purpose and there would be no danger to religious liberty—and thus there would be no violation of the Establishment Clause. Under my proposal, all of the many aid programs to elementary and secondary parochial schools that the Court has invalidated since 1971 would have probably survived constitutional challenge.

How has the Court's approach differed from mine? In every case in which it has disapproved of aid to parochial schools, it has found that the first prong of its test—that the program have a secular purpose—has been met. In some of the cases, however, the Court has condemned the programs because they failed the second prong of its test; i.e., the Court has found that the aid plans might have the primary effect of advancing religion (an effect which, if not prevented by the state, would also produce invalidity under my standard). But, as we shall see, it has been the third prong of the Court's Establishment Clause test—"excessive entanglement" between government and religion—that has effectively posed the greatest obstacle for aid to parochial schools. Since this factor plays no proscriptive role under my proposal, it accounts for the fundamental difference between the Court's approach and mine.

The Court has observed that the major beneficiaries of aid to nonpublic elementary and secondary schools are those operated by the Roman Catholic Church and has found that Catholic schools are "permeated" with religion. The Court has therefore reasoned that in order to insure that government aid does not advance the inculcation of religious doctrine (and thus run afoul of the second prong of its test), the state would have to engage in comprehensive surveillance of the recipient schools. This would foster an impermissible degree of administrative entanglement between church and state (thus failing the third prong of the Court's test). As a consequence, a state that wishes to aid parochial schools is faced with an insoluble dilemma. Since church-related elementary and secondary schools are presumably "permeated" with religion, the Court often requires that even the most neutral forms of aid be continually monitored so as to ensure that they will not be used for religious purposes; but such monitoring engenders "excessive entanglement" and thus renders the program invalid.

## V.

Without cataloguing the school aid cases in detail, I think it is fair to say that application of the Court's three-prong test has generated ad hoc judgments which are incapable of being reconciled on any principled basis. For example, a provision for therapeutic and diagnostic health services to parochial school pupils by public employees is invalid if provided *in* the parochial school, but not if offered at a neutral site, even if in a mobile unit adjacent to the parochial school. Reimbursement to parochial schools for the expense of administering teacher-prepared tests required by state law is invalid, but the state may reimburse parochial schools for the expense of administering state-prepared tests. The state may lend school textbooks to parochial school pupils because, the

Court has explained, the books can be checked in advance for religious content and are "self-policing"; but the state may not lend other seemingly self-policing instructional items such as tape recorders and maps. The state may pay the cost of bus transportation to parochial schools, which the Court has ruled are "permeated" with religion; but the state is forbidden to pay for field trip transportation visits "to governmental, industrial, cultural, and scientific centers designed to enrich the secular studies of students." I hope that these illustrations are sufficiently striking to demonstrate the unpredictability of the Court's approach. Indeed, in an unusually candid recent dictum, the Court forthrightly conceded that its approach in this area "sacrifices clarity and predictability for flexibility"—a euphemism, I suggest, for expressly admitting the absence of any principled rationale for its product.

## VI.

The conceptual chaos forged by the Court's test—effectively attributable to its "entanglement" prong—is not, however, its chief shortcoming. A more fundamental objection is that avoidance of administrative entanglement between government and religion neither should, nor can, represent a value to be judicially secured by the Establishment Clause.

Administrative entanglement between government and religion has sometimes been seen as threatening the values underlying the constitutional separation of church and state because of the fear that religious institutions will capture their public regulators by taking advantage of the widely noted tendency of administrators to develop a mutuality of interest with those they are supposed to regulate. This concern, however, is unfounded, both doctrinally and empirically. First, it has long been held that the Constitution permits the state to regulate church-related institutions even if it provides them no financial assistance whatever. Second, parochial school curricula, for example, have long been regulated, without any significant evidence of the church capturing the state. Thus, while the values underlying the Establishment Clause should forbid the state from abdicating to the church by permitting public funds to be used for religious purposes, they should not prevent meaningful government regulation of church-related institutions.

Another evil, it is often argued, arising from entanglement is that administrative regulation impairs the free exercise of religion. Here, again, there is no real evidence that the regulation of religious bodies which has taken place—albeit in the absence of substantial amounts of aid—has produced this result.

If it did, it would be unconstitutional whether or not the regulation were tied to aid. Although, "as a political matter, aid may prompt constitutional regulation theretofore absent, . . . [t]his consideration is relevant to the question of whether a religious institution should apply for aid; it is not relevant to whether the aid may constitutionally be granted."

Another form of administrative entanglement occurs when the state seeks to distinguish religion from nonreligion in order to grant a religious exemption from burdensome civil regulations. Although government scrutiny of religious beliefs and practices may be a sensitive and unwelcome task, its "necessity arises out of the constitutional language itself, which sets down religion as a subject for special treatment." Here, again, the Court has never doubted that government may become entangled with religion in this way.

In sum, scrupulous avoidance of all administrative "entanglement" between church and state might well require abandonment of virtually all regulation of religious activities, even for such desirable purposes as ensuring minimum educational standards for all school children. Even avoidance of only "substantial" entanglement would probably prevent government from characterizing certain beliefs as religious in order to exempt them from onerous and unnecessary secular rules. This would result either in confining such exemptions to members of long-established churches whose religiosity was universally conceded, or, indeed, in eliminating Free Exercise Clause exemptions altogether. I believe that avoidance of church-state entanglement, at the expense of forsaking legitimate secular pursuits or the more general value of preserving religious liberty, is mandated neither by the Establishment Clause nor good sense.

## VII.

The "entanglement" prong of the Court's Establishment Clause test also contains a somewhat separate element, which may be labeled "political divisiveness," under which government action may be held invalid if it promotes political fragmentation along religious lines. It is somewhat unclear whether the Court is using this "political divisiveness" as an independent test of constitutionality, a "warning signal" calling for stricter application of other tests, or only to reinforce its conclusions. I believe, however, that, like its companion element of administrative entanglement, avoidance of political strife along religious lines neither should, nor can, represent a value to be judicially secured by the Establishment Clause. Indeed, if government were to actually ban religious conflict in the legislative process, this would raise serious questions under those provisions of the first amendment that guarantee political, as well as religious, liberty.

Practical considerations, however, more than doctrinal ones, demonstrate the futility of making "political divisiveness" a constitutional determinant under the Establishment Clause. Surely, legislation is not invalid simply because a religious organization supported or opposed it. Conflict among sectarian groups—whether it arises on the issue of how public funds should be expended or on the question of whether to grant a religious exemption from laws of general application—may well be unfortunate. But such discord is neither meaningfully different nor more dangerous than the disagreements among religious groups that are inevitably generated when government pursues many concededly secular ends. Religious groups have differed concerning a wide variety of political issues—including Sunday closing, gambling, pornography, drug control, gun control, the draft, prohibition, abolition of slavery, racial integration, prostitution, overpopulation, sterilization, abortion, birth control, marriage, divorce, the Equal Rights Amendment, and capital punishment, to name but a few. Undoubtedly, organized churches and other religious groups have markedly influenced the resolution of some of these issues. The participation of such groups in the legislative process may well be relevant in determining whether a law should be subject to scrutiny under the Establishment Clause because it promotes a religious purpose. But if a law serves genuinely secular purposes—or impairs no one's religious liberty by coercing, compromising or influencing religious beliefs—there is no persuasive reason to hold it unconstitutional simply because its proponents and opponents were divided along religious lines.

Furthermore, even if government could or should eliminate political fragmentation along religious lines, the Establishment Clause would be a most ineffective tool for the task. For example, forbidding laws granting aid to parochial schools does not effect a truce, but only moves the battleground. There is every reason to believe that the failure to assist church-related schools antagonizes many citizens who feel that their taxes are being used to subsidize an alien dogma of secularism. Since funding only public schools places parents whose children attend parochial schools at a competitive disadvantage, they will tend to oppose legislation benefitting public schools.

Similarly, Christian groups may lobby for a Sunday closing law, believing that their religious obliga-tion to abstain from work on Sundays places them at a disadvantage in the marketplace. Moreover, it is in their interest, and in the interest of nonreligious people, vigorously to oppose an exemption from the law for Sabbatarians, who might gain a competitive advantage from being open on Sundays. But if the exemption is denied, Sabbatarians will just as vigorously oppose enactment of the Sunday closing law.

In sum, religious antagonism in the political arena, though perhaps regrettable, is a fact of life in our pluralistic governmental system which cannot be effectively suppressed through the Establishment Clause.

## VIII.

To turn now to my principal subject, while it has been the "entanglement" prong of the Court's Establishment Clause test that has plagued the Court's efforts on the question of aid to parochial schools, it is the "secular purpose" prong that is most troublesome in respect to reconciling the seeming antipathy between the Establishment and Free Exercise Clauses. Because this part of the Court's test flatly prohibits any government action that has a religious purpose, it would make virtually *all* accommodations for religion unconstitutional. Since, as we shall see, the primary goal of nearly all accommodations for religion is to avoid burdening religious activity, it is plain that their purpose is to assist religion. Thus, taken literally, the "secular purpose" requirement of the Court's Establishment Clause test would, for example, forbid the exemption of conscientious objectors from military service and Amish school children from compulsory education laws. As we have seen, the Court's interpretation of the Free Exercise Clause rejects these implications of its Establishment Clause test. Indeed, the Court has not only mandated religious exemptions under the Free Exercise Clause but has also strongly indicated its approval of a number of government accommodations for religion that were not constitutionally required.

The Court's apparent inconsistency may be rationalized by concluding that its Establishment Clause principles simply give way in the face of a serious (or even arguably substantial) Free Exercise Clause claim. Indeed, this approach may be endorsed as wisely fulfilling the historic and contemporary aims of both clauses to further religious liberty. But while I do not believe that the Establishment Clause should be read to bar all exemptions for religion, I am also unwilling to totally ignore the Establishment Clause simply because government's purpose is to accommodate religion. Precisely because the Establishment Clause is designed to protect religious liberty, I believe that it should not be automatically read as subordinate to the Free Exercise Clause, but rather as limiting the extent to which government may act in behalf of religion.

My discussion will focus on the Establishment Clause. It makes no attempt to determine, once it is found that a religious accommodation is *permissible* under the Establishment Clause, when such accommodation may be *required* under the Free Exercise Clause. Rather, it concerns the Free Exercise Clause only by confining its scope.

### IX.

My proposal, once again, is that the Establishment Clause should forbid government action that is undertaken for a religious purpose *and* that is likely to result in coercing, compromising, or influencing religious beliefs. Thus, I disagree with the Court's articulated view that religious purpose alone renders government action invalid. Rather, it is only when religious purpose is coupled with threatened impairment of religious freedom that government action should be held to violate the Establishment Clause.

I wish to make clear that my position is not grounded in the idea that government promotion of religion serves secular ends by producing public benefits. If legislation designed to assist religion jeopardizes religious freedom, no public benefit should save it. Conversely, if state satisfaction of the religious needs of either the majority or a minority does not jeopardize any Establishment Clause values that have been identified, it should be held constitutionally permissible regardless of whether it serves some independent secular goal. Thus, the key to an Establishment Clause violation should be whether the government action endangers religious freedom.

To illustrate my view—and specifically to contrast it with prevailing judicial doctrine—I believe that *Epperson v. Arkansas* was wrongly decided. In *Epperson*, the Court held that Arkansas' "anti-evolution" statute, which made it unlawful to teach the theory of Charles Darwin in the public schools, violated the Religion Clauses. The Court rested its conclusion on the ground that it was "clear that fundamentalist sectarian conviction was and is the law's reason for existence." I would not dispute the Court's finding that the statute had a solely religious purpose even if it could be shown that it produced derivative secular benefits such as the promotion of classroom harmony. But to rely on the nonestablishment precept to invalidate a religiously motivated law that creates none of the dangers the Establishment Clause was designed to prevent represents, in my view, an "un-

tutored devotion to the concept of neutrality" between church and state. Conceding that the law in *Epperson* "aided" fundamentalist religions, there was no evidence that religious beliefs were either coerced, compromised or influenced. That is, it was not shown, nor do I believe that it could be persuasively argued, that the anti-evolution law either (1) induced children of fundamentalist religions to accept the biblical theory of creation, or (2) conditioned other children for conversion to fundamentalism. In contrast to other situations to be discussed below, those whose religious interests were not advanced by the law appeared to suffer no *religious* harm. Therefore, while the accommodation for religion in *Epperson* may not have been constitutionally required by the Free Exercise Clause, the law should have survived the Establishment Clause challenge. Even though it satisfied a private religious need, it did not, given the above factual premises, threaten religious liberty.

### X.

Although the Court has seldom explored the tension between the Religion Clauses, the problem has by no means gone unnoticed. It should be helpful in defining the contours of my proposal to contrast it with some of the major scholarly attempts to reconcile the conflict.

Nearly twenty years ago, an influential article by Philip Kurland urged that the Religion Clauses be read together to state a single principle of neutrality, mandating that "government cannot utilize religion as a standard for action or inaction because these clauses prohibit classification in terms of religion either to confer a benefit or to impose a burden." Although there is much to be said for this rule of "religion-blindness," it has, in my view, two serious shortcomings. In requiring government impartiality respecting religion, the rule produces results hostile to religion without serving nonestablishment values and permits forms of aid that subvert historical and contemporary aims of the Establishment Clause.

The neutrality principle produces hostility to religion by flatly prohibiting all solely religious exemptions from general regulations no matter how greatly they burden religious exercise and no matter how insubstantial the competing state interest may be. In advancing the admirable goals of government neutrality and impartiality, it downgrades the positive value that both Religion Clauses assign to religious liberty.

Consider a simple illustration: Suppose that a school regulation requires pupils to wear shorts during gym class for the aesthetic effect of uniform dress and that one child requests an exemption because her religious scruples forbid her to bare her legs. The "religion-blindness" rule would allow a broadly worded exemption for "all children whose modesty makes the wearing of shorts uncomfortable" or for "all children whose parents request exemption." Either of these would protect the religious objector, but so many other children might also take advantage of the exemption that the regulation's aesthetic goal would be destroyed. Even if the school believed that it could exempt children who objected on religious grounds and still achieve its overall aesthetic purpose, such an exemption would constitute an impermissible classification under the neutrality principle. Thus, the school board would seemingly be faced with the choice of either protecting the religious child by abandoning its concededly valid purpose, or compromising the religious child's beliefs even though denying the exemption is unnecessary to serve its purpose. The "religion-blindness" rule would appear to demand these equally unsatisfying alternatives even though granting a religious exemption would neither coerce, compromise, nor influence the religious beliefs of any school children. I doubt that it could plausibly be argued that children would change their religions in order to obtain an exemption, or that the beliefs of those granted the religious exemption would thereby be intensified. Therefore, a religious exemption—admittedly undertaken for nonsecular purposes—would in no way impair religious freedom. Pursuant to my proposal, it would be permitted by the Establishment Clause.

Paradoxically, the neutrality principle not only requires hostility to religion at odds with the values of the Free Exercise Clause, but also permits aid to religion in conflict with values of the Establishment Clause. It would apparently allow the use of tax funds for the purely religious functions of church organizations, so long as the legislative classification is broad enough. For example, suppose the state allocated public funds to all private associations for the purpose of distributing replicas of their insignia to their members. The Rotary Club, the League of Women Voters, and religious groups would all be beneficiaries. Under the "religion-blindness" rule, denial of funds to religious groups would constitute an impermissible religious classification, yet including such groups would designate tax funds to be used to purchase crosses and Stars of David. If our economy were to reach such a stage of collectivization that government fiscal policies so shrunk private sources of funds as to make voluntary support of religion impracticable, there might well then be merit in re-evaluating the historically rooted and contemporarily valued prohibition against state support of strictly sectarian activities. But I do not believe that it has yet been persuasively shown that that time has come.

## XI.

Several scholars have urged that the Establishment Clause is largely designed to implement the Free Exercise Clause, so that when the Religion Clauses clash, the Establishment Clause must be subordinated to the Free Exercise Clause. The leading decision of *Sherbert v. Verner* may be read as supporting this view. In that case, Mrs. Sherbert, a mill worker and a Seventh Day Adventist, was discharged by her employer when she would not work on Saturday, the Sabbath day of her faith, after all the mills in her area adopted a six-day work week. South Carolina denied her unemployment compensation benefits for refusing to accept "suitable work," even though that would require her to work on Saturday. The Court held that this violated the Free Exercise Clause because "to condition the availability of benefits upon [her] willingness to violate a cardinal principle of her religious faith effectively penalizes the free exercise of her constitutional liberties." Under the Court's Establishment Clause test, however, any government action that has a religious purpose is forbidden, and, therefore, a Sabbatarian exemption would appear to be unconstitutional. It seems indisputable that when the state excuses Mrs. Sherbert from taking otherwise suitable work because of her religious scruples, the purpose of the exemption is solely to facilitate her religious exercise.

To avoid the stark impact of its Establishment Clause approach, the Court may have either totally subordinated the Establishment Clause's "no-aid" mandate to the Free Exercise Clause, or simply balanced Mrs. Sherbert's right to Sabbatarianism under the Free Exercise Clause against the "no-aid" principle of the Establishment Clause and found the former weightier. Justice Brennan, author of the *Sherbert* opinion, had previously advocated this approach for resolving the establishment-free exercise conflict: "[T]he logical interrelationship between the Establishment and Free Exercise Clauses may produce situations where an injunction against an apparent establishment must be withheld in order to avoid infringement of rights of free exercise."

If, in a balancing process, the Establishment Clause's prohibition of aid to religion is viewed only as an abstract principle rather than as a means for securing religious liberty, then it is not surprising that the Court found it wanting in *Sherbert*. On the other side of the balance was Mrs. Sherbert's grave, immediate, and concrete injury—the very type of injury that the Free Exercise Clause was meant to prevent. Indeed, if the Establishment Clause is so abstractly viewed, then it is difficult to imagine any situation where it would not be subordinated or outweighed when measured against a colorable free exercise claim.

Under my proposal, the Establishment Clause would not be so viewed. Rather it would serve the underlying values of both Religion Clauses by forbidding laws whose purpose is to aid religion—including exemptions for religion from general government regulations—if such laws tended to coerce, compromise, or influence religious beliefs.

Mrs. Sherbert's exemption would fail this test. First, since those who refused to work on Saturdays for nonreligious reasons, such as watching football games or spending the day with their children, would be denied unemployment benefits under South Carolina's scheme (and could constitutionally be denied them under the Court's ruling), the sole purpose of Mrs. Sherbert's exemption was to aid religion. Second, the exemption results in impairment of religious liberty because compulsorily raised tax funds must be used to subsidize Mrs. Sherbert's exercise of religion.

The situation produced by the Court's decision in *Sherbert* is distinguishable from that in which the state allows all unemployment compensation claimants to refuse work on one day of their choosing in order to pursue whatever outside interests they might have. Even though some claimants might use the day for religious exercise, government has not conditioned the grant of public funds on a religious use, nor in any other way restricted freedom of choice as to how the money will be spent. While taxpayers may rightfully complain if Mrs. Sherbert's exemption is granted on condition that she use it for religious purposes, they may not object to Mrs. Sherbert's religious use of her leisure time. This is analytically the same as a welfare recipient's contributing part of his benefits to his church. Even though the state's money finds its way into the church's coffers, there is no violation of the Establishment Clause because the government has not conditioned the grant on the recipient's promise to use it for religious purposes. The government's secular goal of providing for the basic needs of indigents is served even though a particular recipient decides that one of his basic needs is religion.

Does my proposal—which forbids a religious exemption for Mrs. Sherbert because it would coerce taxpayer's religious beliefs—simply subordinate the Free Exercise Clause to the Establishment Clause?

I think not, because the religious liberty value at the core of both Religion Clauses demands that Mrs. Sherbert's right to freely exercise her religion not encompass the right to governmental assistance which infringes the religious freedom of others.

## XII.

In a provocative article published fifteen years ago, Marc Galanter sought to justify exemptions for religious minorities from general government regulations on the ground that they do not constitute preferential aid to religion forbidden by the Establishment Clause but rather amount to no more than equalizing the position of these minorities with that of the majority. He based his thesis on the persuasive premise that "[w]hatever seriously interferes with majority religious beliefs and practices is unlikely to become a legal requirement—for example, work on Sunday or Christmas." Indeed, the statute involved in Sherbert is illustrative because, by prohibiting any disadvantage against employees who refused to work on Sunday because of their religion, it "expressly save[d] the Sunday worshipper from having to make the kind of choice" imposed on Mrs. Sherbert. Thus, special treatment for religious minorities, Galanter contended, is restorative or equalizing, granting them only "what majorities have by virtue of suffrage and representative government."

One difficulty that I have with this view is that it assumes the validity of certain advantages that religious majorities may create for themselves. But if what the majority obtains "by virtue of suffrage" itself contravenes the Establishment Clause, then providing the same benefit to religious minorities compounds the violation rather than eliminates it. Thus, the devotional Bible reading and Lord's Prayer programs struck down by the Court could not have been cured, in my judgment, by reading from the Torah, the Koran, and works of secular philosophy on selected days of the month. In *Sherbert*, since the exemption for Sunday worshippers granted by South Carolina, as much as the exemption for Mrs. Sherbert mandated by the Supreme Court, served a religious purpose and involved religious coercion in the form of a tax subsidy for religious practice, it too would violate the Establishment Clause under my proposal.

But if the government policy that imposes burdens on minority religions has a secular purpose (as most such regulatory and tax programs do), and is thus itself immune to challenge under the Establishment Clause, I do not believe that Establishment Clause values should be ignored in situations where alleviating the burden or "restoring" the minority to a position of "equality" with the majority results in impairment of religious liberty. For example, even if members of a particular church demonstrated that, largely because of the financial burdens of government taxation, they had inadequate funds to buy vestments, it appears beyond dispute—at least in the absence of the wholly collectivized society hypothesized earlier—that the Establishment Clause should forbid a state subsidy for this purpose. Moreover, even if a zoning ordinance, enacted to serve substantial public goals, excluded churches within many miles of a particular indigent person's home, it is plain that the historical and contemporary Establishment Clause command to avoid taxation in aid of religion should forbid the state's funding his weekly transportation to church.

Similarly, the Establishment Clause should be held to forbid the government's paying chaplains to minister to the religious needs of prisoners and military personnel. It may be that, under a Free Exercise Clause balancing test, the state could not exclude chaplains who volunteer for these purposes. But the Establishment Clause makes it the financial responsibility of the church and not the state to attend to its members' religious needs.

I agree, however, that "restorative or equalizing" accommodations for religion that do not tend to interfere with religious freedom should be permissible, even when such accommodations impose substantial costs of other kinds on those who are not their beneficiaries. For example, if a state were to grant a Sabbatarian exemption from a Sunday closing law, a non-Sabbatarian merchant might well object on the ground that the religiously motivated exemption caused him financial injury because, being forced to close on Sundays, he lost business to Sabbatarian competitors. But even though the non-Sabbatarian store owner probably suffers a far greater monetary loss than any individual taxpayer would suffer from most tax subsidies of religious activities, this *alone* would not produce a violation of the Establishment Clause under my proposal. Similarly, that other accommodations of religious exercise would impose substantial non-monetary costs on nonrecipients would not *itself* invalidate them. For example, granting a draft exemption to a religious objector probably means that a nonbeliever who would otherwise avoid being drafted will be required to serve. Exempting a religious child from the school requirement that she wear shorts in gym class deprives her nonbelieving classmates of the desired total uniformity of dress. Excising evolutionary theory from public school curricula in order to avoid offending devout believers in a religious theory of creation deprives nonbelieving children of meaningful knowledge.

However, these indirect social costs of religious accommodation—in contrast to the tax cost of a religious subsidy—do not themselves threaten the values undergirding the Establishment Clause. They do not tend to coerce, compromise, or influence the nonbeliever's religious beliefs. Unlike the tax cost in *Sherbert*, these indirect social costs are not required to satisfy the believer's needs. The Sabbatarian store owner who seeks to remain open on Sunday does not demand that the non-Sabbatarian be closed on Sunday so that the Sabbatarian may acquire the non-Sabbatarian's customers; they are an unsought benefit, and the Sabbatarian's free exercise claim could be fully satisfied without them. Nor does the religious pacifist need to have another serve in his place; the cost imposed on the nonbelieving draftee does not aid the exempted person's religious beliefs at all. Nor, on the factual premises discussed earlier, is it necessary to the religious tenets of the fundamentalist that nonbelieving children fail to learn about Darwin. In contrast, Mrs. Sherbert claimed a constitutional right to tax funds to subsidize the observance of her Sabbath. The pocketbook injury to nonbelieving taxpayers was required to accomplish this religious end. The cost itself served a religious purpose, rather than resulting incidentally from the accommodation of religious exercise. If accommodations for religion impose religious costs on nonbelievers, then, under my proposal, they are forbidden by the Establishment Clause. But if such accommodations impose only nonreligious costs, then the Establishment Clause should be held to permit—or, indeed, the Free Exercise Clause may be interpreted to demand—that these costs of religious tolerance be paid.

## XIII.

In a most sophisticated effort to resolve the tension between the Religion Clauses, Alan Schwartz, a decade ago, urged that accommodations for religious exercise should survive Establishment Clause challenge unless they result in the "imposition of religion," that is, they *actually influence* individuals to change their religious beliefs. His approach differs from mine in several important respects. First, it would apparently not invalidate a tax subsidy of religion unless it met this criterion. But, as we have seen, the Framers considered taxation in support of churches to be an especially reprehensible form of religious coercion, a view confirmed by the contemporary value of protecting religious freedom. Under the "no imposition" approach, many such subsidies would seemingly be permissible, thus enabling government to finance most private religious activities—as opposed to public activities such as school prayers, which undoubtedly influence religious belief—free of Establishment Clause constraints.

Second, under Schwartz's approach, government action that merely "helps implement a religious or irreligious choice independently made," rather than actually influences religious beliefs, does not amount to imposition of religion, and thus passes the Establishment Clause hurdle. I believe that government programs with no secular purpose that intensify or meaningfully encourage even independently chosen beliefs should be held to violate the Establishment Clause. Otherwise, a modest public reward for regular attendance at the church of one's faith would be permissible.

Finally, Schwartz contends that although aid to religion may induce false claims of religious belief, "the Establishment Clause is not concerned with false claims of belief, only with induced belief." But, as we shall see, at least some initially false claims of belief, particularly those which require for their proof participation in religious exercise, will probably ripen into sincere belief. Indeed, it also seems likely that strong temptations to adopt a particular religion will sometimes produce a sincere belief without any initial bad faith. Thus, government temptations that tend to influence religious choice, like other forms of religiously motivated action that tend to coerce or compromise religious freedom, jeopardize Establishment Clause values and should be proscribed.

## XIV.

As indicated earlier, my proposal to reconcile the tension between the Religion Clauses focuses on when the Establishment Clause permits or prohibits government accommodations for religion. Although it does not speak to when the Free Exercise Clause mandates religious exemptions from secular government regulations, it does assist in the balancing process traditionally employed under the Free Exercise Clause by identifying the state interest that must be weighed against the religious burden imposed. If the Establishment Clause *permits* a religious exemption, the state interest to be balanced against the free exercise claim is that of *maintaining its program without religious exemptions*. If, however, the Establishment Clause *prohibits* a religious exemption, the state interest to be balanced is that of *preserving its entire program*, because only by abandoning it altogether could the free exercise claim be satisfied.

To illustrate, consider the hypothetical regulation requiring school children to wear gym shorts. We have already observed that a religious exemption would in no way coerce, compromise, or influence

religious choice and is thus permissible under the Establishment Clause. In balancing the child's claim for exemption under the Free Exercise Clause, the state's interest would be that of complete uniformity of dress. The free exercise balancing process necessarily involves value judgments that may often be difficult. Whether a more refined analysis than naked interest balancing can be developed is beyond the scope of this discussion. Whatever the optimal approach may be, it would seem most unlikely that the aesthetic interest in complete uniformity could overcome the child's interest in not being compelled to violate her religious beliefs.

Similarly, in *Wisconsin v. Yoder*, which held that the Free Exercise Clause demanded an exemption for Amish children from the state's requirement of school attendance until age sixteen, the Court correctly identified the relevant state interest as that of denying a religious exemption. Unless it could be shown that relieving the Amish of this government-created impediment to fulfillment of their religious tenets would tend to coerce, compromise, or influence religious choice—and it is extremely doubtful that it could—the exemption was permissible under the Establishment Clause. In contrast, in *Sherbert v. Verner* we have seen that my proposal would prohibit the state from granting a religious exemption from the "suitable work" requirement. Therefore, only by abandoning this requirement for *all* claimants as applied to Saturdays (or a day of the claimant's choice) could the state have satisfied Mrs. Sherbert's free exercise claim without running afoul of the Establishment Clause. Under the appropriate Free Exercise Clause balancing test, it seems likely under these circumstances that the state's interest in maintaining its requirement intact would have prevailed.

The draft exemption cases present a further problem. The Court has never held that the Free Exercise Clause requires an exemption for those who object to military service on religious grounds. Indeed, as recently as 1971 in *Gillette v. United States*—holding that the Free Exercise Clause does not require excuse of those whose religious beliefs prohibit participation only in particular wars—the Court strongly suggested that "relief for conscientious objectors is not mandated by the Constitution." The central question for our purposes, however, is whether, contrary to prevailing doctrine, Congress may grant a religious exemption without violating the Establishment Clause.

First, the Court's efforts in *Gillette* to the contrary notwithstanding, an exemption for persons whose objection to military service is based on "religious training and belief" cannot be found to have other than a religious purpose. In *Gillette*, the Court contended that this exemption had a "neutral, secular basis" grounded in "considerations of a pragmatic nature, such as the hopelessness of converting a sincere conscientious objector into an effective fighting man . . . ." But if Congress' aim were simply to exclude those who were especially poor risks for military combat, then its making "religious belief" an absolute ground of incapacity was plainly both under- and over-inclusive. Rather, the Selective Service Act's specific limitation to religious objectors demonstrated on its face—as the Court conceded—Congress' "attempt to accommodate free exercise values" and its "respect for the value of conscientious action and for the principle of supremacy of conscience."

Second, we have already observed that religious exemptions from conscription impose substantial costs on nonbelieving draftees who must take the religious objector's place, but that these "nonreligious" social costs are not themselves enough to condemn the exemption under the Establishment Clause. Nonetheless, they do serve as a warning signal that the advantage for religion may be so great as to impermissibly induce nonbelievers to profess religious belief and ultimately undergo genuine conversions.

The Selective Service Law of 1917, which exempted from combat duty only those religious objectors who belonged to "well-recognized" religious sects, strikingly posed the danger of influencing people to adopt particular religions. The more broadly worded exemption in effect during the Vietnam War era—applying to any person "who, by reason of religious training and belief, is conscientiously opposed to participation in war in any form"—was significantly less likely to induce people to join established churches. In addition, the Court's expansive reading of that provision—making it available "if an individual . . . holds beliefs that are purely ethical or moral in source and content but . . . nevertheless impose

upon him a duty of conscience to refrain from participating in any war at any time"—minimized that danger still further. Still, professing a personal "religion" (as opposed to "essentially political, sociological, or philosophical considerations") was enough to gain the enormous advantage of avoiding combat duty, and therefore would likely influence religious choice. Indeed, since the government was authorized to examine the sincerity of a claimant's religious beliefs, it seems that at least some claimants would be induced to join established churches to corroborate their claims. Even if not, potential draftees seeking exemption would have to formulate a statement of personal doctrine that would pass muster. This endeavor would involve deep and careful thought, and perhaps reading in philosophy and religion. Some undoubtedly would be persuaded by what they read. Moreover, the theory of "cognitive dissonance"—which posits that to avoid madness we tend to become what we hold ourselves to be and what others believe us to be—also suggests that some initially fraudulent claims of belief in a personal religion would develop into true belief. Thus, a draft exemption for religious objectors threatens values of religious freedom by encouraging the adoption of religious beliefs by those who seek to qualify for the benefit.

Finally, in contrast to draft exemption, recall the case of the non-Sabbatarian merchant who coveted the Sabbatarian exemption from the Sunday closing law because he felt that it was more profitable to be open on Sundays than on Saturdays. Perhaps it is possible that some such non-Sabbatarian would be led to misrepresent his religious beliefs to obtain the exemption. But I believe that the intrinsic motivational difference between conscientious opposition to war and the comparatively crass desire to obtain pecuniary gain makes it extremely unlikely that the non-Sabbatarian's actual beliefs would be influenced in the process. Therefore, the Establishment Clause should not bar the accommodation for religion.

## Bibliography

*Establishment and Exercise Clause Tension*

Evans, Bette Novit, *Contradictory Demands on the First Amendment Religion Clauses: Having It Both Ways*, 30 Journal Church & State 463 (1988).

Pfeffer, Leo, *Freedom and/or Separation: The Constitutional Dilemma of the First Amendment*, 64 Minnesota Law Review 561 (1980).

Wheeler, David E., *Establishment Clause Neutrality and the Reasonable Accommodation Requirement*, 4 Hastings Constitutional Law Quarterly 901 (1977).

## D. Establishment Clause Theory

These articles focus upon Establishment Clause premises and policy. Alan Schwarz argues that Establishment Clause cases should be governed by a "no-religious classification" principle. Jesse H. Choper argues that direct or indirect government support of parochial schools does not violate the Establishment Clause, so long as it does not exceed the value of the school's secular educational service. William Van Alstyne uses the United States Supreme Court's decision in *Lynch v. Donnelly* to support his argument that there is a constitutional "drift" of the government in establishing "itself under distinctly religious auspices."

Alan Schwarz, *No Imposition of Religion: The Establishment Clause Value*, 77 YALE LAW JOURNAL 692 (1968)*

The establishment clause of the first amendment has been interpreted to prohibit any aid to religion. The free exercise clause has been interpreted to require that religious exercise be preferentially aided. The coexistence of these interpretations makes conflict between the clauses inevitable. For example, it is arguable that the establishment clause invalidates military service exemptions granted conscientious objectors, while the free exercise clause compels them. Since religious opposition is the only statutory basis for a conscientious objection claim, a religious belief is clearly being preferentially aided. Failure to grant the exemption, however, might violate free exercise.

The Supreme Court has usually decided religion cases on the basis of one clause or the other, without explicitly recognizing the potential conflict between them. Only Justices Brennan and Stewart have spoken to the seeming paradox, Brennan proposing that it be resolved by a subordination of establishment to free exercise, Stewart proposing a less "wooden," "sterile" interpretation of the establishment clause. One commentator has proposed a merger of the two clauses into a united "neutral" principle, but most have favored a subordination or balancing approach. . . .

. . .

Inconsistency between the establishment and free exercise clauses is avoided by merging them into a unified principle; each clause is thereby deprived of any independent content and inconsistency becomes impossible. Professor Kurland urges that both clauses should be construed as a unit to express the single principle that "religion may not be used as a basis for classification for purposes of governmental action whether that action be the conferring of rights or privileges or the imposition of duties or obligations." The Supreme Court has not adopted a no-religious-classification principle. In the *Zorach* and *Arlan's Department Store* cases it upheld preferential treatment accorded religion and its exercise, and in *Sherbert v. Verner* and *In re Jenison*, applying the free exercise clause, the Court invalidated state ac-

* Reprinted by permission of The Yale Law Journal Company and Fred B. Rothman & Company from THE YALE LAW JOURNAL, Vol. 77, pp. 692-737.

tion because preferential treatment had not been accorded religious exercise. . . .

Professor Kurland characterizes a no-religious-classification standard as "akin" to the equal protection clause. It is akin to rather than identical with equal protection, because it forbids all religious classifications instead of forbidding only all unreasonable religious classifications. A pure equal protection test would recognize the legitimacy of values other than perfect equality and consequently would require a determination of the reasonableness of a particular religious classification in terms of other free exercise and establishment values. Since accepting such additional values has resulted in an inconsistent interaction between the religion clauses, however, the use of a pure equal protection test would bring us full circle back to the existing dilemma. A no-religious-classification standard avoids the dilemma by treating the value of perfect equality as one of transcendent significance. Paradoxically, however, because the perfect equality concept is applied only to religious classifications, the standard often in fact discriminates against religious activities, and to that extent thereby subverts the principal value purportedly promoted by the standard. And where application of the standard satisfies the equality value, more significant establishment values are often subverted.

## 1. The Inequality of No Religious Classification

A no-religious-classification standard prohibits government from preferentially aiding religious activity. Aid may only be granted where the religious activity falls within a broader secular classification. The standard thus insists that perfect equality be accorded nonreligious activities, with the result that a legislature may never consider a religious activity to be more worthy than a lawful nonreligious activity having an identical need for aid or protection. Consider application of the standard to an ordinance prohibiting raucous noises within 100 feet of a church, enacted in order to insure tranquility for religious observance. In that form the ordinance would be a religious classification, a religious activity having obviously been singled out for aid. Nor would this infirmity be remedied by extending protection to, say, hospitals and schools, if other activities requiring tranquility have not been included. If all activities with an equal need of protection were included, then the statute would make an activities-requiring-silence classification, which would not conflict with the standard. But short of such total coverage the statute does no more than list the activities to be protected; it provides no overall classification but, rather, separate church, hospital, and school classifications, and thus it seems inescapably to make, inter alia, a religious classification. Thus it would seem that a religious classification could be avoided only by extending protection to all lawful activities, regardless of their worth, which have an equal need of protection. In order to protect religious observance it would be necessary to protect the chess club or perhaps even the lawfully conducted poker game, assuming that both these activities require, for their enjoyment and efficiency, as few distractions as does a religious observance.

Moreover, the standard limits application of the perfect equality value to religious classification; all others are governed by conventional equal protection criteria. A legislature may grant protection to a hospital or school without extending identical aid to the chess game or, at least so long as most secular activities with an equal need for protection are not included, to religious observance; and this nonreligious classification may be made solely on the basis of a judgment of worth, since that factor, like need, is a reasonable basis for discrimination so long as no religious classification is involved. The standard, then, only guarantees that secular activities will benefit if a religious activity is aided; it does not prohibit singling out a particular secular activity for preferential treatment. In prohibiting religious classification and simultaneously allowing hospital, school or chess club classification, the standard, in the name of equality, saddles religion with a disability not shared by secular activities and is thus inconsistent with the goal of equality.

The inequality produced by a no-religious-classification standard is apparently, but only apparently, neutralized by a special immunity granted religion. Unlike other activities, religion may never, regardless of rational reasons therefor, be specially obligated. Even if the standard did provide a special immunity, it is not clear why its price should be disability from special aid. In fact, however, the apparent special immunity is illusory. Application of a general regulatory or criminal law to injurious activity engaged in as a religious exercise would not be a religious classification but an injurious activity classification. Consequently, the standard shields religion only from state action penalizing belief or singling out religiously motivated injurious action for special punishment. But freedom of belief is independently protected by the free speech clause of the first amendment, and purposeful discrimination against religious activity is prohibited by the fifth and fourteenth amendments. Hence, a no-religious-classification standard results in a special disability upon religion without offering any meaningful compensatory special advantage.

## 2. The Equality of No-Religious-Classification

A no-religious-classification standard prohibits preferential aid to religion under all circumstances; it thereby results in inequality. At the same time, however, the standard requires that, if all secular activities with a common characteristic receive aid, religious activities possessing that quality shall also benefit. Thus, if all secular activities requiring tranquility are protected, the religious observance must also be protected. Failure to extend the benefit to the religious activity in that situation would constitute a religious classification. To that extent the standard promotes equality, but in various applications it does so at the expense of a substantial establishment value.

Consider a board of education plan to include in the kindergarten curriculum by way of practice and illustration those activities which most children daily perform in their home lives. Such activities would include eating, bathing, dressing and, in particular communities, praying. A no-religious-classification standard would not only permit but also require that prayer be illustrated and practiced by all the children. The category aided is children's predominant at-home activities, a non-religious classification. The fact that a religious activity is a predominant at-home activity and is consequently aided would, under the standard, be irrelevant. The nonreligious class could not be parsed to exclude the religious activity; parsing would destroy the nonreligious character of the classification and defeat the standard's goal of equality. The class, predominant at-home activities, could therefore not be amended to exclude activities offensive to the religious beliefs of any of the children. An amendment excluding activities offensive to any of the children for any reason, religious or otherwise, would be permissible as a nonreligious classification, but the standard, although permitting, does not require such an exclusion. As a result of the exclusive focus upon the equality value, the standard ignores an establishment value more important than and inconsistent with equality. Thus, in the foregoing hypothetical, a violation of the establishment clause should be found in the imposition of religion by induced prayer whether prayer were given preferred or merely equal treatment.

It might be argued that this illustration sets up something of a straw man since, regardless of the applicability of the religion clauses, compulsory prayer is unconstitutional as a violation of the freedom to believe which is, under the vague teaching of *West Virginia Board of Education v. Barnette*, a right penumbral to freedom of speech. Even if such a penumbral right exists, however, it includes only freedom from coercion, not freedom from propaganda or other influence. Without reference to the religion clauses, the State may be prohibited from coercing belief or adherence to belief, even where the belief in question is patriotism, but nothing in *Barnette* prevents it from attempting to influence belief by propagating patriotism. This is so because although "penumbral radiations" of the free speech clause may prohibit coercing patriotism, that clause does not prohibit the establishment of patriotism. Hence, in order to invalidate a noncoercive prayer program included within a nonreligious classification, it is necessary to ascribe to the establishment clause greater content than Professor Kurland's standard gives it.

If the standard is modified to invalidate all direct government proselytizing, whether or not pursuant to a religious classification, its resulting applications, although less extreme, would still contravene the establishment value. Under such a revised standard, secular aid could and indeed must be granted to religious institutions on a nonpreferential basis where those institutions are as qualified as secular institutions to act as instrumentalities or conduits of a nonreligious government program. Consider a government program subsidizing the construction and operation of privately operated recreation facilities for underprivileged children. The program might properly exclude from participation organizations which are inexperienced in the operation of such facilities or have insufficient resources to finance unsubsidized costs. But the standard requires that religious institutions, if otherwise qualified, be eligible for participation. In practical operation only the established, wealthy sects would qualify. Since recreation facilities are probably as effective a means of proselytizing children as religious tracts, not only would the subsidy, compelled by the standard, have the ultimate effect of imposing religion, thus meeting the criterion of establishment violation proposed in this article, but it would also favor imposition of the beliefs of the dominant, activist religions and hence effect a discrimination between religions.

In the foregoing example a no-religious-classification standard achieves equality at the expense of the establishment value. The resulting equality, moreover, benefits the religious institution, not the religious child. Subsidization of recreation facilities operated by religious institutions is not necessary to avoid discrimination between the religious and nonreligious child. There is no reason to assume that the religious child will not take advantage of a purely secular basketball court. But why should equality between secular and religious institutions—an equality made necessary by a no-religious-classification standard—be a constitutional imperative when discrimination between those institutions does not result in meaningful discrimination between their members? It is true that every organization has a point of view which may be subtly communicated in even the most innocuous activities, and that aid to the institution may advance its propagation efforts. The Constitution, however, does not prohibit the establishment of all points of view, but only of religious beliefs. And while the religious institution may rationally fear preferential, or indeed any aid to the antireligious institution for the reason that aid in any form may promote antireligionism, it seems absurd, except with respect to all-encompassing activities such as education, to equate a nonreligious, secular viewpoint with antireligion, or to characterize it as a competing secular religionism. Since equality between religious and secular institutions is not always necessary to prevent discrimination against religion or its adherents, and since equal treatment may aid a church in its proselytizing function and thus threaten an imposition of religion, the equality goal should not be elevated into a transcendent value underlying the religion clauses.

. . .

## II. THE NO-IMPOSITION-OF-RELIGION STANDARD

### A. Other Establishment Values

The original meaning of the establishment clause is obscure. Madison may have believed in the complete separation of church and state, including a rigid no-aid principle, and may have incorporated that belief into his *Memorial and Remonstrance*. It is doubtful, however, that even Madison intended the first amendment to accomplish such a complete separation, and it is more doubtful that the Congress which adopted and the states that ratified the amendment so intended. Partly because its original meaning is unclear and partly because of a modern jurisprudence which justifies departure from original, specific intent, the Court in interpreting the clause has relied primarily upon the historical and contemporary values which should structure the relationship between religion and government.

It is agreed that the establishment clause prohibits government from intentionally creating an official or preferred religion; at this point agreement ends. Some contend that the clause does not prohibit anything except an official or preferred religion; others that the clause effects a wall of separation, to be breached only by a secular or religious value weightier than the separation principle. The latter position is subsumed under the phrase "no aid to religion."

The validity of the "no-aid" principle is the essential controversy arising under the establishment clause, and the various attempts to create devices to soften the impact of that principle without abandoning it are responsible for the confusion in the area. The question then arises: why shouldn't government aid religion? Several reasons, purportedly of constitutional dimension, have been given.

## 1. Aid Impairs Religious Liberty

The first argument is that aid justifies regulation and regulation impairs free exercise. The argument is neither historically nor juridically correct. Government has always aided religion, nonpreferentially as in fire and police protection, and preferentially as in tax and draft exemptions. These aids have not in fact been accompanied by regulations which impaired free exercise. Moreover, if aid presented a constitutionally significant danger of infringing upon free exercise, nonpreferential as well as preferential aid should be invalid. To the extent that aid authorizes regulation, that regulation could as easily be affixed to one form as the other; yet even the most militant separationists would allow some forms of nonpreferential aid. Most importantly, aid does not justify any greater regulation of free exercise than would be permissible in the absence of aid. Where regulation is vital to a secular interest it may be justified by that secular interest alone; and where regulation is not vital, *Sherbert* and other unconstitutional condition cases demonstrate that it may not be justified by aid. It is true that, as a political matter, aid may prompt constitutional regulation theretofore absent, but the aid has not, in that event, expended the legislature's power—it has only resulted in its exercise. This consideration is relevant to the question of whether a religious institution should apply for aid; it is not relevant to whether the aid may be constitutionally granted.

## 2. Aid Causes Strife

The Court and commentators sometimes refer to avoidance of strife as an establishment clause value from which the no-aid principle is derived. The strife to be avoided is apparently supposed to be caused by the antagonism of religious or irreligious groups who are not aided or who feel that others have received a disproportionate share. Since inequality in aid could, presumably, be remedied by a constitutional requirement of equality and since it is not suggested that unavoidable inequalities in aids to religion present peculiar constitutional dangers, proponents of this view apparently regard the bona fides of the grievance to be irrelevant. It is sufficient that aid does cause strife, whether or not that strife is rational.

To state this proposition is to ridicule it. If avoidance of strife were an independent constitutional value, no legislation could be adopted on any subject which aroused strong and divided feelings. Nor could a constitutional doctrine of strife avoidance be limited in application to legislation which exacerbates religious differences on the ground that those differences are more upsetting than any others. Patently, racial differences are today a far greater cause of strife than differences in religious belief. Would, then, the possibility of exacerbated racial controversy in and of itself invalidate open housing legislation?

Moreover, prohibiting aid to religion does not avoid strife, it merely alters its source. Aid to parochial schools may exacerbate strife by antagonizing Protestants who for the most part would not derive advantages from such an aid program. Failure to aid, however, antagonizes Catholics who pay taxes to support public school education and pay separately to educate their own children at parochial schools. Even if strife avoidance were an independent constitutional value, it would support a no-aid standard only if religious groups generally agreed to a no-aid principle. Since there is no such agreement, both aid and no aid cause strife. Consequently, one must look elsewhere for the source of the no-aid principle.

## 3. Aid Costs Money

Most governmental aids to religion involve an expense which is borne in part by the nonbeliever and the other-believer, either indirectly through their tax bill, as in a subsidy to religion, or directly as in exemption of Sabbatarians from Sunday closing laws. The supposed inequity of this burden often is stated as the reason for the no-aid principle. Justice Black, for instance, writes for the Court in *Everson*, "No tax in any amount, large or small, can be levied to support any religious activities or institutions . . . ," and he cites the Virginia Bill For Religious Liberty for the proposition "'that to compel a man to furnish contributions of money for the propagation of opinions which he disbelieves, is sinful and tyrannical.'"

Emphasis upon pocketbook injury suffered by the nonbeliever or other-believer suggests that the value being invoked is that public moneys cannot be used to support private purposes. Religion, it is assumed, is exclusively a private affair. Ergo, the government may not use public funds to aid religion. The minor premise of this syllogism, however, is false. Religion has significance to an individual in areas which may fairly be called private; it also has significance in areas which are of vital public concern. Successful government in the United States depends upon popular participation in the affairs of government and in a thousand other affairs which are private only because individual and associational participation have made government intervention unnecessary. Some of this vitally necessary participation results from unalloyed self-interest (vote your pocketbook). Much of it, however, requires a sense of the rightness and wrongness of things—a sense indispensable to involvement where immediate self-interest is absent. One need not accept Kant's argument that God exists because true morality cannot exist without God in order to recognize that religion is important if not indispensable to a moral sense, that a moral sense is important to involvement, and that involvement is necessary to democracy. Alexander Meiklejohn makes the point well:

> [T]hinking and feeling, though different from one another, are dependent on each other. What we feel and do about any object determines, and is determined by, what we know and believe about it. Any man or society whose feelings are going in one direction while his ideas are going in another is, in so far, lacking in sanity and heading for breakdown. . . . For some 40 or 50 or 60 per cent of our people, . . . religious belief is . . . the necessary and sufficient source from which our democratic institutions derive their moral validity.

Although religion promotes involvement and therefore serves a public purpose, there may still be reasons for prohibiting government from aiding it. But any such reasons would have nothing to do with public purpose; indeed if they exist, they do so despite rather than because of the relationship between religion and public purpose. And the Supreme Court, when it has directly addressed itself to this matter, has recognized the public aspect of religion rather than simply stating the major premise and conclusion of a defective syllogism. In *Zorach* the Court said, "We are a religious people whose institutions presuppose a Supreme Being"; and in *Engel v. Vitale*, "The history of man is inseparable from the history of religion." Even Justice Rutledge recognized that religion promotes the public welfare; his vehement objection to aid was based upon what he conceived to be its independent dangers.

In any event, does the public purpose doctrine necessarily require a benefit to the state? Why may not satisfaction of a "private" need or desire be a public purpose, when that need or desire will be frustrated without government aid and when the public considers it to be worthy (as it arguably considers

religion)? Before the government can supply food stamps to starving Americans, must it first be shown that the economy will thereby benefit or that crime will be avoided or contagious disease prevented? Or isn't giving food to hungry people a sufficient public purpose?

Once it is recognized that aid to religion is aid for a public purpose, however that phrase is defined, the "why should I pay to support another's religious belief" argument loses all constitutional force. A taxpayer's lack of sympathy with the public use to which his funds are being applied is constitutionally irrelevant. The allocation of resources among competing claims, each serving a public purpose, is essentially a political question, ultimately to be determined by the electoral process, not the Constitution. Constitutional determination requires injury to a constitutional right, and the aid-costs-money basis for the no-aid principle, except as it seeks to rely upon the public purpose doctrine, is not based upon any such injury.

Moreover, despite dicta disapproving of the expenditure of public money for religious use, the Court has not invalidated any aid to religion on that basis. The issue was precipitated in almost crystalline form in *Arlan's Department Store v. Kentucky*. There the Court dismissed for want of a substantial federal question an appeal from a state court decision upholding legislation exempting Sabbatarians from the Sunday closing laws. The sole purpose of the exemption was to aid Sabbatarianism and it caused non-Sabbatarian store owners far more financial injury than any individual taxpayer indirectly suffers through a grant of public funds for a religious purpose. Although the Court may have weighed an establishment clause prohibition against compelling anyone to support another's religion against the Sabbatarians' free exercise claim and arbitrarily concluded that the free exercise claim was weightier, the manner of disposition may indicate that the Court found no constitutional basis for the citizen's interest in not supporting another's religion.

### 4. Aid Impairs Secular Unity

Every level of government has an interest in the unity of its citizens. A shared system of values minimizes dissension and facilitates joint action toward a common goal. The best means of achieving unity is to reserve for government operation those institutions which exert the greatest influence on shaping the values of the population. Perhaps the most important of all such institutions is the educational system. Justice Frankfurter, concurring in *Illinois ex rel. McCollum v. Board of Education*, describes the public school as "[d]esigned to serve as perhaps the most powerful agency for promoting cohesion among a heterogeneous democratic people" and as "a symbol of our secular unity."

Not all aids to religion meaningfully affect secular unity. Some—like exempting Mrs. Sherbert from unemployment compensation requirements—are not relevant to the unity goal. Others—like exempting conscientious objectors from military service and providing army chaplains—may conceivably weaken the unifying tendencies of a secular institution. But the essential purposes of the military as an institution do not include the promotion of unity. Therefore, even complete acceptance of secular unity as a constitutional value need not yield a rigid no-aid standard. Some aids to religion, however, contravene the unity value by weakening secular institutions which significantly promote that value. Aid to parochial schools, for instance, will decrease the enrollment of Catholic children in the public schools and thus impair the unifying tendencies of that institution. And released time, while probably having the effect of increasing attendance of Catholic children at public schools and thus strengthening the institution, impairs its unifying effect.

On what basis, however, is it assumed that secular unity is a constitutional requirement? The state, to be sure, has a corporate interest in unity, but in no other context is a state corporate interest converted into a constitutional requirement. The state has an interest in an educated population. Is compulsory education, then, a constitutional mandate; and is a government program to employ school drop-outs, then, unconstitutional? The Constitution defines permissible governmental interests; it does not require that permissible interests be effectuated nor prohibit a legislature from impairing one in order to serve another permissible interest. The function of choosing between permissible but inconsistent interests, at least in every other context, is assigned to the legislature and ultimately, through the political process, to the people.

Since the state's interest in secular unity does not give rise to a constitutional prohibition against aid, the relationship between any such prohibition and the unity value must be based upon an individual constitutional right. But no such right is apparent. Aid to parochial schools, released time and prayer in the schools all, to one extent or another, impair unity, either by facilitating the segregation of children according to their religious or irreligious beliefs or by recognizing religious differences where there is no segregation. This characterization of the situation invites analogy to Brown v. Board of Education, but here, unlike Brown, there is no state policy to segregate; that result is caused entirely by individual choice. A more appropriate analogy—assuming that religious and racial segregation are analogous—is Griffin v. County School Board. There, the Court invalidated a plan whereby the state subsidized attendance at racially segregated private schools. It did so, however, because of its conclusion that the purpose of the plan was to implement the state's policy of maintaining segregated schools and, significantly, the decree enjoined the subsidy only so long as the county public schools were closed. It cannot be seriously contended that in aiding parochial schools any state has been or would be implementing a state policy to segregate according to religion, rather than respecting private individual choice and implementing a state policy of quality education for all children.

Even if the Constitution were to be interpreted to prohibit all aid which has the effect of impairing racial unity, regardless of state policy, the injury which would prompt such an interpretation is qualitatively different from any injury caused by the impairment of secular unity. In Brown, the evil of segregation was not that it impaired any abstract associational claim. Rather it was the psychological injury caused by a state policy of segregation carrying an implicit judgment of inferiority, coupled with the denial of equal educational benefits, which the Court found to be an inevitable result of racial school segregation. Regardless of the correctness of the Court's psychological and educational conclusions in Brown, they have no bearing on any injury caused by impairment of secular unity. That value by itself protects only the abstract associational claim of togetherness and a claim to have the concept of oneness inculcated through the public school curriculum. Aid to parochial schools, for instance, may result in depriving Protestant children of association with Catholic children, but the Protestant child's loss in no way resembles the injury which the Court in Brown found that segregation works on the Negro. That being the case, why is the Protestant's claim to association with the Catholic to be preferred to the Catholic's claim to disassociation? And why does the Protestant have a constitutional right to have the Catholic exposed to the teaching of oneness? Moreover, if such an associational right exists, why does it exist only with respect to religious differences? The economically deprived student would seem to have a greater associational interest in attending school with the wealthy student than a Protestant does with a Catholic. Yet neither the establishment clause nor any other provision in the Constitution prohibits aid to nonsectarian private schools.

Thus considered, neither the claim to association nor that to disassociation should be constitutionally preferred, and unless we can find a more persuasive establishment value, the state should be free to decide between these antithetical associational values according to which has the greater political support or which best coincides with a corporate state interest. One such interest is unity, but another is excellence in education for all. Yet another basis for a political decision is the religious claim of those wishing disassociation. The Court held in *Pierce v. Society of Sisters* that compulsory *public* school education was unconstitutional. This holding does not compel aid to parochial schools, although as a practical matter many Catholics will "have" to attend public schools if parochial schools are not aided, but the free exercise claim, like the correlative establishment claim precipitated by attendance at "secular" public schools, may properly be considered by a legislature in arriving at its determination.

That secular unity is not and should not be an establishment clause value is finally and perhaps best shown by the results it would authorize. To obtain maximum unity between the Catholic and non-Catholic populations the state would induce (though it cannot compel) Catholics to desert the parochial schools. So long as Catholic education funds hold out, the only inducement with any chance of success would be a system of voluntary religious training in the public schools. Offering religion in the public schools would deprive the parochial school of at least some of the advantages it now offers the religious Catholic, and the more religion offered, the greater the inducement. This solution might make a greater contribution to togetherness and the inculcation of oneness than public schools without religious training. To be sure, religion in the public schools would dilute the maximum togetherness now available to the children who attend them, but that dilution might well be more than made up for by exposing a larger percentage of the Catholic school community to much more togetherness and some more oneness than they now receive. Somehow this solution to the secular unity problem is not appealing. But, if the foregoing analysis is correct, its lack of appeal cannot be explained by its failure to promote secular unity. Rather, it demonstrates that secular unity is not the establishment value we are seeking.

## 5. Aid Impairs Equality Among Religions and Between Religion and Irreligion

Whatever additional content the establishment clause may have, it clearly prohibits discrimination among religions and between religion and irreligion.

To the extent, however, that the agreed principle of no preference is analogous to the equal protection clause, it does not yield a derivative principle of no aid. It merely requires that if aid is granted, the aided category must include all religions and irreligions. So read, the establishment clause requires that aid be granted atheists and agnostics if Protestants and Catholics are aided. It does not, however, require as a condition of aid to religion that institutions or activities which have nothing to do with either religion or irreligion also be aided. A standard which allows aid so long as it is equal necessitates a constitutional definition of "religion" and "irreligion." The definitional problem is troublesome, but that difficulty does not justify rejection of an equal-aid standard since the same difficulty inheres in a no-aid standard. "Religion" must be defined whether the standard be no aid or equal aid.

To substitute an equal-aid for a no-aid principle would not result in identical, and perhaps not even in equal, benefits. Legislators, judges and administrators may, improperly, define religion and irreligion according to their own beliefs, thus discriminating against irreligion and the minority, odd-ball sect. More importantly, identical benefits are often impossible to achieve. To allow each schoolchild in turn to recite a prayer or antireligious statement of his choosing, for instance, while satisfying the value of equal opportunity, would most benefit the majority belief since that belief would realize the most prayer time. Or, to grant financial aid to all religious and irreligious institutions will provide a lesser benefit to the minority sect which may not have the members, finances, organization, or even the desire to utilize the grant. The equality principle, however, does not demand identical benefit. Disparity in resultant benefits is an unavoidable characteristic of any aid program, and the equality principle, as conventionally understood, requires only that all members of the same class (*i.e.*, all religions and irreligions) receive the same opportunities. Indeed, the conventional equality value demands that a religion with a large number of adherents receive a greater share of a government program intended to aid individuals than a minor sect. It is thus apparent that if the establishment clause did no more than incorporate a conventional equal protection value, it would not invalidate equitably allocated aid which produced disparities in benefit.

## B. The No-Imposition Value

The no-preference principle incorporated within the establishment clause is not, however, merely an application of the conventional equality value. It seeks to prevent inequality not only as an independent, ultimate goal, but as a protection against a possible consequence of inequality: an imposition of religion. Failure to divide an aid-to-religion pie into identical segments is not unconstitutional because it results in *A* eating more than *B*; that result may be fair and practicable. The danger lies in the fact that *A* may, and historically has, thrown its pie at *B*, or more accurately, at *B*'s child. If only the equality value were involved, *B*, not wishing pie or not being able to digest it, should not begrudge *A* his piece so long as *B* had the opportunity of participating. But in a pie-throwing contest, keeping ammunition from your opponent is as important as having some yourself.

There are two aspects of the imposition danger—one institutional, the other individual. In both cases, the ultimate fear is that government aid will, directly or indirectly, be used to influence choice of religion, not merely to enhance another's exercise. And it is this fear which causes strife and which makes use of the nonbeliever's or other-believer's taxes so galling. To the individual, the essential danger is that the family's right to determine the religious beliefs of its members, especially its children, will be undermined, either directly by government imposition of religion or indirectly by government aid to the imposition efforts of religious institutions. Regarding religious choice as exclusively a family affair, the no-imposition value, in its individual aspect, resolves into a standard prohibiting all aid which presents a substantial danger of imposition of religion. To the religious or irreligious institution, the essential danger is that government aid will, by intention or otherwise, favor the proselytizing efforts of a competitor. From the institutional point of view, the battle for adherents could, theoretically, be staged under a no-aid standard or under a standard of identical aid. But since it is impossible to aid all proselytization identically, the institutional interest also resolves into a standard which prohibits all aid presenting a substantial imposition danger.

Almost every Supreme Court Justice who has written an opinion involving the establishment clause has identified no imposition as an establishment value. For instance, Justice Black in *McCollum* characterizes the violation as aid which enables "religious groups to spread their faith" in violation of the constitutional prohibition upon aid to "the dissemination of . . . doctrines." And in *Engel* he says, "When the power, prestige and financial support of government is placed behind a particular religious belief, the indirect coercive pressure upon religious minorities to conform to the prevailing officially ap-

proved religion is plain." Justice Frankfurter, concurring in *McCollum*, identifies the violation as government participation in a program of "religious instruction in a faith which is not that of their [the children's] parents," and Justice Stewart, dissenting in *Abington*, states that the violation is "government support of proselytizing activities of religious sects by throwing the weight of secular authority behind the dissemination of religious tenets." The important question, then, is not whether no imposition is an establishment value, but whether the establishment clause contains any other value and, if not, whether the no-imposition value requires a no-aid standard.

As already discussed, it has been asserted that aid to religion imperils the religious liberty of members of the aided institution. Although this assertion is not persuasive, more substantial questions are raised by the related claim that aid imperils the liberties of nonbelievers and other-believers. That claim relies upon the historical fact that the ascendancy of a religious group has often been associated with the denial of civil liberties to nonbelievers and other-believers. Nor is that association of only historical validity. Despite the ecumenical movement, it remains true that the supposedly divine source of most religious dogma gives each dogma a claim to exclusive validity which is basically inconsistent with toleration of other beliefs. And the association is not weakened when a prominent Catholic spokesman asserts that it is the state's duty to promote the true religion, that a Catholic state could not logically permit other groups to engage in "general propaganda," and that constitutional impediments to the view are not insurmountable since "[C]onstitutions can be changed, and non-Catholic sects may decline to such a point that the political proscription of them may become feasible and expedient."

The threat to civil liberties presented by a dominant religious group was clearly a substantial consideration in the adoption of the establishment clause and it fully supports the accepted view that the clause prohibits establishing or preferring a religion. The issue, however, is not exclusive or preferential aid, but any aid. But if equal aid results in unequal benefits and if equal benefits cannot in practice be realized then any aid will increase the power of some churches more than others, and often the church that benefits most is the one which is already closest to dominance. It seems to follow that the best means of avoiding the dangers of dominance is to adopt a no-aid rather than an equal-aid standard. In this context, the real danger of aid to Catholic parochial schools seems to be not that it impairs unity, considered as a state interest, or defeats the Protestant's associational claim, but that it increases the power of the Catholic church, both in absolute terms and in relation to the power of other churches; it is not the Catholic child's absence from a public school that raises constitutional dangers; it is his presence at a parochial school.

The trouble with this position is that it proves too much. The free exercise clause of the first amendment makes religion a constitutional value. Hence, the position must conceive of religion simultaneously as a value and as a threat, the separation principle which includes a no-aid doctrine being necessary to maintain equilibrium between them. But what precisely is this supposed equilibrium? Assume that the now only incipient dangers of religion come closer to fruition as a result of the emergence of a dominant and militant religious group in the United States.

. . .

. . . Therefore, regardless of its source and whether coincidental or not, a no-imposition standard seems to serve the value of affording maximum protection to nonbelievers and other-believers from aid which increases the danger of religion; and it appears unnecessary to resolve definitively the question of whether the establishment clause guarantees nonbelievers and other-believers any greater protection from the incipient dangers of religion than that accorded by an equal-aid standard.

A no-imposition standard, then, is consistent with the value of protecting nonbelievers and other-believers from the incipient dangers of religion in situations where government action induces religious belief and in situations where government action implements an independent religious choice without inducing belief. A much more difficult application is the situation where government action, while not inducing belief, has the effect of broadening belief or increasing its intensity. Aid to parochial schools, for instance, will not ordinarily have the effect of inducing the adoption of Catholicism; increased parochial school attendance will result, but that follows from implementation of a Catholic family's independent desire to have the child receive religious instruction, not from state action creating that desire. Notwithstanding, a parochial school education, made more attractive by the aid, will or may intensify the child's commitment to Catholicism. In determining whether that intensification effect might render the aid an establishment violation, we need not consider the value of exclusive parental choice. Since the family has presumably chosen parochial school education for the very purpose of intensifying the child's religious commitment, its rights have not been impaired. Nor need we consider the value of state neutrality

in the institutional struggle for adherents. That value is primarily concerned with state action which encourages or facilitates poaching, not with action which tends to make poaching more difficult. But, if religion is adverse to the rights of other believers, does not aid which has the effect of intensifying belief increase the danger, and to that extent, is not the value of protecting other believers from the dangers of religion given something less than maximum protection by a no-imposition standard? Justice Douglas may have the dangers of religion in mind when he warns that the "vice" of aid is that it facilitates "a church's efforts to gain and *keep* adherents."

If religion is a threat to the other-believer, the believer's apostasy might be to his advantage. Even on that assumption, however, the practical alternatives are not commitment versus apostasy but nominal versus devout belief. If there were no parochial schools the total Catholic population would not be significantly reduced. The vast majority of people continue, at least nominally, in the religion they were born to. And the occasional instance of apostasy to which a denial of aid might contribute has no constitutional relevance because the threat to the other believer comes from the totality of a religion's membership, not from any particular believer or handful of believers. The question, then, is whether a devout believer is more dangerous than a nominal believer. There is no certain means of resolving this question, but the evidence points to a negative answer. First, those aspects of a religion's dogma which are most threatening to the rights of other believers are also those most easily learned. It is not necessary to go to parochial school to learn that the Jews killed Christ. On the contrary, a parochial school education ideally will tend to illuminate Catholic doctrine and thus eliminate intolerances absorbed through casual, uninformed contact. Second, there is substantial authority for the proposition that religious aggression arises not from religious dogma or teaching, but from psychological factors unrelated to religion. To be sure, religion directs that aggression towards the other-believer, but a nominal belief may channel aggression equally as well as devout conviction. Third, empirical evidence indicates that the devout believer (defined, in part, by frequency of church attendance which in turn correlates with early exposure to religious training) is less authoritarian and less prejudiced than the casual, nominal believer. Argyle concludes that although the atheist is less prejudiced and authoritarian than the Catholic, the devout Catholic is less so than his nominal co-religionist.

But perhaps devout belief and nominal belief are

not the only alternatives to be considered. Even if devout belief is no more-and perhaps less-dangerous than nominal belief, and even if the possibility of outright apostasy is not a significant or benign factor, there still remains the potential for diluting obnoxious religious belief through the cleansing medium of secular public education. In this context, aid to parochial schools would be invalid not because it intensifies belief but because it deprives the state of the opportunity to substitute democratic, scientific and other secular values for obnoxious religious belief. This analysis provides an explanation for the Catholic Church's firm resolve to continue its parochial school system. In view of the enormous cost, discontinuance might be a reasonable alternative if parochial schools provided merely a more intensified religious instruction than would be provided through other, existing Church programs. If, however, the consequence of discontinuance would be the inculcation of irreligion through the public school curriculum, the church schools must be maintained regardless of cost.

If a prohibition upon state aid to parochial schools is based upon the value of diluting religious belief, the no-aid doctrine can in no sense be characterized as a derivative of a neutral separation principle; rather, it imposes an obligation of hostility to religion. If such a constitutional obligation were incorporated in the establishment clause, government could not aid parochial schools—but neither should it allow them to exist. And certainly it could prohibit their existence. But *Pierce v. Society of Sisters* affirms their right to exist. Indeed, if the value served by the denial of aid is the dilution of religion, then denial is for the purpose of opposing religion and is itself an imposition. So considered, denial of aid becomes an establishment violation. Therefore, even accepting the approach that since religion is a danger government may not render aid which increases that danger, that value is afforded maximum protection by a no-imposition standard. A standard of no-aid affords no greater protection and is more consistent with hostility than neutrality.

C. Content and Applications of a No-Imposition Standard

1. Imposition Distinguished from Implementation

A no-imposition standard assumes that the principal purpose of the establishment clause is to guarantee to an individual adult maximum freedom in the determination of his religious or irreligious beliefs, and to protect the primacy of the parents in the determination of their children's religious or irreligious beliefs. Other purposes may be to guarantee governmental neutrality in the institutional battle for adherents and to prohibit aid which increases the dangers of religion to the rights of nonbelievers or otherbelievers. All of these purposes are accomplished by a standard which does no more than prohibit government from compelling or influencing religious choice and from aiding others to influence religious choice.

In some respects a no-imposition standard produces results under the establishment clause which overlap with results reached through application of the free exercise clause. Thus, a statute forbidding Baptist church services would prohibit free exercise and would also influence religious choice. In other respects the overlap is questionable. Compelling a Baptist to attend Seventh-day Adventist services, but allowing him to attend his own, is certainly an act influencing religious choice but—assuming that Baptist dogma allows its membership to attend the services of another sect—may not be a prohibition of free exercise. In still other respects there is no overlap at all. State sponsorship of prayer for those schoolchildren who wish to pray is not a prohibition of the free exercise rights of nonparticipating schoolchildren but does influence their religious choice. A no-imposition standard makes it unnecessary to decide whether particular state action constitutes coercion. Compelling religious participation is certainly an imposition, but so is persuasion, endorsement or any other means of influencing choice.

To be distinguished from imposition is state action which does not influence choice but helps implement a religious or irreligious choice independently made. In rendering such aid the state is expressing a judgment that religion is a worthy activity, and it may be argued that in recognizing worthiness, the state is by design or otherwise encouraging belief and hence influencing religious choice. As a practical matter, however, recognition of worth will not have a substantial imposition effect and will have no effect at all where the religion aided is a minority sect. Exemption of Mrs. Sherbert from South Carolina's unemployment compensation requirement represents a judgment that the exercise of Seventh-day Adventism is more worthy than bowling on Saturdays, but the exemption has no significant effect and arguably no effect at all upon whether someone becomes a Seventh-day Adventist. Similarly, the Sabbatarian exemption from Sunday closing laws does not induce one to become a Jew; draft exemption to conscientious objectors does not normally induce one to become a Quaker; closing the public schools on all religious holidays or on every Wednesday at 2 P.M. does not induce the adoption of religion; and compulsory Sunday closing, while implementing an independent desire to attend church services, has no substantial effect upon the creation of such desire. The availability of preferential aid to religious exercise may, to be sure, induce false claims of religious belief, but the establishment clause is not concerned with false claims of belief, only with induced belief.

Some aids to religion, whether preferential or nonpreferential, may have the effect of intensifying an independently made religious belief. While a parochial school bus subsidy does not induce adoption of Catholicism, it may result in a more intense belief. But, as already noted, action which has the effect of intensifying belief is qualitatively different from action which induces belief; the former supplements while the latter contradicts the establishment values of individual and family determination of religious choice. Perfect neutrality is impossible: implementation of a desire to attend parochial school may intensify belief, but failure to implement defeats religious choice; and since freedom of religious choice, not neutrality per se, is the fundamental establishment value, the neutrality tool is useful only insofar as it promotes that choice.

## 2. Imposition and Balancing

Government implementation of one individual's religious choice may result in the imposition of religion upon another. That was the relationship involved in the released time, and Bible and prayer reading cases. To the extent that the children involved, or their parents, desired religious instruction, there was merely implementation of an independently made religious choice. That implementation, however, may have had an imposition effect on those children whose parents did not desire instruction. For these purposes, it is not necessary to decide whether the Court's psychological conclusions as to factors which influence children were correct, or whether the psychological conclusions of McCollum are consistent with those of Zorach. The important point is that all four decisions are primarily concerned with whether the practices in question would have an imposition effect. Thus, significantly, Justice Douglas said in Zorach that the state could "encourage," "accommodate," or "cooperate" with religious exercise, but could not "persuade or force," that is, could not impose religion. These decisions make clear that implementation and imposition effects are not to be balanced. Religion in the classroom—whether by way of instruction or observance—may fairly be said to advance or implement the majority's free exercise. At the same time, perhaps only a few children were subjected to a threat of religious imposition. A balancing standard, therefore, would

have yielded different results in Abington, Engel and McCollum. But the Court evidently considered that the balance would have been between the majority's worthy but nonconstitutional religious interest and the minority's constitutional right.

A much more difficult problem would arise if the majority could not possibly exercise its religion without an imposition of that religion upon the minority. In that event a true collision between constitutional imperatives would occur and subordination of one claim to the other would obviously be required. Should such a situation exist it is far from certain that the establishment clause would be the one subordinated. In fact, however, if the establishment clause is read to prohibit only an imposition of religion, the likelihood of any collision between free exercise and establishment is substantially reduced and the subordination problem becomes largely theoretical. The instances cited by Justice Brennan, for example, as representing a subordination of establishment to exercise, are situations where there has been no imposition, and hence no establishment violation to be subordinated.

An imposition standard also better explains situations where an aid to religion is purportedly balanced against advancement of a state secular interest. Since Everson and McGowan, which involve this approach, do not identify the evil associated with aid they make intelligent balancing impossible. If the evil is identified as imposition, however, these cases become manageable. Implementation of independent decisions to attend parochial school or Sunday church services does not result in any imposition of religion. Since they are not impositions, they do not raise any establishment question and no balancing is required.

Chief Justice Warren in McGowan almost sees this. After seeking to demonstrate that Sunday closing is secularly motivated, he distinguishes McCollum: "[N]o such coercion to attend church services is present in the situation at bar . . . the alternatives open to non-laboring persons in the instant case are far more diverse." In thus distinguishing McCollum the Court's opinion seems to suggest that even if the state's motivation is secular, a regulation which has the effect of compelling or influencing religious choice is suspect. In other words, a secular motive does not necessarily justify an imposition effect. But if the establishment violation consists of an imposition effect, what relevance does that clause have to a situation where there is no imposition, whether the state's motive be secular or religious? Conversely, where imposition results, only a compelling secular purpose which may not otherwise be accomplished would over-balance the prima facie establishment violation.

### 3. Imposition by Government Distinguished from Indirect Aid to Private Proselytization

Under a no-imposition standard, aid which implements religious exercise without inducing religious belief is lawful. Conversely, any direct government imposition of religion, whether the motivation be secular or religious, is unlawful. Situations in both of these categories may be resolved without use of any balancing technique. There is, however, a third category: government aid, designed to serve a secular interest or to implement religious exercise, which has as an indirect effect the advancement of private proselytizing efforts; and situations arising therein require a balancing standard.

There is a difference between imposition by government and government aid to private proselytization which justifies a per se rule in the former case and a balancing approach in the latter. Direct government imposition is much more effective than private proselytization, and hence much more to be feared and guarded against. The state's traditional role is not that of an interested advocate, frankly attempting to persuade, but of an arbiter of truth. The nonbeliever or other-believer is therefore much more subject to imposition by governmental advocacy, unavoidably disguised as objective truth, than by the blandishments and imprecations of a private institution. Justice Brennan offers an analogous distinction as a means of reconciling *McCollum* and *Zorach*:

> The deeper difference was that the *McCollum* program placed the religious instructor in the public school classroom in precisely the position of authority held by the regular teachers of secular subjects, which the *Zorach* program did not. The *McCollum* program, in lending to the support of sectarian instruction all the authority of the governmentally operated public school system, brought government and religion into that proximity which the Establishment Clause forbids. To be sure, a religious teacher presumably commands substantial respect and merits attention in his own right. But the Constitution does not permit that prestige and capacity for influence to be augmented by investiture of all the symbols of authority at the command of the lay teacher for the enhancement of secular instruction.

That is, in *McCollum* the state associated itself with the religious instruction program sufficiently to assume a proselytizing role whereas in *Zorach* the absence of such association resulted in a characterization of the program as one of state aid to private religious instruction rather than imposition by government.

A striking illustration of the distinction between imposition by government and aid to private proselytization is afforded by a comparison of *Fowler v. Rhode Island* and *McCollum*. In *Fowler* the municipality was not only permitted but required to allow Jehovah's Witnesses use of park facilities to spread their gospel, while in *McCollum* the use of school facilities for religious instruction purposes was held unconstitutional. In both cases aid limited to use of public facilities would have been lawful, especially in *McCollum* since the religious groups there did not intend to proselytize but only to offer religious instruction to their own members. In *McCollum*, however, the state associated itself with the program and thereby influenced attendance, while in *Fowler* the unrestricted range of choices available, the lack of peer pressure and the absence of any aura of state authority precluded the possibility that the state itself was influencing religious choice. This is not to say that aid to private proselytization is a proper purpose. On the contrary, it is never a proper purpose and always creates a prima facie establishment violation, but that violation may sometimes be overcome by a secular purpose, or by a free exercise or equality right, or by a free exercise claim other than the institution's interest in proselytizing. It is interesting to compare *McCollum* and *Fowler* with the practice of allowing religious institutions to instruct their members in public buildings, after hours. In *McCollum* there was state imposition—hence an absolute standard is employed; in *Fowler* there was state aid to private proselytization—hence the imposition effect of the aid is balanced against a countervailing interest, specifically, in *Fowler*, a free exercise and equal protection right. Where, on the other hand, public facilities are used for a nonproselytizing religious purpose and there is no danger of an unintended imposition effect, there is not even a prima facie violation—hence there is no need to find a countervailing interest justifying the aid.

The distinction sometimes made between aid to the institution and aid to the individual often produces results consistent with those obtained pursuant to a no-imposition standard. This occurs primarily because many of the benefits conferred upon individuals on the basis of their religious beliefs are in the form of exemptions from regulatory laws, which are unlikely to present imposition dangers, and because individuals—as individuals—are usually not in the business of proselytizing and hence are not likely to devote the aid they receive directly to a proselytizing use. The distinction, however, has no intrinsic merit; it will achieve correct results only insofar as its applications fortuitously coincide with those reached pursuant to a no-imposition standard. Thus a state grant to individuals who regularly attend church is clearly an imposition of religion and would probably be universally considered an establishment violation, yet it is an aid to an individual, not to an institution.

Conversely, many grants to religious institutions would not present any immediate imposition danger. For instance, state subsidy of parochial school textbook purchases, whether secular or religious books, would not impose religion on the parochial school child. The only immediate effect would be to implement a private desire to obtain a religious education. The difficulty is that an indirect effect of institutional aid which has financial value may be the imposition of religion, since funds freed by the aid may be diverted to a proselytizing use. But such diversion is a possible, if more remote, result of financially significant aid to the individual. Consequently, the institution-individual distinction at best serves only as a rule of thumb indicating the likelihood of diversion into a proselytizing use and adds nothing but obfuscation to a no-imposition standard.

Justice Douglas, concurring in *Abington*, identifies imposition as the evil of aid. Moreover, he sees no constitutional distinction between "the State itself . . . conducting religious exercises" (imposition by government) and aid, direct or indirect, in large or small amounts, to the proselytizing efforts of private institutions. As already noted, there is a significant difference in imposition effect as between government imposition and aid to the proselytizing function, although that difference does not automatically create a constitutional distinction. But, if no such distinction is made, how is fire or police protection justified? Both have financial value and hence may be said to constitute indirect aid to proselytizing efforts of private institutions. They are not necessarily justified by a transcendent equality value. As we have noted, equality must at times be subordinated to establishment in order to avoid direct and substantial imposition effects. Obeisance to equality compels disregard for the difference between aid which presents a likelihood of a substantial imposition effect and aid which presents at most a minimal possibility of a marginal imposition effect; and yet the greater and more likely the effect, the greater the danger the establishment clause is intended to prevent. Therefore, notwithstanding Justice Douglas' view that an establishment is an establishment, it is necessary to include within a no-imposition standard a distinction between government imposition and government aid to religious

institutions not intended to further their imposition efforts but which may be diverted to that purpose. The constitutionality of aid which falls within this latter category must be determined by balancing. Recognition that no imposition is the establishment value, however, allows a more structured application of that inherently uncertain methodology. Although it contributes no new insight into those factors (state secular interest, equality value and free exercise right or claim) which may serve to overcome a prima facie violation, it identifies the nature of that violation and thereby allows for assessments and gradations of the degree of permissible danger.

A number of factors are relevant to an assessment of the imposition danger.

The first and most important is the extent to which the aid will directly serve a proselytizing use. For instance, employment of religious institutions as instrumentalities or conduits of public welfare programs will result in direct aid to their proselytizing function. Proselytization in such situations is not a possible, indirect result brought about by diversion of funds but the probable, perhaps inevitable, consequence of their intended use. A church will more effectively influence religious choice by administering poverty funds than by a millennium of conventional evangelism with exclusively "religious" materials. Most obviously, responsibility for the administration of poverty funds will enable a church to reach a vast audience otherwise unreceptive to its teachings. A few churches will consciously seek to gain new members from that audience, and though most churches will not, some of their individual clergymen will. More significantly, participation will gain for the church an image of "relevance" which in turn will attract members. And, most significantly, independently of any policy of gaining members, most clergymen-administrators believe that those in their charge have spiritual as well as material needs and that failure to satisfy all of those needs is a disservice to the poor. It is theoretically possible to separate material from spiritual service, but that separation is unnatural and requires constant discipline of which few are capable. The clergymen-administrators who fail to maintain that separation are not malevolent evangelists: they are merely well-intentioned human beings unable to perform an unnatural, but constitutionally required duty.

A second relevant factor is the extent to which aid to the proselytizing function, or aid which may be converted into a proselytizing use, may at least theoretically be shared equally by all religious and irreligious groups. An exemption for religious proselytizers from a street vending tax obviously aids the

Jehovah's Witness Church more than the Catholic Church, but that inequality of benefit results from the different proselytizing techniques those churches have chosen to adopt. Every group could, if they chose, benefit equally from the exemption. A property tax exemption, on the other hand, frees more money for proselytizing use to the wealthy church than to the poorer ones, and that discrimination is not a product of choice. An exemption limited to $5,000 of church property would obviously be less discriminatory.

A third factor is the likelihood that aid to a non-proselytizing use will be converted into a proselytizing use and the magnitude of the funds involved. A requirement that the funds granted not be used for proselytization is obviously insufficient. A requirement that the total amount of annual church appropriations for proselytization not be increased would be impossible to administer and constitutionally defective. The only test, and a difficult one to apply, which would sometimes be practicable is whether the activity aided was one which the religious institution was already paying for or was likely to pay for. If, for instance, parochial school children had always themselves paid for their lunches or books, a grant to the institution or the children for those purposes would be less likely to create funds for proselytizing. A grant or loan of a cyclotron to a small denominational college is a clearer case. In considering the magnitude of freed funds, a de minimis concept is obviously called for. One hundred or one thousand dollars will have no meaningful imposition effect.

Applying a balancing standard to grants to religious institutions for public welfare purposes, we thus suggest three factors which point toward an imposition danger: (1) most significantly, a direct aid to a proselytizing function, (2) a variety of aid which many, perhaps most, sects are not economically or organizationally able to participate in, and (3) aid of substantial dollar magnitude which may facilitate diversion of funds for *additional* proselytizing use. Conversely, the only factor to be balanced against the substantial imposition danger is that some religious institutions are effective administrators of such programs. Neither the equality value nor any free exercise claim or right is defeated by denying church participation. Therefore, unless church participation is vital to the success of public welfare programs—because private secular institutions are not equipped to administer them and because there is a compelling need for private rather than public administration—that participation would seem to be violative of the establishment clause.

The case for aid to parochial schools, under a balancing standard which identifies imposition as the establishment danger, is much stronger. Most importantly, parochial school aid does not directly serve a proselytizing function; for the most part, only existing Catholics who wish a religious education are directly affected. The imposition effect, if any, will only result from the possible diversion of funds for a proselytizing use, and it is not at all clear that such diversions will occur. If parochial school facilities are as deficient as alleged, it is not likely that a government subsidy will result in a diminution of institutional appropriations to education. Failure to subsidize might ultimately result in an increase in the percentage of church funds used for education, thereby curtailing funds available for proselytization, but it is also possible that failure to subsidize will make parochial education an impossible financial burden, thereby freeing education funds for proselytizing use. Consequently, while it is true that Catholic schools will benefit far more than other religious schools from an education subsidy, and that the sums involved are very substantial, the likelihood of a significant imposition effect resulting from a subsidy is at best speculative. Offsetting this speculative danger is the obvious state interest in quality education for all children and the parochial school child's equality, free exercise and establishment claims. Therefore, it would appear that a no-imposition standard would validate a parochial school subsidy, and that result is clearly indicated if we may use as a touchstone practices, such as tax exemption, which pose much graver imposition dangers and yet have been held constitutional.

---

Jesse H. Choper, *The Establishment Clause and Aid to Parochial Schools*, 56 California Law Review 260 (1968)*

. . .

*In brief, my proposal is that governmental financial aid may be extended directly or indirectly to support parochial schools without violation of the establishment clause so long as such aid does not exceed the value of the secular educational service rendered by the school.*

---

. . .

## II.

### An Establishment Clause Rationale

A proposal permitting governmental financial assistance to parochial schools not exceeding the value of secular services they render comports with a general rationale for the establishment clause that reflects both contemporary and historical aims.

### A. Historical Support

Although the indistinctness of the precise historical designs of the establishment clause has already been noted, several aims emerge quite lucidly. Its paramount purpose then, like its major concern today, was to safeguard freedom of worship and conscience—in a word, to protect religious liberty. And it is equally clear that this purpose comprehended the intention that "the conscience of individuals should not be coerced by forcing them to pay taxes in support of a religious establishment or religious activities." In other words, as part of the general attempt to safeguard religious belief, the establishment clause sought to protect taxpayers from being forced by the federal government to support religion. This is cogently confirmed by Thomas Jefferson's "Virginia Bill for Religious Liberty" which proclaimed "that to compel a man to furnish contributions of money for the propagation of opinions which he disbelieves, is sinful and tyrannical"; by James Madison's "Memorial and Remonstrance Against Religious Assessments" (whose title is itself revealing) which condemned even forcing "a citizen to contribute three pence only of his property" to support any religious establishment; by Thomas Cooley's *Constitutional Limitations* which found clearly unlawful "under any of the American constitutions . . . [c]ompulsory support, by taxation or otherwise, of religious instruction"; and by many important Supreme Court opinions in the church-state field—majority, concurring, and dissenting. Whatever other historical bases for the establishment ban, it is beyond reasonable dispute that it purported to secure religious liberty, in particular by prohibiting taxation for religious purposes. That historical intent conforms with the contemporary American view that "it is a violation of religious liberty to compel people to pay taxes to support religious activities or institutions."

### B. The Scope of the Establishment Clause

Given this background, the broad philosophy of church-state relations reflected in the nonestablishment precept becomes manifest: Governmental action for *religious* purposes is highly suspect; it is constitutionally objectionable when it impinges on religious liberty either, as I have argued elsewhere, by compromising the individual's religious beliefs, or, as outlined above, by directly coercing the individual to support religion by allocating tax funds for sectarian use. On the other hand, governmental action for *secular* purposes does not fall within the core of the establishment clause's concern—the "nonestablishment guarantee is directed at public aid to the *religious* activities of religious groups."

. . .

## III

### Definition of Secular Purpose

The broad establishment clause rationale described above would generally forbid government expenditures for strictly religious purposes and would bar governmental action for these purposes if infringements of religious liberty followed. On the other hand, it would generally permit the state to act for secular purposes. Thus, it is analytically critical to decide what constitutes a secular purpose and how it should be determined. This is frequently a perplexing inquiry because a law may be enacted for a multiplicity of purposes and may produce a multiplicity of effects. A Sunday closing law, for example, may have the secular purpose of promoting the general welfare by creating a day of respite or the religious purpose of forbidding work to enhance church attendance.

Certain aspects of the problem are quite clear. The fact that religious groups sponsored a law—or even were its sole sponsors—does not make its purpose nonsecular; the Civil Rights Act of 1964 might not have passed without the support of churchmen. Nor, with the rare and limited qualification to be noted below, should existence of a secular purpose turn on judicial examination of legislative motives— a long, forbidden psychoanalytic attempt to find the "*real* reason," articulated or unspoken, for passing a law. Rather, whether government action is secular or religious should generally be determined by the nature of its *independent* or *primary* effect (a term to be illustrated below, and not to be confused with "principle" or "paramount" effect). If the primary effect is to accomplish a nonreligious public purpose, the action should generally be held immune from establishment clause attack. But if the primary effect is to serve a religious end, the action's purpose should not be characterized as secular even though an *ultimate* or *derivative* public benefit may be produced.

### A. Illustrations

Specific instances are necessary to illustrate the

point. It has been maintained that public school prayer recitation and Bible reading serve the secular purpose of producing profound convictions in children, thus making them better citizens. But if such are the effects, they come about only if the primary goal of these practices—the implanting of spiritual and religious beliefs—is achieved; the purported secular ends are derivative from the primary religious effect. Thus, under the analysis suggested above, the purpose of the governmental action is religious.

Sunday closing laws also serve an undeniably religious end by encouraging church attendance in removing the obstacle of having to report for work. But they also produce an independent secular effect— "a Sunday atmosphere of recreation, cheerfulness, repose and enjoyment." And this secular effect is in no way dependent on or derived from the religious impact of the statute.

Governmental actions whose secular benefits flow from the achievement of a primary religious effect must be suspect under the establishment clause. Such actions "employ Religion as an engine of Civil policy." Allowing such actions would literally read the clause out of the first amendment; it would justify government subsidization of that church that the government found best inculcates its members with the deep convictions that make for better citizenship. But governmental action that produces independent secular efforts should generally be unassailable even if an equally necessary or inevitable effect is the benefitting of religion. If not, the fire department could not protect burning churches.

### B. Judicial Determinations

This is not to say that the task of distinguishing primary religious and secular effects is always free of difficulty. But usually it is. Thus, in *Torcaso v. Watkins*, the Court observed that there could be "no dispute about the [religious] purpose or effect" of a requirement that public officeholders declare a belief in God. And in *Engle v. Vitale*, the Court had "no doubt that . . . daily classroom invocation of . . . the Regents' prayer is a religious activity."

On occasion, governmental action with a primary religious effect may be wrapped "in the verbal cellophane" of a secular purpose. Thus, in the *Bible Reading Cases* the state argued secular purpose— "the promotion of moral values, the contradiction to the materialistic trends of our times, the perpetuation of our institutions and the teaching of literature." The Court easily rejected the assertion, agreeing instead with the trial court's finding that the exercises had a religious character.

In such instances, the Court is not—nor should it

be—making the judgment that any secular purpose of the law fails to be paramount over whatever religious end the church obtains by the regulated conduct. For the Court to engage in such an ad hoc balancing process—relying only on the Justices' subjective notions of paramountcy—to treat the problem as "one of degree," is not satisfactory when more objective standards are available. Even where a religious purpose exists, the state's secular purpose need not be dominant or paramount; the existence of a "legitimate" independent primary secular purpose should be sufficient. The determination of "legitimacy" by the Court undeniably involves the making of a not wholly objective judgment. But, unlike the "dominancy-paramountcy" inquiry, it is a judgment of a quite limited nature, mainly disposed of by common sense and observation of the obvious effects of the enactment. Although the inquiry is necessitated by a recognition that a disingenuous legislature can easily find secular purposes to cover any religious interest it wishes to further, such a cover is almost always revealed as cellophane.

A few additional illustrations may be helpful. In 1921, the California legislature appropriated 10,000 dollars for the restoration of the San Diego Mission, resulting in an unquestionable financial benefit of a strictly religious nature to the Roman Catholic Church, which owned and controlled the mission for the use of its parishioners. There was also an independent primary secular effect, however, in no way derived from the religious impact of the action, which could not be fairly characterized as a mere "cover." As the court noted, the missions have significant architectural, historical, and educational value, and the aid therefore served a secular esthetic purpose. Under the proposed analysis, this should generally be adequate to establish constitutional validity. It might be added, as a persuasive rather than a constitutional argument, that it is reasonable to believe that reconditioning the mission would pay financial dividends to the state treasury, by increased tourism, in excess of its cost. The mission case thus involved no possible infringement of religious or conscientious scruples, either directly or through diversion of tax funds to religious purposes.

A municipality should not, however, be permitted to allocate public funds to build houses of worship for the purpose of encouraging church-going people to live in the community. In contrast to the mission restoration example discussed above, which attracted people by appealing to their esthetic and educational interests, this plan would publicly finance the religious needs of individuals in order ultimately to derive a secular goal. Even though the plan might increase the general tax base in the community, thus compensating the public for its religious expenditure, its primary effect—from which the secular end would be derived—would be religious.

Finally, it has been suggested that, as part of a state's mental health budget, funds might be granted to the Roman Catholic Church and the Protestant Episcopal Church to subsidize confession costs because of their therapeutic value. But it would seem here that the purported therapeutic benefit—which we may concede is secular—would come about only as a result of the confessor's having obtained spiritual satisfaction. The exclusive primary effect is religious.

. . .

## IV

### Aid to Parochial Schools

#### A. Secular Purpose

At least some governmental aid to support parochial education serves a primary or independent secular purpose. No one can deny the state's legitimate interest in improving the educational quality of all schools, or the benefits to society in general from education, or even the national defense interest in an enlightened citizenry. The fact is that "parochial elementary and secondary schools educate one out of every eight future citizens of this country, and that the teacher and classroom needs of parochial school systems are possibly even more serious than are those of the public school systems."

Even Mr. Justice Rutledge, in his vigorous dissent in *Everson*, admitted that "it is much too late to urge that legislation designed to facilitate the opportunities of children to secure a secular education serves no public purpose. His position was that the establishment clause forbids state support for "religious training, teaching or observance." I agree. But, "[i]f the fact alone be determinative that religious schools are engaged in education," he could "see no possible basis, except one of dubious legislative policy, for the state's refusal to make full appropriation for support of private, religious schools, just as is done for public instruction." I disagree.

Parochial schools perform a dual function, providing some religious education and some secular education. Government may finance the latter, but the establishment clause forbids it to finance the former. That government money may be used for partial support of church schools does not mean that "it can also be used for the support of our churches, and that we are moving toward a union of church and state in America." Conceding Mr. Justice Jackson's premise that "Catholic education is the rock on

which the whole structure rests," his conclusion does not follow that rendering "tax aid to its Church school is indistinguishable . . . from rendering the same aid to the Church itself."

It must be perceived that by using tax funds to support the secular aspects of parochial education, the state expends no more than would be required either to support parochial school pupils if they attended existing public schools, or to establish additional public schools at various sites for all pupils presently attending parochial schools, neither of which alternatives raises colorable constitutional objection. This point is not made to prove that either the free exercise clause or political fairness demands government aid for parochial schools. Rather, it demonstrates that, where the state affords public money to finance the secular aspects of education in church-related schools, it imposes a tax burden essentially identical with that which it could constitutionally impose for separate secular facilities. To do so in no way violates the historical and contemporary policy underlying the establishment clause against infringing religious liberty through taxation for religious purposes.

In addition, it is possible that, by affording some state aid to nonpublic schools (but substantially less than the per capita public school cost), a net decrease in the tax burden would result; a number of nonpublic pupils who are now shifting to public schools for economic reasons might cease doing so and, as is frequently predicted, many public school children might transfer to parochial or private schools. Of course, this latter argument is not of constitutional scope, because a net increase in tax burden should be equally constitutional if the public aid were limited to the secular aspects of education in parochial schools. Nor could government finance religion in the hope, or even with the assurance, that it would in some way produce a smaller overall tax burden. Economically, the argument is appealing. Constitutionally, however, I know of no dissent from the proposition that it would be a patent use of religion as an engine of civil policy in violation of the establishment clause.

#### B. Discrimination Among Recipient Schools

The proposal contained in this article assumes that any governmental aid will be extended to parochial schools on a constitutionally nondiscriminatory basis. For the legislature to single out, say, Lutheran parochial schools or their students for aid, while refusing to afford equal privilege to other similarly situated church-related or private schools, would be a patent violation of the establishment clause, as would giving aid only to church-related schools while denying it to others similarly situated. The former action would "prefer one religion over another." The latter would "aid all religions as against non-believers."

This is not to say that if aid is to be extended beyond the realm of public schools it must be afforded nondiscriminatorily to all nonpublic schools. The statute in the *Everson* case itself distinguished between nonpublic schools "operated for profit in whole or in part" and those that were not, as does Title III of the Elementary and Secondary Education Act of 1965. Such a classification not based on religion, should not violate the establishment clause. Nor, despite suggestions to the contrary, should such an economic differentiation be held to contravene the equal protection clause of the fourteenth amendment. Perhaps wealth is "a capricious or irrelevant factor" to measure a voter's qualifications or to determine certain rights of those accused of crime. But surely it is not such a factor for the purpose of distribution of public largesse. It has been suggested that equal protection forbids discrimination both for and against Negroes, but never seriously that it makes poverty an equally neutral factor.

It is true that this profit-nonprofit classification turns on the character of the school, which is the immediate recipient of the aid, rather than on the particular needs of each child in attendance, and that some needy students will be enrolled in schools operated for profit while some affluent children will be registered in nonprofit institutions. Although a more perfect system might look to the individual child rather than base its judgment on the assumption that nonprofit schools educate more needy children, this would be much more difficult to administer. In the context of an essentially economic classification, equal protection "is offended only if the classification rests on grounds wholly irrelevant to the achievement of the State's objective." "It is by . . . practical considerations based on experience rather than by theoretical inconsistencies that the question of equal protection is to be answered."

Statutes constitutionally neutral on their face, however, may be invalid in effect. Under a proper statutory definition, for example, the only "nonprofit" school in town may be a parochial school. Absent a judicial finding that the legitimate statutory definition merely camouflaged an illegitimate preference of religion violating the establishment clause, the statute should not be held invalid. A public appropriation for a primary secular purpose should not be void merely because, under an appropriate neutral standard, a religiously controlled institution happens to be the only recipient.

A more difficult issue, but one apparently of no great consequence, arises where an aid statute by its terms names the parochial schools of one church only, or names only parochial schools, and it is unknown from the statute or its available legislative history whether other similarly situated schools exist. The Court could: (a) strike down the statute, thus forcing the legislature to redraft properly if it can; (b) strike down the statute, unless it were shown that there were no others similarly situated; (c) uphold the statute, unless it were shown that there were others similarly situated.

## C. The Compensable Amount

The constitutional principle proposed herein speaks of the secular educational services rendered by the church-affiliated school. Assuming that these services may be isolated, little difficulty arises where their cost is the same to the parochial school as to the public school system. Because government may properly finance the secular education of all children, whatever their religious faith, payment to a parochial school under these circumstances of the same amount that such education costs in the public schools should be immune from establishment clause protest: No tax funds are being expended for strictly religious purposes; no more tax funds are being used than would be if the pupils were in public schools; the church obtains no financial benefit except compensation for the cost of secular services rendered. A fortiori, there is no difficulty if the cost of providing this service in the parochial school is less than it is in the public school system, as is not unlikely, and government pays the parochial school only this lesser amount.

But suppose that the cost of providing secular educational services in the parochial school is less than is the cost in the public school system and government pays the parochial school the latter amount. Although here also no more tax funds are being expended than would be if the pupils were in public schools, the church obtains a net financial benefit. Nevertheless, this should not violate the establishment clause. Literally thousands of church-related agencies offer secular services that are funded—or purchased, if you will—by government. If any organization—profit or nonprofit, religious or nonsectarian—provides a secular service to government at the "going rate," and is able to profit thereby because of low labor costs, efficiency, or any other reason, the Constitution should not be held to prohibit it. In fact, for government to refuse to deal on equal terms with an organization providing public services because that organization is religiously-affiliated might even be seen as a violation of the free exercise clause.

It must be recalled that government assistance to religion which neither infringes religious liberty nor expends tax funds for strictly religious purposes should not be considered violative of the establishment bar. Thus, in the context of the immediate discussion, it is the "cost" to the public and not the "aid" to religion that is determinative. As long as the government receives in full the secular services purchased, the relative cost or profit to religion of supplying those services should have no relevance to the establishment clause. Its prohibition should be satisfied by a showing that the government is getting the secular services it paid for. Consequently, where something costs the government little or nothing, it should make no difference what secular services it receives. For example, the government may allow religious organizations temporarily to use vacant public buildings for strictly religious purposes. Such occasional use of public buildings may substantially "aid" religious groups, and it may save them significant rental fees. But, if the use is not "regular and extended in duration," the "cost" to the public is nil or de minimis, and there should be no establishment breach. It may be argued that, even though the use of the building cost the state nothing, it could charge these religious organizations measurable rental fees. But the establishment clause should not require that government profit at religion's expense. It should merely forbid public expenditures for strictly religious purposes.

Therefore, if the government lends money at a rate of interest equal to or above the government borrowing rate but below the commercial rate, it may so lend to sectarian groups, *even though they use the money for strictly religious purposes*. The church benefits, but at no cost to the state. This should not be confused with government loans for *secular* purposes. Since, as to these, grants would be unobjectionable, loans at any rate are obviously valid. It follows that a state may buy textbooks—even religious ones—at quantity prices and sell them to parochial schools at the discounted price.

Finally, suppose that the cost of providing secular educational services in the parochial school exceeds the cost in the public school system and government pays the parochial school the former amount. Although the church here does not obtain funds that may be used for strictly religious purposes, more tax funds are being expended than would be if the children were in public schools. There should, nonetheless, be no violation of the establishment clause. So long as the state expenditure is in fact for a primary secular goal, no tax funds are being used for strictly religious purposes.

## D. The Permeation Issue

### 1. The Facts

Probably the most complex matter concerning public financial assistance to parochial education is the permeation (or integration) issue. It is frequently contended that "official Catholic doctrine refuses to recognize any distinction between secular and religious teaching." Pope Pius XI and Pope Leo XIII are quoted as ordering "that every . . . subject taught, be permeated with Christian piety," as are Catholic educators, theologians and philosophers. A Lutheran school manual demands "that all areas of the curriculum reflect an adequate philosophy of Christian education." Seventh Day Adventists declare their "endeavor to permeate all branches of learning with a spiritual outlook." After all, it is asked, "if religion is taught only one or two hours a day in church schools, what is the point of maintaining the separate parochial school system?"

But there is less than universal agreement as to the facts. Others familiar with Catholic—and Jewish—parochial school education explain that the pupil there "learns essentially the same arithmetic, spelling, English, history, civics, foreign languages, geography, and science" as is taught in the public schools, but in addition learns religion "and the religious dimensions of secular knowledge." In the Lutheran school system, it is said that "the main features of the public school curriculum are reproduced." In response to a study showing that many "secular course" textbooks used in parochial schools are permeated with religious symbols, concepts, and doctrines, it has been said that the examples "were highly arbitrary and not representative," and that "Catholic educators . . . as a whole, do not favor textbooks in which dabs of spurious religion serve only to distort the essential subject matter. . . ."

Further evidence that secular subjects in parochial schools need be little different than their counterpart public school offerings is found in the fact that, as part of shared time programs, many parochial school students actually take such courses as mathematics, physics, science, foreign languages, music, industrial arts, home economics, and physical education in the public school itself. Catholic educators have observed that "basic instruction" in such courses as literature and history could well be undertaken in shared time programs in the public schools "with the church adding the distinctive note which it can bear to the revelation of God in these areas" in the parochial school. Thus, it is concluded, the reason for maintaining a separate parochial school system is not for the purpose of teaching a wholly different curriculum. Rather, it is to add "the most important of the four R's,'' the feeling being that children attending public schools that taught only secular subjects five days a week would consider religious training unimportant, and that this impression could not be overcome by a few after school hours or Sunday school.

Several facts emerge clearly from the foregoing discussion. First, "permeation" is a word of varied and imprecise meaning. Father Drinan can state as "the undeniable fact that secular instruction in a Catholic school is 'permeated' by a Catholic atmosphere and Catholic attitudes," yet urge that "permeation should avoid every suggestion of quasi-coercion or 'indoctrination.'" Second, the secular courses taught in parochial schools rarely, if ever, mirror exactly the courses taught in the public schools. Third, although "no scientific study has ever been done on the extent of the permeation of sectarian teaching in the instruction in secular subjects in Catholic schools," it is likely that some secular subject courses in some parochial schools are so "permeated" that they are in reality courses of sectarian indoctrination, despite the regulatory power of the state—whether exercised or not; that some courses are completely, bona fide secular; that some courses fall between these extremes. Fourth, the problem of the parochial school secular courses being turned into nothing more than religious instruction is not inherent; no religion demands it, nor constitutionally could a religion demand it if contrary to reasonable state requirements.

## 2. Extent of Permissible Aid

Under the rationale proposed in this article, public financial assistance to parochial education may not exceed the value of the secular educational service rendered. One relatively effortless way of avoiding the whole problem of permeation in this connection is simply to ignore it by taking the position that "the secular character of secular subjects is not changed by a moral or religious permeation"; "that it is impossible to study and interpret man and his activities apart from his moral and religious values"; and that "the National Merit Scholarship competition . . . is clear evidence that students who attend church-related schools receive a secular education as good as that received by students in our public schools." On this reasoning, there would be no prohibition to financing accredited parochial schools on a lump-sum parity with public schools without further investigation.

But this may be too simple. Competitive examinations and sociological studies are not so exact as to determine conclusively that the educational services rendered in parochial schools are as complete and effective and have the same impact from a nonreligious perspective on the overall development of the student as does public school education. Viewed from the basis of per-hour input, it is reasonable to assume that this is not the case, given the parochial school time spent on religious instruction. And it is clear that the state may not subsidize religious instruction or indoctrination, no matter where undertaken.

The establishment clause prohibition against using tax funds for strictly religious purposes appears to require a more careful scrutiny to assure that only the secular aspects of parochial school education will be publicly financed. But to admit "an admixture of religious with secular teaching" is the beginning, not the end, of the inquiry. To concede that "commingling the religious with the secular teaching does not divest the whole [course or activity] of its religious permeation and emphasis," is not to conclude that no part of the course or activity may be aided with public money.

A secular subject parochial school course or activity may concurrently serve independent, dual purposes—that is, full secular value may be obtained for the time and resources expended, and religious interests may also be served. If such is the case, the entire course or activity serves a primary secular purpose—and may therefore be fully financed—the aid to religion notwithstanding. On the other hand, a secular subject parochial school course or activity may partially serve both religious and secular ends. Here, an allocation must be made; only the secular product may be publicly financed. Of course, if a "secular subject" parochial school course or activity is in reality religious instruction, it cannot be publicly funded at all; and if it is exclusively secular in purpose, it may be totally funded.

(a) The Relevance of "Atmosphere."— Before applying this approach, certain other matters should be considered. That the general atmosphere of parochial schools—as created by religious symbols, teachers in religious attire, and compulsory religious exercises and courses—is oriented toward religious goals should not affect the constitutional judgment as to whether the particular course or activity may be publicly funded. The clearly sectarian purpose of these accouterments produces no infringement of religious liberty, since students attend the parochial schools of their own volition. And since public funds are not used to subsidize these items, but only for the proven secular aspects of the educational experience, no expenditure of tax money for religious purposes results.

(b) Judicial Definition of "Religion."—Under the analysis proposed herein, the question whether a particular course or activity serves a primary secular purpose, a primary religious purpose, or mixed purposes must ultimately be for the Court. It "must be ready to define religion, religious teaching and religious commitment." But this would not be a novel exercise for the judiciary.

As has already been noted, the Court has on a number of occasions labeled particular governmental activity religious or secular. In the *Sunday Closing Law Cases*, the Court expressed its willingness and obligation to engage in "close scrutiny" to determine if an action's purpose and "its operative effect" were religious. So, too, should the Court examine challenged parochial school courses and activities when necessary.

In the *Regents' Prayer Case*, which is closely analogous to the question in issue, the Court passed judgment on such public school activities as recitation of the Declaration of Independence (or the Gettysburg Address) and the singing of the Star Spangled Banner—all of which are somewhat religiously "permeated"—and concluded that these exercises were "patriotic or ceremonial" rather than "religious." In the *Bible Reading Cases*, the Court ruled that study of the Bible and religion "as part of a secular program of education" was proper, thus addressing itself to the very matter under discussion here.

It has been argued that it is extremely difficult to distinguish religious from secular textbooks; that "the task of separating the secular from the religious in education is one of magnitude, intricacy and delicacy." But just as the Court, if called upon to do so, must determine whether a public school textbook is religiously indoctrinatory, or whether a public school history course is really religious instruction, it should make the same constitutional judgment in respect to parochial school affairs. When a public school action is found religious the remedy is to enjoin; when a parochial school practice is held religious, to forbid its public subsidization.

The general undesirability of requiring the Court to define what is religious and what is not need not be disputed. But, although the Court "can and must avoid passing on the truth of particular religious beliefs," it cannot escape the former task. "This necessity arises out of the constitutional language itself, which sets down religion as a subject for special treatment." A judicial definition must be fashioned under the "absolutist" theory, which bars all aid to "religion." It must be determined under Professor Kurland's thesis, which forbids classifications in terms of "religion." And it must be faced under the rationale proposed herein.

As has been the case concerning the Court's handling of the issue of religious exercises and activities in public schools, most decisions under the proposed rationale for adjudicating these problems in parochial schools will not be difficult. The Court, guided by common sense and the obvious effects of the activity, rather than by its own "prepossessions," may set the standard in a few cases. If abuses occur, they may be checked by federal or state aid administrators, reviewed by state and lower federal courts, with ultimate review always available in the Supreme Court.

*Pragmatically, the issue should rarely arise, at least in the foreseeable future, for it is highly unlikely, as a matter of political reality, that the total amount of governmental assistance to parochial education will even approach the conceded value of the secular educational services it renders.*

(c) Illustrations.—Keeping this last point in mind, some specific illustrations of problems that could arise under the proposed rationale may be helpful. The second grade arithmetic text assigned in a Catholic parochial school may use sectarian characters, illustrations or examples, phrasing arithmetic problems in terms of rosary beads instead of apples, and using pictures of parochial schools instead of public schools. Or, if the text is "clean," the teacher may use these illustrations. Trumpet instruction may involve an unusual amount of religiously-oriented music, and French language instruction may include a high concentration of religiously-significant words or reading.

Considerations of religious liberty, not present in voluntarily-attended parochial schools, might prevent all or some of this in public schools. But in the examples above, full secular value seems to have been obtained for the time and resources expended, despite the fact that religious interests may also have been served.

(1) Burden of Justification.—Some educators might urge that the above uses of sectarian material did not afford the parochial pupils a secular educational experience completely analogous to that offered in the public schools. If such a case is made, the state or federal financing agency and the recipient parochial school should have the burden of justifying allocation of the full cost of the course to the secular side of the ledger. Although legislative and executive action ordinarily carries a much stronger presumption of constitutionality, the Court has forcefully held that this is not the case when the precious personal freedoms of speech, press, and religion are at stake.

It may seem to some that individual liberty is only indirectly affected when governmental grants to religious bodies are challenged under the establishment clause, thus vindicating use of the usual presumption of constitutionality or something close to it. But the prohibition against the use of compulsorily raised tax funds for strictly religious purposes, central to the concept of nonestablishment as an important guarantor of religious liberty, suggests that here, too, the regular presumption should be modified. Thus, after an opponent of aid initially demonstrates that a parochial school course or activity is in whole or part primarily religious, in the sense used in this article, the obligation of rebuttal should rest with those defending aid. In cases of uncertainty, the issue should be resolved against the public funding.

(2) Examples.—In a parochial school biology text or course, after a full explanation of the theory of evolution, the church's perspective on the matter may also be fully articulated. Or, in the civics course, the concept of racial equal protection may be amplified by presenting both the relevant secular and theological values. Since there would seem to be no constitutional objection to such an objective presentation in the public schools, there should likewise be none here, despite the concurrent religious educational value, and despite the fact that these matters may never be mentioned in the average public school class. They still have significant secular educational value. Even a parochial school course in "religion" itself may so qualify if properly handled.

There is a very fine line, however, between objective presentation and subtle commitment, and this truth is not confined to parochial schools. Some texts used in public schools—and, undoubtedly, some teachers—unintentionally emphasize Humanistic or antireligious values. Undoubtedly, the opposite is also true. Such emphasis will vary from public school to public school, dependent in part on the cultural, religious and racial composition of the students and teachers. To the extent that this is constitutionally permissible, effectively unavoidable, or de minimis in the public schools, it should be similarly unobjectionable in the parochial schools for the purpose of public funding—subject always to the burden of justification discussed above.

A parochial school history course or text may teach that all major events are related to or produced by one of the basic truths of the religion, or may emphasize the contribution of one religion over all others. Parochial school texts in English composition may "stress Catholic religious words and teachings," or a current events class may use a weekly magazine whose articles are "Catholic-oriented." An advanced biology text or course may omit all references to birth control, sterilization, and euthanasia, or specifically reject most parts of evolutionary theory and shift scientific concepts so that they appear to be based on religious tenets. A parochial school geography text may describe only Catholic families in various cultures, or the teacher may ask the students to map all Catholic churches in the state of Nebraska.

Clearly, some or all of these parochial school activities, as well as some referred to earlier, cannot be fully supported with public funds. Either the quantity of religious perspective has deprived the course of full secular educational value, or the quality of sectarian permeation has so slanted the material as to have partially undermined or even fully destroyed its secular content. The very description of these courses and texts appears to state a sufficient case to shift the burden of justifying any quantum of secular value to those defending governmental support.

### E. Allocation

It must be reemphasized that, as a realistic matter, problems of the nature just discussed will arise rarely, as will problems of allocating cost between religious and secular parts of "mixed" parochial school activity. As with the issue of permeation, the burden of justifying both the propriety of the allocation and the method used should be on the government or recipient defendant once the assailant has made the requisite initial demonstration.

Several problems of allocation that have disturbed courts may serve as brief illustrations. The cost of bus transportation to parochial schools, for example, cannot be allocated in "proportional shares as between the secular and religious instruction." The reason is that, as will be amply shown, the activity fully serves an independent secular purpose. Thus, its value, if provided by the parochial school while public school children are bussed at public expense, may be completely listed in the secular services column. No allocation is necessary.

Suppose that public funds are used to construct a building for educational research on the campus of a church-affiliated college, title being vested in the school. If the building is always used for this purpose as contemplated, no allocation problem arises. But suppose, after three years, the building is to be converted into a chapel and utilized exclusively for religious purposes. If in the building's three years as a research center, the total governmental contribution to the college, including the full amount of the grant for the building, did not exceed the value of the secular educational service rendered by the college, the matter is closed. The fact that the building will now be used for religious purposes is irrelevant. The taxpayers have gotten at least full secular value for their contribution. But, if in those three years the total governmental contribution, including the grant, exceeded the value of the college's secular educational services, the building may not be used for religious purposes until the college reimburses the government for the excess amount or some other proper arrangement is made. The science of accounting, with judicial review when appropriate, is neither above nor below the needed task.

. . .

William Van Alstyne, *Trends in the Supreme Court: Mr. Jefferson's Crumbling Wall—A Comment on Lynch v. Donnelly*, 1984 DUKE LAW JOURNAL 770 (1984)*

Although the first amendment belongs to all the states, it especially belongs to Virginia. The most notable antecedent debates occurred here. The seminal contributions by James Madison and Thomas Jefferson originated here. The strongest resolves to protect religious liberty from political interference were memorialized here. My immediate purpose is to comment on one particular case decided last term in the Supreme Court, *Lynch v. Donnelly*, which sustained a municipality's nativity display against a constitutional challenge. I mean briefly to examine the case by the light of an understanding of the first amendment that Jefferson and Madison may have shared. My broader purpose is to suggest the extent to which *Lynch v. Donnelly* may serve as a synecdoche of a larger drift that now appears to be winning acceptance in the Supreme Court.

This trend can be summed up as a movement from one national epigram to another; it is the movement from "E Pluribus Unum" to In God We Trust," from the ideal expressed by our original Latin motto—one nation out of highly diverse but equally welcome states and people—to an increasingly pressing enthusiasm in which government re-establishes itself under distinctly religious auspices. *Lynch v. Donnelly* is the clearest expression to date that acts affiliating government and religion may be deemed consistent with the first amendment, at least if ac-

complished gradually, that is, incrementally. A constitutional neologism has nearly displaced the much different figure of speech, that of a "wall of separation" between church and state, which Thomas Jefferson once used in commemorating the ratification of the first amendment. The neologism is that insofar as most persons are religious, it is altogether natural that government should itself reflect that fact in its own practices. Thus, according to this neologism, it is not helpful to regard the first amendment as having emplaced a wall separating the practices of religion from the practices of government, for it is not walls, but bridges, that the first amendment contemplates. Even the absorption of a dominant religion within government itself may be deemed altogether unexceptionable—as though it were but a part of natural history. It is thus symbiosis, not separation, that the first amendment may be interpreted to accommodate. At least I cannot understand *Lynch v. Donnelly* otherwise, although I think it very far removed from the interpretation of the first amendment originally agreed upon by all nine Justices of the Supreme Court when the issue was first comprehensively addressed, in *Everson v. Board of Education*, nearly forty years ago.

I.

Although there is of course very substantial controversy over the "right" meaning of the religion clauses of the first amendment, there is nonetheless considerable agreement that they originally met with broad support from at least three distinct sources. . . . These diverse inputs were the concerns of voluntarism, separatism, and federalism. The first, voluntarism, was derived largely from the moderate spirit of religious toleration associated with the Quaker tradition of Pennsylvania. The second, separatism, was derived principally from the successful efforts of Madison and Jefferson in Virginia to disentangle the affairs of government from religious establishments, especially in respect to taxes and levies for religious assistance. The third, federalism, was derived from the preferences of other states that—in contrast with Virginia—maintained particular religious establishments, which they were concerned to keep free from the interference of the national government. It was quite consistent with all three concerns that they would converge on a single proposition: Congress should be disabled from legislating on religion. The final form of agreement introduces the first amendment itself: "Congress shall make no law respecting an establishment of religion or prohibiting the free exercise thereof."

Accepted at face value, the concerns of voluntarism, separatism, and federalism were not at odds with one another. They framed no tension; rather, they mutually reinforced a single proposition: Questions of religious choice were not to be the business of the national government. Article VI of the Constitution had already provided that "no religious test shall ever be required as a qualification to any office or public trust under the United States," a provision meant to make it quite clear that "unbelievers or Mohammedans" were not excludable. The motto of the new nation, proposed in a Continental Congress committee report by Franklin, Adams, and Jefferson, and adopted for use in the Great Seal of the United States in 1782, was "E Pluribus Unum." The original legend on new coins, first on continental dollars, then on the fugio cent minted in Philadelphia, in 1787, was "Mind Your Business." The inscription on the obverse side of the Great Seal was "Novus Ordo Seclorum," a New Order of the Ages. The secular separation assured each individual that none need feel alien to this government, whatever his own religion or personal philosophy, for it was to be a temporal government not commingled with a clergy, a theism, or a church. At the same time, this wall of separation—in Jefferson's terminology—assured the several states that they would be immune from attempts by the national government to influence or limit their own religious establishments in any respect.

The resolve to forbid this national government from adopting a religion or reserving its offices for only the religious carried over to the field of international affairs. Whatever the disposition of other nations, each might expect a relationship of amity with the United States, which itself incorporated no religious predisposition against any nation. . . .

So strongly was the principle respected by some that they were to risk quite substantial political opprobrium in its behalf, even where the risk may have seemed unnecessary to undertake. Thus, when Congress resolved to request merely precatory presidential statements of annual thanksgiving, themselves seemingly harmless and altogether uncontroversial gestures unlikely to offend anyone, Washington and Adams easily acquiesced—but Jefferson could not. The practice was doubtless well intentioned, he admitted, but the principle was careless and unsound. "I do not think myself authorized to comply," Jefferson wrote,

> I consider the government of the United States as interdicted by the Constitution from intermeddling with religious institutions, their doctrines, discipline, or exercises. This results not only from the provision that no law shall be made respecting the establishment or free exercise of religion, but from that also which reserves to the States the powers not delegated to the United States. Certainly, no power to prescribe any religious exercise, or to assume authority in religious discipline, has been delegated to the General Government. . . . I do not believe it is for the interest of religion to invite the civil magistrate to direct its exercises, its discipline, or its doctrines; nor of the religious societies, that the General Government should be invested with the power of effecting any uniformity of time or matter among them . . . .
>
> I am aware that the practice of my predecessors may be quoted. But I have ever believed, that the example of State executives led to the assumption of that authority by the General Government, without due examination, which would have discovered that what might be a right in a State government, was a violation of that right when assumed by another. Be this as it may, every one must act according to the dictates of his own reason, and mine tells me that civil powers alone have been given to the President of the United States, and no authority to direct the religious exercises of his constituents.

Madison, as president, did not adhere to Jefferson's example but, even after he had discounted such ceremonial utterances for fasts and festivals as "merely recommendatory" and "absolutely indiscriminate," he acknowledged that in fact they constituted a "deviation from the strict principle" he shared with Jefferson. Similarly, Madison acknowledged that he had been quite mistaken in approving—as a member of the House, in 1789—bills for the payment of, congressional chaplains. . . .

> If Religion consists in voluntary acts of individuals, singly, or voluntarily associated, and [if] it be proper that public functionaries, as well as their Constituents should discharge their religious duties, let them like their Constituents, do so at their own expense.

The feature of tax subsidy was especially offensive to Madison—unsurprisingly, since it was that very practice that he and Jefferson had successfully opposed in Virginia. There, Madison had written that not even "three pence" should be coerced of any person, through taxes, for the propagation of religious views with which he disagreed. The point, reflecting Madison's broader, Virginian, perspective went beyond the abuse of the tax power as such. Thus, although no taxes were involved, and although the matter was obviously not one he needed to interfere with, Madison, as president, vetoed a grant of land made by Congress for what Congress thought a benign use by a Baptist church . . . .

The separation principle, moreover, operated in both directions; it was meant to keep religion from entangling the state as well as to keep the churches free from the state influence that would have been the inevitable concomitant of state financial support. *The Memorial and Remonstrance Against Religious Assessments*, of 1785, inveighed against the risk that "the Civil Magistrate . . . may employ Religion as an engine of Civil policy," and equally against the infusion of any particular religion within government "because it will have a like tendency to banish our Citizens," i.e., to make them aliens to their own government. Competition among religions for position within government must be avoided so that none need fear any other, as each might otherwise seek its own establishment through government or within government.

Voluntarism, then, was the principle of personal choice. Separatism was the principle of non-entanglement. Federalism was the principle of pure state autonomy, immune from national power, respecting policies that affect religion. Laws favoring religious establishments, like laws prohibiting the free exercise of religion, were thus altogether disallowed. The contributing streams of the first amendment were not, in this view, jostling and competitive. Rather, they converged on a single proposition thought eminently suitable for the national government. Citizens from all states, regardless of each state's own internal practices, would be assured of being able to meet on common secular ground to conduct the civil business of a purely civil government. The authority of that government was of enumerated civil powers that incorporated none of a religious provenance or cast, and was constrained from directing or otherwise influencing the voluntarism of private choice. No religious tests of any kind were to be associated with that government, for no sort of favored religion or "national" religion would be appropriate for Congress even to consider. Laws tending to finance religion, like laws tending to prohibit particular religions or to favor preferred religions, were prohibited to the national government in order to leave room for such diverse and separate policies as each state might individually elect. The motto of the country, "E Pluribus Unum," was significant: One nation, a civil and neutral polity, from many states of highly diverse people and practices.

Then, with the abandonment, circa 1834, of the last state-established religions and the subsequent enactment, in 1868, of the fourteenth amendment, a principle originally felt suitable to apply to Congress partly on behalf of the states ultimately became applicable to the states as well. The detachment of government from religion that Jefferson and Madison had originally fought to achieve in Virginia had become a general obligation.

## II.

In their first full address to the subject, in *Everson v. Board of Education*, all nine Justices of the Supreme Court agreed in this view. Indeed, the following summary by Justice Black was faulted by no one on the Court:

The "establishment of religion " clause of the First Amendment means at least this: Neither a state nor the Federal Government can set up a church. Neither can pass laws which aid one religion, aid all religions, or prefer one religion over another. Neither can force nor influence a person to go to or to remain away from church against his will or force him to profess a belief or disbelief in any religion. No person can be punished for entertaining or professing religious beliefs or disbeliefs, for church attendance or non-attendance. No tax in any amount, large or small, can be levied to support any religious activities or institutions, whatever they may be called, or whatever form they may adopt to teach or practice religion. Neither a state nor the Federal Government can, openly or secretly, participate in the affairs of any religious organizations or groups and vice versa. In the words of Jefferson, the clause against establishment of religion by law was intended to erect "a wall of separation between church and State."

Rather, four of the nine Justices, agreeing entirely with Black's view, dissented solely on the separate basis that they, unlike the majority, believed it had not been honored, that is, that the particular law in question was defective. Indeed, it was on the basis of Justice Black's description of the first amendment, rather than on the basis of some different description, that the dissent itself also relied.

Fourteen years later, Justice Frankfurter, who had concurred in *Everson* with Justice Black's sentiments even while dissenting in the particular case, returned to the same theme. "The Establishment Clause," he declared,

withdrew from the sphere of legitimate legislative concern and competence a specific, but comprehensive, area of human conduct: man's belief or disbelief in the verity of some transcendental idea and man's expression in action of that belief or disbelief. Congress may not make these matters, as such, the subject of legislation, nor, now, may any legislature in this country. Neither the National Government nor, under the Due Process Clause of the Fourteenth Amendment, a State may, by any device, support belief or the expression of belief for its own sake, whether from conviction of the truth of that belief, or from conviction that by the propagation of that belief the civil welfare of the State is served, or because a majority of its citizens, holding that belief, are offended when all do not hold it.

Difficult cases still arise, of course, even under the Black-Frankfurter view of the establishment clause. Generally, however, the difficulty of such cases has been limited to circumstances in which the good-faith conduct of civic business has imposed a hard choice on individuals whose personal religion has instructed them in opposition to the law. In such cases, there is a fair question whether the relevant public policy is so pressing that, whatever the strength of the religiously-grounded opposition to it, exceptions will not be tolerable, or whether, to the contrary, respect for religious pluralism counsels a measure of state self-restraint.

At one extreme, criminal prohibitions of homicide, mutilation, or child abuse cannot yield regardless of the intensity of the religious passion that demands such exceptional forms of "free" exercise. At the other extreme, however, the civil polity is not seriously distressed if it excuses those for whom ritual forms of respect for the state are acts of blasphemy. In the latter circumstance, the doubtfulness of the state's policy, the meanness of disallowing conscientious abstention, and the gratuitousness of the damage to the sincerely pious weigh in favor of accommodating sincerely held religious beliefs. The establishment clause as described by Jefferson or Madison and summarized in the quoted excerpts from opinions by Justices Black and Frankfurter is not necessarily hostile to such an accommodation. Therefore the occasional wisdom of accommodation does not constitute an objection to traditional establishment clause doctrine. To the contrary, respect for so modest an accommodation as would be required in these circumstances would be strongly counselled by the free exercise clause. In between these extreme and thus rather obvious cases, the closer and more difficult issues must continue to be addressed without inconsistency with the principles of neutrality and separation.

In sharp contrast to those closer issues and presenting a paradigmatic disregard of the establishment clause in virtually every dimension of its concerns would be a case involving all of the following deliberate acts of government:

1. The overt alignment of government with the particular theology of one, politically dominant, religious sect;
2. The collaboration of government with commercial interests to stimulate consumer purchases by the government's own promotional use of a particular religion's artifacts and mysteries;
3. The propagation under government sponsorship of distinctly religious symbols uniquely associated with one sect's most holy event—the miracle of divine birth of its particular prophet and messiah;
4. The purchase and maintenance through tax levies, and promotional display in outdoor public location each year, of sectarian objects, during the season designated for the Mass or eucharist of one religion's principal sacrament.

The facts of *Lynch v. Donnelly* fit this paradigm exactly. Accordingly, when appropriately petitioned by a natural coalition of plaintiffs, a federal district court enjoined the governmental practice. The state had not merely aided "all" religions but rather had promoted emphatically and exclusively *one* religion. It had not only broken with a general neutrality regarding purely religious doctrine, it had also preferred one religion over others. It had used tax money in support of a religious activity and encouraged belief in, and endorsed, the particular holy day—Christ's Mass—of one sect. It openly participated in the affairs of one church by duplicating in wood and plastic the imagery of a sacred event in order to encourage a general secular, commercial enthusiasm to intensify its holy day. The wall of separation between church and state had clearly been breached by a clear governmental, politicized, symbiotic embrace of one faith's preferred holy day.

. . .

In *Lynch v. Donnelly*, a divided panel in the United States Court of Appeals for the First Circuit affirmed. The Supreme Court, in an opinion by the Chief Justice, with four justices dissenting, reversed both lower court holdings that the municipal purchase, maintenance, and periodic illuminated Christmas display of a purely Christian nativity scene was unconstitutional. The opinion perfunctorily acknowledged the "three-prong" test of the Court's earlier cases, which demands that a challenged statute have a "secular legislative purpose;" that its "primary effect" neither "advance nor inhibit" religion; and that it not promote "an excessive entanglement" with religion. Purporting to apply the "primary effect" prong of this test the Chief Justice observed:

> Of course the creche is identified with one religious faith *but no more so* than the examples we have set out from prior cases . . . . We can assume, *arguendo*, that the display advances religion . . . ; [but] whatever [the] benefit to one faith . . . [,] display of the creche is *no more* an advancement or endorsement of religion than the Congressional and Executive recognition of the origins of the holiday itself as "Christ's Mass" . . . .

> [T]o conclude that the primary effect of including the creche is to advance religion in violation of the Establishment Clause would require that we view it as *more* beneficial to and *more* an endorsement of religion

> . . . . than . . . [specific forms of assistance previously allowed such as textbook loans to parochial schools and bus fare reimbursements, or] *more* of an endorsement of religion than the Sunday Closing Laws upheld in *McGowan v. Maryland* . . . [or the payment of chaplain salaries sustained in *Marsh v. Chambers*].

> We are unable to discern a *greater* aid to religion deriving from inclusion of the creche than from these benefits and endorsements previously held not violative . . . .

Such was the tenor of the analysis under the purported "three-prong" approach; but, given the Chief Justice's warning that the Court would not be "confined to any single test or criterion in this sensitive area" we should assuredly be alert to the possibility that an altogether new test was aborning. What is that test? Apparently it is an *"any more than"* test. Here, in one possible summary, are its parts.

> First, the court must determine whether the government acts that have been questioned plainly sponsor, assist, promote, or advance a particular religion, its specific practices, its distinctive theology, or its establishment.

> Second, assuming that the acts complained of plainly do sponsor, assist, promote, and advance a particular religion, its specific practices, its distinctive theology, and its establishment, the court must then nonetheless also determine whether in doing so, the government has merely acted in a manner consistent with what it has regularly done—or with what Congress has regularly done—in the past.

> Third, unless the court finds that the additional acts are more egregious than other acts of government of a like kind—that is, unless the new acts advance this religion "any more than" government has generally advanced a preferred religion—the court shall sustain the acts in question.

In an artless sense—but in no sense that will withstand even the mildest scrutiny—the *Lynch* case can also be fitted within the literal wording of the "three-prong" test a majority of the Court has declared that it will usually apply to establishment clause claims. The first prong, we recall, is that the law or governmental practice must possess a "secular" purpose. If "secular" is taken merely descriptively, simply as a synonym for whatever things temporal or civil government thinks appropriate to undertake as a temporal and civil government, then the facts of the *Lynch* case do indeed fit a "secular" purpose. That purpose is the government's own decision to identify its own conduct, and the uses of its tax revenues, with the events, values, mysteries, customs, and monotheism of a particular religion—the religion, hardly coincidentally, that is most widely subscribed to nationally as well as locally. The municipal purchase and annual, public, illuminated, tax-supported Christmas display of a nativity scene fit within *that* purpose exceedingly well. By the same gesture, the "primary effect" of the city's practice is without doubt to bring about that secular, that is, governmental, objective. Moreover, because the local government pursues its policy strictly through the uses of its own monies and its own property and does not engage any church to provide the place for its illuminated display, there are obviously no "entanglements" with any church or religious body as such.

Viewed this way, the decision need not have been compromised by the majority opinion's ineffectual attempt to compare the city's illuminated, commercially-manufactured, outdoor nativity scene to the mere inclusion of historic religious paintings in a public museum. Neither need the opinion have been hedged by suggesting that had the nativity scene been unaccompanied by additional Christmas tokens such as Santa and reindeer—additions, incidentally, that embarrass the suggestion that the entire display was otherwise similar to the collection of a public art museum—it might have been unconstitutional. Rather, a square logical fit can be made to the conventional three-prong test, albeit a fit that is at once self-validating and ironic. Essentially, it is the following, as, regretfully, I believe was the real case.

Insofar as the theology, artifacts, and liturgy of a particular religion have already formally been adopted into government itself and made a regular feature of government's own practice, the religion has itself been partly secularized. That is, it has been assimilated into and made a part of the state temporal, and not simply left to the church spiritual. To whatever additional extent other incidents of that religion are similarly annexed and identically made a part of official state practice, the acts that are necessary to do so obviously do serve a "secular" purpose, namely, the appropriation of a particular religion or faith as a practice of government. The events that do this may be individually modest, discrete, and extremely gradual, as has happened in the United States.

This movement, a movement of gradual, secularized Christian ethnocentrism, has tended to elude the establishment clause itself. Originally, in merely marginal, seemingly trivial, and obviously nonjusticiable ways, statesmen and politicians easily commingled religiously colored habits of personal conduct with their deportment in public office. Some no doubt did so naturally, without thinking about it. Others, perhaps somewhat crassly, doubtless saw strong political advantage in making great public display of their piety. The commonplace personal tendency, to identify preferred "religious truths" with national policy, is institutionally irresistible in times of greatest sacrifice, such as war time. Thus, it is scarcely surprising, given the religious antecedents of the abolitionist movement, that the Union cause in the Civil War would be mingled with the assimilation of Christian symbolism, and that Christian theology thus would itself become part of the cause. Recall, for instance, the Battle Hymn of the Republic. That "In God We Trust" was first authorized for use on American coins in 1864, therefore, is scarcely remarkable. That the fuller transition was made during the 1950's, with the alteration of the national motto, the insertion of a common monotheism in the Pledge of Allegiance, and the mandatory insertion of "In God We Trust" on all United States currency and money, is equally unsurprising. Jingoistic desires to paint a vivid contrast in the Cold War, separating ourselves, claiming "God" within "our" government, for sanctimonious contrast with "Godless atheistic" Communism, made the deliberate appropriation of a pervasive religiosity an irresistibly useful instrument of state policy.

In these marginal, gradual, ordinary ways, then, virtually from the beginning the nation has drifted, reidentified itself, and become, like so many others, accustomed to the political appropriation of religion for its own official uses. In exchange, it now purchases religious support. Late arrivals to America may suppose they can take the government's religiosity or leave it, but they are stuck with the reality that clashes so clearly with the first amendment: Ours is basically a Christian-pretending government where they will be made to feel ungrateful should they complain. The gradual but increasingly pervasive installment of compromised religious ritual within government itself thus draws that which was formerly outside to the inside; the prevailing monotheism has been made a commonplace exhibition in state practice, and put to service and supported by the state when felt useful. Additional appropriations from sectarianism may then become logically fitted as part of this "secular" but sectarian state. Distinctly religious practices, insofar as they serve the state, thus by definition have virtually succeeded in satisfying a secular purpose and promoting a secular interest. In this gradual absorptive fashion, then, satisfying the Court's current "test" can scarcely ever be a problem.

### III.

Not so long ago, Justice Powell said that he believed we were now far removed from the dangers that so troubled Jefferson and Madison. It is difficult to agree that that is so and, in any event, the supposition seems scarcely sufficient ground for the Court to modify the first amendment simply to accord with its own confidence. "E Pluribus Unum" should mean something to us all, aspirationally, that we ought not abandon although Congress itself has seen fit to do so. The idea of a civil nation of free people, diverse in their thoughts, equal in their citizenship, and with none to feel alien, outcast, or stranger in relation to civil authority, remains powerful and compelling. The installation of a state theism has not been worthy of the United States. *Lynch v. Donnelly* was itself not a credit to an able and distinguished Court. Both the case and the tendency it represents are disappointing reminders that religious ethnocentrism, as well as religious insensitivity, are still with us. I do not know whether Mr. Jefferson would have been surprised, but I believe he would have been disappointed.

# Bibliography

*Establishment Clause Theory*

Braveman, Daan, *The Establishment Clause and the Course of Religious Neutrality*, 45 Maryland Law Review 352 (1986)

Conkle, Daniel O., *Religious Purpose, Inerrancy and the Establishment Clause*, 67 Indiana Law Journal 1 (1991)

Conkle, Daniel O., *Toward a General Theory of the Establishment Clause*, 82 Northwestern University Law Review 1113 (1988)

Redlich, Norman, *Separation of Church and State: The Burger Court's Tortuous Journey*, 60 Notre Dame Law Review 1094 (1985)

Van Alstyne, William, *What is "An Establishment of Religion"?*, 65 North Carolina Law Review 909 (1987)

## E.  Free Exercise Theory

This final section analyzes the Free Exercise Clause. Paul Marcus analyzes the post-ratification history of the Free Exercise Clause, and attempts to articulate standards governing its application. Jesse H. Choper argues that the Supreme Court "has interpreted the free exercise clause to provide a virtually unique protection for religion, one that is markedly greater than the security that the Constitution provides for speech", and attempts to articulate a new standard governing free exercise claims. Michael M. McConnell criticizes modern developments that have significantly recast free exercise doctrine. Douglas Laycock discusses the meaning of the principle that "government must be neutral toward religion." He argues that those who have tried to define the term neutrality "have produced quite inconsistent definitions."

Paul Marcus, *The Forum of Conscience:*
*Applying Standards Under the Free Exercise*
*Clause*, 1973 DUKE LAW JOURNAL 1217 (1973)*

. . .

Throughout the American experience, the right to
believe in and worship one's own concept of the
Supreme Deity has been said by judges and legislators alike to be a cherished and fundamental right at
the very heart of an individual's freedom. This right
to exercise one's religion is protected under the free
exercise clause of the first amendment and, along
with the rights of free speech and press, occupies a
"preferred position" in the constitutional hierarchy
of protected rights. While the free exercise clause
was held, relatively early, to apply to the states as
well as to the federal government, individuals asserting free exercise claims have generally been successful in neither state nor federal courts.

In passing on these claims, the courts have indicated a sharp theoretical awareness of the fundamental nature of free exercise rights and, through much
of this century, have said that a substantial free exercise claim would only be denied if the state could
demonstrate that it had a compelling purpose for its
statute. Nevertheless, until very recently the courts
consistently found such compelling purposes, no
matter how strong the free exercise argument.

The free exercise "losers" have been Mormons
who served stiff sentences for practicing polygamy,
and independently lost the right to vote; conscientious objectors who could not attend state-run universities, and could not, for a period, become natural-
ized citizens of the United States; Jehovah's Witnesses who, for a time, could be required to pay
flat license fees to sell their religious texts, and still
presumably can be prohibited from having their children sell or distribute religious literature in public;
and Black Muslims, who have had an uphill battle
in asserting the right to discuss and practice their
religion while in prison.

These groups, as well as groups with more unusual views, have historically failed miserably in
their free exercise arguments. As recently as 1957
a commentator reviewing the case law could, with
reasonable accuracy, make the following statement:

> [G]enerally when Congress or a state legisla-
> ture, in the exercise of some constitutional

power, enacts a statute which requires or prohibits some action, and makes the violation a
criminal offense, there is no requirement inherent in the First Amendment that religious
beliefs shall constitute a sufficient excuse or
justification for noncompliance with the terms
of the statute.

In short, Professor Kurland was probably correct
when he stated that, while the courts had generally
been tolerant toward religious minorities, "the caveat must be added that the minority must not be too
small or too eccentric."

Relief in the free exercise area, when granted,
tended to be based on alternative constitutional provisions. Indeed, even in his famous religious freedom-
flag salute opinion, Justice Jackson made it fairly
clear that his primary ground of decision was the free
speech clause rather than the free exercise clause.

It would be safe, therefore, to say that most
courts, and certainly the Supreme Court, had not
expressly resolved a major free exercise claim in
favor of the individual and against the state prior to
1963. Yet, in the short ten-year period since *Sherbert
v. Verner* the law of free exercise rights has changed
remarkably, culminating in *Wisconsin v. Yoder*.

. . .

## FORMULATING STANDARDS UNDER THE FREE EXERCISE CLAUSE

It has never been seriously suggested that rights
under the free exercise clause are any more absolute
than rights under any other section of the Constitution. Just as one may not yell "fire" in a crowded
theater when there is no fire, one may not kill an
unsuspecting person in order to make a religious sacrifice. As with cases arising under the free speech
clause, the question here is one of determining when
legitimate claims of the state or society must prevail
over constitutional rights conferred on the individual.

There has been a remarkable number of simple
cases in which free exercise claims have been raised
where this question is not difficult at all, for it is
clear in each such case that either the free exercise
claim is nonsensical or that the state, on other
grounds, must prevail: where a commercial perfor-
mer argues that he is entitled to perform a copy-
righted musical composition in pursuit of his alleged
religious rights; where a taxpayer refuses to disclose
recipients of his reported charitable deductions when
those donations constituted over 20% of his annual
gross income, on the ground that a disclosure would
unduly interfere with the practice of his religion;
where citizens move to block the public distribution
of fluoridated water on alleged religious grounds,

even though they are not compelled to purchase or use such water; where an employee, on religious grounds, refuses treatment for injuries suffered in the scope of his employment, but still seeks compensation for injuries which were compounded or caused by the refusal of the treatment; or where individuals, acting out of sincere religious beliefs, attempt to physically disrupt the administrative workings of the government.

It is not in such cases as these that the formulation of standards to resolve the conflict between the state's interest and the individual religious interest is so crucial. Rather, it is the close cases, where reasonable men can and do differ, that bare all the competing interests and considerations concerning the rights of individuals and the needs of society. These cases range from situations where persons are held in contempt for refusing to testify before a grand jury, to the Amish farmer who refuses to send his child to school beyond the eighth grade, to the orthodox Jew who may be forced out of his business as a result of a Sunday Closing Law.

With these tough cases one begins to hope, with Professor Wechsler, that the courts' resolutions will be based upon standards or principles which transcend the particular fact situation involved. The Supreme Court has recently begun to formulate such standards, although there remains considerable room for refinement. Before focusing on the application of these standards, it is important to consider briefly other standards used by the courts in deciding free exercise claims in order to note how inconsistent their disposition has been and to appreciate how truly dramatic is the Supreme Court's recent shift.

### Following the Founding Fathers' Wishes

A few relatively early cases held that the courts could only determine the validity of a free exercise claim by looking to the historical setting of the enactment of the first amendment and deciding if the founding fathers would have wished that particular claim to be given free exercise protection. While there has been a wealth of material written concerning the historical setting of the enactment of the free exercise clause, there are severe and relatively obvious problems with such a standard.

For one thing, the setting of the enactment of the first amendment is quite inconclusive as to what the founding fathers had in mind with regard to freedom of religion problems. Moreover, even if a particular problem might have been contemplated at the time, it is no doubt true that different individuals would have resolved it in very different ways.

More importantly, it is quite likely that specific problems which now arise, almost 200 years after the enactment of the first amendment, could not even have been imagined by the founding fathers. Claims for unemployment compensation, or the claims of individuals who argue that they use drugs to practice their religion, are hardly eighteenth century difficulties. Yet, while the particular considerations of eighteenth century men are inconclusive and beyond reach, their purpose of preventing a tyranny by the majority and by the state is as clear and vital today as ever.

Thus, without losing sight of the fundamental purpose underlying the free exercise clause, the courts have properly rejected a wooden analysis of history and instead have sought to develop standards appropriate to twentieth century problems. To have done otherwise would have been to defeat a recognition of a vibrant first amendment.

> [As to the founding fathers' views] concerning religious freedom and nonestablishment, we must inevitably find them encrusted with certain implicit assumptions which were products of prevailing social, political, and economic conditions. Doctrinal formulations designed to achieve certain ends may achieve indifferent or perverse results as the assumptions on which they rest change. As the social, political, and economic milieu evolves, so must the content given the first amendment.

### The Action-Belief Distinction

The distinction between conduct taken pursuant to religious beliefs, and religious beliefs themselves, reached its high point about thirty years ago. Some courts denied free exercise claims holding that even though the state could never interfere with one's religious beliefs, it could, if its regulation were rationally based, interfere with one's actions even if such actions were taken pursuant to the individual's religious beliefs. It was never clear from where the authority for such a distinction came. The Supreme Court never expressly based a holding on the distinction, though there is dicta which would seem to approve of it: "[The free exercise clause] safeguards the free exercise of the chosen form of religion. Thus the amendment embraces two concepts,—freedom to believe and freedom to act. The first is absolute but, in the nature of things, the second cannot be."

The distinction never received widespread approval and, though vestigial references to the doctrine still occasionally appear in free exercise cases, it has been thoroughly discredited by *Sherbert* and *Yoder*. It appears to be somewhat incongruous to make such a distinction when the first amendment speaks in terms of protecting the *exercise* of the religion, not simply the beliefs held under the religion. While it is true that "[t]he language of the First Amendment is to be read not as barren words found in a dictionary but as symbols of historic experience illuminated by the presuppositions of those who employed them," it must also be true that Congress meant *something* when it chose to refer to the free *exercise* of the religion, not simply to the freedom to believe in one's chosen religion. However narrowly defined the term "religion" may be, it must encompass action in addition to belief.

Carried to its logical conclusion, the distinction would become ludicrous, as can be seen by a simple example. Inspired by a determination of the Food and Drug Administration that consumption of unleavened bread may result in stomach disorders, a state enacts a statute forbidding the manufacture or consumption of unleavened bread. A certain faith, however, requires its adherents, as a matter of dogma, to partake of limited quantities of unleavened bread on the annual occasion of that faith's most sacred holy day. The statute, as applied in this context, would be held to violate the free exercise clause. Even though the statute may be a rational exercise of the state's police power, and would only be limiting religious conduct and not religious beliefs, it is difficult indeed to imagine a court sanctioning such a flagrant infringement of religious freedom when a less sweeping prohibition could achieve the same statutory objective.

### Neutral Standards

Immediately after the Sunday closing cases, Professor Kurland wrote of his concern for the relationship of the free exercise clause to the establishment clause. Since that time, a number of commentators have written in response to Professor Kurland's analysis of that relationship. Still Professor Kurland's discussion of the relationship remains the most cogent and significant. Professor Kurland argued that the two religious clauses in the first amendment are inseparable and must be treated as such by the courts, so that the state may not lawfully use religion or religious belief as a standard either for governmental action or inaction. Neither burdens nor benefits may flow from the existence of a particular religion or religious belief; religion must be a neutral factor in formulating and applying regulatory schemes. The state has as little right to promote the religious rights of individuals as it has to infringe them. Thus, when a court invalidates a statute, it may not do so on free exercise grounds unless it is also invalidated as to nonreligious individuals—otherwise the result would be a violation of the establishment clause.

The argument no doubt has a certain straightforward appeal and persuasiveness. As noted in a different context, however, "[t]he problem with the argument is that all the authorities are against him." Those few courts that have seriously considered the questions raised by Professor Kurland have uniformly rejected his contentions. For example, in *Commonwealth v. Arlan's Department Store of Louisville*, the state had created an exception to its Sunday closing law for persons who observed a Sabbath day other than Sunday. The petitioner, a department store seeking to stay open on Sunday, argued that such an exception violated the state's neutrality requirement under the establishment clause. The court's response was succinct: "[T]he exemption does not affirmatively prefer any religion nor amount to the establishment of a religion. Rather, it simply avoids penalizing economically the person who conscientiously observes a "Sabbath other than Sunday."

In essence, the answer in *Arlan's* is that which can be given generally to Professor Kurland: his broad conception of the establishment clause has never been accepted by the American judiciary, perhaps because to give it effect would be to largely emasculate the free exercise clause. This problem is especially visible in the area of religious exemptions from statutes of otherwise general applicability, which the Kurland thesis would not allow on the theory that the exemption constitutes a state-conferred benefit for the religious group involved. Where these exemptions are necessary to prevent the infringement of sincerely held religious beliefs, and where it is determined that a limited exemption would not defeat an overriding state interest of compelling character, the courts have focused on free exercise and granted relief—despite the arguable "benefit" to the religious claimants. The response to the establishment clause objections to these results is that such exemptions merely tailor a statute, enacted without respect to the establishment of religion, so as to accommodate the imperatives of free exercise. Any incidental benefit to a particular religious group thus is attributable not to the statutory enactment or exemption, but to the free exercise limitations upon the legislative power. Only where the classification of "religion" for purposes of triggering the exemption is so narrowly drawn as to exclude those who assert other than traditionally recognized religious convictions do establishment clause considerations tangentially arise. It was this problem that various members of the Supreme Court addressed in *Welsh v. United States*.

In *Welsh*, a case actually decided on statutory rather than free exercise grounds, a conscientious objector had refused to submit to military induction, but his refusal was not based on traditional religious grounds. Justice Black, for a plurality of the Court, held that section 6j of the Universal Military Training and Service Act could properly be construed so as to include Welsh's moral and ethical beliefs so long as these beliefs were held with the strength of traditional religious convictions. Justice Harlan concurred in the result on the ground that a construction other than that put forth by Justice Black would be contrary to the establishment clause, as it would have benefited individuals solely because of their religious beliefs.

Justice White—in a dissent joined by the Chief Justice and Justice Stewart—spoke directly to the establishment contention raised by Harlan. Relying on the argument of Justice Frankfurter in the Sunday closing cases, he stated that to deny an exemption to Welsh because his views were not religious would not result in a breach of the neutrality requirement under the establishment clause. Justice Frankfurter had argued that a state action would lose its presumption of neutrality "only if the absence of any substantial legislative purpose other than a religious one is made to appear.

The three *Welsh* dissenters found at least one such legislative purpose—a practical judgment that religious objectors might be of no use in combat—so that limiting the 6j exemptions to traditional religious views

> would be no more an establishment of religion than the exemption required for Sabbatarians in *Sherbert v. Verner* or the exemption from the flat tax on booksellers held required for an evangelist, *Follett v. McCormick*. Surely a statutory exemption for religionists required by the Free Exercise Clause is not an invalid establishment because it fails to include non-religious believers as well; nor would it be less an establishment if camouflaged by granting additional exemptions for non-religious, but "moral" objections to war.

Thus, two distinct approaches to the "neutrality" problem were advanced in the *Welsh* opinions. The first, embraced by Justice Harlan in his concurring opinion, averts collision with the establishment clause by adopting a sufficiently broad definition of "religion" for free exercise purposes as to negate any inference of favoritism. The second, embodied in Justice White's dissent, insists that "the First Amendment itself contains a religious classification"—. . . a classification which need not be expanded to include nonreligious believers under the rubric of "neutrality." Either approach seems to

bely the necessity of strict neutrality. In the subsequent case of *Gillette v. United States*, however, the Court clearly expressed its preference for Justice White's approach. By an eight to one vote, the Court denied that limiting the section 6j exemption to those opposed to all wars, as distinct from those merely opposed to "unjust" wars, violated the establishment clause.

A final response to the Kurland theory is that exemptions limited to a particular religious group may be all that the free exercise clause *can* require in a particular situation. Free exercise, like free speech, is not an absolute, and thus its imperatives must be balanced against compelling state interests. Consequently, while an exemption limited to a small religious minority might not undermine a state policy advanced in a particular statute, the extension of the same exemption to a much broader array of claimants might well do so. Thus, in limiting an exemption to a particular religious group, the court or the legislature merely recognizes the limits of free exercise rather than advancing the particular religious cause.

Despite the failure of the neutrality theory to gain a toehold in the courts, it is not inconceivable that the expanding scope of free exercise relief might resurrect concern with the potential establishment clause problems. Whether the doctrinal responses to the Kurland theory discussed above would withstand such a renewed attack remains to be seen. If not, it is to be hoped that instances of apparent conflict between the two clauses will not result in automatic subordination of the libertarian objectives of free exercise to a scrupulous preoccupation with establishment problems.

### Direct/Indirect Burdens

In *Braunfeld*, Chief Justice Warren discussed for the first time the importance of the distinction between indirect burdens on free exercise rights and direct burdens. A direct burden results when a religious practice itself is outlawed. A good example of a direct burden would be the criminal prosecution of a polygamist, where it is the actual practice of the religion which subjects the individual to criminal sanctions. An indirect burden was involved in the Sunday closing cases. There, Orthodox Jews were not restricted from practicing aspects of their religion, so long as their businesses were not open on Sundays. Since indirect burdens could be viewed as operating less restrictively on free exercise, it could be argued that the state carried a lesser burden of justification in cases where they were involved.

While it has been argued that this distinction is significant, few cases were actually ever resolved in reliance on it. Indeed, the decisions in the Sunday closing cases themselves were not based on this distinction. The Chief Justice was careful to point out that even as to indirect burdens, the state would have to demonstrate that there was no alternative method of accomplishing its rational purpose which would not infringe on free exercise rights.

Almost two years to a day later the distinction was eliminated for all practical purposes by the Court in *Sherbert*. The burden in *Sherbert* was once again indirect, yet Justice Brennan, for the majority, stated that the state would not only have to demonstrate that there were no alternative ways of accomplishing its purpose, but it would also have to show that its purpose was so compelling as to justify interference with the individual's religious rights. While Justice Brennan avoided expressly overruling *Braunfeld*, certainly the direct/indirect burden distinction with regard to the nature of the showing required by the state was wholly rejected by the majority in *Sherbert*.

### Balancing of Interests

There are two kinds of balancing formulations which have been used by the courts in the free speech and, from time to time, in the free exercise areas. The first is the ad hoc balancing of interests, so called because the court is asked to look to the particular facts involved in the case before it and to weigh the interests of the state therein against the interests of the individual. It then determines if the state's infringement of the individual's rights is justified under such facts.

In balancing interests under the free exercise clause in this fashion, the individual has to make a threshold showing that the case does involve an infringement of his religious rights; at that point the state is called upon to convince the court that its regulation is a rational one. Once both showings have been made, the court proceeds to balance the interest of the state in promulgating the regulation against the individual's interest in taking the restricted action and to determine which interest prevails.

The chief benefit of the ad hoc balancing method is its flexibility, as it enables a judge to consider the circumstances of the particular matter being contested. In this way it is hoped that the courts will be able to avoid rigid, unrealistic approaches to adjudicating sensitive first amendment questions.

The major problem with the pure ad hoc balancing approach is that no matter what sort of guidelines the court utilizes to weigh the interests—and a number of incisive commentators have focused on the kinds of guidelines and interests that ought to be involved in the free exercise area—the approach necessarily is

based upon a consideration of factors in only the specific case. Hence, it is the antithesis of that which Professor Wechsler would hope for: neutral principles that transcend the particular fact situation. That is, "ad hoc balancing by hypothesis means that there is no rule to be applied, but only interests to be weighed." The fact that there is no rule of law to be applied means that a citizen "has no standard by which he can measure whether his interests . . . will be held of greater or lesser weight than the competing interest. . . ." More important, perhaps, is that when the courts balance the interests of an individual citizen against the interest of the state, "it is more than mere coincidence" that the state usually wins. This is especially true in speech cases, for "in non-speech areas . . . public passions do not generally ride as high" as in speech areas; yet, no doubt courts have been, and will continue to be, loathe to turn away the states generally on claims of security, health and welfare.

The second approach has been labeled the "definitional balance." As explained by Professor DuVal,

> [D]efinitional balancing seeks to formulate rules for differentiating between protected and unprotected expression. In formulating this distinction, the interests in freedom of expression must be weighed against competing governmental interests in much the same manner as under the ad hoc balancing test. The outcome of the process, however, is a rule which governs not only the case before the court, but future cases as well. . . . Moreover, the adoption of a rule will make it easier for the courts to resist popular pressures for suppression in particular cases.

Probably the most famous definitional balance took place in *New York Times v. Sullivan*. There, the Supreme Court determined that libel laws violated the first amendment when such laws were applied to render defendants liable for false statements concerning a public official and published without knowledge of falsehood or reckless disregard for the truth.

Professor Nimmer, in referring to *New York Times*, succinctly explains the difference between the two balancing approaches:

> [I]t should be made clear that there was balancing in *Times*, but that it was not ad hoc balancing. There was balancing in the sense that not all defamatory speech was held to be protected by the first amendment. The Court could not determine which segment of defamatory speech lies outside the umbrella of the first amendment purely on logical grounds, and no

pretence of logical inexorability was made. By in effect holding that knowingly and recklessly false speech was not "speech" within the meaning of the first amendment, the Court must have implicitly (since no explicit explanation was offered) referred to certain competing policy considerations. This is surely a kind of balancing, but it is just as surely not ad hoc balancing.

If the Court had followed the ad hoc approach, it would have inquired whether "under the particular circumstances presented" the interest of the defendants in publishing their particular advertisement outweighed the interest of the plaintiff in the protection of his reputation. This in turn would have led to such imponderable issues as: How important was it to the defendants (or possibly to the public at large) that this particular advertisement be published? How "serious" was the injury to the plaintiff's reputation caused by the advertisement?

Thus, for situations in which the law of libel (or invasion of privacy) comes into conflict with the first amendment, the Court was able to define a fixed threshold which must be met by any plaintiff who would overcome the assertion of first amendment rights—that is, a showing of knowing falsehood or reckless disregard for the truth. In this fashion, the need for case-by-case situational balancing was substantially reduced: if the plaintiff cannot make the threshold showing, the Court need go no farther.

The Supreme Court in *Sherbert* and *Yoder* appears to have combined the two approaches in formulating a free exercise balance. The current free exercise test may be stated simply: if the individual demonstrates that his actions are sincerely religious and have been interfered with as a result of a state regulation, the state must demonstrate that it has a compelling interest in the regulation, an interest which could not be promoted by any less restrictive means. If the state makes that demonstration, it prevails in the case; if not, it loses.

The test consists of ad hoc balancing because in each particular case a court must determine if a given state interest is substantial, if a person's rights are indeed religious, and if religious, whether they have been interfered with. It is not purely ad hoc in nature, however, for the Court has defined certain state interests—such as problems of administration and weeding out fraudulent claims—as not substantial in any case, and has further established that even an indirect burden may constitute an infringement of free exercise rights.

The test, having been formulated relatively recently, has not yet experienced any variety of severe problems in reported opinions. It would not be difficult, however, to conjecture criticisms that will be raised. For example, one criticism of the test will surely be that judges and perhaps juries are asked to make an inquiry into a particular individual's religious sincerity. The chief critic of such inquiries was Justice Jackson. In *United States v. Ballard*, the defendant, a member of the "I am" movement, had been prosecuted for fraud. He was convicted of using the mails to solicit contributions, having represented himself to be a messenger of God.

The Court held that it would be violative of the first amendment to inquire into the objective truth or falsity of the defendant's representations, but it would be proper to examine the defendant's state of mind to determine if his representations were fraudulent. Justice Jackson took exception to the latter point.

[A]s a matter of either practice or philosophy, I do not see how we can separate an issue as to what is believed from considerations as to what is believable. . . . If we try religious sincerity severed from religious verity, we isolate the dispute from the very considerations which in common experience provide its most reliable answer.

While this writer is unable to discern why a court could not look to whether a defendant is sincerely religious when it can, for example, determine if a defendant's activities are ideologically motivated rather than commercially motivated, some commentators have argued that Justice Jackson's position has at least limited validity. Professor Giannella, for instance, has suggested that the "no inquiry" theory may serve to limit the government's power to restrict arbitrarily the activities of fringe religions on the grounds that such religions are "spurious." Nonetheless, the Jackson position has never been adopted by the Supreme Court or by many lower courts, and most judges routinely permit evidence to be presented concerning the sincerity of the individual in free exercise actions.

The second criticism of the evolving test concerns the necessity of determining whether particular actions or beliefs are religious for purposes of first amendment protection. Indeed, at least one court has stated, albeit in an indirect fashion, that it is beyond its power to say whether a belief or action is religious for purposes of the first amendment:

Defendants have not argued that the beliefs of Elijah Mohammed Muslims do not constitute a religion. A determination that they do not would be indistinguishable from a comparative evaluation of religions, and that process is beyond the power of a court.

This kind of reasoning is wholly indefensible, for determining what is the exercise of religion for purposes of the first amendment does not differ, in substance, from determining what is speech for purposes of the first amendment—a demanding, but wholly necessary operation. Without any definitional threshold enormous problems would arise in trying to maintain a viable, but not unlimited, free exercise clause.

With regard to the practical problem of defining what is religious for the purposes of the first amendment, a number of commentators have tried, with varying degrees of success, to formulate definitions to assist the courts. For the purposes of this article, we shall employ a short but broad definition. The term religion will be defined here, as in the statutory selective service cases, as any "sincere and meaningful belief, which occupies in the life of its possessor a place parallel to that filled by [commonly accepted notions] . . . of God. . . ."

Although this definition could be susceptible to overly-expansive application, such broad contours may be necessary to forestall the resurrection of establishment clause objections to particularized free exercise exemptions. Moreover, any dubious claim which passes the definitional test only because of its pliancy would be unlikely to possess the substance needed to offset a compelling state interest under the balancing test.

The major inadequacy of the current balancing test, as applied by the Supreme Court, is its failure to encompass a necessary third step which would be essentially ad hoc in nature. The Court takes its first step in determining whether the individual's actions are sincere and religious, and whether they have been infringed by the state. It then takes the second step in deciding whether or not the state has a compelling interest for its action, an interest which could not be promoted by any less restrictive action. At this point some "definitional balancing" may occur, in that certain state interests, such as administrative convenience, may be dismissed as short of "compelling" as a matter of law. If, however, the state interest *is* compelling, the Court stops and the state automatically wins, even if the individual's interest is exceptionally compelling.

The third step proposed here would be to weigh, on an ad hoc basis, the importance of the state's interest against the importance of the individual's interest. Although this added step might render the free exercise standards less predictable in some cases, it is submitted that careful application of the "sincerity" test to the religious claim and the "compelling interest" test to the state's justification will assure maximum desirable predictability in this area by deciding most cases before they reach this third step. Those cases pitting a sincere religious belief against a compelling state interest, the "close" cases, do not lend themselves to the relatively unyielding contours of definitional balancing. Considerations such as whether the individual's practice of his religion would be effectively destroyed and whether the state's interest occupies a priority in its hierarchy of values, among others, would be appropriate in such an added balance.

While the necessity for such an added step cannot be shown from either *Sherbert* or *Yoder*—because in each case no compelling state interest was found—the problem is certainly by no means purely academic. Indeed, in a large number of situations, such as the drug use and vaccination cases, the problem is acute.

For example, in *People v. Woody*, the California Supreme Court recognized the problem in resolving an especially difficult free exercise issue. There, a group of Navaho Indians were arrested for possessing peyote. The Navahos proved that the state's restriction on the use of peyote severely limited their ability to exercise their religion. Though the court found that the state had a substantial interest in controlling the use of drugs, even non-addictive drugs, the convictions were reversed on the ground that the Navahos' interest in practicing Peyotism outweighed the interest of the state in having them abstain from peyote. Under the Supreme Court's two-step approach in *Sherbert* and *Yoder*, the California court would never have reached this result in *Woody*, for as soon as the state demonstrated a compelling interest, the case would have been over. If the state's interest is compelling, the religious practice, regardless of its urgency, cannot prevail under the current test.

Such a result would have been improper in *Woody*, for while the state's interest may have been substantial as a general matter, this was a situation where the defendants' religion was wholly eliminated by a state regulation, a regulation which did not even arguably involve the restriction of unusually harmful drugs. Moreover, the defendants' action did not result in any interference with the rights or interests of others. Thus, on balance, the defendants' interest properly prevailed over the state's.

. . .

## CONCLUSION

The Supreme Court within the last ten years has

expanded the scope and application of the previously dormant free exercise clause, as well as the scope of inquiry into the state interests set up in opposition to free exercise claims. It has been the goal of this Article to focus on the Supreme Court's formulation of standards for adjudicating free exercise questions, and to apply these standards to a wide assortment of important free exercise fact situations. It is hoped that the courts will continue to take a long look at the broad arguments raised by the state and federal governments in this area, for it is only in the context of such vigilant concern for free exercise rights that the statement of John Stuart Mill will become reality for religious minorities:

> [T]he worth of a State, in the long run is the worth of the individuals composing it; and a State which postpones the interest of *their* mental expansion and elevation, to a little more of administrative skill, or that semblance of it which practice gives, in the details of business; a State which dwarfs its men, in order that they may be more docile instruments in its hands even for beneficial purposes—will find that with small men no great thing can really be accomplished; and that the perfection of machinery to which it has sacrificed everything, will in the end avail it nothing, for want of the vital power which, in order that the machine might work more smoothly, it has preferred to banish.

---

Jesse H. Choper, *The Free Exercise Clause: A Structural Overview and an Appraisal of Recent Developments*, 27 WILLIAM & MARY LAW REVIEW 943 (1986)*

## I. INTRODUCTION

The free exercise clause, the second of the two religion clauses in the first amendment, is the focus of this Article. Since the early 1970's, the Burger Court has either promulgated or specifically reaffirmed almost all significant aspects of the doctrine surrounding this constitutional protection for religious freedom. Indeed, the Supreme Court, and the Burger Court in particular, has interpreted the free

exercise clause to provide a virtually unique protection for religion, one that is markedly greater than the security that the Constitution provides for speech.

The purpose of this Article is four-fold: first, to identify several distinct kinds of government action that raise significant problems under the free exercise clause; second, to describe and appraise what the Burger Court has done with respect to this provision; third, to indicate a number of serious difficulties that arise from the Court's pronouncements in this area; and fourth, to suggest a better approach to resolving some of the problems.

## II. NEUTRAL GOVERNMENT ACTIONS IMPLICATING FREE EXERCISE CONCERNS

The first general type of government action that presents a genuine issue under the free exercise clause is a regulation that has a secular purpose but that has an effect or impact that conflicts with the tenets of a particular religion. In this instance, the Court, drawing on a famous dictum in *Cantwell v. Connecticut*, has distinguished between "freedom to believe and freedom to act."

### A. Laws With a Secular Purpose But an Impact on Religious Beliefs

Laws that regulate religious beliefs are very unusual. The Court has said that the Constitution absolutely forbids the federal or state governments from regulating religious beliefs. Probably the best illustration is *West Virginia State Board of Education v. Barnette*, in which several Jehovah's Witnesses challenged the obligation to salute the flag in public schools as being contrary to their religious beliefs concerning the worship of graven images. The Court persuasively reasoned that this was an effort by the State to force someone to embrace or express a belief.

*Barnette* did not rest on the free exercise clause, but rather on the broader first amendment protection of freedom of expression. The rationale, however, is the same. It was repeated within the past decade in *Wooley v. Maynard*, in which the Court considered the claim of a Jehovah's Witness who did not want his license plate to bear the New Hampshire state motto, "Live Free or Die." The Court held that the first amendment freedom of speech barred the State from prosecuting him for covering the motto on his license plate, reasoning that the law was forcing him to embrace or express a belief.

### B. Laws With a Secular Purpose But an Impact on Religious Actions

The Supreme Court's most significant doctrinal pronouncement has come with respect to neutral, secular laws that regulate action. When the impact of such regulations conflicts with the tenets of a particular religion, by requiring persons to do something that their religion prohibits or by forbidding them from doing something that their religion demands, the Burger Court has found an abridgment of religious liberty unless the government satisfies what, essentially, is a test of "strict scrutiny." Unless the government can show an overriding, substantial, compelling, or important interest that cannot be achieved by some narrower, alternative means, the individual is constitutionally entitled to an exemption from the regulation.

A leading Burger Court ruling, *Wisconsin v. Yoder*, illustrates the point. Wisconsin had compulsory education until the age of sixteen. The Old Order Amish have a religious tenet, which the Court accepted as a good faith observance of their faith, that holds that sending Amish children to accredited public schools beyond the eighth grade would corrupt them, make them too worldly, and endanger their salvation. In *Yoder*, therefore, the Amish argued that they were entitled to an exemption from the compulsory education law. The Court, in a virtually unanimous decision, agreed. Weighing all the circumstances, the Court held that the State's interest was not strong enough to require the Amish to engage in conduct that was contrary to their religious beliefs.

A contrast between the facts in *Yoder* and a hypothetical situation substantiates the point that the Constitution protects religion to a significantly greater extent than almost anything else—including the freedoms of expression and association, which we generally believe to be at the core of the democratic process. Suppose that Mrs. Yoder, the mother of these children, decided to run for elective office and urged that having her children out of school for a few months before the end of her campaign, working for her full time, was critical to her election chances. Suppose further that she took her children out of school and that the State attempted to prosecute her under the same Wisconsin statute challenged in *Yoder*. Finally, suppose that Mrs. Yoder then contended at trial that Wisconsin's compulsory education requirement violated her freedom of expression and association because running for elective office is a pristine method of exercising that right. The Court almost certainly would give less than short shrift to that position. Thus, if the argument is made under the free exercise clause, it wins in the Supreme Court, virtually unanimously, yet when the argument is framed in terms of freedom of expression and association it appears to be a certain loser.

In addition to *Yoder*, the other famous decision

that illustrates the Court's doctrinal framework is *Sherbert v. Verner*. That case involved a Seventh-day Adventist who worked in the textile mills in South Carolina. Seventh-day Adventists celebrate their Sabbath on Saturday. The mills had worked five days a week, Monday through Friday, but then had gone to a six-day week including Saturday. Sherbert had said that she could not work on Saturday because of her religious beliefs. She had been fired, and she had sought unemployment compensation. The rule was that she could not get unemployment compensation if she refused "suitable work." Although no textile mill would have employed Sherbert without requiring Saturday work, the state board had concluded that she had refused to accept suitable work and thus had denied her benefits. The Supreme Court held that the free exercise clause requires an exemption from this "suitable work" requirement so that she could receive unemployment compensation.

## III. DEFICIENCIES IN THE BURGER COURT'S APPROACH AND A PROPOSED ALTERNATIVE

The Court's decisions in *Yoder* and *Sherbert* highlight a major difficulty with the Court's approach under the religion clauses, one of both logic and policy. The problem arises from the Burger Court's interpretation of the other religion clause, the establishment clause. This difficulty is especially the result of the most significant part of the Court's approach to finding an abridgment of that provision—the firmly embedded principle that a religious purpose alone will make a law violative of the establishment clause.

As a matter of policy, this doctrine casts great doubt on many deeply ingrained practices in our country. The placement of "In God We Trust" on coins and currency, for example, seems to have no real purpose other than a religious one. Moreover, the proclamations by almost all our Presidents of national days of Thanksgiving to "Almighty God" only seem fairly characterized as having a religious purpose. If one takes seriously the Court's doctrine that a religious purpose alone produces a violation of the establishment clause, these and many other longstanding practices in our society must be held invalid.

How does the Court deal with this conflict between its doctrine and established national policies? Although a majority of the justices have applied this "religious purpose equals invalidity" principle strictly on several occasions, the Supreme Court simply ignores its own articulated test when it wishes to uphold a deeply ingrained national practice that clashes with this doctrine. This tactic was illustrated vividly in *Marsh v. Chambers*, when the court held that Nebraska's payment of $320 per month to a chaplain to open each legislative day with a prayer did not violate the establishment clause.

More directly relevant for purposes of this Article, this principle is subject to even greater difficulty as a matter of logic, because it is at war with the Supreme Court's own doctrine under the free exercise clause. The Court's free exercise clause doctrine not only permits states to give exemptions to aid religion, but sometimes, as the Court's decisions in *Yoder* and *Sherbert* demonstrate, the rule requires states to give such exemptions. On the one hand, the Court has read the establishment clause as saying that if a law's purpose is to aid religion, it is unconstitutional. On the other hand, the Court has read the free exercise clause as saying that, under certain circumstances, the state must aid religion. Logically, the two theses are irreconcilable.

How should this conflict be resolved? When should the Court hold that the free exercise clause requires religious exemption from an ordinary government regulation? There is a simple principle that would resolve all issues under the establishment clause and that would be central in approaching most basic issues under the free exercise clause. Government action should be held to violate the establishment clause if it meets two criteria: first, if its purpose is to aid religion; and second, if it significantly endangers religious liberty in some way by coercing, compromising, or influencing religious beliefs.

Under this approach, *Yoder* was correctly decided. Although an exemption for the Old Order Amish children did serve an exclusively religious purpose, it did not coerce, compromise, or influence anyone's religious beliefs. People were not lining up to join the Old Order Amish so they could get their children out of school before the age of sixteen. In the absence of proof of this kind, the exemption posed no danger to religious liberty, even though it served a religious purpose. Therefore, under my proposed approach, the Supreme Court's decision under the free exercise clause did not violate the establishment clause.

*Sherbert*, however, generates a different conclusion under my approach. The first part of the test yields the same result, because the purpose of giving Sherbert the money was solely to assist her religion. To illustrate, suppose Sherbert had said: "I used to work in the mills Monday through Friday. When they went to Saturday, I refused to work that day and was fired. I want unemployment compensation." When asked why she refused to work on Saturday, suppose she had responded, "Because I am a work-

ing mother with children in school. Having to be away Monday through Friday when they come home from school is bad enough. I want to spend Saturday and Sunday with them. I feel very strongly about this. It is a central part of my life." When asked if this involved her religion, suppose Sherbert had replied: "This has nothing to do with religion." Sherbert would get nowhere in the Supreme Court with the argument that a denial of unemployment benefits under these circumstances violated her constitutional rights, at least under existing doctrine. The Court granted an exemption in *Sherbert* for religion alone.

The second criterion in my approach, however, yields a different result because, unlike the exemption in *Yoder*, the exemption in *Sherbert* required South Carolina to use compulsorily raised tax funds to assist religious ends. Most individuals would agree, in general, both as a matter of historical intent and of contemporary values, that one of the principal purposes of the establishment clause is to prevent government from giving compulsorily raised tax funds to churches, whether a particular taxpayer agrees with those churches or disagrees with them. For the government to a give taxpayer's money to religion, even the religion of that taxpayer's choice, is a pristine violation of the establishment clause. A taxpayer's religious freedom is violated when the government forces support of the taxpayer's own religion, and the violation is even more egregious when the government forces support of someone else's religion. That is the consequence when the government distributes tax funds for religious purposes, in contrast to distribution for secular purposes, which implicates no such claim even when a taxpayer does not like the way government spends the money. I cannot distinguish the payment of funds to Sherbert from the grant of a million dollars to support the Presbyterian Church, which most people would agree is an obvious violation of the establishment clause.

*Sherbert* involved unemployment compensation to the Seventh Day Adventist religion, and *only* for religion. The purpose of the exemption, therefore, was religious. Further, the compelled compensation abridged religious liberty. Both criteria under my proposed approach for finding an establishment clause violation are met. In sum, the Court was doubly wrong in *Sherbert*. Not only was South Carolina's denial of unemployment compensation to Sherbert not a violation of the free exercise clause, it was a violation of the establishment clause for the Court to require the State to grant it to her.

## IV. BURGER COURT VACILLATIONS

The decisions just discussed indicate that the

Burger Court has interpreted the free exercise clause generously. This largess always has had limits, however, and recent evidence suggests that the Burger Court's benevolence may be substantially spent. In almost every Term since the high-water mark for the free exercise clause was reached in 1981, the Court has treated religious freedom claims much less charitably. This Article, then, turns to the recent decisions in which the Court has found adequate government interests under the free exercise clause—that is, interests great enough to survive "strict scrutiny"—when religiously dictated actions and neutral government regulations have clashed.

As is often true in life, two major areas of concern in recent decisions have involved war and taxes. As for war, the Court in *Gillette v. United States* repeated the oft-stated dictum that the government's strong interest in national security does not require an exemption from the draft for people opposed on religious grounds. As for taxes, the Court in *United States v. Lee* upheld the application of the Social Security tax to members of the Old Order Amish faith.

The decision in *Lee* was particularly significant because of its factual similarity to *Yoder*. In *Lee*, a member of the Old Order Amish employed several other members of that religion in his business. The employer had refused to pay Social Security taxes on his employees' wages. Because of a literal interpretation of the Bible, the Amish sincerely believe that a failure to provide for their own aged would be a sin. As a consequence, the Amish forbid both the paying of Social Security taxes, which ultimately are used for government care of the elderly, and the receipt of Social Security benefits. The Court stated that, under these circumstances, the issue was whether requiring the Amish to pay—or whether refusing to grant them an exemption—"is essential to accomplishing an overriding governmental interest." The Court unanimously held that it was, and therefore that the failure to grant an exemption did not violate the free exercise clause.

The result in *Lee* is problematic under the standard of strict scrutiny. The Court's first justification was that mandatory participation in the Social Security system is indispensable to the system's fiscal vitality. At first blush, that is a perfectly plausible position, given the well known financial problems of the Social Security system and the efforts to get greater participation to help solve these difficulties. The Court did cite some statements from congressional reports to this effect, but it certainly did not give the matter much scrutiny. Recall that the Amish religion forbids not merely the payment of Social Security taxes, but also the receipt of Social Security benefits. In light of this fact, Justice Stevens persuasively contended in his separate concurrence that an exemption from both ends of the transaction for the Amish probably would save the government money in the long run.

Problems also arise with respect to the Court's second justification, the lack of any principled way to distinguish *Lee* from cases in which people have claimed religious exemptions from other taxes. In many instances, for example, courts denied exemptions to people who refused to pay a large proportion of their income tax because the proceeds of this tax go to support the Defense Department and they were religiously opposed to war. Such cases, however, are quite easily distinguishable from *Lee*. In *Lee*, nothing indicated that an exemption for the Amish would have caused the Social Security system to suffer any net diminution of revenues. The Amish refused to pay in, but they also refused to take out. The same thing cannot be said when individuals withhold a fixed portion of their income taxes because that portion of the national budget goes for defense and those individuals are religiously opposed to war. In this situation, the government may well have a compelling interest in mandatory participation in the income tax system, because mandatory participation is necessary to the fiscal integrity of the government. That compelling interest, however, was not present in *Lee*.

The highly questionable result in *Lee* indicates the justices' discomfort with their own doctrine, which grants a very special right to people who claim exemption from secular government regulations because of their religious beliefs. The Court appeared to make clear in *Lee* that, in addition to war, it was going to draw a line at taxes, even though this position was very hard to justify under its doctrine.

In 1983, the Court produced a third example of a government interest strong enough to override a free exercise claim. *Bob Jones University v. United States* involved the denial of tax exempt status to several private schools because they engaged in racial discrimination. The Court—without dissent on this point —agreed that there was a "compelling governmental interest" in eradicating racial discrimination in education, and that the government had "no 'less restrictive means' . . . available to achieve" that goal. The justices concluded, therefore, that the government's denial of tax exempt status to these schools did not violate the free exercise clause. Thus, after *Bob Jones University*, the Burger Court had identified three major government interests that will survive free exercise clause challenges: war, taxes, and the national policy against racial discrimination.

Two rulings, subsequent to *Bob Jones University* but prior to the Burger Court's final Term, further indicate the justices' greatly reduced enthusiasm for the "strict scrutiny" approach. Although the first decision, *Estate of Thornton v. Caldor, Inc.*, did not directly implicate the free exercise clause, it is suggestive of the Court's attitude. *Thornton* involved a Connecticut statute that required private employers to give employees a day off on their Sabbath, regardless of the burden or inconvenience either to the employer or to other employees. In a nearly unanimous decision, the Court held that this statute violated the establishment clause. The Court reasoned that the law advanced a "particular religious practice," and that its grant of an "absolute and unqualified right not to work" abridged the constitutional separation of church and state.

The purpose of the Connecticut statute plainly was religious, as were the actions required of Wisconsin and South Carolina by the Court in *Yoder* and *Sherbert*. Under my proposed approach, however, a religious purpose alone is not enough to trigger a violation of the establishment clause. The state action also must pose some meaningful danger to religious liberty. Because the opportunity to be excused from work on one's Sabbath would neither coerce nor influence people to join any religion or a particular religion, and because no use of tax funds for religious purposes was involved, no danger to religious freedom was posed. As a result, the Connecticut statute should be viewed simply as an attempt to accommodate religion, and not as a violation of the establishment clause. The statute certainly imposed a potential cost on employers and employees—a burden or inconvenience to accommodate the religious beliefs of certain fellow workers. As long as the statute did not coerce, compromise, or influence religious choice, however, it should not have been found violative of the establishment clause.

The Court's second decision, *Quaring v. Peterson*, appeared even more threatening to the future vitality of the free exercise clause; indeed, it could fairly be described as a potential coup de grace. That case involved a Nebraska rule requiring photographs on all driver's licenses, as applied to a person who sincerely believed that the Second Commandment's prohibition of "graven images" forbade her to be photographed. The United States Court of Appeals for the Eighth Circuit held that Nebraska's refusal to grant a religious exemption from this rule violated the free exercise clause. The Supreme Court granted certiorari but, with Justice Powell not participating, it affirmed by an equally divided Court, without opinion.

Any reasonable application of the "strict scrutiny" test would produce a result vindicating the free exercise claim in *Quaring*. From the claimant's standpoint, the burden of not having a driver's license obviously was substantial, given the need to have a driver's license for employment purposes and other essential activities. Although the State's interest could not be characterized as frivolous, on the other hand, it surely could not be viewed as anything more than quite modest. For example, some states, including New York, have managed to find rapid means of identification other than a driver's license photograph. The fact that four justices of the Supreme Court would reject the free exercise claim in *Quaring*, therefore, boded poorly for robust enforcement of the free exercise clause in the future.

The product of the Burger Court's final Term, however, flashed a contrary signal. The question presented in *Goldman v. Weinberger*, whether the Air Force may prohibit an Orthodox Jewish psychologist from wearing a yarmulke while in uniform on duty at a military hospital, seemed answerable only in favor of the individual under the test of "strict scrutiny." Although a narrowly divided Court rejected the free exercise claim, it did so by putting the case in a special "military affairs" category, which greatly limited the decision's more general precedential force. Of greater consequence for the continued vitality of the free exercise clause was a majority's invocation of the strict scrutiny approach in *Bowen v. Roy* in holding that a person whose sincere Native American religious beliefs forbade the use of Social Security numbers was entitled to an exemption from the requirement that recipients of food stamps and Aid to Families with Dependent Children furnish their Social Security numbers. The fact that Justice O'Connor, who would have sustained the free exercise claim in *Goldman*, authored the prevailing opinion in *Roy* may be of particular significance in the years ahead.

## V. GOVERNMENT ACTIONS THAT EXPRESSLY DEAL WITH RELIGION

### A. Laws That Treat Religion Adversely

Another kind of government action that raises serious problems under the free exercise clause is a regulation that explicitly singles out a particular religion, or religion generally, for adverse treatment. For example, an ordinance that required Catholics to stay off the streets, or forbade people from attending the church of their choice, would fall into this category. The Burger Court decision that best illustrates the proposition that such laws almost always are forbidden is *McDaniel v. Paty*, which involved a Tennessee statute that disqualified clergy from either serving in the legislature or acting as delegates to a state constitutional convention. Statutes that on their face put one or all religions in a disadvantageous position are quite unusual. *McDaniel* is important not so much for the Court's rationale, which was muddled by several opinions, but rather for the Court's unanimous finding that the law was invalid.

### B. Laws That Prefer Some Religions Over Others

Government action that expressly deals with the subject of religion and effectively grants a preference among religious faiths also raises problems under the free exercise clause. The leading case is *Larson v. Valente*. That case involved a Minnesota statute that imposed registration and reporting requirements on charitable organizations to prevent fraudulent solicitations and related abuses, but that exempted religious organizations that solicited more than fifty percent of their funds from their members. The effect of this statute was to exempt the Catholic Church from the onerous registration and reporting requirements, because it raised more than half of its money from its members, but not to exempt the Unification Church, the followers of the Reverend Moon, because it solicited more than half of its funds from nonmembers. The Court held that the Minnesota statute violated the establishment clause, relying on a famous dictum in *Everson v. Board of Education* that the establishment clause bars the preference of one religion over another.

*Larson* should be seen as a free exercise clause decision parading in anestablishment clause disguise. This criticism of the basis for the Court's ruling is not just caused by a sense of aesthetics; rather, it further illustrates the confusion that the Court has created with respect to establishment clause and free exercise clause doctrine. Regardless of the historical relevance that the establishment clause may have had with respect to official governmental designation of a particular religious denomination for special treatment, the Court admitted in *Larson* that its modern three-prong establishment clause test was not really fashioned for the problem of discrimination or preference among religions. Rather, the Court correctly observed that its establishment clause analysis mainly has been concerned with aid to religion generally. In fact, the Court in *Larson* virtually ignored the purpose and effect prongs of the three-prong test, although it did throw in the entanglement prong at the end of the opinion. The Court reasoned that allowing laws to discriminate among religions would produce politicization of religion, pointing to evidence in *Larson* that showed some real effort in the Minnesota legislature to ensure that the Catholic Church was not subject to the reporting and registration requirements but that the Unification Church was.

The major thrust of the Court's opinion, however, involved using what had become the classic free exercise clause analysis, conceding that discrimination among religions "is inextricably connected with the continuing vitality of the Free Exercise Clause." The Court actually held that discrimination among religions must survive strict scrutiny. *Larson* was an easy case under this free exercise clause/strict scrutiny analysis. The Court was willing to assume that the State had a "compelling" interest in preventing fraudulent solicitation of the public. Strict scrutiny, however, also requires the state to have had no narrower means available, and the Court felt that the "fifty percent rule" was neither necessary nor "closely fitted" to achieving the state goal. Therefore, the Court held the law invalid.

The dissenting justices in *Larson* did not really dispute this application of the doctrine to the facts. Rather, the burden of the dissenting opinion's argument was that the Court's test was too stringent. Moreover, although Justice White did not put it quite this way, he essentially agreed with the point, suggested above, that the majority had imported a free exercise clause test into an establishment clause case. In my view, however, the Court's misstep was in viewing the challenge in *Larson* as raising an establishment clause issue to begin with.

The major disagreement between the majority and dissent concerned whether this law discriminated among religions or simply was a neutral law with a disparate impact on different religious groups. The Court adopted the former view. Justice White argued in his dissent, however, that the Minnesota law did not explicitly distinguish between religions. He pointed out that the law named no churches. Rather, it stated general, neutral characteristics describing which religions would be exempt and which would not.

To agree with the dissent's analysis that this law did not explicitly distinguish between religious sects, however, is not to say how the law should have been treated. Although the Minnesota statute did not specifically give preference to some religions over others, it did expressly deal with the subject of religion, and it resulted in favoring some and disfavoring others. In my view, it should have been as vulnerable—that is, subject to the same level of scrutiny—as a general, neutral law that says nothing about religion but that happens to have an adverse impact on some faiths, like the Wisconsin compulsory education law at issue in *Yoder*.

The problem is that when the Court has invoked the establishment clause, it has applied a much more lenient test to laws that expressly deal with religion and subject some faiths to discriminatory treatment than it has applied under the free exercise clause to general, neutral laws that come into conflict with religious beliefs. In *Gillette v. United States*, for example, the Court applied a less stringent test to a provision in the Selective Service Act that exempted from the draft individuals who, because of religious training and belief, were opposed to "war in any form," but did not exempt individuals who were opposed only to "unjust wars." The Court reasoned that this law did not discriminate on the basis of religious affiliation. That is true. The Selective Service Act did not say, for example, that Quakers are exempt and Catholics are not. The law, however, did plainly discriminate on the basis of the kind of religious beliefs one had—beliefs opposed to all wars rather than beliefs opposed only to unjust wars.

In *Gillette*, the Court treated the "gist of the constitutional complaint" as falling under the establishment clause. The Court characterized the statute as a neutral law with a disparate impact, and ruled that as long as Congress had a "valid secular reason" for the law, that law could survive an establishment clause challenge. The Court readily found a valid secular basis—ease of administration of the draft system. Thus, the Court found no violation of the establishment clause despite the law's discrimination among religious beliefs.

Given the Court's contemporary doctrinal treatment of the religion clauses, *Gillette* may be viewed more helpfully as a free exercise case. And, employing a free exercise clause analysis, the Court may well have decided the case correctly. In reality, the Court did not sustain the draft law merely on the basis of some valid secular purpose. If that were all that the Court had required in *Larson*, for example, it would have had no problem upholding the Minnesota statute challenged in that case. Surely some secular basis is available to distinguish between groups that raise more than fifty percent of their funds from the outside and groups that do not. The religious organizations in the former category reasonably may be thought to pose a greater danger of fraud, which may not provide compelling justification for the classification, but which does represent some valid neutral basis for it.

In reality, I believe that the Selective Service Act survived strict scrutiny in *Gillette*. The powerful government interest in raising an army and the difficulties in administering a draft exemption based on "just war" beliefs may well have justified the conclusion that the statutory discrimination among religious beliefs was based on a compelling or essential or overriding government interest.

In sum, the doctrine in *Gillette*, that a valid secular basis for de facto religious discrimination is enough to sustain it under the establishment clause, plainly supports Justice White's dissent in *Larson*. The *Gillette* doctrine, however, effectively has been abandoned, and rightly so. Laws that explicitly deal with the subject of religion, and result in a preference of some religions over others, fall into a separate category of government action that ought to be treated under the free exercise clause. Although the Court in *Larson* did not purport to analyze the statute in that case under the free exercise clause, it explicitly employed a rationale that does. Both the result and most of the rationale in that case, therefore, were eminently sensible.

---

Michael W. McConnell, *Free Exercise Revisionism and the Smith Decision*, 57 THE UNIVERSITY OF CHICAGO LAW REVIEW 1109 (1990)*

For decades, the Free Exercise Clause of the First Amendment was largely uncontroversial. The great debates over the relation of religion to government in our pluralistic republic—over school prayer, aid to parochial schools, publicly sponsored religious symbols, and religiously inspired legislation—almost without exception were issues of establishment. Government support for religion, not government interference with religion, was the issue.

Not that there was any shortage of free exercise cases or closely divided Supreme Court decisions. And not that there was any dearth of academic critics of the Court's doctrine. But free exercise doctrine in the courts was stable, the noisy pressure groups from the ACLU to the religious right were in basic agreement, and most academic commentators were content to work out the implications of the doctrine rather than to challenge it at its roots.

There was, however, a peculiar quality to the consensus which may or may not have contributed to its stability: the free exercise doctrine was more talk

* Reprinted with permission.

than substance. In its language, it was highly protective of religious liberty. The government could not make or enforce any law or policy that burdened the exercise of a sincere religious belief unless it was the least restrictive means of attaining a particularly important (''compelling'') secular objective. In practice, however, the Supreme Court only rarely sided with the free exercise claimant, despite some very powerful claims. The Court generally found either that the free exercise right was not burdened or that the government interest was compelling. In fact, after the last major free exercise victory in 1972, the Court rejected every claim requesting exemption from burdensome laws or policies to come before it except for those claims involving unemployment compensation, which were governed by clear precedent. This did not mean that the compelling interest test was dead, however. There were many more applications of the doctrine in the state and lower federal courts, and legislatures and executive bodies frequently conformed their decision to its dictates. But at the Supreme Court level, the free exercise compelling interest test was a Potemkin doctrine.

With last April's Supreme Court decision in *Employment Division v. Smith*, all that has changed. By a 5-4 vote (Justice O'Connor concurring on different grounds), the Supreme Court abandoned the compelling interest test, holding that ''the right of free exercise does not relieve an individual of the obligation to comply with a 'valid and neutral law of general applicability on the ground that the law proscribes (or prescribes) conduct that his religion prescribes (or proscribes).''' In other words, ''an individual's religious beliefs [do not] excuse him from compliance with an otherwise valid law prohibiting conduct that the State is free to regulate.'' The Court acknowledged that ''leaving accommodation to the political process will place at a relative disadvantage those religious practices that are not widely engaged in.'' Calling this the ''unavoidable consequence of democratic government,'' the Court stated that it ''must be preferred to a system in which each conscience is a law unto itself or in which judges weight the social importance of all laws against the centrality of all religious beliefs.''

. . .

## C. Precedent

Having dismissed the text as ambiguous and ignored the history, the Court in *Smith* purported to base its decision on precedent. But its use of precedent is troubling, bordering on the shocking. A detailed examination of both those precedents on which the Court relied and those that it distinguished is necessary to reveal the full extent of the liberties the Court took with its earlier decisions.

### 1. Never say never.

The *Smith* opinion states baldly: ''We have never held that an individual's religious beliefs excuse him from compliance with an otherwise valid law prohibiting conduct that the State is free to regulate.'' In *Wisconsin v. Yoder*, however, the Court had stated that ''[a] regulation neutral on its face may, in its application, nonetheless offend the constitutional requirement for government neutrality if it unduly burdens the free exercise of religion.'' Indeed, the *Yoder* Court stated that ''[t]he essence of all that has been said and written on the subject is that only those interests of the highest order and those not otherwise served can overbalance legitimate claims to the free exercise of religion.'' In *Yoder*, the Court called a generally applicable compulsory school attendance law, as applied to Amish children above the eighth grade, ''precisely the kind of objective danger to the free exercise of religion that the First Amendment was designed to prevent.'' The compelling interest test has been applied numerous times since *Yoder*. The Court reiterated the compelling interest test no fewer than three times in the year preceding *Smith*, including two unanimous opinions.

Prior to *Smith*, some Justices disagreed with the precedents holding that the Free Exercise Clause requires exemptions from generally-applicable laws, but none denied the existence of those precedents. Chief Justice Rehnquist and Justice Stevens had authored several separate concurrences and dissents in previous cases taking the Court to task for doing precisely what the *Smith* opinion now denies that the Court had ever done. Even Justice Scalia, fourteen months before writing the *Smith* opinion, stated in a dissenting opinion in an Establishment Clause case that the Court had ''held that the Free Exercise Clause of the First Amendment required religious beliefs to be accommodated by granting religion-specific exemptions from otherwise applicable laws,'' listing four illustrative cases, including *Yoder*. Three of the five Justices in the *Smith* majority signed their names to this statement. What happened in the ensuing fourteen months to change their minds?

### 2. Precedents distinguished.

a) *Yoder*. According to the Court in *Smith*, ''[t]he only decisions in which we have held that the First Amendment bars application of a neutral, generally applicable law to religiously motivated action have involved not the Free Exercise Clause alone, but the Free Exercise Clause in conjunction with other constitutional protections.'' *Yoder* is explained as involving "the rights of parents to direct the religious upbringing of their children." But the opinion in *Yoder* expressly stated that parents do not have the right to violate the compulsory education laws for nonreligious reasons. Thus, according to *Yoder* parents have no right independent of the Free Exercise Clause to withhold their children from school, and according to *Smith* they have no such right under the Free Exercise Clause. How can claimants be entitled to greater relief under a "hybrid" claim than they could attain under either of the components of the hybrid? One suspects that the notion of "hybrid" claims was created for the sole purpose of distinguishing *Yoder* in this case.

But does it serve even that purpose? Why isn't *Smith* itself a "hybrid" case? Whatever else it might accomplish, the performance of a sacred ritual like the ingestion of peyote communicates, in a rather dramatic way, the participants' faith in the tenets of the Native American Church. Smith and Black could have made a colorable claim under the Free Speech Clause that the prohibition of peyote use interfered with their ability to communicate this message. If burning a flag is speech because it communicates a political belief, ingestion of peyote is no less. And even if Smith and Black would lose on a straight free speech claim, following the logic of *Smith*'s explanation of *Yoder*, why shouldn't their claim prevail as a "hybrid" with their free exercise claim? The answer, a legal realist would tell us, is that the *Smith* Court's notion of "hybrid" claims was not intended to be taken seriously.

b) The unemployment cases. The *Smith* Court had even more difficulty distinguishing a line of cases involving unemployment compensation for unemployment caused by religious objections to available work. There have been four such cases, the most recent being a unanimous decision only a year before *Smith*. These cases have generally been considered prime examples of free exercise exemptions from generally applicable laws, because workers are excused from the requirement of accepting any "suitable" employment. Even though workers who decline work for other important, conscientious reasons (for example, because of ideological objections to the work or because of the need to care for a dependent) would not receive unemployment compensation, workers who decline work for religious reasons must be given benefits.

The *Smith* Court began its discussion of these cases by noting that the compelling interest test had not led to the invalidation of any government action "except the denial of unemployment compensation,"

as if that were a coherent distinction. Beyond that, the Court noted that the unemployment compensation cases involved "a context that lent itself to individualized governmental assessment of the reasons for the relevant conduct." The unemployment cases thus "stand for the proposition that where the State has in place a system of individual exemptions, it may not refuse to extend that system to cases of 'religious hardship' without compelling reason." On its face, this is not a very persuasive distinction. Difficulty of administration can fairly constitute at least part of the governmental interest in enforcing the law without exceptions, but is hard to see why this concern should limit the universe of potential claims. Moreover, if this is the distinction, it is hard to see why the compelling interest test does not apply to many contacts other than just unemployment compensation—indeed, to the full universe of claims governed by the due process requirement of "some kind of hearing."

Under this analysis, *most* of the supreme Court's free exercise cases resemble the unemployment compensation cases in that they involve individuated governmental assessments of the claimant's circumstances. In *United States v. Lee*, for example, a procedural mechanism already existed for administering religious objections to social security taxation. In *Lyng v. Northwest Indiana Cemetery Protective Ass'n*, the Forest service was already required to study and consider the impact of the logging road on Native American religious practices as well as on the environment. Indeed, every decision to build a road must be made on a case-by-case basis. In *O'Lone v. Estate of Shabazz*, prison officials had informally accommodated the religious needs of the Muslim prisoners but stopped doing so, apparently because the officials interpreted a prison directive to disallow the accommodation. These cases are typical. In each of them the government "ha[d] in place a system of individual exemptions." The unemployment cases cannot be distinguished on this ground.

Even more strikingly, the "individual governmental assessment" distinction cannot explain the result in *Smith* itself. If *Smith* is viewed as an unemployment compensation case, the distinction is obviously spurious. If *Smith* is viewed as a hypothetical criminal prosecution for peyote use, there would be an individual governmental assessment of the defendants' motives and actions in the form of a criminal trial.

The purported distinction thus has no obvious connection to either the circumstance of *Smith* or to the Court's precedents. Like the distinction of *Yoder*, it appears to have one function only: to enable the

Court to reach the conclusion it desired in *Smith* without openly overruling any prior decisions.

. . .

#### 4. Was there really a compelling interest test?

Notwithstanding all that has just been said about the Court's reliance on precedent, it must be conceded that the Supreme Court before *Smith* did not really apply a genuine "compelling interest" test. Such a test would allow the government to override a religious objection only in the most extraordinary of circumstances. In an area of law where a genuine "compelling interest" test has been applied, intentional discrimination against a racial minority, no such interest has been discovered in almost half a century. Even the Justices committed to the doctrine of free exercise exemptions have in fact applied a far more relaxed standard to these cases, and they were correct to do so. The "compelling interest" standard is a misnomer.

But just because the test was not so strong as "compelling" does not mean that the Court failed to apply heightened scrutiny in its previous decisions. There is no support in the precedents for the Court to replace the prior test with nothing more than the toothless rationality review that is applicable to all legislation. As explained in more detail below, a serious examination of the purported justifications for restricting religious exercise is necessary to separate objective differences from prejudice. Rather than taking the extreme step that it took, the Court should have recast the "compelling interest" test in a more realistic form.

. . .

### III. The Theoretical Argument

Perhaps because of its purported reliance on precedent, the *Smith* opinion does not present a sustained explanation of its theoretical underpinnings. Yet the opinion rests, in the end, not on text or history or precedent, but on the majority's view, revealed in a few key sentences in the opinion, of the proper relation between law and religious conscience. It is unfortunate that Justice Scalia wrote the opinion in this way, for while the argument based on precedent is hopelessly contrived, the theoretical argument is serious and substantial, even if mistaken. It requires careful attention and deserves a thorough response.

Virtually the entire theoretical argument of the *Smith* opinion is packed into this one sentence:

It may fairly be said that leaving accommodation to the political process will place at a relative disadvantage those religious practices that are not widely engaged in; but that unavoidable

consequence of democratic government must be preferred to a system in which each conscience is a law unto itself or in which judges weigh the social importance of all laws against the centrality of all religious beliefs.

The rhetoric of this sentence is certainly impolitic, leaving the Court open to the charge of abandoning its traditional role as protector of minority rights against majoritarian oppression. The "disadvantaging" of minority religions is not "unavoidable" if the courts are doing their job. Avoiding certain "consequences" of democratic government is ordinarily thought to be the very purpose of a Bill of Rights. But the argument reflected in this sentence nonetheless contains ideas that cannot be dismissed so lightly.

The Court's argument has a certain unity, but for purposes of analysis I propose to break it up into five separate but related ideas expressed in this sentence and a few other key passages in the opinion. The first idea is an implied devaluation of the importance of denominational neutrality under the Religion Clauses. Second is the assumption that free exercise exemptions are a form of special preference for religion and that generally applicable laws written from the perspective of the majority are necessarily and by definition neutral. Third is the claim that exceptions under the Free Exercise Clause are a constitutional anomaly. Fourth is that decisions regarding free exercise exemptions are inherently subjective and therefore legislative in character; in other words, courts have no non-arbitrary way to adjudicate conflicts between religious conscience and law. Fifth, and most important, is that it is contrary to the rule of law—it would be "courting anarchy"—for individual conscience to take precedent over law.

#### A. Denominational Neutrality

The *Smith* opinion does not specifically address how one should weigh the evils of disadvantaging religious minorities against those of arbitrary judging and lawlessness. The outcome of the case, however, implicitly suggests that denominational neutrality is of secondary importance. The opinion characterizes the doctrine of free exercise exemptions as a "luxury," suggesting that its purposes, while worthy, are distinctly subordinate. Had this proposition been raised explicitly, the Court would have found much in our constitutional history bearing on the question and might have found it more difficult to reach the balance it struck.

In *Larson v. Valente*, the Court noted that the "clearest command of the Establishment Clause is that one religious denomination cannot be officially preferred over another." This conclusion is confirmed repeatedly in both statements and constitutional enactments of the founding period. Baptist leader John Leland proposed an amendment to the Massachusetts Constitutional forbidding the legislature to "establish any religion by law, [or] given any one sect a preference to another. . . ." In a similar vein, Jonas Phillips, Revolutionary War patriot and founder of a synagogue in Philadelphia, informed the Constitutional Convention by petition that the Jews wished the Constitution to be framed so that "all Religious societies are on a Equal footing." Rhode Island's proposed amendment to the federal Constitution asked that "no particular sect or society ought to be favored or established by law."

The twelve state constitutional free exercise provisions extant in 1789 were different in many respects, but all contained language referring to denominational equality (though in two states this equality was extended only to Christian denominations). New York and South Carolina both specified that the right of free exercise was to be "without discrimination or preference," and Virginia provided that "all men are equally entitled to the free exercise of religion." Other states used words like "every," "all," "no," "equal," or "equally" to make the same point. This idea carried forward to the federal Constitution. Although the language did not survive to the final version, Madison's initial draft of the Free Exercise Clause provided that "the full and equal rights of conscience [shall not] be in any manner, nor on any pretext, infringed." The words "full and equal" help to capture the demand for neutrality among religious that imbued the movement for free exercise protections.

Against this background, it seems the Supreme Court should have given more serious attention to the problem of "plac[ing] at a relative disadvantage those religious practices that are not widely engaged in" before concluding that this consideration is outweighed by other principles less firmly rooted in our constitutional scheme.

Why did the majority feel it necessary to take this position? The reason, I believe, arises not from concerns about the Free Exercise Clause but from concerns about the Establishment Clause. Under the *Smith* Court's conception, courts will not be able to order exceptions from laws of general applicability—but legislatures will. Indeed, the Court declares such exemptions "desirable." The problem, as the Court candidly acknowledges, is that the political branches, being political, will tend to be most solicitous of the value of familiar, popular, and socially acceptable religious faiths. Prior to *Smith*, the Free Exercise

Clause functioned as a corrective for this bias, allowing the courts, which are institutionally more attuned to the interests of the less powerful segments of society, to extend to minority religions the same degree of solicitude that more mainstream religions are able to attain through the political process. The Free Exercise Clause, prior to *Smith*, was an equalizer.

There is, however, an alternative equalizer: the Establishment Clause. If the political branches enact accommodations that tend to benefit mainstream more than fringe religions, the solution could be to strike them down under the Establishment Clause. Rather than ensuring that all religious faiths receive equal solicitude, the courts can ensure that all receive equal indifference. This is the position of some secularists who take a strong position on establishment and a weak position on free exercise. It is evident that the *Smith* majority prefers denominational inequality to an Establishment Clause-driven policy of indifference. Indeed, from the Court's perspective, an activist establishment jurisprudence is no less objectionable than an activist free exercise jurisprudence.

Moreover, the establishment strategy would fail, even if it were desirable. Accommodation can be accomplished by inaction just as it can by action. In other words, the legislatures can simply refrain from passing laws that burden the exercise of religion by mainstream groups, and there is nothing the Establishment Clause can do about this. In the end, the only hope for achieving denominational neutrality is a vigorous Free Exercise Clause.

B. Special Privileges or Neutrality in the Face of Differences?

Throughout the *Smith* opinion, generally applicable laws are treated as presumptively neutral, with religious accommodations a form of special preference, akin to affirmative action. The opinion describes religious accommodations as laws that "affirmatively foster" the "value" of "religious belief." In *Sherbert v. Verner*, Justice Brennan's majority opinion characterized a religious exemption as "reflect[ing] nothing more than the governmental obligation of neutrality in the face of religious differences." In a sense, then, both *Smith* and *Sherbert* are about neutrality toward religion. But which has the correct understanding of neutrality?

To examine this question, I will use the facts of *Stansbug v. Marks*, the first recorded case raising free exercise issues after adoption of the First Amendment. The case arose in the Pennsylvania courts and was decided under state law. The Reporter's summary of the holding of the case was: "A

Jew may be fined for refusing to testify on his Sabbath.'' The entire report of the case as follows:

> In this case which was tried on Saturday, the 5th of April), the defendant offered Jonas Phillips, a Jew, as a witness; but he refused to be sworn, because it was his Sabbath. The court, therefore, fined him 10f; but the defendant, afterwards, waiving the benefit of his testimony, he was discharged from the fine.

We can assume that, in those days of the six-day work week, the courts of Pennsylvania were routinely open for business on Saturday. The decision to operate on Saturday, we may assume, was not aimed at members of the Jewish faith, but was simply a matter of convenience. Nor was the law allowing parties to civil suits to compel witnesses to attend court proceedings, on pain of paying a fine, instituted for the purpose of restricting religious exercise. This is an example of a generally applicable, otherwise valid, law. Is it neutral toward religion?

No, it is not. The courts were closed on Sundays, the day on which the Christian majority of Pennsylvania observed the sabbath. The effect of the six-day calendar was to impose a burden on Saturday sabbath observers (mostly Jews) that is not imposed on others (mostly Christians). It is anything *but* neutral—not because the burden happened to fall disproportionately on Jews, but because the burden was attached to a practice that, among others, defines what it means to be a faithful Jew.

What would neutrality require? Surely it is not necessary to conduct court business on Sunday. Since the vast majority of Pennsylvanians were Christians and observed Sunday as the day of sabbath, that would create needless conflict and administrative costs. It would be more neutral to close on both Saturday and Sunday, the modern solution, but that has significant costs in an era of a six-day work week. And if there were other religious minorities in the Commonwealth who observed the sabbath on other days, Moslems perhaps, then this solution would not work at all. The best, least costly, and most neutral solution is to exempt Saturday sabbath observers from the obligation of testifying on Saturday. Thus, an exemption is not ''affirmative fostering'' of religion; it is more like *Sherbert*'s neutrality in the face of differences.

It may be objected that this example is loaded because the selection of days of rest is fraught with religious significance. The selection of Sunday as the day on which the courts would not operate was itself a religious choice, almost an establishment of the Christian religion. It might be said that an exemption is required in that case only to equalize a situation in which Christians had already been granted a benefit on account of religious practice.

But this objection presupposes that there are decisions that are *not* fraught with religious significance. And perhaps there are—but those decisions will not give rise to free exercise claims. All free exercise claims involve government decisions that are fraught with religious significance, at least from the point of view of the religious minority. In this respect, *Stansbury v. Marks* cannot be distinguished from *Smith*. In *Smith*, the generally applicable law was the prohibition on the use of hallucinogenic drugs. The Native American Church uses peyote as its sacrament. Application of the anti-drug laws to the sacramental use of peyote effectively destroys the practice of the Native American Church. Is this neutral?

No, it is not. Christians and Jews use wine as part of their sacrament, and wine is not illegal. Even when wine was illegal during Prohibition, Congress exempted the sacramental use of wine from the proscription. The effect of laws prohibiting hallucinogenic drugs but not alcohol, or of allowing exemptions from one law but not the other, is to impose a burden on the practice of the Native American Church that is not imposed on Christians or Jews. It is no more neutral than operating courts on Saturday and not on Sunday.

But perhaps this overstates the case. Whether to operate courts on Saturday or Sunday is clearly a decision involving commensurables. Hallucinogenic drugs are far more dangerous than wine. The difference in treatment can be said to be based on objective differences between the effects of the two substances. But is this true? Evidence in the *Smith* case showed that ingestion of peyote by members of the Native American Church is *not* dangerous and does not lead to drug problems or substance abuse. Indeed, it is statistically and culturally associated with resistance to substance abuse. The federal government and twenty-three of the states have approved the use of peyote in Native American Church ceremonies for this reason, and the federal government even licenses a facility for the production of peyote.

If this evidence is valid, then the decision to ban the sacramental use of peyote but not the sacramental use of wine is not based on any objective differences between the effects of the two substances. Rather, it is based on the fact that most ordinary Americans are familiar with the use of wine and consider Christian and Jewish sacramental use harmless and perhaps even a good thing; but the same ordinary Americans consider peyote a bizarre and threatening substance and have no respect or solicitude for the Native American Church. In short, the difference is attributable to prejudice.

The only way to tell whether the difference in treatment between peyote and wine is the result of prejudice of the result of objective differences in the substances is to examine closely the purported governmental purpose. If the purpose is important, and if the means are closely related to the purpose, then the policy is probably based on objective differences. If the purpose is weak or the means only loosely related to the purpose, then the policy is more likely the result of prejudice. This, of course, is a rough description of the compelling interest test. That test, therefore, is not a form of "affirmative[] foster[-ing]" of religion. It is a way to determine whether government decisions that interfere with the religious exercise of religious minorities are in fact neutral.

It should be apparent why a mere absence of attention to religious consequences on the part of the legislature cannot prove that legislation is neutral. In a world in which some beliefs are more prominent than others, the political branches will inevitably be selectively sensitive toward religious injuries. Laws that impinge upon the religious practices of larger or more prominent faiths will be noticed and remedied. When the laws impinge upon the practice of smaller groups, legislators will not even notice, and may not even care if they do notice. If believers of all creeds are to be protected in the "full and equal rights of conscience," then selective sensitivity is not enough. The courts offer a forum in which the particular infringements of small religions can be brought to the attention of the authorities and (assuming the judges perform their duties impartially) be given the same sort of hearing that more prominent religions already receive from the political process.

## C. Constitutional Anomalies

Closely related to the preceding point is the *Smith* Court's claim that the compelling interest test in free exercise exemption cases is "a constitutional anomaly." According to the Court, use of the compelling interest test in cases of racial discrimination or content-based speech regulation

> is not remotely comparable to using it for the purpose asserted here. What it produces in those other fields—equality of treatment, and an unrestricted flow of contending speech—are constitutional norms; what it would produce here—a private right to ignore generally applicable laws—is a constitutional anomaly.

Drawing on analogies from several other fields of constitutional law, including freedom of the press, disproportionate impact cases under the Equal Protection Clause, and content-neutral restrictions on speech, the Court concluded that "the only approach compatible with these precedents" is to hold that "generally applicable, religion-neutral laws that have the effect of burdening a particular religious practice need not be justified by a compelling governmental interest."

It is far from clear what is wrong with the Free Exercise Clause being a "constitutional anomaly." Different clauses of the Constitution perform different functions and have different logical structures. It is hard to see how precedents drawn from other areas of constitutional law can have the effect of foreclosing any particular interpretation of the Free Exercise Clause. The Free Exercise Clause is framed in terms of a substantive liberty; there is no reason to expect it to have the same logic as the Equal Protection Clause. Nonetheless, if the Free Exercise Clause were the only provision of the Constitution that required exceptions from generally applicable laws, this might give cause for reexamination. But it isn't.

. . .

In particular, and contrary to the *Smith* opinion, exceptions from generally applicable laws are an established part of the protections for free speech and press under the First Amendment. Indeed, the very core to the free press clause—the freedom from prior restraints—can be seen as an exemption from a form of regulation that can be applied to virtually every other commercial business. . . .

. . .

## D. The Judicial Role

A major theme of the *Smith* opinion is that the compelling interest test forces the courts to engage in judgments that cannot be made on a nonarbitrary basis. The Court commented that "it is horrible to contemplate that federal judges will regularly balance against the importance of general laws the significance of religious practice." It is better that minority religions will be at "a relative disadvantage," the Court said, than that judges have to "weigh the social importance of all laws against the centrality of all religious beliefs."

The Court illustrated this concern with what it playfully admitted to be a "parade of horribles"—claims for free exercise exemptions from such laws as compulsory military service, health and safety regulation, compulsory vaccination laws, traffic laws, and social welfare legislation including minimum wage, child labor, and animal cruelty laws. Putting aside the fact that many of the Court's "horribles" are far from horrible, and that some of its "horribles" involve anti-religious discrimination and thus are unaffected by the *Smith* holding, this parade is almost risible in its one-sidedness. For every claim that would, if granted, produce a horrible result, there is a claim that *ought* to be granted but will not be after the *Smith* decision.

Consider the fact that employment discrimination laws could force the Roman Catholic Church to hire female priests, if there are no free exercise exemptions from generally applicable laws. Or that historic preservation laws could prevent churches from making theologically significant alterations to their structures. Or that prisons will not have to serve kosher or hallel food to Jewish or Moslem prisoners. Or that Jewish high school athletes may be forbidden to wear yarmulkes and thus excluded from interscholastic sports. Or that churches with a religious objection to unrepentant homosexuality will be required to retain an openly gay individual as church organist, parochial school teacher, or even a pastor. Or that public school students will be forced to attend sex education classes contrary to their faith. Or that religious sermons on issues of political significance could lead to revocation of tax exemptions. Or that Catholic doctors in public hospitals could be fired if they refuse to perform abortions. Or that Orthodox Jews could be required to cease and desist from sexual segregation of their places of worship.

If the Court wishes to consider a parade of horribles, it should parade the horribles on both sides. But while the two parades may be of the same length, they are of very different quality. The judicial system is able to reject claims that would be horrible if granted; believers are helpless to deal with infringements on religious freedom that the courts refuse to remedy.

Challenged by Justice O'Connor's rejoinder that the parade of horribles only "demonstrates . . . that courts have been quite capable of . . . strik[ing] sensible balances between religious liberty and competing state interests," the Court retreated to the proposition that "the purpose of our parade . . . is not to suggest that courts would necessarily permit harmful exemptions from these laws (though they might), but to suggest that courts would constantly be in the business of determining whether the 'severe impact' of various laws on religious practice . . . suffices to permit us to confer an exemption."

The Court's evident hostility to subjective judicial second-guessing of legislative judgments is generally salutary, at least if not taken to extremes. But it raises the question: Why is the Free Exercise Clause a particular target? The author of the *Smith* opinion, Justice Scalia, is reasonably consistent regarding the undesirability of judicial discretion. In most areas of constitutional law, however, the majority of the Court does not hesitate to weigh the social impor-tance of laws against their impact on constitutional rights. There is no particular reason to believe that judgments under the Free Exercise Clause are any more discretionary or prone to judicial abuse than judgments under the Commerce Clause, the Due Process Clause, or the Free Speech Clause, to take a few examples from the current catalog of compelling interest or balancing tests. Unless *Smith* is the harbinger of a wholesale retreat from judicial discretion across the range of constitutional law, there should be some explanation of why the problem in this field is more acute than it is elsewhere.

The *Smith* opinion suggests that the problem with the compelling interest test is that it requires inquiry into whether religious beliefs are "central" to the claimant's religion, which is "akin to the unacceptable 'business of evaluating the relative merits of differing religious claims.'" But is this true? In such cases, the court is not judging the "merits" of religious claims but solely trying to determine what they are. To be sure, the court may get it wrong, but what is the grave injury from that (other than the impact on the case itself)? The court does not purport to be resolving issues of religious interpretation for any purpose other than understanding the nature of the plaintiff's claim, and its misinterpretation carries no weight beyond the courtroom. I agree that courts must be sensitive to the impropriety of second-guessing religious doctrine, but I cannot agree that the possibility of error warrants abandonment of the enterprise.

Even so, Justice Scalia's opinion rightly calls attention to the arbitrariness of judicial balancing under the prior compelling interest test. The opinion is correct that the doctrine was poorly developed and unacceptably subjective. But the opinion proposes to solve this problem by eliminating the doctrine of free exercise exemptions rather than by contributing to the development of a more principled approach. In my judgment, the theory of the Free Exercise Clause (as opposed to its application) offers a principled basis for decision in cases of conflict between law and religious conscience. Judges are not forced into the sort of free-wheeling balancing of incommensurate interests that the majority feared in *Smith*. To be sure, there are hard cases, as there are under any constitutional provision. But there are also easy cases—cases that can be decided without any case-specific balancing whatsoever—and the principles constrain judicial discretion. Indeed, in most free exercise cases no "balancing" is required at all, because the relevant factors are ones of kind rather than of degree.

First, the history of the free exercise principle

shows that governmental interests do not extend to protecting the members of the religious community from the consequences of their religious choices. Both the evangelical advocates of religious freedom and the Enlightenment liberals agreed that the "legitimate powers of government extend only to punish men for working ill to their neighbors." The common pattern of state free exercise provisions prior to 1789 protected religious exercise only to the extent consistent with public "peace" and "safety." As Madison summarized the point, free exercise should prevail "in every case where it does not trespass on private rights or the public peace." Where the putative injury is internal to the religious community, the government generally has no power to intervene, with the narrow exception of injury to children.

. . .

A second principle that emerges from the theory of the Free Exercise Clause is that the government is not required to create exemptions that would make religious believers better off relative to others than they would be in the absence of the government program to which they object. The purpose of free exercise exemptions is to ensure that incentives to practice a religion are not adversely affected by government action. By the same token, government action should not have the effect of creating incentives to practice religion.

. . .

A third principle is that the claims of minority religions should receive the same consideration under the Free Exercise Clause that the claims of mainstream religions receive in the political process. This follows from the principle of denominational neutrality discussed above. To a great extent, the advocates of religious freedom at the time of the founding believed that minority religions would be adequately secured in their rights so long as they were on the "same footing" as the mainstream faiths. To achieve equal rights of conscience, the courts should frame the free exercise inquiry as follows: Is the governmental interest so important that the government would impose a burden of this magnitude on the majority in order to achieve it?

. . .

A court faced with a free exercise claim is not required to determine, in the abstract, how important a governmental purpose is or how central a religious practice is. The court instead must engage in the hypothetical exercise of comparing burdens. The degree of protection for religious minorities should be no less than that which our society would provide for the majority. This should be enough to decide many cases quite easily. Who can doubt that unobtrusive exceptions to military uniform regulations would be made if Christians, like Orthodox Jews, had to wear yarmulkes at all times? Who can doubt that there would be exceptions to social security (or, more likely, no social security at all) if mainstream Christians were forbidden by their religion to participate? Who can doubt that the United States Forest Service would find a way to avoid despoiling Christian worship sites when building logging roads?

Other cases would come out the other way. A country could probably not survive if it allowed selective conscientious objection to war. Nor would it allow trespass or interference with the private rights of others. A government interest is sufficient if it is so important that it is not conceivable that the government would waive it even if the religious needs of the majority so required.

No doubt cases will arise in which these principles are inapplicable or incomplete, and in which the judicial task is more indeterminate. Cases involving children are particularly difficult (as they are when arising under other constitutional provisions). But these principles are sufficient to resolve the large majority of free exercise cases that have come before the Supreme Court in recent years without the need for unconstrained case-by-case balancing. In some instances, the principles suggest that the Court has been plainly wrong in denying free exercise claims. But the broader point is that the Free Exercise Clause, properly understood, does not pose the problem of subjective judicial discretion so feared by the majority in *Smith*.

E. The Rule of Law

The deepest and most important theme of the *Smith* opinion is its perception of a conflict between free exercise exemptions and the rule of law. The Court refers to exemptions as "a private right to ignore generally applicable laws." Elsewhere, it states that to apply the compelling interest test rigorously "would be courting anarchy" and warns against making "each conscience . . . a law unto itself." These fears are an unconscious echo of John Locke, who wrote in his *Letter Concerning Toleration* that "the private judgment of any person concerning a law enacted in political matters, for the public good, does not take away the obligation of that law, nor deserve dispensation."

Viewed through the lens of legal positivism, this concern is wholly out of place in the context of a written constitution with a provision that, by hypothesis, authorizes exemptions. The Court itself concedes that there is nothing inappropriate or "anomalous" about legislation that makes exceptions for religious conflicts. Presumably, legislation of this sort is valid whether it is specific (like laws exempting the Native American Church from the ban on consumption of peyote) or general (like laws requiring employers to make reasonable accommodations of their employees' religious needs). Although the judicial role is broader when the legislation is general, the Court would not say that such legislation is therefore improper or unconstitutional. Why, then, is it problematic for the People to enact a similar provision into constitutional law? From the perspective of legal positivism there is no difference between statutes and constitutional amendments. Both are commands of the sovereign.

If there is nothing wrong with statutory commands of the sovereign that make exceptions from generally applicable laws in cases of conflict with religious conscience, then there should be nothing wrong with constitutional commands of the same sort. To Locke, the right to claim exemptions was tantamount to the right to rebellion, since there was no written constitution expressing the sovereign will in a form superior to legislation, and no institution of judicial review to mediate claims of exemption. To the modern Supreme Court, the claim to exemptions is a routine matter of invoking the supreme law of the land. There is nothing lawless or anarchic about it.

From the perspective of legal positivism, free exercise exemptions do not make each conscience "a law unto itself." An arm of the government, the court, decides in each instance what the reach of the law will be. The Free Exercise Clause draws a boundary between the powers of the government and the freedom of the individual, but that boundary is defined and enforced by the government. The significance of the Free Exercise Clause is that the definition and enforcement of the boundary is entrusted to the arm of the government most likely to perform the function dispassionately and best equipped to consider the specifics of the case. The individual believer is not judge in his own case.

From a natural rights perspective, the Court's concerns about the rule of law are more substantial. According to eighteenth-century legal thought, freedom of religious conscience was not a product of the sovereign's will but a natural and inalienable right. The New Hampshire Constitution of 1784, for example, declared: "Among the natural rights, some are in their very nature unalienable, because no equivalent can be given or received for them. Of this kind are the RIGHTS OF CONSCIENCE." George

Washington addressed the Hebrew Congregation of Newport, Rhode Island, in these words: "It is now no more that toleration is spoken of, as if it was by the indulgence of one class of people, that another enjoyed the exercise of their inherent natural rights." The reason the rights of conscience were deemed inalienable is that they represented duties to God as opposed to privilege of the individual. Thus, the Free Exercise Clause is not an expression of the will of the sovereign but a declaration that the right to practice religion is jurisdictionally beyond the scope of civil authority. This, then, is an anarchic idea: that duties to God, perceived in the conscience of the individual, are superior to the law of the land.

That the idea may be anarchic does not mean that we should dismiss it, for there is reason to believe that this inalienable rights understanding is the genuine theory of the Religion Clauses of the First Amendment. One of the leading expositions of the thinking of the day about government and religion, James Madison's *Memorial and Remonstrance Against Religious Assessments*, makes the point in this way:

> Before any man can be considered as a member of Civil Society, he must be considered as a subject of the Governor of the Universe: And if a member of Civil Society, who enters into any subordinate Association, must always do it with a reservation of his duty to the general authority; much more must every man who becomes a member of any particular Civil Society, do it with a saving of his allegiance to the Universal Sovereign.

Note the contrast between the *Smith* opinion and Madison's *Memorial and Remonstrance. Smith* insists that conscience must be subordinate to civil law; Madison insists that civil law must be subordinate to conscience.

At its very core, the Free Exercise Clause, understood as Madison understood it, reflected a theological position: that God is sovereign. It also reflected a political theory: that government is a subordinate association. The theological and political positions are connected. To recognize the sovereign of God is to recognize a plurality of authorities and to impress upon government the need for humility and restraint. To deny that the government has an obligation to defer, where possible, to the dictates of religious conscience is to deny that there could be anything like "God" that could have a superior claim on the allegiance of the citizens—to assert that government is, in principle, the ultimate authority. Those are propositions that few Americans, today or in 1789, could accept.

Conclusion

. . .

[W]hen the Constitution imposes limits on governmental power, interpretation of those limits in marginal cases is—to borrow some of the *Smith* Court's words—the "unavoidable consequence" of constitutionalism.

---

Douglas Laycock, *Formal, Substantive and Disaggregated Neutrality Toward Religion*, 39 DePaul Law Review 993 (1990)*

A wide range of courts and commentators commonly say that government must be neutral toward religion. There are dissenters in both directions—those who think that government can support religion, and those who pursue separation to the point of hostility. In this Article, I will largely ignore those dissenters. I will assume that neutrality is an important part of the meaning of the religion clauses.

This Article is about the meaning of neutrality. My goal is to clarify the concept, or at least to clarify our disagreements over its meaning. In the course of doing that, I will address a third group of dissenters—those who think that neutrality is meaningless and should be dropped from our discourse.

Those who think neutrality is meaningless have a point. We can agree on the principle of neutrality without having agreed on anything at all. From benevolent neutrality to separate but equal, people with a vast range of views on church and state have all claimed to be neutral.

Consider *Texas Monthly, Inc. v. Bullock*. The Supreme Court said that Texas can not exempt the sale of religious publications from a sales tax that applies to all other publications. Justice Brennan and Justice Scalia fundamentally disagreed on almost every issue in the case, but they both claimed to be neutral. Both of them used the word "neutrality," but neither of them defined it.

Most of us think of ourselves as fairminded, and so we tend to assume that our instinctive preferences are fair, and therefore neutral. Some scholars have tried to define neutrality more carefully, but they have produced quite inconsistent definitions.

. . .

## I. IS NEUTRALITY WORTH DEFINING?

Maybe these conflicting uses of "neutrality" prove that we should abandon the concept. A few years ago, Peter Westen stirred up a great fuss by claiming that equality is an empty concept. Neutrality and equality are near cousins; they have most of the same attractions and most of the same inadequacies. If Westen were right, then neutrality would also be empty.

I am quite sure that Westen was wrong, but he highlighted something important that we too often ignore. Equality and neutrality are not empty concepts, but neither are they self-defining. They are insufficient concepts—insufficient to decide cases without supplemental principles. Let me briefly explain this point, with apologies to those who are familiar with the debate.

A claim to equal or neutral treatment is very different from an outright claim of entitlement. If I go to court claiming a constitutional right to a monthly check from the government, the court will laugh at me. It is up to Congress, and not the courts, to create government benefit programs. But if I go to court claiming a constitutional right to a check on the same terms as someone similarly situated, I may have a serious claim. If Congress has given social security benefits to women in my situation but not to men, I will probably win. My claim to an equal entitlement to benefits is very different from my claim to an outright entitlement to benefits.

. . .

Equality with respect to religion does not even sufficiently specify the classification. Religion may refer to status, to belief, to speech, or to conduct. The principal line of disagreement is different for each of these.

Most of our serious disagreements are about religious conduct, and not about religious status or belief. It is therefore religious conduct that is the principal subject of our inquiry into religious neutrality. Americans have very different intuitions about what it means to say that religious conduct is similarly situated to secular conduct, or what it means to treat religious conduct equally.

In religion as elsewhere, the answers sometimes depend on the second variable—the purpose of the classification. Whether we think religious conduct is similarly situated may depend on whether we are talking about direct regulation of conduct, resolution of private disputes, expenditures of government funds, taxation and tax exemption, and so on through the whole range of ways in which religion and government interact.

The debate over religious conduct also triggers sharp disagreement over the choice between equal treatment and equal impact. This may be the most fundamental source of disagreement about the meaning of neutrality toward religion.

Because neutrality requires so much further specification, it cannot be the only principle in the religion clauses. Nor can it be the most fundamental. We must specify the content of neutrality by looking to other principles in the religion clauses. When we have done that, neutrality should be defined in a way that makes it largely congruent with those other principles. We will often be able to explain the objection to a law by saying either that it restricts the autonomy of religious belief or practice, or that it threatens religious voluntarism, or that it deviates from religious neutrality, and so on.

This variety of explanations is important, and the neutrality explanation should not be omitted. In a nation of immense religious diversity, it is of great symbolic value that government views all manner of religious belief neutrally. That the government aspires to religious neutrality, and that the courts stand ready to hold government to its aspiration, is an important reassurance to religious minorities. We should not abandon or de-emphasize that reassurance. We should not omit neutrality from our set of explanations, even if we also offer other explanations, and even if some readers believe that those other explanations are more fundamental. Neutrality has great explanatory importance.

Neutrality also continues to have operational importance. If neutrality properly understood is largely congruent with other principles of the religion clauses, then any of these principles can be the warning flag that calls attention to a threat to religious liberty. Sometimes the deviation from neutrality will be the most obvious explanation of the danger, and even the most fundamental.

For example, I think neutrality is the most straightforward explanation in the equal access controversy. There is no general right to demand that the government make its property available for religious observance: there is not even such a right in narrow and especially appealing circumstances. The lack of such a right is implicit in *Lyng v. Northwest Indian Cemetery Protective Association*, where the Court refused to stop the government from building a useless road on land owned by the government but sacred to Native Americans. There is no entitlement to special access to government property for religious exercise.

Nevertheless, if the government makes its property available for meetings of nonreligious private groups, then it must make that property equally available to religious groups. This is a classic equality right. The equality or neutrality explanation is the one that best and most directly fits the case. Neutrality is the easiest way to recognize the problem, to decide the case, and to explain the result.

More generally, I doubt that there *is* any single foundational principle from which all the others can be derived. The religion clauses embody several principles, which are largely congruent, but occasionally in tension. The search for solutions is rarely a matter of deciding which principle is more fundamental. The search for solutions is more like an iteration in mathematics. In an iteration, you solve a problem by a series of approximations, each building on the one before, until you have as close an approximation as you need or as close as you can get with reasonable effort. We iterate religion clause problems by considering them in light of each of the relevant principles, including neutrality.

For all these reasons, I think that neutrality is worth defining. To that end, I will sketch the principal conceptions of neutrality toward religion in the cases and the literature, illustrating the differences with examples.

## II. FORMAL NEUTRALITY

By far the best known definition of religious neutrality is Philip Kurland's. In 1961, he tendered the following principle:

> The [free exercise and establishment] clauses should be read as stating a single precept: that government cannot utilize religion as a standard for action or inaction because these clauses, read together as they should be, prohibit classification in terms of religion either to confer a benefit or to impose a burden.

This standard of no religious classifications is closely akin to the equal treatment and equal opportunity side of the affirmative action debate. But the shift of context has enough implications so that a different label is required. I will call this standard formal neutrality. I will not call it Kurland's Rule, because I am not sure he intended it in the way it has come to be understood. But I suspect that if you say "neutrality" to most religious liberty scholars, the first thing that they think of is Philip Kurland and a ban on religious classifications.

Formal neutrality sounds highly plausible until you think through its implications. Its simplicity and apparent even-handedness are appealing. It can explain some important cases, including my argument for the constitutionality of the Equal Access Act.

Yet formal neutrality has been almost universally rejected. No major commentator endorsed it for a generation, and no case has adopted it, although many cases and commentators have applied part of it to particular problems. Now an endorsement has come from a most unlikely source, Professor Mark Tushnet. Hardly anyone else has been willing to apply it universally, because it produces surprising results that are inconsistent with strong intuitions.

The most striking example is historical. The National Prohibition Act forbad the sale or consumption of alcoholic beverages in the United States, but it exempted the use of sacramental wine. Under formal neutrality, the exemption was unconstitutional. The exemption undeniably classified on the basis of religion. It was lawful to consume alcohol in religious ceremonies, but not otherwise.

Now consider Prohibition without the exemption. There would be no violation of formal neutrality; religion would not even be mentioned in the statute. But it would be a crime to celebrate the Eucharist or the Seder. If the free exercise of religion includes anything beyond bare belief, it must be the right to perform the sacred rituals of the faith. A law enacted largely at the behest of Protestants that barred the sacred rites of Catholics and Jews, a law that changed the way these rites had been performed for millennia, could not be reconciled with any concept of religious liberty worthy of the name. That the law was formally neutral and enacted for a secular purpose would be no comfort to the victims.

But facial neutrality would be dispositive to the Supreme Court of the United States. In a stunning opinion handed down after this lecture was delivered, the Court said that government may regulate the Mass for good reasons, bad reasons, or no reasons at all, so long as the regulation is facially neutral and does not single out religion. The Court held that criminal punishment of the central religious ritual of an ancient faith raises no issue under the free exercise clause and requires no governmental justification whatever! The example that I chose because I thought it was beyond reasonable argument has now been decided the other way.

Prohibition as applied to sacramental wine is the exemplar of a large class of cases, in which the exercise of religion requires exemption from laws of general applicability. Such exemptions are now a matter of legislative grace. The Court did not go all the way to Professor Kurland's ban on exemptions for religious exercise. Rather, it said that the Constitution is indifferent to such exemptions—that legislatures may grant or refuse exemptions as they choose.

I will return to the problem of exemptions for religious conduct. For now, I note only that formal neutrality would permit a state to ban the Mass. If it produces such an implausible result in a case at the core of religious exercise, the principle is not off to a good start.

In the Prohibition example, formal neutrality seems to trample religion. But formal neutrality also produces results that many Americans find unacceptably favorable to religion. Consider the case of financial aid to private education. Under formal neutrality, government can give unlimited amounts of unrestricted aid to religious schools, so long as the aid goes to all schools and not to religious schools alone. But formal neutrality does not stop there. Any aid to secular private schools *must* be given to religious schools, on exactly the same terms. To exclude religious schools from the aid program, or to impose restrictions on religious uses of the money, would be to classify on the basis of religion. That would violate formal neutrality.

I do not think that this implication of formal neutrality is beyond the range of reasonable debate. Indeed, I think it captures an important insight. But I also believe that at least some of its results would be unconstitutional.

Stricter separationists react much more strongly. To many American separationists, the possibility that government could fully fund religious education must seem as preposterous as the banning of the Mass. This implication of formal neutrality is wildly inconsistent with the Supreme Court's cases and with dominant understandings of the establishment clause.

As these two examples make clear, formal neutrality has something to offend everybody. As a general standard, it appeals to none of the competing factions in religion clause litigation. But it has had disproportionate influence on our understanding of what it means to be neutral.

### III. SUBSTANTIVE NEUTRALITY

My understanding of neutrality is quite different. Again because we need a label, I will call my proposal "substantive neutrality."

My basic formulation of substantive neutrality is this: the religion clauses require government to minimize the extent to which it either encourages or discourages religious belief or disbelief, practice or nonpractice, observance or nonobservance. If I have to stand or fall on a single formulation of neutrality, I will stand or fall on that one. But I must elaborate on what I mean by minimizing encouragement and discouragement. I mean that religion is to be left as wholly to private choice as anything can be. It should proceed as unaffected by government as possible. Government should not interfere with our beliefs about religion either by coercion or by persuasion. Religion may flourish or wither; it may change or stay the same. What happens to religion is up to the people acting severally and voluntarily; it is not up to the people acting collectively through government.

This elaboration highlights the connections among religious neutrality, religious autonomy, and religious voluntarism. Government must be neutral so that religious belief and practice can be free. The autonomy of religious belief and disbelief is maximized when government encouragement and discouragement is minimized. The same is true of religious practice and refusal to practice. The goal of maximum religious liberty can help identify the baseline from which to measure encouragement and discouragement.

My conception of religious neutrality includes a neutral conception of religion. That is, any belief about God, the supernatural, or the transcendent, is a religious belief. For constitutional purposes, the belief that there is no God, or no afterlife, is as much a religious belief as the belief that there is a God or an afterlife. It is a belief about the traditional subject matter of religion, and it is a belief that must be accepted on faith, because it is not subject to empirical investigation. Serious believers and serious disbelievers are sometimes troubled by this equation of their belief systems, but we cannot make sense of the religion clauses without it. This constitutional conception of religious belief as any belief about religion explains why atheists are protected from persecution, and why the government cannot establish atheism.

Similarly, the deeply held conscientious objection of a non-theist must be treated equally with a similar objection rooted in a more traditional faith. As a plurality of the Supreme Court put it in a statutory context, the relevant category is "all those whose consciences . . . would give them no rest or peace" if they were compelled to comply with government policy. To be sure, there are difficulties in applying that standard to non-traditional sources of conscience. But in a nation with millions of non-believers, no other conception of conscientious objection is even plausibly neutral.

That is a bare sketch of substantive neutrality. The next step is to compare and contrast formal and substantive neutrality. Sometimes the two types of neutrality produce the same result. That is, sometimes we can minimize encouragement or discouragement to religion by ignoring the religious aspects of some behavior and treating it just like some analogous secular behavior.

But often the two understandings of neutrality diverge. Government routinely encourages and discourages all sorts of private behavior. Under substantive neutrality, these encouragements and discouragements are not to be applied to religion. Thus, a standard of minimizing both encouragement and discouragement will often require that religion be singled out for special treatment.

Consider two of the examples I have mentioned so far. To prohibit the consumption of alcohol, without an exception for religious rituals, is to flatly prohibit important religious practices. Such a prohibition would discourage religious practice in the most coercive possible way—by criminalizing it. Many believers would abandon their religious practice; some would defy the law; some of those would go to jail. Such a law would be a massive departure from substantive neutrality.

To *exempt* sacramental wine is not perfectly neutral either. Religious observers would get to do something that is forbidden to the rest of the population, but that observation goes to formal neutrality. Would this special treatment encourage religion? It is conceivable that the prospect of a tiny nip would encourage some desperate folks to join a church that uses real wine, or to attend Mass daily instead of weekly or only at Easter. It is conceivable, but only to a law professor or an economist. Such an exemption would have only an infinitesimal tendency to encourage religious activity. In contrast, withholding the exemption would severely discourage religious activity. The course that most nearly approaches substantive neutrality—the course that minimizes both encouragement and discouragement—is to single out religious uses for an exemption. In this and similar applications, substantive neutrality is akin to the equal impact, equal outcome side of the affirmative action debate.

Prohibition is an easy case under formal neutrality, and an easy case under substantive neutrality. The difference is that substantive neutrality gets the right answer. Formal neutrality, as applied to Prohibition, would lead directly to religious persecution.

Sometimes the two concepts of neutrality seem to converge. In the equal access controversy, I argued that substantive neutrality was best achieved by something close to formal neutrality—that student religious groups should be treated like any other student extracurricular group. To give them special privileges would encourage religion; to exclude them would discourage religion.

But even in that example, some deviations from formal neutrality were required. Most student extracurricular groups have a faculty sponsor, but it is widely agreed that a student religious group should not have a faculty sponsor. To say that the school will sponsor any student group except a religious group is to classify on the basis of religion. Withholding the faculty sponsor violates formal neutrality.

The school prayer cases are the most obvious source of our intuition that public schools should not provide faculty sponsors to student religious groups. But substantive neutrality can explain that intuition. School sponsorship of a religious group commits the government to the success of a religious group, thus encouraging religion and violating substantive neutrality. Moreover, the faculty sponsor will inevitably influence the group's conduct, thus encouraging some forms of religious practice and discouraging others.

It is true that religious groups are in some sense discouraged by being forced to organize and function without the school sponsorship available to all other student groups. But withholding the sponsor does not actively harm religious groups; it does not reduce or divert their own resources, or create obstacles for them to overcome. It merely withholds an intrusive benefit that is widely available to other groups that are in some ways analogous. The hoped-for benefit may turn out to be seriously harmful if the government sponsor changes the course of the religious organization. Withholding this risky benefit is not perfectly neutral, but the deviation from neutrality is considerably smaller than the deviations inherent in sponsorship. Thus, the closest the schools can come to substantive neutrality is to leave such groups alone.

Prohibition and equal access are simple examples. I have not yet gotten to the hard cases, like public aid to religious schools. But even these simple cases illustrate some important points about substantive neutrality.

Most obviously, substantive neutrality is harder to apply than formal neutrality. It requires judgments about the relative significance of various encouragements and discouragements to religion. Absolute zero is no more attainable in encouragement and discouragement than in temperature. We can aspire only to minimize encouragement and discouragement. Because substantive neutrality requires more judgment than formal neutrality, substantive neutrality is more subject to manipulation by advocates and result-oriented judges and law professors.

More important, substantive neutrality requires a baseline from which to measure encouragement and discouragement. What state of affairs is the background norm from which to judge whether religion has been encouraged or discouraged? This question also requires judgment; there is no simple test that can be mechanically applied to yield sensible answers.

A conceivable mechanical standard is to treat religion as though government did not exist. If religion is better off than if government did not exist, it has been encouraged; if it is worse off, it has been discouraged. The only thing to recommend this standard is its intellectual purity; I doubt that it appeals to anyone in the real world.

To take the most obvious example, no one suggests that churches be denied police and fire protection. Police and fire protection are sometimes explained as merely incidental benefits. But to what are they incidental? I am not at all sure that police and fire protection arise as an incident of something else. These services are not incidental; they are provided outright and for their own sake. One might say that police and fire protection for churches is incidental to police and fire protection for everybody else, or for all property in the community. But it is easy to imagine either isolated or concentrated religious properties that would strain that rationale to the breaking point. That rationale also fails to explain why we protect churches against vandalism, embezzlement, and other property crimes that pose no threat to the neighbors.

One of the Supreme Court's better opinions on incidental benefits answers the question I have posed. A permissible benefit is one that is incidental to a larger policy of neutrality. The benefits of police and fire protection are such an incident of neutrality. Police and fire protection are such a universal part of our lives that they have become part of the baseline. To deny police and fire protection would be to outlaw religion in the original sense of that word—to put religion outside the protection of the law. To demand that churches provide their own police and fire protection in a modern society would be to place an extraordinary obstacle in their way—a discouragement that would make religion a hazardous enterprise indeed. To provide such services does not make religion attractive to anyone who is not attracted on the merits. As a practical matter, any encouragement is tiny. The discouraging effect of cutting off basic services greatly exceeds the encouraging effect of providing them.

Similar judgments about the baseline level of government activity are at the heart of the equal access controversy. To deny religious groups a faculty sponsor is neutral in the sense of leaving such groups where they would be if government did not exist. But if government did not exist, there would be no public schools and no classrooms in which groups could meet. The opponents of equal access argued that use of the classroom was a benefit—an encouragement in the terms I have been using—that violated the establishment clause. The supporters of equal access argued that once classrooms were made available to other extracurricular groups, the use of the room was part of the baseline—a background norm that both religious and secular groups could take for granted. Most of the opponents seemed to concede that religious groups could use the streets and parks on an equal basis. Streets and parks are in the baseline by common consent; faculty sponsors are not in the baseline; classrooms are controversial.

The proper background norm about public facilities is related to the background norm about student behavior. If the norm is that students can generally do what they want on their own time, subject only to restraints on harmful or disruptive behavior, then banning religious groups is discouragement. But if the norm is that high school students can do nothing without school sponsorship, then allowing meetings looks like sponsorship, and even endorsement, and excluding them from campus can be characterized as the neutral course of simply declining to sponsor them. Opponents of equal access have looked to basic first amendment principles, and to student free speech cases not involving religion—to cases involving war protest and underground newspapers. They argued that the relevant constitutional norm was that unsponsored students could say what they wanted on school premises.

Unless we carefully think through such issues, we will tend to select our baselines by intuition, and we will give free rein to our political preferences and our prejudices. Our preferences can operate freely because the principle of neutrality by itself is insufficient to define the baseline. Judgments about the state of the world must be brought to bear. Equally important, the other principles of the religion clauses must be brought to bear. We must keep in mind what neutrality is supposed to accomplish. Our goal is not to leave religion in a Hobbesian state of nature, nor to leave it regulated exactly to the extent that commercial businesses are regulated, with no extra burdens and no exemptions. Our goal is to maximize the religious liberty of both believers and nonbelievers.

. . .

## IV. DISAGGREGATED NEUTRALITY

The Supreme Court is rarely content with a broad principle if it can substitute a three-part test. Its most famous formulation of the neutrality requirement is the second part of the *Lemon* test, which says that a

law violates the establishment clause if one of its substantial effects is either to advance or inhibit religion. This formulation began simply as an elaboration of neutrality, but is often disaggregated into a test of no advancement and a separate test of no inhibition. If a law has some substantial effect that advances religion, that may be the end of the case. And there is sometimes a very low threshold for finding effects to be substantial.

In the extreme case of *Aguilar v. Felton*, the Supreme Court invalidated a federal program to provide remedial instruction in math and reading to low income children in private schools. Congress enacted this program in pursuit of neutrality—to provide the same remedial program to disadvantaged children without regard to their religious choices. Why did the Court strike it down? Because the public employees who provided the remedial instruction might be influenced by the religious environment of parochial schools, and under that hypnotic influence, might encourage the children to religious belief. That possibility created a risk of a substantial effect of advancing religion; that risk could be avoided only by close supervision that would excessively entangle church and state. That was the end of the case.

I call this disaggregated neutrality, because it looks only at one side of the balance of advancing or inhibiting. Because absolute zero is not achievable, it is always possible to find some effect of advancing or inhibiting religion. Thus, if you look only at one side of the balance, you can always find a constitutional violation. Some of those who would have government sponsor their faith play the same game on the inhibits side of the balance: if government does not lead school children in prayer, or display religious symbols on major holidays, the public may infer that government is hostile to religion. Therefore, these critics conclude, silence is not neutral.

Substantive neutrality always requires that the encouragement of one policy be compared to the discouragement of alternative policies. The principal effect of *Aguilar* was to greatly increase the cost of providing remedial programs to children in private schools. After *Aguilar*, the government or the school must provide separate off-campus facilities and the children must travel to those facilities and back again. The effect of increasing the cost was to reduce the number of children who could be served. So thousands of our least advantaged citizens are now forced to choose; forfeit their right to remedial instruction in math and reading, or forfeit their right to education in a religious environment. That effect discourages religion, and dwarfs the risk that the government's remedial math or reading teacher might suddenly start proselytizing. By disaggregating neutrality, the Court has lost sight of its original objective.

Another way to disaggregate neutrality is to shift back and forth among different versions of neutrality without explanation. If you think that neutrality with respect to government-imposed burdens means that churches and believers never get an exemption (formal neutrality), but that neutrality with respect to government benefits means that churches can never participate (disaggregated substantive neutrality), you had better have a good explanation. The most obvious explanation is simply hostility to religion. If you have the opposite preferences, you are equally in need of a good explanation.

Voting patterns in the Supreme Court are often disaggregated, sometimes in suspicious ways. Justice Brennan applied formal neutrality to strike down a legislative tax exemption in *Texas Monthly, Inc.*, and he applied disaggregated neutrality to strike down the remedial education program in Aguilar. But he believes the *Constitution* requires exemptions from laws that violate religious conscience, a position consistent with substantive neutrality. Justice Rehnquist takes the opposite position on all three of these issues. Justice Stevens agrees with Brennan on tax exemptions and aid to religious schools, but with Rehnquist on exemptions for conscience. Stevens votes against traditional religions on all three issues, an odd interpretation of religious liberty.

In the Term since this lecture was delivered, the Court has dramatically embraced formal neutrality to uphold taxation and regulation of churches and believers. In *Jimmy Swaggart Ministries*, the Court unanimously held that churches can be taxed, so long as the tax laws do not single out churches for discriminatory rates or incidents of taxation. The Court in dictum suggested that it would apply the same standard to regulation of churches, except where compliance with the regulation would require the church to violate its "sincere religious beliefs." In *Employment Division v. Smith*, the exception for sincere religious belief disappeared by a vote of five to four. The free exercise of religion now means that churches cannot be taxed or regulated any more heavily than General Motors. The only remaining protection is that provided by formal neutrality; religious conduct cannot be singled out for facially discriminatory regulation.

The Court recognized that these holdings burdened the exercise of religion. The *Smith* opinion acknowledged that the conduct at issue was "the 'exercise of religion,'" and that Oregon had subjected this conduct to "an across-the-board criminal prohibition," but it insisted that this prohibition of an exercise of religion did not mean that Oregon was "prohibiting the free exercise of religion." In *Swaggart*, the Court said that the economic burden of paying the tax, and "substantial administrative burdens" of collecting the tax or complying with other regulations, were "not constitutionally significant." The Court found it "undeniable that a generally applicable tax has a secular purpose and neither advances nor inhibits religion, for the very essence of such a tax is that it is neutral and nondiscriminatory on questions of religious belief."

This conception of neutrality is irreconcilable with *Aguilar* and the other cases striking down government payments to religiously affiliated schools. In *Aguilar*, the federally-funded instruction in remedial math and reading was directed on equal terms to poor children in all schools, public and private, secular and religious. But the Court did not say that this "neutral and nondiscriminatory" instruction "neither advances nor inhibits religion." Instead, it found that the government money conferred obvious benefits on religion, and did not say that those benefits were of no constitutional significance.

The Court's current position comes to this: when government demands money or obedience *from* churches, neutrality consists of treating churches just like other subjects of taxation or regulation, and it is irrelevant that the church is worse off than it would be without the tax or the regulation. But when government pays money *to* churches, neutrality consists of not making the churches any better off than they would be without the payment, and it is irrelevant that the churches are treated just like other beneficiaries of the same program.

Whatever explains these results, it is not a consistent understanding of neutrality. I suspect that the Justices are not deciding on the basis of neutrality at all, although they invoke it in their opinions. If they are deciding on the basis of neutrality, they have not defined it in any consistent way. But the inconsistency of the current rules may be only a transitional step on the way to widespread application of formal neutrality as the rule of judicial decision.

. . .

That hypothetical development would greatly reduce the inconsistencies in the Court's opinions. But it would not be a triumph for neutrality. Legislatures would be free to practice disaggregated formal neutrality. They could support religion or burden it, support some religions and burden others, as long as they stated their rules in facially neutral terms. The Court in *Smith* acknowledged somewhat euphemistically that its decision "will place at a relative disadvantage those religious practices that are not widely engaged in." In plain English, this means that churches without political clout may be suppressed, that more powerful churches may be accommodated, and if the principle is extended to the financial aid cases, they may be supported. If the Court's decisions are eventually reconciled in this way, the explanatory principle will not be neutrality, but statism. The majority will be permitted to do anything it can achieve by facially neutral rules, however gerrymandered, and the Court will have largely abdicated its role of protecting religious minorities.

## V. APPLYING SUBSTANTIVE NEUTRALITY

Formal and substantive neutrality are broad categories. But as I noted earlier, religious liberty controversies present a succession of specific problems. It is necessary to search out the most neutral course with respect to each problem. That process will at least clarify our disagreements, and it might provide some basis for principled argument to legislatures and state courts.

Recall my distinction between equality and neutrality: equality refers only to tangible penalties and rewards; neutrality also includes expression of government opinion. It seems to me that we have widespread consensus on both equality and neutrality with respect to religious status, consensus on equality but not on neutrality with respect to religious belief, consensus except for a few exceptional cases with respect to religious speech, and no consensus at all with respect to religious conduct.

That is a glib set of categories; what do I mean by them? First, consensus with respect to status: almost no one any longer openly claims that nonbelievers, or non-Christians, or non-Protestants, should be discriminated against because of their religious affiliation. There are occasional exceptions, such as the recent attacks on Father Healy's appointment to head the New York Public Library. But these attacks are nearly always disguised with pretextual justifications. Moreover, hardly anyone thinks it a proper function of government to denounce the adherents of some religious faiths and laud the adherents of others.

Second, partial consensus with respect to religious belief: we have consensus on equality; no one argues that government should actively penalize some religious beliefs and reward others. But we do not have consensus on neutrality. A vocal minority of lawyers and scholars, and perhaps a majority of the public, believe that government may endorse a preferred religious belief. Some urge generic theism, some the

Judeo-Christian tradition, some Christianity. Whatever their preferred teaching, these people reject the Supreme Court's holdings that government should be neutral with respect to religious belief. And of course, the Supreme Court itself does not seem to take those holdings very seriously.

Third, partial consensus with respect to religious speech: religious speech and political speech are the two core cases of highly protected speech, and they should be treated equally. A long line of Supreme Court cases are consistent with that proposition, and I think there is widespread agreement with those results, although not necessarily with my formulation of the principle. Religious speech in and around public schools is an exceptional case where consensus breaks down. Consensus also breaks down when money is involved, as in the *Texas Monthly* case, in the campaign finance and disclosure laws, and in the restrictions on political speech in the Internal Revenue Code. My principle that religious and political speech should be treated equally could have explained the *Texas Monthly* case, and my principle had some relation to the discordant and troublesome combination of opinions that made up the majority. The more recent decision in *Jimmy Swaggart Ministries* makes it harder to sustain benign readings of *Texas Monthly*. But it remains open to the Court to uphold a tax exemption that includes religious speech in some broader category, such as not-for-profit speech, or religious, anti-religious, and political speech. The relationship between constitutional protections for religious and political speech is now before the Court in the quite different context of judgments against churches for such speech torts as defamation and intentional infliction of emotional distress.

Finally, dissensus with respect to religious conduct. What does it mean to be neutral with respect to conscientious objection to government policy, or religious education, or religious charities, or the management of religious institutions? I am not sure we have consensus that either equality or neutrality is required with respect to religious conduct; we certainly have no consensus on what that means.

Allow me to consider just one of these examples, exemption from facially neutral laws that forbid religious conduct or require people to violate deeply held conscientious beliefs. The Supreme Court repeatedly announced the constitutional right to such exemptions, but enforced it half-heartedly. The Reagan Administration quietly hammered at that right for eight years. Now the Court has wholly repudiated the right.

Scholars are also attacking the right to exemption,

often in the name of neutrality. Two major scholars have recently offered all out attacks on the constitutional right to such exemptions. One is Ellis West, a political scientist at the University of Richmond; the other is William Marshall, a lawyer at Case Western Reserve.

Neither the scholars or the Court goes as far as requiring formal neutrality. Neither claims that exemptions for religion are unconstitutional when the legislature voluntarily grants them. Both rely on the formal conception of neutrality, but both draw back from its full implications, or at least from the claim that it is constitutionally required.

They do not appear to flinch from the full implications of their claim that the Constitution requires no exemptions for religious exercise. I assume that they would permit a state to enact Prohibition without an exception for the Mass or the Seder. The Court says as much in its opinion, and Professor West said as much in response to a question. He also said that if a law forbidding ethnic and religious discrimination in employment had no exception for rabbis, then a synagogue might have to hire a Baptist rabbi. He defended himself on the ground that no state would pass such a law, and that probably the Baptist would be unqualified on some other ground.

The hope that no state would pass such a law is insufficient protection for religious minorities. It is true that Americans are more tolerant than many other populations, in part because of the teachings of the religion clauses. Many religious minorities have assimilated into the general culture and into the political process, and the legislature is unlikely to knowingly victimize these minorities in ways that go to the heart of their faith. That is why Jews and Catholics were protected by an exception to Prohibition.

But the precondition of assimilation and respectability is why Oregon has failed to protect Native Americans' ritual use of peyote. This social precondition is why in the nineteenth century we denied Mormons the right to vote, imprisoned some of their leaders, confiscated all the property of their church, and dissolved its legal existence, until the church changed its practice, its teaching, and its belief on plural marriage. This social precondition is why multi-million-dollar tort judgements threaten the very existence of the Hare Krishnas, the Scientologists, and other so-called "cults." I am not much comforted by the prospect that only small and unfamiliar religions will be persecuted.

Nor am I willing to assume that larger religious minorities are always safe. The Church of Christ is hardly a fringe group in Collinsville, Oklahoma, but it too is threatened with destruction from a huge tort judgment for intangible harm to a disgruntled former member. In this decade, the military attempted to eliminate Jewish officers who wore their *yarmulke* while in uniform. In what appeared to be a fit of unthinking deference, the Supreme Court upheld that practice. Congress intervened with protective legislation, but much harm had been done in the meantime. In retrospect, the Court's refusal to protect yarmulkes was a precursor to its refusal in *Smith* to protect any religious conduct at all.

In times of political excitement, of xenophobia, of outbursts of anti-Catholic or anti-Semitic feeling, almost any kind of law is possible, especially at the state and local level. The question is not merely what the federal government might do in such times, although that is scary enough. It was Congress that persecuted the Mormons, and the federal executive that tried to purge observant Jewish military officers. But we must also consider what state and local jurisdictions with religiously homogeneous populations might do to small and unfamiliar minorities. The point is not that such populations are any less enlightened than other Americans, but simply that the forces of pluralism are more attenuated in homogenous communities. What might Utah, or Arkansas, or Yalobusha County do in times of excitement? We have a bill of rights to be enforced by an independent judiciary in part to get us through such times with minimal damage. To claim that the worst horror stories are unlikely to happen is to miss the point of a bill of rights.

I start with overt hostility because it would be a mistake to assume it away. But hostility is not the only source of law forbidding people to practice their religions, and probably not even the most important. The practice of a small faith may be forbidden just because the legislature did not know about it and never considered its needs. Then the bureaucracy will grind forward, enforcing the rule without regard to exceptional circumstance. This may be what happened to Frances Quaring, who thought the picture on her driver's license was a graven image forbidden by the second commandment. The Frances Quarings of the world may or may not be organized enough to get the attention of the legislature, but a court is required to listen to their complaint and to rule one way or the other.

Of course, inadvertence can interact with hostility, or with an insensitivity that borders on hostility. Consider what might happen when Frances Quaring writes her legislator. She may get a sympathetic response and a legislated exemption. But her legislator may find it so impossible to empathize with her belief that he never seriously considers whether an exemption would be workable. Even if he empathizes, the legislative calendar is crowded, and the original statute having been enacted, all the burdens of legislative inertia now work against an exemption.

For a variety of reasons, therefore, we cannot always rely on legislatures to protect minority religious conduct. Courts are not always better, but they give religious liberty claims a second chance to be heard. If we take seriously the constitutional right to freely exercise religion, we must restore a judicially enforceable right to religious exemption in appropriate cases.

The right to exemptions for religious conduct is more easily explained in terms of religious liberty than in terms of neutrality. But the right is consistent with substantive neutrality, and it can be explained in those terms as well.

As I have already noted with respect to Prohibition, a law that penalizes religious conduct discourages religion. The discouragement is often severe, as when the penalty is criminal punishment or Frances Quaring's loss of the right to drive. But in many of the cases, an exemption for conscientious objectors has only a de minimus tendency to encourage any aspect of religion. The exemption is substantively neutral; the lack of an exemption is not.

Another way to state this is that equal impact comes closer to the proper sense of neutrality with respect to conscientious objection. People with a deeply held conscientious objection to a law are not similarly situated to people without such an objection. To insist on formally equal treatment of objectors and non-objectors is to pursue the same majestic equality that forbids the rich and the poor alike to sleep under bridges.

Substantive equality and equal impact are not wholly equivalent. The difference between them appears in cases where religious belief coincides too closely with self-interest, as in conscientious objection to military service or payment of taxes. The distorting effects of self-interest do not make sincere conscientious objectors similarly situated with non-objectors; denying the exemption still has severe and unequal impact on objectors. The equal impact sense of neutrality would focus on the objectors and presumptively grant the exemption, subject only to the government's proof of a compelling reason to deny it.

But substantive neutrality as I have defined it must also consider the non-objectors. If we grant exemptions from military service or general taxation, on the basis of conscientious objection, we will inevitably encourage religion. I do not refer to the people willing to feign religious belief in order to claim an exemption. There may be millions of these people, and the difficulty of adjudicating their false claims is relevant to the government's claim of compelling interest, but these false claimants are only incidentally relevant to neutrality.

I refer instead to the people who honestly persuade themselves that they have come to hold the religious belief that entitles them to the exemption, or who feel pressured to adopt that belief. Human nature being what it is, there may be millions of these people as well. The lure of exemption creates cognitive dissonance between the individual's desire for the exemption and the belief that makes him ineligible for it. The psychological effort to reduce this dissonance can move his actual belief into conformity with the belief that serves his self-interest.

The problem for religious neutrality is that denying the exemption discourages religious belief in one set of people, and granting the exemption encourages religious belief in another, overlapping, set of people. It is no longer clear that exemption is the more nearly neutral course. If we suspect that the original number of conscientious objectors is small, and that the number of non-objectors seriously tempted by the exemption is large, then denying the exemption appears to be more nearly neutral than granting it. If we have no plausible estimate of which effect is larger, then there may be no basis in substantive neutrality for the courts to second-guess the legislature.

Whatever we do in these difficult cases, the deviation from neutrality is large. Either we will deny the exemption, with severe and unequal impact on the original objectors, devastating to their religious liberty, or we will grant the exemption, and greatly encourage religious belief in the objectors induced by the exemption. The case is hard, and the most nearly neutral course will not be very neutral.

Legislatures can sometimes solve these problems by imposing an alternative burden, designed to accommodate conscience while reducing the self-interested reasons for claiming the exemption. That is part of the logic of the alternative service requirement for objectors to military service, and of the requirement that workers who object to union dues make an equivalent contribution to a charity other than their church. These legislative solutions are not perfect—thousands of Jehovah's Witnesses spent World War II in prison because they objected even to alternative service—but they permit a closer approximation to substantive neutrality. They come from thoughtful legislatures; it is harder to see how courts could create them.

## VI. CONCLUSION

I hope I have at least persuaded you that the meaning of neutrality is not self-evident, and that substantive neutrality is a possible alternative to formal neutrality. Beyond that, I hope I have persuaded you that substantive neutrality is more consistent with religious liberty than is formal neutrality. I have much more work to do to show that a neutral baseline can usually be identified in a principled way across the whole range of interactions between religion and government. But I hope I have persuaded you that the work is worth doing. For that is the path toward maximum religious liberty, neutrally distributed among all kinds of believers and non-believers. And that multifarious formulation is as close as I can come to a single principle that summarizes the religion clauses.

# Bibliography

*Free Exercise Theory*

Esbeck, Carl H., *Tort Claims Against Churches and Ecclesiastical Officers: The First Amendment Considerations*, 89 West Virginia Law Review 1 (1986)

Garvey, John H., *Freedom and Equality in the Religion Clauses*, 1981 Supreme Court Review 193 (1989)

Gordon, III, James D., *Free Exercise on the Mountaintop*, 79 California Law Review 91 (1991)

Kauper, Paul G., *Church Autonomy and the First Amendment: The Presbyterian Church Case*, 1969 Supreme Court Review 347 (1969)

Levy, Leonard W., *The Religion Clauses* (1986)

Pepper, Stephen, *Taking the Free Exercise Clause Seriously*, 1986 Brigham Young University Law Review 299 (1986)

Stone, Geoffrey R., *Constitutionally Compelled Exemptions and the Free Exercise Clause*, 27 William & Mary Law Review 985 (1986)

Tushnet, Mark, *"Of Church and State and the Supreme Court": Kurland Revisited*, 1989 Supreme Court Review 373 (1989)